March 11-15, 2018
New Brunswick, NJ, USA

I0027516

**Association for
Computing Machinery**

Advancing Computing as a Science & Profession

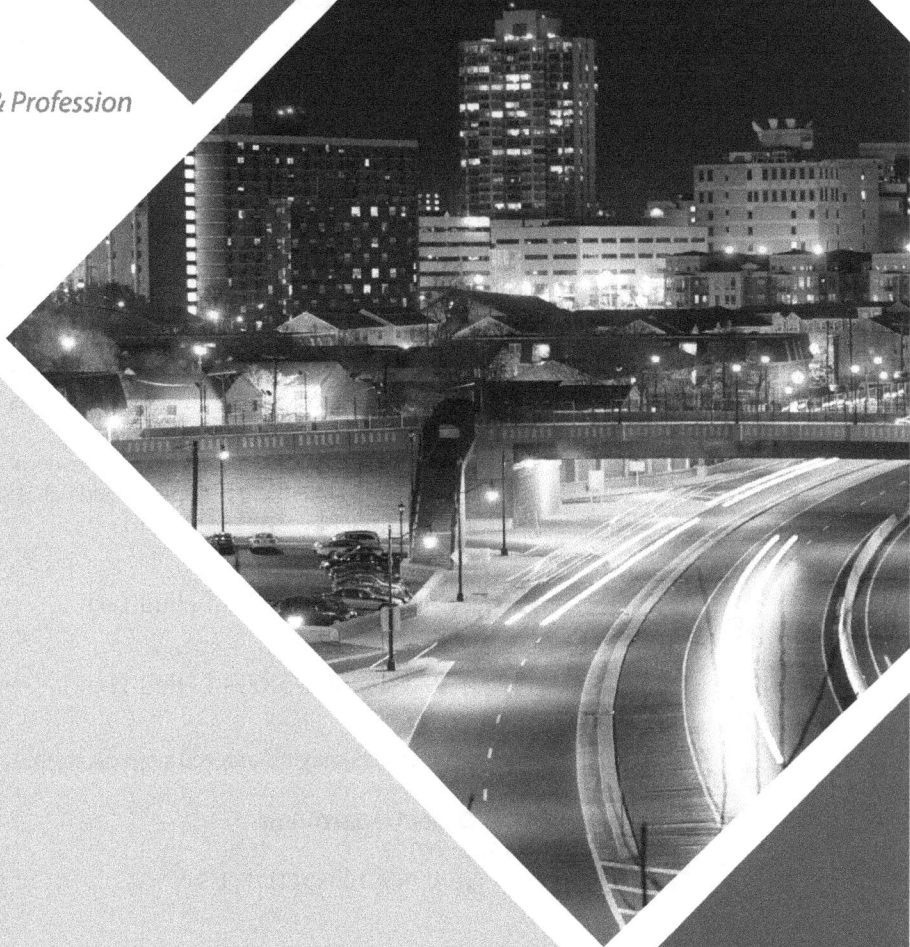

CHIIR'18

Proceedings of the 2018 Conference on
Human Information Interaction & Retrieval

Sponsored by:

ACM SIGIR

In Cooperation with:

ACM SIGCHI

Supported by:

Rutgers University, Google, & Microsoft

**Association for
Computing Machinery**

Advancing Computing as a Science & Profession

The Association for Computing Machinery
2 Penn Plaza, Suite 701
New York, New York 10121-0701

ISBN: 978-1-4503-4925-3 (Digital)

ISBN: 978-1-4503-5877-4 (Print)

Additional copies may be ordered prepaid from:

ACM Order Department
PO Box 30777
New York, NY 10087-0777, USA

Phone: 1-800-342-6626 (USA and Canada)
+1-212-626-0500 (Global)
Fax: +1-212-944-1318
E-mail: acmhelp@acm.org
Hours of Operation: 8:30 am – 4:30 pm ET

Welcome from the CHIIR 2018 General Chairs

It is our great pleasure to welcome you to New Brunswick, New Jersey and the third ACM SIGIR Conference on Human Information Interaction and Retrieval (CHIIR 2018). CHIIR, as you may know, has roots in two previously successful communities: The Information Interaction in Context (IIiX) conference and the Human Computer Information Retrieval (HCIR) symposium, which ran from 2006 and 2007 respectively. These meetings were focused on issues that involved Human Information Behavior (HIB), Interactive Information Retrieval (IIR) and Human-Computer Interaction (HCI). Those roots, as well as decades of research and development on information seeking and other forms of information interaction, human-centered design, and information retrieval are the backbone of CHIIR. At the same time, this vibrant new community has picked up more scholars and themes as it continues to attract new students and professionals, as well as emerging research topics that are evident in this year's program. In fact, CHIIR is one of the few forums that explicitly supports presentation of bold new ideas through its Perspective Papers category. In addition, we have picked up Demos as a new category for presentations this year.

All of these wonderful things could not be possible without a large number of people making significant contributions. We are quite fortunate to have Katriina Byström, Falk Scholer, and Jeff Huang as our Program Chairs this year. These three brave souls took upon a tremendous effort of working with dozens of submissions, reviewers, and meta-reviewers and constructing a high-quality program while coordinating from three different continents. Soo Young Rieh and Preben Hansen, on the other hand dealt with higher than expected load for short papers and still managed to get them reviewed and assessed on time. Even our Doctoral Consortium (DC) this year ended up being quite challenging as we received twice as many submissions as before, but our fine DC chairs Jaceck Gwizdka and Vivek Singh found world-class mentors for these doctoral students. Thanks to our Workshops and Tutorials Chair Xiaojun Yuan, we have a fantastic lineup of tutorials on the first day and workshops on the last day. When the whole program was ready for the conference, it was our Proceedings Chair Roberto Gonzalez-Ibanez who managed to put together these proceedings that you are holding in your hands, or more likely viewing in the ACM Digital Library! We are thankful for having an energetic and resourceful local arrangement committee with Michael Cole as the Treasurer, Fernando Diaz as the Sponsorship Chair, Kaitlin Costello as the Local Organizing Chair, and Sunyoung Kim and Matt Mitsui as the Student Volunteers Chairs. And it was our Publicity Chair Anita Crescenzi, who helped us with not only the outreach efforts, but also with the registration system. Finally, none of these would have happened without the authors and reviewers from more than 30 countries whose contributions are reflected in every aspect of this conference. So, thank you all!

We are fortunate to have two wonderful keynote speakers this year – Pertti Vakkari from the University of Tampere, Finland and Susan Dumais from Microsoft Research, and thank them for their generous acceptance to our invitations to join and engage us. We are grateful for our supporters and sponsors in making this event possible. They include the Rutgers School of Communication and Information, Google, and Microsoft Research. We hope you enjoy all that New Brunswick and CHIIR have to offer and feel engaged, empowered, and enlightened. Looking at this year's program and participation, we can't help but to think how wonderful the path forward is for all of us. Here's to the next three years, thirty years, and beyond of CHIIR. Cheers!

Chirag Shah
CHIIR 2018 General Chair
Rutgers University, USA

Nicholas J. Belkin
CHIIR 2018 General Chair
Rutgers University, USA

CHIIR 2018 Program Overview

We are pleased to welcome you to the third ACM SIGIR Conference on Human Information Interaction and Retrieval (CHIIR, pronounced "cheer"), held in New Brunswick, New Jersey, USA during March 11-15, 2018. CHIIR provides a forum for the dissemination and discussion of research on the user-centered aspects of information interaction and information retrieval. CHIIR focuses on elements such as human involvement in search activities, and information seeking and use in context. CHIIR 2018 follows CHIIR 2017 in Oslo, Norway, and CHIIR 2016 in Chapel Hill, North Carolina, USA.

CHIIR 2018 focuses on user-centered approaches to information access, retrieval, and use, including studies of interactive systems, novel interaction paradigms, new methods, and a range of related areas. Alongside detailed studies on specific information retrieval systems and situations, the program includes real-life research of contextually embedded search tasks. Due to the rapidly increasing use of online and social media-oriented information interaction in all areas of human life - including work, leisure, and education – there has never been a more important time to consider, both empirically and theoretically, the impact and consequences that search options, search strategies, recommendation systems, visualization, social media issues and other aspects of information interaction can have on the development of both individuals and society as a whole.

We are pleased to present the proceedings of CHIIR 2018. The main body of the program consists of Full and New Perspectives papers (ten pages) and Short papers (four pages). We received a total of 57 Full/Perspectives paper submissions, of which 22 were accepted for publication in the proceedings, resulting in an acceptance rate of 38.6%. There are three New Perspectives papers, which are intended to argue systematically for novel ideas or insights concerning approaches, key challenges, or theoretical or methodological issues that have the potential to inspire substantive discussion and lead to significant advances in the field. We also received a total of 60 Short paper submissions, out of which 24 were accepted for publication, an acceptance rate of 40.0%. Full papers are delivered as 30 minute presentations, and short papers as posters in a joint session following short boaster presentations.

In addition to contributed papers, the program features two keynotes by prominent researchers in the CHIIR community, Susan Dumais (Microsoft Research Lab, Redmond, Washington, USA) and Pertti Vakkari (University of Tampere, Finland). We are delighted to be able to present two researchers with such richness of insights and expertise from the ranks of our own. Furthermore, CHIIR 2018 features five Demos, three Workshops, four Tutorials, and a Doctoral Consortium. Thus, the attendees are offered a fabulous range of CHIIR events during the conference.

This grand technical program is a result of the tremendous work of the Organizing Committee, including the Short Papers Co-Chairs, Soo Youg Rieh (University of Michigan, USA) and Preben Hansen (Stockholm University, Sweden); the Doctoral Consortium Co-Chairs, Jacek Gwizdka (University of Texas, Austin, USA) and Vivek Singh (Rutgers University, USA); and the Workshops and Tutorials Chair, Xiaojun Yuan (University at Albany, State University of New York, USA); as well as the 14 Senior Program Committee members and 72 Program Committee members who reviewed submissions. We would like to thank them sincerely for their invaluable efforts.

We would also like to thank the general chairs, Nick Belkin and Chirag Shah (both of Rutgers University, USA), whose interest and support have been essential in all aspects of realizing this conference.

We hope that you find the CHIIR 2018 program stimulating and important for your own purposes, within research and in development. With your engagement, and only then, will the CHIIR community advance in ensuring that research on information interactions promotes individual and societal growth.

Katriina Byström
CHIIR 2018 Program Chair
Oslo Metropolitan University, Norway

Jeff Huang
CHIIR 2018 Program Chair
Brown University, USA

Falk Scholer
CHIIR 2018 Program Chair
RMIT University, Australia

Table of Contents

Session 5: Re-finding in Personal Collections

Session 6: Supporting Efficiency

Keynote Address

Session 7: Investigating Search

Session 8: Searching in Multiple Languages

Short Papers

Demonstrations

Doctoral Consortium

Tutorials

Workshops

CHIIR 2018 Organization

General Chairs:	Chirag Shah & Nicholas J. Belkin *(Rutgers University, USA)*
Program Chairs:	Katriina Byström *(Oslo Metropolitan University, Norway)*
	Jeff Huang *(Brown University, USA)*
	Falk Scholer *(RMIT University, Australia)*
Short Papers Chairs:	Preben Hansen *(Stockholm University, Sweden)*
	Soo Young Rieh *(University of Michigan, USA)*
Doctoral Consortium Chairs:	Jacek Gwizdka *(University of Texas-Austin, USA)*
	Vivek Singh *(Rutgers University, USA)*
Workshops & Tutorials Chair:	Xiaojun Yuan *(University at Albany-SUNY, USA)*
Proceedings Chair:	Roberto González-Ibáñez *(Universidad de Santiago de Chile, Chile)*
Publicity Chair:	Anita Crescenzi *(University of North Carolina-Chapel Hill, USA)*
Local Organizing Chair:	Kaitlin Costello *(Rutgers University, USA)*
Treasurer:	Michael Cole *(LexisNexis, USA)*
Sponsorship Chair:	Fernando Diaz *(Spotify, USA)*
Student Volunteers Chairs:	Sunyoung Kim & Matthew Mitsui *(Rutgers University, USA)*
Webmaster:	Abdurahman Sherif *(Rutgers University, USA)*
Senior Program Committee:	Pia Borlund *(Oslo Metropolitan University, Norway)*
	George Buchanan *(University of Melbourne, Australia)*
	Robert Capra *(University of North Carolina, USA)*
	Abdigani Diriye *(IBM Research Africa, Kenya)*
	David Elsweiler *(University of Regensburg, Germany)*
	Henry Feild *(Endicott College, USA)*
	Luanne Freund *(University of British Columbia, Canada)*
	Diane Kelly *(University of Tennessee, USA)*
	Yoelle Maarek *(Yahoo, Inc., Israel)*
	Daniel Russell *(Google, Inc., USA)*
	Ian Ruthven *(University of Strathclyde, United Kingdom)*
	Catherine Smith *(Kent State University, USA)*
	Mark Smucker *(University of Waterloo, Canada)*
	Paul Thomas *(Microsoft, Australia)*

Program Committee: Omar Alonso *(Microsoft, USA)*

Judit Bar-Ilan *(Bar-Ilan University, Israel)*

Klaus Berberich *(Max Planck Institute for Informatics, Germany)*

Gerd Berget *(Oslo Metropolitan University, Norway)*

Ralf Bierig *(Maynooth University, Ireland)*

Kathy Brennan *(University of North Carolina at Chapel Hill, USA)*

Ed Chi *(Google, Inc., USA)*

Charles Cole *(McGill University, Canada)*

Arjen de Vries *(Radboud University, The Netherlands)*

David Ellis *(Aberystwyth University, United Kingdom)*

Nicola Ferro *(University of Padua, Italy)*

Adam Fourney *(Microsoft Research, USA)*

Ingo Frommholz *(University of Bedfordshire, United Kingdom)*

Norbert Fuhr *(University of Duisburg-Essen, Germany)*

Hua Guo *(Twitter Inc., USA)*

Matthias Hagen *(Bauhaus-Universität Weimar, Germany)*

Morgan Harvey *(Northumbria University, United Kingdom)*

Claudia Hauff *(Delft University of Technology, The Netherlands)*

Daqing He *(University of Pittsburgh, USA)*

Jiyin He *(CWI, The Netherlands)*

Orland Hoeber *(University of Regina, Canada)*

Morten Hertzum *(University of Copenhagen, Denmark)*

Isto Huvila *(Uppsala University, Sweden)*

Peter Ingwersen *(University of Copenhagen, Denmark)*

Sampath Jayarathna *(Cal Poly Pomona, USA)*

Hideo Joho *(University of Tsukuba, Japan)*

Gareth Jones *(Dublin City University, Ireland)*

Joemon Jose *(University of Glasgow, United Kingdom)*

Jaap Kamps *(University of Amsterdam, The Netherlands)*

Jussi Karlgren *(Gavagai & KTH, Sweden)*

Jaana Kekäläinen *(University of Tampere, Finland)*

Claus-Peter Klas *(GESIS - Leibniz Institute for Social Sciences, Germany)*

Rick Kopak *(University of British Columbia, Canada)*

Udo Kruschwitz *(University of Essex, United Kingdom)*

Sanna Kumpulainen *(University of Tampere, Finland)*

Birger Larsen *(Aalborg University Copenhagen, Denmark)*

Dirk Lewandowski *(HAW Hamburg, Germany)*

Christina Lioma *(University of Copenhagen, Denmark)*

Chang Liu *(Peking University, China)*

Jingjing Liu *(University of South Carolina, USA)*

Qiaoling Liu *(CareerBuilder LLC, USA)*

Ying-Hsang Liu *(Charles Sturt University, Australia)*

Andreas Lommatzsch *(Technische Universität Berlin, Germany)*

Irene Lopatovska *(Pratt institute, USA)*

Marianne Lykke *(Aalborg University, Denmark)*

CHIIR 2018 Sponsors & Supporters

Sponsor:

SIGIR
Special Interest Group
on Information Retrieval

In cooperation with:

SIGCHI

Silver Supporter:

RUTGERS
School of Communication
and Information

Supporters:

Google   Microsoft

Information Search Processes in Complex Tasks

Pertti Vakkari
University of Tampere
Fin-33014 Tampere, Finland
Pertti.Vakkari@uta.fi

ABSTRACT

Our understanding of search processes triggered by complex tasks are limited [1]. It is not well known how does the information search process evolve during task performance and how search behavior varies by task process. How do changes in in information needs reflect in search formulation and tactics, in selecting contributing sources and interacting with sources for task outcome? A better understanding of these issues helps in identifying success criteria for various parts of search process. The results contribute also to designing support tools for complex search tasks.

In the talk I analyze information search processes in complex tasks. By task I mean larger tasks, which lead people to engage in search tasks for finding information to advance those tasks [2]. Search process consists of activities from query formulation to working with sources selected for task outcome [3]. I approach task performance from cognitive point of view conceptualizing it as changes in cognitive structures [4,5]. These structures consist of concepts and their relations representing some phenomenon. I analyze how changes in knowledge structures are associated to query formulation and search tactics, selecting contributing sources and working with sources for creating a task outcome. As a result I suggest hypotheses concerning associations between changes in knowledge structures and search behaviors. I present also some ideas for success indicators at various stages of search process.

CCS Concepts/ACM Classifiers

• Information systems ~ Users and interactive retrieval

Author Keywords

Task-based search; Complex tasks; Search process; Task outcome; Cognitive structures; Success criteria

BIOGRAPHY

Pertti Vakkari is Professor Emeritus at the Faculty of Communication Sciences in Information Studies at the University of Tampere, Finland. His work concerns information seeking, task-based information searching, fiction searching, evaluation of interactive information retrieval and outcomes of public libraries.

Vakkari has served as Chairman of Nordic Information Studies Research Education Network, board member of the Nordic Research School for Library and Information Science, member of the Standing Program Committee of the International Conference on Information Seeking in Context (ISIC), and member of the Editorial Board of Information Processing and Managemen and Journal of Documentation. His publications, too numerous to list, include, "Result List Actions in Fiction Search", published in Proceedings of the 15th ACM/IEEE-CS Joint Conference on Digital Libraries, for which he won the Vannevar Bush Award for the Best Paper in 2015.

REFERENCES

1. Belkin, N. et al. (2017). 2nd Workshop on Supporting Complex Search Tasks. In *Proceedings of CHIIR'17*.

2. Vakkari, P. (2003). Task-based Information Searching. *ARIST* 2003, vol. 37. Information Today: Medford, NJ, 413-464.

3. Järvelin, K., Vakkari, P. et al. (2015). Task-based Information Interaction Evaluation. *ACM TOIS* 33(1),3.

4. Ingwersen, P. (1992). *Information Retrieval interaction*. Taylor Graham: London.

5. Vakkari, P. (2016). Searching as Learning. A Systematization Based on Literature. *Journal of Information Science* 42(1):7-18.

ACM ISBN 978-1-4503-4925-3/18/03.
DOI: https://doi.org/10.1145/3176349.3176570

Analyzing Knowledge Gain of Users in Informational Search Sessions on the Web

Ujwal Gadiraju, Ran Yu, Stefan Dietze
L3S Research Center
Leibniz Universität Hannover
lastname@L3S.de

Peter Holtz
IWM (Knowledge Media Research Center)
Leibniz-Institut für Wissensmedien
p.holtz@iwm-tuebingen.de

ABSTRACT

Web search is frequently used by people to acquire new knowledge and to satisfy learning-related objectives, but little is known about how a user's knowledge evolves through the course of a search session. We present a study addressing the knowledge gain of users in informational search sessions. Using crowdsourcing, we recruited 500 distinct users and orchestrated real-world search sessions spanning 10 different topics and information needs. By using scientifically formulated knowledge tests we calibrated the knowledge of users before and after their search sessions, quantifying their knowledge gain. We investigated the impact of information needs on the search behavior and knowledge gain of users, revealing a significant effect of information need on user queries and navigational patterns, but no direct effect on the knowledge gain. Users on average exhibited a higher knowledge gain through search sessions pertaining to topics they were less familiar with.

Our findings in this paper contribute important ground work towards advancing current research in understanding user knowledge gain through web search sessions.

ACM Reference Format:
Ujwal Gadiraju, Ran Yu, Stefan Dietze and Peter Holtz. 2018. Analyzing Knowledge Gain of Users in Informational Search Sessions on the Web. In *CHIIR '18: 2018 Conference on Human Information Interaction & Retrieval, March 11–15, 2018, New Brunswick, NJ, USA.* ACM, New York, NY, USA, 10 pages. https://doi.org/10.1145/3176349.3176381

1 INTRODUCTION

Searching the web for information is among the most frequent online activities. Broder categorized web search queries into having either *navigational, transactional* or *informational* intents [4]. In informational web search sessions, the intent of a user is to acquire some information assumed to be present on one or more web pages.

Recent research in the realm of 'search as learning' (SAL) has recognized the importance of learning scopes and focused on observing and detecting learning needs during web search. Eickhoff et al. investigated the correlation between several query and search mission-related metrics with learning progress [8]. Wu et al. predicted the difficulty of search tasks from query and mission-related

features [22]. Collins-Thompson et al. investigated the aspects of search interaction which are effective for supporting superior learning outcomes [7]. While prior work has focused on improving the learning experience and efficiency during search sessions, the measurement of a user's knowledge gain through the course of an informational search session has not yet been addressed. The importance of learning as an outcome of web search has been recognized. Yet, there is a lack of understanding of the impact of web search on a user's knowledge state. This is a vital cog in the wheel, if web search engines that are currently optimized for relevance can be molded to serve learning outcomes.

Research Questions and Original Contributions. This paper aims at filling this gap by contributing novel insights on the nature of knowledge gain in informational search sessions on the web, and the corresponding behavior of users. By combining qualitative and quantitative analysis, we seek to answer the following research questions.

RQ1: *How does a user's knowledge evolve through the course of an informational search session on the web?*

To further the current understanding of the impact of informational search on a user's knowledge, we recruited 500 distinct users from a crowdsourcing platform and orchestrated search sessions spanning 10 different information needs. By employing scientifically formulated *knowledge tests* to calibrate a user's knowledge before a search session, and assess it after the session, we were able to quantify knowledge gain. We found that nearly 70% of the users exhibited a knowledge gain at the end of a search session corresponding to an information need, with an overall average knowledge gain of almost 20%.

RQ2: *How does the topic and information need in a search session influence a user's knowledge gain?*

We explored the impact of information need on the knowledge gain of users. Our findings revealed that the information need does not directly effect the knowledge gain of users. However, we found a strong negative linear relationship between the knowledge gain of users in an informational search session and their topic familiarity. This suggests that users exhibited a higher knowledge gain in search sessions corresponding to information needs that they were less familiar with.

RQ3: *What is the impact of information need on the search behavior of users in a search session?*

We analyzed the search behavior of users and found a significant effect of the information need on the number of queries entered by users, the number of unique terms in their queries, the number of web pages that users navigated to, and the distinct pay-level domains accessed. Information need also had a significant effect on the amount of time users actively spent on the search results page.

We also found that on average the last queries entered by users were significantly longer than the first queries across all information needs, suggesting an impact of the information consumed through the course of a search session.

2 RELATED LITERATURE

We discuss two main realms of closely related work – studies on the relation between (i) a user's search behavior and knowledge gain, and (ii) a user's search behavior and knowledge state.

2.1 Search Behavior and Knowledge Gain

Some previous works have focused on studying the correlation between learning progress and individual user activity features. Eickhoff et al. [8] investigated the correlation between a number of features of the search session as well as the SERP documents with learning needs related to either procedural or declarative knowledge. Results obtained from an analysis of large-scale query logs showed the distinct evolution of particular features throughout search sessions and the correlation of document features with the actual learning intent. The influence of distinct query types on knowledge gain was studied by Collins-Thompson et al. [7], finding that intrinsically diverse queries lead to increased knowledge gain.

Studies on exploratory search have also investigated a similar set of search behaviors that influence the learning outcome. Hagen et al. [14] investigated the relation between the writing behavior and the exploratory search pattern of writers. The authors revealed that query terms can be learned while searching and reading.In addition, Vakkari [20] provided a structured survey of features indicating learning needs as well as user knowledge and knowledge gain throughout the search process.

The aforementioned prior works consider a limited set of features or address specific learning scenarios and learning types. The generalizability of knowledge gain measures in previous works has not been investigated. In this paper, we extend the current understanding of user knowledge gain in informational search sessions. By simulating real world information needs and search sessions on the Web, we present an analysis of quantifiable knowledge gain.

2.2 Search Behavior and Knowledge State

Authors have also proposed to use features that are extracted from search activity to measure the user's knowledge state in an online learning environment. By matching the learning tasks into different learning stages of Anderson and Krathwohl's taxonomy [2], Jansen et al. studied the correlation between search behaviors of 72 participants and their learning stage [16]. They showed that information searching is a learning process with unique searching characteristics corresponding to particular learning levels. Gwizdka et al. [12] proposed to assess learning outcomes in search environments by correlating individual search behaviors with corresponding eye-tracking measures. Syed and Collins-Thompson [19] proposed to optimize the learning outcome of the vocabulary learning task by selecting a set of documents that consider the keyword density and domain knowledge of the learner.

White et al. [21] investigated the difference between the behavior of domain experts and non-experts in seeking information on the same topic. By analyzing the activity log of experts and non-experts

across different domains, the authors found that the distribution of features such as number of queries and query length differed across the levels of expertise. Zhang et al. [23] explored using search behavior as an indicator for the domain knowledge of a user. Through a small study ($n = 35$), they identified features such as the average query length or the rank of documents consumed from the search results as being predictive. Further, Cole et al. [6], observed that behavioral patterns provide reliable indicators about the domain knowledge of a user, even if the actual content or topics of queries and documents are disregarded entirely.

Other works have focused on detecting task difficulty in search environments based on user activity, where the subjective assessment of task difficulty is highly correlated to the user's domain knowledge [13, 18]. Gwizdka and Spence [13] showed that a searcher's perception of task difficulty is a subjective factor that depends on the domain knowledge and some other individual traits. Arguello [3] proposed to use logistic regression to predict task difficulty in a search environment. Data was collected through a crowdsourcing platform, and the author used search tasks created by Wu et al. [22], which contain task difficulty assessments on multiple dimensions.

The aforementioned works focus on investigating the relation between search behavior and a user's knowledge state. In contrast, we aim to capture the change in knowledge state, i.e. knowledge gain in the learning related search process.

3 OBTAINING SEARCH SESSION DATA

We adopted a crowdsourcing approach and orchestrated search sessions with varying information needs. All interactions of the users during the search sessions were logged. We analyzed the data to further the understanding of user knowledge evolution in informational search sessions on the Web. In this section, we describe the study design and experimental setup.

3.1 Study Design

We recruited participants from CrowdFlower[1], a premier crowdsourcing platform. At the onset, workers were informed that the task entailed 'searching the Web for some information'. Workers willing to participate were redirected to our external platform, *SearchWell*. Figure 1 presents the workflow of participants in the experimental setup orchestrating informational search sessions.

Workers were first asked to respond to a few questions (technically referred to as '*items*') corresponding to a particular topic without searching the Web for answers. The questions took the form of statements pertaining to a topic, and workers had to select whether the statement was 'TRUE', 'FALSE', or 'I DON'T KNOW' in case they were not sure. In this way, we calibrated the knowledge of users corresponding to a given topic. To encourage the workers to respond without external consultation, we informed them that their responses to these questions would not affect their pay. We also encouraged workers to provide responses to the best of their knowledge and avoid guessing. The results of this pre-test were used to calibrate the knowledge of the workers with respect to the topic. We describe the topics and how the knowledge tests were

---

[1]http://www.crowdflower.com/

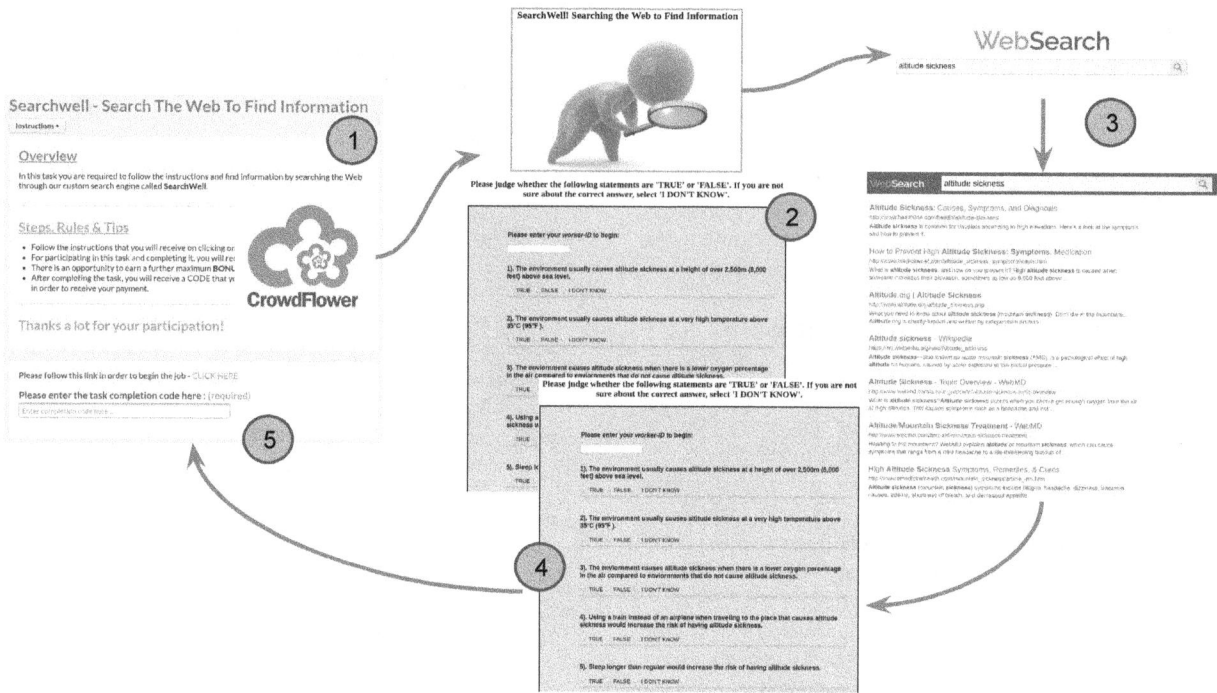

Figure 1: Workflow of participants in the experimental setup orchestrating informational search sessions. (1) Workers are recruited from the CrowdFlower platform, and those willing to participate are redirected to *SearchWell*. (2) Participants are asked to answer a few questions (*knowledge test*) regarding a topic; this is used to calibrate their knowledge before the search session. (3) Participants engage in an informational search session to satisfy a well-defined information need. (4) Participants are asked to complete a post-session test that is identical to the calibration test. (5) Participants receive a completion code, which they enter on CrowdFlower to claim their reward.

created in the following Section 3.2. On completing the knowledge calibration test, workers were presented with their actual task.

Workers were presented an *information need* corresponding to the topic of the calibration test they completed. They were told to use the *SearchWell* platform to search the Web and satisfy their information need. To incentivize workers towards realistic attempts to learn about the topic, we informed them that they will have to complete a final test on the topic to successfully finish the task. Furthermore, workers were conveyed the message that depending on their accuracy on the final test they could earn a bonus payment. We subsequently logged all the activities of the workers (mouse movements, key presses and clicks) within the *SearchWell* platform. Workers were allowed to begin the final test anytime after a search session, which is when a link to the final test was made available. Workers were encouraged to proceed to the next stage only once they felt that their information need was satisfied and when they were ready for the post-session test. On completing the post-session test, workers received a unique code that they could enter on CrowdFlower to claim their reward.

We restricted the participation to workers from English-speaking countries to ensure that they understood the task and instructions adequately [9, 10]. To ensure reliability of the resulting data, we restricted the participation to *Level-3 workers*[2] on CrowdFlower.

---

[2] *Level-3 contributors* on CrowdFlower comprise workers who completed over 100 test questions across hundreds of different types of tasks, and have a near perfect overall accuracy. They are workers of the highest quality on CrowdFlower.

3.2 Topics – Defining Information Needs

We constructed a corpus of topics representing varying scopes of information needs (with some relatively broader than others). Topics were selected randomly from the *TREC 2014 Web Track* dataset[3], and corresponding information needs were defined accordingly. In all cases, the knowledge of users before beginning an informational search session was assessed using pre-tested and evaluated *knowledge tests*. Knowledge tests are scientifically formulated tests that measure the knowledge of a participant on a given topic (for example, the HIV knowledge test [5]).

Knowledge on all given topics was measured using knowledge tests comprising of between 10 and 20 items. The answer options were in all cases 'TRUE', 'FALSE', and 'I DON'T KNOW'. The differences in the number of items reflects our attempt to feature varying scopes of information needs; relatively narrow (e.g., *Carpenter Bees*– 10 items) as well as broad (e.g., *NASA Interplanetary Missions*–20 items). In the construction of all scales, an item pool comprising of more items than finally used was constructed. After a pilot test with 100 distinct participants recruited via CrowdFlower for each of the 10 topics, items that proved to be either too easy (e.g., more than 80% correct answers) or too hard/ambiguous (e.g., more false than true answers) were discarded. Table 1 presents the topics and corresponding information needs considered for orchestrating the informational search sessions. It also shows the internal reliability

---

[3] http://www.trec.nist.gov/act_part/tracks/web/web2014.topics.txt

Table 1: Topics and corresponding information needs presented to participants in the informational search sessions, along with the internal reliability of the corresponding knowledge tests. '$\alpha 1$', '$\alpha 2$' represent Cronbach's α for the pre-session test and post-session test respectively. 'N' is the number of reliable participants after filtering.

Topic	Information Need	$\alpha 1$	$\alpha 2$	N
1. Altitude Sickness	In this task you are required to acquire knowledge about the symptoms, causes and prevention of altitude sickness. (20 items)	0.59	0.79	47
2. American Revolutionary War	In this task, you are required to acquire knowledge about the 'American Revolutionary War'. (10 items)	0.74	0.55	42
3. Carpenter Bees	In this task, you are required to acquire knowledge about the biological species 'carpenter bees'. How do they look? How do they live? (10 items)	0.79	0.58	46
4. Evolution	In this task, you are required to acquire knowledge about the theory of evolution. (12 items)	0.55	0.72	45
5. NASA Interplanetary Missions	In this task, you are required to acquire knowledge about the past, present, and possible future of interplanetary missions that are planned by the NASA. (20 items)	0.80	0.75	42
6. Orcas Island	In this task you are required to acquire knowledge about the Orcas Island. (20 items)	0.91	0.85	39
7. Sangre de Cristo Mountains	In this task, you are required to acquire knowledge about 'Sangre de Cristo' mountain range. (10 items)	0.70	0.52	40
8. Sun Tzu	In this task, you are required to acquire knowledge about the Chinese author Sun Tzu - about his life, his writings, and his influence to the present day. (15 items)	0.81	0.63	37
9. Tornado	In this task, you are required to acquire knowledge about the weather phenomenon that is called 'tornado' (20 items)	0.82	0.62	40
10. USS Cole Bombing	In this task, you are required to acquire knowledge about the 2000 terrorist attack that came to be known as the 'USS Cole bombing'. (10 items)	0.83	0.55	42

(using Cronbach's α) of the pre- and post-session knowledge tests corresponding to each topic. We observe moderate to high values of α in the pre- and post session knowledge tests, suggesting a desirable level of internal consistency.

3.3 Search Environment and Data Collection

We built *SearchWell* on top of the Bing Web Search API. We logged user activity on the platform including mouse movements, clicks, and key presses, using PHP/Javascript and the jQuery library.

To further ensure the reliability of responses and the behavioral data thus produced in the search sessions, we filtered workers using the following criteria.

- Workers who entered no queries in the *SearchWell* system. Since the aim of our work is to further the understanding of how the knowledge state of a user evolves in informational search sessions, we discard those users who did not enter a search query.
- Workers who selected the same option; either 'YES' or 'NO', for all items in the knowledge calibration test or the post-session test.
- Workers who did not complete the post-session test.

We filtered out 80 workers due to the aforementioned criteria, resulting in 420 workers across the 10 topics. The analysis and results presented hereafter are based on these 420 workers alone. For the benefit of further research in this community, the filtered data has been thoroughly anonymized and made publicly available[4]. We henceforth refer to these filtered workers as users in our experimentally orchestrated information search sessions.

4 UNDERSTANDING KNOWLEDGE GAIN

4.1 Measuring Knowledge Gain

We measure the knowledge gain of users in search sessions corresponding to a given information need as the difference between

their knowledge calibration score and the post-session test score[5]. Table 2 presents the average knowledge calibration scores, post-session test scores, and the resulting knowledge gain of users across the search sessions corresponding to different information needs. Across all topics and search sessions, we found that users exhibited an average knowledge gain of nearly 20%. Nearly 70% of all the workers exhibited a knowledge gain, while the remaining workers did not. The standard deviation observed in the knowledge gain of users across all topics is notably high, due to the varying domain knowledge of users. This is evident from the average calibration scores in Table 2. We found that on average, the highest knowledge gain was observed through the search sessions corresponding to the topic, '*Orcas Island*', while the least knowledge gain was observed through those corresponding to the topic, '*Evolution*'. These findings are explored further in the next section.

Table 2: The average knowledge gain of users across the different topics. To enhance readability, the rows have been ordered by ascending knowledge gain *(KG)*.

Topic / Information Need	Avg. Calibration Score *(in %)*	Avg. Post Score *(in %)*	Knowledge Gain *(in %)*
Evolution *(N=45)*	34.07 ± 17.99	48.15 ± 22.49	14.07 ± 18.66
NASA Interplanetary Missions *(N=42)*	38.1 ± 20.53	52.5 ± 17.43	14.40 ± 22.10
Altitude Sickness *(N=47)*	55.88 ± 16.31	70.66 ± 19.11	14.78 ± 17.76
Sangre de Cristo Mountains *(N=40)*	33.25 ± 22.40	49.75 ± 18.10	16.50 ± 22.31
Tornados *(N=40)*	34.44 ± 21.02	53.47 ± 16.28	19.03 ± 22.010
Sun Tzu *(N=37)*	40.54 ± 23.37	60.18 ± 17.15	19.64 ± 21.59
American Revolutionary War *(N=42)*	34.52 ± 25.65	55.95 ± 20.71	21.43 ± 27.31
Carpenter Bees *(N=46)*	45.65 ± 27.08	67.17 ± 20.29	21.52 ± 30.50
USS Cole Bombing *(N=42)*	30.95 ± 25.22	54.37 ± 16.29	23.41 ± 31.30
Orcas Island *(N=39)*	34.74 ± 30.08	65.51 ± 22.04	30.77 ± 30.25
Overall *(N=420)*	38.22 ± 22.96	57.77 ± 18.99	19.56 ± 24.38

---

[4]https://sites.google.com/view/knowledge-gain

[5]We consider the 'I DON'T KNOW' options that were selected, as incorrect responses while computing the knowledge calibration scores and post-session test scores.

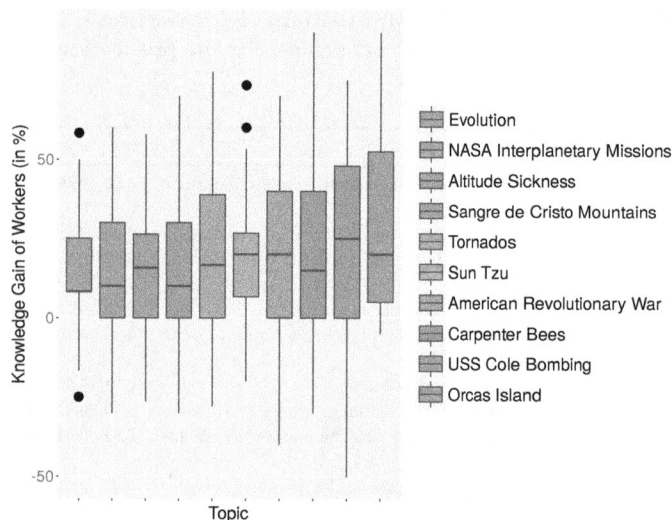

Figure 2: The average knowledge gain of users across the different topics (in ascending order of knowledge gain).

4.2 Topic Familiarity vs. Knowledge Gain

We intuitively reason that users have varying levels of knowledge about a given topic, and their familiarity with the topic influences their behavior in an informational search session [13, 18]. The accuracy of users in a knowledge test corresponding to a topic would therefore be a reflection of their domain knowledge. We build on this notion, and investigate the relationship between the average knowledge gain of users through informational search sessions and their average *topic familiarity*. We compute topic familiarity scores for the different topics, by using the accuracy of users during the creation of knowledge tests. In addition, we argue that the more familiar that a topic appears to be, the less prone users are to selecting the 'I DON'T KNOW' option. Table 3 presents the average topic familiarity scores and the fraction of 'I DON'T KNOW' responses (*%IDK*) corresponding to each topic considered in our experimental setup.

Table 3: The average knowledge gain of users in comparison to the topic familiarity, and the percentage of 'I DON'T KNOW' (IDK) responses to questions in the knowledge test.

Topic/Information Need	Knowledge Gain	Familiarity	% IDK
Altitude Sickness	14.78	52.49	28.67
American Revolutionary War	21.43	40.77	43.57
Carpenter Bees	21.52	42.18	33.57
Evolution	14.07	48.28	31.41
NASA Interplanetary Missions	14.40	51.91	38.61
Orcas Island	30.77	34.69	50.17
Sangre de Cristo Mountains	16.50	44.41	42.15
Sun Tzu	19.64	50.38	40.00
Tornados	19.03	46.2	33.65
USS Cole Bombing	23.41	39.93	48.47

We thereby investigated the relationship between knowledge gain and topic familiarity, along with the %IDK. Using Pearson's

correlation coefficient, we found a strongly negative linear relationship between the knowledge gain of users in informational search sessions and the topic familiarity; $R = -.87, R^2 = .78, p < .001$. This suggests that the more popular a topic is, or the more familiar that users are with a topic, the lesser they tend to learn about the topic in informational search sessions. Thus, we found that 78% of the variance in the knowledge gain of users can be explained by the topic familiarity. This is further corroborated by the moderately positive linear relationship we found between the knowledge gain of users and the fraction of *IDK* responses in the knowledge test; $R = .72, R^2 = .54, p < .05$. An intuitive explanation for this observation is that the lesser a user knows about a topic, the more there is to learn through an informational search session, increasing the scope for knowledge to be gained.

We conducted a one-way between users ANOVA to investigate the effect of topics on the knowledge gain of users. Our findings revealed a lack of significant effect of topics on the knowledge gain of users across the 10 topic conditions.

4.3 User Queries and Click Behavior

4.3.1 User Queries. We found that on average users collectively fired 92 distinct queries across the different topics, and corresponding to the different information needs in each search session. Table 4 presents our findings pertaining to user queries. We note that on average users entered at least 2 distinct queries in a search session, with an average query length of just over 4 terms. Users employed a minimum of 6 unique terms in their queries on average. We conducted a one-way ANOVA to investigate the effect of topic on the number of queries fired by users. We found a significant difference in the number of queries entered by users across the 10 topical conditions at the $p < .001$ level; $F(9, 419) = 3.941$. Post-hoc comparisons using the Tukey-HSD test revealed significant differences in the number of queries entered by users at the $p < .001$ level corresponding to the topic '*NASA Interplanetary Missions*' in comparison to each of '*Altitude Sickness*', '*American Revolutionary War*', '*Carpenter Bees*' and '*USS Cole Bombing*'. Similarly, significant differences were revealed at the $p < .05$ level corresponding to the topic '*NASA Interplanetary Missions*' in comparison to '*Sangre de Cristo Mountains*', and '*American Revolutionary War*' in comparison to '*Evolution*'. On investigating the relationship between the number of queries entered by users and the knowledge gain through a search session, we did not find any significant linear relationship using Pearson's **R**. This suggests that although the information need in a search session influences the number of queries entered by users, there is no measurable effect of the number of queries on the knowledge gain of users.

To analyze the effect of the topics on the number of unique query terms entered by users, we conducted a one-way between users ANOVA. We found a significant difference in the number of unique terms used by users across the 10 topic conditions at the $p < .001$ level; $F(9, 419) = 5.44$. Post-hoc comparisons using the Tukey-HSD test revealed a significant difference in the number of unique terms entered by users corresponding to the topic, '*NASA Interplanetary Missions*' in comparison to each of the other topics except '*Evolution*' and '*Sun Tzu*' at the $p < .001$ level. We did not find a significant linear relationship between the number of unique

Table 4: Queries fired by users in informational search sessions corresponding to different topics. Note that the query length is measured in 'terms'. For readability, the rows have been ordered by an increasing knowledge gain (KG).

Topic/Information Need	KG (in %)	# Distinct Queries (DQ)	DQ Per User	Query Length	# Unique Terms (UT)	UT Per User
Evolution	14.07	140	3.11 ± 2.93	5.62 ± 2.69	437	4.70 ± 1.89
NASA Interplanetary Missions	14.40	160	3.81 ± 4.17	3.58 ± 1.55	671	4.33 ± 3.60
Altitude Sickness	14.78	80	1.70 ± 1.24	4.29 ± 2.56	221	3.57 ± 1.88
Sangre de Cristo Mountains	16.50	72	1.80 ± 1.49	4.31 ± 2.70	238	4.21 ± 2.78
Tornados	19.03	90	2.25 ± 3.68	4.41 ± 2.59	150	9.71 ± 14.81
Sun Tzu	19.64	85	2.30 ± 2.70	8.15 ± 5.52	320	15.98 ± 25.75
American Revolutionary War	21.43	59	1.40 ± 0.76	2.36 ± 0.91	182	3.69 ± 3.73
Carpenter Bees	21.52	75	1.63 ± 1.05	4.74 ± 2.15	164	5.95 ± 5.31
USS Cole Bombing	23.41	71	1.69 ± 1.03	6.25 ± 3.80	177	8.65 ± 11.56
Orcas Island	30.77	91	2.33 ± 2.80	1.93 ± 1.84	144	3.75 ± 10.74
Overall	19.56	92.30	2.20 ± 2.18	4.56 ± 2.63	270.40	6.45 ± 8.20

query terms entered by users and their knowledge gain in search sessions, using Pearson's **R**.

Table 5: A comparison of the first and last query lengths (QL), number of unique terms (UT) in the first and last query entered by users within search sessions.

Topic/Information Need	First QL	Last QL	First UT	Last UT
Altitude Sickness	4.25 ± 2.38	4.38 ± 2.32	3.50 ± 1.58	3.56 ± 1.62
American Revolutionary War	4.73 ± 2.05	5.18 ± 2.37	4.09 ± 1.38	4.55 ± 1.97
Carpenter Bees	5.12 ± 3.29	5.29 ± 2.84	3.59 ± 1.82	3.65 ± 1.64
Evolution	3.00 ± 1.80	5.65 ± 4.75	2.46 ± 1.87	4.15 ± 3.17
NASA Interplanetary Missions	6.96 ± 5.96	6.92 ± 5.16	4.24 ± 3.20	4.80 ± 3.05
Orcas Island	2.58 ± 1.26	3.08 ± 2.06	2.58 ± 1.26	2.83 ± 1.40
Sangre de Cristo Mountains	4.15 ± 1.03	4.08 ± 1.44	4.15 ± 1.03	3.92 ± 1.27
Sun Tzu	6.88 ± 5.86	7.75 ± 6.77	4.31 ± 2.54	4.69 ± 2.89
Tornados	2.30 ± 1.68	3.60 ± 2.33	2.10 ± 1.30	2.90 ± 1.30
USS Cole Bombing	5.29 ± 4.16	5.18 ± 4.15	4.35 ± 3.32	4.41 ± 3.34
Overall	4.53 ± 2.95	5.11 ± 3.42	3.54 ± 1.93	3.95 ± 2.17

4.3.2 Evolution of Query Terms and Lengths.
We investigated how queries from users evolved within a search session corresponding to a given information need. Table 5 presents our findings, considering only those users who entered 2 or more queries in a particular search session. We note that on average across all the topics, the last query entered by users is longer (5.11 terms) than the first query (4.53 terms) entered in the session.

We also note that on average, the number of unique terms in the last query is greater than the number of unique terms entered by users in their first query. A two-tailed T-test revealed that this difference is statistically significant; $t(413) = 3.99, p < .05$. This suggests that as the users consume more information through the course of a search session related to a given topic, their queries tend to become longer.

4.3.3 User Clicks.
We analyzed the clicks of users on results corresponding to each of the queries they entered within search sessions. Table 6 presents our findings with respect to the average number of clicks per user, clicks per query, the average rank of the results that were clicked, and the average interval of time between two consecutive clicks on search results. We note that users clicked on just over 2 search results on average, and on at least 1 result per query on average. In line with prior works that analyzed user behavior with search results [1, 11], we found that users in

the informational search sessions orchestrated in our experiments, typically clicked on top-ranked results (with an average rank of 2.18). The average interval between two clicks by a user in a search session was found to be 0.69 minutes. On investigating the linear relationship between the click interval and knowledge gain of users, we found no significant correlation.

Table 6: The average number of clicks per user, clicks per query, the average rank of the results clicked by users, and the average interval between two consecutive clicks on the search results (in mins) across different topics.

Topic / Information Need	#Clicks Per User	#Clicks Per Query	Rank of Result Clicked	Click Interval
Altitude Sickness	2.49 ± 1.38	1.88 ± 1.36	2.96 ± 2.30	1.32 ± 1.84
American Revolutionary War	2.05 ± 1.59	1.64 ± 1.41	1.84 ± 2.15	0.94 ± 1.58
Carpenter Bees	1.80 ± 1.44	1.32 ± 1.09	1.78 ± 1.53	0.49 ± 0.94
Evolution	3.36 ± 2.84	1.61 ± 1.45	2.66 ± 2.04	0.33 ± 0.69
NASA Interplanetary Missions	2.90 ± 2.09	1.44 ± 1.38	2.64 ± 2.40	0.49 ± 0.72
Orcas Island	2.03 ± 1.94	1.35 ± 1.08	3.17 ± 2.17	0.58 ± 1.01
Sangre de Cristo Mountains	2.38 ± 2.23	1.76 ± 2.11	1.66 ± 1.14	1.14 ± 1.97
Sun Tzu	2.19 ± 1.74	1.37 ± 0.92	1.90 ± 1.28	0.64 ± 1.09
Tornados	1.83 ± 1.50	1.43 ± 1.42	1.65 ± 1.11	0.79 ± 1.28
USS Cole Bombing	1.81 ± 1.47	1.37 ± 1.23	1.52 ± 1.04	0.20 ± 0.50
Overall	2.28 ± 1.82	1.52 ± 1.34	2.18 ± 1.72	0.69 ± 1.16

4.4 Session Duration and Browsing Behavior

4.4.1 Session Length.
We analyzed the session lengths[6] of users and their browsing behavior in informational search sessions corresponding to the different topics. Our findings are summarized in Tables 7 and 8. We found that the average session length of users across the different topics was nearly 5 mins long. To understand the effect of the 10 topics considered on the session length exhibited by users, we conducted a one-way ANOVA. Results revealed no significant effect of the topics on the session length. We also analyzed the relationship between the session length of users and the knowledge gain using Pearson's **R**. We did not find a significant linear relationship between these variables, suggesting that length of a session does not directly influence the knowledge gain of users.

---

[6]For a given topic and user, we measured the session length as the time from which the first query was entered in *SearchWell* by the user after the calibration test, until the time at which the last web page accessed by the user was active before the post-session test. Note that users were allowed to carry out only one search session.

Table 7: The average session lengths (*SL*) of users across different topics, the session length per query, the number of web pages navigated to from the results page (*#Pages Navigated*), the number of web pages navigated to per query entered, and the active time spent on a web page.

Topic / Information Need	Session Length (*SL*) (in mins)	SL Per Query (in mins)	#Pages Navigated	#Pages Per Query	Active Time Per Page (in mins)
Altitude Sickness	4.75 ± 3.48	3.45 ± 2.91	4.74 ± 2.18	3.46 ± 1.93	2.27 ± 1.57
American Revolutionary War	3.88 ± 2.86	3.02 ± 2.22	4.31 ± 1.64	3.36 ± 1.10	2.06 ± 1.37
Carpenter Bees	3.30 ± 2.67	2.19 ± 1.58	4.57 ± 2.13	3.20 ± 1.39	1.72 ± 1.42
USS Cole Bombing	3.96 ± 3.62	2.88 ± 2.98	4.31 ± 2.02	3.03 ± 1.40	1.72 ± 1.24
Evolution	6.79 ± 9.28	2.55 ± 3.12	7.04 ± 5.56	2.87 ± 1.38	1.86 ± 1.29
NASA Interplanetary Missions	6.64 ± 5.68	2.41 ± 2.89	7.79 ± 5.62	2.92 ± 1.79	2.22 ± 1.79
Orcas Island	6.52 ± 12.79	3.30 ± 3.14	5.67 ± 4.66	3.50 ± 2.06	2.25 ± 2.08
Sangre de Cristo Mountains	4.91 ± 4.35	3.29 ± 3.16	5.78 ± 3.37	3.93 ± 2.24	1.90 ± 1.51
Sun Tzu	3.87 ± 4.11	1.99 ± 1.61	5.22 ± 3.19	2.98 ± 1.06	1.82 ± 1.59
Tornados	3.57 ± 3.20	2.64 ± 2.87	5.15 ± 3.71	3.43 ± 1.63	1.85 ± 1.30
Overall	4.82 ± 5.20	2.78 ± 2.65	5.46 ± 3.41	3.27 ± 1.60	1.97 ± 1.52

4.4.2 Navigation. During the search sessions corresponding to the different topics, users navigated to over 5 web pages on average (as shown in Table 8). To understand the effect of the 10 different topics on the navigation behavior of users, we conducted a one-way between users ANOVA. Results confirmed a significant difference in the number of pages users navigated to across the 10 different topic conditions at the $p < .001$ level; $F(9, 419) = 9.154$. Post-hoc comparisons using the Tukey-HSD test revealed that the number of web pages navigated to by users in the search sessions corresponding to the topic of '*Evolution*' was significantly different in comparison to all other topics at the $p < .001$ level. In addition, the number of web pages navigated by users in the search sessions corresponding to the topic of '*NASA Interplanetary Missions*' was found to be significantly more than those pertaining to the topic of '*Altitude Sickness*'. We did not find a significant linear relationship between the number of web pages that users navigated to, and their knowledge gain.

For each query that was entered, users navigated to over 3 web pages on average. We conducted a one-way between users ANOVA to compare the effect of topics on the number of web pages navigated by users across the 10 topic conditions. We found no significant effect of such navigation behavior on the knowledge gain. We also found no significant linear relationship between these two variables using Pearson's **R**.

Next, we investigated the amount of time users actively spent on each web page that they navigated to. We found that on average users spent almost 2 minutes per page. We compared the effect of the topics on the average amount of time that users spent on web pages across the 10 different topic conditions using a one-way between users ANOVA. We found no significant effect across the topic conditions. Using Pearson's **R**, we found a weak positive linear relationship between the amount of active time users spent on web pages and their knowledge gain; **R**= .27, $R^2 = .07, p < .001$. This suggests that the amount of time that users spend actively on web pages within the search session describes around 7% of the variance in their knowledge gain.

4.4.3 Domains and Search Engine Results Pages. We analyzed the pay-level domains (PLDs) of search engine results pages (SERPs) consumed by users during the informational search sessions. PLDs are sub-domains of a public top-level domain, that are acquired by paying for them. PLDs typically indicate that individual user(s) or

organization(s) are likely to be in control. For instance, the PLD for `www.example.com` would be `example.com`. We note that on average, users navigated to 1.64 PLDs from the search results page. To compare the effect of topics on the number of PLDs accessed by users, we conducted a one-way between users ANOVA. We found that there was a significant effect of topics on the number of PLDs accessed by users at the $p < .05$ level; $F(9, 419) = 9.154$. Post-hoc comparisons with the Tukey-HSD test revealed that the users navigated to more PLDs during the search sessions corresponding to the topic of '*Evolution*', when compared to topics '*American Revolutionary War*', '*Carpenter Bees*' at the $p < .05$ level, and '*NASA Interplanetary Missions*' at the $p < .01$ level. However, we did not find a significant linear relationship between the knowledge gain of users and the number of PLDs accessed by them during the informational search sessions.

Next, we investigated the amount of time that users spent on the SERPs. We differentiate between the time users actively spent exploring the snippets on the search results page, and the total amount of time spent including the idle time. We found no significant effect of the topics on the total amount of time that users spent on the search results page on average. We found that users spent almost 40 seconds actively on the search results page on average across all topics. To compare the effect of the topics on the amount of active time spent on the SERP by users, we conducted a one-way between users ANOVA. We found that there was a significant effect of topics on the amount of active time spent by users on the search results page at the $p < .001$ level; $F(9, 419) = 4.066$. Post-hoc comparisons with the Tukey-HSD test revealed that users spent more active time on the results page in search sessions corresponding to the topic of '*NASA Interplanetary Missions*' in comparison to that spent in the topics, '*American Revolutionary War*', '*Carpenter Bees*', '*Sangre de Cristo Mountains*', '*Tornados*', and '*USS Cole Bombing*' at the $p < .01$ level. Similarly, we found that users spent more active time on the SERP in search sessions corresponding to the topic of '*Evolution*' in comparison to '*Sangre de Cristo Mountains*', '*Tornados*', and '*USS Cole Bombing*' at the $p < .05$ level. We did not find a significant linear relationship between the knowledge gain of users and the active time spent on the results page.

We also analyzed the number of web pages that users navigated to directly from the SERP and those that users navigated to from other web pages. We found that the users navigated to nearly 2

Table 8: The average number of pay-level domains (#PLDs) accessed by users during the search session, the amount of time spent on the search engine results page (SERP), the amount of time active on the results page, and the number of pages navigated to from the results page, and other subsequent pages (non-SERPs).

Topic / Information Need	#PLDs	Time Spent on SERP (in mins)	Time Active on SERP (in mins)	#Pages from SERP	#Pages from Non-SERPs
Altitude Sickness	1.89 ± 1.17	9.95 ± 5.75	0.60 ± 0.44	2.11 ± 1.37	0.06 ± 0.32
American Revolutionary War	1.45 ± 0.93	7.92 ± 4.55	0.53 ± 0.44	1.62 ± 1.09	0.10 ± 0.37
Carpenter Bees	1.50 ± 1.12	7.89 ± 4.68	0.55 ± 0.51	1.52 ± 1.12	0.15 ± 0.42
Evolution	2.31 ± 1.74	10.34 ± 7.85	0.91 ± 0.65	2.67 ± 2.57	0.04 ± 0.21
NASA Interplanetary Missions	1.60 ± 1.20	10.43 ± 6.63	0.94 ± 0.97	2.17 ± 1.99	1.05 ± 3.43
Orcas Island	1.51 ± 1.32	11.08 ± 16.20	0.69 ± 0.58	1.92 ± 2.04	0.33 ± 0.69
Sangre de Cristo Mountains	1.58 ± 1.07	8.80 ± 5.00	0.51 ± 0.44	2.28 ± 1.82	0.48 ± 0.74
Sun Tzu	1.73 ± 1.39	8.82 ± 5.43	0.61 ± 0.57	1.89 ± 1.57	0.19 ± 0.46
Tornados	1.50 ± 0.89	7.89 ± 5.19	0.43 ± 0.45	1.68 ± 1.15	0.23 ± 0.61
USS Cole Bombing	1.33 ± 0.81	7.53 ± 4.22	0.46 ± 0.30	1.40 ± 0.87	0.17 ± 0.43
Overall	1.64 ± 1.16	9.06 ± 6.55	0.62 ± 0.53	1.93 ± 1.56	0.28 ± 0.77

web pages from the search results page on average across all topics, while the navigation from a non-results page was less frequent with an average of 0.28 across all topics. To compare the effect of topics on the number of pages navigated to from SERPs and non-SERPs, we conducted between users one-way ANOVAs across the 10 different topic conditions. Results confirmed a significant effect of topics on the number of pages navigated to from the search results page in search sessions at the $p < .05$ level; $F(9, 419) = 2.375$. Post-hoc comparisons with the Tukey-HSD test revealed that users in search sessions corresponding to the '*Evolution*' topic navigated to significantly more pages originating from the search results page when compared to that pertaining to the topics of '*Carpenter Bees*' and '*USS Cole Bombing*'. We also found a significant effect of topics on the number of web pages users navigated to from non-SERPs at the $p < .01$ level; $F(9, 419) = 2.662$. Post-hoc comparisons with the Tukey-HSD test revealed that users in search sessions corresponding to the topic '*NASA Interplanetary Missions*' navigated to significantly more web pages from non-SERPs in comparison to all other topics except '*Orcas Island*' and '*Sangre de Cristo Mountains*' at the $p < .05$ level. This suggests that the nature of topics effects how users navigate from the search results page. Using Pearson's **R** we found no significant linear relationship between the knowledge gain of users and the number of pages navigated from either search result pages or non-SERPs.

4.4.4 PLDs Across Topics. We analyzed the most frequently accessed PLDs during search sessions corresponding to different topics. We found that wikipedia.org was the most accessed PLD, accounting for 47.5% of PLDs accessed across all topics. This was followed by nasa.gov (6.6%) and healthline.com (3.3%). The most number of distinct PLDs accessed by users corresponded to the topic of '*Evolution*', followed by '*Altitude Sickness*' and '*Sun Tzu*'.

4.5 Query Formulation

4.5.1 Query Overlap with Topic Description and Knowledge Tests. We investigated the nature of queries fired by users in the search sessions corresponding to different information needs. First, we analyzed the overlap in the query terms with the terms in the topic description, as well as the questions in the knowledge test. Since users consumed this information prior to beginning the search session, we were interested in analyzing the fraction of query terms

that go beyond the terms in the topic description and knowledge tests. Our findings are presented in Table 9. We note that on average across all topics, almost 11% of the query terms entered by users did not overlap with the topic description or the knowledge tests. Around 55% of the query terms were present in the topic descriptions and nearly 82% overlapped with terms in the knowledge tests on average across all topics. This is understandable, considering that the pre-session calibration test also served as a guide for kindling a realistic information need among the users.

Using Pearson's **R**, we also found a positive linear relationship between the knowledge gain of users and the percentage of query terms fired by them that did not overlap with terms in either the topic description or the knowledge tests; $R = .41, R^2 = .17, p < .001$. This suggests that the nature of the query terms that users enter in the search sessions (in terms of overlap with topic descriptions or knowledge tests) can explain around 17% of the variance in their knowledge gain.

Table 9: Percentage of query terms (%QT) that are distinct with respect to the terms in the topic description TD and knowledge tests KT, and the average query complexity corresponding to the different information needs.

Topic / Information Need	%QT not in TD −(1)	%QT not in KT −(2)	%QT not in (1) or (2)	Query Complexity
Altitude Sickness	9.83	19.23	4.70	19.17
American Revolutionary War	26.19	22.22	22.22	18.12
Carpenter Bees	41.44	28.18	22.65	22.00
Evolution	69.44	11.11	11.11	20.32
NASA Interplanetary Missions	71.11	22.91	5.47	19.95
Orcas Island	31.31	12.62	12.62	22.17
Sangre de Cristo Mountains	68.97	6.90	6.90	19.50
Sun Tzu	56.06	37.29	11.88	20.06
Tornados	55.81	9.30	2.33	19.18
USS Cole Bombing	16.83	10.89	9.90	19.26
Overall	44.70 ± 22.79	18.06 ± 9.69	10.98 ± 6.90	19.97 ± 1.27

4.5.2 Query Complexity. We also analyzed the complexity of the queries fired by users in search sessions corresponding to the different topics. We computed query complexity using the method motivated by Eickhoff et al. [8]. We rely on a listing of over 30,000 English words along with the age at which native speakers typically learn the term compiled by Kuperman et al. [17]. The higher this score, the harder and more specialized a term is assumed to be. We assume the maximum age of acquisition across all query terms as a measure of the query complexity. Table 9 presents the average complexity of the queries entered by users in search sessions corresponding to the different topics. Using Pearson's **R**, we found a positive linear relationship between the knowledge gain of users and their corresponding average query complexity; $\mathbf{R} = .50, R^2 = .25, p < .001$. This suggests that the complexity of queries entered by users during the informational search sessions in our setup, explains 25% of the variance in their knowledge gain.

4.5.3   Evolution of Queries Within Search Sessions. Next, we analyzed the overall evolution of queries entered by users with the search sessions across all topics. Figure 3a presents the number of queries entered by users across all topics corresponding to the query rank. We refer to the sequence number of the query entered by each user in a search session as the *query rank*. For example, a query rank of 5 implies the 5th query that is entered in a given search session by a given user. We observe a power-law distribution, indicating many users fire only a few queries within a search session and that a few users fire many queries.

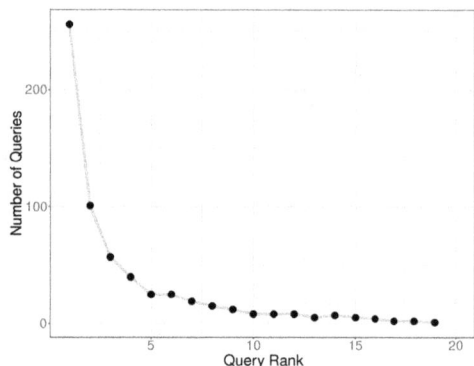

(a) **Number of queries fired by users at a given rank across all topics within search sessions.**

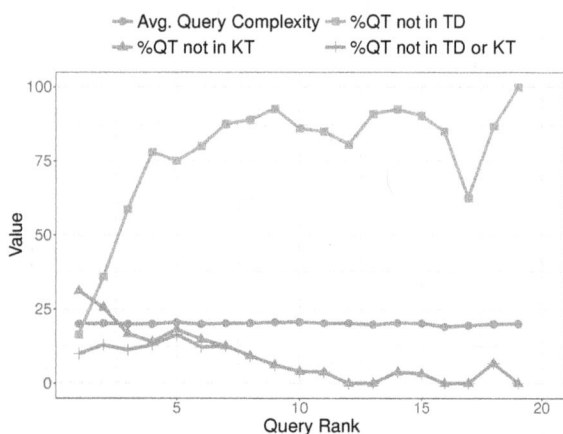

(b) **Evolution of the average query complexity, and overlap of query terms (%QT) with terms in the task description (TD) and knowledge tests (KT) across all topics within search sessions.**

Figure 3: Overall evolution of queries across all topics.

Interestingly, we found that the average complexity of the queries entered by users within the search sessions does not fluctuate significantly over time, with an average query complexity of 20.08 ± 0.38 across the query ranks. We also analyzed the evolution in the overlap of query terms with terms in the task description and knowledge tests corresponding to all topics. As shown in Figure 3b, we found that the overlap of query terms with terms from the topic descriptions decreases with an increasing query rank. Using Pearson's **R**, we found a moderately strong positive linear relationship between the query rank and the *%QT not in TD*; $\mathbf{R} = .63, R^2 = .40, p < .01$. This suggests that 40% of the variance in query term overlap with the terms in the topic description can be explained by the query rank. At the same time, we found that with an increase in query rank the overlap of query terms with terms from the corresponding knowledge tests also increases. This was confirmed by a strong negative linear relationship between the query rank and *%QT not in KT*; $\mathbf{R} = -.87, R^2 = .76, p < .001$, suggesting that over 76% of the variance in the query term overlap with terms in the knowledge tests can be explained by the query rank. The overall trend in the overlap of query terms with terms from either the corresponding task descriptions or knowledge tests *TD or KT* was similarly found to exhibit a strong negative linear relationship; $\mathbf{R} = -.82, R^2 = .68, p < .001$.

Our findings indicate that to formulate their queries through the course of the search sessions, users on average used a decreasing number of terms from the information need presented to them, and an increasing number of terms from the pre-session calibration test they completed.

5   DISCUSSION

5.1   Main Findings

- Through our experimental results, we found that users depicted a higher knowledge gain in informational search sessions corresponding to those topics that are generally less popular[7], resulting in users having a relatively lesser overall *topic familiarity* with the information need. We intuitively reason that the more a user already knows about a given topic, the lesser he/she tends to learn through a search session on the Web.
- We found evidence which affirms that the information need in a search session influences the number of queries entered, the number of pages consumed, and the number of different PLDs accessed by users. However, these factors did not affect the knowledge gain of users through the search session.
- Users navigated to more pages from a search engine result page (SERP) in comparison to non-SERPs. We also found a significant effect of topics on navigation patterns of users; users navigated to more pages from SERPs corresponding to some topics more than they did in case of others. This however, did not have an effect on their knowledge gain.
- We found that the last queries entered in search sessions are significantly longer than the first queries, with more unique terms in the last queries than in the first. This indicates that the knowledge gained through the course of the search session, allows a user to formulate such richer queries.

---

[7]This was estimated by the overall accuracy of 100 distinct responses from crowd workers during the knowledge test formulation for each topic.

We also found that the average complexity of queries entered by users in search sessions is positively correlated to their knowledge gain, such that 25% of the variance in their knowledge gain can be explained by their average query complexity. The amount of active time that users spent on web pages also correlated positively with their knowledge gain, such that the amount of time users spent actively on web pages described around 7% of the variance in their knowledge gain.

- In line with prior works that studied user interaction with search results, we found that workers typically clicked and consumed top-ranked results on the SERP (with an average rank of 2.18).

5.2 Caveats and Limitations

We observed that during the informational search sessions, users enter queries using terms they encountered in the knowledge tests. Although the main purpose of the pre-session tests was to calibrate the knowledge of the users, we also reasoned that the items in the knowledge test could steer users towards the diverse facets of the information need and help shaping realistic search session scenarios. This was confirmed by our findings in Section 4.5.3, where we found that users tend to employ an increasing number of terms from the pre-session calibration test in their queries, through the course of a search session.

We have considered an arguably small set of topics and corresponding information needs for our experiments in this work. However, it is noticeably challenging to create reliable knowledge tests corresponding to each topic in a manner that allows us to measure the knowledge gain of users through search sessions. Nevertheless, we have gathered a substantial amount of data from various search sessions spanning 420 reliable users across 10 topics and representing diverse information needs.

We did not find any impact of the available user demographics on knowledge gain of users across the topics. To control for Type-I error inflation in our multiple comparisons, we used the Holm-Bonferroni correction for family-wise error rate (FWER) [15], at the significance level of $\alpha < .05$.

6 CONCLUSIONS AND FUTURE WORK

In this paper, we presented a study that investigates user knowledge gain through informational search sessions. We quantified the knowledge gain of users by calibrating their knowledge before they began a search session corresponding to a topic, and by assessing their knowledge after the session. We found a significant effect of information need on user queries and navigational patterns, but no direct effect on the knowledge gain. Users exhibited a higher knowledge gain through search sessions pertaining to topics they were less familiar with. Users who spent more active time on web pages depicted a higher knowledge gain. We also found a positive correlation between the average complexity of queries entered by users and their knowledge gain. Our findings revealed deeper insights into the search behavior of users in informational search sessions, and the impact of information needs on knowledge gain.

Based on our work in this paper, we aim to propose a supervised machine learning model in the imminent future, that can predict the knowledge state of a user in an informational search session and measure the knowledge gain through the course of a session. Being able to automatically detect when and how a user acquires new knowledge through web search will be an important step forward, as we move towards building search engines that can serve learning outcomes optimally.

REFERENCES

[1] E. Agichtein, E. Brill, S. Dumais, and R. Ragno. Learning user interaction models for predicting web search result preferences. In *Proceedings of the 29th annual international ACM SIGIR conference on Research and development in information retrieval*, pages 3–10. ACM, 2006.

[2] L. W. Anderson, D. R. Krathwohl, P. Airasian, K. Cruikshank, R. Mayer, P. Pintrich, J. Raths, and M. Wittrock. A taxonomy for learning, teaching and assessing: A revision of bloom's taxonomy. *New York. Longman Publishing. Artz, AF, & Armour-Thomas, E.(1992). Development of a cognitive-metacognitive framework for protocol analysis of mathematical problem solving in small groups. Cognition and Instruction*, 9(2):137–175, 2001.

[3] J. Arguello. Predicting search task difficulty. In *ECIR*, volume 14, pages 88–99, 2014.

[4] A. Broder. A taxonomy of web search. In *ACM Sigir forum*, volume 36, pages 3–10. ACM, 2002.

[5] M. P. Carey, D. Morrison-Beedy, and B. T. Johnson. The hiv-knowledge questionnaire: Development and evaluation of a reliable, valid, and practical self-administered questionnaire. *AIDS and Behavior*, 1(1):61–74, 1997.

[6] M. J. Cole, J. Gwizdka, C. Liu, N. J. Belkin, and X. Zhang. Inferring user knowledge level from eye movement patterns. *Information Processing & Management*, 49(5):1075–1091, 2013.

[7] K. Collins-Thompson, S. Y. Rieh, C. C. Haynes, and R. Syed. Assessing learning outcomes in web search: A comparison of tasks and query strategies. In *Proceedings of the 2016 ACM on Conference on Human Information Interaction and Retrieval*, pages 163–172. ACM, 2016.

[8] C. Eickhoff, J. Teevan, R. White, and S. Dumais. Lessons from the journey: a query log analysis of within-session learning. In *Proceedings of the 7th ACM International Conference on Web Search & Data Mining*. ACM, 2014.

[9] U. Gadiraju, R. Kawase, S. Dietze, and G. Demartini. Understanding malicious behavior in crowdsourcing platforms: The case of online surveys. In *Proceedings of the 33rd Annual ACM CHI Conference*, pages 1631–1640. ACM, 2015.

[10] U. Gadiraju, J. Yang, and A. Bozzon. Clarity is a worthwhile quality–on the role of task clarity in microtask crowdsourcing. In *Proceedings of the 28th ACM Conference on Hypertext and Social Media*, pages 5–14. ACM, 2017.

[11] L. A. Granka, T. Joachims, and G. Gay. Eye-tracking analysis of user behavior in www search. In *Proceedings of the 27th annual international ACM SIGIR conference on Research and development in information retrieval*, pages 478–479. ACM, 2004.

[12] J. Gwizdka and X. Chen. Towards observable indicators of learning on search. In *SAL@ SIGIR*, 2016.

[13] J. Gwizdka and I. Spence. What can searching behavior tell us about the difficulty of information tasks? a study of web navigation. *Proceedings of the Association for Information Science and Technology*, 43(1):1–22, 2006.

[14] M. Hagen, M. Potthast, M. Völske, J. Gomoll, and B. Stein. How writers search: Analyzing the search and writing logs of non-fictional essays. In *Proceedings of the 2016 ACM on Conference on Human Information Interaction and Retrieval*, pages 193–202. ACM, 2016.

[15] S. Holm. A simple sequentially rejective multiple test procedure. *Scandinavian journal of statistics*, pages 65–70, 1979.

[16] B. J. Jansen, D. Booth, and B. Smith. Using the taxonomy of cognitive learning to model online searching. *Information Processing & Management*, 45(6):643–663, 2009.

[17] V. Kuperman, H. Stadthagen-Gonzalez, and M. Brysbaert. Age-of-acquisition ratings for 30,000 english words. *Behavior Research Methods*, 44(4):978–990, 2012.

[18] Y. Li and N. J. Belkin. A faceted approach to conceptualizing tasks in information seeking. *Information Processing & Management*, 44(6):1822–1837, 2008.

[19] R. Syed and K. Collins-Thompson. Retrieval algorithms optimized for human learning. In *Proceedings of the 40th International ACM SIGIR Conference on Research and Development in Information Retrieval*, pages 555–564. ACM, 2017.

[20] P. Vakkari. Searching as learning: A systematization based on literature. *Journal of Information Science*, 42(1):7–18, 2016.

[21] R. W. White, S. T. Dumais, and J. Teevan. Characterizing the influence of domain expertise on web search behavior. In *Proceedings of the second ACM international conference on web search and data mining*, pages 132–141. ACM, 2009.

[22] W.-C. Wu, D. Kelly, A. Edwards, and J. Arguello. Grannies, tanning beds, tattoos and nascar: Evaluation of search tasks with varying levels of cognitive complexity. In *Proceedings of the 4th Information Interaction in Context Symposium*, pages 254–257. ACM, 2012.

[23] X. Zhang, M. Cole, and N. Belkin. Predicting users' domain knowledge from search behaviors. In *Proceedings of the 34th international ACM SIGIR Conference*, pages 1225–1226. ACM, 2011.

Query Priming for Promoting Critical Thinking in Web Search

Yusuke Yamamoto
Shizuoka University
Hamamatsu, Japan
yamamoto@inf.shizuoka.ac.jp

Takehiro Yamamoto
Kyoto University
Kyoto, Japan
tyamamot@dl.kuis.kyoto-u.ac.jp

ABSTRACT

We propose *query priming* to activate careful user information seeking in web searches. Query priming employs query auto-completion (QAC) and query suggestion (QS) to present search terms that stimulate critical thinking and encourages careful information seeking and decision making.

We conducted an online user study using a crowdsourcing service. Analysis of search behavior logs and questionnaire responses confirmed the following. (1) With query priming, participants issued more queries and (re-)visited search engine result pages more frequently. (2) Query priming promoted webpage selection targeted at evidence-based decision making. (3) The query priming effect varied relative to participant educational background.

This study contributes to search interaction design to enhance user engagement in critical thinking in web searches.

CCS CONCEPTS

• **Information systems** → *Search interfaces*; • **Human-centered computing** → *User studies*;

KEYWORDS

Web search, critical thinking, priming effect, human factor

ACM Reference Format:
Yusuke Yamamoto and Takehiro Yamamoto. 2018. Query Priming for Promoting Critical Thinking in Web Search. In *CHIIR '18: 2018 Conference on Human Information Interaction & Retrieval, March 11–15, 2018, New Brunswick, NJ, USA.* ACM, New York, NY, USA, 10 pages. https://doi.org/10.1145/3176349.3176377

1 INTRODUCTION

The web is an important source of information; however, lack of credibility, e.g., fake news disseminated on social networks, is a serious problem. Nevertheless, studies have found that people frequently do not consider the of web information [16, 17]. Therefore, creating information access environments that help people obtain credible information and make effective decisions is important.

Various search support systems have been proposed, such as evidence search systems [13], dispute suggestion systems [7, 22], and systems that visualize credibility-related scores [23]. However,

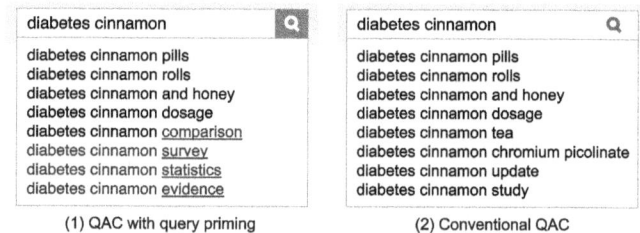

Figure 1: Comparison of QAC with query priming and conventional QAC (prime terms are underlined in this paper so that readers can identify them as manipulated)

such systems are only useful if users understand their purpose and appropriate use. We propose *query priming* whereby terms that promote careful information seeking and effective decision making are suggested. The proposed query priming is based on the priming effect in cognitive science. In cognitive science, the priming effect refers to a stimulus (hereafter *prime*) that activates a mental concept and influences subsequent behaviors [11]. A well-known example of the priming effect is the Florida effect experiment [3]. The experiment involved two groups of students. One group was asked to construct short sentences using words associated with older people, e.g., *worried, Florida, old, gray,* and *wrinkle.* Then, the researchers measured the students' walking speeds, and they found that the walking speed of students who constructed sentences using words associated with older people was statistically faster than that of those who did not consider such words.

Critical thinking is important when evaluating the quality and credibility of information [2]. We design *prime terms* to evoke critical thinking, careful information seeking, and effective decision making. We propose a search user interface (SUI) that displays prime terms in query auto-completion (QAC) or query suggestion (QS) terms. Figure 1 compares QAC with query priming results to conventional QAC results. As shown, we selected familiar prime terms as complementary information for search tasks and integrated them for query priming in SUIs.

We conducted a user study to determine the effect of query priming relative to promotion of critical thinking in web search processes. Our primary contributions are as follows.

- We consider a new query priming concept and propose an SUI that employs query priming.
- Through a user study and analysis, we show that query priming activates search/browsing behaviors that promote webpage selection for evidence-based decision making.
- We found that the effect of query priming varies relative to the educational background of search users.

2 RELATED WORK

2.1 Supporting credibility judgment on the web

Several studies have proposed algorithms to measure the correctness/credibility of web information, such as tweets, claims, and webpages. Pasternack et al. proposed an algorithm to measure information credibility by aggregating multiple sources that support or contradict given information [19]. Dong et al. developed a method to evaluate web page information credibility assuming that credible webpages have few false facts or claims[6]. Castillo et al. proposed a method to automatically assess the credibility level of news propagated through Twitter by analyzing tweets and reposts about news [5].

In addition, some studies focused on helping users assess credibility using qualitative information. Leong et al. developed an algorithm to retrieve evidence information from the web to help users verify the credibility of suspicious statements [13]. DISPUTE FINDER, developed by Ennals et al., highlights suspicious sentences in browsed webpages [7].

2.2 Searcher attitude and bias for careful information seeking on the web

It is known there is a great deal of unverified information on the web; however, several studies have reported that many people accept such information without consideration. For example, Nakamura et al. reported that more than 50% of people inherently perceive webpages retrieved by search engines as somewhat credible [17]. Morris et al. claimed that many people trust information from social network services more than search engine results, even though false information is often spread on social networks [16].

Even if people are aware of suspicious information, they often misjudge its credibility due to the use of incorrect heuristics, i.e., cognitive bias [11]. Leong et al. revealed the existence of domain bias whereby searchers believe that relevant webpages are authorized by specific domains [10]. White et al. studied the relation between beliefs about search topics and search behaviors [20]. They suggested that if a searcher's belief in a search topic is strong, it is difficult to shift the belief after search and browsing.

2.3 Enhancing and Activating effective user search behavior

Some researchers have developed methods to activate and enhance users' search activities. Harvery et al. revealed that providing examples of high-quality queries can help users formulate more effective queries [9]. SEARCH DASHBOARD, proposed by Bateman et al., provides a UI that reflects search behaviors and summarizes search histories [4]. Their experiments indicated that SEARCH DASHBOARD can help users modify their search behavior to improve search performance. Note that these studies focused on explicit feedback to enhance user search skills.

Some researchers have studied methods to change user behavior implicitly to provide better search experiences. Yamamoto et al. suggested that users spend more time viewing search engine result pages (SERP) and webpages if disputed topics are highlighted in web search [22]. Agapie et al. proposed an SUI that places a halo around a query box if a user inputs long queries. They reported that their proposed interface encourages users to input longer queries for better search results [1]. The query priming proposed in this paper is a type of implicit approach to encourage careful search experiences.

3 QUERY PRIMING DESIGN

3.1 Critical Thinking in Web Search Processes

The purpose of query priming is to encourage users to adopt critical thinking when seeking information on the web. Ennis defined critical thinking as logical and reflective thinking to determine what to believe or do [8]. Ennis also claimed that ideal critical thinkers are disposed to: seek reasons, consider the total situation, look for alternatives, and use critical thinking, e.g., deductive reasoning. We expect that, if search users are critical thinkers, to obtain correct and credible information from the web during web search processes, they will behave in the same manner which the information literacy researchers or librarians think is important [14]. Their search behaviors are expected to include: (1) spending more time searching, (2) issuing more queries to obtain appropriate information for decision making, (3) browsing more webpages for comparison, (4) checking evidence to support webpage content, such as the expertise of webpage authors, existence of valid references, and the freshness of webpages, and (5) collecting more evidence to support solid decisions. We designed an SUI with query priming to activate the above behaviors in web search processes.

3.2 Designing Priming Effect in Web Search

The query priming is based on the ideomotor effect, which is a type of priming effect [3]. Here, the basic idea is that search engines present users with terms that encourage careful information seeking during or after issuing queries. To encourage careful information seeking without reducing search engine usability, we consider that query priming terms (hereafter *prime terms*) should satisfy several requirements.

First, for the priming effect to trigger a behavior change, prime terms should evoke critical thinking. Second, the prime terms displayed as complimentary information should not be unusual or unfamiliar. Even if the displayed prime terms are effective, if they are irrelevant to a given search task, they will not encourage a user to proceed with a web search. Third, the prime terms should trigger the priming effect in a variety of users. If possible, users should have several opportunities to look at the terms.

We employ the following approach to achieve the above requirements. To design effective prime terms, we focus on the following dispositions related to critical thinking: *awareness for logical thinking, inquiry-mindset, objectiveness*, and *evidence-based judgment*. We collect terms associated with these four dispositions as prime terms. Furthermore, we collect prime terms that search users capable of critical thinking are likely to use as search queries to guarantee the usability of search engines. We also choose query-independent terms as prime terms such that query priming can be applied to any search topic. To expose search users to the prime terms, we focus on QAC and QS to display prime terms. QAC [15] and QS [12] are very popular search engine features that provide search assistance information displayed close to query boxes. In a web search, a user can issue or modify queries in query boxes.

Therefore, if a search engine displays prime terms using QAC/QS functions, search users are expected to consider such terms.

Screenshots of QAC and QS with query priming are shown in Figure 2. We include the prime terms in the QAC/QS term list. This approach promotes careful information seeking on the web.

3.3 Research Questions

We expect that, if query priming activates critical thinking, user search/browsing behaviors would change both superficially and substantially. Furthermore, if the query priming effect is sustained after using an SUI that includes priming, it is possible that such SUIs can be applied to train critical thinking. However, it is unlikely that query priming will influence all users. Several studies have reported that university-level learning activities foster critical thinking abilities [18]. Thus, we assume that the effect of query priming will depend on pre-existing critical thinking abilities.

To explore the effects of query priming, we consider the following research questions.

- **RQ1:** Does query priming affect users' search and browsing behaviors, such as task completion duration, query issuing count, and page view count?
- **RQ2:** Does query priming change users' perspectives relative to searching and reading webpages to support decision making?
- **RQ3:** After using SUIs with query priming and if query priming affects users, are such effects sustained when SUIs without query priming are used?
- **RQ4:** Do the effects of query priming vary relative to educational background, where university education is assumed to represent critical thinking abilities?

4 PRIME TERM COLLECTION

We used a crowdsourcing service to collect and evaluate prime terms suggested in QAC and QS. In this section, we describe the procedure used to obtain the prime terms.

4.1 Collection of prime term candidates

We adopted two approaches to collect prime term candidates to stimulate critical thinking.

First, we collected terms which people imagined from critical thinkers using Lancers.jp[1], a Japanese crowdsourcing service. We randomly displayed one of the four dispositions described in Section 3.2 to the crowdsourced workers. Then, the workers were asked to write three keywords that describe typical attributes or behaviors that people with the shown disposition recalled. Using this approach, we collected 401 prime term candidates from 74 workers.

Second, we collected query terms that critical thinkers were likely to use when searching for a given topic. In this task, we asked crowd workers to assume that a searcher with one of the four dispositions was searching for each topic listed in Table 1. Then, the workers were asked to write three query terms that the fictional searcher was likely to use together with the search topic using the

[1]Lancers.jp: http://www.lancers.jp

Table 1: Search topics to collect prime term candidates

Search topic
moving company contract, internet service contract, cancer treatment, dieting method, English learning method, overseas study option, buy microwave oven, buy TV, stock trading, apply for credit card

AND operator. Using this approach, we collected 317 prime term candidates from 54 workers.

4.2 Evaluation of prime term candidates

Then, we evaluated the collected prime term candidates.

In this evaluation, we asked crowd workers to imagine that a searcher issued a query containing one of the prime term candidates. Then, the workers evaluated the extent to which they considered the fictional searchers to be critical thinkers. We considered the degree of each evaluation as an association level of each prime term candidate with the critical thinking dispositions.

For each of the four critical thinking dispositions, we targeted the top 20 frequent prime term candidates for the evaluation task. The evaluation task was conducted as follows.

(1) We randomly allocated one of the four dispositions to each worker (here, disposition is denoted d).
(2) For each of the prime term candidates collected by d in Section 4.1, we performed the following (here, prime term candidate is denoted p).
 (a) We asked crowd workers to imagine that a searcher issued a query containing p.
 (b) The workers evaluated the extent to which they felt the searcher would have disposition d using a five-point Likert scale.

The following is an example task description.

> Suppose that a searcher issued the query "<topic> AND comparison" in a web search. Do you feel that the searcher had an objective perspective? Please evaluate the extent to which you feel the searcher had an objective perspective using a five-point scale where -2 is never feel and +2 is feel very intensely. Note that the searcher often includes the term "comparison" in queries even when searching other topics.

In this evaluation task, we allocated 50 workers to each of the four dispositions. Table 2 shows the top five highly-evaluated prime term candidates for each disposition. As prime terms for query priming, we used the 10 terms with the top three rankings that did not have similar terms in this table.

5 METHOD

This section describes the experimental design and the procedure employed in the user study.

5.1 Participants

We recruited 200 participants through Lancers.jp. We excluded 82 participants from the analysis because they did not complete all

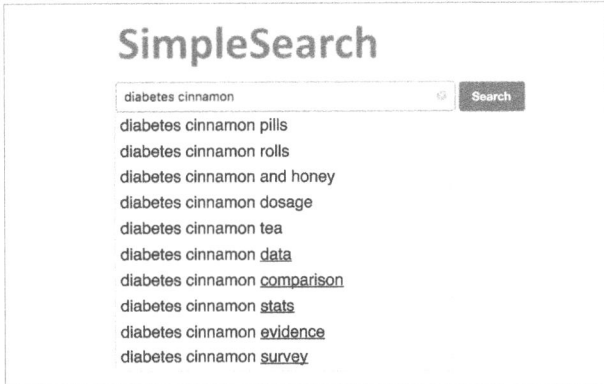

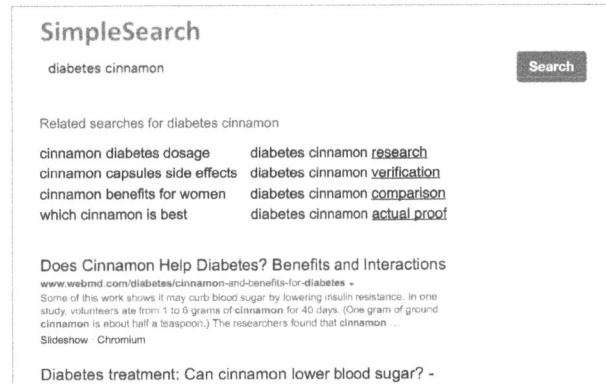

(1) Query priming at a top page (query auto-completion)   (2) Query priming at a SERP (query suggestion)

Figure 2: Screenshot of (1) QAC with query priming and (2) QS with query priming (prime terms are underlined in this paper so that readers can identify them as manipulated)

Table 2: Examples prime term candidates associated with critical thinkers (numbers in parentheses are the mean crowd workers ratings). Underlined terms were used for query priming in the user study.

Disposition type	Top five prime term candidates				
Awareness for logical thinking	principle (1.37)	evidence (1.22)	mechanism (1.22)	process (1.20)	proof (1.18)
Inquiry mind	survey (1.37)	research (1.33)	validation (1.31)	pursuit (1.16)	comparison (0.96)
Objectiveness	comparison (1.27)	stats (1.24)	analysis (0.98)	difference (0.75)	reputation (0.69)
evidence-based judgment	evidence (1.74)	actual proof (1.74)	data (1.56)	promise (1.52)	proof (1.48)

tasks or they unintentionally used other search engines, such as like Google. Thus, we used the data from 118 participants (55 were university educated).

The participants were asked to report how familiar they were with search engines using a five-point Likert scale (-2: completely unfamiliar; +2: completely familiar). We confirmed that most participants were familiar with search engines (*mean*: 1.36, *SD*: 0.73).

Each participant received approximately $4 for their time.

5.2 Tasks

Each participant performed 10 search tasks. As shown in Table 3, we prepared two types of questions for each task, i.e., *open question tasks* and *closed question tasks*. For each open question, the participants were asked to search for answer candidates and to provide one of the candidates as an answer. For each closed questions, they provided a *yes* or *no* response. The task categories included various topics, such as invention, science, and medicine. Note that several answer candidates could be found for each question.

In each task, the participants were asked to use our experimental system to search for answers and find evidential webpages.

Before starting each task, we asked the participants how familiar they were with the task question (five-point Likert scale; -2: completely unfamiliar; +2: completely familiar). On average, the number of the unfamiliar questions (i.e., less than 0) was 8.08 out

Table 3: Search task questions

Type	Question
Open	Who invented the light bulb?
	Who invented the telescope?
	Who invented the steam engine?
	What causes global warming?
	Why did dinosaurs become extinct?
Closed	Does cinnamon help improve diabetes?
	Does vitamin C help prevent pneumonia?
	Does ginkgo leaf help improve tinnitus symptoms?
	Can cocoa decrease blood pressure?
	Does garlic help improve and prevent a common cold?

of 10 ($SD = 1.58$). The mean task familiarity for the 10 tasks was -1.10 on average ($SD = 0.50$). This result confirms that most participants did not know the answers or were not confident of the answers prior to participating in the user study.

5.3 Design and procedure

In this experiment, we adopted a 2x2 between-subjects design to examine the effects of two factors, i.e., educational background and UI condition. The educational background factor had two levels,

Table 4: Participants allocation

UI condition	Educational background	
	University educated	Not university educated
control	29	31
priming	26	32

i.e., *university educated* and *not university educated*. The UI condition factor also had two levels. The first level was *control UI*, which provided conventional QAC/QS functions in a web search, and the second was *priming UI*, which displayed several query primes in QAC/QS expressions. Note that we provide a more detailed explanation of the UI condition in Section 5.4.

We allocated the participants to each UI condition randomly. Consequently, the participants were categorized into the four groups shown in Table 4. After the participants agreed to the consent form on the crowdsourcing website, they moved to our experimental website for the user study. The user study comprised four phrases.

The first was a practice phase. Here, we presented one sample search task to allow participants to become familiar with similar tasks and the search system.

The second phase was the *intervention phase*. In the intervention phase, participants were asked to search for answers to eight of the 10 tasks using the experimental search system. At the beginning of each search task, we presented the following description to introduce the task.

> *Does cinnamon help improve diabetes? Click the "Start search" button and search for an answer using our search system. When you find a satisfactory answer, come back to this webpage and report the answer and decisive evidence URLs (webpages). Here, multiple URLs are acceptable.*

Note that the search process was not time limited. Once a participant found a satisfactory answer for each task, they reported it and the URLs of the webpages that supported the answer (i.e., evidence webpages). In this phase, four tasks were selected randomly for each participant from the open and closed tasks. Note that the task order was randomized in the intervention phase, respectively.

The third phase, i.e., the *plain phase* examined the persistence of the query priming effect. Here, participants searched for answers to two of the 10 tasks (one open and one closed) using a search system wherein QAC/QS functions were disabled. Note that the two tasks did not overlap the eight tasks in the intervention phase and the task order was randomized. Before beginning each task, we presented an introductory description similar to that presented in the intervention phase.

At the end of the experiment, participants were asked to complete a questionnaire (fourth phase). The questionnaire consisted of two sets of questions, i.e., (1) questions about system usefulness and (2) questions about perspectives relative to decision making during the search tasks.

We asked the participants to evaluate system usefulness relative to the following three metrics using a five-point Likert scale (-2: completely useless; +2: completely useful).

QAC/QS to modify input query represents how useful QAC/QS information was to modify the participants' input queries during search tasks.

QAC/QS to consider decision making perspectives represents how useful QAC/QS information was to consider viewpoints for evaluating webpages and answer candidates.

Displayed search result list represents how satisfactory the search results were relative to finding task answers and evidence.

To survey decision-making perspectives, we asked the participants to evaluate the extent to which they considered the following during the search tasks (five-point Likert scale: -2: very little; +2: very much).

Content completeness is the quantity of information in webpages.

Content freshness is the recency of the information in webpages.

Content objectivity is the extent to which participants felt that the content was objective or unbiased.

Content typicality represents how many webpages provided similar information.

Social reputation is the extent to which a webpage had a positive social reputation.

Content author represents who created the webpage content.

5.4 Experimental search system

For the user study, we developed a simple web search system with a UI similar to commonly used search engines, such as Google and Yahoo. The system had a top page and SERPs.

When participants input a query into a search box, the system displayed several query candidates below the search box using the QAC function on both the top and SERPs. If the UI condition was control, the system displayed a maximum of 10 query candidates in the QAC using the input query and the Google Suggest API[2]. If the UI condition was priming, the system replaced half of the Google Suggest queries with queries in which the prime terms in Table 2 were appended to a participant's input query term (Figure 2-(1)).

On SERPs, the system used the Bing Web Search API[3] to provide a list of search results for an given input query. The number of displayed results was set to 150, and each search result comprised a title, a snippet, and a URL. When participants clicked a title, the system opened a webpage in a different browser tab. In addition, the system displayed several queries related to the input query above and below the search results list using the QS function. If the UI condition was control, the system showed a maximum of eight related queries using the Bing Web Search API. If the UI condition was priming, the system replaced half of the Bing-related queries with query primes similar to the QAC function (Figure 2-(2)).

6 RESULTS

We obtained data from 1180 search tasks, and we analyzed the effects of the UI condition and participants' educational backgrounds on participants' search/browsing behaviors and decision making.

---

[2] http://suggestqueries.google.com/complete/search

[3] https://azure.microsoft.com/services/cognitive-services/bing-web-search-api/

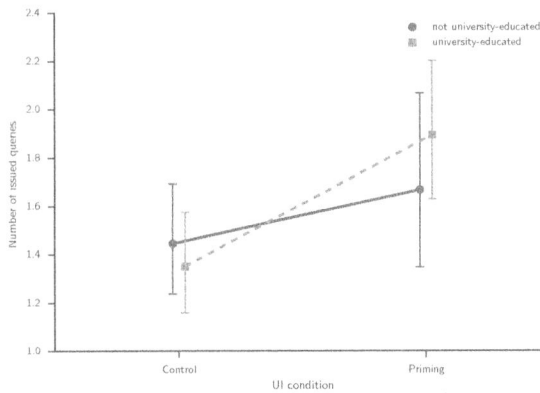

Figure 3: Number of issued queries in each task during the intervention phase divided by educational background and UI condition (error bar means 95% confidence interval)

This analysis was performed for both the intervention and plain phases. Moreover, we studied the effects on participants' search attitudes through an analysis of the questionnaire data.

We employed a non-parametric factorial ANOVA using aligned rank transformation [21] because we did not confirm the normality of the obtained data. All analyses were conducted using the *ARTool* statistical package[4].

6.1 Task performance

To answer RQ1, we first examined the *task completion duration* of each search task, which was measured by monitoring the time required to read the introductory task description and the time required to post an answer and its evidence URLs.

We expected that query priming would make the participants perform search tasks more slowly if the priming promoted critical thinking in the web search process. However, as shown in Tables 5 and 6, we did not find significant effects due to the UI condition and educational background in both the intervention and plain phases.

6.2 Search and browsing Behavior

To answer RQ1, RQ3, and RQ4, we analyzed participants' search and browsing behaviors during each task by examining how carefully they searched for answer candidates.

Query issue count is the number of queries participants issued in each task.

SERP visit count is the number of SERPs participants visited in each task.

Page visit count w/o SERP is the number of webpages participants visited in each task (excluding SERPs).

We found significant effects due to the UI condition and interaction between the UI condition and educational background relative to query issue count in the intervention phase (UI condition: $F_{(1,114)} = 15.8$, $p < 0.001$, partial $\eta^2 = 1.22e-1$; interaction: $F_{(1,114)} = 10.2$, $p < 0.01$, partial $\eta^2 = 8.19e-2$). As shown in Figure 5, regardless of whether the participants were university educated, those using the priming UI issued more queries on average

4 http://depts.washington.edu/madlab/proj/art/

than those using the control UI (university-educated group's *mean*: 1.35 vs. 1.89 in Table 5; not university-educated group's *mean*: 1.44 vs. 1.67 in Table 5). For the interaction between the UI condition and educational background, we conducted a post-hoc simple effect analyses of the query issue count running a Mann-Whitney's U test. The simple effect analyses revealed that the query priming UI for university-educated participants significantly elicited more frequent query issuing than the control UI for ones ($Z = -3.49$, $p < 0.001$, $r = 0.47$). This statistical result indicates that query priming led participants with university education to issue more queries than those without university education in the intervention phase, which displays the primes.

For the plain phase, Table 6 shows that participants using the priming UI issued more queries on average than those using the control UI (university-educated group's *mean*: 1.24 vs. 1.88; not university-educated group's *mean*: 1.31 vs. 1.45). Moreover, the query issue count was affected by educational background and the UI condition (educational background: $F_{(1,114)} = 4.71$, $p < 0.05$, partial $\eta^2 = 4.57e-2$; UI condition: $F_{(1,114)} = 5.46$, $p < 0.05$, partial $\eta^2 = 3.97e-2$). Note that we did not find statistical significance relative to the interaction between the two factors. These results indicate that, if participants used the priming UI in the intervention phase, even after no longer using the UI, they issued more queries than those who used the control UI.

With the SERP visit count, we found significant effects due to the UI condition in the intervention phase ($F_{(1,114)} = 4.56$, $p < 0.05$, partial $\eta^2 = 3.84e-2$). As shown in Table 5, participants using the priming UI visited more SERPs than those using the control UI regardless of educational background (university-educated group's *mean*: 4.72 vs. 6.13; not university-educated group's *mean*: 4.14 vs. 4.90). These results suggest that the query priming UI led the participants to (re-)check a list of search results more frequently after issuing queries or browsing webpages than the control UI.

This trend was confirmed in the plain phase ($F_{(1,114)} = 4.96$, $p < 0.05$, partial $\eta^2 = 4.17e-2$) (university-educated group's *mean*: 3.60 vs. 4.89 in Table 6; not university-educated group's *mean*: 4.30 vs. 5.98 in Table 6). These results suggest that, compared to the control UI, the priming UI led the participants to visit SERPs more frequently even after use of the UI ends.

For the visit count for webpages except SERPs, the participants did not exhibit any difference due to educational background and UI condition, both in the intervention and plain phases.

We can summarize the above results by stating that the priming UI had greater impact on search behavior with the search engines than the control UI. On the other hand, there was no difference between the two UI conditions' effects on browsing behavior outside the search engines.

6.3 Posted evidence

To answer RQ2, RQ3, and RQ4, we examined URLs posted by participants as evidence to support their task answers. We manually checked 309 unique posted URLs (webpages) relative to the following metrics, thereby examining the effects due to query priming on evidence-based decision making.

Number of evidence URLs is how many URLs participants posted as evidence for their task answer in each task.

Table 5: Participant behaviors and submitted answers during each task in the *intervention* phase broken down by educational background (EB) and UI condition (UI) (***: significance level at 0.001, **: 0.01, *: 0.05, and ·: 0.1)

	Metric	University educated		Not university educated		p-value		
		Control	Priming	Control	Priming	EB	UI	Interaction
Task performance	Task completion duration (s)	226.8	239.7	183.4	210.2	0.48	0.48	0.54
Search/browsing behavior	Query issue count	1.35	1.89	1.44	1.67	·	***	**
	SERP visit count	4.72	6.13	4.14	4.90	0.19	*	0.30
	Page visit count w/o SERP	6.06	8.13	5.90	5.97	0.36	0.28	0.40
Submitted evidence	Number of evidence URLs	1.52	1.90	1.47	1.40	*	0.19	*
	Reference validation (%)	49.6	61.1	48.4	53.9	0.41	*	0.41
	Author existence validation (%)	45.7	50.4	33.0	36.3	***	0.12	0.90
	Author expertise validation (%)	20.2	22.7	29.3	35.1	***	0.24	1.00
	TLD validation (%)	8.6	11.1	4.0	3.5	***	0.62	0.30

Table 6: Participant behaviors and submitted answers during each task in the *plain* phase broken down by educational background (EB) and UI condition (UI) (***: Significance level at 0.001, **: 0.01, *: 0.05, and ·: 0.1)

	Metric	University educated		Not university educated		p-value		
		Control	Priming	Control	Priming	EB	UI	Interaction
Task performance	Task completion duration (s)	171.8	228.1	163.8	200.6	0.66	0.12	0.69
Search/browsing behavior	Query issue count	1.24	1.88	1.31	1.45	*	*	·
	SERP visit count	4.30	5.98	3.60	4.89	0.11	*	0.35
	Page visit count w/o SERP	4.95	8.17	5.37	6.70	0.54	0.13	0.37
Submitted evidence	Number of evidence URLs	1.55	1.98	1.50	1.44	*	*	*
	Reference validation (%)	48.3	63.5	53.2	62.5	0.77	0.13	0.54
	Author existence validation (%)	41.4	46.2	43.5	45.3	0.89	0.60	0.79
	Author expertise validation (%)	19.0	32.7	25.8	37.5	0.51	*	0.89
	TLD validation (%)	3.4	15.4	8.1	7.8	0.17	*	·

Author expertise validation is the ratio of tasks where participants posted evidence URLs containing descriptions to confirm if the content authors had expertise in the task topic[5].

Author existence validation is the ratio of tasks where participants posted evidence URLs containing descriptions to confirm if the content authors actually exist[6].

TLD validation is the ratio of tasks where participants posted evidence URLs with credible top-level domains (TLD) suggesting governmental organization or academic organizations[7].

Reference validation is the ratio of tasks where participants posted evidence URLs containing authorized references to support the task answers[8].

For the number of evidence URLs in the intervention phase, we found significant differences due to educational background

and the interaction between educational background and UI condition (educational background: $F_{(1,114)} = 5.45$, $p < 0.05$, partial $\eta^2 = 4.57e\text{-}2$; interaction: $F_{(1,114)} = 4.04$, $p < 0.05$, partial $\eta^2 = 3.42e\text{-}2$). As shown in Figure 4, if participants were university educated, participants using the priming UI posted more evidence URLs than those using the control UI (*mean*: 1.90 vs. 1.52 in Table 5). On the other hand, if participants were not university educated, those using the priming UI gave as many URLs as those using the control UI (*mean*: 1.40 vs. 1.47 in Table 5). The simple effect analyses with a Mann-Whitney's U test indicated that the UI condition factor for university-educated participants approached significance ($Z = -1.68$, $p = 0.094 < .1$, $r = 0.23$). These statistical results suggest that the query priming promoted participants with university education to find more evidence URLs, although the effect was not so statistically significant. On the other hand, we did not confirm that priming would affect those without university education.

This trend was observed for the number of evidence URLs in the plain phase. In the plain phase, the number of evidence URLs was affected by educational background, the UI condition, and the interaction between educational background and UI condition (educational background: $F_{(1,114)} = 4.16$, $p < 0.05$, partial $\eta^2 = 3.52e\text{-}2$;

---

[5]If a content author displayed governmental certificate (medical doctor and lawyer) on their webpage or if the author affiliation was shown as a governmental organization, academic organization, or publicly-listed companies on the webpage, we considered the author demonstrated expertise.

[6]If a webpage showed both a content author's real name and a legitimate affiliation, we considered the author to exist.

[7]We set the following TLDs as credible: *go.jp* (governmental originations in Japan), *.gov*, *ac.jp* (universities in Japan), and *.edu*.

[8]We defined that authorized references were articles published by academic associations or governmental organizations.

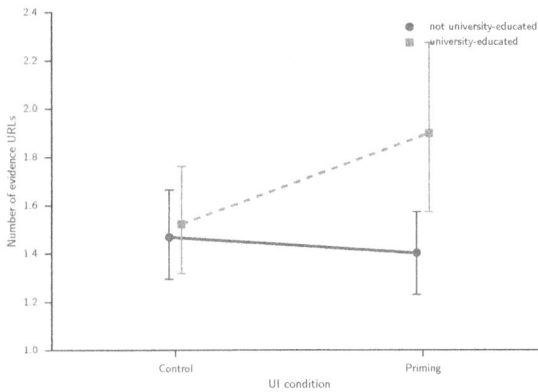

Figure 4: Number of URLs posted as answer evidence in each task during the intervention phase divided by educational background and UI condition (error bar means confidence interval at 95% level).

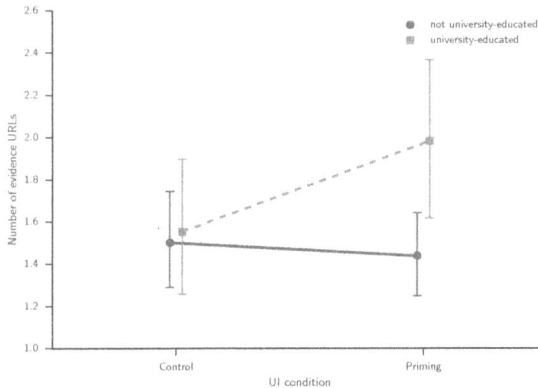

Figure 5: Number of URLs posted as answer evidence in each task during the intervention phase divided by educational background and UI condition (error bar means confidence interval at 95% level).

UI condition: $F_{(1,114)} = 3.99, p < 0.05$, partial $\eta^2 = 3.38$e-2; interaction: $F_{(1,114)} = 5.33, p < 0.05$, partial $\eta^2 = 4.47$e-2). Figure 5 shows that the number of posted evidence URLs when using the priming UI was greater than when using the control UI for only university-educated participants (university-educated group's *mean*: 1.98 vs. 1.55; not-university-educated group's *mean*: 1.44 vs. 1.50). The simple effect analyses with a Mann-Whitney's U test revealed that the UI condition factor for university-educated participants was close to being statistically significant ($Z = -1.93, p = 0.054 < .1$, $r = 0.26$). These results suggest that the priming UI can promote participants to find and post more evidential webpages when using the UI, even after use of the UI ends.

Note that reference validation in the intervention phase was affected by only the UI condition ($F_{(1,114)} = 4.08, p < 0.05$, partial $\eta^2 = 3.46$e-2). Table 5 suggests that, if participants without university education used the priming UI, they posted evidential webpages with validated reference for 5.5% more tasks on average

than those using the control UI (Table 5). Moreover, we found that, if participants with university education used the priming UI, they posted reference-validated webpages as evidence for 11.5% more tasks on average than those using the control UI (Table 5). On the other hand, in the test phase, we did not find a statistical effect due to either educational background or the UI condition relative to the reference validation metric.

With the author expertise validation and TLD validation metrics, we found that the UI condition did not affect these metrics in the intervention phase; however, educational background did affect them (author expertise validation: $F_{(1,114)} = 12.4, p < 0.001$, partial $\eta^2 = 9.82$e-2; TLD validation: $F_{(1,114)} = 11.1, p < 0.001$, partial $\eta^2 = 8.87$e-2). Note that, from these results, we cannot confirm that while participants were using the priming UI, the function difference affected participant attention to author expertise and the TLD of the posted webpages. On the other hand, in the plain phase, a significant effect by the UI condition was observed (author expertise validation: $F_{(1,114)} = 4.16, p < 0.05$, partial $\eta^2 = 3.52$e-2; TLD validation: $F_{(1,114)} = 4.61, p < 0.05$, partial $\eta^2 = 3.89$e-2). The results suggest that, even after the priming UI was no longer used, it affected participant attention to webpage TLD and author expertise, although the effect did not appear while the UI was used.

For the author existing validation metric, we did not observe an effect due to the UI condition in either the intervention or plain phases.

6.4 Questionnaire

To perform a qualitative analysis, we examined the participants' answers to the questionnaire described in Section 5.3. Table 7 shows the average scores for system usefulness and viewpoint in decision making metric (-2: completely disagree; +2: completely agree).

As for the usefulness of QAC/QS for input query modification and the displayed search results, there was no significant effect due to educational background and UI condition, which suggests that participants did not complain about the query priming UI compared to the UI condition. Moreover, we found that the UI condition had significant effect on the usefulness of QAC/QS relative to considering the decision-making perspective ($F_{(1,114)} = 7.88$, $p < 0.01$, partial $\eta^2 = 6.47$e-2). Table 7 shows that, regardless of educational background, participants gave higher scores on this usefulness on average (university-educated group's *mean*: 0.68 vs. 0.94; not university-educated group's *mean*: 0.72 vs. 0.88). From this result, we consider that participants thought that the query candidates provided by the priming UI terms were more useful when investigating appropriate information to answer the task questions than those provided by the conventional QAC/QS UI.

Relative to the decision-making perspective, only the score of the content author viewpoint exhibited a significant difference relative to educational background and interaction between educational background and the UI condition (educational background: $F_{(1,114)} = 9.93, p < 0.01$, partial $\eta^2 = 8.01$e-2; the interaction: $F_{(1,114)} = 5.63, p < 0.05$, partial $\eta^2 = 4.70$e-2). Figure 6 shows that, if participants were university educated, those using the priming UI gave higher scores than those using the control UI (*mean*: 1.11 vs. 0.34 in Table 7). On the other hand, Figure 6 also indicates that,

Table 7: System usefulness and viewpoint for decision making in each task broken down by educational background (EB) and query completion/suggestion type (UI) (***: significance level at 0.001, **: 0.01, *: 0.05, and ·: 0.1).

	Metric	University educated		Not university educated		p-value		
		Control	Priming	Control	Priming	EB	UI	Interaction
System usefulness	QAC/QS to modify input query	1.03	1.08	0.87	1.00	0.61	0.48	0.65
	QAC/QS to consider decision making viewpoint	0.72	0.88	0.68	0.94	0.61	**	0.92
	Displayed search result list	0.93	0.88	1.06	1.16	0.25	0.85	0.73
Viewpoint for decision making	Content completeness	0.90	1.15	0.84	0.88	0.59	0.49	0.91
	Content freshness	0.24	0.04	0.35	-0.19	0.81	·	0.41
	Content objectivity	1.34	1.35	1.03	1.03	·	·	0.74
	Content typicality	1.00	1.15	1.00	1.00	0.56	0.65	0.52
	Social reputation	-0.24	-0.27	-0.29	-0.41	0.93	0.87	0.86
	Content author	0.34	1.11	0.16	-0.25	**	0.84	*

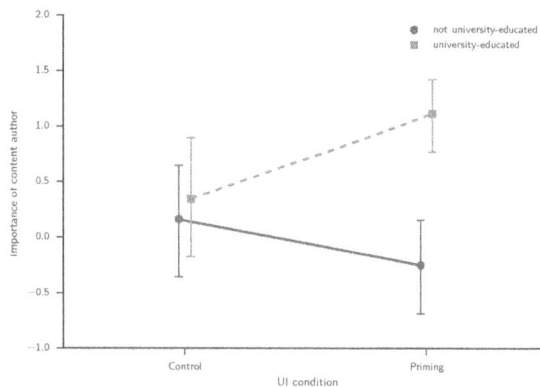

Figure 6: Extent to which participants considered content author in the search task divided by educational background and UI condition (error bar means 95% confidence interval)

if the participants did not have a university education, those using the priming UI gave lower scores than those using the control UI (*mean* -0.25 vs. 0.16 in Table 7). The simple effect analyses with a Mann-Whitney's U test indicated that the UI condition factor for university-educated participants was a certain trend toward significance ($Z = -1.78, p = 0.074 < .1, r = 0.24$). On the other hand, we found that there was no significant influence of the UI condition factor for not-university-educated partisipants. From these results, we consider that there was a trend that the query priming made participants with university education more careful about the content author, while the priming made participants without university education less careful.

7 DISCUSSION

In this section, we discuss answers to RQs 1-5 (Section 1) relative to the results of the user study.

For RQ1 and RQ4, we examined the task performance and search behaviors in a comparison between participants with and without university education. The task performance results demonstrate that both education background and the UI condition did not affect task completion duration (Section 6.1). In addition, the browsing behavior results indicate that query priming did not increase

the page visit count (Section 6.2). If query priming promoted careful information seeking, we expected that participants using the priming UI would spend more time in their search tasks and visit more webpages in order to support their decision; however, the experimental results did not support this expectation.

On the other hand, the search behavior results indicate that the priming UI increased the frequency of issuing queries and (re-)visiting SERPs (Section 6.2). In particular, query priming had greater impact on the frequency of issuing queries for university-educated participants. The questionnaire results indicate that participants that used the priming UI had no complaints about the QAC/QS functions compared to those using the control UI. This questionnaire result denies that the participants using the priming UI issued more queries due to low QAC/QS performance (Section 6.4). From these results, we consider that query priming promoted frequent query issuance and SERP (re-)visits to carefully select which webpages to browse in limited time.

For RQ2 and RQ4, we examined the submitted evidence URLs and the questionnaire relative to the decision-making perspective. The questionnaire results indicate that query priming influenced the content author perspective in decision making (Section 6.4). As shown in Figure 6, if participants used the priming UI, those with university education felt more aware of the content author, while those without university education felt less aware.

However, behavioral results relative to evidence submission tell a different story. As shown in Table 5, the priming UI had no effect on content author factors, such as author existence validation, author expertise validation, and TLD validation. On the other hand, Table 5 indicates that more participants who used the priming UI submitted webpages containing valid references than those using the control UI. Moreover, Figure 4 reveals that university-educated participants using the priming UI submitted more evidential webpages than those using the control UI. From these results, we guess that query priming prompted university-educated participants to seek multiple evidence sources with authorized references even though they were not aware of that.

From the above discussion, we confirm that (1) using the query priming UI changed participant search behavior towards careful information seeking and (2) the effect positively appeared for participants with university education.

For RQ3, we do not insist from the experimental results that the query priming effect was sustained after use of the priming UI ended. Relative to the query issue count and SERP visit count, we observed that the priming UI affected participants during and after the use of the UI (Tables 5 and 6, and Figures 4 and 5). In addition, we observed persistence of the query priming effect on the number of posted evidence URLs for only university-educated participants (Figures 4 and 5). However, the effect on reference validation for the submitted evidence URLs was lost after disabling the QAC/QS functions. Furthermore, for author expertise validation and TLD validation on submitted evidence URLs, although a significant difference between the two UI conditions was observed after the functions were disabled, we did not observe a significant effect of the priming UI when the QAC/QS functions were enabled (Tables 5 and 6). Intuitively, we hypothesized that, if query priming promoted the above two points, the effect would at least appear when the QAC/QS functions were enabled. However, the observed results do not support this hypothesis. Here, one possible interpretation is that the query priming effect would appear with delay. In our user study, participants performed only two tasks in the plain phase compared to five tasks in the intervention phase. Therefore, it is possible that we did not obtain stable results relative to the submitted evidence. In future, we must design and perform a more suitable user study to validate the persistence of the query priming effect. In addition, a laboratory user study is required to examine the effect in detail because we had troubles to prevent some participants from unintentional use of the experimental systems.

8 CONCLUSION

In this paper, we have proposed a new *query priming* concept for QS and QAC towards careful information seeking. A search user interface with query priming presents terms that evoke critical thinking, thereby encouraging users to search for webpages carefully. The results of a user study using a crowdsourcing service indicated that proposed query priming concept changed participants' search behaviors and promoted the issuance of more queries and more frequent visits to SERPs. Furthermore, query priming affected the selection of webpages relative to evidence-based decision making. We found that, among university-educated participants, those using the priming UI collected more evidence with valid references.

Although the user study indicated that the priming UI had some effects while enabled, it did not provide sufficient support relative to the expectation that the query priming effect would be sustained even when the priming UI was not used. In future, we plan to conduct a laboratory study to carefully validate the persistence of the query priming effect.

Most current search tools focus on matching webpages to user information requirements. We believe that our work can support the design of search interactions to encourage careful information seeking and decision making on the web rather than solely relying on machine prediction and judgment.

ACKNOWLEDGMENTS

This work was supported in part by Grants-in-Aid for Scientific Research (17K17832, 16H01756, 16K16156) from MEXT of Japan.

REFERENCES

[1] Elena Agapie, Gene Golovchinsky, and Pernilla Qvarfordt. 2013. Leading People to Longer Queries. In *Proceedings of the SIGCHI Conference on Human Factors in Computing Systems (CHI 2013)*. ACM, New York, NY, USA, 3019–3022.

[2] American Library Association (ALA). 2000. *Information literacy competency standards for higher education.*

[3] John A Bargh, Mark Chen, and Lara Burrows. 1996. Automaticity of social behavior: Direct effects of trait construct and stereotype activation on action. *Journal of personality and social psychology* 71, 2 (1996), 230–244.

[4] Scott Bateman, Jaime Teevan, and Ryen W. White. 2012. The Search Dashboard: How Reflection and Comparison Impact Search Behavior. In *Proceedings of the SIGCHI Conference on Human Factors in Computing Systems (CHI 2012)*. ACM, New York, NY, USA, 1785–1794.

[5] Carlos Castillo, Marcelo Mendoza, and Barbara Poblete. 2011. Information Credibility on Twitter. In *Proceedings of the 20th International Conference on World Wide Web (WWW 2011)*. 675–684.

[6] Xin Luna Dong, Evgeniy Gabrilovich, Kevin Murphy, Van Dang, Wilko Horn, Camillo Lugaresi, Shaohua Sun, and Wei Zhang. 2015. Knowledge-based Trust: Estimating the Trustworthiness of Web Sources. *Proceedings of the VLDB Endowment* 8, 9 (2015), 938–949.

[7] Rob Ennals, Beth Trushkowsky, and John Mark Agosta. 2010. Highlighting Disputed Claims on the Web. In *Proceedings of the 19th International Conference on World Wide Web (WWW 2010)*. 341–350.

[8] Robert H. Ennis. 1987. A taxonomy of critical thinking dispositions and abilities. In *Series of books in psychology. Teaching thinking skills: Theory and practice*, J. B. Baron and R. J. Sternberg (Eds.). W H Freeman/Times Books/ Henry Holt & Co, New York, 9–26.

[9] Morgan Harvey, Claudia Hauff, and David Elsweiler. 2015. Learning by Example: Training Users with High-quality Query Suggestions. In *Proceedings of the 38th International ACM SIGIR Conference on Research and Development in Information Retrieval (SIGIR 2015)*. ACM, 133–142.

[10] Samuel Ieong, Nina Mishra, Eldar Sadikov, and Li Zhang. 2012. Domain Bias in Web Search. In *Proceedings of the Fifth ACM International Conference on Web Search and Data Mining (WSDM 2012)*. ACM, 413–422.

[11] Daniel Kahneman. 2011. *Thinking, fast and slow*. Macmillan.

[12] Diane Kelly, Amber Cushing, Maureen Dostert, Xi Niu, and Karl Gyllstrom. 2010. Effects of popularity and quality on the usage of query suggestions during information search. In *Proceedings of the 28th SIGCHI Conference on Human Factors in Computing Systems (CHI 2010)*. ACM, 45–54.

[13] Chee Wee Leong and Silviu Cucerzan. 2012. Supporting Factual Statements with Evidence from the Web. In *Proceedings of the 21st ACM International Conference on Information and Knowledge Management (CIKM 2012)*. ACM, 1153–1162.

[14] Marc Meola. 2004. Chucking the checklist: A contextual approach to teaching undergraduates Web-site evaluation. *portal: Libraries and the Academy* 4, 3 (2004), 331–344.

[15] Bhaskar Mitra, Milad Shokouhi, Filip Radlinski, and Katja Hofmann. 2014. On user interactions with query auto-completion. In *Proceedings of the 37th international ACM SIGIR conference on Research and development in information retrieval (SIGIR 2014)*. ACM, 1055–1058.

[16] Meredith Ringel Morris, Jaime Teevan, and Katrina Panovich. 2010. What Do People Ask Their Social Networks, and Why?: A Survey Study of Status Message Q&A Behavior. In *Proceedings of the 28th ACM SIGCHI Conference on Human Factors in Computing Systems (CHI 2010)*. ACM, 1739–1748.

[17] Satoshi Nakamura, Shinji Konishi, Adam Jatowt, Hiroaki Ohshima, Hiroyuki Kondo, Taro Tezuka, Satoshi Oyama, and Katsumi Tanaka. 2007. Trustworthiness Analysis of Web Search Results. In *Proceedings of the 11th European Conference on Research and Advanced Technology for Digital Libraries (ECDL 2007)*. Springer, 38–49.

[18] Ernest T. Pascarella. 1989. The development of critical thinking: Does college make a difference? *Journal of College Student Development* 30, 1 (1989), 19–26.

[19] Jeff Pasternack and Dan Roth. 2013. Latent Credibility Analysis. In *Proceedings of the 22nd International Conference on World Wide Web (WWW 2013)*. 1009–1020.

[20] Ryen White. 2013. Beliefs and Biases in Web Search. In *Proceedings of the 36th International ACM SIGIR Conference on Research and Development in Information Retrieval (SIGIR 2013)*. ACM, 3–12.

[21] Jacob O. Wobbrock, Leah Findlater, Darren Gergle, and James J. Higgins. 2011. The Aligned Rank Transform for Nonparametric Factorial Analyses Using Only Anova Procedures. In *Proceedings of the SIGCHI Conference on Human Factors in Computing Systems (CHI 2011)*. ACM, 143–146.

[22] Yusuke Yamamoto and Satoshi Shimada. 2016. Can Disputed Topic Suggestion Enhance User Consideration of Information Credibility in Web Search?. In *Proceedings of the 27th ACM Conference on Hypertext and Social Media (HT 2016)*. ACM, 169–177.

[23] Yusuke Yamamoto and Katsumi Tanaka. 2011. Enhancing Credibility Judgment of Web Search Results. In *Proceedings of the SIGCHI Conference on Human Factors in Computing Systems (CHI 2011)*. ACM, 1235–1244.

Searching as Learning: Exploring Search Behavior and Learning Outcomes in Learning-Related Tasks

Souvick Ghosh, Manasa Rath, Chirag Shah
School of Communication & Information (SC&I)
Rutgers University
4 Huntington Street
New Brunswick, NJ 08901, USA
{souvick.ghosh,manasa.rath,chirags}@rutgers.edu

ABSTRACT

In this paper, we investigate the relationship between searching and learning, by conceptualizing information seeking as a learning process, and learning as an outcome of the information seeking process. We present the participants with four search tasks, each of them designed to represent different cognitive levels of learning. Through quantitative analysis of the participants' Web search logs, we examine how individual search behavior is influenced by different task complexity levels as we present the tasks in a hierarchical order. We also explore how the perceived learning outcomes and processes, and the different learning actions, are related to the levels of cognitive complexity. By analyzing the search logs, self-reports, interview data, and the reports, both quantitatively and qualitatively, we infer that searching and learning are not isolated but co-existing processes. Distinct search patterns and learning outcomes were observed in tasks of different cognitive complexities, and overlapping learning actions were observed for the different tasks.

CCS CONCEPTS

• **Information systems** → **Retrieval tasks and goals**; *Information retrieval*; • **Applied computing** → **Education**;

KEYWORDS

Searching as Learning, Human Information Behavior, Bloom's Taxonomy, Learning Theories, Learning Outcomes

ACM Reference Format:
Souvick Ghosh, Manasa Rath, Chirag Shah. 2018. Searching as Learning: Exploring Search Behavior and Learning Outcomes in Learning-Related Tasks. In *CHIIR '18: 2018 Conference on Human Information Interaction Retrieval, March 11–15, 2018, New Brunswick, NJ, USA.* ACM, New York, NY, USA, 10 pages. https://doi.org/10.1145/3176349.3176386

1 INTRODUCTION

Learning is an important phenomenon that occurs in everyday life. For the most part, we associate learning with an educational environment, as an effect of studying. However, learning is more than a conscious effort to create new knowledge. Learning occurs as we perform our day-to-day activities, from figuring out how to use a new technology to finding a new route to our destination. Learning is closely related to the knowledge structures that human beings possess. Learning can be conceptualized as a process that involves creation or acquisition of new knowledge (constructivist approach to learning). Alternatively, it may involve modifying, accommodating or assimilating new information and experiences into existing knowledge structures [17, 20, 22, 26].

Similarly, various theories and studies in information science literature have tried connecting the search process to the dimension of knowledge [6, 12, 23]. Information seeking can be viewed as a response to problematic situations, which arise due to conflicts between our view of the life-world and any observation that does not fit that typification [23]. A restructuring of our existing knowledge patterns requires more information, which leads to actively seeking information. In other words, information search is a sense-making process [6], bridging the uncertainty (gap in knowledge) between the expected and observed situation. Although searching involves access to different sources of information (bibliographic paradigm), it also involves selection and interaction with information sources, and organization and synthesis of the collected information for successful task completion (constructive paradigm) [26]. Many studies have attempted to explain the observed behavior during such information seeking sessions. In our work, we are interested in exploring how the human information seeking behavior is influenced by the cognitive complexities of the tasks, in a learning environment.

The conceptual similarity between information seeking and learning could be used to better understand how knowledge is constructed and restructured dynamically. Conversely, by using the framework of human cognition, the two concepts of searching and learning can be connected to each other. While this connection has been alluded to in many studies, very few have explicitly studied or articulated the link between these two concepts [11, 26]. In recent years, "Searching as learning" has emerged as an important area of research in library and information science (LIS) as it allows for a better understanding of search behavior using the broader context of human learning. In our study, we investigate how people engage in information seeking behavior, using a taxonomy of learning constructs. By connecting the constructivist approach to learning (i.e., learning as knowledge construction) to the constructive paradigm of information searching (e.g., Kuhlthau's Information Search Process model), we attempt to explain how learning occurs while searching, or how searching facilitates the process of learning [16, 26].

Our study, which uses the framework for learning to explain search behavior and the framework for searching to explore learning outcomes in tasks of different cognitive complexities, is situated within the overall research area on searching as learning [11, 19, 26] and is one of the few studies to use both quantitative and qualitative approaches.

The following three main research questions guide the overall direction and objectives of the research study:

(1) RQ1: What are the different search behaviors that may be observed as people engage in the various tasks associated with the cognitive taxonomy of learning?
(2) RQ2: What is the relationship between the perceived learning processes and outcomes during a search process and the levels of cognitive complexity?
(3) RQ3: What are the different actions, related to learning, which may be observed as the users engage in the various tasks associated with the cognitive taxonomy of learning?

The remainder of the paper is organized as follows: Section 2 presents background and related work, while Sections 3 and 4 explain the experimental methodology and data collection, respectively. We present and discuss our results in Section 5. Section 6 is a discussion of the limitations, and Section 7 presents our key conclusions and outlines the scope for future work.

2 BACKGROUND AND RELATED WORK
2.1 Taxonomy of Educational Objectives

Bloom et al.'s taxonomy of educational objectives [3], introduced in 1956, attempted to develop learning objectives to foster thinkers' in classrooms. In this taxonomy, Bloom proposed a hierarchical order of cognitive domains – Knowledge, Comprehension, Application, Analysis, Synthesis, and Evaluation. Later, Anderson et al. and Krathwohl and Anderson revised the taxonomy to create a two-dimensional framework by separating the noun and verb aspects to knowledge dimension and cognitive process dimension, respectively [1, 15]. The revised taxonomy made significant modifications to how the cognitive process dimension – consisting of Remember, Understand, Apply, Evaluate, Analyze, and Create levels in a hierarchical order, from lowest to highest – interacts with the knowledge dimension (Factual, Conceptual, Procedural, and Metacognitive). While the lowest levels involve additions of new information to our existing knowledge structures, the middle levels involve reshaping and accommodating knowledge, while the highest levels may require deleting and restructuring pre-existing knowledge. The importance of the taxonomy lies in the fact that it views educational goals as not only recalling facts but creating a more comprehensive understanding and application of the learned concepts.

2.2 Information Seeking and Knowledge Building

Given that learning is not just restricted to a classroom environment but can be extended to the world around us, the theories in information science, and the analysis of human information behavior, suggests that learning is an outcome of information seeking. Every person has a view of the world around him or her, certain typifications that we use to model and explain all phenomena around us [23]. Whenever we encounter an anomaly that does not fit our existing model, it creates a problematic situation whose resolution requires more information and knowledge reconstruction. Dervin's [6] sense-making model views information seeking as a way to mitigate the gap (or uncertainty) between the desired and observed situations. Belkin et al. [2] viewed this uncertainty as an anomalous state of knowledge. Similarly, Ingwersen's [12] cognitive model and Wilson's [30] problem solving model suggest a strong relation between human cognition, knowledge, and information seeking. However, human information behavior is not limited to information seeking but can be extended to information searching and information use [31], and may involve various channels for information sharing, as well as different modes of communication.

There exists a rich body of literature that revolves around the triangle of the user, searching, and learning in the field of information science. One of the research directions investigates how users' knowledge impacts search behavior, while the other direction examines information seeking as a collaborative knowledge building environment (KBE), or a process of social learning [7, 25, 27].

2.3 Searching as Learning

The use of information to alter knowledge and cognitive structures can be related to learning in educational environments, and hence, information seeking can be viewed as a precursor to learning. Several studies in LIS literature that have employed the taxonomy of learning to evaluate and classify various search tasks and that required different cognitive processes and demands from users, [9, 13, 14, 28, 32]. Jansen et al. [13] used the taxonomy of cognitive learning to explore the unique information search characteristics specific to learning. Similarly, Rieh et al. [19] explores which search activities can help enhance and support the different cognitive processes. Reynolds [18] looks at how social constructivist educational contexts can help relate collaborative information seeking and learning tasks, while Freund et al. [8] investigates the influence of presentation style and interactivity in learning and knowledge comprehension. Hansen and Rieh [11] summarize the recent advances in the searching-as-learning research and how they can help search experiences to be more oriented towards learning. Furthermore, few studies have provided insights on how Web-searching has contributed as a human learning process in context to the task at hand [21].

It is clear from the review of relevant literature presented above that searching and learning are activities that are connected by knowledge and cognitive dimensions. Therefore, we have used the revised taxonomy of educational objectives to observe and analyze search behavior in the context of learning; and learning outcomes while searching. We also provide insights into the different learning actions [15] that take place at different task complexity levels, focusing on the degree of overlap and uniqueness between the levels.

3 EXPERIMENTAL METHODOLOGY

This section provides a detailed account of the method used to conduct the user study to address our research questions.

3.1 Task Participants

A total of 31 undergraduate students at Rutgers University, comprising 10 males and 21 females, participated in the user study. The participants included 10 sophomores, 8 juniors, and 13 seniors; freshmen were excluded from this study. The academic backgrounds were diverse, with 18 students from STEM and 13 from Arts and Humanities. Only two of the participants identified themselves as non-native English speakers, being native speakers of Spanish and Mandarin. 27 participants out of 31 reported that they had been using Web search for more than five years, and 24 of them reported conducting more than 6 searches per day. The proficiency of the participants in reading and writing English, and their respective search skills, were measured on a 5-point Likert scale (1=Novice, 5=Expert). The average search expertise was 4.16, and the average proficiency in English (reading and writing) was 4.8 and 4.6, respectively.

The study was conducted over a period of two weeks, during which the participants were instructed to perform four search tasks, all of which were based on a common topic and were related to learning. The participants were required to keep a record of the sources that they consulted – along with the details of information obtained from non-Web sources – in an online diary, and to write a report at the end of each task. While it was mandatory for the participants to complete each search task within three days, they could move to the next task immediately after completing the current task. The total time spent to complete this study was five hours on average, as reported by the participants. An exit interview was conducted and a monetary compensation of $40 was paid to each student at the end of the study.

3.2 Study Design

The steps involved in the user study are listed in the following subsections:

3.2.1 Online Orientation. All the students who expressed interest in participating in this user study were asked to fill out a questionnaire based on their academic background. Once their participation was approved, the participants were briefed on what was expected of them and were given an overall description of the research goal and objectives. The participants needed to fill out another questionnaire on demographic and background information, which included their personal details (e.g.: age and gender), Web search experiences, and language proficiency. The researchers guided the participants on how to install and use the Chrome browser plugin Coagmento [10, 24], [1] which was essential to capture the users' search log data, maintain task flow, record the online diary and final reports, and to save responses from pre-task and post-task questionnaires.

---

[1]http://coagmento.org/

3.2.2 Learning-oriented search tasks. In this study, we followed some of the previous research in searching as learning to develop the search tasks [11, 14, 26, 32]. Most designed the search tasks using the cognitive complexity framework from educational theory, grouped under four topic domains where each search task represented a different level of cognitive complexity. Using the revised taxonomy of learning, we developed four task questions, all related to cyber-bullying, which was the single topic for our study. Each task question was created to reflect a particular level of the cognitive process dimension proposed in the revised taxonomy: Remember, Understand, Apply, Analyze, Evaluate, and Create [15]. The participants were provided with an overall task assignment (See Appendix A) simulating a real-life situation: They were the leaders of a student organization tasked with writing a report on cyber-bullying that would be used as part of training materials for school teachers, educators, and decision makers [4].

The following four learning-oriented tasks were designed and given to our participants in the order below:

- Task 1 (Remember and Understand):
  What is cyber bullying? How is it similar or different to other types of harassment (e.g. cyber bullying vs. traditional bullying)? What are some long-term/short-term risks involved with cyber bullying?
- Task 2 (Apply):
  In 2010, Rutgers University witnessed the tragic incident of Tyler Clementi, whose case raised concerns about cyber bullying. Find out more about this case, and possibly some other cases. What does/do this/these case(s) show are some common characteristics of cyber bullying?
- Task 3 (Analyze):
  Having heard some of the recent reports on cyber bullying, what seems to be the main cause of the bullying behavior online? How much is technology and the use of electronic communication associated with cyber bullying? Why?
- Task 4 (Evaluate):
  How effective are some of the currently available strategies to mitigate cyber bullying at schools and university campuses? Why? Which strategy/method do you think is best and why?

It should be noted that the cognitive process dimension of the revised taxonomy comprises six different levels: Remember, Understand, Apply, Analyze, Evaluate, and Create. In our study, we have combined Remember and Understand, the first two levels of cognitive complexity, while removing the final complexity level, Create. As the nature of our tasks was exploratory – which involves open-ended investigation, high levels of uncertainty, vagueness, and multiple facets [28] – we were motivated to merge the two lowest levels of cognitive complexity Remember and Understand, which involves simple fact-finding. Our task required the participants to write a short paragraph based on the findings after each task and to combine them for a comprehensive and coherent final report. We left out the highest complexity level, Create, as the report-writing assignment involves the different components related to it, such as adding newer sections, deleting redundant sentences, and reorganizing the sentences to form a coherent and meaningful structure [32]. We assumed that the assessment of the writing assignment would provide sufficient indicators for the final level.

3.2.3 Information Sources. Information sources are not limited to the online space but can be extended offline as well. In our study, which involved exploration of the learning component involved in search tasks, the participants were instructed to consult three types of sources: Web (i.e., traditional search engines like Google, Bing, etc.), known sources (i.e., friends, family and personal social networks accessible both online and offline), and unknown sources (question-answering forums, information centers, libraries, etc).

While the Web-based information was stored in search logs and captured using the Chrome plugin Coagmento, the offline sources required self-reporting by the participants. Using the online diary, provided as part of our interface, the participants recorded how they consulted the different information sources, any URL which they saved for future referrals, and filled out the details about their offline sources, such as the relationship to the person or group, the question asked, the means of communication, the responses, etc. The details about the three sources are included in Appendix B.

3.2.4 Pre-task and Post-task Questionnaires. To investigate the perceived difficulties and usefulness of each task, and to assess the differences in learning outcomes and experiences, the study required the participants to fill out the pre- and post-task questionnaires before and after completing each task. For our task-related questions, in both the questionnaires, we utilized task measures on task complexity and difficulty, topic familiarity and interests, perceived help of prior knowledge, and the overall gain in knowledge, as these factors are potential indicators of the learning processes and outcomes [5]. Some additional source-related questions were included in the post-task questionnaire, where the participants were asked to select the most and least difficult, and the most and least useful sources. The details of the pre- and post-task questionnaires have been provided in Appendix C.

3.2.5 Exit Interview. Once the participants completed the four tasks, they were asked to meet the researchers for a brief in-person interview, where they were asked questions, both open-ended and specific, about their overall experiences. In the interview, the participants were specifically asked in detail about their perceived learning processes, task-related experiences, and source-related perceptions. The interview allowed us to relate the various search behaviors observed and reported by the participants, and map them to different cognitive dimensions of learning.

4 DATA COLLECTION AND ANALYSIS

In our study, to answer the three research questions, we collected the following types of data: The demographic data of the participants, Web search data (collected using the Chrome browser plugin Coagmento), the pre- and post-task questionnaires collected at the end of each task, the online diary, the exit interview, and the writing assignment. The Web search data was collected using the Chrome plugin Coagmento. The participants were required to install the plugin from Chrome Web store, which once enabled, captured Web log data with time stamps. The data included the search queries, the Web pages that the participants visited, and the amount of time spent on each page. This data was analyzed to identify the breadth of Web searches, the number and diversity of queries, the unique pages visited for each task, the query reformulations, and the dwell time. The responses to the pre- and post-task questions were also saved in the database, and allowed the researchers to assess the learning processes, experiences, and outcomes, as perceived by the participants themselves before and after the task. The online diary, integrated as part of the Web interface, was used by the participants to enter information about their offline search activities and information sources. A rich collection of data, obtained through the online diary and the interview was analyzed qualitatively, provides insight into the search behavior and learning experiences and how the participants consulted the offline sources (known and unknown) in addition to the online sources. Along with the transcribed semi-structured interviews and the retrieved diary data, the contents were coded inductively, based on emerging themes. As this study was exploratory in nature, we were more interested in connecting concepts and seeing potential patterns inductively rather than applying pre-existing concepts to the data [29].

Last, we analyzed the reports that the participants created as part of the writing assignment at the end of each task. The participants wrote their reports using Etherpad, an open-source text editor that allows saving of the writing content and captures other activities performed by the user during the writing task. This includes the entire edit history, copying, pasting, and editing, with playback options. While such rich information content could be used for assessing how the users created knowledge in the final cognitive phase, Create, this was not a part of the current study. In future, we plan to use the reports to identify the atomic actions performed by the user during each task and how they can reflect the construction of knowledge. For this study, we have used qualitative coding of the writing contents to support our quantitative findings.

5 RESULTS

We discuss our results and observations for each of the research questions.

5.1 Search behavior according to the cognitive dimension of learning

The following findings pertain to the first research question, which examines the relationship between search behaviors and levels of learning-related tasks. We identified different search behaviors and examined how they vary as the levels of cognitive complexity changes in the tasks.

Null hypothesis: *"There is no statistically significant influence of the task complexity on the observed search behaviors."*

We performed one-way within-subjects ANOVA (with task complexity level as the independent variable), and post-hoc tests using Tukey's HSD to determine if the null hypothesis was tenable.

5.1.1 Number of unique pages visited. Examining the total number of unique pages visited for each task, we observed that it correlates negatively with the levels of task complexity. The number of unique pages visited was highest for the *Analyze* task followed by the *Remember and Understand* task. However, the difference across tasks was not significant to reject null hypothesis.

5.1.2 Number of unique pages saved. The participants were asked to save the Web pages that they deemed useful for the completion of the task. Similar to the results on the pages visited, the number of unique pages saved did not exhibit any significant correlation with the levels of task complexity. The highest number of pages was saved for the first Remember and Understand task ($M = 3.3, SD = 2.5$), while the lowest was observed for the third task *Analyze* ($M = 2.5, SD = 1.4$).

5.1.3 Number of queries. The number of queries, measured across each task was maximum for *Analyze* task ($M = 9.7, SD = 21.2$) and minimum for *Apply* task ($M = 4.7, SD = 5.6$). The results of one-way ANOVA did not show any statistically significant difference.

5.1.4 Query Length. For our analysis, we measured query length as the average number of words in all the queries submitted for a task. The longest queries were observed in the last task, *Evaluate* ($M = 5.2, SD = 3.66$), while the *Apply* task produced shortest queries ($M = 2.9, SD = 1.6$). The results of one-way ANOVA supported the effect of task complexity on the query length [$F(3, 120) = 3.25, p = 0.02$]. Post-hoc comparisons using Tukey's HSD test confirmed the difference between length of queries between the *Apply* and *Evaluate* tasks (Figure 2).

5.1.5 Query Diversity. Query diversity measures the number of unique query terms used during a search task. We have used stemming to reduce the query terms to their respective base forms without affixes. We observed that the participants used most diverse queries during the third and first tasks associated with the *Analyze* level ($M = 21.5, SD = 37.6$) and the *Remember and Understand* cognitive level respectively ($M = 20.1, SD = 31.4$) (Figure 2). The query diversity was minimal during the second task (i.e., *Apply*) ($M = 12.5, SD = 12.2$), while the final task (i.e., *Evaluate*) produced the second least diverse queries ($M = 15, SD = 17.8$). A one-way within subjects ANOVA was calculated to compare the query diversity for the tasks at varying levels of complexity. However, the results were not significant [$F(3, 120) = 0.77, p = 0.511$].

5.1.6 Query Reformulations. We measured Levenshtein distance between two successive queries [33] and obtained the average query edit distance for each task. This measure was expected to highlight the effect of task complexity on query reformulations. The results of one-way ANOVA showed no effect of task complexity on the average edit distance for the four tasks [$F(3, 120) = 1.1, p = 0.35$]. The edit distance for the *Evaluate* task ($M = 28.2, SD = 34.4$) was the highest while the edit distance for the *Apply* task was lowest ($M = 17.3, SD = 27.5$) (Figure 2). This shows that the participants made more query reformulations during the *Evaluate* task than the *Apply* task.

5.1.7 Average dwell time for each task. The average dwell time measured the time (in seconds) that the participants spent on the Web pages for each task. We observed that the average dwell time was longest for the *Apply* task ($M = 4363.2, SD = 6600$) and lowest for the *Evaluate* task ($M = 2294.5, SD = 3842.9$) (Figure 1). However, the results of one-way within subjects ANOVA did not show any significant difference in average dwell time across tasks

[$F(3, 120) = 1.96, p = 0.1$]. Therefore, we were not able to reject the null hypothesis.

5.2 Learning process and outcomes related to task complexity levels

Our second research question explores how the search tasks influenced the participants' learning processes and outcomes. We relied on the responses to pre- and post-task questionnaires, measured on a five-point Likert scale, to identify the potential patterns exhibited in their learning processes and outcomes. The search task acts as an intervention measure that facilitates learning. We performed Pearson's product-moment correlation coefficient to determine the relationship between various factors, and paired samples t-test to assess the pre-search and post-search assessments of similar factors. We also performed within-subjects ANOVA to investigate the effect of different task complexity levels on the various learning and knowledge outcomes.

Null hypothesis: *"The search tasks do not exhibit any significant difference in the learning processes and their respective outcomes."*

5.2.1 Pre- and post-task topic knowledge. We conducted a paired-samples t-test to compare the perceived pre-task and post-task topic knowledge. There was a significant difference between the pre-task topic knowledge ($M = 2.75, SD = 1.1$) and the post-task topic knowledge for all of the four tasks ($M = 3.71, SD = 1.03$)[$t(123) = 8.5, p < 0.001$], which shows that the participants perceived a 35% increase in topic knowledge. There was also a significant difference in pre-task topic knowledge for the four complexity levels [$F(3, 120) = 15.07, p < 0.001$], with post-hoc comparison using Tukey's HSD confirming the same.

5.2.2 Levels of task complexity and post-task topic interest. The level of task complexity showed some correlation with the post-search interest in the topic ($r = 0.51, p < 0.001$). As the task complexity increased, the participants reported an increase in topic interest after the task. This observation was supported by paired-samples t-test [$t(123) = 4.05, p < 0.001$].

5.2.3 Levels of task complexity and difficulty assessments. The overall difficulty of the task as perceived by the participants was measured as a combination of two difficulty measures: search difficulty and understanding difficulty. The post-task search difficulty and the overall difficulty showed positive correlations to the level of task complexity ($r = 0.202, p = 0.02$ and $r = 0.25, p = 0.006$ respectively). A one-way ANOVA was conducted to evaluate the effect of task complexity on the perceived search difficulty of the task. A significant effect was observed on the pre-task search difficulty assessment for all the four tasks [$F(3, 120) = 3.99, p = 0.01$]. The results indicate that with increasing complexity of the task, the participants found it increasingly difficult to search for answers. Post hoc analysis confirmed that search difficulty of the *Remember and Understand* task ($M = 1.45, SD = 0.58$) differed significantly from the *Apply* ($M = 2.13, SD = 1.003$) and *Analyze* tasks ($M = 2.16, SD = 1.09$).

5.2.4 Task complexity levels and help of prior knowledge. The task complexity levels showed negative correlations with the help of prior topic knowledge, measured before and after performing

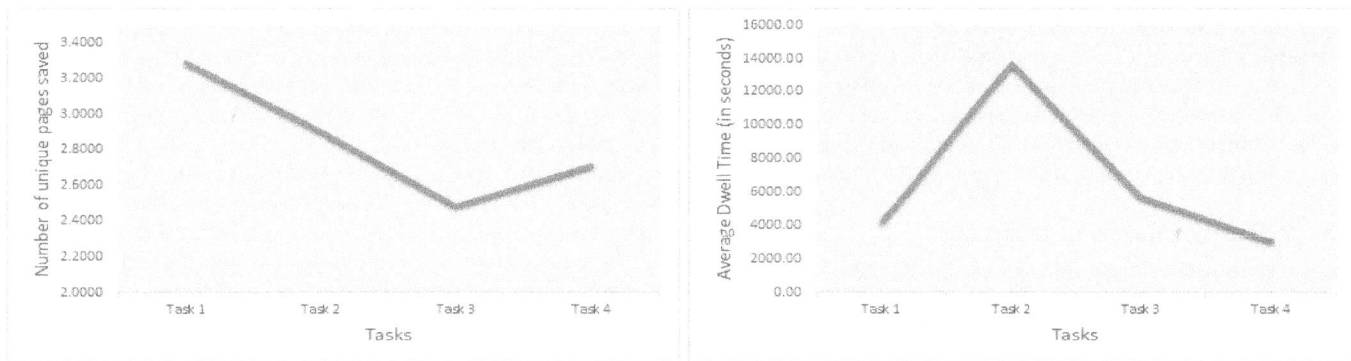

(a) Unique pages saved.

(b) Average Dwell Time.

Figure 1: Page-specific search behaviors based on task complexity levels.

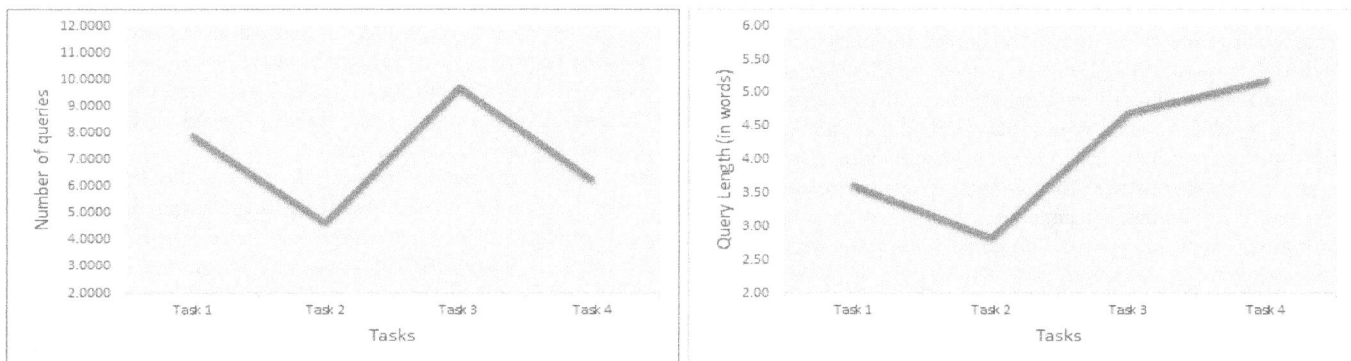

(a) Number of queries.

(b) Query Length.

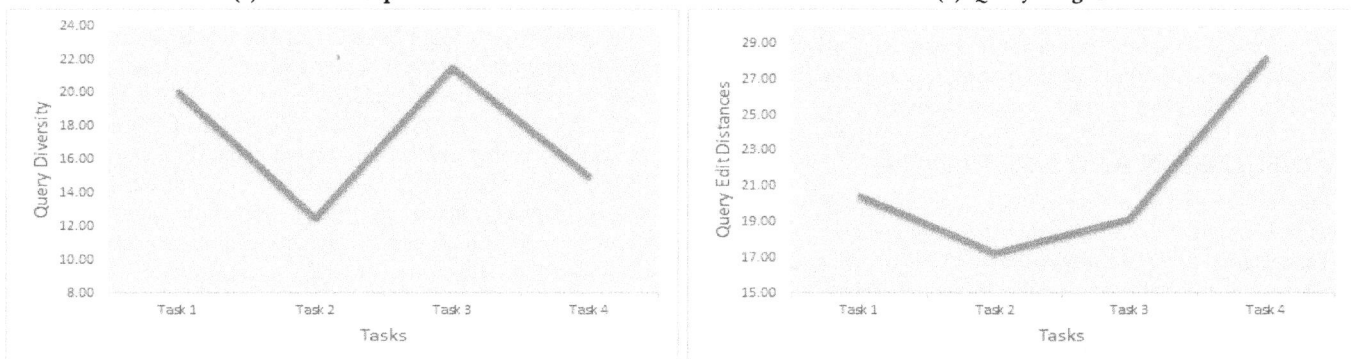

(c) Query Diversity.

(d) Query Reformulations.

Figure 2: Query-specific search behaviors based on task complexity levels.

the task ($r = -0.342, p < 0.01$ and $r = -0.302, p < 0.01$), which signifies that as the task gets more complex, the users felt that their prior topic knowledge was more inadequate. The results of one way within subjects ANOVA highlighted that the pre-task assessment of the help of prior knowledge showed significant difference between task complexities [$F(3, 120) = 7.68, p < 0.001$ and $F(3, 120) = 8.49, p < 0.001$].

5.2.5 Other observations. We also observed a strong correlation between pre- and post-task assessments of prior knowledge help ($r = 0.636, p < 0.001$). This signifies that the users were fairly accurate in their judgment of how much their prior topic knowledge would help them in the task, and hence, their post-search assessments showed a strong relationship to their pre-search assessment.

We also observed a positive correlation between the post-task interest level of the participants and the increase in topic knowledge ($r = 0.69, p < 0.001$). This signifies that the participants' perceived increase in knowledge was influenced by their reported topic interest after each task. Also, the pre- and post-task difficulty assessments for searching and understanding (i.e., how difficult the participants expected seeking and understanding information to be, and how difficult they actually found seeking and understanding information to be) correlated with the reported overall difficulty.

5.3 Actions related to learning

For our third research question, we used a list of twenty action verbs, which were randomized and provided to the participants at the end of each task. The details of the action verbs used can be found in Appendix D. Instead of selecting words belonging to different cognitive complexity levels, we preferred to use an inductive approach. Each verb represents some learning action, and we asked the users to select all those actions that they found associated at the end of each task.

Later we performed word-based clustering using Word2Vec[2] to merge some of the words that were similar and came up with a new list of 15 words. Word2Vec uses a two-layered neural network and a vector space of more than a hundred dimensions, where each word is plotted as a vector. Words that are similar contextually are located at close proximity and can be considered similar. 'Show' was merged with 'Demonstrate' (new category: *Demonstrate*) as they are semantically similar, and similarly, 'Identify' was merged with 'Distinguish' (new category: *Distinguish*), 'Conclude' with 'Infer' (new category: *Conclude*), and 'Plan' and 'Design' with 'Construct' (new category: *Construct*).

In Figure 4, we present the top actions that the users selected for each task. It is interesting to note that the actions Distinguish, Organize and Conclude are most frequent for all the four tasks. The users have also identified List and Define for Task 1 (*Remember and Understand*), Relate and Demonstrate for Task 2 (*Apply*), List and Relate for Task 3 (*Analyze*), and Demonstrate and Relate for Task 4 (*Evaluate*), as the other frequent learning actions.

6 DISCUSSION AND LIMITATIONS

In this study, based on the revised taxonomy of educational objectives, we explored how the learning-oriented exploratory search tasks, designed hierarchically based on the cognitive complexity levels, may be indicative of specific information seeking behaviors. We also examined how the perceived search and learning outcomes and experiences can be linked to cognitive complexity levels. By broadening the scope of information sources to online (Web) as well as offline (known and unknown sources), we aimed to capture a wider range of human information behavior and learning outcomes.

First, in response to our first research questions, we observed different patterns in the Web-related search behavior of the participants. For example, the participants produced longer queries as the task complexity increased. Some other observations – like how a particular task leads to larger number of Websites being visited or saved, or more query reformulations – were found to be not statistically significant and would require further investigations before confirming any hypothesis.

Our second research question helped us to assess the importance of seeking as a learning process. We used the search tasks as an intervention, and assessed the knowledge and learning outcomes, as well as task difficulties and engagements, before and after the tasks. The results, all of which were statistically significant, supports that learning is an important outcome of searching. By comparing the influence of different task complexities on different pre- and post-task assessments, we hypothesize that the increase in topic knowledge decreases as the task gets more complex cognitively. Also, the participants feel less confident about their prior knowledge as they encounter tasks of higher cognitive levels. One interesting observation was how the topic interest increases from the *Remember and Understand* task to the *Apply* task, and from *Analyze* task to *Evaluate* task. While further studies will be needed to explain the decline in topic interests from *Apply* to *Analyze*, the user engagement patterns show some dependence with the task complexity levels.

Last, to answer our third research question, we used a collection of verbs to relate the learning actions with the task complexity levels. The presence of Organize, Distinguish and Conclude in all the three lists highlights the overlap between various learning processes in all the task complexity levels. We suspect that the presence of the writing assignment at the end of each task, for which the users had to organize the information searched and create a coherent paragraph, might have influenced their choice of actions. Nevertheless, the selection of action verbs is an interesting indicator of the perceived learning in each of the cognitive complexity levels.

One participant explained, "I started by searching cyber bullying to find a *definition* for it. Then, in order to *distinguish* it from other forms of harassment, I had to learn more about those other ones, which led to me *classifying* them, and later, the long/short term risks of cyber-bullying. I *listed* those. The whole process required *identifying* terms and the different types of harassment."

We would also like to highlight some of the limitations of this work. The order of the tasks, which followed the hierarchical levels of cognitive complexities, could have helped the participants in their learning tasks and influenced the results. As our task design closely follows the taxonomy of learning, it could have reduced the cognitive workload of the participants and aided them in assimilating and constructing knowledge. The increasing topic knowledge might have caused decrease in Web pages visited and saved, and queries constructed, without causing any decline in task performance. It would be interesting to observe the results by randomizing or rotating the task order and using multiple topics for each task. This would allow us to eliminate some of the extra variables and focus more on the identifiable behavioral patterns by task.

Additionally, our first research question, which looks at information seeking behavior for different task complexity levels, exploited only the Web search logs. Although the online diary content records the interaction of the participants with offline sources (known and unknown), yet it includes more information about the source, the interaction, and the response, with little or no information about the information seeking behavior.

The second research question relies strongly on the self-reports, and lacks any explicit measure for learning outcomes. While self-reports are often good indicators of the learning processes and experiences, we need other measures to validate the claims made

---

[2]https://deeplearning4j.org/word2vec.html

(a) Pre-task topic knowledge.

(b) Post-task topic knowledge.

(c) Pre-assessment of help of prior knowledge.

(d) Post-task search difficulty assessment.

(e) Post-task understanding difficulty assessment.

(f) Post-task overall difficulty assessment.

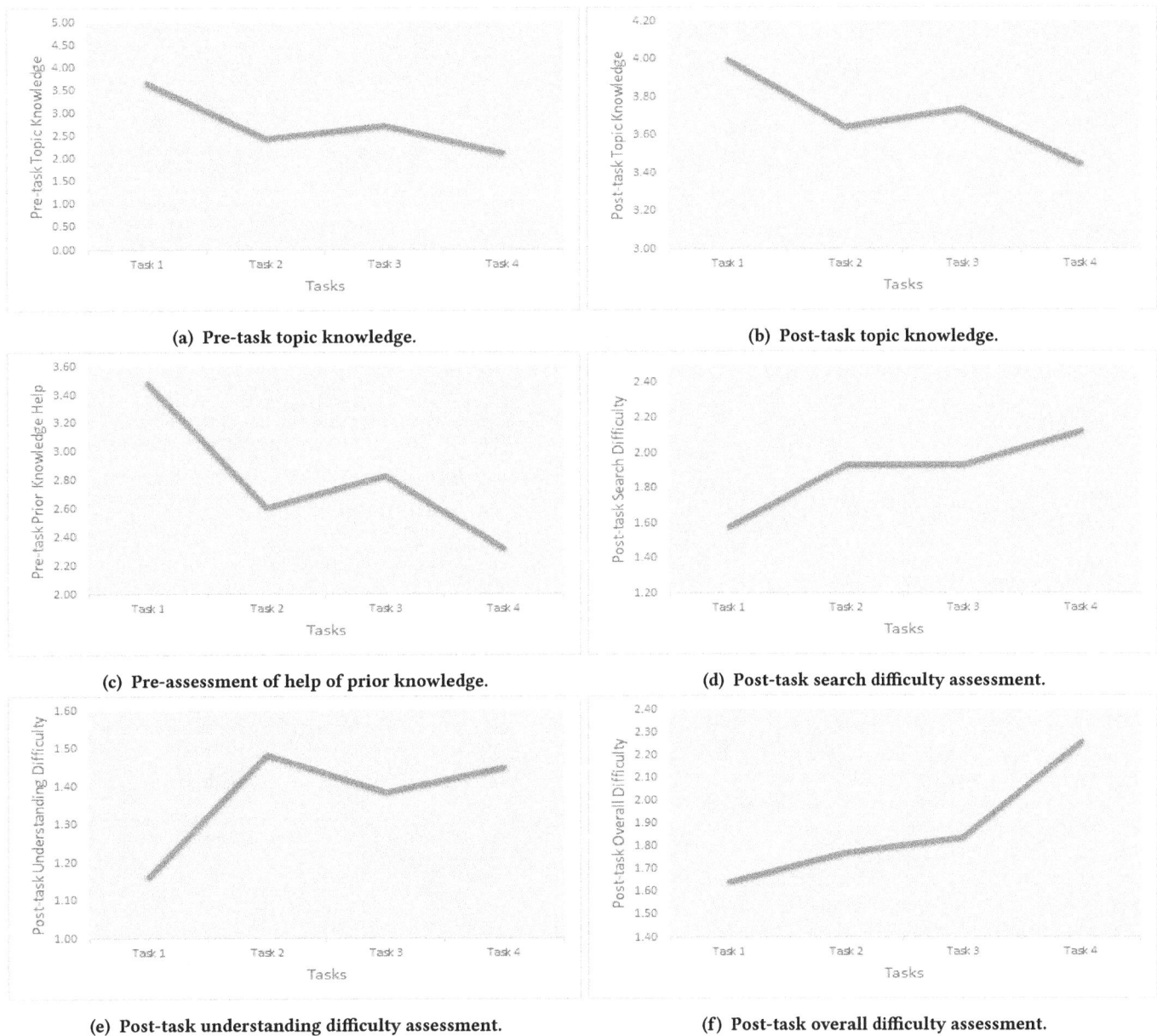

Figure 3: Learning outcomes based on task complexity levels

by the participants. Considering other types of data such as learning assessments may be useful as we attempt to expand our work to advance the research area in the LIS on searching and learning.

7 CONCLUSION AND FUTURE DIRECTIONS

In the study described in this paper, we investigated the differences in information seeking behavior and the learning outcomes of the participants when given four learning-oriented tasks, each belonging to a different cognitive complexity level. By exploring peoples' information seeking behavior and how it may be related to their various cognitive processes, this study offers further insights on how some aspects of searching may be associated with various aspects of learning and cognitive processes. Considering especially the limited number of studies that explicitly discuss this connection of searching and learning, this study attempts to integrate various aspects of searching and learning.

We observed and analyzed the participants' task engagements, search difficulties, and knowledge levels, as they sought information both online and offline for each of the four tasks. Distinct search patterns were observed (like differences in query length) and learning outcomes (like increase in knowledge), which contributes to the recent efforts in LIS to view information seeking and learning as

(a) Task 1 (Remember and Understand).

(b) Task 2 (Apply).

(c) Task 3 (Analyze).

(d) Task 4 (Evaluate).

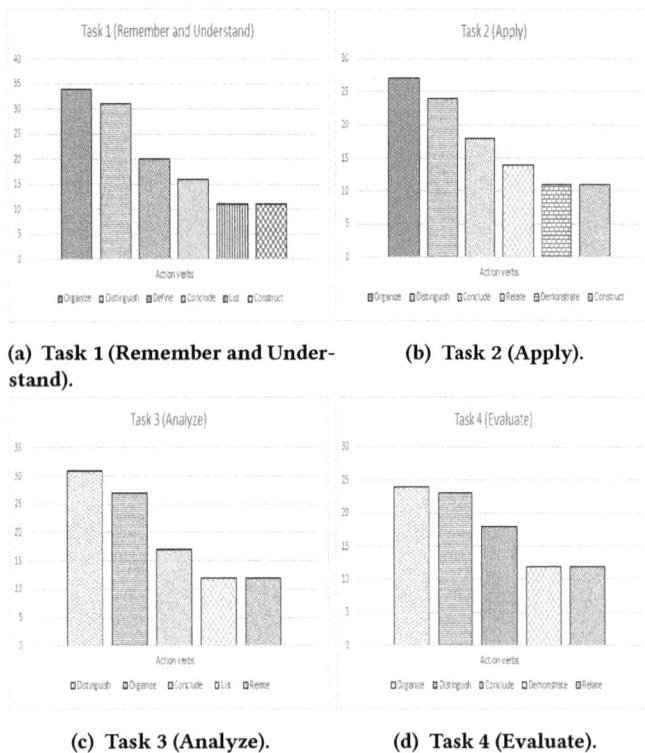

Figure 4: Top learning actions for each task.

co-existing and not isolated processes. We also highlight the overlap in various learning actions in learning-oriented search tasks. We hope that this study contributes to situating searching within the broader context of learning, and in connecting the different learning objectives to search behaviors.

For our future study, we would consider combining the three types of sources into two categories instead: online and offline sources. This would help in eliminating the overlaps between Web-based sources and unknown sources, because our participants heavily incorporated information they found on the Web for the unknown sources. We would also like to explore if participants would utilize offline sources if it is made optional, and what situations warrant the use of known and unknown offline sources. This study also provided us with many useful insights about how participants evaluate and select sources, based on trustworthiness, authenticity, and anonymity, which could be used for future research directions.

8 ACKNOWLEDGEMENT

The work reported here is supported by the Institute of Museum and Library Services (IMLS) grant no. LG-81-16-0025-16. We would also like to thank Matthew Mitsui and SeoYoon Sung, both of who made significant contributions to running this user study.

REFERENCES

[1] Lorin W Anderson, David R Krathwohl, P Airasian, K Cruikshank, R Mayer, P Pintrich, J Raths, and M Wittrock. 2001. A taxonomy for learning, teaching and assessing: A revision of Bloom's taxonomy. *New York. Longman Publishing. Artz, AF, & Armour-Thomas, E.(1992). Development of a cognitive-metacognitive framework for protocol analysis of mathematical problem solving in small groups. Cognition and Instruction 9, 2 (2001), 137–175.*

[2] Nicholas J Belkin, Robert N Oddy, and Helen M Brooks. 1982. ASK for information retrieval: Part I. Background and theory. *Journal of documentation* 38, 2 (1982), 61–71.

[3] Benjamin S Bloom et al. 1956. Taxonomy of educational objectives. Vol. 1: Cognitive domain. *New York: McKay* (1956), 20–24.

[4] Pia Borlund. 2003. The concept of relevance in IR. *Journal of the Association for Information Science and Technology* 54, 10 (2003), 913–925.

[5] Kevyn Collins-Thompson, Soo Young Rieh, Carl C Haynes, and Rohail Syed. 2016. Assessing learning outcomes in web search: A comparison of tasks and query strategies. In *Proceedings of the 2016 ACM on Conference on Human Information Interaction and Retrieval. ACM,* 163–172.

[6] Brenda Dervin. 1983. An Overview of Sense-Making Research: Concepts. *Methods, and Results to Date [on-line] Disponível na Internet na URL http://edfu. lis. uiuc. edu/allerton/96/w1/Dervin83a. html* (1983).

[7] Evren Eryilmaz, Jakko van der Pol, Terry Ryan, Philip Martin Clark, and Justin Mary. 2013. Enhancing student knowledge acquisition from online learning conversations. *International Journal of Computer-Supported Collaborative Learning* 8, 1 (2013), 113–144.

[8] Luanne Freund, Samuel Dodson, and Rick Kopak. 2016. On Measuring Learning in Search: A Position Paper.. In *SAL@ SIGIR.*

[9] Souvick Ghosh and Chirag Shah. 2017. Information seeking in learning-oriented search. *Proceedings of the Association for Information Science and Technology* 54, 1 (2017), 682–684.

[10] Roberto González-Ibáñez and Chirag Shah. 2011. Coagmento: A system for supporting collaborative information seeking. *Proceedings of the Association for Information Science and Technology* 48, 1 (2011), 1–4.

[11] Preben Hansen and Soo Young Rieh. 2016. Recent advances on searching as learning: An introduction to the special issue. (2016).

[12] Peter Ingwersen. 1996. Cognitive perspectives of information retrieval interaction: elements of a cognitive IR theory. *Journal of documentation* 52, 1 (1996), 3–50.

[13] Bernard J Jansen, Danielle Booth, and Brian Smith. 2009. Using the taxonomy of cognitive learning to model online searching. *Information Processing & Management* 45, 6 (2009), 643–663.

[14] Diane Kelly, Jaime Arguello, Ashlee Edwards, and Wan-ching Wu. 2015. Development and evaluation of search tasks for IIR experiments using a cognitive complexity framework. In *Proceedings of the 2015 International Conference on The Theory of Information Retrieval. ACM,* 101–110.

[15] David R Krathwohl and LW Anderson. 2001. A taxonomy for learning, teaching, and assessing: A revision of Bloom's taxonomy of educational objectives (Abridged ed.). (2001).

[16] Gary Marchionini. 2006. Exploratory search: from finding to understanding. *Commun. ACM* 49, 4 (2006), 41–46.

[17] Jean Piaget. 1976. Piaget's theory. In *Piaget and his school.* Springer, 11–23.

[18] Rebecca Reynolds. 2016. Defining, designing for, and measuring "social constructivist digital literacy" development in learners: a proposed framework. *Educational Technology Research and Development* 64, 4 (2016), 735–762.

[19] Soo Young Rieh, Kevyn Collins-Thompson, Preben Hansen, and Hye-Jung Lee. 2016. Towards searching as a learning process: A review of current perspectives and future directions. *Journal of Information Science* 42, 1 (2016), 19–34.

[20] David E Rumelhart and Donald A Norman. 1981. Analogical processes in learning. *Cognitive skills and their acquisition* (1981), 335–359.

[21] Daniel Russell. 2015. Mindtools: what does it mean to be literate in the age of Google? *Journal of Computing Sciences in Colleges* 30, 3 (2015), 5–6.

[22] Daniel L Schacter, Daniel T Gilbert, and Daniel M Wegner. 2011. Semantic and episodic memory. *Psychology,* (2011), 240–241.

[23] Alfred Schütz and Thomas Luckmann. 1974. The Structures of the Life World.(translated by R. Zaner and HT Engelhardt). (1974).

[24] Chirag Shah. 2010. Coagmento-a collaborative information seeking, synthesis and sense-making framework. *Integrated demo at CSCW* 2010 (2010).

[25] Gerry Stahl. 2000. A model of collaborative knowledge-building. In *Fourth international conference of the learning sciences,* Vol. 10. Mahwah, NJ: Erlbaum, 2000a, 70–77.

[26] Pertti Vakkari. 2016. Searching as learning: A systematization based on literature. *Journal of Information Science* 42, 1 (2016), 7–18.

[27] James Waters and Susan Gasson. 2006. Social engagement in an online community of inquiry. *ICIS 2006 Proceedings* (2006), 47.

[28] Barbara M Wildemuth and Luanne Freund. 2012. Assigning search tasks designed to elicit exploratory search behaviors. In *Proceedings of the Symposium on Human-Computer Interaction and Information Retrieval. ACM,* 4.

[29] Tom D Wilson. 1981. On user studies and information needs. *Journal of documentation* 37, 1 (1981), 3–15.

[30] Tom D Wilson. 1999. Models in information behaviour research. *Journal of documentation* 55, 3 (1999), 249–270.

[31] Thomas D Wilson. 2000. Human information behavior. *Informing science* 3, 2 (2000), 49–56.

[32] Wan-Ching Wu, Diane Kelly, Ashlee Edwards, and Jaime Arguello. 2012. Grannies, tanning beds, tattoos and NASCAR: Evaluation of search tasks with varying levels of cognitive complexity. In *Proceedings of the 4th Information Interaction in Context Symposium*. ACM, 254–257.

[33] Li Yujian and Liu Bo. 2007. A normalized Levenshtein distance metric. *IEEE transactions on pattern analysis and machine intelligence* 29, 6 (2007), 1091–1095.

Appendices

A OVERALL TASK ASSIGNMENT

Below is the overall study assignment. Please read carefully. This overall topic should help you guide your 4 tasks as well as your writing process:

You are among the main leaders of a student organization that raises awareness of the issue of cyber bullying. Teachers, educators and policymakers of your local community have recognized your efforts, and they have asked you to write a brief report on cyber bullying. Your report will be used as part of their training materials for the schoolteachers, educators and decision makers who will implement new practices and strategies within the local community.

Your report should be at least 500 words. Concentrate on exploring and answering the 4 task questions when searching and creating your report. Each task answers should contribute to at least one paragraph in your report.

You may add extra paragraphs for a more coherent structure later (optional). You can also copy and use snippets to collect information that you deem useful for writing the report. The report should be organized and written in ways that your readers would be able to understand and use for their implementation of strategies.

B TASK INSTRUCTIONS ABOUT INFORMATION SOURCES

As you are completing the tasks, please make sure to use the three information sources:

- Web (i.e., general search engines like Google, Bing.com or Yahoo!)
- Known people:
  The known people include your close friends, acquaintances, classmates, anyone you know. There are many ways that you can communicate with them about your questions both on and offline. For example, you can 1) Consult in person, (2) Call, text, or email them, (3) Use social media sites like Facebook and Twitter, or (4) Use mobile applications like Slack, WeChat, and SnapChat.
- Unknown people:
  The unknown people consist of those whom you do not know, but still have access to as information sources. This could include various online question-answering sites like YahooAnswers, Reddit, Quora, StackOverflow, answers.com, etc. You can also post your question(s) in public groups you belong to on social media sites such as Facebook. You can also visit information centers, such as libraries, to speak to librarians or assistants at an information center.

C PRE-TASK AND POST-TASK QUESTIONNAIRES

C.1 Pre-task Questions

(1) How much do you know about this topic of the task? (1=nothing, 3=somewhat, 5=I know a lot)
(2) How much do you think your knowledge on this topic will help you with the task? (1=not at all helpful, 3=somewhat helpful, 5=extremely helpful)
(3) How interested are you to learn about this topic of the task? (1=not at all interested, 3=somewhat, 5=extremely interested)
(4) How difficult do you think it will be to seek for information about this topic of the task? (1=not at all difficult, 3=somewhat difficult, 5=extremely difficult)
(5) How difficult do you think it will be to understand the information you find on this topic? (1=not at all difficult, 3=somewhat difficult, 5=extremely difficult)

C.2 Post-Task Questions

(1) How long did it take for you to complete this task in total? (approximately in minutes)
(2) How much do you know about this task topic now? (1=nothing, 3=somewhat, 5=I know a lot)
(3) How much do you think your prior knowledge on this topic helped you with the task? (1=not at all helpful, 3=somewhat helpful, 5=extremely helpful)
(4) Overall, how difficult was this task? (1=not at all difficult, 3=somewhat difficult, 5=extremely difficult)
(5) How difficult was it to seek information about this topic of this task? (1=not at all difficult, 3=somewhat difficult, 5=extremely difficult)
(6) How difficult was it to understand the information you found? (1=not at all difficult, 3=somewhat difficult, 5=extremely difficult)
(7) How much did your interest in the topic increase? (1=not at all, 3=somewhat, 5=extremely)

D ACTION VERB MATCHING

Using the word bank provided below, select five relevant action verbs that best describe the actions you took while engaging in the entire process of the given task (including all aspects such as searching and browsing, consulting with your sources, reading given content/response, and the writing process). Use the description box to elaborate the details of what you did for each aspect (if different). Clicking on appropriate checkboxes will make the selection.

Table 1: List of action verbs.

Distinguish	Plan	List	Critique
Show	Construct	Produce	Organize
Define	Conclude	Judge	Demonstrate
Identify	Argue	Classify	Design
Infer	Solve	Relate	Inspect

Informing the Design of Spoken Conversational Search

Perspective Paper

Johanne R. Trippas
RMIT University
Melbourne, Australia
johanne.trippas@rmit.edu.au

Damiano Spina
RMIT University
Melbourne, Australia
damiano.spina@rmit.edu.au

Lawrence Cavedon
RMIT University
Melbourne, Australia
lawrence.cavedon@rmit.edu.au

Hideo Joho
University of Tsukuba
Tsukuba, Japan
hideo@slis.tsukuba.ac.jp

Mark Sanderson
RMIT University
Melbourne, Australia
mark.sanderson@rmit.edu.au

ABSTRACT

We conducted a laboratory-based observational study where pairs of people performed search tasks communicating verbally. Examination of the discourse allowed commonly used interactions to be identified for Spoken Conversational Search (SCS). We compared the interactions to existing models of search behaviour. We find that SCS is more complex and interactive than traditional search. This work enhances our understanding of different search behaviours and proposes research opportunities for an audio-only search system. Future work will focus on creating models of search behaviour for SCS and evaluating these against actual SCS systems.

KEYWORDS

Conversational Search; Voice Interaction

ACM Reference format:
Johanne R. Trippas, Damiano Spina, Lawrence Cavedon, Hideo Joho, and Mark Sanderson. 2018. Informing the Design of Spoken Conversational Search. *CHIIR '18: 2018 Conference on Human Information Interaction & Retrieval, March 11–15, 2018, New Brunswick, NJ, USA.* ACM, New York, NY, USA, 10 pages. DOI: https://doi.org/10.1145/3176349.3176387

1 INTRODUCTION

With the development of accurate speech recognition and text to speech synthesis, it has become possible to speak simple natural language queries and for an information retrieval (IR) system to verbally respond. However, simply speaking the textual output of a standard search engine result page (SERP) has been found to be insufficient [27]. The underlying components of an Spoken Conversational Search (SCS) system (where communication between user and system is mediated verbally through audio) will need to operate differently from a traditional IR system [36, 37].

Conversational search has been identified as an important new research direction at several meetings including the Second Strategic Workshop on IR [2]. At one recent meeting[1] it was indicated that there is a lack of understanding of search tasks, search result description, and evaluation of SCS. More importantly, the IR community lacks a broader understanding on how users will interact with these highly interactive search systems and which components maybe involved.

In this paper, we provide an insight of conversational search challenges and opportunities, specifically on what search interactions might look like. Note, we focus on audio-only SCS excluding multi-modal or visual interactions. Thus, we designed a study to observe characteristics of spoken interactions and use the observations of the study to examine differences between "conventional text" search and SCS. Hence, this research is not conducted in a (typical) statistical manner but explores the ranges of possibilities or actions in a SCS setting [8].

Radlinski and Craswell [26] define a conversational search system as "...a system for retrieving information that permits a mixed-initiative back and forth between a user and agent, where the agent's actions are chosen in response to a model of current user needs within the current conversation, using both short- and long-term knowledge of the user". With this definition we attempt to place our observations within the context of existing models of information seeking behaviour (e.g., Belkin's Anomalous State of Knowledge (ASK) [6] or Marchionini's Information Seeking Process (ISP) [20]).

Our main contributions are threefold, we identify: *(i)* the impact of the audio channel on interactions between the user and the system, and on search interactions; *(ii)* different levels of system involvement suggesting SCS systems will have to become *actively* involved in a users' search process; *(iii)* new research opportunities linked to the change of the information transfer channel.

In the following section, an overview is provided of our observational experimental setup and the participants. Section 3 describes observations related to the change in modality of interaction (i.e., audio channel) highlighting the importance of understanding the interactivity of this new search paradigm. Then we present observations in Section 4, which have a strong link to search. In Section 5 we provide an overview and discuss the suggested results from the

---

[1]International Workshop on Conversational Approaches to Information Retrieval (CAIR) at SIGIR 2017 https://sites.google.com/view/cair-ws/

made observations. We also suggest ways of differentiating diverse search systems depending on their involvement with the users' search process. The final section provides a conclusion and outlines future work. This paper will provide related work throughout the observations allowing for a better demonstration and integration with our findings.

2 METHODOLOGY

An empirical laboratory study was conducted to investigate the aspects of an SCS system [37]. This study was designed to understand how users communicate in an audio-only search setting and focuses on the issues one could encounter when using such system. Thus, observing how people search in this setting provides initial insight into the interactions which take place. We also consider our observations with existing research and models creating a broader understanding of search in a spoken conversational setting. Thus, we combine previous research with our empirical observations in order to extend the general search expertise.

2.1 Observational Study

The study consisted of a series of sessions, each with two participants, one participant acting as the *seeker* (or user) and the other as the *intermediary*. The seeker received a backstory describing a *task* to find information on a certain topic and had no access to anything to satisfy that information need (such as a computer). The backstories were based on TREC topics (Q02, R03, and T04) and are described by Bailey et al. [4]. The intermediary had access to a search engine through a computer but did not have access to the seeker's backstory. Participants were not able to see each others' facial expressions. All tasks were randomized in order. The roles of the participants were randomly assigned.

The participants had to collaborate with each other in order to satisfy the information need. Before and after each scenario the participants filled out a short questionnaire and at the end of the experiment, a semi-structured interview was conducted. Participants could leave at any time and there were no adverse consequences apart from 90 minutes of the participants' time. All interactions were recorded and transcribed for analysis.[2] This process is described in more detail by Trippas et al. [38].

2.2 Participants

The study involved twenty six participants recruited through a mailing list.[3] Fifteen participants were female and eleven were male. Participants' mean age was thirty (SD=11). Twenty two participants (85%) reported to be a native English speaker and four participants (15%) reported to have a high level of English. Eighteen participants reported that they held either a Bachelor's or Master's degree (69%) and eight participants reported their highest level of degree was awarded at high school (31%). The frequency of main fields of education were Science (19%), Engineering (19%), and Law (11%). The majority of participants were students (73%) or employed (19%). Computer use for over ten years was reported by 85% of our

participants, while 15% reported use for 5-10 years. All participants reported that they used search engines daily with the majority of participants reporting that they used a search engine more than eight times per day (54%).

Participants rated their own search skills on a 5-point scale, where 1=novice and 5=expert. Participants' mean search skills was 3.9 (SD=0.5), with a minimum score of three and maximum of five. Participants reported their usage of intelligent personal assistants, such as Google Now, Siri, Amazon Echo or Cortana. The majority of the participants reported that they had used an assistant a couple of times in the past but did not use it anymore (27%). 19% of the participants reported that they used intelligent personal assistants one to three times per week.

3 NON-SEARCH RELATED OBSERVATIONS

Results are divided into two sections. First, Section 3 presents high level investigations, which are not constrained specifically to search but cover other aspects of SCS, such as communication and cognitive user models. The observations are linked to applicable more general models, which are also applicable to intelligent agents.

Second, Section 4 presents observations, which are framed in the ISP of Marchionini [20], allowing us to introduce our observations in a structured manner.

3.1 One Utterance Consists of Multiple Moves

Complexity appeared to be added in a search process by allowing users to convey their query verbally. In a traditional visual-textual interface, a mouse click or key press are single *moves*. Each action(s) a system needs to take is linked to an atomic move from the user. It could be said that we have a one-action search paradigm (action-response) in a visual-textual setting: if a user provides input (query) the system will respond (results). Search interactions in such a setting can be seen as a linear process.[4]

However, we observed that this paradigm does not hold in a verbal setting. Users were observed describing multiple moves in one utterance. Two such examples are shown in Figure 1. We also observed more than two moves in one utterance; however, this was rather unusual and needs further investigation. These two or more moves in a single utterance increase the complexity of seekers and intermediaries' interactions.

General information seeking behaviour models such as Wilson's information behaviour [41], Marchionini's ISP [20], or Saracevic's Stratified model [29] are too broad and not specific enough and therefore do not provide the necessary information about whether one utterance or interaction may have several moves. Belkin [7] however, describing his work with intermediaries, mentions that one utterance can contain several moves. Yet he does not elaborate on this aspect or on how this may translate in a non-human conversation and how a system should handle this conversation.

Several researchers have proposed ways to incorporate IR through dialogue [25, 31, 32]. Sitter and Stein [31] developed the COnversational Roles (COR) model based on dialogue acts as a general model for information-seeking dialogue combining it with a dialogue plan [3]. The plan is used to guide users through stages of IR

[2]Transcripts of the experiment are available at http://jtrippas.github.io/Spoken-Conversational-Search

[3]The mailing list is maintained by the Behavioural Business Lab at RMIT University, https://orsee.bf.rmit.edu.au/. RMIT University's Ethics Board approval number ASEHAPP 08-16.

[4] Note, this one-action search paradigm could be manipulated by seekers, for example opening several tabs from the SERP.

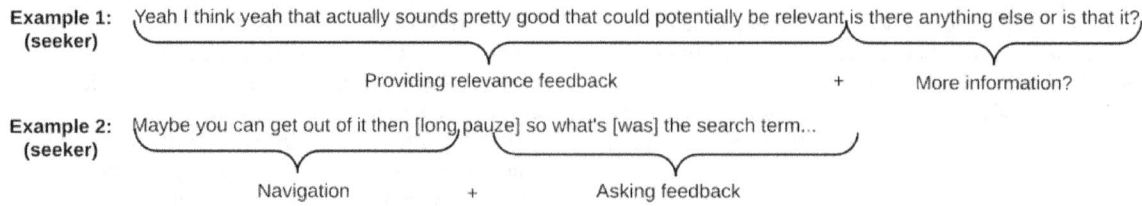

Figure 1: Multiple moves examples.

with two actors. These actors are noted as A (information seeker) and B (information provider) as illustrated in Figure 2. The Figure also provides the main overview of the COR model where the bold lines are the optimal path taken to solve an information need.

The moves (for example from one to two, Figure 2) consist of atomic dialogue acts [33]. By way of illustration, we take Example 2 from Figure 1 and attempts to apply it in the COR model. We can assign the first action of Example 2 to the notion of *request (A,B)* (Number one from the COR model). However, Example 2's second request action cannot be fit into COR's sequential model.

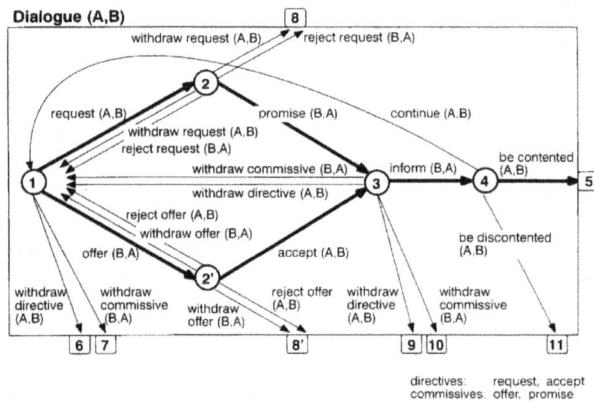

Figure 2: COnversational Roles (COR) model [31].

An alternative approach are scripts from Belkin et al. [10], which are effective interactions between the system and the user on an information seeking strategies (IIS) level [9]. The authors argue that depending on the kind of information need, different interactions may be appropriate. Thus, providing an (ideal) abstraction of the problem allows an understanding of the problem, from which responses (scripts) can be created.

Both the COR model and the scripts enable a form of prediction of which kind of interaction will be necessary following on from a previous move. One could argue that this is a form of advanced slot filling of Spoken Dialogue Systems [22]. Hence, if we could predict and simplify the input given from the user, we may be able to provide appropriate responses generated by the system. Dialogue scripts are a good idea and have worked previously, however, we will need to develop new scripts for this new spoken interaction paradigm.

Other features of the COR model include the flexibility in *mixed-initiative*, meaning that at any given time one of the actors can

decide what happens next or ask questions. Mixed-initiative dialogues allow for a more natural interaction but are more complex for the system to handle [21]. The model also allows for meta-communication by permitting the conversation to go through one of the loops at any point in time.

Allowing users to talk freely to a system will come with challenges from a system's perspective since the system will not be able to control the users' input utterances. The aspect of "freedom of speech" means that the system cannot guide or constrain users' options as easily as in a visual setting. For example, it will be more challenging to provide query refinement options or to check whether a user used the right search terms when browsing images. Simultaneously, it may be challenging from a user's perspective if the system provides multiple moves in one utterance.

However, notwithstanding these difficulties, allowing users this "freedom of speech" may encourage an information need expression that more closely represents their real knowledge gap rather than formulating a query for a box. It is important to keep in mind that this freedom of information need expression may be challenging at first for many users who are accustomed to expressing their need in a search box.

The *naturalness of the interaction* with a SCS system can be an aspect of the evaluation measure which is a measure in Spoken Dialogue Systems [19, 39]. We suggest that one of the aspects of this measure could be users uttering multiple moves in one turn. In a human-human interaction this is a behaviour which is observed and expected, and which the other actor can handle. Therefore, allowing users to utter multiple moves in one turn which the system can handle is likely to lead to positive interactions with the system.

3.2 User and System Model or Memory

> *"The overall approach is based on the idea of cognitive models or images that the components of the system have of one another and of themselves"* Belkin [7, p. 111]

We observed users building cognitive models of their partner during the course of the experiment:

User building model of intermediary: Some examples include seekers creating ideas of which actions intermediaries can perform. In one instance, the intermediary offers a function to the seeker by asking if they would like to open a link in a new tab. The seeker now knows that this is an option of the 'system' and later in that session the seeker requests several links to be opened in different tabs. Later in that session the seeker examines the extent of the function by asking ``Could I open the recyclers recycle uhm in a new tab... if it allows that'' and thus challenges the built intermediary model.

Intermediary building model of user: Other instances were recognized where intermediaries started creating a view of what users may want to hear as output. From the intermediaries we noticed two distinct differences in their utterances. Firstly, intermediaries had formed a cognitive model of *how the information should be presented* to the seeker. For example, through the interaction between the participants, one of the intermediaries was able to form a model of how the seeker preferred to pose queries (this particular seeker posed her queries in a distinctive way with Boolean aspects). As such, the interactions allowed the intermediary to establish a model of how the seeker would form or structure her information and was able to mimic this to satisfy her need.

Secondly, the intermediary had formed a cognitive model about *which information should be presented* to the seeker. In this instance, the intermediary reported names of objects. When the seeker posed another information need, the intermediary checked whether the seeker wanted object names again, even though it was not specified in the seeker's information need. Coincidentally this pair had another search task related to similar objects where the intermediary checked once more whether the seeker wanted the names.

As such, we make a distinction on the system side of how the information should be presented (**form**) and which information should be presented (**content**).

Creating memory over multiple turns/sessions: In this example, the seeker asked for "numbers" (i.e., numerical information) for a particular backstory. In the next task, the intermediary directly asked whether the seeker would like to navigate to the statistics section. This demonstrates an example of creating memory over multiple turns. In an other example, a participant pair had learned from a previous backstory that they could use Google Scholar which the seeker preferred. In the next search task, the intermediary explicitly mentioned that scholarly articles were available for their information need. This demonstrates that memory may be created over multiple sessions as well as multiple turns [26].

Cognitive models are concerned with the cognitive process underlying the search. Much research has been conducted in cognitive IR models [7, 11, 13]. Cognitive models represent search situations at a particular time where the user creates an image of what the system would respond to a particular action. However, the image of this system can change over time. More appropriate to our research is work by Belkin [7] which focuses on the cognitive model of a librarian as an intermediary to a database, particularly at how a librarian forms a cognitive model from the user through dialogue.

We formed the notion that both seeker and intermediary construct *images* or *models* of what the other person can do or which components they have. However, these models are influenced by the seekers' own lens and belief of the world. Similarly Ingwersen and Järvelin [18] mention that a document's author is influenced by their context while the recipient of that document will view it through their lens and belief in their context. Thus, the intended message and the received message may differ. Even though the message itself has been sent across without a noise source [30], the interpretation of the document may vary.

Understanding the cognitive model users form of a system is important for a variety of reasons. For example, understanding what users expect will happen next will allow us to create a system which conforms to the users' model and therefore does not surprise them if something unexpected occur.

We explored the idea of cognitive models of the system; however other ways exist of defining cognitive models [7]. For example, Brooks and Belkin [11] used a reference interview between the intermediary to create a mental model of the user's information need. The idea of using reference interviews to elicit information is not new; however, it could be an interesting "old" approach to a "new" problem. Thus using the conversational interactions would allow us to build a model of the user's information need while utilizing the system's search strategies.

3.3 Decision Offloading and Taking Control

We observed that intermediaries applied many different techniques to deal with the challenge of transferring information through an audio channel. Examples include reading out search results sequentially, summarizing a SERP, or requesting feedback as to whether more information had to be transferred, e.g.

> **Intermediary:** ''Uhm do you want some information about the cinnamon from that company''
> **Seeker:** ''No that is I think that's enough''
> **Intermediary:** ''Ah, what else do we need''

We also noticed that intermediaries became more involved in assisting to express the seeker's information need and taking a leading approach. In the following example, the intermediary *rewrites* the utterance of the seeker into a specific query.

> **Seeker:** ''... cinnamon is from Europe, so I was trying to look uhm is it from Europe or from other places''
> **Intermediary:** ''I look up cinnamon suppliers... in Europe''

We observed intermediaries becoming actively involved in trying to satisfy the seeker's information need by making decisions. These observations suggest that intermediaries have a significant role in deciding which information is transferred. The intermediaries are making decisions as to what information is appropriate to share at a given moment. This may also suggest that intermediaries have to make a *cost-benefit* calculation associated to each strategy in order to decide which one would be more likely to benefit the seeker.

These observations corroborate that, given the high cost of delivering information via a linear channel such as speech, it is not optimal to present everything. The system needs to decide which information it should present at each interaction by continuously estimating the satisfaction of the user.

We also observed seekers explicitly requesting the intermediary to make decisions for them, e.g.: ''uhm do you think that should be enough to know where it actually came from or do you think we should carry on''. It could be suggested that this particular decision offloading example is an artefact of the seeker being aware that there is an intermediary (i.e., human), however, this would be something to explore in a Wizard of Oz setting.

3.4 Effective Information Transfer

Sometimes actors misheard each other (information transfer was not successful) and had to *repair* their conversation. To repair, actors requested a repetition of a previous utterance: ``sorry say that again'' or ``can you repeat that please''. Actors were also observed hesitantly repeating back what the other had said. In other situations, actors interpreted a message incorrectly and were later corrected by the other. Many different instances were noted where the information transfer was disturbed.

The idea of information transfer is a well studied problem. Shannon [30] proposed a model, which shows that a signal can be sent over a noisy channel and the receiver has to construct the signal again with a probability of error (Figure 3). Many researchers have used this model to add probabilities to each of the stages in order to measure the information transfer [12].

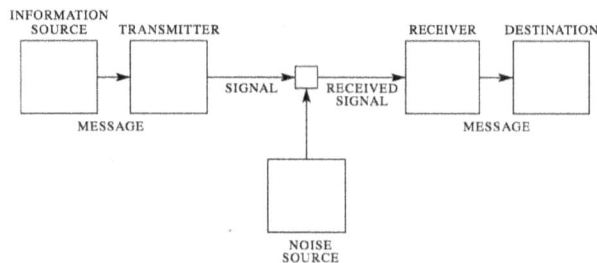

Figure 3: Shannon's general communication system [30].

Moving away from an explicit form of communication (i.e., typing) allows us to express our thoughts more freely. However, this non-explicit communication is prone to more errors in the transfer of the message, adding an extra layer of complexity to search. Meaning that effectively transferring information becomes an even more important feature of search. We expect that effective information transfer will impact greatly how an SCS system will be evaluated. Therefore, including measures of uncertainty of effective information transfer in evaluation metrics will be beneficial.

3.5 Linking Non-search Related Observations

In this section we provided observations which suggest that the audio channel impacts on the interactions between the user and the system. Interacting verbally increases the flexibility of what users can provide as input, which was illustrated with the observation that one utterance can consist of multiple moves. This flexibility also increases the complexity of the belief regarding what a system or user can do (cognitive user model) as there are no conventional interaction paths. Simultaneously, the responsibility for making decisions could be shared between actors or shifted from one to another. However, all this is only possible when the information transfer is successful and effective as shown by Shannon's model [30].

This section also covered some suggested evaluation aspects for SCS, such as measuring the naturalness of a conversation, forming "expected paths" or scripts for cognitive models, or adding a measure of information transfer uncertainty.

4 SEARCH RELATED OBSERVATIONS

We present observations at three stages of the information-seeking process: *Query Formulation*, *Search Result Exploration*, and *Query Reformulation* as defined by Sahib et al. [27]. These stages are equivalent to Marchionini [20]'s *Express*, *Examine*, and *Reformulate*. The model provides broad stages for the collected observations while still providing a structure.

For each of the three stages, we describe the observations and present an analysis of how the observations are explained linking them to existing research and models.

4.1 Query Formulation

We provided the seekers with a backstory for each query, allowing them to verbalize their own information request.[5] In this section we cover the *initial* information requests, i.e., the first iteration of information requests after the user has read the backstory.

Naturalness of Information Request. Participants varied in the way they verbalized their information request: from uttering a query-like expression to describing a detailed and carefully crafted information request. The examples in Table 1 illustrate the range.

Typed queries are usually short [40]. One recent query log analysis by Guy [16] suggested that the average text query length is 3.2 words. Guy [16] also suggested that voice queries are on average longer (4.2 words) stating that the queries are richer in language because they are closer to natural language.

How people formalize a cognitive information gap into a query was modelled by ASK [6]. Once a user has identified a gap, they can start formulating their information need. Taylor [34] proposed four stages of expressing an information need: *Visceral, Conscious, Formalized, and Compromised*. Firstly the need for information (visceral) is formed and its mental description emerges (conscious). The two last stages involve expressing the need (formalized) and then formulating it in a way which can be presented to a search engine (compromised).

Many different expressions of information requests were observed that did not conform to the typical textual query. These information requests included natural language requests, instructions, or additional information to the original information request (Table 1). It could be argued that some of these complexities are observed because users are not restricted to a typical search box and do not have to translate their thoughts into queries as was suggested by Taylor [34]'s stages of information need. We suggest that an SCS information request often will not go through the four stages of information need [34]. Instead SCS information requests will be uttered before they have conformed to textual queries.

Other observations include users wanting to spell keywords in their queries or use advanced search mechanisms such as Boolean syntax. Note that in audio-only settings, allowing spelling may be an important feature, given that typing or copying/pasting keywords are not (or hardly) available.

---

[5]We use the notion of information request because these expressions were often not precise queries but more an explanation of what the users were looking for.

Table 1: Example initial information request utterances.

Example utterance	Characteristic
``Turkish river control''	Query-like
``Which jobs from the United States have been outsourced to India''	Natural language type query
``So the count part in uhm a biscuits that you are get from Europe uhm it contains cinnamon and I want to know where the cinnamon is coming from are there is this uhm is this coming from Europe uhm so how to uhm search for uhm cinnamon Europe biscuits''	Query babbling [24]
``Maybe start of with uhm type in the origins of cinnamon''	Instructions plus query-like
``Can you please search car tyre recycling [long pause] and in the results I am looking for examples of what uhm recycled car tyres are used for''	Instructions plus query-like plus additional information on what to look for in the results (step-wise information request revealment)
``Have Turkish river control projects affected Iraqi water resources [long pause] so we are looking for if dams or irrigation schemes have affected uhm any of the Iraqi people''	Natural language type query plus additional information on what to look for in the results (step-wise information request revealment)
``Uses for old car then the query or, passenger vehicle tyres TYRES (user spells tyres) or in caps tires TIRES (user spells tires) ... and I wanna uhm do a date range so the data is from a recent twelve months, so uses for old car caps or passenger vehicle or tyres TYRES (user spells tyres) caps or tires TIRES (user spells tires) and data in the last twelve months that's the query''	Detailed and carefully crafted information request (teleporting [35]) plus utilizing extra features such as date range from the system

4.2 Search Results Exploration

In the previous stage (Query Formulation) we investigated the first action of the user. In this section we investigate the interactions between the user and the intermediary after this initial utterance.

We investigate the concept of the boundaries between the SERP and the documents. We then cover how both user and intermediary are actively involved in the relevance judgments, followed by what happens when previously encountered results are seen. Finally, we investigate how graphical information can be useful in an audio-only setting.

SERP and Document Boundaries. In traditional IR, the SERP and documents linked from the SERP are thought of as quite different entities. In an SCS system, the differences faded for several seekers during their search.

There were instances where seekers asked intermediaries to access a particular document assuming the intermediary was reading from the SERP. However, the intermediary was already reading from the document in the previous turn without the seeker realizing this –which could be referred to as 'non-hyperlink click' [40]. In other instances, the seeker asked for clarification about information on the SERP thinking the intermediary was reading a document. The lack of visual feedback was a major aspect. As identified earlier, the cost of effective information transfer increased and it may be beneficial for transparency for the seeker to indicate when something is hyperlinked or not.

We also observed intermediaries providing an overall summary of the SERP or document. Some of these summaries covered aspects of multiple documents without the intermediary indicating this to the seeker. This may suggest that incorporating *multi-document*

summarization [5] may be beneficial in transmitting information in an audio-only search setting.

The idea of a SERP (the tool) and the document (the goal) is not distinctively presented in an audio setting.[6] The notion of fading boundaries between the "tool" to get to the relevant document may introduce different cost benefits for the user depending on whether they want to listen more to that particular document. Removing this boundary and provide better integration between the system and the document may have profound impacts on how people perceive "searching" since they may not have to deal with either documents or search engines.

Explicit Relevance Feedback. Relevance feedback allows searchers to provide implicit or explicit feedback about relevant information and these judgments may enhance subsequent searches [28]. Implicit relevance feedback is where users' interactions with the SERP are recorded and integrated in the search. Explicit relevance feedback is where users provide clear feedback on the relevance of items.

Researchers have made the assumption that when a user does not engage with a search result, then that particular result may be irrelevant to the user, or the relevant part is displayed in the SERP. However, in our observations we noted users were actively involved in both rejecting and accepting results and therefore provided explicit relevance feedback.

In a spoken search environment, we observed that explicit feedback was provided by users without prompting them. For example a seeker provided positive feedback by saying: ``Yeah I think yeah that actually sounds pretty good, that could potentially be relevant, is there anything else or is

---

[6]Keeping in mind that search engines now provide cards on the SERP which have become often the goal.

that it?''. We also observed utterances which may be interpreted as negative relevance feedback: ''OK alright that's probably not relevant then so yeah we wanna just find something actually where does the spice cannanon [sic.] cinnamon come from''.

Users were not forced in any way to provide relevance feedback in our experiment; however, they provide it nonetheless. Incorporating such feedback may lead to better performance of the spoken search system and may reinforce users to provide more relevance feedback. We observed that the users who provided relevance feedback and received responses from the retriever provided relevance feedback more often.

Novel vs. Previously Seen Information. Changes in link colour are used to indicate whether a particular link on a SERP has been clicked before or not. The change provides feedback to users on whether they have visited the underlying document, reducing their memory load. We observed several groups indicating that the same search results were displayed: e.g., an intermediaries would state ''I keep on getting the same [search result]'' or ''we're back to that [search result] again''.

Observations suggest that information about whether search results have been already visited or not is also important in an audio-only setting. However, in an audio-only setting this may be more difficult, given that providing visual feedback is not possible.

Interpretation of Graphical Information. Graphical information such as images, charts, or videos are for the majority of search engine users accessible. However, in an audio-only setting accessing graphical information is more challenging. This problem was also observed in previous studies among people with a visual impairment. Abdolrahmani and Kuber [1] indicated that images without description would be inconvenient for people with screen-readers and would lead to increased cognitive load. In our study intermediaries interpreted images and graphs in order to convey the presented information. Most of the interpretations were made of images and graphs in a document. However, we also observed another interpretation of images whereby the intermediary navigated to the image tab on the SERP in order to quickly gather insight of an object which she then described to the seeker. Thus, graphical information will need descriptive information in order to allow for the full potential of audio-only systems.

4.3 Query Reformulation

Automated Repetitive Search. To save time and effort, people try to find ways to automate repetitive tasks into batches (e.g., defining macros) which saves them time and effort instead of performing each task individually. We observed instances of this notion of "automation" during the conversational search setup. One pair wanted to find more information about the health benefits of eating seaweed. The seeker had different seaweed in mind that she wanted to look up and therefore created a short query loop for these different kinds of seaweed as illustrated in Algorithm 1.

Another pair created a repetitive search task with multiple conditions. The seeker wanted to investigate rivers in Turkey and Iraq before searching for dams among those rivers. For each river that

---

Algorithm 1: Automated Repetitive Search (Seaweed)

Result: Which are the health benefits of different seaweeds
1 **foreach** *Seaweed* **do** find health benefits;
2 **else**
3 | Seaweed not relevant to search
4 **end**

---

had a dam, the seeker wanted to know the construction date and water volume. The example is given in Algorithm 2.

Algorithm 2: Automated Repetitive Search (Rivers Turkey)

Result: Did Turkish river control projects affect Iraqi water resources
1 **foreach** *River in Turkey and Iraq* **do**
2 | **if** *They have a dam in Turkey* **then**
3 | **if** *Building date of dam and volume is stated* **then**
4 | Compare river's volume in Iraq before and after building of the dam
5 | **end**
6 | **end**
7 **end**

It could be suggested that seekers had made a plan before starting the search of what their search path was going to be or had formed a model of the intermediary's capabilities. These two examples could be seen as one way of "taking control" over the search interactions as explained in Section 3.3. The seeker has set out a clear path of how they want to search without handing over any decision making responsibilities to the intermediary.

Information Requests Within a Document. We already observed different behaviour in posing initial information requests (Section 4.1), where seekers provided their information need in two steps. First they presented a query-like utterance and then enriching the utterance requesting supplementary information. In addition to providing further information in that initial turn, we also observed seekers providing an information request once they navigated to a SERP/document. Here, seekers requested information about the document that was being inspected by referencing to the given backstory or pieces of information within the document.

In some cases, seekers requested information within the navigated SERP/document with reference to the given backstory, thus, revealing their information need in step-wise fashion.

Seeker: (Initial information request) ''Health benefits of marine vegetation''

Intermediary: ''... It just says a lot of comparing and uhm there are some articles that start to talk about like uhm plankton plants and stuff''

Seeker: ''Uhm do some articles mention the use of marine vegetation as a drug as in like in medicine''

In other cases, intermediaries presented some information from the given document and seekers wanted to know more about a certain entity given in that document.

Seeker: ''Does the data uhm illustrate per capita consumption... by country?''

Intermediary: ''Uhm... the first column... OK this is the list of countries by alcohol consumption measured in equivalent litres of pure ethanol consumed per capita per year''

Seeker: ''Fantastic.. please read out the top ten''

Intermediary: ''Uhm Belarus, Moldova, Lithuania, Russia, Romania, Ukraine, Andorra, Hungary, Czech Republic''

Seeker: ''Where is Australia in the list?''

The notion of "within-document" retrieval is not new and often used by people with the "find" *(Control+F)* function [17]. However, this find function is embedded in the browser and is not part of the search engine. The integration of different search related aspects such as the find function may be important in SCS.

5 SUMMARY

In Sections 3 and 4 we investigated the impact of the audio channel on the interactions between user and system during a search. We also discussed new research opportunities which are a result of the different mode of information transfer (i.e., the audio channel). The observations suggest that SCS has the following *increased complexity and interactivity* between system and user.

Increased complexity. Verbal communication is a major aspect of interacting with this new search paradigm. Since results are no longer displayed but sent through an audio channel which is non-persistent, the complexity of the interaction increases immediately. However, not only is the channel (audio) challenging, but what goes into that narrow channel also becomes increasingly complex. For example, a user is not confined to a search box and can freely express what the system should perform. Our study suggests that the complexity of a system increases by allowing users to express their needs more naturally, for example, by specifying multiple moves in one utterance, uttering non-specified needs, or providing feedback throughout the interactions.

Results also suggested that systems need to make more decisions in this new search paradigm. This increases the complexity of the system and simultaneously the complexity of what users and systems expect the other actor may perform. This then leads to more complicated user- and system models.

Increased interactivity (collaboration). Even though there is an increase in complexity with this new search paradigm, the paradigm also provides new opportunities. Since all results are presented in audio, the idea of static boundaries between the SERP and the documents appears to fade. At the same time, since the user and the system are actively involved in a conversation, this discourse could be used to extract the information need from the user. On the other hand, the user can request, in a more natural manner, information from within a document directly from the system. Thus, integration between search engine and document is important.

Conversation (i.e., interaction) and collaboration are crucial to communicate messages, such as interpreting photos, indicating that documents have been seen before, or explaining the information need. The willingness to collaborate and structure a conversation will be crucial in providing a satisfactory search interaction.

We now discuss the future vision and impact of involvement these search systems may have in the users' search process.

5.1 Existing Search Behaviour Models and SCS

We had aimed to form a clear view of whether any existing information seeking models fit SCS. However, to our knowledge many well-known models such as Belkin's ASK [6] or Marchionini's ISP [20] do not include the system's "responsibility" of interacting with the user. An exception is Saracevic's stratified model [29].

Other models, such as Sitter and Stein's COR model [31] or Belkin's scripts [10], encompass the interaction between two actors. However, these models lack the flexibility of the speech aspect such as multiple moves in one turn. We believe that novel models could be necessary for this new interaction paradigm, allowing for the development of new hypotheses which can be tested to inform the audio search paradigm [12].

5.2 Important Aspects of SCS

We suggest that SCS systems will become more actively involved with the users' search process. This involvement is needed to overcome the imposed complexity of the audio channel. System and user will rely more on aspects such as verifying effective information transfer through feedback. Thus, SCS will require interactivity from both actors while they collaborate on the shared task. Simultaneously, this dialogue allows for supporting and structuring the search from the system while allowing the user freedom to express their needs and wants more naturally.

SCS allows for progressing from an "action-response" search paradigm to a paradigm which has shared responsibilities between actors to succeed in the task. In other words, users have to share their information need and ideally provide direct feedback to the system. Simultaneously the system will have to become more actively involved in deciding which results to present in a narrow audio channel.

SCS allows for single- and multi-participatory search with the system which is similar to collaborative search as previously researched by Evans and Chi [15] or Morris [23]. However, it is widely accepted that people communicate and behave differently between human-human and human-machine communication [14].

5.3 System Differences

The results of this study suggest that SCS is more complex than a "traditional" IR system. Overall, we could argue that we are moving towards a search process where the system is more involved with the users' search process as a whole. The following differentiations can be made:

Passive System. The traditional search system where users have full control over the interactions and decisions. These search systems have many different added components and make decisions for ranking results, query suggestions, or spelling suggestions. Nevertheless, these search systems still leave the majority of the decisions with the users. Simultaneously, not all users (e.g., users with a visual impairment) can make use of these additional features [27]. In addition, the initiative taken in a *Passive System* comes mainly from users. For example, a user submits a query and can resubmit queries, however, the system has limited capabilities to interact with the user in order to elicit the information need. The idea of the one-action search paradigm (action-response) is very much ingrained.

Active System. Search systems become more active due to their involvement with the user, thus shifting away from the passive system as described above. We observed that the interaction between the system and the user becomes important in systems which are based on auditory information transfer. Thus, the system and user have to be engaged with each other in order to effectively transfer information. Simultaneously, the user is not confined to predefined actions (query, mouse-clicks, or pressing enter) and can express their desires more freely. Which means that the system can generate multiple responses to a given action and create a common ground for collaboration. In other words, the "passive" system is becoming more active in the interaction with the user.

Pro-active System. Up till now, the user has initiated a search. The next search paradigm are systems which are actively involved without users having to start the search. Instead, a "Search Engine That Listens (SETL)" could be a system that continuously monitors and listens what the the user does. This way the system can identify information needs/tasks and pro-actively provide content which could support users while satisfying their information need or completing a particular task.

As presented in Figure 4, the essence of search (the Passive System) is not going to change. The idea of posing an information need (by explicitly posing, query extraction through dialogue or extraction through listening) and presenting information will stay. However, it is how users will interact with these systems that is going to change.

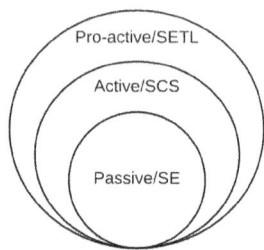

Figure 4: From a passive IR system to a pro-active Search Engine That Listens (SETL).

Examples of Passive and Active Systems. In Figure 5 the information need is expressed in a "search box query" by the seeker. The system ranks all the documents and presents the highest ranked document to the user. As suggested by Taylor [34], the user goes through stages of forming this information need, whereby the last stage is to create a query reflecting their cognitive need.

The observations in this study suggest that people are not expressing their information need exclusively through a "search box query". Instead, users express their need through a more natural language statement. Thus, seekers can benefit from the audio channel to present their information need.

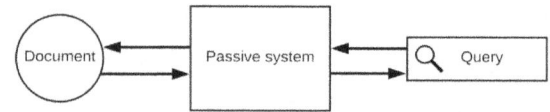

Figure 5: Passive IR with activated components of information need expression.

Simultaneously, the audio channel could also be an advantage on a system level. As suggested by the observations, the boundaries between the SERP and the documents become vaguer. For example, the system could utilize this aspect by not just presenting the highest ranked document, but by generating a summary of similar information in many different documents (multi-document summarization [5] as discussed in Section 4.2) (see Figure 6). Thus, the system would integrate technologies, both existing and non-existing, to create a more advanced interactive search system. Therefore we could suggest that in order to fulfil the difficulties of the audio channel the system may have to become more active and more strongly involved in the users' search process.

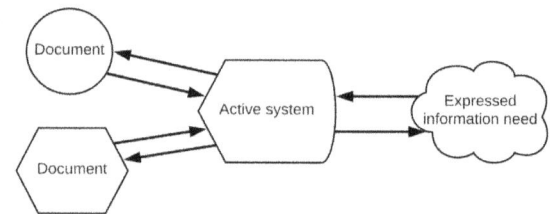

Figure 6: Active IR, combining multiple documents as one representation for the user.

We illustrate that a search system can become actively involved in the user's search process. During this process users may transfer the control they possess in this process. However, both in the passive and active system examples, the system will not be able to act autonomously since the information need may not be completely transferred to the system. This means that we may only be able to have an autonomous search system once the information need extraction can be automated.

6   CONCLUSIONS

This paper explored SCS, an emerging interactive search paradigm wherein all interactions are performed through audio. We conducted an observational study which showed that new information seeking models are needed for SCS. We concluded that this new paradigm is much more complex and interactive than the search scenarios/paradigms covered by existing models. We also suggested several new research opportunities, illustrating that this new search paradigm provides the opportunity to bring together many technologies which have been created into a single integrated model. One limitation is that our results are based on human-human interaction that simulates an ideal situation with search tasks which were designed for a textual setting. We plan to extend our observational experiment into a Wizard of Oz setting in order to understand whether our findings still hold and capture information needs which people would like to solve with this system. Nevertheless, to our knowledge, this is a first major study to provide insight into what SCS may look like.

ACKNOWLEDGMENTS

The authors would like to thank the anonymous reviewers for their constructive comments to improve this paper and the participants who took part in the study. This research was partially supported by Australian Research Council Project LP130100563, Real Thing Entertainment Pty Ltd and Microsoft Research Asia under MSR CORE-12 Project.

REFERENCES

[1] A. Abdolrahmani and R. Kuber. Should i trust it when i cannot see it?: Credibility assessment for blind web users. In *Proc. of ASSETS'16*, pages 191–199. ACM, 2016.

[2] J. Allan, B. Croft, A. Moffat, and M. Sanderson. Frontiers, challenges, and opportunities for information retrieval: Report from SWIRL 2012 the second strategic workshop on information retrieval in Lorne. In *ACM SIGIR Forum*, volume 46, pages 2–32. ACM, 2012.

[3] J. Allen and M. Core. Draft of DAMSL: Dialog act markup in several layers, 1997.

[4] P. Bailey, A. Moffat, F. Scholer, and P. Thomas. User variability and IR system evaluation. In *Proc. of SIGIR'15*, pages 625–634. ACM, 2015.

[5] R. Barzilay, K. R. McKeown, and M Elhadad. Information fusion in the context of multi-document summarization. In *Proc. of ACL'99*, pages 550–557. ACL, 1999.

[6] N. J. Belkin. Anomalous states of knowledge as a basis for information retrieval. *Canadian journal of information science*, 5(1):133–143, 1980.

[7] N. J. Belkin. Cognitive models and information transfer. *Social Science Information Studies*, 4(2-3):111–129, 1984.

[8] N. J. Belkin. A methodology for taking account of user tasks, goals and behavior for design of computerized library catalogs. *ACM SIGCHI Bulletin*, 23(1):61–65, 1991.

[9] N. J. Belkin, P. G. Marchetti, and C. Cool. BRAQUE: Design of an interface to support user interaction in information retrieval. *Information processing & management*, 29(3):325–344, 1993.

[10] N. J. Belkin, C. Cool, A. Stein, and U. Thiel. Cases, scripts, and information-seeking strategies: On the design of interactive information retrieval systems. *Expert Syst. Appl.*, 9(3):379–395, 1995.

[11] H. M. Brooks and N. J. Belkin. Using discourse analysis for the design of information retrieval interaction mechanisms. In *ACM SIGIR Forum*, volume 17, pages 31–47. ACM, 1983.

[12] D. Case. *Looking for information. A survey of research on information seeking, needs and behavior*. Emerald Group Publishing Limited, 2012.

[13] P. J. Daniels. Cognitive models in information retrieval—an evaluative review. *Journal of documentation*, 42(4):272–304, 1986.

[14] L. Dybkjaer, N. O. Bernsen, and W. Minker. Evaluation and usability of multi-modal spoken language dialogue systems. *Speech Communication*, 43(1):33–54, 2004.

[15] B. M. Evans and E. H. Chi. An elaborated model of social search. *Information Processing & Management*, 46(6):656–678, 2010.

[16] I. Guy. Searching by talking: Analysis of voice queries on mobile web search. In *Proc. of SIGIR'16*, pages 35–44. ACM, 2016.

[17] D. J. Harper, I. Koychev, Y. Sun, and I. Pirie. Within-document retrieval: A user-centred evaluation of relevance profiling. *Information Retrieval*, 7(3):265–290, 2004.

[18] P. Ingwersen and K. Järvelin. *The turn: Integration of information seeking and retrieval in context*, volume 18. Springer Science & Business Media, 2005.

[19] D. J. Litman and S. Pan. Designing and evaluating an adaptive spoken dialogue system. *User Modeling and User-Adapted Interaction*, 12(2):111–137, 2002.

[20] G. Marchionini. *Information seeking in electronic environments*. Number 9. Cambridge university press, 1997.

[21] M. McTear, Z. Callejas, and D. Griol. The conversational interface. *New York: Springer*, 10:978–3, 2016.

[22] M. F. McTear. Spoken dialogue technology: enabling the conversational user interface. *ACM Computing Surveys (CSUR)*, 34(1):90–169, 2002.

[23] M. R. Morris. Collaborative search revisited. In *Proc. of CSCW'13*, pages 1181–1192, 2013.

[24] D. W. Oard. Query by babbling: A research agenda. In *Proc. of CIKM'12*, pages 17–21, 2012.

[25] R. N. Oddy. Information retrieval through man-machine dialogue. *Journal of Documentation*, 33(1):1–14, 1977.

[26] F. Radlinski and N. Craswell. A theoretical framework for conversational search. In *Proc. of CHIIR'17*, pages 117–126. ACM, 2017.

[27] N. G. Sahib, A. Tombros, and T. Stockman. A comparative analysis of the information-seeking behavior of visually impaired and sighted searchers. *Jour. of the Amer. Soc. for Inf. Sc. and Tech.*, 63(2):377–391, 2012.

[28] G. Salton and C. Buckley. Term-weighting approaches in automatic text retrieval. *Information processing & management*, 24(5):513–523, 1988.

[29] T. Saracevic. The stratified model of information retrieval interaction: Extension and applications. In *Proceedings of the Annual Meeting-American Society for Information Science*, volume 34, pages 313–327, 1997.

[30] C. E. Shannon. *The mathematical theory of communication*. University of Illinois press, 1949.

[31] S. Sitter and A. Stein. Modeling the illocutionary aspects of information-seeking dialogues. *Information processing & management*, 28(2):165–180, 1992.

[32] A. Stein and E. Maier. Structuring collaborative information-seeking dialogues. *Knowledge-Based Syst.*, 8(2-3):82–93, 1995.

[33] A. Stein, J. A. Gulla, and U. Thiel. User-tailored planning of mixed initiative information-seeking dialogues. *User Modeling and User-Adapted Interaction*, 9 (1-2):133–166, 1999.

[34] R. S. Taylor. The process of asking questions. *Journal of the Association for Information Science and Technology*, 13(4):391–396, 1962.

[35] J. Teevan, C. Alvarado, M. S. Ackerman, and D. R. Karger. The perfect search engine is not enough: a study of orienteering behavior in directed search. In *Proc. of CHI'04*, pages 415–422, 2004.

[36] P. Thomas, D. McDuff, M. Czerwinski, and N. Craswell. MISC: A data set of information-seeking conversations. In *SIGIR 1st International Workshop on Conversational Approaches to Information Retrieval (CAIR'17)*, 2017.

[37] J. R. Trippas, D. Spina, L. Cavedon, and M. Sanderson. How do people interact in conversational speech-only search tasks: A preliminary analysis. In *Proc. of CHIIR'17*, pages 325–328. ACM, 2017.

[38] J. R. Trippas, D. Spina, L. Cavedon, and M. Sanderson. A conversational search transcription protocol and analysis. In *Proc of SIGIR 1st International Workshop on Conversational Approaches to Information Retrieval (CAIR'17)*, CAIR '17, 2017.

[39] M. A. Walker, D. J. Litman, C. A. Kamm, and A. Abella. PARADISE: A framework for evaluating spoken dialogue agents. In *Proc. of EACL'97*, pages 271–280. ACL, 1997.

[40] R. W. White. *Interactions with search systems*. Cambridge University Press, 2016.

[41] T. D. Wilson. Models in information behaviour research. *Journal of Documentation*, 55(3):249–270, 1999.

Style and Alignment in Information-Seeking Conversation

Paul Thomas
Microsoft
Canberra, Australia
pathom@microsoft.com

Mary Czerwinski
Microsoft
Redmond, WA, USA
marycz@microsoft.com

Daniel McDuff
Microsoft
Redmond, WA, USA
damcduff@microsoft.com

Nick Craswell
Microsoft
Bellevue, WA, USA
nickcr@microsoft.com

Gloria Mark*
University of California, Irvine
USA
gmark@uci.edu

ABSTRACT

Analysis of casual chit-chat indicates that differences in *conversational style*—the way things are said—can significantly impact a participants' impressions of the conversation and of each other. However, prior work has not systematically analyzed how important style is in task-oriented, information-seeking exchanges of the sort we might have with a conversational search agent. We examine recordings from the MISC data set, where pairs of "users" and "intermediaries" collaborate on information-seeking tasks, and look for indications of style which can be computed at scale.

We find that stylistic markers identified by Tannen in casual chat do exist in information-seeking dialogue, and that participants can be arranged along a single stylistic dimension: "considerate" to "involved". This labelling for style needs no manual intervention. Furthermore, we find that there is no clear best style; but that differences in style, previously thought to impede communication, are only a problem for shorter tasks. This result is likely due to alignment of conversational style over the course of an interaction.

ACM Reference Format:
Paul Thomas, Mary Czerwinski, Daniel McDuff, Nick Craswell, and Gloria Mark. 2018. Style and Alignment in Information-Seeking Conversation. In *CHIIR '18: 2018 Conference on Human Information Interaction & Retrieval, March 11–15, 2018, New Brunswick, NJ, USA.* ACM, New York, NY, USA, 10 pages. https://doi.org/10.1145/3176349.3176388

1 INFORMATION-SEEKING CONVERSATION

Recent years have seen a dramatic rise in digital personal assistants such as Alexa, Siri, Cortana, and Google Now, as well as "bots"—software agents interacting in natural language—on messaging platforms such as Messenger, Skype, and Sina Weibo. Such conversational agents are attracting more investment, are gaining

*Work carried out at Microsoft.

capabilities, and are being increasingly used[1]. These agents offer a range of services such as device control (e.g., for making calls), closed-domain task completion (e.g., setting reminders or looking up timetables), and factoid lookup. Importantly, they also support *information-seeking conversation*: multi-turn interactions, in natural language, where the user is looking for information rather than trying to complete a small task.

The information retrieval literature has few ways to systematically describe such a conversation. Time, number of turns, or task success are relatively simple to measure but do not describe well the interactant's experience. We must also consider the *style* of a conversation: was it pleasant?, abrupt?, confusing?, courteous? Visual design provides an analogy: a good visual design may or may not improve efficiency or effectiveness, but it will certainly improve the feel of the overall interaction.

For example, Figure 1 provides three extracts from the Microsoft Information-Seeking Converasation collection [25], recorded between pairs of volunteers working on search tasks. Although the same task is being addressed in each case, clearly the participants have different styles. The first is much more formal and concise, the second verbose with more description, and the third more verbose and informal still with "thinking aloud". People may react very differently to these conversations, regardless of the information being discussed or their overall success. There might not be a single "best" style; in fact prior work would suggest that style needs to adapt to different preferences [3] and cultural norms [20].

It is not yet clear just how important style may be for conversational agents, relative to task performance or other factors. However, we argue that conversational style should be considered in design. Consider, for example, a choice between two conversational agents supporting travel, both on the same channel. If either agent can provide the same information, in about the same time, but one is pleasant to deal with while the other is unemotional, or even rude (e.g. abrupt, or confusing), then the first is clearly preferred.

We expect that in the near future, software agents will be able to maintain a conversation to several turns or even several minutes, and that information-seeking tasks will be more important as this capability develops. Our research questions in this work are, therefore: *can we distinguish different conversational styles, in an information-seeking context and when working with an agent? If so,*

[1]See for example http://www.nytimes.com/2015/08/04/science/for-sympathetic-ear-more-chinese-turn-to-smartphone-program.html (Xiaoice); http://venturebeat.com/2016/06/30/facebook-messenger-now-has-11000-chatbots-for-you-to-try/ (Messenger).

User: The two possible treatments for migraine headaches that I want to do first are beta-blockers...
Intermediary: Uh huh
User: ...and calcium channel blockers.
Intermediary: Calcium channel blockers.
Ok, so lets start with beta-blockers.
So, beta-blockers are commonly used for treating high blood pressure and other heart issues and are also prescribed to prevent migraines.

(a) Very efficient and to-the-point—little information about what the intermediary is thinking (participants 23/24).

User: So that's my problem, to discuss beta-blockers, calcium channel blockers and diet an exercise as an option
Intermediary: Ok ... for migraine headaches ... it just says in the ... umm ... it's not even really a result ... it's from migraine.com.
Beta-blockers are commonly used for treating high blood pressure and other heart issues are prescribed to prevent migraines.
Beta-blockers are some times called beta-... eh, well that doesn't matter.

(b) Slightly more verbose language and description of what the searcher is doing—thinking aloud (participants 21/22).

User: I need to research beta-blockers and calcium channel blockers ... um, I guess as to their applicability to migraines ... and their effectiveness to migraines.
And then after that explore other options, if I don't want to take medicines.
I guess I'd just look for beta-blockers.
Intermediary: (LONG PAUSE)
Yeah ... I just go beta-blockers, migraine prevention here ... I'm trying to find a vaguely reputable site to go with ...
(LONG PAUSE)
I found something called American Family Physician that I have never heard of, I want to go back to WebMD—that can kinda be sketchy but should give some sources ...
(LONG PAUSE)
In generally it says beta-blockers work to relax the blood vessels and it is not clear how they work to prevent migraines. ...
It says beta-blockers have been shown to prevent migraines.

(c) Very verbose language and description of what the searcher is doing—lots of thinking aloud and informal language, long pauses (participants 26/27).

Figure 1: Transcripts from the Microsoft Information-Seeking Conversation recordings [25], showing three different styles of conversation.

does conversational style influence perceptions of that conversation? In particular, does similarity or difference in style influence feelings of effort and engagement?

2 CONVERSATIONAL STYLE

Conversational style, the way people behave in conversation, is not well understood in information retrieval. In this study, we follow the work of Tannen, who defines style as "...the use of specific linguistic devices, chosen by reference to broad operating principles or conversational strategies. The use of these devices is habitual and may be more or less automatic" [24, p.188]. "Style" thus includes prosody, word choice, turn-taking, and timing, for example. We distinguish style, the "how", from any topical information transferred, the "what"; we can provide the same information with very different styles [2].

"Style", in various forms, has been considered at length but almost entirely in natural, casual, informal conversation rather than in goal-directed settings or in conversation with agents (human or machine). We discuss some of this work below.

2.1 Involvement and consideration

A key example is long-running work by Tannen [24]. This draws on tape recordings of dinner-party conversation amongst friends, with Tannen as a participant researcher. On the basis of features such as "machine-gun questions", displays of enthusiasm, types and frequency of anecdote, and rate of speech, she identifies a "considerateness-involvement continuum" amongst the guests. There are no firm rules, but speakers in this model are stereotypically divided into two camps or styles. Both styles try to build rapport with an interlocutor, but they do so by emphasising different "rules" of conversation, different aspects of face [6], and different strategies for presentation [12].

Tannen's "high involvement" style is summarised as one which emphasises interpersonal involvement, interest, approval, understanding, and community. It overlaps with Lakoff's "camaraderie" strategy [12] and a need for positive face:

> *When in doubt, talk. Ask questions. Talk fast, loud, soon. Overlap. Show enthusiasm. Prefer personal topics [23].*

The "high consideration" style, on the other hand, is defined by an emphasis on consideration and independence. It overlaps Lakoff's "distance" strategy and a desire to maintain negative face:

> *Allow longer pauses. Hesitate. Don't impose one's topics, ideas, personal information. Use moderate paralinguistic effects. [23]*

Table 1 lists the characteristics of conversational style, on Tannen's summary [23], and the variables we use in this work.

From her analysis of conversations, Tannen suggests that partners with different styles have more trouble communicating. For example, a high-consideration speaker may find a high-involvement speaker to be pushy or a high-involvement speaker may find their opposite partner standoffish: "the use of ... devices that are not understood or expected creates a sense of dissonance, which often leads to negative or mistaken judgements ... This, in turn, leads one to walk away from an encounter feeling dissatisfied or disgruntled." [24]

2.2 Style and agents

If we are building conversational search agents, then many of these aspects of style are under our control. If conversational style, or differences in style, make a difference in this setting then we should consider adapting or monitoring agents accordingly. We are not aware of any work which discusses style in information seeking—this is our goal here—but work in other settings suggests that expressions of agent "personality" and style can make a difference.

Category	Characteristics per Tannen	Variable(s) used here
Topic	Prefer personal topics	Pronoun use (ppron)
	Persistence	Repetition (rept, repu)
	Shift topics abruptly	—
	Introduce topics without hesitance	—
Pace	Faster rate	Rate (wps, wpp, wpu)
	Pauses avoided	Pause length (boplen, poplen)
	Faster rate of turntaking	Pause length (poplen)
	Cooperative overlap	Overlap rate (olap)
Expressive paralinguistics	Pitch shifts	Pitch variation (pv)
	Loudness shifts	Loudness variation (lv)
	Marked voice quality	—
	Strategic pauses	—
Genre	Tell more stories	—
	Tell stories in rounds	—
	Point of stories is emotion of teller	—

Table 1: Tannen's characteristics of conversational style [23], and the variables used in this work. Our variables were selected for ease of automation and do not address genre, but otherwise have good coverage. Variables are detailed in Section 3.2.

People "mindlessly" apply human social rules when interacting with computers, including preferring those which appear to manifest personalities similar to their own [14] and preferring to interact with agents that are more human-like [3]. Evidence from work in human-computer interaction also suggests conversational style is likely to be important in our context. For example, Shamekhi et al. [22] gave crowdsourced workers two "agents", each constructed to exhibit high involvement or high consideration by varying both prosody and script. Participants were asked to respond as the "agents" offered to arrange meetings or ask short questions. Participants tended to prefer the agent whose style matched their own: however, participants' styles were not measured directly, and "agents" followed short, fixed, scripts so interaction was not natural.

3 DATA AND ANALYSIS

We drew on the Microsoft Information-Seeking Conversation data set (MISC) [25] to address the questions above. MISC includes recordings of pairs of volunteer participants working together to solve information-seeking problems: in each pair, one "user" was assigned a sequence of information-seeking tasks but no web access; and one "intermediary" had access to the web on the user's behalf. The two participants were connected by an audio link. This is intended to mimic interactions with systems such as Siri or Cortana, but with a much more natural conversational style.

MISC includes time-series data for each participant and task, including basic prosodic signals and transcripts, which we build on below (Section 3.2). It also includes self-reports for effort, engagement, and opinion of the partner, which we use as dependent variables (Section 3.3). To our knowledge, MISC is the only data set with both recordings and self-reports.

We do not at present consider the effect of style on task completion or accuracy as the data to hand does not let us investigate these questions. All tasks were completed, to some degree, and since some tasks were subjective (finding options to match participants' own preferences) there is no notion of "correctness" to judge against.

3.1 Participants and tasks

MISC includes recordings of 22 pairs of participants, each working on five tasks with a ten-minute limit per task. The first task was a warm-up, and we excluded this from our analysis; thus we analyzed four tasks. The tasks varied in difficulty (availability of information) and complexity (cognitive load, or degree of comparison and synthesis required). Summarising Thomas et al. [25], the tasks were:

Heroism "...you want to find accounts of selfless heroic acts by individuals or small groups for the benefit of others or for a cause." (Low difficulty, low complexity.)

Migraine "...You heard about two possible treatments for migraine headaches, beta-blockers and/or calcium channel blockers, and you decided to do some research about them. At the same time, you want to explore whether there are other options for treating migraines without taking medicines, such as diet and exercise." (Low difficulty, high complexity.)

Olympics "...Find the venues of the 2024 Olympic Games and the 2016 Winter Olympic Games." (High difficulty, low complexity. There was no 2016 winter games, and at the time the venues for 2024 had not been announced.)

Transport "...your task is to decide on the best form of transportation between cities in North America that would be suitable for you [on a three-month holiday by public transport]." (High difficulty, high complexity.)

3.2 Stylistic variables

We considered aspects of conversational style discussed by Tannen [23, 24] and selected variables which reflected these, and which we could extract from the MISC data. As we are interested in the future in analysing conversational style at scale, we preferred variables which could be derived without manual intervention.

For each participant in each task, we derived eleven variables in six categories. One variable records the extent to which a participant spoke about themselves, their partner, or other people:

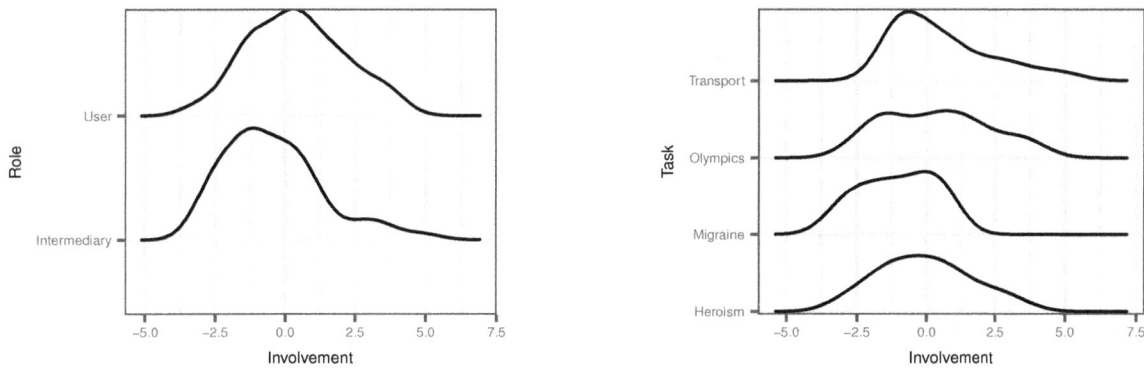

Figure 3: Conversational style is similarly distributed across participant role and task.

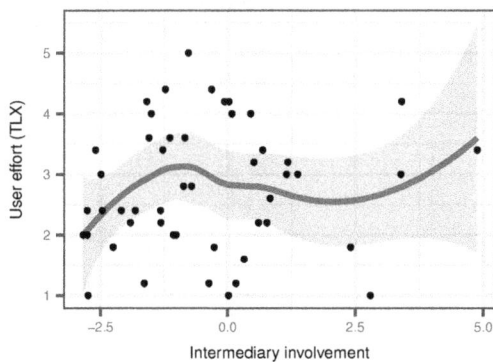

Figure 4: Intermediaries' style (consideration–involvement) and users' reported effort. There is no single "best style" for an intermediary.

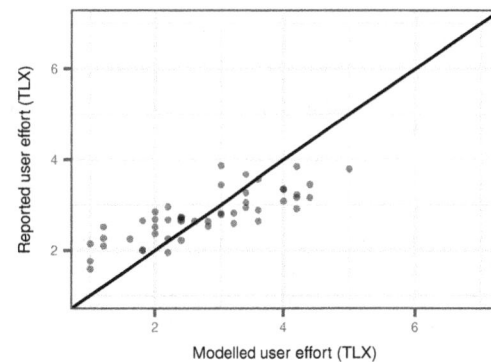

Figure 5: Modelling users' effort as a response to difference in style with random effects per-participant and per-task. Mean error 0.58 points out of 7.

we might believe that an agent should generally show consideration, and that it is inappropriate to display too much enthusiasm.

If there is in fact a "generally good" style, we should design our agents for this. Figure 4 plots intermediaries' style against users' reported effort. There is no apparent correlation, and certainly no "sweet spot" across the range: that is, there is no single "best style". There is no apparent best style either for UES or opinion-of-other (not shown).

4.3 Difference in style

Since there is no single good style, it is possible that effort is at least partly explained by *differences* in style between "user" and "intermediary": that is, that more effort is reported when the two participants have different conversational styles [22, 24]. We test this idea by constructing, for each pair of participants and each task, a difference-in-style variable which is simply the absolute difference between the user's and the intermediary's style on the task. If observations from casual chit-chat [24] and crowdsourcing experiments [22] are borne out here, we would expect reported effort to correlate with difference. This is in fact what we observe.

To investigate the relationship, we built a mixed-effects (linear) model to predict user's effort, as their per-task TLX score, as a response to difference in style. As TLX varies with participant and task, the model also included random effects (both intercept and slope) for both. Model fitting used the lme4 package from Bates et al. [1], in R 3.3.1 [19].

The fitted model is remarkably accurate (Figure 5). The mean error is only 0.58 points on the seven-point scale, and no pattern was apparent in the residuals. The overall (fixed) effect of difference is 0.09: that is, effort is 0.09 points higher for every one-point difference in involvement. The variance due to participant is greater than that due to task, as is common in interactive retrieval. Per-participant effects of difference range from −0.13 to 0.27; per-task effects range from −0.03 to 0.16.[3]

(As an aside, we note that the model would not be useful as a metric or predictor "in the wild": it includes random effects for task, which is not normally observable. As we will see, the model

---

[3] A similar model can be built for intermediaries' effort, with similar effects (fixed effect 0.09; per-participant random effects −0.07–0.30; per-task random effects 0.06–0.15; mean error higher at 0.82). In this study we are interested in the users' experience, not the intermediaries', so we leave further investigations to future work.

is useful for exploring and understanding the relationship between style and effort, and this can lead to design guidelines.)

Direction of difference. Differences in style do make a difference to the "user's" experience. Since the roles of user and intermediary are asymmetric, it is reasonable to ask whether the direction of the difference is significant: that is, does it matter whether it is the user or the intermediary who is more involved? For example, if the intermediary exhibits higher consideration than the user, then she might be seen as courteous; while an intermediary who exhibits higher involvement might be seen as pushy.

We built a version of the model above with two fixed effects, one for the degree to which the intermediary was higher in consideration and one for the degree to which they were higher in involvement. Both were clamped to zero: that is, if the intermediary exhibited higher involvement, then the "higher consideration" variable would be set to zero rather than be negative. This let us model the effect of each direction separately.

The learned model, in this case, had near-identical effects for both "higher involvement" and "higher consideration". This indicates that the *amount* of difference, not the *direction*, is important for perceptions of effort.

Task effects. Although the effect due to task is less than that due to participant, it is still significant. Intercepts range from 2.22 (heroism and Olympics) to 3.35 (transport), as we might expect; but the effect of style differences ranges on both sides of zero. For the heroism and Olympics tasks, difference in style does indeed correlate with effort (effect 0.16). For the migraine task it makes less difference, although differences still increase effort (0.05), and for the transport task we see overall *lower* effort when there is more difference (−0.03).

As possible explanations for this, we note that the migraine and transport tasks are the "high complexity" tasks, which required participants to compare, aggregate, and synthesise information. They are also the tasks which tended to take the longest, even after removing all instances past ten minutes (Figure 6). We consider each of these aspects below.

Complexity and difficulty effects. To examine the effect of task complexity and difficulty, we built a second mixed-effects linear model with fixed effects for style difference; and included a style difference-complexity interaction; and style-difference-difficulty interaction. (That is, the effect of style difference was allowed to vary for each level of complexity and of difficulty). Note that whereas the previous model allowed each task to vary independently, as a random effect, this model postulates a pair of underlying effects and links tasks accordingly. The new model had no random effect for task but retained a random intercept and slope per participant. Final accuracy was good, with mean error 0.58 points, suggesting we have not given up any explanatory power by representing a task by its complexity and difficulty.

Figure 7 plots the fixed effects in the resulting model. We can see again that style differences are most clearly bad for the heroism task, moderate for the Olympics and migraine task, and seem to help the transport task; however we can also see that both increasing task difficulty (left to right) and increasing task complexity (top to bottom) reduces the effect of style mismatch.

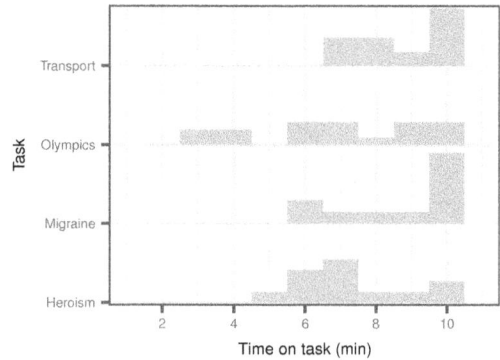

Figure 6: Task times, measured as time of the last recorded conversation. Participants were asked to stop at 10:00 and any longer tasks were excluded (see text). The transport and migraine tasks took considerably longer, typically, than the heroism or Olympics tasks.

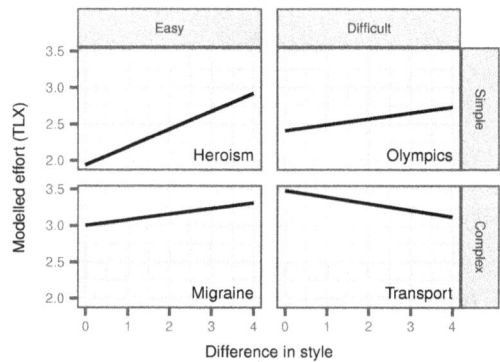

Figure 7: Modelling users' effort as a response to difference in style, complexity, and difficulty (only fixed effects shown). Both complexity and difficulty change the effect of style differences.

It may be that as tasks get more complex and difficult, they require more mental processing and become more "intellective", leading people to focus more on the task content than on factors such as conversational style. Similar effects of task complexity have been noted in a group setting [13]. Another possibility is that as tasks become more difficult, it becomes harder for people to align their styles [10]. As a result, participants may have focussed more on solving the task and less on their and their partner's style, and mismatch could perhaps have become less of an issue.

Task length effects. Since the complex and difficult tasks tended to take longer, we can use similar modelling to examine the effect of time on task. In this case we replace the random effect of task with a fixed effect for time on task, where we use the total time in conversation as a proxy for time on task. Again the result matches closely, with mean error 0.57 on the seven-point scale.

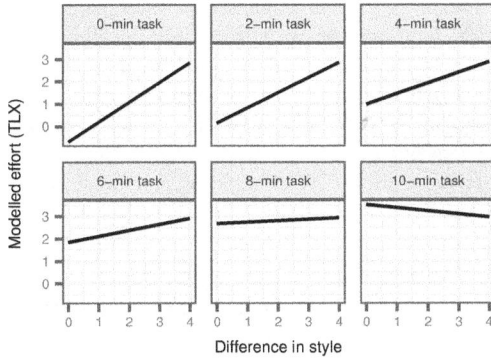

Figure 8: Modelling users' effort as a response to difference in style and time spent on task (only fixed effects shown). As tasks get longer, style differences are less important; past about nine minutes, style differences actually reduce effort.

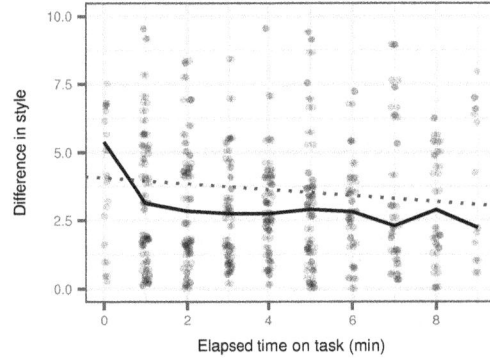

Figure 9: Alignment of conversational style. Solid line shows median difference between "user" and "intermediary", over the course of a task. Dotted line is fixed effect from a mixed-effects model (see text). Alignment is just over 0.11 units per minute on task.

Figure 8 shows the resulting model. For short tasks, up to about six minutes, our model has difference correlating with effort; for medium tasks, it correlates less (and makes no difference for tasks taking about nine minutes); for long tasks, past about nine minutes, it starts to anticorrelate.

If difference in style does become less important as tasks get longer, this anticorrelation may of course be an artefact of our linear model: a linear model cannot represent, for example, a "flattening out" of effect as tasks get longer.

The fact that differences in style do have an effect on experience is congruent with Tannen's model, although to our knowledge it has not been observed before in a search setting. The fact that differences have less impact when tasks are longer, however, warrants further attention and we turn to this next.

5 ALIGNMENT

The effect of task length might be explained several ways. The simplest case is just that "style", as defined here, depends on elapsed time. For example, there is more chance for a measurement to vary given more samples, so the pv (pitch variance) and lv (loudness variance) could be higher for longer tasks due to glitches in the recording or outbursts from the speakers. Similarly, a longer task might involve discussion of more aspects and ppron might vary accordingly. This could lead to more noise in the difference between styles, and therefore less apparent correlation with effort or engagement. However, this simple hypothesis does not hold: neither pv nor lv, the two variance-based variables, correlate with total time on task ($r = -.01$ and $.03$, $t(96) = -.12$ and $.32$, n.s.). Further, of the eleven variables, only one correlates with total time (repu, proportion of utterances with repeated terms: $r = -0.27$, $t(96) = -2.70$, $p < 0.05$). Finally, we see no apparent increase in variability of involvement across task lengths (regressing variance in style on task length to the nearest minute $r = -0.20$, $t(6) = -0.50$, n.s.).

A second possible explanation is that users "got their ear in"—that is, that over time they became more accustomed to their partners' conversational style and it became less of a hindrance. This would

not be observable in the MISC data, except possibly by looking for markers of puzzlement such as "huh?" or frowning.

Alignment. A further possibility is *alignment*. Alignment is the largely unconscious process by which speakers converge on common ways of speaking: for example, by preferring different syntax, lexical choices, articulations, prosodic styles, and even accents [5, 11, 18]. It has been observed in both human-human interaction and human-computer interaction [5], so it is reasonable to expect it in the present case. If MISC participants did align their conversational style over the course of a task, the effect of style mismatch would be reduced.

Evidence for alignment. If there were alignment in MISC, in features such as speech rate or pronoun use, we would see the difference in involvement between "user" and "intermediary" drop during the course of a task, or across the whole series of tasks.

We used the same variables, scaling, and loading as described above to calculate involvement on a minute-by-minute basis for each participant and task. Partial minutes at the end of each task were dropped, and minutes with no utterance were recorded with undefined style.[4] The variation in style is much higher in this version—the underlying variables are not being averaged over the entire task, so cover a greater range—but the overall distribution remains approximately normal.

Figure 9 plots the difference between users' and intermediaries' styles, across all pairs and tasks, minute by minute. Although there is a good deal of variation, the median difference drops a good deal in the first minute and does tend down overall ($r = -0.09$, $t(654) = -2.33$, $p < 0.05$). Again building a linear mixed-effects model with random intercept and slope for each pair, we see a fixed effect of a 0.11-unit drop in difference per minute on the task—i.e., if a typical pair started a task with 3 units of difference in style, this would be reduced to 1.9 units by the 10-minute mark.

---

[4]For example, words per utterance (wpu) is undefined if there is no utterance, and between-own pause length (boplen) is undefined if there is no pause.

We would see this if styles all converged on the same point, as time went on—for example, if fatigue or some quirk of recording caused participants to all adopt the same style over time. There is no evidence of this, however: variance in involvement scores does not decrease across time and in fact is lowest between minutes 3 and 5. Instead, pairs appear to be converging on different styles. This is evidence of alignment over the course of a task: stylistic differences are being smoothed over, consciously or not, by small changes in such factors as rate of speech and use of pronouns.

There is no indication of alignment over longer periods, in the MISC data. That is, there is no overall alignment of style over the whole hour or so of the exercise ($r = 0.01$, $t(654) = 0.19$, n.s.). The MISC protocol had participants work separately after each task, answering questions on their experience, which took a few minutes. It seems likely that this enforced break in conversation, plus the abrupt change of topic when the next task began, meant participants somehow "reset" their adaptations.

Alignment and time on task. Observing alignment partly explains the interaction between time on task, difference in style, and users' reported effort. Spending longer on a task gives more time to align styles, that is to change styles; so a single style computed over the whole task is not as representative. This in turn means this single style is not a good predictor of reported effort, and we would expect to see less effect.

Alignment by role. Since there is evidence that style varies slightly with role, it is possible that alignment also varies—for example, that intermediaries make more effort (even unconsciously) to meet users than vice versa.

Minute to minute, users changed their involvement more than did intermediaries. Median jumps were 2.8 units for users, 1.8 for intermediaries, a significant difference (two-sided $t(441.06) = 5.27$, $p < 0.05$). For both roles, changes in style tended to be in the direction of the partner: that is, if in minute n the participant showed less involvement than their partner, then in minute $n + 1$ they would increase involvement and vice versa (one-sided $t(515) = 2.59$, $p < 0.05$). However, users made larger shifts, closing 46% of the gap minute to minute compared to 18% for intermediaries. This difference was significant (paired $t(48) = 2.20$, $p < 0.05$). This is probably an artefact of the MISC protocol: "users", without any resources to tackle the task themselves, had less to do so may have made greater use of verbal cues to encourage a solution. This also put users in a submissive role, which would result in greater attempts at alignment [4, 9].

6 ENGAGEMENT AND OPINION

The discussion above has focussed on reports of effort as measured by the TLX. We also considered reports of engagement and opinions of the partner.

6.1 Engagement

MISC includes items on engagement for each task and participant, drawn from the User Engagement Scale [16]. The effect of style on engagement is consistent with that on effort, but smaller overall: differences in style are more important to the sense of effort than the sense of engagement.

In particular, there is no single style which maximises engagement; rather, engagement varies with difference in style between the partners. Modelling engagement as a response to style difference, with random effects as in Section 4.3, again gives a good fit (mean error 0.50 units out of seven) but with a smaller effect (0.02 units *less* engagement per unit of style difference, compared to 0.09 units more effort). We observed similar effects of complexity, difficulty, and time, although these effects were smaller all around.

6.2 Opinion

Our third dependent variable is the user's opinion of the intermediary, based on whether they felt understood; whether they felt helped; and whether the intermediary communicated clearly. Again, there is no best style; and other effects are consistent but they are smaller still.

A model of opinion as a response to style difference was remarkably accurate, with mean error only 0.29 units (c.f. 0.58 units for effort). The effects of complexity and difficulty remain, but are smaller still, and the effect of time is negligible.

These items asked about the partner in particular—not the task, or the participant themselves—so smaller effects make sense. They can also be explained by bias in the data, as most responses were 6 or 7 on the seven-point scale.

7 CONCLUDING REMARKS

It is possible to measure the conversational styles adopted by "users" and "intermediaries" in this information-seeking context, and to distinguish differences in a single axis from involvement to consideration. These styles—in particular, differences between the partners' styles—do make a difference to users' reports of effort and engagement.

7.1 Style and style difference

This study focuses on eleven stylistic variables, based on Tannen's description of styles in casual chit-chat [23] but chosen partly for processing convenience. These variables do point to a single factor, which we identify with "involvement". To the best of our knowledge this is the first work to measure involvement in this way, and the first to provide a process for doing so automatically and at scale.

We believe it is also the first study to consider conversational style in information-seeking contexts, and we see a similar pattern to that reported elsewhere. In particular, differences in style contribute to a sense of effort, as reported by the MISC "user" on the NASA task load index. Allowing for per-participant and per-task differences, tasks where partners exhibited similar styles were those which took less effort.

There is also an effect of task complexity and difficulty (differences are less important in more complex or difficult tasks), and of time (overall differences are less important when tasks take longer).

All these effects are also at play for users' engagement, although the effects are smaller, and for users' opinion of their partner, where the effects are smaller still.

7.2 Alignment

The interaction between effort, style, and time on task is at least partly explained by alignment, whereby the user and intermediary work (perhaps unconsciously) to match each others' expressions of involvement or consideration. We see some evidence for this in the MISC data: participants' styles tend to change to close the gap. This makes per-task measures of style less representative for longer tasks. We also see evidence that users, rather than intermediaries, change their expression more. This may be because users were relatively submissive and intermediaries dominant; if so, we would expect the opposite effect for people interacting with software agents.

7.3 System design

These results suggest a few design principles for speech-based, conversational, agents. First, there is no single best style—there is no amount of involvement or consideration which gets uniformly good feedback. Second, it should be possible to monitor a user's conversational style: the variables used here are by no means the only choices, but are all computable at scale and in real-time. Having identified a style, these results suggest adapting to that style will help the user: the same tasks are reported as needing lower effort, and being slightly more engaging, when styles match more closely. This effect is more pronounced when tasks are shorter.

Again, although there are many other possibilities, the variables used here could all be under the control of software systems: speech rate and pauses are easy to adapt, loudness and pitch variation likewise, and dialogue could be varied to include more or fewer personal references.

7.4 Limitations and future work

We note some limitations of the analyses above. Most importantly, the MISC data set was collected from conversations between strangers, working on assigned tasks; it does not reflect how people currently talk to software agents or how people might work on their own tasks (especially shorter tasks). At present, of course, software agents are not capable of carrying on such long conversations nor (outside some experimental systems) are they capable of varying their style in any substantial way; so this limitation is forced on us. The data set is also possibly too small to note subtle effects, and our linear models cannot represent non-linear effects if they exist. Manual inspection of the residuals has not revealed any obvious patterns, however.

The present study is purely descriptive, not experimental. An obvious follow-up would be to measure participants' styles, and adapt an agent to match (or not) before recording effort and engagement; perhaps using a Wizard-of-Oz strategy for dialogue management. This would be an extension of work by Shamekhi et al. [22], for example, with more experimental control and with a more mechanistic notion of "style". We hope to run such experiments in future.

AVAILABILITY

The code used to derive the stylistic variables, the resulting data, and the code used for analysis is available on request.

ACKNOWLEDGMENTS

The variables listed in Section 3.2 build on suggestions from Gregory A. Bennett. Trudy O'Connor contributed to the discussion in Section 5. We thank the MISC participants for their time.

REFERENCES

[1] Douglas Bates, Martin Mächler, Ben Bolker, and Steve Walker. 2015. Fitting linear mixed-effects models Using lme4. *Journal of Statistical Software* 67, 1 (2015), 1–48.
[2] M M Berg. 2014. Modelling of natural dialogues in the context of speech-based information and control systems. PhD thesis, University of Kiel. (2014).
[3] Timothy Bickmore and Justine Cassell. 2005. Social dialogue with embodied conversational agents. In *Advances in natural multimodal dialogue systems*, Jan C J Kuppevelt, Laila Dybkjær, and Niels Ole Bernsen (Eds.). Springer.
[4] Frances R Bilous and Robert M Krauss. 1988. Dominance and accommodation in the conversational behaviours of same- and mixed-gender dyads. *Language & Communication* 8, 3/4 (1988), 183–194.
[5] Holly P. Branigan, Martin J. Pickering, Jamie Pearson, and Janet F. McLean. 2010. Linguistic alignment between people and computers. *Journal of Pragmatics* 42 (2010), 2355–2368.
[6] Penelope Brown and Stephen C Levinson. 1987. *Politeness: Some universals in language use*. Cambridge University Press, Cambridge.
[7] Robert F DeVellis. 2003. *Scale development: Theory and applications* (2nd ed.). Sage, Thousand Oaks, California.
[8] Florian Eyben, Felix Weninger, Florian Gross, and Björn Schuller. 2013. Recent Developments in openSMILE, the Munich Open-Source Multimedia Feature Extractor. In *Proc. ACM Multimedia*. ACM Press, 835–838.
[9] Cindy Gallois, Tania Ogay, and Howard Giles. 2006. Communicaition accommodation theory: A look back and a look ahead. In *Theorizing about communication and culture*, W B Gudykunst (Ed.). Sage, Thousand Oaks, 121–148.
[10] Simon Garrod and Martin J Pickering. 2009. Joint action, interactive alignment, and dialog. *Topics in Cognitive Science* 1, 2 (2009), 292–304.
[11] Vivien Kühne, Astrid Marieke Rosenthal von der Pütten, and Nicole C. Krämer. 2013. Using linguistic alignment to enhance learning experience with pedagogical agents: The special case of dialect. In *Proc. Int. W'shop on Intelligent Virtual Agents*. Springer, 149–158.
[12] Robin Tolmach Lakoff. 1979. Stylistic strategies within a grammar of style. *Annals of the New York Academy of Sciences* 327, 1 (1979), 53–78.
[13] Joseph E McGrath. 1984. *Groups: Interaction and performance*. Prentice-Hall, Englewood Cliffs, NJ.
[14] Clifford Nass and Youngme Moon. 2000. Machines and mindlessness: Social responses to computers. 56, 1 (2000), 81–103.
[15] National Aeronautics and Space Administration Human Systems Integration Division. 2016. TLX @ NASA Ames. (2016). Retrieved January 2017 from https://humansystems.arc.nasa.gov/groups/TLX/
[16] Heather L O'Brien and Elaine G Toms. 2010. The development and evaluation of a survey to measure user engagement. *Journal of the American Society for Information Science and Technology* 61, 1 (2010), 50–69.
[17] J W Pennbaker, R L Boyd, K Jordan, and K Blackburn. 2015. *The development and psychometric properties of LIWC2015*. Technical Report. University of Texas at Austin.
[18] Martin J. Pickering and Simon Garrod. 2004. Toward a mechanistic psychology of dialogue. *Behavioral and Brian Sciences* 27, 2 (2004), 169–225.
[19] R Core Team. 2016. *R: A language and environment for statistical computing*. R Foundation for Statistical Computing, Vienna, Austria. https://www.R-project.org/
[20] Matthias Rehm, Elisabeth André, Yukiko Nakano, Toyoaki Nishida, Nikolaus Bee, Birgit Endrass, Hung-Hsuan Huan, Michael Wissner, I Mayer, and H Mastik. 2007. The CUBE-G approach-Coaching culture-specific nonverbal behavior by virtual agents. *Proceedings of ISAGA* (2007).
[21] William Revelle. 2017. *psych: Procedures for psychological, psychometric, and personality research*. Northwestern University, Evanston, Illinois. R package version 1.7.3.
[22] Ameneh Shamekhi, Mary Czerwinski, Gloria Mark, Margeigh Novotny, and Gregory A Bennett. 2016. An exploratory study toward the preferred conversational style for compatible virtual agents. In *Proc. Int. Conf. on Intelligent Virtual Agents*. Springer, 40–50.
[23] Deborah Tannen. 1987. Conversational style. In *Psycholinguistic models of production*, Hans W Dechert and Manfred Raupach (Eds.). Ablex, Norwood, NJ.
[24] Deborah Tannen. 2005. *Conversational style: Analyzing talk among friends* (new ed.). Oxford University Press, New York.
[25] Paul Thomas, Daniel McDuff, Mary Czerwinski, and Nick Craswell. 2017. MISC: A data set of information-seeking conversations. In *Proc. Int. W'shop on Conversational Approaches to Information Retrieval*.
[26] Italo Trizano-Hermosilla and Jesús M Alvarado. 2016. Best alternatives to Cronbach's alpha reliability in realistic conditions: Congeneric and asymmetrical measurements. *Frontiers in Psychology* 7, Article 769 (2016).

SearchBots: User Engagement with ChatBots during Collaborative Search

Sandeep Avula, Gordon Chadwick, Jaime Arguello, Robert Capra

University of North Carolina at Chapel Hill

asandeep@live.unc.edu,gchadwick10@gmail.com,{jarguello,rcapra}@unc.edu

ABSTRACT

Popular messaging platforms such as Slack have given rise to hundreds of *chatbots* that users can engage with individually or as a group. We present a Wizard of Oz study on the use of *searchbots* (i.e., chatbots that perform specific types of searches) during collaborative information-seeking tasks. Specifically, we study searchbots that *intervene dynamically* and compare between two intervention types: (1) the searchbot presents questions to users to gather the information it needs to produce results, and (2) the searchbot monitors the conversation among the collaborators, infers the necessary information, and then displays search results with no additional input from the users. We investigate three research questions: (RQ1) What is the effect of a searchbot (and its intervention type) on participants' collaborative experience? (RQ2) What is the effect of a searchbot's intervention type on participants' perceptions about the searchbot and level of engagement with the searchbot? and (RQ3) What are participants' impressions of a dynamic searchbot? Our results suggest that dynamic searchbots can enhance users' collaborative experience and that the intervention type does not greatly affect users' perceptions and level of engagement. Participants' impressions of the searchbot suggest unique opportunities and challenges for future work.

ACM Reference Format:
Sandeep Avula, Gordon Chadwick, Jaime Arguello, Robert Capra. 2018. SearchBots: User Engagement with ChatBots during Collaborative Search. In *CHIIR '18: 2018 Conference on Human Information Interaction & Retrieval, March 11–15, 2018, New Brunswick, NJ, USA*. ACM, New York, NY, USA, 10 pages. https://doi.org/10.1145/3176349.3176380

Keywords: Chatbots; Collaborative Search; Intelligent Agents

1 INTRODUCTION

Messaging platforms such as Slack, Yammer, and Facebook Workplace have become commonplace in work environments, allowing distributed workers to communicate and collaborate on shared tasks. These new platforms are different from traditional chat interfaces in their aesthetics and ability to integrate with workplace collaboration technologies such as Github and Google Drive. The increasing popularity of such messaging platforms has also inspired the development of hundreds of third-party *chatbots*. User can engage these chatbots in dialogs to accomplish specific tasks such

as to update a social media status or to schedule a meeting with a group of collaborators. Additionally, there are chatbots that search for information on specific topics such as news, restaurants, and weather. Users engage with these chatbots by sending specific requests (e.g., "@weatherbot New York City"), answering optional follow-up questions required by the chatbot, and then interacting with the search results provided. Much of the consideration of chatbots has focused on their use by *individuals* to accomplish personal tasks or to search for information. However, chatbots are also well-positioned to help groups of users who are working collaboratively on tasks that involve searching for information.

Research on collaborative search has sought to understand how people collaborate during tasks that involve searching for information and to develop tools to support such collaborations. The most prominent approach has been to develop *dedicated systems* for collaborative search [4, 12, 26, 28, 32, 37]. These systems have been designed with the search engine as the centerpiece component, but include additional features that allow users to communicate, share information, and become aware of each other's search activities.

A key finding from research on real-world collaborative search practices is that while people often search in groups, they do so without the use of dedicated collaborative search systems. Instead, they search independently and coordinate using communication tools such as instant messaging, social media, email, and phone [5, 6, 24, 25]. Morris [25] and Hearst [14] highlighted these findings as a rationale to develop lightweight tools for collaborative search that are *directly integrated with existing communication platforms*. Our research in this paper is an answer to this call.

Little prior research has investigated how to integrate collaborative search functions into an existing messaging channel and there are many open questions about how best to do so. In this paper, we present a foray into this design space—we investigate the use of *searchbots* (i.e., chatbots that perform specific types of searches) during collaborative information-seeking tasks facilitated through Slack. Specifically, we investigate searchbots that intervene *dynamically* in the conversation in order to provide contextually relevant search results, and focus on two types of interventions: (1) the searchbot intervenes and *elicits* the information it needs in order to produce search results using a scripted dialogue, and (2) the searchbot intervenes and *directly* produces search results by "inferring" the information it needs from the ongoing conversation.

Two additional findings from prior research in collaborative search motivate the study of *dynamic* searchbots within messaging platforms such as Slack. First, studies have found that chat-based communication is an extremely common activity during collaborative search [37, 38]. Second, studies have found that collaborators often chat about what they are going to search for *before* actually doing so [37, 38]. Oftentimes, this is done to support strategies

CHIIR '18, March 11–15, 2018, New Brunswick, NJ, USA
© 2018 Association for Computing Machinery.
ACM ISBN 978-1-4503-4925-3/18/03...$15.00
https://doi.org/10.1145/3176349.3176380

such as division of labor or to maintain collaborative awareness of each other's plans and actions. In situations where collaborators are willing to let a searchbot monitor their chat, there are opportunities for a searchbot to infer information from the conversation and dynamically contribute.

We report on a Wizard of Oz study that investigates the following three research questions:

RQ1: In our first research question, we investigate the effects of a searchbot (and its intervention type) on participants' collaborative experience. We address this question from two perspectives. First, we focus on participants' self-reported perceptions about the collaboration, such as the level of awareness of each other's activities, level of effort, and level of enjoyment. Second, we focus on objective measures of collaborative effort, such as task completion time, number of messages exchanged, and number of URLs exchanged, which suggests out-of-channel searching and sharing.

RQ2: In our second research question, we investigate the effects of the searchbot's type of intervention of participants' perceptions about the searchbot and their level of engagement with the searchbot. As in RQ1, we address this question from two perspectives. First, we focus on participants' self-reported perceptions, such as their level of annoyance with the intervention, their confidence in the searchbot's ability to help, and their gains obtained from the searchbot. Second, we focus on participants' decisions to engage (or not engage) with the searchbot's results.

RQ3: In our third research question, we investigate participants' general impressions about the searchbot. To address this question, we analyzed participants' responses to two open-ended questions: (1) If the searchbot helped you, how? and (2) If the searchbot did not help you, why not?

2 RELATED WORK

Our work builds on two areas of prior research: (1) collaborative search and (2) dynamic help systems and interruptions.

Collaborative Search: Collaborative search happens when multiple people work together on an information-seeking task. Collaborative search is often investigated with two dimensions in mind: *time* and *space*. The *time* dimension focuses on whether the collaboration happens synchronously or asynchronously, while the *space* dimension focuses on whether the collaborators are co-located or remote. A large body of prior work has focused on understanding collaborative search practices along these two dimensions [24, 25, 34, 35]. In this paper, we focus on *synchronous* collaborative search in situations where the collaborators can only communicate via the Slack messaging platform.

A number of different systems have been developed to support collaborative search, including SearchTogether [26], Co-Sense [28], Coagmento [32], CollabSearch [37], Querium [12], and ResultsSpace [4]. These systems have been designed with the traditional search engine as the centerpiece component, but include additional features for collaborators to communicate, share information, and become aware of each other's search activities. The goal of these additional features is to allow collaborators to coordinate, learn from each other's search paths, avoid duplicating work, and to assist with collaborative sensemaking—becoming aware of collaborators' motivations, actions, and state of knowledge [20, 26]. Systems have also been designed to algorithmically *alter* the ranking of documents

based on collaborators' activities, for example, by using documents shared between collaborators as a form of relevance feedback [30].

Studies have found that these specialized systems provide different benefits during collaborative search, for example, by improving the collaborative experience compared to non-integrated tools [26], by raising the awareness of collaborators' activities [28]; by supporting different strategies adopted by the group (e.g., agreeing on a few relevant items vs. being as exhaustive as possible) [4]; and by reducing communication and coordination efforts [33].

While many different systems have been developed to support collaborative search, these systems have not enjoyed wide-spread use [14]. A survey by Morris [25] found that while collaborative search has become increasingly common, most people use a combination of everyday search and communication technologies to collaborate on search tasks. Morris concluded by suggesting that integrating lightweight search tools into existing communication channels may be a more promising approach than developing dedicated systems for collaborative search.

Prior research has found that people often use social networks such as Facebook and Twitter to engage in *asynchronous* collaborative search, an activity referred to as *social search* [11, 27]. Efron and Winget [9] developed a taxonomy of questions posted on Twitter, and found that a large proportion request factual information that is likely to exist on the Web. This result suggests the possibility of developing search systems that can automatically respond to questions posted on social media and partly motivated the development of the SearchBuddies system [15]. SearchBuddies was designed to embed search results in response to questions posted on Facebook. The embedded search results appeared as a new post in the Facebook thread. A qualitative analysis of people's perceptions found interesting challenges and opportunities for "socially-embedded search engines". For example, users only reacted positively to the embedded search results when they were extremely relevant and non-obvious, or when they complemented another user's answer to the question. To our knowledge, no prior work has investigated how people perceive search systems that intervene in *synchronous* instant messaging conversations.

Dynamic Help Systems and Interruptions: Prior research has investigated the reasons why people avoid systems that intervene to provide assistance. Users avoid help systems due to the cost of cognitively disengaging with the primary task, due to the fear of unproductive help-seeking, due to a failure to admit defeat, or because they are unaware of *how* the help system can provide support [8, 18].

An unwanted intervention can be viewed as an interruption. A large body of research has also focused on understanding how people respond to interruptions while engaged in a task (see Li *et al.* [22] for a review). Studies have found that interruptions can negatively affect task performance [2], cognitive load [16], and emotional state [1]. Research on interruptions has focused on three dimensions: the interruption protocol, timing, and relevance. Early work by McFarlane [23] investigated four interruption protocols: immediate, negotiated, mediated, and scheduled. Negotiated interruptions, which provide mechanisms for easily ignoring the interruption, were the most effective. A wide range of studies have focused on the timing of an interruption. Results consistently show that interruptions during periods of *low* mental workload are less disruptive. In this respect, studies have found that interruptions are less disruptive when they occur early in the task (before the user is deeply engaged) [7] and during sub-task transitions [1, 16, 17]. Finally, studies have found that interruptions that are more relevant to the primary task are less disruptive [7, 17].

Most research on interruptions has focused on interrupting individuals, rather than collaborators working on a common task. As one exception, Peters *et al.* [29] investigated interruptions aimed at one individual while collaborating with another. This study compared interruptions sent at random intervals versus interruptions sent by a human "wizard" monitoring the communication channel. The wizard's interruptions were less disruptive, suggesting that a system with access to the communication channel might be able to predict when to intervene.

3 USER STUDY

To investigate our three research questions, we conducted a Wizard of Oz laboratory study with 27 pairs of participants (34 female and 20 male). Participants were undergraduate students and were recruited in pairs. Each pair of participants collaborated on four tasks that required searching for information (Section 3.2) and were exposed to three searchbot conditions (Section 3.3). Participants used the Slack messaging system to communicate and were also provided with a Google Chrome browser in order to perform any desired searches. Similar to the protocol used by Morris and Horvitz [26], participants were seated in the same room, but did not face each other and were asked not to communicate outside of Slack.

3.1 Study Protocol

Before starting the experiment, the moderator outlined the study protocol, described Slack, and described the basic functionality of a searchbot. Searchbots that intervene do not currently exist in messaging platforms such as Slack. Thus, we believed it was important to explain how searchbots work to our participants. Participants were told that a searchbot is an interactive agent that may *intervene* in a Slack conversation to provide search results after *possibly* asking some questions. Participants were told that searchbots embed search results directly in the chat window and also provide a "click here for more" hyperlink that opens a pop-up browser window. Also, participants were told that the searchbots used in the study were not designed to respond to explicit requests and could only accept input in response to a searchbot-initiated question. Following these explanations, participants interacted with a simple "weatherbot" (designed by us) in order to familiarize themselves with interacting with a searchbot.

As described in more detail below, participants were assigned four tasks that required them to search for information and coordinate towards a solution. Additionally, for each task, each participant was given one "personal preference" they should try to satisfy. Each participant's "personal preference" was *not* known to the other participant. The purpose of these preferences was to emulate a common situation in collaborative search in which collaborators have individual constraints that need to be expressed and accounted for in the final solution. Participants were told that they could use whatever means necessary to search for information—they could interact with the searchbot and/or conduct their own searches.

To familiarize participants with the task format, the first task was always a practice task. Participants were asked to choose three

movies they would like to watch together over the weekend. Before doing so, participants were asked to write down a personal preference they would like to satisfy (e.g., I would like to watch a horror movie.). Participants were then asked to complete the practice task by communicating through Slack and searching on their own (no searchbot intervened). The practice task was the only one in which the participants chose their own personal preference. After completing *each* of the four tasks, participants were asked to complete a post-task questionnaire (Section 3.4). Each participant was given $20 USD for participating in the study. We used Camtasia software to capture participants' screen activity and the Slack API to record all their activity inside of Slack. Additionally, we logged all clicks on the searchbot's results.

3.2 Search Tasks

Participants completed three search tasks in addition to the first practice task: (1) a restaurant-finding task, (2) a local attractions-finding task, and (3) a book-finding task. Each task had a "background story" and asked participants to search for and agree on three different items. Participants were given gender-neutral first names (Jamie and Taylor). For example, the restaurant-finding task had the following background story and objective.

Background/Objective: *Jaime and Taylor went to grad school together in Boulder, Colorado which is about 45 minutes outside of Denver. After graduation, Jamie moved to Denver and Taylor moved to Phoenix. Their new lives have become very hectic, which makes it difficult to keep in touch. However, they are determined to change this because Taylor is coming to Denver for a professional conference. Taylor messaged Jamie regarding meeting soon. Your goal is to pick three potential restaurants to get food.*

Additionally, for each task, each participant was given a personal preference they should try to satisfy during the task. For example, for the restaurant-finding task, one participant (Jamie) was given a constraint on the type of food and the other participant (Taylor) was given a constraint about the location:

Food constraint: *You recently made a life choice to go vegan. To keep yourself in line with this new lifestyle, you have decided to only eat at restaurants that provide good vegan options.*

Location constraint: *You live in downtown Denver (in Capitol Hill). You just sold your car and have been mostly commuting by bike. Since your workplace is about two miles from where you live, you don't have a strong urge to buy a new car immediately. For this reason, you currently like to meet people downtown (in Capitol Hill) and not go anywhere else.*

The personal constraints associated with each task were: restaurants task—location, food preference; local attractions task—location, attraction type; books task—fiction vs. non-fiction, sub-genre. For the two tasks involving location constraints, participants were provided with the constraint description (e.g., as shown above) as well as a map illustrating the location of interest. Different cities were used for these two tasks to avoid learning effects.

3.3 Searchbot Conditions

We custom-designed three different searchbots to match our three tasks: (1) a searchbot for local restaurants, (2) a searchbot for local attractions, and (3) a searchbot for books. Each searchbot required *two* key attributes in order to produce search results. The two key attributes required by each searchbot were designed to match the personal constraints given to participants for the corresponding task—the restaurant searchbot required a location and a food preference, the local attractions searchbot required a location and an attraction type, and the books searchbot required a specification of fiction vs. non-fiction and a sub-genre.

Our study included three searchbot conditions. In the first condition (*no_bot*), there was no searchbot and participants had to use out-of-channel search tools (mostly Google) to find information. In the second condition (*bot_q*), the searchbot intervened and requested the two key attributes needed to produce results using a scripted dialogue, for example: "It looks like you're trying to find local restaurants. What is your location?", "Any food preferences such as Italian, vegetarian, or vegan?". After obtaining the two key attributes, the searchbot produced its search results. The goal of the *bot_q* condition was to mimic a searchbot that is able to intervene and provide relevant information, but does not learn from the conversation and must explicitly request what it needs in order to produce results. In the third condition (*bot_auto*), the searchbot intervened and automatically produced search results without asking for any information. The goal of the *bot_auto* condition was to mimic a searchbot that is able to "learn" from the conversation and directly provide contextually relevant results.

The results provided by the searchbot in the *bot_q* and *bot_auto* conditions were exactly the same for each task. In other words, in the *bot_q* condition, the search results provided by the searchbot were the same regardless of participants' responses to the searchbot's questions. All three searchbots returned 15 results that were pre-fetched from Google Maps for the restaurant-finding and local attractions-finding tasks, and from Goodreads for the book-finding task. Similarly, all three searchbots embedded the top-three results directly into the Slack window and provided a "click here for more" link that opened a pop-up window with all 15 results. For the restaurants and local attractions tasks, the pop-up window also included an interactive map with the search results displayed.

Figures 1a-1c illustrate the look and feel of the local attractions searchbot. Figure 1a illustrates the searchbot's intervention in the *bot_q* and *bot_auto* conditions. Figure 1b illustrates the searchbot's top-three results that were displayed inside of Slack and were visible to both participants. As shown, the results were always followed by a "click here for more" link that opened a pop-up browser window with all the search results (referred to as the landing page). Figure 1c illustrates the landing page, which always included 15 items.

The searchbot was operated by a "Wizard" who had access to the participants' Slack channel and was sitting in a different room. The role of the Wizard was to monitor the conversation and always intervene *immediately* after both participants mentioned their personal preferences in the conversation. By using this point of intervention, we achieved three goals: (1) we maintained a *consistent* point of intervention between the *bot_q* and *bot_auto* conditions, (2) we used a realistic point of intervention for the *bot_auto* condition (a point in which a searchbot would be able to infer the necessary information to produce search results), and (3) we created a situation in the *bot_q* condition in which participants might perceive the searchbot as having "missed" information that would have enabled it to directly produce relevant results. Additionally, we believe that this point in the conversation might often mark a sub-task-transition point (i.e., a point of low cognitive load) in which participants would be less disrupted by the intervention [1, 16, 17]. It should be noted

that it was possible for participants to not "trigger" the searchbot in the *bot_q* and *bot_auto* conditions if they did not mention their personal preferences in the conversation.

Our experimental design involved three search tasks and three searchbot conditions. Each participant pair completed three tasks, with each task combined with one of the searchbot conditions. We used separate Latin Squares to counterbalance the presentation order of the tasks (3 orders) and of the searchbot conditions (3 orders), and then included all 9 combinations of these in our design. Thus, across our 27 participant pairs, the 9 treatment orders were each repeated 3 times.

3.4 Post-task Questionnaire

After completing each of the four tasks, individual participants were asked to complete a post-task questionnaire that had two parts. The first part asked about the participants' collaborative experience and was *always* given to participants. Specifically, we asked questions about the level of collaborative awareness, effort, and enjoyment (Table 1). The second part of the post-task questionnaire asked about participants' experience with the searchbot and was only given to participants in the *bot_q* and *bot_auto* conditions if they actually "triggered" the searchbot during the task by mentioning their personal preferences. Specifically, we asked about the searchbot's point and manner of intervention, the participant's confidence in the searchbot's results, and the gains obtained from the searchbot (Table 2). Additionally, we asked two open-ended (and optional) questions about the searchbot: (1) "If the searchbot helped you in the task, briefly explain how." and (2) "If the searchbot did not help you in the task, briefly explain why not." Excluding the open-ended questions, all questions were asked using agreement statements with a 7-point scale with labeled endpoints (strongly disagree (1) to strongly agree (7)).

Table 1: Post-task questions about collaborative experience.

Theme	Tag	Description
Awareness	aware_browse	During the task, I had a pretty good idea about the information my partner was looking at.
	aware_myprefs	During the task, I was confident that my partner was looking at information that satisfied my own preferences.
	aware_pprefs	During the task, I was confident that I was looking at information that would satisfy my partner's preferences.
Effort	ease_share	It was easy to share information with my partner during the task.
	ease_coord	It was easy for my partner and I to coordinate our search efforts during this task.
	ease_comm	It was easy to communicate my preferences with my partner during this task.
	ease_cons	It was easy for my partner and I to reach consensus during this task.
Enjoyment	enjoy_me	I enjoyed completing this task.
	enjoy_part	I think my partner enjoyed completing this task.

Table 2: Post-task questions about the searchbot.

Theme	Tag	Description
Intevention	distracting	The searchbot intervened at a point that was distracting.
	annoying	When it intervened, the searchbot asked us questions that were annoying.
Confidence	conf_results	When I first saw the information provided by the searchbot, I was confident that it would be useful.
Gains	saved_time	The searchbot saved me and my partner some time.
	useful_info	The searchbot provided us with useful information.
	discover_info	The searchbot helped me to discover new information.
	ideas	The information provided by the searchbot gave me ideas about things to search for on my own.

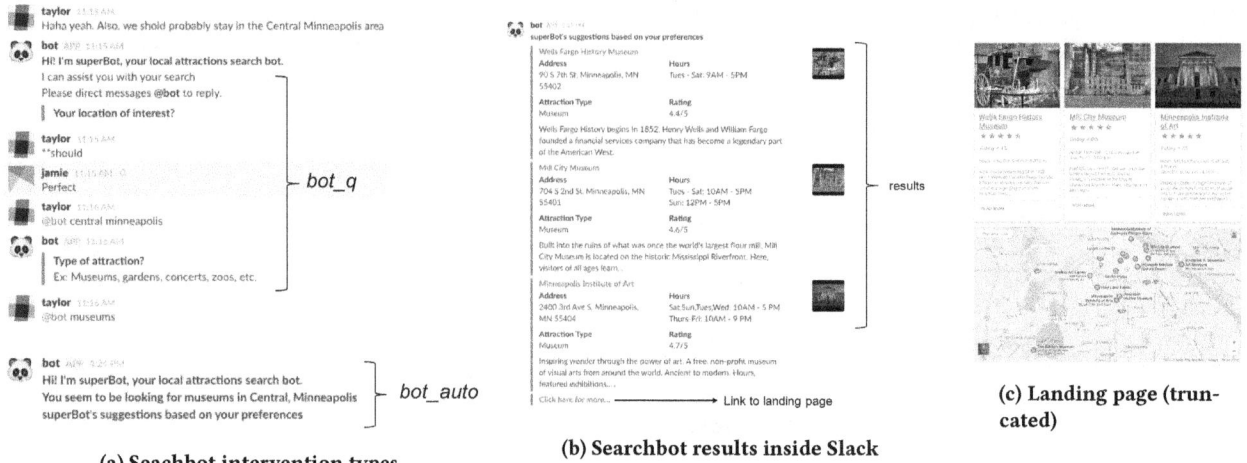

(a) Seachbot intervention types

(b) Searchbot results inside Slack

(c) Landing page (truncated)

Figure 1: Figure 1a shows the searchbot's intervention in the *bot_q* condition (top) and *bot_auto* condition (bottom). Figure 1b shows the top-three search results that were embedded directly into Slack in both *bot_q* and *bot_auto* conditions. Figure 1c shows the top of the landing page that was displayed if a participant clicked the "click here for more results" link.

3.5 Data Analysis

In our experimental design, each participant pair had an opportunity to experience all three searchbot conditions: *no_bot*, *bot_q*, and *bot_auto* (i.e., a within-subjects design). However, it was possible for participants in the *bot_q* and *bot_auto* conditions *not* to "trigger" the searchbot if they did not mention their personal preferences in the conversation. This happened for five sessions in the study (out of $27 \times 2 = 54$ sessions). For these sessions, the participants experienced the *no_bot* condition. Thus, our three searchbot conditions were not equally balanced among participant pairs. To account for this, we used linear mixed-effects regression models in our analyses rather than repeated measures ANOVAs. Mixed-effects models are well-suited for imbalanced, repeated measures data [13]. Also, by using mixed-effect models, we were able to account for random effects due to variations at the participant-pair level ($n = 27$) and at the participant level ($n = 54$). We tested the significance of our mixed-effects overall models by computing the χ^2 statistic using a likelihood-ratio test against a null model (i.e., one without the searchbot condition as a co-variate).

4 RESULTS

Before presenting results for our three research questions, we report on the overall engagement with the searchbot. There were 54 search sessions (27×2) in which participants could trigger the searchbot in either the *bot_q* or *bot_auto* condition. Participants triggered the searchbot in 49 out of 54 sessions (90%). Of these, there were 37 sessions (76%) where at least one participant clicked on a searchbot result. These 37 sessions were almost equally divided between the *bot_q* and *bot_auto* conditions (20 and 17, respectively).

From this preliminary analysis, we can conclude that engagement with the searchbot was fairly high. Additionally, at least in terms of this binary measure of engagement ("interacted" vs. "did not interact"), engagement with the searchbot was roughly equal in the *bot_q* and *bot_auto* conditions. In Section 4.2, we revisit the differences between participants' engagement with the searchbot in the *bot_q* and *bot_auto* conditions (RQ2).

4.1 RQ1: Participants' collaborative experience

To address our first research question, we analyzed participants' responses to the post-task questionnaire section about their collaborative experience, and we also analyzed several measures related to their collaborative effort.

4.1.1 Post-Task perceptions about the collaborative experience. First, we analyze participants' responses to the post-task questions about their collaborative experience. As described in Table 1, these questions focused on three main themes: (1) awareness of each other's activities, (2) effort, and (3) enjoyment. Figure 2 shows the mean of participants' responses for each question across all three searchbot conditions. To analyze the effect of the searchbot condition on participants' responses, we used a linear mixed-effects model (LMM) with nested random effects. The *participant id* was nested within the *participant-pair id*. We ran analyses using both the *no_bot* and *bot_q* conditions as the baseline to test for differences between all pairs of searchbot conditions.

Awareness: Of the three post-task questions about awareness, we found a *marginally* significant effect of searchbot condition on aware_browse ($\chi^2(2) = 5.53$, $p = 0.06$). There were significant differences between the *bot_auto* and *no_bot* conditions ($\beta = 0.56$, S.E. $= 0.26, p < 0.05$) and between the *bot_auto* and *bot_q* conditions ($\beta = 0.59$, S.E. $= 0.28$, $p < 0.05$), with participants reporting greater awareness of their partner's browsing activities in the *bot_auto* condition. Searchbot condition was not a significant predictor for the other two awareness measures (aware_myprefs and aware_pprefs). That said, there was about a 0.5 point difference between the *bot_auto* and *no_bot* conditions for aware_pprefs, with participants reporting greater confidence that they were considering alternatives that would satisfy their partner's preferences in the *bot_auto* condition.

Effort: Of the four post-task questions about effort, we found significant effects of searchbot condition on ease_share ($\chi^2(2) = 12.00, p < 0.01$), ease_comm ($\chi^2(2) = 6.03, p < 0.05$), and ease_cons ($\chi^2(2) = 10.45$, $p < 0.01$). In terms of ease_share, participants reported a greater ease in sharing information in the *bot_q* condition

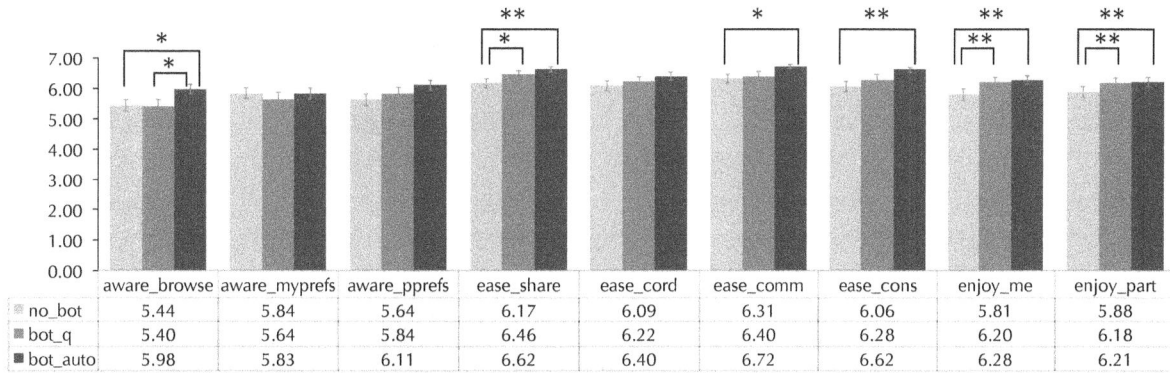

	aware_browse	aware_myprefs	aware_pprefs	ease_share	ease_cord	ease_comm	ease_cons	enjoy_me	enjoy_part
no_bot	5.44	5.84	5.64	6.17	6.09	6.31	6.06	5.81	5.88
bot_q	5.40	5.64	5.84	6.46	6.22	6.40	6.28	6.20	6.18
bot_auto	5.98	5.83	6.11	6.62	6.40	6.72	6.62	6.28	6.21

Figure 2: Post-task responses about the collaborative experience across searchbot conditions. Symbols '*' and '' denote significant differences at the $p < .05$ and $p < .01$ level, respectively.**

($\beta = 0.35$, S.E. $= 0.13$, $p < 0.05$) and the *bot_auto* condition ($\beta = 0.46$, S.E. $= 0.13$, $p < 0.01$) as compared to the *no_bot* condition. In terms of ease_comm, participants reported a greater ease in communicating their preferences with their partner in the *bot_auto* condition ($\beta = 0.42$, S.E. $= 0.17$, $p < 0.05$) as compared to the *no_bot* condition. Similarly, in terms of ease_cons, participants reported a greater ease in reaching consensus with their partner in the *bot_auto* condition ($\beta = 0.63$, S.E. $= 0.19$, $p < 0.01$) as compared to the *no_bot* condition.

Enjoyment: Searchbot condition was a significant predictor for both questions about enjoyment: enjoy_me ($\chi^2(2) = 12.80$, $p < 0.01$) and enjoy_part ($\chi^2(2) = 11.95$, $p < 0.01$). In terms of enjoy_me, participants reported greater levels of enjoyment during the task in the *bot_q* condition ($\beta = 0.54$, S.E. $= 0.17$, $p < 0.01$) and the *bot_auto* condition ($\beta = 0.60$, S.E. $= 0.18$, $p < 0.01$) as compared to the *no_bot* condition. In terms of enjoy_part, participants reported that they perceived their partner to have enjoyed the task more in the *bot_q* condition ($\beta = 0.44$, S.E. $= 0.15$, $p < 0.01$) and the *bot_auto* condition ($\beta = 0.47$, S.E. $= 0.15$, $p < 0.01$) as compared to the *no_bot* condition.

4.1.2 Measures of Collaborative Effort. In addition to analyzing participants' perceptions about their collaboration, we also computed several measures associated with the level of collaborative effort expended during the task. We focused our analysis on four measures: (1) task completion time (in seconds), (2) number of messages exchanged, (3) average message length (in words), and (4) number of URLs exchanged between participants. Figures 3a-3d show the mean value of these measures across all three searchbot conditions. To analyze the effect of the searchbot condition on these measures, we used a linear mixed-effects model (LMM) with *participant-pair id* as a random effects variable. We ran analyses using both the *no_bot* and *bot_q* conditions as the baseline to test for differences between all pairs of searchbot conditions.

Searchbot condition was a marginally significant predictor of the number of URLs exchanged between participants ($\chi^2(2) = 5.65$, $p = 0.06$). Participants exchanged a greater number of URLs in the *no_bot* condition as compared to the *bot_q* condition ($\beta = -0.49$, S.E $= 0.21$, $p < 0.05$). This trend was also present for the *bot_auto* condition, but did not reach significance. Searchbot condition was not a significant predictor for the other three measures. As one

might expect, participants in the *no_bot* condition were forced to search independently "out of channel" and had to share their findings by copy/pasting URLs via Slack.

4.2 RQ2: Searchbot perceptions & engagement

To address our second research question, we analyzed participants' responses to the post-task questionnaire section about the searchbot, and we also analyzed two measures related to their level of engagement with the searchbot.

4.2.1 Post-Task perceptions about the searchbot. First, we analyze participants' responses to the post-task questions about the searchbot, which were given to participants during the 49 sessions in which the searchbot was triggered. As described in Table 2, these post-task questions focused on three main themes: (1) perceptions about the searchbot's intervention, (2) confidence in the usefulness of the searchbot's results, and (3) gains obtained from the searchbot. Figure 4 shows the mean of participants' responses for each question in the *bot_q* and *bot_auto* conditions. To analyze the effect of the searchbot's intervention type on participants' responses, we used a linear mixed-effects model (LMM) with nested random effects. The *participant id* was nested within the *participant-pair id*. The *bot_q* condition was used as the baseline.

Searchbot condition was not a significant predictor of participants' responses for any of the post-task questions about the searchbot. That said, a few trends are worth noting. First, participants found the searchbot's intervention to be slightly more distracting in the *bot_auto* versus the *bot_q* condition. We believe that this is because the top-three search results displayed in the *bot_auto* condition (see Figure 1b) took a much larger portion of the Slack screen than the first question asked by the searchbot in the *bot_q* condition (see Figure 1a). Second, participants were slightly more confident in the searchbot's results in the *bot_auto* versus the *bot_q* condition. We believe that this is because participants were able to immediately see how the searchbot's results were relevant to both of their personal preferences. Finally, participants reported slightly higher gains from the searchbot in the *bot_auto* versus the *bot_q* condition. Participants' responses were slightly higher for saved_time and discover_info. Participants reported gaining *fewer* ideas about things to search for on their own in the *bot_auto* versus

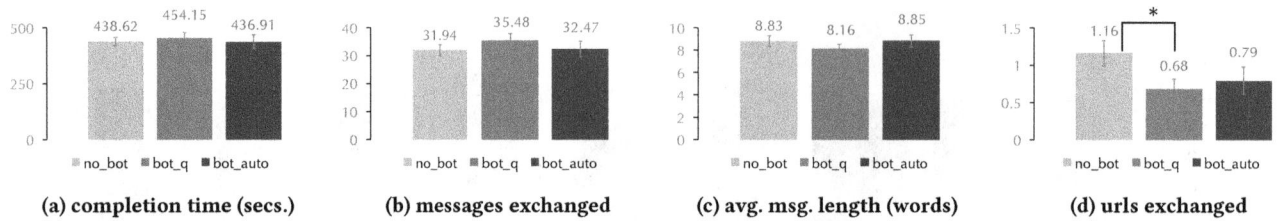

(a) completion time (secs.)   (b) messages exchanged   (c) avg. msg. length (words)   (d) urls exchanged

Figure 3: Objective measures of collaborative effort. Symbol '*' denotes a significant difference at the $p < .05$ level.

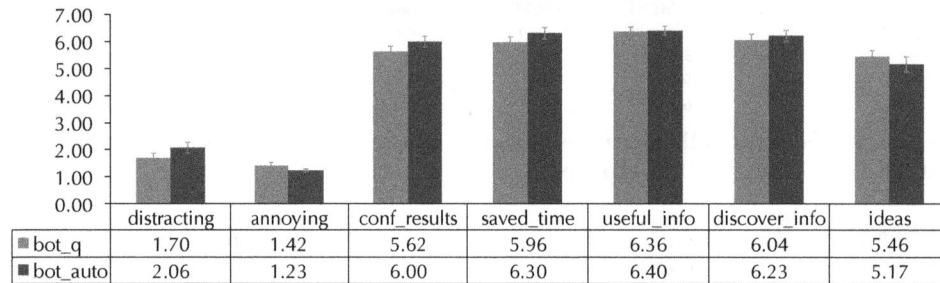

	distracting	annoying	conf_results	saved_time	useful_info	discover_info	ideas
bot_q	1.70	1.42	5.62	5.96	6.36	6.04	5.46
bot_auto	2.06	1.23	6.00	6.30	6.40	6.23	5.17

Figure 4: Post-task responses about the searchbot.

the *bot_q* condition. However, this may simply be because participants were less inclined to search on their own in the *bot_auto* versus the *bot_q* condition.

4.2.2 Measures of Searchbot Engagement. In addition to analyzing participants' perceptions about the searchbot, we also computed two measures associated with participants' level of engagement with the searchbot: (1) the number of clicks (from either participant) on the searchbot's results and (2) the number of items selected by participants (out of three) that came from the searchbot's results.

In terms of both measures, engagement with the searchbot was roughly equal. The number of clicks on the searchbot's results were 2.80 ± 0.52 in the *bot_q* condition and 2.92 ± 0.52 in the *bot_auto* condition. Similarly, the number of searchbot results selected by participants in their final solution were 2.12 ± 0.18 in the *bot_q* condition and 2.00 ± 0.17 in the *bot_auto* condition. To analyze the effect of the searchbot's intervention type on these measures, we used a linear mixed-effects model (LMM) with *participant-pair id* as a random effects variable and used the *bot_q* condition as the baseline. The searchbot's intervention type was not a significant predictor for either measure.

4.3 RQ3: Impressions of the Searchbot

In our third research question (RQ3), we investigate participants' impressions about the searchbot. To address this question, we analyzed participants' responses to the two open-ended questions that were included in the second part of the post-task questionnaire. Recall that this part was given to participants in the *bot_q* and *bot_auto* conditions who actually triggered the searchbot ($n = 98$ out of 108). The first open-ended question asked: "If the searchbot helped you during the task, briefly explain how." The second open-ended question asked: "If the searchbot *did not* help you during the task, briefly explain why not."

To analyze participants' responses, two of the authors conducted two rounds of qualitative coding. During the first round, both authors independently coded participants' responses using open coding and then resolved their codes to derive a closed set of codes.

During the second round, both authors independently re-coded participants' responses using the closed set of codes. Ultimately, the closed set of codes included 11 different codes for the first question and 6 different for the second. A code was assigned to a participant's response only if both authors agreed on the presence of the code during the second round of coding. The Cohen's Kappa (κ_c) agreement during the second round of coding was at the level of "almost perfect" ($\kappa_c > .80$) for 15 codes and "substantial" ($0.60 < \kappa \le .80$) for 2 codes [21]. Participants' responses to the first question were grouped into two categories: (1) motivations for engaging with the searchbot and (2) gains obtained from the searchbot.

Motivations for engaging with the searchbot: Participants reported six motivations for engaging with the searchbot: (1) the task was difficult and I had little prior knowledge (difficult task); (2) the searchbot intervened at an appropriate time, for example, as I was about to start searching (appropriate intervention); (3) the searchbot provided results that matched both of our preferences (relevant results); (4) the searchbot asked us questions that were relevant to the task (relevant questions); (5) the searchbot gave us immediate results without asking any questions (immediate results); and (6) the searchbot provided a limited number of results (limited results). Figure 5 shows the number of responses associated with each code for both *bot_q* and *bot_auto* conditions.

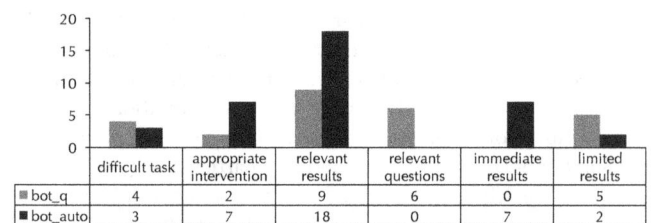

	difficult task	appropriate intervention	relevant results	relevant questions	immediate results	limited results
bot_q	4	2	9	6	0	5
bot_auto	3	7	18	0	7	2

Figure 5: Motivations for engaging with the searchbot.

Our results show five interesting trends. First, participants reported that the task difficulty and their level of prior knowledge

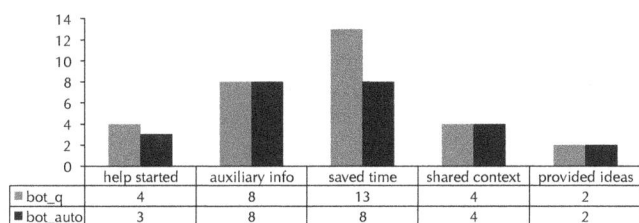

Figure 6: Gains from engaging with the searchbot.

	help started	auxiliary info	saved time	shared context	provided ideas
bot_q	4	8	13	4	2
bot_auto	3	8	8	4	2

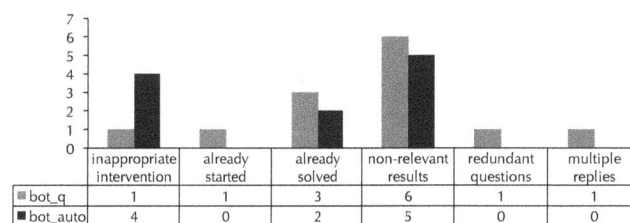

Figure 7: Reasons for not gaining from the searchbot.

	inappropriate intervention	already started	already solved	non-relevant results	redundant questions	multiple replies
bot_q	1	1	3	6	1	1
bot_auto	4	0	2	5	0	0

in the task domain was an important factor in the searchbot's usefulness during the task. Second, participants were more inclined to engage with the searchbot when the intervention came at an appropriate time. Interestingly, this code was more common in the *bot_auto* versus *bot_q* condition (7 vs. 2), suggesting that the intervention was more salient in the *bot_auto* condition. Third, the most common code about why participants engaged with the searchbot was that the search results matched the preferences of both participants ($n = 27$). Interestingly, this code was also more common in the *bot_auto* versus *bot_q* condition (18 vs. 9), suggesting that relevant results were more impressive when the searchbot did not ask questions. Fourth, participants were motivated to engage with the searchbot in both conditions, but for different reasons. In the *bot_q* condition, six participants reported that the searchbot asked relevant questions, while in the *bot_auto* condition, seven participants expressed a positive reaction to the searchbot not asking any questions (immediate results). Finally, a few participants reacted positively to the searchbot producing only a few relevant results.

Gains obtained from the searchbot: Participants reported five gains obtained from engaging with the searchbot: (1) the searchbot provided ideas on how to get started (help started); (2) the searchbot provided auxiliary information such as ratings on items and an interactive map on the landing page (auxiliary info); (3) the searchbot saved us time (saved time); (4) it was useful for my partner and I to be able to see the same search results (shared context); and (5) the searchbot provided ideas about things to search for on our own (provided ideas). Figure 6 shows the number of responses associated with each code for both *bot_q* and *bot_auto* conditions.

Our results show four interesting trends. First, participants reported that the searchbot was useful even if it was not the *only* resource used to complete the task. For example, participants reported that it helped in getting started with the task and provided ideas about things to search for. Second, participants reacted positively to the auxiliary information included in the searchbot's results, such as ratings on items and the interactive map. Third, participants ($n = 21$) reported that the searchbot saved the collaborators time, which re-enforces previous results that it enhanced the collaborative experience. Finally, participants ($n = 8$) also reported that the shared context helped them collaborate more effectively. Participant responses included statements such as: "We were both able to see the museums on the same screen and better agree on the places we wanted to go." and "We could both see the information and did not have to guide each other through different websites.".

Reasons for not gaining from the searchbot: Participants reported six reasons for not obtaining any gains from the searchbot: (1) the searchbot intervened at an inappropriate time (inappropriate intervention); (2) I/we had already started searching on our

own (already started); (3) I/we had already solved the task (already solved); (4) the searchbot's results were not relevant (non-relevant results); (5) the searchbot asked questions about things we had already discussed (redundant questions); and (6) we both replied to the searchbot's questions, but it used the most general (rather than specific) reply. Figure 7 shows the number of responses associated with each code for both *bot_q* and *bot_auto* conditions.

Our results show six interesting trends. First, five participants reported that the searchbot's intervention was not at an appropriate time. One participant reported that it intervened "too early", possibly when the participants were still making sense of the task, and another participant reported that it intervened "in the middle of typing". Interestingly, this code was more common in the *bot_auto* condition, which suggests that the intervention was more salient (and therefore more disruptive) in the *bot_auto* condition. Second, one participant reported that the searchbot was not useful because he/she had already started searching. This result is consistent with prior research which shows that users tend to avoid help systems when it is difficult to cognitively disengage with the current task [8]. Third, as one might expect, the searchbot was not useful when the participants had already solved the task. Fourth, 11 participants reported not gaining from the searchbot because the results were not relevant. Fifth, one participant found it annoying to answer questions about things already mentioned in the conversation. Finally, there was one case where *both* participants replied to the same question from the searchbot, and the searchbot apparently used the wrong input (i.e., the most general response). This result suggests that searchbots that ask questions may need to accommodate (or gracefully ignore) multiple replies from users.

5 DISCUSSION

Research Question RQ1: In terms of our first research question, our results suggest that the searchbot improved participants' collaborative experience. In the *bot_q* and *bot_auto* conditions, participants reported: (1) greater awareness of each other's activities; (2) greater ease in sharing, communicating, and reaching consensus; and (3) greater levels of enjoyment. Additionally, in the *no_bot* condition, participants exchanged a greater number of URLs through Slack. This result suggests that the absence of the searchbot forced participants to search independently and share their findings through Slack.

In terms of the searchbot's intervention type, participants' perceptions of their collaborative experience were *slightly* better in the *bot_auto* versus *bot_q* condition. For one of our post-task measures (aware_browse), there was a significant difference between the *bot_auto* and *bot_q* conditions. For two of our post-task measures (ease_comm, and ease_cons), there were significant differences between the *bot_auto* and *no_bot* conditions, but *no* significant differences between the *bot_q* and *no_bot* conditions.

Our RQ1 results suggest that integrating search tools (e.g., searchbots) into communication channels such as Slack provides some of the same benefits provided by dedicated collaborative search systems [4, 12, 26, 28, 32, 37]. Prior studies involving dedicated systems have found that tools to support chat-based communication are heavily used during collaborative search [37]. In this respect, searchbots have the advantage that they are directly integrated into the communication channel. Additionally, dedicated systems typically include features that raise collaborators' awareness of each other's activities. Prior research has found that these features improve users' experience [26, 28] and reduce communication and coordination efforts [33]. Our results suggest that the shared context provided by a searchbot (i.e., allowing collaborators to see the same information directly in the communication channel) can improve the collaborative experience and reduce the need to search independently and coordinate by copy/pasting URLs.

Research Question RQ2: In terms of our second research question, we did *not* observe strong effects from the searchbot's type of intervention on participants' perceptions about the searchbot and level of engagement with the searchbot. It is important to note that in this particular study, we simulated the *best-case scenario* for both intervention types. In other words, in the *bot_q* condition, the searchbot elicited information that was relevant to the task, while in the *bot_auto* condition, that searchbot "inferred" the needed information in order to provide contextually relevant results. Participants' perceptions about the searchbot were equally positive in both of these best-case scenarios.

Our RQ2 results have two important implications for future work. First, our results suggest that both intervention types (elicitation versus inference) are equally good if they are done well. In the *bot_q* condition, participants were *not* annoyed by having to respond to the searchbot's questions, while in the *bot_auto* condition, participants did not strongly mistrust the searchbot's ability to provide relevant results without eliciting information (perhaps because the results were visibly relevant). This result is consistent with prior research on interruptions, which shows that interruptions that are relevant to the current task tend to be less disruptive [7, 17].

The second implication is that future work is needed to understand the differences between these two intervention types under non-ideal conditions. What is the cost of eliciting information that is not relevant to the task? What is the cost of embedding non-relevant results into the communication channel? What is the cost of eliciting information, if it means the difference between relevant versus non-relevant search results? These are questions for future work. Prior research on different interruption protocols [23] may generate ideas about how a searchbot should intervene given its level of confidence that it has inferred the users' needs.

Research Question RQ3: Our qualitative analysis of participants' responses reveal interesting opportunities and challenges for dynamic searchbots.

In terms of opportunities, participants reported different gains obtained from the searchbot. Participants reported that the searchbot provided relevant results, saved the participants time, helped them get started with the task, generated ideas about things to search for, provided a limited set of relevant results, and provided

auxiliary tools that were useful for the task (e.g., an interactive map). Most importantly, the searchbot provided a shared context that made the collaboration easier. In a large scale user study, Xi and Cool [36] found that *individual* searchers encounter difficulty with seven general processes: (1) getting started, (2) identifying relevant sources, (3) navigating a source, (4) constructing queries, (5) constraining the results, (6) recognizing relevant content, and (7) monitoring the task process. The gains reported by our participants touch upon several of these processes.

In terms of challenges, participants' responses suggest several factors that may influence their decision to engage with a searchbot. Several participants reported engaging with the searchbot because the task was difficult and they had little prior knowledge in the task domain. This result is consistent with prior work which found that users are more likely to engage with search assistance tools during complex tasks [3]. Furthermore, participants' responses clearly indicate that the point of intervention is key. Participants reported avoiding the searchbot because the intervention was too soon (i.e., before they fully understood the task), too late (i.e., after they had completed the task), during the middle of some activity (e.g., while typing), and after participants had already engaged with their own approach to the task (e.g., already searching on their own). Similarly, participants reported engaging with the searchbot because it intervened right as they were about to start searching. These participants' responses echo previous findings from two lines of prior work. Prior work on dynamic help systems has found that people avoid help systems when they do not understand *how* the system can help (e.g., when the intervention happens too soon), or when it is costly to cognitively disengage from the current activity (e.g., after they have already started searching). Similarly, prior work on interruptions has consistently shown that interruptions are less disruptive during periods of low mental workload (e.g., during sub-task transitions) [1, 16, 17].

Practical Concerns: The searchbots that we explored in this paper rely on the ability to monitor a conversation between collaborators and to use the conversational history in order to decide when and how to intervene. There are many privacy, security, and ethical issues that would need to be addressed in such a system. Some of these issues are common to existing systems that monitor an environment in order to provide services (e.g., online email services, home monitoring systems, and sensors in Internet of Things devices). However, the collaborative nature of the searchbot presents additional issues to be considered. For example, it might be advisable to "activate" a searchbot only if all members of the chat channel have enabled it as a feature (i.e., a global setting). In addition, the searchbot could clearly announce itself at the beginning of a conversation and should be "visible" like any other member of the chat channel.

6 CONCLUSION

We reported on a Wizard of Oz user study that investigated the use of a dynamic searchbot during collaborative information-seeking tasks coordinated using the Slack messaging system. The searchbot intervened in two different ways: (1) by eliciting information and (2) by "inferring" the needed information from the conversation and directly providing search results.

In terms of our first research question (RQ1), our results show that the searchbot improved our participants' collaborative experience and reduced the need to search independently. Moreover, participants' perceptions about their collaborative experience were slightly better in the condition where the searchbot intervened by directly providing contextually relevant results (without eliciting).

In terms of our second research question (RQ2), the searchbot's type of intervention did *not* greatly affect participants' perceptions about the searchbot. However, in this study, we simulated the best-case scenarios for both intervention types: the searchbot asked follow-up questions that were relevant to the task and always produced relevant results. Future research is needed to understand the trade-offs between asking potentially non-relevant questions and returning potentially non-relevant results. The manner of intervention may have a greater effect in non-ideal conditions.

In terms of our third research question (RQ3), participants reported different motivations for engaging with the searchbot, different gains obtained from the searchbot, and different reasons for *avoiding* the searchbot. Our results suggest that the point of intervention is key. Participants reported avoiding the searchbot when the intervention was too soon (before understanding the task), too late (after solving the task), or during periods when they were deeply engaged with other tasks. This finding is consistent with prior work on dynamic help systems and interruptions.

The work presented in this paper is an instantiation of a greater area for future research: embedding dynamic search tools into communication channels that are widely used for collaboration. From an IR perspective, many open questions remain: (1) inferring collaborators' needs from their communication, (2) predicting when to intervene, and (3) deciding when and how to elicit information in order to provide relevant results. Outside of IR, the CSCW community has also identified collaborative agents (e.g., intelligent personal assistants, chatbots, and embodied robots) as an important area for research. Recent workshops and panel discussions at CSCW '16 and CSCW '17 have identified important challenges and opportunities for emerging collaborative agents. These include issues about: (1) how agents can integrate into the collaborative process [31], (2) how people coordinate and co-manage the use of an agent [31], (3) the social dynamics involved when people engage with agents in collaborative settings [10, 31], (4) questions about whether people engage with agents as they do with their human collaborators [10], and (5) questions about whether an agent's behavior might influence the way human collaborators interact with each other [19].

Acknowledgements: This work was supported in part by NSF grants IIS-1451668 and IIS-1552587. Any opinions, findings, conclusions, and recommendations expressed in this paper are the authors' and do not necessarily reflect those of the sponsor.

REFERENCES

[1] Piotr D. Adamczyk and Brian P. Bailey. 2004. If Not Now, when?: The Effects of Interruption at Different Moments Within Task Execution. In *CHI*. ACM, 271–278.

[2] Brian P. Bailey and Joseph A. Konstan. 2006. On the need for attention-aware systems: Measuring effects of interruption on task performance, error rate, and affective state. *Computers in Human Behavior* 22, 4 (2006), 685–708.

[3] Robert Capra, Jaime Arguello, Anita Crescenzi, and Emily Vardell. 2015. Differences in the Use of Search Assistance for Tasks of Varying Complexity. In *SIGIR*. ACM, 23–32.

[4] Robert Capra, Annie Chen, Katie Hawthorne, Jaime Arguello, Lee Shaw, and Gary Marchionini. 2012. Design and Evaluation of a System to Support Collaborative Search. In *ASIST*. Wiley.

[5] Robert Capra, Gary Marchionini, Javier Velasco-Martin, and Katrina Muller. 2010. Tools-at-hand and Learning in Multi-session, Collaborative Search. In *CHI*. ACM, 951–960.

[6] Robert Capra, Javier Velasco-Martin, and Beth Sams. 2011. Collaborative Information Seeking by the Numbers. In *Proceedings of the 3rd International Workshop on Collaborative Information Retrieval*. ACM.

[7] Mary Czerwinski, Ed Cutrell, and Eric Horvitz. 2000. Instant Messaging: Effects of Relevance and Timing. In *HCI*, Vol. 2. 71–76.

[8] Garett Dworman and Stephanie Rosenbaum. 2004. Helping Users to Use Help: Improving Interaction with Help Systems. In *CHI*. ACM, 1717–1718.

[9] Miles Efron and Megan Winget. 2010. Questions are content: A taxonomy of questions in a microblogging environment. *ASIST* 47, 1 (2010), 1–10.

[10] Lia Emanuel, Joel Fischer, Wendy Ju, and Saiph Savage. 2016. Innovations in Autonomous Systems: Challenges and Opportunities for Human-agent Collaboration. In *CSCW*. ACM, 193–196.

[11] Brynn M. Evans and Ed H. Chi. 2008. Towards a Model of Understanding Social Search. In *CSCW*. ACM, 485–494.

[12] Gene Golovchinsky, Jeremy Pickens, and Abdigani Diriye. 2011. Designing for Collaboration in Information Seeking. In *HCIR*.

[13] Ralitza Gueorguieva and John H Krystal. 2004. Move over anova: Progress in analyzing repeated-measures data and its reflection in papers published in the archives of general psychiatry. *Archives of general psychiatry* (2004).

[14] Marti A. Hearst. 2014. What's Missing from Collaborative Search? *Computer* 47, 3 (2014).

[15] B. Hecht, J. Teevan, M.R. Morris, and D. Liebling. 2012. SearchBuddies: Bringing Search Engines into the Conversation. In *ICWSM*. AAAI, 138–145.

[16] Shamsi T. Iqbal and Brian P. Bailey. 2006. Leveraging Characteristics of Task Structure to Predict the Cost of Interruption. In *CHI*. ACM, 741–750.

[17] Shamsi T. Iqbal and Brian P. Bailey. 2008. Effects of Intelligent Notification Management on Users and Their Tasks. In *CHI*. ACM, 93–102.

[18] Bernard J. Jansen and Michael D. McNeese. 2005. Evaluating the effectiveness of and patterns of interactions with automated searching assistance. *JASIST* 56, 14 (2005), 1480–1503.

[19] Malte F. Jung, Selma Šabanović, Friederike Eyssel, and Marlena Fraune. 2017. Robots in Groups and Teams. In *CSCW*. ACM, 401–407.

[20] Ryan Kelly and Stephen J. Payne. 2014. Collaborative Web Search in Context: A Study of Tool Use in Everyday Tasks. In *CSCW*. ACM, 807–819.

[21] J. R. Landis and G. G. Koch. 1977. The Measurement of Observer Agreement for Categorical Data. *Biometrics* 33, 1 (1977), 159–174.

[22] Simon Y W L Li, Farah Magrabi, and Enrico Coiera. 2012. A systematic review of the psychological literature on interruption and its patient safety implications. *JAMIA* (2012).

[23] Daniel McFarlane. 1999. Coordinating the interruptions of people in human-computer interaction. In *HCI-INTERACT*. IOS Press, 295–303.

[24] Meredith Ringel Morris. 2008. A Survey of Collaborative Web Search Practices. In *CHI*. ACM, 1657–1660.

[25] Meredith Ringel Morris. 2013. Collaborative Search Revisited. In *CSCW*. ACM, 1181–1192.

[26] Meredith Ringel Morris and Eric Horvitz. 2007. SearchTogether: An Interface for Collaborative Web Search. In *UIST*. ACM, 3–12.

[27] Meredith Ringel Morris, Jaime Teevan, and Katrina Panovich. 2010. What Do People Ask Their Social Networks, and Why?: A Survey Study of Status Message Q&a Behavior. In *CHI*. ACM, 1739–1748.

[28] Sharoda A. Paul and Meredith Ringel Morris. 2009. CoSense: Enhancing Sensemaking for Collaborative Web Search. In *CHI*. ACM, 2007–2012.

[29] Nia Peters, Griffin Romigh, George Bradley, and Bhiksha Raj. 2016. When to Interrupt: A Comparative Analysis of Interruption Timings Within Collaborative Communication Tasks. In *Proceedings of the AHFE 2016 International Conference on Human Factors and System Interactions*. Springer.

[30] Jeremy Pickens, Gene Golovchinsky, Chirag Shah, Pernilla Qvarfordt, and Maribeth Back. 2008. Algorithmic Mediation for Collaborative Exploratory Search. In *SIGIR*. ACM, 315–322.

[31] Martin Porcheron, Joel E. Fischer, Moira McGregor, Barry Brown, Ewa Luger, Heloisa Candello, and Kenton O'Hara. 2017. Talking with Conversational Agents in Collaborative Action. In *CSCW*. ACM, 431–436.

[32] Chirag Shah. 2010. Coagmento-a collaborative information seeking, synthesis and sense-making framework. In *CSCW*. ACM, 6–11.

[33] Chirag Shah. 2013. Effects of awareness on coordination in collaborative information seeking. *JASIST* 64, 6 (2013).

[34] Chirag Shah, Madhu Reddy, and Michael Twidale. 2010. Collaborative Information Seeking (CIS): Toward New Theories and Applications. In *GROUP*. ACM, 321–326.

[35] Chirag Shah and Jennifer Sonne. 2015. Seeking Information in Online Environments: Where, Who, and Why?. In *iConference*.

[36] Iris Xie and Colleen Cool. 2009. Understanding help seeking within the context of searching digital libraries. *JASIST* 60 (2009), 477–494.

[37] Zhen Yue, Shuguang Han, and Daqing He. 2012. An investigation of search processes in collaborative exploratory web search. In *ASIST*. Wiley.

[38] Z. Yue, S. Han, D. He, and J. Jiang. 2014. Influences on Query Reformulation in Collaborative Web Search. *Computer* 47, 3 (2014).

Information Fostering – Being Proactive with Information Seeking and Retrieval

Chirag Shah

School of Communication and Information (SC&I)

Rutgers University

4 Huntington Street, New Brunswick, NJ 08901, USA

chirags@rutgers.edu

ABSTRACT

People often have difficulty in expressing their information needs. Many times this results from a lack of clarity about the task at hand, or the way an information or search system works. In addition, people may not know what they do not know. The former is addressed by search systems by providing recommendations, whereas there are no good solutions for the latter problem. Even when a search system makes recommendations, they are limited to suggesting objects such as queries and documents only. They do not consider providing suggestions for strategies, people, or processes. This Perspective Paper addresses it by showing how to investigate the nature of the work a person is doing, predicting the potential problems they may encounter, and providing help to overcome those problems. This help could be an object such as a document or a query, a strategy, or a person. This whole process is referred to as Information Fostering. Beyond crafting a general-purpose recommender system, Information Fostering is the idea of providing proactive suggestions and help to information seekers. This could allow them avoid potential problems and capture promising opportunities from a search process before it is too late. The current paper presents this new perspective by outlining desired characteristics of an Information Fostering system, envisioning application scenarios, and proposing a set of potential methods for moving forward. Beyond these details, the primary purpose of this paper is to offer a new viewpoint that looks at the other side of the information seeking coin, by bringing together ideas from human-computer interaction, information retrieval, recommender systems, and education.

CCS CONCEPTS

• **Information systems → Personalization**; **Recommender systems**; **Task models**;

KEYWORDS

Information Fostering; Proactive IR; Intelligent Assistants; Task-based Information Seeking

CHIIR'18, March 11–15, 2018, New Brunswick, NJ, USA

© 2018 Copyright held by the owner/author(s). Publication rights licensed to Association for Computing Machinery.

ACM ISBN 978-1-4503-4925-3/18/03...$15.00

https://doi.org/10.1145/3176349.3176389

1 INTRODUCTION

Two of the fundamental problems for information seekers are: not being able to express their needs due to lack of understanding of the task/topic at hand, or the way a resource/system being used works; and not knowing what they do not know [3, 10]. The former is addressed by information retrieval (IR) systems by providing recommendations, whereas there are no good solutions for the latter problem. Even the recommendations made by IR systems are often limited to suggesting information objects only, and do not explore the possibilities of recommending a process/strategy, people, or other forms of suggestions.

In this Perspectives Paper, a novel idea is presented, which looks at the other side of the information seeking coin to address the issues mentioned above. This idea is termed as *Information Fostering*. In a nutshell, it refers to proactively identifying problems and opportunities to not only help information seekers in a more comprehensive way than typically offered by today's IR systems, but also recognize possible questions, answers, barriers, and help that a person may not be even aware of.

The idea of proactively helping in an information seeking situation is not new. It is often studied under the term *Proactive IR* (e.g., [16]). Search systems often pre-fetch information that is likely to be relevant during a search session. But there is one fundamental difference between proactively retrieving information that an information seeker may look for and the concept of *Information Fostering*. The essence of Information Fostering is in trying to understand the larger context of the task in which information seeking may or may not happen, and provide recommendations and help that are more than just queries or documents. This is inspired by the education domain, where learning involves not only getting to right answers, but also the processes that take one to those answers.

The rest of the paper is organized as follows. The idea of Information Fostering is further elaborated in the following section with examples, challenges, and possible ways to address those challenges. Section 3 presents some of the related and relevant works with respect to these challenges. This also sets a context in which the perspective of Information Fostering is described here. Section 4 provides some of the recent works done by various scholars, including the author, trying to address some of the challenges. These works also serve as preliminary investigations into different aspects of Information Fostering for what may come next. To guide the scholars who may want to take on this challenge of Information Fostering, Section 5 provides various methods and ideas for conducting new research in this area. Finally, the paper concludes in Section 6, summarizing this new perspective.

2 INFORMATION FOSTERING SCENARIOS AND EXAMPLES

This section will provide further explanation of what Information Fostering is, could be, and what it would look like implemented in real systems. It starts by showing some of the existing systems that try to cover at least some of the aspects of Information Fostering, and then provides scenarios for ideal systems with the support of Information Fostering.

2.1 Clarifying Information Fostering

Most models for information seeking start with a premise that a person lacks some kind of information [14], or has a need [44] that can be met by obtaining relevant information. Many IR systems are built to address such needs. These systems often even have various mechanisms to help that information seeker when there are problems in obtaining information.

Those interested in the user side have studied this under the names of information seeking/behavior, whereas those interested in the system side have contributed to IR aspects. Then there are scholars who study various interaction elements (information science, HCI) and recommendation aspects (data mining, machine learning). Of course, these are quite broad strokes to paint a picture that depicts human information interaction and retrieval. While definitions and conceptual framings of these terms and areas could be argued, it is clear that

- These studies of information seeking start with the assumption that a person has a need for information;
- When a problem appears in that information seeking process, an intervention/recommendation is presented; and
- These interventions or recommendations are often provided as objects of information, such as documents and queries.

The idea of Information Fostering relaxes all of these assumptions and constraints. A good metaphor is that of a teacher. A good teacher does not simply answer a question by a student; she also shows him how to ask a good question. She does not simply provide an answer; but illuminates a path that the student can follow to reach to that answer. The teacher does not wait for a struggling student to fail; but rather helps him early in the process to ensure that failure does not happen. The *Fostering* part in Information Fostering really emphasizes such characteristics.

2.2 Existing and desired support

While it may be tempting to say that there is no current system or support for Information Fostering, there are indeed several instances one could find in various information systems, albeit at a preliminary level and with shortcomings.

In the late 90s, Microsoft introduced the office assistant feature to its Microsoft Office suite, with the default and the most popular character being *Clippit* (also known as *Clippy*). This feature, through an animated character on screen, monitored a user's activity in an application such as a word processor, and offered proactive help. The reception of this feature was mixed and Microsoft decided to remove it a few years later.

Since the early years of this century, RSS (Really Simple Syndication) feeds have found their way in many applications – desktop-based and mobile – to aggregate and proactively provide content to a user based on his/her interests, preferences, and actions. Variations of RSS have continued their popularity as feeds and notifications of different kinds that push information to people without them actively trying to retrieve it. This is widely used in most social media services such as Facebook and Twitter, as well as news aggregators such as Ozmosys.

More recently, intelligent assistants such as Siri, Google Now, Cortana, and Alexa have provided smarter approaches to offering proactive suggestions to a user based on the given context (e.g., time, location), past needs and assessments, as well as personal preferences. The nature and the amount of proactive support vary greatly, with some of these systems tightly integrated into a person's overall digital life including smarthome and cars, whereas others are glorified IR systems with voice recognition.

In all of these systems or scenarios, the common element is being proactive. While this often helps address the problem of people not knowing what they do not know, there are several drawbacks and shortcomings of such systems. As is evident with *Clippy* example, a proactive suggestion could be perceived more of an annoyance than a help, turning people away from using it even at times when it could be quite useful. In the case of information aggregators or feeds, the recommendations are driven by a person's interests and past assessments, but not necessarily based on the current context or task. In other words, they are less dynamic and less tailored to micro-moments. Finally, even the newer systems, such as Siri, that offer proactive suggestions are limited to the kind of recommendations they make. Siri never suggests that you consult a friend or a colleague as a proactive recommendation.

These realizations lead the author to making a list of an ideal Information Fostering system as enumerated below.

(1) The system should find a good balance between being proactive and invading one's privacy. In other words, offer proactive suggestions in a way that does not hinder one's ongoing task or even take their attention away from it.
(2) The system should consider not only the broad strokes of one's past behaviors and preferences, but also take into account the ongoing activities, assessments, and performance.
(3) The system should make a wide range of recommendations, including information objects (e.g., documents, queries), processes and strategies, as well as people.

In the following subsection, an attempt is made to provide an outlook for such a system in different settings.

2.3 Future scenarios and mockups

This subsection provides a couple of scenarios and mockups to clarify what Information Fostering implementation could look like in typical information seeking situations.

The first one (Figure 1) describes a typical search episode, where an information seeker is looking for information using an IR system and encounters a problem. This is where the system can offer a suggestion. For instance, if the searcher mistypes a query, the system could offer a correction. If the searcher is lost for what would be a good way to complete a query, the system could offer suggestions based on what may be most relevant or how others completed such a query. Assuming the searcher takes such a suggestion, his/her search episode will now be on a new path going forward. An Information Fostering scenario, on the other hand, plays out differently. Here, the system is actively evaluating the current search path that the searcher has taken and tries to predict where it might lead. If it finds a potential problem down the road, rather than waiting for that moment to come, it proactively warns the searcher about this and offers a detour that avoids the problem. This is similar to a GPS navigation unit that is aware of the traffic conditions on the road ahead and offers an alternative route if it finds there to be a problem in the charted path, before the traveler reaches close to that point of congestion.

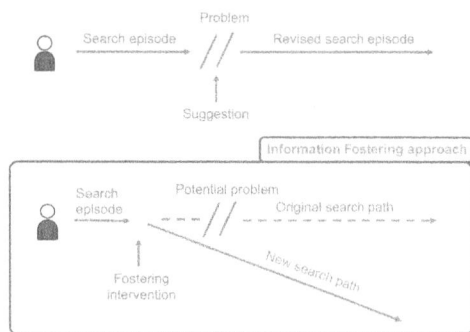

Figure 1: Information Fostering scenario involving an individual information seeker who encounters a problem during a search episode.

Figure 2 provides another scenario. Here, imagine two information seekers working on the same/similar task in the same time-frame. Normally they would go through their search episodes independently, even if they could benefit by working together. There may not be any problems with their individual search episodes, but they could achieve much more if they work with each other. This is an opportunity that is lost, unless someone or something helps make this connection. An Information Fostering system will do just that. It will recognize that there is a potential opportunity here in these two people collaborating, and points it out to them. Assuming they agree to work together, their new search episode is the one that involves collaboration. For an example – the Information Fostering system could recognize that two people working on the same task have different skills or abilities and suggest for them to work together. This asymmetric relationship could be teacher-student, expert-novice, or structured around a specific skillset.

Let us now examine the idea of an Information Fostering system through a real-life scenario. Alice is looking for ideas and things for her grandma's 90th birthday. She starts by searching online – first at a general-purpose Web search engine, and then at an e-commerce site. However, she does not have very clear notion of what this gift may look like, how much she would want to spend, and how she could make this something very special (and not just an off-the-shelf object). An Information Fostering system integrated in her browser quickly realizes this and starts offering suggestions, even as Alice keeps looking around. The system, based on Alice's

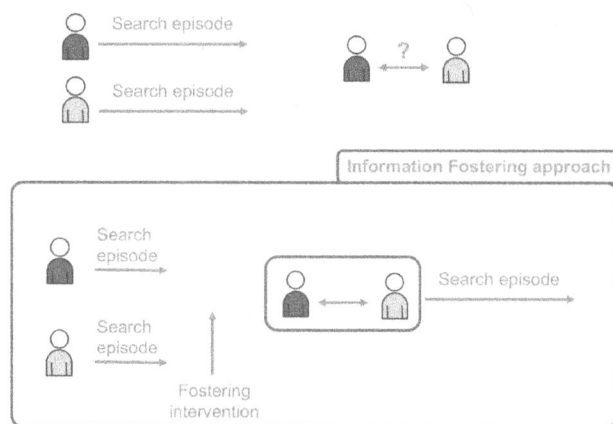

Figure 2: Information Fostering scenario involving two individuals working on the same/similar search task during the same time.

own history and that of the world, offers a strategy to think about finding something based on some significant events that happened in the world during her grandmother's lifetime. That triggers Alice to think about a post-WWII symbolism and how her grandma had talked about it. But Alice does not know enough about that era. Realizing this, the system then offers to connect her to someone who had either lived during that time or has studied it. Alice takes that suggestion and lets the system connect her to a WWII historian. He offers a couple of suggestions. Alice likes one of them – a brooch with an angel symbol to mark the time of peace. Now Alice can focus her searching and look for this particular item. She finally finds it at an antique storefront in an e-commerce site.

Here are the highlights from this scenario: (1) the Information Fostering system is being proactive in offering the suggestions without Alice specifically asking for them; (2) the system is able to use very little data from Alice's ongoing activities, thus addressing the cold start problem; and (3) the recommendations offered include people and strategies, in addition to objects.

A mock-up of this browser-based system is shown in Figure 3 and its various components are described below.

- *Queries*: this component lists potential queries a user may run at a given moment. The queries are found by not simply looking at relatedness as it is done in most query recommendation systems, but also by using task and topic knowledge.
- *Documents*: this component presents a few documents (Webpages) that the user may find useful. They are based on not just what others found to be useful for the same task, but also based on where a user is in the given search process. For instance, if the user is in the beginning stage of a search episode, it may be more appropriate to present documents with broad information. If the task is considered to be complex or obscure, this component will show documents deemed to be explanatory and easier to read (based on automatically computed readability scores and information content).
- *Strategy*: this component provides a combination of queries, documents, and potentially relevant segments. The system

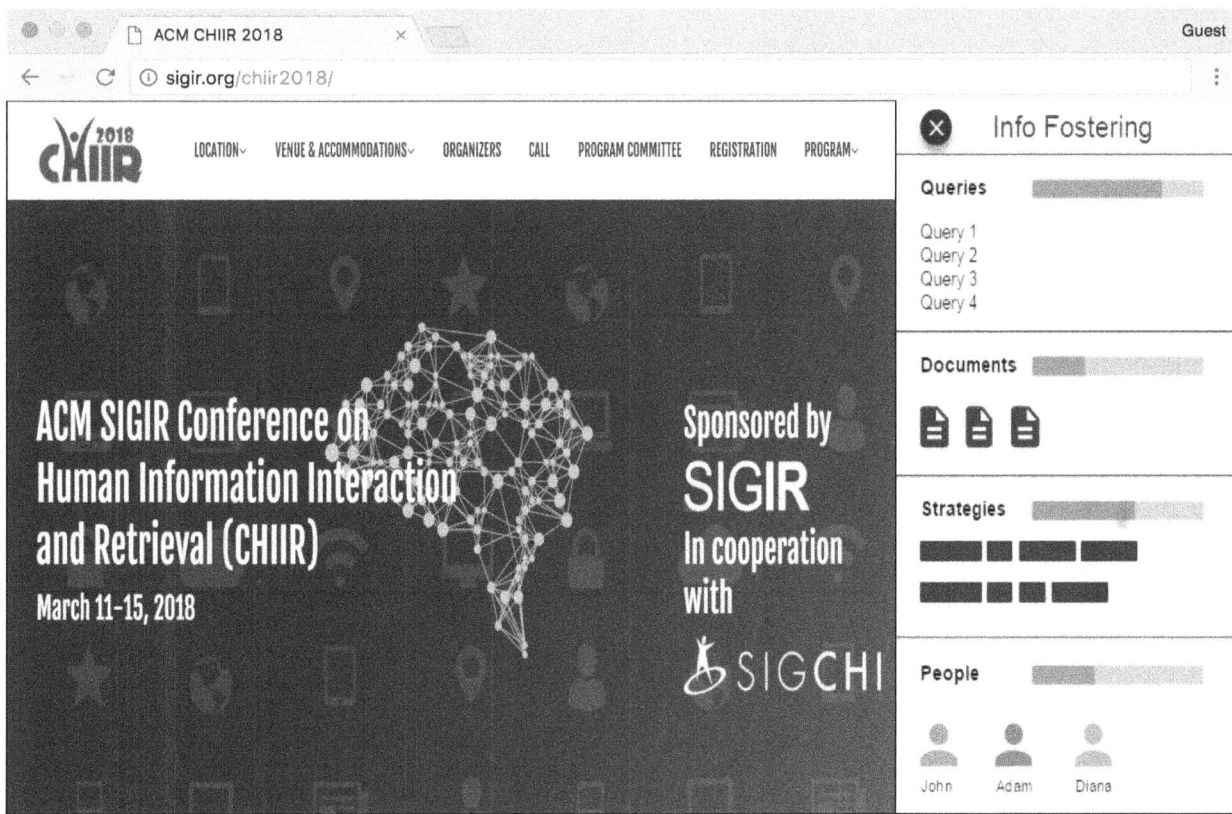

Figure 3: Mockup of an Information Fostering system, embedded in a Web browser.

infers the nature of the task as well as at which stage of the task the user is to guide the strategy recommendations.

- *People*: this component features potential people to collaborate at various stages of the search.

With each of the components, a confidence score is calculated. This score, ranging from 0% to 100%, is one of the outcomes for various techniques/algorithms that make up the Information Fostering system. These scores could be used by the user to decide if he/she wants to take any of the recommendations. Note that the design of this system uses the idea of peripheral awareness [17], which allows one to keep the attention on the ongoing task without being distracted while still having easy access to useful information on the periphery. One could also easily close that peripheral window if he/she wishes not to have such support at all.

Building such an Information Fostering system will require solving a number of problems. There are already several works, including those of the author, that address some of these problems. But all of these have been opportunistic at best. What it means is that these works identified a specific opportunity in information seeking situation where prediction of potential problems could lead to proactive recommendations, but it is not clear if or how any of these approaches could be generalized. To do so, we must approach the problem of Information Fostering top-down, focusing on systematically characterizing its components and thinking

through implications in various scenarios. But first, it is important to understand what is already been done.

3 RELEVANT RESEARCH

3.1 Task characterization and classification

Individuals engage in information seeking activities to accomplish different goals in various contexts and situations. Characterizing goals and contexts of information seeking can inform the design of personalized IR systems that adapt to different types of information problems. One way of exploring goals and contexts is to consider the tasks that motivate information seeking. The relationship between aspects of tasks and information seeking behavior have been discussed and examined in many studies. Various task classifications have been developed to categorize tasks at each or all of the three levels, work tasks, information seeking tasks, and information search tasks.

Campbell [7] focused on objective task complexity and developed a typology of complex tasks using four task attributes: (1) multiple paths to arrive at a desired end-state; (2) multiple desired end-states; (3) conflicting interdependence among paths to multiple desired outcomes; and (4) uncertain or probabilistic linkages among paths and outcomes. Complex tasks can be classified by determining the degree to which a task integrates each attribute and the total number of attributes contained in a task. Bystr´om and J´arvelin

[6] approached task complexity differently by categorizing it based on users' perceptions. They discovered that as the complexity of a task increased, the number of information sources consulted increased, so did the needs for domain knowledge and problem-solving information. Meanwhile, the success of the information seeking process decreased.

Tasks have also been analyzed from the angle of information search tasks, which refer to the activities users perform in IR systems to support their work tasks [15]. Reid [28] classified search tasks into tasks that are internally generated and those that are externally generated. An internally generated task is conceived and executed by the same person, whereas an externally generated task is a task where the task performer is different from the task setter. She argued that a task-oriented test collection is a realistic method of evaluating IR systems because it recognizes the primary importance of the task in user motivation. Gwizdka and Spence [13] suggested that subjective task difficulty is affected by a few factors such as the unique Webpages visited, the dwell time on each page, and the linearity of the navigation paths. The relative importance of these factors in predicting subjective difficulty is also influenced by objective task difficulty.

Li and Belkin [15] addressed the limitation of previous task classifications (e.g., focusing only on one or a few facets of tasks) by developing a faceted classification that comprehensively reflects the characteristics of tasks, and this faceted classification can be used for classifying all levels of tasks (i.e. work, information seeking, and search). This faceted classification scheme captures both the external characteristics of a task (i.e. source, task doer, time, process, product, and goal) and the internal attributes of a task that include task features (i.e. objective complexity and interdependence) as well as users' perception of a task (i.e. salience, urgency, difficulty, complexity, topical knowledge, knowledge of task procedure). This scheme has been widely employed by researchers in designing and characterizing tasks (e.g., [9, 19]) in IR studies. Due to its versatility and comprehensiveness, it will be the classification scheme used for characterize search tasks when a proposal for moving forward is presented later in this paper.

3.2 Recommender systems

Recommender system is defined as an assistant tool that can automate or support a general recommendation process from the system side [38]. During the information seeking process, recommendations from systems can help users filter out part of irrelevant information, decrease their cognitive load, and offer them cues (e.g., queries, terms), answers, and objects (e.g. documents, Web pages) to address their information needs [27]. Therefore, to better support information seeking practices, recommender systems must obtain preferences from people concerning the relevant domain and understand the gaps in their knowledge base based on their information seeking and search behaviors [38]. To reach this goal, both the type and content of recommendations need to be tailored to different tasks, gaps, and goals of information seekers.

The previous studies of recommender systems can be classified into two categories: collaborative filtering (CF) and content-based filtering (CB) [29]. Specifically, CF uses information-filtering techniques in formulating recommendations based on users' previous interactions with systems (e.g., queries issued, page visited and

bookmarked, and search results clicked), whereas CB analyzes a set of documents rated by an individual user and detects content-based similarities between items to infer a user's preferences and needs for recommendations. To facilitate the inference of user's needs and the connections between documents, researchers in this field have employed different data mining techniques (e.g., decision tree, neural network, regression, K-NN, clustering, link analysis) according to different focused features of contents, interactions, and individuals [27].

For both of these two approaches, however, recommendations from previous systems have always been limited to a set of object types, such as queries, documents, images, and videos. These types of objects may be enough for serving navigational search goals of users who have specific known Websites or items in mind. If an information seeker needs to get advice or explore open-ended questions, then the recommender system must gain a deeper understanding of the user's goal and task, go beyond the limits of online resources, and provide more personalized options for them, such as search strategies, people who can answer the questions, or an idea as a starting point for exploration [30]. Under this circumstance, people can acquire the help and strategies (rather than merely objects) offered by proactive recommender systems and better tackle their potential needs and knowledge gaps. This will be one of the important components of an Information Fostering system.

3.3 Proactive information seeking

According to Wilson [45](p.49), information seeking behavior is "the purposive seeking for information as a consequence of a need to satisfy some goal." Guided by different goals and tasks, people often seek and search information in different ways. For example, when seeking to satisfy a navigational goal, an information searcher may directly type in a URL or specific queries. However, for information searchers with undirected, exploratory goals, queries issued in a search engine often need to be broad and cover more potentially relevant topics [30]. In this sense, being proactive in information seeking is to go beyond the immediate, short-term relationship between specific queries and documents, and to try to understand the tasks, topics, and goals of information seekers for better predicting and serving of their potential information needs.

In the relevant literature, the goals and tasks of information seeking have been analyzed mainly in the context of online information search and retrieval. Rose and Levinson [30] investigated the queries issued by users in a search engine and proposed a hierarchical typology of user's search goals. Similarly, drawing on the ideas of the sense-making approach, Savolainen and Kari [32] revealed the discontinuous and dynamic nature of Web searching episodes and developed a conceptual framework of knowledge gaps faced by searchers and corresponding gap-bridging strategies. According to their findings, an understanding of search goals, user's knowledge gaps, and gap-bridging strategies can help tackle the larger problems of representing user goals in an IR system. This could be instrumental in supporting proactive IR.

Besides the goals and gaps, researchers in related fields have also explored the relations between task facets and information seeking and search behavior, aiming at understanding and automatically predicting people's task contexts based on their interactions with information and/or systems. For example, Bystrom and Jarvelin

[6] found that the complexity of task is closely associated with the task doer's information seeking behavior (i.e., types of information needed, information channels used). Liu, Liu, Gwizdka, and Belkin [18] indicate that information searcher's behaviors (i.e., documents dwell time and number of content pages viewed per query) can be used as indicators to predict search task difficulty. In addition to search behavior per se, Mostafa and Gwizdka [26] suggest that various neural signals (i.e., eye movement, EEG, fMRI) can also be employed as indicators to test the hypothesized relations between behavioral markers and search task facets. To support proactive information seeking and retrieval, future studies need to continue exploring the underlying connections between information search behavior, task facets, and other contextual information. And this is what an Information Fostering system should do – understand the relationships among the nature of a search task, various contextual factors during a search episode, and potential problems faced and help to be offered.

4 PAST AND PRELIMINARY WORK

To address the larger problem of creating an Information Fostering framework and a system, one needs to solve several sub-problems. This section provides some details on how several scholars, including the author, have already made reasonable to substantial advancements on these sub-problems.

4.1 Information seeking barriers, failures, and solutions

An information seeking failure is defined as a situation in which an individual could not satisfy his/her information needs at work, at school, or in his/her everyday life. To overcome the limitations of previous works in which only failures in Web searching were considered, the author investigated individuals' failures in information seeking both online and offline. Employing Amazon's Mechanical Turk (MTurk) as a recruiting and surveying platform, the author was able to obtain a diverse pool of 63 participants from various age groups and educational backgrounds. MTurk users are arguably more representative of the general population than academic participants [11].

Data collected from a qualitative survey that gathered 208 real-life examples of information seeking failures and 10 semi-structured interviews with 10 different participants were analyzed using various theoretical frameworks of tasks (e.g., [15]), strategies (e.g., [4]), and barriers (e.g., [8, 31, 37]). The findings indicated that a wide range of external and internal factors caused individuals' failures that were affected by multiple aspects of information seekers' tasks and strategies. These components of information seeking mutually influenced one another and together they led to individuals' information seeking outcomes. Their information needs were often too specific to be fulfilled by the general information available to them. Also, although individuals overwhelmingly chose to search online, the Web might not be the ideal place to look for information in some situations. The respondents often wished to directly seek help from humans after having unsuccessful experiences on the Web. Some of the findings concerning the support individuals wanted are reported in [40, 41]. These studies compiled a list of barriers that users may face in information seeking, and developed a classification of "help" needed by users when having difficulties in finding information, which can be used in the design and data analysis for further research.

4.2 Generative query recommendations

Current work in recommendation in search tasks predominantly focuses on recommending queries from a search log. The possible queries are assumed to be given in advance. User's input is given to the recommendation system; the output is one of these possible queries. However, to gauge the quality of these queries – which are typically user queries – Mitsui and Shah [23] conducted a Mechanical Turk task in which they asked users to guess the query that generated a set of results. The results provided to users represented the first 10 results (i.e., the first page) generated from a real query to Google. It was found that a simple algorithm that output the most frequent words as a query gave more accurate queries than users. This suggests that users may not be able to accurately represent their information needs in a query – and therefore approaches that suggest other users' queries may not yield the most effective recommendations.

Considering this, there are some recent works that employ a generative approach to query recommendation in which completely new queries are generated rather than extracted. In this approach, a typical method is to use the popular topic modeling approach – Latent Dirichlet Allocation (LDA [5]) – to model a user's context as a distribution of topics. This model is trained on an unstructured corpus of text documents and can infer the topic distribution of any given document or set of documents. Given a user's past queries, the author modeled their past queries as a set of topics and recommended the least explored topic that was still relevant to their search, according to a threshold criterion. He then generated multi-word query terms from this topic, using a skipgram model [20] that could create coherent phrases. This was then compared to an existing work that suggested previously issued queries [39]. While the author's method [22] recommended more diverse queries than users, it still strayed from the original topic more so than the competing method, suggesting that a different model incorporating further information (such as task information) should be used to control the query generation process.

4.3 Strategy recommendations

The author has also conducted research in recommending strategies (a sequence of steps involving queries, documents, and relevant information) for exploratory search tasks. These tasks comprise multiple queries and hence lend themselves easily to the problem of Information Fostering. Typical features of an exploratory search task are its open-endedness and the multi-faceted nature of the task, requiring multiple queries [43]. In previous work, the author extracted implicit features of the search process based on the literature, which measured the discovery, creativity, and exploration of the users' search processes. He used these features to recommend trails of search queries to users who were likely to underperform in the future [34]. The recommendations, while a sequence of queries, were "search paths" as defined in by White and Huang [42], which is a series of syntactically related queries. This work was able to accurately predict the performance of a user a few steps ahead within their search, and moreover could offer effective recommendations. The recommendations offered became more effective as the recommendations were given later in the search process. They moreover greatly enhanced user performance, according to quantitative simulations and qualitative judgments of the simulations and user performance. Figure 4 shows the probabilities of helping vs. hurting a searcher through these strategy recommendations at different times. As shown, for the most part the method is able to help the searcher in improving their retrieval effectiveness.

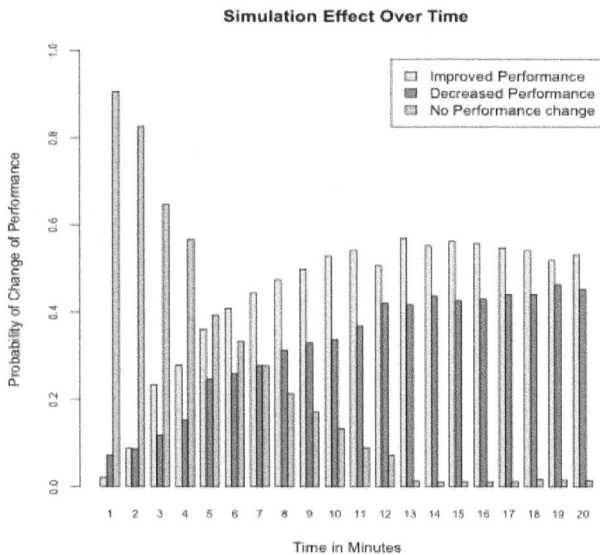

Figure 4: Simulation of help vs. hurt for recommending strategies to searchers.

4.4 Collaborator recommendation

As identified in the previous section, most recommender systems do not go beyond suggesting information objects. However, many studies have found that given a chance, people do want to find others who could work with them or at least help them in their information seeking tasks (e.g., [25]). The author investigated the problem of coming up with a recommendation for a collaborator during a search episode. Using 120 participants in 60 pairs working on an exploratory search task, the author built a model for finding suitable collaborators for an individual during different stages of his/her search. This model was then tested on real-life data obtained from Bing search logs and Internet Explorer browser logs. The data consisted of 8,969 search sessions by 8,051 users who were working on an exploratory search task during the overlapping timeframe. Using the collaborator recommendation model, the newly devised algorithm predicted potential collaborators for each of these searchers and simulated what would happen if they took these recommendations. Figure 5 shows the results of these simulations. As shown in the top graph, using the predicted recommendations for collaboration, the individual searchers would have achieved higher effectiveness (number of useful pages over total number of pages covered) and efficiency (amount of effectiveness per query). The

bottom graph shows the likelihood of helping and hurting someone based on that recommendation at different times. This likelihood calculation can be used as the level of confidence while making a recommendation for a potential collaboration to someone. The details of the method, the model, and the results can be found in [12]. Continuing this thread of research, the author, with his colleagues, has also created new methods [35, 36] for detecting potential roles that collaborators could play in a collaborative search project to optimize the outcomes for their task, once again emphasizing on finding opportunities in an information seeking situation.

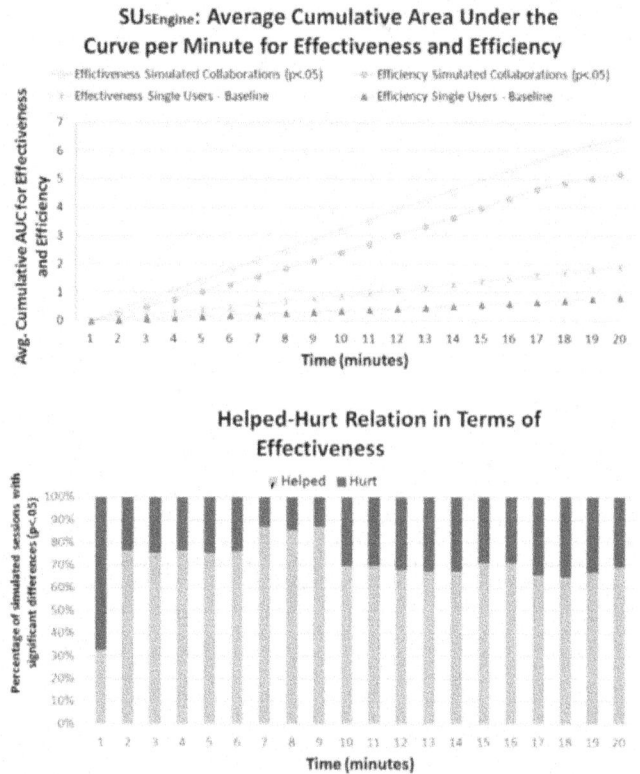

Figure 5: Simulations showing effectiveness and efficiency for recommended collaborations (top) and the likelihood of help vs. hurt (bottom).

5 METHODS FOR MOVING FORWARD

As described earlier, in order to create an Information Fostering or Proactive IR system, we need to understand a great deal about a person's ongoing processes as well as past behaviors. More specifically, we need to extract information about three crucial elements representing one's information interaction: topic, task, and intention/purpose. While there are several possible ways to pursue these goals, this section proposes two different methods – one based on collecting small but rich data to extract task, problems, and help information, and another based on using large-scale data with a more formalized approach from machine learning. The former could be more suitable for an academic environment, whereas the latter could be more appropriate in an industrial setting where large amounts of user data is available.

5.1 Extracting topic, task, problems, and help information

To explicate the topic of a user's information interaction activities, one could use a method described earlier in Section 4.2. In addition to the techniques described in that section, there have been several other approaches one could find in the literature for extracting topic information [1]. On the other hand, extracting task and intention information is considered hard. There have been a few recent efforts to identify an information seeker's intention in a search task [21, 24], but hardly any empirical work on automatically extracting the nature of a search task. Therefore, in this subsection, a short proposal is presented for learning about a person's task using behavioral data. In addition to extracting information about the task, this proposal also covers learning about what problems information seekers face and what solutions could be provided to them that are not just exclusive to the search system they are using. This work will involve building a Task Model as well as a Problem-Help Model.

An appropriate method for building these models is a user study with participants divided in a few (e.g., four) groups based on the kind of task they are assigned. These tasks could be constructed using the faceted task classification presented in Table 9 (p.1834-1835) of Li and Belkin [15]. While the authors in that article identified several facets of a task, many of them may either be not relevant or of no interest. Given the nature of the search scenarios considered here, it is imperative that the tasks will be done by individuals ('Task doer' facet), be unique ('Time → Frequency' facet), and have a single goal ('Goal → Quantity' facet). Also, given the nature of the study design (controlled lab experiments), the tasks will be externally assigned ('Source of task' facet), done in a short time ('Time → Length' facet), and have low interdependence ('Task characteristics → Interdependence' facet). The classification scheme also includes various factors based on user's perception of the task, and are not relevant for designing the tasks. This leaves out the aspects of 'Product', 'Goal → Quality', 'Time → Stage', and 'Task characteristics → Objective task complexity'.

During the lab session, the system will prompt the participant to take a brief questionnaire every time he/she goes to run a new query on a search engine. This can be achieved by modifying an open-source browser-based plug-in such as Coagmento [33].

For this questionnaire, the choices can be drawn from the literature. Existing studies have presented a variety of information seeking barriers/obstacles using varying terminology (e.g., [8, 31, 37]). Individuals frequently face difficulties when looking for information across various disciplines and professions. Barriers may originate from inside an individual (e.g., lack of subject knowledge, searching skills, or patience), be imposed on an individual from outside (e.g., time constraint, restricted access), or be interpersonal (e.g., insufficient support from other people) [31, 37]. Obstacles in finding information can also be profession-specific. For instance, Attfield and Dowell [2] discovered in their study of the field of journalism that product constraints – such as deadline and work-count – often brought challenges to journalists' information seeking. The problems could be deepened by the uncertain nature of writing for news articles. The author has synthesized the literature to generate a list of information seeking barriers [40, 41]. For this study, the list can

be refined to include only problems associated with Web searching. For the "help" needed by individuals when encountering a gap, inspiration can be drawn from the work by Wang and Shah [41] that explored the user-reported remedies in information seeking. The original classification included eight types of support – such as experts and new Web features – that may assist in individuals' information seeking. Only the types that are applicable here should be retained. This results in the following questions and responses to be shown to the user before each query execution.

(1) What problem are you facing right now?
□ Time constraint □ Too much information □ Information is too scattered □ Information is not up-to-date □ Poor quality display of text or graphics □ Information is unreliable □ Information is not available □ Topic is too unclear □ Unable to articulate my information needs □ Unaware of relevant information sources □ Unable to understand the information retrieved □ Other (please write)

(2) What will help you?
□ Query recommendation □ Information source recommendation (e.g., documents, Websites) □ Step-by-step instructions to follow □ A peer/friend to talk to □ An expert to consult □ Other (please write)

The objective of this study is two-fold: using the behavioral data from one's search session, build a task model that could predict various aspects (nature) of the search task; and using the behavior data from one's search session, predict the potential problems as well as possible help at each query execution time (or for a given query segment). Figure 6 outlines these two objectives.

First, using all of the available behavioral data as features and considering task aspects as dependent variables, a prediction model, called Task Model, can be built by doing a multivariate ANOVA (MANOVA) and/or multiple regression analyses. For this analysis, first all the behavioral data from all the sessions (30 minutes/session) should be used. Various model-related parameters including R^2 and η (effect size) will inform about accuracy and robustness of the model. After that, a 10-fold cross-validation can be run to do training-testing on 70-30 data splits. This will provide prediction accuracy results.

Furthering this analysis, various subsets of the available data can be created:

(1) Based on task types (total 4);
(2) Type of behavioral data (three types – interaction logs, mouse movement, eye-tracking); and
(3) Amount of time (e.g., 5 minutes, 10 minutes, 15 minutes, 20 minutes, and 25 minutes).

A number of analyses (at least 4x3x5 = 60) can then be run to see how much and what kind of behavioral data contribute to detecting the nature of a search task. Appropriate exploratory factor analysis and PCA methods can also be used to derive grouping and reduction of variables.

Similar analyses can be performed for building a model that predicts potential problems and help (Problem-Help Model) with the following two differences: (1) Rather than creating subsets of behavior data according to time, they can be created by query segments; and (2) Prediction of "help" can be mediated by "problems" in addition to the behavioral data, which means "problems" will

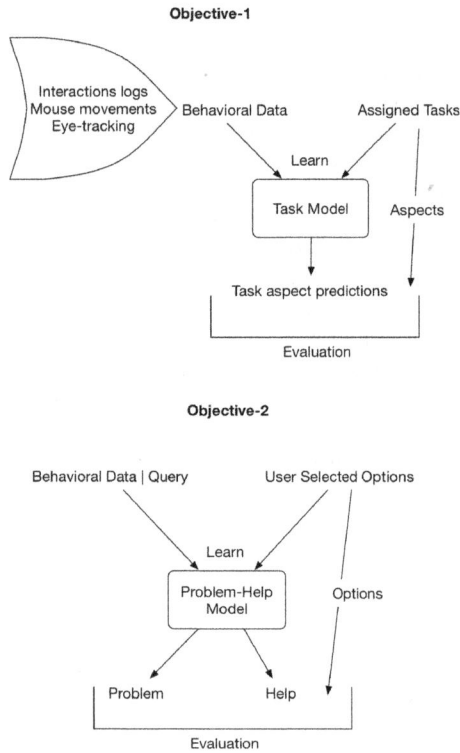

Figure 6: Outline of addressing two objectives for the user study.

possibly serve as an intervening variable, leading to some form of analysis of covariate (ANCOVA).

5.2 Building User, Background, and Activity models

Here is another path forward for building appropriate models that could help an Information Fostering system to project a user's trajectory and make suggestions based on potentially encountering any problems. In order to understand what a user is doing and where that path is heading, three kinds of information is needed: (1) the user's past behaviors; (2) the world knowledge; and (3) the user's current behavior. These three things will be materialized as User Model (M_U), Background Model (M_B), and Activity Model (M_A).

Both M_U and M_A, which are associated with a user's past or current activities, can be represented using the following attributes: Activity, Object, Content, Time-Start, Time-End, Prior, Posterior, and Assessment. Collectively these attributes for various activities/objects from the user's past or the present will capture the knowledge about what the user did before and/or what he/she is trying to do now. Background Model (M_B), on the other hand, can have the following attributes: Activity, Object, Content, Frequency, Duration, Prior, Posterior, and Assessment.

To build these models, data from past lab and field studies involving people's searching and browsing activities can be used. These

datasets will be used to build M_U and M_B, whereas M_A can be built on-the-fly using various behavioral data, such as query issuing, clicks, page visitation, dwell time, etc.

Each of these models contain information for an action, its response, and an assessment. For instance, there could be a data-point about a query (action), a result set (response), and assessment (whether the user clicked on a result or not). Using these attributes, the three models could be represented as the following:

$$M_A = \sum_i (\alpha_i a_i - r_i) \tag{1}$$

$$M_B = \sum_i (\beta_i a_i - r_i) \tag{2}$$

$$M_U = \sum_i (\gamma_i a_i - r_i) \tag{3}$$

Here, α, β, and γ are parameters associated with those models. In order to see if the user's current activity as represented using M_A will lead to something useful or not, we could look at the slope of its corresponding function, given an action a_i. For this, we need to take a partial derivative of M_A with respect to as following.

$$\frac{\partial}{\partial a_j} M_A = \sum_i (\alpha_i a_i - r_i) \frac{\partial}{\partial a_j} (\alpha_0 a_0 + ... + \alpha_j a_j + ... + \alpha_n a_n - r_i)$$

$$= \sum_i (\alpha_i a_i - r_i)\alpha_j \tag{4}$$

This informs us about the slope of M_A along the action that we are considering (a_j). We can then use M_B and M_U to see how this particular action in the user's and/or the world's past was assessed. Based on that, we could predict the chances of the user to take that action and continue on the path. If we determine that there is a good likelihood of the user continuing on that trajectory, we could evaluate where that trajectory could go (next possible actions) and find out corresponding assessments using the same approach as described above. In other words, at a given time, we start looking at various possibilities based on a computed projection of the user's trajectory and assessments from the past behaviors of the user and of the world. If we detect a problem along the way, we could offer the user a different trajectory/strategy that we have calculated to show better promise.

In previous work, the author extracted implicit features of the search process based on the literature, which measured the discovery, creativity, and exploration of users' search processes. He used these features to recommend trails of search queries to users who were likely to underperform in the future [34]. The recommendations, while a sequence of queries, were *search paths* as defined in by White and Huang [42], which is a series of syntactically related queries. This work was able to accurately predict the performance of a user a few steps ahead within their search, and moreover could offer effective recommendations. But this work was limited to using the data about only the participants who did the same task in the controlled lab environment. The proposal presented here allows one to not only scale it up, but also relax the assumption about the nature of the task.

6 CONCLUSION

We lack enough understanding of addressing the problems that information seekers face due to their inability to express their information needs, recognizing a potential problem during a search episode, and identifying support needed that goes beyond what a typical search system could provide. Most recommender systems try to mitigate these problems by suggesting information objects (queries, documents), disregarding a deeper understanding of the task at hand or the possibility of recommendations that involve process/strategy, people, and other forms.

Information Fostering is an idea of being proactive in an information seeking situation by projecting ahead for potential problems and opportunities, and guiding the user to a path that could avoid those problems and/or capture those opportunities before it is too late. Such a path may include recommendations for not only information objects such as queries and documents, but also processes/strategies, and people. A true Information Fostering system may even recommend an information seeker to stop or reconsider a pursuit, like what a good teacher or a friend would do, instead of blindly giving him/her a suggestion for an information object.

In this Perspective Paper, a case was made for this new paradigm that looks at the other side of the information seeking coin – providing relevant information and help/guidance to a person without them explicitly asking or even realizing the need. This was done by reviewing existing systems and literature and outlining what we need next, as well as proposing a couple of methods for moving forward the research agenda. The author believes Information Fostering will provide us the next conceptual leap in the field of human-centered IR, and will become even more relevant as we move further toward conversation-based intelligent assistants for our informational objectives.

7 ACKNOWLEDGMENTS

This work is supported by the National Science Foundation (NSF) grant IIS-1717488.

REFERENCES

[1] J. Allan. Introduction to Topic Detection and Tracking. In *Topic Detection and Tracking: Event-based Information Organization*, volume 12, pages 1–16. 2002.
[2] S. Attfield and J. Dowell. Information seeking and use by newspaper journalists. *Journal of Documentation*, 59(2):187–204, apr 2003.
[3] N. J. Belkin. Anomalous states of knowledge as a basis for information retrieval. *Canadian Journal of Information Science*, 5:133–143, 1980.
[4] N. J. Belkin, P. G. Marchetti, and C. Cool. BRAQUE: Design of an Interface to Support User Interaction in Information Retrieval. *IP&M*, 29(3):325–344, 1993.
[5] D. M. Blei, B. B. Edu, A. Y. Ng, A. S. Edu, M. I. Jordan, and J. B. Edu. Latent Dirichlet Allocation. *Journal of Machine Learning Research*, 3:993–1022, 2003.
[6] K. Byström and K. Järvelin. Task complexity affects information seeking and use. *Information Processing and Management*, 31(2):191–213, 1995.
[7] D. J. Campbell. Task Complexity: A Review and Analysis. *The Academy of Management Review*, 13(1):40–52, 1988.
[8] S. Chowdhury, F. Gibb, and M. Landoni. A model of uncertainty and its relation to information seeking and retrieval (IS&R). *JDoc*, 70(4):5, 2014.
[9] M. J. Cole, J. Gwizdka, C. Liu, R. Bierig, N. J. Belkin, and X. Zhang. Task and user effects on reading patterns in information search. *Interacting with Computers*, 23(4):346–362, 2011.
[10] B. Dervin. Sense-making theory and practice: an overview of user interests in knowledge seeking and use. *Journal of Knowledge Management*, 2(2):36–46, 1998.
[11] J. Erickson, C. S. Mackenzie, V. H. Menec, and D. S. Bailis. The effect of time perspectives on mental health information processing and help-seeking attitudes and intentions in younger versus older adults. *Aging & Mental Health*, 21(3):259–271, 2017.
[12] R. González-Ibáñez, C. Shah, and R. W. White. Capturing collabportunities: A method to evaluate collaboration opportunities in information search using pseudo-collaboration. *JASIST*, 66(9):1897–1912, 2015.

[13] J. Gwizdka and I. Spence. What Can Searching Behavior Tell Us About the Difficulty of Information Tasks? A Study of Web Navigation. *Proceedings of the American Society for Information Science and Technology*, 43(1):1–22, 2007.
[14] P. Ingwersen. Cognitive perspectives of information retrieval interaction: Elements of a cognitive IR theory. *Journal of Documentation*, 52:3–50, 1996.
[15] Y. Li and N. J. Belkin. A faceted approach to conceptualizing tasks in information seeking. *Information Processing and Management*, 44(6):1822–1837, 2008.
[16] Y. Li and Y. Guo. Be proactive for better decisions: Predicting information seeking in the context of earthquake risk. *International Journal of Disaster Risk Reduction*, 19:75–83, 2016.
[17] O. Liechti and Y. Sumi. Editorial: Awareness and the WWW. *International Journal of Human Computer Studies*, 56(1):1–5, 2002.
[18] C. Liu, F. Yang, Y. Zhao, Q. Jiang, and L. Zhang. What does time constraint mean to information searchers? In *Proceedings of the 5th Information Interaction in Context Symposium on - IIiX '14*, pages 227–230, 2014.
[19] J. Liu, C. Liu, J. Gwizdka, and N. J. Belkin. Can search systems detect users' task difficulty? *Proceeding of the ACM SIGIR Conference*, (August 2015):845, 2010.
[20] T. Mikolov, I. Sutskever, K. Chen, G. Corrado, J. Dean, K. Chen, J. Dean, T. Mikolov, and K. Chen. Distributed Representations of Words and Phrases and their Compositionality. In *NIPS'14*, volume cs.CL, pages 3111–3119, 2013.
[21] M. Mitsui, J. Liu, N. J. Belkin, and C. Shah. Predicting Information Seeking Intentions from Search Behaviors. In *Proceeding of the ACM SIGIR Conference*, pages 1121–1124, New York, New York, USA, 2017. ACM Press.
[22] M. Mitsui and C. Shah. Multi-Word Generative Query Recommendation Using Topic Modeling. *Proceedings of the 10th ACM Conference on Recommender Systems - RecSys '16*, pages 27–30, 2016.
[23] M. Mitsui and C. Shah. Query Generation as Result Aggregation for Knowledge Representation. In *Proceedings of the HICSS*, pages 4365–4374, 2017.
[24] M. Mitsui, C. Shah, and N. J. Belkin. Extracting Information Seeking Intentions for Web Search Sessions. In *Proceeding of the ACM SIGIR Conference*, pages 841–844, New York, New York, USA, 2016. ACM Press.
[25] M. R. Morris. A Survey of Collaborative Web Search Practices. In *Proceedings of ACM SIGCHI Conference on Human Factors in Computing Systems*, pages 1657–1660, Florence, Italy, 2008.
[26] J. Mostafa and J. Gwizdka. Deepening the Role of the User. In *Proceedings of ACM CHIIR Conference*, pages 63–70, 2016.
[27] D. H. Park, H. K. Kim, I. Y. Choi, and J. K. Kim. A literature review and classification of recommender systems research, 2012.
[28] J. Reid. A Task-Oriented Non-Interactive Evaluation Methodology for Information Retrieval Systems. *Information Retrieval*, 2(1):115–129, 2000.
[29] F. Ricci, L. Rokach, and B. Shapira. Introduction to Recommender Systems Handbook. In *Recommender Systems Handbook*, pages 1–35. 2011.
[30] D. E. Rose and D. Levinson. Understanding user goals in web search. In *Proceedings of the 13th conference on World Wide Web - WWW '04*, page 13, 2004.
[31] R. Savolainen. Cognitive barriers to information seeking: A conceptual analysis. *Journal of Information Science*, 41(5), 2015.
[32] R. Savolainen and J. Kari. Facing and bridging gaps in Web searching. *Information Processing and Management*, 42(2):519–537, 2006.
[33] C. Shah. Coagmento- A Collaborative Information Seeking, Synthesis and Sense-Making Framework (an integrated demo). In *Proceedings of Computer Supported Cooperative Work (CSCW)*, Savannah, GA, February 2010.
[34] C. Shah, C. Hendahewa, and R. González-Ibáñez. Rain or shine? Forecasting search process performance in exploratory search tasks. *Journal of the Association for Information Science and Technology*, 67(7):1607–1623, jun 2016.
[35] L. Soulier, C. Shah, and L. Tamine. User-Driven System-Mediated Collaborative Information Retrieval. In *Proceedings of ACM SIGIR*, pages 485–494, Gold Coast, Australia, 2014.
[36] L. Soulier, L. Tamine, and C. Shah. MineRank: Leveraging users' latent roles for unsupervised collaborative information retrieval. *IP&M*, 52(6):1122–1141, 2016.
[37] M. Świgoń. Information limits: Definition, typology and types. *Aslib Proceedings*, 63(4):364–379, 2011.
[38] L. Terveen and W. Hill. Beyond recommender systems: Helping people help each other. *HCI in the New Millennium*, (1):487–509, 2001.
[39] H. Vahabi, M. Ackerman, D. Loker, R. Baeza-Yates, and A. Lopez-Ortiz. Orthogonal query recommendation. *Proceedings of ACM RecSys 2013*, pages 33–40, 2013.
[40] Y. Wang, S. Sarkar, and C. Shah. Investigating Information Seekers' Selection of Interpersonal and Impersonal Sources. *Proceedings of ACM CHIIR 2017*, pages 353–356, 2017.
[41] Y. Wang and C. Shah. Exploring support for the unconquerable barriers in information seeking. *Proceedings of the ASIST*, 53(1):1–5, jan 2016.
[42] R. W. White and J. Huang. Assessing the scenic route: measuring the value of search trails in web logs. *Proceeding of the ACM SIGIR*, pages 587–594, 2010.
[43] R. W. White and R. A. Roth. *Exploratory Search: Beyond the Query-Response Paradigm*. Morgan & Claypool Publishers, 2009.
[44] T. Wilson. On user studies and information needs. *Journal of Documentation*, 37(1):3–15, dec 1981.
[45] T. D. Wilson. Human information behavior. *Informing Science*, 3(2):49–55, 2000.

The Role of the Task Topic in
Web Search of Different Task Types

Daniel Hienert*, Matthew Mitsui+, Philipp Mayr*, Chirag Shah†, Nicholas J. Belkin†

*GESIS – Leibniz Institute for the Social Sciences
Cologne, Germany
daniel.hienert@gesis.org,
philipp.mayr.gesis.org

+Department of Computer Science
Rutgers University
New Brunswick, NJ, USA
mmitsui@cs.rutgers.edu

†School of Communication & Information
Rutgers University
New Brunswick, NJ, USA
chirags@rutgers.edu, belkin@rutgers.edu

ABSTRACT

When users are looking for information on the Web, they show different behavior for different task types, e.g., for fact finding vs. information gathering tasks. For example, related work in this area has investigated how this behavior can be measured and applied to distinguish between easy and difficult tasks. In this work, we look at the searcher's behavior in the domain of journalism for four different task types, and additionally, for two different topics in each task type. Search behavior is measured with a number of session variables and correlated to subjective measures such as task difficulty, task success and the usefulness of documents. We acknowledge prior results in this area that task difficulty is correlated to user effort and that easy and difficult tasks are distinguishable by session variables. However, in this work, we emphasize the role of the *task topic* – in and of itself – over parameters such as the search results and read content pages, dwell times, session variables and subjective measures such as task difficulty or task success. With this knowledge researchers should give more attention to the task topic as an important influence factor for user behavior.

CCS CONCEPTS

• **Information systems~Users and interactive retrieval**

KEYWORDS

User Behavior; Web Search; Task; Topic; Session

ACM Reference format:
Daniel Hienert, Matthew Mitsui, Philipp Mayr, Chirag Shah, Nicholas J. Belkin. 2018. The Role of the Task Topic in Web Search of Different Task Types. In *Proceedings of ACM CHIIR '18, March 2018, New Brunswick, NJ, USA.* DOI: 10.1145/3176349.3176382

1 INTRODUCTION

While different models have been proposed for information seeking, in interactive information retrieval (IIR) there is the goal to capture the whole setting with a focus on the interactivity between the *user, system,* and *content.* These elementary concepts of information search are, for example, presented by Tsakkonas and Papatheodorou [22] in their triptych framework. Cole et al. [5] apply usefulness as the overall evaluation criterion for each of these components at different levels. The question here is how useful are the systems' results, processes and the delivered content for the leading task and goal, for sub tasks and information seeking strategies (ISS [2]).

The starting moment in this model is the user's *task* which leads the user behavior. This behavior can be described on the system side by a number of session variables, for example by the number of queries or viewed pages within a search session. The *task type* has been identified as one influencing moment of user behavior that can be measured by session variables [11, 20].

However, there are surely more factors which can be found in the triangle system of user, system, and content that influence or can be indicated by session variables. On the user side, there can be factors such as the user's knowledge about the topic and the task, the ability to search efficiently, her or his learning curve or the expectations of the outcome. On the system side, influencing factors can be, e.g., the quality of search engines or the system's support for query terms suggestions or to save and review interesting results. The content side has been a bit unattended in the past of IIR research – that is, the search topic in itself. Also, it is the main source from where users are extracting information from by reading, understanding, and classifying text, images, videos and other information types from Web pages. From a task's view, content can be targeted by the task type (which particular kind of information needs to be extracted?), but also by the task's topic (from which domain, subject area, theme or thing?).

In this paper, we will address this gap by analyzing data from an experiment with four different task types. The experiment's design is insofar specific that each task type is conducted with two different topics. This allows us to examine in particular the role of the task topic whereby the rest of experiment variables (at least on the task-, system-, and user-side) remains stable. We especially examine the relation between subjective user ratings, e.g., for task difficulty, task success and the usefulness of bookmarked pages and session variables such as task time, number of queries or dwell times on read documents. We focus on the investigation which relationships exist and what are the roles of the task topic for user behavior.

2 RELATED WORK

2.1 The Role of the Task

The idea of a *task* as a motivating moment for the user and as a target variable for the evaluation in interactive information retrieval has gained in importance over the last two decades. Vakkari [23] recites the definition: "A task is an activity to be performed in order to accomplish a goal". Toms [21] gives an outline of the development of the concept "task" and its role in information retrieval. Beside others, an early model of connecting task and search is given by Kekäläinen & Järvelin [10]. They proposed an evaluation model in which the classical lab IR context opened to the information seeking context and work task context. In these contexts, the seeking task and the work task play a major role. Borlund proposed the IIR evaluation model [3] which uses simulated work tasks to simulate information needs and allows the evaluation of IIR systems in a relative controlled environment, but as realistic as possible. Broder [4] suggested an early model for Web search in which he puts the task before the information need. As a first differentiation for task and query types it is differentiated between navigational, informational and transactional queries.

2.2 Different Task Types

Differentiating between *task types* helps to study different characteristics of user behavior. For example, Kellar et al. [11] differentiated between the task types fact finding, information gathering, browsing, and transactions. They found that these task types can be distinguished by different characteristics such as task duration, number of viewed pages, the size of queries and the usage of browser functionality. An information gathering task thereby showed to be more complex than a fact finding task. Toms et al. [20] conducted a user study with the three different task types decision making, fact finding and information gathering. Additionally, they explored the effect of two different task structures: (1) parallel, where multiple concepts on the same level are searched and (2) hierarchical, where a single concept is searched, but with multiple characteristics. Li & Belkin [16] propose a faceted task classification system which describe a task on facets such as the source of task, task doer, time, action, product or goal. Cole et al. [6] found behaviors that could distinguish these facets, and additionally adapted this system and added the facet "level of judgment" for their study.

2.3 Task Topic and Topic Knowledge

Previous research has also largely explored the relationship between *task topic knowledge* and a searcher's behavior. In evaluation campaigns like TREC, topics are used to describe the scenario for a specific information need which may be described as a mixture of task type and topic (e.g. used in the Core/Web Track [7]). In a more accurate sense, the topic describes the subject (area) of a task [13]. This can be rather a broad domain (e.g. health or e-commerce used in [12]) or a very concrete theme or thing (e.g. a person). Kelly states that the topic represents the focus of the task and that the combination of a specific task and topic forms the information need [13]. On the user side, investigations have been done on how user knowledge may influence search behavior. Thereby it can be distinguished between the broader idea of domain knowledge and the more specific idea of topic knowledge [26]. While domain knowledge describes a general awareness about the broader domain, its content and structure, topic knowledge describes familiarity with the explicit topic (e.g. the concrete theme or thing such as a person, animal or other entities) of the described information need. In general, domain knowledge showed to be influential for the user's search behavior [24, 25]. But also knowledge about the concrete topic showed to have an influence on the searcher's behavior [1, 15, 17].

2.4 Subjective Measures and User Behavior

Several works have examined the relationship between subjective measures reported from users and behavioral signals found in log files. Gwizdka and Spence [9] found that variables such as the number of web pages visited or the time spent on each page show correlation to task difficulty for a factual information task on the Web. Gwizdka [8] reports for another experiment that the number of result pages, number of individual pages and number of bookmarks correlate to task difficulty for the two task types fact finding and information gathering. Liu et al. [18] report on the relation between the task type and whole-session in contrast to within-session variables. While whole-session variables describe the session as a whole and can be determined only after a task has finished, within session-variables can be determined at each step of a session and are able to predict task difficulty in real-time. Whole-session variables such as task completion time or number of queries showed a good prediction accuracy to task difficulty. Within-session variables, for example, first dwell time on all SERPs or first dwell time of unique content pages showed a bit lower accuracy for task difficulty prediction. Also, the task type has been shown to influence the prediction level. Kelly et al. [12] conducted an experiment with 20 tasks based on five different complexity levels and four topical domains. They agree that more cognitively complex search tasks require more search activity such as more queries, URL clicks or more time to completion. However, more cognitively complex search tasks were not rated as more difficult by the users and the subjects were equally satisfied with their results across all task types.

3 EXPERIMENT

In this section we describe the tasks, the lab study in which these tasks were conducted, and the session variables we use to analyze the participants behavior from the recorded data. In particular we want to address the following research questions:

1. What is the role of the task topic for session variables used to describe user behavior in search sessions?
2. What is the role of the task topic for the relation between subjective user ratings, session variables and dwell times on content pages?

3.1 Tasks

Four different tasks were designed, located in the discipline of journalism, which try to capture different search problems in this area. Each of these tasks was conducted with two different topics: (1) "Coelacanth" and (2) "Methane Clathrates and Global Warming". Table 1 presents the different tasks for the topic Coelacanth; the same schema was used for the second topic. Tasks are designed based on the task classification system proposed by [16] and modified in [6]. Table 2 gives an overview

Table 1: Search tasks for the topic "Coelacanth"

Assignment 1. Copy Editing (CPE)
Your Assignment: You are a copy editor at a newspaper and you have only 20 minutes to check the accuracy of the six italicized statements in the excerpt of a piece of news story below.
Your Task: Please find and save an authoritative page that either confirms or disconfirms each statement.

Assignment 2. Story Pitch (STP)
Your Assignment: You are planning to pitch a science story to your editor and need to identify interesting facts about the coelacanth ("see-la-kanth"), a fish that dates from the time of dinosaurs and was thought to be extinct.
Your Task: Find and save web pages that contain the six most interesting facts about coelacanths and/or research about coelacanths and their preservation.

Assignment 3. Article Development (REL)
Your assignment: You are writing an article about coelacanths and conservation efforts. You have found an interesting article about coelacanths but in order to develop your article you need to be able to explain the relationship between key facts you have learned.
Your Task: In the following there are five italicized passages, find an authoritative web page that explains the relationship between two of the italicized facts.

Assignment 4. Interview Preparation (INT)
Your Assignment: You are writing an article that profiles a scientist and their research work. You are preparing to interview Mark Erdmann, a marine biologist, about coelacanths and conservation programs.
Your Task: Identify and save authoritative web pages for the following:
Identify two (living) people who likely can provide some personal stories about Dr. Erdmann and his work.
Find the three most interesting facts about Dr. Erdmann's research.
Find an interesting potential impact of Dr. Erdmann's work.

Table 2: Task Description and their task facets

Task Name	Task Facets [16]			
	Product	Level	Goal	Named Items?
Copy Editing	Find facts	Segment	Specific	Yes
Story Pitch	Find facts	Segment	Amorphous	No
Article Development	Produce ideas	Document	Amorphous	Yes
Interview Preparation	Produce ideas	Document	Amorphous	No

of each task type with its task facets. Each participant searched for 2 task types, each task on a different topic. The order of the 2 tasks and 2 topics was additionally flipped, yielding to 16 different configurations.

3.2 Lab Study

A lab study was conducted with undergraduate students from undergraduate journalism courses having completed at least one course in news writing. The 40 participants had to perform two search tasks (one on each topic), the annotation of bookmarks and search intents and had to fill out a number of questionnaires. Their activity was recorded with a Firefox browser plugin and Morae (https://www.techsmith.de/morae.html).

The participants started by filling out a demographic questionnaire and by watching a tutorial video of the Firefox plugin. They then filled out the pre-task questionnaire for topic familiarity, assignment experience and assignment difficulty on a 7-point Likert scale (1="not at all" to 7="extremely"). They then had up to 20 minutes time to fulfill the first search task, although they had the option to finish early. Then they there asked to fill out the post-task questionnaire, rating the difficulty of the task, their successfulness in completing the task, whether they had enough time (1="not at all" to 7="extremely"), and whether they understood the task (1="far too little" to 7="more than enough"), on a 7-point Likert scale.

After the search task, the participants were asked to view the video of their task and to annotate the bookmarks and search

intentions of their queries. In this process participants were asked to rate the usefulness of each bookmark and their confidence in this rating on a 7-point Likert scale from 1="not at all" to 7="extremely".

The same procedure was then conducted for the second search task. In the exit interview, the users were asked about the experience with the two search tasks. Participants received $30 compensation and $10 for best performance awarded to everyone. The whole study process took about 2 hours per user. In this study we use data from 38 participants, 76 valid search sessions, 20 for Copy Editing (CPE), 18 for Story Pitch (STP), 19 for Article Development (REL), 19 for Interview Preparation (INT) tasks and 38 sessions each for the topic Coelacanth and Methane Clathrates.

3.3 Session Variables

To describe the user behavior within a search session, we used a number of session variables following the examples of [12, 18]. We use different categories: (1) Numbers & Frequencies, e.g. action count, (2) ratios, e.g. bookmarks/page visits (3) the overall task time, (4) dwell times, e.g. on content pages, (5) query length, and (6) bookmark dwell times. In [19] different measures for dwell times on content pages were proposed. "Decision time" is the first time within a session the user spends reading on a content page finished by leaving the page e.g. to another tab. "Total dwell time" is the sum of all dwell times the user spends reading a content page. "Total display time" is the whole time span the content page remains open in the browser. In a multi-session experiment Liu & Belkin found that total display time and total dwell time can be a reliable indicator for document usefulness. For category 1 we use the new measures "Number of actions", "Bookmark average first session step" and "First bookmark first session step". Table 3 shows the session variables in detail. Two asterisks at the begin of the variable label indicate a within-session variable.

4 RESULTS

In the following we present the results from the pre- and post-task questionnaire, the rated usefulness of bookmarks and session variables per topic and task type. All values in the presented tables are color-coded. This allows comparison between each task, but also within one task type. Over all tables we use red for higher values and green for lower values. The idea is to instantly see patterns for certain task types or topics.

When dividing data by both task type and topic, there are less than 12 participants per group, making it difficult to perform

Table 3: Session Variables, **=Within-session variable

	Variable	Definition
Numbers & Frequencies	# Actions	Total number of user interactions including queries, page visits, adding/selecting/ closing tabs, save/delete bookmarks, copy&paste text
	# Unique queries	Number of unique user queries
	# SERP visits	Number of SERP visits
	# Unique page visits	Number of unique page visits
	# Page visits	Number of total page visits
	# Unique bookmarks	Number of unique bookmarks
	# Bookmarks	Number of total bookmarks
	****Bookmark average first session step**	The average first session step over all bookmarked pages.
	First bookmark first session step	The session step for the first bookmarked page.
	# Searches without page visits	Number of searches without page visits
Ratios	**Unique pages/unique searches	Ratio of unique pages per search
	**Pages/unique searches	Ratio of pages per search
	Bookmarks/page visits	Ratio of bookmarks per page visit
	Unique Bookmarks/Unique page visits	Ratio of bookmarks per unique page visit
	Unique Bookmarks/Unique queries	Ratio of unique bookmarks per unique page visit
	Bookmarks/Unique queries	Ratio of bookmarks per unique search
TT	Task Time	Time for the whole task
Dwell times	Total time on content pages	Total time on all content pages
	**Average time on content pages	Average time on content pages
	Total time on SERPs	Total time on all SERPs
	**Average time on SERPs	Average time on SERPs
Query length	Total query length	Total query length in characters
	Average query length	Average query length in characters
Bookmark dwell times	**Bookmark decision time	Total decision time on all bookmarks
	**Non-bookmark decision time	Total decision time on pages not bookmarked
	**Bookmark total dwell time	Total dwell time on all bookmarks
	**Non bookmark total dwell time	Total dwell time on pages not bookmarked
	**Bookmark total display time	Total display time on all bookmarks
	**Non bookmark total display time	Total display time on pages not bookmarked

statistical tests for some variables. Hence, some subsequent analyses where we divide both by task and topic, significance testing is absent. However, we provide significance tests where we only divide by one factor such as task or topic, and also for within-session variables (explained in Section 5).

4.1 Pre-task Subjective Measures

In the pre-task questionnaire, subjects were asked for their topic familiarity, experience, and the perceived difficulty level after reading the task assignment. Table 4 shows the average results per task type and topic. *Topic familiarity* with the topic Coelacanths was on average rated with 1.3 ("not at all familiar") and for Methane Clathrates with 2.4 ("low familiarity"). This is a margin of 1.1 towards the topic Methane Clathrates. (significantly different with Mann-Whitney with $p<0.0001$). The *assignment experience* within a task type was rather stable with the rating "slight experience" with 2.80 for Copy Editing, 3.39 for Story Pitch, 2.53 for Article Development and 3.47 for Interview preparation. (from the same population with Kruskal-Wallis test). The perceived *difficulty level* was relatively stable for the two topics within each task type, but diverging between task types with 3.75 ("somewhat difficult") for Copy Editing, 3.39 ("slightly difficult") for Story Pitch, 4.37 ("somewhat difficult") for Article development and 3.89 ("somewhat difficult") for Interview preparation (not significantly different). We can observe that the topic "Coelacanth" seems to be less familiar to subjects than "Methane Clathrates" over all task types. The task "Article Development" with the topic "Coelacanth" was rated most challenging based on topic familiarity, assignment experience, and perceived difficulty.

4.2 Post-task Subjective Measures

After conducting the task, users were asked to fill out a post-task questionnaire for the difficulty and success of the task, the availability of enough time and the understanding of the assignment. Table 5 shows the average results per task type and topic. For *post difficulty*, inverse to the pre-task statements, the topic "Coelacanth" seems to be easier than "Methane Clathrates" over all task types with 2.39 ("low difficulty") for Coelacanths and 2.89 ("slight difficulty") for Methane Clathrates. Post difficulty also diverges between task types with 2.60 ("slight") for Copy Editing, 1.50 ("low") for Story Pitch, 3.16 ("slight") for article development and 3.26 for Interview preparation ("slight"). *Success* was rated better for the topic Coelacanth with 5.61 ("very successful") than for Methane Clathrates ("moderately successful"). The task type Story Pitch was rated with 6.22 ("very successful") and the task Copy Editing with 5.35 ("moderately"), Article development and Interview preparation both with 4.84 ("moderately successful"). *Enough time* was felt moderately for the task type Story Pitch with 4.67 and especially for the topic Coelacanth with 4.90 ("more than enough"). The rest of task types show values around 4 ("enough"). For *comprehension,* we can see high values for the task type Story Pitch with 6.33 ("understood very well") and lower values for Interview preparation with 5.42 ("understood moderately well").

Overall, the task type "Story Pitch" seems to be the easiest task type based on the average measures of difficulty, success, enough time and comprehension. This is followed by "Copy Editing" with a bit lower values. Then comes "Article Development" and most difficult to do was "Interview Preparation".

Table 4: Mean pre-task subjective measures

Task type	Topic	Topic familiarity	Assignment experience	Pre-Difficulty
Copy Editing	Coelacanth	1.56	2.56	3.56
	Methane	2.64	3.00	3.91
Story Pitch	Coelacanth	1.20	3.40	3.50
	Methane	2.13	3.38	3.25
Article development	Coelacanth	1.11	2.33	4.78
	Methane	2.40	2.70	4.00
Interview preparation	Coelacanth	1.20	3.40	3.80
	Methane	2.22	3.56	4.00

Table 5: Mean post-task subjective measures

Task type	Topic	Post-Difficulty	Success	Enough time	Comprehension
Copy Editing	Coelacanth	2.11	5.56	4.56	6.11
	Methane	3.00	5.18	3.64	5.73
Story Pitch	Coelacanth	1.20	6.50	4.90	6.30
	Methane	1.88	5.88	4.38	6.38
Article development	Coelacanth	3.11	5.11	4.00	5.44
	Methane	3.20	4.60	4.10	5.70
Interview preparation	Coelacanth	3.20	5.20	4.20	5.80
	Methane	3.33	4.44	3.89	5.00

Table 6: Session Variables by topic and task type (time values are in seconds;**=Within-session variable)

Task type	Topic	# Actions	# Unique queries	# SERP visits	# Unique page visits	# Page visits	# Unique bookmarks	# Bookmarks	**Bookmark average first session step	First bookmark first session step	# Searches without page visits	**Unique pages/searches	**Pages/searches	Bookmarks/page visits	Unique Bookmarks/Unique page visits	Unique Bookmarks/Unique queries	Bookmarks/Unique queries	Task time	Total time on content pages	**Average time on content pages	Total time on SERPs	**Average time on SERPs	Total query length	Average query length
Copy Editing	Coelacanth	183.78	9.00	25.89	12.56	32.89	6.11	6.67	91.02	21.89	2.44	2.91	6.53	0.28	0.57	0.94	1.01	792.56	372.33	11.32	125.11	P=0.028 4.83	366.33	43.22
	Methane	214.36	9.91	24.55	15.00	40.55	6.55	6.91	107.62	20.27	1.64	3.11	6.57	0.21	0.47	0.71	0.75	1003.73	507.09	12.51	164.73	6.71	560.36	61.64
Story Pitch	Coelacanth	80.80	3.10	13.50	10.40	17.70	5.20	5.30	P=0.001 35.34	11.60	0.20	P=0.003 4.65	P=0.019 10.06	0.36	0.52	2.08	2.18	549.10	375.90	21.24	90.30	P=0.046 6.69	105.20	32.80
	Methane	135.38	7.75	22.75	15.13	30.50	6.25	6.75	65.72	15.38	2.75	3.60	6.87	0.34	0.50	1.15	1.23	814.50	508.00	16.66	183.38	8.06	429.25	50.38
Article development	Coelacanth	174.56	7.67	23.89	14.78	36.67	4.89	5.00	94.76	47.44	1.44	P=0.010 3.70	7.90	0.15	0.38	0.64	0.64	992.56	518.11	14.13	149.22	P=0.002 6.25	337.00	40.44
	Methane	189.50	9.00	34.20	14.60	28.90	6.40	6.50	105.06	26.50	3.50	P=0.044 2.86	7.01	0.29	0.49	0.90	0.90	864.00	394.60	13.65	186.40	5.45	376.10	43.50
Interview preparation	Coelacanth	211.40	10.30	30.50	17.60	58.10	6.90	7.00	102.21	22.20	2.10	3.68	8.52	0.15	0.44	0.87	0.89	908.70	582.60	10.03	190.60	P=0.002 6.25	418.20	35.20
	Methane	161.89	6.33	21.33	15.44	40.89	7.00	7.44	93.48	24.22	1.11	4.16	9.82	0.23	0.52	1.98	2.03	861.67	531.56	13.00	170.11	7.97	276.22	37.44

Table 7: Mean usefulness of bookmarks and confidence in usefulness ratings

Task type	Topic	Usefulness of bookmarks	Confidence in bookmark rating
Copy Editing	Coelacanth	6.04	6.19
	Methane	5.59	5.85
Story Pitch	Coelacanth	6.06	5.87
	Methane	5.71	5.72
Article development	Coelacanth	5.42	5.36
	Methane	5.49	5.57
Interview preparation	Coelacanth	5.78	6.03
	Methane	5.53	5.48

Table 8: Mean dwell times for bookmark and non-bookmark content pages

Task type	Topic	Decision Time		Total dwell time		Total display time	
		Bookmark	Non-bookmark	Bookmark	Non-bookmark	Bookmark	Non-bookmark
Copy Editing	Coelacanth	20.60	P<0.0001 6.31	48.60	P<0.005 11.09	149.93	54.88
	Methane	17.96	9.36	46.18	15.12	167.71	82.12
Story Pitch	Coelacanth	44.13	P=0.039 7.62	57.43	P=0.043 11.42	99.83	P=0.024 52.77
	Methane	27.69	8.02	50.37	10.99	204.28	P=0.043 56.11
Article development	Coelacanth	28.71	8.38	61.84	12.73	282.42	74.85
	Methane	25.43	P=0.002 6.88	35.66	P<0.001 13.66	84.20	65.30
Interview preparation	Coelacanth	22.91	5.13	58.80	9.00	294.24	P<0.001 60.95
	Methane	29.87	6.37	55.22	11.51	138.21	P=0.028 89.15

4.3 Average Values of Session Variables

In Table 6 we show the average results for each session variable for each task ordered by task type and topic. This table gives an overview which values can be expected for different task types. We will not go into detail of every single value. However, as a first impression, for the lowest rated task in difficulty "Story Pitch – Coelacanth" with 1.20, frequencies such as the number of actions, over the number of searches without page visits to average query length and task time are the lowest, ratios are mostly the highest. Total time on content pages and SERPs is low, but average times are high. The other way around, the task "Interview preparation" – with the same topic "Coelacanth" shows high values for frequencies, low ratios, and high numbers for total time on content pages and SERPs.

4.4 Usefulness of Bookmarks

In a separate session after conducting the task subjects then rated the usefulness of individual bookmarks and their confidence in these ratings. Table 7 shows the average rating per task type and topic. Highest rating for the usefulness of bookmarks is for "Story Pitch" and the topic "Coelacanth" with 6.06 ("very useful"), lowest for "Article Development" and "Coelacanth" with 5.42 ("moderately useful"). The differences between the task types were rather low with "Story Pitch" 5.90, "Copy Editing" 5.79, "Interview Preparation" with 5.66 (all three "very useful") and Article Development with 5.46 ("moderately useful").

4.5 Dwell Times on Content Pages

We also computed the average dwell times for bookmark and non-bookmark content pages per task type and topic based on the measures *decision time, total dwell time* and *total display time* proposed by [19], Table 8 shows the results. Decision times for bookmarks are from 17.96s to 44.13s, for non-bookmarks pretty stable from 5.31sec to 9.36s. Total dwell times for bookmarks are from 35.66s to 61.84s, for non-bookmarks from 9.00s to 15.12s.

Total display times for bookmarks are from 84.20s to 294.24s, for non-bookmarks from 52.77s to 89.15s. This means for each dwell time measure bookmarked content pages have a significant higher dwell time than non-bookmarks. This statement is valid for all task topics and types. However, decision times seem to be diverse across task type and topic.

5 Analysis I

Values and colors in Table 6 give a first impression that session variables are also dependent on the task topic, not only on the task type. For example, the number of actions in the task type Story Pitch is different for the topic Coelacanth with 80.80 actions and for Methane Clathrates with 135.38 actions. Or, the task time for Copy Editing is different for Coelacanth with 792.56s to Methane Clathrates with 1003.73s. Therefore in this section we analyze the role of the task topic for session variables and dwell times. We also acknowledge that there is a significant difference in topic familiarity. Moreover, about 26% of participants searching for Methane Clathrates reported a high familiarity (4 or above) while only about 3% reported high familiarity for Coelacanths. We therefore also report findings for only users with low familiarity, analyzing both the full pool of sessions and also those where participants had low topic familiarity.

5.1 Session Variables

As mentioned before, we wanted to compare the mean values for a significant statistical difference between topics of one task type. However, dividing the data set first by task type and then to topics gives very small groups of only up to eleven subjects for each topic. Also because of possible high standard deviations it is hard to find statistical significance. Here, more subjects and data for each topic would be needed. However, some session variables give more than one data point per session and user. In [18] they are called within-session variables because these variables can be gathered also in the middle of a user session. These are mainly 'number of (unique) content pages per query' and 'first (mean) dwell time on content pages or SERPs'.

Unique pages per search and pages per search (n=2,732) showed significant differences for the topic in the task type Story Pitch ($p=0.003$, $p=0.019$) and Article Development ($p=0.010$, $p=0.044$) with a Mann–Whitney test with $alpha=0.05$. We also checked the differences for dwell time on content pages and SERPs and found significant differences in topics for all task types for time on SERPs ($p=0.028$, $p=0.046$, $p=0.002$, $p=0.002$). Each statistical significant difference between topics of one task type is marked with a bold line and p-values on the left side of the table cell in the Tables 6 and 8.

In this experiment, we additionally used the session variable 'bookmark first session step'. We compared the values for all bookmarks (n=490) between topics within a task type. This showed a statistical difference for the task type Story Pitch with $p<0.001$. Altogether, 9 from 20 values of within-session variables show significant differences between topics.

To analyze the influence of topic familiarity, we additionally examined the session variables for all sessions with a topic familiarity of 1-3 ("overall low", n=65 sessions). The mean values remain stable with only slight changes, also, all significant differences between topics remain valid.

5.2 Dwell times

Dwell times for content pages are a good indicators and give better statistical results, because every user's view on a content page is a new data point. Table 8 show the mean values for the different dwell times. Here again we seek for statistical differences between topics in one task type.

For bookmarked pages (n=490) we found significant different dwell times for Story Pitch – Decision Time ($p=0.039$) and Total display time ($p=0.024$), Article Development – Total dwell time ($p=0.002$) and Total display time ($p<0.001$) and Interview Preparation – Total display time ($p<0.001$).

For normal content pages (non-bookmark, n=2,181) we found different dwell times for topics for Copy Editing – Decision Time ($p<0.0001$) and Total dwell time ($p=0.005$), Story Pitch – Total dwell time ($p=0.043$) and Total display time ($p=0.043$), and Interview Preparation – Total display time ($p=0.028$). This means, different dwell times differ dependent on the topic. Here, 10 of 24 values in dwell times show significant differences between topics.

Here again, we analyze the influence of topic familiarity by examining the dwell times for all sessions with a topic familiarity of 1-3. The mean values remain stable with only slight changes. The significance for dwell time differences between topics remained stable for all reported ones without two: Story Pitch – Bookmark decision time and Bookmark total display time.

6 Analysis II

In this section we conduct a number of correlation analyses to find relationships between pre- and post-task measures, session variables, usefulness ratings and dwell times, also dependent on the task type and topic.

6.1 Pre-task Measures

First, we did a correlation analysis from pre-task measures to post-task measures and to session variables (see Tables 9a-c).

6.1.1 Topic Familiarity. For topic familiarity we found only weak overall correlations. For the topic Coelacanth there is a weak correlation to post-difficulty (0.348) which is significantly different to Methane Clathrates by a margin of 0.460. Dividing the data set by task type we found no correlations from topic familiarity to post subjective measures, but depending on the task type to different session variables: for Copy Editing to Average query length (0.562) and for Story Pitch to Number of unique bookmarks (0.514) and Number of bookmarks (0.585).

6.1.2 Assignment Experience. For assignment experience there are also only weak overall negative correlations to other subjective and session variables. The topic Methane Clathrates shows correlations to post-difficulty, average time on SERPs and bookmark decision time which Coelacanth does not. Coelacanth shows a moderate correlation to Comprehension which Methane Clathrates does not.

Table 9: Spearman correlation for pre-task subjective measures with at least significant correlation in one column (in bold different from zero with a significance level of alpha=0.05). Correlation values between Coelacanth and Methane Clathrates significantly different with Fisher's r to z transformation and p<0.05 in bold.

(a) Topic Familiarity

Variable	All	Coe.	Met.	Diff.
Post-Difficulty	0.114	**0.348**	-0.112	**0.460**
# Bookmarks	**0.266**	0.264	0.280	0.016
Average query length	**0.397**	0.123	0.287	0.164
Non bookmark total display time	**0.321**	. 0.038	0.026	0.012

(b) Assignment Experience

Variable	All	Coe.	Met.	Diff.
Pre-Difficulty	**-0.287**	-0.207	**-0.353**	0.146
Post-Difficulty	**-0.334**	-0.227	**-0.464**	0.237
Success	**0.268**	0.220	**0.353**	0.133
Comprehension	**0.347**	**0.404**	0.282	0.122
Confidence in bookmark rating	**0.226**	0.198	**0.250**	0.052
Average time on content pages	0.130	0.109	**0.162**	0.053
Average time on SERPs	0.206	0.079	**0.340**	0.260
Bookmark decision time	0.015	-0.173	**0.262**	0.435
Bookmark total dwell time	0.095	0.026	**0.282**	0.256

(c) Pre-Difficulty

Variable	All	Coe.	Met.	Diff.
Assignment experience	**-0.287**	-0.207	**-0.353**	0.146
Post-Difficulty	**0.310**	0.303	**0.388**	0.085
Success	-0.225	-0.197	**-0.338**	0.141
Comprehension	**-0.286**	**-0.423**	-0.208	0.215
Unique Bookmarks/ Unique queries	-0.128	**-0.336**	0.143	0.480
Bookmarks/ Unique queries	-0.128	**-0.349**	0.144	0.493
Average time on SERPs	0.086	**0.340**	-0.140	0.481

Table 10: Spearman correlation for post-task subjective measures with at least significant correlation in one column (in bold different from zero with a significance level of alpha=0.05). Correlation values between Coelacanth and Methane Clathrates significantly different with Fisher's r to z transformation and p<0.05 in bold.

(a) Post-Difficulty

Variable	All	Coe.	Met.	Diff.
Topic familiarity	0.114	**0.348**	-0.112	**0.460**
Assignment experience	**-0.334**	-0.227	**-0.464**	0.237
Pre-Difficulty	**0.310**	0.303	**0.388**	0.085
Success	**-0.689**	**-0.664**	**-0.676**	0.012
Enough time	**-0.633**	**-0.573**	**-0.631**	0.058
Comprehension	**-0.637**	**-0.710**	**-0.575**	0.135
Usefulness of bookmarks	**-0.469**	**-0.455**	**-0.419**	0.035
Confidence in bookmark rating	**-0.414**	-0.314	**-0.455**	0.141
# Actions	**0.467**	**0.485**	**0.414**	0.070
# Unique queries	**0.323**	**0.421**	0.148	0.273
# SERP visits	**0.385**	**0.426**	**0.302**	0.125
# Unique page visits	**0.356**	0.237	**0.461**	0.224
# Page visits	**0.383**	**0.387**	**0.402**	0.015
# Unique bookmarks	**0.234**	0.180	0.265	0.085
Bookmark average first session step	**0.456**	**0.425**	**0.452**	0.027
First bookmark first session step	0.229	**0.331**	0.115	0.216
# Searches without page visits	**0.233**	0.285	0.092	0.194
Unique pages/ unique searches	-0.078	**-0.341**	0.245	0.586
Bookmarks/page visits	**-0.299**	**-0.378**	-0.240	0.138
Unique Bookmarks/ Unique page visits	**-0.278**	-0.225	**-0.334**	0.109
Unique Bookmarks/ Unique queries	-0.257	**-0.429**	-0.042	0.387
Bookmarks/Unique queries	-0.241	**-0.424**	-0.031	0.394
Task time	**0.556**	**0.500**	**0.548**	0.048
Total time on content pages	**0.358**	0.276	**0.360**	0.084
Total query length	0.291	**0.503**	0.003	0.501
Bookmark total display time	0.270	**0.412**	0.245	0.167
Non bookmark total display time	**0.228**	0.237	0.199	0.038

(b) Success

Variable	All	Coe.	Met.	Diff.
Assignment experience	**0.268**	0.220	**0.353**	0.133
Pre-Difficulty	-0.225	-0.197	**-0.338**	0.141
Post-Difficulty	**-0.689**	**-0.664**	**-0.676**	0.012
Enough time	**0.625**	**0.701**	**0.547**	0.154
Comprehension	**0.537**	**0.695**	**0.422**	0.272
Usefulness of bookmarks	**0.560**	**0.549**	**0.564**	0.015
Confidence in bookmark rating	**0.568**	**0.519**	**0.557**	0.038
# Actions	**-0.318**	**-0.387**	-0.216	0.171
# Unique queries	-0.202	**-0.354**	-0.004	0.350
# SERP visits	**-0.329**	**-0.452**	-0.192	0.260
Bookmark average first session step	**-0.340**	**-0.408**	-0.230	0.178
First bookmark first session step	-0.280	**-0.447**	-0.112	0.335
Unique pages/ unique searches	0.081	**0.349**	-0.242	**0.591**
Unique Bookmarks/ Unique queries	0.170	**0.369**	-0.056	**0.425+**
Bookmarks/Unique queries	0.170	**0.357**	-0.034	**0.391+**
Task time	**-0.456**	**-0.501**	**-0.385**	0.115
Total time on content pages	**-0.270**	-0.279	-0.215	0.064
Total query length	-0.189	**-0.366**	0.050	**0.416+**

(c) Enough time

Variable	All	Coe.	Met.	Diff.
Post-Difficulty	**-0.633**	**-0.573**	**-0.631**	0.058
Success	**0.625**	**0.701**	**0.547**	0.154
Comprehension	**0.434**	**0.513**	**0.359**	0.154
Usefulness of bookmarks	**0.520**	**0.551**	**0.461**	0.090
Confidence in bookmark rating	**0.399**	**0.348**	**0.378**	0.030
# Actions	**-0.543**	**-0.529**	**-0.538**	0.008
# Unique queries	**-0.436**	**-0.513**	**-0.381**	0.132
# SERP visits	**-0.462**	**-0.467**	**-0.470**	0.003
# Unique page visits	**-0.356**	-0.176	**-0.455**	0.279
# Page visits	**-0.431**	**-0.458**	**-0.434**	0.024
Bookmark average first session step	**-0.511**	**-0.485**	**-0.498**	0.013
First bookmark first session step	-0.197	**-0.378**	-0.022	0.356
# Searches without page visits	**-0.264**	**-0.313**	-0.178	0.135
Unique pages/unique searches	0.203	**0.467**	0.000	**0.467**
Bookmarks/page visits	**0.371**	**0.420**	**0.375**	0.045
Unique Bookmarks/ Unique page visits	**0.347**	0.285	**0.395**	0.110
Unique Bookmarks/ Unique queries	**0.372**	**0.521**	0.261	0.260
Bookmarks/Unique queries	**0.362**	**0.499**	0.271	0.228
Task time	**-0.705**	**-0.616**	**-0.759**	0.143
Total time on content pages	**-0.535**	**-0.452**	**-0.577**	0.124
Total time on SERPs	**-0.271**	-0.219	-0.220	0.001
Total query length	**-0.450**	**-0.547**	**-0.334**	0.213
Average query length	**-0.348**	**-0.338**	-0.206	0.132
Bookmark total dwell time	-0.259	-0.212	**-0.404**	0.192
Non bookmark total dwell time	0.128	**0.361**	0.010	0.351
Bookmark total display time	**-0.400**	**-0.625**	**-0.365**	0.260
Non bookmark total display time	-0.284	-0.103	**-0.483**	**0.380+**

(d) Comprehension

Variable	All	Coe.	Met.	Diff.
Assignment experience	**0.347**	**0.404**	0.282	0.122
Pre-Difficulty	**-0.286**	**-0.423**	-0.208	0.215
Post-Difficulty	**-0.637**	**-0.710**	**-0.575**	0.135
Success	**0.537**	**0.695**	**0.422**	**0.272+**
Enough time	**0.434**	**0.513**	**0.359**	0.154
Usefulness of bookmarks	**0.399**	**0.469**	0.313	0.156
Confidence in bookmark rating	**0.338**	**0.417**	0.236	0.181
# Page visits	**-0.232**	-0.228	-0.248	0.020
Task time	**-0.310**	**-0.418**	-0.200	0.218
Total time on content pages	**-0.280**	**-0.320**	-0.190	0.130
Non bookmark total dwell time	0.080	**0.358**	-0.228	0.586
Bookmark total display time	-0.218	**-0.352**	-0.178	0.174

(e) Usefulness of bookmarks

Variable	All	Coe.	Met.	Diff.
Post-Difficulty	**-0.469**	**-0.455**	**-0.419**	0.035
Success	**0.560**	**0.549**	**0.564**	0.015
Enough time	**0.520**	**0.551**	**0.461**	0.090
Comprehension	**0.399**	**0.469**	0.313	0.156
Confidence in bookmark rating	**0.662**	**0.748**	**0.554**	0.194
# Actions	**-0.321**	**-0.380**	-0.234	0.147
# SERP visits	**-0.250**	**-0.344**	-0.167	0.177
# Page visits	**-0.282**	**-0.367**	-0.223	0.144
Bookmark average first session step	**-0.244**	**-0.308**	-0.143	0.165
Bookmarks/page visits	0.256	0.300	0.285	0.014
Task time	**-0.466**	**-0.610**	**-0.317**	0.293
Total time on content pages	**-0.376**	**-0.493**	-0.248	0.245
Average time on SERPs	**0.323**	0.282	**0.476**	0.194
Total query length	**-0.239**	**-0.321**	-0.134	0.186
Average query length	-0.227	-0.024	**-0.230**	0.206
Bookmark total dwell time	**-0.323**	-0.290	**-0.455**	0.165
Bookmark total display time	**-0.396**	**-0.544**	**-0.396**	0.148

6.1.3 Pre-Difficulty. Also for pre-difficulty we found only weak overall correlations. Coelacanth shows negative correlations to ratios unique bookmarks/unique queries and bookmarks/unique queries which Methane Clathrates does not with a margin of nearly 0.5.

6.2 Post-task Measures

Following this line, we conducted a correlation analysis from subjective measures of the post questionnaire and from the usefulness ratings of bookmarks to session variables. Tables 10a-e show the summarized results.

6.2.1 Post-Difficulty. For post-difficulty there are strong overall correlations to other post-questionnaire measures such as to success (-0.689), enough time (-0.633) and comprehension (0.637). There are also moderate correlations from post-difficulty to the usefulness of bookmarks (-0.469) and confidence in the bookmarks (-0.414). From task difficulty to session variables we have found moderate correlations to the number of actions (0.467), bookmark average first session step (0.456) and task time (0.556). Additionally, we can find a number of weak correlations to other session variables.

For different *topics* the correlations to subjective measures, number of actions, bookmark average first session step, and task time are stable. However, other session variables such as bookmarks/unique queries or total query length differ.

For different *task types* we find for Copy Editing a correlation to Ratio unique pages/unique searches (0.561). For Story Pitch to task time (0.723), total time on content pages (0.572) and total time on SERPs (0.516). For Article Development there are no correlations and for Interview preparation to searches without page visits (0.460), task time (0.694) and total time on SERPs (0.579).

6.2.2 Success. Success is also strongly correlated to other of post-questionnaire measures such as enough time (0.625) and comprehension (0.537). There is also a high correlation to usefulness of bookmarks (0.560) and confidence in bookmark rating (0.568). We found a moderate negative correlation from success to task time (-0.456) and some weak correlation to other session variables. The topics differ on session variables such as unique bookmarks/unique queries.

6.2.3 Enough Time. Enough time correlates moderately to strongly to a number of other subjective measures and session variables. The two topics here are relatively stable, only between unique pages/unique searches there is a margin up to 0.467.

6.2.4 Comprehension. Comprehension shows moderate to strong correlations for enough time and post-difficulty. Here, a lot of correlations are moderately and significant for Coelacanth, but not for Methane Clathrates.

6.2.5 Usefulness of Bookmarks. Usefulness of bookmarks is weakly to moderately correlated to the post-questionnaire measures post-difficulty (-0.469), success (0.560), enough time (0.520), and comprehension (0.399) and strongly correlated to the confidence in the rating (0.662). For *session variables,* there is a moderate correlation to task time (-0.466) and several other weak correlations.

If we divide the data set by *topic*, we find for Coelacanth a strong negative correlation of -0.610 to task time, and moderate negative correlations -0.544 to bookmark total display time and of -0.493 to total time on content pages. For the topic Methane

Clathrates correlations to task time and total time on content show a weaker correlation with a difference around 0.3.

If we divide the data by *task type*, we can find for Copy Editing correlations to average query length (-0.500). For Story Pitch to task time (-0.577), total time on content pages (-0.608) and bookmark total display time (-0.567). For the type Article Development we find correlations to task time (-0.546) and average query length (-0.509). No correlations were found for the task type Interview preparation.

We also tested with sessions of topic familiarity 1-3. Then the significant difference test between topics failed for values marked with a plus in the tables 10b Success, 10c Enough Time, and 10d Comprehension.

7 DISCUSSION

7.1 Pre-task Subjective Measures

The factor of *topic familiarity* in this experiment had an overall weak effect on the number of bookmarks and a nearly moderate effect on query length. This means user behavior is influenced slightly by making more bookmarks and moderately by entering longer queries for those who felt they had more familiarity with a topic. For the topic Coelacanth, topic familiarity showed a weak influence to post difficulty with 0.348, for Methane Clathrates it did not. Also, the different task types showed no influence from topic familiarity to post-difficulty. We additionally checked session variables and dwell times for the influence of topic familiarity. This showed only minor changes in mean values and most significant differences between topics remain intact. For the *experience in the assignment* there is a weak negative correlation to pre- and post-difficulty around -0.28 to -0.33. For the *pre-difficulty* measure we found a weak correlation to post difficulty (0.31) and a weak negative correlation to comprehension (-0.28). No overall session variables were influenced by the pre-task difficulty. This means, in this experiment the perceived difficulty before the task has only a slight influence on perceived difficulty after the task and on task success. All in all, pre-task measures here have only a weak effect on task behavior and post-task ratings. Only topic familiarity to query length has a nearly moderate effect.

7.2 Post-task Subjective Measures

7.2.1 Task Difficulty and User Effort. The correlation analysis for post-task measures showed that *task difficulty* is correlated to a number of session features which in general measure the *user effort* to conduct the task. The variable task time is a general feature which can represent user effort for a task and shows a solid correlation with 0.556. A novel tested measure in this study is the number of overall actions which shows a stable correlation of 0.467 and describes the number of all interactions the user does. More fine-grained features representing user effort are number of SERP visits and number of page visits with still moderate correlation around 0.38. Some other session variables representing user effort show still weak correlations such as total time on content pages (0.35) and total query length around 0.29. Most of these features have also been found to correlate with task difficulty in related work [e.g. 8, 12, 18]. Action count, task time and bookmark average first session step showed stable correlations also for both task topics. However, these correlations cannot be found in all task types. It seems intuitive that more user effort results in the subjective impression that the task is more difficult. However, the correlation is not so strong for every task type that there is a direct one-to-one relationship. So, also other factors seem to influence the subjective task difficulty level.

7.2.2 Task Difficulty and Task Success. In this experiment, we found a strong negative correlation of -0.689 between task difficulty and task success. This means, the more difficult a task felt, the less successful it was rated. Again, this sounds intuitive, and there seems to be a strong overall relationship between difficulty and success. Session variables which correlate with both concepts are task time, first bookmark first session step and bookmark average first session step. Task time for both has a moderate correlation (0.556 vs. -0.456) and can describe the overall effort as described above. Two new features Bookmark average first session step has a correlation to task difficulty with 0.456 and to success with -0.340. These feature describe when in the session (e.g. sooner or later described in action steps) on average the bookmarks are saved. They can describe in a simple manner when first results for a task are found.

7.2.3 Task Difficulty and Usefulness of Content Pages. We also found a moderate correlation of -0.469 between task difficulty and of 0.560 between success and the usefulness of bookmarked web pages. This means, the more useful the bookmarked web pages were seen, the less difficult and more successful the task was rated. This is a clear indication that the usefulness of the bookmarked content (the task's results) has an influence on the task difficulty and success. This is surely an intuitive notion; however, the usefulness of the content has not yet been taken into account so far as to measure the success and the difficulty of a task. For sure this aspect has been discussed on a model basis [e.g. 22, 5] and has been researched for decades on the basis of the relevance of the content to a user query. But, the usefulness of the content in relation to a task measured over a whole user session is still a different issue.

7.2.4 Dwell Times. Related work has found that dwell times on content pages can be used to predict document usefulness under consideration of the task type and also the specific user [14]. In [19] decision time, total dwell time and total display time were examined in two different task types: a dependent task and a parallel task. While total dwell time and total display time were good predictors for usefulness in each individual task, decision time was not. The authors argued that in the parallel task the sub tasks only changed in their topic and users could reuse some useful documents.

7.2.4.1 Aspect Threshold. Also in this experiment different types of dwell times show significant differences between bookmarked (and usefully rated) pages and those which were not bookmarked. Decision time and total dwell times are relatively stable for non-bookmarking pages over all tasks and topics. So, for decision time there is a range from 5.13s to 9.36s for non-bookmarking and from 17.96s to 44.13s for bookmarked pages. A certain threshold, e.g. of 14s, here can surely predict those pages which will be bookmarked by the user. The same is true and even enforced for total dwell time: there is a range from 9.00s to 15.12s for non-bookmarking pages and from 35.66s to 61.84s for bookmarked pages. A threshold of e.g. 20sec could surely predict those pages which will be bookmarked. The picture is not that clear for total display time. Here, time span

are overlapping between the span of bookmarked and non-bookmarked pages: from 52.77s to 89.15s for non-bookmarked and from 84.20s to 294.24s for bookmarked. And, for each task the times are significantly different for bookmarked and non-bookmarked pages.

7.2.4.2 Aspect Usefulness of Bookmarks. In this experiment, over all tasks we found weak to moderate negative correlations between usefulness of bookmarks and dwell times, e.g. for bookmark total display time. This is in contrast to related work [e.g. 19], where longer dwell times correlate with higher usefulness ratings. However, other correlations seem to be dependent on the topic. For the topic Coelacanth we find a strong negative correlation to task time and a moderate to total time on content pages which cannot be found for the topic Methane Clathrates. We have to mention that in this experiment we have only usefulness ratings for bookmarked pages, not for every content page. This might influence the correlation analysis for these session variables. However, other session variables such as total time on content pages are available for every content page. We also tested for the relationship between usefulness of bookmarks and different task types. Here, we also find different results. For the task type Story Pitch there is a moderate to strong correlation for task time and time on content pages which could not be found for the other task types.

7.3 Task Type and Task Topic

The mean values for different session variables in Table 8 and correlations in Table 10 give a first indication that user behavior is not only dependent on the task type, but also on the task topic.

In the section 'Analysis I' we found a number of session variables that show significant differences between the two topics in one task type, e.g. bookmark first session step or pages/search. Especially, different dwell time measures show significant differences between topics. There are two reasons for that: (a) in some cases (e.g. for Story Pitch with the task level 'Document segment') we found that high decision times originate from individual web pages with a lot of text on it. So, users need up to several minutes for the extraction of the relevant information for the task. (b) In other cases, users spend more time on average on all content pages.

In the section 'Analysis II' we looked for overall correlations between subjective measures and session variables. This can be set in contrast to correlations found by dividing the dataset by task type or topic. For example, *topic familiarity* only showed a weak correlation for the topic Coelacanth, but not for Methane Clathrates and not for different task types. For correlations to *task difficulty* the session variables action count, task time and average first session step showed stable correlations for both topics, but not for each task type. Other correlations to post-difficulty are dependent on the topic. For the *usefulness of bookmarks* a number of correlation can be found for the topic Coelacanth (-0.610 to task time, -0.544 to bookmark total display time and -0.493 to total time on content pages) which are weaker for Methane Clathrates.

8 CONCLUSION

In this work we analyzed data from an experiment with four different task types and additionally two different topics for each task type. User behavior was measured with session variables and dwell times. We mainly conduct two analyses: (I) a comparison of mean values and (II) a correlation analysis from subjective user rating such as task difficulty, task success and usefulness of bookmarked pages to session variables. From the analysis and the discussion we conclude the following points:

- *Topic familiarity* in this experiment overall only played a minor role because both topics were fairly unfamiliar to subjects. But topic familiarity was dependent on the task topic.

- *Task difficulty* is moderately correlated to *user effort* and can be measured with a number of session variables such as task time, number of actions, or more specifically with features such as number of SERP visits or number of content pages. The correlation between user effort and task difficulty seems to be dependent on the task type and topic.

- Session variables measuring user behavior are also dependent on the task type and task topic.

- *Task success* and *task difficulty* are strongly negatively correlated, and task success can be measured with session variables such as task time and with session variables dependent on the topic.

- *Task success* and the *usefulness of bookmarks* interpreted as the task's result are nearly strong related. This means the content's usefulness plays an important role for the task's success.

- *Usefulness of bookmarks* is weakly to moderately correlated to certain dwell times and dependent on the task type and topic.

- A *threshold* can be used to distinguish between *useful (bookmarked) pages* and other content pages. Decision time and total dwell time can be used as within-session variables independent of the task type and topic.

- *Decision time* on web pages can be dependent on the text size on the page and how easy it is to extract the relevant information for the user. This is dependent on the task type and topic.

Therefore the *task type*, but also the *task's topic* has an important influence on user behavior. The task type influences how users are searching; the task topic influences what results are presented by the search engine. The search results influence dwell times, and nearly all session variables. This influences at the end the perceived task success and difficulty.

If researchers are using only one topic in their task description, this can massively influence the results in a free Web search task. A good solution for this issue has been applied by Kelly et al. in their study [12] who used four domains (health, commerce, entertainment, science & technology) and different topics tailored to study participants in the sense of Borlund's Simulated Work Task [3].

Acknowledgements This work was partly funded by the DFG grant no. MA 3964/5-1 and by the NSF grant no. IIS-1423239.

REFERENCES

[1] Allen, B. 1991. Topic Knowledge and Online Catalog Search Formulation. *The Library Quarterly*. 61, 2 (1991), 188–213. DOI:https://doi.org/10.1086/602333.

[2] Belkin, N.J. et al. 1995. Cases, Scripts, and Information-Seeking Strategies: On the Design of Interactive Information Retrieval Systems. *EXPERT SYSTEMS WITH APPLICATIONS*. 9, (1995), 379–395.

[3] Borlund, P. 2003. The IIR evaluation model: a framework for evaluation of interactive information retrieval systems. *Information research*. 8, 3 (2003).

[4] Broder, A. 2002. A Taxonomy of Web Search. *SIGIR Forum*. 36, 2 (Sep. 2002), 3–10. DOI:https://doi.org/10.1145/792550.792552.

[5] Cole, M. et al. 2009. Usefulness as the criterion for evaluation of interactive information retrieval. *Proceedings of the Workshop on Human-Computer Interaction and Information Retrieval* (2009), 1–4.

[6] Cole, M.J. et al. 2015. User Activity Patterns During Information Search. *ACM Trans. Inf. Syst.* 33, 1 (März 2015), 1:1–1:39. DOI:https://doi.org/10.1145/2699656.

[7] Collins-Thompson, K. et al. 2015. *TREC 2014 web track overview*. DTIC Document.

[8] Gwizdka, J. 2008. Revisiting search task difficulty: Behavioral and individual difference measures. *Proceedings of the American Society for Information Science and Technology*. 45, 1 (2008), 1–12. DOI:https://doi.org/10.1002/meet.2008.1450450249.

[9] Gwizdka, J. and Spence, I. 2006. What Can Searching Behavior Tell Us About the Difficulty of Information Tasks? A Study of Web Navigation. *Proceedings of the American Society for Information Science and Technology*. 43, 1 (2006), 1–22. DOI:https://doi.org/10.1002/meet.14504301167.

[10] Kekäläinen, J. and Järvelin, K. 2002. Evaluating information retrieval systems under the challenges of interaction and multidimensional dynamic relevance. *Proceedings of the 4th CoLIS conference* (2002), 253–270.

[11] Kellar, M. et al. 2007. A Field Study Characterizing Web-based Information-seeking Tasks. *J. Am. Soc. Inf. Sci. Technol.* 58, 7 (May 2007), 999–1018. DOI:https://doi.org/10.1002/asi.v58:7.

[12] Kelly, D. et al. 2015. Development and Evaluation of Search Tasks for IIR Experiments Using a Cognitive Complexity Framework. *Proceedings of the 2015 International Conference on The Theory of Information Retrieval* (New York, NY, USA, 2015), 101–110.

[13] Kelly, D. 2009. Methods for Evaluating Interactive Information Retrieval Systems with Users. *Found. Trends Inf. Retr.* 3, 1–2 (Jan. 2009), 1–224. DOI:https://doi.org/10.1561/1500000012.

[14] Kelly, D. and Belkin, N.J. 2004. Display Time As Implicit Feedback: Understanding Task Effects. *Proceedings of the 27th Annual International ACM SIGIR Conference on Research and Development in Information Retrieval* (New York, NY, USA, 2004), 377–384.

[15] Kelly, D. and Cool, C. 2002. The Effects of Topic Familiarity on Information Search Behavior. *Proceedings of the 2Nd ACM/IEEE-CS Joint Conference on Digital Libraries* (New York, NY, USA, 2002), 74–75.

[16] Li, Y. and Belkin, N.J. 2008. A faceted approach to conceptualizing tasks in information seeking. *Information Processing & Management*. 44, 6 (2008), 1822–1837. DOI:https://doi.org/https://doi.org/10.1016/j.ipm.2008.07.005.

[17] Liu, J. et al. 2013. Examining the effects of task topic familiarity on searchers' behaviors in different task types. *Proceedings of the Association for Information Science and Technology*. 50, 1 (2013), 1–10.

[18] Liu, J. et al. 2010. Predicting Task Difficulty for Different Task Types. *Proceedings of the 73rd ASIS&T Annual Meeting on Navigating Streams in an Information Ecosystem - Volume 47* (Silver Springs, MD, USA, 2010), 16:1–16:10.

[19] Liu, J. and Belkin, N.J. 2010. Personalizing Information Retrieval for Multi-session Tasks: The Roles of Task Stage and Task Type. *Proceedings of the 33rd International ACM SIGIR Conference on Research and Development in Information Retrieval* (New York, NY, USA, 2010), 26–33.

[20] Toms, E.G. et al. 2008. Task Effects on Interactive Search: The Query Factor. *Focused Access to XML Documents: 6th International Workshop of the Initiative for the Evaluation of XML Retrieval, INEX 2007 Dagstuhl Castle, Germany, December 17-19, 2007. Selected Papers*. N. Fuhr et al., eds. Springer Berlin Heidelberg. 359–372.

[21] Toms, E.G. 2011. Task-based information searching and retrieval. *Interactive Information Seeking, Behaviour and Retrieval*. I. Ruthven and D. Kelly, eds. facet publishing. 43–59.

[22] Tsakonas, G. and Papatheodorou, C. 2006. Analysing and Evaluating Usefulness and Usability in Electronic Information Services. *J. Inf. Sci.* 32, 5 (Oktober 2006), 400–419. DOI:https://doi.org/10.1177/0165551506065934.

[23] Vakkari, P. 2003. Task-based information searching. *Annual review of information science and technology*. 37, 1 (2003), 413–464.

[24] White, R.W. et al. 2009. Characterizing the Influence of Domain Expertise on Web Search Behavior. *Proceedings of the Second ACM International Conference on Web Search and Data Mining* (New York, NY, USA, 2009), 132–141.

[25] Wildemuth, B.M. 2004. The effects of domain knowledge on search tactic formulation. *Journal of the American Society for Information Science and Technology*. 55, 3 (2004), 246–258. DOI:https://doi.org/10.1002/asi.10367.

[26] Zhang, X. et al. 2013. Task topic knowledge vs. background domain knowledge: Impact of two types of knowledge on user search performance. *Advances in Intelligent Systems and Computing*. Springer Verlag. 179–191.

Juggling with Information Sources, Task Type, and Information Quality

Yiwei Wang, Shawon Sarkar, Chirag Shah
Rutgers University
New Brunswick, New Jersey
{yiwei.wang,shawon.sarkar,chirags}@rutgers.edu

ABSTRACT

This paper examines how individuals judge the accuracy, adequacy, relevance, and trustworthiness of different types of impersonal and interpersonal information sources and how task type influences their evaluation process. 53 participants from diverse backgrounds recruited via Amazon's Mechanical Turk performed four simulated information seeking tasks. This study analyzed the data collected from participants' self-reported information seeking experiences in online logbooks and follow-up semi-structured interviews with 23 participants by applying both qualitative and quantitative methods. The findings suggest that task type and information source type affect individuals' information quality judgment, and they perceive websites are more accurate than interpersonal sources, though the latter can be trustworthy. Moreover, their understanding of the type of information also affects their quality judgment. For example, they prefer factual information to opinions in some situations.

KEYWORDS

Information seeking behaviors; Information quality judgment; Information sources

ACM Reference format:
Yiwei Wang, Shawon Sarkar, Chirag Shah. 2018. Juggling with Information Sources, Task Type, and Information Quality. In *Proceedings of 2018 Conference on Human Information Interaction & Retrieval, New Brunswick, NJ, USA, March 11–15, 2018 (CHIIR '18)*, 10 pages.
https://doi.org/10.1145/3176349.3176390

1 INTRODUCTION

Information seeking activities occur when individuals purposefully look for information to satisfy a goal [38]. When seeking information, a person may ask another person, such as a friend or colleague, or he/she may look for the information in online databases, Websites, in books, or other physical documents. With the rapid advent of advanced technologies and mobile devices, today, a significant amount of information is being created and is directly available to the public through a variety of sources and channels. People now have abundant information choices in their everyday lives,

and therefore, they can acquire information from multiple sources – from traditional print resources, from different online sources available on the Internet, as well as from human sources.

Although how and where people look for information, especially on the Internet, is an extensively researched topic in the areas of information seeking and retrieval, researchers often tend to choose one type of source (e.g., online sources or human sources) to study. Also, very few studies have had in-depth investigation of how information seekers choose and evaluate one source over the others from a wide array of sources available to them. Previous studies have discussed the criteria individuals adopt when selecting information sources, such as perceived accessibility, availability, and quality of the source [42]. There are also constraints, individual differences, and other environmental factors associated with information seekers' selection of sources, such as their past search experience and time constraints [18, 36]. Fidel and Green [14] revealed a number of factors that contribute to the accessibility of information sources. Similar to accessibility, information source qualify also has different dimensions (e.g., accuracy, adequacy). However, it is not entirely clear how individuals evaluate the quality of an information source on various dimensions. In this era of user-generated data, information is available to people in unfiltered formats of varying quality. This has increased concern about the quality of the information and information sources, in particular for open Web sources. Moreover, as information is available through multiple media in various formats, such as audio, visual, and textual, individuals sometimes have difficulty evaluating and understanding information in these formats [20, 27]. Thus, the uncertainty about quality and increasing quantity of information raises the importance of evaluating and selecting good quality information sources to achieve information goals. It is essential to learn how information seekers perceive qualify of information sources to provide help accordingly. Information literacy may have become a crucial issue now more than ever before. The Association of College and Research Libraries [1] has defined information literacy as "a set of abilities requiring individuals to recognize when information is needed and have the ability to locate, evaluate, and use effectively the needed information." An information literate individual should not only be able to determine and access information, but also be able to "evaluate information and its sources critically" [1]. Meanwhile, there are the ever-present concerns about peoples' limitations in judging the quality of information and its sources [28, 31].

Using both quantitative and qualitative methods, the study reported in this paper examines how individuals judge the quality of different types of information sources and source contents on four dimensions - *accuracy, adequacy, relevance,* and *trustworthiness.* 53 participants' reports of their information seeking experiences in a semi-structured logbook and 23 follow-up interviews present how and why individuals' source selection is connected to these quality evaluation criteria. This study fills the gap in previous research in several aspects. First, it gave little constraint to participants' information seeking by allowing them to use a variety of information sources that would be available to them in normal circumstances. This created an environment that was arguably closer to individuals' natural information seeking environment than research limited to certain information sources. Second, this study explored the relationships among various information quality dimensions, information source types, and two task types. Third, this study utilized Amazon's Mechanical Turk, a crowd-sourcing platform to recruit participants with diverse backgrounds, and thus went beyond studying information seeking behaviors in academic or professional contexts. The rest of this paper is structured as follows. In the next section, a review of the literature related to information sources and information quality has been presented to establish the background and motivation of the present study. The method and findings have been reported in sections 3 and 4, followed by a discussion of the results and limitations of the study. The paper concludes in section 6 with a brief summary of the merit of this study along with a suggested scope for future studies.

2 LITERATURE REVIEW

Previous research has investigated various aspects related to information seeking behaviors such as information needs, tasks, goals, information seeking strategies, information sources, information qualify assessment, and individual differences (e.g., [6, 11, 13, 41]). Information seeking behaviors are influenced by contextual factors related to seekers such as domain knowledge, cognitive abilities, intentions, and the nature of search tasks [18]. The source of information, the information seeker, and the task or problem that brings about an information need are three main attributes of an information seeking episode [40]. Previous studies have identified different strategies employed by individuals during information seeking episodes. Xie [39] identified two dimensions or strategic actions of information seeking strategies – methods and resources. Methods are the techniques information seekers employ to look for information, such as scanning and searching, and resources include information sources and information [39]. Since many seekers may start with a vague idea about what information they want [7], they may use multiple information strategies within one information seeking episode, depending on their goals and tasks (e.g., [8]). Within each seeking strategy, information seekers may also use multiple information sources, such as human sources - friends and colleagues, books, and online sources [2]. Information seekers' selection and use of information sources are important strategic actions that demonstrate seekers' information seeking process [32, 39].

2.1 Information Sources

An information source is defined as a depository that carries and provides knowledge (i.e., [40]). Information sources can be categorized into two broad categories: impersonal or non-relation sources (e.g., online sources, search engines, physical documents, etc. non-human sources), or interpersonal or relational sources

(e.g., friends, colleagues) via a variety of online or offline channels through which individuals access sources [2, 29, 40, 42]. Although information source and information channel are two distinct concepts, past studies have used both terms synonymously (see, for example [10, 15, 16]). However, according to Xu et al. [40], information channels are the mode of communication through which content is delivered from information source to seeker, such as through face-to-face, phone, or e-mail interactions. Agarwal et al. [2] differentiated between an information source and an information channel based on Xu et al.'s [40] definition of channel. They categorized information sources into two – interpersonal and impersonal, and defined two dimensions of channel through which these two sources can be accessed: physical-electronic dimension – the use of a physical or electronic medium for information transfer, and synchronous-asynchronous dimension – the synchronicity of communication or connection [2]. To design this study, a third dimensionality has been added to the previously identified two methods of accessing information – mediation/no mediation – that is, the involvement of any mediated entity. Together, with the interpersonal-impersonal classification of sources and the combination of the three dimensions, an information source classification schema has been created with two broad categories:

Impersonal sources refer to nonhuman sources where information seekers do not have any direct interaction with a person to get information [2, 29]. It is passive and one-directional. This includes Websites, online databases, existing online forum posts, physical books, and so on.

Interpersonal sources refer to human sources where information seekers get information from a person through a direct both-way communication, whether via face-to-face or technology-mediated interactions [29]. This includes friends, family members, coworkers, etc., accessed on a variety of online or offline channels.

Under these two broad categories, there are 11 sub-categories or types of information sources, of which 6 are impersonal sources: (a) book or manual, (b) electronic copies of journals or books, (c) online databases/catalogs, (d) pre-posted entries in forums, blogs, or Q&A, (e) professional Websites, (f) Web search engines; and 5 are interpersonal sources: (g) e-mail, (h) face-to-face, (i) online chatting or mobile texting, (j) posting on online forum, or social networking sites, and (k) phone. For each interpersonal source sub-category, colleagues, friends, relatives, or other people are listed as human sources with whom seekers interact. For example, face-to-face interaction with a friend is interpersonal, physical, synchronous, and non-mediated source, whereas reading others' comments on online forums without replying to them is impersonal, electronic, asynchronous, and mediated source.

2.2 Quality Judgment Criteria

Previously, researchers have studied how and why seekers select one information source over another (e.g., [14, 25, 40, 42]). Two models of information seeking have gained prominence in the literature: the principle of least effort and the cost-benefit models. In the principle of least effort model, seekers look for sources that are readily available and need less mental or financial effort (e.g., [4, 12, 15]). In this model, seekers prefer accessibility over source quality. The cost-benefit model proposes that information seekers select an information source or channel based on their assessment of expected benefits and costs [2, 5, 16]. Agarwal et al. [2] and Zimmer et al. [42] found that source quality and accessibility are equally significant. Additionally, individuals tasks at hand also have an effect on information seeking and source picking. For example, if the task or problem is important or complex, the seeker may put more effort into obtaining quality information or consult people rather than documentary sources [9, 40].

Given equal accessibility, seekers tend to choose the source with higher perceived quality [42]. Therefore, among the criteria adopted by users, information quality is an important factor of information source selection. The literature has identified several dimensions, such as accuracy, specificity, timeliness, topicality, novelty, understandability, relevancy, reliability, usefulness, and scope [2, 40, 42]. These quality characteristics are not mutually exclusive, and there are overlaps among these concepts. For example, Xu et al. [40] found out that reliability, topicality, understandability, and novelty are closely associated with relevancy. Moreover, other researchers have identified different dimensions of source quality, and also define concepts of these dimensions differently, including or excluding some from their quality judgment criteria.

In this study, Taylor's [35] concept of quality has been used as a framework to judge information sources. Taylor [35] defined quality as "a user criterion which has to do with excellence or in some cases truthfulness in labeling." This study used accuracy, trustworthiness, adequacy, and relevance as quality judgment criteria. When judging the quality or value of information, there is often confusion between assessing a source and/or evaluating the information that the source contains. For example, when assessing the trustworthiness of information, trust can be attributed to a friend as an information source and/or the information gained from the friend. To maintain broadness, this study does not differentiate between information source quality and content quality.

In the past, researchers have often studied information seeking behaviors and the selection of information sources of various special populations, such as engineers [3], new employees in an organization [24], or Chinese business managers [22]. Rieh [26] suggested that users devoted great efforts in judging Web information source quality. Morrison [24] investigated information seeking behaviors of newcomers in an organization and the relationship between their satisfaction and performance. She found out that newcomers usually tend to go to experienced peers and direct supervisors when looking for information. Lin's [22] findings show that the Chinese business managers prefer to use internal sources rather than external sources, and prefer personal as opposed to impersonal sources. They also indicated that source reliability is the most fundamental characteristic affecting source use. Kang, Höllerer, and Donovan [19] explored factors that influence individuals' perceptions of microblog credibility. Other than content, visual cues such as design and layout were also found to be important in influencing credibility assessment.

Results reported from previous works of information sources are somewhat inconsistent probably due to the different types of work or information seek tasks examined as well as different contexts investigated. Studies on how individuals define various dimensions of information quality and evaluate different sources along those dimensions are scarce. To address these shortcomings, this paper investigates how individuals perceive information quality dimensions and evaluate the quality of the information sources based on these dimensions. Specifically, this work explores the relationships among individuals' understanding and evaluation of the accuracy, adequacy, relevancy, trustworthiness of information sources and their selection and use of those information sources, in context of their tasks. Participants' ratings of sources along the four dimensions coupled with qualitative analysis of the logbook and interview data are employed to present and explain those relationships.

2.3 Research Question

Based on the literature review, this study explored the following research question:

RQ: How do individuals' selection and use of information sources influence their evaluation of the adequacy, accuracy, relevance, and trustworthiness of information sources?

The merit of this work is threefold. First, past studies investigated accessibility and quality of information sources irrespective of source types, or focused only on Web sources. This study contributes to the literature by theorizing and exploring the relationships between information quality dimensions and different types of information sources. Second, as mentioned above, past studies on information sources have observed mostly specialized user groups or populations. This study investigates a diverse group of people from different educational and professional backgrounds as well as demographics. Moreover, this study provides insights into how individuals perceive the accuracy, adequacy, relevance, and trustworthiness of information sources, which will provide implications for information systems in providing accurate information and boosting user satisfaction.

3 METHOD

3.1 Recruitment and Participants

To invite participants outside of a specific academic or professional context, this study recruited 53 participants from Amazon's Mechanical Turk (hereafter MTurk). MTurk is an online crowd-sourcing platform where individuals and businesses (known as Requesters) can hire other individuals (known as Workers) to finish tasks that require human intelligence (e.g., surveys, usability testing). MTurk has the following advantages in participant recruitment. First, it provides access to one of the most diverse participant pools, as anyone with an MTurk account worldwide can select work to finish and get compensated [23]. Second, MTurk participants remain anonymous throughout the study because all contacts and payments are mediated through the MTurk Website; they are only identified by their MTurk IDs. Third, the recruitment process is semi-automated. Participants who do not finish tasks on time will not have access to the tasks after the deadline, and the unfinished tasks will automatically be reopened for others to complete. In recent years, MTurk has been increasingly used by researchers in social sciences to collect research data [34]. Hauser and Schwarz [17] suggested that MTurk Workers are more attentive to instructions than are college students.

In the present study, 53 participants comprised 26 males and 27 females. Their average age was 35.8 (SD=11) and ranged from 19 to 65. Participants were predominately college educated (67.9%). Only participants residing in the United States were recruited this time to reduce languages issues and time differences. They came from a variety of professional or educational backgrounds, including software engineering, biology, retail, painting, and firefighting. A few of them were self-employed or full-time MTurkers who do MTurk tasks for a living.

3.2 Task Design

Four simulated exploratory information seeking tasks were designed and assigned to participants. Each task came with a scenario that helped participants place themselves in the context of that task. Task scenarios were inspired by a qualitative survey conducted on MTurk that collected individuals' failures in information seeking (see [36]). This study also consulted Wildemuth and Freund's [37] guideline to include attributes of exploratory information seeking tasks. Specifically, exploratory tasks should introduce some ambiguity and include multiple facets to trigger exploratory and dynamic search behaviors, while maintaining the standardization required for a study. Two types of tasks producing two types of products (i.e., intellectual, decision/solution [21]) were designed. In Task One (T1) and Task Three (T3), participants were asked to prepare arguments for a debate related to one of two controversial topics. In Task Two (T2) and Task Four (T4), they were asked to look for a hybrid car for purchase or two apartments for rent, respectively. T1 and T3 are intellectual tasks (i.e., tasks that produce ideas or findings) while T2 and T4 are everyday life decision making tasks. Task descriptions were provided in a previous work (see [30]) so they are not included here for brevity.

3.3 Study Design

This study was carried out in two stages. In the first stage, each participant was given access to an online logbook that presented the tasks and questions guiding them to write about their information seeking experiences. They had up to two days to finish the tasks and logbook entries. The reasons of setting this time limit will be provided in the Pilot Tests section. MTurk Workers usually aim to finish tasks and get paid as quickly as possible so they are not likely to devote much cognitive effort unless specific requirements are given [43]. Therefore, they were instructed to utilize at least three different strategies to look for their desired information for each task. At least one of the three should have included interpersonal source(s) (i.e. human-to-human interaction online or offline). Although giving these two requirements may have limited their natural search activities, these restrictions were considered necessary to guide MTurk participants. After submitting the logbook responses, participants were invited to have a half-hour semi-structured follow-up interview with a researcher. 23 of them agreed to be interviewed through *GoToMeeting*, a web-hosted conferencing software. Both stages were finished remotely, which permitted the study to recruit participants from all over the United States. Each participant was paid $15 for completing the tasks and logbook, and an extra $10 for being interviewed. Considering that exploratory information seeking tasks could be time-consuming, although participants were encouraged to put in their best efforts, they were told that they were not expected to spend more than an hour on each task or thoroughly complete a task. They were not required to finish the

tasks in one sitting. Detailed study procedure is reported in the next two sub-sections.

3.3.1 Logbooks. The first stage of this study (tasks and logbook) was posted as a Human Intelligence Task (HIT) on MTurk. Participants who resided in the U.S. were allowed to sign up and start the study. On the main task page, a link to a semi-structured logbook was provided to each participant to detail their information seeking experiences. The logbook method utilized here is very similar to the diary method frequently used by information science researchers. It is called a logbook in this paper to differentiate it from the typical diaries kept by participants for a relatively longer period of time (from a week to a year) in other studies (e.g., [33]).

This study aimed to have participants finish the tasks in naturalistic settings and to set as little constraint as possible in terms of the devices used and information sources consulted, to motivate natural behaviors. Thus, participants were not restricted to using a specific device or source when looking for information. The downside of this was the difficulty of recording their activities. Self-administered logbook was chosen here because it allowed participants to report their whole experience, particularly the activities that would not otherwise have been easily accessible to researchers (e.g., face-to-face communication). Also, participants could write in the logbook at any time and they were encouraged to record their activities immediately after they occurred. Compared to interviews, this method captures the details that may soon be forgotten.

In their logs, participants were asked to describe their information seeking strategies, the barriers they encountered (if any), their findings, and whether they considered each strategy successful. Information seeking strategies were categorized as a two-dimensional concept based on methods and sources [39]. Methods are the actions undertook by participants to interact with information such as browsing or searching. Sources include information, information objects, and humans with whom participants interact [39]. In other words, participants wrote down the sources consulted and the methods employed to access and use those sources. For instance, one participant wrote down *"I first texted my friend who I knew has owned multiple hybrid cars,"* the method is texting while the source is this participant's friend.

Other than the open-ended descriptive questions, they also rated the accuracy, trustworthiness, relevance, and adequacy of the information/information sources on a five-point scale and explained their ratings. Participants were given two days following their acceptance of the tasks on MTurk to work on the tasks and write in their logbooks. Their partial responses were automatically saved by the system so they could leave at any time and start up again at their previous stopping point. Here are several examples of the questions asked in the logbook:

- Please describe step-by-step the first strategy you adopted to look for information, including but not limited to the sources you consulted (e.g., people, Websites) and the questions asked or keywords entered if it was an online search.
- What difficulties did you encounter when using this strategy?
- Do you think you succeeded in finding the information you needed with this strategy? Why? ...

3.3.2 Semi-structured Interview. Logbooks are limited in capturing the full picture of some situations. Because filling out the logbook was not an iterative process guided by a researcher and participants were not always sure about what details to report, they sometimes failed to record important elements such as their reasons for choosing certain sources. Follow-up interviews were arranged to solicit in-depth explanations of participants' experiences. For example, if a participant gave a low rating for the accuracy of the information without giving a reason, the researcher was able to ascertain the reason in the interview. Interviews also helped researchers verify if their interpretations of participants' narratives reflected what participants really meant. The interview was created as another HIT on MTurk. Due to the restrictions set by MTurk, participants could only sign up for one HIT at a time and they are not obligated to participate in any follow-up tasks. In other words, participants got paid after they finished the logbook and they could choose to be interviewed or not. An invitation was sent to each participant via MTurk after they finished their logbooks. Those who signed up also provided their time preference for the interview. Next, each interview participant was given a link to a GoToMeeting page where the audio interview would take place. All they needed to do was visiting the link at their scheduled interview time and a researcher would be waiting on the other end. GoToMeeting was chosen here because it did not require participants to install anything on their end, which simplified the interview process. The researcher in charge of an interview reviewed participants logbook responses before the interview so questions could be tailored to each participant. Below are sample questions asked in the interviews:

- Regarding your response to the first task, you said, *"some sites are more opinion than facts."* Is that the reason you rate accuracy and trustworthiness pretty low? Could you elaborate on that?
- What do you mean by facts? Could you give me an example?
- Regarding your response to the third task, cellphone and safety, you did a Google search as your second strategy, and gave high ratings because *"a lot of information was from very reputable sources."* How do you define *"reputable sources?"*

3.3.3 Pilot Tests. Three rounds of pilot tests with three to five participants in each round were conducted to test the study procedure and instruments. In the first round, five days were given to each participant to finish the tasks and logbook, though they could submit at any time within that five days. Five days were considered more than plenty so participants could work without feeling a time pressure. However, unlike many other studies on MTurk in which responses could be obtained fast, the first completed logbook was submitted ten days after the study was open. It was found out later during a follow-up interview with an experienced MTurk Worker that many MTurk participants accept multiple tasks at a time and usually work on the tasks that are due soon first. When they were given five days, they would assume that they had plenty of time and left this task till the last minute. As a result, they might realize on the last day that this task would not be finished quickly and gave up. The task would be open for other people to sign up but the same thing might happen again. Longer time limits turned out to be not useful when participants did not start right after accepting the tasks.

After two more rounds of pilot tests, it was decided that two days provided enough pressure that triggered participants to start soon but also left them a decent amount of time to finish everything.

4 DATA ANALYSIS AND RESULTS

At the end of the tasks and interviews, 53 participants submitted a total of 636 information seeking episodes related to four tasks (one reported strategy was counted as one episode). They reported their choices of information sources, the channels through which they consulted the sources, their ratings on four information quality dimensions on 5-point scales, and explanations behind their ratings. As reported in the literature review, a coding scheme was developed based on Agarwal's [2] classification of source/channel types to categorize the sources reported by participants. Two coders first classified the sources reported in 10% of the data independently and achieved satisfactory inter-coder reliabilities for source classification (Cohen's Kappa=.91). After resolving the disagreements, each then coded half of the remaining data. A mixed-method approach was taken to analyze the data. In the quantitative analysis, descriptive statistics and ordered logistic regression were used to analyze information sources and users' self-reported ratings for each task type and for the whole dataset. The qualitative analysis attempts to explain the relationships between users' selected information sources and their ratings on four information quality dimensions generated from the quantitative analysis based on the explanations they provided in their logbook and interview responses.

4.1 Quantitative Analysis

After coding information sources for each episode, a frequency analysis for all source variables and quality dimensions was performed in order to understand the data distribution. The data has been analyzed first, from a holistic point of view, and initial observations were made concerning the frequency of information sources chosen by the seekers in each task type, as well as in all four tasks. After that, observations that were more granular were made for each task, source, and the quality dimension. Tables 1 and 2 present the descriptive statistics of information quality and source types for each type of task.

As mentioned above, the intention for quantitative analysis was to explore the relationship between users' source quality judgment and the selection and use of information sources, particularly, the relationships between individuals' understanding and evaluation of the adequacy, accuracy, relevancy, and trustworthiness of information sources and their selection and use of those information sources in contexts of the tasks at hand. To explore the influences of the sources over the evaluation ratings, the study created ordered logistic regression models using information source types as predictors and participants' ratings of accuracy, adequacy, relevance, and trustworthiness of information sources as response variables. The ordered logistic regression was used because the dependent variables were ordinal – the orders of the categories were meaningful, however, the real distance between categories was unknown. There were four evaluative measures for information quality – accuracy, trustworthiness, relevance, adequacy – and each has users' ratings in five categories 1 = "not at all"; 2, 3 = "somewhat"; 4, and 5 = "very"

Table 1: Information Source Usage for Each Task Type

	Intellectual tasks		Everyday decision-making tasks	
	Task 1	Task 3	Task 2	Task 4
Number of Sessions	159	159	159	159
Impersonal Sources	117	109	112	119
Electronic copy	5	3	0	0
Online knowledge base	4	5	0	0
Online posts	6	2	6	1
Websites	102	89	98	113
Search engine	80	75	79	48
Interpersonal Sources	45	51	52	50
Email	0	1	0	4
F2F	21	14	13	7
Chatting texting	6	11	7	6
Phone	6	9	20	24
Posting online	10	10	4	5

Table 2: Frequencies of Each Rating Value Given to Each Source Type

Source	Task Type		Accuracy					Adequacy					Relevance					Trustworthiness				
		Scale	1	2	3	4	5	1	2	3	4	5	1	2	3	4	5	1	2	3	4	5
Impersonal	Everyday	T2	1	4	21	44	42	4	9	26	27	46	1	4	12	28	67	3	7	19	31	52
		T4	2	5	27	41	44	8	11	19	27	54	2	6	12	29	70	2	8	28	39	42
	Intellectual	T1	3	6	27	48	33	3	15	25	36	38	1	3	11	34	68	4	11	20	40	42
		T3	1	8	25	32	43	2	14	21	28	44	2	4	8	30	65	2	10	23	27	47
Interpersonal	Everyday	T2	7	1	16	13	15	9	7	13	7	16	5	3	8	11	25	6	2	12	11	21
		T4	16	3	9	10	12	19	2	4	12	13	15	4	2	13	16	12	3	8	9	18
	Intellectual	T1	4	7	18	9	7	6	7	11	8	13	2	2	8	15	18	5	7	11	10	12
		T3	10	6	16	13	6	10	11	13	12	5	6	4	14	15	12	8	5	13	12	13

as dependent variables. Ten information source variables (five impersonal and five interpersonal sources) were used as predictors. All of them were categorical, with 0 and 1 levels where 1 indicated that the participants used the source during that information seeking episode, and 0 indicated that they did not use the source. For each type of task (everyday life and intellectual), regression models were created using one information source type and one information quality criterion in each model.

All the assumption tests necessary for the ordered logistic regression were performed to check whether the data were qualified to provide reliable results. Proportional odds logistic regression models were generated to account for the proportional odds assumption in the given regression model. Although the data fulfilled the assumption of proportional odds (i.e., that each independent variable had an identical effect at each cumulative split of the ordinal dependent variable), two or more independent variables were highly correlated with each other, thus multicollinearity became a problem. Therefore, separate regression models with single independent variable were computed.

Ordered logistic regression helped to determine which of the independent variables had statistically significant effect on the dependent variables. Therefore, the resulted models were analyzed and odds ratios and p-values were calculated to understand the significant effects ($p < 0.05$). Table 3 presents a portion of statistically significant results ($p < 0.05$) from the ordered logistic regression model and reports the values of the coefficients and odds ratios. In ordered logistic regression, a coefficient value indicates how much the dependent variable is expected to increase (if the coefficient is positive) or decrease (if the coefficient is negative) when that independent variable increases by one. For example, for a one unit increase or decrease in one independent variable, i.e., going from 0 (not used) to 1 (used) or vice versa, the odds of "very(5)/4" accurate/adequate/relevant/trustworthy versus "somewhat(3)/2" or "2/not at all" accurate/adequate/relevant/trustworthy were greater, given that all of the other variables in the model were constant. On the other hand, odds that an event occurred were the ratio of the number of participants who used the source to the number of participants who did not.

The results are briefly summarized as follows:

Table 3: Portion of Results from Ordered Logistic Regression Models

Statistically significant odds ratios with the p-value < 0.05 are marked with *

Predictor Sources	Task type	Accuracy coeff	Accuracy odds ratio	Adequacy coeff	Adequacy odds ratio	Relevance coeff	Relevance odds ratio	Trustworthiness coeff	Trustworthiness odds ratio
Impersonal sources	Everyday	0.7794	2.1802*	0.6296	1.8769	0.7013	2.0164*	0.2994	1.3490
	Intellectual	1.1878	3.2798*	0.4455	1.5613	0.8184	2.2668*	0.6501	1.9158
	All	1.2613	3.5299*	0.9553	2.5995*	1.1798	3.2537*	0.5632	1.7564*
Electronic copies	Everyday	0	0	0	0	0	0	0	0
	Intellectual	0	0	0	0	0	0	0	0
	All	0.7291	2.0732	0.4915	1.6347	-0.0765	0.9263	0.4913	1.6344
Online databases and catalogs	Everyday	0	0	0	0	0	0	0	0
	Intellectual	1.0284	2.7965	-0.0998	0.9050	1.0767	2.9349	0.5160	1.6753
	All	1.0348	2.8146	0.5541	1.7404	0.2454	1.2782	0.7402	2.0964
Online posts	Everyday	-0.0934	0.9108	0.1648	1.1791	0.4533	1.5735	-0.4558	0.6339
	Intellectual	-0.2182	0.8039	-0.6127	0.5419	0.1676	1.1825	-0.7284	0.4827
	All	-0.2510	0.7781	-0.3057	0.7366	-0.0765	0.9264	-0.4941	0.6101
Websites	Everyday	0.7680	2.1555*	0.8813	2.4140*	0.7146	2.0434*	0.5426	1.7205
	Intellectual	0.9909	2.6936*	0.6999	2.0136*	0.7077	2.0293*	0.6739	1.9618*
	All	1.1334	3.1061*	0.9874	2.6843*	1.1338	3.1074*	0.6138	1.8474*
Search engine	Everyday	0.4237	1.5276	-0.0869	0.9168	0.2785	1.3211	0.2840	1.3285
	Intellectual	1.0697	2.9144*	0.8134	2.2555*	0.7749	2.1703*	0.7548	2.1271*
	All	0.5530	1.7384*	0.3379	1.4020*	0.5501	1.7335*	0.3136	1.3684*
Interpersonal sources	Everyday	-0.8600	0.4231*	-0.9762	0.3767*	-0.6716	0.5109*	-0.5073	0.6021
	Intellectual	-1.3459	0.2603*	-0.6591	0.5173*	-0.8061	0.4466*	-0.8129	0.4436*
	All	-1.2389	0.2897*	-1.0919	0.3356*	-1.1047	0.3313*	-0.6635	0.5150*
Email	Everyday	0	0	0	0	0	0	0	0
	Intellectual	0	0	0	0	0	0	0	0
	All	-1.0636	0.3452	-0.5495	0.5772	0.2346	1.2645	1.8435	6.3188
F2F	Everyday	-1.2700	0.2808*	-1.2872	0.2761*	-1.5678	0.2085*	-0.6491	0.5225
	Intellectual	-08998	0.4067*	-0.3951	0.6736	-0.7136	0.4899	-0.4649	0.6282
	All	-0.9791	0.3756*	-0.7055	0.4938*	-1.0009	0.3676*	-0.3858	0.6799
Chatting texting	Everyday	-0.6155	0.5404	-1.4559	0.2332*	-0.5385	0.5836	-0.1342	0.8744
	Intellectual	-1.4469	0.2353*	-1.9312	0.1450*	-1.2910	0.2750	-1.5244	0.2178*
	All	-1.2057	0.2995*	-1.4358	0.2379*	-0.7820	0.4575*	-0.7475	0.4736*
Phone	Everyday	0.3632	1.4379	0.1583	1.1715	0.9378	2.5545	0.1329	1.1421
	Intellectual	-7848	0.4562	0.0282	1.0286	-0.8608	0.4228	-0.9043	0.4048
	All	-0.1352	0.8736	-0.2053	0.8144	-0.1630	0.8496	-0.0484	0.9528
Posting online	Everyday	-0.3545	0.7015	-1.0657	0.3445	-0.9584	0.3835	-0.5431	0.5809
	Intellectual	-1.2713	0.2805	-1.0648	0.3448	-0.2102	0.8104	-0.7781	0.4593
	All	-1.3863	0.2500*	-1.2224	0.2945*	-0.8930	0.4094*	-0.9990	0.3683*

(1) Impersonal sources positively affect the accuracy and relevance of information sources for all types of tasks, and adequacy and trustworthiness regardless of task type.
(2) Interpersonal sources negatively affect the adequacy, accuracy, and relevance of information sources for all types of tasks, and the trustworthiness of information sources for intellectual tasks as well as when task type is not considered.
(3) Websites (e.g., Kelley Blue Book) positively affect the accuracy, adequacy, and relevance of information sources for all types of tasks.
(4) Websites positively affect the trustworthiness of information sources for intellectual tasks as well as when all information seeking episodes were considered regardless of task type.

(5) Search engines positively affect the accuracy, adequacy, relevance and trustworthiness of information sources for intellectual tasks as well as when all sessions were considered regardless of task type.
(6) Face-to-face communication negatively affects the accuracy of information sources for all task types as well as the adequacy and relevance for everyday life tasks, and regardless of task type.
(7) Online chatting or texting negatively affect the accuracy, adequacy, trustworthiness, and relevance of information sources regardless of task type.
(8) Online chatting or texting also negatively affect the accuracy, adequacy and trustworthiness in intellectual tasks alone and the adequacy in everyday life tasks as well.

(9) Posting on online forums negatively affects the accuracy, adequacy, relevance and trustworthiness of information sources regardless of task type.

Overall, participants mostly used impersonal sources (231 times for everyday life tasks and 226 times for intellectual tasks). Among impersonal sources, they used professional Websites (e.g., Kelley Blue Book) most frequently to look for information (see Table 1 for the frequencies of each source type used). Regarding task type influence, the study could not find much difference in participants' ratings for impersonal sources across task type. Most participants rated all impersonal sources highly compared to interpersonal sources (3-5), irrespective of task type, and they scarcely gave them a low rating (1-2). On the contrary, there are some observable variations regarding participants' ratings for interpersonal sources. Notably, they rated interpersonal sources relatively higher regarding accuracy, adequacy, relevance, and trustworthiness for everyday life tasks compared to intellectual tasks (see Table 2).

4.2 Qualitative Analysis

As the statistical analyses have shown, interpersonal sources generally negatively affect all quality dimensions of information sources. In particular, chatting/texting and posting online have negative effects on the ratings of all criteria when task type is not considered and face-to-face communication negatively affects all but trustworthiness. Participants explained in their narratives that they usually relied on one or a few people's opinions or knowledge, which were hardly adequate because of their limited personal experiences (e.g., P4: *"They mostly had Toyota Priuses so it was difficult to have a great understanding of the hybrid market and what exactly is available."*) Although posting on online forums would have generated more information, it would also have taken more time so not enough information was collected on time (e.g., P50: *"Not enough people responded to provide adequate results."*) Also, interpersonal sources might not be as focused as expected and irrelevant topics could easily come up, which affected relevance of the information received (e.g., P51: *"There wasn't much information included with the person's answer and opinion, and the answer quickly went off topic."*) When considering each task type separately, texting and online chat's negative effects in intellectual tasks become more obvious, influencing the accuracy, adequacy, and trustworthiness of information. This is probably because that chatting and texting may be more suitable for obtaining a quick answer. Intellectual tasks (in this study, preparing for debate topics) require more domain specific knowledge or scientific evidence that could not be easily obtained by texting or chatting, particularly from non-experts. Participants often believed that the information offered by other people was just opinion from one or several non-experts, so the accuracy and adequacy were doubtful (e.g., P30: *"There is no scientific evidence to back any of this up"*; P02: *"Mainly this was one person's opinion on the topic, so it gets rated slightly lower"*).

Interestingly, in some cases, not receiving high quality information did not mean that the source was not trustworthy. Participants frequently asked people they trusted, though that trust did not necessarily make the information accurate or adequate (e.g., P01: *"This is simply anecdotal and based on his experience and earlier research. Without being able to check facts for myself, I cannot really confirm the accuracy or adequacy of the information. I do trust my friend though, so the information is most likely good."*) There were also participants who mix trustworthiness of information sources with other criteria. For those participants, asking a person they trusted was equal to obtaining information of good overall quality (P06: *"I trust most of the people I spoke to, and their information is likely accurate for the most part".*)

In contrast, impersonal sources, particularly Websites, usually had higher ratings. Participants did not seem to be concerned about the quality of online information. Some participants even suggested that since there are so many Web users, the wrong information online could easily be detected and corrected. For instance, P13 considered the information from Planned Parenthood accurate because *"anyone who would be against that information would already brought up with them and made them correct it"*. Also, due to the considerable amount of online information available, information may be easily cross-checked by visiting multiple sites, and looking at different sites was effortless compared to consulting human sources (e.g., P10: *"I mean everything is in outside verifiable. I can always Google the claim outside."*) Some participants indicated their preference of the Websites that cited outside sources, particularly peer-reviewed research articles (e.g., P14: *"It provides citations supporting each argument, with links to scholarly articles, scientific research, or legal opinions as justification – it's not just someone's opinion, but there is peer reviewed research you can use to support each argument."*, and P37: *"I noticed that the information that was on the site had a lot of outside resources cited and specifically linked to, and the resources that they had, I felt were very trustworthy."*) In contrast, they rated Websites like *Craigslist* low for accuracy and trustworthiness because *"it's hard to tell a person's true intentions on craigslist"* (P19).

Task type did influence participants' judgment of information quality along certain dimensions. For the everyday life tasks (T2 & T4), participants were more likely to look for a community of people with similar interests to help verify the information found online. Unlike intellectual tasks in which participants perceived the accuracy of information provided by interpersonal sources to be low, everyday life tasks sometimes reflected participants' appreciation of other people's opinions (e.g., P30: *"There's actually a large community for the type of vehicle. They would suggest maybe a list, check your local store, check this Website, check that Website"*; P34: *"I asked my group on Facebook. Their responses kind of verified that it was a decent area to live than the other areas."*)

5 DISCUSSION

From the data analysis some interesting observations emerge. A few of the observations are evident and have confirmed results from similar studies done in the past. However, there are some subtle observations that can be important for understanding users' perception of information quality, as well as the relationship among information sources, perceived quality, and task types.

The study found that information seekers used impersonal sources, especially professional Websites, more than any other sources for all task types. Since the participants had to complete the tasks in a two-day time frame, time did affect their selection of sources, and as impersonal sources are easily available irrespective of time and place, they preferred impersonal sources. Some participants mentioned that they were unable to contact car dealers during the weekend to seek information. Furthermore, some impersonal sources were more likely to be perceived as relevant and accurate than interpersonal sources. Individuals believed in databases like Scopus as precise and reliable sources – that resources provided by these databases come from scholars or other domain experts (e.g., P10: *"These are peer-reviewed scientific studies that I can trust thoroughly for using the scientific method instead of biased articles"*). While there are shared concerns and doubts about the quality of online information, and lack of quality assurance mechanism on the Internet, participants generally considered internet sources to be trustworthy. They did not share the same concerns regarding online information quality as researchers, and they seemed to be confident in judging online sources' quality.

One surprising rationale emerged from the qualitative analysis is that some users think that since there are so many Web users, false information would easily be detected and corrected. Some participants also mentioned cross-checking of information by visiting multiple sources. There were also participants who gave high ratings only when a Website cited outside sources. Some participants thought the information was accurate because of the Website's design, user-friendliness, and readability. This echoes [19] that visual cues are influential in individuals' quality judgment. Moreover, task type influenced participants' selections of information sources and quality judgment. For the everyday life decision-making task (T2 & T4), participants looked for other people with similar interests to help verify the information found online. Meanwhile, they tended to distrust anyone who were on the business' side (e.g., salesperson, apartment manager): P13: *"This interaction did nothing to get me my needed information. I cannot trust a salesperson to give totally relevant information because they're trying to sell a car."* For the intellectual tasks, they rated highly those Websites that produced balanced and neutral arguments for both sides of the issue.

Participants gave quite a few low ratings to interpersonal sources on all quality dimensions. One main reason for this is their understanding of the nature of information. Most participants did not consider opinion as knowledge or accurate information and opinions could be associated with emotions (e.g., P49: *"There was too much passion and heated arguments for the information to be reliable and logical. No one cited any facts, but rather depended on their ideology."*) For the intellectual task, people also found biased information that lowered the perceived accuracy (e.g., P40: *"She only talked about the bad stuff. I generally trust my mother, but she's too biased in this situation to be a really good source, though she brings up some okay points."*). Moreover, the data reveals that interpersonal sources might not be as focused as expected and irrelevant topics can easily come up while directly conversing with a known source, a friend or colleague. A conversation about a task topic could soon turned into chatting on random topics. For that reason, face-to-face communication and online chatting or texting negatively affect accuracy, adequacy, and relevance of information sources. While some participants could differentiate between accuracy and trustworthiness and did not take the information provided by a trusted source for granted, other participants also mixed trustworthiness of information sources with other criteria. This may be affected by participants' education or information literacy. Further research is needed to explore the reasons behind these phenomena.

The findings offer several implications. First, although individuals predominantly relied on Web sources, interpersonal sources served as useful complements to Web sources in some cases. Participants counted on others' experiences to help in decision-making and verify the information found online. Designers may take this aspect into consideration in system design. For example, in addition to returning documentary sources, systems may also recommend platforms for users to seek a second opinion from others. Second, the fact that anyone could create information online did not concern participants in this study because it indicates that anyone could also correct information online. A systematic evaluation of online information related to a topic is needed to verify if this claim stands for a particular topic. For now, it is still critical to inform Web users the strategies for evaluating online information and the importance of doing so to prevent them from over-trusting online sources. Third, individuals' selection and evaluation of information sources could be varied greatly by task type. It is important for both information system designers and information service providers to understand users' task at hand to provide help accordingly.

This study has some limitations. First, four simulated search tasks performed by the participants might not be related to their daily lives. This might have affected participants' information seeking behaviors in some scenarios. For example, a few participants mentioned that if they had to do the decision-making tasks in real life, they would have contacted a car dealer or an apartment manager, but they chose not to do so because they did not want to waste other people's time. However, most participants did mention in the interviews that they would do the same if they were doing the tasks for real. Second, participants were required to use at least three strategies and at least one interpersonal source, which might not reflect their real information seeking behavior. While the benefit was likely to outweigh the drawback in this study because of the characteristic of MTurk participants, future studies conducted in other context may consider offering less constraints. Third, this study is based on participants' self-reported data, and as with other research with self-reported data, it is prone to some biases. In the future, other data collection methods such as collecting log data and photo taking may also be added to the design. Finally, although participants were from various professional backgrounds, the extent to which this sample could represent the general population is unknown. It is possible that MTurk Workers are more tech-savvy than the general population.

6 CONCLUSIONS

Using both quantitative and qualitative methods, the study reported in this paper examined how individuals judge the *accuracy, adequacy, relevance,* and *trustworthiness* of different types of information sources and source contents. This paper also considered whether task types played any role in peoples' evaluative judgment processes. Briefly, first, individuals use various evaluative criteria to evaluate information sources, though they sometimes also mixed different criteria. Second, their judgment varied by the information source type. For impersonal sources, they look for cues such as overall organization, creator, and readability as identifiers to evaluate the source. On the other hand, for interpersonal sources, they rely on connections they can trust. Third, task type affects users' evaluation of sources. For intellectual tasks, people look for balanced, neutral, or factual information from both impersonal and interpersonal sources. Conversely, for everyday decision-making tasks, people want opinionated information from interpersonal sources in addition to information from impersonal sources. Fourth, irrespective of researchers' general disbelief for information online, for the most part individuals consider online information mostly accurate and trustworthy compared to interpersonal sources. Last, individuals like to consult multiple sources to verify the quality of information.

Overall, this study presents the subtlety and complexity of users' information quality judgment process in relation with task type and information source type. It is important to differentiate between various task types and source types to obtain a clearer picture of individuals' information quality judgment and source selection. A typical information seeker seems to be juggling these three balls – sources, tasks, and quality assessment – while seeking, retrieving, and using information. In future, the study could be expanded with additional task types to further investigate these observations.

ACKNOWLEDGMENTS

The work reported in this paper is supported by the U.S. Institute of Museum and Library Services (IMLS) grant #LG-81-16-0025-16.

REFERENCES

[1] ACRL. 2000. Information literacy competency standards for higher education. *Community & Junior College Libraries* (2000), 16.
[2] Naresh Kumar Agarwal, Yunjie Calvin Xu, and Danny CC Poo. 2011. A context-based investigation into source use by information seekers. *Journal of the Association for Information Science and Technology* 62, 6 (2011), 1087–1104.
[3] Thomas J Allen. 1988. Distinguishing engineers from scientists. *Managing professionals in innovative organizations: A collection of readings* (1988), 3–18.
[4] Claire J Anderson, Myron Glassman, R Bruce McAfee, and Thomas Pinelli. 2001. An investigation of factors affecting how engineers and scientists seek information. *Journal of Engineering and Technology Management* 18, 2 (2001), 131–155.
[5] Susan J Ashford. 1986. Feedback-seeking in individual adaptation: A resource perspective. *Academy of Management journal* 29, 3 (1986), 465–487.
[6] Nicholas J Belkin. 1990. The cognitive viewpoint in information science. *Journal of Information Science* 16, 1 (1990), 11–15.
[7] N J Belkin. 1997. An overview of results from Rutgers investigation of interactive information retrieval. *Proceedings of the 34th Annual Clinic on Library Applications of Data Processing* 70 (1997), 45–62.
[8] Nicholas J. Belkin, Pier Giorgio Marchetti, and Colleen Cool. 1993. BRAQUE: Design of an interface to support user interaction in information retrieval. *Information Processing & Management* 29, 3 (1993), 325–344.
[9] Katriina Byström. 2002. Information and information sources in tasks of varying complexity. *Journal of the American Society for Information Science and Technology* 53, 7 (2002), 581–591.
[10] Donald Case. 2007. *Looking for information. A survey of research on information needs, seeking and behavior.* Academic Press, New York, NY.
[11] Colleen Cool and Nicholas J. Belkin. 2002. A classification of interactions with information. *Emerging frameworks and methods. Proceedings of the Fourth International Conference on Conceptions of Library and Information Science (COLIS4)* June (2002), 1–15.
[12] Mary J Culnan. 1985. The dimensions of perceived accessibiiity to information: Implications for the delivery of information systems and services. *Journal of the American Society for Information Science* 36, 5 (1985), 302–308.
[13] David Ellis. 1989. A behavioural approach to information retrieval system design. *Journal of documentation* 45, 3 (1989), 171–212.
[14] Raya Fidel and Green Maurice. 2004. The many faces of accessibility: Engineers' perception of information sources. *Information Processing and Management* (2004), 563–581.
[15] P G Gerstberger and T J Allen. 1968. Criteria used by research and development engineers in the selection of an information source. *Journal of Applied Psychology* 52, 4 (1968), 272.
[16] Andrew P. Hardy. 1982. The selection of channels when seeking information: Cost/benefit vs least-effort. *Information Processing and Management* 18, 6 (1982), 289–293.
[17] David J Hauser and Norbert Schwarz. 2016. Attentive Turkers: MTurk participants perform better on online attention checks than do subject pool participants. *Behavior research methods* 48, 1 (2016), 400–407.
[18] Ingrid Hsieh-Yee. 2001. Research on Web search behavior. *Library & Information Science Research* 23, 2 (2001), 167–185.
[19] Byungkyu Kang, Tobias Höllerer, and John O'Donovan. 2015. Believe it or not? Analyzing information credibility in microblog. *Proceedings of the 2015 IEEE/ACM International Conference on Advances in Social Networks Analysis and Mining* 53 (2015), 611–616.
[20] Kyung-Sun Kim and Sei-Ching Joanna Sin. 2011. Selecting quality sources: Bridging the gap between the perception and use of information sources. *Journal of Information Science* 37, 2 (2011), 178–188.
[21] Yuelin Li and Nicholas J Belkin. 2008. A faceted approach to conceptualizing tasks in information seeking. *Information Processing & Management* 44, 6 (2008), 1822–1837.
[22] Yang Lin, Charles Cole, and Kimiz Dalkir. 2014. The relationship between perceived value and information source use during KM strategic decision-making: A study of 17 Chinese business managers. *Information Processing and Management* 50, 1 (2014), 156–174.
[23] Winter Mason and Siddharth Suri. 2012. Conducting behavioral research on Amazon's Mechanical Turk. *Behavior research methods* 44, 1 (2012), 1–23.
[24] Elizabeth Wolfe Morrison. 1993. Newcomer information seeking: exploring types, modes, sources, and outcomes. *The Academy of Management Journal* 36, 3 (1993), 557–589.
[25] Charles A O'Reilly III. 1982. Variations in decision makers' use of information sources: The impact of quality and accessibility of information. *The Academy of Management Journal* 25, 4 (1982), 756–771.
[26] Soo Young Rieh. 2002. Judgment of information quality and cognitive authority in the Web. *Journal of the American Society for Information Science and Technology* 53, 2 (2002), 145–161.
[27] Soo Young Rieh. 2009. Credibility and cognitive authority of information. *Encyclopedia of Library and Information Sciences, Third Edition* (2009), 1337–1344.
[28] Soo Young Rieh and Nicholas J Belkin. 2000. Interaction on the Web: Scholars' judgement of information quality and cognitive authority. *Proceedings of the 63rd Annual Meeting-American Society for Information Science* 37 (2000), 25–38.
[29] Diane Liang Rulke, Srilata Zaheer, and Marc H Anderson. 2000. Sources of managers' knowledge of organizational capabilities. *Organizational behavior and human decision processes* 82, 1 (2000), 134–149.
[30] Shawon Sarkar, Yiwei Wang, and Chirag Shah. 2017. Investigating relations of information seeking outcomes to the selection and use of information sources. *80th Annual Meeting of the Association for Information Science and Technology* 54 (2017), 347–356.
[31] Reijo Savolainen. 2008. Source preferences in the context of seeking problem-specific information. *Information Processing & Management* 44, 1 (2008), 274–293.
[32] Reijo Savolainen. 2016. Information seeking and searching strategies as plans and patterns of action. *Journal of Documentation* 72, 6 (2016), 1154–1180.
[33] Chirag Shah and Chris Leeder. 2016. Exploring collaborative work among graduate students through the C5 model of collaboration: A diary study. *Journal of Information Science* 42, 5 (2016), 609–629.
[34] Daniel B Shank. 2016. Using crowdsourcing websites for sociological research: The case of Amazon Mechanical Turk. *The American Sociologist* 47, 1 (2016), 47–55.
[35] Robert Saxton Taylor. 1986. *Value-added processes in information systems.* Greenwood Publishing Group, Westport, CT.
[36] Yiwei Wang and Chirag Shah. 2017. Investigating failures in information seeking episodes. *Aslib Journal of Information Management* 69, 4 (2017), 441–459.
[37] Barbara M Wildemuth and Luanne Freund. 2012. Assigning search tasks designed to elicit exploratory search behaviors. In *Proceedings of the Symposium on Human-Computer Interaction and Information Retrieval.*
[38] T. D. Wilson. 2000. Human information behavior. *Informing Science* 3, 2 (2000), 49–55.
[39] Hong Iris Xie. 2002. Patterns between interactive intentions and information-seeking strategies. *Information Processing and Management* 38, 1 (2002), 55–77.
[40] Yunjie Xu, Cheng Yian Tan, and Li Yang. 2006. Who will you ask? An empirical study of interpersonal task information seeking. *Journal of the American Society for Information Science and Technology* 57, 12 (2006), 1666–1677.
[41] Yan Zhang, Yalin Sun, and Yeolib Kim. 2017. The influence of individual differences on consumer's selection of online sources for health information. *Computers in Human Behavior* (2017), 303–312.
[42] J. Christopher Zimmer, Raymond M. Henry, and Brian S. Butler. 2007. Determinants of the use of relational and nonrelational information sources. *Journal of Management Information Systems* 24, 3 (2007), 297–331.
[43] Guido Zuccon, Teerapong Leelanupab, Stewart Whiting, Emine Yilmaz, Joemon M. Jose, and Leif Azzopardi. 2013. Crowdsourcing interactions: Using crowdsourcing for evaluating interactive information retrieval systems. *Information Retrieval* 2 (2013), 267–305.

Looking for the Movie Seven or Sven from the Movie Frozen? A Multi-perspective Strategy for Recommending Queries for Children

Ion Madrazo Azpiazu, Nevena Dragovic, Oghenemaro Anuyah, Maria Soledad Pera

People and Information Research Team (PIReT)

Boise, Idaho

ionmadrazo,nevenadragovic,oghenemaroanuyah,solepera@boisestate.edu

ABSTRACT

Popular search engines are usually tuned to satisfy the information needs of a general audience. As a result, non-traditional, yet active groups of users, such as children, experience challenges composing queries that can lead them to the retrieval of adequate results. To aid young users in formulating keyword queries that can facilitate their information-seeking process, we introduce *ReQuIK*, a multi-perspective query suggestion system for children. *ReQuIK* informs its suggestion process by applying (i) a strategy based on search intent to capture the purpose of a query, (ii) a ranking strategy based on a wide and deep neural network that considers both raw text and traits commonly associated with kid-related queries, (iii) a filtering strategy based on the readability levels of documents potentially retrieved by a query to favor suggestions that trigger the retrieval of documents matching children's reading skills, and (iv) a content-similarity strategy to ensure diversity among suggestions. For assessing the quality of the system, we conducted initial offline and online experiments based on 591 queries written by 97 children, ages 6 to 13. The results of this assessment verified the correctness of *ReQuIK*'s recommendation strategy, the fact that it provides suggestions that appeal to children and *ReQuIK*'s ability to recommend queries that lead to the retrieval of materials with readability levels that correlate with children's reading skills.

CCS CONCEPTS

• **Information systems** → **Query suggestion**; *Query intent*; • **Social and professional topics** → **Children**; • **Human-centered computing** → *User studies*;

KEYWORDS

Query suggestions; children; search intent; dataset

ACM Reference Format:

Ion Madrazo Azpiazu, Nevena Dragovic, Oghenemaro Anuyah, Maria Soledad Pera. 2018. Looking for the Movie Seven or Sven from the Movie Frozen? A Multi-perspective Strategy for Recommending Queries for Children. In *Proceedings of 2018 Conference on Human Information Interaction & Retrieval (CHIIR '18)*. ACM, New York, NY, USA, 10 pages. https://doi.org/10.1145/3176349.3176379

1 INTRODUCTION

As one of the largest communities that search for online resources, children are introduced to the Web at increasingly young ages [9]. However, popular search tools are not explicitly designed with children in mind nor do their retrieved results explicitly target children. Consequently, many young users struggle in completing successful searches, especially since most search engines do not directly support, or offer weak support, for children's inquiry approaches [16]. As stated in [45], this is an important issue to address since early experiences influence skill development in making proper use of resources for personal and educational growth.

As described in the book Search Engine Society, "Children growing up in the 21st century have only ever known a world in which search engines could be queried, and almost always provide some kind of an answer, even if it may not be the best one" [20]. Even though children, as inexperienced users, struggle with describing their information needs in a concise query [12], they still expect search engines to retrieve relevant information in response to their requirements, or at least suggest better choices for a successful search. As part of their capabilities, search engines often suggest[1] queries to aid users in better defining their information needs. In fact, a recent study conducted by Gossen et al. [17] shows that children pay more attention to suggested queries than adults. Unfortunately, these suggestions are not specifically tailored towards children and thus need improvement [44]. While multiple query suggestion modules have been developed to automatically generate queries that capture users' needs [3, 50], only a small number of them specifically target children. To address this problem, along with a need for more children-related tools, we introduce *ReQuIK* (**Re**commendations based on **Qu**ery **I**ntention for **K**ids), a query suggestion module tailored towards 6-to-13 year old children.

The main goal of *ReQuIK* is to provide query recommendations that explicitly consider diverse and ambiguous users' information needs. Prior to generating recommendations for a given child-initiated query, *ReQuIK* takes advantage of the *search intent module* presented in [9], which is used to capture the intended meaning of the query. In doing so, *ReQuIK* can deal with long natural language queries or queries that include common patterns children use when searching the web, which are difficult for search engines to process and properly handle. Even when the search intent of a query is identified, it is not enough to trigger the retrieval of suitable materials for each user, since the interests of children can vary depending on their age. To capture a wide range of potential suggestions, *ReQuIK* emulates a popular *query generation* strategy. Thereafter, *ReQuIK* identifies suitable suggestions by using a multi-perspective approach based on raw text analysis and a number of textual traits specifically associated with children content. These traits analyze

---

[1]*Suggestion* and *recommendation* are used interchangeably in this manuscript.

usage of children words, popular culture terms, entities and diminutives in queries. By applying a multi-perspective approach based on deep learning, the proposed query suggestion module is able to learn distinctive characteristics that portray adults and children queries, and use that knowledge to predict which queries are the most child-friendly among the ones in a candidate set. To guarantee diversity among the recommended queries, *ReQuIK* uses a content similarity strategy that groups together queries that are topically similar and excludes suggestions that refer to the same topic, i.e., queries that would retrieve the same type of resources. We are aware that suggested queries could retrieve resources that children may not easily comprehend due to their high reading difficulty [36]. In order to minimize this situation, *ReQuIK* prioritizes query suggestions that will potentially lead to easier-to-read resources.

Due to the lack of datasets that capture children search activities, we dedicated research efforts to creating one. To do this, we deployed an ad-hoc search framework which interacts with the Bing *api* and facilitates the archival of search sessions. We conducted an experiment with 97 children, ages 6 to 13, who were given research/informational and factual search tasks by their teacher. As a result, we gathered close to 600 queries, which we used for development and evaluation purposes. Thereafter, we verified the validity of *ReQuIK* based on both offline and online experiments, using the aforementioned dataset, which demonstrate that not only does *ReQuIK* suggest queries that are children oriented, but it also leads to resources that are of the adequate reading level.

To the best of our knowledge, *ReQuIK* is the only available system that can be coupled with existing engines to generate query recommendations for children, favoring those that can lead to easier-to-read resources. *ReQuIK* suggests queries that initiate the retrieval of child-related topics and materials, which can lead to improving search engines' performance. The design of the proposed tool explicitly considers different patterns children use while searching the Web to adequately capture the intended meaning of their original queries. For example, if a child submits the query *"elsa"*, *ReQuIK* aims to prioritize query suggestions such as *"elsa coloring papers"* or *"elsa dress up games"* that correlate better with topics of interest to children rather than *"elsa pataky"*, as suggested by Google[2], which is more appealing to mature users. Other contributions of our work include (i) a novel ranking model inspired by a deep-and-wide architecture that, while successfully applied for ranking purposes [7, 49], has never been used in the query suggestions domain, (ii) a strategy to overcome the lack of queries written by children by taking advantage of general purpose children-oriented phrases, and (iii) the aforementioned newly created dataset, which will be made available to the research community[3].

2 RELATED WORK

Creating an appropriate query that leads to retrieving relevant information is challenging for young users. Previous studies state that the performance of a web search engine is poorer when retrieving documents in response to queries targeting information for children than for queries oriented to content of more traditional users [42]. Query recommendations can help children by providing queries that can be used to initiate a search.

Current research on children's query suggestions is limited, with a simple query to ACM Digital Library for "children query suggestions" or "children query recommendations" retrieving five distinct research works from among the top-20 results. Existing research includes the one conducted by Duarte et al. [12], who rely on a bipartite graph constructed using tags and URLs to suggest children queries. The authors enhanced their proposed strategy, as discussed in [42], by considering topical and language modeling features, such as a topic-sensitive Page Rank and a children-related vocabulary distribution. Besides examining tags assigned at Delicious to retrieve web pages, Eickhof et al. [13] consider high-level semantic categories (inferred from Wikipedia and the DMOZ.org taxonomy) associated with tags, and treat them as expansion terms. The aforementioned approaches, however, rely primarily on tags to make their suggestions, which can be poorly defined due to the lack of quality control on user tags which can be inherently noisy. Furthermore, these tags are often provided by adults, instead of children, which explains why the vocabulary used to describe online resources for children might not correlate with the terms used by children. The work conducted by Vidinli and Ozcar [46] focuses on suggesting queries in within an educational search environment. The proposed strategy analyzes a number of features to determine the most suitable queries, among the candidates, that should be recommended, given a child-generated query. Unfortunately, the majority of the features are computed as a result of query-log examination, which is a constraint as query logs generated by K-12 students are rarely accessible.

To the best of our knowledge, the studies done in [24, 38, 47] are the only ones that do not use tags or query logs for generating children query suggestions. Instead, the authors in [38] use bigrams extracted from websites that contain text generated by children and Simple.Wikipedia.org, a collection of documents written for users whose second language is English. As opposed to the strategy in [38], which depends upon a pre-defined set of topical categories, *ReQuIK* relies on a dynamic clustering to ensure diversity of recommended queries. The module presented in [47] creates query suggestions that are semantically different but conceptually similar to a child-initiated query. To do so, the authors consider result set overlap generated by pairs of queries (a given query and a possible suggestion) and term overlap between the queries, and prioritize suggestions including n-grams in Simple Wikipedia or include terms in a pre-defined children vocabulary.

Even if with a different purpose, the work of Eickhoff et al. [14] is similar ours, given that they also aim at distinguishing between children and non children content. In their work, the authors use aesthetic features of websites as discriminators of children-related content, features that are not useful for classifying queries.

Similar to the approach in [24], *ReQuIK* emulates Ubersuggest's query generation strategy to create a set of queries to recommend. However, while the query suggestion strategy discussed in [24] depends on a regression model that combines multiple features, such as children vocabulary, phrasing patterns, popular culture terms related to children, and the popularity of the terms among children, *ReQuIK* adopts a multi-perspective suggestion approach that considers a different and larger set of traits to infer if a query is child-related, as well as content of the query itself. What distinguishes *ReQuIK* the most, among its counterparts, is its ability to simultaneously combine text pattern analysis as well as varied query traits to identify suitable child-related query suggestions.

---

[2] As verified on May 19, 2017.
[3] The dataset can be found in https://doi.org/10.18122/B2WQ5T.

Algorithm 1 Generating Query Suggestions

```
Input: A query Q written by a child, a trained ranking
model RM, wordId dictionary WD, number of suggestions to
generate k
candidates = empty set
scoredCandidates = empty list
suggestions = empty list
Q' = searchIntent(Q)
candidates = generateCandidates(Q')
for each candidate CQ in candidates do
    features = generateFeatures(CQ)
    wordIds = getWordIDs(CQ,WD)
    score = calculateScore(wordIds, features, RM)
    scoredCandidates = scoredCandidates + <CQ, score>
end for
sort(scoredCandidates)
for each candidate <CQ,score> in scoredCandidates do
    if suggestions is empty then
        suggestions = CQ
    else
        if CQ is not similar to any query in suggestions and
readability(CQ)<8 then
            suggestions = suggestions + CQ
        end if
    end if
    if |suggestions| ≥ k then
        break
    end if
end for
```

---

3 REQUIK

In this section, we describe the design of *ReQuIK* (see pseudocode in Algorithm 1). Along with the description of each strategy used in *ReQuIK*, we provide a step-by-step example (denoted **R.I.A**, ReQuIK in action) using Q_E: *"I want the trol song"*, a query written by a child, which is also part of the sample introduced in Section 4.1.1. This running example aims to further showcase the practical application of *ReQuIK*. Note that for Q_E, Google neither offers possible query suggestions nor leads to the retrieval of resources that explicitly target younger audiences, as illustrated in Figure 1, which further aids our case in advocating for the existence of query recommendation strategies solely for children.

3.1 Search Intent

As described by Bilal et al. [5], to adequately serve children, search engines must address the fact that children are seldom successful in formulating succinct queries. In fact, researchers have observed that children tend to use long (natural language) queries, as opposed to keyword queries, when performing online searches [10]. Unfortunately, the longer the query, the less likely a web search engine is to retrieve relevant resources in response to it, which can be very frustrating for young users [10]. Furthermore, children tend to misspell words and use writing patterns that differ from those of adults. For example, children can include the word "amazzzzing" instead of "amazing" in a query to emphasize something is really amazing. To best satisfy children needs, *ReQuIK* relies on *QuIK*, the search intent module for children presented in [9], which addresses common patterns detected in children writing, including: use of diminutives, exaggerated and trendy terms as well as higher percentage of misspellings when compared to adult users. In doing so, it transforms an initial query Q into a simplified keyword query Q'

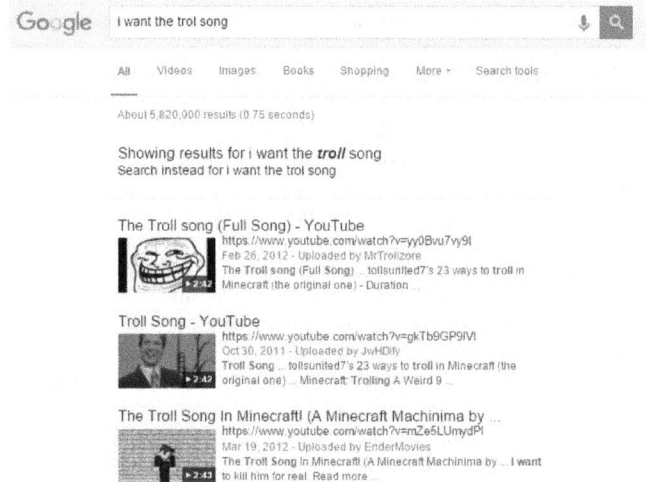

Figure 1: Screenshot of documents retrieved by Google for the query *"I want the trol song"*

that (i) captures the information need meant to be expressed by a child and (ii) can be adequately processed by search engines.

R.I.A. The search intent module employed by *ReQuIK* transforms Q_E into Q'_E "troll song", which suitably captures the intended meaning of Q_E, i.e., troll song from the popular movie Frozen. The search intent module solves two problems observed in Q_E: (i) removing terms that are superfluous for capturing the meaning of the query, i.e. *"I want the"*, and (ii) fixing the spelling error on *"trol"*.

3.2 Candidate Generation

Having identified the information need of a young user expressed in a query Q and created a shorter, more concise query Q', *ReQuIK* generates a set of candidate queries, i.e., queries that could possibly be suggested to a user, by emulating the algorithm of Ubersuggest[4] [1], a popular query suggestion tool based on Google auto complete API. The advantage of adopting such a strategy is that it quickly finds keywords based on what users search for on the Internet, creating multiple possible queries [4]. Bypassing the use of static query logs or probabilistic models allows *ReQuIK* to offer up-to-date candidate queries, since the aforementioned auto-complete strategy is constantly updated by online search trends.

R.I.A. Submitting Q'_E to the candidate generator creates more than 200 candidate suggestions, including queries related to children, such as *"troll song from dora"* and *"troll song frozen"* as well as queries that seem intended for more mature users, such as *"troll song no copyright"* and *"troll song hitler"*.

3.3 Ranking model

Not all the candidate queries generated in Section 3.2 are necessarily targeted towards children' needs, reading abilities, and interests. Consequently, to identify suitable suggestions among the candidates, *ReQuIK* takes advantage of a novel model (see Figure 2) that we created by combining two architectures, a *deep model* and a

---

[4]Ubersuggest queries Google autocomplete API multiple times with the initial query followed by each letter of the alphabet in order to retrieve multiple query candidates.

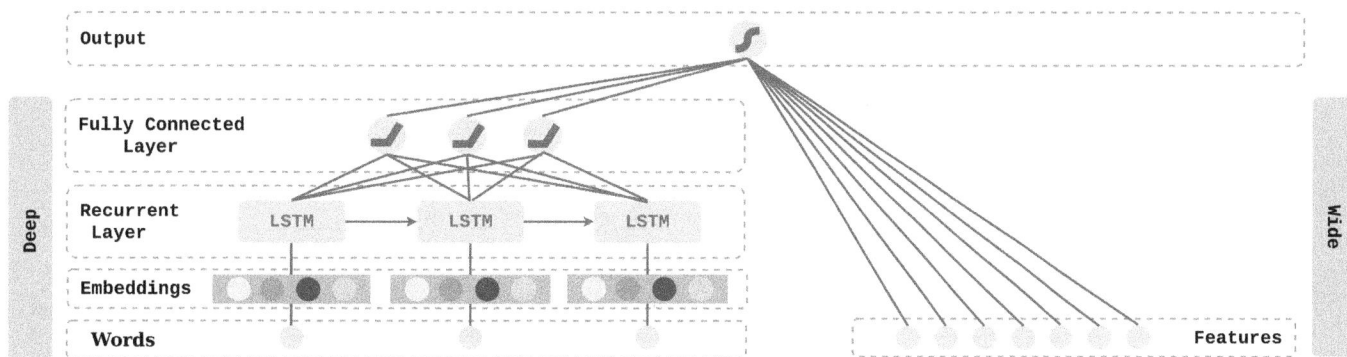

Figure 2: Ranking Model Architecture

wide model, inspired by the app recommendation model recently developed by Cheng et al. [7]. We discuss below insights and benefits of each architecture when applied to child-related tasks, as well as how we combine them into a single model for ranking purposes.

3.3.1 Wide Model: Learning what makes a query child-like. The wide model incorporates a set of manually-created features that are meant to capture traits often observed on child-related queries. These features are a result of an extensive analysis of children-related sentences (sampled from online sources for children). The wide model is composed of a vector $x_{feats} \in \mathbb{R}^f$, consisting of f features. Those features along with their computations are shown in Table 1, while their descriptions are provided below. Due to space constraints, Table 1 only includes the final set of features considered by *ReQuIK*. However, it is worth mentioning that we conducted an empirical analysis to identify the best subset of features to be used as a part of the ranking process. For example, features based on readability levels calculated by readability formulas such as Gunning FOG [2] and Dale-Chall [6] were overlooked in favor of the features based on an enhanced version of Spache [39] readability formula, which more adequately captures the level of difficulty of web resources.

Trendy Terms: Queries generated by young users contain a large amount of children-related trendy terms, such as names of movies, popular singers, computer games etc. By examining the presence of such terms in a candidate query Q, *ReQuIK* is able to determine if Q is appealing to children or not. (See Table 1-A.)

Entities: Based on a conducted analysis on queries generated by children, we identified a considerable use of entities (e.g., person, location, organization, etc.). For this reason, *ReQuIK* examines the presence of entities as one of the criteria to help decide how likely Q is related to children's interest. (See Table 1-B.)

Children Dictionary: In developing *ReQuIK*, we created a children dictionary using text collected from child-related websites. The use of such a collection of terms is of crucial importance since it best describes appropriate terms children use. Based on this, we concluded that young users use a narrower and unique vocabulary when expressing their needs. Therefore, we analyze the average frequency of terms in Q that are included in our children dictionary to enable *ReQuIK* to decide if the Q is tailored towards adults or children. Note that, this dictionary will be made available to the research community on this project's website upon the publication of this manuscript. (See Table 1-C.)

Flesch-Kincaid: Another criteria that targets a simplicity of Q is based on the well-known readability formula, i.e., Flesch-Kincaid [15], which provides the grade level of Q and enables *ReQuIK* to decide if a young user can comprehend Q. (See Table 1-D.)

Enhanced Spache: As a complement to the Flesch-Kincaid readability assessment, *ReQuIK* uses a feature based on an enhanced Spache formula. As an enhancement of a regular Spache [39] to obtain a greater accuracy, we expanded existing Spache dictionary of common words with children dictionary previously created. The combination of two dictionaries was necessary for considering more reliable and up-to-date trends of kids' vocabulary. This criteria increases the level of detection of words used by children in Q and enables *ReQuIK* to differentiate adult and child-related candidate queries. (See Table 1-E.)

Difficult Terms: *ReQuIK* uses a criteria generated based on the frequency of non-children [5] terms in Q to further separate adult and child-like queries. (See Table 1-F.)

3.3.2 Deep Model: Learning from text. Manual analysis of queries can lead to identifying distinctive features such as the ones mentioned in Section 3.3.1, however, some patterns can be impossible to detect upon simple observation or empirical analysis. Deep learning enables learning directly from raw data, so that new, unexpected features can be inferred automatically allowing the model to grasp patterns that humans are unable to find. The deep neural network is composed of one input layer and 3 hidden layers. The output layer is shared with the wide model and is therefore described in Section 3.3.3. Each of the other layers are described as follows:

Input Layer. The input of the neural network is represented as $x_{words} \in \mathbb{Z}^k$ where x_{words} is a vector k identifies representing a sequence of words. After analyzing the distribution of length of the queries we gathered, we fixed k at 15, a sufficient length to capture 95% of queries in our sample.

Embedding Layer. The embedding layer's role is to convert each word identifier into a dense representation that will capture the semantics of the word. For doing so we define an embedding function $Q : wordId \rightarrow \mathbb{R}^\alpha$, where α is the embedding size, that converts a word id to an embedding of length α. This function is based on a lookup table $S \in \mathbb{R}^{v \times \alpha}$, where v represents the vocabulary size. The embedding function Q returns a row from S

---

[5]We treat as "non-children" terms that do not appear or have low frequency on our children dictionary.

Feature ID	Feature Name	Description
A	Trendy Terms	$tt(q) = \frac{\sum_{i=1}^{\|q\|} t(q_i)}{\|q\|}, t(q_i) = \begin{cases} 1, & \text{if } q_i \text{ is recognized as a trendy term} \\ 0, & \text{otherwise} \end{cases}$ To determine if q_i is a child-related trendy term, *ReQuIK* examines its existence in children related pages on well-known websites, such as Amazon.com and CommonSenseMedia.org.
B	Entities	$et(q) = \frac{\sum_{i=1}^{\|q\|} e(q_i)}{\|q\|}, e(q_i) = \begin{cases} 1, & \text{if } q_i \text{ is recognized as an entity by Stanford NER tool [35]} \\ 0, & \text{otherwise} \end{cases}$ To determine if q_i is an entity, *ReQuIK* uses well-known CoreNLP tools.
C	Children Dictionary	$ct(q) = \frac{\sum_{i=1}^{\|q\|} c(q_i)}{\|q\|}, c(q_i) = \begin{cases} 1, & \text{if } q_i \text{ is included in a children dictionary} \\ 0, & \text{otherwise} \end{cases}$ We created our own children dictionary, comprised of 100,000 non-stop lemmatized terms, extracted from texts retrieved from a sample of various children-related websites.
D	Flesch-Kincaid	$FK(q) = 0.39\left(\frac{total\ words}{total\ sentences}\right) + 11.8\left(\frac{total\ syllables}{total\ words}\right) - 15.59$ In our case *total words* is the total number of words in q_i and *total sentences* is always equal to 1.
E	Enhanced Spache	$ES(q) = (0.121 \times AvgLengthOfq) + (0.082 \times NumberOfUniqueUnfamiliarWordsInq)$ We implemented Enhanced Spache formula by updating the existing dictionary of common words with the children dictionary in C.
F	Difficult terms	$dt(q) = \frac{\sum_{i=1}^{\|q\|} d(q_i)}{\|q\|}, d(q_i) = \begin{cases} 1, & \text{if } q_i \text{ is recognized as a difficult term} \\ 0, & \text{otherwise} \end{cases}$ *ReQuIK* treats q_i as a difficult term if it is not included in the children dictionary, or Spache dictionary of common words, or trendy terms list in A

Table 1: Criteria description, where q represents a query, q_i is the ith non-stop word, lemmatized term in q, and $|q|$ is length of non-stop-words in q. Each computed criteria score is normalized to fit a 1-5 scale

that corresponds to the provided word id. This function is applied to all the word ids in the input sequence creating a new matrix $H_1 \in \mathbb{R}^{k \times \alpha}$ that will be the input of the next layer. The matrix S is initialized using a random uniform distribution within $[-1, 1]$ and will be trained together with the weights of the neural network.

Recurrent Layer. Recurrent neural networks have been successfully used for processing sequential information [33]. A text document can be seen as a sequence of words, where each word depends on information provided by previous words, making it adequate for a recurrent neural network. The third layer of *ReQuIK*'s ranking deep neural network takes advantage of Long Short Term Memory cells (LSTM) [21], a recurrent cell specially suited for textual documents given its capability to remember long term information. Given a word embedding and a state vector $l_s \in \mathbb{R}^\beta$, where β refers to the number of LSTM units, each LSTM cell generates a output $l_{out} \in \mathbb{R}^\beta$. These outputs are concatenated to create a vector $h_2 \in \mathbb{R}^{\beta * k}$, which will be the input of the next layer.

Fully Connected Layer. A fully connected layer is one of the most common layers in a neural network. This layer computes a weighted sum over all the outputs of the previous layer. More precisely, given the vector h_2 produced by the LSTM layer, this layer computes the following operation:

$$h_{deep} = \text{relu}(Wh_2 + b) \quad (1)$$

where $h_{deep} \in \mathbb{R}^\gamma$ is the output of this layer, $W \in \mathbb{R}^{(\beta * k) \times \gamma}$ is a matrix of weights, $b \in \mathbb{R}^\gamma$ a bias vector. γ is a parameter that determines the number of neurons in the layer and *relu* refers to Rectified Linear Unit [32] which corresponds to the activation function that is applied to the result of the weighted sum.

3.3.3 Output Layer: Combining both models. The last layer of the ranking model is the one responsible for combining the aforementioned deep and the wide models. This enables *ReQuIK* to

incorporate the benefits of both a wide and a deep model, being capable of learning patterns from text automatically, while also using human crafted features that consider traits related to children queries. For doing this we first concatenate h_{deep} and x_{feats} to create a new vector $h_{comb} \in \mathbb{R}^{\gamma+f}$. Similar to the fully connected layer in the deep model, a weighted sum of all the values is computed, to create an output:

$$y' = \text{sigmoid}(W_{comb}h_c comb + b_{comb}) \quad (2)$$

where $y' \in \mathbb{R}^c$ is the prediction of the neural network, $W_{comb} \in \mathbb{R}^{(\gamma+f) \times c}$ is a weight matrix, $b_{comb} \in \mathbb{R}^{\gamma+f}$ a bias vector, c the number of prediction classes (2 in our case) and a sigmoid as activation function. Note that the prediction vector y' is composed of real values, enabling to use the same model for both prediction and as a scoring function for ranking the candidate queries.

3.3.4 Training. To produce relevant predictions, a neural network needs to be trained. This process involves fitting several variables that include, weights, biases and embedding values. For fitting those values a loss function is minimized using input/output pairs from a training dataset. For doing so, we take advantage of Cross Entropy function as a loss function, defined as follows:

$$H_{y'}(y) = -\sum_i y'_i \log(y_i) \quad (3)$$

where y' is the prediction created by the neural network and y is the target ground truth using one-hot encoding. For minimizing the error, we took advantage of the Adaptive Movement Estimation (Adam) [31] optimization technique.

The performance of a neural network is affected by its parameters. To identify the optimal α, β, and γ, we sweep possible values and found that the best combination for this task is $\alpha = 128; \beta = 128; \gamma = 128$. Thus, this is the parameter set used in all the experiments reported in this paper.

R.I.A. Using its ranking strategy, *ReQuIK* assigns a rating to each of the candidate query recommendations generated for to Q'_E. Based on the predicted ratings, queries like *"troll song from dora"* and *"troll song frozen"* are prioritized over queries such as *"troll song no copyright"*, which more likely better capture topics of interest for more mature audiences.

3.4 Readability

We observed that among the list of top-N child-related queries, not all of them lead to the retrieval of documents matching the reading skills of 6 to 13 year old children. This is of high importance for the recommendation process, since children are not able to comprehend resources above their reading capabilities. To determine what queries will most likely retrieve documents with suitable reading levels, *ReQuIK* applies the Flesch-Kincaid formula [15]. Queries that lead to the retrieval of resources associated with readability levels that are greater than readability levels expected for a child are excluded from the list of queries to be suggested[6]. Note that we treat 8 as an appropriate children grade level since it corresponds to reading level of 13 year old user.

Relying on this filtering strategy enables *ReQuIK* to identify suitable suggestions based not only on query content itself, but also on the readability levels of documents that would potentially be retrieved using those queries to initiate the search process.

R.I.A. ReQuIK further filters candidate queries to ensure that recommendations shown to its users most likely trigger the retrieval of documents they can understand. Based on the average readability scores of the top-N documents retrieved in response to *"troll song frozen"* and *"troll song no copyright"*, which are 6.7 and 11.3, respectively, *ReQuIK* retains the former and excludes the latter from the set of possible query recommendations.

3.5 Diversity

To guarantee that generated suggestions cater to diverse user interests, *ReQuIK* excludes from the set of top-N query recommendations candidate suggestions that are, to a degree, similar to each other. *ReQuIK* applies the Semantic Similarity algorithm developed by Yuhua Li et al. [34], which provides WordNet-based scores that are used to determine if any two suggestions are semantically the same, i.e., would trigger the retrieval of similar resources. In this context, two suggestions are treated as similar if their similarity score is above a threshold. By applying this topical filtering strategy, we select top-k[7] diverse suggestions from the ranked list generated in Section 3.4. For doing so, the first suggestion S_1 is always included in the final set of suggestions. Each subsequent candidate suggestion S_n is compared to the suggestions already in the final set. Thereafter, S_n is included only if it yields similarity scores of at most 0.7[8] with respect to the already-selected suggestions.

R.I.A. In the last step of its process, *ReQuIK* selects not only highest-rated and readability-level suitable queries, but also queries that offer topical diversity and thus target a wide range of users. For example, using its similarity-based filtering, *ReQuIK* treats *"troll song frozen"* and *"troll song frozen movie"* as highly similar and excludes the latter from the set of suggestions to be presented to the users. Lastly, the final set of suggestions generated by *ReQuIK* in response to the initial child-query Q_E includes *"troll song frozen"* and *"troll song from dora"*. These suggestions not only capture different information needs but do so in a keyword fashion that enable search engines to retrieve more relevant and suitable results for 6-13 year olds.

4 EXPERIMENTAL RESULTS

In this section, we detail the results of the offline and online studies conducted to demonstrate the correctness of *ReQuIK*'s methodology and the relevance of its generated query recommendations.

4.1 Evaluation Framework

We discuss below the datasets and query suggestion strategies used for comparison purposes.

4.1.1 Dataset & Other Resources. Obtaining children-related data is not a simple task, especially due to children protection regulations that make sharing this type of data highly restrictive. While other researchers have used queries extracted from existing query logs like the popular AOL [11], the extraction strategy may be limited and not always identify queries written by children, as some writing patterns are common among both children and adult queries. To address this issue, given that neither datasets that can be used to evaluate query recommendations for children nor query logs comprised only of children queries are publicly available, we created our own dataset[9].

Search Environment. In order to construct a dataset, we developed an online search framework that emulates the behavior and appearance of Google, and enables us to gather search sessions[10] of children and archive information such as: query typed, selected query suggestions (if available), clicked URLs, and timestamps. We made the appearance of this framework similar to that of a popular search engine, given children's preference to use well-known engines, as opposed to the counterparts designed for them, e.g., KidzSearch. The search framework contains an initial page that a teacher can configure based on the grade of his/her class.

Gathering Queries. In order to get children to use the search framework, we collaborated with elementary schools in the Idaho (USA) area. We asked K-9 teachers to propose their students information discovery tasks, for which they used our framework to create queries. For determining the type of tasks we followed the strategy used by Gwizdka et al. [19] and included both: research/informational tasks such as *Find information about fire belly toads* or *Find information about tigers* and factual tasks such as *How long do toads live* or *When does summer start*. Each teacher started the class with specific questions, however, children were later allowed to find information about things of their interest. A total of 97 children between the ages of 6 and 13 participated in the study, generating 591 unique queries.

Even though *ReQuIK*'s objective is to recommend children queries, for development and assessment purposes we also required a set of non-children queries. Thus, the resulting dataset, denoted *ReQqs*, includes the aforementioned 591 queries labeled *children-queries* and 591 queries randomly selected among the ones in the Yahoo's query log dataset [48] labeled *adult-queries*.

---

[6]To determine which candidate query cq potentially retrieves resources with reading levels above the expected ones, we compute and average the reading levels of the top-3 resources retrieved in response to cq.

[7]We set $k = 4$ to emulate the number of suggestions often offered by search engines.

[8]We experimentally set 0.7 as the similarity threshold.

---

[9]The process of gathering and archiving children queries was supervised by the Institutional Review Board at Boise State University in order to ensure children-related ethical and legal concerns were met.

[10]Information obtained from a child's search session is anonymous.

Other Data Sources. Due to the limited amount of children query-logs in ReQ_{qs}, we gathered ReQ_{corp}, a sample of 1,061,666 sentences for development and training purposes. In creating ReQ_{corp}, we extracted sentences from websites oriented to children, including Dogo [8], Spaghetti [40], Toy Insider [43], Raising Children [37], Kidzvuz [30], Kids-in-mind [23], and Edutaining-kids [28]. We also included in ReQ_{corp} sample sentences from Wikipedia in order to provide negative, i.e., non-children, examples.

4.1.2 Comparison Strategies. In the following sections, we discuss the results of a number of experiments conducted to demonstrate the need for a query suggestion modules specifically designed with young users in mind and showcase the correctness and effectiveness of *ReQuIK*. To give context to such results, we compared the performance of *ReQuIK* with that of a number of baseline and state-of-the-art strategies. We examine (the queries suggested by) *Google*, *Yahoo*, and *Bing*, given that children favor well-known search engines when performing information discovery tasks [5]. Given that we argue for the need of techniques tailored for children, we also consider a number of search engines designed exclusively for children, including: *AskKids*[27], *Kidzsearch*[29], *Ipl2*[22], *KidRex*[26], and *SweetSearch* [41]. We also include in our experiments CQS [38] (discussed in Section 2), which is a state-of-the-art alternative for generating queries tailored to children.

4.2 Usefulness of the Search Intent Module

In addition to the results reported in [9], which demonstrate the performance of the search intent module, we conducted an experiment for measuring the impact this module has for query recommendation. For doing so, we submitted each of the child-written queries in ReQ_{qs} to a number of popular search engines. Thereafter, we determined for which of these queries, the corresponding search engine provided suggestions.

As shown in Table 2, there is a consistent decrease in the number of children queries that can be handled by search engines, in terms of providing suggestions given a child-initiated query. This fact is evidenced in both commercial search engines and state-of-the-art systems such as CQS. Unlike its counterparts, *ReQuIK* is able to provide suggestions for 94% of the queries considered in this study, which is a clear indicator that taking advantage of a search intent module is beneficial not only to enhance the document retrieval process [9] but also the query recommendation process. While in Table 2 we report results on search engines favored by children, it is important to mention that those percentages remain so, even on search engines designed specially for children. This is anticipated, since many of the search tools for children are powered by Google's safe search (e.g., Ask.forkid.co) or do not offer query suggestions (e.g., Cybersleuth-kids.com and Kiddle.co). CQS is only able to generate suggestions for 57% of the children-generated queries in ReQ_{qs}, due to its candidate generation strategy that struggles with identifying suggestions for queries longer than four-grams.

Google	Bing	Yahoo!	Kidsearch	CQS	ReQuIK
46%	36%	65%	76%	57 %	94%

Table 2: Percentage of queries that trigger a recommendation in each compared system

4.3 Effectiveness of the Recommendations

As previously mentioned, there is a lack of datasets comprised of children queries and gathering and sharing children data to create such datasets is not trivial due to time and privacy concerns. Unfortunately, queries on ReQ_{qs} are not sufficient to train a deep neural network (i.e., ranking) model. In order to amend this issue, we train *ReQuIK*'s ranking model using children and non children oriented sentences in ReQ_{corp}. We hypothesize that these sentences are similar enough to a search query, permitting the modeled knowledge to be transferable to the query suggestion context. Therefore, to showcase the correctness of *ReQuIK*'s ranking strategy, we conducted two experiments. The first one measures the performance of the model in predicting whether a sentence is oriented for children or adults, and the second one measures how well this knowledge is transferred to the task of ranking children query suggestions.

	Wide	Deep	Wide and Deep
Accuracy	0.68	0.92	0.94

Table 3: Performance of diverse ranking strategies

For the first task we trained the model described in Section 3.3 using sentences from ReQ_{corp}. Note that sentences from Wikipedia were randomly sampled to make it comparable to that of the children data sources, which resulted in an evenly balanced dataset. We used a 10-cross-fold-validation framework for computing prediction accuracy, which was measured and averaged for each fold. This procedure was applied using the 3 different submodels with the aim of demonstrating the validity of combining both the wide and deep models. As reported in Table 3, the wide and deep model outperforms all its counterparts with a statistically significant improvement using a pairwise t-test with a confidence value $p < 0.05$.

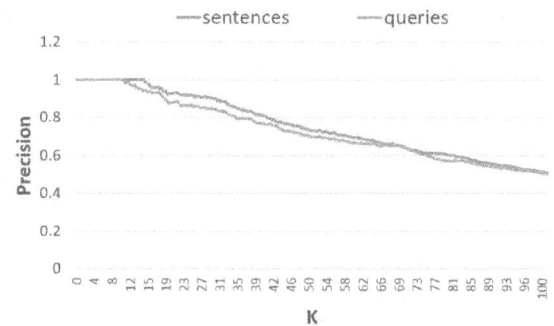

Figure 3: *Precision@K*, where *K* is defined as the percentage of queries and sentences analyzed. We define *K* as a percentage, as the raw counts of sentences and queries are not comparable otherwise

In order to demonstrate how this model can be translated to a more real query suggestion ranking environment we conducted an experiment where we ranked both sentences from ReQ_{corp} and queries from ReQ_{qs} using the model trained on sentences of ReQ_{corp}. Figure 3 illustrates the *Precision@K*, where *Precision* is measured as the ratio of children queries/sentences among the *K* considered and *K* indicates the proportion of ReQ_{qs} and ReQ_{corp} examined. As shown in the figure, the model achieves similar results for both the sentences and the queries, proving that a model trained over sentences can be translated to the context of ranking queries.

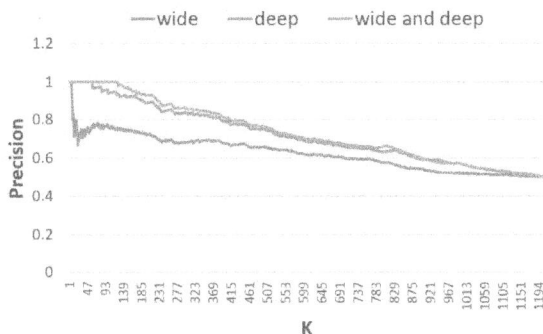

Figure 4: Model assessment based on *Precision@K*, **where** *K* **is the number of queries examined**

To further demonstrate the validity of each submodel (i.e., wide, deep, and wide and deep), we conducted an experiment using each of them. Figure 4 illustrates the *Precision@K*, in this case measured as the ratio of children queries among the top-k analyzed, for $K \in$ 1..1194. The wide and deep model outperforms both other models, followed closely by the deep model. The first adult result appears in position 123, 59, and 9, for the combined model, the deep model and the wide model respectively. Even if the suggestions of the wide model might look poor, Figure 4 illustrates that it complements the deep model improving the overall ranking.

It is worth mentioning that upon manual examination, we noticed that most of the queries in *ReQqs* labeled as "non-children" and ranked high by *ReQuIK* refer to content that could have been searched by children. For example, *"naruto shimpuden cheats"* ranked in 64th position by the deep and wide model refers to a videogame that could be equally of interest for young or mature audiences, and thus it is treated by *ReQuIK* as a false positive.

4.4 Suitability of Retrieved Documents

We conducted another experiment to verify the suitability of the documents retrieved in response to queries suggested by *ReQuIK* and to highlight the need of readability based filtering. For conducting this experiment, we generated suggestions for the child queries in *ReQqs* using popular search engines, children search engines, and *ReQuIK*. We treat as *suitable* documents that have readability levels matching the reading skills expected of children ages 6 to 13.

As children "systematically go through retrieved resources and rarely judge retrieved information sources" [18] we averaged the readability scores computed for the top-3 documents retrieved in response to each of the top-2 query suggestions generated by each evaluated strategy. For measuring readability, we use the well-known Flesch-Kincaid formula [15], which considers various textual features, such as term sentence length.

The results in Table 4 show that documents retrieved by *ReQuIK*'s recommendations are in general easier to read and understand than the ones retrieved by other search engines, even those that explicitly target children, or CQS [38]. This is evidenced by the fact that the average readability score of documents retrieved by recommendations of popular search engines is above 11 in all cases, while for *ReQuIK* is 7.7. This correlates with the grade level of a 13

ReQuIK	Google	Bing	Yahoo!	CQS
7.71	12.46	19.96	11.42	11.82
AskKids	**Ipl2**	**Sweet Search**	**KidRex**	**Kiddle**
13.3	10.9	12.3	12.7	12.83

Table 4: Average readability of top-3 documents retrieved for test query recommendations

year old child, usually in 7th or 8th grade, for which the results have been filtered for, demonstrating the benefits of a readability filtering strategy as part of the query suggestion process.

We are aware that Kiddle does not offer query suggestion, however, being the premier search engine for children [25], it needed to be part of this comparison. For this reason, we analyze the readability level of the top results retrieved by Kiddle for the children queries in *ReQqs*. Kiddle achieves an average readability of 12.83 on retrieved document, which is comparable to the one obtained by the engine that powers it, Google. These results provide further evidence for the need for query recommendation tools for children that lead to the retrieval of resources children can read and understand.

4.5 Online Assessment of ReQuIK

To further validate the performance of *ReQuIK*, we conducted an online survey intended to quantify the effectiveness of *ReQuIK* from a user's perspective. For doing so, we included in the survey 10 queries randomly selected among the ones written by children in *ReQqs*. These queries were not included among the ones used to train our wide and deep model presented in Section 3.3.3. To ensure diversity among sampled queries, we included unigrams and n-grams queries. We also considered question-type queries, which tend to be used by children. For each sampled query, we generated top-N suggestions using *ReQuIK*, a popular commercial search engine (Google), a popular children search engine (Kidzsearch), and CQS [24], the system discussed in Section 2, which explicitly provides children query suggestions. Note that some of the sampled queries were misspelled, as they are written by children. We purposefully left these queries as they were originally written, in order to be able to consider the effect of misspelled query terms and measure its impact on the suggestions offered by each strategy.

For each sampled query, we selected the top-2 suggestions from among the list of suggestions provided by each strategy, including *ReQuIK*. These suggestions were randomly merged into a list, which was then presented to a group of independent appraisers: teachers. Following Institutional Review Board guidelines, we recruited a cohort of teachers from 5 schools in Boise, Idaho. This gave us a total of 11 teachers that participated in this study. We considered teachers as ideal appraisers for this experiment, given that they know what children are particularly interested in and are trained on the needs of children; making them capable of offering knowledgeable judgments. In the survey, we used a practical scenario, which prompted the teachers to select the best two suggestions for each query that would lead a child to locate child-friendly and interesting web-pages from their view-point. We treated their selections as the *gold standard*.

We collected 181 responses for the survey (i.e., 10 teachers selected at most two suggestions for each of the 10 sampled queries), a snapshot of which is shown in Figure 5. For performance analysis we use accuracy of each query suggestion strategy *S*, computed as the fraction of suggestions selected by a teacher for a given query over the total number of suggestions generated by S. Based on the analysis of the collected responses, which we illustrate in Figure 6, we observe that appraisers favored suggestions created by search engines and recommendation modules that target children, i.e., *ReQuIK* and Kidzsearch, rather than the ones generated by general purpose engines, i.e., Google. We should mention that except for the case of unigram queries, *CQS* is consistently outperformed by the remaining considered strategies. We believe this is caused by the "novelty" of the majority of the queries included in the survey, which refer to contemporary topics of interest to children (such as names and characters in recent Disney movies), when *CQS* suggestions are based on pre-trained probabilistic models that may not account for the probability of occurrence of such query terms.

We observed that for queries that could have been formulated by either children or more mature audiences, Google has an advantage. For example, for the query *"how do seahorses swim"* suggestions offered by Google were preferred almost exclusively over suggestions generated using any of the counterparts in this study. We hypothesize that this is due to the fact that Google's suggestions are based on common query formulations, which in this case leads to better suggestions, as they do not necessarily have to focus on the retrieval of child-related resources. On the other hand, we observed that for other queries, bias towards children content, as in the case of Kidzsearch, *CQS*, and *ReQuIK*, positively affected the suggestion-selection process. For example, for the query *"Elsa"*, the top-2 suggestions generated by using Google were *"Elsa Pataky"* and *"Elsa Hosk"*, which are names of two popular celebrities. The suggestion most likely to be preferred by a child–as per teacher responses–is *"Elsa and Anna"*, which was not included among the top-2 suggestions of Google, but was presented as the top suggestions using *ReQuIK*.

ReQuIK achieved the highest accuracy, as it consistently offered child-friendly suggestions for unigram, bigram and n-gram queries. Based on a paired t-test, the improvement in the *overall* performance of *ReQuIK* with respect to each of its counterparts is statistically significant with $p < 0.05$.

5 SCOPE AND LIMITATIONS

We highlight below limitations we encountered in designing *ReQuIK*; which we could not address due to the project scope.

ReQuIK is a query recommendation system for children. The project is intended to explore the personalization aspect of the query recommendation task for children. Therefore, common tasks performed in traditional query recommendation systems, such as candidate generation or topic filtering do not suppose a novelty by themselves, and thus, are not extensively explored in this paper. We are also aware that both Flesch-Kincaid and Spache are simple readability formulas, which sometimes lack precision, an issue that is usually highlighted when the text is short. This constraint for short documents is common for all readability formulas and to solve it is out of scope for this project.

ReQuIK is a system that is meant to integrate and complement existing search engines, as opposed to function as a standalone tool. Consequently, tasks that are usually performed by the search engine itself, such as document retrieval and ranking, are omitted from the assessment of this project.

Due to project scope, the presented online experiment is meant to gather initial feedback on the quality of *ReQuIK*'s suggestions, as the

Query Suggestions for Children

Imagine "Sven" is a young child using a search engine. To start a search, Sven uses the phrases below. In each case, which two suggestions will lead Sven to find child friendly and interesting web pages?

* Required

Sven wrote "Math", I would encourage him to use: *

☐ math games played for germany national-sports

☐ mathway

☐ math games

☐ math playground

☐ math games played for brazil national-sports

☐ math riddles for kids

☐ mathletics

☐ math worksheets for kids

Figure 5: Snapshot of online survey presented to teachers for overall assessment of *ReQuIK* and other strategies

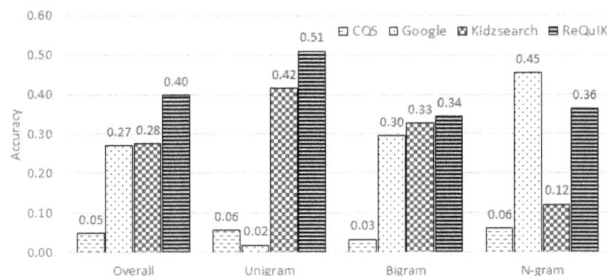

Figure 6: Comparison of query recommendation systems

experiment is based only on a small set of sampled queries. Given the promising results, we will conduct further online assessments.

Finally, user interaction and perceived usability of *ReQuIK*, as well as its effectiveness in terms of offering suggestions that lead to child friendly websites, are beyond the scope of this work, but will be addressed as future work (see Section 6).

6 CONCLUSIONS AND FUTURE WORK

In this paper, we presented *ReQuIK* a multi-perspective query recommendation system specifically tailored to facilitate information-seeking tasks for children. *ReQuIK* takes advantage of multiple strategies that inform the process of generating query suggestions and prioritize queries that are of interest to children. For assessing the performance of the system we conducted a study in collaboration with teachers of four different schools in the area of Idaho, where 97 students used our framework to complete factual and research/informational search tasks assigned to them by their teacher. We also conducted a user study to gather feedback from the teachers themselves. Using the set of queries written by children, we conducted a number of empirical analysis and demonstrated the validity of our proposed strategy and its value, in terms of offering up-to-date suggestions aimed at helping children with their information-seeking needs.

The technical contributions associated with our research work include (i) introducing a strategy which takes advantage of a search intent for capturing the purpose for which the query was written, (ii) creating a novel wide and deep neural network which considers both the raw text and traits frequently associated with child-related queries, (iii) employing a strategy to train a model based on children/non-children oriented resources that transfers well to the query suggestion context, (iv) explicitly considering the readability levels of both the query and results retrieved by the candidate suggestions, favoring the ones that leads to the retrieval of content that will be easier to read, (v) using a whole pipeline that considers multiple perspectives for candidate query generation, and (vi) creating a dataset comprised of children and non-children queries that can be used by the research community at large for children-related research.

In the future, we will extend the candidate query suggestion process by also considering phrases extracted from children corpora provided it evolves over time. In addition, we are aware that the range of 6 to 13 years can be too broad, as the interest of a 6 year old child are not the same as that of a 13 year old. Therefore, we plan to extend *ReQuIK* so that it is able to generate recommendation for more specific age ranges. Moreover, we plan to extend the manner in which resource readability is computed, to account for information beyond text, such as the different aesthetics of web pages, which can impact the level of complexity of resources. Finally, while in this paper we evaluated *ReQuIK* (and other query suggestions modules), in terms of offering queries that are suitable for children, in the future, we plan to conduct a user study to verify the degree to which *ReQuIK* leads to the retrieval of children-related resources and facilitates information discovery tasks for children.

ACKNOWLEDGMENTS

This work has been supported in part by the National Science Foundation Award Number 1565937.

REFERENCES

[1] Ubersuggest. http://ubersuggest.io, Accessed: 2017-05-18.
[2] J. Albright, C. de Guzman, A. Acebo, D. Paiva, M. Faulkner, and J. Swanson. Readability of patient education materials: implications for clinical practice. *Applied Nursing Research*, 9(3):139–143, 1996.
[3] A. Anagnostopoulos, L. Becchetti, C. Castillo, and A. Gionis. An optimization framework for query recommendation. In *ACM WSDM*, pages 161–170, 2010.
[4] Backlinco. How to find long tail keywords. http://backlinko.com/long-tail-keywords, Accessed: 2017-05-18.
[5] D. Bilal and R. Ellis. Evaluating leading web search engines on children's queries. In *Human-Computer Interaction. Users and Applications*, pages 549–558. Springer, 2011.
[6] J. S. Chall and E. Dale. *Readability revisited: The new Dale-Chall readability formula*. Brookline Books, 1995.
[7] H.-T. Cheng, L. Koc, J. Harmsen, T. Shaked, T. Chandra, H. Aradhye, G. Anderson, G. Corrado, W. Chai, M. Ispir, et al. Wide & deep learning for recommender systems. In *Deep Learning for Recommender Systems workshop*, pages 7–10, 2016.
[8] Dogo. News, book, and movie reviews for kids by kids. https://www.dogonews.com, 2017.
[9] N. Dragovic, I. Madrazo Azpiazu, and M. S. Pera. Is sven seven?: A search intent module for children. In *ACM SIGIR*, pages 885–888, 2016.
[10] A. Druin, E. Foss, L. Hatley, E. Golub, M. L. Guha, J. Fails, and H. Hutchinson. How children search the internet with keyword interfaces. In *SIGCHI*, pages 89–96, 2009.
[11] S. Duarte Torres, D. Hiemstra, and P. Serdyukov. An analysis of queries intended to search information for children. In *IIiX*, pages 235–244, New York, NY, USA, 2010. ACM.
[12] S. Duarte Torres, D. Hiemstra, I. Weber, and P. Serdyukov. Query recommendation for children. In *ACM CIKM*, pages 2010–2014, 2012.
[13] C. Eickhoff, T. Polajnar, K. Gyllstrom, S. D. Torres, and R. Glassey. Web search query assistance functionality for young audiences. In *Advances in Information Retrieval*, pages 776–779. Springer, 2011.
[14] C. Eickhoff, P. Serdyukov, and A. P. de Vries. Web page classification on child suitability. In *ACM CIKM*, pages 1425–1428. ACM, 2010.
[15] R. Flesch. A new readability yardstick. *Journal of Applied Psychology*, 32(3):221, 1948.
[16] E. Foss, A. Druin, R. Brewer, P. Lo, L. Sanchez, E. Golub, and H. Hutchinson. Children's search roles at home: Implications for designers, researchers, educators, and parents. *JASIST*, 63(3):558–573, 2012.
[17] T. Gossen, J. Höbel, and A. Nürnberger. A comparative study about children's and adults' perception of targeted web search engines. In *SIGCHI*, pages 1821–1824, 2014.
[18] L. Graham and P. T. Metaxas. Of course it's true; i saw it on the internet!: critical thinking in the internet era. *Communications of the ACM*, 46(5):70–75, 2003.
[19] J. Gwizdka and D. Bilal. Analysis of children's queries and click behavior on ranked results and their thought processes in google search. In *ACM CHIIR*, pages 377–380, 2017.
[20] A. Halavais. *Search engine society*. John Wiley & Sons, 2013.
[21] S. Hochreiter and J. Schmidhuber. Long short-term memory. *Neural computation*, 9(8):1735–1780, 1997.
[22] Ilp2. Search engine. http://www.Ilp2.com, 2017.
[23] K. in mind. Data source for kids. https://www.kids-in-mind.com, 2017.
[24] S. Karimi and M. S. Pera. Recommendations to enhance children web searches. *ACM RecSys*, 2015.
[25] L. Keating. Kiddle search engine is the google for kids. http://www.techtimes.com/articles/136639/20160225/kiddle-search-engine-kids.htm, Accessed: 2017-05-18.
[26] Kidrex. Safe search for kids. http://www.KidRex.org, 2017.
[27] A. kids. Search engine. http://www.askkids.com, 2017.
[28] E. Kids. Data source for kids. http://www.edutainingkids.com, 2017.
[29] KidzSearch. Web search engine for kids. http://www.kidzsearch.com, 2017.
[30] Kidzvuz. Data source for kids. https://www.kidzvuz.com, 2017.
[31] D. Kingma and J. Ba. Adam: A method for stochastic optimization. *arXiv preprint arXiv:1412.6980*, 2014.
[32] A. Krizhevsky, I. Sutskever, and G. E. Hinton. Imagenet classification with deep convolutional neural networks. In *Advances in Neural Information Processing Systems*, pages 1097–1105, 2012.
[33] S. Lai, L. Xu, K. Liu, and J. Zhao. Recurrent convolutional neural networks for text classification. In *AAAI*, pages 2267–2273, 2015.
[34] Y. Li, D. McLean, Z. A. Bandar, J. D. O'shea, and K. Crockett. Sentence similarity based on semantic nets and corpus statistics. *IEEE TKDE*, 18(8):1138–1150, 2006.
[35] C. D. Manning, M. Surdeanu, J. Bauer, J. Finkel, S. J. Bethard, and D. McClosky. The Stanford CoreNLP natural language processing toolkit. In *ACL System Demonstrations*, pages 55–60, 2014.
[36] J. Palotti, G. Zuccon, and A. Hanbury. The influence of pre-processing on the estimation of readability of web documents. In *ACM CIKM*, pages 1763–1766, 2015.
[37] RaisingChildren. Data source for kids. http://raisingchildren.net.au, 2017.
[38] M. Shaikh, M. S. Pera, and Y.-K. Ng. Suggesting simple and comprehensive queries to elementary-grade children. In *IEEE/WIC/ACM WI-IAT*, volume 1, pages 252–259, 2015.
[39] G. Spache. A new readability formula for primary-grade reading materials. *The Elementary School Journal*, 53(7):410–413, 1953.
[40] Spaghetti. Book reviews by kids for kids. http://www.spaghettibookclub.org, 2017.
[41] Sweetsearch. A search engine for students. http://www.sweetsearch.com, 2017.
[42] S. D. Torres, D. Hiemstra, I. Weber, and P. Serdyukov. Query recommendation in the information domain of children. *JASIST*, 65(7):1368–1384, 2014.
[43] Toyinsider. Data source for kids. http://www.thetoyinsider.com, 2017.
[44] A. Usta, I. S. Altingovde, I. B. Vidinli, R. Ozcan, and Ö. Ulusoy. How k-12 students search for learning?: analysis of an educational search engine log. In *ACM SIGIR*, pages 1151–1154, 2014.
[45] N. Vanderschantz, A. Hinze, and S. J. Cunningham. "sometimes the internet reads the question wrong": Children's search strategies & difficulties. *JASIST*, 51(1):1–10, 2014.
[46] I. B. Vidinli and R. Ozcan. New query suggestion framework and algorithms: A case study for an educational search engine. *Information Processing & Management*, 52(5):733–752, 2016.
[47] A. Wood and Y.-K. Ng. Orthogonal query recommendations for children. In *iiWAS*, pages 298–302, 2016.
[48] Yahoo! Academic Relations. L13 - yahoo! search query tiny sample. http://webscope.sandbox.yahoo.com/catalog.php.
[49] H. Zamani, M. Bendersky, X. Wang, and M. Zhang. Situational context for ranking in personal search. In *WWW*, pages 1531–1540, 2017.
[50] Z. Zhang and O. Nasraoui. Mining search engine query logs for query recommendation. In *WWW*, pages 1039–1040, 2006.

Improving Exploration of Topic Hierarchies: Comparative Testing of Simplified Library of Congress Subject Heading Structures

Jesse David Dinneen
School of Information Management
Victoria University of Wellington
jesse.dinneen@vuw.ac.nz

Banafsheh Asadi
Ilja Frissen
Fei Shu
Charles-Antoine Julien
School of Information Studies
McGill University

ABSTRACT

Many large digital collections are organized by sorting their items into topics and arranging these topics hierarchically, such as those displayed in a tree view. The resulting information organization structures mitigate some of the challenges of searching digital information realms; however, the topic hierarchies are often large and complex, and thus difficult to navigate. Automated techniques have been shown to produce significantly smaller, simplified versions of existing topic hierarchies while preserving access to the majority of the collection, but these simplified topic hierarchies have never been tested with human participants, and so it is not clear what effect simplification would have on the exploration and use of such structures for browsing and retrieval. This study partly addresses this gap by performing a comparative test with three groups of university students (N=62) performing ten topic hierarchy exploration tasks using one of three versions of the Library of Congress Subject Headings (LCSH) hierarchy: 1) the original LCSH hierarchy, acting as a baseline, 2) a shallower version of 1), and 3) a narrower version of 2). A quantitative analysis of measures of accuracy, time, and browsing shows that participants using the simplified trees were significantly more accurate and faster than those using the unmodified tree, and the narrower, balanced tree was also faster than the shallower tree. These results show that automated topic hierarchy simplification can facilitate the use of such hierarchies, which has implications for the development of information organization theory and human-information interaction techniques for similar information structures.

CCS CONCEPTS

• **Human-centered computing** → *Empirical studies in HCI*; *User studies*; *Information visualization*; • **Information systems** → Document topic models;

KEYWORDS

Organization of information, topic hierarchies, trees, browsing, comparative testing, Library of Congress Subject Headings (LCSH)

ACM Reference Format:
Jesse David Dinneen, Banafsheh Asadi, Ilja Frissen, Fei Shu, and Charles-Antoine Julien. 2018. Improving Exploration of Topic Hierarchies: Comparative Testing of Simplified Library of Congress Subject Heading Structures. In *CHIIR '18: 2018 Conference on Human Information Interaction & Retrieval, March 11–15, 2018, New Brunswick, NJ, USA*. ACM, New York, NY, USA, Article 4, 8 pages. https://doi.org/10.1145/3176349.3176385

1 INTRODUCTION

To successfully use current tools for searching digital information users must generally possess or acquire the vocabulary used by the authors of the relevant documents, express their information need with this vocabulary, and avoid problems of polysemy that plague textual information retrieval systems. These demands can be partly mitigated by topic hierarchies that users can browse to discover domain vocabulary and retrieve documents [1, 2, 21, 25], but real-world topic hierarchies are large and sparsely populated by their collection, making them difficult to use for retrieval and exploration. Julien et al. [18] describe an automated approach to simplify topic hierarchies by reducing the number and nesting of sub-topics, and without losing access to the removed topics' documents, but the benefits and drawbacks of such approaches have yet to be tested experimentally.

This paper presents the first results of an experimental test of the effects of structural simplification on hierarchy exploration as described by Julien et al. [18]. Human participants performed tasks using different versions of the Library of Congress Subject Headings (LCSH), which is the dominant topical vocabulary in North-American, widely used by English-language academic libraries across the world. The LCSH structure is a case study of a working, evolving, large topical hierarchy containing over 240K topics, and is currently used by hundreds of thousands university students, faculty, and staff; works focusing on LCSH-organized collections therefore have the potential to improve topic and searching tools. In the following sections, we explicate the problem area by reviewing relevant literature, detail the study's research questions and methodology, and review and discuss the results of the study.

1.1 Topic Hierarchies

Textual information retrieval over unstructured text collections entails inherent limitations. For example, when facing unsatisfactory search results, users may need to formulate multiple queries, consider long lists of often irrelevant items, and possess or hope to stumble upon adequate search vocabulary; this can be frustrating and time consuming [9]. There is therefore a growing interest towards supporting more exploratory search, especially when searchers are seeking information in unfamiliar domains where they may not initially possess adequate search vocabulary, and information structures allow for such exploration [1, 2, 21, 25].

Drawing upon information foraging theory [27] to model the human-information interaction process [e.g., 4], Julien et al. [18] characterize the exploration of topic hierarchies as a series of decision points whose options are either to expand a topic (i.e., reveal narrower terms), return to a previously visited topic, or continue extracting value from the current topic (i.e., viewing its documents). Topic hierarchies are often very large; however, the algorithm provided by Julien et al. [18] reduces the number of decisions and their difficulty, which should facilitate the navigation and exploration of topic hierarchies.

Julien et al. [18] describe an algorithm that aims to mitigate the issues of navigating large topic hierarchies by opportunistically modifying a topic hierarchy by exploiting one of their known common features: topics' document access follow a skewed distribution such that a small group of topics provides access to most of the documents while most topics are assigned to very few documents. Skewed distributions are found in various knowledge domains [10, 26] and are common in organized information [19, 23, 30]. Capitalizing on this trend, the simplification algorithm presented by Julien et al. [18] reduces the size and depth of a collection's topic hierarchy by pruning the topics that are not representative of that collection.

The simplification described by [18] is achieved in two ways. First, to reduce the number of browsing decision points a compression operation reduces the depth of the structure by removing those topics that provide access to relatively little or no documents of their own. Second, to facilitate the remaining decisions the algorithm performs a pruning operation to ensure a manageable number of related topic choices per broader topic: it removes narrower topics that provide access to a statistically marginal proportion of the collection's documents. The combination of compression and pruning was shown to have dramatic effects on the topologies or shapes of the Medical Subject Headings (MeSH) and the LCSH hierarchies: the simplified hierarchies are significantly smaller, in terms of size, breadth, and depth, while still providing access to over 95% of their respective collections. This is significant for such large topic structures are known to be difficult to use by untrained users; indeed, the National Library of Medicine (NLM) has admitted to the need for online tools to facilitate the exploration of the MeSH topic structure [5].

Although the approach taken by Julien et al. [18] is statistically promising, it has potential benefits and drawbacks to exploratory searching and browsing, and these have not been identified. Thus it remains unclear if human participants can effectively use the simplified topic structures with minimal effort and what effect the simplification has on participants' information behavior during exploration. This study begins to address these gaps in knowledge.

1.2 Related Studies

To our knowledge, the problem of automatically modifying a topic structure for the purpose of human-information interaction has received scant attention. Many prior works concern the generation and modification of topic hierarchies or similar structures, however. Although the initial data and objectives differ from the present study, perhaps the most closely related prior work is a reconstruction of the Dewey Decimal Classification (DDC) for automatic text classification [30], in which the authors balance the hierarchy so that documents are evenly distributed among the topics. This line of research contrasts with prior topic structure browsing applications that assume searchers will use the same structure as professional subject indexers [15, 20, 22, 28, 31, for example].

Additional works have focused on automated or semi-automated techniques to mitigate the scalability and cost of manual topic indexing in various domains, for example by providing vocabulary suggestions from the DDC to improve the consistency and number of access points in social media tags [12], and on the evaluation of such techniques [13]. The potential of such techniques has created questions concerning the value of manual indexing: while human-indexed terms, without structure, can be as effective as some automatic processes in some contexts [29], a detailed review of prior works shows conflicting results that suggest little or no advantage to manual term indexing in many contexts [24]. Works such as these are concerned with comparing the use and value of manual and automatic processes for creating topic hierarchies, whereas the present study is an investigation into the effects of automated modifications to existing topic hierarchies, whether created manually or automatically, on users' exploration of such hierarchies. Our assumptions are that a hierarchy of topics, no matter how it was created, can facilitate information exploration, and that its structure should be designed to favor its navigation by humans.

The topic structure modification approach provided by Julien et al. [18] is analogous to non-linear degree-of-interest value (DOI) approaches [e.g., 11]. However, such approaches assume the DOI decreases linearly with distance between nodes (i.e., browsing decision points). The assumption of Julien et al. [18], maintained also in the present study, is that unlike the physical world, distance in the digital world entails marginal *travel cost*; therefore, our DOI value considers that the few topics that are highly representative of the collection are more interesting to users than most other topics, which provide little or no access to the collection. There are other non-linear DOI distortion interfaces [16], but none use the distribution of the collection to reshape a topic hierarchy for the purpose of facilitating document retrieval.

Finally, Julien and Tirilly [17] further enhanced the simplification algorithm presented by Julien et al. [18] by increasing access to documents not accessible from multiple topics. While that enhancement is promising for increasing the quality of the resulting topic tree, its added prohibitive computational costs currently prevent its real-time use when simplifying large hierarchies, and so it is not tested here.

2 RESEARCH QUESTIONS

The outcomes of exploratory searching or browsing tasks are difficult to define [3], but we consider two outcomes of exploratory browsing in a topic structure to be: 1) the user finds valuable documents about a topic, and 2) the user acquires new domain vocabulary by reading topic labels and their relations with other topics. The simplified LCSH topic trees produced using the approach given by [18] are promising with regards to outcome (1): their overall shape suggests they are easier to browse since (a) their users must make fewer browsing decisions before reaching the boundaries of a shallower tree, and (b) each decision is made from a more predictable and smaller number of related topics. It is tempting to assume that a smaller structure with little or no loss of document access is likely to benefit users, but the approach does have drawbacks regarding outcome (2) – i.e., users may be exposed to fewer topic labels and thus acquire fewer terms from the relevant vocabulary – and these may outweigh the benefits of a smaller hierarchy to outcome (1).

As the pruning threshold increases, a larger proportion of topics progressively disappear. Although access to the collection is preserved during this, the process does radically change the topic structure. The logic of the hierarchy is always respected (i.e., broader topics remain broader than any of their descendants) but the distances, in terms of number of topics, between remaining dense topics is greatly reduced. It is therefore possible that the remaining topic labels force too large of a semantic distance between a topic and its narrower topics, which may make it difficult for users to quickly grasp how a topic is related to its parent, siblings, or children.

This report therefore seeks to answer the following research questions:

RQ1 Do users attempting to complete topic structure exploration tasks perform better (e.g., more frequently successful and in less time) with a simplified topic tree? What are the independent effects of compression and pruning on performance?

RQ2 What are the effects of the simplification on users' information behavior (e.g., number of topics inspected)?

Answers to these questions will suggest if the simplified trees are an improvement on the unmodified tree for exploration and if they have negative effects on users' information behavior.

3 METHODOLOGY

The objective of this study is to isolate potential effects of hierarchy simplification on users' task performance and information behavior during information exploration. Towards this we performed a between-subject experiment where 3 groups of 20 randomized, remote participants perform without supervision the same 10 topic-location tasks using one of three versions of a topic hierarchy according to their group: 1) the unmodified hierarchy acting as a baseline, 2) a compressed version of 1), or 3) a pruned version of 2). This design controls variability from users by randomly assigning each participant to a single, adequately large group, and variability from tasks by having participants perform the same tasks in different, random orders, which reduces variability to our independent variable: topic hierarchy modification. This section describes the data set, variables, tasks, participants, procedure, and hypotheses used.

3.1 Data set used

Maintained by the Library of Congress (LC) since 1898, LCSH is a controlled vocabulary (CV) that has been continuously evolving for the creation of topical access points and their assignment to bibliographic records. Despite perennial criticisms centered on cost, scalability, and consistency, LCSH is the standard CV used to organize the collections of most academic libraries in the United States and throughout the world. LCSH is therefore a promising case study of a widely implemented, large, and mature general knowledge topic model or thesaurus.

A collection organized using LCSH is comprised of two data sources: 1) bibliographic records that are indexed by topic with at least one topical LCSH string, and 2) the LCSH *authority* records that contain the *established* topical LCSH strings and their broader topics, which define the topical LCSH hierarchy. Our data set is comprised of 1) a collection of 122,197 bibliographic records from a major North American university's Science and Engineering library, and 2) its roughly 205,000 LCSH authority records. The domain of science was selected as an extreme test for this study since it offers the deepest and most connected portion of the LCSH structure [19, 32].

3.2 Independent variable: topic tree

LCSH authority records contain broader/narrower term relationships, but the LCSH system was not originally conceived as a hierarchical thesaurus; therefore, original work is required to connect the topic branches to form a structure that can be displayed as a tree view. Julien et al. [19] retrofitted LCSH into a topical hierarchy to enable its presentation as seen in this study. The process extracts the LCSH strings assigned to the bibliographic collection, which are matched to an authority record to place each bibliographic record in the LCSH hierarchy. Topics in LCSH (and similar structures like MeSH) have multiple immediate broader terms (i.e., parent topics), which requires duplicating narrower terms and their descendants under each parent (called *multiple inheritance*). The outcome of this data set preparation is a subset of the LCSH topical structure represented as a true hierarchy or *tree* that contains the collection; this topical structure serves as the initial, unmodified baseline LCSH tree, herein referred to as the *initial tree*.

To assess the effect of compression and pruning, two simplified trees are tested against the initial: 1) a strictly compressed tree, and 2) a fully simplified tree that is both compressed and pruned. The compressed-only tree is herein referred to as *C95* to indicate that retained hierarchy level assignments must make up at least 5% of the documents accessible from it and all its descendants. The third, fully simplified tree is a further modification of C95 that is also pruned using a 0.2% threshold, herein referred to as *C95P02* (i.e., compression 95%, pruning 0.2%). This entails that narrower terms are retained if they provide at least 0.2% additional access to the collection as compared to their larger, retained sibling topics. These thresholds are selected to produce the most dramatic structural changes to LCSH while having minimal effect on access to the collection, as demonstrated by Julien et al. [18]. Therefore, the

Table 1: A statistical comparison of the shape of the tested topic trees.

	Initial	C95	C95P02
Narrower terms per parent (mean)	1.5	1.5	1.3
Balance (SD^{-1} of narrower terms)	0.24	0.19	0.45
Depth (mean)	17.4	8.6	9.0
Size (unique topics)	21,658	19,064	8,007
Size (total tree topics including duplicates)	2,555,589	970,807	482,216

Table 2: Tasks (10) tested in random order and their respective targets' depths in each tree.

Target	Initial	C95	C95P02
Crops	5	4	4
Culture	1	1	1
Geometry	6	5	6
Grain drying	8	7	7
Hjelmslev planes	9	8	9
Nanotechnology	4	4	4
Personality	7	5	5
Source refondening	n/a	n/a	n/a
Transportation engineering	4	3	3
War	2	2	2

experiment's *independent variable* is: topic tree (3 levels: initial; C95; C95P02).

Table 1 describes the tested trees in terms of their *mean breadth* (i.e., narrower terms per parent), *balance* (i.e., predictability of the number of narrower terms per parent as expressed by the inverse of its standard deviation or SD^{-1}), *mean depth*, and *size*, which is defined in terms of unique topics and total tree topics including duplicate topics resulting from multiple inheritance. It shows that C95 is significantly shallower than the initial tree, and C95P02 is shallower, narrower, more balanced, and clearly smaller than the other trees.

Figure 1 illustrates the structural differences between the three trees using collated screenshots of the testing engine where the same topic and sub-topic have been expanded in all three trees. The initial and C95 trees have a greater number of narrower terms per topic than C95P02, which is clearly smaller given that it is fully visible while the others would require scrolling. C95P02's improved balance is reflected by encountering a smaller and relatively consistent number of narrower terms at each decision point, while the smaller depth of both modified trees entails that users are asked to perform fewer browsing decisions before encountering the boundaries of the topic hierarchy. Taken as a whole, Table 1 and Figure 1 suggest that the independent variable levels differ adequately to enable testing the effect they may have on the performance and behavior of participants performing the following tasks.

3.3 Tasks

An obvious assumption is that browsing for a target topic (hereafter called *target*) in a very large tree versus the same target in a much smaller tree would necessarily favor the smaller of the two; although intuitive, it may be that the structural modifications to simplify the LCSH hierarchy have in fact lessened its semantic expressivity and discoverability. The initial, unmodified LCSH tree might be systematically favored if task targets were strictly absent topics pruned in C95P02, but this may not be true given that the targeted semantic regions might in fact be deeply buried in the much larger initial LCSH tree. Therefore, this initial experiment tests only topic targets that are present in all three trees, while future experiments will consider targets as semantically equivalent topical regions where the same collection documents are found.

Table 2 displays the ten chosen tasks and their shallowest depths in each tree (i.e., the minimal number of steps required to reach the

target). Task design controlled for topic depth by asking participants to find broad topics near the root (e.g., *culture*, depth 1) and specific topics found deeper in the tree (e.g., *Hjelmslev planes*, a geometric concept, depth 9). Two tasks (5 and 6) required finding a target seen previously along the path to an earlier task's target. Tasks were randomized for each participant, but tasks 5 and 6 always came after the tasks that would provide the initial sighting. An impossible task was designed to test participants' information behavior in terms of search resilience that consisted of a seemingly credible but invented term, *Source refondening*, not covered by LCSH.

3.4 Participants

We recruited 62 fluent English-speaking university students (64% undergraduate, 36% graduate students) who were not familiar with LCSH and have English as one of their first languages. Selected participants were sent instructions to download the testing software to run on their own machine when they had the time to do so. Fifty-one participants (82%) agreed to provide their demographic data. Of these, 60% are female, 40% study science and engineering, 40% study information studies, and 20% study other topics (e.g., literature, economics, nursing, environmental science, law). The group's mean age was 22.8 years (SD 4.2). Familiarity with LCSH could make tasks unrepresentatively easy, but 96% of our participants reported that they are either not at all familiar with LCSH or they have simply never used it before. The prevalence of participants with little or no knowledge of LCSH, including those in information studies, may be indicative of the lack of widely available and usable tools to help users find information by navigating and exploring its structure of related topics.

3.5 Instrumentation and Procedure

Traditional tree views were chosen for displaying the topic trees because of the likelihood that they would be instantly recognized by participants and usable with little training. Participants downloaded the software, packaged in a single executable file, and ran it on their computers running Windows XP or newer. The download links provided in email randomly assigned each participant to one of the three tested trees (i.e., initial, C95, or C95P02) until each group consisted of at least 20 participants. The testing software presents pages sequentially, like an *install wizard*, to the participant:

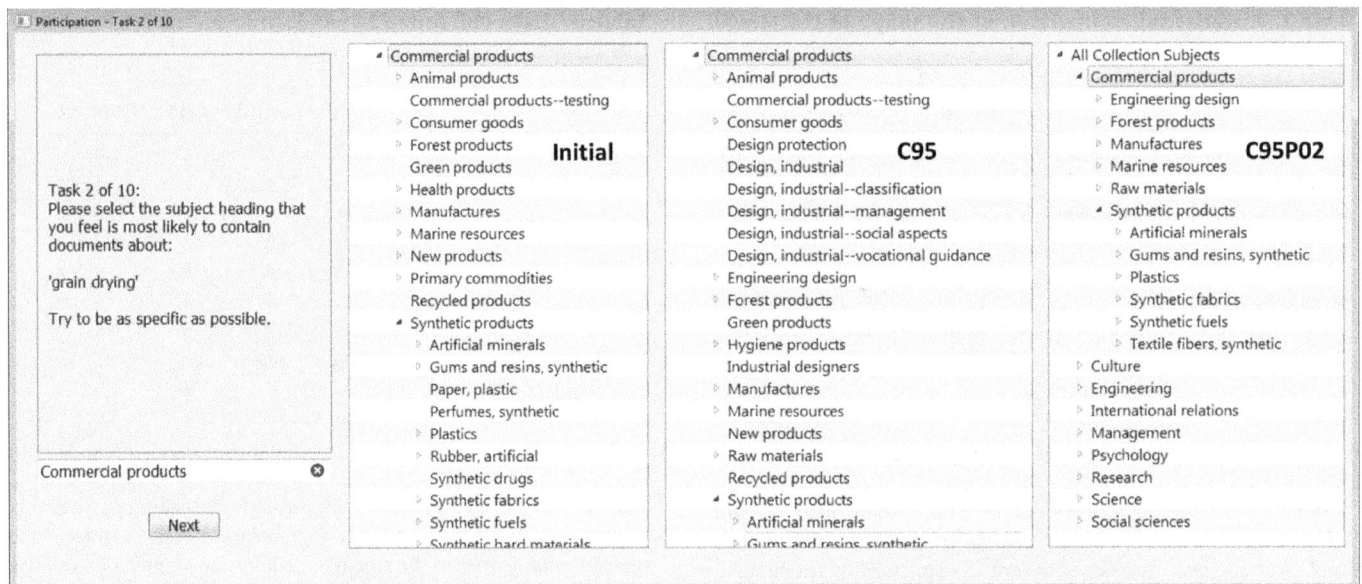

Figure 1: Collated screenshots of testing engine interface showing structural differences between the tested trees. Each participant sees and performs tasks using only one of the three trees, randomly assigned, and is not made aware of the other trees. Participants complete tasks by selecting terms in the tree using the mouse; a selected term appears for review in the text box (left), which does not allow input (e.g., keyword searching is not possible).

(1) Greets them and presents the consent form (consent is required to proceed).

(2) Offers a guided learning task to experience working with the system and browsing the tree during their participation, and asks them to complete their participation in a single, uninterrupted sitting.

(3) Asks the participant to complete the 10 browsing tasks listed in Table 2. Participants complete tasks using one of the three tree versions (Initial, C95, or C95P02) and are not made aware of the other versions. Tasks are completed by using the mouse to find and select a target topic in the displayed LCSH tree, and clicking the *next* button to proceed. Blank answers were accepted but regarded as incorrect during analysis. Tasks were randomized for each participant as described below.

(4) Presents two questionnaires (see Figure 2) that assess the participant's experience in performing the tasks (e.g., Nasa Task-Load Index (TLX) [14] and Technology Acceptance Model (TAM) questionnaires [7, 8]).

(5) Transfers the collected task and questionnaire data via secure File Transfer Protocol (sFTP) to the researchers' server.

(6) Tells the participant how to collect a $15 remuneration for their participation.

(7) Thanks the participant and exits the application.

Since participants could download and run the software on their own systems, task completion was possible in a natural setting relying on participants' own aptitudes and pace (i.e., there was no experiment administrator present to potentially add performance pressures). The testing software was developed using open-source tools, including Python 3.5 and the Qt 5 graphical framework to provide a recognizable graphical user interface. Three versions were compiled using PyInstaller to provide executable binaries of the experiment software, each implementing one of the three tree versions (i.e., initial, C95, and C95P02). The test data is saved to JSON-formatted text file that is sent to the researchers' server using secure FTP.

3.6 Dependent Variables

The data collected consists of post-test questionnaire responses, participants' task answers, and click events with timestamps. These enable measuring the participants' task success (achieved by selecting the correct topic as a task answer), the amount of time taken to complete each task, and the information behavior exhibited during each task, defined here as the topic browsing events *selecting*, *expanding*, and *contracting* topics in the tree. This simple and restrictive definition of information behavior was chosen to make clear any broad differences in behavior between the trees, and is consistent with the information foraging conception of information behavior [27] since it measures movement between *patches* of information (in this case, the LCSH topic labels). Conversely, a lack of significant differences would indicate that such a definition of information behavior is not sensitive enough to capture differences in behavior. The results of the post-tests (see procedure step 4 and Figure 2) are not presented in this report.

3.7 Pilot Testing

Piloting of the experimental procedure was first conducted in a controlled environment using three successive, live participants who were recruited within our department, observed by the researchers,

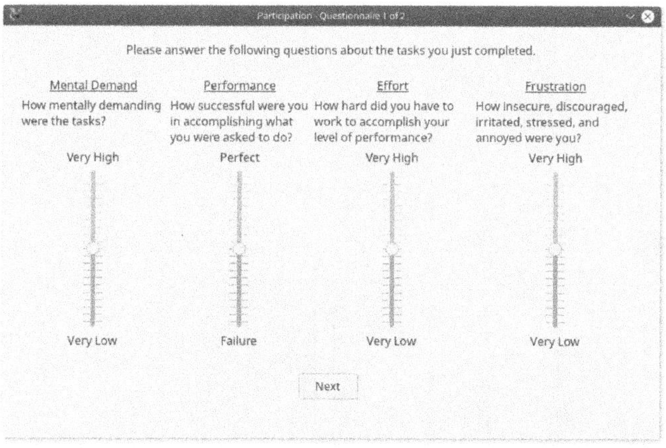

Figure 2: Screenshot of testing engine post-test questionnaire.

and recorded by screen capture software. Each of the three participants tested one of the three tested trees (i.e., initial, C95, or C95P02). The resulting data were then verified, and as minor usability issues were identified appropriate modifications to the testing engine and procedure were made until the experiment software was deemed ready to be run asynchronously without researcher intervention. The pilot suggested the entire process would require 15-60 minutes from each participant, depending on which version of the tree they would be randomly assigned.

3.8 Hypotheses

Corresponding to the research questions posed above, the following hypotheses are formulated for statistical verification. RQ1 will be answered by measures of task time and success; therefore, the following null hypotheses were tested:

> $RQ1_{TimeNull}$: There is no difference between participants' performance in terms of task time between the three trees.
> $RQ1_{AccNull}$: There is no difference between participants' performance in terms of task success between the three trees.

RQ2 is answered by counting the number of topics selected by participants across the three trees as tested by the following null hypothesis:

> $RQ2_{BrowseEventsNull}$: There is no difference between the number of topics selected by participants across the three trees.

4 RESULTS

4.1 Data analysis

Group means were calculated for the following three dependent measures (see panels of Figure 3):

> *Correct answers*: percentage of the ten tasks that the participants answered correctly (i.e., task success). In this preliminary analysis we regard a correct answer only as one providing the exact topic target sought in a task, and an incorrect answer as one providing any other topic or no topic. This is a simple approach that does not consider answers close to

the target as being partly correct. A more fine-grained evaluation of answer performance (e.g., distance in the hierarchy from the ideal answer) will be the subject of future analysis, but it is first helpful to know if there are broad differences in performance between the LCSH trees.

> *Mean completion time*: average time participants took to complete each of the 10 questions.

> *Mean number of events*: average number of events the participants produced in each of the 10 questions.

Collapsing results across tasks allows for a preliminary assessment of general differences between the three conditions (i.e., the three trees). This makes the analysis less sensitive to the effects of specific tasks, which will be the subject of a future report.

4.1.1 Statistical tests. Collapsing each dependent variable's results across tasks makes the data suitable for a one-way Analysis of Variance (ANOVA) with *Tree* as the grouping variable to distinguish between the three LCSH trees (i.e., Initial, C95, and C95P02).

In terms of the percentage of correct answers (left panel), there is an obvious difference between the three conditions. While the Initial tree produced low performance (3.2%), C95 (24.3%) and C95P02 (30.5%) produced substantially elevated performance. An ANOVA confirmed that there was a significant effect of *Tree* ($F(2, 58) = 13.3$, $p < 0.001$). Follow up, Bonferroni corrected, two-sample t-tests showed a significant difference between Initial and C95 ($t(38) = 4.68$, $p < 0.0167$), between Initial and C95P02 ($t(38) = 5.19$, $p < 0.0167$), but not between C95 and C95P02 ($t < 1$).

The average time it took to complete the tasks was different across the trees. The Initial tree produced the longest (98s) completion times, followed by C95 (79s), while the C95P02 tree produced completion times that were only half as long (47s) as the Initial tree. An ANOVA confirmed that there was a significant effect of *Tree* ($F(2, 58) = 3.33$, $p = 0.043$). Bonferroni corrected, two-sample t-tests showed a significant difference between Initial and C95P02 ($t(38) = 3.78$, $p < 0.001$), but not between Initial and C95 ($t(38) = 1.12$, $p = 0.27$) or C95 and C95P02 ($t(40) = 1.38$, $p = 0.18$).

Despite the shorter task completion times, the average number of events was higher for the truncated trees than for the Initial tree, but this difference was not statistically significant ($F(2, 58) = 1.17$, $p = 0.32$).

5 DISCUSSION

RQ1 asked if users attempting to complete topic hierarchy exploration tasks perform better with a simplified LCSH tree. The results do not allow the rejection of $RQ1_{TimeNull}$ or $RQ1_{AccNull}$: participants' task success is significantly better with either simplified trees, while participants are significantly faster when using C95P02 compared to the initial tree. These results show that compression (as provided by C95) offers measurable task success advantages over the initial LCSH, and that the added pruning operation produces an additional time advantage.

Although the differences in time between the initial and C95 and between C95 and C95P02 weren't statistically significant, the clear overall trend (i.e., the decreasing times across the trees) suggests that compression does reduce time somewhat and that adding pruning to the compression reduces this further. A similar trend

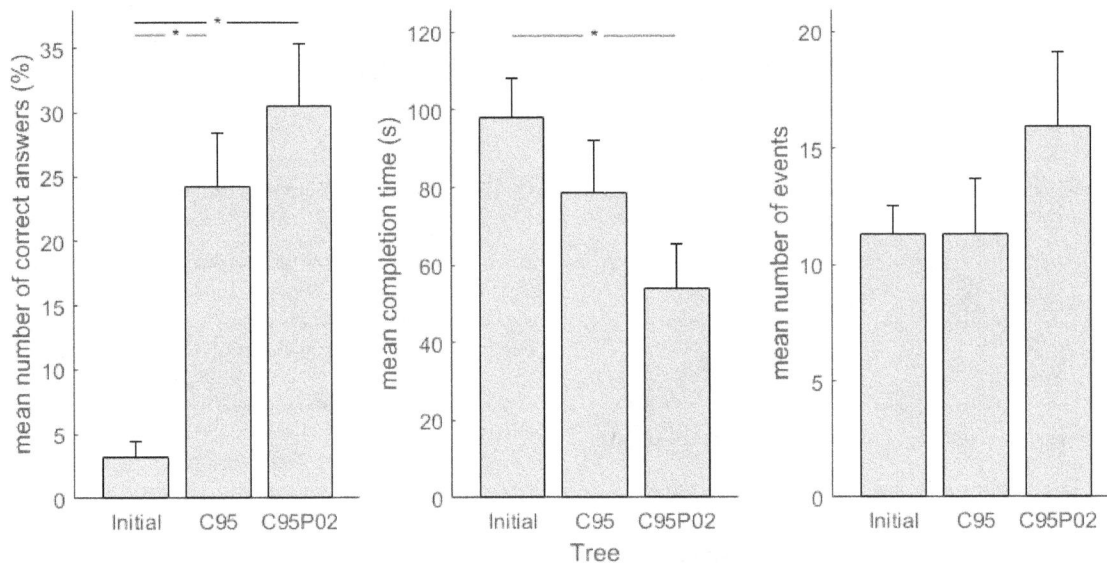

Figure 3: Bar chart of mean number of correct answers, completion time, and number of events across the three LCSH trees. Error bars represent standard errors of the mean. Horizontal lines with asterisks highlight significant differences.

can be seen in the measurement of task success, despite no significant difference between C95 and C95P02. This confirms that the modification approach of Julien et al. [18] improves aspects of topic hierarchy use relevant to performance (i.e., success and time).

RQ2 asked what are the effects of the simplification on users' information behavior. The results do not allow rejection of RQ2-BrowseEventsNull, meaning that participants selected equivalent numbers of topics across the three trees. This may suggest that our definition of information behavior is not sensitive enough to measure differences, which will be the subject of future analysis using additional logged usage data, but this lack of difference is nevertheless interesting since one would expect fewer browsing events when using the smaller tree, C95P02. This suggests that removing superfluous semantic information (e.g., by pruning those topics that provide little document access) does not discourage interaction with and exploration in the tree, and perhaps conversely that the semantic information provided by the pruned topics is not solely responsible for encouraging interaction with the tree.

The consistent information behavior across the trees also suggests users of information structures may have a limited capacity to select and inspect topics, and for our participants this capacity was exhausted by all three trees. This comparable behavior resulted in poorer outcomes and longer task times when using the initial tree, however. This may be because the initial tree forces users to perform a greater number of more difficult browsing decisions among greater, less predictable numbers of narrower topics.

Taken together, our findings show that the tested topic tree modifications improve topic hierarchy exploration and do not create semantic gaps between the remaining topics that would hinder navigation. This is promising but further testing is required to generalize to other organized collections and tasks. Although there are reports of semantic structure simplification techniques [6], as

far as we can gather, the present study is the only one that tests a topic hierarchy simplification approach with human participants.

6 LIMITATIONS

Our results warrant further testing in different experimental contexts to generalize beyond the LCSH structure and collection used and the specific tasks tested. Indeed, the tested simplification techniques may produce different results in other knowledge domains beyond science and engineering whose topic network might be arranged significantly differently (e.g., collections from the humanities), but its potential is promising given that organized collections in general are distributed within their organizing structure according to power laws.

This concise report reports measures of performance and browsing across all tasks, and so does not identify the effects of individual tasks. A future full-length report will include such analyses. Additionally, asynchronous data collection entailed that participants performed tasks remotely and unsupervised, and thus could be distracted, which may influence task times and thus warrants further analysis.

Finally, as our participants were unfamiliar with LCSH, it remains unclear if structure simplification would have a different effect on users experienced or familiar with the LCSH tree. Given the size of LCSH (2.5 million terms in the unmodified, Initial tree, as seen in 1) we find it unlikely that many people are familiar with even a small portion of it, but intend to control for prior knowledge in a future study to confirm this.

7 CONCLUSION

Representing a collection's structure as a hierarchy is a promising approach for improving topical exploration since it permits its visual representation and interaction, for example as widely-used tree views found in digital file management software, to allow systematic top-down navigation from broad to narrower topics. These trees may be pruned and compressed to make them more balanced in their presentation [18], but the efficacy and effect of such modifications on users' interactions with such hierarchies was previously unknown.

The study presented here found that performing such modifications on an LCSH tree improved participants' success in completing retrieval tasks, and decreased the time they spent completing these tasks. Modification also had no effect on their overall information behavior (i.e., their interaction with the tree): removing superfluous semantic information (e.g., by pruning those subjects that provide little document access) did not discourage interaction with and exploration in the tree.

These results suggest that comparable large information structures could be modified with similar positive results, but requires further research to generalize across organizing structures and collections. Near-future work will include fine-grained analysis of the collected data to isolate results of the *impossible* and the *previously seen topic* tasks, which may partly explain the differences in mean task times reported in this report. Additional promising directions for further study include extending the use of information foraging in understanding the exploration of topic hierarchies, for example by investigating how hierarchy modifications may be changing information *scents* [e.g., in line with the approach of 4].

ACKNOWLEDGMENTS

This research is supported by the National Science and Engineering Research Council of Canada (NSERC), the Fonds de recherche du Québec – Société et culture (FRQSC), and in kind contributions from McGill libraries.

REFERENCES

[1] Nicholas J Belkin, Robert N Oddy, and Helen M Brooks. 1982. ASK for information retrieval: Part I. Background and theory. *Journal of Documentation* 38, 2 (1982), 61–71.
[2] Nicholas J Belkin, Robert N Oddy, and Helen M Brooks. 1982. ASK for information retrieval: Part II. Results of a design study. *Journal of Documentation* 38, 3 (1982), 145–164.
[3] S.-J. L. Chang. 2005. *Chang's Browsing*. Information Today, Medford, NJ, 69–74.
[4] Ed H Chi, Peter Pirolli, Kim Chen, and James Pitkow. 2001. Using information scent to model user information needs and actions and the Web. In *Proceedings of the SIGCHI conference on Human factors in computing systems*. ACM, 490–497.
[5] Dan Cho. 2014. MeSH on demand tool: An easy way to identify relevant MeSH terms. (2014). Retrieved September 29, 2017 from https://www.nlm.nih.gov/pubs/techbull/mj14/mj14_mesh_on_demand.html
[6] Michel Crampes and Michel Plantié. 2014. Visualizing and Interacting with Concept Hierarchies. In *Proceedings of the 4th International Conference on Web Intelligence, Mining and Semantics (WIMS14)*. ACM, 5.
[7] Fred D Davis. 1989. Perceived usefulness, perceived ease of use, and user acceptance of information technology. *MIS Quarterly* (1989), 319–340.
[8] Fred D Davis, Richard P Bagozzi, and Paul R Warshaw. 1989. User acceptance of computer technology: a comparison of two theoretical models. *Management science* 35, 8 (1989), 982–1003.
[9] Marian Dörk, Carey Williamson, and Sheelagh Carpendale. 2012. Navigating tomorrow's web: From searching and browsing to visual exploration. *ACM Transactions on the Web (TWEB)* 6, 3 (2012), 13.
[10] Leo Egghe. 2005. *Power laws in the information production process: Lotkaian informetrics*. Emerald Group Publishing Limited.
[11] George W Furnas. 1986. Generalized fisheye views. In *CHI '86, Proceedings of SIGCHI Conference on Human Factors in Computing Systems*, Vol. 17. ACM, Boston, MA, 16–23.
[12] Koraljka Golub, Marianne Lykke, and Douglas Tudhope. 2014. Enhancing social tagging with automated keywords from the Dewey Decimal Classification.

Journal of Documentation 70, 5 (2014), 801–828.
[13] Koraljka Golub, Dagobert Soergel, George Buchanan, Douglas Tudhope, Marianne Lykke, and Debra Hiom. 2016. A framework for evaluating automatic indexing or classification in the context of retrieval. *Journal of the Association for Information Science and Technology* 67, 1 (2016), 3–16.
[14] Sandra G Hart and Lowell E Staveland. 1988. Development of NASA-TLX (Task Load Index): Results of empirical and theoretical research. *Advances in Psychology* 52 (1988), 139–183.
[15] Marti A Hearst and Chandu Karadi. 1997. Cat-a-Cone: an interactive interface for specifying searches and viewing retrieval results using a large category hierarchy. In *ACM SIGIR Conference on Research and Development in Information Retrieval*, Vol. 31. ACM, Philadelphia, PA, 246–255.
[16] Jeffrey Heer and Stuart K Card. 2004. DOITrees revisited: scalable, space-constrained visualization of hierarchical data. In *Proceedings of the Working Conference on Advanced Visual Interfaces*. ACM, 421–424.
[17] Charles-Antoine Julien and Pierre Tirilly. 2013. Exact versus estimated pruning of subject hierarchies. In *Proceedings of the Association for Information Science and Technology*, Vol. 50. Wiley Online Library, 1–10.
[18] Charles-Antoine Julien, Pierre Tirilly, Jesse David Dinneen, and Catherine Guastavino. 2013. Reducing subject tree browsing complexity. *Journal of the Association for Information Science and Technology* 64, 11 (2013), 2201–2223.
[19] Charles-Antoine Julien, Pierre Tirilly, John E Leide, and Catherine Guastavino. 2012. Constructing a true LCSH tree of a science and engineering collection. *Journal of the Association for Information Science and Technology* 63, 12 (2012), 2405–2418.
[20] Flip Korn and Ben Shneiderman. 1995. Navigating terminology hierarchies to access a digital library of medical images. (1995).
[21] Frederick Lancaster. 1986. *Vocabulary control for information retrieval* (2 ed.). Information Resources, Arlington, VA.
[22] X Lin. 1999. Visual MeSH. In *Proceedings of 22nd international conferences on research and development in information retrieval*. SIGIR '99, Berkeley, CA, 317–318.
[23] Tie-Yan Liu, Yiming Yang, Hao Wan, Hua-Jun Zeng, Zheng Chen, and Wei-Ying Ma. 2005. Support vector machines classification with a very large-scale taxonomy. *ACM SIGKDD Explorations Newsletter* 7, 1 (2005), 36–43.
[24] Ying-Hsang Liu and Nina Wacholder. 2017. Evaluating the impact of MeSH (Medical Subject Headings) terms on different types of searchers. *Information Processing & Management* 53, 4 (2017), 851–870.
[25] Gary Marchionini and Ben Shneiderman. 1988. Finding facts vs. browsing knowledge in hypertext systems. *Computer* 21, 1 (1988), 70–80.
[26] Mark EJ Newman. 2005. Power laws, Pareto distributions and Zipf's law. *Contemporary Physics* 46, 5 (2005), 323–351.
[27] Peter Pirolli and Stuart Card. 1999. Information foraging. *Psychological Review* 106, 4 (1999), 643.
[28] Nihar Sheth and Qin Cai. 2003. *Visualizing mesh dataset using radial tree layout*. Technical Report. Indiana University, Bloomington, IN.
[29] Nina Wacholder and Lu Liu. 2008. Assessing term effectiveness in the interactive information access process. *Information Processing & Management* 44, 3 (2008), 1022–1031.
[30] Jun Wang and Meng Chen Lee. 2007. Reconstructing DDC for interactive classification. In *Proceedings of the sixteenth ACM conference on Conference on information and knowledge management*. ACM, 137–146.
[31] Kwan Yi and Lois Mai Chan. 2008. A visualization software tool for Library of Congress subject headings. In *Proceedings of 10th Int. Conf. of International Society for Knowledge Organization: Culture and identity in knowledge organization*. 170–176.
[32] Kwan Yi and Lois Mai Chan. 2010. Revisiting the syntactical and structural analysis of Library of Congress Subject Headings for the digital environment. *Journal of the Association for Information Science and Technology* 61, 4 (2010), 677–687.

Fixation and Confusion – Investigating Eye-tracking Participants' Exposure to Information in Personas

Joni Salminen
Qatar Computing Research Institute,
Hamad Bin Khalifa University; and
Turku School of Economics
jsalminen@hbku.edu.qa

Bernard J. Jansen
Qatar Computing Research Institute,
Hamad Bin Khalifa University
jjansen@acm.org

Jisun An
Qatar Computing Research Institute,
Hamad Bin Khalifa University
jan@hbku.edu.qa

Soon-Gyo Jung
Qatar Computing Research Institute,
Hamad Bin Khalifa University
sjung@hbku.edu.qa

Lene Nielsen
IT University of Copenhagen
lene@itu.dk

Haewoon Kwak
Qatar Computing Research Institute,
Hamad Bin Khalifa University
hkwak@hbku.edu.qa

ABSTRACT

To more effectively convey relevant information to end users of persona profiles, we conducted a user study consisting of 29 participants engaging with three persona layout treatments. We were interested in confusion engendered by the treatments on the participants, and conducted a within-subjects study in the actual work environment, using eye-tracking and talk-aloud data collection. We coded the verbal data into classes of informativeness and confusion and correlated it with fixations and durations on the Areas of Interests recorded by the eye-tracking device. We used various analysis techniques, including Mann-Whitney, regression, and Levenshtein distance, to investigate how confused users differed from non-confused users, what information of the personas caused confusion, and what were the predictors of confusion of end users of personas. We consolidate our various findings into a confusion ratio measure, which highlights in a succinct manner the most confusing elements of the personas. Findings show that inconsistencies among the informational elements of the persona generate the most confusion, especially with the elements of images and social media quotes. The research has implications for the design of personas and related information products, such as user profiling and customer segmentation.

ACM Reference format:

J. Salminen, B.J. Jansen, J. An, S.-G. Jung, L. Nielsen, and H. Kwak. 2018. Fixation and Confusion: Investigating Eye-tracking Participants' Exposure to Information in Personas. In *CHIIR '18: Conference on Human*

CHIIR '18, March 11–15, 2018, New Brunswick, NJ, USA
© 2018 Association for Computing Machinery.
ACM ISBN 978-1-4503-4925-3/18/03...$15.00
https://doi.org/10.1145/3176349.3176391

Information Interaction and Retrieval, March 11-15, 2018, New Brunswick, NJ, USA. ACM, NY, NY, USA, 10 pages.
DOI: https://doi.org/10.1145/3176349.3176392

1 INTRODUCTION

Personas are fictitious information representations of core user groups [1]. They are used by professionals in marketing, product development, system design, and corporate decision making [2] [3] [4] [5]. Traditionally, personas have been created using manual methods, such as ethnography and interviews [6]. While these methods result in deep user insight, their feasibility is reduced by time and cost, making personas unavailable for many organizations with tight product deadlines or limited budgets. More recently, researchers have looked into automating the persona generation process, which is based on information on real user behavior in social media whose collection and processing has been automated [7] [8] [9] [10] [11].

While social media benefits persona generation in many ways, the task of compressing social media data into simple persona presentations is not a trivial one. First, among all information elements (e.g., demographics, psychographics, etc.), one has to choose the right elements for a particular user or use case. Second, one needs to determine how this information is presented to be helpful for the end users of personas, while minimizing negative cognitive effects, such as information overload and confusion. Achieving these goals requires an in-depth understanding of how users perceive an interface or system and what are their cognitive reactions to it. Such questions are best addressed by experimental studies, measuring constructs such as confusion, defined here as a state of cognitive disorientation. In particular, earlier studies have found that end users can react to personas with disbelief and perception of inconsistency [12] [13] [14], perceptions that are conceptually similar to confusion.

This research reports the interaction between automatic personas and users' cognitive state, although we believe the findings are applicable to personas generated by any method. Particularly, we are investigating the relationship between users and their perceived confusion. Our research questions are:

- How do confused users differ from non-confused users in terms of their eye fixation patterns?
- Which areas of automatic personas cause the most confusion?
- What are the most powerful predictors of confusion?

To answer the questions, we analyze the eye-tracking data from a user study consisting of 29 participants. For the first question, we first look at the quantity and duration of fixations between the groups. Then, we examine the structural differences between the transition paths from one area of interest (AOI) to another. AOIs are commonly used in eye-tracking studies to connect fixation observations to particular areas of the screen. After this, we look deeper into the participants' interactions to see what caused confusion. We do this by a mixed method approach, combining qualitative and statistical techniques, and present then our findings. Finally, we conclude by discussing the measurement and analysis of confusion from eye-tracking data in user studies and its implication for the design of personas, both automatically generated and traditionally developed, and related artifacts such as user profiles.

2 RELATED LITERATURE

Granka et al. [15] note that most of eye-tracking user studies are in fact focused on analyzing cognitive information processing, e.g. what the users are thinking of and what information they are paying attention to. The general problem is how to identify positive or desired cognitive states (i.e., interest) from negative ones (e.g., confusion), as the former indicate good designs and the latter bad ones. Earlier research has shown users may experience confusion relating to several reasons, such as poor information designs [16]. Adopting the eye-mind hypothesis [17], confused users should pay more attention to their points of confusion. The basic metrics relate to fixation quantity, duration, and screen position.

A fixation is defined as a relatively stable state of the eye, focusing on particular gazepoint, and lasting 100-600ms [18] [19]. Saccades, in turn, are shorter, rapid eye movements between fixations. Together the two form scanpaths [20]. Fixations capture the direction of a user's attention and therefore indicate where information acquisition and processing are possibly taking place [15]. In addition, fixations are related to the depth of information processing and its level of difficulty [21]. For example, Golberg and Kotval [16] found that an intentionally poorer user interface resulted in significantly more fixations than a better design. In a similar vein, long fixation durations may indicate participant confusion [16].

The studied persona profile layout is divided into AOIs, so that each fixation is targeting a specific area of interest that matches its coordinates (x, y). AOIs are commonly used to identify user's interest in the examined layout [15]. For example, listings on a search results page, or different focal elements in e-commerce site could be defined as AOIs by researchers [22] [23]. Scanpaths between different AOIs are seen as records of visual attention [24]. For example, a longer scanpath can be indicative of less efficient searching due to a poor layout, as users are resorting to more cognitive effort to find what they are looking for [25]. Albeit comparing scanpaths of different groups is generally seen more difficult than pairwise comparison [15], some approaches have been developed. For example, Eraslan et al. [26] introduced the scanpath trend analysis (STA) algorithm. Moreover, in experimental eye tracking studies, it is common to record the cognitive processes of participants through the talk-aloud method to enable deeper analyses [27]. Analyzing the talk-aloud records gives an understanding of users' the state of the mind, as they are explicitly telling about their perceived mental state [28].

There are also studies that attempt to predict cognitive states from eye-tracking data using neural networks. In their pioneering work, Yamada et al. [29] define four emotion states as inputs for neural network learner, inferring these from individuals' voice signals. Harada et al. [30] propose a model for assessing the level of distraction, especially focused on drivers, and Grace et al. [31] explore the use of neural networks for detecting drowsiness and distraction in driving. Kuperberg and Heckers [32] investigate using neural networks for classification of schizophrenia.

However, inferring confusion from eye-tracking data is quite complicated because of three reasons: first, the fixation patterns tend to be complex, consisting of users' eye fixation jumping from one area of the screen to another. Beyond basic metrics, such as number and duration of fixations, one also should consider the sequence of AOIs that intuitively should matter for the prediction (assuming that gazing behaviors between confused and non-confused participants are different; see e.g. Eraslan et al. [35] for discussion). Second, earlier research has shown that basic features, such as duration spent fixated on an AOI can be interpreted differently depending on the use case and user in question. For example, the longer duration can indicate confusion in information retrieval tasks [24], i.e. individuals are having a tough time making sense of the information, but in website browsing, a higher fixation duration can indicate stronger interest [23]. Granka et al. [15] argue that in some tasks where the high focus is required, long fixation might not indicate confusion but the opposite.

Third, the problem lies in getting from the high-dimensional sequence and duration representation of confused users into a well-defined and evaluated predictive model. The users' eye fixation pattern should reveal they are confused, but this pattern is not easily analyzable by traditional methods [24]. Overall, the relative nature of this problem implies that general rules about the relationship between fixation durations and patterns with confusion cannot be easily formulated. Rather, we suggest that such relationships are better off being predicted from the data, given that we have labeled data on confusion, such as when cognitive measures are retrieved by the talk-aloud method [36]. Even though prior research has provided indications for the relationship between confusion and eye fixations, this relationship is not well known. We aim at targeting this research gap.

3 METHODOLOGY

3.1 Data collection

We conducted an eye-tracking user study to test different persona profile layouts for automatic persona generation (APG) which is both a system and a methodology for generating behaviorally accurate personas [7-11]. Personas are imaginary representations of core customers of a company or other organization [4]. They can be created automatically by retrieving social media data via application programming interfaces (APIs), and processing this data with non-negative matrix factorization and topic modeling [7] [8] [10]. This process has been described in detail in earlier work [7-11], and we refrain from repeating it here. An example of an automatically generated persona is shown in Figure 1.

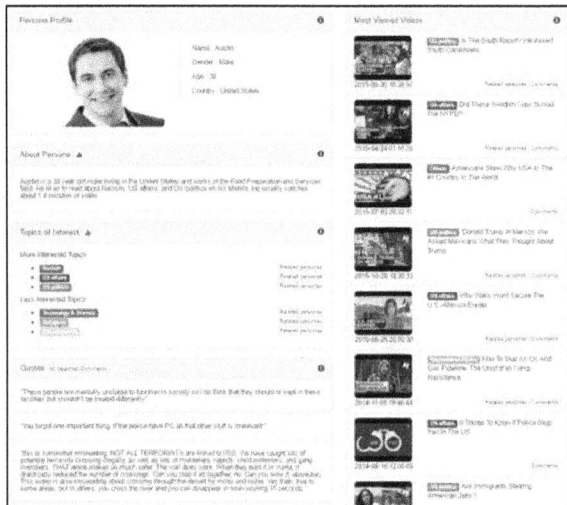

Figure 1: Example of automatically generated persona. It (he) has a picture, name, demographic information, topics of interest, descriptive quotes, and most viewed video content.

In particular, we wanted to know how many and what kind of images should be used in the automatically generated persona profiles. Previous persona literature does not provide an answer to this question, as there are only a few studies focused on persona images [37] [35] [36], none of which are measuring confusion. Therefore, we conducted the user study and chose eye-tracking as the form of data collection. The participants included 29 individuals working at the case company using our APG system, a large media company based in Doha, Qatar. The study consists of all 29 participants without grouping them, and all participants are exposed to the same layouts listed in Figure 2 (within-subjects design). Table 1 includes information about the participants.

Table 1: Information on the eye-tracking study participants.

	Male	Female	Total
Avg. age (years)	28.5	30.2	32.6
Avg. exp. in news industry (years)	7.1	7.5	7.3
Producers	11	7	18
Editors	3	5	8
Others	1	2	3
Total	15	14	29

We set up the eye-tracking device (EyeTribe, which comes with a cloud-based software for data processing) with desktop computers in the company's premises and, during five working days, conducted eye-tracking trials with the participants. We had each participant undergo three treatments (see Figure 2) at a random sequence and simultaneously collected talk-aloud data to connect the eye-tracking observations to cognitive processes of the individuals [17]. The participants were free to spend as much as time as they wanted with each treatment; after they were done, they clicked forward to the next one. The order of treatments was randomized. We recorded the voice-aloud comments during the experiment, and analyzed them later by dictionary-based cognitive discourse analysis (CDA) [40], in which we paid attention to verbal cues from the participants' speech to detect confusion.

During the experiment, the participants were encouraged to express their cognitive states as they were looking at the screen ("Where are you looking at? What do you see?"). We then adopted CDA [40] to code each AOI in terms of confusion expressed by the participant (e.g., "not understanding why three pictures are shown" indicated confusion targeting the images, and "seems confusing, not sure what quotes mean" targeting quotes). Following this technique, we paid attention to verbal cues of confusion when coding the perceived confusion expressed by the participants during the experiment. The cue words included e.g. "confusing", "did not understand", "difficult to say", etc. Table 2 includes examples of the confusion instances and cue words.

Table 2: Examples of confusion cue words used in coding.

Perceived confusion = TRUE	Cue words
"seems confusing, not sure what quotes mean"	Confusing, not sure
"there are different pictures, I don't understand"	Don't understand
"lost on here - conflicted profile"	Lost, conflicted
"weird information about videos - how are they related?"	Weird, how
"not sure what to think of the picture"	Not sure
"doesn't make sense"	Does not make sense

When a cue is found, the instance is coded as 1 (TRUE). If the notes lack cues, the instance is coded as 0 (FALSE). The coding is done for each treatment of each participant based on the talk-aloud transcripts made during the eye tracking sessions.

We coded the confusion for each participant in each trial and verified the coding reliability by inter-rater test (Cohen's Kappa 0.86). In addition to the fixation observations, collected with the EyeTribe system, and the confusion coding, we asked background information from each participant, including age, gender, and experience in the industry. Treatments used in the study are shown in Figure 2.

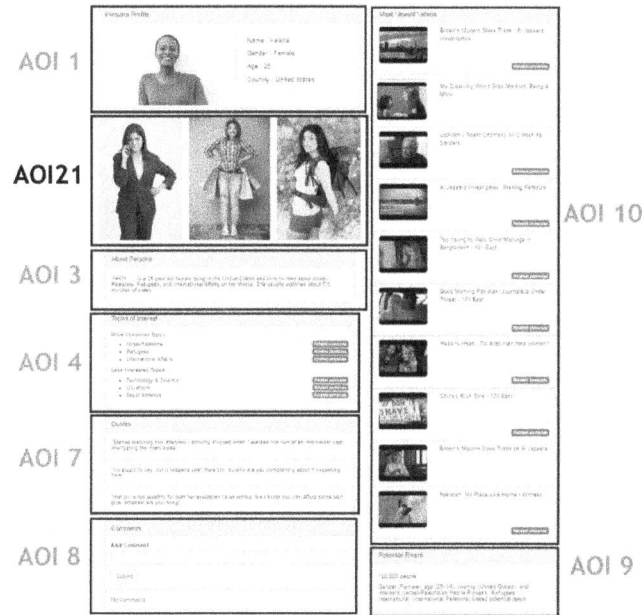

Figure 2: The tested layout. Between the three treatments, everything else was equal except T2 and T3 (in picture) had contextual pictures (AOI 21) added. As can be seen, different parts of the screen are defined as areas of interest (AOIs)

Automatic personas include six sections: *persona profile* with photo, name, age, gender, and country (AOI 1); *textual description* about persona (AOI 3); *topics of interest* the persona is most and least interested in (AOI 4); *descriptive quotes* aggregated from real social media users (AOI 7); *content* the persona has most interacted with (AOI 10); and *total audience size* retrieved from Facebook Marketing API [2] with the corresponding targeting criteria (AOI 9). T2 and T3 also included additional contextual pictures (AOI 21) that were manually added to explore their effect on users' stated confusion. In terms of other content, the treatments were identical.

3.2 Description of data

To select meaningful metrics for our study, we adopt Goldberg and Kotval's [16] suggested metrics. For temporal aspect, we are looking at fixation duration and dwell times. For spatial aspect, we look at heatmaps generated by the eye-

---

[2] https://developers.facebook.com/docs/marketing-apis/

tracking software, as well as the length of fixation and transition paths. Table 3 describes the studied variables.

Table 3: Data variables for quantitative analysis.

Variable	Description
Number of fixations	The number of fixation observations recorded by the measurement device. The sampling frequency of the device was 50Hz.
Avg. duration of fixations	The average duration of fixations. A fixation duration is typically 100-600ms [18] [19].
Total duration of fixations	Sum of fixation durations (e.g., by participant, treatment, AOI).
Number of transitions between AOIs (i.e., *transition paths*)	Indicates fixation movement from one AOI to another. The number of transitions can be computed by eliminating fixations targeting the same AOI repetitively from the total number of fixations (e.g. A1 → A1 → A2 would transform into A1 → A2).
Background information	Questionnaire answers: role (producer / editor / other), age (young / mature); gender (male / female); experience (novice / experienced).
Perceived confusion	Indication if the participant expressed confusion during a given treatment (TRUE/FALSE).

The measures applied in our study are commonly used in eye tracking studies to analyze the data. For example, Cowen et al. [41] analyze the number of fixations and total fixation duration. The number and duration of fixations (dwelling time) are commonly used in eye tracking studies to evaluate user engagement and sense of relevance [42]. In addition, Eraslan et al. [35] point out that individual variables, such as gender and user expertise tend to influence eye-tracking patterns, so we also include them.

Note that we are using fixations, but not saccades. Transition paths are different from the fixations paths; the former capture the movement from one AOI to another, while the latter includes also repetitive fixations to an AOI. It is important to examine both, as they might reveal different information about the viewing behavior of the user. In particular, a transition path is a higher-level description of viewing pattern than fixation path that includes also the repeated views on the same AOI. Fixation path is equal to the number of fixations subtracted by 1 (the start state).

Finally, the confusion data is available for each trial of each participant (T-P); and for each AOI at each trial of each participant. We use both levels of coding depending on the question we are answering to. If T-P level data suffices to answer a question, we prefer using it since the AOI-level data is sparser.

However, for questions dealing with the AOI-level impact on confusion, we must use that level data.

4 FINDINGS

4.1 How do confused users differ from non-confused users?

There are 29 participants with usable data, of which 23 (79%) expressed confusion and 6 (21%) did not. The confusion varies greatly by treatment, and most confusion was expressed in T3 (60% of all confusion observations), the least in T1 (19%). Out of all participants, 8 (28%) expressed confusion in two or more treatments. Therefore, we find that the participants do differ by perceived confusion. Figure 3 shows the observed confusion among the participants.

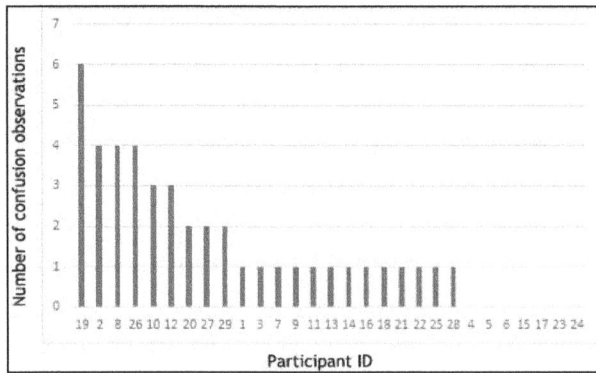

Figure 3: Observed confusion among participants. Confusion is calculated by each AOI of each participant in each trial. Not that a participant can express confusion toward several AOIs per trial.

As can be seen, there are both confused and non-confused participants. Confusion is calculated by each AOI of each participant in each trial. The maximum number of confusion observations per participant is six, and minimum zero. The average is 1.48 confusion observations per participant. Table 4 shows basic eye-tracking metrics between the confused and non-confused users.

Table 4: Basic eye-tracking metrics comparing confused and non-confused users. The confusion is calculated by participant and trial.

	Confused	Non-confused
Avg. number of fixations	885	766
Avg. dur. of fixations (ms)	336	363

The difference of fixation durations between confused and non-confused users is small (confused have ~8% longer fixation duration). In turn, the confused have ~16% more fixations than non-confused, warranting further inspection. We do this by carrying out a Mann-Whitney-Wilcoxon test, in which we compare confused group (number of fixations from each confused trial of each participant) with the non-confused group,

with the null hypothesis that there is no statistically significant difference.

It is clear from the test that there is a significant difference between the two groups (p-value = 0.012). This implies the number of fixations is statistically different across the two groups (p<0.05). The number of fixations for non-confused is smaller on average than for confused. Thus, we find evidence of differences and proceed to explore the data further.

4.2 How do confused and non-confused users differ by their fixation paths?

To answer this question, first, we measure the average length of transition paths. This is done by eliminating repetitive fixations targeting any given AOI, revealing the "bare" transition path between participants and AOIs (e.g., fixation path for a participant P1: A1 → A1 → A2 will become transition path P1: A1 → A2). Table 5 shows the average of transition paths of confused and non-confused users.

Table 5: Average length of transition paths in AOIs.

	Confused	Non-confused
Avg. length of transition paths	162.5	140.2

The transition paths are longer with the confused group (calculated as P-T), indicating they are "jumping" from one AOI to another more often. To find out if this difference is statistically significant, we conduct a Mann-Whitney-Wilcoxon test. It is clear from the results (p-value = 0.3091) that there is no significant difference between the two groups on the length of transition paths. Yet, based on standard deviations, the lengths of confused ($\sigma=82.28$) are more spread out than those of non-confused ($\sigma=61.37$), giving some indication of more sporadic behavior.

We are also interested in knowing if the paths vary by content, i.e., their AOI states. For this purpose, we use the Levenshtein distance to compare paths turned into strings against one another [43]. Such sequence alignment techniques are commonly used in measuring eye-tracking paths [44] [15].

First, we build four similarity matrices: M0, comparing all participants' fixation sequence strings to one another; M1, comparing confused participants to one another; M2, comparing non-confused participants to one another; and M3, comparing confused participants with non-confused participants. We then average the pairwise comparisons of each matrix to produce an overall score of fixation path similarity within a group. The results are shown in Table 6.

Table 6: Similarity between Confused and Non-confused fixation paths.

Similarity matrix	Fixation path similarity
Confused	660
Non-Confused	559
Compared Confused with Non-confused	628
All	604

As shown in Table 6, these are non-normalized edit-distances (i.e., Levenshtein distance). Here, the score refers to the number of operations needed to substitute one fixation path to another. For example, 660 means that 660 operations (i.e., delete, insert or substitute) are needed to change the fixation path to another fixation path. Thus, the higher the distance is, the less similar a pair of two participants are. From the fixation path similarity numbers, we observe that the confused are most different from one another, and non-confused are most similar to one another. Moreover, non-confused are more different relative to confused than to other non-confused. However, interestingly, confused are more different to one another than to non-confused. This seems to suggest that confusion is sporadic, i.e., consisting of random rather than systematic patterns. In addition, the relative differences are quite large (the confused are 17.9% more dissimilar than the non-confused). Figure 4 illustrates the similarity matrices.

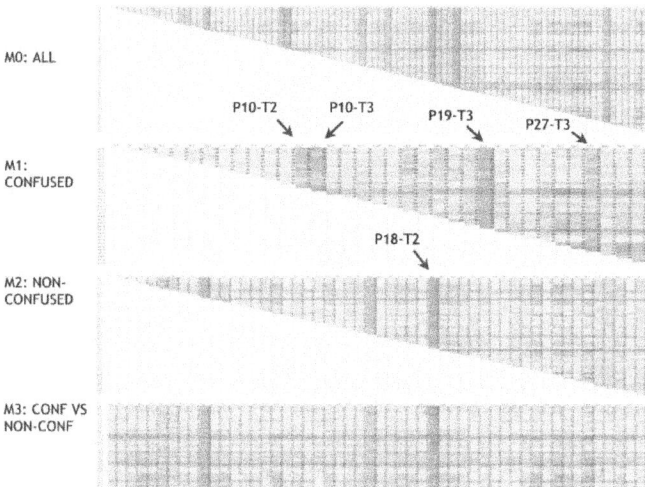

Figure 4: Levenshtein distance matrices; each column and row maps into each user's fixation path. Red indicates higher distance, green closer. Yellow is in between. In this matrix, each participant is compared with all the other participants once (e.g., comparing P1 and P2 in P1 row means we do not repeat the comparison with P2 column).

From Figure 4, we can detect some individual differences. Very distinct fixation paths from all others could indicate measurement errors. For example, P18 (T2) is distinctly different from other non-confused (red vertical line in M2). The transition path of this participant is displayed in Figure 5.

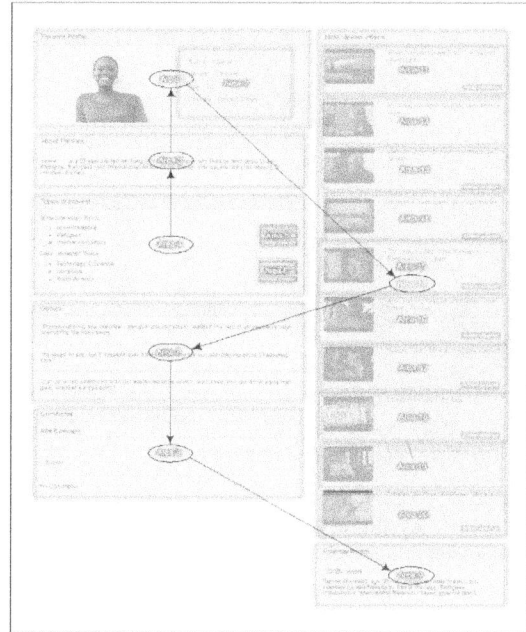

Figure 5: Transition path of P18 (male, 39, other). The line is drawn from the center of one AOI to another and thus does not depict the actual scanpath.

We can observe that, uncommon to most participants who start from the top-left of the screen and the move down and to topics of interest and then to right-side column videos, this participant firstly focused on topics of interest, and then moves upward. From confused ones, P10 (T2 and T3), P19 (T3), and P27 (T3) clearly differ from the others (red vertical lines in M1 in Figure 4). Table 7 shows the dissimilarity of these fixation paths.

Table 7: The most dissimilar fixation paths. Difference is from the mean Levenshtein distance of other confused participants.

Participant/Treatment	Avg. distance	Diff. from mean
P10-T2	702	+6%
P10-T3	720	+9%
P19-T3	736	+12%
P27-T3	692	+5%

In this case, we observe some individual patterns in Levenshtein distances of grouped users. For example, the Mann-Whitney test shows that the distribution of dissimilarity scores from P19-T3 is significantly different the distribution of others (W = 18295, p-value < 2.2e-16). Thus, one can use the dissimilarity matrix as a basis of visualization, and then explore the visible differences between statistical and qualitative means. Both group-level and individual insights can be found by analyzing the distance matrix.

4.3 Which areas of personas profiles cause the most confusion?

Next, we investigate the relationship between confusion and areas of interest. Figure 7 shows confusion observations by AOIs.

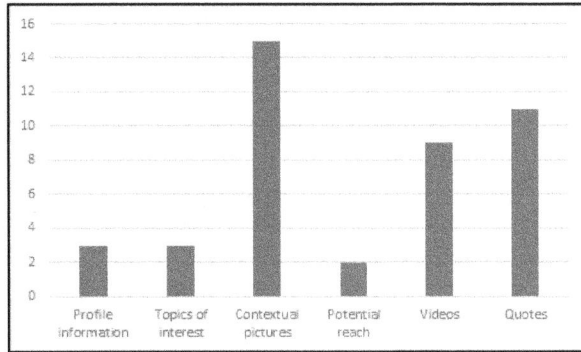

Figure 7: AOIs with the most confusion. AOIs without confusion observations are not included.

Contextual pictures were the target of most confusion (35%), (see Figure 8 – A), followed by persona quotes (26%) (Figure 8 – B) videos (21%) (Figure 8 – C), and topics of interest (7%) (Figure 8 – D). Yet, the number and duration of fixations indicate that videos are most looked at. Two areas in the layout did not gather any confusion: Description which includes the textual description for the persona, and the Comments section are largely ignored.

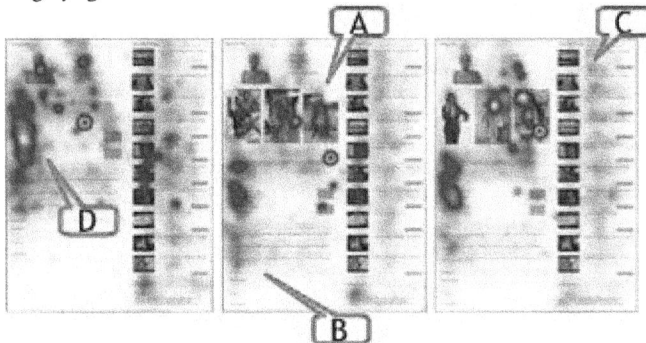

Figure 8: Heatmaps of visual attention of participants (includes all participants). Brighter color indicates more fixations.

From the heatmaps in Figure 8, we can see that in T2 (middle) and T3 (right), which overall had the strongest confusion, the attention seems to focus on a) the extra pictures and b) topics of interest. Confusion was also highest for the extra pictures among the AOIs, indicating a relationship between confusion and number of fixations. In contrast, quotes and videos, which also had a substantial share of confusion, were paid less attention to. It, therefore, seems that confusion targeting each AOI should be evaluated relative to the attention it is receiving.

For this purpose, we compute the "confusion ratio", a metric which we invented here, to evaluate the relative intensity of confusion per AOI: this is calculated by dividing the amount of

time targeted by confused users to an AOI with the amount of time from non-confused users targeting the same AOI. That is, if the ratio is high, the relative confusion of that AOI is higher than otherwise. Table 8 shows the results of the calculations.

Table 8: Confusion ratio. The order of the rows is based on the number of confusion observations.

AOI	Confusion ratio	Name of AOI
A21	1.160	Contextual pictures
A7	1.711	Quotes
A10	1.072	Videos
A1	1.144	Profile information
A4	2.422	Topics of interest
A9	2.189	Potential reach

We can see that the "ranking" of AOIs in terms of confusion changes from the ranking with pure observations (Figure 7) when we account for fixation duration targeting that same AOI. This captures the fact that time spent in AOIs is not equally distributed. Thus, even though contextual pictures have the largest share of confusion observations, their confusion ratio is actually lower than for potential reach, which is rarely looked at but makes users more confused when it is being looked at. Videos, in turn, have a low confusion ratio because they are looked at often, but the relatively lower number of participants found them confusing. Figure 9 shows the average dwell time (sum of fixation durations) of confused and non-confused participants.

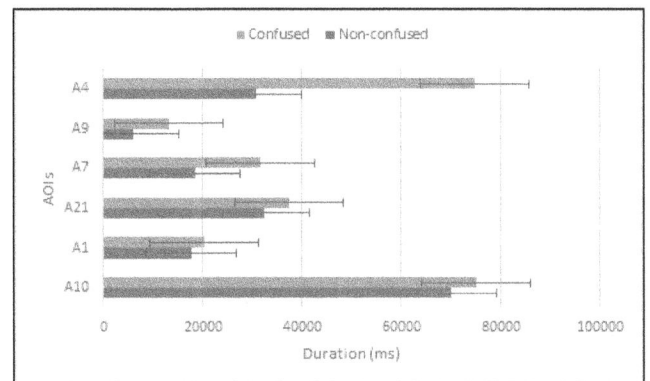

Figure 9: Average dwell times per AOI by confused and non-confused users. The line on each bar indicates standard error. Topics of interest (A4) have the clearest difference, and it is also ranked highest by confusion ratio metric.

4.4 Reasons for confusion

For any type of user study focusing on confusion and informativeness, it is useful to know why users were confused so that proper conclusions can be drawn for informing information design. For this purpose, we also highlight reasons to why the participants expressed confusion (Table 9)

Table 9 Examples of confusion reasons.

AOI	Explicated reason for confusion
Contextual pictures (A in Fig. 8)	"confused – don't get the photos" (P13); "don't understand why these photos are there" (P8)
Quotes (B in Fig. 8)	"confused; talks about video maybe [means] something on the refugee situation international community" (P2)
Videos (C in Fig. 8)	"looking at the videos – can't find stories tie into the topics" (P18)
Topics of interest (D in Fig. 8)	"[the persona is] not interested in South America although closer to her location" (P29)

We can thus see that there are various underlying reasons for confusion. For example, conflicting information. The photos that represented other, similar individuals were perceived confusing. The participant could not understand the linkage of them being similar to the person depicted in the mugshot ("[I am] a little confused, all different women" (P14). One participant assumed they are "pictures of her friends" (P19). In other cases, information definitions are not clear to the user ("don't know what the quote section is; don't know if it's about her or by her" (P8)). Overall, the findings suggest that AOIs are processed relative to one another, so that inconsistent information becomes a major source of confusion.

In addition, confusion coding revealed insights useful for system development, e.g. that "potential reach" was not understood by the news producers the same way as marketers would understand it (i.e., as potential audience size), but instead as the reach of the persona. Consequently, we clarified the definitions of the titles accordingly in the system (see Figure 10).

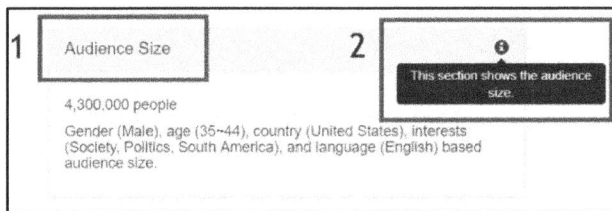

Figure 10: Example of changes made based on the user study. Users did not understand potential reach, so we decided to change to "audience size" (1), which is a more unambiguous term. Additionlly, we included tooltip definition (2).

Finally, some users questioned the topics chosen for topic classification ("I feel international affairs is too broad unless I knew more about what exactly she's interested in -- too vague") (P19). For example, the concept of *Human story* raised some questions. This goes to show that when defining topics for data

analysis of labels for user interfaces, researchers should ensure they are "speaking the same language" as the end users.

4.5 What are the best predictors of confusion?

To answer this question, we use a binary classification model to test the predictive power of the variables. Binary classification can be used for mapping instances between certain classes/groups to determine the best predictors for a given result, in this case confusion. In our case, the variables are the previously mentioned variables we are working with. The accuracy of the model is expressed by AUC (Area Under the Curve) metric. Table 10 shows the AUC scores of each variable.

Table 10 Accuracy of variables; higher is greater accuracy.

Predictor	AUC
Length of transition path (T3)	0.66
Experience Group	0.65
Number of fixations	0.64
Age Group	0.61
Total duration of fixations	0.60
Gender	0.56
Length of transition path (T1)	0.54
Avg. duration of fixations	0.53
Role	0.51
Length of transition path (T2)	0.49

The most predictive factors are a) Age Group, b) Experience Group, c) Length of transition path (for Treatment 3 with extra pictures), and d) Number of Fixations. The proposed model, based on these four variables, gives a good accuracy, giving the right prediction about 8 times out of 10 (AUC=0.812). We conclude that the four most significant factors are good predictors of user confusion. To examine the influence of user-level variables more closely, we plot them in one visualization. We choose T3 as a filter because it has the most confusion observations (Figure 11).

Finally, because the binomial classification model predicts but does not provide significance analysis beyond the AUC metric, we conduct a regression analysis. As the results of the binomial model indicate that the Treatment 3 (T3) is an important factor for confusion, we test each treatment separately. Since there are only 29 subjects, we used the stepwise regression method to get the final model by reducing non-significant variables.

To choose the variables for the reduced model, we are using a procedure called backward selection that finds any significant variable by Akaike information criteria (AIC) by dropping one variable at a time and seeing which one minimizes the AIC most, and moving forward until the AIC change is insignificant.

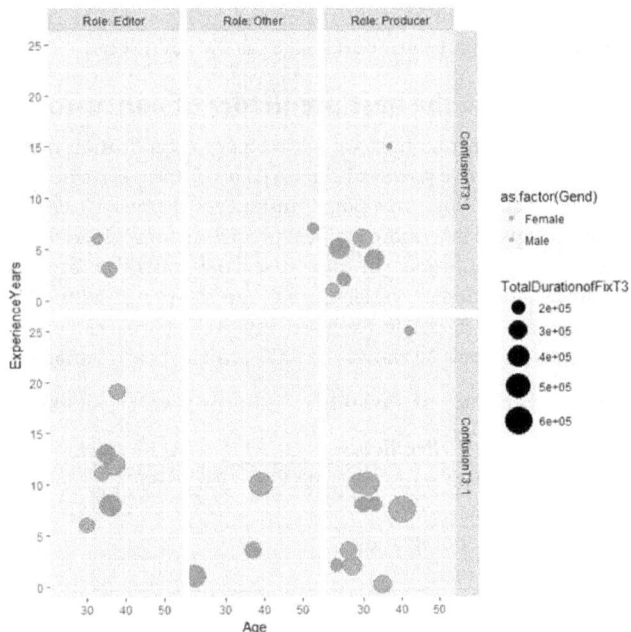

Figure 11: Confusion of participants by background information. It seems that mature males are most prone to confusion in this case.

We thus start from a large number of variables, including background information, fixation information, as well as calculated metrics (e.g., transition path length), and find that the number of fixations has a significant positive relationship with confusion, and the relationship holds across treatments (T1: p-value = 0.041; T2: p-value = 0.059; T3: p-value = 0.037). This corroborates our previous analysis comparing confused and non-confused users in terms of number of fixations. The results of the regression analysis for T3 are shown in Table 11.

Table 11: Reduced regression model for T3.

	Estimate	**Std. error**	**Z**	**Pr(>|z|)**
(Intercept)	-7.93e+00	4.23e+00	-1.88	0.061
No. of fixations	3.440e-02	1.663e-02	2.068	0.039*
No. of transitions	1.000e-01	6.496e-02	1.540	0.124
Total duration	-3.78e-05	1.996e-05	-1.90	0.058
Transition ratio	-4.98e+01	2.52e+01	-1.97	0.048*
Experience	2.627e-01	1.611e-01	1.631	0.103

'' 0.05 significance*

The number of fixations is a significant variable in predicting confusion. Another significant variable in T3 is the transition ratio (total number of transitions/total number of fixations), which provides information on how frequently the user switched from one AOI to another relative to overall fixation

activeness. Total duration (i.e., dwell time) is close to being significant but is not at 5% significance level. Background variables (gender, age, role) were eliminated from the reduced model as they did not improve the explanatory power of the model.

5 CONCLUSION AND DISCUSSION

Overall, our study responds to the call of Blascheck et al. [36] for correlating eye tracking, think-aloud, and other data for analysis of users' cognitive states. We find that personas seem to raise a considerable amount of confusion. Confusion mostly relates to pictures and quotes. While we did not find significant differences in duration of fixation paths between confused and non-confused users, a positive relationship between the number of fixations and confusion is implied both by regression analysis and binomial classification. The fixation paths of confused users are longer and more varied than those of non-confused users. In addition, the binomial classification showed that the most notable predictors for confusion were age, experience, and the number of transitions and fixations. These results confirm earlier findings on the impact of user-level characteristics on users' mental state [35]. In particular, it seemed that older men had more trouble with the more complex layout, supporting findings that gender and age play a role in information processing [45] [46].

The study provides several practical insights for persona development, especially when automated. Most importantly, consistency is a problem when automatically generating quotes and pictures. This concern has also been raised in earlier persona literature [12], and we dub it here as the *consistency problem*. From the explicit feedback, we can see that perceived inconsistency between different informational elements is associated with confusion. Confusion arising from inconsistency could be reduced e.g. by contextualization of the data (i.e., presenting numbers or diversity in the underlying group the persona is based on), and manual verification of different informational elements to ensure they make sense. Consistency is more acute when integrating data from different sources, such as quotes from different users or social network. Further research could find ways to measure and improve consistency automatically, which would help improve the information design of personas profiles.

Finally, we found confusion to vary highly across AOIs, and introduce a metric, confusion ratio, that takes into consideration the relative difference of attention paid to each AOI (dwell time) when determining the criticality of the confusion for the users. By considering this relativity, AOIs that appear confusing can be actually less confusing than what the absolute numbers claim.

We find the talk-aloud technique useful because it helps finding both evidence for confusion for a given user-trial and the reasons behind confusion, supporting quantitative and qualitative analysis. Yet, it is not a perfect technique, as the individuals may differ in their accounts, so that not all users are equally vocal about their experience confusion. In addition, talk-aloud may influence the actual viewing behavior. Therefore, we suggest corroborating talk-aloud records with more robust data analysis in future works.

REFERENCES

[1] A. Cooper, *The Inmates Are Running the Asylum: Why High Tech Products Drive Us Crazy and How to Restore the Sanity*, 1 edition. Indianapolis, IN: Sams - Pearson Education, 2004.

[2] J. Pruitt and J. Grudin, "Personas: Practice and Theory," in *Proceedings of the 2003 Conference on Designing for User Experiences*, New York, NY, USA, 2003, pp. 1–15.

[3] J. Pruitt and T. Adlin, *The Persona Lifecycle: Keeping People in Mind Throughout Product Design*, 1 edition. Amsterdam; Boston: Morgan Kaufmann, 2006.

[4] L. Nielsen and K. Storgaard Hansen, "Personas is applicable: a study on the use of personas in Denmark," in *Proceedings of the SIGCHI Conference on Human Factors in Computing Systems*, 2014, pp. 1665–1674.

[5] L. Nielsen, *Personas-user focused design*, vol. 15. Springer Science & Business Media, 2012.

[6] L. Nielsen, K. S. Nielsen, J. Stage, and J. Billestrup, "Going Global with Personas," in *Human-Computer Interaction – INTERACT 2013*, 2013, pp. 350–357.

[7] S.-G. Jung, J. An, H. Kwak, M. Ahmad, L. Nielsen, and B. J. Jansen, "Persona Generation from Aggregated Social Media Data," in *Proceedings of the 2017 CHI Conference Extended Abstracts on Human Factors in Computing Systems*, New York, NY, USA, 2017, pp. 1748–1755.

[8] J. Salminen *et al.*, "Generating Cultural Personas From Social Data: A Perspective of Middle Eastern Users," presented at the The Fourth International Symposium on Social Networks Analysis, Management and Security (SNAMS-2017), Prague, Czech Republic, 2017.

[9] J. An, H. Kwak, and B. J. Jansen, "Validating Social Media Data for Automatic Persona Generation," presented at the The Second International Workshop on Online Social Networks Technologies (OSNT-2016), 13th ACS/IEEE International Conference on Computer Systems and Applications AICCSA 2016. 29 November - 2 December, 2016.

[10] J. An, K. Haewoon, and B. J. Jansen, "Personas for Content Creators via Decomposed Aggregate Audience Statistics," presented at the Advances in Social Network Analysis and Mining (ASONAM 2017). July 31., 2017.

[11] J. An, H. Kwak, and B. J. Jansen, "Towards Automatic Persona Generation Using Social Media," presented at the The Third International Symposium on Social Networks Analysis, Management and Security (SNAMS 2016), The 4th International Conference on Future Internet of Things and Cloud. 22-24 August, 2016.

[12] C. N. Chapman and R. P. Milham, "The Personas' New Clothes: Methodological and Practical Arguments against a Popular Method," *Proceedings of the Human Factors and Ergonomics Society Annual Meeting*, vol. 50, no. 5, pp. 634–636, Oct. 2006.

[13] T. Matthews, T. Judge, and S. Whittaker, "How Do Designers and User Experience Professionals Actually Perceive and Use Personas?," in *Proceedings of the SIGCHI Conference on Human Factors in Computing Systems*, New York, NY, USA, 2012, pp. 1219–1228.

[14] K. Rönkkö, M. Hellman, B. Kilander, and Y. Dittrich, "Personas is Not Applicable: Local Remedies Interpreted in a Wider Context," in *Proceedings of the Eighth Conference on Participatory Design: Artful Integration: Interweaving Media, Materials and Practices - Volume 1*, New York, NY, USA, 2004, pp. 112–120.

[15] L. Granka, M. Feusner, and L. Lorigo, "Eye Monitoring in Online Search," in *Passive Eye Monitoring*, R. I. Hammoud, Ed. Springer Berlin Heidelberg, 2008, pp. 347–372.

[16] J. H. Goldberg and X. P. Kotval, "Computer interface evaluation using eye movements: methods and constructs," *International Journal of Industrial Ergonomics*, vol. 24, no. 6, pp. 631–645, Oct. 1999.

[17] M. A. Just and P. A. Carpenter, "Eye fixations and cognitive processes," *Cognitive Psychology*, vol. 8, no. 4, pp. 441–480, Oct. 1976.

[18] W. Barfield and T. A. Furness, *Virtual Environments and Advanced Interface Design*. Oxford University Press, 1995.

[19] L. Granka and K. Rodden, "Incorporating eyetracking into user studies at Google," in *Workshop Position paper presented at CHI*, 2006.

[20] D. D. Salvucci and J. H. Goldberg, "Identifying Fixations and Saccades in Eye-tracking Protocols," in *Proceedings of the 2000 Symposium on Eye Tracking Research & Applications*, New York, NY, USA, 2000, pp. 71–78.

[21] B. Follet, O. Le Meur, and T. Baccino, "New Insights into Ambient and Focal Visual Fixations using an Automatic Classification Algorithm," *i-Perception*, vol. 2, no. 6, pp. 592–610, Aug. 2011.

[22] D. Beymer, P. Z. Orton, and D. M. Russell, "An Eye Tracking Study of How Pictures Influence Online Reading," in *Human-Computer Interaction – INTERACT 2007*, 2007, pp. 456–460.

[23] E. Cutrell and Z. Guan, "What Are You Looking for?: An Eye-tracking Study of Information Usage in Web Search," in *Proceedings of the SIGCHI Conference on Human Factors in Computing Systems*, New York, NY, USA, 2007, pp. 407–416.

[24] J. H. Goldberg and J. I. Helfman, "Scanpath Clustering and Aggregation," in *Proceedings of the 2010 Symposium on Eye-Tracking Research & Applications*, New York, NY, USA, 2010, pp. 227–234.

[25] C. Ehmke and S. Wilson, "Identifying Web Usability Problems from Eye-tracking Data," in *Proceedings of the 21st British HCI Group Annual Conference on People and Computers: HCI...But Not As We Know It - Volume 1*, Swinton, UK, UK, 2007, pp. 119–128.

[26] S. Eraslan, Y. Yesilada, and S. Harper, "Scanpath Trend Analysis on Web Pages: Clustering Eye Tracking Scanpaths," *ACM Transactions on the Web*, vol. 10, no. 4, pp. 1–35, Nov. 2016.

[27] T. Blascheck, K. Kurzhals, M. Raschke, S. Strohmaier, D. Weiskopf, and T. Ertl, "AOI hierarchies for visual exploration of fixation sequences," 2016, pp. 111–118.

[28] P. Balatsoukas and I. Ruthven, "An eye-tracking approach to the analysis of relevance judgments on the Web: The case of Google search engine," *J Am Soc Inf Sci Tec*, vol. 63, no. 9, pp. 1728–1746, Sep. 2012.

[29] T. Yamada, H. Hashimoto, and N. Tosa, "Pattern recognition of emotion with neural network," in , *Proceedings of the 1995 IEEE IECON 21st International Conference on Industrial Electronics, Control, and Instrumentation, 1995*, 1995, vol. 1, pp. 183–187 vol.1.

[30] T. Harada, H. Iwasaki, K. Mori, A. Yoshizawa, and F. Mizoguchi, "Evaluation model of cognitive distraction state based on eye-tracking data using neural networks," in *2013 IEEE 12th International Conference on Cognitive Informatics and Cognitive Computing*, 2013, pp. 428–434.

[31] R. Grace *et al.*, "A drowsy driver detection system for heavy vehicles," in *17th DASC. AIAA/IEEE/SAE. Digital Avionics Systems Conference. Proceedings (Cat. No.98CH36267)*, 1998, vol. 2, p. I36/1-I36/8 vol.2.

[32] G. Kuperberg and S. Heckers, "Schizophrenia and cognitive function," *Current Opinion in Neurobiology*, vol. 10, no. 2, pp. 205–210, Apr. 2000.

[33] R. Chai *et al.*, "Classification of EEG based-mental fatigue using principal component analysis and Bayesian neural network," in *2016 38th Annual International Conference of the IEEE Engineering in Medicine and Biology Society (EMBC)*, 2016, pp. 4654–4657.

[34] S.-K. Jang, S. Kim, C.-Y. Kim, H.-S. Lee, and K.-H. Choi, "Attentional processing of emotional faces in schizophrenia: Evidence from eye tracking," *J Abnorm Psychol*, vol. 125, no. 7, pp. 894–906, 2016.

[35] S. Eraslan, Y. Yesilada, and S. Harper, "Eye tracking scanpath analysis techniques on web pages: A survey, evaluation and comparison," *Journal of Eye Movement Research*, vol. 9, no. 1, Dec. 2015.

[36] T. Blascheck, M. John, S. Koch, L. Bruder, and T. Ertl, "Triangulating User Behavior Using Eye Movement, Interaction, and Think Aloud Data," in *Proceedings of the Ninth Biennial ACM Symposium on Eye Tracking Research & Applications*, New York, NY, USA, 2016, pp. 175–182.

[37] J. E. Nieters, S. Ivaturi, and I. Ahmed, "Making Personas Memorable," in *CHI '07 Extended Abstracts on Human Factors in Computing Systems*, New York, NY, USA, 2007, pp. 1817–1824.

[38] F. Long, "Real or imaginary: The effectiveness of using personas in product design," in *Proceedings of the Irish Ergonomics Society Annual Conference*, 2009, vol. 14.

[39] C. G. Hill *et al.*, "Gender-Inclusiveness Personas vs. Stereotyping: Can We Have it Both Ways?," 2017, pp. 6658–6671.

[40] T. Tenbrink, "Cognitive Discourse Analysis: accessing cognitive representations and processes through language data," *Language and Cognition*, vol. 7, no. 1, pp. 98–137, Jul. 2014.

[41] L. Cowen, L. J. s Ball, and J. Delin, "An Eye Movement Analysis of Web Page Usability," in *People and Computers XVI - Memorable Yet Invisible*, Springer, London, 2002, pp. 317–335.

[42] M. Lalmas, H. O'Brien, and E. Yom-Tov, *Measuring User Engagement*. Morgan & Claypool Publishers, 2014.

[43] A. Levenshtein, "Binary codes capable of correcting deletions, insertions, and reversals," *Soviet Phys. Dokl.*, vol. 10, pp. 707–710, 1966.

[44] C. M. Privitera, "The scanpath theory: its definition and later developments," presented at the Human Vision and Electronic Imaging XI, 2006, vol. 6057, p. 60570A.

[45] J. Meyers-Levy and D. Maheswaran, "Exploring Differences in Males' and Females' Processing Strategies," *Journal of Consumer Research*, vol. 18, no. 1, pp. 63–70, 1991.

[46] L. Lorigo, B. Pan, H. Hembrooke, T. Joachims, L. Granka, and G. Gay, "The influence of task and gender on search and evaluation behavior using Google," *Information Processing & Management*, vol. 42, no. 4, pp. 1123–1131, Jul. 2006.

The Lifetime of Email Messages: A Large-Scale Analysis of Email Revisitation

Tarfah Alrashed*
Massachusetts Institute of Technology
Cambridge, MA, USA
tarfah@mit.edu

Ahmed Hassan Awadallah
Susan Dumais
Microsoft Research
Redmond, WA, USA
{hassanam,sdumais}@microsoft.com

ABSTRACT

Email continues to be one of the most important means of online communication, leading to a number of challenges related to information overload and email management. To better understand email management practices in detail, we examine the distribution of visits to emails over time. During their lifetime, emails may be visited one or more times, and with each visit different actions may be taken. Emails that are revisited over time are especially interesting because they represent an opportunity to improve email management and search. In this paper, we present a large-scale log analysis of email revisitation, the activities that people perform on revisited email messages (e.g. responding to, organizing or deleting messages, and opening attachments), and the strategies they use to go back to these emails. We find that most emails have a short lifetime, with more than 33% having a lifetime of less than 5 minutes. We also find that deleting is the most common action taken on messages visited once, and that responding and organizing are more common for messages visited more than once. We complement the log analysis with a survey to understand the motivation behind revisits and the types of emails that are revisited. The survey results show that 73% of the visits are to find information (e.g. a link or document, instructions to perform a task, or answers to questions), while 20% of revisits are to respond to the email. Our findings have implications for designing email clients and intelligent agents that support both short- and long-term revisitation patterns.

KEYWORDS

Email interaction, email revisitation, email lifetime

ACM Reference Format:
Tarfah Alrashed, Ahmed Hassan Awadallah, and Susan Dumais. 2018. The Lifetime of Email Messages: A Large-Scale Analysis of Email Revisitation. In *Proceedings of 2018 Conference on Human Information Interaction & Retrieval (CHIIR '18)*. ACM, New York, NY, USA, 10 pages. https://doi.org/10.1145/3176349.3176398

*Research was conducted at Microsoft Research.

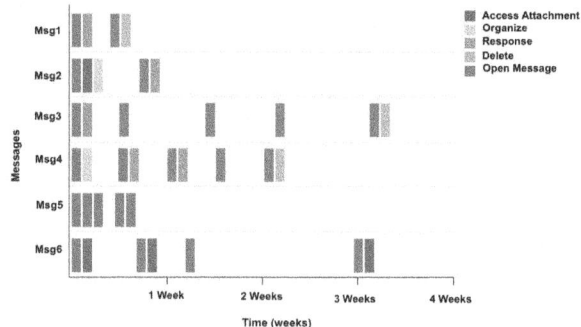

Figure 1: An illustration of activities on email messages over time.

1 INTRODUCTION

Email is one of the most familiar mediums of communication. It has evolved over time to also support task management and serve as a personal repository of information, leading to a number of challenges related to information overload and email management [11], in both work and personal settings. People use different strategies for managing personal and work accounts. They tend to create more structure in their work accounts, where they organize their emails into categories and folders, but they create fewer folders in personal account and rely to search to find emails [4].

Every message we receive in our mailbox goes through a journey. That journey starts with opening a message and ends with deleting, responding, archiving, or no further interaction. During its journey, the message undergoes a sequence of actions. This journey represents the lifetime of that email. Most emails have a short lifetime, never visited or visited once, and some have a longer lifetime, visited more than once (revisited). To better understand and characterize how and why people interact with emails over time, we investigate email revisitation behavior. Different users have distinct mailbox characteristics. For example, the distribution of the type of emails they receive may vary (e.g., instructions, information about an event, shared document or resource, etc.), and hence, their interactions with those emails vary. Users interact with their emails in different ways as well [7, 22]. Some users like to read all the email and reply to each immediately, others triage emails and return to important ones later. To go back to important emails, people use a variety of strategies - some users flag such emails or mark them as unread to facilitate quick visual scanning, others place them in folders or delete them, and some do nothing and use search to get back to important emails.

Figure 1 shows an illustration of email activities for different messages. Each row represents a unique email message and the x-axis shows a user's interaction with that message over time. Different colors represent different actions taken on the email (e.g., blue is "Open Message"), as discussed in more detail in section 3.3.2. The figure shows that different messages have distinct revisitation patterns. Some messages are revisited within short intervals and others remain relevant for a longer period of time. Some messages receive revisits in a small number of bursts, while others are revisited periodically. Some messages are revisited to retrieve information from the message body or attachments, other messages are revisited because the recipient needs to take an action against the message (e.g., reply, delete, etc.).

In this paper, we present a detailed study of the lifetime of an email through the lens of email revisiting behavior. We present a large-scale log analysis of one hundred thousand anonymized users of Outlook Web Access. We complement the log analysis with a survey to gain more insights into the motivation for the observed user behavior. Previous research has studied email and specifically email search [1, 10, 14, 17], however less work has focused on analyzing the journey that different emails go through by examining how and why people go back to emails. The research presented in this paper differs from previous work in several ways. We use large-scale log analysis to analyze interaction patterns in work email accounts. We examine the lifetime of emails by analyzing email revisitation patterns using two complementary methods: a large-scale log analysis, which captures the email activities and patterns, and a survey, which helps complement the log analysis. The research questions we address through our analysis are:

(1) *What are the characteristics of email revisitation?* We examine email revisitation using different dimensions: the number of visits, the inter-visit interval, the lifetime of revisited emails, and the distribution of actions on emails.

(2) *Why do users go back to emails?* We want to understand the type of emails that are most likely to be revisited, the intent behind these visits, and the actions performed on these emails.

(3) *How do users find emails they want to revisit?* In particular, we want to understand what strategies people use to re-find these emails (e.g., search or browse), and if this is influenced by the lifetime of emails.

2 RELATED WORK

Email is one of the most important means of online communication as well as a way to manage tasks and archive personal information. As the volume of email grows, challenges related to email management and retrieval increase [3]. In the research described in this paper, we examine how people interact with email messages over time, with a special focus on understanding how and why people revisit email messages. Two lines of prior work are especially relevant, one on email management and organization and the other on large-scale log analysis of email interaction.

2.1 Email Management and Organization

Most previous studies of email management strategies were based on small samples and used qualitative methods such as interviews, surveys, or diaries. In their pioneering work, Whittaker and Sidner

[22] investigated how people manage and organize their email. They identified three user types based on their strategies for managing email overload: no filers (search for emails), filers (put emails into folders), and spring cleaners (occasionally organize their emails). More than a decade after the original paper, Fisher et al. [7] and Grevet et al. [9] conducted qualitative studies based on Whittaker and Sidner strategies. They found that these strategies were still evident and that email overload was still an issue in both work and personal settings.

Increasingly people have multiple email accounts, and prior work has examined how people manage both work and personal email. Smith et al. [18] conducted a qualitative diary study with 16 participants, in which they found that more than half of their participants had two email accounts. A later study by Capra et al. [2] showed that 84% of participants had separate accounts to help manage boundaries between work and personal life. These two types of accounts had different characteristics: respondents reported more frequent use of keeping behaviors and larger mail boxes in their work accounts. Cecchinato et al. [4] used a diary study to investigate email management and search strategies. They found that people manage their personal and work accounts differently, and use different retrieval strategies. Work accounts were more structured, and email was generally retrieved through the folder structure, whereas people had fewer folders in personal accounts and relied more on search to find email.

Our research also examines email interaction behavior, but we focus on work email and use large-scale log analysis, as opposed to small studies. We also examine in greater detail the journey that individual emails go through by analyzing email revisitation behavior using data from both log analysis and a survey.

2.2 Large-Scale Log Analysis of Email Interaction

One of the earliest naturalistic log studies of re-finding in email was conducted by Elsweiler et al. [6]. They examined a variety of email interactions such as selecting messages, opening folders, sorting or changing views and searching. Using a small amount of labeled data, they developed models to identify re-finding behavior from email logs and described how various interface features were used in re-finding. Whittaker et al. [21] carried out a larger-scale field study of 345 users using an web-based email client who conducted over 85,000 re-finding actions. They investigate different re-finding strategies, and found that although users who create complicated folders do use them for email retrieval, this approach did not improve retrieval success. On the other hand, both search and threading support more effective retrieval. Kalman and Ravid [13] conducted a study of email management strategies on thousands of users over a period of 8 months using a popular email web client add-in. They showed that people use a wide variety of strategies to manage their emails, many more than had been identified in earlier studies.

More recently, both Koren et al. [15] and Grbovic et al. [8] investigated email re-finding strategies using larger-scale log analyses of popular web email clients. They found that search is an increasingly important alternative to tagging emails and creating folders. Ai et al. [1] and Narang et al. [17] also used large-scale log analysis to investigate interaction patterns in work email accounts. Ai et al. [1] examined the actions that people perform on emails after searches and compared re-finding in email search with web search. Narang et al. [17] also examined the activities performed on messages following searches, and how this related to the characteristics of people's mailboxes and email organization strategies. They found that people with larger mailboxes search more, and people who organize less tend to search more.

Re-finding previously seen information is a frequent activity that goes beyond email [5]. Re-finding has been studied in the context of Web search and browsing, and in desktop search. Teevan et al. [19] showed that about 80% of web-page visits are re-visits and 39% of all queries issued to a search engine are to re-find something seen before. Tyler and Teevan [20] provided key insights into the behavior people employ when re-finding. Dumais et al. [5] showed that email is the by far most common type of information that people re-find in a desktop search application, and that more than half of the items re-found using search are more than a month old.

Our research is similar to this line research in that we are also investigating user's email activities. We extend prior work by studying email revisitation, regardless of whether it is accomplished by searching or browsing (which we find to be much more common). We focus on investigating enterprise email behavior, since accessing email makes up a large proportion of users' information seeking efforts within enterprises [16]. We also look more broadly at the lifetime of email messages from the time they are first read to the time they are deleted, responded to, archived or abandoned. And, we use complementary techniques (large-scale log analysis and a survey) to provide a more complete picture of how and why people revisit emails.

3 METHODOLOGY

We studied email revisitation using two complementary techniques: a large-scale log analysis and a survey. The log analysis provides valuable information about general patterns in email usage. We used a sample of email action logs from a popular email client. We analyzed user behavior along different dimensions to understand email revisitation. We also developed a survey to better understand properties of email revisitation that are not possible to study using log analysis. The survey allowed us to examine the intent behind revisitation and the relation between email content and revisitation behavior. In this section, we describe these data sources, and the measures we considered through out our analysis.

3.1 Log Data

We analyzed a sample of the anonymized email logs from Outlook Web Access over a four months period from February 1, 2017 to May 31, 2017. The email web client can be used on both desktop and mobile with multiple browsers. The typical configuration has a folder list on the left and a search box is on the top left, the message list in the middle, and the message reading pane on the right.

Our sample included emails from enterprise users only (as opposed to consumer Web email users). The logs do not provide access to the text of the email message, headers or email search queries. The email log contains actions performed against messages with timestamps and other metadata. In order to capture revisitation

behavior in email logs, we only considered active users, specifically those who were active for more than 75% of the workdays within those four months. A user is considered active on a given day if she performs at least one action (e.g., reply, read) on that day. Our sample contained one hundred thousands active users who performed about 800 million actions during four months. The actions are described in section 3.3.2. Since our analysis focused on the lifetime of emails by analyzing email revisiting behavior, we focused on actions against revisited email messages.

3.2 Survey

We conducted a survey to investigate the intent behind email revisits, and types of information users were looking for in revisited emails. The survey was distributed to a random set of employees within Microsoft who were based in the USA. 395 respondents completed the entire survey, while 3 additional respondents provided partial responses (response rate: 13%, completion rate: 99%). In our analysis, we only consider the 395 who completed the survey in its entirety. 74% of the respondents were male, and were distributed across a wide age range ranging from under 20 to more than 60. Respondents came from a diverse set of roles within the company including: software development, program management, sales, marketing, legal, human resources, administrative assistance, IT support, finance, retail, etc.

The survey was structured into several sections, and like the log data, focused on work emails. In the first section, we asked our respondents about their general email behavior, such as the email client(s) that they use, and the number of emails that they typically receive during a work day.

In the second section, we asked our respondents to recall the last time they went back to an email they had seen before, and briefly describe what the email was about and why they went back to it. We also asked them whether they were successful in re-finding that email, and how long it took them to find it.

In the third section, we asked about characteristics of revisited emails. Specifically we asked respondents to estimate how long ago they received that email (e.g., in the last few hours, today, this week, this month, etc), and what the email was about (e.g., information about an event, instructions to perform a task, an email asking them to do something, etc).

In the fourth section, we asked respondents about their motivation in revisiting the email (e.g., did they go back to the email to find information, to respond, or to organize). We also asked them about the type of information they were looking for (e.g., an email that contained an attachment, instructions to perform a task, etc.).

In the fifth section, we asked respondents about the strategy they used to re-find the email they recalled (e.g., search, browse, or filter for flagged/unread emails). We also asked about attributes that used to find the message (e.g., sender name/email) and whether they had previously revisited the email. In addition, we asked whether they anticipated that they would need to go back to that mail when they first read it, and if so what technique they used to facilitate getting back to that email (e.g., flag/mark as unread, move to a folder, etc.). Lastly, we asked a few optional demographic questions.

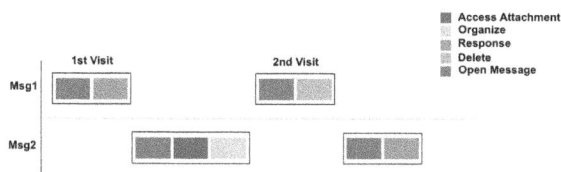

Figure 2: A simple illustration of how we defined email visits and revisits. For a given user, each row represents a message that the user interacts with, and for every message, each set of consecutive actions represents a visit.

3.3 Measures

In order to understand the lifetime of emails, we analyze email revisitation behavior. We examine: (1) characteristics of emails that are revisited, (2) why users revisit emails by analyzing the distribution of email actions (from logs) and types of emails (from surveys), (3) how users get back to revisited emails (browse or search). We start by defining email visits/revisits, and then describing the actions we considered on email messages, the types of email messages, and email revisitation strategies. We describe each of these measures in more detail below.

3.3.1 Email visits and revisits.

Definition 1. An *email visit* is a sequence of consecutive actions performed by a user on an email, which are not interleaved with actions on other emails. An *email revisit* occurs when a user returns to the email after interacting with other messages.

Figure 2, which is a magnification of Figure 1, shows a simple illustration of this. Each row represents a unique message, and all messages belong to one user. The user "visits" Msg1, opens it and then responds to it. Then the user "visits" Msg2, opens it, accesses an attachment and then organizes it. The user then "revisits" Msg1 and opens, then deletes it. This is a revisit to Msg1 because there were intervening actions on another message, Msg2 in this case – that is, they went to another message and came back to (revisited) Msg1. Note that our definition of a visit requires an unbroken sequence of interactions on the same message. We realize that actions performed on one email could be interleaved with actions performed on another. We opted for treating these as multiple visits. One direction of future research could focus on organizing related visits into higher-level hierarchies similar to the work on segmenting search sessions into missions, tasks and goals [12].

The lifetime of an email starts with the user's first interaction with a message (typically opening the message) and ends with their last interactions with the message. We divide users' actions on messages into visits, and analyze the actions taken on messages within these visits, the interval between visits, the type of email messages, and the strategies used to revisit them.

3.3.2 Actions on email messages.
In email, unlike web search, several actions of different types can be performed on a message (e.g., read, reply, move, etc.). In our analysis, we considered the ten most common actions present in the log data sample described in Section 3.1. Table 1 shows these ten actions grouped into higher level categories of actions – open, delete, response, and organize

Table 1: Groups of Message-Related User Actions

Group	Actions
Open Message	StartReadingDisplayPane
Delete	DeleteMessage
Response	Reply, ReplyAll, Forward
Organize	Flag, FlagComplete, MarkAsUnread
Access Attachment	OpenAttachment, EditAttachment

Table 2: Enterprise Email Classification Used for our Survey

Email Type	Description
Commitment	Email committing to do something
Communication	Informal communication with a colleague
Event	Information about an event
Instructions	Instructions to perform a task
Receipt	Receipt or confirmation (e.g., flight)
Request	Email asking someone to do something
Resources	Email sharing resources or documents
Status	Status update
Task	Email asking me to do something
Other	Other types of emails

message, and access attachment. Open message occurs when a message is clicked and its content is shown in the reading pane. Delete occurs when the user deletes an email message. Three actions are used to respond to email messages, and these actions are (Reply, ReplyAll, and Forward). Three actions are used to organize messages in different ways, these actions are (Flag, CompleteFlag, and MarkAsUnread). Delete can be considered as a type of organization activity, but we consider it separately because it is so common. Lastly, two actions are used to access email attachments (OpenAttachment and EditAttachment). We summarize the actions that people take on messages by computing the proportion of total email actions that each activity group accounts for. We further analyze the distribution of actions by the number of visits and the interval between visits.

3.3.3 Types of emails.
To better understand email revisits, we study different revisitation patterns in light of the intent behind sending that email. To characterize the intent behind work emails, we classify work emails into several main types listed in Table 2. These types were derived from analyzing the free text responses to a survey question asking the respondents to describe the work emails that they needed to go back to. The types cover machine-to-human emails such as receipts, confirmations, events, etc. as well as human-to-human emails such as sharing a status update, assigning a task, requesting a resource, sharing instructions, etc.

This is not a complete taxonomy of work email types but it gives us some insights on how the content of the email could affect revisitation patterns. Analyzing the types of emails that are revisited enables us to answer questions like: are emails that contain requests, or attachments more likely to be revisited?

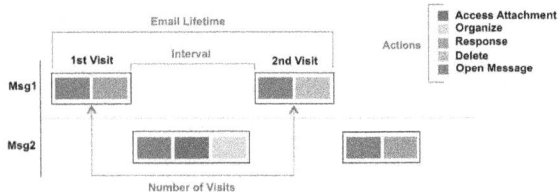

Figure 3: An illustration of the four dimensions we investigate when analyzing email revisits: number of visits, inter-visit interval, email lifetime, and actions taken on revisited emails.

3.3.4 Revisitation strategies. People use several strategies to go back to (revisit) emails that they have previously seen. Understanding the ways users revisit their emails, and how this might be affected by various email properties, is important in understanding email revisitation. We examine two revisitation strategies: searching and browsing. Searching occurs when a user explicitly types a query and accesses a message from the search results. Browsing occurs when a user browses messages in the inbox or navigates to a folder or a category to access the message. We also analyze revisitation strategies for emails with short and long lifetimes, and investigate the actions taken on messages that were found by searching or browsing.

4 RESULTS

In this section, we address our research questions. First, we characterize email revisits. Then, we address our second research question "why do users go back to their email?". Lastly, we address our third research question "how do users go back to their emails?".

4.1 Characterizing email revisits

In order to understand the lifetime of emails, we consider several dimensions that might influence general interaction and revisitation patterns. Figure 3 shows the four dimensions we investigate: number of visits, inter-visit interval, lifetime of revisited email, and actions taken on revisited email. Although we focus on revisited emails, we also examine the distribution of actions on emails that are visited only once and compare it with the distribution of actions on emails that are revisited.

4.1.1 Distribution of number of visits. As described in Section 3.3.1, we first divide users' interactions into visits and compute the number of visits each message receives. Most emails are visited only once, but about a third are visited two or more times. Figure 4 (top) shows the distribution of number of visits for messages that are revisited. The x-axis shows the number of visits and the y-axis shows the relative frequency of occurrence for each on a log-scale. The distribution of the number of visits for revisited emails is heavily skewed to the right. The average number of visits is 10.7 but the the median is only 4. Of the revisited emails, 25% are visited only twice and 64% are visited five times or less. The proportion of messages drops quickly as the number of visits they received increases; leaving only a small percentage of messages receiving large number of visits. Now we move on to study the time between subsequent visits on the same message.

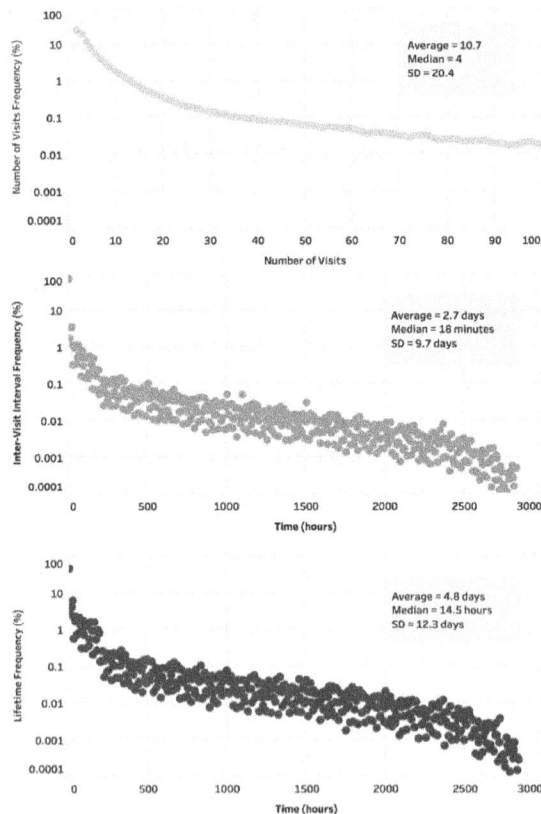

Figure 4: Distribution of number of visits (top), inter-visit interval for revisited emails (middle), and lifetime of revisited emails (bottom).

4.1.2 Distribution of inter-visit intervals. The distribution of time intervals between visits for revisited emails is shown in Figure 4 (middle). The x-axis shows the inter-visit intervals in hours and the y-axis shows the relative frequency of occurrence for each time interval on a log-scale. Again the distribution is heavy tailed – most revisits happen within a very short time from the previous visit (short-term revisits), while a much smaller number of revisits happen several months after the previous visit (long-term revisits). The average inter-visit interval is about 64 hours (2.7 days) and the median is 18 minutes. Further examination of the log data revealed that short-term revisits are more frequent and usually happen when the users are scanning their emails moving back and forth in the message list or when they are interleaving visits to different messages (e.g., read an incoming email and then go back to the previous email to respond or take other actions). The difference between short and long-term revisits has implications for designing methods to support revisiting behavior. Long-term revisits may be well supported by search or organizing into folders or marking; short-term revisitation may be better supported with quick access to recently viewed messages.

4.1.3 Distribution of email lifetimes. As described above, we define the lifetime of an email as the time between a user's first and last interactions with the email. Figure 4 (bottom) shows the

Table 3: Ratios of Actions for Emails Visited Once and Revisited

Action Group	Likelihood Ratios (Revisited/Visited once)
Open Message	3.1
Access Attachment	2.7
Response	1.1
Organize	1.1
Delete	0.4

distribution of lifetimes for revisited emails. Again, we see a heavy-tailed distribution. The average email lifetime is about 115 hours (4.8 days) and the median is 14.5 hours. In our analysis, we find that most emails have a short lifetime - 36% of emails have a lifetime of 5 minutes or less, 43% of emails have a lifetime of 1 hour or less, and 63% of emails have a lifetime of 5 days or less. This temporal distribution could be used as a feature to email ranking functions.

4.1.4 Distribution of actions. To analyze the distribution of actions, we computed the proportion of total email actions that each action group accounts for across all other actions in the dataset. Although we focus on revisited emails, we start by comparing the distribution of actions for emails that are visited once and those that are revisited.

Table 3 shows the ratio of different actions for emails that are revisited compared to those that are only visited once. All actions except delete occur more in revisited emails than in emails visited once. Messages visited only once are 2.5 times more likely to be deleted (ratio 2.5 = 1/0.4). This is expected, since when a message is deleted it is less likely to be visited again. On the other hand, messages that are visited more than once are 3.1 times more likely to be opened and 2.7 times more likely to be accessed for attachments compared with messages visited only once. Revisited messages are also somewhat more likely to be responded to or organized. If users know that they will go back to the emails when they receive them, then they are not likely to delete those emails.

4.2 Why do users revisit their emails?

To answer this question, we analyze the users' intent behind their email revisits and what actions they perform after they revisit the email. Log data provides insights about the actions performed on emails after they are revisited and survey data give us insights about the intent behind email revisits and the types of emails that are revisited. For the log data, we further partition the result by the dimensions described in the previous section – number of visits, inter-visit intervals, lifetime of emails, and type of email.

4.2.1 Actions on revisited emails / Intent. In this section, we examine both actions taken on revisited emails and the intent behind email revisitation. First, we analyze the actions taken on revisited emails broken down by number of visits, and the inter-visit interval. Finally, we investigate revisit intent using our survey data.

Actions vs. Number of Visits. To better understand why users revisit their emails, we analyze actions taken on revisited emails (e.g., did the user go back to a specific email to reply or to open an attachment?). Figure 5 shows the distribution of actions over

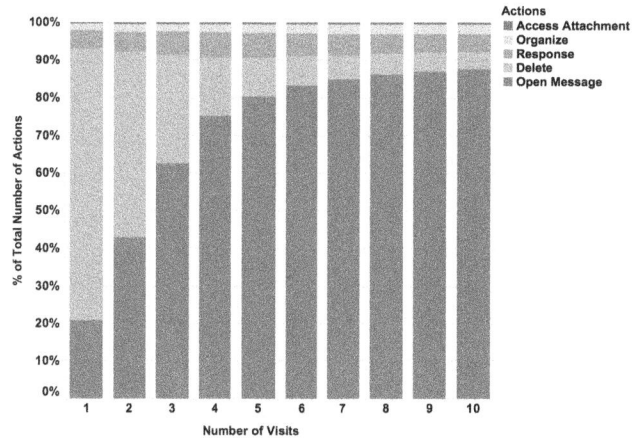

Figure 5: Distribution of actions over number of visits.

number of email visits (for number of visits between 1 and 10). Note that this figure shows the distribution of actions for email that were visited once and revisited emails (2 or more visits). The most common action for emails that are visited once or twice is delete, and the most common action for emails visited more than twice is open. The proportion of delete action decreases with the increase of the number of visits. On the other hand, the proportion of open message actions increases with the number of visits, which we expect to see since users need to open their emails every time they visit them. It is interesting to see that response actions increase with number of visits until the fourth visit, then decrease after that. We also observe a small increase in the proportions of both organizing a message and accessing attachments from emails as the number of visits increases. It appears that responding to an email is most likely to happen within the first four visits to that email, and after that organizing or access to attachments are more common.

Actions vs. Inter-visit Intervals. As we discussed earlier, different emails exhibit different revisitation patterns, some of the revisits happen within a short amount of time, and others occur over a longer period of time. Different actions might be taken for emails revisited within a short interval versus longer ones. We analyze the distribution of actions over the interval between visits. Figure 6 shows the distribution of actions over inter-visit interval (in days) for the first seven days. For emails that are revisited within one day delete and open message are both common. For emails revisited after more than one day, the most common action by far is open. We also find a slight increase in the response percentage with an increase of the inter-visit interval. Open message and access attachment decrease a bit with emails that are revisited more than four days apart.

In Figure 7, we zoom into the action distribution of actions over inter-visit interval (in hours) within six hours. Of the deletes that happened within one day (shown in Figure 6), more than half happened within an hour. We also notice that if emails are revisited after more than an hour users are less likely to delete these emails (10-15%). The other actions (response, organize, and access attachment) increase slightly as the inter-visit interval increases. Observe the overall similarity of patterns seen in Figure 6 and 7. They both

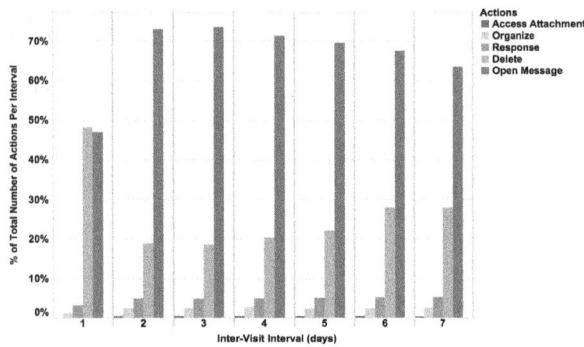

Figure 6: Distribution of actions over inter-visit interval in days (messages revisited within 7 days).

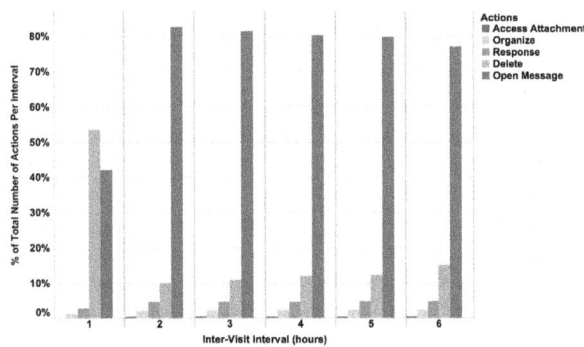

Figure 7: Distribution of actions over inter-visit interval in hours (for messages revisited within 6 hours).

show different proportions in the first day (Figure 6) or the first hour (Figure 7) compared to intervals above one day or one hour. That is because; the vast majority of deletes happen after very short revisits, which affects the proportions of the other actions.

Revisit Intent. In the previous section, we studied actions that are taken on a message during a revisit. In this section, we study the intents that lead a user to revisit a message. In the survey, we asked respondents why they went back to the email they recalled revisiting - was it to find some information, to do something with the email (e.g., reply, forward), to organize or clean up the email (e.g., flag, delete), or something else. Table 4 shows the distribution of the email revisit intents. Most of the emails (73.4%) were revisited to find some information, 20.6% to respond to the email, only 0.6% went back to the emails to delete it or organize it, and 5.4% revisited emails to do something else. For respondents who went back to their emails to find some information (73.4%), we further investigated the type of information they were looking for. Giving our respondents a list of types, as shown in Table 5, we found that 24.1% of the email revisits were to find instructions, 22% were to look for a document (e.g., attachment, link), 16.3% were to find an answer to a question, 10.2% were status updates, 9% were to find a solution to a problem, and other intents occurred less than 5% of the time.

4.2.2 Types of revisited emails. We are interested in understanding the influence that the type of email has on revisitation patterns.

Table 4: Distribution of Email Revisit Intents

Revisit Intent	Percent
Find information in the email	73.4%
Do something with the email (e.g., reply, forward)	20.6%
Organize or clean up their email (e.g., flag, delete)	0.6%
Other	5.4%

Table 5: Distribution of Types of Information Users were Looking for in Emails that were Revisited

Type of Information	Percent
Instructions to perform a certain task	24.1%
A document (e.g., attachment, link)	22.0%
An answer to a question that was previously asked	16.3%
status update	10.2%
A solution to a problem	9.0%
A task request to you	4.9%
A person/customer (e.g., contact information)	2.0%
An appointment/event	2.0%
Machine generated message (e.g., reservation)	0.8%
Other	8.6%

For example, do users go back to emails that contain instructions more often than emails about an event? In the survey, we used a general classification of work email types listed in Table 2, and asked respondents what the email that they went back to was about. Table 6 shows the distribution of the types of revisited email.

38.2% of revisited emails were about sharing resources or documents, 17.3% were emails containing instructions on how to perform a task, 11.9% were emails that asked users to do something, 9.9% were status updates, 5.1% were emails that asked someone else to do something, 3.6% contained information about an event, 2.4% were committing to do something, 1.8% were communicating with a colleague, 0.9% of them were containing receipt or a confirmation, and 7.5% did not fit into our classification. From the previous section we found that 73.4% of users go back to emails to find information, which explains why the two common types of emails are those sharing resources or documents (38.2%), and containing instructions on how to perform a task (17.3%).

4.3 How do users revisit their emails?

To better understand email revisitation behavior, we analyzed the strategies people used to revisit emails, and how effective those strategies were. Before we describe strategies for revisiting email, we briefly summarize the success and effort required to do so. 95.5% of our respondents said they found the email successfully, and most found it quickly (48.4% found it in less than a minute, 41.3% in less than 5 minutes, and 9% needed more than 5 minutes). Respondents indicated that they had previously revisited 62.9% of these messages.

The vast majority of respondents said they used search to revisit the email - 71.6% said they used search to go back to the email, 20.9% said they browsed through their emails (11% browsed in their inbox and 9.9% browsed in a folder/category), only 1.5% filtered for flagged

Table 6: The Distribution of Email Types from Table 2

Email Type	Percent
Resources	38.2%
Instructions	17.3%
Task	11.9%
Status	9.9%
Request	5.1%
Event	3.6%
Commitment	2.4%
Communication	1.8%
Receipt	0.9%
Other	7.5%

or unread emails, and 6% used other strategies. For respondents who used search we also asked about the type of queries they issued - 75.3% said they used keywords that were in the message body or title, 66.1% of them used sender name or email, 14.2% used the recipient name or email, and 7.9% use date/time range that they believe the message was sent in.

Finally, we wanted to understand whether users anticipated that they would need to go back to emails when they first read them. Our survey showed that 62.3% of users anticipated they would revisit these emails. Although the majority of respondents knew that they would revisit these emails in the future, 38.5% of them did not do anything to help facilitate getting back to these emails, 27.4% moved them to folder, and 19.2% flagged/marked them as unread. Note, however, that deleting other messages is another way to make it easier to re-find content by reducing the size of the inbox.

4.3.1 Revisit Strategy vs. Message Lifetime. In our survey, we asked respondents how long ago they received the email that they revisited. 29% said they received it more than a month ago, 27.5% within the same month, 23% within the same week, 6% the day before, 6% the same day, 2.4% the last few hours, 1.5% the last few minutes, and 4.5% could not recall when they had first seen it. It is interesting to note that 56.5% of the revisited emails were received more than a week ago, and the main strategy our respondents said they used was search (71.6%). It appears that when we asked respondents to think of an email that they had revisited, they tended to think about older emails that they used search to get back to. They did not think of the many revisits that occur over short intervals (that are evident in the log data) as "revisits".

Using the log data, we examined the distribution of message lifetime (in hours), for messages received within 24 hours, for searching and browsing; the results are shown in Figure 8. We find that users are more likely to browse when the message was received within three to four hours, and more likely to search for messages received more than 4 hours ago. We also analyze the distribution of revisiting strategies over the lifetime of revisited emails over days. Observe that a large portion of browsing happens for messages received within the first day as shown in Figure 9. The portion of the messages revisited through browsing drops significantly for messages older than one day and remains constant for messages up to one week old, and drops again for messages older than one week.

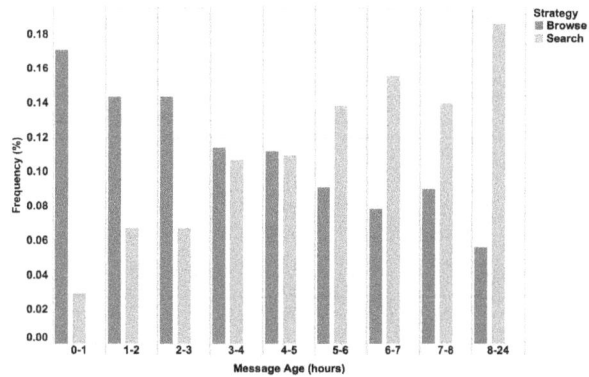

Figure 8: Distribution of message lifetime in hours for both revisit strategies (for messages received within 24 hours).

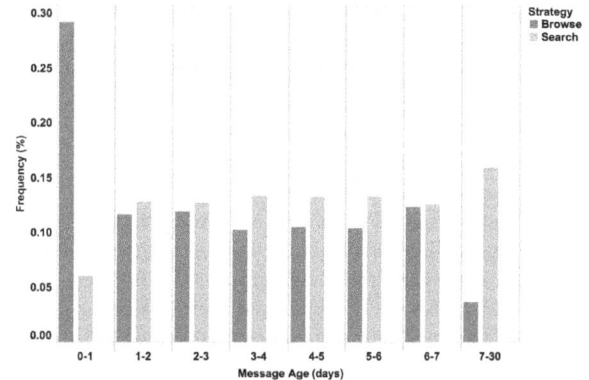

Figure 9: Distribution of message lifetime in days for both revisit strategies (for messages received within 30 days).

4.3.2 Revisit Strategy vs. Action taken on Message. In this section, we examine the differences in the actions that people take on messages depending on whether the message was revisited by searching or browsing. The top actions taken on messages after browsing are in order: open message, delete, response, organize, access attachment. After searching, the top actions taken are: open message, response, delete, organize, and access attachment. For both strategies, open message is the most frequent action, and organize and access attachment are the least frequent actions. An important difference is that delete is proportionally more frequent after browsing while response is more frequent after searching.

Table 7 shows the likelihood ratios for different actions after browsing or searching. Organizing and deleting are more likely after browsing (ratio: 2.9 and 2.3 respectively). On the other hand, responding is significantly more likely after a search (ratio:0.5), and reading a message is slightly more likely after a search (ratio:0.8). Managing content is roughly the same regardless of revisit strategy (ratio:1.0). Accessing attachments occurs roughly the same proportion of the time regardless of the strategy used to revisit the message (only 3% more likely after browsing). This suggests that people browse through their inbox to triage mail, deleting some and filing others. On the other hand, when they search for a message

Table 7: Likelihood Ratios Of Actions After Browsing or Searching

Action	Likelihood ratio (Browse/Search)
Organize	2.9
Delete	2.3
Access Attachment	1.0
Open Message	0.8
Response	0.5

they have seen before, they are more likely to read or respond the messages.

5 DISCUSSION

In this paper, we examined the journey that emails go through from the time they are first read to the time they are last viewed using two complementary methods. We analyzed 800 million email actions from a sample of 100 thousand people, and conducted a survey of almost 400 people to provide insights about search intents, success and strategies. We *characterized* email interaction patterns for work emails with a focus on revisitation (regardless of whether emails are revisited via search or browsing).

The analysis presented in this paper is just a first step toward understanding the lifetime of email messages and revisitation behavior. There are several directions of future work to extend the work presented in this paper both in terms of developing a deeper understanding of the lifetime of different messages by further investigating techniques that people use to facilitate revisiting emails (e.g., flagging or tagging messages, marking messages as unread, moving messages to folders, etc.) and designing email clients and intelligent assistants that help users with going back to messages. In this section, we highlight some of the key findings and discuss their implications as well as directions for future work and conclude with a discussion of the limitations of this work.

Revisits and Lifetime: Most emails are visited only once. For these emails, the most common action is delete, accounting for 72% of actions. Most emails that are visited once are deleted without having been opened. Delete is 2.5 times more likely in emails that are only visited once. This suggests that, on average, people quickly triage their email by deleting emails. On the other hand, for emails that are revisited, the most common action is open/read message. Opening messages is 3 times more likely in revisited emails and opening attachments is 2.7 times more likely.

Although most emails receive only one visit, more than a third of emails are revisited at least once. The median number of visits is 4, while the average is 10.7. This reflects that some emails receive a much larger number of visits (see Figure 4). The proportion of emails are revisited and the steady increase in the the volume of messages make supporting people in getting back to emails increasingly important.

We also found out that the lifetime of most emails is very short. For example, 63% of emails had a lifetime of 5 days or less and 36% of emails had a lifetime of 5 minutes or less. The distribution of the email lifetimes was also skewed with an average email lifetime of 4.8 days and median of 14.5 hours. This temporal distribution could

be leveraged to provide a better ranking functions for email search or caching of most recently visited emails.

The emails that have longer lifetime exhibit interesting revisitation patterns. Figure 1 illustrates some of these patterns, where we see some messages receiving visits in a small number of bursts while other are revisited periodically. Additionally, some emails are revisited over short periods of time, while others are revisited over longer periods in regular intervals or irregular intervals. Deeper understanding of these patterns and how they can be leveraged to support revisiting and re-finding messages is an interestingness direction for future work. This temporal distribution (in combination with previous interaction patters on emails) could be used as a signal to email ranking functions.

Types of Revisitation: Our analysis uncovered two distinct types of email revisitation: short- and long-term revisits. Most revisits occur shortly after an email is first read – this is salient in Figures 6 and 7. Other revisits are longer term and have longer inter-visit intervals. This distinction between types of revisitations is also evident in the actions that people take on the emails. Very short-term revisits often result in a message being deleted. This is similar to messages that receive a single visit where users quickly triage their messages by deleting some of them. Revisits that happen after more than an hour are less likely to result in a message being deleted. For revisits that occur after an interval of one day or more), the most frequent action, by far, is opening the message. The other actions taken on emails (response, organize, and access attachment) increase slightly as the inter-visit interval increases.

Short-term and long-term revisits also impact the strategy users employ to get back to the message. This is evident in Figures 8 and 9 which show that users are more likely to browse when the message was received within three to four hours, and more likely to search for messages received more than 4 hours ago. The difference between short and long-term revisits has implications for designing methods to support revisiting behavior. Short-term revisitation may be supported with UX elements that enable quick access to recently viewed messages. On the other hand, long-term revisiting might be supported by improving search ranking techniques to assist with retrieving previously seen messages.

Revisit Intent: From the survey, we find that most longer-term revisits are to find information (74%) or to take some action on the email (20%). Such information varied from a status update, information about an event, instructions to perform a task, etc. Our analysis also showed that although 62.3% of users knew that they would go back to emails when they first read them, 38.5% of users did nothing to help them re-find the items and relied on search instead. This suggests that there is an opportunity to provide better support for going back to previously seen messages. For example, we can build a model to predict which emails are most likely to be revisited and the actions that will be taken on these emails. Predicting such behavior can provide new means to support getting back to relevant emails.

Limitations: Finally, we should discuss some limitations of the work presented. We used two complementary techniques for this research: a large-scale log analysis and a survey. Log-based studies allow us to characterize how people interact with email, but provide limited insights into the intentions of the users as they interact with emails. As a result, our insights related to revisit intents were limited to the survey data. Our log data sample comprises logs recorded for a hundred thousand active users over a 4-month period of time. The logs could be segmented along different dimensions (e.g., demographics, industry type, etc.) to better understand revisitation behavior varies depending on such segmentation. We leave the study of the impact of these segmentations on the user behavior to future work.

On the other hand, the tremendous scale of log-data allowed us to study the behavior of a large number of users from different industries and backgrounds, this is typically harder to achieve with survey-based or observational analysis. Our survey targeted a smaller number of subjects (relative to the log-data size) from one organization. To partially address this, we included participants from various job roles (e.g., sales, legal, HR, software development, etc.) in our survey. Additionally, our survey design required participants to recall the last time they revisited an email and answer questions about this particular event. While recollecting specific events is more accurate than asking about general patterns, the retrospective methodology can still run the risk of inaccurate or incomplete recollections. Since we asked respondents to recall the last occurrence of a frequent event, the vast majority of them (85.3%) reported no difficulty in recalling the last message they needed to go back to. However, they seemed to interpret "revisit" as referring to older emails (~80% of them reported receiving the email more than 24 hours ago). They did not think of the many short-term revisits that are evident in the log data as revisits. Despite the limitations, the log-based and survey-based studies provided complimentary insights on user behavior but additional research (e.g., involving an *in situ* survey) will be required to better align the findings from the two studies.

6 CONCLUSION

We sought to understand the lifetime of email messages by investigating email revisitation behavior, and understanding why people want to get back to messages and how they do so. We found that while most messages have a short lifetime, many messages remain relevant for a longer time period. We also studied the intents that lead people to go back to messages that they have seen before, and found that finding information and responding to email are the most common reasons. We also found that the strategy used to revisit (search or browse) depended on the age of the email and the intent behind the revisit. Understanding the lifetime of an email message could have implications on understanding how people interact with their email and designing email clients and intelligent agents to help people with managing and organizing their messages. Our future work will aim to develop deeper understanding of the lifetime of an email and explore applications that would better support email revisits.

REFERENCES

[1] Q. Ai, S. Dumais, N. Craswell, and D. Liebling. 2017. Characterizing email search using large-scale behavioral logs and surveys. In *Proceedings of the 26th International Conference on World Wide Web (WWW '17)*. Perth, Australia, 1511–1520. https://doi.org/10.1145/3038912.3052615

[2] R. Capra, J. Khanova, and S. Ramdeen. 2013. Work and personal e-mail use by university employees: PIM practices across domain boundaries. *Journal of the Association for Information Science and Technology* 64, 5, 1029–1044. https://doi.org/10.1002/asi.22815

[3] D. Castro, Z. Karnin, L. Lewin-Eytan, and Y. Maarek. 2016. You've got mail, and Here is what you could do with it!: Analyzing and predicting actions on email messages. In *Proceedings of the Ninth ACM International Conference on Web Search and Data Mining (WSDM '16)*. San Francisco, CA, USA, 307–316. https://doi.org/10.1145/2835776.2835811

[4] M.E. Cecchinato, A. Sellen, M. Shokouhi, and G. Smyth. 2016. Finding email in a multi-account, multi-device world. In *Proceedings of the 2016 CHI Conference on Human Factors in Computing Systems (CHI '16)*. 1200–1210. https://doi.org/10.1145/2858036.2858473

[5] S. Dumais, E. Cutrell, J. J. Cadiz, G. Jancke, R. Sarin, and D. C. Robbins. 2016. Stuff I've Seen: A system for personal information retrieval and re-use. In *ACM SIGIR Forum*, Vol. 49. 28–35. https://doi.org/10.1145/2888422.2888425

[6] D. Elsweiler, M. Harvey, and M. Hacker. 2011. Understanding re-finding behavior in naturalistic email interaction logs. In *Proceedings of the 34th international ACM SIGIR conference on Research and development in Information Retrieval*. 35–44. https://doi.org/10.1145/2009916.2009925

[7] D. Fisher, A. J. Brush, E. Gleave, and M. Smith. 2006. Revisiting Whittaker & Sidner's "email overload" ten years later. In *Proceedings of the 2006 20th anniversary conference on Computer Supported Cooperative Work (CSCW '06)*. Banff, Alberta, Canada, 309–312. https://doi.org/10.1145/1180875.1180922

[8] M. Grbovic, G. Halawi, Z. Karnin, and Y. Maarek. 2014. How many folders do you really need?: Classifying email into a handful of categories. In *Proceedings of the 23rd ACM International Conference on Conference on Information and Knowledge Management (CIKM '14)*. Shanghai, China, 869–878. https://doi.org/10.1145/2661829.2662018

[9] C. Grevet, D. Choi, D. Kumar, and E. Gilbert. 2014. Overload is overloaded: Email in the age of Gmail. In *Proceedings of the SIGCHI Conference on Human Factors in Computing Systems (CHI '14)*. Toronto, Ontario, Canada, 793–802. https://doi.org/10.1145/2556288.2557013

[10] M. Harvey and D. Elsweiler. 2012. Exploring query patterns in email search. *Advances in information retrieval* (2012), 25–36.

[11] A. Jerejian, C. Reid, and C. Rees. 2013. The contribution of email volume, email management strategies and propensity to worry in predicting email stress among academics. In *Computers in Human Behavior*, Vol. 29. Elsevier, 991–996. https://doi.org/10.1145/2661829.2662018

[12] R. Jones and K.L. Klinkner. 2008. Beyond the Session Timeout: Automatic hierarchical segmentation of search topics in query logs. In *Proceedings of the 17th ACM Conference on Information and Knowledge Management (CIKM '08)*. 699–708. https://doi.org/10.1145/1458082.1458176

[13] Y.M. Kalman and G. Ravid. 2015. Filing, piling, and everything in between: The dynamics of E-mail inbox management. In *Journal of the Association for Information Science and Technology*. Toronto, Ontario, Canada, 2540–2552. https://doi.org/10.1002/asi.23337

[14] J.Y. Kim, N. Craswell, S. Dumais, F. Radlinski, and F. Liu. 2017. Understanding and modeling success in email search. In *Proceedings of the 40th International ACM SIGIR Conference on Research and Development in Information Retrieval (SIGIR '17)*. Perth, Australia, 265–274. https://doi.org/10.1145/3077136.3080837

[15] Y. Koren, E. Liberty, Y. Maarek, and R. Sandler. 2011. Automatically tagging email by leveraging other users' folders. In *Proceedings of the 17th ACM SIGKDD international conference on Knowledge discovery and data mining (KDD '11)*. San Diego, CA, USA, 913–921. https://doi.org/10.1145/2020408.2020560

[16] U. Kruschwitz and H. Charlie. 2017. Searching the Enterprise. *Foundations and Trends in Information Retrieval* 11, 1 (2017), 1–142.

[17] K. Narang, S. Dumais, and Q. Ai. 2017. Large-scale analysis of email search and organizational strategies. In *Proceedings of the 2017 Conference on Conference Human Information Interaction and Retrieval (CHIIR '17)*. 215–223. https://doi.org/10.1145/3020165.3020175

[18] H. Smith, Y. Rogers, and M. Underwood. 2003. Managing personal and work email in the same box: overcoming the tensions through new metaphors. *Proceedings of the Home Oriented Informatics and Telematics (HOIT '03)* (2003).

[19] J. Teevan, E. Adar, R. Jones, and M.A.S. Potts. 2007. Information re-retrieval: repeat queries in Yahoo's logs. In *Proceedings of the 30th annual international ACM SIGIR conference on Research and Development in Information Retrieval*. 151–158. https://doi.org/10.1145/1277741.1277770

[20] S.K. Tyler and J. Teevan. 2010. Large scale query log analysis of re-finding. In *Proceedings of the 3rd ACM International Conference on Web Search and Data Mining*. 191–200. https://doi.org/10.1145/1718487.1718512

[21] S. Whittaker, T. Matthews, J. Cerruti, H. Badenes, and J. Tang. 2011. Am I wasting my time organizing email?: A study of email refinding. In *Proceedings of the SIGCHI Conference on Human Factors in Computing Systems (CHI '11)*. Vancouver, BC, Canada, 3449–3458. https://doi.org/10.1145/1978942.1979457

[22] S. Whittaker and C. Sidner. 1996. Email overload: Exploring personal information management of email. In *Proceedings of the SIGCHI Conference on Human Factors in Computing Systems (CHI '96)*. Vancouver, British Columbia, Canada, 276–283. https://doi.org/10.1145/238386.238530

"Other Times It's Just Strolling Back Through My Timeline": Investigating Re-finding Behaviour on Twitter and Its Motivations

Florian Meier
Science, Policy and Information Studies
Department of Communication and Psychology
Aalborg University Copenhagen
Denmark
fmeier@hum.aau.dk

David Elsweiler
Information Science Group
I:IMSK
University of Regensburg
Germany
david.elsweiler@ur.de

ABSTRACT

Returning to previously viewed or possessed information — re-finding — is a core information seeking behaviour that has been studied in diverse contexts including physical environments, personal computer filing systems, web search and email. Despite being designed for real-time and ephemeral content, recent studies have shown that re-finding of older content is performed in social media applications too. To better understand why this is and how re-finding can be better supported, in this work we describe the results of a large-scale web-based survey which queried 606 Twitter users on how and how often they re-find, as well as the motivations for this behaviour. Our main contribution is the qualitative analysis of these motivations and motivations sourced via two existing studies, resulting in a coding scheme documenting the breadth and frequency of different social media re-finding tasks. We discuss how this classification can be used in (i) the design of task-based evaluations, (ii) the detection and interpretation of re-finding in click-stream data and (iii) the design of social media search systems.

KEYWORDS

Personal Information Management; Re-finding; Social Media; Twitter; Survey

ACM Reference Format:
Florian Meier and David Elsweiler. 2018. "Other Times It's Just Strolling Back Through My Timeline": Investigating Re-finding Behaviour on Twitter and Its Motivations. In *CHIIR '18: 2018 Conference on Human Information Interaction & Retrieval, March 11–15, 2018, New Brunswick, NJ, USA*. ACM, New York, NY, USA, 10 pages. https://doi.org/10.1145/3176349.3176392

1 INTRODUCTION

Social media (SM) are increasingly embedded in everyday life and have become a primary information source for many. A recent *Pew Research Center* study reveals that 62% of U.S. adults use SM to inform themselves about recent news and current affairs [19]. This emphasis on new, up-to-date information is reflected in the design of services such as Twitter, which focus on the newest posts to support diverse real-time information needs e.g., live discussions of TV shows or emergency relief during disasters [42, 43]. A growing body of literature suggests, however, that SM content can have longer lifespans and users would benefit from additional *wayback machine*-like functionality to search for older posts [1]. Despite limited explicit interface support, users often attempt to re-access older content with SM applications, which function as information silos [30, 34, 38, 57]. Studying how people manage and search for personally relevant information has a long research tradition in the field of Personal Information Management (PIM) dating from studies of physical desktop organisation [31]. Despite this tradition and our growing understanding of how people archive and re-access SM content, we know little about the situations surrounding re-finding on SM: what people seek, how often they require to do so and the motivations for re-finding. Unlike other domains, such as web search [8], mobile search [12] or problem contexts like long-lasting and complex exploratory search scenarios [29, 32, 55] — and even re-finding in other contexts, where several efforts have been made to structure the breath of people's information needs into tasks — no classification exists characterising the kinds of re-finding tasks people perform on SM platforms.

Our contributions in this article are threefold: (i) we report on the findings of a survey, which characterises re-finding behaviour on Twitter by providing insights into the frequency with which people try to re-access previously consumed Tweets, the factors affecting re-finding, as well as the strategies people employ when re-finding. (ii) We qualitatively analyse user descriptions of their motivation for re-finding from three sources to understand the spectrum of re-finding reasons and present the resulting coding scheme characterising diverse motivations. (iii) Based on our results we present recommendations for the design of re-finding tasks in task-based PIM experiments, explain how our results can be used to inform the analysis of SM click-stream data and outline design implications for social search and SM platforms.

2 RELATED WORK

The following sections outline two primary bodies of related work: (i) PIM literature focusing on studies providing insights into re-finding behaviour and re-finding on SM in particular. (ii) Diverse task classifications demonstrate how the research community and practitioners can benefit from an understanding of user needs and tasks when designing search systems, analysing log data or conducting interactive IR experiments.

2.1 PIM and Re-finding

Re-finding — the behaviour exhibited to reacquire previously seen information — is a core PIM activity [3, 24]. Re-finding is common and has been studied in many contexts and with different types of information including paper documents [31], photos [52], digital files on the desktop [2], emails [11, 16, 53] and websites [10, 41, 48]. Other work has studied behaviour across multiple applications and types of information [5, 13, 25]. Quite recently, motivated by the increasing importance of SM, researchers have started to study SM content, such as Facebook posts or Tweets, as PIM objects [34, 57].

The PIM community has unearthed numerous re-finding behaviours and factors influencing re-finding. The evidence shows that how and why information is kept are two factors which influence later retrieval. Others include the type of information (email vs. website), specific properties (e.g., uniqueness), meta-data (e.g., author and date) and perceived value [2, 5, 28, 52]. Two dominant re-finding strategies are (i) to locate information spatially (*orienteering*), which is characterized by narrowing in on the target item via browsing or navigation and (ii) logical finding (*teleporting*), which attempts to re-locate the target directly often with detailed search queries [2, 53].

An investigation of the motivations for using the RT feature revealed evidence of PIM-related behaviour on Twitter. Participants reported using the RT feature to keep Tweets with the intention of future re-access [7]. A similar study investigating the motivations for using the favourite feature (now like) discovered that bookmarking Tweets for later retrieval was the second most common use case [35]. Gorrell and Bontcheva also investigated how the favouriting feature is used [18]. Machine learning experiments were used in an attempt to predict whether a favourite is intended as bookmark, like, for self-promotion, to signal agreement or show gratitude. Elsweiler and Harvey analysed data from an experience sampling study which aimed at finding out about motivations for using Twitter's search function discovering that up to 40% of user-reported reasons for using the Twitter search were related to finding previously seen Tweets [15]. Teevan, Ramage and Ringel Morris used quantitative log data to study peoples Twitter search behaviour [49]. They characterised repeated queries — which in other contexts are taken as hints for re-finding intentions — as monitoring behaviour, concluding, somewhat contradictory to the previous study, that Twitter search is not frequently used for re-finding tasks [49]. To date, only one study has explicitly investigated re-finding on SM platforms using click-stream analysis [34]. The results indicate that although Twitter focuses on real-time information, older content is viewed with regularity. Moreover two strategies were identified which people employ to re-find older Tweets: (i) re-locating Tweets by scrolling down the timeline and (ii) re-locating Tweets on the profile sites of other users. Both behaviours indicate a dominance of orienteering based re-finding approaches. The data show that searching for Tweets directly accounts for less than 4% of all re-finding actions. Thus, not only is there conflicting evidence with

respect to the frequency with which people re-access Twitter content and doubt with respect to the strategies taken to do so, but we know little about the motivations for SM re-finding.

Researchers from other communities studying social media behaviour, however, provide some clues as to motivations for returning to SM content. Users of Facebook and Pinterest, for example, regularly return to previously viewed content often to curate their on-line presence, a task referred to as *Impression Management* [22]. A large body of literature deals with the phenomenon of regret deletions in SM – a *repair strategy* where SM users delete messages because they regret revealing private information or expressing views they no longer hold [45, 58]. Moreover some platforms are per se perceived as personal lockers or archives which are used to reminisce in past content or manage personal information collections [30, 57]. Zhao et al. analyse Facebook's role as tool for the creation of personal collections used not only for self-presentation, but also as a means to reminisce or re-experience memories [57]. Linder, Snodgrass and Kerne study how Pinterest users utilise the platform for creative processes and idea generation [30]. They found that during ideation people regularly return to older created or viewed pins. Recently, Oh and colleagues studied the use of hashtags on Instagram in the context of the *Weekend Hashtag Project*. They observed users re-tagging older posts with the hashtag #WHP in order to update these older posts and thus be able to take part in the most recent contest [38].

While these studies all shed light on diverse motivations for returning to SM content, no comprehensive classification of motivations — especially with respect to Twitter — exists. Our work fills this gap by deriving a classification of Twitter re-finding motivations and tasks. Task classifications are ubiquitous in many other domains and important for academics and practitioners alike, as the following section shows.

2.2 Task Classifications in Interactive Information Retrieval (IIR) Research

Search tasks are completed by cognitive actors (users) as a means to obtain information [23]. Classifications of search tasks in IIR are numerous and are often delineated based on type or characteristic [26]. Type-based examples focus on what people are trying to achieve and include the differentiation of look-up, learn and investigate information seeking tasks [32] and distinguishing between decision, fact-finding, information gathering and exploratory search tasks [50, 54]. Characteristic-based classifications, on the other hand, delineate tasks by property, such as specificity [40], complexity [9], some characteristic of the user performing the task [4] or a combination of other features. Li and Belkin classify, for example, tasks along three different character facets: generic facets (e.g., source of task, goal), common facets (e.g., objective task complexity) and user facets (e.g., subjective task complexity, difficulty, knowledge of the topic) [29]. Further specialised classifications exist for particular usage contexts, such as web [8] or mobile [12] search. A comprehensive collection of research papers related to search tasks in IIR can be found via the *Repository of Assigned Search Tasks* (RepAST) [54].

Classifications, such as those reviewed above, are important because they inform the design of IIR systems [26, 54], help to

4.4 Which of the following best applies?

When you want to find a Tweet again, do you...

	strongly disagree	disagree	neutral	agree	strongly agree
tend to search for it in your own timeline?	○	○	○	○	○
tend to search for it in your favourites list?	○	○	○	○	○
tend to look in the persons timeline, you can remember tweeting it?	○	○	○	○	○
tend to use the Twitter searchbox and initiate a query?	○	○	○	○	○
tend to use a general purpose search enige (like Google)?	○	○	○	○	○
tend to look in a particular store (e.g. browser bookmark, software (Pocket, Evernote...), E-mail inbox, Word document, paper printout, RSS-Feed)	○	○	○	○	○

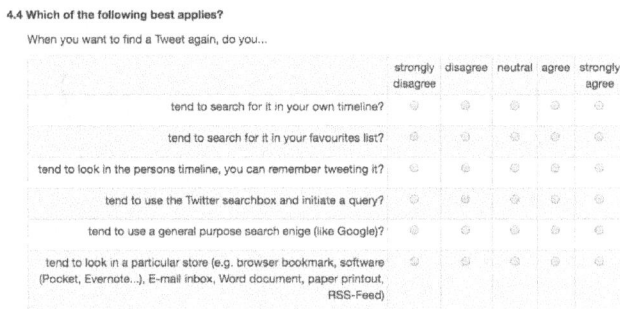

Figure 1: Example question from the survey in which participants had to tick which strategies they tend use for re-finding Tweets.

study and model search behaviour [21], as well as evaluate search systems and user interfaces [17]. Appropriate task classifications are especially important during IIR experiments and evaluation scenarios as poorly or inadequately designed tasks can impact search behaviour in such studies, confound results or complicate the analysis [26].

In contrast to the extensive efforts to delineate tasks in IIR, in PIM search task classifications are rare. Due to their highly personalized nature, task-based studies in PIM are hard to design [17]. Therefore, standard approaches to search in PIM often simplify the problem by considering it as a known-item search [27] or by adopting task types from information seeking scenarios which do not properly mirror re-finding problems [10]. Elsweiler and Ruthven took a more nuanced approach, distinguishing between lookup, item and multi-item re-finding tasks and additionally considering the time that has passed since the initial encounter of the information [17]. Other studies reveal re-finding with certain types of information which can also be used for task design. Barreau and Nardi report three different types of information re-found by their participants: ephemeral, working and archival information [2]. Bergman and Whittaker contrast information along four dimension: type, actionable vs. informative, uniqueness and accumulation [3].

In summary, the first body of reviewed literature reveals the growing importance of SM as an information source and as a place for storing information. We nevertheless have limited understanding of how people behave in these situations, how often such situations arise and, importantly, why they arise. The second body of literature shows that search task classifications have improved IIR evaluation and offer a better understanding of user behaviour. Equivalent classifications in PIM are lacking. By deriving a coding scheme, characterising the motivations for SM re-finding, we can help to create tasks that adequately reflect the re-finding needs of SM users. To obtain a wide range of re-finding motivations we combine descriptions of re-finding tasks from three different data sources. We introduce these data sources and outline our methodology in detail below. In a first step, however, we add to knowledge of how and how often people re-find Twitter content by presenting results from one of the data sources, a web-based survey on Twitter usage.

3 METHODOLOGY AND DATA ANALYSIS

We achieve our research aims by combining data collected via three separate studies. The primary source is a survey questioning 606 Twitter users on their keeping and re-finding behaviours when using the platform. The structure of the survey as well as its quantitative results are presented in section 3.1 and section 4 respectively. Free-form comments from the survey are supplemented by re-finding motivations from two additional experience sampling studies:[1]

- Elsweiler and Harvey collected motivations for performing Twitter searches, of which a proportion were explicitly classified as re-finding tasks [15]. We include these re-finding descriptions in our analysis.
- To complement their naturalistic log study, Meier and Elsweiler employed a heuristic algorithm to detect re-finding actions [34]. Participants verified these actions and provided descriptions of what they were trying to find and why.

In total we qualitatively analyse 372 re-finding motivations following an approach blending the steps of content analysis and grounded theory explained in section 3.3. The results of this analysis are presented in section 4.2. Below we present the details and the structure of the Twitter survey.

3.1 Twitter-Survey

To attain a comprehensive overview of how people engage in PIM related activities on Twitter we designed a web-based questionnaire consisting of 37 items divided into five parts: (i) Demographics and general Twitter usage (ii) Favouriting behaviour (iii) Keeping Twitter content (iv) Re-finding Twitter content (v) Summary questions. In addition to basic demographic information, part (i) questioned respondents on their general Twitter usage (e.g., how often they use the service, how often they check their timeline, as well as account statistics e.g., number of posted Tweets, number of followers etc.). Favouriting/liking is the dominant feature with respect to bookmarking and re-accessing Tweets [35]. Part (ii) questioned users on the usage of this feature. Part (iii) and (iv) focused on Twitter keeping and re-finding behaviours. Finally, two questions established opinion on the adequacy of Twitter's features for PIM.

The survey comprised of three question types: (i) frequency-based questions, typically presented at the beginning of every question block, queried participants on the frequency with which they tend to exhibit certain behaviours. Such questions were answered on a 7-point likert-scale ranging from *never* (1) to *multiple times per day* (7) mirroring the answer format from another Twitter survey [39]. (ii) Follow-up questions were presented in every question block to respondents who stated to exhibit certain activities at least rarely (2). These questions were introduced by the prompt: *Which of the following best applies?* followed by options on a scale ranging from *strongly disagree* to *strongly agree* (See Figure 1 for an example). (iii) Free-form questions gathered qualitative insights on motivations for engaging in specific PIM activities. To overcome problems of memory bias, participants were asked to visit their Twitter profile and copy-paste recently favourited and re-found Twitter messages.

---

[1]We thank David Elsweiler, Morgan Harvey and Florian Meier for sharing their data with us.

(n=606)	min	max	median	IQR
Tweets posted (n)	0	73940	118	1013
Followee Count (n)	0	33 000	28	124
Follower Count (n)	0	20 000	50	173
Favourites Count (n)	0	55 600	5	40

Table 1: Twitter account statistics for all survey participants.

3.2 Participants

606 Twitter users participated in the web-based survey, which was distributed via (i) internet fora, social media and mailing lists, resulting in a snowball sample of 103 participants and (ii) the on-line survey platform TellWut.com, resulting in a crowdsourced sample of 503 Twitter users. 65.3% of respondents were female and were mostly young (37.1% were aged 19-29). TellWut.com offered access to participants with broader age-range with more younger (<19) and older (>49) participants being recruited this way. 5.6% of respondents were younger than 19 and 18.8% were older than 49. Participants were mostly well-educated, with more than half (51.9%) having achieved or working towards a Bachelor's degree.

Respondents reported diverse use of Twitter. 74.8% had been using the service for at least a year with only 7.3% being fairly new to Twitter. The Twitter web interface was the principal means to access the service (89.6%), although 37.6% of respondents reported additionally using the Twitter mobile application. This contrasts Twitter's official usage statistic, which claims that over 80% of requests come from mobile phones [51]. Our data show that users tend to use both options, most likely depending on the tasks they wish to achieve. Other applications for accessing Twitter (e.g., TweetDeck) feature infrequently (<10%). Table 1 shows Twitter account statistics for the respondents, revealing highly skewed long-tailed distribution for all variables. In addition to using Twitter, participants reported having a Facebook (92%) and Pinterest (37.1%) account. For most participants Twitter is only one platform in their SM ecology [56].

3.3 Quantitative and Qualitative Data Analysis

The likert-scale questions were analysed using basic descriptive statistics. To test for differences between groups of users (e.g., participants who keep Tweets regularly vs. participants who reported never needing to do so) we checked if the percentile (95%) of the confidence interval of the differences of bootstrapped means exhibit the null effect (in this case the differences of *means* = 0) as proposed in [36]. If the null effect cannot be observed the distributions of two groups differ from each other significantly.

Our qualitative data analysis approach is based on Schreier's toolbox for qualitative content analysis [44]. Schreier argues that all "forms of qualitative content analysis that are mentioned in the literature are reconstructed not as discrete versions of the method, but as variations on specific steps in the course of structured qualitative content analysis" [44]. The toolbox guides researchers through the qualitative analysis process. This led to us choosing a three-stage coding process, consisting of *Open Coding, Axial Coding, Selective Coding*, from the Grounded Theory Methodology as basic strategy to inductively build a coding scheme. The precise steps we took to analyse the re-finding motivations were as follows: First, we

randomly sampled 50 re-finding motivations from the pool of all statements, which three researchers analyzed in an open coding process. *Open Coding* is characterised as assigning codes to interesting aspects of each user reported reason and involves "breaking down, examining, comparing, conceptualising and categorising data" [46]. In a second stage — *Axial Coding* — the coders met, discussed their results and rearranged the codes in a bottom-up fashion into higher-level categories or concepts. An affinity diagram helped identify relationships or criteria of demarcation between concepts. The outcome of this stage was a complete coding scheme containing a set of codes and categories reflecting the motivations for re-finding Tweets at a useful level of abstraction. The aim of the final stage — *Selective Coding* — is to determine a core category. Although this coding process was not fully achieved, the identified motivations can be classified into two main groups according to the general information properties which characterize Tweets as information items or items with need for further action. To test the quality and reliability of the coding scheme, we again randomly sampled 50 re-finding motivations to be coded by three coders according to the developed coding schema from which an inter-rater agreement was calculated. As multiple codes can be applied to a single motivation and multiple coders were involved in the coding process the calculation of the inter-rater agreement took the mean of pairwise Kappa (κ) coefficients to calculate an overall Kappa value $\kappa_{OVERALL}$ as proposed by Hallgren [20]. In a first run only weak agreement of $\kappa_{OVERALL} = 0.51$ was achieved thus Mayring's guidelines for revising coding schema were applied [33]. Mayring recommends discarding dimensions or sub-categories when categories are too detailed. We used the revised coding scheme in a second test phase taking the same approach with a new sample of 50 randomly selected reasons which resulted in a moderate agreement ($\kappa_{OVERALL} = 0.74$). Finally, the revised coding scheme was applied by the lead author to code all re-finding statements. The result is described in section 4.2.

4 RESULTS

The following sections present results regarding re-finding behaviours and motivations for engaging in re-finding.

4.1 Re-finding Behaviour

73.4% participants reported having had the need to return to a previously seen Tweet. The proportion of respondents stating that they wanted to keep a Tweet of interest is even higher (77.3%). This can partially be explained by users who keep a collection of favourable or memorable Tweets by curating favourited Tweets in their favourites list [35]. It seems logical that people who keep more often also re-find more frequently, which is indicated by a positive correlation ($\rho = 0.36$) between the two variables as shown in Figure 2(b).

For 43.9% of the respondents re-finding is an event that occurs only *rarely*. However, at least 8.4% of participants stated that they re-find Tweets on a weekly basis or even more frequently. A positive correlation ($\rho = 0.39$) between *Re-finding Frequency* and *Re-finding Frequency Own Tweets* indicates that people do not only return to Tweets from their stream but also re-find Tweets they posted themselves. Returning to self-posted Tweets is a frequently mentioned motivation for re-finding (see code (7)).

(a)

(b)

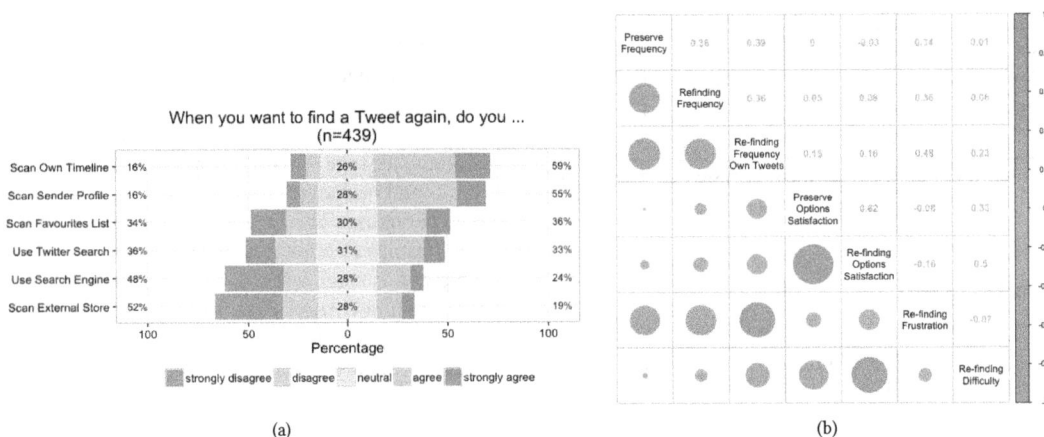

Figure 2: Re-finding strategies (2(a)) and correlation matrix (2(b)) of important variables.

31.9% of respondents disagree with the statement that re-finding on Twitter is an easy task, although a strong response bias can be noticed due to 43.1% of participants checking *neutral*. Although this means that many people were unsure whether re-finding is difficult, there is evidence that it can be frustrating. 58.3% of respondents reported having been frustrated by challenging or unsuccessful re-finding task in the past. Interestingly, perceived difficulty and frustration are uncorrelated. 20% judge the re-finding facilities Twitter offers to be *poor* or *very poor* but again 47.2% provided a neutral answer. Participants who rated Twitter's facilities for preserving Tweets as *good* or *very good* rated the re-finding facilities accordingly ($\rho = 0.62$). As shown in Figure 2(a) the most commonly reported re-finding strategies were scanning one's own timeline (59%) and scanning the profile sites of other users i.e the Tweets they have posted (55%). This reveals the dominance of orienteering-based strategies with users narrowing in on the target items by browsing and navigation. Other re-finding methods, such as those requiring prior keeping behaviour or searching for Tweets directly (*teleporting*) were reported less often. These results are in-line with the log-study findings in [34].

Differences in behaviour are observed, however, when comparing the behaviour of people who claim never to keep Tweets for future retrieval (n=59) and those who did (at least rarely, n=380). A significant stronger agreement for using the re-finding methods *Scan External Store*, *Scan Favourites List* and *Scan Own Timeline* can be found among the group of participants who stated to preserve Tweets of interest at least rarely (see Figure 3).

We also observe differences in the strategies employed depending on the way participants answered with respect to the perceived re-finding difficulty, the level of frustration reported and how various re-finding options were rated. Overall, participants who stated that re-finding is easy (i) tend to rate the re-finding options as *good* or *very good* (see Figure 2(b), $\rho = 0.50$) (ii) have not experienced frustration (see Figure 2(b), $\rho = -0.07$) and (iii) are more likely to use all re-finding options available (see Figure 3). The evidence suggests that participants who use multiple strategies when re-accessing previously seen Twitter content characterize re-finding

as an easy task, which is well supported by Twitter and thus have never been frustrated.

The analysis of our survey responses paints a similar picture to what has been reported previously: Twitter content is not always ephemeral and Tweets can be of relevance for much longer than their initial appearance in the stream. Multiple participants express a need to keep and re-find Tweets, even the need to return to Tweets they posted themselves. Re-finding tasks can be easy and straightforward. However, our analysis shows that they can also be difficult and frustrating. The two main strategies identified in a previous study for re-accessing Tweets — scanning the own timeline and scanning the profile site of other users — are also the two dominant strategies for the participants in our survey [34]. Re-finding using Twitter search happens only rarely, which is in line with Teevan et al. [49], as well as Meier and Elsweiler's observations [34]. Finally our data suggest that when employing

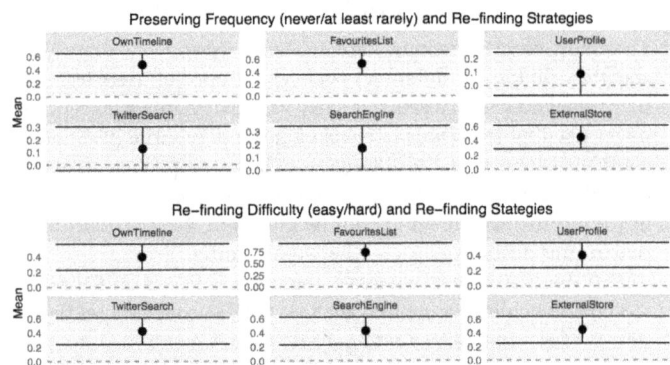

Figure 3: Bootstrapped means ($B = 10000$) for detecting group differences. Error bars indicate the 95% percentile of the differences of the bootstrapped means. If the error bars don't touch or cross the red line (null effect) a significant difference in the distribution between two groups can be observed.

multiple strategies re-finding is easier and less frustrating for users. Now we know how often people re-find and which strategies are used. We nevertheless know little about the motivations driving these behaviours. We turn our attention to this in the next sections.

4.2 Re-finding Motivations

In total, 372 descriptions of re-finding motivations were analysed qualitatively as described in section 3.3. The process resulted in 522 codes being assigned (on average 1.4 codes per reason). Three re-finding motivations had a maximum of five codes. Figure 4 visualizes the usage frequency of different codes, as well as the intersection of different codes that were frequently assigned in combination. Table 2 shows the final coding scheme. To ease the comparison of codes and their allocation, each reason is assigned a unique reference number shown in round brackets (e.g (R5)). Codes are referenced using a similar notation, e.g., (1.1) refers to Code 1.1, which describes re-finding motivations that are related to writing and posting Tweets.

Motivations can be thought of as either actionable or informative [3]. Information is actionable when it requires the user to act or respond. This is typical, for example, for emails as they often require the user to reply. Contrastingly, web-pages discovered during web search are mostly informative as they are typically consumed without the user needing to act in a specific way. It is not always possible, however, to draw a clear distinction. Tweets are informative most of the time, but in some cases may also require user action. Codes in categories (1) and (2) represent actionable motivations. Codes in categories (3), (4) and (5) represent informative motivations. Codes (6) and (7) are auxiliary codes, which do not fit into Bergman and Whittaker's distinction. In the sections to come each code is explained in detail.

4.2.1 (1) Administrative Motivations. Code category (1) *Administrative Motivations* describes re-finding behaviour with administrative or management motivation. The four sub-codes associated with this category were applied in total 97 times. Sub-code (1.1) *Tweet Composing* covers cases whereby participant responses linked re-finding to composing or posting Tweets. Target Tweets were sometimes authored by users themselves. Such explanations included efforts to verify a Tweet's formulation, e.g., its spelling

1	Administrative Motivations	(5) 97
1.1	Tweet Composing	23
1.2	Monitoring/Checking Status	22
1.3	Specific Use	36
1.4	Time Management	11
2	Social Motivations	70
2.1	Share on Platform: RT	9
2.2	Generic Sharing	61
3	Sentimental Motivations	(7) 82
3.1	Entertainment	37
3.2	Nostalgia/Memory	22
3.3	Re-experience Other Sentiments	16
4	Informational Motivations	(44) 131
4.1	Specific Detail/Item	55
4.2	Specific Topic	32
5	Media Re-finding	94
5.1	Links	53
5.2	Pictures/Videos	24
5.3	Quotes/Comments	17
6	Multi-item Re-finding	20
7	Own Tweets	27
		$\sum = 522$

Table 2: Coding Scheme for Re-finding Reasons.

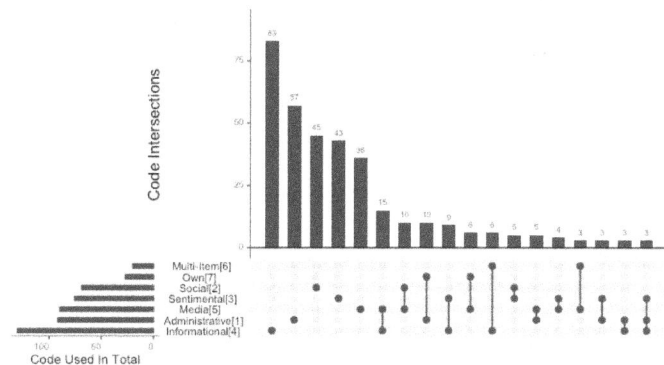

Figure 4: Codes from Table 2 and their combined usage.

(R4,R250) or veracity: "Check if the tweeted information was stupid or not" (R243), sometimes concluding that posted information was too sensitive or personal for their followers and thus deleting it. This *Regret Deletion* behaviour is well-documented in SM research [45, 58], where Tweets are typically re-accessed shortly after initially posting the Tweet. Due to the short time-period elapsed between interacting with and relocating the content, it is debatable whether this should actually be considered as re-finding. The term re-visit might be more appropriate. Other explanations for returning to self-posted Tweets included to avoid duplicates or to replicate intentionally: "I want to see whether I tweeted a given picture already" (R86), "to copy the content because I cannot remember it and lazy to write it again" (R40). These reasons were also assigned code (7) *Own Tweets*. Figure 4 confirms that sub-codes (1.1) and (7) were applied commonly 10 times.

Other reasons coded with code (1.1) had target Tweets posted by other users, such as "I want to reply to the person [...]" (R279) or "[...] reply to a tweet that I hadn't originally had the time to" (R161). (R161) moreover exhibits a further administrative dimension captured by sub-code (1.4) *Time Management*. In reasons with this code users argue their motivation for returning to a Tweet was a lack of time during the initial encounter. 11 reasons were coded with time constraint sub-code (1.4). Examples include: "[...] I might also look back on a conversation that had not previously been finished"

(R226), "I was looking at the link earlier and decided to visit later when I had more time" (R23) or "Something that I've seen whilst quickly checking twitter e.g. on the bus on waiting for something that I want to review in more detail" (R66). The reasons indicate that checking the most recent updates often occurs in situations, whereby users lack sufficient time to allocate necessary attention during Tweet consumption. Users defer the evaluation of Tweets until they have more time. In such cases people sometimes forget about these Tweets, a problem Bergman and Whittaker refer to as the *Deferred Evaluation Problem*, which leads to the evaluation being postponed or cancelled [3]. Our descriptions contained such cases: "[...] got distracted doing something else and forgot about it until later on" (R206). Here Twitter has the additional problem that Tweets lack a reminding function, which files retained on the desktop or emails kept in the inbox provide [2, 31].

A further administrative motivation, coded with sub-code (1.2) *Monitoring/Checking Status*, is returning to Tweets to check for replies or to evaluate their success by checking the number of likes or re-tweets received: "wanted to see if there were any replies" (R67); "looking for responses [...]" (R250).

Finally, sub-code (1.3) *Specific Use* relates to re-finding descriptions mentioning a specific follow-up action, performed once a Tweet has been re-found. One example is to use the re-found Tweet in a conversation or discussion: "Needed it in discussion [...]" (R361) and "Use it for later in work / discussions" (R79). A further action is keeping the re-found Tweet or its content by transferring it to a more frequently visited external store: "I remembered that Max tweeted something about a nice building inside the campus. I wanted to save the image" (R260).

4.2.2   (2) Social Motivations. 70 statements were tagged with code (2) or a sub-code there of. These identify Tweet sharing as a major motivation for Twitter re-finding. Driven by social incentive, people re-locate Tweets either to re-tweet (sub-code (2.1)) or to share by another means, such as email or simply by showing others on their mobile phone (sub-code (2.2)). Example reasons mentioning the use of on-platform functionality for sharing Tweets (code (2.1) *Share on Platform:RT*) include: "want to re-tweet them" (R210) or "I wanted to refind the tweet containing a ted-talk I started watching earlier in the afternoon. The aim being to favourite and then retweet it" (R251). In many cases participants did not explicitly mention a specific sharing method. These descriptions often contain verbs like *to share* or *to show* accompanied by a receiver: "want to share them with someone" (R166) or "if it's something i want to share with someone else not on twitter" (R104). In only a few cases users did explicitly mention a specific method for sharing in this case Twitter and Facebook simultaneously.

4.2.3   (3) Sentimental Motivations. To relive feelings or certain emotional states can be a motivator for re-finding Tweets. In our data 82 statements described a sentimental motivation. Sub-code (3.1) *Entertainment* was the most frequently applied code in this category, representing people re-finding Tweets to be re-entertained: "because it's funny" (R233) or "i remember a joke i found funny" (R323). People justify their motivation by making topical references to what they found amusing: "was looking for a tweet I had seen joking about former yahoo ceo scott thompson's fake computer science degree" (R132) or "Was talking to someone about ADHD,

and wanted to share with them a funny tweet i'd seen once before. had to search google's index of twitter to find it" (R347).

The second sentimental dimension (sub-code (3.2)) characterizes re-finding as memory related, often with a nostalgic emphasis. People return to "something worth remembering" (R49) or re-find a Tweet to "bring back memories" (R165). Recollecting and reminiscing is achieved by re-visiting Tweets connected to those episodes and often relates to self-posted Tweets (code (7) *Own Tweets*). Driven by nostalgic intentions users reported traversing their timeline to browse past Tweets. It seems in these cases people do not have a specific target Tweet, but achieve feelings of nostalgia via multiple Tweets: "For general interest (e.g., I wonder what I said in that argument, I wonder what my first tweet was, I wonder what photos I have posted etc.)" (R36) or "Other times it's just strolling back through my time line to find things I'd retweeted just to enjoy them again (usually not a specific tweet in mind)" (R54). The second statement describes re-finding Tweets as meandering through one's own timeline for hedonistic reasons, which are satisfied by seeing posted pictures or re-tweeted Tweets. Certain statements with this code highlight elements of self-reflection: "i like to see things that i have posted in the past to see how much i have changed" (R201). Self-reflection is closely related to the concept of *Impression Management* i.e. the presentation of self introduced in Eric Goffman's sociological theory that has been adopted to SM [22, 57]. These examples emphasize that re-finding on Twitter is not limited to one single re-finding target, but certain re-finding needs can only be satisfied by looking at multiple Tweets.

The final code in this category, sub-code (3.3) *Re-experience Other Sentiments* covers descriptions mentioning emotional experiences that users attempt to achieve when re-finding: "to inspire me" (R237), "uplifting or good message" (R238) or "it's a sentiment i wanted to see again for inspiration when things were getting tough" (R341).

4.2.4   (4) Informational Motivations. Code category (4) represents the most dominant category and describes the informational content users seek. Figure 4 visualizes this dominance and shows that codes from category (4) are typically assigned in isolation. Information can mean a specific detail or item (sub-code (4.1)). This can mean a number, date or hashtag or simply information about a specific topic e.g., sports, music or personal finance (sub-code (4.2) *Specific Topic*). Participants looking for specific information commented on re-finding in the following ways: "looking for the name of the guy who does recsys user studies" (R308), "friends bday/anniversary" (R324) or "the hashtag i wanted to use in a tweet I was about to send" (R167). Statements not mentioning a specific information item but referencing a certain topic and thus generic information on this topic were tagged with sub-code (4.2), e.g., "good workout routine or recipe" (R187) or "i would like to make these cookies." (R185). To re-visit Tweets containing recipe information was a rather common re-finding motivation. Despite it being impossible for a single Tweet to contain a whole recipe and it is likely that a contained link was the re-finding target, when a link was not mentioned explicitly sub-code (5.1) was not applied. In cases where the description contained neither a reference to a specific item nor a specific topic, we applied the top level code (4), which, as Table 2 shows, was the case for 44 statements. Examples include: "if there was information that was important for me" (R29), "Because they contain some relevant information that I don't remember; it is very much like knowing that an information is written down in a specific book/chapter, and you can look it up whenever you need to" (R202). Reason (R202) portraits Twitter as a long-time medium with characteristics of an archive or silo, in which information is stored safely and can be retrieved at will. This user does not seem to perceive difficulties in returning to previously seen Twitter content nor the need to keep Tweets in an separate store for faster and less challenging retrieval. This contradicts recent work analyzing Tweets form large corpus showing that of the Tweets aged six years old or older, one-third were no longer accessible, indicating that information on the platform is definitely not permanent [37].

4.2.5 (5) Media Re-finding. Another common re-finding motivation is the aim to locate a previously seen Tweet containing media content, e.g., a link (sub-code (5.1)), photo or video (sub-code (5.2)) or quote (sub-code (5.3)). 94 re-finding reasons (25.3%) contained a reference to a specific type of media. Such descriptions tended to contain keywords such as *link, reference, picture* in the descriptions: "if there's an interesting picture or link that I want to investigate further" (R236) or "Trying to find a link to a video that I remember one of my friends had posted. Pretty sure I saw it on Twitter." (R70). Statements explicitly mentioning textual media such as jokes, quotes or comments include: "it was a catchy saying" (R93) or "want to find interesting quote again" (R284). Sometimes a whole thread of comments or a conversation was the target. These were additionally assigned code (6) *Multi-item re-finding* together with sub-code (5.3): "i might also look back on a conversation that had not previously been finished" (R226) or simply "To recall a conversation" (R292).

4.3 Discussion and Implications for Future Research

The coding scheme presented in Table 2 reveals diverse motivations for relocating previously seen Twitter content. We discuss the implications of our findings with respect to three areas: (i) the development of appropriate re-finding tasks for task-based PIM experiments (ii) the analysis and interpretation of SM click-stream data (iii) the design of social search and SM systems.

4.3.1 Re-finding Motivations and Task Development. Appropriately designed re-finding tasks are essential to conduct task-based experiments to understand user behaviour and evaluate how changes to SM interfaces support users complete specific objectives e.g., re-find content. Our coding scheme can assist with the design of such tasks.

When designing experiments, we know from other domains (e.g., [6, 26]), that ecological validity is crucial and including tasks, which simulate the diversity of behaviours exhibited in the wild is an important aspect of this. The coding scheme derived in this work reflects this diversity in the context of SM re-finding; representing different reasons for both actionable and informative tasks. The frequency information provided offers insight into the prominence of different task types. Our data suggest that to realistically model re-finding tasks, most tasks should be informational in nature with a single target Tweet. Our results suggest, however, that to evaluate re-finding features holistically, it is insufficient to utilise tasks with

a single target Tweet alone; researchers must also include tasks involving multiple targets, such as when seeking conversations or pictures from a specific account, which our quantitative results demonstrate lead to differing search strategies being applied by the user. Participant descriptions, moreover, illustrate diverse means of re-finding ranging from browsing one's own timeline, to narrowing in on a target user and browsing temporally to using an external search engine that indexes Twitter content. Thus, the aim of laboratory evaluations in this context should be to simulated diverse situations, which engender diverse search strategies.

Another important dimension to consider is that of time. The elapsed time since the initial encounter of an information item is known in other contexts to influence how a re-finding tasks will be perceived [14], what the user remembers to drive the search [3], as well as the re-finding strategy employed [10]. The task descriptions hint at diversity in elapsed time in SM re-finding tasks. For example, returning to Tweets to check spelling errors most likely occurs soon after posting. Other short-lapse tasks included "Looking for a tweet that i just read 30 secs ago. Why is this so hard? I have lots of tweets and it just seems to be lost" (R11), demonstrating that short time lapses do not necessarily equate to simple tasks. Our data also shows that users re-find Tweets, which have been viewed some time ago: "Wanted to find a post about an inspirational website (graphic design) which I saw on Twitter a few weeks ago" (R362). This observation, combined with corroboratory evidence in [34], suggests that when creating experimental tasks, researchers should not only consider diversity in task type, but attempt to diversify the time elapsed since interacting with the target Tweet(s).

Another time-related aspect — code (1.4) *Time Management* — reveals that users often check their Twitter stream in situations whereby attention is limited making a full relevance decision impossible and leading to *deferred evaluation*. We have discussed that people can forget about potentially relevant Tweets in these cases until an information need is triggered via an external event: "looking for a link I had previously seen in my feed. Abt US politics, don't recall exact issue. Checked bc something else reminded me that I had seen it and became curious" (R310). Such situations could also be simulated in task-based PIM experiments by having a first phase where participants check their Twitter feed via a mobile client and use the desktop client in a re-finding session or vice versa.

4.3.2 Re-finding Motivations and Click-stream Data Analysis. Analyses of click-stream data studying SM re-finding behaviour have used a second click on a Tweet in a subsequent session as proxy for identifying re-finding actions [34]. Our results suggest this approach to be less than ideal as many of the reported descriptions would be omitted using this proxy.

Re-finding motivations tagged with codes from category (1) *Administrative Motivations* especially those assigned the sub-codes (1.1) or (1.4) reveal that interacting with and subsequently re-finding Tweets can occur within a single session. Whether this is to return to a Tweet to correct a spelling mistake or relocate an informational Tweet read a few moments earlier, returning to Tweets within the same session happens frequently. Whether this should be referred to as re-finding is perhaps debatable. Given the short-time elapse, the term *re-visit* seems more appropriate for such tasks. However, if researchers wish to identify all activities related to re-finding in transaction logs, re-visits should be taken into consideration. Furthermore, our results suggest that many re-finding actions may be completed without a second click on a target Tweet. Re-finding self-posted Tweets or multiple Tweets from a conversation most likely are poorly identified using a re-click proxy. It seems, therefore, that a re-click proxy underestimates re-finding. Finally, another shortcoming of Meier and Elsweiler's work relates to the fact that they ignored interactions as they only recorded user clicks with the desktop client and neglected interactions with mobile clients [34]. All actions dealing with impression management, start from the premise of a previous action and can fill in for the missing information of mobile devices and also implicitly mean a later return to those messages. Future log analysis should account for our considerations when analysing re-finding behaviour.

4.3.3 Re-finding Motivations and the Design of Social Media Systems. Growing evidence exists for SM services being used as information silos despite being designed for real-time information and social interaction. We believe this should lead to designers of SM platforms considering user PIM needs when building new or re-designing existing platforms. About 70% of our respondents hold the opinion that Twitter's features for returning to previously viewed content should be improved. Our questionnaire responses show users who exhibit keeping behaviour also use the stores they keep Tweets in for future retrieval. This means improving keeping facilities also improves re-finding. One option would be to improve the favourite/like feature by providing more structure to the list or implementing a reminder function, which reminds users of previously kept Tweets so users do not file and forget re-finding targets, as previous studies have shown seems to be the case [34].

Although scrolling down the own profile page is not the only option to locate self-posted Tweets [45] as other options, such as searching for using your own Twitter handle exist, *teleporting* strategies are not favoured by users. Moreover, the auto-complete function also biases behaviour by immediately suggesting a user-profile page thus hindering users from adding additional query terms [34]. After all, users show a clear preference for orienteering-based re-finding strategies. Especially when re-finding Tweets from other senders users re-locate the re-finding target among this user's posted Tweets. One option to assist and quicken re-finding in this context would be to highlight potential re-finding targets in the senders stream. Users could also benefit from others options like to let re-finding targets re-appear among fresh Tweets on the users stream. Tweets could re-appear either en bloc similar to the *In case you missed it*-feature or completely interleaved into the stream. Similar concepts have proven to be successful in the context of web search [47].

Recently Alonso and colleagues have begun to integrate way-back machine-like functionality into a social search system to fulfil the need to go back in time and look at older (potentially already viewed) content [1]. Their approach of archiving data over time and mining relevant links shared by trusted users, cannot only be used for selecting high quality content but also help with identifying fake news. Returning to a Tweet to check the trustworthiness of the source, could be an additional motivation, which however did not explicitly come up in our studies probably because this theme

had it's rise during the U.S. presidential elections in 2016 when the phase of data collection had already been finished.

5 SUMMARY AND CONCLUSION

In this work we have presented the results of a large-scale web-based survey, which queried 606 Twitter users on the frequency with which they exhibit PIM behaviours on Twitter as well as their motivations for doing so. We complemented the responses with qualitative data from two additional sources. Our analyses provide yet more evidence that SM content can offer lasting utility with many users needing to return to previously viewed content. Responses to our questionnaire reveal a dominance of orienteering-based strategies (primarily scanning one's own timeline (59%) and the posted Tweets of other users (55%)), aligning with the interpretation of Twitter click-stream data [34]. The main contribution of the work, however, is the classification of re-finding motivations to provide the first comprehensive list of motivations and reasons on why Twitter users — and SM users in general — return to previously viewed and/or created SM content. We qualitatively analysed 372 re-finding statements from three different sources to derive a coding scheme covering the broad range of heterogeneous reasons for re-finding reported by the participants. This coding scheme demonstrates that re-finding can be influenced by numerous dimensions including time (shot-time re-finding/within session vs. after a long time), type of author (posted by oneself or by others), attached media or number of re-finding targets (single- vs. multi-item re-finding). Some of the participants interpret Twitter as a long-term information silo, where information is stored and easily accessible. However this might not be the case in all re-finding scenarios. On the one hand re-finding can be very straightforward and directed towards a specific target e.g., a Tweet with a certain link. On the other hand re-finding actions can be undirected where the journey is the reward; users stroll through their own posted Tweets in order to take a trip down the memory lane. Despite Twitter, at least in comparison to Facebook, having only limited features to build and manage one's on-line presence, users regularly retrieve self-posted Tweets to fulfil the need for nostalgic experiences, learn about themselves and how they and their lives have changed over time. The role Twitter takes in a user's SM ecology especially with respect to the self-representation and how this relates to re-finding should be investigated further in the future. We have demonstrated how our coding scheme offers utility in different contexts: (i) The design of tasks for lab-based interactive IR/PIM studies and the evaluation of SM search systems (ii) The analysis and interpretation of SM click-stream studies and (iii) The (re-)design of SM platforms to better support their users PIM needs.

REFERENCES

[1] Omar Alonso, Vasileios Kandylas, Serge-Eric Tremblay, Jake M. Hofman, and Siddhartha Sen. 2017. What's Happening and What Happened: Searching the Social Web. In *Proc. of WebSci '17*. ACM, New York, NY, USA, 191–200.

[2] D. Barreau and B. A. Nardi. 1995. Finding and Reminding: File Organization from the Desktop. *SIGCHI Bull.* 27, 3 (1995), 39–43.

[3] O. Bergman and S. Whittaker. 2016. *The Science of Managing Our Digital Stuff.* The MIT Press, Cambridge, London.

[4] Dania Bilal. 2001. Children's use of the Yahooligans! Web search engine: II. Cognitive and physical behaviors on research tasks. *JASIST* 52, 2 (2001), 118–136.

[5] R. Boardman and M. A. Sasse. 2004. "Stuff Goes into the Computer and Doesn't Come out": A Cross-tool Study of Personal Information Management. In *Proc. of CHI'04*. ACM, New York, NY, USA, 583–590.

[6] Pia Borlund. 2003. The IIR evaluation model: a framework for evaluation of interactive information retrieval systems. *Information Research. An International Electronic Journal* 8, 3 (2003).

[7] Danah boyd, Scott Golder, and Gilad Lotan. 2010. Tweet, Tweet, Retweet: Conversational Aspects of Retweeting on Twitter. In *Proc. of HICSS'10*. IEEE, Washington, DC, USA, 1–10.

[8] Andrei Broder. 2002. A Taxonomy of Web Search. *SIGIR Forum* 36, 2 (Sept. 2002), 3–10.

[9] Katriina Byström and Kalervo Järvelin. 1995. Task Complexity Affects Information Seeking and Use. *Inf. Process. Manage.* 31, 2 (March 1995), 191–213.

[10] R. Capra and M. Perez-Quinones. 2005. Using Web Search Engines to Find and Refind Information. *Computer* 38, 10 (2005), 36–42.

[11] David Carmel, Guy Halawi, Liane Lewin-Eytan, Yoelle Maarek, and Ariel Raviv. 2015. Rank by Time or by Relevance?: Revisiting Email Search. In *Proc. of CKIM'15*. ACM, New York, NY, USA, 283–292.

[12] Karen Church, Mauro Cherubini, and Nuria Oliver. 2014. A Large-scale Study of Daily Information Needs Captured in Situ. *TOCHI* 21, 2 (2014), 10:1–10:46.

[13] S. Dumais, E. Cutrell, JJ Cadiz, G. Jancke, R. Sarin, and D. C. Robbins. 2003. Stuff I've Seen: A System for Personal Information Retrieval and Re-use. In *Proc. of SIGIR'03*. ACM, New York, NY, USA, 72–79.

[14] David Elsweiler, Mark Baillie, and Ian Ruthven. 2011. What Makes Re-finding Information Difficult? A Study of Email Re-finding. In *Proc. of ECIR'11*. Springer, Berlin, 568–579.

[15] David Elsweiler and Morgan Harvey. 2015. Engaging and maintaining a sense of being informed: Understanding the tasks motivating twitter search. *JASIST* 66, 2 (2015), 264–281.

[16] D. Elsweiler, M. Harvey, and M. Hacker. 2011. Understanding Re-finding Behavior in Naturalistic Email Interaction Logs. In *Proc. of SIGIR'11*. ACM, New York, NY, USA, 35–44.

[17] David Elsweiler and Ian Ruthven. 2007. Towards Task-based Personal Information Management Evaluations. In *Proc. of SIGIR'07*. ACM, New York, NY, USA, 23–30.

[18] Genevieve Gorrell and Kalina Bontcheva. 2016. Classifying Twitter favorites: Like, bookmark, or Thanks? *JASIST* 67, 1 (2016), 17–25.

[19] Jeffrey Gottfried and Elisa Shearer. 2016. News Use Across Social Media Platforms 2016. (2016). http://www.journalism.org/2016/05/26/news-use-across-social-media-platforms-2016/

[20] Kevin A Hallgren. 2012. Computing Inter-Rater Reliability for Observational Data: An Overview and Tutorial. *Tutorials in quantitative methods for psychology* 8, 1 (2012), 23–34.

[21] Jiyin He and Emine Yilmaz. 2017. User Behaviour and Task Characteristics: A Field Study of Daily Information Behaviour. In *Proc. of CHIIR'17*. ACM, New York, NY, USA, 67–76.

[22] Bernie Hogan. 2010. The Presentation of Self in the Age of Social Media: Distinguishing Performances and Exhibitions Online. *Bulletin of Science, Technology & Society* 30, 6 (2010).

[23] Peter Ingwersen and Kalervo Järvelin. 2006. *The Turn: Integration of information seeking and retrieval in context*. Vol. 18. Springer Science & Business Media.

[24] W. Jones and J. Teevan. 2007. Introduction. In *Personal Information Management*, W. Jones and J. Teevan (Eds.). University of Washington Press, Washington, 3–20.

[25] W. Jones, A. Wenning, and H. Bruce. 2014. How do people refind files, emails and web pages? In *Proc. iConference'14*. 552–564.

[26] Diane Kelly, Jaime Arguello, Ashlee Edwards, and Wan-ching Wu. 2015. Development and Evaluation of Search Tasks for IIR Experiments Using a Cognitive Complexity Framework. In *Proc. of ICTIR'15*. ACM, New York, NY, USA.

[27] Jinyoung Kim and W. Bruce Croft. 2009. Retrieval Experiments Using Pseudo-desktop Collections. In *Proc. of CIKM'09*. ACM, New York, NY, USA, 1297–1306.

[28] B. H. Kwasnik. 1991. The Importance of Factors that are not Document Attributes in the Organisation of Personal Documents. *Journal of Documentation* 47, 4 (1991), 389–398.

[29] Yuelin Li and Nicholas J. Belkin. 2008. A Faceted Approach to Conceptualizing Tasks in Information Seeking. *Inf. Process. Manage.* 44, 6 (2008), 1822–1837.

[30] Rhema Linder, Clair Snodgrass, and Andruid Kerne. 2014. Everyday Ideation: All of My Ideas Are on Pinterest. In *Proc. of CHI'14*. ACM, New York, NY, USA, 2411–2420.

[31] Thomas W. Malone. 1983. How Do People Organize Their Desks?: Implications for the Design of Office Information Systems. *TOIS* 1, 1 (1983), 99–112.

[32] Gary Marchionini. 2006. Exploratory Search: From Finding to Understanding. *CACM* 49, 4 (April 2006), 41–46.

[33] P. Mayring. 2014. *Qualitative content analysis: theoretical foundation, basic procedures and software solution*.

[34] Florian Meier and David Elsweiler. 2016. Going Back in Time: An Investigation of Social Media Re-finding. In *Proc. of SIGIR'16*. ACM, New York, NY, USA, 355–364.

[35] F. Meier, D. Elsweiler, and M. L. Wilson. 2014. More than Liking and Bookmarking? Towards Understanding Twitter Favouriting Behaviour. In *Proc. of ICWSM'14*. The AAAI Press, Washington.

[36] Robert A. LaBudde Michael R. Chernick. 2008. *Bootstrap Methods. A Guide for Practitioners and Researchers*. John Wiley & Sons, Inc., New York, NY, USA.

[37] Mainack Mondal, Johnnatan Messias, Saptarshi Ghosh, Krishna P. Gummadi, and Aniket Kate. 2016. Forgetting in Social Media: Understanding and Controlling Longitudinal Exposure of Socially Shared Data. In *Proc. of SOUPS'16*. USENIX Association, Denver, CO, 287–299.

[38] Changhoon Oh, Taeyoung Lee, Yoojung Kim, SoHyun Park, and Bongwon Suh. 2016. Understanding Participatory Hashtag Practices on Instagram: A Case Study of Weekend Hashtag Project. In *Proc. of CHI EA'16*. ACM, New York, NY, USA, 1280–1287.

[39] M. Ringel Morris, J. Teevan, and K. Panovich. 2010. What Do People Ask Their Social Networks, and Why? A Survey Study of Status Message Q&A Behavior. In *Proc. of CHI'10*. ACM, 1739–1748.

[40] Jean-François Rouet. 2003. What was I looking for? The influence of task specificity and prior knowledge on students' search strategies in hypertext. *Interacting with computers* 15, 3 (2003), 409–428.

[41] Sargol Sadeghi, Roi Blanco, Peter Mika, Mark Sanderson, Falk Scholer, and David Vallet. 2015. Predicting Re-finding Activity and Difficulty. In *Proc. of ECIR'15*. Springer, Cham, 715–727.

[42] Takeshi Sakaki, Makoto Okazaki, and Yutaka Matsuo. 2010. Earthquake Shakes Twitter Users: Real-time Event Detection by Social Sensors. In *Proc. of WWW'10*. ACM, New York, NY, USA, 851–860.

[43] Steven Schirra, Huan Sun, and Frank Bentley. 2014. Together Alone: Motivations for Live-tweeting a Television Series. In *Proc. of CHI'14*. ACM, New York, NY, USA, 2441–2450.

[44] Margrit Schreier. 2014. Ways of Doing Qualitative Content Analysis: Disentangling Terms and Terminologies. *Forum: Qualitative Social Research* 15, 1 (2014).

[45] Manya Sleeper, Justin Cranshaw, Patrick Gage Kelley, Blase Ur, Alessandro Acquisti, Lorrie Faith Cranor, and Norman Sadeh. 2013. I Read My Twitter the Next Morning and Was Astonished: A Conversational Perspective on Twitter Regrets. In *Proc. of CHI'13*. ACM, New York, NY, USA, 3277–3286.

[46] Anselm Strauss and Juliet Corbin. 1996. *Grounded Theory: Grundlagen qualitativer Sozialforschung*. Beltz, Weinheim.

[47] J. Teevan. 2007. The Re:Search Engine: Simultaneous Support for Finding and Re-finding. In *Proc. of UIST'07*. ACM, New York, NY, USA, 23–32.

[48] J. Teevan, E. Adar, R. Jones, and M. A. S. Potts. 2007. Information Re-retrieval: Repeat Queries in Yahoo's Logs. In *Proc. of SIGIR'07*. ACM, New York, NY, USA, 151–158.

[49] J. Teevan, D. Ramage, and M. R. Morris. 2011. #TwitterSearch: A Comparison of Microblog Search and Web Search. In *Proc. of WSDM'11*. ACM, New York, NY, USA, 35–44.

[50] Elaine G. Toms, Heather O'Brien, Tayze Mackenzie, Chris Jordan, Luanne Freund, Sandra Toze, Emilie Dawe, and Alexandra MacNutt. 2008. *Task Effects on Interactive Search: The Query Factor*. Springer Berlin Heidelberg, Berlin, Heidelberg, 359–372.

[51] Twitter. 2016. Twitter Usage/Company Facts. (2016). https://about.twitter.com/company

[52] Steve Whittaker, Ofer Bergman, and Paul Clough. 2010. Easy on that trigger dad: a study of long term family photo retrieval. *Personal and Ubiquitous Computing* 14, 1 (2010), 31–43.

[53] Steve Whittaker, Tara Matthews, Julian Cerruti, Hernan Badenes, and John Tang. 2011. Am I Wasting My Time Organizing Email?: A Study of Email Refinding. In *Proc. of CHI'11*. ACM, New York, NY, USA, 3449–3458.

[54] Barbara Wildemuth, Luanne Freund, and Elaine G. Toms. 2014. Untangling search task complexity and difficulty in the context of interactive information retrieval studies. *Journal of Documentation* 70, 6 (07 10 2014), 1118–1140.

[55] Barbara M. Wildemuth and Luanne Freund. 2012. Assigning Search Tasks Designed to Elicit Exploratory Search Behaviors. In *Proc. of HCIR'12*. ACM, New York, NY, USA, Article 4, 10 pages.

[56] Xuan Zhao, Cliff Lampe, and Nicole B. Ellison. 2016. The Social Media Ecology: User Perceptions, Strategies and Challenges. In *Proc. of CHI'16*. ACM, New York, NY, USA, 89–100.

[57] Xuan Zhao, Niloufar Salehi, Sasha Naranjit, Sara Alwaalan, Stephen Voida, and Dan Cosley. 2013. The Many Faces of Facebook: Experiencing Social Media As Performance, Exhibition, and Personal Archive. In *Proc. of CHI'13*. ACM, New York, NY, USA, 1–10.

[58] Lu Zhou, Wenbo Wang, and Keke Chen. 2016. Tweet Properly: Analyzing Deleted Tweets to Understand and Identify Regrettable Ones. In *Proc. of WWW'16*. Geneva, Switzerland, 603–612.

"I just scroll through my stuff until I find it or give up": A Contextual Inquiry of PIM on Private Handheld Devices

Amalie Enshelm Jensen
Caroline Møller Jægerfelt
Sanne Francis
Department of Communication & Psychology
Aalborg University Copenhagen
Copenhagen, Denmark

Birger Larsen, Toine Bogers
Science, Policy and Information Studies
Department of Communication & Psychology
Aalborg University Copenhagen
Copenhagen, Denmark
{birger|toine}@hum.aau.dk

ABSTRACT

While ownership and usage of handheld devices such as smartphones and tablets continues to grow at a rapid pace, we do not have complete picture of how people manage personal information on these devices. The few existing studies have typically used interview or survey methods to focus on personal information management (PIM) practices on smartphones. We present the results of an exploratory contextual inquiry study of PIM practices aimed at providing a structured, naturalistic overview of PIM on both smartphones and tablets. We find that people use multiple complementary strategies to acquire different types of information on their devices, and that people rely strongly on automatic chronological ordering instead of organization by subject, although this pays off most for smaller information collections. Deletion of information is strongly influenced by usefulness and personal attachment. Finally, we find that people strongly prefer browsing over search when retrieving information from their devices.

ACM Reference Format:
Amalie Enshelm Jensen, Caroline Møller Jægerfelt, Sanne Francis, and Birger Larsen, Toine Bogers. 2018. "I just scroll through my stuff until I find it or give up": A Contextual Inquiry of PIM on Private Handheld Devices. In *CHIIR '18: 2018 Conference on Human Information Interaction & Retrieval, March 11–15, 2018, New Brunswick, NJ, USA.* ACM, New York, NY, USA, 10 pages. https://doi.org/10.1145/3176349.3176394

1 INTRODUCTION

Ownership and usage of handheld devices such as smartphones and tablets continues to grow at a rapid pace: in 2017, ownership of handheld devices was estimated at 2.32 billion smartphone users and 1.23 billion tablet users worldwide with an expected growth of 18-23% by 2020 [13, 14]. Handheld devices have also come to play a major role in our information behavior, with Google reporting that since 2015 over half of all searches come from mobile devices [11].

However, while there have been several studies on how people move around with their smartphones [3], which apps are used in which context(s) [1, 12], and what people search for [10], we

still know surprisingly little about how people manage personal information on their handheld devices. Buttfield-Addison et al. [6] were among the first to investigate the emergent role tablets play in *personal information management* (PIM) for information and knowledge workers. They focused in particular on the collection and management of personal information and found that a variety of apps are used to store information, typically for longer periods of time. Zhang and Liu [26] performed a similar study with Chinese college students about how they use their smartphones for PIM. They found that PIM behavior on smartphones diverges significantly from laptops and desktop computers, and concluded that support for mobile PIM is still lacking in many respects.

Both studies, however, used a combination of questionnaires, interviews, and focus groups to study PIM practices, which makes them prone to recall bias and less suited to uncovering tacit knowledge. What is missing is a structured, naturalistic investigation of PIM on both smartphones and tablets. We take a first step towards addressing this research gap by investigating the PIM practices of users with their private handheld devices through a contextual inquiry (CI) study. In particular, we focus on the main types of information managed throughout the first four PIM stages identified by Jones [16]: *acquisition, organization, maintenance,* and *retrieval.* We cover the *usage* phase only tangentially, because it is the phase that has received the most research attention so far, as argued above. We aim to answer the following research questions:

RQ1 What type of personal information is managed on private handheld devices?

RQ2 What strategies for acquisition, organization, maintenance and retrieval are used in PIM on private handheld devices?

RQ3 What challenges, if any, do people experience when managing personal information on their private handheld devices?

The rest of this paper is organized as follows. We discuss relevant related work in the next section. Section 3 describes the methodology used in our CI study of PIM behavior on handheld devices. Section 4 describes our findings with regard to the different types of information that people manage on their devices. Sections 5-8 describe the different phases of PIM: acquisition, maintenance, organization, and retrieval. Finally, we conclude in Section 9.

2 RELATED WORK

Personal information management (PIM) refers to the practice and the study of the activities that people perform in order to acquire, organize, maintain, retrieve and use personal information for everyday use [16]. Malone [18] was one of the first to study PIM as manifested in physical desk organization. He found that desks are organized both to enable retrieval of desired information as well as serve as a reminder of things to do. Since then, Jones has arguably had a big influence on the field by defining the different stages of PIM: acquisition, organization, maintenance, retrieval, and usage of information. These stages describe how information is managed in a user's *personal space of information* (PSI), which comprises all physical and digital information items under the user's control [16]. This PSI is made up of multiple *personal information collections* (PICs), which represent separate collections of information consciously controlled by the users, such as the notes in a note-taking app, a smartphone's photo albums, or an e-mail inbox [16].

Our work in this paper focuses on the different PIM stages on handheld devices and how they affect the user's PICs, which are often tied to specific apps. This cross-app(lication) approach is similar to the work by Boardman and Sasse [4], who examined cross-tool PIM and found that users employ a rich variety of strategies both within and across PIM tools. With regard to the information managed using handheld devices, we follow the typology of personal information proposed by Whittaker [23]. He distinguished between *action-oriented* information items, which require some kind of action from the user, such as e-mails and work-related documents, and purely *informative* items that do not, such as personal documents and photos. The remainder of this section covers general work on smartphone usage as well as work focused on the PIM practices using smartphones and tablets.

2.1 General smartphone usage

The popularity of smartphones has resulted in a large number of studies on how people interact with their smartphones. For instance, Becker et al. [3] describe the results of a series of studies of mobility patterns of smartphone usage, while Andone et al. [1] analyzed age and gender differences in smartphone usage through a longitudinal survey study. They found that both female and younger participants used their smartphones more frequently and for entertainment and communication purposes, while older participants tend to use it as a classic phone. Other studies have produced similar findings [12, 19]. Mobile search has also been examined in detail by, e.g., Church et al. [10] and Carrascal and Church [8]. The latter found there is a strong relation between mobile search and app interactions both before and after search, suggesting a need for tighter integration.

2.2 PIM using smartphones

While holistic studies of all PIM phases on smartphones are rare, work has been done on specific information types or PIM's individual stages. Capra [7], for instance, focused on the acquisition phase with a specific focus on the transfer of information between electronic devices, including smartphones. He found that—with regard to saving information found on the Web—almost all participants reported using bookmarks and over half sent self-addressed emails. Bota et al. [5] focused exclusively on self-addressed e-mails and found that to-dos and reminders were the most popular type of information contained in such e-mails.

Leino et al. [17] examined how to-do lists are used for organizing information on smartphones. While list-creation and note-taking practices varied, their general conclusion was that users commonly run into problems when acquiring and organizing large amounts of information on their smartphone. In a study of management of

digital photography collections, Whittaker et al. [24] found that organization schemes not created by the user were often a barrier to successful retrieval. This could be an additional problem for information organization on smartphones due to the increased availability of automatically organized photo collections, based on geographical and temporal information.

Finally, Zhang and Liu [26] examined the PIM practices of Chinese college students and found significant differences between smartphones and computers. Taking screenshots and sending self-addressed e-mails and messages were popular information acquisition strategies for smartphone users. Information was most commonly organized by location, accessibility, frequency of use, and salient visual characteristics. Finally, they also found that search functionality typically lacks in-app access and that, as a result, retrieval of relevant information is often problematic.

2.3 PIM using tablets

The role that tablets (can) play in PIM is still unclear. So far, only Buttfield-Addison et al. [6] have investigated the use of tablets in PIM by information and knowledge workers in a multi-year study. They found that tablets are commonly used for acquiring information scraps and micro-notes in a variety of apps. These scraps are often kept for long periods of time, because storage capacity is rarely an issue. This contrasts Müller et al.'s findings for general users, who use their tablets mostly for entertainment.

3 METHODOLOGY

To study the PIM practices of owners of private handheld devices, we used *contextual inquiry* (CI), a qualitative method for understanding and gathering information about how people perform certain tasks in context. Through CI, users can be observed in their own environment or context while performing their tasks, as researchers can learn from them by asking for explanation and clarification. To achieve this, CI is based on three principles, according to Raven and Flanders [21]: (1) data must be gathered in the participant's own *context* or environment; (2) the inquiry is a *partnership* between the participant and the researcher to explore issues and behavior together, as opposed to a traditional interview; and (3) data collection is based on an exploratory approach with a pre-defined *focus* instead of a pre-determined agenda or set of questions.

There are multiple reasons for preferring CI over more traditional methods such as surveys, interviews or observations. One such reason is the ubiquity and high usage frequency of private handheld devices. We suspect that this means that many types of interactions have become so routine and 'invisible' to the user that they would be hard-pressed to recall them or make them explicit. CI is better at uncovering such tacit knowledge according to Holtzblatt and Jones [15] as surveys and interviews can suffer from recall bias. They can also fail at adequately capturing context in which a user performs their tasks, which is an important factor in studying PIM [9, 24]. Finally, observation is often not able to provide a deep enough understanding of why and how people operate, which the partnership element of CI addresses [15, 21].

Raven and Flanders [21] distinguish between three different implementations of CI. *Work-based interviews* and *post-observation inquiries* are similar in that observation of the participant takes place while they are engaged in an activity. However, in some situations the activity in question takes place sporadically or over a period of time, such as when a user goes days without using an app and then using it several times in an hour. To investigate this kind of activity, *artifact walkthrough* is used. Here, the researcher asks participants to demonstrate or recreate a specific activity or process [21]. We used artifact walkthroughs to investigate the PIM practices on handheld devices, because many activities take place either sporadically or over a longer period of time. A drawback of this approach is that that tasks are set by the research, which could lead to biased results. To ensure a focus on the different information types and PIM stages in the CI, we used a task-based approach, where each participant was given the opportunity to re-create a situation or process.

3.1 Participants

Due to the qualitative nature of CI and temporal constraints, we aimed for a small number of participants to conduct in-depth inquiries with into their PIM practices. We used snowball sampling to recruit participants from the authors' own network in Denmark, with the only eligibility requirement being the private ownership of at least one handheld device. Table 1 presents an overview of our five participants. For all participants, their smartphone was their main device, which they reported typically using between 1 to 6 hours per day. Tablets were not used on a daily basis.

Table 1: Demographics of our CI participants, all of whom had the Danish nationality.

ID	Age	Gender	Occupation	Smartphone	Tablet
A	26	Male	IT support	Android	iOS
B	24	Female	Student	iOS	-
C	24	Male	Student	iOS	-
D	37	Male	SME owner	iOS	iOS
E	29	Female	PR manager	iOS	-

Our artifact walkthroughs resulted in over six hours of recorded material for all participants combined. While our participants do not span a wide age range, they do all fall within the age group of 18-44 years old that has most embraced handheld devices [20], so there is no clear-cut reason to expect their behavior to be atypical. Our small sample size prohibits us from generalizing to the larger population. However, our study is exploratory in nature, so we do not expect this to harm the external validity of our findings and recommendations with a view to inspiring future work.

3.2 Materials

Each CI session was conducted in the home environment of each participant. We focused on private handheld devices as opposed to work devices to capture the richest behavior. Each session was recorded using a dedicated recording device. One week before each CI session took place, participants were sent an information letter to explain the goal of the study and the procedure that would be followed. This included listing the aspects of their PIM practices we were interested in investigating, as well as the kind of information we would like to record through screenshots. This included apps used by the participant, (deleted) photos, (deleted) screenshots, open browser tabs, website bookmarks, (deleted) e-mails, and (deleted) notes. We suspected that providing this information could lead to participants deleting or hiding information relevant to our study. We therefore emphasized that all data would be treated confidentially and that it was not the information itself we were interested in, but rather the way they managed this information. Participants were in constant control of their own devices and were only asked to show us information they were comfortable with sharing. Participants were asked to sign a secured consent form reiterating this before their CI session started. This study was conducted as part of a Master's thesis, which are not subject to approval by Aalborg University's IRB. However, all procedures and materials had to be explicitly approved by the supervisor.

3.3 Design and Procedure

3.3.1 Pilot testing. All sessions were conducted in English and consisted of an introduction, the artifact walkthrough, and wrapping up the session. We pilot-tested with a single participant not included in the main study in order to fine-tune and time the inquiry protocol as well as test the tasks and questions. One of the things that we learned from pilot testing was the increased need to emphasize that we also wanted to look at deleted information as a part of PIM's maintenance phase. This was added to the information letter as a result, as well as the estimated duration of 1.5 hours. In addition, we updated the phrasing of certain questions so they were easier to relate to for participants.

3.3.2 Artifact walkthrough. Two researchers were present during each artifact walkthrough session, one of which conducted the inquiry according to the pre-determined protocol, while the other took notes, supplied follow-up and clarification questions, kept track of time, and recorded the session. We provided the participants with simple tasks to perform so the participant could demonstrate or recreate a specific activity or process [21]. Instead of relying on user-provided tasks, we provided the tasks ourselves, both to allow for comparison between participants as well as staying true to the third principle of CI of picking a pre-determined focus. Without such a focus, our setup would be reduced to a more traditional observation study. Below, we describe the main foci and tasks of each session stage[1]. Participants were asked to think aloud during each task and we asked for screenshots to be taken during the process where relevant.

Introduction. After introducing the participant to the purpose of the study and obtaining informed consent, we asked them questions about how many devices they owned and how much time they spend on them respectively. We validated this using each device's overview of battery usage per app for the last week and asked participants to identify which apps were used for PIM activities. We recorded the top five apps for later reference. Participants were also asked whether this overview was representative.

Acquisition. In the acquisition stage, we asked participants to perform two tasks to demonstrate their acquisition practices. The first task focused on online acquisition as participants were asked to go through the steps of finding new clothes online to wear at a wedding that they could purchase at a later date. We asked participants follow-up questions about how frequently they used screenshots,

---

[1] The complete protocol is available at http://toinebogers.com/?page_id=788.

bookmarks, open browser tabs, and self-addressed e-mails and text messages to acquire information in general, and whether certain types of information were more frequently combined with specific acquisition methods. Finally, participants were also asked how they decided which information to keep.

The second task asked them to imagine how they would capture non-digital information. We asked participants follow-up questions about how frequently they used photos, audio or video recordings, electronic notes, and self-addressed e-mails and messages to acquire such information. We also inquired about the influence of the information type and the context in which it is encountered.

Organization. The four tasks in the organization stage centered around different information types: apps, e-mails, photos and notes. The first task required people to download a free app from the their phone's app store and show the researcher how they would organize it on their device. Our follow-up focus was on the general organization scheme(s) they used to organize their apps. If they stated apps were organized by frequency of use, we contrasted this with the app usage overview from the introduction stage.

For the second task, we sent each participant an e-mail and asked them to imagine they were concert tickets and show us how they would typically process such an e-mail. We specifically focused on their preference for different organization features, such as the use of folders and tags, and organization styles, such as broad vs. shallow or task vs. topic.

The third task focused on photos and asked users to launch their preferred photo app and demonstrate how and whether they used different features to organize their photos and screenshots, such as folders, tags, and flags.

The fourth and final task was related to note-taking and organization and similar in setup to the photo task. In addition to focusing on the organization of notes we also inquired about the way participants organized their information within their notes, i.e., through the use of lists and markup features.

Maintenance. In the maintenance stage, we asked our participants to explain how (often) and why they delete, update, or re-organize information from their device(s) as they went through four tasks. The first task focused on open browser tabs as we asked them to explain if they use them as reminders, and why and when they open and close them.

The other three tasks focused on deletion of photos, e-mails, and notes respectively, as we asked participants how and when they decide which photos and e-mails to delete or keep. Finally, we asked participants what kind of information (e.g., apps, notes, e-mails, photos) they update and re-organize and when and how.

Retrieval. In the retrieval stage, we asked participants to complete three different tasks. The first task focused on retrieving photos from their device(s), one from around three months ago and another from about a week ago. We asked them to reflect on the difference in retrieval strategies in terms of information type, and whether they used geotags, favorite bookmarks, or manually created folders to retrieve their photos.

Task two asked the participants to re-find an e-mail containing tickets to an event and contrasted this with an e-mail they received in the past week. Again, we focused on which features they used to

retrieve these e-mails and asked them to reflect on the (potential) difference in retrieval strategies.

For the third task we had participants re-find information on the Web that they had acquired within the last week. If this information was still in an open browser tab, they were asked to find a two-month-old screenshot of Web-based information (to make them use a different strategy as well). We asked participants to explain which features they used to re-find said information, such as open browser tabs, bookmarks or screenshots, as well as in which context they would use these strategies.

Closing. We wrapped up the CI session by summarizing the main findings for the participant to allow for correction, and by asking relevant clarification questions to increase internal validity.

4 TYPES OF PERSONAL INFORMATION

Past PIM studies have typically focused on the types of personal information that are commonly managed in desktop or laptop environments, such as files, e-mails, and bookmarks [4]. Because of the different nature and affordances of handheld devices, we draw a different distinction between information types managed on handheld devices, inspired by relevant related work [6, 26]. To answer RQ1, we examined the PIM behavior with five different information types: e-mails, photos, screenshots, notes, and apps. Where relevant, we use Whittaker's distinction between action-oriented and informative items to highlight differences in behavior.

4.1 E-mail

All participants spent time on managing their e-mails using their smartphone, which is consistent with the findings by Müller et al. [19]. Participants often used several e-mail accounts corresponding to different contexts, such as work and private life. Some participants used different apps for these different accounts to more easily separate them. E-mail is commonly used for action-oriented information, supporting previous findings of Whittaker [23]. Participants reported using e-mail "*[...] for important things*" (participant D), such as "*[...] mail from Siemens [...] where I have to change my password*" (participant D), "*[...] an email from my lawyer*" (participant D), "*work-related information*" (participant E), and "*[...] job applications that my friends have emailed me to use for inspiration [...]*" (participant E). However, participants also reported receiving occasional e-mails of a more informative nature, such as spam and news letters. In contradiction to earlier work [6], neither tablet user managed their e-mail on their tablets, with one of them not even having "*[...] set up my private mail on the iPad.*" (participant D).

4.2 Photos

Photos were also a popular type of information for our five participants, who had stored 824, 528, 9, 6,116, and 1,410 photos on their smartphone respectively at the time of the contextual inquiry. They either stored their photos in "*[...] the photo app that the phone was born with ...*" (participant A) or in "*[...] iCloud [...] every time it is charged.*" (participant D). Many photos were of an informative, long-term nature, which is reflected in their content: "*Both vacation photos, selfies, quotes, recipes [and] good memories for a recent trip to Paris.*" (participant E). Action-oriented photos were also common, but served a more short-term purpose: "*The pictures that I [...] have here are more of temporary character that I need to do something with, such as upload on [...] social media, or a screenshot to remind me of something*" (participant C). This indicates that different photos serve different purposes, with participants balancing short-term, action-oriented photos in the same app as long-term, informative photos. Our two tablet users did not seem to use them for managing photos: participant D was found to "*only have 51 [photos] and 43 of them are screenshots*", while participant A never used his tablet for taking photos.

4.3 Screenshots

Screenshots are another common type of information, that almost exclusively serve as action-oriented information. Participants acquired such screenshots across a variety of applications, such as content "*[...] received on Snapchat [that] I have taken a screenshot of*" (participant B), browser screenshots of websites to be revisited later (participant C), and e-mail screenshots meant to remind the participant "*[...] to do something about the information at a later point*" (participant C). As is evident from these examples, screenshots typically serve as reminders of some future intended action. Only one of the two tablet users collected screenshots and had acquired 43 screenshots (participant D). Most of these were of "*[...] things I want, for example interior to my new house or something for the car*". Participant D clarified that the majority of these screenshots were taking for shopping purposes.

4.4 Notes

While all five participants kept notes on their smartphone, the number of notes varied considerably between participants: participant C had only 9 notes, whereas participant D had acquired 153 notes. Participants kept notes for both action-oriented and information-oriented purposes to a similar degree. For instance, note-taking apps were commonly used to create lists for grocery shopping, party planning, items to buy, and things to experience in different cities. One participant also used notes "*to make a draft for a mail or message or to prepare an important call*" (participant E). Notes of a more informative nature typically contain "*really important information that I need to remember*" (participant E), such as passwords, names of doctors, and explanations of food certification labels, as "*for example fish should be labeled by the MCS certificate in order for it to be healthy and not contain all sorts of pesticides*" (participant E).

Tablets were, perhaps surprisingly [6], not popular for taking notes. Participant A never used his tablet for note-taking, whereas participant D only had 9 notes on his tablet. Notes taken on the tablet also commonly took the form of lists. However, participant D remarked that the intended usage context has an influence on which device is used to create the note. For example, when making a list of things to buy at IKEA, he would "*actual[ly] have the smartphone with me so I can access it when I am in IKEA*", whereas "*the iPad is more for plans I make and re-use at home*". This is in line with the findings by Müller et al. [19], who found that tablets tend not to be used outside of home.

4.5 Applications

Smartphone and tablet apps provide the majority of the interaction and functionality on handheld devices. To get an overview of app usage without the risk of recall bias, we asked users to show us an overview of the battery usage per app for the last week, where we only recorded apps that used more than 5% battery power. This threshold was based on pilot testing observations. Based on this overview, we identified four main categories of apps: (1) socializing & interaction, (2) browsing the Web, (3) entertainment, and (4) utilities. This overview was not intended to be representative of our participants' general behavior or of the general population. Different activities in different weeks are likely to impact app usage. Apps that are used frequently, but in short bursts may also have a less prominent position in the battery usage list. Instead, we used this overview to compare our participants' answers to their actual behavior.

In general, participants thought that the app ordering in the battery usage overview on their devices was accurate. The biggest deviations arose from background usage. For instance, participant A's high usage of Google Maps (which falls under 'Utilities') was due to the app's use of location services in the background, which inflated the battery usage of the app, even though actual on-screen usage of the app was much lower.

Socializing & Interaction. A considerable share of action-oriented app usage for the purposes of socializing and interaction with others. Social media apps, such as Facebook, Instagram, and Snapchat, were commonly used for "*follow[ing] different people and their lives*". Snapchat was the most singular in its purpose as it was used exclusively for communicating with friends. Several participants reported using Instagram for other purposes as well, such as following trends and "*finding inspiration for food, where I use it a lot to go into the profile of different food bloggers and find recipes*" (participant E). Facebook was used for many different purposes, from news consumption, planning and managing events with friends, and keeping track of birthdays. In contrast to smartphone usage, tablets were hardly ever used for socializing and interaction.

Browsing the Web. The degree to which smartphones were used to browse the Web varied from participant to participant, with some participants having no significant browsing activity and others spending 27% of their time using the Web browser app on their smartphone, typically for following the news or general information seeking. Using Web browser apps, such as Safari or Google Chrome, to explore the Web was by far the most popular tablet activity, which is in line with the findings by Müller et al. [19]. Participants searched for a variety of information, such as "*things I want for example interior to my new house or something for the car*" (participant D), information about yoga classes, cars, risotto recipes, and hammock-making tutorials.

Entertainment. Music streaming was a commonly mentioned entertainment use of smartphones, with participant B placing Spotify in her dock for easy access. Movie streaming apps such as Netflix, YouTube and Plex were also commonly used. Surprisingly, and in contrast to the findings of Müller et al. [19], both tablet users did not appear to use their tablets for entertainment purposes based on battery usage alone. However, participant D did mention using the tablet's Web browser to stream TV from the Danish Broadcasting Service's website. This shows the value of not relying on battery usage alone, as certain interaction patterns may be obscured.

Utilities. Not all utility apps play a role in PIM behavior and their background operation can be misleading when examining only battery usage. Commonly used utility apps for PIM included Google

Maps and the calendar app, which is used for managing appointments and setting reminders, such as "*last day with Ungdomskort (= Youth Travel Card) so I will remember to renew it*" (participant B). Other apps that serve PIM purposes were password managers, address books, wishlist and note-taking apps, Google Drive, and QR code scanners. The two tablet users in our inquiry did not use any utility apps on their tablets for PIM purposes.

5 ACQUISITION

The first phase in PIM deals with the acquisition of information: when user encounter information, do they decide to consume it immediately, ignore it, or keep it and add it to their PICs [16]? In our CI study we distinguish between the acquisition of digital and non-digital information.

5.1 Digital information

Screenshots. Screenshots were a popular acquisition strategy and often serve as reminders to many of our participants: "*If I know I'll have to find it again, I'll just take a screenshot that includes the title and website.*" (participant D). Screenshots were often combined with other acquisition strategies. On several occasions, participants kept information in multiple places: "*I would go to a website I know and then take a screenshot if I think it might be something I want to buy. And then I would keep the browser tab open.*" (participant A) and "*I have a screenshot of a website with the rollerblades, and it is also in the reading list.*" (participant C). This suggests that different strategies complement each other, possibly to maximize their future retrieval chances due to the static nature of images.

Browser tabs. For some users, leaving Web pages open in browser tabs serves as a temporary acquisition and storage strategy: "*I open new tabs so I can look at it later, and then I can do something with it. I purchase it or save it more permanent, like taking a screenshot, or note down the link.*" (participant C). These open browser tabs often function as reminders for things to buy (participant A), recipes to prepare (participant C), or other action-oriented purposes. Other participants preferred open browser tabs to screenshots for the sake of convenience when they had to return to and act upon the information in question, as they could "*[...] go directly to the stuff I was looking at instead of looking at the screenshot and typing in the information again.*" (participant A). Finally, some participants also admitted to keeping information in open browser tabs because they were interrupted or simply forgot to close them: "*[...] I can see that right now I have 14 tabs open [...] I think it is mostly because I forget to close it [...]*" (participant D).

Self-addressed texts and e-mails. Similar to earlier work by Bota et al. [5] and Capra [7], self-addressed e-mails and messages were also a common way of acquiring and transferring information for our participants. For example, one participant stated that "*[...] I have used both email and Messenger to send stuff to myself [...] for example to copy links from stuff I want to add to my birthday wish list and sent the links to myself via Messenger.*" (participant D).

Bookmarks. Using bookmarks to acquire and keep information was not done by all participants. While participant C saw website bookmarks as a permanent way of keeping information, participant B stated she did not even know where to find the bookmarking function. Our inquiries also showed that bookmarking websites was a strategy used not only to acquire information found on the Web, but also within social media apps. For instance, participant C stated that "*[...] you can also save something directly in the app [Instagram] like a bookmark [...]*", while another reported to "*[...] just save them [information items] in Pinterest. You can Pin whatever you like to save.*" (participant A). The visual affordances of bookmarking directly in apps such as Instagram and Pinterest may explain why bookmarks are rarely used in browser applications, where the information is kept only as a link.

5.2 Non-digital information

Photos. Taking photos was a common method of acquiring non-digital information by all participants, because it is fast and can serve as a visual reminder. Interestingly, two participants stated they preferred using Snapchat for taking photos instead of their device's native photo app, "*[...] because then I can write a text that is on the picture if I need to know the model or any other information about the item.*" (participant B). This suggests that being able to annotate the acquired information is important to some users. In contrast to photos and note-taking, audio and video recording was rarely used by our participants. Acquiring information by taking photos was not done using tablets by our participants.

Note-taking. Note-taking is another popular strategy for acquiring non-digital information, mostly because of its speed as is clear from the following statements: "*Notes are something that I use for quickly writing things, so it shouldn't take too long*" and "*[i]t is basically just space where I can jot down thoughts when I do not have a computer to write them down*" (both participant B). A possible challenge is that participants are not always reminded of their notes, hindering future retrieval: "*[...] sometimes I forget it even though it is in a note, because I am not reminded [...]*" (participant D).

6 ORGANIZATION

The organization of information deals with classifying, naming, grouping, and placing information in different locations to ease later retrieval from the participant's PICs [16].

6.1 Subject

All five participants used folders to organize their apps by subject (or category) on their smartphone, while only one participant did the same on his tablet. Whenever possible, participants would come up with their own labels for these folders such as "*Clothes sales*" (participant B) or "*Fitness*" (participant E). However, some participants found it challenging to come up with representative labels, as expressed by participant A: "*I have this folder called 'Random? [on the second page] that I have created myself where I just put stuff I don't know where else to put*". This may be to avoid the cognitive effort required to decide upon an organization structure, as argued by Malone [18]. Participant B grouped related apps together without placing them in a folder: "*[...] then I have the Notes, Calculator and Watch close to each other which may well remind of each other in some way. It is practical stuff.*".

In contrast to previous work by Whittaker and Sidner [25], a majority of our participants did not use folders to organize their smartphone e-mail. Only participant C used folders to collect e-mails related to major topics or events to improve future retrieval and keep his inbox 'clean'. Tagging was not used by our participants for e-mail, notes, or photos.

Only two participants had manually created folders to organize their photos and screenshots; the others relied on the automatic folders created by their device's native photo app. Those participants that did create photo folders explained that it was "*so they are easier to find*" (participant D). An example is the folders labeled 'Photos for home', which contained "*[...] photos that I took on vacations that I would like to print and put up at home.*" (participant D). This suggests that folders are usually created for photos that need to be acted upon.

None of our participants organized the notes on their smartphones by subject. Instead, they were content with the automatic chronological organization performed by their note-taking app(s) as it supports their retrieval process. However, this does contradict Whittaker et al. [24], who argued that users do not remember organization schemes they have not created themselves.

6.2 Frequency of use

All participants organized their most frequently used apps on the front page of their smartphones and tablets, while folders were usually reserved for the other smartphone pages. The 'dock' bar in iOS was another place where frequently-used apps were placed: for two participants the dock held their most frequent apps. Judging frequency of use was not that straightforward: participants A, B and E all claimed to organize their front page apps by frequency of use, but could not explain the presence of several rarely-used apps on their front page.

6.3 Accessibility

In addition to placing frequently-used apps on the front page, several participants also reported organizing apps by accessibility, as "*[...] it saves me a swipe to get to them.*" (participant C). Placing apps within easy reach of their thumb was also common: "*[...] down here [in the bottom row on the front page] ...*" (participant B) and "*[...] in the bottom, right corner ...*" (participant D). Some participants expressed frustration with having more frequently-used apps than they had space for on-screen, something also reported by Voit et al. [22]. A final observation is that occasionally participants would start re-organizing their apps during the CI process to improve their accessibility and bring their actual app organization more in line with the organization principles they claimed to adhere to.

6.4 Acceptability

While perhaps not a main organizing principle, several participants stated that social or behavioral acceptability influenced how they organized their apps and occasionally overruled other principles, in particular for which apps ended up in the dock (participants B, D and E). For instance, participant D deemed Snapchat to be "*a little too informal*" and socially too unacceptable to keep it in plain view in the dock. Participant E felt the same about apps, such as Instagram, Snapchat, and Tinder: "*Tinder is just a no-go to have in there [the dock], that would be too offensive.*"

Behavioral acceptability—whether a participant deemed a certain type of action or organization principle personally acceptable—was also mentioned as an influence by participant E: "*I have an idea that social media shouldn't take up too much of my time, so I like that they*

are not placed on the front page to avoid constantly being reminded of their existence.". When reflecting on the same issue, participant B started moving her social media apps off the front page and into a separate folder on another page during the session.

6.5 Aesthetics

Organizing apps by color was not a common principle for our participants, but two participants did prioritize laying out the apps in visually attractive manner without empty spaces or too many app pages. For example, participant D stated that he "*[...] would not like it if there was some space randomly left empty.*".

6.6 Status

Some participants used status markers to organize their information inside apps, such as flags or marking as favorites or unread. Marking items as favorites was typically reserved for photos that "*[...] I use commonly or that I for example intend to use as the background cover on my phone or a new profile picture*" (participant E). Important e-mails were usually marked as unread or flagged to highlight the need for some type of action: "*I use it as an indicator of having to perform an activity, so when I leave the email app I can see the red notifications which will remind me that there is still something in there that I have to do something about.*" (participant D).

6.7 Time

A majority of participants relied on the automatic chronological ordering that many smartphone apps provide. For instance, participant B elaborated that "*[...] it is nice that the phone organizes my notes chronologically*". Two participants did not appear to use anything but the reverse chronological installation order to organize their apps. While more research is needed, it appears this is related to the number of installed apps, as retrieval from a small set of apps is less impacted by the absence of a dedicated organization scheme. This also seemed to be a guiding principle in adopting organization schemes for e-mail: participants with a small number of e-mails in their inbox were more likely to rely on chronological ordering or search to find what they needed. All of the above suggests that participants do find automatic organization helpful, despite findings to the contrary by Whittaker et al. [24].

6.8 Habit

One organization principle that emerged from our CI sessions that, to the best of our knowledge, has not been mentioned before in PIM literature is organization out of habit. Four out of five participants stated that their current organization structure is partially out of habit. For instance, participant A mentioned that after some initial organization effort, the structure has mostly stayed the same: "*[...] when I first got my phone I organized and dragged apps to the front page that I used a lot but it has looked like this for two years now.*". While this could also be interpreted as a lack of maintenance, we have included it under organization, because habitual organization preferences also appear to carry over between devices. For instance, participant D stated that he had "*[...] only had three iPhones and they have all been organized like this.*".

7 MAINTENANCE

The maintenance phase in PIM deals with updating and optimizing the system(s) that take care of our PICs [16]. In particular, we focus on when and how people modify their systems' organization and what prompts them to keep or delete information.

7.1 Modifying

While the overall organization structure is decided on when the device is new, information is modified continuously by moving items to folders, updating incorrect information and renaming folders.

Moving information. As mentioned earlier, most participants decide upon the organization of their PICs on their handheld devices right after it is purchased. One participant claimed this was probably "*[...] because when it is new it is not completely loaded with information, so it is easier to make a completely new structure*" (participant E). Afterwards, even after transitioning to a new device, this organization is rarely fundamentally altered so it stays familiar. This familiarity ensure future retrieval success, or as participant A puts it: "*I know where all my apps on the front page is placed so I can easily locate them.*". When participants do move information around or re-organize, it is typically because the current location is inconvenient, such as app placement on the smartphone. In other cases, apps were moved to become more visible and hopefully nudge the participant into increasing certain behavior, as when participant B explained that she moved her step counting app because "*maybe I will use it more then and I would like to look at how active I am.*". Other apps were moved to place them more closely to related apps. Newly downloaded apps were also commonly moved to an appropriate location; this also holds for newly received e-mails.

Updating information. Due to their different nature, not all information types are updated with equal frequency. While photos, screenshots, and e-mails are never updated due to their static nature, notes lend themselves to more frequent updates. Lists were often mentioned by participants as dynamic notes, such as grocery lists for "*stuff I need to buy at the store*" (participant A), wish lists, or lists for "*travel planning I update that if I do some research about the destination*" (participant E). Apps are also updated by most participants when newer versions are made available, although it is contingent on available storage space.

Renaming information. Participants did not frequently mention renaming information, such as created notes or folders. Only if the contents of a folder changed, would they consider this. Some of this renaming took place during the CI session, but this is likely to have been influenced by their participation in the CI session.

7.2 Keeping & deleting

Some information was never deleted by participants. Notes containing recipes or passwords might be modified, but were always kept. While some participants deleted old shopping lists, participant B did not and instead updated a single shopping list note continuously. To some participants, including participant C, website bookmarks "*[...] are permanent, I do not delete them.*". The deletion of e-mails depended on the type of account: work e-mails were deleted less often than e-mails from private or study accounts, because their "*[...] study email is going to be deleted anyway when I finish school, [...] so I do not really care about that.*" (participant C). Private e-mail

account attracted more spam and mailing lists, which explains the higher deletion activity. Photos were commonly kept by four out of five participants, but more on smartphones than on tablets. This deletion aversion appears to be due to 'deleter's remorse': "*I am afraid that I want a photo back that I have deleted.*" (participant C).

Usefulness. The most commonly mentioned reason for deleting information was usefulness: once information was no longer of use or relevant to active tasks, then most participants stated they would delete it. This holds for all information types: e-mails, photos, screenshots, notes, and apps. Irrelevant e-mails, such as spam, mailing lists and newsletters were hardly ever kept for long. Photos that were too similar to each other were often deleted, as well as screenshots that had served their purpose as a reminder. With regard to notes, shopping lists, drafts and study-related notes were most commonly deleted after they served their purpose.

Open browser tabs were also closed after they had outlived their usefulness. For example, participant C stated: "*[...] the other day I was researching something and then I had a bunch of tabs open, and that was fine instead of putting them into the reading list, cause I did not need them at a later-later day, just later the same day. So my "OCD brain" could handle them in there, because I knew they were going away in a few days.*". Three participants also closed browser tabs, because they believed it would save them battery.

Task completion. Completing a task was a common reason for deleting the information associated with that task and provided participants with positive feedback, as expressed by participant B: "*I would delete stuff in the list when I have done it. And when I have done everything on my list, I will delete the note completely. It gives me a good feeling when I can delete stuff in a to do list.*". However, deletion of such information does not always take place right away. For instance, participant D hangs on to screenshots until "*[...] after a few months when I am sure the screenshots no longer are needed*".

Personal attachment. Most of the participants explicitly mentioned finding it difficult to delete photos, notes, and e-mails because of their sentimental value. For example, when observing participant C's e-mail folders, he expressed that "*some emails in the folders are important and some are for nostalgic purposes.*". Participant B mentioned that some notes were difficult to delete, such as a note containing "*[...] a list of things I like because I wanted to remind myself what I find important*". Participants also indicated that many of their photos had sentimental value, making them harder to delete. In contrast, screenshots rarely suffer from this problem as they are action-oriented items that lose their importance after the completion of the related task.

Cleaning. Some users deleted photos if they started to clutter up their native photo app: "*I do not like pictures to clutter up in my photo gallery, my brain cannot handle that and it annoys me [...]*" (participant C). Another type of maintenance that one participant performed was cleaning the unread-information notifications that appear in red circles at the top-right corner of iOS apps. Participant D stated that he liked "*'[...] the feeling of 'cleaning out', similarly I can't stand having red notifications on apps*".

Boredom & effort. Several participants expressed that they often did not delete irrelevant information, because they found it boring or too much effort. For instance, participant A elaborated "*I don't* close [browser tabs] due to laziness." and participant D stated it "would take so much time, I think I have around 6,000 photos and 3,000 of them could probably be deleted [...]". However, when irrelevant information is encountered accidentally, it is typically deleted: "[...] occasionally when I just stumble upon them, it is not systematic in any way." (participant E). This is in line with previous work by Jones [16], who found that users tend to keep everything in order to avoid the cognitive and emotional difficulties involved in the deletion process.

Storage capacity. Available storage capacity on their device played a role in whether to delete information for several of our participants. As expressed by participant C: "[...] it is not a space issue, so I do not need to think about it, and I do not need to remove stuff to get room for more stuff, so it does not matter if it is there or not.". Similarly, participants in need of more storage capacity would delete unused or irrelevant apps and photos: "[...] if I don't have enough storage capacity, then I just go through my photos [...] and then I consider what I can delete." (participant E). The kind of photos that would be deleted were typically photos of "[...] old outfit[s] [...] photos of my friends sleeping or similarly irrelevant." (participant E).

8 RETRIEVAL

The retrieval phase deals with remembering, recalling and recognizing information from a person's PICs, and as such depends strongly on the information need and context which initiate the search as well as the amount of information available [16].

8.1 Search

Device search. The device search function which sifts through all accessible information on the handheld device was not used by most participants. Four out of five participants forgot this functionality even existed and preferred browsing as their retrieval strategy: "[...] just scroll through my stuff until I find it or give up" (participant A). Only one participant used device search occasionally when "[...] there is something I can't find, but I know I have" (participant D).

In-app search. In-app search was used by all participants, especially for e-mail. In general, search was used as a first step to restrict the set of possibly relevant results "so the amount of mails I have to skim through are more decreased" (participant E). Participants would then scroll and browse through the results to find the e-mail(s) they were looking for. Another multi-stage process was be to first locate e-mails previously flagged or marked as unread, after which scrolling down would lead the participant to the desired e-mail. In-app search was also used for retrieving notes, but rarely for photos due to perceived performance issues there.

Conversational search. Conversional search was not popular. Only one participant used the voice recognition functionality to search for destinations and plan routes using Google Maps, because "[...] when driving [...] it finds the location faster than I can write it" (participant D). However, even this participant avoided using Siri, Apple's voice-controlled intelligent personal assistant, because "it commonly misinterpret[s] what I am saying".

8.2 Browsing

Location. Many participants eschewed searching when they knew the location of the desired information item; in those cases they simply navigated to that location and scrolled to the relevant item. For instance, participant D was very aware of the location of his apps: "I think I could close my eyes and tell you where every one of the apps in the first four rows is placed without looking.". The same holds for open browser tabs: if people remembered having certain information open in a browser tab, they would scroll through their open browser tabs instead of using Web search to re-find the information. This confirms the findings of Aula et al. [2], who reported open browser tabs to be a common retrieval strategy in the desktop environment as well.

Time. As mentioned earlier in Section 6.7, a majority of participants used the automatic chronological ordering provided by smartphone apps to organize their information. Scrolling through these lists in reverse chronological order was also a common retrieval strategy, as explained by participant A, who would "use this time function where I can sort by date. And then I would just scroll down to that specific time.".

Visual features. Finally, visual orientation was useful retrieval strategy for some participants, especially for app retrieval. For those participants that preferred taking screenshots as visual reminders, their presence then made it easier for them to navigate to the desired item(s). However, in situations of information overload, such as having too many screenshots, the usefulness of this strategy was greatly reduced. Marking e-mails using flags was also seen as a useful visual boon to retrieval; participant D expressed that the flags "[catch] my eye while scrolling [and] I don't have to skim the title of every mail but just look for the flag.".

9 DISCUSSION & CONCLUSIONS

In this paper, we have presented the results of an exploratory contextual inquiry study of PIM practices using private handheld devices. Our small sample size, especially for tablet usage, prohibits us from drawing any representative conclusions, but there are common, relevant patterns in PIM behavior across our small sample of participants that could serve to inspire future, larger studies.

Through our artifact walkthrough sessions, we answered RQ1 and found that the main information types managed on smartphones are e-mails, photos, screenshots, notes, and apps. Action-oriented use of these information types commonly focused on setting up reminders of things to do or buy through photos and screenshots, but important e-mails and notes were also managed frequently on smartphones. The frequent use of screenshots and photos has design implications for the OS of handheld devices: the use of OCR for instance could make large collections of screenshots more searchable, if users remember part of the text on the screenshots. Although analyzing battery usage cannot paint a complete picture, it did provide us with discussion material in the sessions and showed that app usage on smartphones typically involved communication, browsing the Web and entertainment. For our tablet users, only screenshots were commonly managed on their devices and app usage centered mostly on browsing the Web.

We answered RQs 2 and 3 by analyzing the different PIM stages during the CI sessions. Our participants used multiple complementary acquisition strategies. Bookmarks were not commonly used on smartphones, but taking screenshots and photos of digital and non-digital information was common practice. Note-taking was often used to manage many different types of lists, but did not serve as great reminders, in contrast to photos and screenshots.

App organization was done in different ways—by subject, frequency of use, and ease of accessibility—although there occasionally was a disconnect between participants' principles and practice. Novel organization principles uncovered in our study were by social and behavioral acceptability, and force of habit. Perhaps surprisingly, other information types were not commonly organized by subject; instead, chronological ordering was very popular for photos, screenshots, notes, and e-mails, although its success depended heavily on the amount of information. Reminders were often set up through the use of flags, favoriting, and marking as unread.

Our results show that notes and apps are most frequently updated. Interestingly, some participants would adjust their organization structure during the CI sessions after becoming aware of imperfections, which is a drawback of the method. In general information on smartphones was deleted after task completion or outliving its usefulness, although personal attachment to photos, notes and e-mails often got in the way of deletion.

Echoing the title of this paper, participants overwhelmingly preferred to browse and scroll their way to desired information, often only resorting to search as a filter on the initial set of items to examine. People relied strongly on their memory of location, time and visual characteristics to help them re-find information. This has design implications for operating systems for handheld devices, such as how users currently browse reminder screenshots and how this could be better supported. An example could be a feature that detects when a users is scrolling through a collection of screenshots and informs the users that they can try searching for some of the known words in the screenshot they are looking for to streamline the retrieval process.

9.1 Future work

We believe our exploratory study using CI to study PIM practices provides valuable knowledge about PIM practices on handheld devices. However, our (out of necessity) small sample size hurts generalizability and the most fruitful avenue for future work would be to repeat our study on a larger sample, either using CI or other methods more suited to collecting large(r)-scale data.

Due to the fact that only two users possessed both a smartphone and tablet, our findings about tablet use for PIM are wholly incomplete. Future work should focus specifically on the role tablets play in PIM practices, building upon our work and that of Buttfield-Addison et al. [6].

During our inquiries, we experienced several times that the device's operating system strongly influenced the possibilities for and restrictions on PIM practices. Our small sample size prohibited us from drawing any meaningful conclusions about this, but future work could productively focus on the PIM-related affordances of the device OS to uncover the relationship between the two.

In our study, we treated photos as a type of personal information. Photos, however, can serve multiple purposes and more research is needed to better understand the contexts in which photos serve as personal information on handheld devices. Finally, cross-device management of personal information—such as transferring, synchronizing and backing up personal information—is another phenomenon that has seen little research attention in the past.

REFERENCES

[1] Ionut Andone, Konrad Błaszkiewicz, Mark Eibes, Boris Trendafilov, Christian Montag, and Alexander Markowetz. 2016. How Age and Gender Affect Smartphone Usage. In *Proceedings of UbiComp '16*. ACM, New York, NY, USA, 9–12.

[2] A. Aula, N. Jhaveri, and M. Käki. 2005. Information Search and Re-access Strategies of Experienced Web Users. In *Proceedings of WWW '05*. ACM, New York, NY, USA, 583–592.

[3] Richard Becker, Ramón Cáceres, Karrie Hanson, Sibren Isaacman, Ji Meng Loh, Margaret Martonosi, James Rowland, Simon Urbanek, Alexander Varshavsky, and Chris Volinsky. 2013. Human Mobility Characterization from Cellular Network Data. *CACM* 56, 1 (2013), 74–82.

[4] Richard Boardman and M. Angela Sasse. 2004. "Stuff Goes into the Computer and Doesn't Come out": A Cross-tool Study of Personal Information Management. In *Proceedings of CHI '04*. ACM, New York, NY, USA, 583–590.

[5] Horatiu Bota, Paul N. Bennett, Ahmed Hassan Awadallah, and Susan T. Dumais. 2017. Self-Es: The Role of Emails-to-Self in Personal Information Management. In *Proceedings of CHIIR '17*. ACM, New York, NY, USA, 205–214.

[6] Paris Buttfield-Addison, Christopher Lueg, Leonie Ellis, and Jon Manning. 2012. "Everything Goes into or out of the iPad": The iPad, Information Scraps and Personal Information Management. In *Proceedings of OzCHI '12*. 61–67.

[7] Robert Capra. 2009. A Survey of Personal Information Management Practices. In *Proceedings of the 2009 ASIS&T Workshop on PIM*. 2–5.

[8] Juan Pablo Carrascal and Karen Church. 2015. An In-Situ Study of Mobile App & Mobile Search Interactions. In *Proceedings of CHI '15*. ACM, New York, NY, USA, 2739–2748.

[9] Duen Horng Chau, Brad Myers, and Andrew Faulring. 2008. What to Do when Search Fails: Finding Information by Association. In *Proceedings of CHI '08*. ACM, New York, NY, USA, 999–1008.

[10] Karen Church, Barry Smyth, Keith Bradley, and Paul Cotter. 2008. A Large Scale Study of European Mobile Search Behaviour. In *Proceedings of MobileHCI '08*. ACM, New York, NY, USA, 13–22.

[11] Jerry Dischler. 2015. Building for the next moment. *Google Inside AdWords*. Available at https://adwords.googleblog.com/2015/05/building-for-next-moment.html. (5 May 2015). Last accessed August 11, 2017.

[12] Trinh Minh Tri Do, Jan Blom, and Daniel Gatica-Perez. 2011. Smartphone Usage in the Wild: A Large-scale Analysis of Applications and Context. In *Proceedings of ICMI '11*. ACM, New York, NY, USA, 353–360.

[13] eMarketer. 2017. Number of smartphone users worldwide from 2014 to 2020 (in billions). *Statista – The Statistics Portal*. Available at https://www.statista.com/statistics/330695/number-of-smartphone-users-worldwide/. (2017). Last accessed August 8, 2017.

[14] eMarketer. 2017. Number of tablet users worldwide from 2014 to 2020 (in billions). *Statista – The Statistics Portal*. Available at https://www.statista.com/statistics/377977/tablet-users-worldwide-forecast/. (2017). Last accessed August 8, 2017.

[15] Karen Holtzblatt and Sandra Jones. 1993. *Contextual Inquiry: A Participatory Technique for System Design*. Lawrence Erlbaum Assoc., Hillsdale, NJ, 177–210.

[16] William Jones. 2008. *Keeping Found Things Found: The Study and Practice of Personal Information Management*. Morgan Kaufmann.

[17] Juha Leino, Sanna Finnberg, and Kari-Jouko Räihä. 2010. The Times They Are A-changin': Mobile PIM is Leaving the Paper Trail Behind. In *Proceedings of BCS '10*. British Computer Society, Swinton, UK, UK, 259–268.

[18] Thomas W. Malone. 1983. How Do People Organize Their Desks?: Implications for the Design of Office Information Systems. *ACM Trans. Inf. Sys.* 1, 1 (1983), 99–112.

[19] Hendrik Müller, Jennifer L. Gove, John S. Webb, and Aaron Cheang. 2015. Understanding and Comparing Smartphone and Tablet Use: Insights from a Large-scale Diary Study. In *Proceedings of OzCHI '15*. ACM, 427–436.

[20] Nielsen. 2016. Millenials are Top Smartphone Users. Available at http://www.nielsen.com/us/en/insights/news/2016/millennials-are-top-smartphone-users.html. (15 November 2016). Last accessed August 8, 2017.

[21] Mary Elizabeth Raven and Alicia Flanders. 1996. Using Contextual Inquiry to Learn about your Audiences. *ACM SIGDOC Asterisk Journal of Computer Documentation* 20, 1 (1996), 1–13.

[22] K. Voit, K. Andrews, and W. Slany. 2009. Why Personal Information Management (PIM) Technologies are not Widespread. In *Proceedings of the 2009 ASIS&T Workshop on PIM*. 60–64.

[23] Steve Whittaker. 2011. Personal Information Management: From Information Consumption to Curation. *ARIST* 45, 1 (2011), 1–62.

[24] Steve Whittaker, Ofer Bergman, and Paul Clough. 2010. Easy on that Trigger, Dad: A Study of Long-Term Family Photo Retrieval. *Pers. Ubiquitous Comput.* 14, 1 (2010), 31–43.

[25] Steve Whittaker and Candace Sidner. 1996. Email Overload: Exploring Personal Information Management of Email. In *Proceedings of CHI '96*. ACM, New York, NY, USA, 276–283.

[26] Pengyi Zhang and Chang Liu. 2015. Personal Information Management Practices of Chinese College Students on Their Smartphones. In *Proceedings of Chinese CHI '15*. ACM, New York, NY, USA, 47–51.

Augmentation of Human Memory: Anticipating Topics that Continue in the Next Meeting

Seyed Ali Bahrainian
Faculty of Informatics, Università della Svizzera italiana
(USI), Lugano, Switzerland
bahres@usi.ch

Fabio Crestani
Faculty of Informatics, Università della Svizzera italiana
(USI), Lugano, Switzerland
fabio.crestani@usi.ch

ABSTRACT

Memory augmentation is the process of providing human memory with information that facilitates and complements the recall of an event in a person's past. Recently, there has been a lot of attention on processing the content of meetings for later reuse, such as reviewing a meeting for supporting failing memories, keeping in mind key issues, verification, etc. That is due to the fact that meetings are essential for sharing knowledge in organizations.

In this paper, we propose four novel time-series methods for predicting the topics that one should review in preparation for a next meeting. The predicted/recommended topics can be reviewed by a user as a memory augmentation process to facilitate recall of key points of a previous meeting. With the growing number of meetings at an organization that one may attend weekly and with the growing number of topics discussed, forgetting past meetings becomes eminent, hence recommending certain topics to the user in order to prepare the user for a future meeting is beneficial and important.

Our experimental results on real-world data, demonstrate that our methods significantly outperform a state-of-the-art Hidden Markov Model baseline. This indicates the efficacy of our proposed methods for modeling semantics in temporal data.

ACM Reference format:
Seyed Ali Bahrainian and Fabio Crestani. 2018. Augmentation of Human Memory: Anticipating Topics that Continue in the Next Meeting. In *Proceedings of 2018 Conference on Human Information Interaction & Retrieval, New Brunswick, NJ, USA, March 11–15, 2018 (CHIIR '18)*, 10 pages.
DOI: https://doi.org/10.1145/3176349.3176399

1 INTRODUCTION

Human memory is a critically important cognitive ability that we constantly rely on for carrying out various tasks in our daily lives [12]. However, some times due to the volume and intensity of information that we are exposed to on a typical working day, or due to our lack of adequate attention, or due to aging, this critical cognitive ability fails to recall important events in our past. In a workplace environment, failing to recall important work-related events can result in frustration and disappointment. Discussions

may be repeated over and over again and the work cycle may be prolonged. This can result in a waste of time, energy and resources, in addition to bringing misunderstandings to the workplace. In a study by Jaimes et.al. [14], common issues that people forget regarding a past meeting were studied. Among several investigated issues, inability of participants to recall a significant amount of a previous meeting's content (i.e. dialogue) after a week time is noteworthy.

Augmentation of human memory in a workplace environment has been proposed as a solution in preventing failure to recall past events [8, 14]. Jaimes et.al. [14], proposed a framework for memory cue based retrieval of meeting content. Moreover, Lamming et.al. [10] studied memory problems in a workplace environment and designed a system referred to as "memory prosthesis". Automatically recorded data of user activities could be later retrieved by their system for remembering things, specially those that the user did not think were needed to be remembered at the time. They explain further that context-sensitive reminders can be shown to the user for reminicing past work-related memories. From a somewhat different perspective of personal lifelog management, [8] also proposed a memory augmentation tool with multimodal memory cues. They explain that "being reminded of information in a work situation (e.g. previous meetings with an individual)" could be an application of their system. Their work among other similar works, rely on the advent of various wearable data capture devices (e.g. wearable video/audio recorder or biophysical sensors) which has recently created great opportunities to utilize the collected data for various human-aid applications such as support of failing memories and memory augmentation.

Using summarization tools for memory augmentation, as opposed to searching keywords has been proposed, by arguing that in many cases a user may not remember enough about a past meeting to even be able to formulate a query [1]. In such settings a summary of the meeting can reminisce the faint memories of that meeting. At the same time, [18] shows that extractive summaries provide a more efficient way of navigating meeting content than simply reading through the transcript and using audio-video records, or navigating by keyword search. As a result of the two rationales, other work on processing meeting content [32] have focused on extracting summaries from a meeting transcript including extraction of Latent Dirichlet Allocation (LDA) [7] topics for producing summaries. In support of meeting summaries, [13] explains that "users absorb information in summaries more quickly than in full text, despite some loss of accuracy". They study meeting summarization by focusing on user needs such as highlighting the most important decisions made in a meeting. Motivated by these studies we aim at predicting the continuation of LDA topics of previous meetings in a future meeting to address yet another users need: preparation for the next meeting.

The Remembrance Agent [22] is an interesting framework for aiding human memory in a proactive fashion. In a subsequent work, Rhodes et. al. [23] defined a class of memory aid tools with the goal of Just In Time Information Retrieval (JITIR). These tools were "software agents that proactively present on a wearable head-up display potentially valuable information based on a person's local context.

Addressing users' near-future information needs, has been also studied in the context of personal assistants such as Google Now, Microsoft Cortana or Apple's Siri. These systems offer proactive experiences [25] that aim to recommend *the right information at just the right time*" [26].

In this paper, we focus on proactive augmentation of human memory [3] with respect to the content of previous meetings in a workplace environment, by reminding a user of relevant topics of previous meetings that will be important in the next meeting. We use two real-world datasets of weekly meetings of ten groups of people. In these datasets, we recorded real workplace meetings of each group (where a group consisted of two individuals) over a span of an entire month (in the case of the first dataset) and over 6 weeks (in the case of the second dataset). We compare various methods for predicting the topics of a conversation that will be continued from the previous meetings, which should therefore be reviewed by the people involved in that meeting to prepare next meeting. To the best of our knowledge, this is the first work that aims at augmenting human memory by predicting the continuation of intermittent topics in consecutive meetings.

The main contributions of this paper are:

C1: we propose the idea of augmenting human memory by predicting the topics of one's next meeting.

C2: to address the above problem, we develop four new methods for performing this task. These methods are all based on a probabilistic word embedding model that tracks each word in all its different contexts (i.e. co-occurrence with other words) over consecutive meetings.

The organization of this paper is as follows: Section 2 presents the background and related work motivating this research work. Section 3, describes the theory of the novel methods that we developed for predicting the topics that one should review in preparation for one's next meeting. In Section 4, we compare the proposed methods against the baseline method, in a benchmark based on their predictive performance. Section 5 elaborates on some important points regarding our study. Finally, Section 6 concludes this paper and gives insight into future work.

2 BACKGROUND AND RELATED WORK

2.1 Augmentation of Human Memory in Workplace Meetings

Psychology of human memory has comprehensively studied how human memory recalls events or forgets them. One groundbreaking work in this domain was the proposal of the *forgetting curve* in 1885 by Ebbinghaus [9]. The forgetting curve (which is an exponentially decreasing curve) shows that a human forgets on average about 77% of the details of what he has learned for the first time

after just six days. This motivated our goal in augmenting human memory to assist one in recalling more details of her past events. Also, this notion of exponential forgetting was previously used by information retrieval researchers [16] to develop a probabilistic recency-based model, for modeling the strength of memories of people in recalling their visits of places logged on websites such as Tripadvisor or Yelp. We also use an exponential forgetting factor in our models.

Different meeting search, browsing, and summarization systems have been developed for aiding people to reuse content of meeting at a later time [14, 27]. As an example, [14] proposed a video summarization tool that summarizes and indexes a meeting's video recording. The system then allows users to use various types of queries and memory cues to find certain content in the meeting. Tucker et.al. [27] investigated several meeting browsing systems. They state that most meeting browsers have ignored semantic techniques such as topic tracking.

This is while other research shows that extractive summaries [13, 18] and in particular LDA topics extracted from meetings [32] provide users with an efficient and effective way of browsing meeting content. Thus far, focusing on a user's informational needs when going through previous recorded meetings has been mostly limited to taking a user's search keywords as feedback or highlighting the decisions made during a meeting. However, one common informational need of a user can be to use the previous meetings for preparing a future meeting. Therefore, there is a need for tracking topics and semantic information to produce summaries which are important for the near future of a user. Addressing such need is the focus of this paper.

Many meeting summarization and browsing systems have been developed in the past including those specifically designed for memory aid and others for mere search and navigation. Due to space limitations we only mentioned some of them. Analogously to these systems, we have also developed a meeting memory augmentation tool that we have already deployed for aiding people's memory in their workplace meetings at an organization [1, 2]. This system takes as input transcriptions of audio recordings of one's conversations and images taken automatically by a wearable camera at fixed time intervals. Both media types are time synchronized. The tool then processes the data by modeling the topics of the transcribed conversations, connecting the topics with their corresponding images. Figure 1 shows a demo of this tool presenting an LDA topic and its corresponding image. Through pressing a button the system will display the next or previous topic. As mentioned earlier, topic models have been used before for summarizing conversations and meetings [1, 32].

Moreover, the studies[13, 18] show that extractive summaries provide a more efficient way of navigating meeting content than simply reading transcript and using audio-video record, or navigating via keyword search. Similarly, minute taking in meetings although useful, requires more work from the user side, both for writing and later reading it. Additionally, in certain situations (e.g. less formal meetings) such facilities may not be available. Furthermore, if a user needs to know about a topic in more details, our tool uses LDA to trace back the words of a topic, to the spoken sentences where the topic was extracted from.

Buttons
Symbols
Readability
Understand
People
Meaning
Communicate
Difficulty
Visual
Practice

Figure 1: Sample output of our memory augmentation tool

However, the drawback of most memory augmentation tools is that with the growing number of meetings that one participates in and with the growing number of topics discussed, there are thousands of topics to be reviewed every week in preparation for future meetings that might touch only a part of the many topics discussed in previous meetings.

2.2 Representations of Text Documents: Topics and Beyond

In the previous section we discussed that our goal in this study is *predicting the topics that one should review in preparation of one's next meeting* given her previous meetings. Note that we did not state our goal as predicting the topic of one's next meeting due to the fact that in most situations future events are unpredictable. For instance, in our dataset of conversations it occurred between two individuals that before their last meeting one of them had been sick. Therefore, for the first time out of all their conversations he talked about his sickness and a new topic was introduced in their conversation. Predicting such future events is virtually impossible. Hence, our goal is only to predict which topics will continue from previous meetings, not predicting the unpredictable.

In the literature [31], topic models are defined as hierarchical Bayesian models of discrete data, where each topic is a set of words, drawn from a fixed vocabulary, which together represent a high level concept. According to this definition Latent Dirichlet Allocation (LDA) [7] was introduced. Here, we use LDA topics for carrying out our experiments. However, our proposed methods are generic enough that any vector representation of documents could be used and predicted by the methods. This advantage of our models is very important because there are many human-centered studies such as [29] which produce various textual summaries of conversations. The only requirement for using our models is to have a vector containing a set of words where each word is associated with a corresponding probability score showing the strength of its presence in a given document. In this paper, similarly to [32], we use LDA as summaries. Use of LDA topics as representations of documents is theoretically motivated and endorsed by previous related work on temporal compression of recordings of conversations [28]. Tucker et al. [28] present and compare various speech

compression techniques including audio speed-up methods and excision methods. Speed-up methods are simply based on increasing the speed of audio playback to achieve a certain temporal compression rate, while excision methods are removal of insignificant utterances and words from the transcripts of speech signals. Their study showed that excision methods outperform speed-up methods in representing an audio recording of a conversation that humans understand. Thus, since LDA topics are also an excision method they could be useful and understandable by humans. Additionally, LDA enables a potential user to refer back to the sentences that contributed to a topic, if she wanted to review part of a previous meeting in greater detail.

Recently, there has been interesting work on mapping semantically related words to nearby positions in the vector space in an unsupervised way. Some example approaches are the well known word2vec model [17], Glove [19], in addition to other probabilistic word embedding methods such as [30] which uses a Gaussian distribution for modeling each word. In this paper, we build on the same concept by using a Gaussian Mixture Model (GMM) for modeling each word in each of its contexts. We define a context of a target word as a word co-occurrence in the same vicinity. For example, the word 'book' can mean making a reservation or it can also mean a bound collection of pages depending on the context. Finally, we note that a temporal topic model such as the Dynamic Topic Model [6] is not a suitable option to be included in our benchmark, because: (1) it assumes that all topics are present over all time slices of a given dataset, (2) its not capable of tracking textual representations of conversations other than topics.

3 METHODOLOGY

In this section, we present four new different methods as well as the baseline method for predicting the topics to be reviewed in preparation of one's next meeting. In our research of methods that can effectively predict the continuing topics over time, we devised various methodologies. One of the methods we designed assigns average weights to all words across all consecutive meetings, and disregards the passage of time. On the contrary, we designed two other methods, one which increases the weights of most recent words, and another which, increases the weights of more established (i.e. persistent) words. Additionally, we developed an evolutionary method that combines both recency and establishment effects, while estimating weights for each of these effects over time. We elaborate on the details and rationale behind each of these time-series methods in the following subsections.

Finally, we use the Hidden Markov Models (HMM) [21] as the state-of-the-art baseline for unsupervised multi-variate time-series prediction, and compare its performance against our proposed methods. HMMs have shown strong results in predicting multivariate time-series in different applications [33] and are commonly considered as the state-of-the-art in a number of domains. Reference [20] enlists a number of papers that describe domains where HMMs hold the state-of-the-art performance. We elaborate on the HMM baseline approach in the last subsection of this section.

3.1 The CorrAv Effect

We model each word from each meeting using a Gaussian Mixture Model (GMM) with K components, where each component c_i represents a context word for the target word being modeled. We define a context word as a word which co-occurs with the target word in one or more sentences of the meeting. Thus, we obtain the following equation density function f_w:

$$f_w(\vec{x}) = \sum_{i=1}^{K} p_{w,i} \mathcal{N}(\vec{\mu_{w,i}}, \sigma w, i)$$

$$= \sum_{i=1}^{K} \frac{p_{w,i}}{\sqrt{2\pi|\sigma_{w,i}|}} e^{-\frac{1}{2}(\vec{x}-\vec{\mu_{w,i}})^T \Sigma_{w,i}^{-1}(\vec{x}-\vec{\mu_{w,i}})} \qquad (1)$$

where $p_{w,i}$ is the probability of a component modeling a certain context with $\sum_{i=1}^{K} p_{w,i} = 1$, $\mu_{w,i}$ is the probability of the position of the i_{th} component and σ_w models the uncertainty of the context. We learn the parameters of $GMM_{i,n}$ for word i from meeting n to compute probability of each context of each word in each meeting. This will lead to computing $p_{w,i,n}$ which is the probability of word w in its i_{th} context from the n_{th} meeting.

Finally, we formally define the CorrAv effect as follows: given the topics of your last n consecutive meetings, we would like to predict which topic continues in the $(n + 1)_{th}$ meeting. Lets say we have a vocabulary v of all the words occurring in the first n meetings. We construct a word vector containing the average probability of presence of all words in each of their contexts in v. Finally, we use the following equation to compute the aggregate probability of word w in a certain context under the CorrAv effect:

$$P_{w,c} = \sum_{n=1}^{N} \sum_{w_i \in v} \frac{BM25_{w,n} * P(w_{i,c,n})}{(n)} \qquad (2)$$

where n is the meeting sequence number, $P(w_{i,c,n})$ is the probability of word w under component c (i.e. context c), derived from the n_{th} meeting. The resulting constructed word vector is an average representation of probability of all words present in all n meetings. Finally, $BM25_{w,n}$ is the weight of the word w in meeting n computed using the probabilistic algorithm BM25 [24] in each of the previous meetings.

Using Equation 2, we learn a reference vector for each word in each context across all previous meetings. As it will be explained later in Section 4.1, our dataset contains LDA topics extracted from the first n meetings whose continuation in the $(n + 1)_{th}$ meeting should be predicted. For each given topic whose continuation should be predicted, we construct a new word vector derived from the reference vector. That is due to the fact that in the reference vector we have computed each word in all its contexts. However, words have different meanings or contexts, and an LDA topic model puts together words that often reflect the same context. Therefore, we have to select relevant contexts for each topic whose continuation is being predicted. We search through each given LDA topic and identify context words of a target word that have the highest probability in the LDA topic. Subsequently, from the reference vector we add the probability of each word in its identified topic to the new vector that we construct. We name this new vector

the $Vector_t$ where t refers to the LDA topic whose continuation should be predicted, meaning that for each topic t we construct a unique vector of contextual words. We emphasize again that $Vector_t$ contains all the words in v with the difference that if a word w is present in topic t we use the context probability of the word which best suites the context of t, and otherwise we assign it the highest context probability.

The last step is to compare a $Vector_t$ with a topic t to make the prediction. Other previous work [17] have used element-wise dot product of word vector distributions as an energy function which would show how similar two vectors are and could be used for predictive tasks. However, we take a different approach by computing the correlation between two vectors as a measure of similarity. This is inspired by the underlying belief in topic models and word embeddings that words have certain meanings in certain contexts. Thus, looking at the words co-variance can better capture a context similarity or difference.

As a result, we compute the Pearson correlation of $Vector_t$ with the topic t to make the prediction. The result of this step, is a ranked list of all of the t topics from the first n meetings based on this correlation value. According to the CorrAv effect, the topics highly correlating with the average probability of all words are those that are most likely to continue in the $(n + 1)_{th}$ meeting, hence the naming. We use the Pearson correlation metric defined as $P_{X,Y} = \frac{COV(X,Y)}{\sigma_X \sigma_Y}$, where $P_{X,Y}$ is the Pearson correlation of two populations X and Y, COV is the co-variance and σ is the standard deviation. Pearson correlation is a measure which captures the linear dependence between two populations X and Y, and returns a correlation score ranging from '-1' to '1'. In particular, it returns '1' if the two populations are identical, '0' if the two populations have no correlation, '-1' if the two populations are uncorrelated. In our use case, the Pearson correlation can capture the dependence between a topic t and a learned $Vector_t$.

Finally, we require a threshold for accepting a topic as a continued topic which needs to be reviewed. To determine an effective threshold we use n-fold cross validation. That is, we iteratively leave out each set of four meetings (for a single group) and compute the threshold which minimizes the Mean Squared Error (MSE) of prediction on the remaining folds. Then, using the computed threshold, we evaluate the left-out fold. In Section 4, we show how this method performed in our experiments.

3.2 The Recency Effect

The recency effect assigns higher weights to the contextual words of the most recent previous meetings. Then it identifies those topics which are most correlated with the word vectors computed based on the recency effect.

We follow the same problem definition described in Section 3.1. All steps for computing GMMs for each word are the same as explained in Section 3.1. The only difference of this model with CorrAv is that the computed probability scores are higher for words spoken in the most recent meetings. Therefore, after computation of GMMs instead of using equation 2, we compute the $P_{w,c}$ according to the following equation:

$$P_{w,c} = \sum_{n=1}^{N} \sum_{w_i \in v} \frac{BM25_{w,n} * P(w_{i,c,n}) * e^{(n-1+\lambda)}}{(n)} \qquad (3)$$

where n is the meeting sequence number, $P(w_{i,c,n})$ is a the probability of word w under component c (i.e. context c), derived from the n_{th} meeting. $BM25_{w,n}$ is the weight of the word w in meeting n computed using the probabilistic word ranking algorithm BM25 in each of the previous meetings. The $e^{n-1+\lambda}$ is the rate with which recent words from recent meetings are assigned higher weight. As explained earlier in Section 2.1, psychology research [9] has shown that forgetting is an exponential function of time. Thus, we compute the variable λ according to the forgetting rate of 77% shown by the psychology study. As a result of this computation λ is set to 1.125. Further exploration of this variable remains a future work and in this work we only rely on the findings of psychology research.

Using equation 3 we model each word in its various contexts in a temporal fashion, meaning that contextual co-occurrences of words are weighted differently in time.

Subsequently, all steps explained for the CorrAV method after Equation 2 were also applied in the case of recency modeling.

3.3 The Establishment Effect

The establishment effect, identifies topics containing words that have been frequently used or are in other words established. This method assigns a higher weight to words that have persisted from previous meetings. Therefore the establishment effect is the opposite to the recency effect, as it assigns higher weights to more persistent words.

Again, we refer to the problem definition stated in Section 3.1. We compute the GMMs for each word in the same way as explained in Section 3.1. The only difference of this model with CorrAv is that the computed probability scores are weighted higher for words which have been persistent over time. Therefore, after computation of GMMs instead of using equation 2, we compute the $P_{w,c}$ according to the following equation:

$$P_{w,c} = \sum_{n=1}^{N} \sum_{w_i \in v} \frac{BM25_{w,n} * P(w_{i,c,n}) * e^{-(n-1+\lambda)}}{(n)} \qquad (4)$$

where n is the meeting sequence number, $P(w_{i,c,n})$ is a the probability of word w under component c (i.e. context c), derived from the n_{th} meeting and $BM25_{w,n}$ is the weight of the word w in meeting n computed using the probabilistic word ranking algorithm BM25 in each of the previous meetings. The $e^{-(n-1+\lambda)}$ is the rate with which established words are assigned higher weight. As explained earlier in Section 2.1, psychology research[9] has shown that forgetting is an exponential function of time. Therefore, the rationale in the establishment effect is that if a word persisted in meetings of two individuals over time, we could weight this remembered word higher by the exponential forgetting factor. Similar to the recency model we compute the variable λ according to the forgetting rate of 77% shown by the psychology study. As a result of this computation λ is set to 1.125.

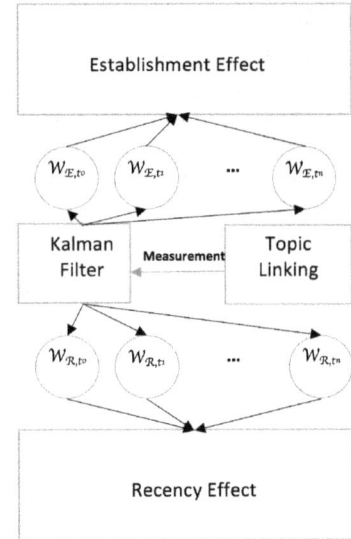

Figure 2: K2RE Method's Architecture

Analogously to the CorrAv and recency effects, all steps explained for the CorrAv method after equation 2 are also applied in the case of the establishment method.

3.4 K2RE

This method is a hybrid that combines the recency and establishment effects. It dynamically estimates the weights of each of these effects for each meeting and corrects itself over time. We refer to this method as *Kalman combination of Recency and Establishment (K2RE)*. It utilizes the Kalman filter [15] to estimate the Recency and Establishment weights over time. By measuring the meeting behavior of a group in terms of establishment and recency, K2RE adapts itself to data of each group. In the following, we first present a general overview of K2RE and then elaborate on its details. Figure 2 illustrates the components of the K2RE method. This method integrates scores from the recency and the establishment effects, described in Sections 3.2 and 3.3, using a linear interpolation.

The linear interpolation for a meeting at time slice t is defined as:

$$K2RE_t = w_{E,t} * Score_{establishment} + w_{R,t} * Score_{recency} \qquad (5)$$

where $Score_{establishment}$ and $Score_{recency}$ are computed by the establishment and the recency effects, respectively. Furthermore, $w_{E,t}$ and $w_{R,t}$ are establishment weights and recency weights computed by the Kalman filter at time t, such that:

$$w_{E,t} + w_{R,t} = 1 \qquad (6)$$

This means that at each time slice t each of the two effects will be given a weight, either equally or if one effect is assigned a higher weight, the other will receive a lower weight.

The Kalman filter is always initialized by assigning equal probability of 0.5 to both $w_{E,t}$ and $w_{R,t}$.

$$f(n) = \begin{cases} X^{G} = A^{G} f_{t-1} + \varepsilon_t{}^{G} & t = 2, \ldots, T \\ z_t = H^{G} f_t + w_t{}^{G} & t = 1, \ldots, T \end{cases}$$

where f_t is the system state at time t, A^{G} denotes the transition of the dynamic system from $t-1$ to t, H^{G} describes how to map state f_t to to an observation (i.e. measurement) z_t and both $\varepsilon_t{}^{G}$ and $w_t{}^{G}$ are mutually independent Gaussian noise variables with co-variances R_t and Q_t respectively. The superscript G in the system of equations explains that we compute these equations per each group. The dynamic system, then evolves over time and updates itself proportional to the Kalman gain.

Now that we explained the Kalman filter module and how it computes the weights for recency and establishment effects, we explain the topic linking module and describe how the measurement process explained in the Kalman filter equations works.

In our previous work [4], we introduced a topic model for tracking the evolution of intermittent topics over time. In other words, this model tracks the evolution of topics that may occur discretely over time, such that a topic does not need to be necessarily present over all time slices. In the topic linking module shown in Figure 2 we use a component of the mentioned topic model. This component links together similar topics over time. As explained, the linking of a topic may be discrete or continuous under this model (i.e. a topic may be present over all time slices or it may skip some time slices). We briefly explain the model in the following. The general idea is to form a Gaussian random walk in a Markovian state space model. The Markov assumption enforces probabilities of a hidden state at time t to be computed merely dependent on the previous time slice and not all the previous states. We utilized this assumption to compute topic chains that capture the evolution of a topic discretely over time. If two topics over two different time slices are similar according to the following criterion, they will be linked.

$$\beta_{t,k} | \beta_{t-m,1..k} \sim \mathcal{N}(\beta_{t-1}, \sigma^2 I) \qquad (7)$$

where $\beta_{t,k}$ is topic k at time slice t, $m \in (1, .., n)$ with n being the number of previous time slices (meetings) and σ is the maximum variance allowed from the mean of a topic in the previous time slice. By assigning a very small value to σ, the model links two topics that are highly similar. Furthermore, the Baum-Welch [5] algorithm learns the forward and backward probabilities of the transitions among the topics. We used this model as a component of K2RE for linking the topics that are similar across different meetings. The model takes as input the topics from the first n meetings whose continuation in the $(n+1)_{th}$ meeting is to be computed.

After linking similar topics over every two consecutive meetings, the topic linking module computes the recency rate of the topics for meeting n by computing the number of topics from the meeting $n-1$ that have been present in the meeting n divided by the total number of topics in the same meeting. This measurement is given as the observation matrix to the Kalman filter for each meeting which we explained above. Subsequently, the Kalman filter computes the evolution of recency and establishment weights using the Kalman filter equations presented above. Furthermore, using Equation 6, similarly to the recency and establishment methods, a K2RE reference vector is generated.

Moreover, analogously to the other three previous methods, all steps for computing word vectors and computation of Pearson correlation as an energy function are performed.

3.5 Hidden Markov Model Baseline

HMMs [21] have been extensively used for modeling multivariate time series and predicting next states.Therefore, in this paper we also use HMM to predict the continuing topics as a baseline for our benchmark.

The architecture we use does not allow transitions between topics in the same time slice but it enforces connections between topics over consecutive time slices. This is set using the transition matrix. Additionally, the HMM we implement uses a Gaussian kernel. Using the Baum-Welch algorithm the model is trained. For determining the number of HMM output states, similarly to [33], we use the Bayesian Information Criterion (BIC) to find the optimal number of output states given the data of each set of four meetings. Finally, after training the HMM model with the topics of the first n meetings we measure the likelihood of each of the topics that we want to predict its continuation under the trained model. The result is a likelihood score per topic. We normalize the likelihood scores by dividing each of them by the maximum likelihood score. Finally, similarly to the previous models described in Section 3 we compute the optimal classification threshold using n-fold cross validation.

4 EXPERIMENTAL RESULTS

4.1 Datasets Description

4.1.1 First Dataset. Our first dataset consists of recordings of workplace meetings of 10 groups of people. Each group consisted of two members. For each group, the audio of 4 consecutive meetings over four weeks were recorded. Our dataset is real-world and captured in the wild, meaning that the involved participants were asked to simply have their usual meetings with no regulations imposed. Out of the 10 groups, data of 3 groups were used as a development set, to design our models. The remaining 7 groups were used as a test dataset. In the following, we report the statistics of the test dataset.

Participants: overall, there were 14 unique participants recruited for this study. For recruiting participants, we looked for groups of two people who usually had a weekly work-related meeting. No restrictions were imposed on the meetings from our side. Thus, we were able to collect a real-world dataset of workplace meetings. Due to the nature of this dataset (involving participants and being real-world) capturing it took a long time. All participants signed consent forms to be recorded.

Converting audio to text: subsequently, we transcribed all audio recordings of the meetings using an online professional transcription service[1] at a cost. The transcription error according to the website is 1%.

Basic statistics: Some important statistics of our dataset are presented in Figure 3. We note that by comparing the number of unique words in all 4 meetings combined and average number of words per each meeting, we observe how focused the topics of the 4 consecutive meetings are. As an example, by looking at statistics

[1] www.rev.com

of group 7 we observe that the number of unique words used in all four meetings is almost half of the average number of words per-meeting. In general, Figure 3 shows the variability in the statistics of meetings and the behavior of the different groups.

The average number of days in between every two consecutive meetings for all the 7 groups when rounded down to full days was 8.

Topic extraction: as explained earlier, we extract LDA topics from the texts. For this purpose, we treat every full sentence in the text as a document and extract LDA topics from all of them. Since the number of topics (K) discussed in two different meetings might vary, it is important to estimate the number of topics per each meeting. For this purpose, similar to the method proposed in [11], we went through a model selection process. This consists in keeping the LDA Dirichlet parameters (commonly known as α and η) fixed, we assign several values to K and computed an LDA model each time. Subsequently we picked the model that satisfied:

$$\operatorname*{argmin}_{K} logP(W|K)$$

In Figure 5 we show an example of model selection to find the optimal number of topics for a randomly selected meeting from our dataset. As we can see in the plot, for this meeting the optimal number of topics is 10. We repeated this process for each meeting to find the optimal number of topics for that meeting. Figure 1 shows a real sample topic about "interface design" from our dataset.

Labeling the extracted topics: In order to obtain ground-truth labels for the topics of the first 3 meetings that continue in the 4th, we asked a human assessor to label the topics of the first three meetings for every set of four meetings. The goal was to label the topics of the first three meetings from each set by examining whether a topic was also discussed in the fourth meeting or not. Therefore, by looking at the topics of the last meeting, the human annotator determines if any of the topics of the first three meetings continued in the last meeting. Hence, there are two possible labels to assign to each topic, i.e., 'continued' and 'not continued'. This is the ground truth for evaluation.

The assessor is given instructions on how to label the topics. These instructions include putting more emphasis on the top 30 words in each topic to take a decision. That is due to the fact that at the end, the users of our system usually look at the top words of each topic to understand it. On the other hand, using a k-nearest-neighbors implementation, information on the top 5 neighbors of each of the topics from the first three meetings in the last meeting is provided to the human assessor to simplify the annotation task. This is while the assessor is asked to take a final decision on the label, based on his own understanding. The assessor assigned to each set of the meetings is familiar with domain knowledge necessary to label it.

Statistics of labeled dataset: subsequently, our goal is to correctly predict the topics that have continued over time. After the topics of all first 3 meetings were labeled based on whether or not they are continued in the $4th$ meeting, the resulting number of labeled topics to be predicted was 205. Our goal is to correctly predict the assigned labels. The dataset of the labeled topics is unbalanced with 60% of the topics continued (positive class) and 40% that did

not continue (negative class). Due to the bigger size and variation of this dataset, in most of the experiments that we conducted in the evaluation section this dataset was used.

4.1.2 Second Dataset. Our second dataset is recorded and prepared with the same process as the first dataset. Thus, we skip the redundant explanations about the preparation process and merely highlight the differences. The two main differences of this dataset compared with the first dataset is the smaller size which is 3 groups, and the higher number of meetings recorded for each group which is 6. Hence, we use this dataset to analyze the effect of more number of consecutive meetings on the prediction models. Figure 4 presents some basic statistics of this dataset. Given the space limitations, we used this dataset only in Subsection 4.3.1 where we tested the effect of the number of meetings over time. The average length of a meeting in this dataset is 35.6.

We prepared this dataset by labeling the topics of the first 3 meetings which will continue in the 4th meeting, then labeling the topics of the first 4 meetings which continue in the 5th meeting and finally labeling all the topics of the first 5 meetings which will continue in the 6th meeting. The number of labeled topics from the first 3 meetings whose continuity in the 4th meeting was labeled is 85 with 48 being continued and 37 not continued. Furthermore, the number of topics from the first 4 meetings was 112 where 65 constituted the continued class and 47 the discontinued class. Finally, the number of topics extracted from the 5 first meetings was 139 of which 70 were continued and 69 discontinued.

4.2 Evaluation Metrics

We performed a rigorous testing of all the four methods presented in Section 3 and compared them against the baseline method. For evaluation, we used standard information retrieval evaluation metrics, namely, precision, recall, F_1 measure and Mean Average Precision (MAP).

Our choice of evaluation metrics is influenced by two factors. First, we used metrics that are commonly used in the information retrieval community for prediction tasks. Second, since we are dealing with an unbalanced dataset, it was important to use metrics such as MAP or F_1 which work well even on unbalanced datasets.

Additionally, for the seven sets of meetings in our test data we always performed a 7-fold cross validation by iteratively leaving one set out and evaluating it using the threshold value learned from the remaining folds.

4.3 Evaluation

All presented experiments, except the experiment on *number of meetings over time* in Subsection 4.3.1, are using the first dataset. In our first experiment, we compute precision and recall values of all the proposed methods and compare them with the HMM baseline. Table 1 shows precision values at different levels of recall and for all decision thresholds. The values are obtained from per-group interpolated precision-recall curves. The table shows that the K2RE method outperforms other methods as well as the HMM baseline in terms of precision at all levels of recall. We also observe that on low levels of recall the second best performing method is the establishment effect. Additionally, we observe that on higher levels of recall the recency effect performs as the second best method.

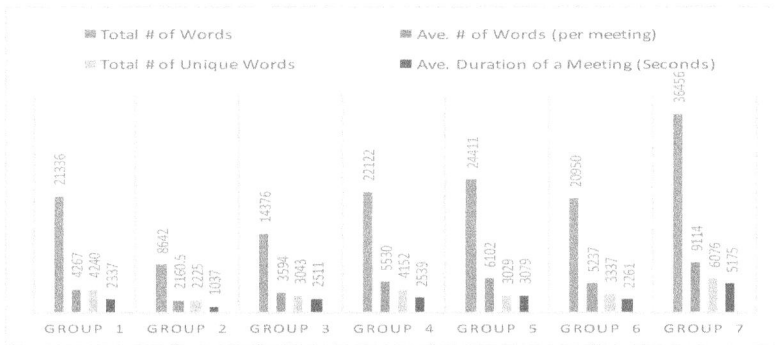

Figure 3: Statistics of the First Dataset

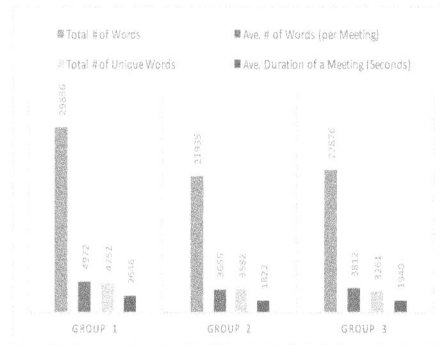

Figure 4: Statistics of the Second Dataset

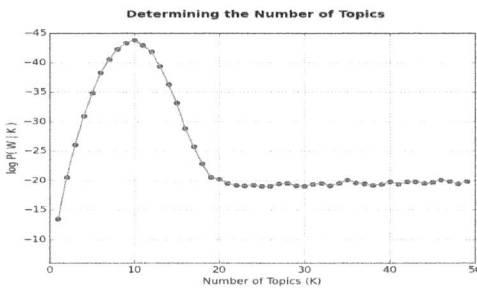

Figure 5: Model selection results for a randomly selected meeting from our dataset. The plot shows the log-likelihood of the data under different number of topics, K.

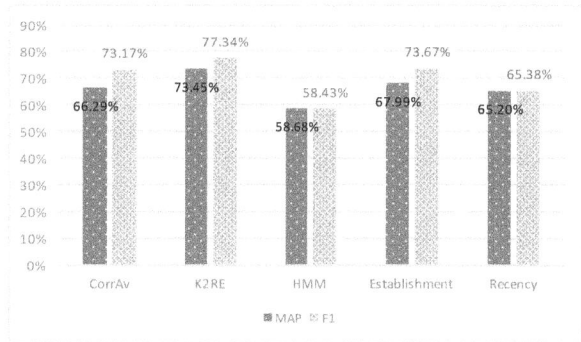

Figure 6: Comparison of our novel methods against the HMM baseline in terms of MAP and F_1 measure on the first dataset

In the second experiment we computed MAP as well as the F_1 measure and reported it in Figure 6. The F_1 measures are computed on the dataset using 7-fold cross validation for each of the seven groups. We can observe through this experiment that K2RE significantly outperforms the HMM baseline. We confirmed the significance in performance difference using a two-tailed paired t-test with the p-value of less than 0.05. Furthermore, the performance of the CorrAv, establishment, and recency effects were confirmed to be statistically significant in terms of the F_1 measure against the HMM baseline. We also present a comparison between all the methods with respect to F_1 measure and MAP in Table 2.

4.3.1 Effect of Parameters. In this subsection we analyze the effect of some parameters that influence our presented models.
Data Sample Sizes
Second, we show the effect of different sizes of training data on MAP, since MAP is more indicative of the changes in models for all decision thresholds. Figure 7 shows the results of this experiment. We computed the MAP measure for 2, 4, 6 and 7 groups respectively. The result of the same metric for all 7 groups which is the full size of the first dataset was also presented in Figure 6 which we also include here for easy comparison. We can observe from the graph that the performance of our *K2RE* method is stable and superior to other methods for different numbers of groups being tested. Moreover, we generally see that almost all methods show the same behavior across the different data sample sizes. The only exception is the MAP value of the recency effect for 2 groups, that for the first time shows a

higher performance than the establishment method. In our analysis of the data, we observed that one of the two groups is having mostly brainstorming meetings where they discuss different ideas for a project and they change ideas at a high pace. Although, we observe through this experiment, as well as the one presented in Figure 6, that for a larger number of groups on average, the establishment effect is a stronger model for predicting the continuation of topics, we also observe that there are cases where recency is a better model. This also proves the need for developing the K2RE method which can at all times adapt itself to the meeting behavior of a group being analyzed. The evolutionary K2RE method is clearly a stronger model than the others and as the number of groups being analyzed increases, its efficacy compared with the other models is more visible. Furthermore, another observation from Figure 7 is that the MAP value of the K2RE method starts to converge as the size of the dataset reaches 4 groups and higher.
Number of meetings over Time
Third, we analyze the effect of sequentially adding meetings to predict the continuation of topics from previous meetings to the next meeting over time. To achieve this goal we used *the second dataset* which consists of 3 groups with 6 meetings recorded for each group. In this experiment, we use the first 3 meetings of each group to train the models. As in the case of the previous experiments we aim to predict those topics of the first 3 meetings

Table 1: Precision of all methods at different Recall levels for all decision thresholds, derived from per-group interpolated precision-recall curves on the first dataset

Recall (%)	Prec. CorrAv (%)	Prec. Establish. (%)	Prec. Recency (%)	Prec. K2RE (%)	Prec. HMM (%)
10	79.16 %	84.04 %	78.15 %	**87.25 %**	68.53 %
20	74.12 %	81.18 %	75.77 %	**85.46 %**	66.62 %
30	71.88 %	72.02 %	73.98 %	**80.10 %**	66.62 %
40	69.66 %	70.41 %	73.98 %	**79.03 %**	66.62 %
50	69.49 %	70.41 %	71.55 %	**77.28 %**	66.62 %
60	68.78 %	70.41 %	70.08 %	**77.15 %**	66.62 %
70	67.04 %	69.46 %	70.08 %	**76.63 %**	66.28 %
80	66.60 %	68.18 %	69.83 %	**74.15 %**	65.81 %
90	66.60 %	66.87 %	68.30 %	**73.15 %**	65.81 %
100	66.40 %	66.04 %	66.48 %	**70.25 %**	64.28 %

Table 2: A comparison of our proposed methods against the HMM baseline on the first dataset

	CorrAv	Establish.	Recency	K2RE	HMM
F_1 Measure (%)	73.17	73.67	65.38	**77.34**	58.43
MAP (%)	66.29	67.99	65.20	**73.45**	58.68

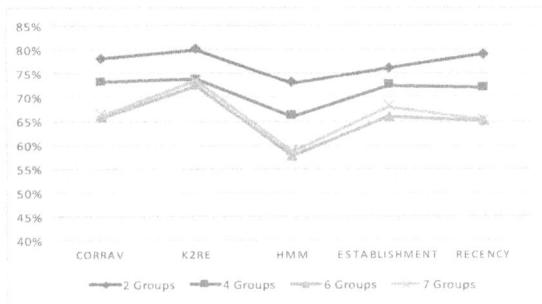

Figure 8: A Comparison of All Methods in terms of MAP, by sequentially adding meetings. This Experiment was performed on the second dataset.

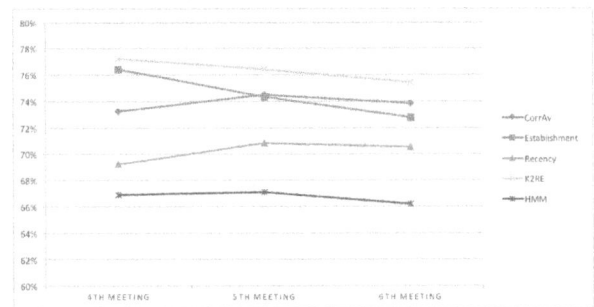

Figure 7: A Comparison of All Methods using the MAP Measure, on different Data Sample Sizes from the first dataset: 2 Groups, 4 Groups, 6 Groups and 7 Groups.

that will continue in the 4th. However, we then continue with predicting those topics of the first 4 meetings that will continue in the 5th meeting and so on. We measure the performance of the models in terms of MAP. As a result of this experiment we present Figure 8 with results of prediction on the 4th, the 5th and the 6th meetings for all three groups. As we see in the figure, the K2RE method shows better performance compared with all other methods over time. The performance of the establishment effect in terms of MAP drops over time, while the CorrAv method stays more robust in this sequential analysis. This is a consequence of how this method is conceived. This experiment confirms that the dynamic K2RE method, is robust against a higher number of meetings over time.

5 DISCUSSION

By investigating the results of our evaluation presented in the previous section, we observe that:

The K2RE method clearly outperforms other methods as well as the HMM baseline in all experiments that we conducted, and is therefore the superior model in our benchmark.

The establishment effect is the second best method and it outperforms the recency effect.

The recency effect is clearly a weaker method also compared with the CorrAv method. However, we observed that in the case of some groups the recency effect was better than CorrAv and establishment effects in modeling the continuation of topics over time. By observing the establishment and recency effects perform very differently on data from different groups, and also by observing that the CorrAv method (which correlates with the average of the two aforementioned methods) always performs reasonably well, we believed that, if we design a model that could learn to perform a weighted average and adapt itself to the input data, this model is likely to outperform all other proposed models. Our results confirm that this belief and intuition was correct.

The K2RE method benefits from the fact that it distinguishes two different effects which are also opposite to one another, and weighs each effect differently over time, while the HMM baseline tries to find a generic solution without considering any different effects that maybe present in the data.

Our goal in designing the proposed models was to develop intuitive time-series algorithms for modeling user behavior, specifically regarding conversations and meetings. The broader vision and strategy that we tried to incorporate into the K2RE method, was that people often have the tendency to repeat the same behavior, but we also sometimes have the willingness to explore a different one. Hence, modeling this contrast between establishment and recency or, in other terms, repetition and exploration, was an important strategy that not only proved to outperform all other tested methods, but may also be useful in other domains and with other types of user data. The concept behind K2RE may be also used in personal assistants, to track user behavior over time and provide the user with the right information just in time the user might need them.

Finally, we would like to add that in a parallel study using ten participants [2], we have achieved results indicating that on average an individual who reviewed her past meetings using our memory augmentation tool (see Section 2), could recall significantly more details of a meeting compared with when she did not use the tool.

Hence, we believe that further development of such technologies is effective in assisting people to recall their past important meetings.

6 CONCLUSIONS

In this paper, we introduced the problem of predicting topics to be reviewed in preparation of one's next meeting to augment one's memory as a just-in-time-IR approach. For this purpose, we proposed four different novel methods and compared them against an HMM baseline which has been extensively used in the literature for multivariate time series prediction tasks and is the state-of-the-art in a number of domains [20]. We showed through extensive experimentation that the dynamic K2RE method, that combines recency and establishment effects, significantly outperformed all other methods as well as the HMM baseline. The developed methods could be implemented as a part of a proactive memory augmentation system that aids people in their every day lives. The benchmark presented in this paper could be a foundation for future studies and further development of such technologies.

There are a few interesting directions for future work. One interesting future work would be adapting the K2RE method to other user intent and context tracking domains and compare it with other methods in those domains. For example, analyzing datasets which current personal assistants such as Microsoft Cortana or Google Now gather (that track user behavior to anticipate their information needs) could be a possibility.

REFERENCES

[1] Seyed Ali Bahrainian and Fabio Crestani. 2016. Cued Retrieval of Personal Memories of Social Interactions. In *Proceedings of the First Workshop on Lifelogging Tools and Applications (LTA '16)*. 3–12.

[2] Seyed Ali Bahrainian and Fabio Crestani. 2017. Are Conversation Logs Useful Sources for Generating Memory Cues for Recalling Past Memories?. In *Proceedings of the 2Nd Workshop on Lifelogging Tools and Applications (LTA '17)*. 13–20.

[3] Seyed Ali Bahrainian and Fabio Crestani. 2017. Towards the Next Generation of Personal Assistants: Systems that Know When You Forget. In *Proceedings of the ACM SIGIR International Conference on Theory of Information Retrieval, ICTIR 2017, Amsterdam, The Netherlands, October 1-4, 2017*. 169–176.

[4] Seyed Ali Bahrainian, Ida Mele, and Fabio Crestani. 2017. Modeling Discrete Dynamic Topics. In *Proceedings of the Symposium on Applied Computing (SAC '17)*. 858–865.

[5] Leonard E. Baum and George R. Sell. 1968. Growth transformations for functions on manifolds. (1968).

[6] David M. Blei and John D. Lafferty. 2006. Dynamic Topic Models. In *Proceedings of the 23rd International Conference on Machine Learning (ICML '06)*. 113–120.

[7] David M. Blei, Andrew Y. Ng, and Michael I. Jordan. 2003. Latent Dirichlet Allocation. *J. Mach. Learn. Res.* 3 (2003), 993–1022.

[8] Yi Chen and Gareth JF Jones. 2010. Augmenting human memory using personal lifelogs. In *Proceedings of the 1st augmented human international conference*.

[9] Hermann Ebbinghaus. 1885, translated in 1913. Memory: A Contribution to Experimental Psychology.

[10] Mik Lamming et.al. 1994. The Design of a Human Memory Prosthesis. *Comput. J.* (1994), 153–163.

[11] Thomas L Griffiths and Mark Steyvers. 2004. Finding scientific topics. *Proceedings of the National academy of Sciences* (2004).

[12] Morgan Harvey, Marc Langheinrich, and Geoff Ward. 2016. Remembering through lifelogging: A survey of human memory augmentation. *Pervasive and Mobile Computing* (2016), 14–26.

[13] Pei-Yun Hsueh and Johanna D. Moore. 2009. Improving Meeting Summarization by Focusing on User Needs: A Task-oriented Evaluation. In *Proceedings of the 14th International Conference on Intelligent User Interfaces*. 17–26.

[14] Ro Jaimes, Kengo Omura, Takeshi Nagamine, and Kazutaka Hirata. 2004. Memory cues for meeting video retrieval. In *In Proceedings CARPE 04*. 74–85.

[15] Rudolph Emil Kalman. 1960. A New Approach to Linear Filtering and Prediction Problems. *Transactions of the ASME–Journal of Basic Engineering* 82, Series D (1960), 35–45.

[16] Wen Li, Carsten Eickhoff, and Arjen P de Vries. 2016. Probabilistic Local Expert Retrieval. In *Advances in Information Retrieval*. 227–239.

[17] Tomas Mikolov, Ilya Sutskever, Kai Chen, Greg S Corrado, and Jeff Dean. 2013. Distributed representations of words and phrases and their compositionality. In *Advances in neural information processing systems*. 3111–3119.

[18] G. Murray. 2007. Automatic Summarization of meeting. In *PhD thesis, University of Edinburgh, UK*.

[19] Jeffrey Pennington, Richard Socher, and Christopher D Manning. Glove: Global Vectors for Word Representation.

[20] Marcin Pietrzykowskiand and Wojciech Salabun. 2014. Applications of Hidden Markov Model: state-of-the-art. In *International Journal of Computer Technology and Applications*.

[21] Lawrence R. Rabiner. 1989. A tutorial on hidden Markov models and selected applications in speech recognition. Vol. 77. 257–286.

[22] Bradley Rhodes and Thad Starner. 1996. Remembrance Agent: A continuously running automated information retrieval system. In *The Proceedings of The First International Conference on The Practical Application Of Intelligent Agents and Multi Agent Technology*. 487–495.

[23] B. J. Rhodes and P. Maes. 2000. Just-in-time Information Retrieval Agents. *IBM Syst. J.* 39 (2000), 685–704.

[24] Stephen Robertson, Hugo Zaragoza, and others. 2009. The probabilistic relevance framework: BM25 and beyond. *Foundations and Trends® in Information Retrieval* 3, 4 (2009), 333–389.

[25] Milad Shokouhi and Qi Guo. 2015. From Queries to Cards: Re-ranking Proactive Card Recommendations Based on Reactive Search History. In *Proceedings of the 38th International ACM SIGIR Conference on Research and Development in Information Retrieval (SIGIR '15)*. 695–704.

[26] Yu Sun, Nicholas Jing Yuan, Yingzi Wang, Xing Xie, Kieran McDonald, and Rui Zhang. 2016. Contextual Intent Tracking for Personal Assistants. In *Proceedings of the 22Nd ACM SIGKDD International Conference on Knowledge Discovery and Data Mining (KDD '16)*. 273–282.

[27] Simon Tucker and Steve Whittaker. 2004. Accessing multimodal meeting data: Systems, problems and possibilities. In *International Workshop on Machine Learning for Multimodal Interaction*. 1–11.

[28] Simon Tucker and Steve Whittaker. 2006. Time is of the Essence: An Evaluation of Temporal Compression Algorithms. In *Proceedings of the SIGCHI Conference on Human Factors in Computing Systems*. 329–338.

[29] S. Tucker and S. Whittaker. 2008. Temporal Compression Of Speech: An Evaluation. *IEEE Transactions on Audio, Speech, and Language Processing* (2008).

[30] Luke Vilnis and Andrew McCallum. 2014. Word representations via gaussian embedding. *arXiv preprint arXiv:1412.6623* (2014).

[31] Chong Wang, David Blei, and David Heckerman. 2008. Continuous time dynamic topic models. *Proc. of UAI* (2008).

[32] Lu Wang and Claire Cardie. 2011. Summarizing Decisions in Spoken Meetings. In *Proceedings of the Workshop on Automatic Summarization for Different Genres, Media, and Languages (WASDGML '11)*. 16–24.

[33] Jihang Ye, Zhe Zhu, and Hong Cheng. 2013. What's your next move: User activity prediction in location-based social networks. In *Proceedings of the 2013 SIAM International Conference on Data Mining*. SIAM, 171–179.

Characterizing Search Behavior in Productivity Software

Horatiu Bota
University of Glasgow
Glasgow, Scotland, UK
h.bota.1@research.gla.ac.uk

Adam Fourney
Microsoft Research
Redmond, Washington, USA
adamfo@microsoft.com

Susan T. Dumais
Microsoft Research
Redmond, Washington, USA
sdumais@microsoft.com

Tomasz L. Religa
Microsoft Corporation
Redmond, Washington, USA
toreli@microsoft.com

Robert Rounthwaite
Microsoft Corporation
Redmond, Washington, USA
robertro@microsoft.com

ABSTRACT

Complex software applications expose hundreds of commands to users through intricate menu hierarchies. One of the most popular productivity software suites, Microsoft Office, has recently developed functionality that allows users to issue free-form text queries to a search system to quickly find commands they want to execute, retrieve help documentation or access web results in a unified interface.

In this paper, we analyze millions of search sessions originating from within Microsoft Office applications, collected over one month of activity, in an effort to characterize search behavior in productivity software. Our research brings together previous efforts in analyzing command usage in large-scale applications and efforts in understanding search behavior in environments other than the web. Our findings show that users engage primarily in command search, and that re-accessing commands through search is a frequent behavior. Our work represents the first large-scale analysis of search over command spaces and is an important first step in understanding how search systems integrated with productivity software can be successfully developed.

KEYWORDS

Environment specific retrieval, command search

ACM Reference Format:
Horatiu Bota, Adam Fourney, Susan T. Dumais, Tomasz L. Religa, and Robert Rounthwaite. 2018. Characterizing Search Behavior in Productivity Software. In *CHIIR '18: 2018 Conference on Human Information Interaction & Retrieval, March 11–15, 2018, New Brunswick, NJ, USA*. ACM, New York, NY, USA, 10 pages. https://doi.org/10.1145/3176349.3176395

1 INTRODUCTION

In a 2007 column, Don Norman argued that graphical user interfaces would struggle to scale under the increasing complexity of software applications, and that scaling could be achieved by embracing rich

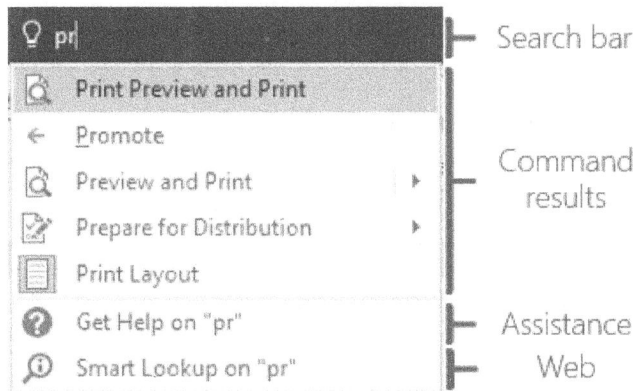

Figure 1: Searching for *"print"* in Microsoft Word.

search experiences [19]. This transformation was predicated on search interfaces gaining, or strengthening, an ability to directly execute actions in addition to retrieving documents. In the intervening ten years, rich search experiences, combining document retrieval with action execution, are now available across a variety of surfaces, including: web search engines, operating systems, and feature-rich applications. For example, on both Bing.com and Google.com, the query [*stopwatch*] both summons an interactive stopwatch, and retrieves documents about this timepiece. Likewise, on both the Windows 10 and macOS operating systems, the query [*bluetooth*] both accesses the device's Bluetooth settings, and optionally retrieves web pages about Bluetooth technology. Finally, users of both Microsoft PowerPoint and Adobe Photoshop can issue the query [*crop*] to either execute the application's crop command, or to retrieve documentation about this tool.

Core to these experiences, and to Norman's vision, is that search systems effectively respond to queries where the searcher's intention is to perform some action (web-mediated, or otherwise). Such search intents were first observed in the query logs of the AltaVista search engine [4, 21], and have varyingly come to be known as *transactional queries* [4], or *resource interact(ion)* queries [21]. Historically, transactional queries represent a minority of all web searches.

More recently, researchers have begun characterizing search interactions occurring via the virtual assistants that are integrated into modern operating systems [7, 15]. In this environment, log analysis has shown that roughly half of all queries result in the direct execution of an action (e.g., setting an alarm) [15]. As such, virtual assistants represent a mid-point along a spectrum of search systems that support direct execution of transactional queries.

In this paper, we provide the first large-scale log-based characterization of search interactions within the context of productivity software, namely Microsoft Office (Figure 1). Microsoft Office, and similar in-application search experiences (e.g., [3, 16]), represent an extreme point along the aforementioned spectrum – an understudied search environment where most queries are intended to execute an action. To investigate this environment, we analyze the queries of a million Microsoft Office users, engaging in millions of search sessions over a one month period in 2017. With these data, we address the following research goals:

(RG1) **Describing search behavior:** In particular, we answer the following questions with respect to search in productivity software: **(1.1)** How is search distributed across queries, accessed commands and users? **(1.2)** What types of search do users engage in and how frequently? **(1.3)** How do users engage in different types of search activity? Specifically, we want to characterize how users engage in command and control search in contrast to informational search.

(RG2) **Describing search abandonment:** Users frequently abandon their sessions without clicking on results returned by the search system. We set out to contrast abandoned search to searches in which commands are executed, and we highlight properties of search results and rankings that potentially influence abandonment.

(RG3) **Describing re-ranking methods:** The use of behavioral signals in improving search results ranking is widespread in modern web search [2, 25]. Therefore, we explore methods of using historical user interaction data and simple user engagement metrics in re-ranking command lists, with the intent of improving ranking quality in rich application search.

The rest of this paper is structured as follows: We review prior research, then describe the search experience that is integrated into many Microsoft Office products. We describe the specific instrumentation data we analyzed, and present results that address our research objectives. We conclude with a discussion of the implications of our findings for the development of in-application search experiences.

2 RELATED WORK

This work builds on three distinct threads of prior research which we review here. We begin by discussing transactional queries in the context of web search, and their generalizations to other domains. We then review research that characterizes command invocations in feature-rich software. Finally, we review past and ongoing efforts to integrate rich search experiences into feature-rich software.

2.1 Transactional Queries

Transactional queries were first characterized by Andrei Broder as web searches whose "*intent is to perform some web-mediated activity*" [4]. Broder interpreted this definition quite broadly, including queries intended to initiate e-commerce, as well as those intended to access phone directories, weather services, and other on-line databases. Upon examining 400 searches performed on the AltaVista web search engine, Broder reported that 30% of all queries met this definition. Other work has consistently placed transactional queries in the minority of all web searches, though the precise proportion varies by search engine [20], and by query topic [13].

In follow-up work [21], Rose and Levinson proposed a refinement to Broder's taxonomy, subdividing transactional queries into four subcategories. Relevant to this work is the subcategory "*interact*", whose queries include those where the searcher's "*goal is to interact with a resource*" (e.g., a weather service, or a unit converter). Again using AltaVista search logs, Rose and Levinson reported that between 4.6% - 6.0% of all queries met this narrower definition.

Web search engines have since moved to directly support Rose and Levinson's *interact* queries by presenting tailored experiences directly on search engine results pages. In 2011, Chilton and Teevan reported that the Bing.com search engine supported nearly 100 such experiences [5]. Separately, Stamou and Efthimiadis studied donated search logs, and reported that 27% of web searches were intended to trigger these types of quick answers [22]. These trends prompted Don Norman to observe that "*more and more, we type commands (into search engines), not search items*", and to further describe search as the "*modern command language*" [19].

Importantly, Norman's observations were not confined to web search: desktop search, email search, and an early version of Microsoft Office search are explicitly mentioned in [19]. Broder's definition of transactional queries naturally generalizes to these environments by simply lifting the constraint that the intended activities be web-mediated. Through this lens we consider work by Jiang et al., who analyzed queries posed to the Cortana virtual assistant [15], the successor of desktop search on the Windows 10 operating system. Jiang et al. reported that roughly half (47%) of all queries result in the direct execution of an action (e.g., setting an alarm, or playing a song) and thus meet the generalized definition of transactional queries. Moreover, this figure may understimate the prevalence of transactional queries, as it excludes utterances that have a transactional intent, but which fall outside the capabilities of the virtual assistant [7, 24]. In this paper, we extend this generalization of transactional queries, and Broder's query taxonomy, by characterizing search behaviors in Microsoft Office – one of several well-known applications to recently allow commands to be triggered through in-application search.

2.2 Command Invocations in Software

As noted above, Norman characterized search as the "*modern command language*" [19], and, in doing so, drew a direct comparison to a prior generation of command-line interfaces. Command-line systems have themselves been the subject of extensive study [10–12], and there are several relevant findings that we report here. First, as with web search [14], command invocations are known to follow an inverse power law distribution, with the most common commands occurring exponentially more often than less popular commands [11, 12]. Second, though each user will tend to frequent a small set of commands, there is little overlap in the command vocabularies between users [11]. Finally, even when users have the same commands or intentions in mind, they will often use different words or terminology to describe these intentions to the system,

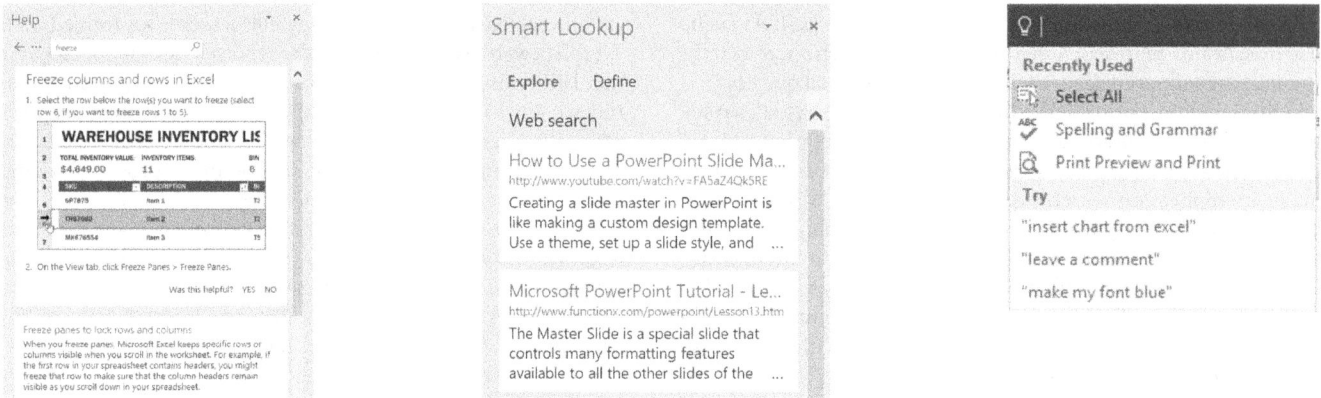

(a) Interface side panel displaying help documents retrieved by the search system for the query *"freeze"* in Excel.

(b) Interface side panel displaying web search results for the query *"slide master tutorial"* in PowerPoint.

(c) Search interface displaying three of the most recently used commands and query suggestions, as shown before query input in Word.

Figure 2: Example (a) help search results, (b) web search results and (c) no-query interactions.

posing problems for command-line interfaces and search systems alike [10]. In this paper, we touch on each of these points, as they relate to commands issued in Microsoft Office via a search interface.

Graphical user interfaces (GUIs) are also command languages – albeit visual rather than textual. To this end, research has found that the aforementioned properties of command-line interfaces also apply to GUIs [17], and to the web search queries that users issue to support their use of those systems [6]. This has spawned work on two fronts: First, numerous command recommendation systems have been been developed to help with command discovery, and to broaden users' command vocabularies [9, 18, 26]. Second, to address the vocabulary problem, researchers have proposed integrating search experiences into graphical interfaces, including Microsoft Office, so that a user's free-text queries can be more flexibly matched to system commands. We describe these search systems next.

2.3 In-Application Search

Search is becoming a popular method of accessing commands, settings, and other functionality in modern feature-rich applications. In addition to Microsoft Office, Adobe's creative products now feature a universal in-application search experience [16]. Likewise, the macOS operating system has long offered a search field in the system-wide help menu, providing its users with a means of searching and executing commands found in the top few levels of any application's menuing system [3]. Similarly, search is the primary means of accessing settings in the Chrome web browser, and on all modern operating systems and platforms (Windows, macOS, iOS, Android, etc.)

Embedded in each of these in-application experiences is the need to return relevant commands, settings, and documents in response to user queries. In GUIs, there is often very little text associated with each command or setting, aggravating the aforementioned vocabulary problem, and limiting the effectiveness of simple ranking algorithms that depend on term or character overlap [6]. In the literature, several systems address this retrieval problem. For example, Fourney et al. [8] leveraged web search queries, together with on-line software tutorials, to better map keywords to system

commands. Likewise, Adar et al., improved command search by learning a command-to-word embedding from millions of on-line tutorials [1]. In this work, we demonstrate how behavioral data can be used to improve command ranking.

In summary, our work extends prior research by characterizing transactional queries and command invocations in the context of a widely deployed suite of software applications. As such, our findings are derived from a comprehensive analysis of in-application query logs, and our work is the largest such study of its kind. We begin by providing a review of search functionality in Microsoft Office.

3 SEARCH IN MICROSOFT OFFICE

Microsoft Office is a collection of productivity software developed for knowledge workers, with millions of active users each month. Recent versions of Office[1] include a unified search interface that allows users to issue free-form text queries to either find and quickly access commands, search through Office help documentation or retrieve Web results directly in the application interface. The unified search functionality is provided through a search box that prompts users to *"Tell me what you want to do"*, located above the application command menu (the *ribbon*).

In this paper, an in-application *"search"* starts when the user activates the query input area (the *search box*), and ends when the user clicks one of the results returned by the system, or deactivates query input by clicking outside the search area. This section provides an overview of search in Microsoft Office, and describes the types of results returned by the system.

3.1 Result Types

Three types of results are accessible through Office search: commands, help documents and web results. We describe each below.

Command Results. Figure 1 shows an example of a Microsoft Word user issuing the query *"pr"* to the search system. Up to five command results are displayed immediately underneath the search box, and are updated continuously as users type. Results are ranked

---

[1] Starting with Microsoft Office 2016.

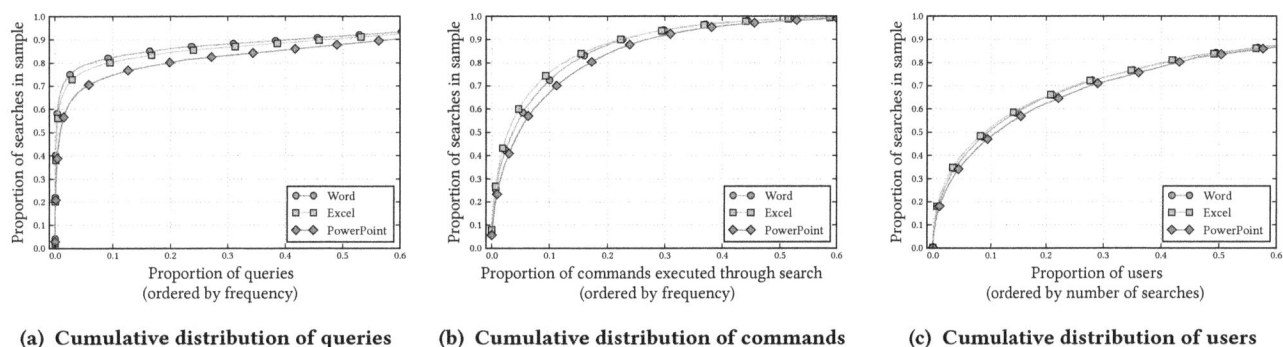

(a) **Cumulative distribution of queries** (b) **Cumulative distribution of commands** (c) **Cumulative distribution of users**

Figure 3: Distribution of queries and commands executed via search functionality

by their relevance to the user query, and need not be lexically similar to command names.

Command results returned by the search system can be of three sub-types : **(i)** *action* commands that initiate a process (for example, the *"Print"* command opens an additional dialog that users need to navigate in order to complete their task); **(ii)** *flag* commands which toggle a binary feature (such as the *"Bold"* command) without requiring any additional action from the user; **(iii)** *menu* commands which, on user click, open an additional side menu containing related sub-commands that the user can browse and click – in Figure 1, menu commands are displayed with a chevron icon on the right of their label. In addition, commands returned to users are disabled (greyed-out, not clickable) if the active system state is incompatible with their execution (e.g., the *Group* command is greyed-out when no items are selected for grouping). We investigate the role these command types serve in influencing search behavior in §5.5.

Help Results. Office search allows users to quickly retrieve help documentation using free-form text queries. Unlike commands, help results are not displayed directly beneath the search bar, but in a side panel where the user can refine their query and navigate returned documents. To activate the help search side panel, users need to click on the *"Get Help"* button shown below the command results list, as shown in Figure 1. Figure 2a shows an example of the help search side panel for the query *"freeze"* in Microsoft Excel.

Web Results. Users can also retrieve and display web documents directly in the application interface through Office search. The interaction pattern is similar to accessing help documents, in that web results are displayed in a side panel, where the user can explore returned documents. The web search side panel is activated by clicking on the *"Smart Lookup"* button below the command results list. Figure 2b shows an example of web documents returned for the query *"slide master tutorial"* in Microsoft PowerPoint.

3.2 Zero-query Interactions

After activating the search box, but before any query input, the search results area is populated with query suggestions (Figure 2c, bottom), and up to 5 of the most recent commands previously found and executed through search (Figure 2c, top).

3.3 Abandoned Search

Search sessions are regularly abandoned, with the user deactivating the search box (e.g., by clicking outside the search interface) without interacting with any of the results returned by the system. We explore abandonment in the context of in-application search in section 5.5 in more detail, but we highlight here the two types of search abandonment we observed in our analysis: **(i) abandoned (query)**: search sessions in which the user explicitly types a query in the search box and decides not to interact with any of the results returned by the system; and **(ii) abandoned (zero-query)**: search sessions in which the user activates the search area, but does not issue a query or interact with the search interface (e.g., recently used commands) before deactivating the search menu. We highlight these two types of abandonment (*with* and *without* query) because they are driven by different underlying user expectations with regard to system functionality.

4 DATA

To understand search in productivity software and address our specific research goals, we make use of Office instrumentation logs, which include: **(i)** *information about the user*: anonymized user identifier; **(ii)** *information regarding application context*: application version number, users' system locale and language settings; **(iii)** *information about search sessions*: timestamps, user-typed queries, result rankings shown to user, and clicks.

From the instrumentation logs, we extracted English-language queries performed by Microsoft Office users who reside in the United States. Although search functionality is available in most Office products[2], we focus our analysis on three of the most popular applications in the suite: Word, Excel and PowerPoint. In addition, our data was obtained from a single Office build version, to ensure consistency of features available to users over incremental releases of Microsoft Office. Our data covers search events over a four week period, from the 29th of May to the 25th of June 2017. Finally, from these data, we randomly sampled one million users and their millions of queries.

5 RESULTS

We begin this section by describing the properties of query, command and user distributions in Office search (§5.1). We structure

---

[2]Version 16 and higher.

our results by providing a comparison between different types of in-application search (§5.2 – §5.4), followed by a closer look at characteristics of abandoned search (§5.5); lastly, we describe ways of using behavioral data to improve command ranking quality (§5.6).

5.1 Query, Command and User Distributions

Similar to Web search [14], the distribution of queries observed in Office search is long-tailed, with a small number of query strings accounting for a large proportion of the search events, across applications. Figure 3a shows the cumulative distribution of distinct query strings observed in our sample, ordered by frequency. Roughly 10% of query strings account for 80% of searches in our sample. This trend is consistent across Office applications, suggesting that productivity search is similar across the three applications we studied. Figure 3b shows the cumulative distribution of *commands executed* via the search functionality. Similarly, the top 10% most popular commands executed via search account for roughly 70% of all search-issued commands – although the shapes of the two distributions suggest a heavier tailed query distribution. Finally, Figure 3c displays the cumulative distribution of searches across users, showing that the most active 10% of users account for roughly 50% of the searches in our sample.

5.2 Engagement Across Result Types

When users issue search queries in Office, the results may include commands, a link to Office help, or a link to Web search results. Among these three, command execution is the most likely outcome; command results are clicked 6.4 times as often as help documentation, and 32 times as often as web search. This indicates that most searches in Office are transactional, and are used to access — or re-access — commands.

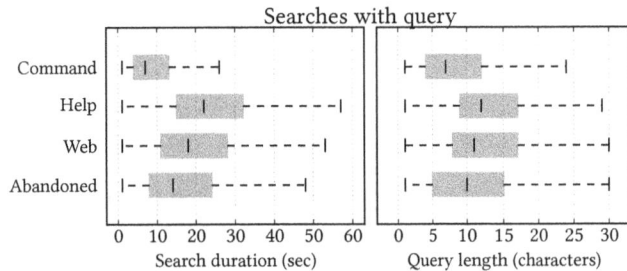

Figure 4: Search session durations and query length.

Figure 4 shows the distribution of search session duration and query length across types of search outcomes. Search session duration is the duration in seconds between search bar activation (e.g., by a user click on the search bar) and search bar deactivation (e.g., by a user clicking on one of the results), and query length is the number of characters in the query at search bar deactivation.

The median duration of search sessions that terminate with a command execution is 7 seconds, whereas the median duration for search sessions that terminate with the activation of help or web search panels is 22 and 17 seconds respectively. Similarly, command search queries have a median length of 6 characters, whereas help or web search queries have median lengths of 12 and 11 characters respectively. These differences highlight that informational

intent (i.e., the combination of help and web results) is typically expressed through longer queries and takes longer to formulate than command search. However, there is only a weak positive correlation between session duration and query length (*Pearson's* $r = 0.39, p < 0.001$), suggesting that the typing effort is not the only factor behind the differences we observed. We now contrast command search to informational search in more detail.

5.3 Command (Transactional) Search

Given that command access is the most frequent search intent in Microsoft Office, we take a closer look at this activity. Table 1 shows the top 10 most frequent queries for each of the three applications in our dataset. Though each of these queries was explicitly typed by the searcher, user behavior is influenced by queries *previously* suggested via the no-query experience (as described in §3.2). These *primed queries* are over-represented in our dataset, and are denoted with †. We note that *primed queries* are abandoned at a much higher rate than other queries (%Abandoned), perhaps indicating users are exploring the system, rather than satisfying actual search needs. We discuss abandonment in detail in §5.5.

It is interesting to note that previous work on command execution in large-scale applications has shown a strong overlap among users in their access of the most popular commands, and low overlap for commands in the torso or tail of the corresponding command distribution [11, 17]. In contrast, our analysis of in-application search shows that there is low overlap in queries across users (%Users column; similarly reported with respect to command usage in [17]) – even with respect to the top searches – even though queries often directly match the names of commands. One possible interpretation is that users are leveraging in-application search to access idiosyncratic commands in their command vocabularies.

In addition to frequency, we report the proportion of *users* who issued each query (User Rank). This metric provides an indication of how popular a given query is across users. We highlight two examples: the query *"undo"* for Word, although it is the 5th most popular query by number of issues, it is the 15th most popular by the number of users who have issued the query at least once. Similarly, the query *"group"*, for PowerPoint, ranks 10th most popular by frequency of issues, but 17th most popular by number of users who have submitted it to the search system at least once. This shows that a smaller number of searchers make frequent use of these queries. We discuss these re-access and re-finding patterns in §5.4.

Finally, queries used to access commands vary widely. Table 2 presents a different perspective on command access, by showing the three most frequent commands executed through search, along with the five most popular queries used to retrieve these commands, and their relative frequency. There is less variation in the queries used to retrieve commands such as *"Print"* in Word or *"Crop"* in PowerPoint, where the command name also maps directly to the query used most frequently to retrieve it – 80% of retrievals of the *"Crop"* command being achieved via the query *"crop"*. On the other hand, Table 2 also shows examples of commands that are retrieved by a more varied set of queries, such as *"Line Spacing"* in Word or *"Orientation"* in PowerPoint. Because these commands require parameters (e.g., the amount of spacing between lines), users, in addition to using the command name as a query, may

Query	Most Popular Command	% Search Volume	% App Sessions	% Users	% Abandoned	% Requery	# Query Rank	# App Rank	# Users Rank
			Microsoft Word						
print†	PrintDefault	4.06%	5.95%	7.21%	71.99%	27.20%	1	1	1
write an essay†	Researcher	1.48%	2.36%	3.14%	99.48%	12.98%	2	2	2
word	WordCount	1.20%	1.12%	1.22%	2.86%	58.14%	3	5	6
spell	Proofing	1.00%	1.54%	1.77%	2.49%	27.78%	4	3	4
undo	Undo	0.88%	0.81%	0.85%	3.26%	60.22%	5	12	15
share my document†	Collaborate	0.84%	1.43%	1.96%	99.90%	4.28%	6	4	3
find	Find	0.80%	1.12%	1.17%	6.61%	40.05%	7	6	7
water	Watermark	0.80%	1.05%	1.13%	5.96%	41.69%	8	8	8
sp	Proofing	0.76%	1.10%	1.23%	2.52%	33.73%	9	7	5
page	PageNum	0.60%	0.81%	0.97%	12.11%	32.90%	10	11	12
			Microsoft Excel						
header	HeaderAndFooter	2.09%	3.04%	3.32%	6.88%	39.17%	1	1	1
free	FreezePanes	1.70%	1.96%	2.11%	8.25%	52.57%	2	3	3
print	PrintDefault	1.44%	2.19%	2.53%	16.21%	32.90%	3	2	2
sort	Sort	1.18%	1.29%	1.44%	11.85%	53.38%	4	8	7
find	Find	1.07%	1.35%	1.27%	7.35%	54.82%	5	5	9
insert	InsertSheetRows	1.06%	1.14%	1.24%	23.88%	55.58%	6	10	10
freeze the top row†	FreezePanes	0.93%	1.43%	1.92%	99.78%	20.93%	7	4	4
insert row	InsertSheetRows	0.85%	0.93%	1.06%	8.62%	52.43%	8	11	12
freeze	FreezePanes	0.80%	1.16%	1.41%	13.41%	32.94%	9	9	8
insert a table†	InsertList	0.79%	1.34%	1.79%	99.77%	13.77%	10	7	6
			Microsoft PowerPoint						
crop	Crop	2.76%	2.33%	2.47%	20.55%	64.18%	1	2	3
start presentation†	StartSlideshow	2.17%	3.76%	4.57%	99.55%	15.55%	2	1	1
change slide background†	FormatBackground	1.31%	2.19%	2.72%	99.42%	16.98%	3	3	2
portrait	Orientation	1.19%	1.94%	2.41%	7.27%	18.72%	4	4	4
de	DesignerPane	0.94%	1.04%	1.12%	4.15%	52.11%	5	6	7
master	SlideMaster	0.84%	1.02%	0.97%	1.61%	53.58%	6	7	11
des	DesignerPane	0.71%	0.82%	0.88%	2.59%	50.38%	7	12	13
design	DesignerPane	0.67%	0.90%	0.97%	6.05%	41.81%	8	9	10
change layout of slide†	MasterStyle	0.64%	1.09%	1.37%	99.66%	14.24%	9	5	5
group	Group	0.64%	0.69%	0.77%	35.03%	51.79%	10	15	17

Table 1: Head queries per application. Priming queries are marked with the (†) symbol.

Microsoft Word			Microsoft Excel			Microsoft PowerPoint		
Command Name	Query		Command Name	Query		Command Name	Query	
Proofing	spell	28.07%	FreezePanes	free	39.69%	Orientation	portrait	24.38%
	sp	18.51%		freeze	14.87%		orientation	6.65%
	spe	15.27%		fre	13.30%		landscape	5.02%
	spelling	6.35%		fr	11.82%		change to portrait	3.94%
	spell check	6.25%		freez	4.34%		change orientation	3.20%
WordCount	word	42.96%	HeaderAndFooter	header	56.65%	DesignerPane	des	23.29%
	word count	20.13%		footer	13.71%		design	19.80%
	wor	12.15%		head	9.03%		de	16.39%
	wo	4.86%		foo	3.71%		desi	8.33%
	character count	4.40%		foot	3.23%		d	6.10%
LineSpacing	line	14.94%	InsertSheetRows	insert row	33.72%	Crop	crop	81.16%
	spacing	6.80%		insert	27.15%		cr	12.42%
	single space	6.61%		insert a row	5.82%		crop picture	0.60%
	double space	6.19%		inser	4.67%		finish crop	0.39%
	double	4.78%		insert rows	3.64%		crop image	0.34%

Table 2: Most frequently used queries for executing top three most frequent commands executed through search.

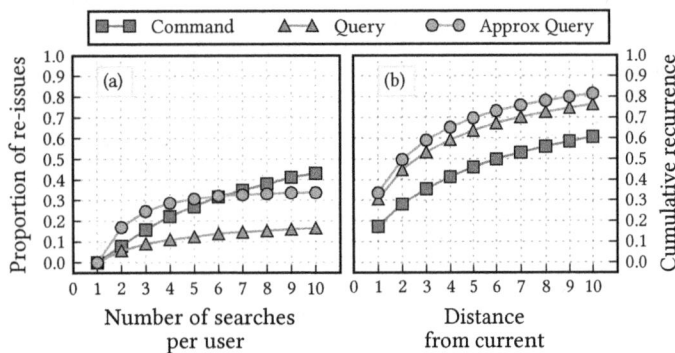

Figure 5: Search recurrence.

also specify parameters of the command as part of their queries. This behavior is informative for the development of search systems for productivity software, where command outcomes, rather than command descriptions are used for search (e.g., users issuing the query "blue text" rather than "change font color").

5.4 Re-finding

Re-finding is an important aspect of search. As in Web search, where up to 39% of searches are driven by accessing previously retrieved resources [23], re-finding is frequent in Microsoft Office search. Not only do searchers frequently make use of the recently used commands list, they repeatedly issue the same queries. Table 1 shows, for a given query, the proportion of searches for which users had previously issued the same query within our sampling period (% Requery). There is variation among users and queries with respect to their re-querying rate, but on average, the priming queries are the least re-issued by users (and most likely to be abandoned).

The aforementioned view of re-querying is muddied by the fact that people varied in their use of the Office applications in general, and of the in-application search experience in particular (i.e. people with more sessions or queries had more opportunities for re-accesses). Figure 5(a) shows the proportion of re-accesses, but partitions users into cohorts based on the total number of queries they issued during the month we studied. We distinguish three separate re-access types: re-executing a command found through search (*"Command"*), re-issuing a query to the search system (*"Query"*) or re-issuing a prefix or an extension of a previously issued query – for instance, the queries *"pr"* and *"prin"* – (*"ApproxQuery"*). For each of these types of search engagement, Figure 5(a) shows the distribution of re-access over repeated use of the search system. It is interesting to note that, for users with three distinct searches in our sample, the proportion of repeated queries is 9%, but the proportion of repeated commands is 17%, and that of approximately repeated queries is 26%. This suggests that users learn approximately equivalent queries (e.g., a set of prefixes) for accessing the same commands.

We also examine the distance (i.e. the number of search activations) between re-access instances. In this view, we include only search sessions that are indeed instances of re-access for a given user. As seen in Figure 5(b), 30% to 35% of repeated queries are identical to, or are approximations of, the previous query issued by the user. Moreover, a history window of 5 queries is sufficient to

explain 70% of approximate query re-issues. Conversely, command re-access is distributed more evenly across the five most recently executed commands, primarily because the recently used command list provides easy access to these commands. Even so, almost 20% of the commands that are re-executed through search are repeats of the most recently executed command, and the top five most recent commands account for roughly 45% of command repeats. We now take a closer look at factors influencing search abandonment.

5.5 Search Abandonment

Like in web search [22], searches in Office are frequently abandoned. Abandonment can occur when a user inputs a query and elects not to click a result, or when a user activates the search bar without issuing a query and elects not to click on a recently used command or suggestion. In either case, a user may fail to click on a result either because the intended command is not listed, or, importantly, because it is present but the active system state is incompatible with its execution (i.e. the command is greyed-out). For example, in PowerPoint an object must be selected for the *Crop* and *Group* commands to be enabled, and thus the corresponding queries *"crop"* and *"group"* have high abandonment rates compared to similar queries (20.55% and 35.03% respectively, as seen in Table 1). We return to these system state errors, and their role in search abandonment, later.

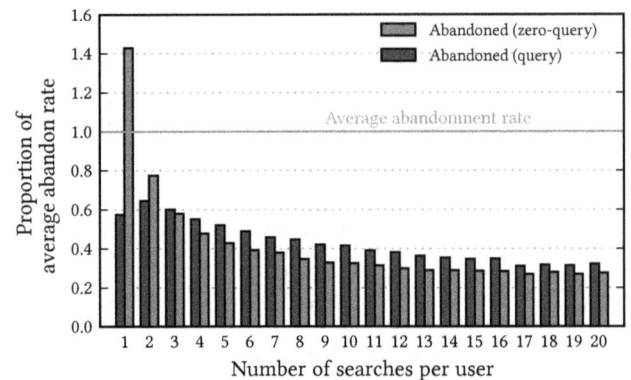

Figure 6: Distribution of search abandonment over user groups partitioned by the number of search instances.

In our data, abandonment is twice as common in the zero-query condition than in cases when users type at least one character into the search box. Users just exploring the search bar as a novelty item or mistakenly activating the search bar through click or keyboard shortcut might partially explain abandonment without query input. Figure 6 shows the distribution of search outcomes over groups of users with repeated search access, sorted from users who have used search functionality a single time (left) to users who have used search functionality exactly 20 times (right) over the time period we observed in our sample. It is interesting to note that the relative proportion of abandoned search decreases with repeated system use, as users either populate their recently used command list with relevant or frequently accessed commands, or they learn and adapt to the capabilities of the search system. We now take a closer look at search abandonment after query input.

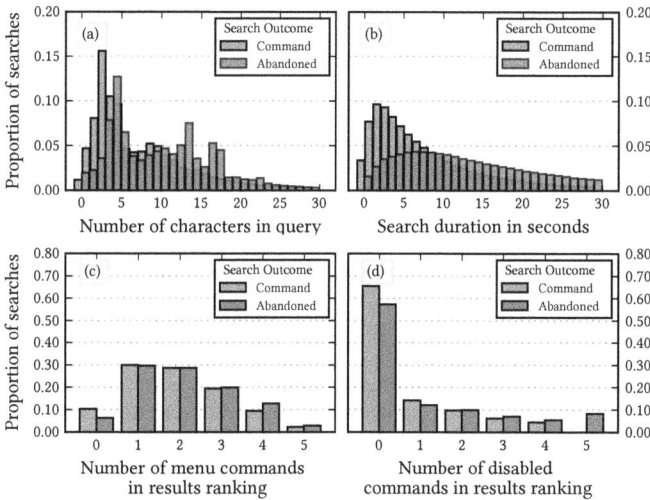

Figure 7: **Differences between command search and abandoned (query) search.**

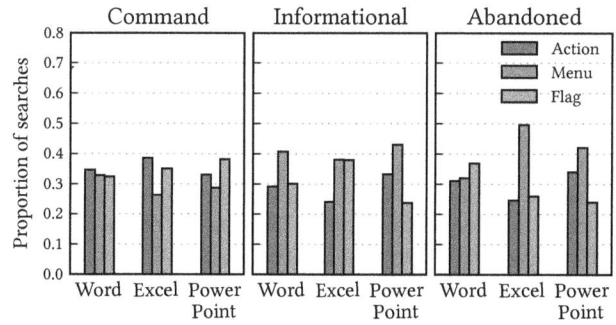

Figure 8: **Distribution of search outcomes over command types, controlling for how often each command type is displayed at top rank.**

5.5.1 Differences between command and abandoned search.

Understanding the characteristics of abandoned search in contrast to successful command search is critical to developing rich search functionality that meet users' expectations and needs. Figure 7 shows differences between command and abandoned search with respect to query length (7a), search session duration (7b), number of menu results shown in the search ranking, (7c) and number of disabled results shown in the search ranking (7d). The first row in Figure 7 shows differences in search session properties, such as query length and duration. Overall, for abandoned search sessions we observe longer queries (median query length 10 characters) and longer search duration (median duration 14 seconds) than for command search. This suggests that, in the case of abandoned sessions, users express more complex needs to the system, and that search properties, such as query length and duration, can be used to identify searches in which users are struggling and perhaps pre-empt abandonment by offering additional support.

The second row of Figure 7 shows differences based on the number of menu type results shown in the ranked list of commands, and the number of disabled results in the ranking. In both cases, abandoned search sessions typically display more menu type results and more disabled items – almost 8% of abandoned searches do not lead to a command execution simply because all items returned to the user are disabled due to system state (e.g., searching for *"crop"* when no items that can be cropped are selected). It is worth noting that showing a disabled command is arguably better than not showing it at all, which might leave the user uncertain about whether the command exists, or if the system understood the intent of the query. Overall, these findings suggest that the types of commands returned to the user have an effect on search behavior and we further investigate the role of result type in search abandonment.

5.5.2 Command types and search abandonment.

Command results returned by the search system in Microsoft Office are not uniform with respect to their user interaction patterns. Section 3.1

reviews the different types of command results returned to users: *action*, *flag* or *menu* commands. Given that, overall, a majority of user clicks on command results are issued on the top-ranked result, in this section we inspect the effects of top-ranked command type on user search behavior.

The type of command displayed at top rank in the search results returned varies with both user intent and with the distribution of command types available in each of the applications we explored. Table 3 shows the distribution of command types shown at top rank. Although there is some variation across applications, the most common types of results returned at top rank are *action* commands and *menu* commands.

	Action	Flag	Menu
Word	49.88%	10.88%	39.24%
Excel	44.45%	13.16%	42.40%
PowerPoint	34.89%	21.29%	43.82%

Table 3: **Distribution of command types displayed at top-rank.**

Figure 8 shows the distribution of search outcomes over command types, normalized by the relative frequency of command types at the top rank for each application. Given this normalization, in a uniform setting, each command type (i.e. bar color) should account for $1/3^{rd}$ of the search outcomes. However, our results show that menu commands are more frequent at top rank in the case of abandoned and informational search. This finding suggests that the menu command type might influence users decision to abandon their searches or seek additional support. One hypothesis that may explain this behavior is that relevant command results may not be readily apparent to the user until they take the additional action of opening the sub-menu, and that not all users will take this additional step. Another hypothesis is that menu commands reflect more complex or obscure tasks, which may pose challenges in both query formulation and task execution. As such, it is not the menu result that leads to abandonment, but rather the more complex task the user is engaged in. Even so, our findings suggests that extracting sub-commands from deeper menu hierarchies and displaying sub-commands directly in the search results list might benefit users trying to complete multi-step actions through search.

5.6 Re-ranking Results

In this section, we report on the application of command re-ranking strategies informed by behavioral data. We evaluate our re-ranking strategies in an off-line setting, using log data, by interpreting clicks as positive relevance labels. There are two aspects of result re-ranking that we discuss here: re-ranking *strategy*, by which we refer to the reordering of commands returned to users based on simple metrics; and re-ranking *selection*, by which we refer to the process of selecting *queries* that might benefit from results re-ranking. Informed by our analysis of user engagement with Office search, we consider the following strategies:

Result type re-ranking. Based on our observation that searches in which *menu* commands are top-ranked seem to be abandoned at a higher rate, we re-rank results by explicitly placing menu commands below *action* or *flag* items in the ranking.

Per-query command click-through rate. User engagement with the search system allows us to observe command execution frequency and click-through rate for a given query. For a query and a list of results relevant to the query, we re-rank commands in descending order of their per-query click-through rate.

Overall command click-through rate. Similar to the previous strategy, we can compute global command click-through rates for individual commands, as a measure of how useful a command is overall. Given a list of results, we re-rank commands in descending order of their global click-through rate.

To evaluate the strategies outlined above, we split our data into training and test folds (each fold covering a non-overlapping period of two weeks). We use training data for two purposes: firstly, to compute overall and per-query command click-through rates; secondly, we use the training fold to select which *queries* (and corresponding rankings) potentially benefit from re-ranking. Selecting which result lists to re-rank is not trivial, given that more than 70% of searches retrieved optimal rankings (i.e. clicked command returned at top rank), and as such, re-ranking these searches would likely deteriorate the quality of their results. Thus, we compare two different methods to select instances of search in which to deploy our re-ranking strategies.

Historical query selection. We use training data to select *queries* that generated clicks on lower ranked results, on average, and we apply our re-ranking strategies only to those queries, as observed in our test data. Using this filtering method, we select 16.34% of the searches in our test fold for re-ranking.

Oracle query selection. Given that our logs contain the clicked result rank, we can identify all searches in which clicks were not issued on the top-ranked result, and apply re-ranking strategies to these searches. This selection method is not feasible in a real-world setting, where click rank is not know beforehand, but is an informative baseline with respect to the effectiveness of our re-ranking strategies. Using this filtering method, we select 29.46% of the searches in our test fold for re-ranking.

Table 4 shows the distribution of clicks over ranks for our re-ranking strategies. The existing system ranker returns the clicked result at top rank in more than 70% of searches in our test data. Even so, all re-ranking strategies we explored increase the proportion of clicks at top-rank. Simply placing *menu* type results lower in the ranking increases the proportion of top-rank clicks by 0.6% to

Selection	Strategy	Clicked result rank				
		1	2	3	4	5
	No re-ranking	70.54%	15.93%	7.18%	3.85%	2.50%
Historical	Result type	71.17%	12.47%	7.21%	5.28%	3.87%
	Overall click-through	74.66%	12.52%	6.47%	3.83%	2.51%
	Per-query click-through	77.93%	12.29%	5.32%	2.68%	1.78%
Oracle	Result type	76.77%	7.48%	5.76%	5.63%	4.36%
	Overall click-through	82.65%	7.25%	5.08%	3.20%	1.82%
	Per-query click-through	83.18%	9.47%	4.24%	1.99%	1.12%

Table 4: Distribution of clicks over ranking positions.

6%, in historical and oracle re-ranking query selection, respectively. Together with our analysis of command types and their role in abandoned search, our findings suggest that placing menu items lower in the ranking does not deteriorate the quality of results returned to the user, and might even prevent abandonment. We hypothesize that users willing to navigate menu hierarchies to locate their intended command will do so even when the menu result – which collapses the relevant menu hierarchy – is at a lower rank; the converse might not be true, with users looking for quick access to an action (or flag) command perhaps being less inclined to review the sub-menu contents of top-ranked menu results in order to locate their intended command, and maybe more likely to abandon their search. We leave testing this hypothesis for future work.

Overall, the most effective re-ranking metric we explored is *per-query command click-through rate*. Re-ranking based on this metric increased top-rank clicks by 7% to 13% over historical and oracle query selection methods, respectively. Even though integrating behavioral signals into search results ranking is widespread in search algorithms for the web [2, 25], their application to in-application command search is under-explored and our work provides an overview of simple re-ranking strategies based on user interaction data as a first step towards integrating behavioral signals into command and control search.

6 CONCLUSIONS

Rich search experiences have become available across a variety of surfaces: from the web, to personal information repositories, feature-rich applications and operating systems. These novel search experiences transform both the way users engage with complex applications, and their expectations of search systems in general.

Our study provides a characterization of user behavior in an under-studied area of information access: search in productivity software. Millions of users actively engage with productivity software each month. As search interactions become integrated into their workflows, understanding search behavior is necessary for developing systems that can effectively respond to users' queries.

Users primarily engage in finding commands through the search interface available in Microsoft Office (***RG1.2***). The distributional properties of observed queries are similar to other search domains, in that a large proportion of search volume is generated by a small proportion of queries (***RG1.1***). However, our results show that, unlike command access, there is low overlap in queries across users – even for frequently observed query strings. One possible interpretation is that users are leveraging in-application search to access idiosyncratic commands in their command vocabularies. We also show that queries used to access commands vary widely, and that action outcomes (e.g., *"portrait"*) rather than command names (e.g., *"change orientation"*) are commonly used to retrieve parameterized commands (**RG1.3**). Users frequently engage in command re-access through search, not only by using the zero-query interface available in Microsoft Office, but by explicitly re-issuing queries to the system. For frequent users of search, on average, more than 26% of queries are approximate repetitions of a previously issued query. Moreover, up to 70% of repeated queries occur within a window of five most recent user queries. Together with our characterization of observed queries, our findings regarding re-access are informative for the development of command retrieval systems (**RG1**).

Identifying instances of search in which users are unable to access intended commands is a crucial element of improving search quality. Our work on abandonment shows that successful command search and abandoned searches vary with respect to their behavioral properties, such as query length and search duration, and with respect to result ranking characteristics, such as the number of disabled or menu commands shown in the results list (**RG2**). Furthermore, we indicate that different command types influence search outcomes, and show that menu commands are prevalent at top rank in abandoned searches. Our findings suggest that ranking sub-commands, as opposed to collapsible menus, directly in the results list might benefit users trying to execute multi-step actions.

Finally, our work on re-ranking commands using metrics derived from historical interaction data shows that behavioral signals can be used to improve command rankings (**RG3**). More work is required to merge previous efforts on command recommendation and the use of behavioral data in command retrieval, and through our study we provide a direction for future endeavors in this space.

7 ACKNOWLEDGMENTS

We would like to thank Madeline Kleiner for insightful discussions which helped to shape this research in its early stages, and motivate many of the research questions that were pursued in this paper.

REFERENCES

[1] Eytan Adar, Mira Dontcheva, and Gierad Laput. 2014. CommandSpace: Modeling the Relationships Between Tasks, Descriptions and Features. In *Proceedings of the Symposium on User Interface Software and Technology (UIST '14)*. ACM, New York, NY, USA, 167–176.

[2] Eugene Agichtein, Eric Brill, and Susan Dumais. 2006. Improving Web Search Ranking by Incorporating User Behavior Information. In *Proceedings of the Conference on Research and Development in Information Retrieval (SIGIR '06)*. ACM, New York, NY, USA, 19–26.

[3] Apple Inc. 2017 (accessed September, 2017). *OS X Yosemite: Onscreen help in OS X*. https://support.apple.com/kb/PH18780.

[4] Andrei Broder. 2002. A Taxonomy of Web Search. *SIGIR Forum* 36, 2 (Sept. 2002), 3–10.

[5] Lydia B. Chilton and Jaime Teevan. 2011. Addressing People's Information Needs Directly in a Web Search Result Page. In *Proceedings of the Conference on World Wide Web (WWW '11)*. ACM, New York, NY, USA, 27–36.

[6] Adam Fourney. 2015. *Web Search, Web Tutorials & Software Applications: Characterizing and Supporting the Coordinated Use of Online Resources for Performing Work in Feature-Rich Software*. Ph.D. Dissertation. University of Waterloo, Waterloo, Ontario, Canada. http://hdl.handle.net/10012/9502

[7] Adam Fourney and Susan T. Dumais. 2016. Automatic Identification and Contextual Reformulation of Implicit System-Related Queries. In *Proceedings of the Conference on Research and Development in Information Retrieval (SIGIR '16)*. ACM, New York, NY, USA, 761–764.

[8] Adam Fourney, Richard Mann, and Michael Terry. 2011. Characterizing the Usability of Interactive Applications Through Query Log Analysis. In *Proceedings of the Conference on Human Factors in Computing Systems (CHI '11)*. ACM, New York, NY, USA, 1817–1826.

[9] C. Ailie Fraser, Mira Dontcheva, Holger Winnemöller, Sheryl Ehrlich, and Scott Klemmer. 2016. DiscoverySpace: Suggesting Actions in Complex Software. In *Proceedings of the Conference on Designing Interactive Systems (DIS '16)*. ACM, New York, NY, USA, 1221–1232.

[10] G. W. Furnas, T. K. Landauer, L. M. Gomez, and S. T. Dumais. 1987. The Vocabulary Problem in Human-system Communication. *Commun. ACM* 30, 11 (Nov. 1987), 964–971.

[11] Saul Greenberg. 1993. *The Computer User As Toolsmith: The Use, Reuse, and Organization of Computer-based Tools*. Cambridge University Press, New York, NY, USA.

[12] Stephen José Hanson, Robert E. Kraut, and James M. Farber. 1984. Interface Design and Multivariate Analysis of UNIX Command Use. *ACM Trans. Inf. Syst.* 2, 1 (Jan. 1984), 42–57.

[13] Bernard J. Jansen and Danielle Booth. 2010. Classifying Web Queries by Topic and User Intent. In *Extended Abstracts on Human Factors in Computing Systems (CHI EA '10)*. ACM, New York, NY, USA, 4285–4290.

[14] Bernard J. Jansen, Amanda Spink, and Tefko Saracevic. 2000. Real Life, Real Users, and Real Needs: a Study and Analysis of User Queries on the Web. *Information Processing & Management* 36, 2 (2000), 207 – 227.

[15] Jiepu Jiang, Ahmed Hassan Awadallah, Rosie Jones, Umut Ozertem, Imed Zitouni, Ranjitha Gurunath Kulkarni, and Omar Zia Khan. 2015. Automatic Online Evaluation of Intelligent Assistants. In *Proceedings of the Conference on World Wide Web (WWW '15)*. ACM, New York, NY, USA, 506–516.

[16] Julieanne Kost. 2016 (accessed September, 2017). *In-Application Search in Photoshop CC 2017*. http://blogs.adobe.com/jkost/2016/11/in-application-search-in-photoshop-cc-2017.html.

[17] Benjamin Lafreniere, Andrea Bunt, John S. Whissell, Charles L. A. Clarke, and Michael Terry. 2010. Characterizing Large-scale Use of a Direct Manipulation Application in the Wild. In *Proceedings of Graphics Interface (GI '10)*. Canadian Information Processing Society, Toronto, Ont., Canada, 11–18.

[18] Justin Matejka, Wei Li, Tovi Grossman, and George Fitzmaurice. 2009. CommunityCommands: Command Recommendations for Software Applications. In *Proceedings of the Symposium on User Interface Software and Technology (UIST '09)*. ACM, New York, NY, USA, 193–202.

[19] Don Norman. 2007. The Next UI Breakthrough: Command Lines. *ACM Interactions* 14, 3 (May 2007), 44–45.

[20] Daniel E. Rose. 2006. Reconciling Information-Seeking Behavior with Search User Interfaces for the Web. *Journal of the American Society for Information Science and Technology* 57, 6 (2006), 797–799.

[21] Daniel E. Rose and Danny Levinson. 2004. Understanding User Goals in Web Search. In *Proceedings of the Conference on World Wide Web (WWW '04)*. ACM, New York, NY, USA, 13–19.

[22] Sofia Stamou and Efthimis N. Efthimiadis. 2010. Interpreting User Inactivity on Search Results. In *Proceedings of the 32nd European Conference on Advances in Information Retrieval (ECIR'10)*. Springer-Verlag, Berlin, Heidelberg, 100–113.

[23] Jaime Teevan, Eytan Adar, Rosie Jones, and Michael A. S. Potts. 2007. Information Re-retrieval: Repeat Queries in Yahoo's Logs. In *Proceedings of the Conference on Research and Development in Information Retrieval (SIGIR '07)*. ACM, New York, NY, USA, 151–158.

[24] Gokhan Tur, Anoop Deoras, and Dilek Hakkani-Tür. 2014. Detecting Out-Of-Domain Utterances Addressed to a Virtual Personal Assistant. In *Proceedings of Interspeech*. ISCA - International Speech Communication Association. https://www.microsoft.com/en-us/research/publication/detecting-out-of-domain-utterances-addressed-to-a-virtual-personal-assistant/

[25] Gui-Rong Xue, Hua-Jun Zeng, Zheng Chen, Yong Yu, Wei-Ying Ma, WenSi Xi, and WeiGuo Fan. 2004. Optimizing Web Search Using Web Click-through Data. In *Proceedings of the Conference on Information and Knowledge Management (CIKM '04)*. ACM, New York, NY, USA, 118–126.

[26] Longqi Yang, Chen Fang, Hailin Jin, Matthew D. Hoffman, and Deborah Estrin. 2017. Personalizing Software and Web Services by Integrating Unstructured Application Usage Traces. In *Proceedings of the Conference on World Wide Web (WWW '17)*. International World Wide Web Conferences Steering Committee, Republic and Canton of Geneva, Switzerland, 485–493.

Better Together: An Interdisciplinary Perspective on Information Retrieval

Susan T. Dumais
Microsoft Research
Redmond, Washington, USA
sdumais@microsoft.com

ABSTRACT

The success of information retrieval systems depends critically on *both* the ability of systems to efficiently and effectively retrieve information, and to support people in articulating their information needs and making sense of the results. This interdisciplinary, user-centered perspective on information systems motivated my early work on Latent Semantic Indexing (LSI), which sought to mitigate the disagreement between the vocabulary that authors use in writing and searchers use to express their information needs, and continues to shape my research today. Over the last two decades, search has become a core fabric of people's everyday lives, driven by advances in understanding context, natural language, and speech. I will illustrate how new capabilities in email and virtual assistants are driven by advances in both algorithms and user modeling. As we look forward to new types of information systems that anticipate information needs, interact via richer dialogs, and integrate physical and digital information, it is more important than ever to understand and support information seekers using interdisciplinary methods and perspectives.

CCS Concepts/ACM Classifiers

• Information systems → Users and interactive retrieval; Information systems → Web searching and information discovery; Human-centered computing → Human computer interaction (HCI)

Author Keywords

Information retrieval; Human-computer interaction; Behavioral log analysis; Interdisciplinary research

BIOGRAPHY

Susan Dumais a Distinguished Scientist and Deputy Director of the Microsoft Research AI Lab, and an adjunct professor at the University of Washington. Prior to joining Microsoft, she was at Bell Labs where she worked on Latent Semantic Analysis, techniques for combining search and browsing, and organizational impacts of new technology. Her current research focuses on user modeling and personalization, email search, contextual search, and large-scale behavioral log analysis. Susan has published widely in the fields of information retrieval, human-computer interaction, and cognitive science. She has worked closely with several Microsoft product groups (Bing, Windows Desktop Search, SharePoint, and Office Online Help) on search-related innovations, and holds several patents on novel retrieval algorithms and interfaces. She is Past-Chair of ACM's Special Interest Group in Information Retrieval (SIGIR), and serves on academic, government and industry review panels. She is an ACM Fellow, was elected to the CHI Academy, the National Academy of Engineering (NAE) and the American Academy of Arts and Sciences (AAAS), and received the SIGIR Gerard Salton Award for Lifetime Achievement in IR, the ACM Athena Lecturer Award, the Tony Kent Strix Award and the Lifetime Achievement Award from Indiana University Department of Psychological and Brain Science.

CHIIR '18, March 11–15, 2018, New Brunswick, NJ, USA
© 2018 Copyright is held by the owner/author(s).
ACM ISBN 978-1-4503-4925-3/18/03.
DOI: https://doi.org/10.1145/3176349.3176571

Here and Now: Reality-Based Information Retrieval

Wolfgang Büschel
Interactive Media Lab
Technische Universität Dresden
bueschel@acm.org

Annett Mitschick
Interactive Media Lab
Technische Universität Dresden
annett.mitschick@tu-dresden.de

Raimund Dachselt
Interactive Media Lab
Technische Universität Dresden
dachselt@acm.org

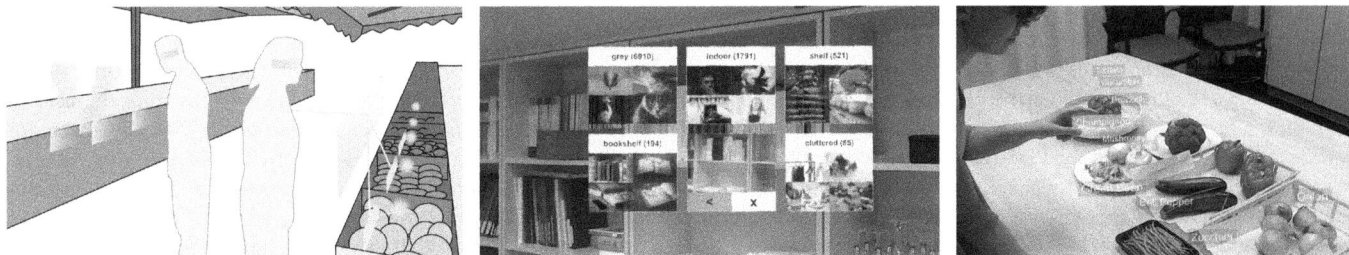

Figure 1: Left: Basic concept of RBIR illustrated by the envisioned scenario of grocery shopping. Center: Our situated photograph Image Retrieval prototype, showing a photograph taken by the user (yellow, in the middle) and extracted tags. Result pictures retrieved from pixabay.com. Right: Recipe search prototype, showing tagged groceries as input for a recipe search.

ABSTRACT

Today, the widespread use of mobile devices allows users to search information "on the go", whenever and wherever they want, no longer confining Information Retrieval to classic desktop interfaces. We believe that technical advances in Augmented Reality will allow Information Retrieval to go even further, making use of both the users' surroundings and their abilities to interact with the physical world. In this paper, we present the fundamental concept of Reality-Based Information Retrieval, which combines the classic Information Retrieval process with Augmented Reality technologies to provide context-dependent search cues and situated visualizations of the query and the results. With information needs often stemming from real-world experiences, this novel combination has the potential to better support both Just-in-time Information Retrieval and serendipity. Based on extensive literature research, we propose a conceptual framework for Reality-Based Information Retrieval. We illustrate and discuss this framework and present two prototypical implementations, which we tested in small user studies. They demonstrate the feasibility of our concepts and inspired our discussion of notable challenges for further research in this novel and promising area.

CCS CONCEPTS

• **Information systems → Search interfaces**; • **Human-centered computing → Mixed / augmented reality**;

KEYWORDS

Reality-based Information Retrieval, Augmented Reality, Spatial User Interface, Immersive Visualization, In Situ Visual Analytics

ACM Reference Format:
Wolfgang Büschel, Annett Mitschick, and Raimund Dachselt. 2018. Here and Now: Reality-Based Information Retrieval. In *CHIIR '18: 2018 Conference on Human Information Interaction & Retrieval, March 11–15, 2018, New Brunswick, NJ, USA*. ACM, New York, NY, USA, 10 pages. https://doi.org/10.1145/3176349.3176384

1 INTRODUCTION & BACKGROUND

Searching for information plays a dominant role in the everyday life of people of the so-called "information age". We rely on search engines to fulfill our information needs, which might be more or less abstract or specific, highly depending on the real-world context or completely in the digital domain, with a practical impact or just out of sheer curiosity. Originally, information retrieval was exerted in the physical world, for example in a library, by asking other people, and reading public notifications. Later, it has long been (and is still) performed on desktop computers, fixed at a single location as a gateway to a virtual environment containing the digital information sources. These traditional search interfaces force the user to abstract information needs to specify the query and to "translate" the results back to match his or her real-world demands. Today, with the dissemination of powerful mobile devices and appropriate bandwidth, search has gone mobile. Statistics show that today more web searches take place on mobile devices than on computers[1].

1.1 Understanding Mobile Search & Information Needs

Since the beginning of the smartphone era, a large number of short- and long-term studies have been conducted to investigate mobile

[1] Google Blog, May 2015: https://adwords.googleblog.com/2015/05/building-for-next-moment.html

search behavior and mobile information needs. The most comprehensive one to date is a 3-month-study of daily information needs with 100 users by Church et al. [14]. It shows that *"daily information needs are highly varied, intricate, and dynamic"* and highly influenced by contextual factors. A preceding study [15] showed that most information needs occurred when participants were mobile, i. e., away from desk, traveling, on-the-go. They distinguished *geographical* needs, needs related to *Personal Information Management (PIM)*, like schedules, contacts, etc., and *informational* needs, that is, *"focused on the goal of obtaining information about a topic"*. The majority of information needs (mobile and non-mobile) were *informational*, and 64% of informational intents arose in a mobile context [15]. Still, a large extend of research on mobile search interfaces is focused on geographical or PIM-related needs, incorporating the user's context (location, time, activity, social context, etc.) to adapt the search interface or visualize results, e. g., map-based interfaces [31], and informational needs are addressed to a lesser extend. Approaches that deal with the various informational needs (e. g., how-to's, facts, explanations, advice) either focus on the advancement of input modalities and interaction techniques for complex, explicit queries, like [4, 32, 45], or they try to limit the extent of required input as much as possible. For example, they use reasoning to derive implicit information from background knowledge [37], provide automatic query-term extraction from Web content [55], or use question-answering systems [45] to extent given keywords and provide natural language answers. Of course, both strategies are driven by the limited capabilities of mobile devices for query formulation, e. g., text input by touch keyboard or speech input, or visual input by camera [22]. Other research is focused on situation-aware filtering or ranking of search results [8] taking into account the limited display size of mobile devices.

1.2 The Potential of AR-based Information Retrieval

We believe that in the future, Information Retrieval (IR) will not only be location-based but actually *return to happen in the real world*. It will be tightly interwoven with the physical world itself in what we call *Reality-based Information Retrieval* (RBIR). With the help of Augmented Reality (AR) technology, we aim to decrease the gulfs of execution and evaluation [27] for a broad range of search applications by providing Natural User Interfaces based on the situated visualization of search stimuli, queries, and results. In a few years, AR glasses are likely to become mainstream and to be a common form factor in a "post-smartphone era". Search facilities will be a vital part of such versatile devices, not only because of the constant need for information in mobile contexts but also because of the novel opportunities to satisfy it much better. One of these opportunities is the concept of Just-in-time Information Retrieval (JITIR) [48], proactively retrieving information "based on a person's local context in an easily accessible yet non-intrusive manner", which is very similar to the idea of "finding what you need with zero query terms (or less)" envisioned in [2]. JITIR heavily relies on modeling the user's context (e. g., location, time, application usage, individual preferences and interests, and nearby objects) and situationally matching it to the environment. So far, it has seen limited use in mobile AR settings (e. g., [1]).

In addition to that, a focus of current research in Human-computer Information Retrieval concentrates on the understanding of *serendipity*, *"an unexpected experience prompted by an individual's valuable interaction with ideas, information, objects, or phenomena"* [43], leading to unforeseeable, but much more valuable insights. According to [41], some strategies can stimulate serendipity, like *"going out and about"* to experience new things one might not have come across otherwise, or *"keeping [...] eyes and ears open to things happening"* in order to recognize or to be receptive for connections. More than any other digital environment, AR is able to support serendipity in information access by fusing virtual and physical information artifacts, suggesting contextual information [1], and assisting the user to *"follow up on potentially valuable opportunities"* [41]. Furthermore, studies investigating mobile search activities showed that *"interactions with the material world tend to create more information needs and information seeking behaviors than virtual interactions"* [12]. Therefore, we believe that examining how to combine IR and AR to better integrate Information Retrieval into the physical world is a promising field of research.

In our endeavor to pave the way for a new generation of immersive, in-the-wild IR systems, we seek to close the gap between both research fields, Augmented Reality and Information Retrieval. Thus, our main contributions in this perspective paper are as follows:

(1) We present the general and novel concept of *Reality-based Information Retrieval* (RBIR),
(2) and suggest a conceptual framework for the design of future RBIR systems by integrating Natural Interaction and Situated Augmentations into the classical information retrieval model.
(3) We report on two implemented prototypes which we tested in small-scale user studies that demonstrate the feasibility of our ideas, and
(4) derive and discuss future challenges of RBIR.

2 ENVISIONED SCENARIOS AND BASIC CONCEPT

We illustrate the basic concept of Reality-based Information Retrieval with the following scenario:

Alice and Bob are at the market place to buy groceries. Although they have a broad idea on what they plan to cook, they are not sure about the dessert. They use the new Reality-based Information Retrieval system with its lightweight AR glasses (see Figure 1, left). As they look at the different fruits and vegetables, small indicators light up, showing that the system has additional information ready for them. Going nearer, virtual tags appear floating above exotic fruits in addition to the physical price tags. The tags tell the couple that these are kumquat and provide information about their origin and the supply chain. Bob and Alice select the fruit's tag to search for kumquat recipes. The recipes appear scattered in front of them, showing the most relevant results closer to them. Organically, clusters of related recipes form. Bob selects a recipe with an interesting preview picture and gets nutrition and allergy information. He notices that a graph of other required ingredients is visualized, connecting the kumquats with beets and avocados at a different booth. Surprised that there are recipes with both kumquats and beet, Bob wants to find other such recipes. He adds the beets to the search query; most recipes fade out while some light up. While looking at other fruits and vegetables, Alice remembers that they had a delicious avocado dessert last week. She wants to share the recipe with others. She connects it to the avocados, allowing future market visitors to find the dish and get inspired just like her.

We also envision other use cases for RBIR, e. g.,

- Image retrieval: *Anne searches for pictures to decorate her living room by virtually placing relevant results from an image database on her wall. The RBIR application extracts visual features from the surrounding for content-based image retrieval to filter the result set of relevant images, e. g., regarding dominant colors.*

- Literature search: *Alex draws a book from a bookshelf of his housemate and searches for related publications of the author. The RBIR application identifies the book and its metadata. The writing on the book cover is augmented by virtual controls as overlays which Alex physically touches to start a search. Results are presented in the bookshelf in front of him.*

- Video retrieval: *Currently watching a soccer game, Phil searches for soccer videos with scenes showing similar positions of the players for comparison. The RBIR application analyses the relative positions and motion vectors of the identified players on the field and suggests similar recordings.*

The scenario and short examples illustrate our concept of *Reality-based Information Retrieval* from the user's point of view. Locations and objects in the physical world regularly trigger information needs in our daily lives. Thus, the fusion of virtual and physical information artifacts and the application of JITIR could lead to unexpected, but valuable information. Addressing this, information about the physical world, as well as associated abstract content, is digitally connected to these objects or locations and accessed by the means of AR technology. Users wear mixed reality headsets or smart glasses. They get context-specific suggestions for search terms, e. g., in form of tags virtually attached to real world objects. The basis for these tags can be manifold: Low-level (visual) features from an image analysis, higher-level meaning derived from object recognition, or even information explicitly attached by other users or supplied by smart things. Making use of these sources, the users build search queries addressing their information needs. Retrieved documents are then presented, can be browsed, and allow for relevance feedback. To seamlessly integrate the system into the users' routines, the visualizations of tags, queries, and results should all be designed to prevent visual overload or the occlusion of important real-world information. Furthermore, all interaction steps are to be supported by natural interaction techniques that allow users to benefit from, e.g., proprioception, and minimize cognitive load.

3 RELATED WORK

Although some application-specific approaches do exist, as of yet little work has been done to address issues in the intersection of the fields of IR and AR. Ajanki et al. [1] developed a prototype system which retrieves information relevant to contextual cues, i. e., people identified using face recognition techniques and objects with attached markers, to be presented with AR techniques on a handheld or head-mounted display. A similar approach was presented in [30]: face recognition techniques were used to retrieve video snippets from a personal lifelog to immediately show previous encounters

with the person the user is currently looking at. General visual cues as input parameters were addressed in work from the field of Mobile Visual Search [22], showing the feasibility of content-based query term extraction from photos taken of objects in the environment [21, 59]. Other perceptive and contextual cues have been addressed, with Mobile Audio Search (involving technologies like speech recognition, audio fingerprinting, query-by-humming) and Location-based Mobile Search leading the way [58]. On the other side, ongoing research deals with the challenges of data integration and provision, e. g., using linked data and Semantic Web technologies for Augmented Reality [42, 61], to exploit the huge amount of publicly available interlinked information.

Another interesting field of related work is the realization of information retrieval in a virtual reality (VR) setting, involving 3D information exploration and browsing. Work like [13, 46, 62] informs the design of AR interaction and visualization techniques for query and result interaction even if it lacks the aspect of registration in the real world.

Placing information and labels in AR according to their connection to the real world has been subject to extensive research published in the last few years [23, 29, 39, 40, 47] and the concepts of *In Situ Visual Analytics* [20] and *Situated Analytics* [17] bring visual analytics into AR environments. The tightness of the coupling between virtual and physical world characterizes the different strategies: the spectrum ranges from a very weak coupling like in the concept of 2D information spaces in 3D mixed reality environments [19, 20], to a very tight coupling like in the concept of *embedded data representations* [57].

The design space of AR applications and the extent of research in the field of AR (cf. [50] for an overview) forms the basis of our conceptual framework for the novel paradigm of *Reality-based Information Retrieval*.

4 A CONCEPTUAL FRAMEWORK FOR REALITY-BASED IR

In the following we present and discuss our conceptual framework for *Reality-Based Information Retrieval* (RBIR). We base this framework on the general model of the Information Retrieval process as described in various forms [10, 25, 49]. Figure 2 shows our concept as an adaptation of the system-oriented IR model described in [25]. In contrast to other models, e. g., those based on cognitive IR theory [28], it is ideally suited to emphasize and delineate the two aspects *Interaction* and *Representation*. In that model, a user's *Information Need* is formulated as a machine-understandable *Query* that is matched against the internal representation of the source documents (*Indexed documents*) which form the database. The result, a usually sorted set of *Retrieved documents*, then either satisfies the information need or leads to a reformulated or new query or an abort. The processes of *Query formulation* and *Feedback*[2] form the *Interaction* side of the front-end to the IR system, the *Query* itself and the set of *Retrieved documents* form the *Representation* side. To integrate the aspects of Augmented Reality to form a conceptual model of *Reality-Based Information Retrieval*, we adopted the three

---

[2]Of course, user feedback in terms of Relevance Feedback can also be used to adapt matching parameters or even indexing parameters within a dynamic IR system. This is not in the scope of this paper.

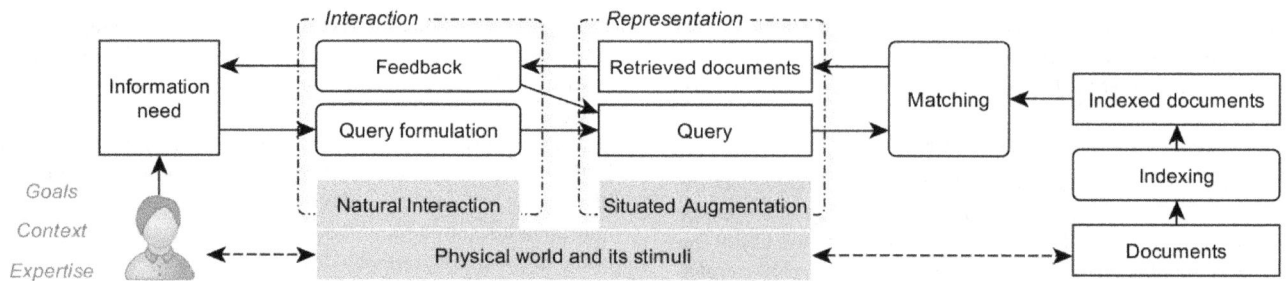

Figure 2: Conceptual model of Reality-based Information Retrieval. We extend the IR model from [25] by adding the user and three aspects of AR: the physical world, situated augmentations, and natural interaction.

elements of an AR application described by Billinghurst et al. [7]: real physical objects, virtual elements and interaction metaphor. These three components are represented in Figure 2 as *Physical world* (i. e., real physical objects), *Situated augmentation* (i. e., virtual elements), and *Natural interaction* (i. e., interaction metaphor).

The user, depicted on the left side, is an integral part of the physical world and can be described with parameters such as over-all *Goals* (from which a certain information need arise), *Context* (which both may trigger or influence an information need), and *Expertise* (which affects the user's ability to identify and specify an information need). These parameters are influenced by past or present real world experiences. On the other side, the content of documents (or information objects in general) which the user wants to retrieve represent parts of the physical world or are at least associated with them. The *Indexing* process involves an analysis of these associations and representations in combination with the (predicted) information need of the user.

4.1 The Physical World

Embedding the IR process into the physical world is one of the key aspects of Reality-Based Information Retrieval. Sensory input from the real world, mainly visual and auditory stimuli, are one of the main triggers for information needs: We want to know which song is playing on the radio, are interested in the name of an actor on a movie poster, or require nutrition information for a product in the super market. We focus mainly on visual and auditory input as these are best supported by today's hardware and also have the highest bandwidth. However, in the future, other input channels (e. g., smell) could also come into play.

4.1.1 Physical World Stimuli. Both specific real-world objects and the environment in general provide the contextual cue and input for the users' queries [1]. We differentiate several classes of *physical world stimuli* (inpired by commonly used abstraction levels in Content-based Image Retrieval [16]):

(1) *Low-level* features that can be directly extracted from the in-put stream. Visual examples are dominant colors and textures, acoustic examples are loudness or pitch.
(2) *Mid-level features* that are usually based on classification or pattern detection processes, such as object classes or materials, based on their visual appearance like texture, shape, surface reflectivity, etc. Acoustic examples are instrumental features and distinguishing music from spoken content.

(3) *High-level concepts* that include identities derived from low- and mid-level features and background knowledge, e. g., specific people or devices, a specific piece of music, speaker recognition (who is it) and recognized spoken content (what is said).
(4) *Associated data and services* that are either provided by a (smart) object itself or are externally hosted and logically connected to an object, e. g., user-generated content connected to an object or location, social media channels about or related to the object, etc.

These classes also show a progression from physical to human-defined properties. As such, the first two and sometimes the third class are openly observable features while the latter needs instrumentation (i. e., active beacons) and/or external databases.

4.1.2 Contextual Cues. The interpretation of the scene and its objects can be dependent on the context. We differentiate between context free cues, which are usually low-level features (e. g., color), cues with a weak context (e. g., knowledge about general settings such as "office" helps to identify object classes), and those with a strong context (including, e. g., the exact location, beacons, or QR codes). A deep contextual knowledge can facilitate sensemaking and is also the gate to attached data and services, making for a more powerful system than achievable by context free data only. However, information about the context may be missing, limited, or misinterpreted. As such, Reality-based Information Retrieval systems should at least support a fall back to context-free cues if the use case allows for it.

4.1.3 Output. The physical world is not only the source for information needs and query input. By appropriation of existing displays or *embedded physicalizations* [57] (i. e., physical objects used for in-situ data representation), the physical world can also be used to visualize queries or result sets, or even give acoustic feedback. Furthermore, using the physical world as output enables collaborative search scenarios, making it easier to share and discuss information or results, or direct users to particular artifacts. We see embedded physicalizations as an optional feature for Reality-based Information Retrieval to enhance user experience, but its realization should be considered carefully regarding privacy issues.

4.2 Situated Augmentation for Reality-based IR

The registration of content in 3D forms the connection between the physical and virtual world. Aligning virtual objects with related physical objects (locally) or the physical world (globally) makes them intuitively understandable and easier to interpret. For content that is semantically related to the environment, White and Feiner introduced the term *Situated Visualization* [56]. In this case, the connection between presented information and the location is characterized by the congruence or intersection of their meaning. Here, we use the term *Situated Augmentation* to emphasize that it should not be restricted to visual representation. Within our framework for RBIR we propose three concepts for Situated Augmentation as described in the following.

(1) Situated Stimulus. We define a *Situated Stimulus* as the representation of real-world object properties (see above) as input for a search query. Ideally, but not necessarily, they would correspond to the psychological stimuli from the physical world that trigger an information need. The simplest form of visualization for situated stimuli are labels placed in the scene. It is important that the user mentally associates them to the objects or environments that they belong to. Such a connection can be visually supported by placing the labels near the corresponding object or linking them with lines (cf. for example Figure 1, right). Additional visual variables can be used to encode, e. g., the type of the underlying property. More advanced visualizations include example pictures or highlighting of the corresponding physical object.

There are two strategies to dynamically create situated stimuli in an AR scenario: (a) processing the whole scene (either 2D or 3D) in front of the user to find Regions-of-interest (ROI) and identify visible physical objects in the camera's field-of-view [24] or (b) analyzing the users gaze points to detect and extract ROI [54] and identify and label objects in the visual focus. Using 2D or 3D information to solve these tasks depends on the technical abilities of the used AR device. The second strategy has the advantage of significantly reducing the complexity of object detection by narrowing down the search area according to users interests. Nevertheless, the first strategy seems better suitable to support serendipity.

(2) Situated Query Representation. The visualization of the queries depends on their complexity and the requirements of the use case. In a very simple case where single situated or only a few equally weighted stimuli are used as search input, no further query visualization may be needed except a feedback which stimuli are used to form the query (e. g., by highlighting the label).

For more complex queries consisting of several terms which are, e. g., individually weighted and/or combined with logical operators, a 2D virtual user interface [19] showing the selected terms and their relation can be used to provide an overview of the request and also allow for editing it. In Figure 3 we illustrate a conceivable example for a 2D query representation based on the *Filter/Flow* metaphor by Young and Shneiderman [60] to visualize boolean queries. Other visualization techniques developed for classical 2D representation would be suitable as well. Spatial visualization of a query in 3D provides the opportunity to give weight to the connection between query components and the physical world (e. g., as a network [6]), but regarding data overload and visual cluttering it should be considered carefully.

Figure 3: Example illustration of an AR application using the Filter/Flow model from [60] for boolean query formulation.

(3) Situated Result Representation. Of course, the representation of search results plays a very important role in a RBIR application. AR provides a number of possibilities determined by

(1) the intrinsic order/structure of the result set(s) (e. g., ordered by relevance, hierarchy, certain properties like timestamp, etc.)
(2) the reference to the real-world (e. g., placing visualizations relative to the user, i. e., body-referenced, or relative to the environment by augmenting vertical or horizontal surfaces) [50], and
(3) the mapping of the result space (e. g., using metaphors like a bookshelf, 3D shapes in free-space [62], or local coordinate systems like the space above a table [11]).

Although the results may also be presented on a 2D virtual user interface with its "advantages in efficiency, speed, precision and reduction of clutter" [19], the opportunity to map parameters to the physical world, e. g., using distance to the user to represent relevance of individual results , and the ability to move within or relative to it has proven benefits (e. g., [5, 11]).

4.3 Natural Interaction for Reality-based IR

Various interaction techniques have been proposed for AR [7], ranging from traditional input devices, such as keyboard, mouse, and touch screen to advanced 3D interaction methods and natural interaction techniques. Regarding our envisioned application scenarios, the use of traditional input devices such as keyboard and mouse is not suitable. However, an additional touch-enabled device such as a smartphone could simply provide text input or serve as a handy device for pointing, selecting or data transfer [38]. Furthermore, several ideas of purpose-built devices for interaction in AR have been proposed [34, 53]. Other interaction modalities applicable in an AR environment are voice input, free-hand gestures, tangible input, body motion, and gaze, in summary also referred to as *natural interaction techniques*. Gaze is by far the most unobtrusive and discreet input modality when we think of use cases in public space. Based on the elementary interaction tasks in the IR process (see Figure 2), we distinguish four Natural Interaction tasks within RBIR as described in the following.

(1) Natural Query Specification. A query can be submitted to an IR system in the form of

(a) text, like keywords, tags, natural language, artificial query language, commands, etc.
(b) key-value pairs, e. g., for property-based or faceted search,

(c) one or more examples, in case of Query-by-Example / similarity-based search, or

(d) via associations, e. g., in browsing scenarios.

Of course, the most natural and efficient input modality for text is voice input [26], but it has its drawbacks regarding privacy issues, social acceptance, and in noisy environments. This is to a great extend also the case for free-hand gestures [35, 36] and body motion [51] as interaction modalities. We believe that gaze input in combination with additional hardware like a smartphone or smartwatch for confirmation [52] and manipulation is most applicable for the above mentioned query modalities (b)-(d), so long as query formulation can be down-scaled to a selection task. This in turn means that the user should be able to select from a range of items, i. e., a set of possible values for properties or facets (b), a set of examples for similarity-based search (c) and a set of linked items for exploration/browsing (d). These items can be virtual, but also and more particularly physical (physical world stimuli), e. g., picking a color from a surface, capturing a part of the scene as visual example (a query-by-photograph metaphor [3]) or browsing through a taxonomy of recognized higher concepts. Certainly, this only works if the system is able to provide items or the physical world contains according stimuli.

(2) Natural Result Exploration and Interaction. Depending on the concrete reference and mapping of the result representation (see above), we envision *spatial interaction techniques* as proposed in [33] or gaze-supported multimodal interaction like [52] for natural result exploration. Spatial interaction involves a much more intense immersion. Locally or globally registered information spaces can be explored by physical movement of the user, e. g., determining the level of detail by the distance and the type of information by the angle to the object [33]. We also imagine unobtrusive wearable input devices like smartwatches, ring devices [18] or other novel devices [34] for casual interaction with even large result sets using zooming, panning, sorting, and filtering techniques.

(3) Natural User Feedback. Interacting with a result set is of course an implicit form of giving relevance feedback. Thus, any above mentioned modality could serve as input for user feedback, especially gaze [63] and spatial interaction [33], e. g., coming closer to an item gives it more weight, literally turning one's back on an item excludes it from the relevant results. Additionally, we imagine to rearrange results as a form of relevance feedback using motion and gestures or additional devices. We propose the idea of *metaphorical relevance feedback* using or establishing relations between results and the physical world, e. g., by explicitly placing results onto or near physical-world objects that symbolize a certain usage like a trash basket (removal), a notice board (keeping), or a personal device (taking along).

(4) Natural Annotation. Beyond the rather implicit user feedback described above, we also envision a natural way for the user to annotate physical stimuli, situated stimuli as well as retrieved results, resp. the connection between stimuli and results. Of course, the user benefits from his/her personal annotations. They support sensemaking but also serendipity in the sense of "remembering and drawing on previous experiences" as one of the key strategies [41]. Furthermore, like in the envisioned scenario in Section 2 we

also imagine social interaction or loose collaboration. User annotations left in AR may inspire other users or help them discover new aspects or connections.

Creating and leaving annotations in AR necessitates interaction techniques that allow the user to register them to the environment, in either a specific or abstract way. Precisely placing virtual artifacts in the real world is typically a very cumbersome task. In order to achieve a rather casual interaction, placing annotations and thus connecting them to physical stimuli should be supported by semantic and contextual cues, e. g., annotations could "snap" to their location according to their meaning and the user's context.

5 EXPERIMENTS WITH REALITY-BASED IR

To show the general feasibility of our proposed concept for Reality-based Information Retrieval, we implemented two prototypes. Both implementations described below realize different information retrieval concepts in AR for the Microsoft HoloLens device[3], using its build-in functions for image processing, augmentation and interaction. We also tested these prototypes in short, preliminary studies to collect feedback for further design iterations.

5.1 Case Study I: Situated Photograph Image Retrieval

Our first prototype realizes the basic concept of situated photograph queries in AR for image retrieval. It incorporates the usage of a photograph metaphor based on [3] to extract visual information from the environment as query parameters. The implementation is quite simple: performing an air-tap gesture the user takes a photograph of the center of the visible scene, which is displayed as a query object in the middle of a 2D canvas located in free space in front of the user (see Figure 1, center). This implements the three main aspects of RBIR: *Natural interaction techniques* to formulate a query based on some *physical, real-world stimuli* and *situated augmentations* enriching the user's environment. The picture is sent to the Microsoft Computer Vision REST API[4] to retrieve automatically assigned tags. The tags are then used to retrieve preview images from the Pixabay API[5]. The retrieved images are displayed as preview images around the initial query image and labeled with the corresponding tags. The actual query, i. e., searching for images with specific tags, is executed by tapping on a tag, thus making use of the same techniques to interact with digital and physical objects. A second 2D canvas serves as result visualization, which can be freely placed on available surfaces by the user using gaze direction and air tap. This result canvas shows the sorted set of images retrieved from the Pixabay API using one or more selected tags (see Figure 4). The user can also take multiple photos and thus create multiples query canvases to combine tags corresponding to different objects. Selecting one of the preview images replaces the original photo with the chosen image which is then used as query source, allowing the user to iteratively browse through pictures.

---

[3]Microsoft HoloLens: https://www.microsoft.com/hololens
[4]Microsoft Cognitive Services:
https://docs.microsoft.com/en-us/azure/cognitive-services/computer-vision/home
[5]RESTful interface for searching and retrieving free high-quality images from Pixabay, see https://pixabay.com/api/docs/.

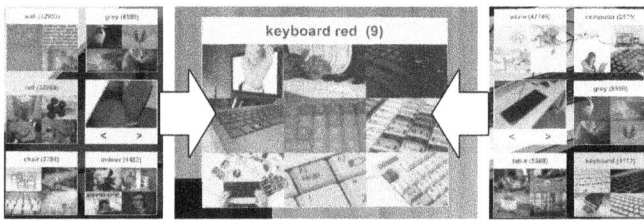

Figure 4: Aggregation of the tags "red" (left) and "keyboard" (right) from different photographs to build a combined query (middle). Result pictures retrieved from pixabay.com.

Evaluation: We conducted a qualitative user study to evaluate the usability of situated photograph queries as a basic interaction technique for RBIR. Seven male students from the local university, aged between 22 and 26 years, took part. A series of tasks was chosen to provoke interaction between the user and the application. Every task consisted of one or two keywords that the user should search for. The task was considered complete when the keyword(s) were active on the result canvas. Simple tasks were set at the beginning to facilitate getting started. In order to follow and later reproduce the participants' actions during usability testing, all discrete user activities (e. g., taking pictures, tapping a preview image for browsing) were logged. Users were asked to "think aloud" and give statements about the application whenever they encountered a special situation or problem. These statements were recorded using a camcorder. In a follow-up questionnaire we assessed the application using the System Usability Scale (SUS) [9].

During the study we could observe two opposing ways of interacting with the prototype, which was confirmed by an analysis of the logs: (1) using the photograph technique only as an initial query and browsing through tags by selecting preview images (*browsing*) and (2) using the photograph technique repeatedly to refine a query (*non-browsing*). While non-browsing participants performed fewer interactions per minute (average of 4.8 versus 5.4), the average time spent using the application was also lower (26 min.) compared to browsing participants (38 min.). In total, non-browsing participants performed fewer interactions (average of 124 versus 209) to solve the tasks. This possibly results from the fact that browsing often incorporates rather quick jumping from one picture to the next, which involves comparatively many tapping interactions in a short period of time. The browsing strategy was more time consuming and involved more interactions compared to a non-browsing behavior. Additionally, the analysis of the questionnaire also indicates that browsing participants needed more effort (2.3 versus 1.7), especially for "getting the right keywords", and felt less pleasure (3.4 versus 4.3) when using the application. The perception of usefulness varies regarding the provided features, but the average differences are small (3.9 versus 3.6). Although differences in the SUS score between the groups of participants are generally not big (72.5 for browsing versus 79.4 for non-browsing), it is worth noting that browsing participants rated the application lower in 7 of the 10 statements compared to non-browsing participants.

Although general implications should not be made, we observed that browsing participants were less aware of the room and used it less during their interaction with the application. Participants who

recognized their environment and its possibilities were not only more effective but also more confident. This insight encouraged our work on a succeeding experiment (described in the following) where we decided to provide visual guidance to the user in order to support the awareness of the environment and physical stimuli.

5.2 Case Study II: Recipe Search

For our second prototype we were inspired by the food search scenario presented earlier. The concept behind this prototype is that food, e. g., fruits and vegetables, is augmented with labels. The user then selects such tags to form a search query. As results, a set of recipes containing the selected ingredients are presented. In contrast to the first prototype, we opted against the user explicitly taking photographs. Instead, the concept is to have the current camera image automatically analyzed in the background, showing tags as they are generated and thus better supporting serendipity. In reference to our framework, the tags are examples for *mid-level features* that represent object classes, either specifically (e. g., "apple") or more generally (e. g., "meat"). For improved reliability and stable results necessary for the evaluation, we decided to pre-generate the tags for the prototype instead of using an actual computer vision API. The recipe search is implemented using the Food2Fork web API[6], which returns a list of recipes with ingredients, preview images, and other metadata.

Figure 5: First-person mixed reality capture of the Recipe Search prototype showing the tags in the foreground, the result visualization (left) and the query (right) in the background. Result data retrieved from Food2Fork.com.

The visualization is graph oriented, with tags being connected to the corresponding real-world location and also to the query that they are a part of. This helps to show the spatial relations between keywords and results. Extending this, it would be feasible to also visually link result ingredients to the search query. The query as well as the results are shown on spatially positioned 2D canvases that automatically turn towards the user. Similar to the first prototype, interaction is based on gaze pointing and the air tap gesture of the HoloLens. Users can select tags to add them to

---

[6]Food2Fork: https://food2fork.com/about/api

the query or, when tag and canvas are next to each other, simply drag them to the canvas.

Evaluation: We tested our second prototype with four usability experts (three male, one female, aged 26 to 34). To this end we prepared a large table in our lab with 13 different fresh vegetables and fruits, their arrangement resembling a real market place. All goods where digitally annotated with their type. After signing informed consent, the participants received a short introduction to the use case and the prototype. They then had the chance to freely explore the system for approximately 10 minutes, looking up recipes based on selections of the augmented ingredients presented on the table. As in the first study, the participants were encouraged to voice their opinion and talk about positive and negative aspects as they encountered them (*think-aloud*). Afterwards, they filled out a questionnaire consisting of nine 5-point Likert items on usability and five items on serendipity, based on the *Serendipitous Digital Environment scale* (SDE) [44].

The experts reported a high usability: For instance, learnability was rated with an average score of 4.5 out of 5, and confidence in using the application was rated 4 out of 5. Our participants reported a medium level of serendipity, e. g., partly agreeing that it invites examination of its content (3.5 out of 5). We believe that the study setting and its limited scope negatively affected serendipity. In their comments, the experts provided valuable feedback on several potential problems of the prototype for real world use. This feedback, in combination with the results of the first study, informs the challenges that we present in the following section.

6 CHALLENGES

In this section we identify open research challenges, informed both by our review of related literature and our own experiences with our prototypes. We believe that addressing these challenges will be the key to future successful RBIR.

A main challenge is to clarify if existing retrieval models are suitable for RBIR. While we believe that current models can be applied, incorporating extended context models and considering the imprecise nature of the user input will be beneficial. Subsequently, new evaluation methodologies should be examined to suitably measure effectiveness while considering the serendipitous nature of the interface. Approaches like the *Serendipitous Digital Environment scale* [44] might be promising starting points. Additionally, there are some technical challenges, which are not specific to RBIR but still need to be addressed. They include the weight and battery life of the devices and the availability of a reliable, low-latency communication infrastructure. Also, object detection and registration of virtual content in the scene is an ongoing research challenge.

In the following we would like to highlight some challenges we think are crucial for the success of RBIR:

Reliable Stimulus Detection & Identification: Currently, there is no system that accurately classifies arbitrary objects and their properties in real time, let alone on a mobile device. We believe that local pre-computation, e. g., finding regions of interest or determining the scene context, combined with cloud-based object classification could be promising for the use case of RBIR. However, stimulus detection is not only a question of computer vision. It is just as important to assess the user's attention to objects or environmental features as a form of relevance feedback. In this context, having a reliable user model allows to estimate what a user might be interested in and how to correctly interpret stimuli. On the other hand, we believe that unexpected (i. e., wrong) results could actually improve serendipity by presenting new and surprising opportunities, as long as the system as a whole still feels reliable.

Visibility & Subtlety: Designing suitable and effective visualizations for the queries and results in 3D is a major challenge. In particular, there are two conflicting goals regarding the choice of visualization. On one hand, the aim is to design augmentations that stand out well enough to be recognized even in cluttered environments. A specific goal has to be supporting the mental model of the user, in this case the association between real objects and virtual content. Here, in contrast to many other AR applications, not only spatial cues but also, e. g., a similar color could be used to link stimuli to objects. On the other hand, augmentations need to be seamlessly integrated as to not obfuscate or occlude important features of the physical world. This is especially important in RBIR, assuming a system that runs in the background for extended periods of time. There has been a lot of research on, e. g., label placement in AR, however, achieving not only optimal visibility but also a visually calm presentation that does not lead to visual overload is still challenging.

Limited Interaction Capabilities: Working with our prototypes, not all users were able to reliably use the air tap gesture. Also, the concept of a gaze directed pointer, similar to a traditional mouse pointer, was not always clear. While these and similar problems are general challenges of spatial input for AR, a specific question for RBIR is how to achieve the expressiveness and flexibility of traditional, desktop based searches. For instance, we do not believe that a system could solely rely on contextual information taken directly from the environment. Instead, the explicit input of search strings will also sometimes be necessary. Speech-to-text is one approach for text input with AR headsets, however especially with IR systems, questions of privacy remain (see below). Another challenge are complex, facet-based searches that usually require complex menus. For such information needs, a successful RBIR system should not be significantly harder to use than regular systems.

Perspicuity & User Control: Typically, IR systems are a black box for the user. In the future, when they affect decisions in our daily lives even more directly, an understanding of the factors leading to the results is even more important. Thus, it is a challenge to design Reality-based IR in such a way that the users feel in control. Support for easy relevance feedback is one particular way to keep the *human in the loop*. Building on that, it is important to clearly visualize the system state and how the user's input (e. g., their relevance feedback) influences the IR process.

Accessibility & Inclusion: Often, it is assumed that every user can interact with a designed system, when in reality accessibility is lacking. For example, in AR there is a very strong reliance on visuals with little regard for alternative forms of output, excluding visually impaired users. Similarly, RBIR assumes physical navigation and spatial input that may not be feasible for users with motor impairments. Being locked out from using future general purpose RBIR systems could become a serious problem. However, exclusion can also happen on other levels, through the language or the metaphors that the system uses or by the type and form of presentation of the results. Thus, it is an important research challenge to come up with a system design that is inclusive for all user groups, independent of factors such as age, cultural background, or abilities.

Privacy: A person's search history allows to derive detailed knowledge of their interests and is as such highly sensitive information. Privacy in RBIR is an even bigger concern because of the combination with real-time location tracking, gaze information, and other metadata. However, another challenge is to support privacy not only against search providers but also bystanders and shoulder-surfing attacks. Very explicit forms of interaction, e. g., voice input or gestures, may leak information about the search interests of a user. AR headsets, while single user, may also allow others to perceive parts of their content and, in comparison to smartphones, can not be easily shielded by the user.

Filter Bubbles & Discriminating Algorithms: The risk of any user-model is to only show things that the user knows, expects, or wants. This stands in direct opposition to our goal of serendipity. While problematic even in today's systems, it could become even worse in AR. There, these Filter Bubbles would extend to the real world with differing opinions being hidden from the user. Furthermore, recent developments show that many IT companies do not shy away from using their influence on their users to shape public opinion. Thus, even explicit discrimination or the suppression of information in the physical world by search engine providers would become a scary possibility in the future. Similarly, there have been examples of algorithms discriminating against groups of people, be it by malice or ignorance of the developers. How to support the creation of open and transparent platforms that are resilient to these effects is another research challenge for RBIR.

User-generated Annotations. User-generated annotations in AR may refer to a physical stimulus in its specific representation (e. g., the physical book in the shelf) or the abstract concept of it (e. g., avocados in general). Automatically detecting the reference of an annotation is a particular challenge which might profit from other users' annotations, machine learning techniques, and extensive domain knowledge. Furthermore, the physical world is subject to changes, artifacts move or exist only temporally. And finally, user-generated content shared in a virtual community also involves the questions of how to create, filter and manage them, including the danger of misuse and malpractice, a complex challenge requiring synergies from multiple disciplines.

7 CONCLUSION

In this perspective paper, we introduced the concept of Reality-based Information Retrieval (RBIR). Since information needs are often stimulated by the user's surroundings, we combined the Information Retrieval process with Augmented Reality by extending the IR model with the notions of the physical world, Natural Interaction, and Situated Augmentations. With intuitive user interfaces for spatial, in-situ visualizations of search stimuli, queries, and results, RBIR has the potential to support serendipitous Just-in-time Information Retrieval. We presented a conceptual framework for

the design of RBIR systems and reported on two implemented prototypes, which we tested in small-scale user studies. These studies show the feasibility of our ideas and allowed us to derive challenges specific to RBIR. We aim to address these challenges and hope that our work can spark a discussion about future IR systems interwoven with the physical world.

8 ACKNOWLEDGMENTS

We would like to thank Philip Manja for his contributions, including his work on the first prototype. This work was funded in part by grant no. 03ZZ0514C of the German Federal Ministry of Education and Research (measure Twenty20 – Partnership for Innovation, project Fast).

REFERENCES

[1] Antti Ajanki, Mark Billinghurst, Toni Järvenpää, Melih Kandemir, Samuel Kaski, Markus Koskela, Mikko Kurimo, Jorma Laaksonen, Kai Puolamäki, Teemu Ruoko-lainen, et al. 2010. Contextual information access with augmented reality. In *Proc. 2010 IEEE Int. Workshop MLSP*. IEEE, 95–100.
[2] James Allan, Bruce Croft, Alistair Moffat, and Mark Sanderson. 2012. Frontiers, Challenges, and Opportunities for Information Retrieval: Report from SWIRL 2012 the Second Strategic Workshop on Information Retrieval in Lorne. *SIGIR Forum* 46, 1 (May 2012), 2–32. https://doi.org/10.1145/2215676.2215678
[3] Jürgen Assfalg, Alberto Del Bimbo, and Pietro Pala. 2002. Three-Dimensional Interfaces for Querying by Example in Content-Based Image Retrieval. *IEEE Trans. Vis. Comput. Graphics* 8, 4 (Oct. 2002), 305–318. https://doi.org/10.1109/TVCG.2002.1044517
[4] Juhee Bae, Vidya Setlur, and Benjamin Watson. 2015. GraphTiles: A Visual Interface Supporting Browsing and Imprecise Mobile Search. In *Proc. MobileHCI '15*. ACM, New York, NY, USA, 63–70. https://doi.org/10.1145/2785830.2785872
[5] Robert Ball, Chris North, and Doug A. Bowman. 2007. Move to Improve: Promoting Physical Navigation to Increase User Performance with Large Displays. In *Proc. CHI '07*. ACM, New York, NY, USA, 191–200. https://doi.org/10.1145/1240624.1240656
[6] Daniel Belcher, Mark Billinghurst, SE Hayes, and Randy Stiles. 2003. Using Augmented Reality for Visualizing Complex Graphs in Three Dimensions. In *Proc. ISMAR '03*. IEEE CS, Washington, DC, USA, 84–93. https://doi.org/10.1109/ISMAR.2003.1240691
[7] Mark Billinghurst, Adrian Clark, and Gun Lee. 2015. A Survey of Augmented Reality. *Found. Trends Hum.-Comput. Interact.* 8, 2-3 (March 2015), 73–272. https://doi.org/10.1561/1100000049
[8] Ourdia Bouidghaghen, Lynda Tamine-Lechani, and Mohand Boughanem. 2009. Dynamically Personalizing Search Results for Mobile Users. In *Proc. FQAS '09*. Springer-Verlag, Berlin, Heidelberg, 99–110. https://doi.org/10.1007/978-3-642-04957-6_9
[9] John Brooke. 1996. SUS: a "quick and dirty" usability scale. In *Usability Evaluation in Industry*. Taylor and Francis.
[10] Michael K. Buckland and Christian Plaunt. 2000. On the Construction of Selection Systems. *Library Hi Tech* 12 (06 2000).
[11] Wolfgang Büschel, Patrick Reipschläger, Ricardo Langner, and Raimund Dachselt. 2017. Investigating the Use of Spatial Interaction for 3D Data Visualization on Mobile Devices. In *Proc. ISS '17*. ACM, New York, NY, USA, 62–71. https://doi.org/10.1145/3132272.3134125
[12] Juan Pablo Carrascal and Karen Church. 2015. An In-Situ Study of Mobile App & Mobile Search Interactions. In *Proc. CHI '15*. ACM, New York, NY, USA, 2739–2748. https://doi.org/10.1145/2702123.2702486
[13] Patrick Chiu, Andreas Girgensohn, Surapong Lertsithichai, Wolf Polak, and Frank Shipman. 2005. MediaMetro: Browsing Multimedia Document Collections with a 3D City Metaphor. In *Proc. MULTIMEDIA '05*. ACM, New York, NY, USA, 213–214. https://doi.org/10.1145/1101149.1101182
[14] Karen Church, Mauro Cherubini, and Nuria Oliver. 2014. A Large-scale Study of Daily Information Needs Captured in Situ. *ACM Trans. Comput.-Hum. Interact.* 21, 2, Article 10 (Feb. 2014), 46 pages. https://doi.org/10.1145/2552193
[15] Karen Church and Barry Smyth. 2009. Understanding the Intent Behind Mobile Information Needs. In *Proc. IUI '09*. ACM, New York, NY, USA, 247–256. https://doi.org/10.1145/1502650.1502686
[16] John Eakins, Margaret Graham, and Tom Franklin. 1999. Content-based Image Retrieval. In *Library and Information Briefings*.
[17] Neven ElSayed, Bruce Thomas, Kim Marriott, Julia Piantadosi, and Ross Smith. 2015. Situated Analytics. In *2015 Big Data Visual Analytics (BDVA)*. 1–8. https://doi.org/10.1109/BDVA.2015.7314302

[18] Barrett Ens, Ahmad Byagowi, Teng Han, Juan David Hincapié-Ramos, and Pourang Irani. 2016. Combining Ring Input with Hand Tracking for Precise, Natural Interaction with Spatial Analytic Interfaces. In *Proc. SUI '16*. ACM, New York, NY, USA, 99–102. https://doi.org/10.1145/2983310.2985757

[19] Barrett Ens, Juan David Hincapié-Ramos, and Pourang Irani. 2014. Ethereal Planes: A Design Framework for 2D Information Space in 3D Mixed Reality Environments. In *Proc. SUI '14*. ACM, New York, NY, USA, 2–12. https://doi.org/10.1145/2659766.2659769

[20] Barrett Ens and Pourang Irani. 2017. Spatial Analytic Interfaces: Spatial User Interfaces for In Situ Visual Analytics. *IEEE Comp. Graph. Appl.* 37, 2 (2017), 66–79. https://doi.org/10.1109/MCG.2016.38

[21] Xin Fan, Xing Xie, Zhiwei Li, Mingjing Li, and Wei-Ying Ma. 2005. Photo-to-search: Using Multimodal Queries to Search the Web from Mobile Devices. In *Proc. MIR '05*. ACM, New York, NY, USA, 143–150. https://doi.org/10.1145/1101826.1101851

[22] Bernd Girod, Vijay Chandrasekhar, David M Chen, Ngai-Man Cheung, Radek Grzeszczuk, Yuriy Reznik, Gabriel Takacs, Sam S Tsai, and Ramakrishna Vedantham. 2011. Mobile visual search. *IEEE Signal Process. Mag.* 28, 4 (2011), 61–76.

[23] Raphael Grasset, Tobias Langlotz, Denis Kalkofen, Markus Tatzgern, and Dieter Schmalstieg. 2012. Image-driven View Management for Augmented Reality Browsers. In *Proc. ISMAR '12*. IEEE Computer Society, Washington, DC, USA, 177–186. https://doi.org/10.1109/ISMAR.2012.6402555

[24] Yulan Guo, Mohammed Bennamoun, Ferdous Sohel, Min Lu, and Jianwei Wan. 2014. 3D Object Recognition in Cluttered Scenes with Local Surface Features: A Survey. *IEEE Trans. Pattern Anal. Mach. Intell.* 36, 11 (Nov 2014), 2270–2287. https://doi.org/10.1109/TPAMI.2014.2316828

[25] Djoerd Hiemstra. 2009. Information Retrieval Models. In *Information Retrieval*. John Wiley & Sons, Ltd, 1–19. https://doi.org/10.1002/9780470033647.ch1

[26] Ronghang Hu, Huazhe Xu, Marcus Rohrbach, Jiashi Feng, Kate Saenko, and Trevor Darrell. 2016. Natural language object retrieval. In *Proc. CVPR '16*. 4555–4564. https://doi.org/10.1109/CVPR.2016.493

[27] Edwin L. Hutchins, James D. Hollan, and Donald A. Norman. 1985. Direct Manipulation Interfaces. *Hum.-Comput. Interact.* 1, 4 (Dec. 1985), 311–338. https://doi.org/10.1207/s15327051hci0104_2

[28] Peter Ingwersen and Kalervo Järvelin. 2005. *The Turn: Integration of Information Seeking and Retrieval in Context (The Information Retrieval Series)*. Springer-Verlag New York, Inc., Secaucus, NJ, USA. https://doi.org/10.1007/1-4020-3851-8

[29] Daisuke Iwai, Tatsunori Yabiki, and Kosuke Sato. 2013. View management of projected labels on nonplanar and textured surfaces. *IEEE Trans. Vis. Comput. Graphics* 19, 8 (2013), 1415–1424.

[30] Masakazu Iwamura, Kai Kunze, Yuya Kato, Yuzuko Utsumi, and Koichi Kise. 2014. Haven'T We Met Before?: A Realistic Memory Assistance System to Remind You of the Person in Front of You. In *Proc. AH '14*. ACM, New York, NY, USA, Article 32, 4 pages. https://doi.org/10.1145/2582051.2582083

[31] Matt Jones, George Buchanan, Richard Harper, and Pierre-Louis Xech. 2007. Questions Not Answers: A Novel Mobile Search Technique. In *Proc. CHI '07*. ACM, New York, NY, USA, 155–158. https://doi.org/10.1145/1240624.1240648

[32] Amy K. Karlson, George G. Robertson, Daniel C. Robbins, Mary P. Czerwinski, and Greg R. Smith. 2006. FaThumb: A Facet-based Interface for Mobile Search. In *Proc. CHI '06*. ACM, New York, NY, USA, 711–720. https://doi.org/10.1145/1124772.1124878

[33] Jens Keil, Michael Zoellner, Timo Engelke, Folker Wientapper, and Michael Schmitt. 2013. *Controlling and Filtering Information Density with Spatial Interaction Techniques via Handheld Augmented Reality*. Springer, Berlin, Heidelberg, 49–57. https://doi.org/10.1007/978-3-642-39405-8_6

[34] Konstantin Klamka and Raimund Dachselt. 2015. Elasticcon: Elastic Controllers for Casual Interaction. In *Proc. MobileHCI '15*. ACM, New York, NY, USA, 410–419. https://doi.org/10.1145/2785830.2785849

[35] Jarrod Knibbe, Sue Ann Seah, and Mike Fraser. 2014. VideoHandles: Replicating Gestures to Search Through Action-camera Video. In *Proc. SUI '14*. ACM, New York, NY, USA, 50–53. https://doi.org/10.1145/2659766.2659784

[36] ByoungChul Ko and Hyeran Byun. 2002. Query-by-Gesture: An Alternative Content-Based Image Retrieval Query Scheme. *J. Vis. Lang. Comput.* 13 (2002), 375–390.

[37] Jihoon Ko, Sangjin Shin, Sungkwang Eom, Minjae Song, Dong-Hoon Shin, Kyong-Ho Lee, and Yongil Jang. 2014. Semantically Enhanced Keyword Search for Smartphones. In *Proc. WWW '14 Companion*. ACM, New York, NY, USA, 327–328. https://doi.org/10.1145/2567948.2577331

[38] Ricardo Langner, Ulrich von Zadow, Tom Horak, Annett Mitschick, and Raimund Dachselt. 2016. *Content Sharing Between Spatially-Aware Mobile Phones and Large Vertical Displays Supporting Collaborative Work*. Springer International Publishing, 75–96. https://doi.org/10.1007/978-3-319-45853-3_5

[39] Gang Li, Yue Liu, and Yongtian Wang. 2017. Evaluation of Labelling Layout Methods in Augmented Reality. In *Proc. VR '17*. 351–352. https://doi.org/10.1109/VR.2017.7892321 00000.

[40] Jacob Boesen Madsen, Markus Tatzgern, Claus B Madsen, Dieter Schmalstieg, and Denis Kalkofen. 2016. Temporal Coherence Strategies for Augmented Reality Labeling. *IEEE Trans. Vis. Comput. Graphics* 22, 4 (April 2016), 1415–1423. https:

//doi.org/10.1109/TVCG.2016.2518318

[41] Stephann Makri, Ann Blandford, Mel Woods, Sarah Sharples, and Deborah Maxwell. 2014. "Making my own luck": Serendipity strategies and how to support them in digital information environments. *J. Assn. Inf. Sci. Tec.* 65, 11 (2014), 2179–2194. https://doi.org/10.1002/asi.23200

[42] Tamás Matuszka. 2015. The Design and Implementation of Semantic Web-Based Architecture for Augmented Reality Browser. In *The Semantic Web. Latest Advances and New Domains*. Springer, 731–739. https://doi.org/10.1007/978-3-319-18818-8_46

[43] Lori McCay-Peet and Elaine G. Toms. 2015. Investigating serendipity: How it unfolds and what may influence it. *J. Assn. Inf. Sci. Tec.* 66, 7 (2015), 1463–1476. https://doi.org/10.1002/asi.23273

[44] Lori McCay-Peet, Elaine G. Toms, and E. Kevin Kelloway. 2015. Examination of relationships among serendipity, the environment, and individual differences. *Information Processing & Management* 51, 4 (2015), 391 – 412. https://doi.org/10.1016/j.ipm.2015.02.004

[45] Taniya Mishra and Srinivas Bangalore. 2010. Qme!: A Speech-based Question-answering System on Mobile Devices. In *Proc. HLT '10*. Association for Computational Linguistics, Stroudsburg, PA, USA, 55–63. http://dl.acm.org/citation.cfm?id=1857999.1858006

[46] Munehiro Nakazato and Thomas S Huang. 2001. 3D MARS: immersive virtual reality for content-based image retrieval. In *Proc. ICME '01*. 44–47. https://doi.org/10.1109/ICME.2001.1237651

[47] Jason Orlosky, Kiyoshi Kiyokawa, Takumi Toyama, and Daniel Sonntag. 2015. Halo Content: Context-aware Viewspace Management for Non-invasive Augmented Reality. In *Proc. IUI '15*. ACM, New York, NY, USA, 369–373. https://doi.org/10.1145/2678025.2701375

[48] Bradley J Rhodes and Pattie Maes. 2000. Just-in-time Information Retrieval Agents. *IBM Syst. J.* 39, 3-4 (July 2000), 685–704. https://doi.org/10.1147/sj.393.0685

[49] Cornelis J. Van Rijsbergen. 1979. *Information Retrieval* (2nd ed.). Butterworth-Heinemann, Newton, MA, USA.

[50] Dieter Schmalstieg and Tobias Hollerer. 2016. *Augmented reality: principles and practice*. Addison-Wesley Professional.

[51] Kimiaki Shirahama and Kuniaki Uehara. 2011. Query by Virtual Example: Video Retrieval Using Example Shots Created by Virtual Reality Techniques. In *Int. Conf. on Image and Graphics '11*. 829–834. https://doi.org/10.1109/ICIG.2011.158

[52] Sophie Stellmach, Sebastian Stober, Andreas Nürnberger, and Raimund Dachselt. 2011. Designing Gaze-supported Multimodal Interactions for the Exploration of Large Image Collections. In *Proc. NGCA '11*. ACM, New York, NY, USA, Article 1, 8 pages. https://doi.org/10.1145/1983302.1983303

[53] Zsolt Szalavári and Michael Gervautz. 1997. The Personal Interaction Panel – a Two-Handed Interface for Augmented Reality. *Computer Graphics Forum* 16, 3 (1997), C335–C346. https://doi.org/10.1111/1467-8659.00137

[54] Norimichi Ukita, Tomohisa Ono, and Masatsugu Kidode. 2005. Region Extraction of a Gaze Object Using the Gaze Point and View Image Sequences. In *Proc. ICMI '05*. ACM, NY, USA, 129–136. https://doi.org/10.1145/1088463.1088487 00005.

[55] Nayuko Watanabe, Masayuki Okamoto, Masaaki Kikuchi, Takayuki Iida, Kenta Sasaki, Kensuke Horiuchi, and Masanori Hattori. 2011. *Designing Mobile Search Interface with Query Term Extraction*. Springer, Berlin, Heidelberg, 67–76. https://doi.org/10.1007/978-3-642-23854-3_8

[56] Sean White and Steven Feiner. 2009. SiteLens: Situated Visualization Techniques for Urban Site Visits. In *Proc. CHI '09*. ACM, New York, NY, USA, 1117–1120. https://doi.org/10.1145/1518701.1518871

[57] Wesley Willett, Yvonne Jansen, and Pierre Dragicevic. 2017. Embedded Data Representations. *IEEE Trans. Vis. Comput. Graphics* 23, 1 (Jan 2017), 461–470. https://doi.org/10.1109/TVCG.2016.2598608

[58] Xing Xie, Lie Lu, Menglei Jia, Hua Li, Frank Seide, and Wei-Ying Ma. 2008. Mobile Search With Multimodal Queries. *Proc. of the IEEE* 96, 4 (April 2008), 589–601. https://doi.org/10.1109/JPROC.2008.916351

[59] Tom Yeh, John J. Lee, and Trevor Darrell. 2008. Photo-based Question Answering. In *Proc. MM '08*. ACM, New York, NY, USA, 389–398. https://doi.org/10.1145/1459359.1459412

[60] Degi Young and Ben Shneiderman. 1993. A graphical filter/flow representation of Boolean queries: A prototype implementation and evaluation. *J. Am. Soc. Inf. Sci.* 44, 6 (1993), 327–339. https://doi.org/10.1002/(SICI)1097-4571(199307)44:6<327::AID-ASI3>3.0.CO;2-J

[61] Stefan Zander, Chris Chiu, and Gerhard Sageder. 2012. A Computational Model for the Integration of Linked Data in Mobile Augmented Reality Applications. In *Proc. I-SEMANTICS '12*. ACM, New York, USA, 133–140. https://doi.org/10.1145/2362499.2362518

[62] Qi Zhang, Simon Zaaijer, Song Wu, and Michael S. Lew. 2014. 3D Image Browsing: The Planets. In *Proc. ICMR '14*. ACM, New York, USA, Article 511, 3 pages. https://doi.org/10.1145/2578726.2582613

[63] Yun Zhang, Hong Fu, Zhen Liang, Zheru Chi, and Dagan Feng. 2010. Eye Movement As an Interaction Mechanism for Relevance Feedback in a Content-based Image Retrieval System. In *Proc. ETRA '10*. ACM, New York, NY, USA, 37–40. https://doi.org/10.1145/1743666.1743674

A Study of Immediate Requery Behavior in Search

Haotian Zhang
School of Computer Science
University of Waterloo
haotian.zhang@uwaterloo.ca

Mustafa Abualsaud
School of Computer Science
University of Waterloo
m2abuals@uwaterloo.ca

Mark D. Smucker
Department of Management Sciences
University of Waterloo
mark.smucker@uwaterloo.ca

ABSTRACT

When search results fail to satisfy users' information needs, users often reformulate their search query in the hopes of receiving better results. In many cases, users immediately requery without clicking on any search results. In this paper, we report on a user study designed to investigate the rate at which users immediately reformulate at different levels of search quality. We had users search for answers to questions as we manipulated the placement of the only relevant document in a ranked list of search results. We show that as the quality of search results decreases, the probability of immediately requerying increases. We find that users can quickly decide to immediately reformulate, and the time to immediately reformulate appears to be independent of the quality of the search results. Finally, we show that there appears to be two types of users. One group has a high probability of immediately reformulating and the other is unlikely to immediately reformulate unless no relevant documents can be found in the search results. While requerying takes time, it is the group of users who are more likely to immediately requery that are able to able find answers to questions the fastest.

CCS CONCEPTS

• Information systems → Users and interactive retrieval;

KEYWORDS

Immediate requery; Query abandonment; User study

ACM Reference Format:
Haotian Zhang, Mustafa Abualsaud, and Mark D. Smucker. 2018. A Study of Immediate Requery Behavior in Search. In *CHIIR '18: 2018 Conference on Human Information Interaction & Retrieval, March 11–15, 2018, New Brunswick, NJ, USA.* ACM, New York, NY, USA, 10 pages. https://doi.org/10.1145/3176349.3176400

1 INTRODUCTION

Today's search engines are typified by interfaces that allow a search user to issue a text query and then receive a list of search results. The moment the search engine results page (SERP) is displayed, the user begins processing that page with a goal of making one of three decisions:

(1) Click a search result to navigate to its page for viewing.
(2) Abandon the query, but continue the search by reformulating the query to produce a new search results page.
(3) Abandon not only the query but also the search. The next interaction with the search engine will not be a continuation of the current search.

Modern web search engines not only return organic search results, but also advertisements and other possible interaction mechanisms, for example, other suggested queries. In this paper, we limit our discussion to an abstract search engine that only returns organic search results in a ranked list, and where each search result is displayed with a summary to aid the user in deciding on the result's relevance.

To distinguish the abandonment in choice 2 from the abandonment in choice 3 above, we term choice 2 an *immediate requery*, i.e. a query reformulation without any clicks on search results. While a user performing an immediate requery does not click on any search results, the user will spend some time to view the search results and reformulate the query.

An immediate requery means that the user effectively places zero value on the search results. Even if the search results may contain relevant results, the immediate requery means that the user has spent time on the page but remains unsatisfied. If a user found significant value in the search result summaries, we assume the user would either click on a search result or abandon the query satisfied. Given the apparent loss in value to the user that results from an immediate requery, it is important to understand what conditions make immediate requeries likely. In particular, how good do search results need to be to have at least one click and avoid being treated as worthless with an immediate requery?

We conducted a controlled user study to investigate the relationship between search results quality and immediate requeries. In our study, we asked participants to find the answers to a set of questions. The questions were selected to be simple to answer given a good search engine, but unlikely for our study participants to already know the answers. For example, one question was "How long is the Las Vegas monorail in miles?" We varied the quality of the search results by placing one relevant document at varying ranks. We selected the non-relevant search results to appear somewhat plausible as search results for the given question, but to also be clearly non-relevant on inspection.

We found that in our study:

- Users make their decisions to requery or click quickly. The median time from query to immediate requery was 7.7 seconds.
- The probability of an immediate requery increases as the user has to search further down the ranked list to find a relevant document. In particular, the probability of an immediate

requery approximately doubles when the topmost relevant document is at rank 2 rather than at rank 1.
- The time it takes users to make a decision of whether to requery or not, appears to be independent of search results quality.

We also found that there may be two classes of user behavior for the examination of search results. One group, the majority, focuses on the top of the ranked list to make their decision about whether to requery or not. The other group appears to be more likely to examine the whole ranked list. The group more likely to immediately requery is able to find answers faster than the group less like to immediately requery.

We next review related work, then detail our experiment, report results, and finally conclude the paper.

2 BACKGROUND AND RELATED WORK

Hearst [12, Section 3.5.5] synthesizes research on web search behavior to suggest that a common strategy for users to follow is to "issue general queries, get information about the results, reformulate based on information seen in the results, and then navigate to promising-looking links or else give up." As part of this common strategy, it has long been recognized that some search users will decide to immediately reformulate their query without clicking on any search results. While terminology describing this behavior varies, commonly it is referred to as *query abandonment*. Joachims and Radlinski [16] termed "abandonment" to be "the user's decision to not click on any of the results." Likewise, Radlinski et al. [24] defined *abandonment rate* to be "the fraction of queries for which no results were clicked on." Unfortunately, "query abandonment" also sounds similar to what a user does after clicking on a result and deciding to reformulate a query. Indeed, Wu and Kelly [31] defined query abandonment to be "the point at which a person decides to stop his/her current query and enter a new one."

To avoid confusion, we define an *immediate requery* to be when a user enters a query, and then without clicking on any of the search results, the user reformulates the query to continue their search. For our notion of a modern search engine, clicking on a search result is the user interface action that allows the user to navigate to the result and view it in its entirety. We expect that users will, in most cases, view some search result summaries/snippets even if they do not click on them.

Li et al. [18] highlight that there is both good and bad query abandonment. Good query abandonment occurs when users find, for example, the answer they were looking for in the search results summaries or located somewhere on the SERP. Bad abandonment is associated with the user being dissatisfied with the search results. In our study, we are focused on bad abandonment caused by poor quality in search results.

There are a host of reasons why users may abandon queries. Stamou and Efthimiadis [29] classified query abandonment reasons into two categories: intentional causes and unintentional causes. The intentional causes include, for example, spelling or syntax changes to the query, checking whether search results have changed since the last time they issued the same query, and understanding the meaning of the query by looking at its results. The unintentional causes include, for example, no results returned, results are irrelevant, repetition of previously seen results, and interrupted search.

In an another study, Stamou and Efthimiadis [28] examined two types of post-query search abandonment: 1) pre-determined (when the user plans to find answers from the result snippets without clicking at any result), and 2) post-determined (when the user plans to click on a result but decides not to after viewing the SERP). They found that 27% of queries were abandoned due to a pre-determined intentions, and nearly half of the post-determined queries were abandoned due to dissatisfaction with the SERP.

Diriye et al. [9] found that 27% of SERP abandonment is not due to satisfaction nor dissatisfaction with results. The reasons of abandonment were: users came up with a better query before they viewed the SERP (13%), users found search results not sufficiently important (3%), and the user got interrupted by some factor (1%) (e.g., network failed and tab closed). Some 10% of the reasons fell into a catch-all "other" category.

Wu and Kelly [31] found three factors that may influence query abandonment. The first factor was the properties of search results. The proportion and relative location of relevant results determines the quality of SERPs and further affect query abandonment. The second factor was the properties of query. Users can learn new vocabulary from current query result and as a result they issue a new query. The last factor was the properties of the search task. Some users requery each time a subtask is fulfilled.

Several researchers have used eye-tracking as part of their studies on how users interact with search results. Granka et al. [11] showed that users spend more time and attention to top ranked results, and that they generally work top to bottom when looking for relevant documents. In addition to spending more time on top ranked results, researchers have also found that users are biased towards clicking on top results [14, 15, 19].

Klöckner et al. [17] classified users into two groups based on how they processed search results. One group followed a "strictly depth-first" strategy where they work down the ranked list one result at a time. The remaining participants followed either "partially breadth-first" or "extreme breadth-first" strategies. A partial breadth-first strategy is reflected by looking ahead a few results and making comparisons between the results to determine what to click on. The extreme breadth-first approach involves studying all of the search results before deciding which to click on.

Like Klöckner et al., Aula et al. [1] found users to follow either an "economic" or "exhaustive" strategy for processing search results. In Aula et al.'s study, about 6-7 summaries were visible at a time on the computer screen, and *economic* users would scan at most the first three results before acting. The *exhaustive* users would examine more than half of the visible summaries and sometimes even scroll to see the remaining summaries before acting. Aula et al. [1] found that the *economic* searchers had more computer experience and would fixate for shorter periods on each result.

Dumais et al. [10] found three groups of users and following the convention of Aula et al. [1], named the groups: "economic-results", "economic-ads", and "exhaustive". Dumais et al.'s study involved a commercial search engine and the two *economic* groups differed in how they examined advertisements. A significant difference between the economic and exhaustive groups was the amount of time spent examining result summaries. The *economic* users spent between 8.7 and 9.9 seconds while the *exhaustive* users spent 14.6 seconds on average. Some users may display exhaustive behavior as a result of being dyslexic, for MacFarlane et al. [21] have found that dyslexic users are more likely to backtrack and reread material.

Lorigo et al. [20] investigated how a SERP's components such as result summaries can affect clicking behavior. In their study, participants used a web search engine to find answers to various short questions. Eye tracking data of participants using the web search was collected and analyzed. Using this data, the authors found that the relevance of the top 3 documents in the list can be a useful indicator to whether users will further explore the rest of the list. If the first 3 documents of the SERP are non-relevant, most users will end their exploration of the list. Eye tracking data provided insight on participants reading behavior of the SERP. In particular, they found that users generally tend to skim document summaries.

A large-scale cursor/mouse tracking study by Huang et al. [13] found that users tend to hover over 4 documents before deciding to requery. In contrast to Lorigo et al. [20] and Huang et al. [13], Cutrell and Guan [7] report that users view the first 8 results before deciding to requery.

Wu et al. [32] conducted a user study in which participants had to complete several search tasks. Each task consisted of using a web search engine to find an answer to exploration-type questions that often require multiple queries and multiple page visits. They manipulated their SERP according to two within-subject variables: Information Scent Level (ISL) and Information Scent Pattern (ISP). ISL was defined as the number of relevant documents appearing in the first SERP of the task, and ISP as the distribution of four relevant documents in the SERP. Both ISL and ISP included 3 categories. Low, medium, and high for ISL and persistent, disrupted, and bursting for ISP. These categories addressed different qualities of the SERPs. The authors found that around 42% of users abandoned their queries without any click on low ISL SERPs (where only the first document is relevant), and 13% of users requery on medium ISL SERPs (where only the top 3 documents are relevant). Only 1.6% of uses requery on high ISL SERP (where only the top 5 documents are relevant). For tasks under ISP, they found no big difference in SERP abandonment between persistent ISP (relevant documents at rank 1, 2, 5, and 8) and disrupted ISP (relevant documents at rank 1, 2, 3, and 4). Persistent ISP and disrupted ISP had 10% and 12% SERP abandonment rate respectively. Bursting ISP (relevant documents at rank 4, 5, 6, and 7) had 20% rate of SERP abandonment.

Finally, there has been considerable recent work in the simulation of user behavior for information retrieval evaluation [3, 6]. Much of this work attempts to model user behavior with search engines so that the models can be used to make accurate predictions of user behavior and gain received from the search engine [4, 5, 25, 27, 30].

Of particular note, many researchers have looked at modeling a user's decision to either stop processing search results, or when to stop and reformulate the query to get new, and hopefully better search results [8, 22, 23, 26].

3 METHODS AND MATERIALS

In this section, we describe the details of our experiment. To measure the effect of search results quality on users' requery behavior,

we created a controlled within-subjects laboratory user study. After giving their consent to participate, each participant in our study was asked to find the answer to 12 questions using our custom search engine. We designed the search engine to manipulate the search results and control the placement of one relevant document in the 10 displayed search results. We carefully instrumented the search engine to allow us to record detailed user interaction data. We next describe the search tasks, how we manipulated the search results to vary their quality, how we measured user behavior, and the study design.

3.1 Search Tasks

We asked each participant to search for answers to 12 questions. Table 1 shows the 12 questions including a practice question. For each search task, we provided participants with a single question and asked them to use our search engine to find an answer to the question. Participants could enter as many queries as they wanted and spend as much time as needed to find the correct answer. We designed the questions to meet the following requirements: (i) Most participants should not already know the answer, and thus, participants would be forced to search to find an answer. (ii) The question should be straightforward, non-confusing, and be able to be answered easily with the help of a modern search engine. (iii) Each question should only have one standard answer. (iv) The question should make it easy for us to find plausible non-relevant search results as well as a relevant web page that contains the answer.

After completing our study, we found that question 12 failed to meet the requirement that participants be able to easily answer it, for only 28% answered it correctly. In hindsight, we see that question 12 was tricky. Michael Jordan was selected to play in the All-Star Game 14 times but only played 13 games in total due to an injury. Many participants gave an answer of 14 games instead of 13. In addition, some participants had trouble with question 6 (78% accuracy), and this was because they entered the start of the lyrics as the answer rather than the song's title. All other questions had greater than 90% accuracy.

3.2 Search Interface

The search interface used for all study tasks is shown in Figure 1. The interface design was similar to that of common commercial search engines, except it did not include any means to get more than 10 results per query. Participants could enter their search queries using the search bar and trigger the query by either clicking on "Search" button or pressing "Enter" keystroke. The question of the current task that participants need to search an answer for was always visible and shown next to the search bar. The question was also shown during the pre-task. Clicking on the help button would trigger a pop-up showing the help information on how to use the interface. Subjects were asked to use this search interface to find an answer for each question and were allowed to submit multiple queries and click on multiple documents if they wished. To accurately measure clicks and time spent in the SERP and in the documents, we disabled right-clicks and opening documents in new tabs. Participants needed to use the back button on the browser to return back to the SERP after clicking and viewing a document.

ID	Question	Answer	Triggered Query Words
P	What is the weight of Hope Diamond in carats?	45.52	N/A (practice question)
1	How long is the Las Vegas monorail in miles?	3.9/4 miles.	Las, Vegas, monorail
2	Find out the name of the album that the Mountain Goats band released in 2004.	We Shall All Be Healed	Mountain, Mountian, Goats, Goat, album
3	Which year was the first Earth Day held?	1970	Earth, Day
4	Which year was the Holes (novel) written by Louis Sachar first published?	1998	Holes, hole, louis, sachar, Novel
5	Find the phone number of Rocky Mountain Chocolate Factory located in Ottawa, ON?	(613) 241-1091	Rocky, Mountain, Chocolate, Factory, Ottawa
6	What is the name of opening theme song for Mister Rogers' Neighbourhood?	Won't You Be My Neighbor?	Mister, Rogers, Roger, Roger's, Neighbourhood, opening, theme, song
7	Which album is the song Rain Man by Eminem from?	Encore	Rain, Man, Eminem
8	How many chapters are in The Art of War book written by Sun Tzu?	13	Art, War, Sun, Tzu
9	What is the scientific name of Mad cow disease?	Bovine Spongiform Encephalopathy (BSE)	Mad, Cow, Disease
10	How many campuses does the University of North Carolina have?	17	University, North, Carolina, Campus, campuses, UNC
11	Which Canadian site was selected as one of United Nations World Heritage Sites in 1999?	Miguasha National Park	United, Nations, World, Heritage, UN
12	How many times did Michael Jordan play the NBA All-Star Games?	13	Michael, Jordan, NBA, All-Star, Star

Table 1: The study's 1 practice and 12 search task questions and their corresponding answers and trigger query words.

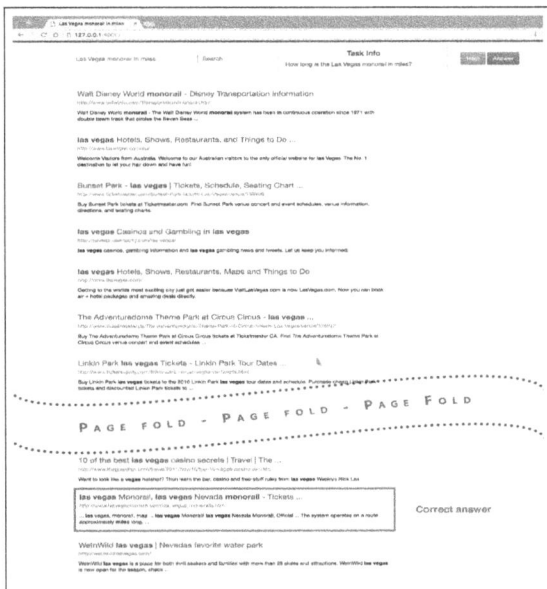

Figure 1: The search interface for all tasks. The interface has a search bar, help button and answer button. The SERP shows a maximum of 10 documents with no further results available. Here, a manipulated SERP is presented and the correct document is placed at the rank 9. In general, the results at ranks 8-10 were not visible without scrolling.

3.3 Quality of Search Results

Our search engine only provided 10 search results in response to a query. With 10 search results and simple binary relevance, there are 1024 (2^{10}) possible ways to construct search results to vary their quality. In this paper, a relevant document contains the answer to the user's question and a non-relevant document does not contain the answer. To simplify our study, we decided to focus on the placement of a single relevant document in a ranked list of 10 search results. Placing the single relevant document at ranks 1 through 10 gave us 10 different rankings where the assumption was that as the relevant document was placed lower in the ranking, the lower the search quality would be to the user. We also produced a ranking where all 10 documents were non-relevant, which we call an "All Bad" SERP. Finally, we also had a control condition where the search results were the actual results produced by the Bing search API[1] in response to the user's query.

All the results shown in manipulated SERPs contained at least one keyword from the question. Relevant, or *correct*, documents provided a straightforward answer to the user's question that should be easy for the user to find. Non-relevant, or *incorrect*, documents contain keywords from the question, and may be related to the question in some way, but their overall topic is clearly non-relevant. A non-relevant document does not contain the answer.

We found all documents and their snippets by issuing queries to the Bing search API. For documents with the correct answer in their snippets, we manually removed the answer from the snippets to force the user to click on the document and find the answer from its content. We only controlled the snippet content for the

---
[1]https://azure.microsoft.com/en-ca/services/cognitive-services/bing-web-search-api/

manipulated SERPs. The control SERP (Bing) used snippets directly from the Bing API.

In order to make the manipulated SERPs look realistic and reasonable, and to prevent participants from having any suspicion or confusion regarding the SERP, the incorrect documents were selected from queries related to the corresponding factoid question. Take, for example, the "Las Vegas Monorail" question shown in Figure 1 (ID 1 in Table 1). For this question, a somewhat realistic but unrelated query would be "Las Vegas Casino" or "Las Vegas Hotel". Both queries have the phrases "Las Vegas" but are not relevant to "Las Vegas monorail". We used such queries to retrieve incorrect documents for all 12 questions.

We constructed the SERPs in this fashion for participants to think the results were real, but to also make it clear there were many non-relevant documents in the results. We wanted to trigger immediate requeries while also studying the effect of rank on immediate requery behavior.

3.4 Triggering Manipulated SERPs

As described above, we had 11 manipulated SERP tasks (one relevant document at ranks 1-10, and all non-relevant documents). We wanted to be careful to only show the study participant the manipulated SERP if the participant entered a query that could reasonably be an attempt to use a search engine to find an answer to the given question. For each question, we constructed a list of keywords that if any of them were entered by the participant as part of their query, they would trigger the manipulated SERP. If the participant entered a query lacking all of the selected keywords, we would send the query to the Bing search API and return organic results. Table 1 shows the trigger keywords for each question.

For each search task, the participant can only trigger the manipulated SERP once. All further queries will not trigger the manipulated SERP, regardless of what the query terms are. All queries following the display of a manipulated SERP produce live, organic results from the Bing search API.

After analyzing the search logs for manipulated SERP tasks, we found that only 2 participants on 2 different tasks failed to trigger the manipulated SERP with their first query. The first user entered "canadian heratige site 1999" as their first query for task # 11, with the wrong spelling of the word "heritage". None of the query terms are triggers. The second user entered an empty query for task # 3 and our system returned an empty SERP. Both of these two users successfully triggered a manipulated SERP with their second query. For both of these two users, we skip their first query and analyze their data from the query that triggered a manipulated SERP.

For the control search task, all queries are sent to the Bing search API, and its results are shown to the participant.

3.5 Measurements

Our goal is to investigate the requery behavior of users given SERPs with different quality. More specifically, how much time users spend before they abandon a SERP and issue a new query and probability of an immediate requery on SERPs of different quality. To collect all necessary data to achieve these goals, we designed our interface to record all user actions and system responses (clicks, keystrokes, query submission, SERP appearance, etc.) and their corresponding timestamps in the client time to allow us to compute time spent between any two actions. Any time that a participant spent on the help page, was excluded from all measurements.

The time spent before an immediate requery is measured from the time the SERP loads following a query to the time they select the query box to reformulate their query. In 5 cases, a participant clicked the search button without reformulating their query, and in these cases, the time from query to the time they clicked the search button is counted as the length of time for the immediate requery.

The time to submit an answer is measured from the display of the search interface to the moment the participant submits their answer.

The time of a participant's "first click" on a result in a SERP is measured from the time the SERP loads following a query to the time of the first click on one of a SERP's results.

The time to formulate or reformulate a query was measured from the time of a participant's first keystroke in the query box to the time they submit the query.

3.5.1 Time on documents. For the manipulated SERPs, we already know the rank of correct (relevant) and incorrect (non-relevant) documents in the list. We can easily measure how long the participants spend on correct documents and incorrect documents.

For the organic SERPs returned by Bing, we performed a post-study analysis to manually check every web page clicked by participants. We classified these clicked documents into three categories.

- **Correct**: The document contains the correct answer.
- **Incorrect**: The document is non-relevant or does not contain the correct answer in linked to pages.
- **Not sure**: The document content does not include the correct answer, but the answer can be found by navigating the page links. To get to the answer, participants would need to click on some links from the document to get to the page where the answer is written.

After manually checking clicked documents from Bing SERPs and categorizing each document, we measure the time users spend on documents of each category.

3.6 Study Procedure and Design

The study was run in a closed computer laboratory using desktop machines with the same monitor size and specifications. The computer monitors had a screen resolution of 1680 × 1050 pixels. The Google Chrome browser was used to access the study.

After receiving participants' informed consent, we collected participants' demographics and information on their search engine usage and experience before the start of the study. Instructions on the study tasks and expectations were provided before the study. We mention that "You can enter as many queries as many times as you want." in the instructions to encourage participants to query. Cell phone usage was prohibited and complete attention during the study was expected of participants. We explained to participants that they were not allowed to use other search engines to find answers. A short quiz was used to ensure participants read and understood the study's tasks and instructions. Participants were not allowed to proceed to the study until all quiz questions were answered correctly.

We provided a practice page of the search interface and asked all participants to familiarize themselves with the interface by searching for an answer to a practice question (Table 1, ID "**P**"). All search results returned by the system during the practice phase were organic Bing results. Participants proceeded to their first task after completing the practice task. Completion of the practice task and all further tasks were done by providing a written answer to the task's question.

Each search task included a pre-task and a post-task questionnaire. During the pre-task, we showed the current question and asked participants about their prior knowledge of the current question topic. The post-task questionnaire asks the participants about their confidence in their answer. We asked participants on their feedback and overall experience with an end-of-study questionnaire.

3.6.1 Balanced Design. The study involved 12 tasks and 60 participants. We used a 12 × 12 Graeco-Latin square to create a fully balanced design and randomize SERP quality treatments and experimental conditions. As mentioned before, there are 12 different SERPs including 11 manipulated SERPs and one control Bing SERP. The 12 different SERPs composed one block. Each block balanced the order of tasks and the rank positions of correct documents. By randomizing the columns and rows, this process creates five separate 12 × 12 Graeco-Latin Squares - for all the 60 participants.

3.7 Participants

After receiving ethics approval from our university's office of research ethics, we recruited participants through posters placed in different departments of the university. The study involved 73 participants in total, but only 60 participants' data was used for our analysis. We removed data of 13 participants due to pilot testing and technical issues. After careful examination of the 60 participants' data, we did not find any irregularities and thus did not clean or modify their data before the analysis. Each of the 60 participants completed their 12 tasks in a balanced order, yielding a total of 720 tasks, 660 were manipulated SERP tasks, and 60 were non-manipulated organic Bing SERP tasks (control).

Participants' age ranged between 18 and 48 years old (mean = 23.6). There were 34 male and 26 female participants. Of these participants, 54 of them were from science, technology, engineering, or math, 1 from arts, and 5 did not specify their major.

Each participant was compensated $15 with an advertised payment of $10 for participation and a $5 bonus for answering at least 10 out of 12 questions correctly. However, regardless of participant performance, we paid all participants the full $15. This payment structure was designed to motivate good performance while not harming any person who might not have been able to answer 10 questions correctly. 58 participants answered 10 or more questions correctly. One participant answered 9 questions correctly, and one participant only answered 8 questions correctly.

4 RESULTS AND DISCUSSION

In our study, participants used a search engine to find answers to 12 questions. For 11 search tasks, we manipulated the search results quality. For one of the search tasks, which acted as a control, participants received results directly from the Bing search API. For

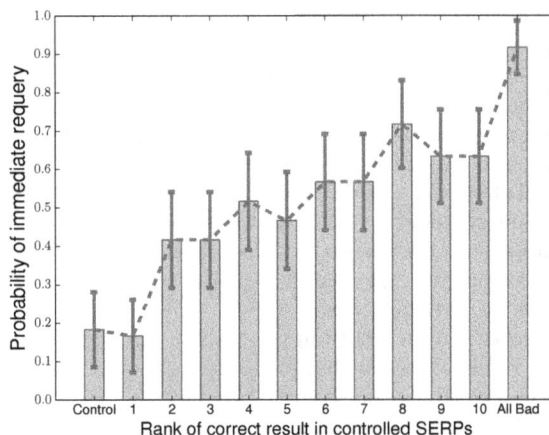

Figure 2: The probability of immediate requery for the 12 different SERP conditions. The control condition's search results are from the Bing search API. The "All Bad" condition means that all 10 search results are non-relevant. The error bars are 95% confidence intervals.

the manipulated SERPs, any queries that followed the manipulated SERP provided results from the Bing search API. As explained in Section 3.3, the manipulated SERPs included 1 single correct document, placed in different ranks from 1 to 10, or 0 correct documents.

Figures 2, 3, 4, and Table 2 show our main results. In Figure 2, we see that as the rank of the relevant document goes from rank 1 (top of page) to rank 10 (bottom of page), the probability of an immediate requery increases. The highest probability for an immediate requery, 0.92, occurs when all of the search results are non-relevant, and this rate is a statistically significant difference from the other conditions. The control condition's search results, which are Bing API search results, have a probability of immediate requery of only 0.18, which is, for all purposes, the same as we saw for a relevant result at rank 1. The probability of immediate requery at rank 1, 0.17, is significantly different than at rank 2, 0.42.

Figure 3 shows that the time it takes a user to decide to immediately requery appears to be independent of the search results quality. Figure 4 shows the distribution of all times to immediate requery. The median time for an immediate requery is a fast 7.7 seconds, and the average time is 9.2 seconds. A log-normal distribution fitted to this data has a mean of 2.0 and a standard deviance of 0.68.

We also measured the time from a query to a participant's first click on the search results. Figure 5 and Table 3 show the time from a query to the first result click for ranks 1-10. We can see a very linear increase in the time it takes participants to scan the ranked list of results from rank 1 to rank 4. The median time from query to a click on rank 1 is only 3.1 seconds, and then it takes approximately 2 seconds more for each rank up to rank 4, which takes 10.4 seconds to reach. Participant's behavior on ranks 5-7 is different with these median times taking 8.5, 11.4, and 11.3 seconds. Finally, for the ranks that require the participant to scroll to reach, ranks 8-10, we see that participants appear to scan these upward

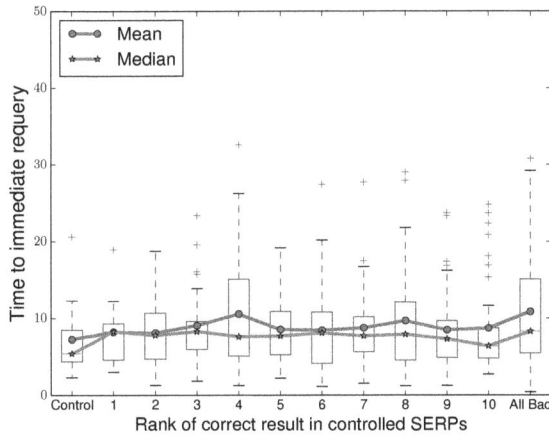

Figure 3: Time to immediate requery without any document clicks on the manipulated SERPs and organic Bing SERPs using the triggered query.

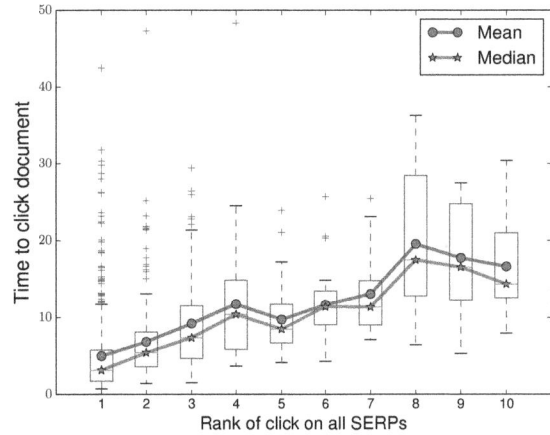

Figure 5: Time from query to the first result click at different ranks on all SERPs.

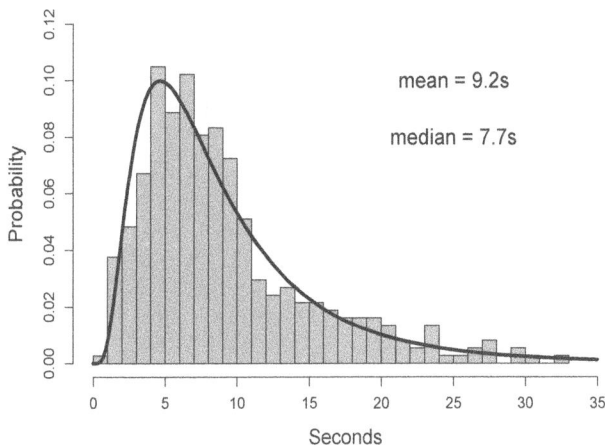

Figure 4: The distribution of time to immediate requery on the manipulated SERPs and organic Bing SERPs. A log normal curve fit to the data is also shown.

Rank of Correct Document	Freq.	Prob. Immediate Requery [95% CI]	Seconds to Immediate Requery [95% CI]
Control (Bing API)	11	0.18 [0.09, 0.28]	7.3 [4.1, 10.5]
1	10	0.17 [0.07, 0.26]	8.2 [5.2, 11.2]
2	25	0.42 [0.29, 0.54]	8.1 [6.2, 10]
3	25	0.42 [0.29, 0.54]	9.1 [7.0, 11.1]
4	31	0.52 [0.39, 0.64]	10.5 [7.9, 13.2]
5	28	0.47 [0.34, 0.59]	8.5 [6.9, 10.2]
6	34	0.57 [0.44, 0.69]	8.4 [6.5, 10.4]
7	34	0.57 [0.44, 0.69]	8.7 [7.0, 10.5]
8	43	0.72 [0.60, 0.83]	9.7 [7.7, 11.6]
9	38	0.63 [0.51, 0.76]	8.5 [6.8, 10.2]
10	38	0.63 [0.51, 0.76]	8.7 [6.8, 10.6]
All Bad Results	55	0.92 [0.85, 0.99]	10.9 [8.9, 12.8]

Table 2: The frequency, probability and time to immediate requery with corresponding 95% Confidence Interval on the controlled SERPs (cf. Figures 2 and 3).

Rank of Correct Document	Median Time To Click	Mean Time To Click [95% CI]
1	3.1	5.0 [4.5, 5.5]
2	5.4	6.8 [6.0, 7.7]
3	7.3	9.2 [8.0, 10.4]
4	10.4	11.7 [9.5, 13.9]
5	8.5	9.7 [8.6, 10.9]
6	11.4	11.6 [10.1, 13.2]
7	11.3	13.1 [10.8, 15.3]
8	17.5	19.6 [14.6, 24.5]
9	16.6	17.8 [14.5, 21.0]
10	14.4	16.6 [14.0, 19.3]

Table 3: Time in seconds to first click on a result at different ranks (cf. Figure 5).

from rank 10 to 9 to 8 with median times of 14.4, 16.6, and 17.5 seconds, respectively.

As reviewed in the related work section (Section 2), past eye-tracking research also shows that users tend to linearly scan search results. But if users are linearly scanning the results, why does the time to immediately requery appear to be independent of the rank of the relevant document? One possible explanation is found in the other eye-tracking research that largely shows that users scan the first 3 or 4 results before deciding to requery. Our participants appear to be able to scan ranks 1-3 in 7.3 median seconds and our median time to immediately requery is 7.7 seconds. Unfortunately,

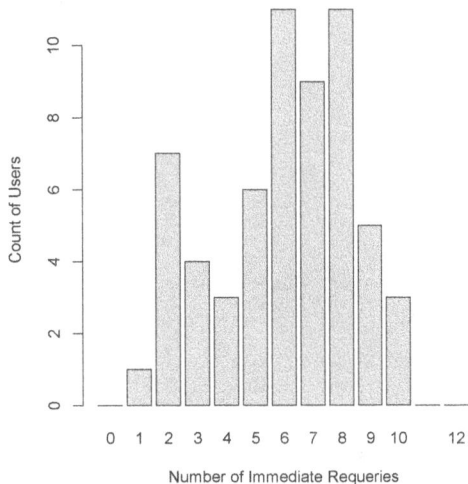

Figure 6: Distribution of immediate requeries for all participants.

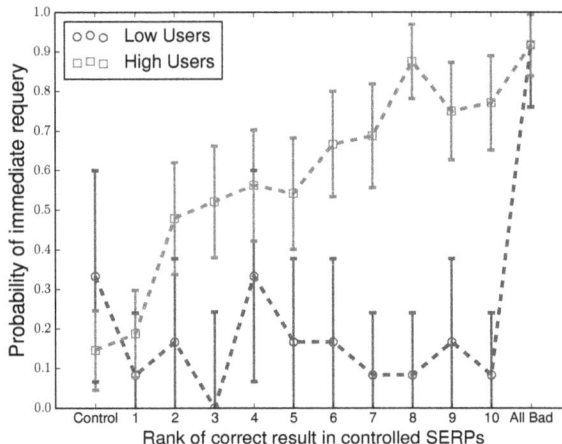

Figure 7: The probability of immediate requery for the 12 different SERP conditions for two different groups of participants (cf. Figure 2). The "Low Users" issued immediate requeries for 3 or fewer of the 12 search tasks. The "High Users" each had 4 or more immediate requeries. The error bars are 95% confidence intervals.

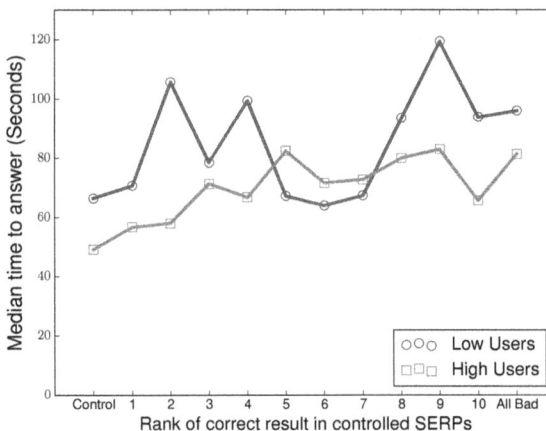

Figure 8: The median time from starting a task to answer a question for different groups of users.

this does not explain why we see participants clicking at ranks 5-10, for if participants stopped their scans at ranks 3 or 4, they should never see the relevant documents at lower ranks to click on them.

Given past eye-tracking research that has shown there to be two different classes of searchers, i.e. economic and exhaustive searchers (see Section 2), we looked closer at the individual behavior of the study participants.

Figure 6 shows the distribution of number of immediate requeries per participant. While our analysis is limited by the number of participants and the number of search tasks, it appears that we have one group of participants who have a low rate of immediately requerying (≤ 3 immediate requeries), and other group that immediately requery much more frequently (≥ 4 immediate requeries). As such, we label each participant as either having a low or high probability of immediately requerying and looked at the behavior of each group.

Figure 7 shows the probability of immediately requerying for the *low* vs. *high* groups. As can be seen, the *low* group's probability of immediately requerying stays low until they are faced with search results that are all non-relevant. In contrast, the *high* group's probability of immediately requerying grows quickly as the rank of the relevant document goes from 1 to 10. It appears that the *low* group are *exhaustive* searchers while the *high* group are likely *economic* searchers.

If we believe that search users optimize their search behavior to find answers as quickly as possible [2], then the majority of participants who appear to be *economic* in their search behavior, should find answers faster in spite of their higher probability for immediately requerying. Indeed, we find that participants who are more likely to immediately requery to be able to find answers faster. The mean time to answer for the participants likely to immediately requery (*high*) is 85.9 seconds and the mean time for

the participants with *low* probability of immediately requerying is 111.6 seconds, and this difference is statistically significant by a two-tailed, Student's t-test (p=0.0005). While this difference is significant, it is possible that the *high* group's performance is the result of many additional factors that correlate with a higher probability for immediately requerying.

Figure 8 shows the median time to answer a question for the *low* and *high* groups of users across the 12 search conditions. While the data is noisy because of the limited size of the *low* group, we see that for the control condition, and when the relevant document is at ranks 1-4 and 8-10, the *low* participants take longer than the high

Rank of correct document	Median
Bing	57.6
1	59.7
2	60.7
3	72.2
4	69.6
5	77.9
6	71.1
7	72.5
8	81.5
9	89.5
10	70.2
All Bad	85.9

Table 4: For all participants, the median time in seconds from starting a task to answering a question for the different search conditions.

	Mean	Standard Error	Median
Correct doc time	22.9	0.7	16.1
Incorrect doc time	20.3	1.7	9.7
Not sure doc time	35.2	3.2	27.4

Table 5: Time in seconds to view types of documents.

group. We also see that for the mid-ranks of 5-7, the *low* users have slightly faster times to answer than the *high* group. For comparison, Table 4 reports the median time to answer for all participants.

What seems to be happening is that the *low* group wastes time looking at more results for results at ranks 1-4 than is necessary to select the relevant document. When the relevant document is at ranks 5-7, the group of participants with a *high* probability of immediately requerying has apparently stopped scanning at rank 3 or 4 and immediately requeried. Meanwhile, the *low* group, which is exhaustively scanning results finds the relevant document at ranks 5-7 without needing to incur the cost of an immediate requery. Strikingly, the *high* group appears to be able to keep the time to answer nearly uniform for ranks 5-10 and "All Bad", for while they have to take time to immediately requery, we know from the control condition that participants find the answer quickly with the Bing search results.

The cost of an immediate requery is actually quite low. First there is the sunk cost of examining the current results, which we reported earlier as a median time of 7.7 seconds. The median time for a user to reformulate their query was 3.2 seconds. The median time to reach rank 1 in the search results is only 3.1 seconds. Thus, assuming the reformulated query can find a relevant document at rank 1, users with a high probability of immediately requerying should be able to cap their median cost to reach a relevant document at approximately 14 seconds, which is more than the cost to reach relevant documents at ranks 5-7, but less than the cost to reach ranks 8-10, and this seems to explain their behavior and our results.

4.1 Document Review Time

Table 5 shows the mean, standard error of the mean, and median time users spent reading documents in the three different categories we defined in Section 3.5.1. Given that this sort of user data typically follows a log-normal distribution, the median time is usually more informative than the mean. We see that participants are able to quickly realize their mistake in clicking on an incorrect (nonrelevant) document. After clicking on an incorrect document, they return back to the search results in only 9.7 seconds. The median times on correct and "not sure" documents are longer than for incorrect documents.

4.2 Study Limitations

A limitation of our work is that we only studied one type of search task. Our study participants needed to find answers to simple questions. Other search tasks may result in different behavior. For example, when our study participants experienced a SERP with only 1 relevant document at rank 1, we only saw a 17% immediate requery rate, which is considerably different than the 42% that Wu et al. [32] found (see Section 2). Likewise, when our topmost relevant document is at rank 4, we found that 52% of participants would immediately requery while Wu et al.'s "bursting" pattern had only a 20% rate. We think these differences in results are likely the result of the different types of search tasks that our two studies used. Our study had participants search for a single answer to a simple question. On the other hand, Wu et al. had many search tasks that would involve attempting to find many relevant documents. It appears that the search task can change immediate requery behavior.

A potential concern of our study would be if participants noticed the manipulation of search results. Our study provided a means for participants to supply open ended feedback after each search task as well as at the end of the study. Some participants commented that they were surprised that our search engine would not return Wikipedia search results at rank one when they included keywords such as "wiki" in their queries. One participant noted that our search engine seemed to be sensitive to the order of words in the query. Thus, while participants may have noticed some behavior different from commercial search engines, they did not specifically make mention of our manipulated behavior, and we did not notice any behavior that would indicate that they understood how the results were manipulated.

5 CONCLUDING DISCUSSION

There are many reasons for immediate requeries and not all of them are bad. In this paper, we focused our study on immediate requeries caused by poor quality results. Ignoring good reasons for abandonment, conventional wisdom holds that search engines should strive to minimize the fraction of queries that result in an immediate requery.

We expected to find that as the search results quality decreased, that the rate of immediately requerying would increase, and we did find this to be the case. Based on our results and others' eye-tracking studies, it appears that immediately requerying in web search is largely caused by the topmost relevant search results appearing at ranks lower than 3 or 4.

What we did not expect to find were a group of participants who were more likely to immediately requery, and that these participants would find answers faster than participants who stayed with the search results. In other words, being quick to immediately requery may actually be an efficient strategy for use of web search engines, which would explain why we saw a majority of participants employ this technique.

Unfortunately, these results mean that modifications to a search engine that lowers the rate of immediate requeries, may actually hurt user performance if the modification forces users to stick with bad results rather than quickly move to better results.

Indeed, it would seem that an important function of web search engines is to help users quickly find a query that delivers relevant documents at ranks 1 to 3. The faster a search engine can guide a user's query reformulations to the "right query", the faster the user will find relevant results.

Traditional evaluation of search engines focuses on the single list of search results produced by a query. Unfortunately, looking only at the quality of a search engine's ranking, focuses attention primarily on the minority of users who have a low probability of immediately requerying. In our study, it does not seem to matter to the majority of participants if a relevant document is at rank 5 or rank 10, both are considered to be worthless. It is important to keep in mind that for different or more complex search tasks, we might expect user behavior to differ from what we observed.

If only the top 3 or 4 results matter to a majority of users, as information retrieval researchers, we will need to both work to help users zero-in on the right query and to find ways to evaluate a search engine's ability to help users with this process of querying and repeated reformulation.

ACKNOWLEDGMENTS

The idea for this research was in part a result of a sabbatical that Mark Smucker spent at Microsoft, and the conversations he had with Ryen White, Susan Dumais, Paul Bennett, and others during the sabbatical. This work was supported in part by the Natural Sciences and Engineering Research Council of Canada (Grants CRDPJ 468812-14 and RGPIN-2014-03642), in part by Google, and in part by the University of Waterloo.

REFERENCES

[1] Anne Aula, Päivi Majaranta, and Kari-Jouko Räihä. 2005. Eye-Tracking Reveals the Personal Styles for Search Result Evaluation. In *Human-Computer Interaction – INTERACT 2005 (LNCS)*, Vol. 3585, 1058–1061.

[2] Leif Azzopardi. 2011. The economics in interactive information retrieval. In *SIGIR*, 15–24.

[3] Leif Azzopardi, Kalervo Järvelin, Jaap Kamps, and Mark D. Smucker. 2011. Report on the SIGIR 2010 workshop on the simulation of interaction. *SIGIR Forum* 44 (January 2011), 35–47. Issue 2.

[4] Feza Baskaya, Heikki Keskustalo, and Kalervo Järvelin. 2012. Time Drives Interaction: Simulating Sessions in Diverse Searching Environments. In *SIGIR*, 105–114.

[5] Ben Carterette, Evangelos Kanoulas, and Emine Yilmaz. 2011. Simulating simple user behavior for system effectiveness evaluation. In *CIKM*, 611–620.

[6] Charles L.A. Clarke, Luanne Freund, Mark D. Smucker, and Emine Yilmaz. 2013. Report on the SIGIR 2013 Workshop on Modeling User Behavior for Information Retrieval Evaluation (MUBE 2013). *SIGIR Forum* 47, 2 (Jan. 2013), 84–95.

[7] Edward Cutrell and Zhiwei Guan. 2007. What are you looking for?: an eye-tracking study of information usage in web search. In *SIGCHI*, 407–416.

[8] Arjen P. de Vries, Gabriella Kazai, and Mounia Lalmas. 2004. Tolerance to Irrelevance: A User-effort Oriented Evaluation of Retrieval Systems without Predefined Retrieval Unit. In *RIAO*, 463–473.

[9] Abdigani Diriye, Ryen White, Georg Buscher, and Susan Dumais. 2012. Leaving so soon?: understanding and predicting web search abandonment rationales. In *CIKM*, 1025–1034.

[10] Susan T. Dumais, Georg Buscher, and Edward Cutrell. 2010. Individual differences in gaze patterns for web search. In *IIiX*, 185–194.

[11] Laura A. Granka, Thorsten Joachims, and Geri Gay. 2004. Eye-tracking analysis of user behavior in WWW search. In *SIGIR*, 478–479.

[12] Marti A. Hearst. 2009. *Search User Interfaces* (1st ed.). Cambridge University Press.

[13] Jeff Huang, Ryen W White, and Susan Dumais. 2011. No clicks, no problem: using cursor movements to understand and improve search. In *SIGCHI*, 1225–1234.

[14] Thorsten Joachims, Laura Granka, Bing Pan, Helene Hembrooke, and Geri Gay. 2005. Accurately interpreting clickthrough data as implicit feedback. In *SIGIR*, 154–161.

[15] Thorsten Joachims, Laura Granka, Bing Pan, Helene Hembrooke, Filip Radlinski, and Geri Gay. 2007. Evaluating the Accuracy of Implicit Feedback from Clicks and Query Reformulations in Web Search. *ACM TOIS* 25, 2 (2007), 1–27.

[16] Thorsten Joachims and Filip Radlinski. 2007. Search Engines That Learn from Implicit Feedback. *Computer* 40, 8 (Aug. 2007), 34–40.

[17] Kerstin Klöckner, Nadine Wirschum, and Anthony Jameson. 2004. Depth- and breadth-first processing of search result lists. In *SIGCHI extended abstracts*, 1539–1539.

[18] Jane Li, Scott Huffman, and Akihito Tokuda. 2009. Good Abandonment in Mobile and PC Internet Search. In *SIGIR*, 43–50.

[19] Lori Lorigo, Maya Haridasan, Hrönn Brynjarsdóttir, Ling Xia, Thorsten Joachims, Geri Gay, Laura Granka, Fabio Pellacini, and Bing Pan. 2008. Eye tracking and online search: Lessons learned and challenges ahead. *JASIS* 59, 7 (2008), 1041–1052.

[20] Lori Lorigo, Maya Haridasan, Hrönn Brynjarsdóttir, Ling Xia, Thorsten Joachims, Geri Gay, Laura Granka, Fabio Pellacini, and Bing Pan. 2008. Eye tracking and online search: Lessons learned and challenges ahead. *JAIST* 59, 7 (2008), 1041–1052.

[21] Andrew MacFarlane, George Buchanan, Areej Al-Wabil, Gennady Andrienko, and Natalia Andrienko. 2017. Visual Analysis of Dyslexia on Search. In *CHIIR*, 285–288.

[22] David Maxwell, Leif Azzopardi, Kalervo Järvelin, and Heikki Keskustalo. 2015. Searching and Stopping: An Analysis of Stopping Rules and Strategies. In *CIKM*, 313–322.

[23] Teemu Pääkkönen, Jaana Kekäläinen, Heikki Keskustalo, Leif Azzopardi, David Maxwell, and Kalervo Järvelin. 2017. Validating simulated interaction for retrieval evaluation. *Information Retrieval* (2017), 1–25.

[24] Filip Radlinski, Madhu Kurup, and Thorsten Joachims. 2008. How Does Click-through Data Reflect Retrieval Quality?. In *CIKM*, 43–52.

[25] Mark D. Smucker and Charles L.A. Clarke. 2012. Time-based calibration of effectiveness measures. In *SIGIR*, 95–104.

[26] Mark D. Smucker and Charles L.A. Clarke. 2016. Modeling Optimal Switching Behavior. In *CHIIR*, 317–320.

[27] Mark D. Smucker and Charles L. A. Clarke. 2012. Modeling User Variance in Time-Biased Gain. In *HCIR*. ACM, 1–10.

[28] Sofia Stamou and Efthimis N Efthimiadis. 2009. Queries without clicks: Successful or failed searches. In *SIGIR 2009 Workshop on the Future of IR Evaluation*. 13–14.

[29] Sofia Stamou and Efthimis N. Efthimiadis. 2010. Interpreting User Inactivity on Search Results. In *ECIR*, 100–113.

[30] Paul Thomas, Alistair Moffat, Peter Bailey, and Falk Scholer. 2014. Modeling Decision Points in User Search Behavior. In *IIiX*, 239–242.

[31] Wan-Ching Wu and Diane Kelly. 2014. Online search stopping behaviors: An investigation of query abandonment and task stopping. *Proceedings of the Association for Information Science and Technology* 51, 1 (2014), 1–10.

[32] Wan-Ching Wu, Diane Kelly, and Avneesh Sud. 2014. Using information scent and need for cognition to understand online search behavior. In *SIGIR*, 557–566.

Exploring Document Retrieval Features Associated with Improved Short- and Long-term Vocabulary Learning Outcomes

Rohail Syed
School of Information
University of Michigan
Ann Arbor, Michigan
rmsyed@umich.edu

Kevyn Collins-Thompson
School of Information
University of Michigan
Ann Arbor, Michigan
kevynct@umich.edu

ABSTRACT

A growing body of information retrieval research has studied the potential of search engines as effective, scalable platforms for self-directed learning. Towards this goal, we explore document representations for retrieval that include features associated with effective learning outcomes. While prior studies have investigated different retrieval models designed for teaching, this study is the first to investigate how document-level features are associated with actual learning outcomes when users get results from a personalized learning-oriented retrieval algorithm. We also conduct what is, to our knowledge, the first crowdsourced longitudinal study of *long-term* learning retention, in which we gave a subset of users who participated in an initial learning and assessment study a delayed post-test approximately nine months later. With this data, we were able to analyze how the three retrieval conditions in the original study were associated with changes in long-term vocabulary knowledge. We found that while users who read the documents in the personalized retrieval condition had immediate learning gains comparable to the other two conditions, they had better long-term retention of more difficult vocabulary.

ACM Reference Format:
Rohail Syed and Kevyn Collins-Thompson. 2018. Exploring Document Retrieval Features Associated with Improved Short- and Long-term Vocabulary Learning Outcomes. In *CHIIR '18: 2018 Conference on Human Information Interaction & Retrieval, March 11–15, 2018, New Brunswick, NJ, USA.* ACM, New York, NY, USA, 10 pages. https://doi.org/10.1145/3176349.3176397

1 INTRODUCTION

Recent work in information retrieval has focused on models, algorithms, and evaluation methods at the intersection of general Web search with learning-oriented intents [6, 18] to investigate different dimensions of the concept of search as learning. For example, some studies have investigated and demonstrated the evident demand for using Web search engines for accomplishing learning or discovery goals [2, 7, 13]. Other studies have investigated the use of Web search engines to accomplish learning goals and possible links between search behavior and learning outcomes [1, 6, 9, 23]. Additional research also investigated effects of search behavior on learning outcomes but through more indirect measures of learning, such as classifying users as beginners or experts and observing their behaviors [10, 22].

Learning outcomes have also served as the specific basis for a retrieval objective or framework within educational applications. Prior work by Collins-Thompson and Callan on the REAP system [5] demonstrated how a system could automatically crawl, filter, curate, and retrieve a set of Web documents to accommodate learning a predefined set of words from context within an intelligent tutoring system. However, this framework did not extend to supporting a real-time search engine for finding personalized learning-oriented documents for arbitrary topics or ad-hoc queries. One of the first studies to introduce a retrieval model whose objective specifically aimed at optimizing learning outcomes was the study by Syed and Collins-Thompson [19], later extended in [20]. In that study, the authors ran a large-scale crowdsourced user study to investigate actual changes in knowledge states of participants before and after they were provided personalized documents to read [20]. They demonstrated that their personalized retrieval approach could achieve better learning gains per unit of effort compared to a commercial search engine baseline.

That work, however, did not explore which specific features in documents or document sets being retrieved were likely to help or hinder learning, and we know of little work in general on that question. Such features might include the number and density of accompanying images, the difficulty of the text, the length of paragraphs, and so on. In this work, we study an extensive set of features based on a dataset from the original study by Syed and Collins-Thompson to determine what features best predict different learning outcomes, as well as a few other important learning-related variables such as time spent reading. We also assess the long-term retention of those who took part in the original study by Syed and Collins-Thompson [20] by conducting a delayed post-test with a subset of those users.

The main contributions of this work are as follows: (1) We investigate a comprehensive set of document, document-set and user interaction features for their association with a variety of short-term and long-term learning measures on a vocabulary learning task; (2) using predictive models based on these features and outcomes, we show that even models without user-specific information are somewhat effective at predicting which documents are likely to be associated with improved learning, with user-specific features further improving model fit; (3) We conduct the first study of long-term retention in the context of Web search for learning; and (4) We investigate temporal changes in knowledge state from three stages of learning (pre-test, immediate post-test, delayed post-test) and connect these outcomes to properties of the original study conditions. Finally, we discuss the implications of our findings for further improving search-as-learning frameworks.

2 RELATED WORK

A number of prior studies have investigated different aspects of how Web search can be, and is, used for learning [2, 7, 10, 14, 22, 24]. Several large-scale query log studies have investigated how search interaction features, including queries issued, pages visited, time spent and more, varied between experts and non-experts [10, 22] and between expert and non-expert website *content* [14]. Work by Kim et al. [14] also found evidence of users exhibiting "stretch reading" behavior where they choose to read documents significantly higher than their own expected understanding level. A recent study by Verma et al. [21] also found that readability of a document showed a negative correlation with how easily users could find relevant content on the page. This suggests that certain features of Web page content could have an effect on which pages a user chooses to visit when learning, and their ability to find relevant information on that page.

Short-term learning. While such studies are useful in understanding estimated changes in a user's domain expertise, they did not directly assess actual learning outcomes of participants engaging in a learning task. There have been quite a few studies that have investigated this [1, 6, 9, 12, 20, 24]. Several studies have examined how users in largely unconstrained search environments exhibit different search behaviors, which in turn may link to changes in assessed learning outcomes [9, 12, 24]. Other studies assessed changes in knowledge state as a function of search behavior and documents that were selected or preferred by the user, e.g. via exploring intrinsically diverse results [6], scanning multiple documents first, ordering and then reading them [1], or simply providing a custom set of documents without taking query input at all from the user [20]. Furthermore, very few studies that have explicitly assessed Web search and its intersection with learning outcomes have tried to directly optimize the utility of search results for learning [5, 20]. One of the primary goals of this study is to explore how document properties, used as features in robust regression models, are associated with actual learning outcomes, and predictive of future learning outcomes as part of optimal content retrieval by search-for-learning systems.

Long-term learning. Despite the importance of long-term retention as a learning goal, few, if any, studies to our knowledge have considered search engines aimed at long-term retention of knowledge, or long-term gains in knowledge. In practice, learning is a continuous process, constantly engaged as a function of information that we observe and cognitively process [4]. While the distinction between short and long-term learning has been established for quite some time [3], its application to a search retrieval framework would be a novel and critical contribution. Recent work by Eickhoff et al. [10] investigated how users' domain expertise changes over time in a large-scale query log analysis, but did not measure actual knowledge of the users at any stage. Earlier work by Wildemuth [23] assessed how Web search tactics and behaviors changed during a nine-month span in the context of an educational course. The author investigated different search patterns and differences in actual learning outcomes at three separate temporal stages. While this offered useful insight into how search behavior may change with changes in knowledge, it did not give insight as to what properties of the documents were influencing these changes, nor did it investigate different retrieval algorithms and their possible effect on the learning changes. In this study, we conduct the first

crowdsourced longitudinal study to assess a participant's long-term retention of knowledge, based on measured learning outcomes from an earlier user study of vocabulary learning. We investigate what document and user variables may be associated with long-term changes in knowledge state and how different document retrieval algorithms may influence the strength of these changes.

3 DATASETS

To conduct our analysis, we used a dataset provided from earlier work by Syed and Collins-Thompson [20], who conducted a large-scale crowdsourced user study to evaluate the effectiveness of their retrieval models for personalized learning. They tested their approach on 10 topics, with 40 participants in each condition, yielding a total of 863 judgments after enforcing quality control filters. Participants first completed a pre-test consisting of 10 multiple-choice questions on definitions of related vocabulary keywords. They were then provided a personalized set of documents that they had to read and were finally given a post-test, identical to the pre-test.

In this study, we only consider participants who were shown different personalized sets of documents, as this allows us to compare changes in document features to changes in knowledge state. This reduced dataset contains 283 records, with each record containing data about a unique participant, including their prior and post knowledge scores for each of the 10 keywords, the time they spent in the reading section, and the set of documents they were provided (and read).

In addition to analysis on this dataset, we investigated the effect of a variety of features on robust, or long-term, learning outcomes by conducting a follow-up crowdsourced test. As we could not control which participants would return, especially since it had been nearly nine months since the original study, we did not get long-term data for all 863 participant records, though we were still able to gather a reasonable number of records. In the following section, we will first investigate the features that best predict different measures of learning outcomes along with time spent reading. We will then give an analysis of data for long-term learning outcomes and their relationship to document and user features.

4 ANALYSIS

Overall, we considered a set of document features that included features pertaining to image use, vocabulary difficulty, word count and content structure (described in Section 4.1). A complete list, including user-dependent features, can be found in Table 1. In this section we analyze the relationships between these features and a variety of measures of learning (Section 4.2). We fit and analyze models restricted to user-independent features (Section 4.3) and then with all features (Section 4.4).

4.1 Choice of Features

We chose document and user features based on various concepts investigated in earlier studies [8, 11, 16, 20, 21, 25]. Broadly, the features we chose can be grouped as follows:

1. **Image content.** Some studies have found that providing plain-text filtered documents (with images removed) improves learning outcomes [11] over the original document, possibly suggesting a negative effect of image use in Web documents on learning. However, other studies found positive

Type	Group	Feature	Description
D	Effort	*WordCount*	Total number of unigrams in the document.
D	Effort	*KeyCount*	Total number of keywords in the document.
D	Effort	*DocumentCount*	Total number of documents in the set. This feature ranges from 1 to 10.
D	Effort	*WordsPerDocument*	Ratio of *WordCount* to *DocumentCount*.
D	Effort	*DocumentAgeDifficulty*	85th percentile Age-of-Acquisition score for the document. Uses the expanded set of scores from the study by Kuperman et al. [15].
D	Effort	*WeightedWordCount*	Each unigram is assigned its corresponding "age" from the Age-of-Acquisition dataset. These scores, for each occurrence of each unigram in the document, are summed.
D	Effort	*AverageParaLength*	Average length of each paragraph in the document. Computed as count of all unigrams in all HTML <p> tags divided by total instances of <p> tags.
D	Images	*ImageCountTag*	Total instances of the HTML <img> tag that appeared in the document.
D	Images	*ImageCountManual*	Total instances of non-advertising and non-navigational images that appeared in the document. Counted manually.
D	Images	*ImageToText*	Ratio of *ImageCountTag* to *WordCount*.
D	Links	*OutboundLinks*	The count of all outbound links.
D	Keywords	*KeywordDensity*	Computed as the count of occurrences of any of the N keywords $k_1, \ldots, k_N$ divided by the count of all words (i.e. *WordCount*).
D	Keywords	*WeightedDensity*	Same as *KeywordDensity* except the denominator is the *WeightedWordCount* feature.
U+D	Keywords	*IncorrectKeysRatio*	Total occurrences of keywords that the participant got wrong in their pre-test, divided by the total occurrences of any keyword in that document.
U+D	Keywords	*IncorrectSemanticRatio*	First compute *SRel* scores: the relevance of each keyword instance in a document computed as the average Word2Vec similarity [17] of its five surrounding words (both ahead and behind). *IncorrectSemanticRatio* is the sum of all *SRel* scores for keywords the participant got wrong on the pre-test, divided by the total sum of *SRel* scores.
DS	Keywords	*LogWeightedDensity*	Same as *WeightedDensity* except that instead of simply summing the values over the set of documents, each successive document's value of *WeightedDensity* was reduced by a DCG discount factor of $\log_2(p + 1)$ where p is the rank in the set of documents.
DS	Images	*Set_ImageToText*	Set-level calculation of *ImageToText*.
DS	Effort	*Set_AvgParaLength*	Set-level calculation of *AverageParaLength*.
DS	Keywords	*Set_KeyDensity*	Set-level calculation of *KeywordDensity*.
DS	Keywords	*Set_WeightDensity*	Set-level calculation of *WeightDensity*.
U+DS	Keywords	*Set_IncorrectRatio*	Set-level calculation of *IncorrectKeysRatio*.
U+DS	Keywords	*Set_IncorrectSemsRatio*	Set-level calculation of *IncorrectSemanticRatio*.
U+DS	Keywords	*ExpectedKnowledge*	Expected knowledge computed as a personalized sigmoid function of keywords [20].
U		*PriorKnowledge*	Sum of initial correct answers to the vocabulary terms needed to be learned.

Table 1: Set of features that were considered. "U" are User features that involve prior data about the User's knowledge. "D" are Document features that require only individual document data. "DS" are Document Set features based on treating the set of documents as a single bag-of-words. The "D" features values were aggregated by summation, since learning outcomes were measured against sets of documents.

association of image use and learning, when used appropriately [16] and a positive association with the fraction of images in documents and the ability of users to find relevant content [21].

2. **Keyword content.** Prior work has found that optimizing document selection by difficulty-weighted keyword density improved multiple measures of learning outcomes [20] in a vocabulary learning task where the system determined the set of keywords that a participant had to learn. We also investigate other keyword features like the count of occurrences of keywords unknown to the user relative to all keywords.

3. **Effort.** Prior work has suggested that too much effort on the part of users can be overwhelming and, according to

Cognitive Load Theory, could hurt learning outcomes [8]. On the other hand, having "desirable difficulties" [3] has been found to improve learning outcomes. We consider effort as functions of document count, word count and reading-difficulty-weighted measures of content.

4. **Embedded links.** Several studies have found that embedded links in documents can disturb the linearity of the learning process [25] and can add extra cognitive load [8], potentially hurting learning gains.

4.2 Measures of Learning Outcomes

We now evaluate the following measures of learning outcomes, on the provided sets of $K = 10$ vocabulary questions, with Pre_k as prior knowledge of keyword k, $Post_k$ as corresponding post knowledge and r_k as vocabulary difficulty level of k:

Learning Gains (LG). As a simple measure of learning growth we compute the total instances where a participant did not know a keyword to be learned in the pre-reading test and did know the definition in the post-reading test.

$$LG = \sum_{k=1}^{K} \begin{cases} 1 & Pre_k = 0 \text{ and } Post_k = 1 \\ 0 & \text{otherwise} \end{cases}$$

Difficulty-Weighted Gains (DWG). This meausure is essentially the same as Learning Gains but we weight the learning gains of each keyword by the vocabulary difficulty level associated with it. These difficulty scores are retrieved from the expanded dataset from work by Kuperman et al. [15]. By weighting the learning gains by vocabulary difficulty, we can capture the intuition that learning more difficult words like 'luciferase' and 'eclogite' may require different features than those required for learning easier words like 'minerals' or 'soils'.

$$DWG = \sum_{k=1}^{K} r_k \begin{cases} 1 & Pre_k = 0 \text{ and } Post_k = 1 \\ 0 & \text{otherwise} \end{cases}$$

Realized Potential Gains (PG). This is a measure of the participant's actual Learning Gain relative to their maximum possible Learning Gain. Specifically, for a set of 10 vocabulary terms being tested, we have:

$$PG = \frac{LG}{10 - \sum_{k=1}^{10} Pre_k}$$

Participants who had perfect prior knowledge (10/10) were omitted from analysis as they could not have theoretically shown any improvement.

Final Knowledge (FK). This is a much simpler measure of learning outcome where we take the linear sum of the participant's final test scores, regardless of their prior performance. Specifically, we have:

$$FK = \sum_{k=1}^{K} Post_k$$

Learning Hindrance (LH). While previous measures of learning outcomes assessed positive learning outcomes, it is also important to understand features that may *hinder* learning. We consider Learning Hindrance to be the total keywords that a participant got wrong in the pre-test and got wrong again on the post-test, indicating that they were unable to learn the definition. Specifically, we have:

$$LH = \sum_{k=1}^{K} \begin{cases} 1 & Pre_k = 0 \text{ and } Post_k = 0 \\ 0 & \text{otherwise} \end{cases}$$

Total Reading Time (TR). While this is not technically a measure of learning, it is an important measure to analyze as it can help determine what document and user features influence how much or how little time people are willing to spend when engaged in a learning task. This is measured as the total time (ms) a user spent reading the set of documents they were provided.

4.3 Prediction without User Data

There are many scenarios in Web search where it may be difficult or impossible to obtain an accurate assessment of a user's prior knowledge, especially for any arbitrary topic. Thus, here we investigate document features that are completely independent of the user ("D" and "DS" type properties only) and assess how well robust regression models trained on these features can predict learning outcomes. These models could facilitate learning-oriented retrieval for situations where a Web search framework has access to document data but not to a user's prior knowledge.

In selecting the features for each model, we applied a stepwise algorithm using AIC (Akaike information criterion) to reduce the likelihood of overfitting to unnecessary features. We used min-max scaling to normalize the predictor and dependent variables in all models. To reduce the effect of any specific influential points on model fitting, we fit all the models with robust regression. We tabulate the trained models and averaged 10-fold cross-validated correlations in Table 2.

The results from Table 2 show that even without any features about the user, we can still get reasonably strong correlations between predicted learning outcomes and actual outcomes. For learning gains, the Difficulty-Weighted Gains tend to show substantially better improvement over the unweighted gains. On the other hand, the Final Knowledge state variable shows a much stronger correlation as does the Learning Hindrance variable. We visualize the trained models for Difficulty-Weighted Gains, Final Knowledge and Learning Hindrance in Figure 1.

For the selected features, all positive measures of learning showed positive weights for ImageCountManual and negative weights for ImageCountTag, suggesting that, in general, Web pages having more relevant images tend to be associated with better actual learning outcomes with the opposite being true for irrelevant images (such as ads and navigational icons), possibly due to their distracting to the user. This is consistent with existing work in this area that has suggested that having images in learning material has been found to both help and harm learning outcomes, depending on the study[8]. All measures of learning gains showed a negative relationship with the total number of links in the document, which is consistent with what we would have expected from theory (Section 4.1). However, it is not entirely clear why Final Knowledge shows a positive relationship with total links. We also observe that both unweighted and weighted learning gains measures were positively affected by weighted keyword density, at the individual document level. This is consistent with the results from [20] that found that document sets produced by greedy document-level optimization for weighted keyword density outperformed commercial baseline results in terms of learning gains. However, we also found that at the set level, the weights for weighted density were negative. This disparity may be due to the document-level features being computed as sums across all documents in the set, thus making the DocumentCount feature an implicit feature in document-level weighted density. This suggests that at the set level, keyword density should be rewarded but weighted keyword density should be penalized. The positive learning outcomes from the earlier study [20] could be attributed to the fact that set-level weighted density was also strongly negatively correlated to features like ImageCountTag and OutboundLinks, so that optimizing towards weighted density could have indirectly brought out higher quality documents.

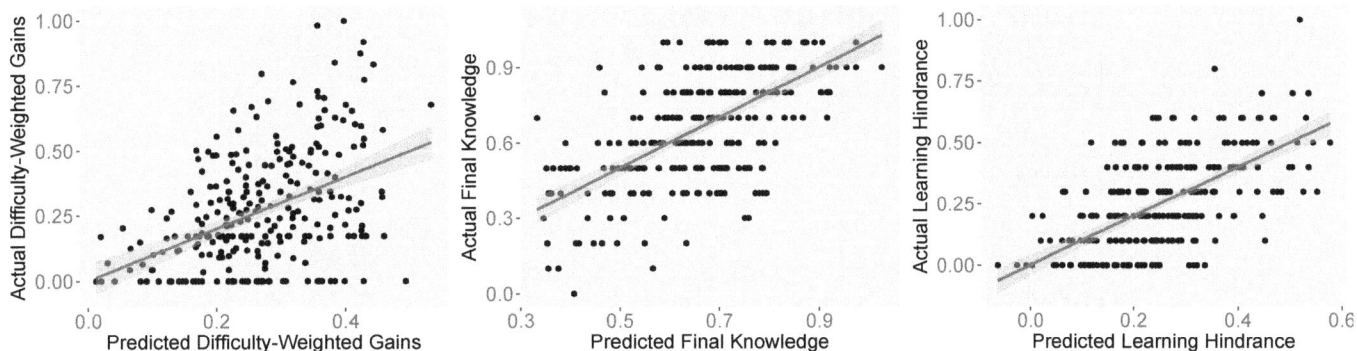

Figure 1: Predicted and actual learning measures trained on non-user features.

Feature	LG	DWG	PG	FK	LH	TR
WordCount		0.4379	3.6121		-0.5535	-2.8926
WeightedWordCount			-3.5873			2.3241
AverageParaLength			-0.2336	-0.2755	0.3486	
ImageCountManual	0.2904	0.3224	0.5441	0.2996	-0.2738	0.1544
OutboundLinks	-0.2394	-0.3990		0.2681	-0.1498	0.3157
KeywordDensity	-2.4830	-1.9237	-1.9809			
WeightedDensity	1.7599	1.8847	2.1748			
DocumentAgeDifficulty		0.3747	-0.2834	-0.2651	0.3308	
ImageToText						
ImageCountTag	-0.3068	-0.2283	-0.6259	-0.2909	0.2688	0.1498
KeyCount		-0.4071				
LogWeightedDensity	0.5371					
DocumentCount	0.4221					0.0864
WordsPerDoc					0.4481	
Set_AvgParaLength	0.1492	0.1832	0.2393	0.1142	-0.1181	0.2591
Set_ImageToText				-0.2189	0.1909	-0.2600
Set_KeyDensity	1.5808	2.0079	1.6829	-0.3255	0.2626	
Set_WeightDensity	-1.5624	-1.8801	-2.1677			
Performance	**LG**	**DWG**	**PG**	**FK**	**LH**	**TR**
Correlation (model prediction vs actual)	0.3296	0.3611	0.3436	0.5810	0.6117	0.2376

Table 2: Trained normalized features for different dependent variables. Values for corresponding features are learned coefficients in the robust regression model. LG = Learning Gains; DWG = Difficulty-Weighted Gains; PG = Potential Gains; FK = Final Knowledge; LH = Learning Hindrance; TR = Total Reading Time (ms).

We find a similar tradeoff when it comes to average paragraph length, with the set-level average (micro-averaged across documents) being positively correlated with all measures of learning, suggesting less segmentation of the text can be an indication of higher-quality content for learning. However, we also note that the document-level average showed the opposite trend for Potential Gains and Final Knowledge, possibly suggesting that average paragraph lengths should be longer but there should be fewer documents overall.

Finally, we note that the models are not simply capturing the intuition that having more documents results in stronger gains. The "DS" set-level features are mostly ratio features which are invariant to proportional increases in the amount of content but

are dependent on the *relative* changes of different types of content. Adding or removing documents to a set would give no guarantee of increasing or decreasing these values (e.g. Set_AvgParaLength had nearly 0 correlation with DocumentCount). If we excluded all the "DS" features, the new correlated strength decreased by about 16.3% averaged across the six models and if we consider *only* DocumentCount as a feature, the drop is substantially higher at 38.9%, suggesting that the models explain more than just exposure to more content is associated with higher learning outcomes.

4.4 Predicting with User Data

We have seen that in the absence of user-dependent features, we were able to train robust regression models on multiple measures

Feature	LG	DWG	PG	FK	LH	TR
WordCount						-2.5116
WeightedWordCount						1.8478
AverageParaLength	-0.1523				0.1066	
ImageCountManual	0.3077	0.3867	0.5178	0.2353	-0.2154	
OutboundLinks						
IncorrectSemanticRatio			0.7476			0.6536
KeywordDensity	-0.4643	-0.5915	-2.2101	-0.5441	0.3250	-0.2334
WeightedDensity			2.2856			
DocumentAgeDifficulty			-0.4410			
ImageToText						
IncorrectKeyRatio	0.3443	0.3578		0.3933	-0.2410	-0.5565
ImageCountTag	-0.1759	-0.2824	-0.5097	-0.1426	0.1231	0.2191
KeyCount						0.3497
LogWeightedDensity	0.3261	0.4702		0.3570	-0.2283	
DocumentCount						0.2834
WordsPerDoc						
ExpectedKnowledge	-0.1199			-0.1757	0.0839	-0.2341
Set_AvgParaLength	0.1466			0.1098	-0.1026	0.2404
Set_ImageToText	-0.2745	-0.1738	-0.3182	-0.2347	0.1921	-0.1901
Set_KeyDensity		1.4125	1.3909			
Set_WeightDensity		-1.4657	-1.7781			
Set_IncorrectRatio	-0.6198	-0.2546	-0.4914	-0.6803	0.4338	
Set_IncorrectSemsRatio	0.4063			0.4612	-0.2844	
PriorKnowledge	-0.3694	-0.3889	0.3289	0.7584	-0.6414	0.3565
Performance	**LG**	**DWG**	**PG**	**FK**	**LH**	**TR**
Correlation (model prediction vs actual)	0.4571	0.5091	0.3908	0.7156	0.7499	0.2650
Robust correlation with PriorKnowledge	0.3744	0.3397	0.2731	0.6657	0.7361	-0.0563

Table 3: Trained normalized features for different dependent variables (considering *all* possible features). Values for corresponding features are learned coefficients in the robust regression model.

of learning, resulting in observed trends that were commensurate with findings from existing literature. Now we attempt to further augment the power of these results by including all the features from Table 1 in our model. Repeating the same feature selection and model fitting process as before, we have the results in Table 3.

We first note that including all features improved the cross-validated correlations for all measures of learning, and for some quite substantially. This is not unexpected, given that we are adding signals which have a naturally strong correlation to most measures of learning already. For example, regardless of other properties, the user's prior knowledge could be expected to have a strong negative correlation with Learning Gains since users with higher prior knowledge naturally have less opportunities for improvement. Indeed, we trained the set of six learning measures against a robust model containing *only* PriorKnowledge as a predictor and found substantially strong correlations from that alone (last row of Table 3). However, training against the full set of features did show significant improvement in predicting Learning Gains, Difficulty-Weighted Gains, Potential Gains and especially Total Reading, which had almost no correlation with PriorKnowledge.

As such, there are definitely advantages to incorporating both user features and document features for better results.

Using all features, we see similar trends to those we saw before: (1) all measures of learning outcomes had positive coefficients for the count of relevant images, and those measures that had count of all images as a significant feature had negative weights; (2) weighted keyword density again shows conflicting association with learning outcomes at the set level vs. the sum of document level; (3) we see a similar effect that we discussed earlier with average paragraph lengths as well as with total embedded links.

However, we also notice some new effects and features. First, the ImageToText ratio feature was in the original models, but was not significant for most of the features. In this set of all features, the set-level ImageToText feature has significant negative weight for *all* measures of learning, suggesting that in general, while more images might be helpful, there needs to be an overall balance between how many images there are per unit of text. Second, the ratio of counts of unknown keywords to all keywords is a positive predictor of better learning outcomes at the document level. However, it shows the opposite trend at the set level, either suggesting that in aggregate a set of documents should *not* have stronger coverage of unknown keywords (that need to be learned). The reasons for this require further study.

In aggregate, this enhanced set of features has given us trained models that do show expected improvements over the document-features-only models and much of the same observations remain valid in these new models as well. While Syed and Collins-Thompson [20] demonstrated strong improvements in learning efficiency (learning gains per unit of effort), the models introduced here may lead to improvements in learning effectiveness (learning gains or final knowledge state) or strong reductions in learning hindrance.

5 LONG-TERM RETENTION

We now describe a crowdsourced longitudinal study of long-term retention, or *robust learning*, in which a subset of users who participated in an initial learning and assessment study also completed a delayed post-test nine months later, in order to study how much of their original word learning they had retained over time.

5.1 Study design

Our experiment used the same platform, Crowdflower, as the study by Syed and Collins-Thompson [20], as well as the original crowd response dataset from that study. Our study design included three pages of multiple-choice question tests for three topics out of the ten total that were originally tested. Afterwards, participants completed a Likert-scale survey of the perceived importance of various "learning factors" [1] on learning outcomes.

We limited this delayed post-reading assessment to only three topics to prevent participants from having to take too many tests and possibly having fatigue influence the results. We retained explicit quality control measures by adding gold standard test questions in each of the three tests that participants had to pass and we randomized the order in which the assessments appeared. Unfortunately, while the Crowdflower platform allows us to see the unique worker's ids after an experiment has terminated, they do not allow us to have this information during the experiment, nor do they allow us to specifically request certain workers. As such, we had to rely on chance that we would get repeat participants and further on chance that some of those repeat participants would have participated in one of the three selected topics. To maximize the number of data points we could get, we chose the three topics that had the lowest number of unique participants[1].

In the original study [20], we gathered a total of 1200 data points (judgments). In this study, we accumulated a total of 600 judgments from the crowd, within which we found 36 unique repeat participants who had taken part in the original study (out of a maximum of 116 from the set of three topics we chose) and there were 83 unique (participant, topic) tuples that matched the original dataset. After filtering out those who did not answer all the gold standard test questions correctly, we ended up with 81 unique tuples. We performed the subsequent analysis on this dataset, matched against the original dataset. For notation purposes, we consider "pre-test" to be the pre-reading test results from the original study, "post-test" to be the post-reading test results from the original study and "delayed-test" to be the test results from the (later) crowdsourced study described here.

Difficulty Split	Lower Difficulty	Higher Difficulty	p-val
Robust Gains (Long-term)	1.025	1.000	0.867
Retained Gains	0.457	0.765	0.002
Retained Knowledge	2.395	2.296	0.733
Net Retained Knowledge	1.815	1.160	0.067
Learning Prior	2.753	2.469	0.093
Learning Gains (Short-term)	0.679	1.296	<.001

Table 4: Averages for the two splits for each robust measure along with two short-term measures indicates better opportunity for gains in difficult terms.

Measure	Web	NP	P	p-val
Robust Gains	1.960	2.000	2.136	0.809
Retained Gains	1.280	1.059	1.409	0.856
Retained Knowledge	4.440	4.706	4.955	0.706
Net Retained Knowledge	2.520	2.941	3.545	0.439
Post-Test	6.360	6.471	6.364	0.966
Delayed-Test	5.560	6.118	6.091	0.764

Table 5: Averages of short- and long-term knowledge state measures, broken down by retrieval models.

5.2 Robust learning outcomes

We consider the following measures of robust, or long-term, learning outcomes: (1) robust learning gains; (2) robust retention of learning gains; (3) robust retention of post-test knowledge and (4) robust change in post-test knowledge[2]. We define these measures as follows:

(1) **Robust Learning Gains.** Computed as the sum of keywords that a participant did not know in the pre-test and did know in the delayed-test.

(2) **Retained Gains.** Computed as the sum of keywords a participant learned (as defined by Learning Gains in Section 4) and that they still knew in the delayed-test.

(3) **Retained Knowledge.** Computed as the sum of keywords that a participant did get correct in the post-test and still got correct in the delayed-test.

(4) **Net Retained Knowledge.** Computed as signed sum of retentions in post-test knowledge (retention is positive if participant got the keyword correct in post-test and again in delayed-test; retention is negative if participant got the keyword correct in post-test and wrong in delayed-test).

5.2.1 Variation by Keyword Difficulty. We first analyze how the average robust measures compare when considering the averages of the lowest-difficulty keywords only versus the averages of the highest-difficulty keywords only. We split the set of ten keywords into sets of five by a median split on their Age-of-Acquisition scores [15]. We then compute each of the robust measures as well as the pre-test scores on each of the sets and perform a Kruskal-Wallis test to test for significance. The results are presented in Table 4.

---

[1]This increased the likelihood of getting more complete sets of (participant, topic) tuples across all topics.

[2]In this section, *robust* learning refers to participant learning that is retained over the long term, not to be confused with the robust regression estimation method used in our predictive models.

We find that of the four robust measures, Retained Gains and Net Retained Knowledge showed significant differences in means: (lower mean = 0.457, higher mean = 0.765, p=.002) and (lower mean = 1.815, higher mean = 1.160, p=.067)[3] respectively. This suggests that in general, of the keywords participants were able to learn and remember, more of these were likely to be difficult ones. On the other hand, the opposite trend with Net Retained Knowledge suggests that overall participants were also more likely to *forget* the meanings of more difficult keywords. This shows an interesting balance where participants who retained short-term learning gains tended to retain acquired knowledge of more difficult terms better. However, in cases where they forgot newly-learned terms, they tended to lose acquired knowledge more with difficult terms as well. In aggregate, there appears to be more forgetting than retaining with difficult terms, suggesting that participants with better post-test knowledge of easier terms will likely show a better net retention of that knowledge even after a considerable time delay.

Another interesting finding is that the Robust Gains split was unaffected by difficulty but the short-term learning gains were strongly improved by higher difficulty (almost twice as much). We also observe that the averages of these measures suggest a negative relationship (i.e. lower short-term gains in easier terms led to better long-term gains of easier terms and vice versa for difficult terms). This may be explained by the fact that more difficult keywords are likely those that are more unfamiliar and novel to the learner and this novelty may facilitate better immediate recall but not long-term retention. Conversely, learning unknown but easier keywords may be less likely to cause learning gains as just a function of recall.

Related to the concept of *desirable difficulties* [3], it is possible that the easier keywords that were unknown to the participant were those that were difficult to learn but not so much that they inhibited long-term retention. This is supported by the Net Retained Knowledge results, where easier keywords showed substantially better net change in delayed-test knowledge. These results suggests that in personalizing document selection, it is important to incorporate the difficulty of unknown words.

5.2.2 Variation by Retrieval algorithm.

We now analyze whether there were differences in robust learning outcomes depending on the search model a user was assigned in the original study. There were three possible models: (1) commercial search engine (**Web**); (2) non-personalized retrieval (**NP**) and (3) personalized retrieval (**P**). In our long-term dataset, each condition had roughly similar, but small, sample sizes (n=25, n=34, n=22) respectively. The **NP** and **P** algorithms exclusively considered a measure of difficulty-weighted keyword density as the document selection criteria, with **P** also incorporating information about the participants' prior knowledge and **NP** assuming zero prior knowledge for all participants. Details on these algorithms are provided in the original study [20].

We found that omnibus Kruskal-Wallis tests between these three models showed no significant differences for each of the four robust measures (Table 5), suggesting that in aggregate the choice of retrieval model didn't have significant impact on robust learning outcomes. However, if we split these features again by difficulty, we find some significant differences. In particular, both Robust Gains and Retained Gains showed significant differences (p<.05) when comparing only **Web** and **P** on higher difficulty keywords (Figure 3). In both cases, **P** outperformed **Web** (by 85% and 92% respectively),

---

[3]This significance was strengthened to p<.05 when normalizing by post-test knowledge

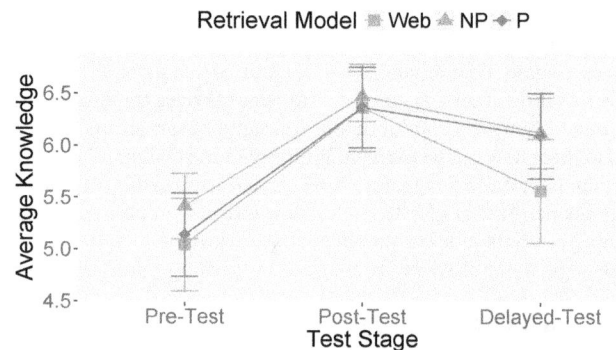

Figure 2: **Average changes in knowledge state (number of keywords correct) over three periods of assessment for each retrieval model.**

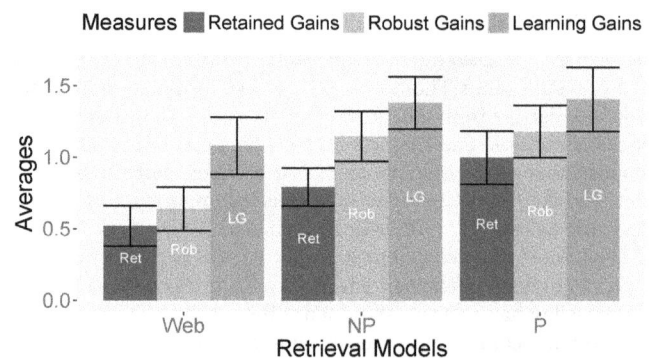

Figure 3: **For higher-difficulty keywords, the Personalized model (P) led to significantly better long-term retention of learned keywords than the baseline Web model.**

suggesting that the personalized algorithm introduced in [20] produced significantly better long-term improvements in knowledge of more difficult terms, including better retention of short-term gains on such terms.

We also observe some interesting variations in measures of final knowledge state. In particular, observe in Table 5 that the post-test final knowledge state showed very small differences across each of the models, suggesting that regardless of the retrieval model, the final knowledge state mostly ended up the same. However, in the delayed-test knowledge state, while there was consistent evidence of forgetting, this effect was distinctly stronger in **Web**, which was the commercial search baseline (Figure 2). This suggests that the other two models, proposed in [20] actually did demonstrate not just evidence of short-term improvements but very possibly evidence of long-term improvement as well.

Overall, we find that the personalized document retrieval model (Model **P**) showed substantially better ability compared to a commercial Web search model (Model **Web**) to help participants achieve long-term understanding of more difficult keywords and retain short-term learning gains of such keywords as well. We further find that, though not significant, the commercial model produced relatively stronger overall forgetting from post-test to delayed-test.

Feature	Robust Gains			Net Retained Knowledge			Retained Gains		
	Lower	Upper	Corr	Lower	Upper	Corr	Lower	Upper	Corr
ImageCountManual	2.912e+01	2.919e+01	-.0875	**3.265e+01**	**2.623e+01**[*]	-.1901·	2.811e+01	2.972e+01	-.0595
OutboundLinks	1.016e+03	9.165e+02	-.0699	**7.299e+02**	**1.15e+03**[*]	**.2777**[*]	9.234e+02	9.765e+02	.1015
IncorrectSemanticRatio	**3.138e+00**	**4.614e+00**†	**.3930**!	**4.545e+00**	**3.531e+00**·	**-.3292**†	**3.21e+00**	**4.409e+00**[*]	**.4114**!
KeywordDensity	4.044e-01	4.128e-01	.0923	**4.455e-01**	**3.788e-01**[*]	-.1363	3.832e-01	4.23e-01	.0257
WeightedDensity	5.67e-02	5.801e-02	.0949	**6.3e-02**	**5.28e-02**[*]	-.1506	5.375e-02	5.942e-02	.0262
IncorrectKeyRatio	**3.214e+00**	**4.723e+00**†	**.3937**!	**4.632e+00**	**3.633e+00**·	**-.3154**†	**3.288e+00**	**4.513e+00**[*]	**.4032**!
KeyCount	5.541e+02	5.191e+02	-.1047	**5.81e+02**	**4.941e+02**·	**-.2731**[*]	5.32e+02	5.347e+02	.0840
LogWeightedDensity	2.993e-02	3.065e-02	.0870	**3.353e-02**	**2.766e-02**†	-.1983·	2.858e-02	3.128e-02	-.0079
ExpectedKnowledge	**9.48e+00**	**9.276e+00**[*]	-.1915·	9.4e+00	9.329e+00	-.1952·	**9.481e+00**	**9.298e+00**·	.0093
Set_KeyDensity	3.945e-02	4.104e-02	.0310	**4.647e-02**	**3.525e-02**†	**-.3245**†	3.89e-02	4.116e-02	-.0631
Set_WeightDensity	5.456e-03	5.667e-03	.0286	**6.494e-03**	**4.809e-03**†	**-.3195**†	5.409e-03	5.668e-03	-.0696
Set_IncorrectRatio	**3.445e-01**	**5.035e-01**[*]	**.3200**†	**5.169e-01**	**3.694e-01**[*]	**-.4056**!	3.687e-01	4.727e-01	**.3151**†
Set_IncorrectSemsRatio	**3.375e-01**	**4.974e-01**[*]	**.3324**†	**5.112e-01**	**3.623e-01**[*]	**-.4074**!	3.667e-01	4.639e-01	**.3079**†
PriorKnowledge	**6.147e+00**	**4.553e+00**!	-.5270!	**4.378e+00**	**5.932e+00**!	**.4689**!	**5.964e+00**	**4.83e+00**!	**-.4452**!
Survey Features									
Novelty	**3.618e+00**	**4e+00**[*]	.0421	**4.081e+00**	**3.636e+00**[*]	-.0797	**3.571e+00**	**3.981e+00**·	.0494
	Signif. codes: 0 '!' 0.001 '†' 0.01 '*' 0.05 '·' 0.1 ' ' 1								

Table 6: For each dependent variable (DV), "Lower" and "Upper" columns contain mean values for different features when considering either the subset of less than median of the DV or above median respectively. The third column "Corr" is the Pearson's correlation between each feature and each DV. Bold values are significant features at particular significance levels.

5.2.3 Analysis of median split. In this section, we consider how each measure of robust learning differs, on average, with each of the features from Table 1 when considering two subsets of data, split on the median value of the corresponding robust measure. For space reasons, we only included features that showed significant differences or significant correlation. We tabulate the results in Table 6 and include the averages, the overall correlation of the feature with the measure, and the associated significance levels of both the splits and the correlations.

The first observation we make from these findings is that both Robust gains and Retained gains exclusively only showed significant differences on measures pertaining to the user's prior knowledge. This suggests that while short-term learning gains may be influenced by user-independent document features, neither long-term gains nor retention of short-term gains seem to be affected similarly. However, unlike what we saw in Section 4, here we note that both the set-level and sum of document-level features show the same, strong positive sign, suggesting that for robust learning gains and retention of short-term gains, we should optimize strongly towards documents with better coverage of unknown keywords relative to known keywords. We also did find an intuitively strong correlation between total keywords and total words (r=.835, n=283), suggesting that the keyword density of unknown keywords will also likely be a factor positively influencing robust learning outcomes.

Conversely, for Net Retained Knowledge we found a more interesting picture. It was interesting to find that all measures of unknown keyword ratios showed negative but relatively weaker correlations. This makes sense when we consider that Net Retained Knowledge measures not just the retention of previously unknown words but also retention of words that were already known at the time of the pre-test. As such, giving preference to more unknown keywords gave less focus to the participants reinforcing keywords

that they may have known only partially at the time, possibly leading to this negative correlation.

We also find that the overall keyword and weighted keyword density measures showed significant and negative correlations at both the document-level and set-level. This suggests that, contrary to what we observed in Section 4, robust retention of knowledge is hurt by providing too many units of knowledge (instances of keyword) in a small amount of text. We also find that Net Retained Knowledge was improved by pages that had more embedded links and those with a lower count of relevant images. This illustrates a tradeoff: whereas these directional features had a negative relationship to short-term learning, they have a positive relationship to long-term retention.

We observe that participants who reported higher ratings for content novelty as an important feature for learning showed significantly better Robust Gains and Retained Gains, suggesting that those who believe more strongly in the importance of content novelty also tend to achieve better Robust Gains and Retained Gains.

6 DISCUSSION

We now discuss implications and extensions of our work as it relates to search support of both short- and long-term learning.

Short-term learning. We found that short-term measures of vocabulary learning gains are typically improved by: (1) having a lower set-level coverage of unknown keywords versus all keywords; (2) having more contextually relevant images while not having too many total images relative to total word count and (3) having a higher set-level keyword density. We found that we could train robust regression models for predicting learning gains reasonably well with a set of document, user and document-set features.

Long-term learning. Due to the nature of the crowd platform used in our experiments, we could not guarantee that we would get return participants from the original study. However, it turned out that from 600 original responses, we got 81 return participants, as represented by unique (participant ID, topic) tuples that matched against the original dataset. We found evidence that participants who were provided documents chosen exclusively by personalized difficulty-weighted keyword density in the original study showed almost 92% higher Retained Gains of difficult keywords after a nine-month delay compared to those who got documents from a commercial Web search engine.

IR for Learning. These results extend the findings from the original study [20] that optimizing purely for difficulty-weighted density improves learning outcomes not only in the short term, but also in the long term. This provides strong support for the utility of efficient, robust document retrieval models to support personalized vocabulary learning at scale.

We also consider some of the limitations of this study. In the study that produced the initial dataset, the authors assumed that a participant's knowledge of a particular term may be modeled as a binary variable (1 if answered correctly and 0 otherwise). More refined and continuous measures of learning would likely give us more accurate knowledge levels that could result in better fitted models. In the robust learning study, we note that the results are based on a relatively small sample size due to the nature of the delayed post-test design. In future work we plan to consider other possible platforms that may be more amenable to more refined longitudinal analysis with a larger study population.

7 CONCLUSION

This study analyzed how features of documents and user knowledge related to multiple types of learning outcomes, both short-term and long-term, on a contextual vocabulary learning task. We also presented trained regression models for a variety of learning outcome measures that allowed us to analyze the relative importance of document and user features in predicting learning and retention. We primarily focused on features that could be automatically and quickly computed, to enable these models to be applied at scale in a large variety of possible applications. We also provided a second set of models, specifically trained on non-user features to accommodate realistic scenarios where a user's prior knowledge of an arbitrary topic is not known.

Beyond analyzing short-term learning outcomes, we were able to analyze long-term learning outcomes for a subset of users from the original study who completed a delayed post-test approximately nine months after the initial post-test. Due to the smaller sample size of this subset, we did not provide trained models but we did provide median split analysis of long-term learning outcomes against each feature of the full feature set. Finally, we investigated how different retrieval models were associated with changes to a user's vocabulary knowledge state in the immediate and delayed test stages and found evidence that the personalized retrieval model introduced in [20] provided documents that resulted in almost double the long-term learning gains for higher-difficulty terms compared to corresponding results for a commercial search baseline.

Acknowledgements. We thank the anonymous reviewers for their comments. This work was supported in part by the Michigan Institute for Data Science (MIDAS), and by the Institute of Education Sciences, U.S. Department of Education, through Grant R305A140647 to the University of Michigan. The opinions expressed are those of the authors and do not represent views of the Institute or the U.S. Department of Education.

REFERENCES

[1] Mustafa Abualsaud. 2017. *Learning Factors and Determining Document-level Satisfaction In Search-as-Learning.* Master's thesis. University of Waterloo.

[2] Peter Bailey, Liwei Chen, Scott Grosenick, Li Jiang, Yan Li, Paul Reinholdtsen, Charles Salada, Haidong Wang, and Sandy Wong. 2012. User task understanding: a web search engine perspective. In *NII Shonan Meeting on Whole-Session Evaluation of Interactive Information Retrieval Systems, Kanagawa, Japan.*

[3] Elizabeth Ligon Bjork, Jeri L Little, and Benjamin C Storm. 2014. Multiple-choice testing as a desirable difficulty in the classroom. *Journal of Applied Research in Memory and Cognition* 3, 3 (2014), 165–170.

[4] Bertram C Brookes. 1980. The foundations of information science Part I. Philosophical aspects. *Journal of Information Science* 2, 3-4 (1980), 125–133.

[5] Kevyn Collins-Thompson and Jamie Callan. 2004. Information Retrieval for Language Tutoring: An Overview of the REAP Project. In *Proceedings of the 27th Annual International ACM SIGIR Conference on Research and Development in Information Retrieval (SIGIR '04).* ACM, New York, NY, USA, 544–545.

[6] Kevyn Collins-Thompson, Soo Young Rieh, Carl C. Haynes, and Rohail Syed. 2016. Assessing Learning Outcomes in Web Search: A Comparison of Tasks and Query Strategies. In *Proceedings of the 2016 ACM on Conference on Human Information Interaction and Retrieval (CHIIR '16).* ACM, New York, NY, USA, 163–172.

[7] Cathy De Rosa. 2006. College students' perceptions of libraries and information resources: A report to the OCLC membership. OCLC.

[8] Diana DeStefano and Jo-Anne LeFevre. 2007. Cognitive load in hypertext reading: A review. *Computers in Human Behavior* 23, 3 (2007), 1616–1641.

[9] Geoffrey B Duggan and Stephen J Payne. 2008. Knowledge in the head and on the web: Using topic expertise to aid search. In *Proceedings of the SIGCHI Conference on Human Factors in Computing Systems.* ACM, 39–48.

[10] Carsten Eickhoff, Jaime Teevan, Ryen White, and Susan Dumais. 2014. Lessons from the Journey: A Query Log Analysis of Within-session Learning. In *Proceedings of the 7th ACM International Conference on Web Search and Data Mining (WSDM '14).* ACM, New York, NY, USA, 223–232.

[11] Luanne Freund, Rick Kopak, and Heather O'Brien. 2016. The effects of textual environment on reading comprehension: Implications for searching as learning. *Journal of Information Science* 42, 1 (2016), 79–93.

[12] Bernard J Jansen, Danielle Booth, and Brian Smith. 2009. Using the taxonomy of cognitive learning to model online searching. *Information Processing & Management* 45, 6 (2009), 643–663.

[13] Terry Judd and Gregor Kennedy. 2010. A five-year study of on-campus Internet use by undergraduate biomedical students. *Computers & Education* 55, 4 (2010), 1564–1571.

[14] Jin Young Kim, Kevyn Collins-Thompson, Paul N. Bennett, and Susan T. Dumais. 2012. Characterizing Web Content, User Interests, and Search Behavior by Reading Level and Topic. In *Proceedings of the Fifth ACM International Conference on Web Search and Data Mining (WSDM '12).* ACM, New York, NY, USA, 213–222.

[15] Victor Kuperman, Hans Stadthagen-Gonzalez, and Marc Brysbaert. 2012. Age-of-acquisition ratings for 30,000 English words. *Behavior Research Methods* 44, 4 (2012), 978–990.

[16] Richard E Mayer. 1997. Multimedia learning: Are we asking the right questions? *Educational Psychologist* 32, 1 (1997), 1–19.

[17] Tomas Mikolov, Kai Chen, Greg Corrado, and Jeffrey Dean. 2013. Efficient estimation of word representations in vector space. *arXiv preprint arXiv:1301.3781* (2013).

[18] Soo Young Rieh, Kevyn Collins-Thompson, Preben Hansen, and Hye-Jung Lee. 2016. Towards searching as a learning process: A review of current perspectives and future directions. *Journal of Information Science* 42, 1 (2016), 19–34.

[19] Rohail Syed and Kevyn Collins-Thompson. 2017. Optimizing search results for human learning goals. *Information Retrieval Journal* (2017), 1–18.

[20] Rohail Syed and Kevyn Collins-Thompson. 2017. Retrieval algorithms optimized for human learning. In *Proceedings of the 40th International ACM SIGIR Conference on Research and Development in Information Retrieval.* ACM, 555–564.

[21] Manisha Verma, Emine Yilmaz, and Nick Craswell. 2016. On Obtaining Effort Based Judgements for Information Retrieval. In *Proceedings of the Ninth ACM International Conference on Web Search and Data Mining.* ACM, 277–286.

[22] Ryen W White, Susan T Dumais, and Jaime Teevan. 2009. Characterizing the influence of domain expertise on web search behavior. In *Proceedings of the Second ACM International Conference on Web Search and Data Mining.* ACM, 132–141.

[23] Barbara M Wildemuth. 2004. The effects of domain knowledge on search tactic formulation. *Journal of the American Society for Information Science and Technology* 55, 3 (2004), 246–258.

[24] Wan-Ching Wu, Diane Kelly, Ashlee Edwards, and Jaime Arguello. 2012. Grannies, tanning beds, tattoos and NASCAR: Evaluation of search tasks with varying levels of cognitive complexity. In *Proceedings of the 4th Information Interaction in Context Symposium.* ACM, 254–257.

[25] Joerg Zumbach and Maryam Mohraz. 2008. Cognitive load in hypermedia reading comprehension: Influence of text type and linearity. *Computers in Human Behavior* 24, 3 (2008), 875–887.

Switching Languages in Online Searching: A Qualitative Study of Web Users' Code-Switching Search Behaviors*

Full Paper[†]

Jieyu Wang
Department of Information Systems
University of Maryland, Baltimore County
U.S.A.
wajieyu1@umbc.edu

Anita Komlodi
Department of Information Systems
University of Maryland, Baltimore County
U.S.A.
komlodi@umbc.edu

ABSTRACT

The availability [1]of information in many languages on the Web allows multilingual searchers to search in multiple languages at the same time. Few studies have examined how multilingual web users seek information in two or more languages online, specifically how they switch languages in order to get satisfying search results. This research investigates native Chinese web users' code-switching (Chinese-English) search behaviors in their information seeking process through diary studies interviews. Results indicate that they usually switch languages when they need translation, search for domain knowledge, news and entertainment information, and academic resources, go online shopping, seek personal health information, and need social networking. Findings highlight when the participants need prompt information, they search in Chinese in order to get an immediate understanding. They seek information in English for better resources, which can offer them appropriate information and help them search effectively. We also find that these multilingual users use situational code-switching when the search tasks require them to switch languages in order to get effective and sufficient search results. The role of each language is different in the situational code-switching. When web users switch languages due to emotional or attitude changes associated with complex social or cultural context, they use metaphorical code-switching in order to get satisfying search results. The study aims to provide implications for website design concerning multilingual web users' code-switching search strategies, habits, and needs.

CCS CONCEPTS

•**Information systems**→ **Information retrieval**; *Specialized information retrieval* → Multilingual and cross-lingual retrieval

CHIIR'18, March 11-15, 2018, New Brunswick, NJ, USA.
© 2018 Association of Computing Machinery.
ACM ISBN 978-1-4503-4925-3/18/03...$15.00.
DOI: https://doi.org/10.1145/3176349.3176396

KEYWORDS

Situational and metaphorical code-switching; information seeking behaviors; culture; socio-linguistics; web information accessibility

1 INTRODUCTION

A large number of the potential users of the Internet are multilingual. Overall, only 40% of the world population is monolingual, whereas 60% of the world population is bilingual, trilingual or multilingual [11]. A European Commission survey suggested that 56% of the respondents speak two languages in Europe [11]. According to the U.S. Census Bureau, 18% of the population is bilingual or multilingual in the United States [25]. In this study we focused on Chinese native searchers who search in English. Though it is hard to investigate how many non-native English web users use English websites (L2 users), it was estimated there were over 200 million Chinese users who use English on the Internet [13].

Code-switching refers to the switching of languages during conversation. It was defined as "an individual's use of two or more language varieties in the same speech event or exchange" [29]. Code-switching phenomena have been studied by social scientists for decades. Researchers have defined and analyzed code-switching in different social contexts [9, 22, 4, 29]. Discourse-related code-switching between one's native languages and second/foreign languages as one dominant type of code-switching has been extensively studied in sociolinguistics [24, 20, 28]. However, little research has been done to study how users with multilingual backgrounds search for information by code-switching between their native languages and second/foreign languages in order to get satisfying results.

In this study we investigate Chinese native speaker web users' code-switching search behaviors between their native Chinese language and their English foreign language when they search online. This work explores when, how, and why multilingual web users switch languages when they search for information and the roles of the two languages they use.

2 RELATED WORK

Our research focuses on multilingual web users' code-switching information seeking behaviors when they seek information online and aims to find out the functions of these code-switching in their online searching and the impact of factors such as web accessibility, language proficiency and translation, and cultural elements on multilingual web users' code-switching behaviors.

2.1 Code-Switching in Socio-Linguistics

Code-switching is one of the most important concepts in the social-linguistic field. "Code-switching can be defined as an individual's use of two or more language varieties in the same speech event or exchange" [29]. Blom and Gumperz[6] introduced the definition of situational switching and metaphorical switching. Situational code-switching happens when there are "clear changes in the participants' definition of each other's rights and obligation" [6]. Alfonzetti[3] in her article mentioned one example of situational code-switching. One speaker talked about the topic about recent politics by using the language of Standard Italian. Then she changed her topic by using the language of Sicilian as the hint of topic change. Researchers considered this type of code-switching as "code selection or language choice" [29]. This concept can also be applied into information retrieval. When users search for information online in Chinese for a specific topic and then switch to English due to their change of ideas and this behavior results in situational changes, we consider this is a situational code-switching search behavior. In this case, each search language has its own role and expected search results.

Metaphorical code-switching "is a change in language that does not signal a change in the definition of the fundamental speech event" [29]. Moreover, its "message elements are tied by syntactic and semantic relations equivalent to those that join passages in a single language, the relationship of language usage to social context is much more complex" [9]. It is a result of a change in attitudes and norms associated with a specific language. For example, family members will talk about school or work stuff in a high prestige language during dinner time. One who is working in his company will prefer to use the high prestige language to communicate with peers, while he would switch to a low prestige language while talking about his family issues [10]

2.2 Code-Switching in Online Interactions

Only a few researchers have studied multilingual web users' code-switching behaviors online. For instance, Kötter[14] has studied German-English code-switching phenomena in an online environment. He analyzed 29 language students' code-switching discourses which were presented on MOO, an online learning website. These language students were from a German university and a North American university. The German students were learning English and the US students were learning English. The researcher analyzed electronic transcripts of eight meetings between the German and American teams and the students' questionnaire data. They found that learners on MOO requested more clarification, explanation and reformulation from their language partners than what the learners did in other face-to-face discourse studies. Results revealed different ways and reasons that these student switched languages. When they encountered difficult words in the language they were learning during their

communication, the American students preferred their German partners' translation rather than their German partners paraphrasing in German. The German students preferred to request their American partners to paraphrase the difficult words or repeat the words.

Bilingual postings on social media can also be classified as code-switching [17]. Multilingual web users switched languages to display and better represent their identities and to limit their audience by languages. Code-switching, or using non-native languages on Facebook were even considered to be presumptuous because these actions showed that their non-native language proficiency was higher than others'.

Facebook users with multilingual backgrounds also switch codes by posting bilingual/multilingual posts and comments on the website [26]. Through observing 83 active Facebook users' status updates and interviewing 10 users with multi-lingual backgrounds, the researchers found that audience, locality and context were three important factors that impacted users' language selections. Even though Facebook offered translational functions for users' posts and comments, multilingual users still tried to use their native languages to limit their audience to family members and a circle of friends because Facebook could not offer the translation of certain languages. Locality was one important factor that affected their language selections. Non-native English users in their native countries tended to prefer to use their native languages other than English on Facebook. Non-native English users in native English speaking countries were likely to use English more often than their native languages. Context also impacted users' language selections on Facebook. When the context of the posts or comments was in English, users tended to respond in English. If the context of the posts and comments was in languages other than English, they tended to use the languages other than English. Users with high language proficiency in English and their native languages frequently code-switched from their native language to English in their posts and comments on Facebook.

2.3 Factors That Impact Code-Switching Information Seeking Behaviors

Previous research has examined code-switching in searching but it only identified that this behavior exists, no significant analysis of the types of code-switching actions and scenarios has been completed. Access to information on the Web, language proficiency, and cultural impacts were three of the most important factors that were identified.

2.3.1 Accessibility of Web Information. Web information accessibility impacts multilingual users' searching behaviors [16]. There were more websites available for better represented language groups than underrepresented language groups on the internet. The non-native multilingual web users did not get as much benefit as the represented language groups. As the number of non-native English web users increased, the challenges of web languages, content, and search tools appeared. Factors such as content-creation, link-setting, and link-following behavior would contribute to the under-representation of non-English languages on the web [5]. User satisfaction was not only related to users' cognitive searching process but also related to the availability of the alternative information in other languages that the website offered. This situation encourages multilingual web users switch codes from their underrepresented native languages to English when they cannot find enough information on non-English websites

Moreover, non-native English web users had less accessibility to a website if the information on the website was not offered in their native language [15]. Furthermore, the way that non-native speakers with high domain knowledge searched for information was similar to that of native speakers. But if non-native English users' domain knowledge was not sufficient, their search was language-sensitive. Therefore, multilingual web users' language proficiency and domain knowledge may influence their information seeking behaviors of code-switching..

2.3.2 Language Proficiency and Translation. Not only domain knowledge plays a role in non-native English users' information retrieval, but also language skills are the factors that influence users' code-switching information seeking behaviors [7]. Users with language-related majors, such as social sciences, anthropology, politics and international relations, were more likely to search and switch multiple languages. Users whose majors were medicine, dentistry and biology rarely searched in languages other than their native languages. Language abilities had an impact on multilingual users' information seeking. Users with multilingual backgrounds were likely to benefit more than users with monolingual backgrounds during their cross-language code switching searching process. Furthermore, the functionality of cross-language information retrieval tools, for example, Google translation functionality, was helpful to users who searched in languages other than their native language.

Multilingual users preferred to view the translated version of web pages in their third languages while reading the original versions of web pages in their second languages [19]. When language unfamiliarity increased, the use of Google translation also increased. They also found that users were more confident about the results for easy queries rather than hard queries. They concluded that users' language skills impacted their multilingual search experience and effectiveness.

2.3.3 Cultural Impact. Language tools and domain knowledge impact multilingual web users' code-switching search behaviors. Meanwhile, cultural elements also perform a role in multilingual users' information searching behaviors, Kralisch and Mandl [16] did a lab-experiment to explore how factors such as culture, language, and medical knowledge influence web users' information categorization and search options. In this 2x2 study British and Malaysian groups were native speakers of the website's language. Russian and German groups were other language speakers.. They found that due to the low level of the participants' medical knowledge, all groups preferred visual cues rather than verbal cues. Furthermore, they concluded that culture influences the users' information categorization, their attitudes, and their searching behavior the most. They found that in the card sorting activity the Malaysian and British groups' behaviors were close to each other, and the behaviors of the Russian and the German group were similar. Language mainly affected the users' opinions about the ease of use and usefulness of the website.

Even though the research summarized above has studied users' language selection behaviors, few studies have been done to explore when, how and why multilingual web users switch languages when they seek information online. We attempt to explain how multilingual users interact with different languages in order to satisfy their information needs.

3 Methods

The purpose of this study was to explore how multilingual web users interacted with information in order to satisfy their information needs in daily life. It aimed at examining when and why web users searched for information by using two or more languages for the same search task and how users switched languages when they interacted with information. The study specifically investigated the roles of the languages that users selected when they seek information online.

3.1 Participants

To address the research goal above, native Chinese Internet users who spoke English as a second or foreign language were selected to participate in the study. The participants were recruited by phone and email messages. This group of participants represented a large proportion of internet users in the world. Chinese was the second popular internet language that used by 704.5 million users online in 2016, while the most popular language was English, whose web users were 872.9 million [12]. In terms of countries, China had 641.6 million internet users in 2016, which ranked No. 1 in the world [12].

Questionnaires were used to collect participants' demographic and background information. Demographic questionnaires in hardcopies were sent to the participants. Ten participants took part in the study, ranging from 21 to 40 years old with a mean of 32. Six of them were female and four of them were male. The participants' English language proficiency ranged from intermediate to advanced according to their TOFEL (80 - 105) or IELTS (6 to 7) scores. They all have stayed or traveled internationally from several days to several years. Moreover, the participants were chosen from a variety of disciplines, such as geography, linguistics, communication, economy, life sciences, information systems, and computer science. Meanwhile, all the participants obtained more than six years of computer experiences.

3.2 Dairy Studies

Participants were asked to record their searching code-switching episodes for three weeks. After the diaries were recorded, the participants were interviewed about the code-switching episodes. The purpose of this method was to capture the participants' experiences of code-switching episodes in their daily life. These captured episodes were then unpacked in the interviews. In order to ensure that the participants captured code-switching episodes in their diaries, email/phone call reminders were sent to them weekly. Their diaries were reviewed each week to ensure detailed information was captured. The researcher also discussed the diaries with the participants weekly while their memory of the event was fresh. This study was approved by the university IRB office and consent forms were signed by the participants..

3.3 Interview

Interviews were conducted to uncover the natural process of users' information seeking. The researchers tried to conduct the interviews in as natural an environment for the participants as possible. For example, university participants were asked to search for information in labs or offices in the way they usually do. Professional participants were asked to seek information at home or in their offices using their own computers. The interviews mainly asked the participants to demonstrate several code-switching information seeking episodes which they reported in the diaries. Context-related factors were captured and analyzed when the participants searched for information. The interviews lasted about one hour. Data were collected by taking notes and pictures of participants at work and audio recording.

3.4 Data Analysis

The interviews were transcribed and analyzed using qualitative data analysis methods. They were first coded to identify preliminary concepts of interest. Following this step, axial coding was used to identify and group code-switching episode characteristics. The method of constant comparison was used as new transcripts were added and the more recently emerging concepts and categories were compared to those previously identified [8, 21].

4 RESULTS AND DISCUSSION

Initial diary reports showed that users whose native language was Chinese and second/foreign language was English, switched languages when seeking information online. The participants reported that they switched languages daily or 4-5 times per week. These multilingual users switched languages because when looking for information related to translations, shopping, travel, entertainment, domain knowledge, academic resources, networking and medical information.

The in-context interview data not only revealed the categories of code-switching, but also investigated how factors, such as web accessibility, language and translation tools, and social and cultural elements, impact multilingual users' language switching in online searching. Different functions of code-switching, for example, situational code-switching and metaphorical code-switching were identified based on the findings. The results describe multilingual web users' code-switching search patterns in the context of their searching behavior.

4.1 Categories of Code-Switching

Fifty episodes about language switching between English and Chinese during the participants' information seeking process have been collected from self-reported diaries and in-context interviews. In these episodes, around 200 code-switching search examples have been presented. These episodes have been grouped

according to different categories, such as language, news and entertainment, travel, domain knowledge, academic resources, and daily life information such as personal health, shopping, investment, social network information (Table 1).

Table 1: Categories of Code-Switching

Categories of Code-Switching	No. of Episodes
Language and translation	6
News and entertainment	9
Travel	7
Domain knowledge	9
Academic resources	8
Daily life information	11

Half of the participants reported in six episodes that they did code-switching searches related to language issues. They needed English translation for certain Chinese terms. They also needed to understand the meaning of certain words within different cultural contexts. For example, Participant One in the interview explained that he tried to look for the translation of "土(earth)". He was confused by the meaning of "mud" in English. He had to switch languages in order to find the appropriate translation in English.

Eight participants reported in nine episodes that they switched languages when they seek news and other entertainment information for translation purposes or to get quick information because Chinese content is faster to be processed for them as they are Chinese natives.

"I searched for people, locations, events in Chinese to get the information more quickly, for example, some movie stars from news. I wanted to know more about his biology. So I looked up the "Bai Du BaiKe" (Chinese wiki), instead of Wikipedia" (I-P2).

Participant One, Three, and 10 indicated that they searched in Chinese in order to find corresponding English movies, songs, famous people's names.

"I found out the name in one language based on the name in the other language" (D-P2).

Six participants expressed in seven episodes that they switched languages when they seek travel information, for example, places' English translation, air tickets, reviews and recommendations. Participant Two did metaphorical switching in order to find quick Chinese information about the place.

"When I'm going to travel to some places, I tend to search the English name and "中文(Chinese)", so I can get a full description of this place more quickly. And read some Chinese reviews and recommendations" (D-P2).

Domain knowledge is one of the important fields that multilingual web users code switched during their searching online. Five participants mentioned in nine episodes that they tried to switch languages in their domain knowledge related to their majors or work to get quick information from Chinese websites and sufficient information from English websites.

"I have searched for the exhibition information from Chinese websites. Then I went to related English websites to get more detailed information as supplemental resources" (I-P7).

"When I need a quick information about a term, I will find out its Chinese translation and search for the Chinese term" (D-P5).

Six participants addressed in eight episodes that they code-switched their searching in order to find accurate and sufficient academic information and resources, for example, researcher papers, university information, biomedical conferences, and reviews for textbooks.

"When we wrote a literature review, we had to find out enough papers related to our thesis...we cannot find Chinese papers only, so we also typed in English to find international papers or articles" (D-P10).

"When I wanted to participated in the lung cancer conference, I first search in Chinese "肺癌(lung cancer)". The Chinese papers and conferences came out. Since there are little information about international conferences, I secondly searched in English for the topic. This time I got international conferences, which included USA conferences and European conferences" (D-P6).

The participants also reported code-switching episodes about their needs in daily life, for example, searching for medical information, shopping and food information, visa information, investment information, jobs and even social networking.

"I searched both in English and Chinese for some medical terminologies to better understand them" (D-P2).

"I searched for the English term with regard to a Chinese term in order to buy the corresponding product on English websites" (D-P2).

"I wanted to know my old friend's information..I searched for a Chinese friend who lives in the US now. First, I typed her Chinese name and found some old information about her. I was not satisfied about the results. So I changed the language to English. This time the results came out, which were all her current information" (D-P6).

In summary, the participants indicated that the information retrieved from Chinese search engines and English search engines was different. They needed to retrieve all these results to get satisfying search results. Sometimes they chose to search in Chinese in order to get quick information due to their high native language proficiency. They chose to search in English to get adequate information.

4.2 Functions of Code-Switching

4.2.1 Situational Code-Switching in Language and Translation, Web Information Accessibility, and Culture.

Situational code-switching occurred when the participants searched for information in one language and switched to the other language because the topic needed the participant to change languages in order to get appropriate search results. Each language had its own role and corresponding search results.

Situational code-switching occurred in three types of code-switching scenarios we identified. The first of these concerns translation, when searchers encounter terms or longer text they are unfamiliar with in English and have to turn to translation tools

to find the Chinese meaning or they did not know about the English terms when they search so that they had to translate their ideas into English. In this situation their needs to translate encouraged them to switch languages.

Participant Eight used situational code-switching when she searched for academic information in different languages. She first went to bing.com and started with English "public relations" because her assignment was in English. Then she viewed the English results. She found some English results have lots of terminologies that she did not understand, which was likely related to her intermediate English language proficiency. Thus, next step she searched in Chinese on the Chinese website (Baidu) because her search needs required a change in the topic, which defined this code-switching as a situational one. She explained that sometimes she would use Google translate or other translation tools to translate her search terms. Once she retrieved the Chinese information, she understood some knowledge about this term. She explained the different roles of languages in this situational code-switching as follows.

"English is the official language. I chose English because it's better for me to write down my assignments. It's more direct. But I met with the problem. So I switched the language (to Chinese). Chinese is my native language. It's better for me to understand" (I-P8).

We found similar situational code-switching in Participant One's language episodes. He tried to search for an English movie in his lab based on the Chinese translation of that movie since he only knew the movie's Chinese name. He used his iPad to search for the movie's Chinese name "末路狂花" on Baidu.com, the most popular search website in China. He retrieved diverse search results from this searching, most of which were in Chinese. Some results presented the original English name "Thelma & Louise" of the movie in the information they provided. Thus, the participant copied this English topic to search in Google for get more information for this movie. In this case his information needs required him to first search in Chinese and then in English. The searching situation has been changed. Each language has its own role. He stated the search process and the roles of languages as follows.

"I found some information like the poster (by searching in Chinese). But of course the posters they will have English names. In this case, Chinese is the key word and English is the result" (I-P1).

The second type of situational code-switching happened when the participants tried to search for accurate information by switching languages. Due to the limited web information accessibility on their native language websites, they realized that their native language websites could not offer them enough information. They preferred to switch to English websites and get accurate and sufficient information. Their needs to get more information enabled them to code-switch from their native language to English.

Participant Three, who was an office manager, pointed out that when he searched for technical solutions about computers, which was related to his domain knowledge, he searched in Chinese first because Chinese was his native language so that he could get fast information. But then he switched to English because he had no problem reading English in his domain knowledge and   he believed that the accessibility of effective information on English websites was much more easier than that of Chinese websites. He pointed out that some information on Chinese websites was out dated and inaccurate. His search needs required him to change his search situation from Chinese websites to English websites. He explained the different roles of the languages. He first searched for "电脑黑屏(screen black)" on Baidu because it was his native language. He thought it would be easier for him to understand the steps about how to fix the broken desktop. But he did not find appropriate results. He believed this was due to the reason that the information on Chinese websites was over dated. Therefore, he turned to English websites and searched in English queries "computer down screen black" and got the latest search results.

"This morning our office desktop's screen is totally black. I searched for that in Chinese, but it did not work. So I switched the key words in English" (I-P3).

Participant Seven used situational code-switching for the purposes of better web information accessibility. She is the CEO of an educational company teaching students music. She searched for information about festival exhibitions in other countries. She first searched in Chinese "艺术节" (art festival)on Baidu. She explained that Chinese is her native language. It is more direct and convenient for her to get the information. When the information she retrieved was not enough and could not satisfy her information needs, she switched to English. She then typed "art festival" on Baidu. She mentioned that most of the time she needed translation tools such as Google translate or Baidu translator when she switched the search terms into English due to her intermediate English language proficiency. When she viewed the English results, she used Baidu translator to translate the English content on the webpage because there were lots of terminologies she could not understand. She illustrated the roles of languages in her search.

"The role of Chinese would be, it's more direct. The English information is more sufficient and broader" (I-P7).

We found situational code-switching due to web information accessibility and translational purposes in Participant Five's episodes. He searched for information of a travel destination. He first typed English word "Ammen" on Google because he learned this place in English. From the results he found Chinese information about this place. He then clicked on the Chinese result. He explained the role of Chinese as follows.

"It's easier. It's my native language. My first language is first to absolve" (I-P5)

He then expressed he could not find the information he needed on the Chinese website, for example, public transportation from the airport to the city center. He then gave up with this Chinese website and switched back to the English results. Situational code-switching emphasizes different roles of languages. In this case Chinese was convenient for the participant to get information. However, the Chinese information was not sufficient for the participant. Instead, the role of English was to offer him sufficient travel information. He switched from Chinese to English due to the task requirement and the searching situations have been changed.

"I will switch to English Wikipedia and start looking for it. There is much more information here. So I would be able to find some information about the transportation and much more about the history, too. Usually Chinese information will be really short, concise and gives me a general picture of what's going on" (I-P5).

The third type of situational code-switching was related to linguistic/cultural factors. The participants were multilingual which meant they had the abilities to search for information in different linguistic/cultural context and compare the information to get satisfying search results.

Participant Four was a linguist who translated Chinese poems into English. In her office she searched for poems of Li Bai, who was a famous poet in Chinese history both on Chinese and English websites. First she searched for Chinese information on Baidu, which is a popular search website in China. She explained that these Chinese sources offered her related information. Later she went to Google for an academic translation tool "汉典" (Chinese dictionary) to find appropriate search queries about the poem content. Then she returned to Google to search for this poet's English translation name and the poems. She pointed out that it was because the information on Chinese and English websites about poems or poets was different from cultural and historical perspectives. She would like to search both in Chinese and English to compare eastern and western researchers' reviews and critique from different cultural and historical perspectives. This is a typical example of situational code-switching because her information needs required her to search both in English and Chinese. She expressed her opinions as follows.

"On English websites there is some of the information which might be a little different from the Chinese. And also the research, the research from the different perspectives by the Chinese researchers and those translators from the western countries are analyzing the same poem in different ways or analyzing the same poet in a specific cultural or historical context in different ways" (I-P4).

Participant Five is a professor who teaches Geography to Chinese students. However, his domain knowledge is in English. Therefore, he expressed that he often searched for related theories by using situational code-switching in order to better coordinate and compare different domain knowledge in different cultural context.

"I will also type in Chinese so that I can get an idea in Chinese... Usually these kinds of (English) terms won't have Chinese translation. So I would look for how other Chinese people talk about it " (I-P5).

4.2.2 Metaphorical Code-Switching in Mixed Language Queries, Domain Knowledge, and Attitudes

Metaphorical code-switching occurred when participants changed their attitudes, emotions, and quoted certain norms while they seek information online. Some episodes, especially the ones related to news, reviews, quotations, emotions, contained metaphorical code-switching. The participants who used this code-switching expressed their attitudes or emotional changes by using different languages according to the complex social and cultural context.

Queries in mixed languages meant the participants used two languages in the same query. They were one of the most important metaphorical code-switching that these multilingual web users used in their online searching because they needed quick information retrieved from Chinese websites. Meanwhile, they also searched for English information from different social perspectives other than Chinese resources. Mixed language queries (especially the second half query languages, e.g., "Trump 选举结果") were social/lingual context hints about multilingual web users' attitudes and language choice during their searching.

Participant Three searched for American election results in his laptop in the activity room on the floor where he lives. He typed "Trump 选举结果 (election results)" on Google because he initially learned his name in English.

"Basically I learned this guy's name in English. So I am kind of call him or address him in English instead of Chinese translation "特朗普". That is the reason that I naturedly typed "Trump" instead of in Chinese translation" (I-P3).

However, he preferred to read Chinese news because he wanted the very quick Chinese translation of the results instead of long English interpretation of the election in English, which had been found on most English web pages. It was quicker for him to get the information in Chinese. The second part of his query "选举结果" showed his social attitude and language choice, which meant he preferred to view the Chinese search results. He explained why he used metaphorical code-switching by typing a mixed language query in English and Chinese in the following answer.

"Because I want the Chinese information. I don't want English interpretation of the result. So I want the Chinese result. I typed in "选举结果" and got some Chinese results." (I-P4)

Participant Two searched for travel information with metaphorical code-switching search terms. The queries included both English and Chinese key words. She typed the place's Chinese name and English together on Google, for example "普吉岛 (Fuji) English" in order to find English information. "English" in the second half mixed language query was the hint that she tried to search for English information and select English results. She explained the reason that her query had both Chinese and English.

"Usually I know the Chinese name of the destination, but I don't know the English. (The Chinese) is just my experience or I heard from my friends....I want to get more information and more pictures about this place (on Google)" (I-P2).

She also explained that sometimes she searched for the place's Chinese name on Google and got the Chinese results from BaiduBaike (Chinese wiki). Even though BaiduBaike was based on Chinese, it happened to have some original English information, for example, the English name of the place. Then she copied the English name of that place from BaiduBaike and pasted the English on Google.

Metaphorical code-switching could also be found in other participants' language choices. The participants expressed they used metaphorical code-switching to show their feeling of being comfortable, seek emotional support, and have a sense of belonging.

Participant Six expressed her feeling towards searching and reading in English and Chinese when the information on English and Chinese websites was both sufficient and accurate. She is a life scientist. She often searched for medical information about her domain knowledge in English on baidu.com. For example, she first searched for "lung cancer therapy" on Baidu. Then she retrieved both English and Chinese results. By reading the results, she figured out the right Chinese translation of the English search terms. Then she copied the Chinese and pasted it as a new query on Baidu and retrieved Chinese results. Even though the search website could retrieved both English and Chinese results, she preferred the Chinese results because she felt comfortable reading the Chinese results. In this case her attitude determined her action that she switched English to Chinese. She described her searching as follows.

"I searched for 'lung cancer therapy' on websites for the project. But you know, sometimes your search results include Chinese papers and they are advanced. At this time, I change my key word into Chinese, and tried to find out the whole paper in my native language because by doing so, my time was saved because it's easier to read Chinese. What's more, I grasped the knowledge more deeply by better understanding the language." (I-P6)

The participants used metaphorical code-switching from English to Chinese so as to seek emotional support or a sense of belonging during their information seeking process.

Participant One is an international Ph.D. student. He searched for his textbook first in English and then searched in Chinese in order to get Chinese reviews about the book. He first went to Google to search in English as he explained that the text book was in English. He addressed that because the system language of his iPad's is Chinese, Google automatically displayed some Chinese results. His search purpose was to view the reviews of this book both in English and Chinese. For English reviews he went to Amazon, which offered lots of customer reviews. Even though he got enough search results, he still preferred to know what Chinese people commented on this book. He expressed that since he grew up in China, he would like to see the attitudes of the Chinese audience towards this textbook. Then he clicked on the Chinese result page of Google. He found there were not so much reviews of this book in Chinese. He made a conclusion that this book was not popular in China. This metaphorical code-switching represented one's seeking for support in a different cultural context and demonstrated his sense of belonging.

"You know some of the thinking patterns of Chinese and English people are different. And since I finished my college in China, I would like to find out what Chinese people think about it" (I-P1).

Our analysis through situational and metaphorical code-switching indicated that situational code-switching happened when the participants changed topics and information needs during their searching. They code switched metaphorically to display different social/linguistic context hints, feelings and attitudes towards different languages.

5 CONCLUSIONS AND FUTURE WORK

This study aims to explore when and how multilingual web users switch languages when they seek information on the web. Its contributions are based on the detailed analysis of nine multilingual users' code-switching behaviors while searching where little research has been done before. Moreover, the study provides implications for website designers concerning multilingual users' code-switching search strategies, habits, and needs.

Because all the participants are Chinese, the results may not be generalized to all multilingual web users. However, this work provides detailed method design and the context of multilingual web users' code-switching behaviors when they seek information online. These results may transfer to similar situations. Multilingual web users in similar situations can benefit from the specific design implications from this research.

In our previous study we explored the criteria that the participants applied to judge a website's credibility by analyzing the participants' questionnaires and the impact of user personality in websites credibility judgment, and discussed about multilingual web users' code-switching behaviors during their online searching [1, 2, 27]. Now we have started the eye-tracking data collection and analysis about multilingual web users' code-switching search patterns during their online searching. The participant's fixation length and count data in the AOI areas have been collecting. The controlled lab-based eye-tracking study allows us to understand specific features of users' eye movements. We hope these eye movement recordings can help us explore where on web pages searchers focus when searching in their native vs. a foreign language and how the reading patterns differ.

ACKNOWLEDGMENTS

We thank our participants for their contribution.

REFERENCES

[1] Rahayu Ahmad, Anita Komlodi, Jieyu Wang, and Karoly Hercegfi. 2010. The impact of user experience levels on web credibility judgments. In *Proceedings of the 73rd ASIS&T Annual Meeting on Navigating Streams in an Information Ecosystem - Volume 47* (ASIS&T '10), Vol. 47. American Society for Information Science, Silver Springs, MD, USA, , Article 6 , 4 pages.

[2] R. Ahmad, J. Wang, K. Hercegfi, and A. Komlodi. 2011. Different people different styles: impact of personality in web sites credibility judgment. In *Human Interface and the Management of Information*, M. J. Smith & G. Salvendy (Eds.). Springer, New York, NY, 521-527.

[3] Giovanna Alfonzetti. 2002. Italian-dialect code-switching in Sicily. In *Code-Switching in Conversation: Language, Interaction and Identity*, P. Auer (Eds.).Taylor & Francis, 198.

[4] P. Auer. 1998. *Code-Switching in Conversation*. London, Routledge.

[5] B. Berendt and A. Kralisch. 2009. A user-centric approach to identifying best deployment strategies for language tools: the impact of content and access language on Web user behavior and attitudes. *Inf. Retr.*, 12, 3, 380-399.

[6] J. P. Blom and J. J. Gumperz.1972. Social Meaning in Linguistic Structures: Code-switching in Norway. In *Directions in Sociolinguistics*, J. J. Gumperz and D. Hymes (Eds.). Holt, Rinehart, and Winston, New York, 407-434.

[7] P. Clough and I. Eleta. 2010. Investigating language skills and field of knowledge on multilingual information access in digital libraries. *International Journal of Digital Library Systems*, 1, 1, 89- 103.

[8] J. Corbin and A. Strauss. 2008. Basics of Qualitative Research: Techniques and Procedures for Developing Grounded Theory (3rd. ed.). Sage, Thousand Oaks, CA.

[9] J. J. Gumperz. 1982. *Discourse Strategies*. Cambridge University Press, Cambridge, UK.

[10] J. J. Gumperz and D. H. Hymes. 1986. Directions in Sociolinguistics: The Ethnography of Communication. Basil Blackwell, Oxford, UK.

[11] Ilanguages Organization. 2016. Multilingual People. Retrieved from http://ilanguages.org/bilingual.php

[12] Internet Live Stats. 2016. Internet Users by Country. Retrieved from http://www.internetlivestats.com/internet-users-by-country/ China

[13] B. B. Kachru. 2005. *Asian Englishes Beyond the Canon*. Hong Kong University Press, Hong Kong.

[14] M. Kötter. 2003. Negotiation of meaning and code-switching in online tandems. *Language Learning & Technology*, 7, 2, 145-172.

[15] A. Kralisch and B. Berendt. 2005. Language-sensitive search behavior and the role of domain knowledge. *New Review of Hypermedia and Multimedia*, 11, 2, 221-246.

[16] A. Kralisch and T. Mandl. 2006. Barriers to information access across languages on the internet: Network and language effects. In *Proceedings of the 39th Annual Hawaii International Conference*, IEEE, Kauai, Hi, 3, 54b-54b.

[17] Jessica Lingel, Mor Naaman, and Danah M. Boyd. 2014. City, self, network: transnational migrants and online identity work. In *Proceedings of the 17th ACM conference on Computer supported cooperative work & social computing* (CSCW '14). ACM, New York,NY,USA,1502-1510. DOI=http://dx.doi.org/10.1145/2531602.2531693

[18] V. Marian and A. Shook. 2012, October 31. The Cognitive Benefits ofBeingBilingual.Retrievedfrom http://dana.org/Cerebrum/2012/The_Cognitive_Benefits_of_Being _Bilingual.

[19] Jennifer Marlow, Paul Clough, Juan Cigarrán Recuero, and Javier Artiles. 2008. Exploring the effects of language skills on multilingual web search. In *Proceedings of the IR research, 30th European conference on Advances in information retrieval* (ECIR'08), Craig Macdonald, Iadh Ounis, Vassilis Plachouras, Ian Ruthven, and Ryen W. White (Eds.). Springer-Verlag, Berlin, Heidelberg, 126-137.

[20] Y. Maschler. 1998. On the transition from code-switching to a mixed code. In *Code-switchingin Conversation: Language, interaction and identity*, P. Auer (Eds.). Routledge, NewYork, 125-150.

[21] S. B. Merriam. 2009. *Qualitative research: A guide to design and implementation*. John Wiley & Sons, San Francisco, CA.

[22] C. Myers-Scotton. 1993. Social Motivations for Code-switching: Evidence from Africa. Clarendon, Oxford, UK.

[23] Peggy Nzomo, Victoria L. Rubin, and Isola Ajiferuke. 2012. Multi-lingual information access tools: user survey. In Proceedings of the 2012 iConference (iConference '12). ACM, New York, NY, USA, 530-532. DOI=http://dx.doi.org/10.1145/2132176.2132276

[24] C. O. Serra. 1998. Discourse connectives in bilingual conversation: The case of an emerging Italian-French mixed code. In Code-switching in Conversation: Language, interaction and identity, P. Auer (Eds.). Routledge, New York, 101-124.

[25] U.S. Census Bureau. 2013. Language Use and English-speaking Ability.Retrievedfrom https://www.census.gov/prod/2003pubs/c2kbr-29.pdf

[26] J. Wang and S. Joardar. 2015. Cultural capital at work in Facebook users' selection of different languages. In Cross-Cultural Design: Applications in Mobile Interaction, Education, Health, Transport and Cultural Heritage, P. L. P. Rau (Eds.). Springer, NewYork, NY, 101-109.

[27] Jieyu Wang and Anita Komlodi. 2016. Understanding Users' Language Selection: Code-switching in Online Searches. In Proceedings of the 2016 ACM on Conference on Human Information Interaction and Retrieval (CHIIR '16). ACM, New York, NY, USA, 377-379. DOI: https://doi.org/10.1145/2854946.2854955

[28] L. Wei. 1998. The 'why' and 'how' questions in the analysis of conversational code-switching. In *Code-switching in Conversation: Language, interaction and identity*, P. Auer (Eds.). Routledge, New York, 156-179.

[29] K. A. Woolard. 2004. Code-switching. In A Companion to Linguistic Anthropology. A. Duranti (Eds.). Blackwell, Oxford, 73-94.

A Comparative User Study of Interactive Multilingual Search Interfaces

Chenjun Ling
Department of Computer Engineering
Santa Clara University
cling@scu.edu

Ben Steichen
Department of Computer Science
California State Polytechnic
University, Pomona
bsteichen@cpp.edu

Alexander G. Choulos
Department of Computer Science
Purdue University
achoulos@purdue.edu

ABSTRACT

While the number of polyglot Web users across the globe has increased dramatically, little human-centered research has been conducted to better understand and support multilingual user abilities and preferences. In particular, in the fields of cross-language and multilingual search, the majority of research has focused primarily on improving retrieval and translation accuracy, while paying comparably less attention to multilingual user interaction aspects. By contrast, this paper specifically focuses on multilingual search user interface preferences and behaviors, through a lab-based user study involving 25 participants interacting with a set of four different interactive multilingual search user interfaces. User preference results confirm that multilingual search users generally have strong preferences towards interfaces that provide clear language separation, and that the traditional approach of interleaving results, as typically used in prior research, is least preferred. In addition, an analysis of user interaction behaviors shows that multilingual users make significant use of each of their languages, and that there are several interaction behavior differences depending on interface and task type.

KEYWORDS

Multilingual Search; Multilingual Interfaces; Human–Computer Information Retrieval; Eye Tracking

ACM Reference format:
Chenjun Ling, Ben Steichen, and Alexander G. Choulos. 2018. A Comparative User Study of Interactive Multilingual Search Interfaces. In *CHIIR '18: Conference on Human Information Interaction and Retrieval, March 11-15, 2018, New Brunswick, NJ, USA.* ACM, NY, NY, USA, 10 pages.
DOI: https://doi.org/10.1145/3176349.3176383

1 INTRODUCTION

With the unrelenting worldwide increase in Internet penetration rates, nearly 40% of the world's population is connected to the Internet today[1]. Asia, the Americas, and Europe are the top three contributors, making up 48.4%, 21.8%, and 19% respectively[1]. With this dramatic increase in online population numbers, there has been a similar increase in the diversity of Web users.

One key aspect of diversity lies in user language abilities, with a significant number of Web users being polyglots, i.e. people who are proficient in more than one language. For example, recent surveys in China have shown that out of those with junior secondary education qualifications or above, 67.4% of Chinese graduates had studied at least one foreign language, among which as many as 93.8% had studied English [1,2]. Likewise, in the European Union, an average of 94.6% of secondary education pupils learn English in general programs, and an average of 64.7% even learn two or more languages[2]. This growth of polyglots is evident throughout the world, and it is generally acknowledged that there are many more people who are proficient in English as a second language than as a native language[3].

This byproduct of globalization generates new challenges for adapting information access systems to different user abilities and preferences, especially in terms of supporting Web search and browsing tasks across different languages. In recent surveys, it was found that the majority of polyglots frequently use multiple languages for searching and browsing the Web [3,4]. This behavior is in part due to the fact that some languages are vastly underrepresented in terms of content, despite large user populations. For example, statistics by Web Technology Surveys[4] indicate that 52.1% of all current websites are written in English, whereas Chinese language websites only account for 2% of all current websites, even though 22% of online users are from China[1]. There is hence a pressing need to research and develop novel multilingual search systems that directly support polyglot users in searching and browsing the Web across multiple languages.

One of the greatest unexplored challenges regarding multilingual search lies in how to best support polyglot users from an interface and interaction perspective. While many current systems technically already support multiple languages, they typically tend to emphasize distinctions between languages, often requiring users to switch between systems, or at least conduct separate searches to obtain results from more than one language source. This extra effort reduces the probability that a user will perform a search involving multiple languages, which may result in less relevant results being retrieved (especially

---

[1]www.internetlivestats.com/internet-users/

[2]Eurostat Foreign language learning statistics: ec.europa.eu/eurostat/statistics-explained/index.php/Foreign_language_learning_statistics

[3]www.britishcouncil.org/learning-research-english-next.pdf

[4]w3techs.com/technologies/overview/content_language/all

given the language imbalance discussed above). To conquer these shortcomings, there has been significant initial progress in building systems that can retrieve information from multiple languages. In particular, cross-language search systems have been developed to allow users to search for information in a language that is different from the query language [8]. However, there has been a distinct lack of research on the user interaction aspects of multilingual search, especially in terms of how to design interactive multilingual search result interfaces.

By contrast, the objective of this paper is to specifically evaluate different interactive multilingual search interface designs, to get a better understanding of how to best support polyglot Web users and their multiple language skills. Specifically, we ask the following research questions:

- (RQ1) What type(s) of interactive multilingual search interface designs are preferred by polyglot users?
- (RQ2) What are the interaction behaviors of polyglot users with interactive multilingual search systems?
- (RQ3) Do different interactive multilingual search interfaces and/or task types lead to different user behaviors?

In order to answer these research questions, this paper provides the first in-depth comparative analyses of user behaviors and preferences with respect to four different multilingual search user interfaces, through a lab-based user study involving 25 participants.

2 RELATED WORK

2.1 Multilingual Search

In the area of multilingual search, the majority of research has been concerned with the concept of *cross-language information retrieval (CLIR)* [8], focusing primarily on translation and retrieval effectiveness through focused campaigns such as the Cross-Language Evaluation Forum (CLEF)[5].

The user interaction aspect of multilingual search and CLIR has received comparably less attention, with a few notable exceptions focusing specifically on query elicitation and translation, e.g. as presented in [5,6,8], as well as part of the interactive CLEF (iCLEF) campaigns[6] (e.g. [9,10]). For example, Petrelli et al. [5] found that automated translation of user queries, together with optional user editing capabilities ('delegate' mode), was more effective and satisfactory than if a user was forced to choose between different translations ('supervised' mode). Oard et al. [6] found that auto query translation aids were generally considered advantageous to a user's interaction experience. Marlow et al. [7] studied the effect of language ability on the use of Google translation for multilingual search. They found that for unfamiliar languages, users reported an increased use of translation tools, while for familiar languages, users tended to write translated queries by themselves. Similarly, Petrelli et al. [11] and Chu et al. [12] found that participants with relatively

low secondary language skills indicated a significant need for translation tools. Likewise, a qualitative study by Chu et al. found that during the query elicitation phase, participants indicated that it is important provide a simple and intuitive user interaction functionality, specifically an automatic machine translation solution with user ability to edit and keep track of queries [13].

While these initial works have provided important guidelines regarding query elicitation and translation, there remains a particular lack of research regarding the design of multilingual Web search result pages. For displaying multilingual search results, three main types of interfaces have been used in prior work, primarily for prototyping purposes. The most commonly used interface type to date consists of an 'Interleaved' approach, whereby results from all languages are merged into a single result list (either through round-robin or based on specific aspects such as collection size [14]). A second common type of interfaces takes a 'Tabbed' approach [10,15], whereby retrieval results are split by language through different tabs, which users can use to switch between languages. Thirdly, several more recent multilingual systems have adopted a 'Panels' approach, which displays results in separate panels per language on a single page (e.g. 2lingual[7], ollito[8], [3,13]).

In terms of examining the respective benefits, tradeoffs, and preferences regarding different types of interfaces, there has been very limited research. In our prior work, we studied different types of multilingual search result pages using static interfaces, i.e. interfaces that did not allow users to type their own search queries [3]. In that study, we included the abovementioned 'Interleaved', 'Tabbed', and 'Panels' interfaces, as well as a fourth interface called 'Universal', which displayed search results from different languages in vertical blocks. The study uncovered several interesting initial results, particularly the finding that users seemed to prefer strict language separation (e.g. as provided by 'Panels'), rather than displays that showed results in a single list.

In this paper, we aim to extend and corroborate our findings presented in [3], by investigating fully functioning interactive multilingual search systems. In particular, while the work in [3] aimed to ensure that all variables, apart from interface layout, remained fixed (such as the search queries and their translations), the static nature of the study may have lacked in ecological validity, and thereby may have led to biased preferences. In this paper, we investigate to what extend user preferences may change if interactive features are enabled. In addition, while the static interfaces in [3] did not allow us to perform any analysis of general or interface-specific interaction behaviors, the study presented in this paper conducts such an in-depth study with interactive prototypes, aiming uncover user interaction behaviors with multilingual search systems.

---

[5]CLEF (now Conference and Labs of the Evaluation Forum): www.clef-initiative.eu/
[6]iCLEF: nlp.uned.es/iCLEF/

[7]2lingual : www.2lingual.com/
[8]ollito: www.ollito.com/

2.2 Monolingual Aggregated Search Interfaces

In terms of comparing different interactive search interface designs, more research can be found in the area of monolingual aggregated search, which is concerned with aggregating and displaying results from multiple verticals (e.g. news, images, etc.).

For example, several interactive aggregated search interfaces are compared by Bron et al. [16]. Their 'Tabbed' interface presents each result collection separately arranged in labeled tabs, similar to the 'Tabbed' design in multilingual search [3]. On the other hand, their second interface is similar to the abovementioned 'Universal' [9] interface, as it displays result collections separately in contiguous blocks (e.g. news result block, followed by image results block, followed by Web results) [16]. Through an interactive user study, Bron et al. [16] found that the 'Tabbed' interface was more suitable to zoom in and look into the details of one single result source, while the 'Universal'-style interface was especially useful for simultaneously exploring multiple sources.

Similarly, Sushmita et al. [18] compared a 'Universal'-style interface to a 'Panel'-style interface [10], which showed results from each collection in separate panels. Their findings showed that participants bookmarked slightly more pages in the 'Universal'-style interface, even though both interfaces had similar click frequencies.

Likewise, Thomas et al. [19] compared four different monolingual interactive aggregated search interfaces in the government meta search domain, including a 'Tabbed', an 'Interleaved'-style (called 'Merged'), a 'Panels'-style (called 'Side-By-Side'), and a 'More Results' interface. The 'Tabbed' and 'Panels' interfaces were similar to the corresponding 'Tabbed' and 'Panels' interfaces used in [16] and [18]. The 'More Results' interface showed the main source results on one page, with an additional side-section on the same page that pointed to additional results from other sources. Results in this paper showed that users preferred interfaces that provided more information up-front. Conversely, the 'More Results' interface was least preferred because no indication was given as to which other sources had relevant results.

As previously mentioned, aggregated monolingual search interfaces typically focus on aggregating results from different verticals, such as images, news (typically also accompanied by images), and video (e.g. [16,18]). It thereby makes different result sources much easier to distinguish from each other due to increased visually saliency. It is thus interesting to investigate whether findings from interactive aggregated search interfaces would still hold in multilingual search.

3 EXPERIMENTAL SETUP

As mentioned in the previous section, this paper focuses specifically on studying and comparing different types of interactive multilingual search interfaces. This section first describes in detail the four different interfaces that were designed and developed for our study. These interfaces were based on the techniques identified from prior work, and in particular extending the static multilingual interfaces presented in [3]. This is followed by a description of the experimental platform, study tasks, and user study and analysis procedure.

3.1 Interfaces Used in the Study

3.1.1 Tabbed Interface. As shown in Figure 1, the 'Tabbed' interface allows users to change between lists of results in different languages through tabs. The language tabs reflect the languages that the user is proficient in (up to 4 languages), as determined through the pre-questionnaire. As with each of the other interfaces described below, the 'Tabbed' interface automatically translates (using the Microsoft Translator API[11]) the user's query to the language of the currently selected tab. For example, in Fig. 1, a user with English and Chinese proficiency has typed an English query "recipes for chocolate pudding", and has then chosen the Chinese Tab to view Chinese results, which are retrieved using the auto-translated query "巧克力布丁的食谱". Translations can also be edited, as recommended in prior work [6], and several translation alternatives are provided as suggestions to the user. Each result page displays a single monolingual ranked list, which contains 12 results (retrieved using the Bing Search API[12]). At the bottom of the page, participants can click 'previous' and 'next' buttons to view more search results.

Figure 1: Tabbed Interface

3.1.2 Panels Interface. The 'Panels' interface (Figure 2) displays one or more panels on a single result page, with each panel displaying results in a different language. The number of languages (and hence panels) per page is determined by the user through the use of checkboxes (up to 4 languages). A user may choose to view results in each of his/her languages, or only focus on one single language.

---

[9] In Aggregated Search research, e.g. [16,18,19], 'Universal'-style interfaces are typically called 'Blended'. In our paper, such interfaces are referred to as 'Universal' (based on Google's original naming of aggregated search features - googlepress.blogspot.com/2007/05/google-begins-move-to-universal-search_16.html), in order to better distinguish it from other interfaces that are technically also blended, such as 'Interleaved' (not used in Aggregated Search)

[10] Typically referred to as 'Non-Blended' in Aggregated Search research [18,19]

[11] datamarket.azure.com/dataset/bing/microsofttranslator - While there are many different machine translation techniques and tools, this was not the focus of this study. The Microsoft Translator API supports a large number of language pairs, and it was found to work sufficiently well for the topics used in the study tasks.

[12] datamarket.azure.com/dataset/bing/search

To make sure that the same number of results is displayed for each result page, and to ensure consistency across interfaces (e.g. 'Panels' having the same number of results per page as 'Tabbed'), the number of results per language equals to 12 divided by the number of languages. For example, if a user has selected 4 languages, each individual panel will contain 3 results. Conversely, if only one language is chosen, the result list is equivalent to the 'Tabbed' interface, i.e. 12 results for the chosen language. Each panel is headed by the (editable) auto-translated query according to the respective language, and the results within each panel can be navigated with 'previous' and 'next' buttons.

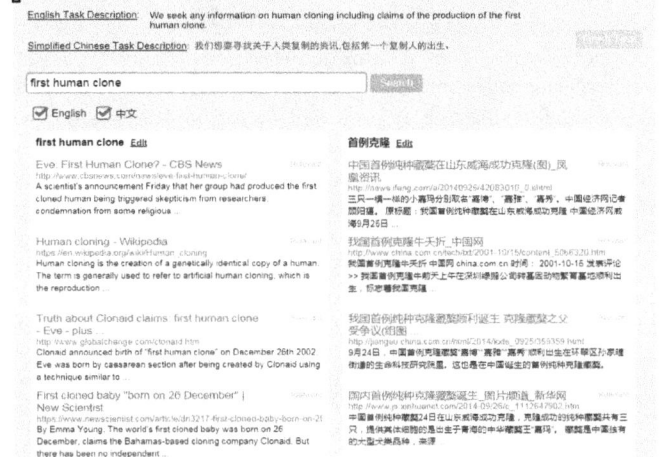

Figure 2: Panels Interface

3.1.3 Interleaved Interface. As shown in Figure 3, the 'Interleaved' interface has a single result list, with Web search results from different languages being interleaved. Checkboxes again allow users to select/deselect results in specific languages, and all (editable) auto-translated queries are shown together above the interleaved list. The number of results per page is again 12. For example, if a user has selected 2 languages (as in Figure 3), there will be 6 results per language, with result 1 being in the user's first language, result 2 being in the user's second language, result 3 again in the first language, etc.

Figure 3: Interleaved Interface

3.1.4 Universal Interface. The 'Universal' search interface also presents a single result list similar to the 'Interleaved' interface. However, results from each language are grouped together into blocks, rather than interleaved with each other. For example, as shown in Figure 4, when a user selects 2 languages, a block of 6 results in the user's first language are shown above a block of 6 results in the user's second language.

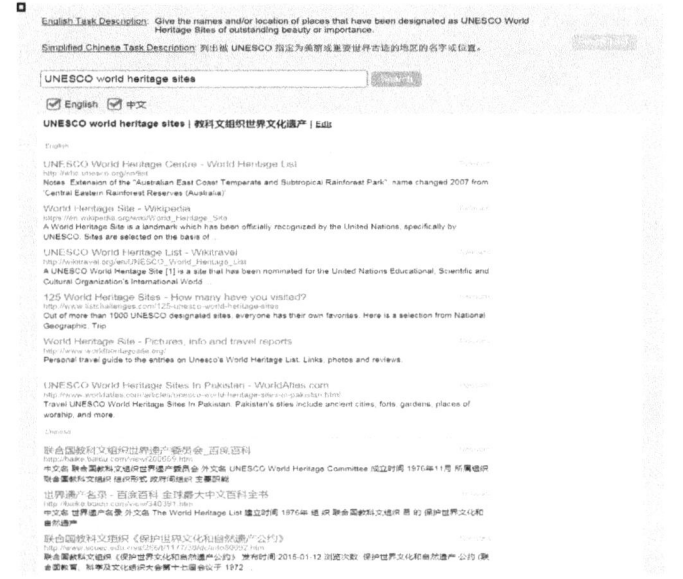

Figure 4: Universal Interface

3.2 Platform and Participants

We conducted a lab-based study using a purpose-built experimental platform (built using PHP and MySQL), running on a desktop computer with a 24-inch monitor. In addition, user eye gaze was tracked using a Tobii X3-120 eye tracker, which is a remote eye tracker providing unobtrusive tracking.

Experiment participants were recruited through campus mailing lists, and were required to have 'some proficiency'[13] in at least two out of a set of 7 languages (English, French, German, Spanish, Italian, Simplified Chinese, Traditional Chinese). Each participant was given a gift voucher worth 20 USD, and the average time to complete the entire study was approximately 90 minutes.

3.3 Task Questions

Each user was presented with a total of 12 tasks (Table 1), which were to be completed using the 4 interfaces (3 tasks per interface, counterbalanced across participants/interfaces). These tasks were sourced from CLEF (2006-2011) and TREC (2012-2014) campaigns, representing a variety of general Web search topics. The tasks were manually categorized into the following three different task type categories (using the definitions/categorization schemes in [20]): *Doing*, *Fact Finding*, and *Learning* tasks, and all topic descriptions were manually translated to the seven supported languages prior to the study using native speakers.

Before performing assigned tasks with each interface, participants first performed a practice task (the same practice task was used for each interface).

---

[13] Having 'some proficiency' was defined as 'you must have some reading/writing ability' in the language.

Table 1: Task Questions and Question Types

Question	Type
Find recipes for making chocolate puddings.	Doing
You want to know how a .csv file can be imported in excel.	Doing
You want to buy Yves Saint Laurent boots. You want to find places to buy, reviews, etc.	Doing
Rock climbing for beginners only publications which specifically provide information on climbs that are not difficult or give instructions on rock climbing for beginners are of interest.	Doing
What is the current price of oil?	FactFinding
Give the names and/or location of places that have been designated as UNESCO World Heritage Sites of outstanding beauty or importance.	FactFinding
What conditions trigger asthma in children?	FactFinding
How high above ground level is the ozone layer?	FactFinding
Look for information on the existence and/or the discovery of remains of the seven wonders of the ancient world.	Learning
Find publications providing general introductions to food allergies and the prevention of such allergies.	Learning
We seek any information on human cloning including claims of the production of the first human clone.	Learning
In what sports are drugs used illegally?	Learning

3.4 Procedure

There were five main steps each participant followed in the experiment. These five steps were i) calibrating the eye tracker ii) completing an initial questionnaire, iii) performing tasks, iv) completing mid-study questionnaires, and v) completing a post-study questionnaire.

The first part was a demographic questionnaire that included self-reported language proficiency in terms of reading, listening, and writing ability. Proficiency was measured on a scale from 1 to 4, with 1 corresponding to very limited proficiency, and 4 corresponding to native proficiency.

Next, users interacted with the previously described interfaces. More specifically, for each interface, users performed one practice task, followed by 3 tasks. For each task, participants were asked to issue their own queries to look for information on the given topic, with the topic being displayed in all of the participant's languages. Participants were also asked to mark any results they found relevant or helpful in learning about or solving the task, using buttons placed next to each result (see Fig. 1-4). These markings were recorded by the experimental platform, along with task times, queries issued, as well as documents viewed (i.e. results clicked/opened). Participants were free to move on to the next task if they felt that they had received sufficient relevant information on the task (in line with similar studies in aggregated search [16,18,19]).

Upon completion of all 3 tasks with one interface, a mid-study questionnaire was presented, which asked users to indicate their perceived level of search support provided by the interface.

Lastly, after having interacted with all 4 interfaces, a post-study questionnaire asked participants to indicate their overall comparative impressions, including i) which interface was 'easiest to use', ii) which interface they 'preferred the most', and iii) which

interface they 'disliked the most'. In addition, participants were asked to indicate their reasoning for particular preferences/dislikes.

3.5 Data Analysis

To understand multilingual user behaviors and preferences, we analyzed both user interaction data and user preference data. For each of these analyses, we will report statistical significance as determined through Chi-squared tests or ANOVA tests (as well as Bonferroni-corrected posthoc tests).

In addition, we analyzed several types of data captured through eye tracking, including number of fixations, fixation rate, fixation duration, and saccade length (see Table 2 for feature descriptions).

Table 2. Eye-Tracking Features

Feature	Description
Fixation number	Total number of eye gaze fixations
Fixation time	Total fixation time spent
Fixation rate	Fixation number divided by time interval (e.g., fixations per second)
Saccade length	Distance between fixations

4 RESULTS

In this section, we will first present participant demographics (section 4.1), followed by the results for user preference ratings (section 4.2). Next, we will present results for interaction behaviors (e.g. task time, number of queries, etc. – section 4.3). Lastly, we will present a detailed analysis of differences in interaction behaviors between the different interfaces, including analyses of eye gaze data for each interface, as well as influences of different task types (section 4.4)

4.1 Participant Demographics

In total, 36 participants took part in the study, of which responses were retained from 25 after filtering out cases of recording errors.

The 25 retained participants had an age range of 19-55, and, in accordance with the study requirements, were all proficient in at least two languages. 18 participants indicated that they were proficient in two languages, 5 participants were proficient in three languages, and 2 participants in four languages. The most common first languages were English (16), Chinese (8), and German (1). The most common second language was Spanish (10), followed by English (9), French (4), and Chinese (2). All participants indicated native proficiency in their first language, and the majority of participants indicated high proficiencies (level 3 or 4) in their second language across reading, writing, and listening (22/18/20 respectively).

4.2 User Preferences (RQ1)

As previously mentioned, user preferences were gathered through a comparative post-study questionnaire (i.e. after all tasks with all interfaces had been completed), as well as mid-study questionnaires (after all tasks for an individual interface were completed).

In the post-study questionnaire, participants generally indicated clear preferences/dislikes towards specific interfaces, with the interface type having a statistically significant effect on all post-study questionnaire answers. As shown in Figure 5, the

'Panels' interface was strongly considered to be the 'easiest to use' compared to all other interfaces ($p<0.001$), and the comparatively 'most preferred' ($p<0.001$) interface. The 'most disliked' interface was the 'Interleaved' interface ($p<0.01$).

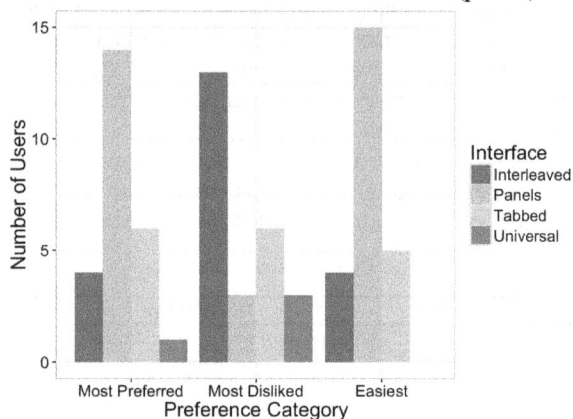

Figure 5: Post-study questionnaire results. 'Panels' is considered the 'most preferred' and 'easiest to use' by most participants, while 'Interleaved' is the 'most disliked'.

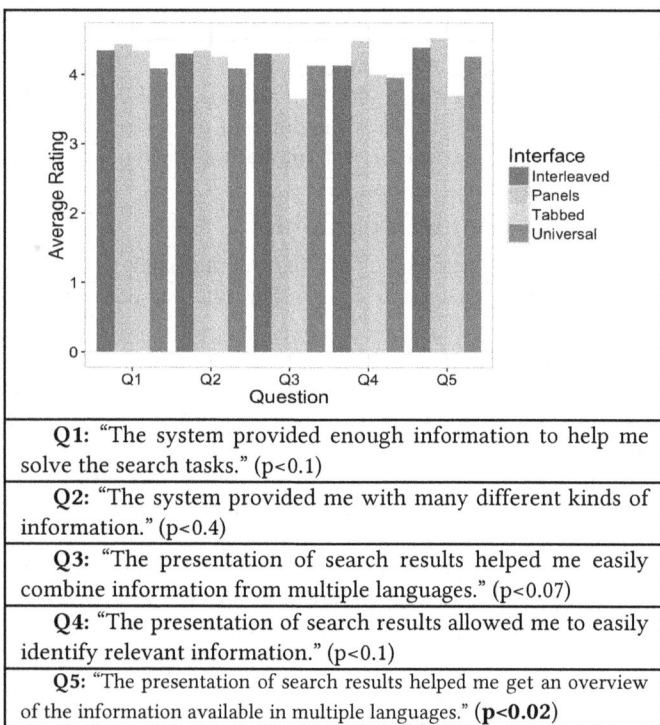

| **Q1:** "The system provided enough information to help me solve the search tasks." ($p<0.1$) |
| **Q2:** "The system provided me with many different kinds of information." ($p<0.4$) |
| **Q3:** "The presentation of search results helped me easily combine information from multiple languages." ($p<0.07$) |
| **Q4:** "The presentation of search results allowed me to easily identify relevant information." ($p<0.1$) |
| **Q5:** "The presentation of search results helped me get an overview of the information available in multiple languages." (**$p<0.02$**) |

Figure 6: Mid-study questionnaire results. Ratings indicate the level of agreement with the statement (1=strongly disagree, 5=strongly agree).

For the mid-study questionnaires (i.e. after having finished all tasks with one particular interface), results similarly indicated differences between interfaces, although less pronounced, as shown in Figure 6. In particular, differences between interfaces were found to be statistically significant for Q5 ('getting an overview'), and marginally significant for Q3 ('helping combine information'). Moreover, through Bonferroni-corrected post-hoc

tests, it was found that the 'Panels' interface was considered to be particularly good at 'getting an overview' compared to the 'Tabbed' and 'Universal' interfaces ($p<0.05$ and $p<0.09$ respectively).

Additional analyses with respect to participants' proficiency levels did not yield any statistically significant results, suggesting that the preferences were not influenced by participants' language skills in their secondary languages. However, as previously mentioned, language proficiencies of participants were not well distributed (the vast majority of participants indicating a proficiency level of 3 or higher in their secondary language), hence requiring further research with a participant base that includes lower second language proficiencies.

4.3 General User Behavior (RQ2)

4.3.1 Query behavior

We analyzed user queries in terms of two criteria, namely i) number of queries, and ii) languages used for queries.

There were 557 queries in total, most of which were entered in the main search box. Surprisingly, only 3 users used the edit query function to revise auto-translations, editing a total of only 4 queries. On average, participants issued 1.86 queries per task, and 22.28 queries for the whole study session.

In order to analyze users' language choices, we divided queries into 3 types, depending whether the query contained a user's first language (L1), a secondary language (L2), or both L1 and L2 (Mix). There was a statistically significant difference (Figure 7) in terms of language use ($p<0.001$), with participants performing L1 queries more often than L2 queries, and rarely using mixed-language queries. Nevertheless, as shown in Figure 7, it is noteworthy that the number of L2 queries was still high (approximately half as many as L1 queries). However, there were 6 out of 25 participants who only used L1 during their whole study session.

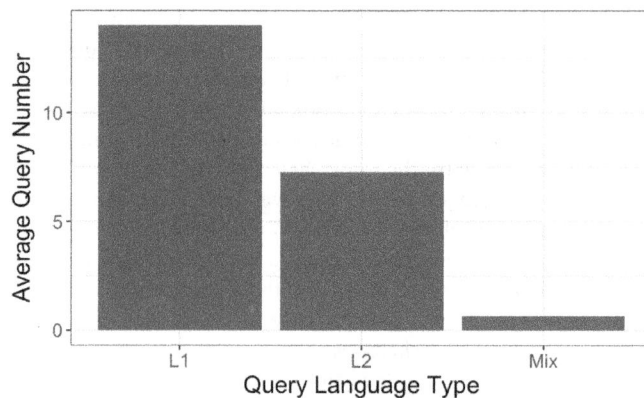

Figure 7: Average query number per language (Mix indicates the use of multiple languages within a single query)

When analyzing query language changes within all 300 tasks (25 users * 4 interfaces * 3 task types), we found that (as Table 3) during a total of 240 tasks (80%), participants only used a single language for querying, i.e. only L1, only L2, or only Mix (with L1, a user's first language, being the most popular). Conversely, during 60 tasks (20%), participants switched between languages for querying (e.g. starting with L1 queries, then switching to L2).

Table 3. Query language changes within tasks

Query Pattern	Language Sequence	Percentage	Percentage Sum
No Change	L1 only	62%	80%
	L2 only	16%	
	Mix only	2%	
Change	L1 -> L2	10.67%	20%
	L2 -> L1	3%	
	L1 -> Mix	1%	
	Mix -> L2	0.33%	
	Multiple switches	5%	

4.3.2 Result viewing and marking behavior

In addition to queries, we also analyzed the number of documents viewed by participants (i.e. result links that participants had clicked on), as well as the number of documents that participants had marked as relevant to the task.

On average, participants clicked on 7.98 documents per task. When breaking down by language, the number of documents viewed in participants' L1 was slightly higher at 4.54 compared to L2 at 3.42. However, this difference was not found to be statistically significant. Compared to the query results above, participants made more use of each of their languages during tasks, with participants choosing to click on results in each of their languages during 44% of the tasks. Conversely, only during 38% of tasks did participants click on results in only their L1.

The average number of documents marked as relevant was 6.25, and, similar to the above results on documents viewed, there was only a small difference between L1 and L2 (average of 3.43 vs 2.82). Again, this difference was not statistically significant. Participants very often marked results as relevant in each of their languages (74% of tasks). Conversely, only during 20% of tasks did participants mark results in only their L1 as relevant.

4.3.3 Use of language checking/unchecking and tabbing

As discussed in section 3.2, three interfaces ('Panels', 'Interleaved', 'Universal') allowed users to check/uncheck languages during their searches (e.g. to only search/display results in L1). Participants only made use of this functionality during practice tasks (where they were explicitly explained the functionality and instructed to try it), and not at all during the actual tasks. The number of tab switches for 'Tabbed' was also low, with only an average of 1 tab switch per user per task.

4.4 Influence of Interface and Task types (RQ3)

4.4.1 Comparison of Interface Types

Overall, participant behavior differences in terms of average task time, number of queries, number of documents viewed, and number of documents marked as relevant were not found to be statistically significant ($p<0.08$/$p<0.31$/$p<0.14$ respectively). Likewise, no difference was found in terms of query lengths. However, there appeared to be a common trend (and near statistical significance) towards longer task times, higher number of queries, and higher number of documents marked as relevant for the 'Tabbed' interface compared to all other interfaces (see

Figure 8 for task time). While 'Interleaved', the most disliked interface, showed the shortest task time, this was not found to be statistically significant.

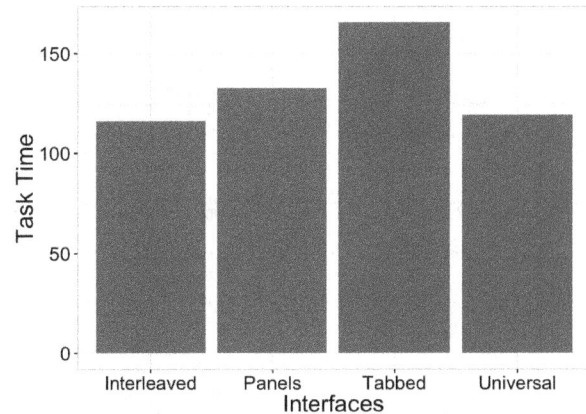

Figure 8: Average task time per interface

Three eye-tracking variables, namely fixation number, fixation time, and saccade length, did show statistically significant differences with respect to interface ($p<0.0085$/ $p<0.0003$/$p<0.002$ respectively), confirming the trends observed in the above behavior differences. In particular, the distributions (Figure 9) were similar to task time, where 'Tabbed' had the highest value.

Through post-hoc tests, it was found that participants had a much higher fixation number on the 'Tabbed' interface compared to the 'Universal' interface ($p<0.01$). For fixation time, 'Tabbed' had statistically significantly longer fixation time than 'Interleaved' ($p<0.05$) and 'Universal' ($p<0.008$). Regarding saccade lengths, however, the 'Tabbed' interface had shorter length compared to 'Interleaved', 'Panels' and 'Universal' ($p<0.06$/$p<0.005$/$p<0.005$). Additionally, 'Panels' also had longer saccade length compared to 'Interleaved' ($p<0.04$). Fixation rate did not yield any statistically significant differences for interface type ($p<0.05$), but 'Tabbed' still appeared to have the highest values. Again, these measures confirm the aforementioned trends that the Tabbed interface required users to spend more time. values. Again, these measures confirm the aforementioned trends that the Tabbed interface required users to spend more time.

In addition to statistically comparing the raw eye gaze measures, we also generated visual heat maps for the four interfaces[14]. More specifically, we generated 'first glance' heat maps, which visualized participants' initial fixations before performing their first result view click[15].

---

[14] These maps were generated from the number of eye gaze fixations from all the participants who had indicated two languages. Heat maps across participants with different numbers of languages cannot be overlaid given the slightly different overall page lengths and layouts. The number of participants with more than two languages was very low, hence these participants were not analyzed separately.

[15] Overall heat maps from users' entire interactions (i.e. beyond 'first glance') yielded very similar results.

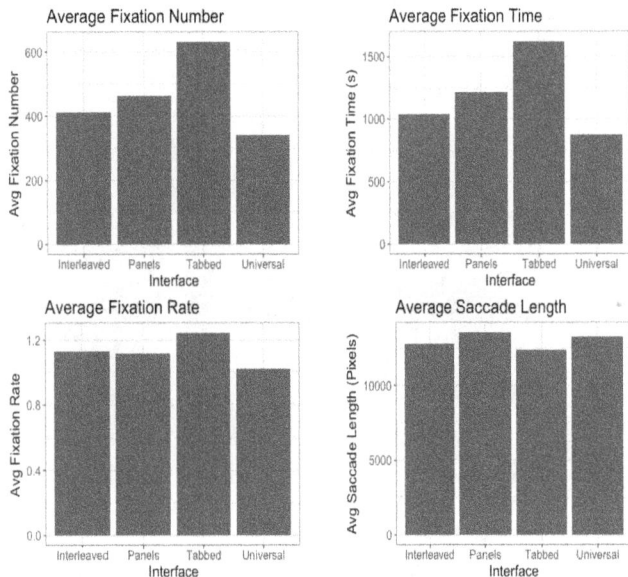

Figure 9. Eye tracking features per interface

The heat maps shown in Figure 10 are constructed through gradient colors from green to red, which represent eye fixation counts from low to high. The heat maps generally follow the same pattern as found in monolingual search research, showing a strong skewing towards the top few results. This meant that for 'Universal', L2 results received relatively less attention (although not resulting in statistically significantly lower document views). The heat map for the 'Panels' Interface reveals that participants frequently checked the top results for both 'L1' and 'L2', suggesting that both panels were regarded as equally important. This pattern also explains the higher saccade lengths found above.

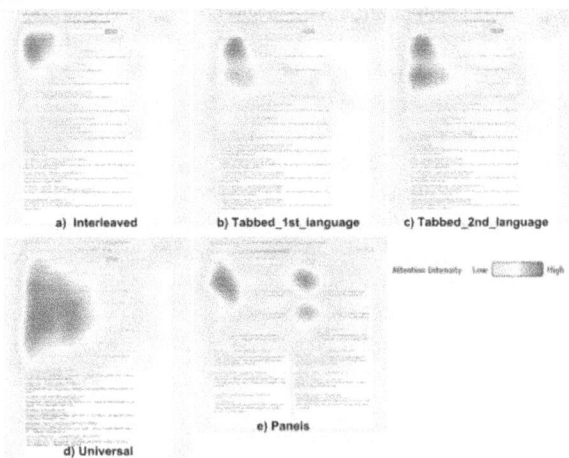

Figure 10. First glance heat maps

4.4.2 Influence of Task Type on User Behavior

Lastly, a series of additional analyses was conducted to investigate the influence of task type (*Doing/Fact Finding/Learning*), as well as any interaction effects between task type and interface type. A statistically significant effect was

found for task type on task time ($p<0.001$), with *Learning* tasks generally taking longer than both *Fact Finding* and *Doing* tasks.

In addition, there was a statistically significant difference regarding the number of L1 queries with respect to task type ($p<0.003$), with *Learning* tasks having a higher number of L1 queries than *Doing* and *FactFinding* tasks. Interestingly, there was no statistically significant difference in the number of L2 queries ($p<0.35$) or Mix queries ($p<0.31$) with respect to task type. Figure 11 illustrates this influence of task type on the use of L1, L2, and Mix queries. As can be seen in this graph, participants used a higher number of L1 queries during *Learning* tasks (particularly compared to *Doing* tasks), whereas the number of L2 queries was more stable.

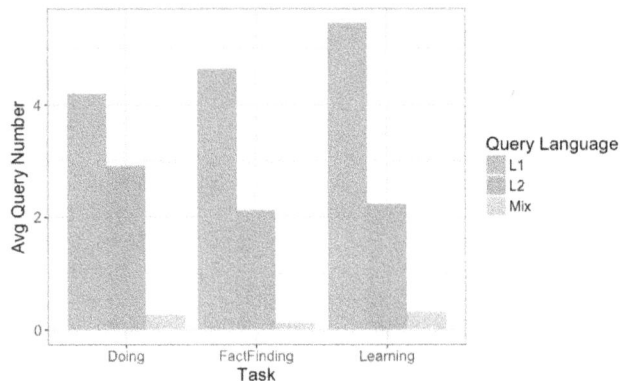

Figure 11. Average query number per language per task type

Related to this, we found that participants changed the query language less during *FactFinding* tasks compared to both *Doing* tasks ($p<0.003$) and *Learning* tasks ($p<0.01$). Similar results were found for the number of documents marked as relevant. However, no statistically significant differences could be found.

Lastly, there were no interaction effects between task type and interface type for any of the measures.

5 SUMMARY AND DISCUSSION

In this section, we will summarize the key findings from our study regarding interface-specific user preferences and interaction behaviors (RQ1 and RQ3), as well as general interaction behaviors found across all interfaces (RQ2). We will compare these results to prior work, provide further insights and recommendations based on participants' free text responses (given as part of the post-study questionnaire), and discuss implications for designing multilingual search interfaces.

The 'Panels' interface was by far the most preferred interface, and it was regarded as providing the best 'overview of information'. Additionally, when analyzing participants' free text responses, it was found that the 'Panels' interface was considered 'very organized' due to the 'clearly separated languages'. Participants reported that this made it easier to differentiate between the different languages, allowing one to focus on one language at a time. In addition, compared to the 'Tabbed' interface, which actually had the clearest language separation, participants liked that the 'Panels' interface still allowed the viewing of results in each language without any additional interface actions (e.g. clicking between tabs). This strong preference for the Panels interface is much more pronounced than in related monolingual aggregate search [16,18,19], hence suggesting that the combination of results in multiple languages is different from the combination of different verticals in traditional aggregated search (e.g. Web and image results). This may stem from strong saliency differences in traditional monolingual aggregate search (e.g. image results having a strong visual saliency compared to textual Web search results), which different multilingual results are lacking. In addition, this preference for 'Panels' is even more pronounced than in our prior work that used only static multilingual interfaces [3]. However, several users still reported some issues interacting with the 'Panels' interface. In particular, some users did not feel comfortable having to 'move their eyes around too much' to view different language panels when reading. In terms of behavioral differences, this increased gaze effort is supported by the saccade lengths found in the eye tracking analysis, which showed that the panels interface does induce longer saccades (although not increasing task times).

The 'Interleaved' interface, which interleaves results from different languages in a single ranked list, was found to be the 'most disliked' interface. In participants' free text comments, it was noted that the proximity of the different languages made it difficult for participants to 'transfer their reading mode' and thus they 'could not focus' and 'felt confused'. This may again be due to the aforementioned lack of saliency differences between different multilingual results, leading to extra cognitive effort for participants to 'code-switch' between languages. However, despite its general unpopularity, there were still some users who preferred the 'Interleaved' interface, stating that they thought it was 'faster to read'. This individual user differences may hence partially explain why there were no major behavioral differences (e.g. for task time) between 'Interleaved' and other interfaces.

While interfaces with clear language separation were generally preferred, the 'Universal' interface, which separates languages in vertical blocks, had the lowest vote for the most preferred, and the lowest number for the most disliked (hence evoking no strong reaction either way). Several participants noted that L2 results were too far down the list, meaning that they were sometimes not noticed. Nonetheless, the interface did not suffer from the strong general dislike that the 'Interleaved' interface received, which is different from prior findings with static interfaces [3]. It therefore appears that, if used in an interactive setting, 'Universal' is generally the preferred 'vertical result list' interface.

The most controversial interface was 'Tabbed', as it was voted second for 'easiest' and 'preferred' interface, yet also second for 'most disliked'. It appears therefore that there are clear differences between users. Some participants preferred 'Tabbed' to all other interfaces because of the ability to fully switch between languages (and hence having more results in the desired language on one page). However, others disliked it compared to all other interfaces because they had to switch manually between languages, which made it difficult to get an overview. In terms of behavioral differences, there were several trends suggesting that

a 'Tabbed' interface leads to longer task times, an increased number of queries, an increased number of documents marked as relevant, as well as a higher number of fixations and fixation durations. These trends echo similar results found for monolingual aggregate search [16], where it was found that 'Tabbed' interfaces generally afforded looking deeper into the details of individual result sources, while other 'Universal' (called 'Blended') interfaces afforded getting a quick overview of multiple sources.

In terms of general user interaction behaviors, there were several interesting findings across all interfaces. First of all, most participants made significant use of each of their languages during the study session, reinforcing the general motivation for providing systems that explicitly support multilingual users. While participants made less use of their L2 during querying, they did view and mark L1 and L2 documents almost to an equal degree. This suggests that when users choose to enter queries in a particular language (e.g. due to higher proficiency or personal preference), they are often still interested in viewing results in their other languages. This again confirms the usefulness of search result pages that integrate results from multiple languages. Interestingly, participants in our study did not make much use of query editing capabilities as recommended in prior work [12], nor language selection/deselection. This finding suggests that users prefer to simply reissue a new overall query, rather than interacting with a subpart of the multilingual result page. Participants' eye gaze behavior for each of the interfaces was generally similar to monolingual search result page results, with top results receiving comparably higher numbers of fixations. A notable pattern was shown for the 'Panels' interface, where participants gave equal priority to each individual panel. This suggests that horizontal panel placement may not be of great importance when presenting multilingual result pages.

While we also analyzed the effect of task type, we did not find many statistically significant differences. Most notably, we found that for *Learning* tasks, users issued an increased number of queries, and this increased number appeared to be mostly additional L1 queries. Conversely, for *Doing* and *FactFinding* tasks, which require less effort in general, the distribution between L1 and L2 was more balanced. This suggests that when users go beyond an initial overview of results (often sufficient for *Doing* and particularly simple *FactFinding* tasks), they tend to stick with their L1. Therefore, it may be sufficient to display only L1 results beyond the first result page. This would be similar to aggregated search practices in modern search engines, which often do not display aggregated pages beyond the first result page.

Lastly, across all interfaces, many participants noted in free text comments that it was important to clearly mark the language of individual or groups of results, e.g. through explicit labels. This need for clarity may have contributed to the general dislike of the 'Interleaved' interface, as it is lacking clear signifiers as to the language of each result. In addition, some participants indicated that they sometimes did not notice the different language sections, or completely forgot that other languages were available. This was particularly noted for the 'Universal' interface, suggesting that result blocks in secondary languages should potentially be 'slotted' higher in the vertical search result list in order to get noticed. This may take the form of modern aggregated search interfaces, where different verticals are slotted into a 'main list' dynamically. This variation of the 'Universal' interface warrants further research, as it may help users better notice the different languages, while still maintaining a clear language separation, which was generally found to be beneficial.

6 CONCLUSIONS AND FUTURE WORK

While the population of multilingual Web users across the globe has increased dramatically, there has been a distinct lack of research on how to best support multiple language abilities, particularly in terms of multilingual search result pages. In this paper, we have evaluated four interactive multilingual search interfaces designed specifically with multilingual users in mind.

Overall, it was found that clear language separation was strongly preferred, whereas an 'Interleaved' approach was least preferred. The findings from this interactive study thereby extend similar results found in studies that used static interfaces, and further present a compelling case for changing how multilingual search interfaces are built. In particular, while prior research in Multilingual Information Access has traditionally been confined to 'Interleaved' or 'Tabbed' presentation approaches, our studies have shown that these approaches are in fact often the least preferred by multilingual users. In terms of interaction behaviors, we found that users made significant use of each of their languages during search sessions. In particular, participants viewed and marked documents as relevant to a similar degree in each of their languages.

Lastly, there are several areas of future work to improve upon the interface approaches presented in this paper. For example, it was found that the 'Universal' interface, which presents blocks of results for each language in a single vertical list, sometimes suffered from participants missing lower language blocks (which was also confirmed by eye tracking results). A possible alternative to this approach worth exploring is therefore to "slot" result blocks in secondary languages higher up in the result list, similar to monolingual aggregate search interfaces, e.g. where blocks of image or news results are slotted in at various stages in a main search result list. While this may result in higher visibility for secondary languages, determining the ranking and/or number of results within different blocks will require further research. Likewise, further research is necessary in terms of determining potential causes for individual user preferences, e.g. some participants particularly liking/disliking the 'Tabbed' interface. This may involve the investigation of the effect of individual user characteristics, similar to studies on individual differences in the area of monolingual aggregate search [21]. Likewise, since the participant population in our study mostly reported high L2 proficiencies, further research is needed to determine the effects

of different levels of user proficiency on preferences and interaction behaviors.

REFERENCES

[1] SGO (the Steering Group Office for Survey of Language Use in China). 2006. *Findings and Documents of Survey of Language Situation in China.* Beijing: Language Press.

[2] Wei, R., & Su, J. 2012. The statistics of English in China. *English Today,* 28(03), 10-14.

[3] Steichen, B., & Freund, L. 2015. Supporting the Modern Polyglot: A Comparison of Multilingual Search Interfaces. *In Proceedings of the 33rd Annual ACM Conference on Human Factors in Computing Systems.* ACM, 3483-3492.

[4] Steichen, B., Ghorab, M.R., Lawless, S., O'Connor, A., and Wade, V. 2014. Towards Personalized Multilingual Information Access-Exploring the Browsing and Search Behavior of Multilingual Users. *In Proceedings of the International Conf. on User Modeling, Adaptation, and Personalization,* 435-446.

[5] Petrelli, D., Levin, S., Beaulieu, M., and Sanderson, M. 2006. Which user interaction for cross-language information retrieval? *Journal of the American Society for Information Science and Technology,* 57, 5 (2006), 709–722.

[6] Oard, D.W., He, D., and Wang, J. 2008. User-assisted query translation for interactive cross-language information retrieval. *Information Processing & Management.* 44, 1 (2008), 181–211.

[7] Marlow, J., Clough, P., Recuero, J.C., and Artiles, J. 2008. Exploring the effects of language skills on multilingual web search. *In Proceeding of 30th European Conference on Advances in information retrieval,* (2008), 126–137.

[8] Peters, C., Braschler, M., and Clough, P. 2012. Multilingual Information Retrieval: From Research To Practice, chapt. 4, *Springer Science & Business Media,* (2012).

[9] Gonzalo, Julio, and Douglas W. Oard. "The clef 2002 interactive track." *In Workshop of the Cross-Language Evaluation Forum for European Languages,* pp. 372-382. Springer, Berlin, Heidelberg, 2002.

[10] Oard, Douglas W., and Julio Gonzalo. "The CLEF 2003 interactive track." *In CLEF,* pp. 425-434. 2003.

[11] Petrelli, D., Levin, S., Beaulieu, M., & Sanderson, M. (2006). Which user interaction for cross-language information retrieval? Design issues and reflections. *Journal of the Association for Information Science and Technology,* 57(5), 709-722.

[12] Chu, P., Komlodi, A., & Rózsa, G. (2015). Online search in english as a non-native language. *Proceedings of the Association for Information Science and Technology,* 52(1), 1-9.

[13] Chu, P., & Komlodi, A. (2017, May). TranSearch: A Multilingual Search User Interface Accommodating User Interaction and Preference. *In Proceedings of the 2017 CHI Conference Extended Abstracts on Human Factors in Computing Systems* (pp. 2466-2472). ACM.

[14] Braschler, M. 2004. Combination Approaches for Multilingual Text Retrieval. *Information Retrieval,* 7, 1-2 (2004), 183–204.

[15] Amato, G., Debole, F., Peters, C., and Savino, P. 2008. The MultiMatch Prototype: Multilingual/Multimedia Search for Cultural Heritage Objects. *In International Conference on Theory and Practice of Digital Libraries,* (2008), 385–387.

[16] Bron, M., van Gorp, J., Nack, F., Baltussen, L.B., and de Rijke, M. 2013. Aggregated Search Interface Preferences in Multi-session Search Tasks. *In Proceedings of the 36th international ACM SIGIR conference on Research and development in information retrieval,* (2013), 123–132.

[17] Capstick, J., Diagne, A.K., Erbach, G., Uszkoreit, H., Leisenberg, A., and Leisenberg, M. 2000. A system for supporting cross-lingual information retrieval. *Information processing & management.* 36, 2 (2000), 275–289.

[18] Sushmita, S., Joho, H., Lalmas, M., and Villa, R. 2010. Factors Affecting Click-through Behavior in Aggregated Search Interfaces. *In Proceedings of the 19th ACM international conference on Information and knowledge management,* (2010), 519–528.

[19] Thomas, P., Noack, K., and Paris, C. 2010. Evaluating Interfaces for Government Metasearch. *In Proceedings of the third symposium on Information interaction in context,* (2010), 65–74.

[20] Freund, L. 2013. A cross-domain analysis of task and genre effects on perceptions of usefulness. *Information Processing & Management.* 49, 5, 1108-1121, 2013.

[21] Brennan, K., Kelly, D., and Arguello, J. The effect of cognitive abilities on information search for tasks of varying levels of complexity. In Proc. of the 5th Information Interaction in Context Symposium (IIiX '14), 165-174. 2014.

Collaborative Information Seeking through Social Media Updates in Real-Time

Karthik Bhat
Institute for Computing and Society
United Nations University
Macau SAR, China
ksbhat@unu.edu

Andrés Moreno
Institute for Computing and Society
United Nations University
Macau SAR, China
amoreno@unu.edu

Michael L. Best
Institute for Computing and Society
United Nations University
Macau SAR, China
mikeb@unu.edu

ABSTRACT

This paper describes co-located collaborative information seeking in the context of the Social Media Tracking Centre (SMTC) in Ghana. The SMTC was operational for three days during the Presidential elections in Dec 2016. The SMTC's role was to collaboratively find and verify novel, actionable, and relevant information on social media and escalate it to the authorities to use that information to ensure a transparent and peaceful election process. We performed a qualitative analysis of semi-structured interviews with the volunteers at the SMTC as well as its managing team. We present, in this paper, the importance of volunteer motivation and co-location in the success of the SMTC, as well as the users' feedback on the collaborative tool, informing future design, derived from our analysis.

CCS CONCEPTS

• **Human-centered computing** → **Empirical studies in collaborative and social computing**; • **Information systems** → *Collaborative filtering*; *Social networking sites*;

KEYWORDS

Collaborative Information Seeking, Social Media Monitoring, Crisis Monitoring, Co-location, Motivation, Aggie

ACM Reference format:
Karthik Bhat, Andrés Moreno, and Michael L. Best. 2018. Collaborative Information Seeking through Social Media Updates in Real-Time. In *Proceedings of Conference on Human Information Interaction & Retrieval, New Brunswick, NJ, USA, March 11–15, 2018 (CHIIR'18)*, 4 pages.
https://doi.org/10.1145/3176349.3176869

1 INTRODUCTION

Social media monitoring has become popular in the field of crisis monitoring and response, as updates from social media users can be used by emergency services to increase their situational awareness [8]. Social media monitoring can relate to the field the collaborative information seeking (CIS) as it involves teams seeking meaning from information retrieved from social media platforms.

CIS "is just as much about making coherent sense of information as it is about finding extant information. In a collaborative context, information is typically distributed unevenly across actors, and they may interpret the information known to them in different ways or be unable to make coherent sense of it" [6]. This definition fits social media monitoring activities with the caveat that there may not be *extant* information, but the *possibility* of relevant, timely and actionable information. The quick changes in the relevance and actionability of real time information make "collaborative grounding" [6] crucial to the work of the social media monitors. Human organizations and software platforms should push for collaboration and sharing of information as the search task proceeds to avoid individual monitors not benefiting from others' work, and to avoid taking collaboration for granted [6].

This paper presents the CIS in the context of a Social Media Tracking Centre (SMTC) during the Presidential elections of 2016 in Ghana. It adds to CIS literature by addressing the motivation to participate in CIS and the importance of co-location as expressed by the interviewees who participated in the SMTC. It also comments on software features designed to assist collaboration, and then discusses potential improvements to the software to inform future platform design for collaboration.

2 BACKGROUND

Foster [3] defines the field of CIS as "the study of the systems and practices that enable individuals to collaborate during the seeking, searching and retrieval of information". Hertzum [6] expands the scope of this definition by combining it "with the collaborative-grounding activities involved in making this information part of the actors' shared understanding of their work". This definition better captures the importance of communication, and information sharing to establish a shared understanding of knowledge. It also allows for group processes during social media monitoring events to be studied as a collaborative information seeking environment.

CIS research has focused on the usage of existing tools for collaboration [2], and applications of CIS in different domains like healthcare [11] and education [7]. Various tools have also been developed specifically for collaboration such as CoSearch [1] and TeamSearch [10] for searching online for digital content, and Co-agmento [13] for "collaborative information seeking, synthesis and sense-making". More recently, research has been directed towards new areas, including assisting collaboration in humanities research [4] and investigating the influence of mood and emotions during collaborative tasks [5]. However, literature has been found lacking with regards to the usage of CIS tools in social media monitoring, and situational awareness during critical events. Conversely, social media monitoring has not yet been studied as a CIS context.

This paper addresses this gap in the literature. We have performed a qualitative analysis of the interviews of volunteers who participated in the CIS at the SMTC and its managing team to understand the factors that affect the collaboration in a real time information seeking setting: co-location of collaborators, and motivation to participate. This addresses one of the gaps in CIS literature brought out by Shah [14]: "motivations are not identified in the context of situations in which collaborative information searching occur". We also comment on affordances of the collaborative platform used by the volunteers and suggest improvements that could inform future design of collaborative tools for social media monitoring.

3 SMTC: SETTING OF THE CIS

During the Ghanaian presidential elections of 2016, a local NGO conducted CIS for election-related events by recruiting volunteers from local institutes to work at an SMTC. The SMTC was an organization with four volunteer teams and one managing team comprising of members of the NGO. Three of the teams, namely the *tracking*, *veracity* and *escalation* teams, were co-located in a single room. The fourth team, namely the *embedded* team, acted as liaisons between the SMTC and different partner organizations. The tracking team's role was to read incoming information and forward useful information to the veracity team as 'incidents'. The veracity team would then try to establish the veracity of these incidents. If the information was true, this was passed on to the escalation team, who would contact members of the embedded team in the most relevant government organization to act on this information.

The SMTC members used Aggie[1] to monitor social media and to coordinate and organize the monitoring process. Aggie is an open source web application for aggregating social media and other digital resources to track incidents during real-time events such as elections or natural disasters. It allows organizations to extract key data from social media posts through automatic aggregation and manual expert filtering. The volunteers were trained to use Aggie for 15 hours spread over 5 sessions. They were given introductions to Aggie, the working of an SMTC and the roles of each team. The trained volunteers could collaborate, verbally or using Aggie, to add social media information to incidents and follow up on the resolution of incidents by virtue of their co-location.

Aggie is designed for collaborative information seeking among the different roles. Features provided to the tracking team assist them in filtering reports according to several criteria, e.g., date, author, keyword. Aggie also ensures each member is assigned a unique set of reports to analyze (a 'batch' of reports), with each report assigned to no more than one user. Aggie provides the co-located teams with flags and the ability to assign other users to follow up on the 'incidents' to assist in collaboration.

4 METHOD

We have used qualitative methods of data collection and analysis. The qualitative data was collected between 6th and 8th December,

2016. We conducted semi-structured interviews with the volunteers (17) who consented to be interviewed. We also interviewed members of the embedded team (4) and the SMTC managing team (3) all of whom were employees of the Ghanaian NGO that was hosting the SMTC. Additionally we interviewed media experts (3) from different organizations before the elections to understand their opinion on the role of social and traditional media platforms in news reporting during the elections. In total, we conducted 27 interviews. The interviews were conducted in English. Despite self-selection, the volunteers who were interviewed represented a balanced sample of all volunteers as they had worked in all shifts, and had worked in all co-located teams of the SMTC.

The volunteers were interviewed for about 15 minutes, and were asked about their most and least successful strategies for finding incidents and the different roles they performed at the SMTC. The members of the managing team were interviewed for about 30-60 minutes, and were asked about their experience organizing the SMTC, and their reflections on its success. One of the authors present at the SMTC also recorded observations that informed the research and findings.

The interviews were audio and video recorded, and later transcribed. One of the authors conducted the interviews, and some of the transcription was split among two of the authors. The rest of the transcription was done by a research assistant hired in Ghana. We used Template analysis [9] to analyze these transcripts. The transcripts were first open-coded by one author who did not conduct the interviews. The initial codes were reviewed by the other authors, and some emerging themes were discussed. The interviews covered a range of topics spanning different aspects of the research plan. For this paper, we combined some emerging themes from the first round of coding into broader themes (e.g. 'technology', 'curiosity', 'impact' were combined as 'motivation'), and re-coded the interviews with these as a template. The findings we present in this paper are borne out of these themes.

5 FINDINGS AND DISCUSSION

The interviewees covered a variety of topics in their responses. First, we focus on some factors that the interviewees said were critical to the success (finding 159 election-related incidents from the 300717 collected reports) of the SMTC. Then we present findings on the design of Aggie as a collaborative tool, and the features the interviewees said they found useful or lacking.

5.1 Success Factors

The interviewees spoke of factors that positively influenced the collaboration at the SMTC, and its operation as a social media monitoring entity during the elections.

5.1.1 Co-location of teams. The authors observed first-hand, and learned from the interviews, some collaborative practices that emerged by virtue of the co-location of the volunteers at the SMTC. In this regard, the interview with the SMTC coordinator was the most informative, due to his capacity as the information seeking instigator. He spoke of two practices that worked very well: **vocal coordination**, and **live feedback**.

When asked what he felt resulted in the successful operation of the SMTC, he said, that "*team communication... went really really*

---

[1]Screenshots and documentation can be found at http://getaggie.org

well". He exemplified this statement by saying:

"I realized that some people would call out and say, 'who is working on this incident?' because he may be trying to create a new incident and he wants to be sure that no one else is working that. At some point it was too noisy. Maybe I felt it ought to be quiet, but realized it was working for them because of the cross-communication... so that went really well... in terms of knowledge sharing"

He added that, in addition to the inter-team communication, the co-location also assisted with easy feedback channels, by saying:

"... point where someone comes up to the monitors and says, 'hey, you guys have to tag this well. You have to do this well because it is making us work twice' ... When they saw something they didn't keep it until the end of review, they will tell them right there, 'do that and fix that because it is giving us issues'. The feedback system really worked well and enabled the other team to pick up and work with the data they have gathered"

There is extensive literature on the two factors that inform the classic way of organizing collaborative activities: location and time. Twidale and Nichols [17] first depicted the existing collaborative platforms on these two dimensions. Some existing research suggests that collaboration involving benefiting from others' actions is often asynchronous and remote [14]. Teasley et. al.[16], on the other hand, situated teams in a "warroom setting" to assist communication and assist benefiting from each others' interactions. They explain how the teams in their study performed much better in co-located situations, terming it as "radical collocation" and asserting that such warroom-like co-location greatly increased productivity.

Collaboration in tasks is successful when there is a diversity among the people [12]. To take advantage of this, the volunteers at the SMTC were asked to switch roles at certain points of time, so that there was variety in their responsibilities, and a variety in people performing the tasks. Teasley et. al., [16] observed how the proximity of the team members allowed them to overhear each other, and help if someone was having difficulty in some task. The information seeking instigator at the SMTC observed a similar phenomenon occur during the CIS: when the volunteers changed roles, they helped each other with the expertise they had gained in their previous roles.

Ultimately, communication in some form is essential for good collaboration. In the SMTC, this communication was efficient due to the co-location of the volunteers, who could talk to each other and call each other's attention. It removed barriers for communication, and further proved conducive for fluid work practices that could be modified for better productivity with no communication overhead. Therefore, we posit that in a short-term, time-sensitive setting of a critical event, co-location assists fast knowledge sharing, and consequently, better CIS.

5.1.2 Motivation to participate in CIS. The interviewees mentioned various reasons why they participated in the SMTC. Their motivations can be classified based on two broad factors: **social impact** and **use of new technology**.

The anticipated social impact of their work appears to have motivated the volunteers to participate in the CIS at the SMTC. One such motivating factor was the ability not just to find and act on information, but also to verify the information, and disseminate corrections to the public. One of the interviewees expressed,

"...I enjoyed every minute of... what we were doing. I also self-found that it is a very great way to inform the public. Especially in countries where elections are taking place, [situation] can be sensitive, and anytime [false] information is spread to people, it can easily affect them and also be a threat to others... With processes and with system[s] like Aggie, [it] would make people and communities that are voting to be safe and to be sure [of their safety], and also encourages people to ... turn out to vote."

Similarly, the interviewees were also motivated by the sense of contributing towards upholding the country's democracy by counteracting fake news and rumors. One volunteer stressed on this by saying *"... the SMTC program was quite beneficial to the election process in Ghana... greatest thing about it is that ordinary people can actually contribute to something which... can shape elections in Ghana and I think it is something magnificent"*.

Using, and learning about, new technologies was a big motivating factor for the volunteers who were mostly students in a technological entrepreneurship program. One interviewee told us when he heard *"that people are using technology to solve some... problems with elections-related issues"*, he was *"very, very happy... wanted to learn how a technology tool is going to help monitor social media"*. Another interviewee saw this as a *"step in the right direction"* towards integrating new useful technology. She further explained, *"... with systems and programs like Aggie, it is a clear indication of how technology can be used for good."*.

The volunteers were not political experts but had been in Ghana for long enough to understand the local political situation. This situational knowledge was very important in our time-critical information seeking. The information received by the SMTC was rich with geographical information, political references, and sometimes was even completely false. We suggest that this local immersion and knowledge contributed to the effectiveness of the SMTC.

We posit that these motivations to participate in the CIS were a major factor in the success of the SMTC. Spatharioti and Cooper [15] say that "simple tasks such as image labeling often feel monotonous and lead to worker disengagement". While the same can be said of the tracking team's task of clicking a button to read 15 text-based reports for hours on end, we observed no sense of disengagement and we actually found that attempts to preclude monotony by switching tasks was met with resistance. This resistance, we suggest, was born out of the workers' motivation to ensure safe elections. Switching tasks, to them, meant a loss of productivity and a waste of developed expertise, as opposed to a welcome respite from a repetitive task. Existing research [15] on crowdsourced work on Mechanical Turk suggests that "task variety is a key factor in worker motivation". Our findings, in the SMTC setting, suggest that intrinsic motivation is a bigger factor than task variety.

5.2 Platform Design for CIS

Aggie, as mentioned, has some features to assist in collaboration within and among the different teams at the SMTC. For the tracking team, the most polarizing feature of Aggie was the ability to filter reports when perusing 'batches' of reports. By nature, the feature was meant to filter out unwanted information, and provide perceivably useful information. The volunteers, however, felt that filtering out unwanted information would result in a failure on their part to read through *all* incoming content for information. One volunteer defended this approach by saying

"*...I didn't use that [filtered batch] like most of the times and the reason I didn't use that was because I realized, I believed am suppose to like go through everything. So reducing it to whatever I want to, won't be the most efficient way to search. So I allowed it to give me everything and I go through.*"

One volunteer said that "*the flow or the momentum that you are working with is disrupted*" when using filters. Narrowly defined filters could result in no more than one or two batches of unread reports thereby forcing the volunteers to stop and reset the filters after analyzing those few batches, disrupting their rhythm.

Volunteers also found the ability to filter out 'retweets', essentially repeated information on the platform, beneficial in addition to the ability to filter out old, and therefore potentially useless information and find new information.

Aggie was aggregating information across social media platforms such as Facebook and Twitter. Both these platforms have different affordances, with lots of interviewees opining that Facebook was uninformative, and Twitter's 'retweets' were bothering them as noise. This did lead to some interesting ad-hoc practices at the SMTC, such as some volunteers taking on the sole responsibility of reading Facebook reports, in order to allow others to see more useful ones. However, social media aggregation platforms like Aggie could, in the future, cluster retweets together, and/or cluster all social media reports with the exact same information together, to allow for easier useful-information gathering.

Like reports, the created incidents could also be filtered by criteria like date, location, and tags. Contrarily to the ability to filter reports, the ability to filter incidents was well received by the veracity team members. When talking about how they used the filtering feature to verify incidents, the volunteers spoke of its usefulness in determining duplicate incidents. One volunteer spoke of how they used the 'location' assigned to a relevant tweet to filter out the duplicates as, "*...some people could use different wording...for the name of the incident. So the best thing is use the location [filter] and all of them pop up, and you can actually find if it is the same incident*".

The "radical collocation" has disadvantages noticed both by Teasley et al. [16] and at the SMTC: the communication causes noise and consequently, in Teasley's study, distraction. The information seeking instigator felt that at some point, the SMTC got too noisy; but acknowledged that it didn't affect the productivity of the volunteers. The issue at the SMTC was the lack of a feature in the collaborative platform that provided the user a knowledge of others' actions. In retrospect, a design solution that may have reduced the amount of cross communication is a live-ticker of other collaborators' actions. This may, to some extent, have reduced the number of volunteers asking for updates from others.

6 CONCLUSION AND FUTURE WORK

In this paper, we described a real time collaborative information seeking task in the context of the Social Media Tracking Centre during the Presidential elections of Ghana in December 2016. A group of volunteers used Aggie: a tool for social media aggregation, to collect and organize their workflow in a co-located setting. The

volunteers were involved in a workflow involving gathering information from various social media sources, establishing the veracity of the information, and eventually using the gained knowledge to assist government organizations in resolving situations.

We described the collaborative information seeking performed by the different teams at the SMTC. We also provided an overview of the affordances of Aggie to assist in collaboration. We then presented our findings that emphasized on two factors that contributed to the productivity of the CIS: co-location to assist timely collaborative grounding, and motivation to participate in this real time information seeking during the elections, and discussed the volunteers' feedback on some features of Aggie.

The space of social media monitoring tools and practices has not yet been studied under the lens of collaborative information seeking. This provides ample opportunity for future research to analyze, and consequently inform design of social media monitoring platforms. Such lens could also assist in designing training and establishing collaborative practices for monitoring critical events in real-time.

REFERENCES

[1] Saleema Amershi and Meredith Ringel Morris. 2008. CoSearch: a system for co-located collaborative web search. In *Proceedings of the SIGCHI Conference on Human Factors in Computing Systems*. ACM, 1647–1656.

[2] Robert Capra, Gary Marchionini, Javier Velasco-Martin, and Katrina Muller. 2010. Tools-at-hand and learning in multi-session, collaborative search. In *Proceedings of the SIGCHI Conference on Human Factors in Computing Systems*. ACM, 951–960.

[3] Jonathan Foster. 2006. Collaborative information seeking and retrieval. *Annual Review of Information Science and Technology* 40, 1 (Jan. 2006), 329–356.

[4] Lisa M. Given and Rebekah Willson. 2015. Collaboration, Information Seeking, and Technology Use: A Critical Examination of Humanities Scholars' Research Practices. In *Collaborative Information Seeking*. Springer International Publishing, 139–154.

[5] Roberto González-Ibáñez. 2015. Affective Dimension in Collaborative Information Seeking. In *Collaborative Information Seeking*. Springer International Publishing, 193–208.

[6] Morten Hertzum. 2008. Collaborative information seeking: The combined activity of information seeking and collaborative grounding. *Information Processing & Management* 44, 2 (March 2008), 957–962.

[7] Jette Hyldegård. 2006. Collaborative Information Behaviour - exploring Kuhlthau's Information Search Process Model in a Group-based Educational Setting. *Inf. Process. Manage.* 42, 1 (Jan. 2006), 276–298.

[8] Muhammad Imran, Carlos Castillo, Fernando Diaz, and Sarah Vieweg. 2015. Processing Social Media Messages in Mass Emergency: A Survey. *ACM Comput. Surv.* 47, 4 (June 2015), 67:1–67:38.

[9] Nigel King. 2004. Using templates in the thematic analysis of text. In *Essential guide to qualitative methods in organizational research*, Catherine Cassell and Gillian Symon (Eds.). SAGE Publications, Ltd, London, 256–70.

[10] Meredith Ringel Morris, Andreas Paepcke, and Terry Winograd. 2006. Teamsearch: Comparing techniques for co-present collaborative search of digital media. In *Horizontal Interactive Human-Computer Systems, 2006. TableTop 2006. First IEEE International Workshop on*. IEEE, 8–pp.

[11] Madhu C. Reddy and Bernard J. Jansen. 2008. A model for understanding collaborative information behavior in context: A study of two healthcare teams. *Information Processing & Management* 44, 1 (Jan. 2008), 256–273.

[12] Chirag Shah. 2009. Toward collaborative information seeking (CIS). *arXiv preprint arXiv:0908.0709* (2009).

[13] Chirag Shah. 2010. Coagmento-a collaborative information seeking, synthesis and sense-making framework. *Integrated demo at CSCW* 2010 (2010).

[14] Chirag Shah. 2010. Collaborative Information Seeking: A Literature Review. In *Advances in Librarianship*, Anne Woodsworth (Ed.). Vol. 32. Emerald Group Publishing Limited, 3–33. DOI: 10.1108/S0065-2830(2010)0000032004.

[15] Sofia Eleni Spathariotis and Seth Cooper. 2017. On Variety, Complexity, and Engagement in Crowdsourced Disaster Response Tasks. In *Proceedings of the 14th International Conference on Information Systems for Crisis Response And Management*. Albi, France, 489–498.

[16] Stephanie Teasley, Lisa Covi, Mayuram S. Krishnan, and Judith S. Olson. 2000. How does radical collocation help a team succeed?. In *Proceedings of the 2000 ACM conference on Computer supported cooperative work*. ACM, 339–346.

[17] Michael Twidale and David Nichols. 1996. Collaborative browsing and visualisation of the search process. In *Aslib Proceedings*, Vol. 48. 177–182.

How to Evaluate Humorous Response Generation, Seriously?

Pavel Braslavski
Ural Federal University
pavel.braslavsky@urfu.ru

Vladislav Blinov
Ural Federal University
vladislav.blinov@urfu.ru

Valeria Bolotova
Ural Federal University
lurunchik@gmail.com

Katya Pertsova
University of North Carolina
pertsova@email.unc.edu

ABSTRACT

Nowadays natural language user interfaces, such as chatbots and conversational agents, are very common. A desirable trait of such applications is a sense of humor. It is, therefore, important to be able to measure quality of humorous responses. However, humor evaluation is hard since humor is highly subjective. To address this problem, we conducted an online evaluation of 30 dialog jokes from different sources by almost 300 participants – volunteers and Mechanical Turk workers. We collected joke ratings along with participants' age, gender, and language proficiency. Results show that demographics and joke topics can partly explain variation in humor judgments. We expect that these insights will aid humor evaluation and interpretation. The findings can also be of interest for humor generation methods in conversational systems.

KEYWORDS

computational humor; conversational systems; evaluation; crowdsourcing

ACM Reference Format:
Pavel Braslavski, Vladislav Blinov, Valeria Bolotova, and Katya Pertsova. 2018. How to Evaluate Humorous Response Generation, Seriously?. In *Proceedings of 2018 Conference on Human Information Interaction & Retrieval (CHIIR '18).* ACM, New York, NY, USA, 4 pages. https://doi.org/10.1145/3176349.3176879

1 INTRODUCTION

There is a rapid proliferation of natural language interfaces – chatbots, intelligent assistants, conversational agents. These interfaces are used for a variety of tasks – from ordering pizza to serving as an intelligent companion or even a confidant of the user. The technology behind such applications as Apple's Siri or Microsoft's Cortana is changing the style of human interaction with mobile devices, cars, consumer electronics, smart homes, etc. This interaction becomes more emotional, personal, and even intimate. Sense of humor is an important quality of a conversational agent: humor makes a human-computer conversation more engaging, helps to establish a

more trusting relationship between the user and the agent, creates a feeling of agent's empathy and personality. The need for humor is evident from the users' requests to personal assistants: "tell me a joke" is a very frequent request [10]. A humorous response is a good option for out-of-domain requests [4], it can soften the negative impact of inadequacies in the system's performance [5] and is a good option if the system is not able to generate an appropriate response.

The sense of humor of modern mobile personal assistants is seemingly based on a relatively small number of hand-crafted stimulus–response pairs, which leads to repetitions. Ideally, a personal assistant should be able to produce fresh and funny responses for a wide variety of input utterances. Thus, it becomes crucial to evaluate what users find funny. Automatic evaluation of dialog systems that relies on proximity metrics to reference utterances received a great deal of attention thanks to end-to-end training of conversational systems. As a recent study showed [12], outcomes of such evaluation do not correlate with human judgments well. Automatic methods for evaluation of humorous responses should be even worse due to diversity of potentially funny responses in a given context. Subsequently, a controlled lab evaluation remains the main viable option so far. Humor evaluation is challenging since the perception of humor is highly subjective and is conditioned on the situation and the socio-cultural background. Our preliminary small-scale evaluation experiments have shown that assessors' agreement is very low [6].

In this follow-up study, we attempt to investigate the problem of humor evaluation on a larger scale using crowdsourcing. The main idea of the study is to analyze personal characteristics of the assessors and estimate the contribution of these characteristics to variations in judgments. We collected a set of 30 two-turn jokes from different sources. Almost 300 people – volunteers and paid Mechanical Turk workers – took part in the online evaluation. Along with joke ratings, we collected assessors' age, gender, language proficiency, self-assessed sense of humor, and Big5 personality traits[1].

We conclude that crowdsourcing platforms are an efficient and appropriate option for humor evaluation. Annotators' demographics such as age and language proficiency can partly explain their disagreement. Although gender does not affect average humor scores, certain topics are appreciated by men and women differently. Comparison of obtained ratings with those based on evidence from joke sources (e.g. likes and retweets in case of funny tweets) suggests that we cannot straightforwardly reuse the same humor scores in different settings. We expect that these new insights will help to

---

[1]Due to limited space we do not report the Big5-related analysis of results in the paper.

design better humor evaluation methods and interpret their outcomes. The findings can also be used to improve humor generation strategies in conversational systems.

2 RELATED WORK

Our experimental design is similar to psychological humor appreciation studies. For example, a widely adopted 3 WD (*Witzdimensionen*) test assesses an individual's perception of jokes and cartoons along three basic humor types: incongruity-resolution, nonsense, and sexual humor [18]. While psychological tests aim at revealing individual humor-related traits based on a fixed set of stimuli, our goal is to reliably evaluate humorous content from an average user's point of view.

Jester dataset [7, 16] contains over 5 million ratings of 100 jokes from 150K users on a continuous [−10, +10] scale. Jokes were collected 'from friends and newsgroups' with filtering out 'highly offensive jokes'. However, the main focus of Jester was on the joke recommendation algorithm, rather than on specific issues of humor evaluation. Both users and jokes were treated as a 'black box'.

In computational humor studies, humorous vs. serious content is usually considered as such based on its source: for example, humor collections vs. news [15, 23]. Another approach relies on expert opinion. For example, humor scores of tweets related to a TV show in the *#HashtagWars* collection reflect the choice of the show's editorial staff [17].

There are two main approaches to evaluating computer–generated humor. In one of them, users evaluate their overall experience of using the system and the system's sense of humor in particular [11, 15, 22]. The second approach is to evaluate individual automatically-generated jokes on a rating scale [9, 20, 21]. Many of these studies rely on crowdsourcing [19, 21, 22], but unfortunately they do not report crucial details about the evaluation process. Humor evaluation experiments mentioned above also do not take into account the demographics of assessors and their personal traits.

3 EXPERIMENTAL DESIGN

The online questionnaire consisted of an introduction followed by three sections: 1) demographics; 2) Big5 test plus two sense of humor self-assessment items; and 3) 10 screens with three dialog jokes on each to evaluate, 30 jokes in total.

We collected demographic information about age range, gender, and English proficiency. To obtain Big5 factor scores we used the Ten Item Personality Measure (TIPI) [8]. Additionally, participants were asked to assess two items related to their humor appreciation and productivity on a 7-point scale:

(1) *I laugh often; it is easy to make me laugh.*
(2) *I usually pun, tell jokes or funny anecdotes in a social situation.*

We collected 30 two-turn dialog jokes from several sources: Jester dataset, Siri, *Jokes & Riddles* category of Yahoo!Answers[2], Reddit's *funny* subreddit[3], tweets from funny Twitter accounts[4], as well as automatically retrieved answers to Yahoo!Answers questions from our previous experiments [6]. The breakdown of the collection

---

[2]https://answers.yahoo.com/dir/index?sid=396546041
[3]https://www.reddit.com/r/funny/
[4]These accounts were obtained through various lists, such as http://www.hongkiat.com/blog/funny-twitter-accounts/

Table 1: Joke sources, average scores, and rank correlations with rankings in source data

Source	Count	Avg. score	Spearman's ρ
Jester	7	2.32	0.57
Siri	3	1.76	–
Yahoo!Answers	5	1.73	0.05
Automatically generated	5	1.80	0.97
Reddit	5	2.37	0.80
Twitter	5	1.82	-0.30
Total	30	2.01	

by joke source is shown in Table 1.[5] In the case of Siri we went through image results for a query [siri jokes] and picked up funny question/answer pairs that have no references to Siri herself. When composing the collection we tried to maintain topical variety. In addition, we tried to pick jokes of varying levels of funniness based on ratings presented in the original sources – points on Reddit, thumbs up & down on Yahoo! Answers, likes and retweets on Twitter, and user ratings in Jester data. Note that the Jester dataset contains 'canned jokes' only; Siri jokes can also be assigned to the same category due to the popularity of the application and its limited joke inventory. Other jokes are closer to spontaneous conversational jokes: the odds are high that the assessors have not seen them before. See [1] for distinction between canned and conversational jokes.

The jokes were presented to participants on 10 screens, three jokes at a time. The order of the screens and jokes were the same for all participants. The jokes were judged on a four-point scale, with corresponding emoticons in the evaluation interface: not funny at all (1, ☺), can be better (2, ☺), funny (3, ☺), and hilarious (4, ☺).

Volunteers were recruited via online social networks. Paid workers were recruited through the Mechanical Turk (MT) crowdsourcing platform. MT workers were required to have a US locale and were offered 0.3$ per HIT.

4 RESULTS AND DISCUSSION

4.1 General Trends

Overall, 167 volunteers and 112 MT workers took part in the experiment.[6] Table 2 reports the breakdown of total 279 participants by age, gender, and English language proficiency (see #-columns).

As can be seen from the Table, the population has a skew towards younger people (under 30); however, the next two age groups (31–40 and 41-50) are fairly well presented in the sample. The population is gender-balanced, although we undertook no special efforts to ensure it. Almost all MT workers reported being English native speakers, whereas volunteers' self-reported proficiency in English is more diffuse.

Self-assessed humor appreciation/productivity levels do not correlate with joke scores.[7] It means that self-reported sense of humor cannot be used for unbiasing the joke scores.

---

[5]The complete list is available at http://bit.ly/HumorEval
[6]We rejected MT workers who spent less than five seconds per page or used only two out of four levels on the evaluation scale.
[7]However, the correlation is high in a group of 15 participants who assessed *both* their humor appreciation and productivity as very high.

Table 2: Average joke scores and number of participants by group (MT – MT workers, V – volunteers)

	Group	MT	# MT	V	# V	All	# All
Age Group	18–30	2.05	46	2.07	77	2.06	123
	31–40	1.89	37	2.04	54	1.98	91
	41–50	1.80	18	2.02	29	1.94	47
	51–60	1.84	10	1.97	6	1.89	16
	61+	1.73	1	3.33	1	2.53	2
Sex	Male	1.92	52	2.01	82	1.97	134
	Female	1.95	60	2.10	85	2.04	145
Language	Average	–	–	2.16	15	2.16	15
	Good	2.25	5	2.10	69	2.11	74
	Bilingual	2.11	3	2.06	39	2.07	42
	Native	1.91	104	1.95	44	1.92	148
	Global	1.93	112	2.06	167	2.01	279

Table 2 summarizes average joke scores for each group of participants. According to an independent-sample t-test, the difference between average scores of volunteers and MTurk workers for 30 jokes is not statistically significant.

Mean assessments by men and women are slightly but insignificantly distinct. This result supports numerous psychological studies that find no gender-specific differences in sense of humor. There are still gender-specific topical preferences: studies suggest that men are more likely to enjoy aggressive and sexual humor, whereas women like 'nonsense' humor more (see references and discussion in [13]). Our data support these hypotheses, see section 4.2.

Average joke scores decrease whith age. This is in line with some psychological studies suggesting that decline in cognitive abilities in the elderly may be associated with lower comprehension of humor (but greater humor appreciation at the same time). Some studies suggest that *humor type preferences* change with age (see details in [13]).

We can also observe a monotone decrease of average scores with increase in language proficiency, which is surprising at first glance. According to [3], most frequent cases of failed humor appreciation by non-native speakers are connected with the failure to understand the meaning of words and their connotations. Grasping word ambiguities is crucial in our experiment since many jokes in our collection involve some kind of wordplay. We hypothesize that participants had no time pressure to comprehend the jokes in contrast to real-life conversations (volunteers spent more time assessing the jokes, see below). Non-native speakers may also be less aware of 'canned' jokes.

Figure 1 shows average time spent on assessment along with average joke scores by MT workers vs. volunteers on each out of 10 screens of joke triples. The score bars demonstrate again that volunteers and MT workers assess jokes in a very similar way. The time chart shows that MT workers complete tasks faster; there is less variation in time intervals. This observation can be explained again by MT workers' language proficiency and their more professional attitude. The discrepancy of time spent on the first page between volunteers and MT workers can be explained by the fact that this is the shortest page out of 10 (three jokes make up 230 characters), the jokes on this page are quite simple (i.e. no tricky wordplay), and volunteers are very enthusiastic at

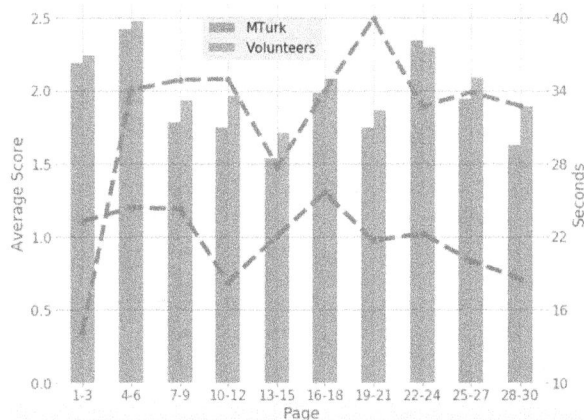

Figure 1: Time spent (line, right y-axis) and corresponding average scores (bars, left y-axis) for joke triples.

the very beginning of the experiment and less so at the end. There is seemingly no 'fatigue effect' towards the later pages that some volunteers reported in private conversations. It is interesting to note that time spent per page and average triple scores are oppositely correlated in volunteers (-0.21) and MT workers (0.47).

4.2 Individual Jokes

In this section we make observations about the specific jokes. For example, below is the joke with the highest variation in ratings:

Q: *Why did 10 die?*
A: *He was in the middle of 9/11.*

It is obvious that jokes about the tragedy of 2001 may seem inappropriate to many people. The greatest difference between average scores (0.97) can be observed between the groups of native speakers and participants with an average knowledge of English.

Despite the fact that men and women assess jokes in a similar way, their judgments are quite different on some jokes. Here's the joke which shows the largest difference (0.50) between men's and women's scores:

Q: *What is the meaning of life?*
A: *All evidence to date suggests it is chocolate.*

It can be assumed that women are more responsive to some topics, *sweets* in particular. This is confirmed by experiments on author profiling that list *chocolate* among most distinctive 'female words' [2]. The claims that men prefer cynical or violent humor is partially supported by the fact that male participants assessed the *9/11* joke 0.32 points higher than female participants.

The third column in Table 1 contains average scores by joke source. A rather low score of three Siri jokes is not necessarily indicative of her sense of humor in general. Two of these jokes used rather highbrow or complex words (the third one is the *chocolate* joke mentioned above):

Q: *What is the meaning of life?*
A: *I Kant answer that. Ha, ha.*

Q: *Why did the chicken cross the road?*
A: *I am not perspicacious about the peregrinations of poultry.*

Their low scores support the findings reported in the literature that funnier jokes tend to use more common, easily recognizable words [14, 19]. The third column in Table 1 shows rank correlations between joke 'source' rankings and rankings based on average scores obtained in our experiment. Original Yahoo! Answers jokes were ranked based on a difference of thumbs up & down counts. Automatically matched jokes were annotated by three assessors on a four-point scale in our previous experiment [6]. Reddit posts were ranked based on their points; tweets were ordered according to normalized scores (defined as a sum of retweets and likes divided by the number of an account's followers). The outcomes are mixed: in case of automatically matched jokes and Reddit, the rankings are very close; in case of Yahoo!Answers and Twitter, the ordering is quite different (negative rank correlation of tweets can be partially explained by the aggressive normalization – maybe popular accounts post inherently funnier tweets). Almost identical ranking of automatically matched jokes in both experiments can be explained by a very similar experimental design. We can assume that if one is interested in relative ranking of jokes rather than in obtaining absolute scores for individual jokes, a small group of assessors may be sufficient (though they will have a low agreement).

We took a closer look at the Jester jokes and compared score distributions for seven jokes in Jester data vs. our experiment. We mapped Jester's continuous values to our four-point scale and calculated Kullback-Leibler divergence (with Jester being the reference distribution). The KL-scores range from 0.04 (almost perfect coherence) to 0.48; average score over seven jokes is 0.26. The following joke has the highest divergence score:

Q: *How many programmers does it take to change a lightbulb?*
A: *NONE! That's a hardware problem.*

Figure 2 compares the Jester scores for this joke to those obtained in our experiment. We can explain the discrepancies by the negative effect of a 'canned' joke – it sounds a bit dull in 2017 (recall, the first version of Jester went online in 1998). This observation as well as low-rank correlations with 'original' scores discussed earlier cast doubt on the success of transferring joke ratings between different domains and re-using old jokes.

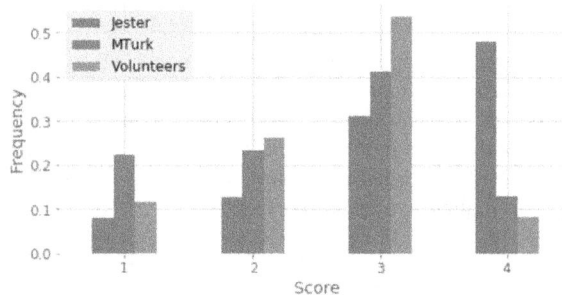

Figure 2: Distribution of joke #4 scores by Jester users/MTurk workers/volunteers (Jester continuous ratings mapped to four-point scale).

5 CONCLUSIONS AND FUTURE WORK

The results show that paid crowdsourcing workers and volunteers assess jokes in a very similar way. Thus, we can conclude that crowdsourcing is a viable and efficient option for humor evaluation. The findings also suggest that age, gender, and language proficiency can partly explain variation in funniness scores. We expect that these new insights will help to design humor evaluation and interpret its outcomes. They can also be directly applied to humor generation in conversational systems.

In the future, we are going to analyze the impact of personality traits on humor evaluation. It is expected that Big5 can better reflect the annotator's humor appreciation level. We will also focus on how joke topics influence subjects' scores. We plan to include education level as an additional feature in our future experiments.

REFERENCES

[1] Salvatore Attardo. 1994. *Linguistic Theories of Humor.* Walter de Gruyter.
[2] Angelo Basile et al. 2017. N-GrAM: New Groningen Author-profiling Model. In *CLEF'2017 Evaluation Labs and Workshop.*
[3] Nancy Bell and Salvatore Attardo. 2010. Failed humor: Issues in non-native speakers' appreciation and understanding of humor. *Intercultural Pragmatics* 7, 3 (2010), 423–447.
[4] Jerome R Bellegarda. 2014. Spoken Language Understanding for Natural Interaction: The Siri Experience. In *Natural Interaction with Robots, Knowbots and Smartphones.* 3–14.
[5] Kim Binsted. 1995. Using humour to make natural language interfaces more friendly. In *AI, ALife and Entertainment Workshop.*
[6] Vladislav Blinov, Kirill Mishchenko, Valeria Bolotova, and Pavel Braslavski. 2017. A Pinch of Humor for Short-Text Conversation: an Information Retrieval Approach. In *CLEF.* 3–15.
[7] Ken Goldberg, Theresa Roeder, Dhruv Gupta, and Chris Perkins. 2001. Eigentaste: A constant time collaborative filtering algorithm. *Information Retrieval* 4, 2 (2001), 133–151.
[8] Samuel D Gosling, Peter J Rentfrow, and William B Swann. 2003. A very brief measure of the Big-Five personality domains. *J. Res. Pers.* 37, 6 (2003), 504–528.
[9] Bryan Anthony Hong and Ethel Ong. 2009. Automatically extracting word relationships as templates for pun generation. In *CALC.* 24–31.
[10] Jiepu Jiang et al. 2015. Automatic online evaluation of intelligent assistants. In *WWW.* 506–516.
[11] Peter Khooshabeh et al. 2011. Does it matter if a computer jokes. In *CHI.* 77–86.
[12] Chia-Wei Liu et al. 2016. How NOT To Evaluate Your Dialogue System: An Empirical Study of Unsupervised Evaluation Metrics for Dialogue Response Generation. In *EMNLP.* 2122–2132.
[13] Rod A. Martin. 2007. *The Psychology of Humor: An Integrative Approach.* Elsevier.
[14] Rada Mihalcea and Stephen Pulman. 2007. Characterizing Humour: An Exploration of Features in Humorous Texts. In *CICLing.* 337–347.
[15] Rada Mihalcea and Carlo Strapparava. 2006. Learning to laugh (automatically): Computational models for humor recognition. *Computational Intelligence* 22, 2 (2006), 126–142.
[16] Tavi Nathanson, Ephrat Bitton, and Ken Goldberg. 2007. Eigentaste 5.0: constant-time adaptivity in a recommender system using item clustering. In *RecSys.* 149–152.
[17] Peter Potash, Alexey Romanov, and Anna Rumshisky. 2017. SemEval-2017 Task 6: #HashtagWars: Learning a Sense of Humor. In *SemEval.* 49–57.
[18] Willibald Ruch. 1992. Assessment of appreciation of humor: Studies with the 3WD humor test. *Advances in personality assessment* 9 (1992), 27–75.
[19] Dafna Shahaf, Eric Horvitz, and Robert Mankoff. 2015. Inside jokes: Identifying humorous cartoon captions. In *PKDD.* 1065–1074.
[20] Oliviero Stock and Carlo Strapparava. 2005. HAHAcronym: a computational humor system. In *ACL (demo).* 113–116.
[21] Alessandro Valitutti et al. 2013. "Let Everything Turn Well in Your Wife": Generation of Adult Humor Using Lexical Constraints.. In *ACL (2).* 243–248.
[22] Miaomiao Wen et al. 2015. OMG UR Funny! Computer-Aided Humor with an Application to Chat. In *ICCC.* 86–93.
[23] Diyi Yang, Alon Lavie, Chris Dyer, and Eduard Hovy. 2015. Humor Recognition and Humor Anchor Extraction. In *EMNLP.* 2367–2376.

Strategies for Finding and Evaluating Information about Personal Finance Topics: The Role of Government Information

Kathy Brennan
University of North Carolina at Chapel Hill
Chapel Hill, NC, USA
25brennan@gmail.com

Diane Kelly
University of Tennessee, Knoxville
Knoxville, TN, USA
dianek@utk.edu

ABSTRACT

In this paper, we present work-in-progress results from the stimulated recall portion of a U.S.-based lab study that investigated the influence of financial knowledge and cognitive abilities on the search performance, relevance assessments, and mental workload of adults searching the Internet for personal finance topics. Participants were asked to retrospectively think aloud while viewing screen recordings of one of their search tasks. Qualitative, inductive coding was applied to transcribed interviews. An early theme about government websites and information emerged in the data analysis and that is the topic of this paper. For all three tasks, participants prioritized and valued information from U.S. government websites over that of commercial websites, which seems to contradict recent national surveys indicating low levels of trust in government information sources and the government in general. Our findings suggest that for certain topics, especially those associated with high levels of uncertainty, people might resort to more basic search and evaluation behaviors.

ACM Reference format:
Kathy Brennan and Diane Kelly. 2018. Strategies for Finding and Evaluating Information about Personal Finance Topics: The Role of Government Information. In *CHIIR '18: Conference on Human Information Interaction and Retrieval, March 11-15, 2018, New Brunswick, NJ, USA*. ACM, NY, NY, USA4 pages.
DOI: https://doi.org/10.1145/3176349.3176883

1 INTRODUCTION AND BACKGROUND

For most people, financial well-being depends on the ability to make sound, informed decisions about many aspects of personal finance. This is particularly true in the United States (U.S.), where the crux of major financial decisions such as paying for education, housing, and retirement is left up to consumers. In addition, the array of financial concepts and products is broad and complex. This is especially true in the area of consumer loan products such as mortgages and student loans in the U.S., where consumer debt holdings are currently more than $10.4 Trillion[1].

Recent reports indicate that the most common information source consumers use when making decisions about borrowing and credit is the Internet, ahead of close associates, financial planners, accountants, and lawyers [1]. This is problematic, given the non-regulated, open nature of the Internet. While there is no shortage of unbiased, accurate information available online about many personal finance topics, there is also a proliferation of misinformation spread by alternative financial services (AFS) providers seeking to exploit consumers' lack of financial knowledge. Uncertainty about how and where to find the best information online can lead consumers to inadvertently follow online financial guidance that is incomplete, inaccurate, or inappropriate for addressing their specific financial circumstances.

While there are many studies about how people search for information and make relevance judgments on the Web (c.f.e. [2, 3]), few studies have addressed evaluating information in the context of personal finance information. Research in information science related to more general personal finance contexts is also very limited, focusing primarily on stock and bond investing [4, 5]. Furthermore, most of these studies have been conducted in countries outside the U.S. [6, 7] where financial products can differ.

Studies from consumer finance and behavioral economics provide general insights about consumers' debt-related information behaviors. An analysis by Kerr and Dunn [8] found that the size of credit card balances was positively associated with credit information search. A secondary analysis of data from the U.S. Survey of Consumer Finance found that *search effort*, defined as the extent and length of search, was associated with interest rates charged on home mortgages [9]. These findings from consumer finance and behavioral economics posit ideas of what may drive consumer behavior, however, it is important to keep in mind that they were developed from analyses of large government or proprietary corporate data sets. Thus, it is difficult to translate results from these studies to interface and system design.

The purpose of the current study is to increase our knowledge in IIR about consumers' information search and evaluation behaviors for personal finance topics and more specifically, consumer loan-related information. In this paper, we

---

[1] Federal Reserve Bank of New York, 2017 Q1 Results

report as work-in-progress initial findings from the stimulated recall portion of the study which addressed the following research questions, *What are users' strategies for finding and evaluating information on the internet about different kinds of financial loans?*

2 METHOD

A lab study was conducted (IRB #17-0077) with 47 participants who were recruited via the staff and faculty email list at the University of North Carolina. The intention behind recruiting from the staff and faculty email list was to draw a sample of participants who would have at least basic experiences with personal finances from having generated earned income regularly from employment. Participants were also required to be native-English speakers. As the result of errors during data collection, we had to discard the data from three participants. The final sample (N=44) consisted of 31 females and 13 males. The average age was 32.6 (SD=13.229), with ages ranging from 18 to 62 years. Three participants were high school graduates, nine had some college but no degree, three had obtained Associate's degrees, 15 had Bachelor's degrees, and 14 had post-graduate degrees. Two participants were self-employed, six were full-time students, 10 worked part-time, and 26 worked full-time. Participants held a number of positions including Pharmacy Technician, House Staff Member, Facilities Support, and Librarian.

The study took place in two separate sessions held on different days. During the first session, participants completed three search tasks, as well as several questionnaires about their experiences. Their search interactions were logged and their eye gazes were tracked. At the end of this session, they completed stimulated recall of their last search task. During the second session, participants completed instruments measuring their cognitive abilities and financial knowledge. In this report, we focus on results from the stimulated recall portion of the first session.

The search tasks [2] were designed as simulated search situations [10]. They centered around information searching situations related to three different kinds of financial loans: payday loans, reverse mortgages, and student loans. The goal of each task was the same: to find "reputable, trustworthy webpages" that would help the participant understand the financial product as well as find information out about more specific elements of each type of loan. Tasks were rotated and lasted about 12 minutes each. Participants were instructed to bookmark all webpages viewed and rate each one using a four-point scale, ranging from *not relevant* to *very relevant*.

Stimulated recall data were captured using Morae screen and audio recording, for the last task that each participant completed; 15 participants conducted their last search task on payday loans, 15 on the reverse mortgage task, and 14 on student loans. Stimulated recall was conducted only on the last search task to reduce memory burden on participants for thinking back

through the task and also to keep the first session within a 75-minute timeframe. The instructions presented in Figure 1 were read aloud to introduce this portion of the study to participants. The 44 recorded sessions were transcribed by a professional transcription service into text format.

During this next section of the study, I'm going to play back a screen recording of the actions you took during the last task you completed. While you watch this recording, I would like for you to state aloud why you took the actions shown on the screen and what you were thinking when you took those actions. I would like to walk me through the decision-making processes you underwent as you searched. There are no right or wrong answers here. I am simply looking for your thoughts as you review the steps you took during the experiment. Even minor thoughts will be helpful to this study.

Figure 1. Stimulated recall instructions to participants

Procedures for coding and analyzing the data followed guidance from the literature [11] for qualitative thematic analysis. A 20% sample of the data was used to create a codebook and then those codes were applied to the remainder of the sample. A hierarchical coding system was developed with top-level nodes that categorized data related to the elements of the research question -- finding and evaluating information, financial knowledge, and cognitive abilities. Subordinate nodes emerged from the data at varying levels of granularity.

3 FINDINGS AND DISCUSSION

In this section, we present a general overview of participants' activities for finding and evaluating information and then focus on the prominent theme of government information. In terms of finding information, participants talked about their tactics and strategies for starting the search tasks, their search goals and the outcomes of those goals, the kinds of information they found, and how they dealt with uncertainty during the search process. To evaluate information, participants' processes included approaches for understanding the financial products, determining which websites would provide them the best information to answer their questions, reading through websites they selected, and making decisions about the relevance of the websites. One theme that emerged prominently across both categories for finding and evaluating information was related to the importance of U.S. government websites and information. Of the 44 participants in the interview sample, 38 (86%) mentioned U.S. government websites and government-sponsored information as part of their information searching and evaluation processes.

3.1 Strategies for Finding Information

When starting their searches, participants shared their thoughts about the kinds of information sources they wanted to avoid and those they wished to find. Advertisements that showed on the top of the SERP were frequently singled out as results to be avoided. Participants also said they wished to avoid

---

[2] Available at https://www.dropbox.com/s/yd8qcsgb4lu56cx/Search_Tasks.pdf?dl=0

banks and lenders at the early stages of their search process when they were interested in finding general information such as product definitions and background. In terms of information they said they wanted to find for completing the tasks, nine participants said they intentionally looked for government websites or information at the beginning of their search processes. One participant explained his strategy for starting his search on the student loan task this way: *"One of the first things I wanted to do instead of going to the .coms was to go to ed.gov because what better way to start searching then (on) something that's sponsored by the government?"* (P21). Another said, *"then I found a .gov site so I said, 'Well that's probably a good place to start'"* (P29). Other participants chose to start their searches on government websites once those websites appear on the SERP: *"a government site came up in search results, so I figured that was a good place to start"* (P02).

These comments suggest that participants relied heavily on a basic search strategy of identifying websites hosted by the federal government as those with the *.gov* top-level domain[3] (TLD) and prioritized information from those websites over information from websites with *.com* and *.org* TLDs and sites from the two states mentioned in the tasks – Virginia and North Carolina. Only one participant (P38) shared about an intentionally more sophisticated approach on the reverse mortgage task which entailed searching for regulations about reverse mortgages on the North Carolina Commissioner of Banks website.

Each task provided examples of the kinds of information that would be useful to find, such as advantages and disadvantages of the financial product, special programs for paying off loans, local institutions to use for borrowing money, and possible information resources to call upon with any questions they might have in the future. Most participants simply matched their search activities to these task descriptions, using the parameters of the tasks as goals, rather than devising more sophisticated search strategies based on their own knowledge of the task topic. An example of a more sophisticated search strategy was one employed by P08, who, instead of using the task parameters like a search checklist, began his search by looking for approaches to reducing the interest rates of existing student loans through refinancing.

Unlike at the beginning of the search process when participants may have avoided information from banks, during the latter parts of the search tasks participants did view banks and other lending institutions for product specifics. There was no lending institution mentioned more than once or twice, however, which stood in contrast to the frequent mentions of four government websites: 11 participants mentioned the Federal Trade Commission (FTC), 8 mentioned U.S. Housing and Urban Development (HUD), 7 mentioned Consumer Finance Protection Board (CFPB), and 3 mentioned U.S. Department of Education. Participants sought these government websites to answer specific questions about financial products and to confirm information they found on commercial websites. Participants also said they used government websites when they wanted to find additional information from what they had already found. In some instances, the information was definitions about key aspects of financial products in the tasks, legal ramifications of the financial products, or to get a *"secondary perspective"*. Participants also consulted these sites to test the exhaustiveness of their findings, *"I was just trying to see what else was there, if there was something different than what I had looked for"* (P17) and *"I was just checking to see if there's any more information that I didn't find out on the other site"* (P31).

Participants shared their feelings of uncertainty at different points during the tasks and the different kinds of tactics and strategies they used for addressing uncertainty. Participants who were uncertain about what to query would get their query terms from the task language, use the auto-complete drop-down suggestions on Google, or simply use the name of the financial product as the query (e.g., "reverse mortgage"). When uncertain about what to search for next, participants examined the *related searches* suggestions at the bottom of the SERP, read through the task parameters, scanned the SERP for ideas, or clicked through several of the links on the SERP and skimmed webpages for ideas.

3.2 Strategies for Evaluating Information

When talking about their evaluation behaviors, a number of participants expressed the need to learn general information and background about the financial product in the task. When selecting the kinds of websites that could provide the best information for completing their tasks, participants identified government websites and information as reliable, trustworthy, and unbiased, such as one participant who said, *"I look down (the SERP) and typically I'm trying to find government sources and skip the commercial sources. Just because I want unbiased sources and not, you know, somebody that has an interest in a slant on the information"* (P35). Adjectives used to describe government websites and information are shown in Table 1, in order by the number of participants who mentioned each. Participants valued the government as a source of credible, reliable, trustworthy information that would provide relevant information on its websites, especially for personal finance topics. *" . . . I know that with financial stuff, the government websites are really helpful"* (P32).

Table 1. Words Describing Government Websites and Information (By Number of Participants)

Reputable (9)	Legitimate (2)	Unbiased (2)
Reliable (6)	Neutral (2)	Comprehensive (1)
Trustworthy (5)	Official (2)	Credible (1)
Useful (4)	Professional (2)	

Participants prioritized government websites and information sources in their relevance criteria over other sites and sources. Some participants' statements clearly indicated this prioritization, such as: *"Well, **the first reason** I thought it was*

---

[3] The use of the *.gov* domain by organizations is restricted to U.S. federal agencies and are administered by GSA (See https://www.dotgov.gov/dotgov-web/policy/policy_final_rule.xhtml?_m=8)

relevant was it was a government resource" (P22) and *". . . **the first thing** I clicked on was a government website. I feel like this is a reliable resource"* (P26). In other cases, participants used their previous knowledge about specific government agencies to predict the quality of information on a website. For example, when the FTC website showed in the screen recording, P25 said he knew that it was *"definitely going to be pretty reliable, like better than Credit.com or PaydayLoanInfo.org."*

Participants made statements and comments about government websites that reflected possible beliefs about how the federal government conducts website marketing differently than commercial websites. For instance, one participant said *"they don't gain revenue off of clicks,"* (P21) and another surmised that government organizations are *"presumably not paid by the lender"* to create website content about reverse mortgages (P16). One participant said he went to government websites because he believed he would find low-cost options for financial advising.

4 CONCLUSIONS

In this paper, we presented initial findings from the stimulated recall portion of a larger study that investigated the influence of financial knowledge and cognitive abilities on the search performance, relevance assessments, and mental workload of adults searching the Internet for personal finance topics. This work-in-progress presented how people described their strategies for finding and evaluating information on the internet about financial loans. This is one of the first studies in IIR to investigate users' search and evaluation behaviors in the domain of personal finance.

We found that when searching for and evaluating information about personal finance scenarios whose possible outcomes could be widely divergent and financially significant, participants seemed to use behaviors that involved finding the most basic and neutral information. In the absence of finance-specific vocabulary, participants' principle strategies for finding information included using task language or basic product names for their search queries. Participants' uncertainty about online financial information sources led them to rely on their general trust of government consumer agencies and avoid commercial websites, often using clues from the SERP for ideas on what to search. Principle strategies for evaluating information included first learning basic details about the financial products and then prioritizing government information in their relevance criteria. Better support of users on complex topics such as these might include developing search engines and algorithms that rank information on quality and accuracy, or by creating user interfaces specifically tailored to present financial information with key characteristics (e.g., interest rates, loan terms, penalty fees) prioritized in the display.

Another direction for research relates to our findings about the role of government websites and information in our participants' activities. A majority of participants emphasized the importance of finding websites and information sources created by the U.S. federal government. Of the 44 participants, 38 (86%) mentioned U.S. government websites and government-sponsored information as part of their information searching and

evaluation processes. This theme stands out in light of recent national surveys that have found public trust in the government at historically low levels [12] and that people's trust in government information sources ranks lower in comparison to other sources of information such as libraries and local news organizations [13]. Evidence from this study supports notions of user confidence in government information as it relates to providing reliable, trustworthy information about consumer loans. It may be the case that consumers are able to discretize government sources of information based upon the context of their information needs in ways that enable them to choose which information to trust and from which government agencies. In the context of personal finance-related information needs, particularly related to consumer loans, the findings of this research demonstrate the importance of the federal government as playing a central role in the information infrastructure of consumers. Similar to Freund and Berzowska [14], it also suggests a need for deeper understanding of how people use government information, though in the context of personal finance.

ACKNOWLEDGMENTS

This work was conducted as part of the first author's doctoral dissertation work at the UNC-Chapel Hill. The authors wish to thank Jaime Arguello, Rob Capra, Javed Mostafa, and Jaceck Gwizdka for feedback as members of the first author's dissertation committee as well as the School of Information and Library Science at UNC for its support of this research.

REFERENCES

[1] Jesse Bricker, Lisa Dettling, Alice Henriques, Joanne Hsu, Kevin Moore, John Sabelhaus, Jeffrey Thompson, and Richard Windle. 2014. Changes in U.S. Family Finances from 2010 to 2013: Evidence from the Survey of Consumer Finances Board of Governors of the Federal Reserve System, Washington, DC.
[2] Soo Young Rieh. 2002. Judgment of information quality and cognitive authority in the Web. In *JASIST, 53*, 2, 145-161.
[3] Anastasios Tombros, Ian Ruthven, and Joemon M. Jose. 2005. How users assess Web pages for information seeking. In *JASIST, 56*, 4, 327-344.
[4] Elizabeth M. Mezick. 2002. Investing wisely: Individual investors as information seekers. In *Journal of Business & Finance Librarianship, 7*, 3-23.
[5] Lisa G. O'Connor. 2012. The information seeking and use behaviors of retired investors. In *J Libr Inf Sci, 45*, 1, 3-22.
[6] Kirsty Williamson and Dimity Kingsford-Smith. 2010. Empowered or vulnerable? The role of information for Australian online investors. In *Can J Inform Lib Sci, 34*, 1, 39-81.
[7] Simangaliso Biza-Khupe. 2014. Credit Search. In *The Journal of Applied Business and Economics, 16*, 3, 116-134.
[8] Sougata Kerr and Lucia Dunn. 2008. Consumer search behavior in the changing credit card market. In *Journ Bus & Econ Stats, 26*, 345-353.
[9] Jinkook Lee and Jeanne M. Hogarth. 1999. Returns to information search: Consumer mortgage shopping decisions. In *Journal of Financial Counseling and Planning, 10*, 1, 49-67.
[10] Pia Borlund. 2003. The IIR evaluation model: A framework for evaluation of interactive information retrieval systems. In *Inform Res, 8*, 152.
[11] Johnny Saldana. 2009. *The Coding Manual for Qualitative Researchers.* SAGE Publications, Thousand Oaks, CA.
[12] Pew Research Center. 2017. *Public trust in government remains near historic lows as partisan attitudes shift.* Pew Research Center.
[13] John Horrigan. 2017. *How people approach facts and information.* Pew Research Center.
[14] Luanne Freund and Justyna Berzowska. 2010. The goldilocks effect: Task-centred assessments of e-government information. In *Proc of ASIST*, 1-10.

What Sources to Rely On? Laypeople's Source Selection in Online Health Information Seeking

Yu Chi, Daqing He, Shuguang Han, Jie Jiang
University of Pittsburgh
Pittsburgh, PA, USA
{yuc73;dah44;shh69;jij48}@pitt.edu

ABSTRACT

In this study, we examined what sources laypeople would select (i.e., visit and adopt) to resolve their health-related information needs, and how different health conditions affect the selection. Twenty-four college students participated in this user study, where they were asked to search for two separate health issues respectively: multiple sclerosis and weight loss. The search logs were collected and analyzed afterwards. We classify the online information sources on both website level and webpage level, and a webpage classification scheme based on genre is proposed. Results suggest that users' selection of sources depends on different types of health issues in terms of urgency and complexity. Health-specific webpage is a popular source and highly adopted for both tasks, but it is particularly helpful for urgent and complex health conditions. Search engines could facilitate users to navigate among scattered health information and support concerns regarding common health issues.

KEYWORDS

source selection, health information seeking, source classification

ACM Reference Format:
Yu Chi, Daqing He, Shuguang Han, Jie Jiang. 2018. What Sources to Rely On? Laypeople's Source Selection in Online Health Information Seeking. In *Proceedings of ACM SIGIR Conference on Human Information Interaction and Retrieval (CHIIR'18)*. ACM, New Brunswick, NJ, USA, 4 pages. DOI: https://dx.doi.org/10.1145/3176349.3176881

1 INTRODUCTION

A nationwide project conducted by the Pew Research Center revealed that 72% of US Internet users had the experience of looking for health-related information through online channels [1]. Different from the general information seeking behaviors, looking for health information has two unique characteristics. Firstly, understanding health-related information often requires users to master a certain amount of domain-specific knowledge [10], particularly when they encounter the resources full of domain-specific terminologies. Secondly, users care more about the quality of the obtained health information since they might eventually take actions based on such information. As a result, it is common for users to navigate

through multiple resources before choosing the best ones. Fortunately, the continuing development of the Web has made it possible for users to access a variety of online health information resources, which include online forums (e.g., PatientsLikeMe) and specified websites (e.g., MedlinePlus) [12].

However, diverse health information resources bring challenges to users too. It is true that users can seek for high quality answers to their health issues by comparing among the different sources, but they are increasingly facing the scattered information across multiple sources, and each requires a different level of prerequisite knowledge. This is particularly problematic for laypeople who might not have the adequate knowledge.

We are interested in understanding how people seek for online health information, particularly their source selection behaviors. Our motivation is that, through analyzing sources they selected, we can better understand the current online health information environment, and could potentially devise automated machine learning algorithms to assess the information quality. With an increasing trend of observing health information seeking behaviors from laypeople, we specifically target on laypeople rather than health professions and experts, which are known to behave differently to newbies [2].

Health information seeking is not a new topic. Instead, it has been studied in several previous works [10, 12]. Compared to the past works, our research has the following novel contributions. Firstly, existing studies on users' selection of online health information sources were mainly based on surveys, which neglect search context since the surveys were distributed after the happening of an actual search. Our study devised a live search system and asked users' in-situ search experience [3]. Secondly, participants in prior studies were often asked to select among a set of preselected resources instead of allowing them to examine the sources freely in their search tasks. Our study, on the contrary, puts users in a realistic search environment and does not impose any restriction over their source selection process, although we do employ controlled user study as our research method.

Specifically, this paper explores the following research questions:

RQ1: What types of online sources do laypeople select for health-related information seeking tasks?

RQ2: Do different health conditions affect laypeople' source selection behaviors?

2 METHODOLOGY

To address the above two research questions, we conducted a controlled user study under the approval of IRB with well-designed search tasks. The details of the user study are presented below.

2.1 User Study

Tasks. Two search tasks were selected: one on multiple sclerosis (T1-MS) and the other on weight loss (T2-WL). Each task consists of three sequential subtasks: 1) seeking the general description of the symptoms (locating information); 2) identifying differences among different types of conditions (differentiating information); and 3) generating in-depth treatment suggestions (making decisions). T1-MS is adapted from [9] and T2-WL is designed by the authors. There are two reasons for us to choose these two tasks. Firstly, they are different in terms of complexity and urgency [11]. Participants' responses from our study also confirmed our hypothesis. T1-MS is significantly more urgent ($t = 5.845$, $p < .001$) and more complex ($t = .6.646$, $p < .001$) than T2-WL according to the results of 5-point Likert scale. Secondly, prior work suggests that the Internet is the first source for people with MS concerns [5], and weight loss/diet is a hot topic among college students when searching for online health information [7]. Therefore, adopting these two tasks would be closer to realistic information needs.

Procedure. Upon arrival, the participants were asked to fill in a questionnaire about their background (e.g., age, education). Then they are introduced with our experimental search system, on which they can freely search, click and view webpages. Our system is wrapped around Google search API, and it returns Google search results with our behavioral logging functions for follow-up usage log analysis. During the introduction of our system, the participants were given a training task to get familiar with our system, and they were explicitly informed that their behaviors such as queries and clicks would be logged and analyzed afterward. Participants could highlight certain text in any webpage and click the *"save to workspace"* button to save it. They could save as many snippets as possible, which would be used for them to generate reports after the search. During the actual search, each participant were assigned to the two tasks in different rotations to avoid sequential bias. The participants were given 21 minutes to complete the three subtasks for each task. After finishing both two tasks, a follow-up interview was conducted. The whole study took approximately 1.5 hours.

2.2 Data Collection

2.2.1 User Study Data.

In total 24 college students (15 females and 9 males, ranging from 18-33 years old) were recruited as convenient samples from University of Pittsburgh (17) and Carnegie Mellon University (7). 17 of them were undergraduates and the remaining were graduate students. They all reported themselves as experienced (M= 4.25/5, SD=.124) and frequent (M= 4.79/5, SD=.104) web searchers. We applied two screening criteria to make sure all the participants were from our target population (i.e., laypeople): 1) we excluded people from health or medicine related domains; and 2) we only recruited people who have conducted online health information seeking within the last 12 months [8]. Therefore, most of our participants have searched for health-related information very recently (in last week: n=15, 62.8%; last month: n=8, 33.3%; last six months: n=1, 4.2%). The majority of them also reported searching on weekly (n=8, 33.3%) or monthly (n=8, 33.3%) basis. In total, we collected 48 complete search logs (144 search sessions) from 24 participants. Our data collection contains 5,298 clicked webpages, among which 965 (18.21%) were saved into the workspace.

2.2.2 Classifying Online Health Information Sources.

In order to perform analyze on the collected health information resources, we need a classification schema those health information resources. Due to the lack of a widely-adopted classification scheme, we developed our own at both the broad level (Website level) and the specific level (Webpage-level, see Table 1). The mapping from one source to a website category is based on the automated analysis of domain names, and the mapping to webpage category is obtained through manual content analysis by two coders.

Website type classification. Domain names are designed to represent the resources distributed in various hosts and network systems with a string of characters usually separated by dots as its structure. Top-level domain name (TLD) is the last part of the domain name in the US websites. If a domain name is outside of US, its TLD would be the second last in the URL. From TLD, one can tell the entity, administrator and the intended use of a website [6]. For example, the TLD of *https://www.ncbi.nlm.nih.gov/pubmed/* is *.gov*, indicating the website is held by governmental entities. This study adopted 5 TLDs, including .com, .edu, .org, .net, and .gov.

Webpage type classification. Researchers [4] often distinguish webpages through topic (e.g., health vs. sport) and genre (e.g., online news vs. online forums). In our study, the topic is restricted to health. Thus, we classify a webpage based on its genre. We defined a set of 9 genre types, and each webpage was mapped to a genre through a human manual coding by two coders. To generate the base codes, two coders separately open-coded the transaction log of the first participant. Seven types of webpages emerged, and the two coders achieved a very good agreement (Cohen's Kappa = 0.891). In the afterward debriefing, two coders discussed on the controversial records and two more types were added. Table 1 provides the final nine genre types. All the examples in the talbe are from the participants' search logs.

3 RESULTS

3.1 Website-level Source Selection Patterns

Figure 1 illustrates the distribution of the top-level domains among the sources selected by the participants. The left chart describes the share of the TLDs among the visited pages, and the right chart shows the distribution of the adopted (i.e., saved) sources. Clearly, dot com (.com) is the most popular domain of the selected source, accounting for 76% (4,015) of the visited sources (5,298) and 64% of the adopted sources (965). Interestingly, 19% (992) of the visited sources come from non-commercial entities with the domain name .org. This percentage is even higher for the adopted sources (269, 28%). This reveals that the websites maintained by the non-commercial entities, such as non-profit organizations and open-source projects are important online sources, and participants perceived the information from these sources as helpful ones. The rest domains (i.e., .edu, .gov and .net) only account for 5% visited sources and 8% adopted sources, showing that these sources are less selected for resolving laypeople's health information needs.

3.2 Webpage-level Source Selection Patterns

The treemap in Figure 2 summarizes the distribution of different types of webpages among all the participants' visited sources and adopted sources. The size of each block is determined by its share.

Table 1: Classification Scheme for Webpage Types and the Corresponding Examples

Code	Webpage Type	Description	Example Webpages
SERP	Search result page	A search engine result page for a given query.	Google Search Result Pages
HSP	Health-specific page	A webpage that offers focused information around one specific health issue, whose content is often contributed by professionals.	National Multple Sclerosis Society (in T1-MS); EveryDiet (in T2-WL)
WBP	Wiki-based page	A wiki page that collects voluntary creation from general users.	MEpedia (in T1-MS); Wikipedia (in T2-WL)
ALP	Academic literature	A Webpage with its main content as academic literature.	PLOS ONE (in T1-MS); NCBI (in T2-WL)
PP	Personal webpage	A webpage sharing authors' personal ideas and experiences; Self-portrayals, personal homepages with informal content.	Health Central (in T1-MS); MyFitnessPal (in T2-WL)
NAP	News article page	A webpage filled with long reviews, reports, news feed or photos.	The New York Times (in T1-MS); The Global and Mail (in T2-WL)
SNS	Social network service	A webpage supports interactions among users. Through the interactions, users may seek for questioning, answering, emotional support, human experiences etc. Wiki-based pages are excluded as its core is to co-edit instead of interaction.	myMSteam (in T1-MS); Quora (in T2-WL)
ECP	E-commerce page	A webpage with main purpose of profiting from products and supporting online purchase.	Swiss Medica Clinic (in T1-MS); ASCENT FOOD FOR ATHELETS (in T2-WL)
OEP	Online education page	A webpage with the main goal for online education with tutorials (in digital print, video, and etc.).	University of Maryland Medical Center (in MS); Harvard T.H. Chan-School of Public Health (in WL)

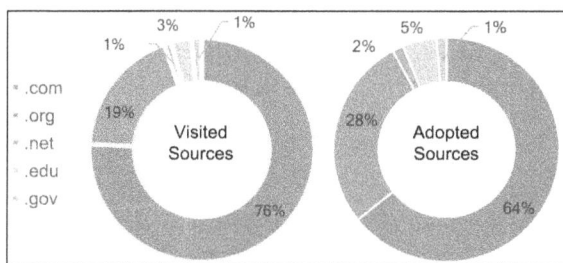

Figure 1: Distribution of the top-level domains among the users' visited sources (left) and saved sources(right)

For example, the largest chunk in the visited sources is HSP (health-specific page), which is mainly contributed by health professionals. Similarly, HSP is also the most adopted source. Participants visited 2,364 health-specific pages in total, and among these pages, they saved 659 pages (27.88%).

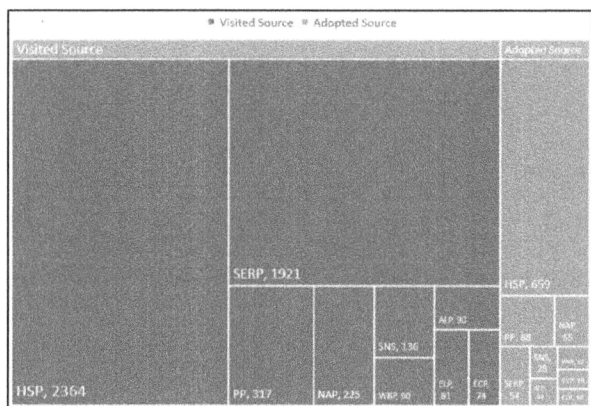

Figure 2: Distribution of different types of webpages among all the users' visited sources and saved sources

The second most visited page is search result page (SERP). Participants in total visited 1,921 SERP, accounting for 36.26% of the

selected sources. However, only 54 of them were saved, suggesting participants didn't directly digest information from SERPs, which makes sense since SERP only contains snippets of the result pages, and are also hard to provide detailed information. Other types of pages were not as frequent as HSP or SERP. There were 317 clicked personal pages (27.76% were saved) and 225 news articles (24.44% were saved). The social-based webpages, including SNS and WBP were not commonly clicked and saved. Moreover, among the 136 SNS pages visited, only 20.59% of them were saved, which is even lower than the saving rate of e-commerce webpages (19/74=25.68%). The result suggests that SNS webpages usually do not provide useful information for the tasks.

3.3 Task Types and Selection of Webpages

We further explored whether users' visited sources and adopted sources vary among tasks. Figure 3 shows a comparison of source selection between T1-MS (left in blue) and T2-WL (right in red). The darkness of the blue/red bars represents the portion of the adopted sources among the visited sources.

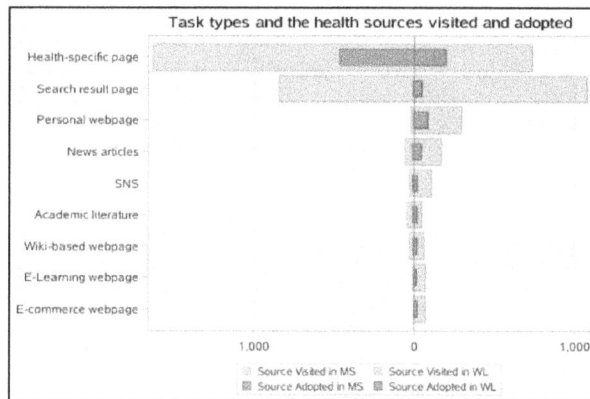

Figure 3: Comparison of the types of visited and adopted webpages in two tasks: T1-MS (left) and T2-WL (right)

As shown in Figure 3, health-specific page (HSP) was the most popular source in both tasks, especially in the MS task. In MS, 60.96% of the participants' visited pages were HSP, and 28.37% of the visited HSP were saved into workspace, accounting for as much as 89.38% of all saved MS sources. The second most visited source was the search result page (SERP). However, only 8 SERP among the 847 visited SERP were saved, suggesting that the search engine mainly works as a navigational portal in MS. The rest sources together shared 7.39% of the visited sources.

However, participants' selection of sources was much more diverse in WL. The most visited source was SERP (1,074, 40.98%), and 4.28% of them were saved, which was much higher than that in MS. Health-specific page was the second most visited sources (27.93%) but the first most adopted (43.84%). It is worth to note that personal webpages (PP) rose to be a popular source in WL, which accounted for 11.21% of the visited sources and 18.34% of the adopted. The rest sources were more evenly distributed than they were in MS.

4   DISCUSSION

Information from government and educational institutes are less selected as expected. Websites of government and educational institutes are usually considered to be more reliable. Indeed, in our post-task interviews, the domain name was reported as an important factor when judging the website reliability. However, in our recorded user logs, websites from .edu and .gov together only accounts for 4% of visited sources and 6% of adopted sources. This might because both websites provide less *useful* health information-either regarding the amount or the ease of understanding for laypeople. It is also possible that the participants only click top-ranked search results without paying attention to the domain names.

Health information source selection depends on health conditions. Based on our user study results, we find that laypeople are more likely to trust health professionals' information on serious diseases, e.g., multiple sclerosis, while they would adopt advice from other general users on common health issues, e.g., weight loss. Specifically, we found that the health-specific webpage created by the health professionals is the most selected source in MS while the amount decreases significantly in WL. This finding aligns with a previous study from Synnot et al. (2016). On the contrary, when searching for the weight loss information, a relatively high portion of personal webpages was selected, and treated as useful judging from its high adoption rate. One potential reason is that people tend to share their knowledge and experience in less serious health conditions. Though there are also personal webpages sharing individuals' experience and advice about MS, it is not as often as that in WL. Further analysis will test how heavily the sharing behavior affects the selection of the sources.

Search engines play important navigational roles for scattered health information. Figure 3 suggests that online health information for serious disease is more centralized, whereas information of other common health issues is decentralized across multiple resources. Unlike in the MS tasks, participants in the WL tasks saved webpages from scattered webpages. According to our user study, search engines tend to play more important roles in organizing the scattered information in the WL task. Users sometimes

even directly saved search result pages as a type of information source in this task.

Social network-based online sources are rarely used for health issues. Though the social interaction-based sources (e.g., health forums or Facebook) become more important in other tasks, they are rarely found to be useful in this study. A recent study by Zhang et al. [12] discovered that SNSs were more likely to be selected for factual finding tasks. We will further study this topic in the future. Also, it is hard to tell if the controlled research settings affected the usage of social-based online sources. Participants were informed that their behaviors would be recorded and analyzed afterward, so it was possible that they consciously avoided using personal SNS accounts when collecting relevant information.

5   CONCLUSION

This study examined laypeople's selection of sources when searching for health information. In the search for some serious conditions, e.g., multiple sclerosis, laypeople tend to rely on health-specific information generated by professionals. However, when seeking information about weight loss, their selection of online information is more diverse. The findings suggest that search engines could consider the source type as a factor when recommending results to the users. Also, more attention should be paid to the quality of some highly selected sources, such as the health-specific webpage. One limitation is the generalizability of the results to other laypeople other than college students recruited in the current study.

REFERENCES

[1] Pew Reseach Center. 2013. Health Fact Sheet. *Pew Res. Cent. Internet Sci. Tech* (2013).
[2] Christoph Hölscher and Gerhard Strube. 2000. Web search behavior of Internet experts and newbies. *Computer networks* 33, 1 (2000), 337–346.
[3] Jiepu Jiang, Daqing He, Diane Kelly, and James Allan. 2017. Understanding Ephemeral State of Relevance. In *Proceedings of the 2017 Conference on Conference Human Information Interaction and Retrieval.* ACM, 137–146.
[4] Ioannis Kanaris and Efstathios Stamatatos. 2009. Learning to recognize webpage genres. *Information Processing & Management* 45, 5 (2009), 499–512.
[5] Ruth Ann Marrie, Amber R Salter, Tuula Tyry, Robert J Fox, and Gary R Cutter. 2013. Preferred sources of health information in persons with multiple sclerosis: degree of trust and information sought. *Journal of Medical Internet Research* 15, 4 (2013).
[6] Heather N Mewes. 1998. Memorandum of Understanding on the Generic Top-Level Domain Name Space of the Internet Domain Name System. *Berkeley Technology Law Journal* (1998), 235–247.
[7] Christine Percheski and Eszter Hargittai. 2011. Health information-seeking in the digital age. *Journal of American College Health* 59, 5 (2011), 379–386.
[8] Susan L Perez, Debora A Paterniti, Machelle Wilson, Robert A Bell, Man Shan Chan, Chloe C Villareal, Hien Huy Nguyen, and Richard L Kravitz. 2015. Characterizing the processes for navigating Internet health information using real-time observations: a mixed-methods approach. *Journal of medical Internet research* 17, 7 (2015).
[9] Joseph Sharit, Jessica Taha, Ronald W Berkowsky, Halley Profita, and Sara J Czaja. 2015. Online information search performance and search strategies in a health problem-solving scenario. *Journal of Cognitive Engineering and Decision Making* 9, 3 (2015), 211–228.
[10] Ryen W White, Susan T Dumais, and Jaime Teevan. 2009. Characterizing the influence of domain expertise on web search behavior. In *Proceedings of the second ACM international conference on web search and data mining.* ACM, 132–141.
[11] Yan Zhang, Ramona Broussard, Weimao Ke, and Xuemei Gong. 2014. Evaluation of a scatter/gather interface for supporting distinct health information search tasks. *Journal of the Association for Information Science and Technology* 65, 5 (2014), 1028–1041.
[12] Yan Zhang, Yalin Sun, and Yeolib Kim. 2017. The influence of individual differences on consumer's selection of online sources for health information. *Computers in Human Behavior* 67 (2017), 303–312.

Active Viewing: A Study of Video Highlighting in the Classroom

Samuel Dodson
University of British Columbia
dodsons@mail.ubc.ca

Ido Roll
University of British Columbia
ido.roll@ubc.ca

Matthew Fong
University of British Columbia
mfong@ece.ubc.ca

Dongwook Yoon
University of British Columbia
yoon@cs.ubc.ca

Negar M. Harandi
University of British Columbia
negarm@ece.ubc.ca

Sidney Fels
University of British Columbia
ssfels@ece.ubc.ca

ABSTRACT

Video is an increasingly popular medium for education. Motivated by the problem of video as a one-way medium, this paper investigates the ways in which learners' active interaction with video materials contributes to active learning. In this study, we examine *active viewing* behaviors, specifically seeking and highlighting within videos, which may suggest greater levels of participation and learning. We deployed a system designed for active viewing to an undergraduate class for a semester. The analysis of online activity traces and interview data provided novel findings on video highlighting behavior in educational contexts.

CCS CONCEPTS

• **Information systems** → **Video search**; • **Applied computing** → **Interactive learning environments**; **Annotation**;

KEYWORDS

active viewing, video search, learning, highlighting

ACM Reference Format:
Samuel Dodson, Ido Roll, Matthew Fong, Dongwook Yoon, Negar M. Harandi, and Sidney Fels. 2018. Active Viewing: A Study of Video Highlighting in the Classroom. In *CHIIR '18: 2018 Conference on Human Information Interaction & Retrieval, March 11–15, 2018, New Brunswick, NJ, USA.* ACM, New York, NY, USA, 4 pages. https://doi.org/10.1145/3176349.3176889

1 INTRODUCTION

Video is an increasingly popular medium for education. Video offers many advantages, such as the opportunity for self-paced learning. Given the benefits of video based learning, many blended, flipped, or hybrid courses employ video lectures. Video is not perfect, however. Watching video often creates a passive learning experience for students. Motivated by the problem of video as a one-way medium, this paper investigates the ways in which learner's interaction with video materials contribute to active learning.

Theories of active learning [e.g., 4] argue that effective learning takes place while students engage and interact with the educational

materials, such as textbooks and video lectures. When studying reading, nonlinear navigating and annotating can be used as indicators of active reading [1]. For evaluating video viewing, we examine *active viewing* behaviors, specifically seeking and highlighting within videos, which may suggest greater levels of participation and learning. By "seeking" we mean moving to a new part of the video. Previous studies have shown that video navigation behaviors are associated with active information seeking and engaged learning [5, 9]. Nonetheless, it is largely unknown how video highlighting constitutes an active viewing experience.

Recently, Fong et al. [6] presented ViDeX, a system that supports video highlighting. Although the design of the system was assessed, the ways in which active viewing features are used was not examined. Consequently, we are left with the following research questions: (i) How are video seeking activities associated with highlighting behaviors? (ii) How do active viewing behaviors contribute to learning? (iii) What are the appropriate affordances of video interfaces for engagement?

To answer these questions, we deployed ViDeX to an undergraduate class for a semester. The analysis of online activity traces and interview data provided novel findings on video highlighting behavior in educational contexts. For instance, the type of content (i.e., textual or visual) was an important determinant of highlighting behavior. The users of the highlighting features relied more often on semantic cues of the Transcript than visual cues of the Filmstrip.

2 RELEVANT WORK

For online learning to be effective, students must have access to tools that facilitate active learning. For example, in the video medium, this could be done by supporting aggregation and visualization of viewer interactions to facilitate navigation [7, 9]. In other mediums, a common way that learners interact with information is by commenting, highlighting, tagging, or otherwise annotating. Annotation is a type of information interaction that has been found to have a positive relationship with learning outcomes, such as recall, comprehension, and engagement [2, 3, 15]. Consequently, many digital reading environments have been designed to support active reading by providing annotation [e.g., 11, 17]. Tashman and Edwards [16] define active reading as "reading activities that involve more interaction with the reading media than simple sequential advancement through the text."

While annotation is a well-established information practice in text environments, it is less common when viewing video. This may be because there are few video viewing systems that enable this functionality, although there are exceptions [e.g., 10]. The lack of systems that allow for annotation may be due to the difficulty designing systems that enable video annotation in a user-friendly way. Hayles [8] discusses the challenge of translating information practices for learning activities from one medium to another, arguing that some functionality of the particular practice is both lost and gained in the process. As a result, the design of video based learning systems must not simply borrow practices from other media without considering the differences between media.

While active reading is specific to text, we can learn from the developments of digital reading environments to develop new approaches to encourage active viewing. Highlighting is one of the most popular types of annotation in text environments [13]. This is, perhaps, because of the low cognitive load required to emphasize content, which does not distract from the individual's primary task. The popularity of highlighting may also be due to learners' assumption that highlighting has positive effects on their reading processes and outcomes. By supporting highlighting in video, we can attempt to translate a common text based practice and test its effectiveness in video based learning environments.

3 VIDEX

ViDeX is a system designed for active viewing through content interaction and personalization. Encouraging information interactions similar to the more familiar practice of annotating text, ViDeX aims to make interacting with video intuitive. ViDeX currently supports the ability to highlight intervals of video and text. We created ViDeX to explore the effectiveness of highlighting video. We recognize that annotation is an important way in which many individuals learn and interact with information in other media, and suspect that viewers may benefit from similar tools. While commenting exists in many video viewing systems, highlighting is a unique feature.

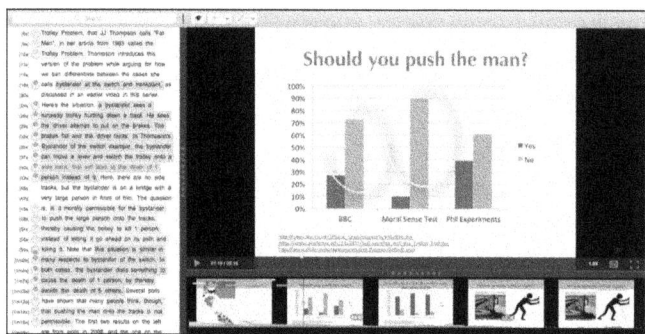

Figure 1: A screenshot of ViDeX, displaying the Transcript (far left) and Filmstrip (bottom).

The ViDeX interface is comprised of three elements: the Player, the Filmstrip, and the Transcript. The Filmstrip provides users with a visual summary of the video, allowing users to skim the video content. The Filmstrip itself is a sequence of thumbnails, where each thumbnail represents a segment of the video. By placing the cursor across the width of each thumbnail, the picture in the thumbnail changes according to the linear mapping between the width of the thumbnail and the part of the video it represents. This allows the user to preview the visual content that the video represents.

To highlight, users must either drag and select across the Filmstrip or Transcript to first select a span of content, and subsequently select a highlight color using the toolbar above the Player. Highlighting creates a strip of color along the top edge of the Filmstrip in addition to the corresponding text in the Transcript.

The Transcript brings the user a textual representation of the video. Each word in the Transcript is associated with a time in the video. Consequently, selections and highlights in either the Filmstrip or the Transcript are synchronized. Any actions made in one widget transfers to the other.

4 METHODS

We evaluated engagement with ViDeX using a mixed-method approach, employing log data analysis and interviews, over the course of a semester in an undergraduate chemistry class. Quantitative log data were used to identify patterns of information interaction. Qualitative interview data were used to better understand and explain these patterns. Students enrolled in the class were provided with videos related to lectures and labs. The videos ranged in length from 3.93 to 12.92 minutes (M=8.73 minutes, SD=2.94 minutes). One of the authors visited the class at the beginning of the semester to introduce students to ViDeX and invite them to participate in the study by using the system to watch videos assigned by their instructor. Using ViDeX was not a class requirement nor was watching the videos. The videos were also available on YouTube, so students could watch the content without participating in the study. Participants were not compensated for using ViDeX.

All relevant system events were logged, including video events (such as loading, playing, and seeking) and highlighting events (such as color, source, and span of each highlight). All data were anonymously logged. To allow students time to familiarize themselves with the system and its novel features without affecting our analysis of typical usage, we analyzed data starting a month after the start of the semester. By the end of the semester, 6,995 system events from 28 participants were logged. A limitation of the study was the relatively small sample size. The log data were analyzed, using R, with an exploratory data analysis approach. We treated system events as independent in our data analysis.

In addition to logging system events, we also collected qualitative data through interviews with students from the class at the end of the semester. One of the authors recruited six participants for one-on-one and small group semi-structured interviews of about ten minutes each. The interviews explored participants' typical use of ViDeX and their learning practices with and without ViDeX. Interviewees were paid a $15.00 honorarium for their time.

5 RESULTS & DISCUSSION

In this section, we explore students' viewing and highlighting behaviors. We supplement the quantitative analysis with feedback we received from interviewees about their typical use of ViDeX throughout the semester.

5.1 Highlighting

Of the 28 participants whose interactions with the system and content were logged, five (18%) highlighted at least once. In total, these five participants created 51 highlights. All but one of the participants highlighted in more than one login session. The highlights varied in color, length, and location within the videos. The median length of highlight spans was 6.23 seconds (M=11.55, SD=13.15), and ranged from 0.16 to 54.69 seconds. Most highlights (n=29, 56.86%) were less than ten seconds and only 6 (11.76%) were longer than thirty seconds. Unlike previous studies of text highlighting [14], we did not find that some participants engaged in heavy highlighting of the content (so called "happy highlighters").

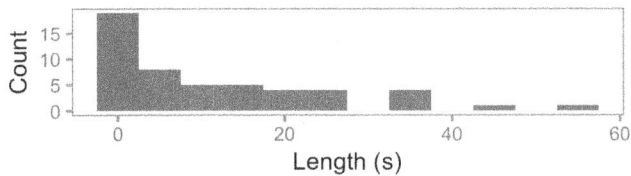

Figure 2: Highlight length in seconds showing that 56.86% of highlights were less than ten seconds and only 11.76% were longer than thirty seconds.

To highlight, the user selects content by clicking and dragging content via either the Filmstrip or the Transcript then chooses a highlight color using the toolbar above the Player. Few selections became highlights. While students made 942 selections, only 51 highlights were created. One reason for this may be the interface itself. The select-and-highlight sequence may not have been very intuitive or visible to most users. At the end of the semester, four of the six interviewees explained they did not know they could highlight using ViDeX, which is surprising given that ViDeX was demoed at the beginning of the semester. Highlighting may have been used more if students had known about it, especially considering all interviewees reported taking notes. The four interviewees that did not highlight explained that they either took notes using a word processor, with a paper notebook, or by taking screenshots.

Of the highlights that were created, many appeared to be used as bookmarks. 56.86% (n=29) of the highlights were less than ten seconds. This suggests that students were placing bookmarks in the video more than selecting spans of content, such as highlighting full sentences or paragraphs in the Transcript. One of the interviewees explained that he used highlights as bookmarks for spans of video to watch later. He would replay the bookmarked video to learn more about a keyword. Using highlights exclusively as bookmarks is somewhat surprising, since highlights have been found to have additional functions in text [e.g., 12].

Given that students mainly highlighted content using the Transcript, why did they use the highlights as bookmarks and not for other types of functions that are common when annotating text? This tendency may suggest that students were indeed strategic about their behavior. Even when highlighting text, students realized that this activity is done in the context of video. A bookmark highlight is sufficient to locate the area of interest. By clicking and jumping to a highlight, they were able to bring the playhead to the area of interests, and play the relevant segment of video. The majority (n=26, 50.98% of highlights were also jumped to by clicking within the highlighted span of content. The actual number of

highlights that were jumped to is likely higher, because students may have clicked just before the highlighted span, especially for short highlights that are difficult to click. Indeed, 86.27% highlighted spans were viewed again.

Notably, while most selections were made using the Filmstrip (n=764, 81.00%), all but two highlights were created with the Transcript. Students' preference to highlight using the Transcript may be explained in a similar way: highlighting was used mainly to bookmark keywords, rather than emphasize the full extent of visual content of interest. As highlighting was based on textual information, the Transcript was the natural place for highlighting.

Another important aspect of highlights is their location relative to the playhead position, which represents the current playing frame of video content. Approximately two-fifths of the highlights were created within 10 seconds of the playhead (see Figure 3). Highlights were created behind (n=8, 15.69%) and ahead (n=23, 45.10%) of the playhead. The behavior of highlighting close to and far from the playhead was consistent across participants. Highlighting ahead of the playhead suggests that students may have been skimming the text to identify important content to highlight and guide their future information interaction. This pattern, again, is consistent with the role of highlights as bookmarks described above.

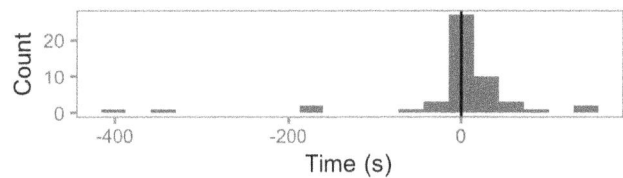

Figure 3: Highlight relative to playhead position. 39.22% of highlights were created within 10 seconds of the playhead.

How information is communicated through video may affect highlighting and seeking. An interviewee explained that he would have highlighted more frequently if the videos had more "show how" rather than "tell how" information. When communicating embodied knowledge, the Transcript would likely contain less textual and more visual information, requiring the student to watch the video to fully understand the context of what is being communicated.

5.2 Seeking

Students used the Filmstrip and Transcript to seek to information differently. The Filmstrip was used for navigation of visual content, such as seeking through the video to find a specific PowerPoint slide, whereas the Transcript was used for scanning for keywords and highlighting. Given that the content was video lectures, it is not surprising that 76.6% of all seeks were made using the Filmstrip. Interviewees explained that the Filmstrip was useful for searching for visual content. The interviewees, for example, explained they would seek through the video for specific PowerPoint slides and transitions to new slides. Once they found the slide they sought, the interviewees explained they would copy the information using a word processor, a paper notebook, or by taking screenshots

It seems that the two user interface elements were used for different types of information seeking, suggesting that seeking video and text support different information needs. The median seek distance using the Filmstrip was 18.27 seconds, whereas the median seek using the Transcript was 108.03 seconds. The Filmstrip seeks may have been used to fine-tune the current playhead location: for example, seeking backwards to repeat the last few spoken words or jumping forwards to search for a transition to a new PowerPoint slide. In contrast, Transcript seeks were often larger and occasionally made across the entire length of the video. This may have been the result of finding important textual information while ignoring the current position of the playhead. Indeed, the Transcript allowed students to navigate and highlight the content without watching it. An interviewee explained he would scan the Transcript from top to bottom for keywords to identify which segments of video to watch. Unlike the Filmstrip, the Transcript was used for both navigation and highlighting. Thus, it comes as little surprise that when jumping to highlights, the Transcript was used more often (79.7%) than the Filmstrip (20.3%).

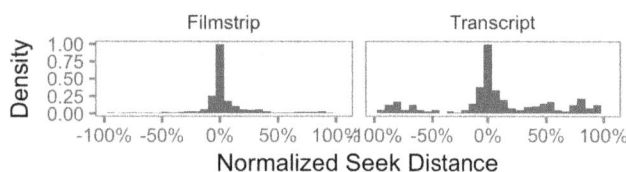

Figure 4: Jumping direction and distance by user interface element. The Filmstrip was used for shorter jumps than the Transcript.

6 CONCLUSION

The results suggest that students made strategic use of the textual and visual user interface elements. We see two main differences with regard to students' interaction with textual information (using the Transcript) and visual information (using the Filmstrip). Most seeks were made using the Filmstrip. This is likely because of the rich cues aided seeking to visual changes in the video, such as PowerPoint slide changes, and since students are used to seeking video using the horizontal bar beneath it in other video viewing environments, such as YouTube. Highlighting, on the other hand, was conducted primarily via the Transcript. Similarly, when jumping to highlights, the Transcript was used most often.

A more careful analysis suggests a specific use for highlights — that of bookmarks for future watching, based on textual keywords. This is suggested by seeing that students (i) highlighted very short spans, (ii) did so using the Transcript, and (iii) highlighted far away from the current location of the playhead. This interpretation is supported by students' interviews. One explanation for these patterns is that students brought in their work habits, using the tools in familiar ways and not making use of the linked nature of these two elements in ViDeX. It is possible that better integration of the two elements, such as a vertical Filmstrip adjacent to the Transcript, would help learners see the connection between the two. However, another possibility is that this behavior demonstrates a desired and adaptive behavior. Students knew that they could use both elements for seeking, and they were strategic about which element to use.

The different patterns may make sense, given the different goals of seeking. It is important to remember that the videos used in this study were highly verbal, which invites this kind of behavior. In that case, the fact that ViDeX supported different uses of its elements to achieve different goals may suggest a useful implementation.

To summarize, we identified strategic use of textual and visual user interface elements for different types of information interactions (short and long seeking, jumping to highlights, and highlighting). Specifically, we found that highlighting of video is very different from highlighting text. For one, it does not seem to be very intuitive. Also, these highlights tend to be shorter, while typical text highlights often select phrases, sentences, or paragraphs. Video highlights also appeared to serve only one function, unlike text highlights. Further research and support for learners are needed to better understand how to make video highlighting a more effective tool for interaction with video content.

REFERENCES

[1] Mortimer J Adler and Charles Van Doren. 1972. *How to read a book*. Simon & Schuster, New York, NY.
[2] Thomas H Anderson and Bonnie B Armbruster. 1984. Studying. In *Handbook of Reading Research*. Pearson, New York, NY, 657–679.
[3] David C Caverly and Vincent P Orlando. 1991. Textbook study strategies. In *Research and Advanced Technology for Digital Libraries*. International Reading Association, Newark, DE, 86–165.
[4] Michelene T H Chi and Ruth Wylie. 2014. The ICAP framework: linking cognitive engagement to active learning outcomes. *Educational Psychologist* 49, 4 (2014), 219–243.
[5] Suzanne L. Dazo, Nicholas R. Stepanek, Robert Fulkerson, and Brian Dorn. 2016. An empirical analysis of video viewing behaviors in flipped CS1 courses. *ACM Inroads* 7, 4 (Nov. 2016), 99–105.
[6] Matthew Fong, Gregor Miller, Xueqin Zhang, Ido Roll, Christina Hendricks, and Sidney Fels. 2016. An investigation of textbook-style highlighting for video.. In *Graphics Interface*. 201–208.
[7] Philip J. Guo, Juho Kim, and Rob Rubin. 2014. How video production affects student engagement: an empirical study of MOOC videos. In *Proceedings of the First ACM Conference on Learning @ Scale Conference (L@S '14)*. ACM, New York, NY, 41–50.
[8] N Katherine Hayles. 2005. *My mother was a computer: digital subjects and literary texts*. University of Chicago Press, Chicago, IL.
[9] Juho Kim, Philip J. Guo, Carrie J. Cai, Shang-Wen (Daniel) Li, Krzysztof Z. Gajos, and Robert C. Miller. 2014. Data-driven interaction techniques for improving navigation of educational videos. In *Proceedings of the 27th Annual ACM Symposium on User Interface Software and Technology (UIST '14)*. ACM, New York, NY, 563–572.
[10] Scott LeeTiernan and Jonathan Grudin. 2001. Fostering engagement in asynchronous learning through collaborative multimedia annotation. In *INTERACT*. 472–479.
[11] Chunyuan Liao, François Guimbretière, and Ken Hinckley. 2005. PapierCraft: a command system for interactive paper. In *Proceedings of the 18th Annual ACM Symposium on User Interface Software and Technology*. ACM, New York, NY, 241–244.
[12] Catherine C Marshall. 2009. *Reading and writing the electronic book*. Morgan & Claypool Publishers, San Rafael, CA.
[13] Ilia A Ovsiannikov, Michael A Arbib, and Thomas H McNeill. 1999. Annotation technology. *International Journal of Human-Computer Studies* 50, 4 (1999), 329–362.
[14] Frank Shipman, Morgan Price, Catherine C Marshall, and Gene Golovchinsky. 2003. Identifying useful passages in documents based on annotation patterns. In *Research and Advanced Technology for Digital Libraries*. Springer, Berlin, Germany, 101–112.
[15] Michele L Simpson and Sherrie L Nist. 1990. Textbook annotation: an effective and efficient study strategy for college students. *Journal of Reading* 34, 2 (1990), 122–129.
[16] Craig Tashman and W Keith Edwards. 2011. Active reading and its discontents: the situations, problems and ideas of readers. In *Proceedings of the SIGCHI Conference on Human Factors in Computing Systems*. ACM, New York, NY, 2927–2936.
[17] Craig Tashman and W Keith Edwards. 2011. LiquidText: a flexible, multitouch environment to support active reading. In *Proceedings of the SIGCHI Conference on Human Factors in Computing Systems*. ACM, New York, NY, 3285–3294.

Noisy Signals: Understanding the Impact of Auditory Distraction on Web Search Tasks

Morgan Harvey
CIS Department
Northumbria University
Newcastle upon Tyne, UK
morgan.harvey@northumbria.ac.uk

Matthew Pointon
CIS Department
Northumbria University
Newcastle upon Tyne, UK
m.pointon@northumbria.ac.uk

ABSTRACT

More than half of all searches are now submitted on mobile devices, which can (and often are) used in various potentially distracting situations, such as travelling on a noisy train or when walking down a busy street. Research suggests that walking has negative effects on search performance and behaviour and that auditory distractions can impact on user input and affect perception of task duration. In this work we conduct a user study (n=16) using a simulated distracting condition to investigate how auditory distractions change perceived and objective search performance and behaviour. Our results suggest that noisy environments induce stress on users, causing them to feel additional perceived time pressure, leading to a reduced ability to identify task-relevant documents and a compulsion to finish the search task quickly.

KEYWORDS

mobile search; distraction; search experience; cognition; user study; experimentation

ACM Reference Format:
Morgan Harvey and Matthew Pointon. 2018. Noisy Signals: Understanding the Impact of Auditory Distraction on Web Search Tasks. In *Proceedings of Conference on Human Information Interaction & Retrieval (CHIIR'18).* ACM, New York, NY, USA, 4 pages. https://doi.org/10.1145/3176349.3176871

1 INTRODUCTION

Since 2016 the number of Google searches made using mobile devices exceeds that of desktop machines [3], meaning that such devices are now our primary means of searching the web. They are used by around half of all users for everyday Information Retrieval (IR) tasks such as searching for real estate, jobs and getting information about health problems and government services [14]. However, unlike "traditional" desktop machines, they are commonly used on public transport, while walking from place to place [8, 9, 13] or in social contexts [2] - all situations where there is the potential for significant auditory distraction.

Distractions encountered during walking on a busy street, driving, and using public transport can preoccupy users [11], reducing their effectiveness in interacting with a UI [1, 9] and resulting in a larger number of misspelled and underspecified queries [12, 13]. A large body of work has considered how distraction affects user input on mobile devices, including how attention is diverted from the interface when following a pre-defined, but otherwise uncontrolled, route through a city. This was found to cause significant impairment when compared with a "non-social laboratory condition" [11].

Recent work, in which participants were subjected to simulated conditions (a treadmill and pre-defined indoor route), investigated how ambulatory distraction (walking) affects web search [4, 5]. Participants in the distracted conditions were found to objectively perform worse than those who were not distracted and perceived increased time pressure and stress. Very little work has considered how another common type of distraction - noise - impacts on user behaviour for mobile tasks. The only work to date, by Hoggan et al. [7], investigated a number of novel interfaces, including a haptic interface and one based on auditory signals, for simple touchscreen typing tasks. Participants performed the tasks whilst on a noisy and bumpy subway and were found to perform progressively worse as the noise level increased.

When people use their devices in context they process auditory information more efficiently when relevant auditory and visual stimuli are presented from the same, rather than different, spatial locations [15]. More specifically, they can be distracted when audio and visual stimuli appear to be disconnected. Research from psychology suggests that sounds that have affective impacts can modulate time perception - those that are arousing and hard to ignore increase perceived task duration [10]. Studying the combined effects of auditory distraction and task completion will not only have key applied implications, but will also evaluate how well users are able to recover from auditory distraction, which is not well addressed [6].

In contrast to previous work, we consider how auditory distractions impact user performance for specific search tasks, as opposed to simple typing and button selection tasks, and on the participants' perceptions of this impact. To aid in both repeatability and realism, our studies involve a *simulated* context in which participants are exposed to a pre-recorded audio track of common loud and distracting sounds. The results for participants placed in this context are compared with results from those under exactly the same experimental set up but with no auditory distractions (a quiet room). As people frequently also use tablets to access the web on the go, we conduct experiments with both tablet and phone devices.

Our main research questions are:

- Do auditory distractions impact on search performance for common search tasks?
- How do users perceive these distractions and are they aware of their effects on their own search performance, if indeed there are any?

2 METHOD

We conducted a laboratory experiment with 16 participants drawn from a large European University (a mixture of academic staff, support staff and post-graduate students), of whom 10 were male and who had a modal age range of between 25 and 30. There were two independent variables: the type of *device* (tablet or phone) and whether or not participants were subjected to simulated *auditory distractions*.

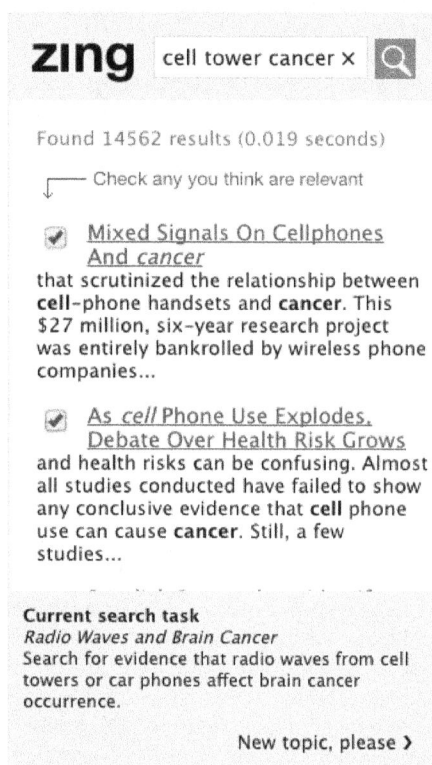

Figure 1: zing search interface on an Apple iPhone 5. Checkboxes used to indicate relevance.

We developed a simple mobile search interface named *zing*, shown in Figure 1, which mimics a standard SE interface by showing 10 links in descending order of relevance together with snippets for each. The interface allowed participants to enter search terms and indicate (via checkboxes) which documents they thought were relevant. It showed the current task (TREC topic) at the bottom of the screen and allowed participants to progress to the next topic at any time. The interface also prompted users to fill in pre- and post-topic questionnaires to survey their perceptions about the task and their self-assessed post-task performance, satisfaction, perceived time pressure and focus/involvement on the task. Half of the

participants completed their first two topics on a phone, moving on to the tablet for their final two topics, while the other half began with the tablet.

We created simulations of typical auditory distractions using a dictaphone with a wind-protected boom microphone around a major UK city, capturing everyday sounds (i.e. trains, cars, road works, people talking etc.). The audio was synchronised, layered and composed into sequences using a piece of editing software (Adobe Audition CC 2017) and we created four sequences for each search activity. Participants in the auditory distractions group conducted the experiment under the same seated conditions as those in the baseline, however speakers were placed on either side of them through which the audio sequences were played continuously throughout the tasks. The volume of the speakers (and the computer playing the audio) was the same for all participants and, as task sequence was randomised, so too was the audio sequence experience by each participant for the four tasks.

We used a standard test collection: AQUAINT[1] together with the 50 TREC 2005 Robust track topics, of which four[2] were randomly chosen from a subset of those which are neither too difficult nor too easy. Indexing and searching was provided by Apache SOLR. [3] Each participant was given the same 4 topics (tasks) in a random order with a per-task time limit of 15 minutes and alternated between the two *device* conditions. Participants were asked to imagine they wanted to learn more about the subject of each topic for a short report and were requested to select 3–5 documents they thought were relevant.

3 RESULTS

Before the experiment was described to participants, they filled in a short pre-study questionnaire asking them about their use of mobile devices and search engines as well as how difficult they would expect it to be to search on a phone or a tablet in various contexts, including in a noisy environment. All participants reported using a search engine and a smartphone several times a day and all but one stated they used their device to search the web at least daily. Half (n=8) reported using them at least daily on public transport and 9 said they used them daily in "in a noisy and distracting social situation (e.g. a pub or café)".

3.1 Pre-task perception

Before each task, participants filled in a questionnaire about their prior topic knowledge, their interest in it and expected difficulty (clarity of task, overall difficulty, difficulty in finding relevant documents, and difficulty in knowing when to finish). For the first three questions there was little variation between the two groups, with all participants being moderately interested in the topics (mean=3.12) but, on average, not very knowledgeable about them (mean=2.06) and clear on what they had to do (mean=4.19). All participants said they expected using a mobile device to search the web while sitting still to be easy, very easy or trivial, however two expected doing

[1]We removed duplicate documents in a pre-processing step, to provide a better and more familiar user experience.
[2]Topics 362, 367, 404 and 638.
[3]http://lucene.apache.org/solr/

the same in a noisy environment to be difficult and none thought it would be trivial under such conditions.

Condition	Sitting (baseline)	Distracting
Overall difficulty	2.32*	2.73*
Finding rel. docs.	2.5	2.5
When to finish	2.9*	3.2*

Table 1: Mean pre-task difficulty responses. * indicates significant difference (t-test, p < 0.05).

As shown in table 1, there were some interesting differences by condition for the other questions. Participants in the group subjected to the distracting environment expected the task to significantly more difficult than those given the baseline condition. They also expected it to be significantly more difficult to determine when they had collected enough information for the task. However, despite this, there was no significance difference in how difficult the two groups expected it to be to identify relevant documents.

3.2 Post-task perception

Immediately after each task the interface presented participants with a post-task questionnaire (see Table 2 for selected questions).

#	Question
Q1	I felt time pressure when completing this task
Q2	I needed to work fast to complete this task
Q3	Overall, I thought this was a difficult task
Q4	It was difficult to find relevant information on this topic
Q5	It was difficult to determine when I had enough information to finish the task
Q6	It was important to me to complete this task quickly
Q7	While I was working on this task, I thought about how much time I had left
Q8	While I was working on this task, I thought about how well I was doing
Q9	I blocked out things around me when I was completing the search task

Table 2: Selected post-task questions.

As shown in Table 3, there were a number of significant differences in the responses between the two groups and some questions for which responses were, perhaps surprisingly, not different. Despite all participants being given the same amount of time for the tasks, it is clear from Q1, Q2, Q6 and Q7 (all significant differences) that those in the distracting audio condition felt under much more time pressure. Even so, they did not perceive the task to be any more difficult than those under the baseline condition (Q3) and did not find it any more difficult to locate relevant information (Q4). In agreement with their pre-task perceptions, however, they did find it significantly more difficult to determine when they had enough information to complete the task (Q5). It seems the considerable additional perceived time pressure made the distracted participants more concious and concerned about their own performance (Q8), even though they thought they were not significantly less able to block out the world around them (Q9).

Condition	Sitting (baseline)	Distracting
Q1	2.61*	3.49*
Q2	2.34*	2.68*
Q3	2.72	2.89
Q4	3.05	3
Q5	3.62*	4.14*
Q6	2.61*	3.83*
Q7	2.47*	3.19*
Q8	3.72*	4.47*
Q9	3.57	3.38

Table 3: Mean post-task questionnaire responses. * indicates significant difference (t-test, p ≪ 0.01).

3.3 Task Performance

To objectively evaluate search performance, we rely on a number of metrics: the average number of hits (relevant documents) returned per search query; the mean average precision (MAP); the number of documents bookmarked per user per topic; the number of those that are relevant; the ratio of documents bookmarked that were relevant; the number of documents read per query; the average query length; and the average query duration per task. The results of these analyses are shown in Table 4.

Condition	Sitting (baseline)	Distracting
Hits/query	3.23	3.04
MAP	0.106	0.094
Bookmarks/topic	2.75	2.82
# relevant	1.82	1.21
(ratio relevant)	0.63	0.45
# documents read	1.59	1.2
# query terms	3.61	3.52
Query duration (s)	42	37

Table 4: Objective performance measures by condition.

Although none of the objective performance measures differed significantly by condition, there are a number of fairly large and interesting differences which, given larger sample sizes, may become significant. It seems that condition had little impact on the participants' ability to construct queries as both groups achieved similar numbers of average hits and MAP values. However, when we look at the participants' ability to identify relevant documents, it seems that the auditory distractions may have had an effect. Despite the fact that the "distracted" users actually bookmarked more documents per topic on average, fewer of these were relevant than those bookmarked by the participants in the baseline group. This means that, on average, the baseline group were able to identify a relevant document 65% of the time, while the other group only managed this is 45% of cases. The baseline group read more documents, submitted longer queries and spent a little longer querying than the other group. Linear modelling indicates that both Q4 and Q5 are significant predictors of task performance (in terms of number of relevant documents bookmarked).

4   DISCUSSION AND CONCLUSIONS

In this work we sought to investigate how everyday auditory distractions commonly experienced by mobile searchers (e.g. noisy public transport, pub and café environments, roadworks, etc.) impact on their searches. We conducted a user study with a total of 16 participants, 8 of whom were seated in a quiet, distraction-free environment (the baseline group), while the other 8 (the distracted group) were subjected to pre-recorded audio tracks to simulate such environments. The participants were given a set of four different search tasks to perform on the mobile devices and were asked to complete pre- and post-task questionnaires for all four tasks, which were presented at random to mitigate ordering/fatigue effects.

Our results suggest that the auditory distractions had a number of significant effects on the perceptions of the people in the distracted group. Mostly notably, the conditions seemed to induce a feeling of time pressure, even though it was never necessary to impose any kind of time restriction on any of the participants. The distracted group felt significantly more rushed and felt they had to complete the task more quickly than those in the baseline group, although strangely this did not appear to make them consider the task to be any more difficult. This result ties in with the work of Noulhiane et al. [10] who found that certain distracting sounds have the ability to increase perceived duration and, thus, perceived task duration. It may be that this result is also due to the somewhat irritating nature of the disruptive sounds and may, therefore, be due to the wishes of participants to complete the tasks quickly so that they can minimise the amount of time they are exposed to the spatially-discordant stimuli [15].

In keeping with their pre-task perceptions, the distracted users felt - in comparison with the baseline group - that it was significantly more difficult to determine when they had enough information to complete the task, although did think it more difficult to find relevant information. Despite this, the objective performance results suggest that it was indeed more difficult for the distracted users to ascertain whether or not a document was relevant, as they had lower success in determining relevance, albeit not significantly so. This may be because they spent less time on the tasks and read fewer documents, likely due to the additional perceived time pressure. However, the level of distraction from the audio may also have made it more difficult for them to concentrate on what they were reading and/or recall what they had already seen.

Comparison with the results of Harvey and Pointon [4, 5], who investigated distracting in the form of walking on a treadmill and navigating an obstacle course, suggest that auditory distractions are different from ambulatory ones. While the effects on querying performance are not so great, auditory distractions induce a much greater increase in time perception (and corresponding stress caused) and a decrease in the ability of participants to evaluate the relevance of documents.

4.1   Future Work

This research provides us with an initial understanding of the impact auditory distractions can have on search, however, there are a number of potential possibilities for future research to build on this. Although many of the differences between the groups in terms of perception were significantly different, the differences in objective performance, although at times seemingly quite large, were not significant. This may be a result of the relatively small cohort size and, therefore, an obvious extension to this work would be to increase the number of participants. In addition, more specific analysis could be performed to try to determine whether or not there are specific sounds that are more distracting than others and whether or not there is a fatigue effect. Alternatively, as some participants suggested, the opposite may be true - initial expose to the audio is distracting, however, after some time, people grow accustomed to the stimuli and are able to "tune it out". Finally, it may be interesting to experiment with a third, more naturalistic, condition (like that used in the work of Hoggan et al. [7]) in which participants perform searches out "in the wild". Although, unlike the work presented here, the obvious issue with this is that it would not be possible to guarantee that all participants are exposed to the same stimuli, making any generalisation of results difficult.

REFERENCES

[1] Andrew Bragdon, Eugene Nelson, Yang Li, and Ken Hinckley, *Experimental analysis of touch-screen gesture designs in mobile environments*, Proceedings of the SIGCHI Conference on Human Factors in Computing Systems, ACM, 2011, pp. 403–412.

[2] Karen Church and Nuria Oliver, *Understanding mobile web and mobile search use in today's dynamic mobile landscape*, Proceedings of the 13th International Conference on Human Computer Interaction with Mobile Devices and Services, ACM, 2011, pp. 67–76.

[3] Samuel Gibbs, *Mobile web browsing overtakes desktop for the first time*, https://www.theguardian.com/technology/2016/nov/02/mobile-web-browsing-desktop-smartphones-tablets, 2016, Accessed: 04 October 2016.

[4] Morgan Harvey and Matthew Pointon, *Perceptions of the effect of fragmented attention on mobile web search tasks*, ACM SIGIR Conference on Human Information Interaction & Retrieval (CHIIR), 2017.

[5] ———, *Searching on the go: the effects of fragmented attention on mobile web search tasks*, Proceedings of the 40th International ACM SIGIR Conference on Research and Development in Information Retrieval (New York, NY, USA), SIGIR '17, ACM, 2017, pp. 155–164.

[6] Helen M Hodgetts, François Vachon, and Sébastien Tremblay, *Background sound impairs interruption recovery in dynamic task situations: Procedural conflict?*, Applied Cognitive Psychology **28** (2014), no. 1, 10–21.

[7] Eve Hoggan, Andrew Crossan, Stephen A Brewster, and Topi Kaaresoja, *Audio or tactile feedback: which modality when?*, Proceedings of the SIGCHI conference on human factors in computing systems, ACM, 2009, pp. 2253–2256.

[8] Anne Kaikkonen, *Full or tailored mobile web-where and how do people browse on their mobiles?*, Mobility, ACM, 2008, p. 28.

[9] Min Lin, Rich Goldman, Kathleen J Price, Andrew Sears, and Julie Jacko, *How do people tap when walking? an empirical investigation of nomadic data entry*, International Journal of human-computer studies **65** (2007), no. 9, 759–769.

[10] Marion Noulhiane, Nathalie Mella, S Samson, R Ragot, and Viviane Pouthas, *How emotional auditory stimuli modulate time perception.*, Emotion **7** (2007), no. 4, 697.

[11] Antti Oulasvirta, Sakari Tamminen, Virpi Roto, and Jaana Kuorelahti, *Interaction in 4-second bursts: the fragmented nature of attentional resources in mobile hci*, ACM CHI, ACM, 2005, pp. 919–928.

[12] Richard Schaller, Morgan Harvey, and David Elsweiler, *Entertainment on the go: finding things to do and see while visiting distributed events*, IIiX, ACM, 2012, pp. 90–99.

[13] ———, *Out and about on museums night: Investigating mobile search behaviour for leisure events*, Searching4Fun WS at ECIR, 2012.

[14] Aaron Smith et al., *Us smartphone use in 2015*, Pew Research Center **1** (2015).

[15] Charles Spence and Liliana Read, *Speech shadowing while driving: On the difficulty of splitting attention between eye and ear*, Psychological science **14** (2003), no. 3, 251–256.

A Study of Search Practices in Doctoral Student Scholarly Workflows

Sharon Favaro Ince
Seton Hall University
University Libraries
South Orange, NJ, USA
sharon.ince@shu.edu

Christopher Hoadley
New York University
Steinhardt School of Culture,
Education, and Human Development
New York, New York, USA
chiir18@tophe.net

Paul A. Kirschner
Open University of the Netherlands
Psychology and Educational Sciences
Heerlen, Netherlands
Paul.Kirschner@ou.nl

ABSTRACT

Search, especially library search, is a distinct part of the research process which can be taught and supported separately from the scholarly processes of knowledge creation. We interviewed eight early career researchers (ECRs) composed of doctoral students or recent graduates about their overall scholarly workflows including not only search but also social networking around scholarly information and production of scholarly works. Evidence suggests that search itself is less discrete and library-centric than prior models may have suggested, and that students use both social resources and non-library technologies to discover and locate scholarly works. We argue that taking a workflow-centric and collaboration-centric view, rather than a search-centric view, should inform design of tools and training for search of scholarly resources.

CCS CONCEPTS

• **Information systems** → **Users and interactive retrieval**; • **Human-centered computing** → *Empirical studies in collaborative and social computing*;

KEYWORDS

Search; Academic librarianship; Scholarly workflow; Information Literacy; Graduate Students

ACM Reference Format:
Sharon Favaro Ince, Christopher Hoadley, and Paul A. Kirschner. 2018. A Study of Search Practices in Doctoral Student Scholarly Workflows. In *Proceedings of ACM SIGIR Conference on Human Information Interaction and Retrieval (CHIIR '18)*. ACM, New York, NY, USA, Article 4, 4 pages. https://doi.org/10.1145/3176349.3176877

1 INTRODUCTION

Traditionally libraries were central for scholars searching for information and held distinct tools for searching and browsing, as well as being the source for the holdings. Increasingly, new search tools, social media, and non-library websites containing academic papers are widely used. In some cases, non-library websites are not only the first point of access, but often the only point of access,

bypassing direct contact with the library. Recent literature names Google Scholar®and ResearchGate®[9] as the main sources for early-career researchers (ECRs) to locate information. One of the reasons for the shift away from library search is because 'Google is easy and the library is complicated' [5]. One reason why the library may be perceived as 'complicated' is because information retrieval is based on cataloging, classification, and librarians' interpretations of the literature rather than the searcher's [2]. Additionally, the librarian has, in the past, 'served as the mediator' between information resources and the user but may not always be the case now; libraries are resource-centric rather than reader-centric [1].

With this shift in search tools, it is import to examine where and why ECRs choose alternative services to conduct research. Looking at ECRs are important for three reasons. First, they are emblematic of scholars who are learning not only their domain but also the information and digital literacies necessary to conduct scholarship. Thus they help expose tensions and trajectories of how search is used in the academy. Second, ECRs are opportunistic and malleable in terms of their workflows; while senior scholars tend to settle into established practices with established tools, ECRs are more open to new technologies, new forms of scholarship, and new workflows that knit them together. Finally, ECRs are in a vulnerable and important phase in the pipeline of researchers. Current work helps demonstrate that early career scholars are not generally incorporated in libraries' models of information literacy or digital literacy, and that students entering doctoral programs are often ill-prepared for using libraries as part of knowledge generation [1, 6, 7]

Reader-centric systems for early career scholars not only need to have high usability as described in the literature; they also need to take into account how reading is constituted differently as part of the practices of knowledge building. If we take a consumption/ingestion model of reading, learning, and scholarship, 'reader-centric' looks a lot like traditional search and browse. On the other hand, if we consider the 'reader' to be an active scholar, not only encountering information but generating new knowledge, both in the sense of constructivist learning as a student, and in the sense of participation in networked communities of scholars, then we have to look at the practices and workflows of these scholars across the whole information problem solving lifecycle [4]. For example, the literature has described the difference between 'searching' and 'browsing' as one of intentionality and systematicity [8]. These distinctions are less clear when discussing modern workflows with ECRs. In the next section, we describe our empirical study of ECRs and how their use of digital tools and their scholarly workflow help illustrate a broader model of what it means for them to 'search'.

2 METHODS

We recruited eight early-career researchers (people in doctoral programs and recent graduates up to three years post-PhD) in Education and Social Sciences from four US universities and one European university for a 45 minute semi-structured interview held by phone, video conference call, or in-person. The participants received a copy of the 24 questions beforehand which covered the use of libraries, information literacy, information management, knowledge management, and scholarly communication; follow-up questions were asked for clarification. The interviews were audio recorded and transcribed. This paper reports on the analysis of the results related to search (which comprised both locating known and discovering unknown resources).

We examined the interviews for common concepts, tools, and search strategies. Additionally, we looked at types of training students received prior to doctoral program and during the program. We used descriptive coding [11] to identify digital tools used for locating known works as well as discovery and organization; and process and axial coding [11] to examine practices in scholarly workflows. A case study research method was used to analyze each participant as a case, followed by a cross-case analysis [12] to look for common themes across participants. This paper presents a subset of that analysis.

3 FINDINGS

3.1 Library-provided vs. freely available tools

Participants were asked to identify the first place they look for scholarly information. Seven participants identified Google Scholar as the starting place for information and one noted the library search box. Participants were also asked separately how they keep up with new information (what librarians traditionally think of as 'alerting'). This question was intended to capture either browsing or more serendipitous forms of search, as well as any more intentional and systematic alerting on narrow queries. Tools mentioned by participants are listed below in Table 1.

We see that search and keeping up with new information use different but overlapping tools. Participants were much more likely to use library-provided tools for locating known works than for discovery (alerting or uncovering unknown works), but even here non-library tools like Google Scholar are heavily used. While our interviews did not specifically explore the difficulties participants might have with library-provided tools, several discussed some of these issues. When participants did use library databases, it was often for the purpose of retrieving works for which the citation was already known.

> "Yeah, using library databases. That's one thing you have to figure out in order to get your dissertation done... how to find information in there. Then from there, I think, Google Scholar can be really helpful in finding something... Giving yourself a thread to pull on."

The participant then went on to discuss using Zotero® and Google Scholar and citation chasing (backward and forward reference chaining, i.e., finding who a known paper cites or who cites the known paper) as ways to locate individual articles or books, but

Table 1: Prevalence of tool use for search and alerting

Search tools		Alerting tools	
Tools	Users	Tools	Users
Google Scholar	8	Google Scholar	6
WorldCat	5	Journal alerts	4
Rejects library search	4	Twitter	3
Library discovery	3	Listservs	2
Citation chasing	3	Mendeley	1
Zotero	2	Google news	1
Twitter	2	Follow people	1
Email	2	ResearchGate	1
ERIC	2	Email account for alerts	1
Facebook group(s)	2	Conference reviewing	1
Google search	1	Research group sharing	1
Senate	1	Subscription to journal	1
Pubmed	1		
SciHub	1		
Gehat	1		

returning to the library databases for access. This participant also was the only one to specifically mention asking librarians for assistance in locating and accessing specialized information, such as GIS and geographic data. Another described how he avoided using the library search altogether by using sites for sharing papers via fair use or piracy. In response to being asked "Do you ever go directly to the library site?" he said,

> "Not usually. I usually go... Usually there's a moment of login through Google Scholar that doesn't...For some reason, the login doesn't maintain on my browser. I'll often end up having to sign in through the Library to gain access and things like that. The truth is, and this might be interesting for you, I often access articles if it's quicker, I'll use a pirating site. I'll use Sci-Hub."

One participant described her preference for Google Scholar due to the breadth of the results. Names of familiar scholars were used as a cue to prioritizing search results.

> "When I used to use the library system it used to take a lot more to search. It wasn't, you know how Google does it after you put in the keywords and it gives you everything, right? In the library you have to select much more. I guess When you think about it that's probably a more focused way of trying to find the things, but what can sometimes end up happening if you're not familiar with the same terminology that the library is using you don't get a large swath of results. On Google Scholar even if I got some of those that were not exactly what I was looking for, I get a wider range to choose from. It's like being able to scroll through the various results, and each result gives you a little bit more information on what it is, and if I'm already familiar with some of the authors then I can see that quickly."

Another participant described using Google Scholar's free-text format as both a retrieval tool and a query refining tool. Her use shows a privileging of more-cited literature, which traditional library tools do not easily support.

> "It's actually through Google Scholar that I have the easiest time narrowing down my search term. I often go by keywords, and then I start to snowball search. I see what I can find in terms of the keywords. What are the top hits that they often go by citation counts? I start looking by the articles that have the most citation counts."

3.2 Search, collaboration, and learning

Several participants discussed the importance of embedding search in social information-seeking behaviors and in learning behaviors. This dovetails with participation in networked scholarly communities, whether virtual (distal) or face-to-face (proximal).

> "Right now I use Google Scholar. I also, that's my primary way of doing it. Then I also put out questions on Twitter because I have a big academic community and network on Twitter. I sometimes put out a question saying, 'Hey, does anyone have any recommendations for stuff to read about this?' I also get a bunch of answers. Sometimes I know specific people in my network who I think would know about these things, so I directly contact them either by Email or on Twitter itself and say, 'Hey, I know this is something that you do. Do you know anybody, or have you recommend things I should read?' All of that."

This quote demonstrates that some ECRs are using diffuse, online social networks to aid their search. Other participants used more proximal, tight-knit social networks to support their learning and research process:

> "I knew that I could do a search, but I also knew that my colleague, is the absolute expert in [subtopic]. If anybody would know what's good, he would know what was good. What he was able to do for me was also give me stuff that wasn't available in any databases. He was like, 'Hey, talk to my grad student. She's doing her dissertation. See if she's willing to share her proposal.' She ended up being willing to share her proposal. Or, 'Here's this paper that we currently have in preparation. You could totally share this with the student that's in your independent study.' He'll also point me to a really common move for me. Then I might go into those papers and see who they cite and back my way into that literature base. There's sometimes where I'll start with the Google Scholar. If I know I'm looking for something super targeted, I'll often ask somebody."

One common feature in both of these quotations is that the participants link information seeking with the value of recommendations from other scholars. The openness to recommendations could be taken simply as an enhanced search strategy, but could also be interpreted as a learning strategy as these ECRs deepen their knowledge through the literature. If the goal were purely information seeking, they might have used library staff for help, but

reliance on professional networks and colleagues indicates a more socially embedded practice of increasing expertise.

The choice of tools for search is influenced by how the results of those searches are used in other parts of the scholarly workflow, especially when collaborating with others either for information sharing or for collaborative work. In this sense, the search tool can be conceived of as part of a socio-technical systems 'ensemble' [10] described as "the commitments, additional resources such as training, skilled staff, and support services, and the development of organizational arrangements, policies, and incentives to enable the effective management and use of new technologies." When we look at our participants' descriptions of search, the ensemble which includes tools as well as commitments, training, staff and services come into view as connected to the whole workflow of scholarship, well beyond search. For example, one participant describes part of her Google-based workflow thus:

> "I do have some Google Scholar alerts. I also use Mendeley. I used the Zotero in my master's work previously, and then currently, I use Mendeley. Our university liaison librarian who's in charge of our program, she did a little workshop and then she helped me set it up, because I was doing a research project for my advisor. Mendeley also has the alert. Then there are just some mentors that I follow, and I look at who they're citing."

Another participant described his work as similarly crossing collaboration tools:

> "Yeah. Google Docs, Dropbox, Slack ... I've been using Padlet a little bit, and something that I ... Well, no. I guess that wouldn't be relevant, but I started using Hypothes.is, but just a little bit, but not for the research. It's more for a learning thing."

To summarize, our results show that ECRs in our sample use a variety of 'search' tools, and tend to emphasize tools that are not traditional library databases. They use those tools for a combination of searching for known works and discovery. Their workflows for search and discovery are socially embedded in their participation with both proximal and distal scholarly networks (e.g., fellow grad students in the program vs. academic twitter). These workflows serve a dual purpose of information problem solving and learning. Within our sample, discussion of the library-provided centered on document access but also demonstrated that even for this function scholars were able to circumvent the library if it proved inconvenient compared to other tools on the open Web resources.

4 DISCUSSION AND IMPLICATIONS

ECRs in Education use non-library tools such as Google Scholar, social media and people as tools (e.g., email, following people, reviewing for conferences, etc.) for searching information. Search occurs not as discrete activity but is embedded in larger workflows. A mix of tools, many of which are not provided by libraries, are used. This workflow has similar patterns to the social scientist workflow identified by de Tiratel [3] before social networking grew to prominence. In this study, finding information consisted of consulting with others, citation tracking, use of current information, and only

Table 2: Search workflow comparison

de Tiratel (2000)	Current study
consults with colleagues and experts	consults with colleagues and experts
—-	use of social media for extended networks
citation tracking	citation tracking via Google Scholar
use of current information	use of freely available tools
use of library to obtain previously identified material	use of library for known material or pirate sites for previously identified material
—-	information funneled to collaboration platforms

using the library for known items. In Table 2 is a comparison of the current workflow and de Tiratel's 2000 model.

One of the most prominent tools is Google Scholar as seven of eight participants use it to find information, and as the front end access point of the library via library-provided metadata (the Google Scholar 'library links' feature). All participants noted their use of Google Scholar and all but one who mentioned using Google Scholar have their preferences set to take advantage of this, although we have no clear indication of how much or how often this is used as the primary retrieval workflow (as opposed to searching library provided tools for known resources). Some participants, however, did mention that this is their only interaction with the university library.

If we ask why one tool is so widely used, we see a variety of advantages Google Scholar provides. Some are related to ease of use (e.g., simpler to locate known citations, provides links to full papers on the open web if available) or advanced search features like ranking by number of citations or citation chasing. However, many features of Google Scholar support either social interaction or links to the larger workflow. Search completion and open text search helps ECRs learn the terminology of a domain. Author pages facilitate establishing the social context of individual works. And Google Scholar allows either saving references internally or easily exporting to reference managers such as Zotero, Mendeley, or Endnote, or supporting construction of bibliographies in a variety of bibliographic styles. Beyond these features, we do see our participants using other freely available tools to directly support sharing and learning. Certainly, generic social media is mentioned (e.g., twitter), but the use of collaboration tools such as hypothes.is (a group- or public-facing shared annotation tool), slack (a workgroup collaboration tool), or the collaboration features of cloud-based reference managers Mendeley and Zotero reinforces the idea that for many of these subjects, search is tightly embedded in a larger workflow that is usually collaborative.

Returning to where we started, this data sheds light on how to think beyond a resource-centered or library-centered view of how scholars, especially ECRs, use search. Our data confirmed prior findings [5, 9] showing a shift away from traditional library search tools. The picture emerging from our data makes sense when considering a workflow of scholarship that includes not only information search and retrieval but the whole lifecycle of scholarly production, including learning from and about literature. Seeing search as an activity that can occur deliberately or opportunistically at a variety of times in the research process helps explain why young scholars are turning from library tools to Google Scholar. But the pastiche of tools used by these young scholars shows that even Google does not support the entire workflow; our participants described using tools to support search but also sharing and socially embedded querying as part of a longer term participation in professional communities, and they explicitly link search to their own learning. If we are to design tools to better support scholarly search, we need to consider the entire ensemble [10], including the human and policy relationships that shape scholarly workflows as not only an opportunity to produce research but also to produce learning.

ACKNOWLEDGMENTS

The authors would like to thank Dean John Buschman, Seton Hall University Libraries; the members of the NYU dolcelab (Lab for Design of Learning, Collaboration, and Experience); and the anonymous reviewers for helpful suggestions.

REFERENCES

[1] J. M. Budd. 1995. User-centered thinking: Lessons from the reader-centered theory. *RQ* 34, 4 (1995), 487–496.

[2] J. M. Budd. 1996. The complexity of information retrieval: A hypothetical example. *Journal of Academic Librarianship* 22, 2 (1996), 111–117.

[3] S. R. de Tiratel. 2000. Accessing information use by humanists and social scientists: A study at the Universidad de Buenos Aires, Argentina. *Journal of Academic Librarianship* 26, 5 (2000), 346–354.

[4] S. Favaro and C. Hoadley. 2014. The changing role of digital tools and academic libraries in scholarly workflows: A review. *Nordic Journal of Information Literacy in Higher Education* 6, 1 (2014), 6–22.

[5] L. Hagund and P. Solsson. 2008. The impact on university libraries of changes in information behavior among academic researchers: A multiple case study. *Journal of Academic Librarianship* 34, 1 (2008), 52–59.

[6] C. Harris. 2011. The case for partnering doctoral students with librarians: A synthesis of the literatures. *Library Review* 60, 7 (2011), 599–620.

[7] S. Ince, C. Hoadley, and P. Kirschner. submitted. The Role of Libraries in Information and Digital Literacy Skills for Doctoral Students. (submitted).

[8] S. Keenan and C. Johnston. 2000. *Concise dictionary of library and information science.* Gale Group.

[9] D. Nicholars, C. Boukacem-Zeghmouri, B. Rodriguez-Bravo, J. Xu, A. Watkinson, A. Abrizah, and M. Swigon. 2017. Where and how early career researchers find scholarly information. *Learned publishing* 30, 1 (2017), 19–29.

[10] W. Orlikowsky and C. S. Iacono. 2001. Desperately seeking "IT" in IT research — a call to theorizing the IT artifact. *Information Systems Research* 12, 2 (2001), 121–134.

[11] J. Saldana. 2015. *The coding manual for qualitative researchers.* SAGE.

[12] R. K. Yin. 2015. *Case Study Research.* SAGE.

Investigating Everyday Information Behavior of Using Ambient Displays: A Case of Indoor Air Quality Monitors

Sunyoung Kim
Rutgers University
New Jersey, USA
Sk1897@comminfo.rutgers.edu

ABSTRACT

With the advent of the Internet of Things (IoT), people are increasingly gathering and using information through ambient displays every day. While this everyday information behavior has become a common mode of human information behavior, little is known about the factors that constitute such practices to inform the design of information dashboards. Drawing from 729 user reviews of indoor air quality monitoring stations posted to Amazon.com as a case, this study investigates the process through which people gather and use information from an ambient display as everyday information behavior. By using sense-making theory as an analytical framework, we illustrate key themes that constitute ways in which people make sense of information through everyday information behaviors of ambient display use.

ACM Reference format:
Sunyoung Kim. 2018. Investigating Everyday Information Behavior of Using Ambient Displays: A Case of Indoor Air Quality Monitors. In CHIIR '18: Conference on Human Information Interaction and Retrieval, March 11-15, 2018, New Brunswick, NJ, USA. ACM, NY, NY, USA, 4 pages.
DOI: https://doi.org/10.1145/3176349.3176880

1 INTRODUCTION

Information behavior is a term used to describe ways in which human beings interact with information "in relation to sources and channels of information, including both active and passive information seeking, and information use" [18]. "Active" and "passive" refer, respectively, to whether the individual does anything actively to acquire information, or is passively available to absorb information but does not seek it out [1]. Everyday information gathering is as important as active information seeking because people absorb much information naturally every day without expending energy to acquire it.

With the advent of new technologies, smart devices, and the Internet of Things, our living environments are increasingly becoming saturated with different types of digital devices and ambient displays. Consequently, the ways people seek information are changing. Moreover, smart environments make available a stream of real-time contextual information about the quality of our daily life and surroundings. Smart environments allow people to passively absorb information as part of daily routines without much effort or intention. Such information behavior is part of traditional everyday life information seeking as it focuses on the legitimate nature of information seeking in "the non-work context", such as health or hobbies, within everyday contexts "without explicit effort for acquisition" [14]. While everyday information behavior of using an ambient display is becoming a popular mode of information behavior, there has been little research to understand the factors that constitute such behavior. To that end, this study, through an analytical lens of sense-making theory, aims to elicit the factors that constitute everyday information behavior, using a device to monitor indoor air quality as an exemplary ambient display.

Indoor air quality (IAQ), as defined by the US Environmental Protection Agency, refers to "the air quality within and around buildings and structures, especially as it relates to the health and comfort of the building occupants" [6]. IAQ is an important determinant of health, as people in modern societies spend the majority of their time indoors, over 65% being in their residence [6]. An increasing body of evidence about a strong correlation between IAQ and health risks [16] has fueled the growing availability of IAQ monitoring stations (i.e., Awair[1], Foobot[2], Netatmo[3], See Figure 1) that make available the information about the current IAQ status to the residents. Consequently, researchers have started examining various aspects relating to the use of the instruments, such as measurement accuracy, behavioral effects, and influences on IAQ [10,17]. Yet another crucial research question requiring more attention is the conceptualization of everyday information gathering behaviors through the use of ambient displays.

Using 729 user reviews of three indoor air quality monitoring stations posted to Amazon.com, we conducted content analysis through the theoretical lens of sense-making theory to investigate how everyday information gathering is constructed, performed, and used. We found that increased health concerns relating to respiratory diseases or allergies are a vital trigger to IAQ information needs. Then, the reliability and interpretability of IAQ information posed gaps in making sense of the information, which can be overcome by observation of information over time and checking data accuracy with other compatible devices. Finally, the process of gap-bridging results in various outcomes of information seeking and use, including emotional anxiety relief and behavioral changes to remove indoor air pollutants. This work is a preliminary study of understanding everyday information behavior of using an IAQ monitoring device, and so we plan to investigate other ambient displays to contribute to our understanding of everyday information behavior.

---

[1] Awaire, https://getawair.com/
[2] Foobot, https://foobot.io/
[3] Netatmo, https://www.netatmo.com/en-US/site/

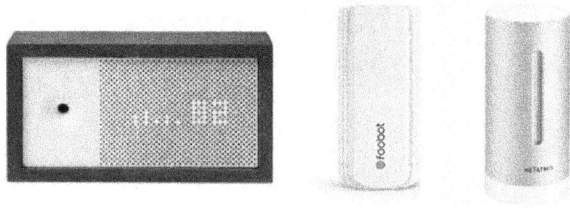

Figure 1: IAQ monitoring stations: Awair, foobot, and netatmo (from left to right)

2 LITERATURE REVIEW

2.1 Approaches to Information Behavior

Historically, the study of information behavior has been dominant in library and information science research. Major approaches to information behavior include information seeking and problem solving to study purposive behavior within a problem-solving framework to models of general problem solving (e.g., [3]); everyday life information seeking to refer to non-work or citizens' information needs and seeking [14]; and information foraging to understand how users search for information [13].

However, none of these approaches alone can completely explain human behavior in relation to everyday information behaviors of using an ambient display. The advent of pervasive and smart technologies has stimulated reconsideration of information behavior, broadening the approach from generic human-information behaviors to paying special attention to the communication patterns within people's particular situation or world to contribute to our understanding of information behavior.

2.2 Ambient Display: IAQ Monitor

Air pollution is recognized as one of the leading causes of death worldwide [4]. A growing body of scientific evidence indicates that indoor air pollution within homes and other buildings can be worse than outdoor air pollution even in the largest and most industrialized cities. Traditionally, IAQ measurements have been carried out using sophisticated and expensive equipment. In the past few years, however, there has been an explosion of low-cost IAQ sensors entering the market. Technologies are being developed not only to measure IAQ [18] but also to raise awareness of indoor air pollution and foster healthier everyday life; such developments are coming from industry and academia [7,8]. As interactive computing systems have been increasingly designed to allow people easy access to knowledge relating to health concerns associated with IAQ and to improve IAQ, it is critical to understand information behavior.

2.3 Sense-Making Theory and Gap-Building

The sense-making theory is a communications model that has been applied to information seeking and use studies [5]. It is established as a theoretical framework to understand everyday life information seeking, including both purposive (goal-oriented) and non-purposive information behaviors. This theory considers information seeking as a dynamic process situated in a specific space and time within a sociocultural context with four metaphors, including situation, gap, bridge, and outcomes [14]. In the sense making approach, the person is facing a "gap" (i.e., a sense-making need) that arises out of a context-laden "situation." Through the process of "gap-bridging," people seek information that leads to "outcomes" [11]. This theoretical framework is pertinent to understanding the dynamics of everyday information behavior in that it provides guidance to posit contextual questions as to how people interpret information to make sense of it. Therefore, this study examines the factors that constitute everyday information behavior of interacting with ambient displays using these metaphors as a theoretical lens.

3 METHODS

3.1 Data Collection

A total of 1028 Amazon.com reviews of three indoor air quality monitoring stations that had more than 100 reviews were scraped in July 2017. We chose to use Amazon.com's review corpus for this study because these reviews provide an unsolicited evaluation of the instruments and are a potentially rich source of descriptions of general uses of the instruments. Content analysis of web reviews has been used to understand reviewer opinions. No identifying information about reviewers was collected.

3.2 Content Analysis

First, the reviews were checked to ensure that they were related to the actual experience of using the instruments. Thus, reviews that were short or un-descriptive (e.g., "good product" or "Don't buy it") were excluded from further coding. The remaining reviews (N= 729, 71%) were used for analysis.

We analyzed the reviews using a thematic analysis to reveal patterns across data sets that are important to the description of a phenomenon and are associated with our research question. In particular, we applied both inductive and deductive approaches informed by grounded theory and other theory-driven qualitative analysis methods, such as thematic analysis [11,15]. That is, we inductively analyzed the data to allow for the themes to emerge, while we deductively reflected the emerged themes on the four constructs of the sense-making theory, including situation, gap, bridge, and outcomes. We examined if the emerged themes are compatible with the constructs; the emerged theme was categorized as the construct if the emerged theme fell under a subset of any of the constructs, and was introduced as a new theme if not. The final set of the themes has become the analytical framework through which we can understand the relationships among different themes and codes. We integrated all concepts through building relationships across the themes.

4 FINDINGS

Most emerged themes are associated with the key constructs of a sense making theory to elaborate on the process through which people gather and use IAQ information. In what follows, we describe the process of IAQ information gathering and use.

4.1 Situations to Trigger Information Needs

A "situation" is constructed by a set of contextual circumstances that provoke needs for information. Questions that elicit data on a person's experiencing of a situation include: "what issue were you dealing with?", "what led you to confront this issue?" and "what did you hope to achieve?" [7]. In the context of monitoring IAQ, the situation is made up of various needs to know about IAQ.

Concerns about IAQ are on the rise, triggering information needs about IAQ. The findings demonstrate that health- and space-related issues are the key factors that contribute to seeking IAQ information. The most common contextual cue is the increased health concerns relating to respiratory diseases or allergies. People who suffer from respiratory issues or allergies seek to learn the potential sources of the problem, and polluted indoor air has been known to have serious health effects on the respiratory system. Because many air pollutants are invisible and impossible to detect with human senses, it is very difficult with human perception to detect the changes in air quality. Therefore, people in search of IAQ information may end up purchasing IAQ monitors as a technical intervention.

"As one of the people who suffered from all sorts of nasal-related illnesses, I was one of the first ones to buy this device."

"I'm hoping maintaining healthy air quality will help with the wide range of allergies and health issues between my fiancé, myself and the 2 cats and 2 dogs."

Having a newborn or a young child with respiratory concerns (e.g., asthma) in the house is a critical trigger to the increased attention to IAQ. Since young children are particularly vulnerable to poor air quality, parents make an effort to ensure the quality of the indoor environment. With the current advancement of technology, an IAQ monitoring station is a plausible solution to cope with the problem, triggering the purchase of IAQ monitors.

"I bought it a week before my new baby girl arrived."

"As a mom of a 2 years old having health troubles since birth I was looking for a device that could help me understand what is surrounding our environment."

In addition, the change of a physical space has been identified as a spatial trigger. When people move to a new region where outdoor air quality is known to be poor or when people move in to a new house with new furniture, painting, and household materials, information needs for IAQ surge. Uncertainty about the quality of the dwelling environment triggers information needs about IAQ.

"As an active woman, concerned by the threat of downtown NY pollution, I was looking for an easy way of keeping an eye on my indoor environment."

"I moved into a newly renovated home and suddenly had an allergic reaction. It subsided and returned. I was hoping this device would help me identify the VOC levels in the home."

4.2 Gaps in Sense-Making

Ambient displays are designed to support serendipitous information gathering. With having an IAQ monitor installed in a residential space, people have easy and causal access to IAQ information as part of their daily practices. For example, they can glance at the display unintentionally whenever they pass by it as if checking the time on a clock or looking at a mirror with no purpose. However, we found that having easy access to IAQ information does not guarantee that people make sense of the IAQ condition. We identified two significant gaps that prevent people from making sense of IAQ information, namely *interpretability* and *reliability*.

The first is *interpretability* of the presented information. Most IAQ monitors represent the current state of IAQ using a colored graph (e.g., green meaning healthy and red meaning unhealthy) with numeric measures (i.e., the number of particles in the air). Many people reported that it is difficult, if not impossible, to interpret the information as meaningful knowledge. Because health concerns are a key trigger of IAQ information needs, people have sought to interpret the information associated with health concerns. However, the current ways of presenting IAQ information do not support these needs, as it lacks information relating to a healthcare context.

"I think the information is not of a value. What does it mean? How does it impact health or so is not clear."

"Interpretation is a bit confusing. I'm not an air-expert so numeric display of CO_2 or VOC can't be easily understood... I wish is if the device told me what the VOCs means... It's really unclear how to interpret the value of the VOC measure e.g. 300 ppb vs. 600 ppb vs. 1200 ppb. I would love to see the meaning behind it."

An equally critical issue is *reliability* of the available information. Due to the fact that there is no means to measure the accuracy of IAQ information presented on the instrument, people easily doubt its reliability once they experience a negative event with the use of the instrument. Example events include a drastic change of IAQ when nothing has happened or the presented IAQ information is not compatible with other resources.

"I started to suspect that it the measurements were not accurate when I started to see significant swings in the readings, especially for CO_2 and VOC, with no significant changes in my home environment."

"My smoke alarm at home was going gang busters and it didn't detect anything. So I'm not entirely convinced of its accuracy anymore"

As such, making the information just easy to access via an ambient display does not satisfy information needs nor guarantee valuable information. In what follows, the strategies to overcome, or "bridge", these two gaps are reported.

4.3 Bridging the Gap

"Bridging" is the process used to move across the gap when making sense of a situation. For example, bridging might involve actions that can influence cognitive or affective shifts, or influence values and stories or narratives. A question to elicit bridges is "what answers helped you better understand the issue?" [7].

A strategy to cope with the issue of *interpretability* is to observe the trend of IAQ information over time. It enables people to identify the repetitive IAQ patterns relating to the potential sources or solutions of indoor air pollution, as well as establishing empirical knowledge of what different IAQ conditions mean and their relationship with indoor activities. This experience is then used to interpret what the IAQ information means in relation to health concerns. Furthermore, building knowledge of the relationship between the IAQ status and its meaning helps improve its reliability, too. *"Since I started using the device, it's given me practical and reliable data about my home's air quality in real-time, as well as sets of graphs and trends that show air quality history."*

"I find it very sensitive. Turn on the overhead fan, and the dust monitor will kick up. Open the window and CO_2 will go down."

A strategy to overcome the issue of *reliability* other than building knowledge is to compare the IAQ information with other devices. While this is a costly option, those who are serious about IAQ willingly invested to ensure the reliability of IAQ data.

"I wanted to make sure that I could trust this because my 4-year-old suffers from asthma. This device seems grossly inaccurate. I've now checked it against other devices, and all of the air quality measures seem off (CO2, VOC and particulate)."

"The data from this device is crap. VOC is a min of 125 and the other data is way off compared to professionally tested levels in my home."

4.4   Outcome

"Outcome" describes the ways in which people put information into use. The process of gap-bridging results in various outcomes of information seeking and use. In sense making, the outcomes of information use are referred to as helps or hurts. Empirical examples of "outcomes" include "got ideas, understandings", "got pleasure and confirmation" and "got connected to others" [7].

We identified *emotional* and *behavioral* outcomes from information behaviors of IAQ. First, emotional outcome refers to one's reassurance and relief from emotional anxiety or concerns about poor IAQ and its negative influence on health. This outcome was the most prevalent type and many people reported relief from emotional distress as long as they retain confidence in the reliability of the information.

"I placed the unit nearby my newborn's bed for monitoring environment, and overall I feel much more secured about the air conditions."

"Before, all I could do at best is a 'sniff test'. Since I have placed it in our apartment, it has helped us gain immense insight as to how our behavior affects our air quality and vice versa."

Once establishing empirical knowledge of what different IAQ conditions mean and their relationship with indoor activities, people start to change their behaviors, some of which have become daily habits, which we call behavioral outcomes. Increased awareness and knowledge about IAQ was a substantial factor in motivating people to alter their behavior to improve air quality.

"I found that some rooms were getting to potentially unhealthy CO2 levels, and that my office had too high of a dust level. This encouraged me to include a higher amount of ventilation throughout the house"

"It cultivated some good habits such as reinforcing us to open our windows after each meals we've cooked, or when to mopping and vacuuming the floor."

5   DISCUSSION AND CONCLUSION

This case study reports the preliminary findings of the process through which people gather and use information from an ambient display as everyday information behavior, using IAQ monitoring instruments as a case. By using sense-making theory as an analytical lens, we identified key themes that constitute ways in which people make sense of information through everyday information behaviors of ambient display use. The findings demonstrate that merely making information available does not guarantee that people make sense of information. Thus, several strategies were employed for bridging gaps. However, further study is required as only one type of ambient display was studied.

As a next step, we plan to further investigate everyday information behaviors of ambient display usage to understand how people interact with such instruments in daily practice. We are hopeful that this study provides a step toward understanding the factors that constitute human information behaviors and informs the design of novel information dashboards.

REFERENCES

[1]   Bates, M.J., 2002. Toward an integrated model of information seeking and searching. The New Review of Information Behaviour Research, 3, pp.1-15.

[2]   Brand-Gruwel, S., Wopereis, I. and Vermetten, Y., 2005. Information problem solving by experts and novices: Analysis of a complex cognitive skill. Computers in Human Behavior, 21(3), pp.487-508.

[3]   Byström, K. and Järvelin, K., 1995. Task complexity affects information seeking and use. Information processing & management, 31(2), pp.191-213.

[4]   Cohen, A.J., Brauer, M., Burnett, R., Anderson, H.R., Frostad, J., Estep, K., Balakrishnan, K., Brunekreef, B., Dandona, L., Dandona, R. and Feigin, V., 2017. Estimates and 25-year trends of the global burden of disease attributable to ambient air pollution: an analysis of data from the Global Burden of Diseases Study 2015. The Lancet, 389(10082), pp.1907-1918.

[5]   Dervin, B., 1998. Sense-making theory and practice: an overview of user interests in knowledge seeking and use. Journal of knowledge management, 2(2), pp.36-46.

[6]   EPA, An Introduction to Indoor Air Quality, available from https://www.epa.gov/indoor-air-quality-iaq/introduction-indoor-air-quality, 2016

[7]   Jang, J., Dworkin, J. and Hessel, H., 2015. Mothers' use of information and communication technologies for information seeking. Cyberpsychology, Behavior, and Social Networking, 18(4), pp.221-227.

[8]   Jiang, Y., Li, K., Tian, L., Piedrahita, R., Yun, X., Mansata, O., Lv, Q., Dick, R.P., Hannigan, M. and Shang, L., 2011, September. Maqs: A mobile sensing system for indoor air quality. In Proceedings of the 13th international conference on Ubiquitous computing (pp. 493-494). ACM.

[9]   Kim, S. and Paulos, E., 2010, April. InAir: sharing indoor air quality measurements and visualizations. In Proceedings of the SIGCHI Conference on Human Factors in Computing Systems (pp. 1861-1870). ACM.

[10] Kim, S., Paulos, E. and Mankoff, J., 2013, April. inAir: a longitudinal study of indoor air quality measurements and visualizations. In Proceedings of the SIGCHI Conference on Human Factors in Computing Systems (pp. 2745-2754). ACM.

[11] Miles, M.B. and Huberman, A.M., 1994. Qualitative data analysis: An expanded sourcebook. sage.

[12] Naumer, C., Fisher, K. and Dervin, B., 2008, April. Sense-Making: a methodological perspective. In Sensemaking Workshop, CHI'08. Pirolli, P. and Card, S., 1999. Information foraging. Psychological review, 106(4), p.643.

[13] Savolainen, R., 1995. Everyday life information seeking: Approaching information seeking in the context of "way of life". Library & information science research, 17(3), pp.259-294.

[14] Strauss, A. and Corbin, J., 1998. Basics of qualitative research techniques. Sage publications.

[15] Sundell, J., 2004. On the history of indoor air quality and health. Indoor air, 14(s7), pp.51-58.

[16] Wang, Z., Calderón, L., Patton, A.P., Sorensen Allacci, M., Senick, J., Wener, R., Andrews, C.J. and Mainelis, G., 2016. Comparison of real-time instruments and gravimetric method when measuring particulate matter in a residential building. Journal of the Air & Waste Management Association, 66(11), pp.1109-1120.

[17] Wilson, T.D., 2000. Human information behavior. Informing science, 3(2), pp.49-56.

[18] Zhi, S.D., Wei, Y.B. and Yu, Z.H., 2017, July. Air Quality Monitoring Platform based on Remote Unmanned Aerial Vehicle with Wireless Communication. In Proceedings of the International Conference on Future Networks and Distributed Systems (p. 26). ACM

Supporting Information Task Accomplishment: Helpful Systems and Their Features

Jingjing Liu
University of South Carolina
1501 Greene Street
Columbia, SC 29208
jingjing@mailbox.sc.edu

Yuan Li
University of North Carolina at Chapel Hill
100 Manning Hall
Chapel Hill, NC 27599
yuanli@email.unc.edu

ABSTRACT

We investigated systems and their features that help people use retrieved information to accomplish their information tasks. Participants were 32 college students who first recalled a recently accomplished task, and then worked on a task that they would need to finish. They answered questionnaire questions about what systems and features are helpful for task accomplishment. Our results discovered multiple helpful systems and features, which have implications on designing search systems for better helping accomplish tasks.

KEYWORDS

Task accomplishment; task outcome; helpful system features

ACM Reference format:
J. Liu and Y. Li. 2018. Supporting information task accomplishment: Helpful systems and their features. In *Proceedings of ACM SIGIR Conference on Human Information Interaction and Retrieval (CHIIR'18)*. ACM, *March* 2018, 4 pages. DOI: https://doi.org/10.1145/3176349.3176875

1 INTRODUCTION

Information searching has become more and more indispensable in modern society. In real life, information search is rarely an insulated activity. Instead, it is generally driven by some tasks that arouse the information need, usually aims at accomplishing the tasks by using located information, and is frequently accompanied by or intertwined with other activities, such as information saving, note taking, and so on. For example, to write a course paper, a student searches library databases for useful resources, saves the found information, maybe also takes notes, and later uses the sources write the course paper. Searching in this case is caused by and targets at writing the paper. In the meantime, it is accompanied by saving sources and taking notes. It is followed by using the information to write the paper.

Information use is another component in information behavior models such as Wilson's [10] model. In the Information Retrieval (IR) research community, tasks involving information use are called "work tasks", in comparison with "search tasks" that focus on searching only [3]. The concept of work task context implies that it is not enough for search systems to support only searching,

but that they should support searchers' information use for task accomplishment in a more comprehensive sense.

Researchers in the Interactive Information Retrieval (IIR) area have long realized the importance of tasks as the context for information search. However, only recently have few studies started to examine work task outcome and the relationship between search task and work task, which reflect the relationship between information search and information use [4-7, 9].

Still, research effort has rarely been spent to explore system features that support information use and task accomplishment. This is true especially thinking from the user's perspective, eliciting real users' opinions through user studies, asking questions in the context of real tasks instead of asking general questions in surveys. The current research aims at filling the gaps by exploring the following research questions:

RQ1. What system features are helpful for people to accomplish their work tasks?

RQ2. Do system features helpful for task accomplishment vary across tasks, or task types?

2 RELATED LITERATURE

Search engines have attempted to provide more functions to help with user tasks than returning search results. Google Notebook[1], and Yahoo! Search Pad[2] are examples to help save search results or notes. Unfortunately, these functions have either been shutdown or not attracting much use. Regardless, these functions were primarily information saving related instead of information use techniques. It remains an open area of great potential that search systems are equipped with features supporting information use.

Some research explores how search engines support tasks. For example, search engines have been used as language tools for checking spelling, grammar, and definitions [2]. Brandt et al. [1] designed an interface that embedded a task-specific search engine in the development environment, which was shown to significantly reduce the cost of finding information and thus enabled programmers to write better code more easily. However, the above mentioned are either low-level, simple tasks for which search engines are good at providing answers, or purpose/activity specific for which the search engines are built in the activity (e.g., programming) interface. It remains unknown how other users like the search engines to help with their tasks that are of more variety.

---

[1] https://en.wikipedia.org/wiki/Google_Notebook

[2] http://www.businessinsider.com/yahoo-releases-search-pad-the-automatic-search-assistant-2009-7

In recent years, researchers in the IIR field [5, 6, 8, 9] have attempted to examine user information interaction from a more holistic perspective by putting search tasks in the context of work tasks. Kumpulainen and Järvelin [4, 5] found that when seeking information, people use multiple sources and channels, including web search engines, literature databases, websites, biodatabases, etc. They suggested that information integration is needed for system development. Vakkari and Huuskonen [9] examined how the effort that participants spent on searching is associated with their search performance and task outcomes in an essay-writing task. They found that the effort in the search process degraded search precision but improved the essay writing task outcome. Through examining users' search on Internet and their use of the located information in report writing, Liu and Belkin [6] found that some measures used typically in evaluating search performance, e.g., the number of viewed useful webpages, the number of issued queries, etc., were not correlated with the performance of report writing. Instead, they found that the performance of report writing positively correlated with users' effectiveness of finding useful webpages and their time allocated to writing. In a following study, Liu and Belkin [7] found that those users with different levels of task knowledge performed differently in different tasks: higher-level knowledge users tended to perform better in the parallel-structured task (subtasks in parallel with each other) than in the dependent-structured task (some subtasks dependent upon the completion of others); in comparison, lower-level knowledge users tended to perform better in the dependent task than in the parallel. A common finding in all these studies is that information search and information use are two different activities whose performances are not even correlated. This strongly endorses the importance of researching and designing systems for supporting information *use* to achieve the accomplishments of work tasks.

3 METHOD
3.1 Participants
Thirty-two students (20 female, 12 male) from the first author's university participated in this study. They were recruited by student email listserv from randomly selected academic departments. There were 23 undergraduates and 9 graduate students. Their average age was 23 years. Each participant received $15 remuneration upon completing the experiment session.

3.2 Tasks
In order to help the users to be more engaged when interacting with search systems and other applications (e.g., MS Word) regarding information searching, saving, and using, this study used participants' own real life tasks.

Each participant dealt with two work tasks, which they were asked to think of at the beginning of each session. Both tasks should involve information search, and importantly, have concrete task outcome(s). The tasks could be school, work, or life related. Specifically, the first task was a recall of a recently finished task. Participants were guided by a questionnaire to describe what the task was, how it was finished, and what system features were helpful for accomplishing the task, etc. The second task was a to-be-finished task. They were asked to work on it using the desktop

computer in the lab. A post-task questionnaire asked participants about helpful system features for their task accomplishment.

Since all tasks were participants' own tasks, the 64 (32*2) tasks we collected are all different from each other. More detailed description of the tasks and their types is presented in Section 4.

3.3 Procedure and data collection
Participants were invited individually to an on-campus information interaction lab for the experiment. The lab had a Windows desktop computer, equipped with high-speed cable Internet connection. The computer had two monitors: a main monitor for searching and working on tasks, and a side monitor for questionnaires.

Upon arrival, each participant was first given a paper version consent form to read through and sign. Then they completed a background questionnaire on the side monitor. Next, participants were shown the questionnaire for Task 1. They were asked to recall a real-life task that they had recently finished and to describe how they finished it. In the questionnaire, participants rated, on a 7-point scale, their levels of interest in and knowledge of the task, how difficult it was to find information, and to finish the task, etc. Participants also answered open-ended questions about system features that helped them to find and save information, and to accomplish the task. Task 1 took about 20-30 minutes.

Participants then worked on Task 2, which was a task that they had in mind and needed to complete. A pre-task questionnaire asked them to describe the task, rate their levels of interest in and knowledge of the task, predicted difficulty of finding information and of accomplishing the task. Participants were given up to 30 minutes to work on the task. They were encouraged to work on it as they would do in their life if not coming to the experiment. They were allowed to freely use any sources and tools/software that were accessible and available on the computer to finish the task. Subsequently, a post-task questionnaire was presented for the participants re-rating their levels of interest and knowledge about the task, their experienced difficulty of searching for information and of finishing the task. They also answered questions about system features that were helpful for finding and saving information, as well as for completing the task. The whole experiment session took about one hour.

3.4 Data analysis
We coded participants' responses to the question of what system features were helpful in using the found information to finish their tasks. The two authors first coded all participants' responses individually, and then discussed until an agreement was reached for every response.

4 RESULTS & DISCUSSION
4.1 Task overview
As mentioned earlier, participants' tasks were all different. Since participants were college students, it is reasonable to see that a great portion of the self-identified tasks (81%; 52 out of 64) was academic related (AC): some of them were scholarly (SC), which involved in-depth research, such as writing a literature review or a course paper; others were non-scholarly (NS), which did not

involve in-depth research, such as learning the Photoshop program. In contrast, only a small amount of tasks (19%; 12 out of 64) were non-academic (NA) related, such as writing a blog about vegan make-up companies. Table 1 presents an overview of the frequencies and examples of these task types.

Table 1. Tasks of different types: frequency and examples

Task type	Freq.	Example
NA	12	*Write a blog about vegan make-up companies*
AC-NS	8	*Learning the Photoshop program and editing a photo for a class requirement*
AC-SC	44	*Write a ten pages paper on solar energy materials with references as one of the course requirements*
Total	**64**	--

4.2 Helpful system features

We asked participants about helpful system features in general without any specification. Their responses covered many different types of systems, including search systems, browsers, and Microsoft Office applications (e.g., Word, Excel), etc.

Of special interest to us are search systems and their features. Meanwhile, other systems (in this paper, we use the label "system" in a broad sense that includes applications) and their features could have implications on search system design for better assisting task accomplishment. Therefore, we report all system features, and divide them into two categories: one for search systems and their features, and the other for other systems and their features[4].

4.2.1 Search systems and their features

Table 2 shows helpful search systems' features identified by participants for accomplishing their work tasks, with corresponding frequencies and task types in which these features appeared. The reported features were not only about finding the information (information search), but also about generating task outcomes (information use), which were rarely examined by previous studies. All the reported features spread across various aspects: search general features, search tips, querying, SERP features, information source features, as well as features in specific systems (e.g., some databases, and Youtube).

Although not appropriate for statistical significance tests in the current study, an overview of the features' appearance frequency could provide a sense of what features were most "favored" by the participant group. The most favored feature was the system providing pre-prepared citations, which appeared 8 times. This was particularly for academic related, especially scholarly tasks (AC-SC), perhaps because AC-SC tasks typically require references.

Another interesting point is that although most of the tasks were academic or even scholarly related, the participants were found to have much use of commercial search engines (in

comparison to library sources), and reported many features that belong to search engines. These include the simplicity and speed of search (Google), query auto-completion, and (YouTube) providing a "share" function with the URL for easy copy/paste. These would be good design references for other systems.

Table 2. Helpful search systems and their Features

Aspect	Helpful Feature	Freq.	Task type (freq.)
Search general feature	(Google) simplicity of search	1	AC-SC
	(Google) speed of search	1	AC-SC
Search tips	allowing quotation mark to search exact word(s)	1	AC-SC
Querying	query auto-completion	1	AC-SC
SERP (mainly search engines)	SERP distinguish result types (journal articles) and source types (forums) to help filter out unhelpful results	2	NA AC-NS
	SERP highlighting keywords in the snippets	2	AC-NS AC-SC
	providing snippets	1	AC-SC
	SERP providing URL for copy/paste	2	NA AC-SC
	option to filter (by subject, resource type, etc.)	2	AC-SC (2)
	returning plentiful results	1	AC-SC
	more reliable sources being at the top	1	AC-SC
	access to specific types of references (non-profit)	1	AC-NS
	having results from .org/.gov which are more credible	1	AC-SC
	the ability to search for abstracts and reviews as well as the original materials	1	AC-SC
Database	(side bar) pre-prepared citations	8	AC-SC (7) AC-NS (1)
	allowing to save article links in the system	1	AC-SC
	option to email articles	1	AC-SC
Information sources	full text available	2	AC-SC
	peer-reviewed sources available	2	AC-NS (2)
	articles being more credible	1	AC-SC
Youtube	(youtube) "share" function that provides the URL	2	AC-SC NA

4.2.2 Other systems and their features

Table 3 shows other helpful systems/applications and their features, along with the appearance frequencies and corresponding task types. These features are relevant to webpages, Microsoft applications such as Word and Excel, Photoshop, email, notebook, and general computer features.

---

[4] Although it is possible that some participants may lack knowledge about system features, the current study aims at exploring what the users think and therefore all features identified by the participants were reported.

Of particular interest to us are those features that have implications for search system design. One system with highe frequency in Table 3 was MS Word, and the feature was that it enables placing ideas and located (webpage) links together.

Table 3. Other helpful systems and their features

Aspect	Helpful system feature	Freq.	Task type (freq.)
General	copy/paste (citations, urls, texts, etc.)	6	AC-SC (5) NA (1)
	scroll down	1	AC-SC
General	search within a page	2	AC-SC AC-NS
Webpage/ browser	webpage saving/bookmark	8	AC-SC (4) AC-NS (1) NA (3)
	back button (to SERPs)	1	NA
	webpage/article having list of references to other sources	3	AC-SC (3)
	clear webpage layout	2	AC-SC (2)
	helping credibility judgment (e.g., too many pictures or less credible sources)	1	AC-SC
	saving HTML files quickly	1	NA
Word	placing ideas and located links together	8	NA (2) AC-SC (4) AC-NS (2)
	Formatting function	2	AC-NS, AC-SC
	using MS Word at the same time as searching	1	AC-SC
Excel	excel charting	1	NA
	excel freeze cell feature	1	NA
Photoshop	internal search available	1	AC-NS
Email	email the ideas	2	AC-SC (2)
Blog	write and post blogs	1	NA
PDF	highlighting function	1	AC-SC
	adding text in (PDF) margin for notes for later	1	AC-SC
Others	deliver information through interlibrary loan	1	AC-SC
	writing down information in a note book	1	NA

This implies a design direction for search systems to meet users' expectation by letting users store ideas and locate sources more conveniently, possibly somewhere in the search systems, for future use of these ideas and sources to complete tasks. Furthermore, this feature applies to all three types of tasks, indicating that the feature could be considered by various types of search systems for helping with different types of tasks.

One other feature, "writing it down in a notebook", is similar as the above in that they both addressed note taking. Although the user meant to take notes in the paper note book, we thought this feature also important since it not only indicates that users took notes during the search process, but also tells that users took notes in a way that is convenient for them. For developing possible note taking or saving features for helping task completion, search systems especially those with touch screens might consider making this feature more like a paper note book.

There are other interesting features. For example, one other popular feature was copy/paste sources and texts (not necessarily in Word). The implication of this feature for search system design could be that search systems make it easier for users to copy/paste by providing a one-click button to copy texts or URL. Another feature was emailing the ideas. The implication could be that search systems provide a function/feature, maybe through clicking a button, to easily email (by the system) ideas to the users, rather than the users going to their own email systems.

5 CONCLUSIONS

Through a user study, this research examined what systems and features help users accomplish their real life tasks. Our findings show that the most favored search system features were pre-prepared citations, mostly for academic work. Search engines were also widely used for academic work, and their features such as query auto-completion were reported helpful. Other systems and their functions included storing notes or sources in MS Word, copy/paste, emailing, and so on. The results have implications on designing search systems that help task accomplishment.

ACKNOWLEDGMENTS

This research was partially supported by a USC ASPIRE grant. We thank Samantha Hastings for her support and Hassan Zamir for his help with data collection. We also thank the reviewers for their constructive comments.

REFERENCES

[1] Joel Brandt, Mira Dontcheva, Marcos Weskamp, and Scott R. Klemmer. 2010. Example-centric programming: Integrating web search into the development environment. In *Proceedings of the SIGCHI Conference on Human Factors in Computing Systems (CHI '10)*. ACM Press, New York, NY, 513-522. DOI: 10.1145/1753326.1753402

[2] Adam Fourney, Meredith Ringel Morris, and Ryen W. White. 2017. Web search as a linguistic tool. In *Proceedings of the 26th International Conference on World Wide Web (WWW '17)*. 549-557. DOI: 10.1145/3038912.3052651

[3] P. Ingwersen and K. Järvelin. 2005. *The turn: Integration of information seeking and retrieval in context*. Heidelberg: Springer.

[4] S. Kumpulainen and K. Järvelin. 2010. Information interaction in molecular medicine: Integrated use of multiple channels. In *Proceedings of the third symposium on Information interaction in context (IIiX'10)*. ACM Press, New York, NY, 95-104. DOI: 10.1145/1840784.1840800

[5] S. Kumpulainen and K. Järvelin. 2012. Barriers to task-based information access in molecular medicine. *JASIST* 63, 1(Jan. 2012), 86-97. DOI: 10.1002/asi.21672

[6] J. Liu and N. J. Belkin. 2012. Searching vs. writing: Factors affecting information use task performance. *ASIS&T* 49, 1 (2012), 1-10. DOI: 10.1002/meet.14504901127

[7] J. Liu and N. J. Belkin. 2014. Multi-Aspect Information Use Task Performance: The Roles of Topic Knowledge, Task Structure, and Task Stage. *ASIS&T* 51, 1 (2014), 1-10. DOI: 10.1002/meet.2014.14505101031

[8] Y. Li, and N. J. Belkin. 2008. A faceted approach to conceptualizing tasks in information seeking. *Information Processing & Management*, 44, 1822-1837. DOI: https://doi.org/10.1016/j.ipm.2008.07.005

[9] P. Vakkari and S. Huuskonen. 2012. Search effort degrades search output but improves task outcome. *JASIST* 63, 4(2012), 657-670. DOI: 10.1002/asi.21683

[10] T. D. Wilson. 2000. Human information behavior. *Information Science* 3, 2 (2000), 49-55.

How do Information Source Selection Strategies Influence Users' Learning Outcomes?

Chang Liu   Xiaoxuan Song

Department of Information Management, Peking University

5 Yiheyuan Road, Haidian Dist., Beijing, China, 100871

{imliuc, songxiaoxuan}@pku.edu.cn

ABSTRACT

Learning-related type of tasks has attracted much research attention recently but it is still not clear what factors would influence users' learning outcomes and how. In this study, we conducted a user experiment to assess searchers' learning outcomes and examine how information source selection strategies would influence their learning outcomes. In this experiment, thirty-two college students conducted search for two types of learning tasks: receptive tasks and critical tasks. Participants were asked to write down what they knew about the task before and after the search. For data analysis, we proposed a comprehensive assessment method, which used both quantitative measures (i.e. knowledge points, knowledge facets, knowledge scope, etc.) and qualitative measures to assess users' learning outcomes. Our results demonstrated that searchers' information source preferences influence their learning outcomes; i.e., encyclopedia-preferred sessions had better relevance of written summaries in receptive tasks and Q&A preferred sessions led to better relevance in critical tasks. Furthermore, searchers had two types of information source selection strategies: task-adaptive strategy and non-task-adaptive strategy. The results showed that searchers with task-adaptive strategy could gain better learning outcomes, e.g. knowledge points, facets, scope, depth, relevance and analyticity. This study highlighted the importance of information source selection strategies in learning-related type of tasks, and knowing how to select suitable information sources for different types of tasks may benefit the learning outcome for searchers.

ACM Reference format:

Chang Liu and Xiaoxuan Song. 2018. How do Information Source Selection Strategies Influence Users' Learning Outcomes? In *CHIIR '18: Conference on Human Information Interaction and Retrieval, March 11-15, 2018, New Brunswick, NJ, USA*. ACM, NY, NY, USA, 4 pages.
DOI: https://doi.org/10.1145/3176349.3176876

1 INTRODUCTION

Users have different types of goals when conducting search. Learning-related goal is an important type of search tasks for users. Current search systems are designed for users to find relevant information, not to optimize learning outcomes [1-3]. In order to design better search systems to help searchers with learning-related tasks, we need to better understand how the learning occurred during search, and how would users construct and reconstruct new knowledge during search [2, 4]. With respect to the assessment of learning outcomes, previous studies have proposed several methods to assess learning outcomes. For example, Hersh et al. [5] assessed information obtained of medical students after searching based on their ability to answer questions from a short-answer test. The test questions were designed to have specific answers and assessed by correctness of answers. Willoughby et al. [6] calculated the score of written essay about the assigned question after searching according to the number of acceptable factually correct statements or phrases. Wilson and Wilson [4] measured depth of learning of users' written summaries based on Bloom's taxonomy [7]. The measurement of depth of learning included quality of facts, interpretation of data into statements, use of critique, emphasizing respectively usefulness, analyzing, evaluating to users' written summaries. Similarly, Collins-Thompson et al. [8] assessed users' learning outcomes as the cognitive learning scores using post-search written test which consisted of six learning assessment questions. Each question addressed one of Bloom's learning levels [7] such as remembering, understanding, applying, analyzing, evaluating, and creating. It would be more comprehensive to use both quantitative measures and qualitative measures to assess searchers' learning outcomes.

Besides assessing learning outcomes, it is also important to explore what factors would influence searchers' learning outcomes. Previous studies have demonstrated that domain knowledge and search behavior could influence users' learning outcomes. Willoughby et al. [6] investigated the effects of domain knowledge and using information from the Internet as a resource to essay performance. They found searching information from the Internet could enhance essay performance for Internet groups much better than no-exposures-to-the-Internet groups. However, it was significant only for those participants who had high domain knowledge, those who had low domain knowledge had no difference on whether using information from the Internet as a resource. Wilson and Wilson [4] also found that participants with more topic knowledge produced texts with higher quality and covered more topics in their summaries. Collins-Thompson et al. [8] investigated the relationship between search behavior and learning outcomes. The results showed that searchers who spent more time reading

CHIIR '18, March 11–15, 2018, New Brunswick, NJ, USA.
© 2018 Association for Computing Machinery.
ACM ISBN 978-1-4503-4925-3/18/03...$15.00.
DOI: https://doi.org/10.1145/3176349.3176876

documents were more likely to receive higher scores on their writing summaries. However, not much research has examined how users' information source selection behavior would influence searchers' learning outcomes.

In this study, we conducted a preliminary study on users' information source preferences and strategies, and how such strategies would influence their learning outcomes. First, the study identified several source preferences and examined their relationships with learning outcomes in different types of learning-related tasks. Second, we examined whether searchers' sources preferences would vary for different types of tasks. Thirdly, we examined whether different source selection strategies would lead to different learning outcomes. Specifically, we have three research questions:

RQ1: What is the relationship between source preferences and searchers' learning outcomes?

RQ2: Do searchers have different source selection strategies for different types of learning-related tasks?

RQ3: How do searchers' source selection strategies influence their learning outcomes?

2 METHOD

2.1 User Experiment

We conducted a user experiment to assess users' learning outcomes and analyze how information source would influence users' learning outcomes. Thirty-two college students at Peking University participated in this experiment. They majored in various subjects, e.g. humanities, social science, information science and engineering, and medical domains. During the experiment, each participant was asked to conduct search on the computer in our lab for four learning-related tasks. We constructed two types of learning-related tasks according to the first two levels of Cognitive Learning Mode [9] classification: receptive tasks (Task 1 and 2) and critical tasks (Task 3 and 4). Receptive task is defined as understanding, remembering and reproducing what is taught, such as facts, concepts, procedures and principles, critical task as criticizing and evaluating ideas from multiple perspectives. Two tasks for each type were

constructed, and an example of each task is shown below (In this preliminary study, we took these two tasks for data analysis). The sequence of tasks was rotated using Latin Square to reduce the learning and fatigue effects for the participants.

- Receptive Task (T1): "Anti-haze mask task": The haze is getting worse and worse, and you insistent demand of mask. Before buying a mask, you want to know what types of masks are available, and the differences between different types of masks, and which masks are suitable for young people.

- Critical Task (T3): "Youth soccer task": Your cousin in junior high considers joining the school soccer team. Most of the relatives support this idea. But others suggest that soccer is a dangerous sport with potential health risks. His parents inquire your opinion on advantages and disadvantages of playing soccer for a long time, and should children join the soccer team?

After reading the task description and before searching, participants were asked to write down what they have already known about the tasks in the pre-search questionnaire on their own, without referring to any external reference; during the search, they could write/copy/paste/reorganize related information to answer the questions raised in the search tasks in the notepad file; after the participants completed search, they were asked to close all the webpages and notepad files, and write down what they knew about the question again in the post-search questionnaire on their own. During search, users' interactions with the computer were recorded by Morae Recorder 3.3.

2.2 Assessment of Users' Learning Outcomes

In this study, we used both quantitative and qualitative methods to assess the knowledge state of the written summaries by participants after searching, and regarded participants' post-knowledge state as the learning outcomes. For quantitative assessment, we first extracted all the knowledge points from users' written texts and then summarized these knowledge

Table 1: The assessment indicators of learning outcome

Learning outcome Indicators		Rating	Description
Quantitative measures	Knowledge points	------	The number of knowledge points
	Knowledge facets	------	The number of knowledge facets
	Knowledge scope	------	Calculated as the number of knowledge facets divided by the total number of knowledge facets for the task
	Depth of knowledge	------	Calculated as the number of knowledge points divided by the number of knowledge facets
Qualitative measures	Relevance	0	The written summary is completely irrelevant to search task with no useful information.
		1	The written summary is relatively broad to search task with a little bit of useful information.
		2	The written summary is full relevant to search task with a wealth of useful information.
	Analyticity	0	No in-depth analysis about issues (i.e. the discussion of distinction, advantages, disadvantages, etc.)
		1	Preliminary simple analysis about issues (i.e. the discussion of distinction, advantages, disadvantages, etc.)
		2	Relatively detailed analysis about issues (i.e. the discussion of distinction, advantages, disadvantages, etc.)
	Opinion	0	No opinions about issues.
		1	Have users' own opinions about issues.

users' written texts and then summarized these knowledge points into different knowledge facets to represent the scope of knowledge they gained after searching. The extraction of knowledge points and classification of knowledge facets were conducted through manual coding by two independent coders. When disagreements raised, an independent third encoded the inconsistent data. We then calculated four measures based on the knowledge points and knowledge scope, i.e. number of knowledge facets, number of knowledge points, breadth of knowledge scope, and depth of knowledge. For knowledge quality, we manually assessed three measures by two coders: relevance, analyticity, and opinion, adapted from [4]. The assessment indicators and their descriptions are shown in Table 1.

For the coding of knowledge points, two coders achieved Fleiss k of 0.841 and 0.883 respectively for T1 and T3. There were eight knowledge facets mentioned in T1: model, material, function, appearance, characteristic, recognition, use and price; and twelve knowledge facets mentioned in T3 including skeleton muscle, brain, organ, soft tissue, system adjustment, other physical damage, physical exercise, learning, character, communication, interest and motion protection. For qualitative measures, i.e. relevance, analyticity and opinion, the two coders achieved Fleiss k of 0.671, 0.735 and 0.95 respectively in above three aspects of knowledge.

2.3   Information Source Preferences

In this study, we focused on the sources where searchers acquire new information from during search. From all the webpages that searchers visited during search sessions, we extracted those that users recorded information from in the notepad by replication, transcription, user personal reorganization, etc. Therefore if the visiting to a webpage was followed by a notepad writing or checking activities, then this web page was considered as an information source for the searcher.

Among the 64 sessions that we analyzed in this study, there were 237 unique webpages that could be considered as information sources for participants. These webpages can be classified to five types according to source of websites, the percentages showed that Q&A platform websites and Encyclopedia websites were two main source types for the participants in our study.

- Professional websites (8.9%): professional academic medical domain websites and the medical information related websites that were designed for the public;
- Encyclopedia websites (25.7%): online encyclopedia websites, such as Wikipedia;
- Q&A websites (46.8%): websites of knowledge communities in which users would ask and answer questions;
- News websites (13.1%): websites releasing various of news;
- Other websites (5.5%): beyond the four types above, such as personal blog websites.

Further, in order to clarify users' information source preference in each session, we conducted K-means clustering based on the

percentages of each type of websites per session. All the sessions were clustered into two groups: "encyclopedia preferred sessions" and "Q&A preferred sessions", as shown in Table 2.

Table 2: The clustering results of source websites

Cluster	Mean percentage of encyclopedia websites	Mean percentage of Q&A websites	Number of sessions
1	56%	13%	33
2	5%	72%	31

The percentages of professional websites, news websites and other websites were very low, and there were no significant differences between two clusters, we did not show their percentages in the table. Cluster 1 is "encyclopedia preferred session" (N=33), and the mean percentage of encyclopedia websites is 56%; cluster two is "Q&A preferred session" (N=31) and the mean percentage of Q&A websites in this cluster is 72%. We then analyzed how users' source preferences in sessions would relate to their learning outcomes in the results part.

3   RESULTS

3.1 Source Preferences and Learning Outcomes

We first investigated the relationship between source preferences with users' learning outcomes per session in two types of tasks using two-way ANOVA tests. The results (shown in the left figure of Fig.1) revealed that in participants who had encyclopedia preference have significantly better relevance of written summaries in receptive tasks than in critical tasks; on the contrary, participants with Q&A preference could perform better in critical tasks than receptive tasks significantly. We also found that knowledge facets and scope of written summaries were benefited from encyclopedia preference in receptive tasks significantly (shown in middle and right figures of Fig.1). In critical tasks, even if there were not much difference on knowledge facets and scope between encyclopedia preference and Q&A preference, the means of knowledge facets and scope were also relatively high for the sessions with Q&A preference.

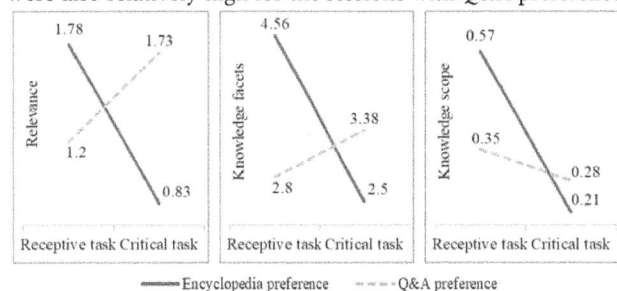

Figure 1: Information source preferences influence learning outcomes in different types of tasks

3.2 Information Source Selection Strategies

We further examined whether users' source preference would change in different tasks. For each participant, we compared whether their source preference in different search sessions was the same. If the source preferences were the same for the two types of tasks, then the information source selection strategy of this participant was classified as "non-task-adaptive"; if the source preferences were different, then the information source selection strategy of this participant was described as "task-adaptive". The results (in Table 3) showed that 21 participants adopted *task-adaptive strategy*; specifically, all of them were "encyclopedia-preferred" in receptive learning tasks, and "Q&A-preferred" in critical learning tasks. On the other hand, for other searchers, regardless of task type, six kept encyclopedia preference and five kept Q&A preference. We claimed this type information source selection strategy as *non-task-adaptive strategy*.

Table 3: The distribution of source selection strategies

Source selection strategies	Task-adaptive	Non-task-adaptive	
		Encyclopedia preference	Q&A preference
Number of participants	21	6	5

3.3 Information Source Selection Strategies and Learning Outcomes

In this section, we conducted Mann-Whitney U tests to examine which source selection strategy would gain better learning outcomes. The results showed (in Table 4) that searchers with task-adaptive strategy had significantly more knowledge points and facets, broader knowledge scope and deeper depth of knowledge than those with non-task-adaptive strategy. At the same time, participants with task-adaptive strategy performed remarkably better in relevance and analyticity of written summaries after searching than those with non-task-adaptive strategy. However, no significant difference in proposing personal opinion was found between two information source strategies.

Table 4: source selection strategies influence learning outcomes

Learning outcomes	Task-adaptive strategy	Non-task-adaptive strategy	Comparison
Knowledge points	12.43(34.40)	8.73(66.59)	**p=0.041***
Knowledge facets	4.10(2.38)	3.09(3.99)	**p=0.047***
Knowledge scope	0.44(0.04)	0.33(0.05)	**p=0.048***
Depth of knowledge	3.13(2.04)	2.31(2.21)	**p=0.035***
Relevance	1.83(0.19)	1.23(0.66)	**p<0.0001***
Analyticity	1.36(0.58)	0.82(0.73)	**p=0.015***
Opinion	0.67(0.23)	0.64(0.24)	p=0.81

4 DISCUSSION and CONCLUSION

We examined the relationship between information source strategies and searchers' learning outcomes. For leaning outcomes, we used quantitative measures and qualitative measures to assess. For source strategy, we first classified website types that searchers acquired new knowledge from, and identified two types of information source preferences in search sessions using cluster analysis: encyclopedia preferred and Q&A preferred. When examining source preferences with their

learning outcomes by sessions, we found encyclopedia preferred sessions could gain better learning outcome in receptive tasks, and Q&A preferred sessions had better learning outcome in critical tasks. This may be due to the differences of task types and websites content itself. Receptive task corresponds to remembering and understanding in the learning process [2]. The encyclopedia websites contain more comprehensive factual information with clear structure and more accumulated knowledge on a particular subject. Users could understand the knowledge in a relatively short time on encyclopedia websites, so these websites should be good source for receptive tasks. But in critical tasks, users need to apply, analyze and evaluate knowledge beyond the factual information acquisition [2], and the discussions or opinions shown on Q&A platforms may generate more inspiration for searchers, so searchers who were Q&A preferred had better learning outcomes in critical tasks.

We further analyzed whether searchers would change their information source preference according to the task types, and found two types of source selection strategies: task-adaptive strategy and non-task-adaptive strategy. Searchers who took task-adaptive strategy had better learning outcomes in knowledge points, facets, scope, depth, relevance and analyticity than those with non-task-adaptive strategy. The results of this preliminary analysis demonstrated that source types where searchers acquire information could influence their learning outcomes, and whether the searcher could adapt their source strategy according to the types of tasks they are working on is very important, especially for learning-related tasks. We will further analyze the factors that influence users' source preferences or strategies, and how to guide searchers for the suitable type of information source they may need according to the type of tasks in our future studies.

REFERENCES

[1] Gwizdka, J., Hansen, P., Hauff, C., He, J., & Kando, N. (2016). Search as Learning (SAL) Workshop 2016. International ACM SIGIR Conference on Research and Development in Information Retrieval, 1249-1250.

[2] Rieh, S. Y., Collins-Thompson, K., Hansen, P., & Lee, H. J. (2016). Towards searching as a learning process. Journal of Information Science, 42(1), 19-34.

[3] Rieh, S. Y., Gwizdka, J., Freund, L., & Collins - Thompson, K. (2015). Searching as learning: novel measures for information interaction research. Proceedings of ASIS&T 15', 51(1), 1-4.

[4] Wilson, M. J., & Wilson, M. L. (2013). A comparison of techniques for measuring sensemaking and learning within participant-generated summaries. JASIS&T, 64(2), 291–306.

[5] Hersh, W. R., Elliot, D. L., Hickam, D. H., Wolf, S. L., & Molnar, A. (1995). Towards new measures of information retrieval evaluation. Proceedings of SIGIR95', 164-170.

[6] Willoughby, T., Anderson, S. A., Wood, E., Mueller, J., & Ross, C. (2009). Fast searching for information on the internet: the impact of domain knowledge. Computers & Education, 52(3), 640-648.

[7] Bloom, B. S., Engelhart, M. D., Furst, E. J., Hill, W. H., & Krathwohl, D. R. (1956). Taxonomy of educational objectives: the classification of educational objectives. Of Educational Goals' Handbook Cognitive Domain, 1(15), 58-60.

[8] Collins-Thompson, K., Rieh, S. Y., Haynes, C. C., & Syed, R. (2016). Assessing Learning Outcomes in Web Search: A Comparison of Tasks and Query Strategies. Proceedings of CHIIR 16', 163-172.

[9] Lee, J. (2015). Does higher education foster critical and creative learners? An exploration of two universities in south Korea and the USA. Higher Education Research & Development, 34(1), 131-146.

Personalizing Information Retrieval Using Search Behaviors and Time Constraints

Chang Liu
Peking University
imliuc@pku.edu.cn

Jingjing Liu
Univ. of South Carolina
jliujingjing@gmail.com

Zengwang Yan
Peking University
yanzhangzeng@pku.edu.cn

ABSTRACT

Studies have examined how time constraints influence search behaviors; however, no effort has been spent on how time constraints may help predict document usefulness for personalization purposes. This study aims to fill this gap by researching the relationships between time constraints, search behaviors, and usefulness judgments. A controlled lab experiment was conducted with 40 participants searching for four tasks of two types (fact finding and information understanding), under two time conditions (with or without time constraints). Results show that time constraints and usefulness had interaction effects on first dwell time; while usefulness had positive relationship with total dwell time. Results indicate that knowing time constraints helps predict document usefulness from dwell time. The findings provide implications on personalization in information search.

ACM Reference format:

Chang Liu, Jingjing Liu, and Zengwang Yan. 2018. Personalizing Information Retrieval Usig Search Behaviors and Time Constraints. In *CHIIR '18: Conference on Human Information Interaction and Retrieval, March 11-15, 2018, New Brunswick, NJ, USA*. ACM, NY, NY, USA, 4 pages. DOI: https://doi.org/10.1145/3176349.3176878

1 INTRODUCTION

Context is an important factor that influences users' information search behavior and personalization of information retrieval systems. With the fast development of the Internet and mobile devices, users may often turn to search engines for information needs required to be addressed in a given short time period. Recently, some studies have examined the effects of time related contextual factors, including time pressure [4][6], time constraints [9][10], system delay [5], slow search [3][15], and urgent information needs [13], on search experience and behaviors. Some studies have also manipulated time perceptions and considered that into the evaluation of time-related searches [12].

The previous studies have found that when given time constraints, users' perceived time pressure and task difficulty were good predictors of their satisfaction with search strategies [4], rated higher levels of task difficulty, were less satisfied with their performance, and engaged in more metacognitive monitoring [6]. Studies have also found that time constraints did not affect searchers' assessment of task difficulty, but lowered their pre-

search confidence, evaluation of search performance, knowledge acquisition, and affective states [10]. Other studies examining search behaviors found that participants with time pressure issued queries more frequently, viewed fewer documents per query and spent less time examining documents and Search Engine Result Pages (SERPs) [5].

Some studies examined decision making and document selection in the situation of time limitation. Weenig & Maarleveld [17] found that participants did not adapt to time constraints through acceleration, but rather took more time on each item. Liu & Wei [9] also showed that searchers often adopted economic style of search on SERPs when there were no time constraints, but were more cautious and selective when given time constraints. However, no research has examined the effects of time constraints on document usefulness.

In IR research, dwell time has been an important source predicting document usefulness. These studies, with different experiment settings, have generated seemingly conflicting findings regarding the relationship between document reading time and preference/relevance judgment. Some studies (e.g. [14]) found reading time had a strong positive correlation with user's rating of interestingness of the articles or the retrieved document's usefulness, while [7] found that the length of time that a user spent viewing a document was not significantly related to the user's subsequent relevance judgment.

Researchers further suggest that contextual factors should be taken into account as a mediating variable to the relationship between document usefulness and user behaviors. White & Kelly [18] explored the effects of two factors of user and task on dwell time and document usefulness. They found that tailoring display time threshold based on task information improved implicit relevance feedback algorithm performance. Liu & Belkin [9] found that in multi-session tasks, users' task phase and topic knowledge prior knowledge could help interpret document usefulness from first dwell time (the time duration that users first view a document until first exiting the document). Vakkari, Luoma, & Ntinen [16] also confirmed such non-linear relationship between dwell time and the interest level when selecting fiction books, in which they found the most time was used for judging borderline cases compared with more valuable or valueless cases. Liu, Belkin and Cole [8] modeled user search behavior in search sessions in four different search tasks to infer document usefulness and then using such information to personalize search results. Many contextual factors have been considered in the above studies; however, no research has considered the effect of time constraints on the relationship between dwell time and document usefulness.

The current study aims to examine whether searchers' dwell time/decision time on assessing the search result content pages with various levels of usefulness would be accelerated or decelerated when given time constraints or under time pressure. Specifically, we had the following research questions:

(1) Do time constraints affect the relationship between document usefulness and search behaviors during users' first-time dwelling of content pages?

(2) Do time constraints affect the relationship between document usefulness and search behaviors during users' total dwelling of content pages?

2 METHODOLOGY

2.1 Participants

A lab-based user experiment was conducted to collect data for investigating the research questions. Forty undergraduate students (20 females and 20 males) from Peking University participated in the experiment. Among them, 5 were first-year, 11 were second-year, 15 were third-year and 9 were final year. Their ages were between 18 to 23. With respect to the computer expertise: most of them (N=29) rated themselves as "competent", some (N=9) rated as "proficient", and two rated as "advanced beginners", whereas none rated themselves as "novices" or "experts".

2.2 Tasks

In this study, we constructed two types of search tasks according to the first two cognitive process dimensions of Anderson and Krathwohl's Taxonomy of Learning: Remember—retrieving, recognizing, and recalling relevant knowledge from long-term memory (so called Fact Finding tasks) and Understanding—constructing meaning from oral, written, and graphic messages through interpreting, exemplifying, classifying, summarizing, inferring, and explaining (so called Information Understanding tasks) [1]. Each type consists of two tasks with two different topics, one is health-related and the other is encyclopedia knowledge related. Task descriptions were:

FF1 (Fact Finding 1): You heard that India has very interesting wedding traditions, and now you want to search for the following aspects of Indian Wedding: Wedding dresses, painted hands, and the type of food served.

FF2 (Fact Finding 2): One of your friends said he was bitten by a rove Beetle, and felt very itching, and the wound festered after scratching. You were quite worried about this type of beetles. You want to search what is rove beetle? Is it poisonous? What should you do if you see a rove beetle? If bitten by a rove beetle, how should we treat?

IU1 (Information Understanding 1): Your nephew is considering trying out for a football team. Most of your relatives are supportive of the idea, but you think this sport is dangerous and are worried about the potential health risks. Specifically, what are long-term health risks faced by teen football players?

IU2 (Information Understanding 2): Doric column is a distinctive architectural form in Ancient Greece architecture. Please search information about the general characteristics and representative works of Doric column, and whether Doric column has any influence on Chinese architecture? If so, what are the representatives?

2.3 Time Conditions

There were two experiment conditions regarding the time to finish a task: time constraints (TC), and no time constraints (NTC). In the NTC condition, participants were told beforehand that they could stop searching whenever they thought enough information had been collected for the task in their notebook file. Participants in the TC condition were informed beforehand that they had a restricted time of 5 minutes to finish a search task. This limit was determined according to psychology studies (e.g. [20]), being set as less than 50% of the average time in a pilot study (average task completion time was more than 10 minutes) done before the experiment, for the purpose of generating severe time pressure.

Each participant conducted searching in both conditions: two search tasks (one FF and one IU) in the TC condition and another two search tasks (one FF and one IU) in the NTC condition. To eliminate the possible carryover effect given this within-subjects design, participants were given a 5-minute break after they completed two search tasks in one time condition and before they switched to the other time condition. The order of search tasks and time conditions was systematically balanced using a 2x2 Graeco-Latin Square design.

2.4   Procedure

Participants were invited individually to an information interaction lab to finish the experiment. They were asked to search for four assigned tasks on a desktop computer. After signing the consent form, they first filled out a background questionnaire and were then given a training task to warm up. During search, participants were asked to respond to each task by typing or copying/pasting useful information for the task into a notebook file. After reading the task description and before working on each task, they filled out a pre-search questionnaire about their topic familiarity and expected task difficulty; after the task, they were provided the replay of their clicked documents during the search session, and were asked to provide the usefulness score (0-not useful at all; 1-somewhat useful; 2-very useful) to each content page. Then they were given a post-task questionnaire to evaluate their own search performance. After having finished all four tasks, an exit questionnaire assessed participants' overall search experience. We used Morae Recorder 3.0 to record searchers' interactions with the computer and the computer screen unobtrusively.

2.5 Search behavioral variables

In this study, we took the definitions of dwell time from Liu & Belkin [11]. Given that searching was intertwined with other activities such as working in the notebook file, first dwell time is defined as the first period of time the user reads a page, starting from when the user opens a page for the first time to when she leaves the document for the first time. Total dwell time is defined as the sum of all time periods that the user reading a document.

Besides dwell times, we also considered users' wheel activities, including the amount of scroll down, the amount of scroll up, the amount of total scrolling, and the number of times they changed scrolling directions. These scrolling activities were counted during users' first dwell time and total dwelling time respectively.

3. RESULTS and DISCUSSION

Users assessed a total of 767 content pages. Among them, 220 content pages were assessed as very useful (usefulness score=2), 249 pages as somewhat useful (usefulness score=1), and 298 as non-useful (usefulness score=0). The three-way relationship between time constraints, document usefulness, and users' interactions during their first-time and total dwelling on content pages were examined using General Linear Model (GLM). The original interaction data were not normally distributed, so we transformed data for each variable using Box-Cox [25], and the transformed data were used in the following analysis. In this part, we first present the results on the relationship among time constraints, document usefulness and interactions during first-time dwelling period, and then report their relationships during total dwelling period.

3.1 Time Constraints, document usefulness, and first-time dwelling behaviors

As is shown in Table 1, document usefulness and time constraints had significant main effects first-dwell time. Specifically, the more useful the page, the more the first-dwell time users spent; and users in NTC spent more first-dwell time than those in TC.

Table 1 Summary of the F(p) values of factors (obtained from GLM analyses) on user interactions during first dwelling of content pages

	Usefulness	Time Constraints	Usefulness * Time Constraints
BC-First-DwellTime*	**9.24** **(0.000)**	**5.89** **(0.015)**	**2.75** **(0.065)**
BC-First-WheelTotal	**4.95** **(0.007)**	2.11 (0.147)	0.04 (0.96)
BC-First-WheelDown	**4.76** **(0.009)**	3.08 (0.08)	0.048 (0.953)
BC-First-WheelUp	0.007 (0.993)	0.549 (0.459)	1.10 (0.335)
BC-First-WheelChange	0.008 (0.992)	1.40 (0.237)	0.836 (0.434)

(*Note: BC-variable stands for Box-Cox transformation of the data)

Meanwhile, there was also a significant interaction effect between usefulness and time constraints on first-dwell time (Fig.1). Specifically, in TC, users first-dwell time on somewhat useful pages were similar to or a bit longer than that in NTC. It seems that users tried to accelerate their reading speed when given time constraints; however, their reading speed could not be easily increased on somewhat useful pages because it was probably hard for them to decide if it was useful or not. This finding is consistent with previous studies [9][15], which suggested that users often spent most time on exploring somewhat useful pages during their first visit to the content pages.

Regarding the wheel activities, document usefulness had significant main effects on the amount of total first wheel scrolling, and first scrolling down. Fig.3 shows that the more useful the page, the fewer the scrolls, especially downward scrolling. Time constraints did not show significant effects on wheel activities, nor did the interaction between usefulness and time constraints. This all indicate that predicting document usefulness from first-dwell time may need to consider the time constraints condition, and predicting document usefulness from wheel scrolling during first-dwell period, especially downward scrolling, may not need to consider the time constraints condition.

3.2 Time Constraints, document usefulness, and total dwelling behaviors

As shown in Table 2, document usefulness had significant main effects total-dwell time, total-wheelup and total-wheelchange. Specifically, the more useful the page, the more total-dwell time, the more total-wheelup, and the more total-wheelchange users had. Time constraints had significant main effects on total-dwell

time, total-wheeltotal, total-wheeldown, and total-wheelchange. Users in NTC had more wheel activities, wheels down, and total wheel change than those in TC. Fig.2 & Fig.4 show the relationships between usefulness, time constraints, total dwell time, and sum of wheels during dwell total dwelling time. With respect to the number of wheels, even though they also follow a linear relationship with document usefulness, the pattern was different from that during first dwell time. During first dwelling period, the more useful the page, the fewer the scrolls; during total dwelling period, the more useful the page, the more the scrolls.

Table 2 Summary of the F(p) values of factors (obtained from GLM analyses) on user interactions during total dwelling of content pages

	Usefulness	Time Constraints	Usefulness * Time Constraints
BC-Total-DwellTime	**79.77** **(0.000)**	**40.45** **(0.000)**	0.48 (0.619)
BC-Total-WheelTotal	1.91 (0.149)	**14.629** **(0.000)**	1.084 (0.339)
BC-Total-WheelDown	0.85 (0.427)	**16.957** **(0.000)**	0.765 (0.466)
BC-Total-WheelUp	**7.31** **(0.001)**	3.2 (0.072)	1.39 (0.249)
BC-Total-WheelChange	**8.732** **(0.000)**	**6.28** **(0.012)**	1.46 (0.233)

Meanwhile, no significant interaction effect between document usefulness and time constraints were detected on any of these interactions during the total dwelling period. Compared with the first-dwelling period, predicting document usefulness from the total-dwell time does not seem to need considering the time constraints condition as with the first-dwell time, since the total dwell time and usefulness score showed linear correlation, no matter whether there were time constraints or not.

4. CONCLUSIONS

In this paper, we examined the relationship among time constraints, document usefulness, and search behaviors on content pages during two dwelling periods: first-dwelling and total dwelling. The results showed that wheel activities were not in general influenced by the condition of time constraints in indicating document usefulness, so was total dwell time. However, in indicating document usefulness, first dwell time was found to be influenced by the time condition, as was shown by the interaction effect between usefulness and time constraints. Since total dwell time could not be captured until a search episode is completed, but first dwell time could be captured during a search, knowing the time constraint condition is important in helping predict document usefulness from first dwell time. On the other hand, it seems that users may need assistance in judging somewhat useful pages when there were time constraints. Our findings have implications on designing search systems that are personalized according to time constraint conditions.

ACKNOWLEDGEMENT

This project is funded by National Nature Science Foundation of China (NSFC) #71303015.

REFERENCES

[1] Anderson, L. W. & Krathwohl, D. A. (2001). A taxonomy for learning, teaching and assessing: A revision of Bloom's taxonomy of educational objectives. New York: Longman.

[2] Box, G. E. P., Cox, D. R. (1964). An Analysis of Transformations. *Journal of the Royal Statistical Society, 26*(2), 211-252.

[3] Burton, R., & Collins-Thompson, K. (2016). User Behavior in Asynchronous Slow Search. *The International ACM SIGIR Conference* (pp.345-354). ACM.

[4] Crescenzi, A., Capra, R., & Arguello, J. (2013). Time Pressure, User Satisfaction and Task Difficulty. *Proceedings of ASIS&T 13'*.

[5] Crescenzi,A., Kelly, D., and Azzopardi, L. (2015). Time Pressure and System Delays in Information Search. *SIGIR '15.*

[6] Crescenzi,A., Kelly, D., and Azzopardi, L. (2016). Impacts of Time Constraints and System Delays on User Experience. *Proceedings of CHIIR'16.*

[7] Kelly, D., & Belkin, N.J. (2004). Display time as implicit feedback: Understanding task effects. *Proceedings of SIGIR 04'* (pp. 377–384).ACM.

[8] Liu, C., Belkin, N. J., & Cole, M. J. (2012). Personalization of search results using interaction behaviors in search sessions. *Proceedings of SIGIR 12'* (pp.205-214). ACM.

[9] Liu, C., & Wei, Y. (2016). The impacts of time constraint on users' search strategy during search process. Proceedings of the Association for Information Science & Technology, 53(1), 1-9.

[10] Liu, C., Yang, F., Zhao, Y., Jiang, Q., & Zhang, L. (2014). What does time constraint mean to information searchers?. Information Interaction in Context Symposium (pp.227-230). ACM.

[11] Liu, J., & Belkin, N. J. (2010). Personalizing information retrieval for multi-session tasks: The roles of task stage and task type. *Proceeding of SIGIR 2010'*, Geneva, Switzerland, July (Vol.66, pp.26-33).

[12] Luo, C., Zhang, F., Li, X., Liu, Y., Zhang, M., & Ma, S., et al. (2016). Manipulating Time Perception of Web Search Users. *CHIIR 16'* (pp.293-296). ACM.

[13] Mishra, N., White, R. W., Ieong, S., & Horvitz, E. (2014). Time-critical search. *Proceedings of SIGIR 14'* (pp.747-756). ACM.

[14] Morita, M., & Shinoda, Y. (1994). Information filtering based on user behavior analysis and best match text retrieval. *SIGIR 94'* , 272-281.

[15] Teevan, J., Collins-Thompson, K., White, R. W., Dumais, S. T., & Kim, Y. (2013). Slow Search: Information Retrieval without Time Constraints.

[16] Vakkari, P., Luoma, A., & Ntinen, J. (2014). Books' interest grading and dwell time in metadata in selecting fiction. *Information Interaction in Context Symposium (pp.28-37).* ACM.

[17] Weenig, M. W., & Maarleveld, M. (2002). The impact of time constraints on information search strategies in complex choice tasks. *Journal of Economic Psychology, 23*(6), 689-702.

[18] White, R. W., & Kelly, D. (2006). A study on the effects of personalization and task information on implicit feedback performance. *CIKM 2006'*, Arlington, Virginia, USA, November (Vol.92, pp.297-306). DBLP.

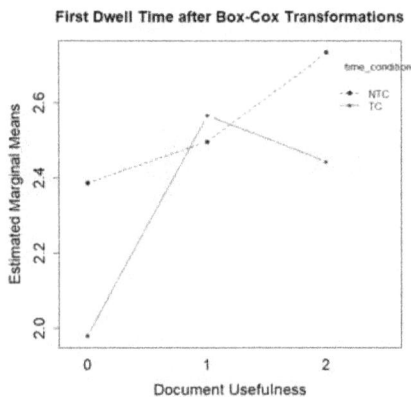

Fig. 1. Relations between usefulness, time constraints, and first dwell time

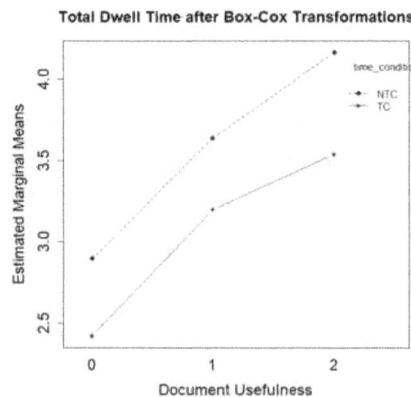

Fig. 2. Relations between usefulness, time constraints, and total dwell time

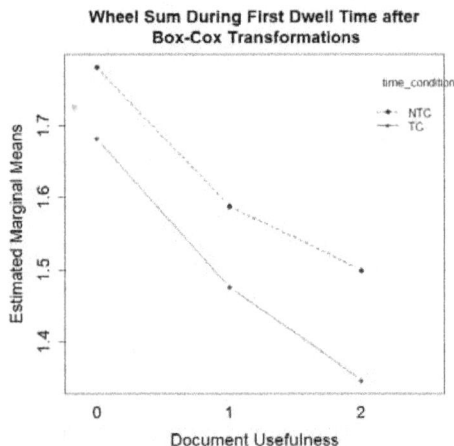

Fig. 3. Relations between usefulness, time constraints, and wheel sum during first dwell time

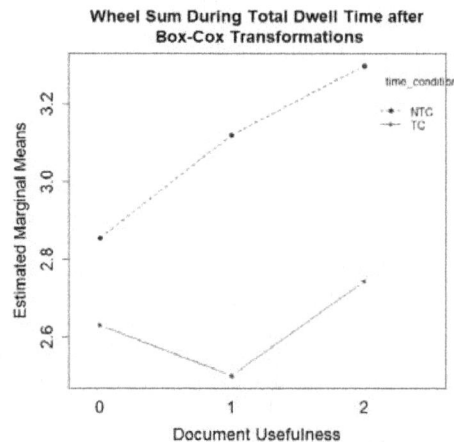

Fig. 4. Relations between usefulness, time constraint, and wheel sum during total dwell time

Personification of the Amazon Alexa: BFF or a Mindless Companion?

Dr. Irene Lopatovska
School of Information
Pratt Institute
144 W. 14 st., New York, NY 10011
ilopatov@pratt.edu

Harriet Williams
School of Information
Pratt Institute
144 W. 14 st., New York, NY 10011
hwilli13@pratt.edu

ABSTRACT

The conversational nature of intelligent personal assistants (IPAs) has the potential to trigger personification tendencies in users, which in turn can translate into consumer loyalty and satisfaction. We conducted a study of Amazon Alexa usage and explored the manifestations and possible correlates of users' personification of Alexa. The data were collected via diary instrument from nineteen Alexa users over four days. Less than half of the participants reported personification behaviors. Most of the personification reports can be characterized as mindless politeness (saying "thank you" and "please" to Alexa). Two participants expressed deeper personification by confessing their love and reprimanding Alexa. A new study is underway to understand whether expressions of personifications are caused by users' emotional attachments or skepticism about technology's intelligence.

KEYWORDS

Intelligent Personal Assistants, Digital Personal Assistants, Voice-Powered Personal Assistants, Conversational agent, Amazon Echo, Amazon Alexa, personification, anthropomorphizing

ACM Reference format:

I. Lopatovska and H. Williams. 2018. Personification of the Amazon Alexa: BFF or a mindless companion?. In *Proceedings of ACM CHIIR conference, New Brunswick, NJ USA, March 11-15, 2018 (CHIIR'18)*, 4 pages. DOI: 10.1145/3176349.3176868

1 INTRODUCTION

The idea of digital (also referred to as "intelligent") personal assistants (IPAs) is not new and traces back to the 1980th concepts of Apple's Knowledge Navigator, AT&T's PersonaLinks [26], and devices like IBM Simon and Apple Newton that were produced in the 1990s and aimed to assist users with managing calendars and notes, connecting to the network and other simple tasks [32].

The current generation of IPAs, including Google Assistant, Apple Siri, Microsoft Cortana, and Amazon Alexa, is designed to perform similar tasks and more through the natural language voice-control interfaces. The ability to "speak" to people often leads to attribution of human-like properties to the IPA systems [12]. Such attributions inspire researchers to examine user tendencies to personify this technology and even link personification to higher user satisfaction with IPAs [30, 25]. We expanded this line of inquiry by conducting a qualitative study of Amazon Alexa usage and explored the manifestations and possible correlates of users' personification of this technology.

2 RELEVANT LITERATURE

Personification, also frequently referred to as anthropomorphizing in the literature, can be defined as attribution of "humanlike properties, characteristics, or mental states to real or imagined nonhuman agents and objects" [11]. Research in the field of personification traces its roots in the works of Hume, Darwin, Feuerbach, and Freud and usually examines various forms of human interaction with animals, machinery and computers [31]. A number of authors address the question of why humans attribute humanlike qualities to nonhuman agents. Epley, Waytz, and Cacioppo [11] argue that personification of animals or objects serves three functions: 1) to make sense of a situation by projecting a person's own behaviors or thoughts onto an unfamiliar person/object, 2) to reduce the feeling of uncertainty in a situation by predicting the behavior of the other agents in it, and 3) to establish social connections. Epley, Akalis, Waytz, and Cacioppo [10] examined the link between loneliness or social disconnect and personification and found that "social disconnection leads people to seek companionship from nonhuman agents". Multiple studies suggest that people who are lonely are more likely to create relationships with pets or machines [16, 27] and that, in turn, a personified nonhuman agent can decrease the feeling of loneliness (for example, Banks, Willoughby, and Banks [2] found that a robotic dog did indeed decrease loneliness in nursing home residents).

Contrary to the "purposive" definition of personification by Epley et al. [11], Nass and Moon [22] and Nass, Steuer, and Tauber [24] describe personification as a mindless activity or an automatic reflex that can be triggered by the proper social cues. The authors call this behavior "overlearned politeness". Nass and Moon [22] observed that people are more polite in direct face-to-face interactions with other humans than indirect interactions. The researchers observed the same interaction tendencies towards computers despite people's universal denial that computers have "feelings" or warrant polite treatment: "The social rule that dictates insincere responses (the 'politeness' rule) automatically came into play as soon as the computer asked about itself" [22].

Humans seem to find it easier to interact with technology that resembles some of their characteristics, so it is not surprising that popularity and usability of many modern technologies, including IPAs, is predicated on their anthropomorphic characteristics and abilities to support social interactions [4]. Characteristics of behavioral realism aim to improve system functions and experiences [14].

Some of the technology design features that contribute to the illusion that the device has "consciousness, intentions, and emotional states" [11] include but are not limited to "faces" [23], voices [8], movement [20], and voices with social speech patterns [22]. Some of the personification triggers are further refined for gender, ethnicity and other factors, and are aimed to elicit different responses in users [23]. For example, Nass and Moon [22] conducted experiments in which "the generally positive praise from a male-voiced computer was more compelling than the same comments from a female-voiced computer".

Breazeal [4] developed a classification of technology based on the type of personification experience it elicits, including socially evocative, social interface, socially receptive, and sociable. Socially evocative technology uses cues that encourage people to personify it and interact with it. An example of such technology is the Tamagotchi toy that has features (such as a baby-like face) that trigger children to nurture the toy. Social interface technology uses "human-like social cues" to interact with humans for the purpose of making the interaction easier for the human. Examples of social interfaces include avatars that are designed to deliver information and, in some instances, "understand" the verbal message from a human and return the requested information or behavior. Socially receptive technology "learns" from humans, increasing its vocabulary or gestures by copying and predicting human behaviors in order to aid its users (e.g. machine learning). The highest level of social interaction is represented in sociable technology that aims to "read" human cues, learn and expand in order to improve its own functioning [4]. In the context of developing conversational agents, Cassell [6] emphasized the following system requirements: a) ability to recognize verbal and non-verbal input, b) ability to generate verbal and non-verbal output, c) support conversational norms (e.g. turn-taking, feedback), and others.

Amazon Alexa can be described as a social interface that uses "human-like social cues and communication modalities in order to facilitate interactions with people" and relies on the "shallow" social model of a person [4]. Its conversational functions are limited and do not fully meet Cassell's requirements [6]. Alexa does not learn, and does not have internal goals beyond the task given to it by its owner. It resides on a stationary device, Amazon Echo, with no "face". However, due to its speech features and ability to produce humorous responses, it is not unreasonable to expect that this device would trigger some kind of personification response from users, even if it is a shallow one. A recent study explored the levels of user personification of Alexa, the factors affecting personification and user satisfaction by analyzing the content of user reviews of the Echo/Alexa posted on the Amazon.com website [25]. Results indicate that over half of the reviewers include the personified name "Alexa" and reference the device with the object pronouns. The authors

found that personification of Alexa is associated with increased levels of satisfaction, even in cases when owners experience technical problems with the device. The study also suggests that reviewers from multiple-member households are more likely to personify the device than reviewers who live alone, a finding that goes against earlier work on increased personification tendencies in lonely people [2]. Turk [30] discusses the manifestations and causes of IPAs' personification. The author observes that users tend to interact with IPAs similarly to how they interact with pets or friends, and even say "please", "thank you" or "I love you" to Alexa. Turk [30] hypothesizes that such emotional interactions with Alexa suggest the presence of human longing for social connections that is satisfied by technology personification. Purington [25] and Turk [30] illustrate the dominance of the quantitative approach to studying IPA's personification.

3 METHODS

In order to understand users' perspectives on their interactions with Alexa and examine users' accounts of personification behaviors, we designed a qualitative study. The study data were collected primarily through the structured online diary, which participants were asked to complete once a day for four days. The diary method is commonly used in information interaction research and enables researchers to examine user behaviors with technology in their daily lives [3, 9, 17]. The decision to use a structured diary instrument was made in order to minimize time- and effort-related burdens on participants and collect comparable data across all study participants [15]. Participants were asked to fill out the diary once a way and identify the types of interactions with Alexa, their rate of success, user satisfaction and memorability as well as personification language they reported using with Alexa. Parents of young participants were asked to fill out the diary based on their children's accounts, as well as parents' own observations of children interactions with Alexa. The diary was recorded on two work days (Friday and Monday) and the weekend (Saturday and Sunday). In addition to the diary, participants were asked to fill out an online demographic questionnaire and share information about their Alexa ownership. The study was approved by the IRB. The details on the study instruments and procedures can be found in Lopatovska et. al. [18]

The study recruited a sample of 19 heterogeneous participants from nine households using a snowball sampling technique. Post hoc, the participants, ranging from 4 to 55 years of age, were grouped into three categories: children 4-10 years old (6), younger adults 20-39 years old (7) and older adults 40-60 years old (6). Twelve (63%) participants reported being professionally employed (e.g. two nurses, a lawyer, and a professor), 5 (26%) were students, and 2 (10%) were unemployed or declined to respond. Six households reported having one Alexa, two households reported having two devices and one reported three devices in their homes. Six households have had their Alexa(s) for at least 3-12 months, two households had Alexa for less than 3 months and only one household had their Alexa for more than a year. Seven (36%) participants reported using Alexa very frequently, 8 (42%) said that they used it very infrequently, and 4 (21%) respondents reported medium usage. The most frequent Alexa uses reported by the participants included quick information searches (17), entertainment (15), and control of other devices (9).

4 RESULTS AND DISCUSSION

The total of 127 interactions with Alexa were reported over the course of four days. The most frequent types of interactions included quick weather checks (N=39) and music-playing requests (N=29). Other types of interactions (e.g. use of Alexa to control other devices, check facts or news) were reported less frequently. Participants also reported an overall high satisfaction (N=124) and positive memorable experiences (N=33) with Alexa even for interactions that it did not produce desirable outcomes. The patterns of Alexa usage suggest that the interaction experience is more important to the users than its outcome.

In order to examine whether Alexa generates personification behaviors, we examined instances when participants referred to Alexa as if it had human-like qualities and analyzed the non-command language that participants reported in their "conversations" with Alexa. Of the nineteen study participants, eight (42%) participants, representing different age groups, reported seventeen instances of behaviors that could be described as personification. Analysis of participants' comments revealed 12 instances of "thank you" responses, 9 mentions of Alexa as a "she", two responses of "please" and one "good afternoon" greeting to Alexa. Four participants mentioned that while they do not converse with Alexa, they talk to Apple SIRI as if it was human. All participants who expressed personification signs were part of the multi-person households, confirming the findings of Purington, Taft, Sannon, Bazarova, and Taylor [25], but going against the hypothesis that lonely people are more likely to personify [10, 16]. Length of Alexa ownership or frequencies of its use did not seem to affect personification tendencies.

We attribute most of the recorded personification responses to what Nass and Moon [22] call "over-learned social behaviors", or social mindless responses that humans say to each other without hearing or meaning anything by the response. We noted that all ages, except the very young, engaged in mindless responses, including three middle-aged participants, two ten-year-olds and two older participants. It is possible that the very young participants did not direct any social responses towards Alexa due to not-yet-established social manners. It is also possible that children realize that Alexa does not react to politeness or impoliteness, and therefor treat Alexa rudely (a hypothesis that is supported by previously reported parents' accounts [29]). Further investigation into reasons behind presence and lack of social mindless responses in various age groups is needed.

Within the group of seven personifying participants, two provided responses that might indicate levels of personification that went beyond over-learned politeness. One person (age 53) told Alexa she loved it, and another one (age 24) chastised Alexa for not accomplishing its task. We see two possible explanations for such higher-level personification behaviors including: a) purposeful treatment of technology as human [10, 11] and observations about human longing for social connections [30] or b) purposeful testing of its intelligence to highlight its limitations and nonhuman nature. The second explanation follows Mori's [21] discussion of the "uncanny valley" phenomenon that refers to human tendencies to create a distance with technology that appears unnervingly human [21]. Using the "uncanny valley"

explanation, users' expressions of affection might in fact be expressions of mockery aimed at demeaning technology and emphasizing its inferior nonhuman performance. Several websites are dedicated to "funny things to ask Alexa" and provide users with "tricky" questions that point to Alexa's limited conversational abilities [13].

Several participants' responses reinforce the notion of participants' awareness of Alexa's nonhuman nature and limitations:

P1: [Alexa] couldn't respond to my child's questions (what's my brother's name);

P2: She had some silly responses in relation to the questions we asked.

Affective expressions towards Alexa might also signal users' tendencies to test the system that they do not fully understand and that "fools" them to believe it is more "human" than it actually is [19]. The fact that participants requested Alexa to tell jokes only six times also points to participants' awareness of technology's limitations for social interactions. Further in-depth analysis of users' reasoning behind the expressions of extreme personification is needed to understand whether such expressions manifest emotional attachments or skepticism towards human-like technology or some of its features.

5 CONCLUSIONS

Our findings did not confirm high levels of IPAs' personification suggested by some previous work [25, 30]. Only seven of the nineteen participants reported personifying behaviors during Alexa interactions. The majority of these behaviors can be categorized as overlearned social mindless responses [22] or "shallow" interactions [4]. Only two reported behaviors could be characterized as higher-level personification, and none of these behaviors were associated with children. Factors that attribute to some users' personification tendencies need further investigation. We did not, for example, find that heavier users or users who owned Alexa for a longer period of time were more likely to personify it than infrequent users or new owners. Similar to Purington et al. [25], we found that participants from multi-person households were more likely to personify than participants from the single-person households, possibly confirming that mindless politeness is more prevalent in a group than a lonely setting. Unlike Purington et al. [25], however, we did not find a link between user satisfaction with Alexa and its personification, as all users reported high levels of satisfaction with Alexa even when it failed to deliver the desirable outcome (for example, play a song).

The study had a number of limitations, mainly reliance on a small sample and self-report data. A new larger study is underway, collecting logfile and observational data on user interactions with Alexa. So far, the new study findings confirm our diary results pertaining to the tendency of the majority of the users to non-personify or make fun of Alexa, with very few users developing deep engagement with this technology (e.g. sharing their life stories with it). We plan to expand the old and share the new findings in the areas of a) over-learned mindless personification and b) high-level personification as an expression of emotional attachment or skepticism.

Personification is a double-edged sword: it can lead to long-term attachments to objects or it can cause frustration when the object does not live up to expectations or becomes too human-like [5, 7, 21, 19]. Finding the right balance might translate into more successful IPA products and happier users.

ACKNOWLEDGMENTS

We would like to thank the following student researchers for the contributions to the project: Katrina Rink, Ian Knight, Kieran Raines, Kevin Cosenza, Harriet William, Perachya Sorscher, David Hirsch, Qi Li, and Adrianna Martinez

REFERENCES

[1]   Amazon. 2017. Echo & Alexa Devices. Retrieved from https://www.amazon.com/Amazon-Echo-And-Alexa-Devices/b?ie= UTF8&node=9818047011

[2]   Marian R. Banks, Lisa M. Willoughby, and William A. Banks. 2008. Animal-assisted therapy and loneliness in nursing homes: Use of robotic versus living dogs. *J. Am. Med. Dir. Assoc.* 9, 3 (Mar. 2008), 173-177. DOI: 10.1016/j.jamda.2007.11.007.

[3]   Karley Beckman, Sue Bennett, and Lori Lockyer. 2014. Reconceptualizing technology as a social tool: A secondary school student case study. In *Proceedings of World Conference on Educational Multimedia, Hypermedia and Telecommunications 2014.* EdMedia2014, AACE, Chesapeake, VA, 1554-1559.

[4]   Cynthia Breazeal. 2003. Toward sociable robots. *Robot. Auton. Syst.* 42 (2003), 167-175. Retrieved from http://robotic.media.mit.edu/wp-content/uploads/sites/14/2015/01/Breazeal-RAS-03.pdf.

[5]   Elizabeth Broadbent. 2017. Interactions with robots: The truths we reveal about ourselves. *Annu. Rev. of Psychol.* 68, 1 (Jan. 2017), 627-652. DOI: 10.1146/annurev-psych-010416-043958.

[6]   Justine Cassell. Tim Bickmore, Lee Campbell, Hannes Vihjalmsson & Hao Yan. 2000. Human Conversation as a System Framework: Designing Embodied Conversational Agents. In Embodied Conversational Agents. Justine Cassell. (ed) MIT Press: 29-63

[7]   Jesse Chandler and Norbert Schwarz. Use does not wear ragged the fabric of friendship: Thinking of objects as alive makes people less willing to replace them. *J. Consum. Psychol.* 20, 2 (2010), 103-228. DOI: 10.1016/j.jcps.2009.12.008.

[8]   Mick P. Couper, Roger Tourangeau, and Darby M. Steiger. 2001. Social presence in web surveys. In *Proceedings of the CHI 2001 Conference on Human Factors in Computing Systems.* ACM, New York, NY, 412-417. DOI: 10.1145/365024.365306.

[9]   Stefanie Elbeshausen, Thomas Mandl, and Christa Womser-Hacker. 2015. Collaborative information seeking in the context of leisure and work task situations: A comparison of three empirical studies. In *Collaborative Information Seeking*, Preben Hansen, Chirag Shah, and Claus-Peter Klas (Eds.). Springer, Cham, 73-98. DOI: 10.1007/978-3-319-18988-8_5.

[10] Nicholas Epley, Scott Akalis, Adam Waytz, and John T. Cacioppo. 2008. Creating social connection through inferential reproduction: Loneliness and perceived agency in gadgets, gods, and greyhounds. *Psychol. Sci.* 19, 2 (2008), 114-120. DOI: 10.1111/j.1467-9280.2008.02056.x.

[11] Nicholas Epley, Adam Waytz, and John T. Cacioppo. 2007. On seeing human: A three-factor theory of anthropomorphism. *Psychol. Rev.* 114, 4 (2007), 864-886. DOI: 10.1037/0033-295X.114.4.864.

[12] Friederike, Eyssel, Dieta Kuchenbrandt, Simon Bobinger, Laura de Ruiter, and Frank Hegel. 2012. 'If you sound like me, you must be more human': on the interplay of robot and user features on human- robot acceptance and anthropomorphism. In *Proceedings of the seventh annual ACM/IEEE international conference on Human-Robot Interaction* ACM, 125-126. '

[13] Hayden. 2016. 101 Fun Things to Ask Alexa. Retrieved from http://thingstoaskalexa.com/index.php/2016/03/10/101-fun-things-to-ask-alexa/.

[14] Kerstin Heuwinkel. 2012. Framing the Invisible – The Social Background of Trust. In *Your Virtual Butler: The Making-of.* Robert Trappl (ed). Springer, 16-26. doi: 10.1007/978-3-642-37346-6_3

[15] Masumi Iida, Patrick E. Shrout, Jean-Philippe Laurenceau, and Niall Bolger. 2012. Using diary methods in psychological research. In *APA Handbook of Research Methods in Psychology: Vol. 1. Foundations, Planning, Measures, and Psychometrics*, H. Cooper (Ed.). American Psychological Association, Washington, D.C., 277-305. DOI: 10.1037/13619-016.

[16] Lee A. Kirkpatrick, Daniel J. Shillito, Susan L. Kellas. 1999. Loneliness, social support and perceived relationships with God. *J. Soc. Pers. Relat.*, 16, 4 (Aug. 1999), 513-522. DOI: 10.1177/0265407599164006.

[17] Irene Lopatovska, Megan R. Fenton, and Sara Campot. 2012. Examining preferences for search engines and their effects on information behavior. In *Proc. Am. Soc. Info. Sci. Tech.* American Society for Information Science and Technology, Baltimore, MD, 49, 1 (Oct. 2012), 1-11. DOI: 10.1002/meet.14504901110.

[18] Irene Lopatovska, Katrina Rink, Ian Knight, Kieran Raines, Kevin Cosenza, Harriet William, Perachya Sorscher, David Hirsch, Qi Li, and Adrianna Martinez, (in print). Talk to me: exploring interactions with the Amazon Alexa. *J. of Librarianship & Info. Sci.*

[19] Ewa Luger and Abigale Sellen, 2016. Like Having a Really Bad PA: The Gulf between User Expectation and Experience of Conversational Agents. In *Proceedings of the 2016 CHI Conference on Human Factors in Computing Systems* ACM, 5286-5297.

[20] Carey K. Morewedge, Jesse Preston, and Daniel M. Wegner. 2007. Timescale bias in the attribution of mind. *J. Pers. Soc. Psychol.* 93, 1 (2007), 1–11. DOI:http://dx.doi.org/10.1037/0022-3514.93.1.1.

[21] Masahiro Mori. 1970. The uncanny valley. *Energy* 7, 4 (1970), 33-35. Translated by Karl F. MacDorman and Takashi Minato.

[22] Clifford Nass and Youngme Moon. 2000. Machines and mindlessness: Social responses to computers. *J. Soc. Issues* 56, 1 (Spring 2000), 81-103. Retrieved from http://ldt.stanford.edu/~ejbailey/02_FALL/ED_147X/Readings/nass-JOSI.pdf

[23] Clifford Nass, Youngme Moon, and Nancy Green. 1997. Are computers gender-neutral?: Gender stereotype responses to computers. *J. Appl. Soc. Psychol.* 27, 10 (May 1997), 864-876. DOI: 10.1111/j.1559-1816.1997.tb00275.x.

[24] Clifford Nass, Jonathan Steuer, and Ellen R. Tauber. 1994. Computers are social actors, In *Proceeding CHI '94 Proceedings of the SIGCHI Conference on Human Factors in Computing Systems.* ACM, New York, NY, 72-78. DOI: 10.1145/191666.191703.

[25] Amanda Purington, Jessie G. Taft, Shruti Sannon, Natalya N. Bazarova, and Samuel Hardman Taylor. 2017. Alexa is my new BFF: Social roles, user satisfaction, and personification of the Amazon Echo. In *Proceedings of the 2017 CHI Conference Extended Abstracts on Human Factors in Computing Systems.* ACM, New York, NY, 2853-2859. DOI: 10.1145/3027063.3053246.

[26] Marina Roesler, and Donald T. Hawkins. 1994. Intelligent Agents: Software Servants for an Electronic Information World (And More!). *Online* 18, 4, 18-20,22,24-26,28-30,32.

[27] James A Serpell. 1991. Beneficial effects of pet ownership on some aspects of human health and behavior. *J. Roy. Soc. Med.*, 84 (Dec. 1991), 717-720. DOI: 10.1177/014107689108401209.

[28] Lee Sproull, Mani Subramani, Sara Kiesler, Janet H. Walker, and Keith Waters. 1996. When the Interface is a Face. *Hum-Comput. Interact.* 11, 2 (1996), 97-124. DOI: 10.1207/s15327051hci1102_1.

[29] Alice Truong (2016, June 9). Parents are worried the Amazon Echo is condition their kids to be rude. *Quartz.* Retrieved from https://qz.com/701521/parents-are-worried-the-amazon-echo-is-conditioning-their-kids-to-be-rude/

[30] Victoria Turk. 2016. Home invasion. *New Sci.* 232, 3104–3106 (Dec. 2016), 16-17. Retrieved from http://www.sciencedirect.com/science/article/pii/S0262407916323181.

[31] Adam Waytz, Joy Heafner, and Nicholas Epley. 2014. The mind in the machine: Anthropomorphism increases trust in an autonomous vehicle. *J. Exp. Soc. Psychol.* 52 (May 2014), 113-117. DOI: http://dx.doi.org/10.1016/j.jesp.2014.01.005.

[32] Pei Zheng and Lionel Ni. 2006. *Smart Phone and Next Generation Mobile Computing.* Elsevier, Amsterdam.

Predicting Zika Prevention Techniques Discussed on Twitter: An Exploratory Study

Soumik Mandal, Manasa Rath, Yiwei Wang
Rutgers University
New Brunswick, New Jersey
{soumik.mandal,manasa.rath,yiwei.wang}@rutgers.edu

Braja Gopal Patra
University of Texas Health Science Center at Houston
Houston, Texas
brajagopal.cse@gmail.com

ABSTRACT

Social media platforms are widely seen as a valuable medium to spread a wide range of information including charitable causes and health awareness. But given the flexibility provided by the social media platforms, it is important to ensure that the right kind of information is delivered to the right audience when needed. The pilot study presented in this paper considered a sample of Zika related tweets that were classified into different prevention techniques. The classification categories were drawn from the guidelines by CDC. Training a logistic regression model on the annotated data we found the accuracy to be 72%. The findings are significant in studying the effectiveness of social media platforms in spreading the right kind of information in time. This in turn can be useful in informing health care officials to take necessary steps with the help of real-time communication for such unfortunate events in future.

KEYWORDS

Zika prevention; Health analytics; Social media; Logistic regression

ACM Reference format:
Soumik Mandal, Manasa Rath, Yiwei Wang and Braja Gopal Patra. 2018. Predicting Zika Prevention Techniques Discussed on Twitter: An Exploratory Study. In *Proceedings of 2018 Conference on Human Information Interaction & Retrieval, New Brunswick, NJ, USA, March 11–15, 2018 (CHIIR '18)*, 4 pages.
https://doi.org/10.1145/3176349.3176874

1 INTRODUCTION

The past decade has witnessed the rapid growth and widespread usage of social media platforms such as Facebook and Twitter. Kaplan and Haenlein [7] defined social media as a group of Internet-based applications - such as blogs and social networking sites (SNS) - that "allow the creation and exchange of user-generated content" (p. 61). Nearly two-thirds of American adults use social media for a variety of purposes such as consuming news, sharing health-related information, and dating [13]. The number of social media users is also increasing by millions each day. As a result, social media as a form of collective wisdom has given rise to citizen sensing and is generating trends in topics of a wide range (e.g.,

health, politics, and entertainment industry) [1]. The literature has shown that the data gathered from social media sites can be used to make quantitative predictions of future outcomes and outperform traditional methods such as surveys and opinion polls [1, 2]. Social media data also reduces the time lag associated with traditional survey-based methods due to its real-time nature. Social media data is particularly helpful in epidemiological surveillance of health-related trends (e.g., disease, drug use, drug reaction). Traditional methods are costly, slow, and may be biased compared to social media data [15]. Employing machining learning techniques allow official organizations to be informed about what is known and discussed by the general public on social media platforms.

In this work, we focus on tweets discussing the surveillance and prevention of Zika virus, one of the deadliest viruses spread by mosquitoes. As a popular micro-blogging service that limits users' posts to 140 characters long, Twitter motivates brief and frequent mobile status updates. Specifically, we collected a set of tweets posted by official Zika accounts and utilized machine learning techniques (e.g., logistic regression, J48) to explore how accurately they could be classified into five Zika prevention techniques proposed by the U.S. Center for Disease Control and Prevention (CDC)[1]. The remainder of the paper is structured as follows. Next section introduces background and motivation of this study which is followed by details of data collection, preprocessing, and labeling categories. The data analysis and evaluation methods are introduced afterwards. Finally, the conclusion and future work are drawn.

2 BACKGROUND

Zika virus is primarily transmitted to people through the bites of infected Aedes species mosquitoes. Its negative effect can be serious in some cases, causing Guillain-Barre syndrome or miscarriage [3]. Zika virus may also be transmitted from a pregnant woman to her fetus, leading to birth defects such as microcephaly [14]. In early 2015, rooted from Brazil, an epidemic of Zika fever triggered by the Zika virus started to spread to countries in America and several islands in the Pacific and Southeast Asia. A year after, World Health Organization (WHO) declared the epidemic a public health emergency of international concern. The arrival of the Zika virus in the U.S. caused much concern among public which prompted the CDC to come up with ten Zika response planning tips to spread the awareness of Zika virus and prevention techniques that could prevent the spread of the virus. The ten prevention tips[2] are listed as follows:

- Vector Control and Surveillance

---

[1] https://www.cdc.gov/
[2] https://www.cdc.gov/zika/index.html

- Public Health Surveillance
- Laboratory Testing and Support Services
- Prevention of Sexually Transmitted Zika Virus Infections
- Prevention of Blood Transfusion- Transmitted Zika Virus Infections
- Maternal and Child Health Surveillance Response
- Rapid Birth Defects and Monitoring and Follow Up
- Travel Health News
- Clinical Outreach and Communication
- Risk Communication/Community Outreach

The outbreak also elicited extensive discussion on social media platforms such as Twitter and Facebook, which may have facilitated information sharing but also caused misinformation and fear to spread [10]. It is important to monitor what kind of information is covered on social media platforms and to help official organizations amend misinformation. For instance, previous research on Ebola outbreak in 2014 suggested that more than half of the tweets contained misinformation during the outbreak and more importantly, such tweets had a larger potential reach than the accurate ones [11]. Similar studies on Zika-related tweets found misconception on Zika vaccine [4]; potential misalignment between public concern and the concern of the authorities [5]. In this study, we are taking a closer examination on the latter to understand the public awareness on the prevention methods of the epidemic. More specifically, we are interested in how the prevention tips proposed by the CDC are discussed by Zika-related accounts on Twitter. Following are the research questions of our study:

- **RQ1**: What are the prevention techniques and tips most discussed on Twitter?
- **RQ2**: How accurately can we predict the Zika prevention techniques and tips discussed on Twitter?

3 METHOD

Our methodology consists of collecting the tweets from the official Zika prevention and intervention accounts; creation of categories and labeling the tweets; and data analysis using machine learning techniques. 1448 tweets were collected from 13 official Twitter accounts (e.g., ZikaCampaign, zikapedia) related to Zika using NodeXL[3] in the month of April 2017. The Twitter accounts were chosen carefully by focusing on only those accounts that were created specifically for spreading Zika awareness. Some of these accounts were bot accounts, which were designed to spread others' tweets based on the hashtag Zika. The decision of collecting tweets based on accounts rather than hashtags was primarily for two logistical concerns. First, gathering data by hashtags would only return the most recent tweets. Whereas, by focusing on individual accounts, it was possible to collect past tweets, especially from the period (in 2016) during Zika epidemic spread. Second, we hope to learn how the tweets from official accounts (such as WHO, CDC) vary from that of general twitteraties in a future work. For each tweet, the following set of features were also collected for current study as well as future work include: time stamp, timezone, and the user who tweeted.

---

[3]https://nodexl.codeplex.com/

3.1 Preprocessing and Labeling Data

The data cleaning process consisted of the following steps:

First, all the tweets containing less than four tokens (including hashtag, URL etc.) were removed, as they were unlikely to express anything meaningful.

Next, all the non-ASCII characters (such as ©, ®, ™ etc.), URLs, hyperlinks, @ and special characters were removed. Although it can be argued that URLs may contain useful information, however, we are not capturing that for this study.

Following that, we began to remove the non-English tweets. Since Zika was prevalent mostly in South America, a significant fraction of the tweets was in non-English language (mostly Spanish). To filter the tweets in English from the rest, we employed an English lexical database, WordNet [8], where each tweet was parsed into a stream of tokens, and the root forms of the tokens were checked for presence in the dictionary. The probability (p) of each tweet being a non-English one was calculated as:

$$p_i = \frac{(Number\ of\ tokens\ out\ of\ the\ database)_i}{(Total\ number\ of\ tokens)_i}$$

If the probability p_i for the tweet t_i is calculated as > 0.5, we marked the tweet as non-English tweets and hence removed from the dataset. The reason behind employing the fraction, rather than a stricter approach (e.g., presence of a single non-English word) was that a large fraction of the tokens in the tweets was proper noun and therefore, were not part of the dictionary. Hence, employing a more lenient approach mitigated the problem of mistakenly marking an English tweet as non-English one. Thus, we separated 668 English tweets from the rest.

Finally, we checked for duplicates and retweets. In total, we found 127 duplicate tweets which were removed. Thus at the end of preprocessing stage we were left with only 541 unique English tweets ready for annotation.

Since, the dataset we had at the end of preprocessing stage was really small for a 10-class classification problem, it was decided to convert the classification task into a 5-class one. For this purpose, the CDC-proposed prevention techniques were merged into five broader categories:

- *Surveillance of potential victims and follow-up* (C1)
- *Surveillance of vector* (C2)
- *Prevention of the disease (including sexual transmitted virus and infection from blood transfusion)* (C3)
- *Travel health news* (C4)
- *Public outreach/community outreach* (C5).

The labeling of tweets to one of these categories was performed at two levels: At first, the annotators were asked to separate the tweets that belonged to any of the above 5 categories from the others. If, a tweet was found relevant to one of the 5 categories, it was marked as "*yes*", otherwise as "*other*". In the second round, those tweets marked as "*yes*" at first-go were categorized into one out of the five categories (C1-C5). We assume the mutual exclusivity of the tweet categories based on the limitation of tweet size. Unlike other forms of text corpus, the length of tweet too small (maximum 140 characters) to belong to more than one categories. Following are examples of tweet for each category:

- **C1**: "Follow-up of 11 infants with Zika virus identifies neurological impairments."
- **C2**: "Mosquitoes can pass #Zika to their offspring."
- **C3**: "How You Can and Can't Catch the #Zika Virus"
- **C4**: "Federal agency offers travel guidelines on Zika virus."
- **C5**: "Health care: Zika Virus Conference to be Held in Washington DC This March."
- **C6** (*Other*): "Senate pass #Zika bill."

The two-level coding scheme was employed in coherence with the two research questions. Also, we felt the sequential labeling procedure would give a better understanding of the categories than a combined six-class labeling among the annotators. Two annotators were employed for the labeling task. Their inter-coder agreement was calculated to be 81% for the first level (all the 5 categories vs others) and 61% for the second level. The lower agreement on second level annotation indicates the difficult nature of the classification problem. We analyzed distribution of the data and discovered that 56% of the dataset consisted of tweets related to prevention and rest of the tweets belonged to the "*other*" category.

3.2 Feature Selection and Classification

Two sets of features were collected from the dataset.

3.2.1 Vector Space approach: Following the success of vector space model in text mining and information retrieval purposes [9], we used the same approach in our analysis. The vector representations of tweet words were obtained from a word2vec model, *GloVe* [12] (global vector for word representation). The advantage of employing *GloVe* over traditional word2vec model was three-fold.

First, the models in *GloVe* framework were pre-trained on existing datasets (one on Wikipedia data, two on common data crawls and one on Twitter). For this experiment, we downloaded the Twitter-one from the repository, which was pre-trained on 2 billion tweets, 27 billion tokens, and 1.2 million vocabularies. Since the training sample was so large and this model was pre-trained on tweet specific data, it is more suitable for any text mining research on Twitter data.

Secondly, *GloVe* allows more flexibility in specifying the dimension of feature space. For the twitter crawl, the dimension values allowed by the *GloVe* were 25, 50, 100 or 200.

And lastly but most importantly, the distance (Euclidean or cosine similarity) between two-word vectors in *GloVe* provides an effective method for measuring the linguistic or semantic similarity of the corresponding words. Thus, at this step, we generated a vector representation for each word in the tweets.

Next, the word vectors were converted to tweet vectors by taking the normalized summation of all the word vectors in a tweet as shown below:

$$\vec{t_i} = \frac{1}{N_i} \sum_{j=1}^{N_i} \vec{w_{ij}}, \; and \; \vec{w_{ij}} = \vec{0} \; if \; w_{ij} \notin GloVe$$

where w_{ij} = j^{th} word in i^{th} tweet and N_i = number of words in i^{th} tweet.

Consequently, at the end of this stage, we had 50 features for each tweet along with its class labels.

Table 1: Accuracy comparison of the selected classifiers

Accuracy	J48	JRip	Logistic Regression
Number of correctly classified instances	308	310	382
Number of incorrectly classified instances	233	231	159

Table 2: Evaluation of logistic regression model

Class Label	Precision	Recall	F-Measure
C1	0.782	0.775	0.751
C2	0.692	0.563	0.621
C3	0.769	0.632	0.694
C4	0.816	0.585	0.681
C5	0.700	0.233	0.350
C6	0.665	0.847	0.739
Weighted Avg.	0.715	0.706	0.696

3.2.2 Bag-of-words and Cosine Similarity: Next, we extracted six bag-of-words (B_1, B_2, B_3, B_4, B_5, and B_6) from the dataset, one for each of the six categories (including *others*). At this stage, the stop words were identified based on their frequencies in the text and removed before further processing. Next, each bag was represented as a vector. Thus, at the end of this stage, we had six vectors ($\vec{B_1}$, $\vec{B_2}$, $\vec{B_3}$, $\vec{B_4}$, $\vec{B_5}$, and $\vec{B_6}$), one for each bag-of-words we collected from the training set.

Next, we calculated the distance between each tweet and the bag of words vectors by using cosine similarity. For each tweet t_i the distance between $\vec{t_i}$ and $\vec{B_i}$ was calculated as:

$$Similarity(\vec{B_i}, \vec{t_i}) = cos\theta = \frac{\vec{B_i}.\vec{t_i}}{|\vec{B_i}||\vec{t_i}|}$$

Thus, in this process, we extracted six more features for each tweet. Finally combining these six similarity scores with the previous 50 features, we transformed our dataset into 541×57 feature space (541 number of tweets) including class labels.

3.3 Constructing Models and Evaluation

With the combined features, classification of tweet categories was performed using the Weka v 3.9.0 [6]. We used three different types of classifier, e.g., a rule-based classifier (using JRip), a tree-based (using J48) and a function-based (using logistic regression) to train our model. A ten-fold cross-validation was performed to test the accuracy of the models. A comparison of the performance of the three models is shown in Table 1.

As the values in Table 1 depict, the accuracy of the rule-based and tree-based model were nearly identical at around 57%, whereas the logistic regression model performed far better than these two. Out of the 541 instances, it correctly identified 382 instances thus achieving an accuracy of 70.61%. We also employed a Linear SVM on the dataset. However, the accuracy was found to be far lower than the other classifiers, and hence it is not reported here.

A detailed accuracy of each class in logistic regression model was shown in Table 2. It suggests that logistic regression performed reasonably well achieving a weighted F-measure of 0.696. It was largely successful in classifying the tweets that belonged to C1 and

C6 classes, moderately successful for C2, C3 and C4 classes, and mostly unsuccessful for the C5 class. This can be attributed to the class imbalance problem of the dataset, out of 541 tweets only 30 instances were belonged to class C5. A pairwise t-test performed on the accuracy of the classifiers from Weka Experimenter showed that the logistic regression model performed significantly better than the rule-based model, whereas no significant difference was found between the accuracy of rule based and tree based model. To deal with the class imbalance issue, the supervised preprocessing technique, *Synthetic Minority Over-sampling Technique* (SMOTE) was used to introduce 20 synthetically created data points that were labeled as C5. Using the logistic regression function, we found the accuracy of the classifier improved to 72.95%. Although the way SMOTE introduced the synthetic variables was somewhat naive, however, the purpose here was not to achieve higher-accuracy but to demonstrate that the lower-accuracy of the classifier was because of the dataset and not due to feature selection.

4 FINDINGS

The results showed that logistic regression model outperformed the others and achieved decent accuracy for most of the classes. We think it has to do with the nature of the classification problem. SVM or Linear SVM is inherently known to be deterministic in nature (although it can be used with Platt's model for probability score) while logistic regression is probabilistic. In this study, the classification problem we are trying to address is better suitable for a probabilistic classifier than a deterministic one due to the subjective nature of the labeling scheme. This can also explain why the logistic regression performed better than any other models we tried. A possible workaround worth pursuing may be SVM with non-linear kernel, e.g., RBF, which we plan to investigate in future. In the result of logistic regression model, the low accuracy for class C5 could be attributed to the class imbalance issue since C5 only accounted for 9% of the data. By introducing synthetically generated data points, the effect of class imbalance problem was reduced.

Nonetheless, this work has a couple of important implications:

- First, the distribution of tweets suggest that for an epidemic like Zika, people are going to discuss about prevention techniques as much as they will cover other aspects of the disease (news of someone getting infected, misinformation etc). Hence, one cannot rely solely on the social media network to get important prevention tips.

- Secondly, people were discussing more on surveillance of potential victims and their follow up than the surveillance of the vector (mosquitoes). This could imply that people have less faith on the later mechanism.

- Lastly, low volume of tweets on public outreach may be a cause of concern for medical practitioners and public health institutes such as CDC.

This work has several limitations. First, our final dataset for data analysis is too small for a six-class classification problem. Since we aimed for collecting tweets posted by official Zika accounts and historical tweets posted during the time of the epidemic and Twitter API has restriction on collecting old data, we were not able to get a large amount of data. Second, we derived our class labels from the CDC-proposed prevention techniques, which is the first of its kind

to our knowledge, therefore we could not refer to any previous literature on coding scheme. We hope to consult domain experts in the future to standardize the coding scheme. Third, tweets not relevant to Zika prevention techniques represented a considerable portion of the dataset. Also, another possible workaround may be to explore more probabilistic classification scheme.

5 CONCLUSION AND FUTURE WORK

In the work reported here, we collected tweets related to Zika epidemic and explored the extent to which machine learning techniques could be used to classify tweets into various prevention categories as proposed by CDC. This approach is useful during the outbreak of a disease in informing official health organizations about what and how the public is discussing a disease on social media platforms. Our primary findings are summarized as follows. First, almost half of the Zika related tweets were not about any prevention techniques. Second, distribution of tweets among the five prevention categories is not equal. There were more tweets on surveillance and monitoring of potential victims than the other topics. Third, logistic regression classifier performed significantly better than the other classifiers possibly due to the nature of the dataset. We hope to continue this project in the future by 1) extending the dataset by searching for other official accounts, 2) further improving the classifier, 3) using the improved model on a bigger dataset that span across larger time-frame and 4) including time-series analysis on the categories to trace users' change of topics and interests throughout the span of epidemic.

REFERENCES

[1] S. Asur and B. A. Huberman. Predicting the future with social media. In *Web Intelligence and Intelligent Agent Technology (WI-IAT), 2010 IEEE/WIC/ACM International Conference on*, volume 1, pages 492–499. IEEE, 2010.

[2] K.-Y. Chen, L. R. Fine, and B. A. Huberman. Predicting the future. *Information Systems Frontiers*, 5(1):47–61, 2003.

[3] T. Dos Santos, A. Rodriguez, M. Almiron, A. Sanhueza, P. Ramon, W. K. de Oliveira, G. E. Coelho, R. Badaró, J. Cortez, M. Ospina, et al. Zika virus and the guillain-barré syndrome–case series from seven countries. *New England Journal of Medicine*, 375(16):1598–1601, 2016.

[4] M. Dredze, D. A. Broniatowski, and K. M. Hilyard. Zika vaccine misconceptions: A social media analysis. *Vaccine*, 34(30):3441, 2016.

[5] E. M. Glowacki, A. J. Lazard, G. B. Wilcox, M. Mackert, and J. M. Bernhardt. Identifying the public's concerns and the centers for disease control and prevention's reactions during a health crisis: An analysis of a zika live twitter chat. *American journal of infection control*, 44(12):1709–1711, 2016.

[6] G. Holmes, A. Donkin, and I. H. Witten. Weka: A machine learning workbench. In *Intelligent Information Systems, 1994. Proceedings of the 1994 Second Australian and New Zealand Conference on*, pages 357–361. IEEE, 1994.

[7] A. M. Kaplan and M. Haenlein. Users of the world, unite! the challenges and opportunities of social media. *Business horizons*, 53(1):59–68, 2010.

[8] A. Kilgarriff. Wordnet: An electronic lexical database, 2000.

[9] C. Manning, P. Raghavan, and H. Schütze. Introduction to information retrieval/christopher d, 2009.

[10] M. Miller, D. Banerjee, R. Muppalla, D. Romine, D. Sheth, et al. What are people tweeting about zika? an exploratory study concerning symptoms, treatment, transmission, and prevention. *arXiv preprint arXiv:1701.07490*, 2017.

[11] S. O. Oyeyemi, E. Gabarron, and R. Wynn. Ebola, twitter, and misinformation: a dangerous combination? *Bmj*, 349:g6178, 2014.

[12] J. Pennington, R. Socher, and C. D. Manning. Glove: Global vectors for word representation. In *Empirical Methods in Natural Language Processing (EMNLP)*, pages 1532–1543, 2014.

[13] A. Perrin. Social media usage. *Pew Research Center*, 2015.

[14] S. A. Rasmussen, D. J. Jamieson, M. A. Honein, and L. R. Petersen. Zika virus and birth defects–reviewing the evidence for causality. *N Engl J Med*, 2016(374):1981–1987, 2016.

[15] A. Sadilek, H. A. Kautz, and V. Silenzio. Modeling spread of disease from social interactions. In *ICWSM*, pages 322–329, 2012.

A Two-Stage Model for User's Examination Behavior in Mobile Search

Jiaxin Mao[†], Yiqun Liu[†*], Noriko Kando[‡], Zexue He[#], Min Zhang[†], Shaoping Ma[†]

[†]Department of Computer Science & Technology, Tsinghua University, Beijing, China
[‡]National Institute of Informatics, Tokyo, Japan
[#]Beijing Normal University
yiqunliu@tsinghua.edu.cn

ABSTRACT

With the rapid growth of mobile search, it is important to understand how users browse the mobile SERPs and allocate their limited attention to each result. To address this problem, we introduce a two-stage examination model that can separately capture the position bias with a skimming model and the attractiveness bias with an attractiveness model. The effectiveness of the proposed model is validated by using a dataset that contains explicit examination feedbacks from users. We further investigate user's examination behaviors by analyzing the model parameters learned via EM algorithm. The results reveal some interesting findings such as how the skimming behavior is dependent on the previous examination sequence and what factors are associated with the attractiveness of search results on mobile SERPs.

CCS CONCEPTS

• **Information systems** → **Users and interactive retrieval**; *Retrieval on mobile devices*;

KEYWORDS

Mobile Search, User Behavior Analysis, Examination, Selective Attention

1 INTRODUCTION

A good understanding of how users interact with the search engine may significantly contribute to improving its functionality. Among all kinds of user interactions, user's examination behavior on the search engine result page (SERP) draws much attention from the IR community. Many previous studies used eye-tracking to investigate examination behavior and found the *position bias* that user's attention are systematically biased towards the top-ranked results [5, 13]. Follow-up eye-tracking studies further showed that user's examination patterns are affected by a variety of factors such as the vertical types [11] and visual saliency of search results [9]. Combining with the *Examination*

---

[*]Corresponding author

Hypothesis [13], which assumes that a user will click on a result on SERP when she has examined it and consider it as relevant or useful, these findings on examination behavior help us to accurately interpret the click-through data as implicit relevance feedbacks [5] and contribute to the improvement of result ranking.

With the rapid spreading of smartphones, understanding user's search behaviors on mobile phones become increasingly important. Because the user interfaces (UIs) of mobile devices are different from those of desktop computers, user's examination behaviors on these two platforms are different [6]. Knowing how users allocate their limited visual attention to mobile SERPs may be arguably more crucial because the mobile SERPs often contain information cards and knowledge graph results [7] that can provide users with sufficient information without requiring them to click. In these cases, examination is the only indicator of result usefulness and therefore an important feature to separate the *good abandonment* [14], where the information need is satisfied without any click, from the bad abandonment, where no relevant results are returned. Recently, Lagun et al. [7, 8] also used eye-tracking devices to inspect examination behaviors in mobile search. Besides characterizing the position bias in the mobile search environment, they showed that the browser viewport can be used as a measurement of user attention.

In this work, we want to further investigate and characterize user's examination behaviors in mobile search. Inspired by the previous work by Liu et al. [10], we propose a two-stage examination model for mobile search. Based on the assumption that the user will first *skim* a result and then decide whether or not to put more effort to *examine* the result based on its *attractiveness*, the two-stage model consists two components: a *skimming* model that captures user's browsing patterns on mobile SERPs and an *attractiveness* model that model the attractiveness of each search result. We use EM algorithm to fit the proposed models on a dataset collected in a carefully designed user study and investigate user examination behavior by analyzing the parameters of the fitted models.

Our study is different from the previous studies on this topic (e.g. [6–8]) in the following aspects: First, instead of using an eye-tracking device to record the fixation time on each result as a signal for examination, we collected user's *explicit examination* feedbacks. Liu et al.'s investigation in desktop settings [10] has shown that while the *examination* of the result is a necessary condition for click, the *skimming* event captured by eye-fixations does not always imply the examination or "reading" event measured by user's explicit examination feedbacks in retrospect. We assume that in mobile search, a thorough examination is necessary not only for making click decisions but also for processing the information on information card or knowledge graph results, so we adopt users' feedbacks as measures for examinations in our study. Second, rather than building a *discriminative* model to *estimate* examinations using features such as mouse movement for desktop search [10] and viewport time for mobile search [8], we construct a *generative* model, attempting to *explain* why some results are more likely to be examined by users. Because of these differences, our study is complementary to existing studies. We hope the findings in this study can shed new light on the understanding of user's examination behavior in mobile search.

2   A TWO-STAGE EXAMINATION MODEL

The basic assumption behind the two-stage examination model is that to examine a result on the SERP, the user will first *skim* the result and if the result is attractive to her, she will then put more effort to *examine* it. This assumption can be described in a more formal way:

$$(S_i = 1) \wedge (A_i = 1) \Leftrightarrow E_i = 1 \tag{1}$$

Here $S_i = 1$ means the user skimmed result i, $A_i = 1$ means result i is attractive, and $E_i = 1$ means the user examined result i.

We further assume that the probability of skimming $P(S_i)$ is determined by user's browsing patterns on mobile SERPs and independent of the content and appearance of the result and therefore independent of the probability of attractiveness $P(A_i)$. So the examination probability can be written as:

$$P(E_i = 1) = P(A_i = 1)P(S_i = 1) \tag{2}$$

We hope that the skimming model can model the position bias of examination while the attractiveness model can capture the attractiveness of the heterogeneous results in mobile search.

In this study, we use three different skimming models:

Rank model: $P(S_i = 1) = \gamma_{r_i}$, the skimming probability is determined by the rank of result i.

Position model: $P(S_i = 1) = \gamma_{y_i}$, the skimming probability is determined by the result i's Y position on the SERP. We use a binning method to estimate γ_{y_i}: each result is grouped into a bin according to its Y position on the SERP. The width of each bin is 160 pixels.

UBM model: The User Browsing Model (UBM) was originally introduced by Dupret and Piwowarski [3] to model user's examination and click behaviors in Web search. It assumes that the user will browse the SERP in a top-down order and the probability of examining a result depends on the rank of the results and the distance with the last previous clicked result. We use it to model the skimming probability as the following: $P(S_i = 1) = \gamma_{r_i, d_i}$, where r_i is the rank of result i, d_i is the distance in rank between result i and the last examined result.

For the attractiveness model that gives $P(A_i)$ for each result independently, we use a logistic regression model that maps a set of features x_i to $P(A_i)$:

$$P(A_i = 1) = \frac{1}{1 + exp(-x_i \cdot \beta)} \tag{3}$$

The features used to build the attractiveness model are shown in Table 1. We will further analyze how these features affect the result attractiveness and the overall performance of the two-stage model in Section 3.

Table 1: Features used in the attractiveness model.

Groups	Features	Descriptions
Content	height	The height of the result (in pixels).
	char_length	The length of the text content of the result, measured in number of characters.
	hl_length	The number of highlighted characters in the result.
	anchor_num	The number of hyperlink anchors in the result.
	image_num	The number of images in the result.
Visual	visual_saliency	The average/ sum/ standard deviation of the visual saliency map [4] of the result.
	edge_density	The average/ sum/ standard deviation of the edge density [2] of the result.
Annotation	relevance	The 4-level relevance annotation of the result.
	click_necessity	The 3-level click-necessity annotation of the result

We treat E_i as observable variables while S_i and A_i as latent variables in the two-stage examination model because only the explicit feedback for examination (E_i) was collected in the user study (See Section 3.1 for more details). Because of the existence of the latent variables, we use EM algorithm to fit the model [1]. For the attractiveness model, we estimate its parameters β in the M-step by using the logistic regression solver provided in scikit-learn [2] package.

3   EXPERIMENTS

3.1   Data Collection

We conducted a user study to collect a dataset [3] that contains participants' explicit examination feedbacks in mobile search.

The user study involves 20 search tasks and 43 participants. Each search task is defined by a query sampled from the query log of a commercial mobile search engine in China [4]. We wrote a background story for each query to create a simulated work task situation [1] for the participants. We also use each query to crawl four SERPs from four popular mobile search engines in China. Because the search tasks cover a wide range of topics, the crawled search results cover a variety of vertical types such as Image, Video, and Knowledge Graph. All the participants are college students aged from 19 to 23. 20 of them are female and 23 are male. All the participants are native Chinese speakers and reported that they were familiar with search engines and smartphones.

In the user study, we required each participant to use an Android Smartphone with a 5-inch, 1280×720, touchscreen to complete the 20 search tasks. For each search task, our experiment system would show one of the four crawled SERPs to the participants. While no further query reformulation is allowed in the user study, the participant could freely browse the SERP and click the results on them until she thought that she had completed the search tasks. The task order and the origins of the SERP were rotated to balance the impressions for each SERP and prevent potential order effect on participants' search behaviors. After the participant completed each search task, the experiment system would show the SERP again and asked the participant to provide binary explicit examination feedbacks ($E_i \in \{0, 1\}$) for all the results on the SERP and 4-level usefulness feedbacks for the examined results. The method of getting examination feedback is

---

[1] The derivation of the EM algorithm is similar to UBM model. We omit it here because of the limited space.
[2] http://scikit-learn.org/
[3] The dataset will be open to public after the reviewing.
[4] All the search tasks, instructions, and apparatus in the user study are in Chinese.

similar to that adopted by Liu et al. [10] in desktop settings. We acknowledged the limitation that the explicit examination feedbacks may be further affected by the position bias in the feedback process. But we chose not to randomize the result order in the feedback process because it would make the participant more likely to forget which results were actually examined by her during the search process.

After collecting the user behavior dataset, we also asked professional assessors to make 4-level relevance annotations and 3-level click necessity annotations [12] for the search results because we want to use them as features for the attractiveness model to inspect their relationship with the result attractiveness and examination probability.

In this way, we collected 860 search sessions. 919 distinct search results were shown 10,021 times in these search sessions. 2,765 result impressions were annotated as examined ($E_i = 1$). On average, 3.215 results were examined by the participants in each session.

3.2 Examination Prediction

Based on the collected data, we test whether the proposed two-stage examination model can effectively model the examination probability of mobile search results. To measure the performance in examination prediction, we use a 10-fold cross validation on our dataset to compute the log-likelihoods and perplexities of different examination models.

We measure the performance of the two-stage models that combine both the skimming models and attractiveness models. To show the advantage of building a two-stage generative model to separately model the position bias and attractiveness bias, we use a discriminative logistic regression model (LR) as baseline. The features used to build the baseline are the attractiveness features in Table 1 along with the the rank (r) and Y position (y) of the results. To test whether adding attractiveness models can improve the examination prediction performance, we further compare the log-likelihood and perplexity of the two-stage model against the corresponding skimming model.

The results are shown in in Table 2. We can see that: 1) except for the Position+Attr. Model, the other two models with different feature combinations outperform the logistic regression baselines, demonstrating the proposed generative models can better explain user's examination behaviors. 2) except for only using the visual features to build the attractiveness model, adding the attractiveness model as a component in the two-stage examination model significantly improves its performance.

3.3 Model Analysis

By analyzing the parameters of the fitted skimming and attractiveness models, we can characterize the position bias on examination in mobile search in different aspects.

For the skimming models, we show the γ parameters in the Position models and UBM models in Figure 1 and Figure 2. From Figure 1, we spot a sharp decreasing in γ_y within the initial viewport (first 4 bins, [0, 640 pix]), suggesting that in mobile search the position bias within the initial viewport is stronger. From Figure 2, we can see how the skimming probability is conditioned on previous examinations. The darker cells in the first column ($d = 1$) indicate that the user is more likely to skim a result that is right

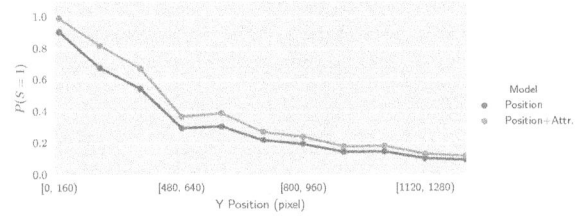

Figure 1: The skimming probability parameters γ_y estimated by Position and Position+Attr. models. The width of each bin is

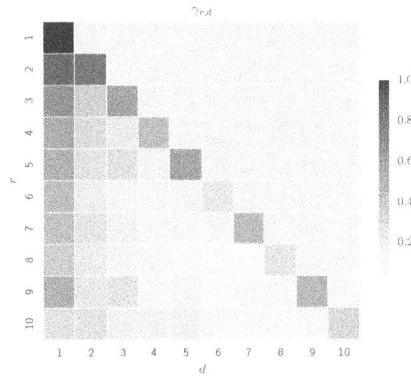

Figure 2: The skimming probability parameters $\gamma_{r,d}$ estimated by UBM+Attr. model.

below an examined result, while the darker cells along the diagonal ($d = r$) suggest that the user is more likely to skim a result if she has not examined any result yet.

For the attractiveness models, we show the β parameters of the UBM+Attr. models in Table 3. From this table, we can see that: 1) As expected, the height, character length, and highlighted character length is positively correlated with result attractiveness; 2) Both the visual saliency feature and the edge density feature have a positive correlation with result attractiveness. Users are more likely to examine a result with higher visual saliency. 3) Relevance is positively correlated with result attractiveness, suggesting relevance has an influence on the decision of putting more effort to examine the result or not. 4) Click necessity annotation is negatively correlated with attractiveness. This indicates that the results with low click necessities (e.g. knowledge graph and instant answer results) can indeed attract more attention from users. The top 3 most attractive and unattractive results according to $P(A_i = 1)$ computed by the attractiveness model of UBM+Attr. model are shown in Figure 3. The top 3 most attractive results are all federated results that consist of information from different sources while the top 3 most unattractive results are all query suggestions with four related queries.

4 CONCLUSIONS

To conclude, in this work, we introduce a two-stage examination model in mobile search. Using a dataset with explicit examination feedbacks from users, we show that the proposed model can

Table 2: The performance of the two-stage examination models measured in log-likelihood (*LL*) and perplexity (*Perplexity*). */ indicates the performance is significantly different from the baseline (LR) at $p < 0.05/0.01$ level. +/++ indicates the of the two-stage model is significantly different from the corresponding skimming model at $p < 0.05/0.01$ level.**

Feature groups:	Skimming model		Content		Visual		Content+Visual		Content+Visual+Annotation	
Eval. Metric:	*LL*	*Perplexity*	*LL*	*Perplexity*	*LL*	*Perplexity*	*LL*	*Perplexity*	*LL*	*Perplexity*
LR	-	-	-4.555	1.595	-4.547	1.594	-4.522	1.590	-4.490	1.584
Rank	-4.395	1.572	-4.369(**/++)	1.567(**/++)	-4.383(**/-)	1.569(**/-)	-4.361(**/++)	1.565(**/++)	-4.332(**/++)	1.560(**/++)
Position	-4.492	1.589	-4.481(*/+)	1.586(-/++)	-4.482(*/-)	1.587(-/-)	-4.472(-/-)	1.585(-/+)	-4.447(-/++)	1.580(-/++)
UBM	-4.183	1.539	-4.161(**/+)	1.535(**/++)	-4.172(**/-)	1.537(**/-)	-4.153(**/+)	1.533(**/++)	-4.122(**/++)	1.528(**/++)

Table 3: The parameters (normalized β) of the attractiveness model of UBM+Attr. model. We omit the the parameters that are not significantly different from zero at $p < 0.01$ level with '-'.

β	Content	Content+Visual	All
intercept.	1.834	0.077	-0.503
height	1.460	0.787	0.701
char_length	1.742	1.600	1.192
hl_length	2.049	1.718	0.378
anchor_num	-0.559	-0.242	-0.409
image_num	-2.661	-2.528	-1.387
avg. visual_saliency		0.526	0.412
sum. visual_saliency		0.883	0.688
std. visual_saliency		-0.564	-0.095
avg. edge_density		-	0.836
sum. edge_density		1.063	0.931
std. edge_density		1.185	0.628
relevance			1.605
click_necessity			-0.530

(a) Top 3 attractive results

(b) Top 3 unattractive results

Figure 3: Top 3 most attractive/unattractive results according to the attractiveness model of UBM+Attr. model.

effectively estimate the examination probability of each search result by separately capturing the position bias and attractiveness bias. We further analyze the parameters of the fitted models to characterize user's examination behaviors in mobile environment in different aspects such as how the skimming is conditioned on previous examinations and what features are associate result attractiveness in mobile search

We acknowledge the limitation of this study that we only use the explicit examination feedbacks from the participants in a small scale laboratory user study. For the future work, we can: 1) utilize eye-tracking device to investigate user's skimming (short fixation time on a result) and examination (long fixation time, reading sequence) behaviors; 2) collect a larger dataset that use remotely collected viewport data as signals for skimming and examination.

ACKNOWLEDGMENTS

This work was supported by Tsinghua University Initiative Scientific Research Program(2014Z21032), National Key Basic Research Program (2015CB358700), Natural Science Foundation (61532011, 61472206) of China and Tsinghua-Samsung Joint Laboratory for Intelligent Media Computing.

REFERENCES

[1] Pia Borlund. 2000. Experimental components for the evaluation of interactive information retrieval systems. *Journal of documentation* 56, 1 (2000), 71–90.

[2] John Canny. 1986. A computational approach to edge detection. *IEEE Transactions on pattern analysis and machine intelligence* 6 (1986), 679–698.

[3] Georges E Dupret and Benjamin Piwowarski. 2008. A user browsing model to predict search engine click data from past observations.. In *SIGIR'08*. ACM, 331–338.

[4] Jonathan Harel, Christof Koch, and Pietro Perona. 2007. Graph-based visual saliency. In *Advances in neural information processing systems*. 545–552.

[5] Thorsten Joachims, Laura Granka, Bing Pan, Helene Hembrooke, and Geri Gay. 2005. Accurately interpreting clickthrough data as implicit feedback. In *SIGIR'05*. Acm, 154–161.

[6] Jaewon Kim, Paul Thomas, Ramesh Sankaranarayana, Tom Gedeon, and Hwan-Jin Yoon. 2016. Understanding eye movements on mobile devices for better presentation of search results. *JASIST* 67, 11 (2016), 2607–2619.

[7] Dmitry Lagun, Chih-Hung Hsieh, Dale Webster, and Vidhya Navalpakkam. 2014. Towards better measurement of attention and satisfaction in mobile search. In *SIGIR'14*. ACM, 113–122.

[8] Dmitry Lagun, Donal McMahon, and Vidhya Navalpakkam. 2016. Understanding mobile searcher attention with rich ad formats. In *CIKM'16*. ACM, 599–608.

[9] Yiqun Liu, Zeyang Liu, Ke Zhou, Meng Wang, Huanbo Luan, Chao Wang, Min Zhang, and Shaoping Ma. 2016. Predicting search user examination with visual saliency. In *SIGIR'16*. ACM, 619–628.

[10] Yiqun Liu, Chao Wang, Ke Zhou, Jianyun Nie, Min Zhang, and Shaoping Ma. 2014. From skimming to reading: A two-stage examination model for web search. In *CIKM'14*. ACM, 849–858.

[11] Zeyang Liu, Yiqun Liu, Ke Zhou, Min Zhang, and Shaoping Ma. 2015. Influence of vertical result in web search examination. In *SIGIR'15*. ACM, 193–202.

[12] Cheng Luo, Yiqun Liu, Tetsuya Sakai, Fan Zhang, Min Zhang, and Shaoping Ma. 2017. Evaluating Mobile Search with Height-Biased Gain. In *SIGIR'17*. ACM.

[13] Matthew Richardson, Ewa Dominowska, and Robert Ragno. 2007. Predicting clicks: estimating the click-through rate for new ads. In *WWW'07*. ACM, 521–530.

[14] Kyle Williams, Julia Kiseleva, Aidan C Crook, Imed Zitouni, Ahmed Hassan Awadallah, and Madian Khabsa. 2016. Detecting good abandonment in mobile search. In *WWW'16*. 495–505.

The Paradox of Personalization: Does Task Prediction Require Individualized Models?

Matthew Mitsui
Department of Computer Science
Rutgers University
mmitsui@cs.rutgers.edu

Jiqun Liu, Chirag Shah
School of Communication & Information
Rutgers University
{jl2033,chirags}@rutgers.edu

ABSTRACT

We explore the gap between 1) statistically significant relationships between task and browsing behavior and 2) predicting task type from such behaviors. Previous literature has shown relationships between Web browsing behavior and person's corresponding search task. We find statistically significant browser features for detecting task - comparing the features to previous literature - and apply this knowledge to task classification of search sessions. Even though significant features improve prediction over baselines, it is not by much. We suggest that a more subtle treatment of such features should go beyond statistical significance. In some cases, considering personal patterns may be required for effective prediction.

CCS CONCEPTS

• **Information systems → Task models**; **Retrieval tasks and goals**; *Personalization*;

KEYWORDS

interactive information retrieval; task type; prediction; statistical significance; user behavior

ACM Reference Format:
Matthew Mitsui and Jiqun Liu, Chirag Shah. 2018. The Paradox of Personalization: Does Task Prediction Require Individualized Models?. In *CHIIR '18: 2018 Conference on Human Information Interaction Retrieval, March 11–15, 2018, New Brunswick, NJ, USA*. ACM, New York, NY, USA, Article 4, 4 pages. https://doi.org/10.1145/3176349.3176887

1 INTRODUCTION

Interactive Information Retrieval (IIR) research has recognized that Web search sessions are not just single-query, single-response episodes. Decades have been dedicated to understanding search tasks that people work on, ultimately to help searchers. Since searchers use the web, studies have found relationships between Web browsing behavior and search tasks (e.g., [8, 12]), showing statistical differences in behaviors between different task types. Can an algorithm that knows these differences predict a user's task from behavior? If it can determine a searcher's goal, for instance, it

can use that knowledge to assist an underperforming user (e.g., by tailoring search results or suggesting a page or a person to contact).

Studies often demonstrate statistical differences in behaviors, leaving task prediction to future work. Can these differences be simply inserted in a task prediction model? One possible roadblock is a lack of replication: significant findings that were due to chance. Yet if findings can be replicated, what else could prevent successful prediction? One possibility is *individual differences*. Suppose a study shows reading speed differentiates fact-finding and exploratory tasks. Consider a "speed-reader" - someone with higher than average reading speed. Task affects her reading speed, yet she still has high reading speed for most tasks. A prediction algorithm using reading speed may still misclassify this user. Individual differences (e.g., in reading pattern and topic knowledge) can significantly affect user behavior and related task classification [14], so applying individual characteristics may improve task prediction.

Given the above research gaps, we seek to link statistically different behaviors to task prediction, asking two research questions:

- **RQ1:** Do statistically significant differences in browsing behaviors for different task types replicate in larger datasets (not collected in a controlled laboratory setting)?
- **RQ2:** Can statistically significant differences in browsing behaviors help create a general model or personalized model to accurately classify searchers' tasks?

We show that the answer to RQ1 is yes, and the answer to RQ2 is mixed. We suggest that testing for general statistical significance, while useful, is not sufficient for building accurate live prediction systems to support IIR. Our investigations also suggest that sometimes, individual differences may matter for predictive models.

2 TASK TYPES AND USER BEHAVIOR

Users' behaviors are heavily influenced by their search tasks, embedded in work task flows or associated with problematic situations [2]. Task modeling has gained attention in the information seeking and information retrieval (IR) communities, since task serves as a theoretical framework for understanding user behavior. Researchers have classified and studied different aspects of user task. Ingwersen [7] proposed an intention-driven model of a task, such as whether the task was well- or ill-defined. Other task classifications have arisen, for instance categorizing the task's objective complexity [3] or more unified, generalized faceted classifications [10].

In IIR research, some researchers have linked behavioral measures to aspects of the user's task, such as those aspects above. Researchers typically study a task's relationship to features that are noninvasively capturable while a person is browsing, e.g., from their personal computer's Chrome browser. Several groups have found significant differences between task type and behaviors such as query length, session time, and number of URLs per query [8, 12]. Similar relationships exist for task complexity rather than type [1, 9]. Other work has additionally explored relationships between eye tracking behavior, physiological factors, and task features [5, 6]. Furthermore [11] discovered that incorporating task type into a traditional relevance feedback technique can improve retrieval performance for session-based tasks. These works suggest that behaviors are indicative of task type and that knowing the task improves retrieval performance. A predictive task-based model that uses behavior to improve retrieval in real time has yet to be built. Addressing our RQs will help determine how possible this is.

3 METHOD AND DATASET

Studies on statistical significance are usually in small lab settings. To address our research questions, we analyze the data from the TREC 2014 Session Track [4]. The purpose of the track was to accelerate research on information retrieval over sessions instead of on ad-hoc retrieval. The session data was collected from users recruited through Mechanical Turk, comprising a total of 260 users conducting 1,257 search sessions over 60 controlled tasks/topics. TREC topics were controlled by task type as defined in [10], in particular controlling for the product and goal that represent ends or aims of tasks. In the data, the product of a search task is either "intellectual" - producing new ideas or findings - or "factual" - locating facts or data. The goal, similar to the ill-defined or well-defined information need [7], is either "specific" or "amorphous". This produces 4 possible pairings of product and goal, in turn categorized as "known-fact search" ("factual"/"specific") , "known-subject search" ("factual"/"amorphous"), "interpretive search" ("intellectual"/"specific"), and "exploratory search" ("intellectual"/"amorphous"). These types are uniformly distributed - 15 unique prompts per task type.

Lab studies typically consist of populations of a few dozen users, with each conducting 1-2 multi-query sessions. TREC Session has the controlled topics of a user study but a much larger number of users, some of which conducted many sessions. In our analyses, each whole session is a data point (at most 1,257 data points). True IIR task prediction should be done in the middle of a session, and we acknowledge this shortcoming. This is a proof of concept for prediction, starting with the ideal scenario with complete information about a person's task (namely, the whole session).

3.1 Statistical Significance of Features

To compare statistically significant relationships in TREC to those of a laboratory study, we need to simulate the conditions of a lab study. When using all sessions for analysis, certain significant relationships may hold (or fail to hold) because some users are overly represented in the data. Some users performed 1 search session, but 10 users, for instance, each performed over 40 sessions.

In task-related lab studies like [12], tasks are assigned uniformly among participants. If there are 40 participants, 4 tasks, and 1 session per participant, each task is assigned to 10 unique participants. TREC contains 260 users and 4 task types. To simulate conditions where tasks are uniformly assigned, we simulated random trials in which each user was randomly assigned one of their existing sessions. Each random sample contained all 260 users and therefore

260 sessions. Each sample was constrained to have uniform assignment - 65 users assigned to each task type - thus simulating lab study conditions. We simulated 10,000 such samples. 194 users only conducted 1 session, so the random assignment was only performed for the remaining 66 users, which we address in the future work. Sessions with undefined users were assumed to belong to unique users with only 1 session. Since we were interested in the task type, product, and goal, we compare our findings to [8, 12]. While their features are not exhaustive, to our knowledge this is some of the only work directly comparing task type to whole session behaviors.

3.2 Classification: Single Model vs. Personalized Models

To examine prediction, we sliced the dataset in 2 ways. First, we used 1,021 sessions (called our "full" dataset). 236 sessions have no current or final query and cannot be applied in our problem setting [4]. The 1,021 sessions include the 260 users above. Our second data slice contained only "active" users - the 10 users who conducted at least 40 sessions. The first slice was used to explore general classification performance, and the active user data was used to explore building personalized models for predicting task. A single general model was built on all data for classification. 1 model was built for each person (10 models) when performing personal modeling, with training on some of their sessions and testing on the rest. Therefore, several data points per user (we chose 40) were needed. Training/testing split was 80/20 in all cases.

As shown in Table 4, we utilize features from [8, 12] to determine whether the significant features entail good classification performance. We wanted to compare our findings to accepted associations discovered between user and task but do not need to restrict our features to these. We incorporated several other whole-session features: 1) The number of terms per query (including and excluding stopwords), the number of queries without clicks, and the number of URLs per query - each examined for its relationship to task complexity [1]. 2) The total number of unique query terms in a session (further associated with different levels of cognitive complexity [9]). The unique URL and query measures of [9] would've assumed the task is given. 3) Total and average dwell times on content pages and SERPs, and total actions (queries, SERP views, and page views).

4 RESULTS
4.1 Statistical Significance of Features

Each of Tables 1-3 shows probability that a sample's p-value reaches the critical threshold - e.g. $P(p < .05) = \frac{\#trials\ where\ p < .05}{10,000}$. If $P(\cdot)$ is above the critical value ($P(p < .05) > .05$), this suggests that significant findings are not due to chance and that the feature is a significant indicator. Otherwise, it may not be significant. Positive results could corroborate or disconfirm findings from past studies. We grant that 194 users' task assignments stayed constant in the simulations, eliminating true randomness. Therefore, some results may be artificially high or low. Yet if there is a true effect of task on these behaviors, we should expect critical thresholds to be hit often, regardless of randomness or lack thereof. Similarly if there is no effect, we expect values to be low.

Table 1: Probabilities of significant differences between specific and amorphous goals. Cited significance values are in the second column. We conducted the Mann-Whitney U test.

Feature	Significant? [12]	$P(p < .05)$	$P(p < .01)$
Completion time	No	0.661	0.107
# pages visited	No	0.6278	0.122
# queries	No	0.219	0.008

Table 2: Probabilities of significant difference between factual and intellectual tasks (using the Mann-Whitney U test).

Feature	Significant? [12]	$P(p < .05)$	$P(p < .01)$
Completion time	$p < .05$	0.076	0.001
# pages visited	$p < .01$	0.102	0.004
# queries	No	0.261	0.012

Table 3: Probabilities significant difference between the 4 task types. Results use the Kruskal-Wallis H test.

Feature	Significant? [8]	$P(p < .05)$	$P(p < .01)$
# queries	Yes	0.087	0.005
# SERP views	No	0.041	0.001
% time view SERP	Yes	0.002	0
SERP views/q	Yes	1e-4	0
Time view SERP/q	No	0.453	0.103

Tables 1-3 directly compare [12]'s findings on task product and goal. [12] suggested that there are no significant relationships for goal, but our results suggest otherwise. Completion time, number of pages visited, and number of queries meet our $P(p < .05)$ threshold by a large margin: 0.661, 0.6278, and 0.219 respectively. Completion time and number of pages visited additionally meet the $P(p < .01)$ threshold by 0.107 and 0.122. We hence have evidence that these features are significant indicators of goal. Similarly, our results for product differ from the expected. Completion time, number of pages visited - declared significant by [12] meet the $P(p < .05)$ threshold by small margins of 0.102 and 0.261. Number of queries - not expected to be significant - meets the $P(p < .05)$ and $P(p < .01)$ thresholds by 0.076 and 0.012. For task type (Table 3), significance values are for the most part much lower or flipped entirely. Total SERP dwell time per query, not deemed significant by [8], reaches both thresholds by 0.453 and 0.103. The number of queries (deemed significant) only reaches the $P(p < .05)$ threshold at a rate of 0.087. Lastly, we found that extra features (see Section 3.2) meet our thresholds rather strongly. Among them, query length without stopwords meets it for product ($P(p < .05)$=0.999, $P(p < .01)$=0.9745). Likewise for pages per query for goal ($P(p < .05)$=0.868, $P(p < .01)$=0.350) and query length for task type ($P(p < .05)$=0.994, $P(p < .01)$=0.907).

Several features from [8, 12] may help distinguish task types, though the particular useful features may not be as expected. Our findings do not make or break a framework; further investigation is required. We omitted a more rigorous test for the validity of p-values [13] beyond the scope of this work, but we will later discuss how it can robustly discover statistically significant differences. Our

analysis served as replication, but it also provides a starting point for feature selection for task classification, discussed next.

4.2 Classification: Single Model vs. Personalized Models

We compare several classifiers (described in Table 4) to random and most frequent class baselines, drawing the following conclusions:

Classification performance with a general classifier is better than chance, but not by much - Most classification algorithms improve over their respective baselines, and this agrees with our previous findings that some features show significant differences with respect to product, goal, and type. Performance gains are found for our full list of features and [8, 12]. Yet the gains over a conservative baseline are small. The largest gains in accuracy for each label were 0.524 for goal (0.524-0.503=0.021 [+4.2%]), 0.549 for product (0.549-0.522=0.027 [+5.2%]), and 0.268 for type (0.268-0.252=0.016 [+6.3%]) on full data. These are not reliable for real-time prediction, and this is when simply classifying whole sessions.

Classification accuracy is greatly boosted when predicting the user - In exploring why batch classification performance is poor, we considered an alternate problem: identifying a session's user instead of its task. If accuracy improvement is greater for predicting user than predicting task, predicting user is much easier. This suggests that a user has very distinctive patterns separating herself from other users, and perhaps treating users uniformly with a single classifier is not best. We verified this may be the case, using a single 10-class classifier. In contrast to < 10% improvement previously, accuracy improves a staggering 105% from .209 to .430.

Prediction accuracy is (sometimes) affected by the quantity of data per user and the label being predicted - When predicting goal, adding personalization does not seem to justify potential performance gains (0.521-0.498=0.023 [+4.6%]) over a single model (0.524-0.503=0.021 [+4.2%]). For predicting product, a collection of personalized models may actually perform worse (0.505-0.499=.006 [+1.2%]), regardless of whether all users are active (0.527-0.507=0.02 [+3.9%]) or not (0.549-0.522=0.027 [+5.2%]). However, for the entire task type, personalization seems to provide benefits. With active users, there is overall improvement for personalization for task type, regardless of whether using the features of [8, 12] (0.254-0.244=0.01 [+4.1%]) or additional features (0.283-0.272=0.011 [+4.0%]). When there are overall many data points per user, the percent gain in accuracy is also greater (0.283-0.240=0.043 [+17.9%]) than when many users have sparse data (0.268-0.252=0.016 [+6.3%]).

5 CONCLUSION AND FUTURE WORK

We have laid groundwork for future investigations into predicting task type. We investigated whether statistically significant relationships found in IIR experiments could necessarily be used for accurate models classifying task type of sessions. With a larger dataset of controlled tasks, we verified that the wisdom of past literature could illuminate links between browser behaviors and task type, but the findings may not be the ones we expected. We applied significant features and others to a simple task classification task as a first step to live task prediction. We achieved mixed results, but our analyses hinted that more data per user may be important for certain predictions. Users have personal behavior patterns; not all

Table 4: Accuracy for several algorithms: AdaBoost (ADA), Naive Bayes (GNB), k-nearest neighbors (KNN), and Support Vector Machine (SVM). Baselines are a most frequent (MFQ) and stratified random (STR) baseline. Datasets are the full dataset or active users. Either 1 model is trained on all data (Personalized=No) or 10 models are trained on active users (Personalized=Yes). Best performers for each row are boldfaced, and significance values are against the best baseline in that row. (*=p<.05,**=p<.01)

Dataset	Target	Feature set	Personalized	ADA	GNB	KNN	SVM	MFQ	STR
Full	Goal	[8, 12]	No	0.500	0.491	**0.506**	0.493	0.479	0.503
Full	Goal	All	No	**0.524****	0.507	0.501	0.500	0.479	0.503
Full	Product	[8, 12]	No	0.532	0.533	**0.549****	0.547	0.522	0.497
Full	Product	All	No	0.514	0.523	0.530	**0.535***	0.522	0.497
Full	Type	[8, 12]	No	0.259	0.250	**0.264****	0.257	0.250	0.252
Full	Type	All	No	0.256	0.262	0.267	**0.268****	0.250	0.252
Active	Goal	[8, 12]	No	0.468	0.477	0.478	0.494	0.483	**0.498**
Active	Goal	All	No	0.511	0.495	0.502	**0.514***	0.483	0.498
Active	Product	[8, 12]	No	0.470	0.492	0.501	0.501	0.504	**0.507**
Active	Product	All	No	0.497	0.502	**0.527****	0.487	0.504	0.507
Active	Type	[8, 12]	No	0.238	0.232	0.236	0.244	0.231	**0.251**
Active	Type	All	No	**0.272****	0.232	0.253	0.247	0.231	0.251
Active	Goal	[8, 12]	Yes	0.493	**0.514***	0.483	0.451	0.434	0.498
Active	Goal	All	Yes	0.497	**0.521****	0.476	0.435	0.434	0.498
Active	Product	[8, 12]	Yes	**0.505**	0.481	0.469	0.457	0.466	0.499
Active	Product	All	Yes	**0.501**	0.480	0.487	0.467	0.466	0.499
Active	Type	[8, 12]	Yes	0.228	**0.254***	0.229	0.202	0.196	0.240
Active	Type	All	Yes	0.262	**0.283****	0.254	0.197	0.196	0.240
Active	User ID	[8, 12]	No	0.303	0.233	0.348	**0.430****	0.209	0.138
Active	User ID	All	No	0.309	0.303	**0.390****	0.378	0.209	0.138

users are the same. This may not matter for task goal, but individual differences may provide gains when predicting task type.

This work has a methodological shortcoming. Due to data limitations, 194 users' tasks were fixed when randomly sampling the remaining 66, not making true random samples. Our 10,000 samples were not independent; they all contained the same user population, even though some tasks were randomly assigned. In truly random samples of unique users assigned to controlled tasks, we could use a vigorous p-curve test created by [13]. It compares a distribution of p-values (e.g., from numerous studies or numerous independent samples) to a baseline to see if a set of findings is truly significant.

Future work must explore more ground. First, features with a more personal component could be incorporated, such as reading speed or pages and queries per second. TREC data does not contain eye tracking behavior - another obvious feature. Second, for live classification, more granular session behavior can be used. Information seeking literature like [14] discusses "moves" and "strategies" people take when seeking, so perhaps some patterns across time could be incorporated. Yet we think this work is an insightful first step to task classification, and later to task prediction.

6 ACKNOWLEDGMENTS

This work is supported by the National Science Foundation (NSF) grant IIS-1717488.

REFERENCES

[1] Kathy Brennan, Diane Kelly, and Jaime Arguello. 2014. The Effect of Cognitive Abilities on Information Search for Tasks of Varying Levels of Complexity. In *Proceedings of the 5th Information Interaction in Context Symposium*. ACM.

[2] Katriina Byström and Preben Hansen. 2005. Conceptual framework for tasks in information studies. *Journal of the Association for Information Science and Technology* 56, 10 (2005).

[3] D. J. Campbell. 1988. Task Complexity: A Review and Analysis. *Academy of Management Review* 13, 1 (1988).

[4] Ben Carterette, Evangelos Kanoulas, Mark Hall, and Paul Clough. [n. d.]. Overview of the TREC 2014 Session Track. ([n. d.]).

[5] Michael J. Cole, Chathra Hendahewa, Nicholas J. Belkin, and Chirag Shah. 2015. User Activity Patterns During Information Search. *ACM Trans. Inf. Syst.* (2015).

[6] Ashlee Edwards and Diane Kelly. 2017. Engaged or Frustrated?: Disambiguating Emotional State in Search. In *Proceedings of the 40th International ACM SIGIR Conference on Research and Development in Information Retrieval*. ACM.

[7] Peter Ingwersen and Kalervo Järvelin. 2005. *The Turn: Integration of Information Seeking and Retrieval in Context (The Information Retrieval Series)*. Springer-Verlag New York, Inc.

[8] Jiepu Jiang, Daqing He, and James Allan. 2014. Searching, Browsing, and Clicking in a Search Session: Changes in User Behavior by Task and over Time. In *Proceedings of the 37th International ACM SIGIR Conference on Research & Development in Information Retrieval (SIGIR '14)*. ACM.

[9] Diane Kelly, Jaime Arguello, Ashlee Edwards, and Wan-ching Wu. 2015. Development and Evaluation of Search Tasks for IIR Experiments Using a Cognitive Complexity Framework. In *Proceedings of the 2015 International Conference on The Theory of Information Retrieval (ICTIR '15)*. ACM.

[10] Yuelin Li and Nicholas J. Belkin. 2008. A faceted approach to conceptualizing tasks in information seeking. *Information Processing and Management* (2008).

[11] Chang Liu, Nicholas J. Belkin, and Michael J. Cole. 2012. Personalization of Search Results Using Interaction Behaviors in Search Sessions. In *Proceedings of the 35th International ACM SIGIR Conference on Research and Development in Information Retrieval (SIGIR '12)*. ACM.

[12] Jingjing Liu, Michael J. Cole, Chang Liu, Ralf Bierig, Jacek Gwizdka, Nicholas J. Belkin, Jun Zhang, and Xiangmin Zhang. 2010. Search Behaviors in Different Task Types. In *Proceedings of the 10th Annual Joint Conference on Digital Libraries*. ACM.

[13] Uri Simonsohn, Leif D. Nelson, and Joseph P. Simmons. 2014. P-curve: A key to the file-drawer. *Journal of Experimental Psychology: General* 143, 2 (2014).

[14] Barbara M Wildemuth. 2004. The effects of domain knowledge on search tactic formulation. *Journal of the Association for Information Science and Technology* (2004).

QWERTY: The Effects of Typing on Web Search Behavior

Kevin Ong
RMIT University
kevin.ong@rmit.edu.au

Kalervo Järvelin
University of Tampere
kalervo.jarvelin@uta.fi

Mark Sanderson
RMIT University
mark.sanderson@rmit.edu.au

Falk Scholer
RMIT University
falk.scholer@rmit.edu.au

ABSTRACT

Typing is a common form of query input for search engines and other information retrieval systems; we therefore investigate the relationship between typing behavior and search interactions. The search process is interactive and typically requires entering one or more queries, and assessing both summaries from Search Engine Result Pages and the underlying documents, to ultimately satisfy some information need. Under the Search Economic Theory (SET) model of interactive information retrieval, differences in query costs will result in search behavior changes. We investigate how differences in query inputs themselves may relate to Search Economic Theory by conducting a lab-based experiment to observe how text entries influence subsequent search interactions. Our results indicate that for faster typing speeds, more queries are entered in a session, while both query lengths and assessment times are lower.

CCS CONCEPTS

• **Information systems → Users and interactive retrieval**; • **Human-centered computing → Text input**;

KEYWORDS

Search Economic Theory, Text Input, Web Search Behavior

ACM Reference Format:
Kevin Ong, Kalervo Järvelin, Mark Sanderson, and Falk Scholer. 2018. QWERTY: The Effects of Typing on Web Search Behavior. In *Proceedings of Conference on Human Information Interaction & Retrieval, New Brunswick, NJ, USA, March 11–15, 2018 (CHIIR'18)*, 4 pages.
DOI: http://dx.doi.org/10.1145/3176349.3176872

1 INTRODUCTION

Interactive Information Retrieval (IIR) researchers seek to understand the interactions between an information seeker and an information retrieval system [7]. Modeling IIR interactions is a nontrivial process as many factors can contribute to differences in the search behavior. The search process itself is an iterative sequence of actions that often requires multiple queries to acquire the desired amount of relevant information for an underlying information need to be resolved. In IIR, the focus is on the interaction between a human and a search system. The interaction can take place over three modalities, such as search by using/viewing images, speaking [17] or traditionally by typing into a search box. In this paper we focus on typing.

Nowadays, searchers expect rapid responses from search engines [15]. However, the amount of useful information gathered during the search process is also dependent on how well searchers are able to translate their search inputs (such as typing), into useful information output [2]. IIR is a collaborative effort between the searcher and the system to answer an information need. However, research efforts have mainly focused on the changes in human search behavior as a response to system response delays [4, 12], rather than on the effort exerted by both humans and systems as part of the search process. Maxwell and Azzopardi [12] observed that as total time on queries increases, then more time will be spent on assessing the returned Search Engine Result Pages (SERPs). Query cost is inevitably tied to searcher's own input interactions on the search interface itself.

Typing behavior has received renewed research attention recently [6, 10, 11] but not within the IIR community. In this paper, we study the relationship between typing speed and search behavior, and how an individual's search and typing behavior may be used as a factor for explaining IIR behavior.

2 RESEARCH QUESTIONS

The main research question studied in this work is:

> "What is the relationship between a user's typing speed and their search behavior?"

The search process arises in order to satisfy some information needs, and SET suggests that when query costs increase, more time will be spent on assessments. We investigate if typing speed can be used as an indicator to understand the differences that might contribute to different query-assessment trade-offs, by considering the following specific research questions.

RQ1, *What is the relationship between typing speed and the number of queries and assessment time per query?* Azzopardi et al. [2] postulated that user search interactions can be modeled by an economic theory. We seek to understand how the cost of typing can be incorporated into such a model.

RQ2, *Will a faster searcher type more characters per query?* As the effort to type is lower for faster searchers, we seek to understand if they will choose to issue queries that are longer.

RQ3, *Do differences in typing speed for different topics reflect a user's topic interest and familiarity?* Past work found that changes in searchers' behavior can be measured from their emotion and typing behavior [5, 10]. Informed by Kelly and Cool [9], we seek to understand how topic interest and familiarity may be associated with differences in the typing behaviors of searchers.

3 BACKGROUND

Past work on SET and typing behavior revealed how different search costs may give rise to different search behaviors. Using the Interaction-Cost hypothesis [1], we propose that query cost based on typing effort can be used as a factor to explain the trade-offs between alternative search strategies in IIR.

SET proposed that differences in query costs will result in changes in search behavior [1]. The search process is a combination of inputs (Q, A) per search session, where

- **Q** is the number queries that a user will issue,
- **A** is the number of assessments per query.

A refers to both assessments of SERPs and web documents. The combination of (Q, A) will be dependent on the relative cost of a query against the cost of assessing a web page. The cost estimations can either be interaction-based [2] or time-based [12]. Under the interaction-based approach [2], the combination of (Q, A) produces a cumulative gain (CG), which can be measured as

$$g(Q, A) = \alpha * Q^{\beta} * A^{(1-\beta)}$$

where the parameter α represents how well a searcher can convert their interactions into finding relevant documents, and β is the relative cost of **Q** to **A**.

Maxwell and Azzopardi [12] studied the effect of query cost on search behavior by subjecting users to two forms of delays: five seconds SERP response delays, or five seconds document download delays. They found that when total querying time increased, document assessments increased. Similarly, when both SERP response and document download delays were introduced, users spent more time examining documents.

Typing Salthouse [14] studied the effects of age and skills on typing behavior, and found that experience but not age influenced typing speed. A skilled typist is formally trained on typing on keyboards. In subsequent work, John [8] suggested a baseline of 30–60 Words Per Minute (WPM) as an average typing speed on a standard keyboard. There has been renewed interest in typing [6, 10, 11]. Lim et al. [10] studied the effects of emotion on typing behavior and found that highly stressed users spent longer on tasks and clicked more rapidly but typed more slowly and were more error prone. Feit et al. [6] studied 30 participants aged 20 – 55 and found that non-skilled typists can attain the same level of typing speed and accuracy compared to skilled typists (58 vs 59 WPM). Logan et al. [11] found that skilled typists typed at 45 WPM when composing text. In general, previous research [6, 11] found non-skilled typists typed as well as skilled typists, unlike earlier works [8, 14]. This suggests that the growing computer literacy over the decades might have narrowed the gaps between these two groups of typists.

4 METHOD

To investigate the relationship between typing and search behavior, a user study was carried out.

Searchers: 36 searchers (18 males and 18 females) aged from 18–47 with a mean age of 26 were recruited via opportunistic sampling at a local campus library. While 13 participants reported that English was not their first language, all participants were confident in reading and typing in English. A 15" Macbook laptop was provided for the experiment, and participants were asked if they were familiar with the type of keyboard; half reported that they were unfamiliar with the keyboard provided. The participants were told they had 45 minutes in total to complete six topics, and were compensated at the end of the experiment with a $20 voucher for participation.

Data: Data were collected as part of a larger experiment where individual search interactions were collected [13]. Participants were given two attempts at an initial typing test. The test allowed the participants to familiarize themselves with the keyboard. They were then asked to conduct searches for six provided informational search tasks. Unknown to the participants, the initial SERPs were controlled by varying quality of search results on the first page [13].[1] Search results for any query reformulations per task were obtained from a live commercial search engine. Participants were asked to carry out the tasks as they would on a normal web search engine. Task order was rotated and counterbalanced with different types of initial starting conditions. They were able to enter as many queries as they liked, and were asked to find as many relevant search results as they needed to satisfy the search task. Participants were free to distribute their time as they saw fit and were not pressed to complete each task within a set time frame. Total time remaining was provided to the participants if requested, but was otherwise not indicated.

Participants could mark a search result as relevant within the SERP itself by clicking a checkbox, without having to open the underlying document (which they could do, should they choose to). Participants were also given both a pre-task questionnaire on topic interest and familiarity, and post-task questionnaire on topic difficulty for each task.

Logging: To capture typing behavior, a search engine interface was created to log the typing speed of each query using JavaScript. The following interactions were logged:

- The number of queries issued.
- The average task typing speed, measured in WPM. This is the number of keystrokes divided by five, between the first and last key presses within the time taken, as described by John [8].[2] It is inclusive of all non-character keystrokes, such as backspaces and other non-characters.
- The number of key press errors: backspaces and other non-characters.
- The number of documents clicked and marked by the participants as relevant.
- The amount of time spent typing and assessing SERPs and documents.

Task-searcher pairs (i.e. search interactions performed by each searcher on each task) are classified into three groups based on

---

[1]The initial starting conditions did not influence the final number of documents saved ($F = 0.2$, $p = 0.95$).
[2]The division is for the average number of characters in an English word.

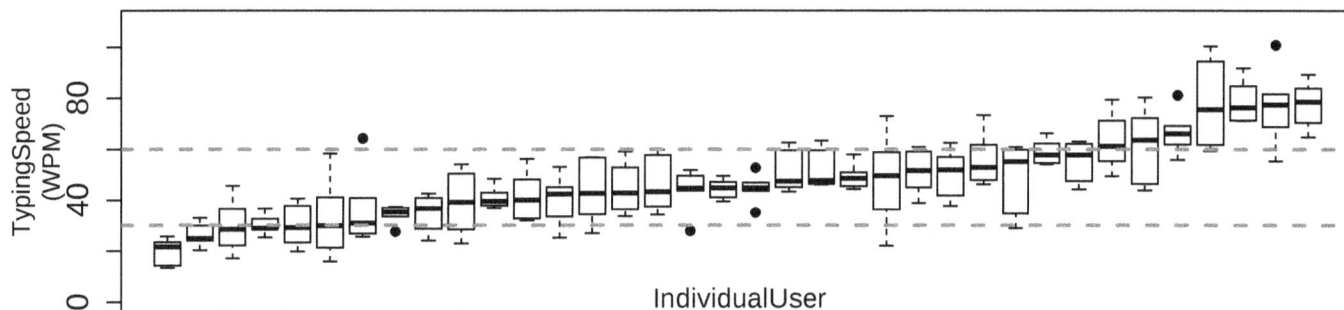

Figure 1: Typing speed of each individual user across their search tasks

their average on-task WPM. The following thresholds were proposed by John [8]: fast (>60 WPM), average (30–60 WPM) and slow (<30 WPM).

5 RESULTS

The data from the user study was analyzed based on individual task-searcher combinations (i.e. search interactions performed by each searcher on each task) because we conjectured that typing speed might also vary with both topic familiarity and interest [9, 16]. There were 213 task responses in total. Three tasks from two searchers were removed due to non-logging issues.

Figure 1 shows the average task typing speed on each topic across all six topics, for all 36 participants . Two horizontal, red dashed lines mark the boundary at 30 and 60 WPM. Some typists had consistent typing speeds (shorter boxes) while others varied substantially (taller boxes). This figure shows that typing speed varies significantly across individuals ($F = 8.1, p < .0001$) and that an individual's typing speed is dependent on the topic that the task-searcher is working on. The mean speed across all task-searchers was 48 WPM with a SD of 17.5.

Time-based and interaction-based measurements are recorded in Table 1. Chi-Square (X^2) or ANOVA (F-score) values are recorded for each relevant variable. A follow-up Tukey's honest significance difference (TukeyHSD) test is conducted at $p < 0.05$ for values analyzed with ANOVA. Values that are significantly different from two other categories using TukeyHSD pairwise tests are bold.

Across three speed categories, there were 38 slow, 128 average, and 47 fast task-searchers ($X^2 = 69.2, p < .001$). For those who were familiar with the laptop keyboard, there were 14 slow, 63 average, and 30 fast task-searchers ($X^2 = 35.1, p < .001$). For task-searchers who were not, there were 24 slow, 65 average, and 17 fast task-searchers ($X^2 = 38.1, p < .001$). Regardless of familiarity with the keyboard, more than 60% were average task-searchers. The differences in rates of yes/no familiarity responses within each speed group were not significant (slow: $X^2 = 2.63, p = 0.1$; average: $X^2 = 0.03, p = 0.9$; fast: $X^2 = 3.60, p = 0.06$).

For time-based response measures, fast task-searchers spent significantly less time issuing queries ($F = 77.1, p < .001$) and assessing documents and SERPs ($F = 4.9, p < .001$) than the other types of task-searchers. On the interaction-based response measures, the slow, average and fast task-searchers typed 24.3, 45.9 and 72.8 WPM respectively ($F = 370.0, p < .001$). Fast task-searchers

Table 1: Mean or median ($\bar{x}$) (and standard deviations, SD) of searchers' interactions per task. Significant differences (ANOVA) denoted by: *p < 0.05, **p < 0.01, ***p < 0.001. Values for pairwise comparisons (TukeyHSD; p < .05) are bold.

	Categories of task-searchers			X^2
	Slow (<30 WPM)	Average (30-60 WPM)	Fast (>60 WPM)	
Number of task-searchers	38	128	47	69.2***
Familiarity with keyboard provided	Yes: 14 No: 24	Yes: 63 No: 65	Yes: 30 No: 17	35.1*** 38.1***

Time-based (per query)				F
Typing Time / Query (in sec)	22.2 (10.6)	10.9 (5.7)	**5.2** **(2.1)**	77.1***
Assessment Time / Query (in sec)	79.4 (40.3)	73.2 (44.3)	**54.3** **(28.1)**	4.9***
Total Time / Query (in sec)	101.6 41.9	84.1 44.9	**59.6** 28.3	11.4***
Interaction-based (per query)				F
On-Topic Typing / Query (WPM)	**24.3** **(4.2)**	**45.9** **(8.2)**	**72.8** **(10.7)**	370.0***
Typed Characters / Query	42.5 (20.1)	37.3 (16.5)	**29.2** **(9.9)**	7.7***
Error Characters / Query	11.0 (13.2)	7.2 (7.4)	**3.6** **(4.6)**	12.0***
Output Characters / Query	31.6 (10.7)	30.2 (12.9)	25.7 (7.9)	3.3*
Documents Marked / Query	3.4 (2.2)	3.9 (2.9)	4.3 (3.3)	0.9
Documents Clicked / Query	1.1 (1.3)	1.0 (1.2)	0.6 (1.0)	2.9
Total Interaction counts				F
Number of Queries	**1.7** **(0.9)**	**2.4** **(1.4)**	**3.3** **(2.1)**	13.1***
Documents Marked (in total)	5.4 (3.8)	8.6 (8.0)	**12.5** **(10.1)**	8.5***
Documents Clicked (in total)	1.6 (1.8)	2.4 (2.9)	1.7 (2.8)	1.7
Self report				F
Age	26.9 (5.6)	26.5 (7.8)	**23.1** **(4.3)**	4.9**
Topic Interest	$\bar{x} = 7$ (2.4)	$\bar{x} = 6$ (2.7)	$\bar{x} = 6$ (2.2)	0.5
Topic Familiarity	$\bar{x} = 3$ (2.4)	$\bar{x} = 4$ (2.4)	$\bar{x} = 3$ (2.2)	0.07
Topic Difficulty	$\bar{x} = 4$ (2.3)	$\bar{x} = 4$ (2.4)	$\bar{x} = 4$ (2.3)	2.4

also typed significantly shorter queries ($F = 7.7, p < .001$) and were also less error-prone ($F = 12.0, p < .001$) than both average and slow task-searchers. Fast task-searchers entered significantly greater number of queries ($F = 11.1, p < .001$), while the average numbers of documents marked did not vary significantly between groups ($F = 0.9, p = 0.435$). However, fast task-searchers marked more documents than both average and slow task-searchers in total ($F = 8.5, p < .001$). Regarding demographic data, fast task-searchers are significantly younger at 23.1 years on average, compared to 26.5 and 26.9 for average and slow task-searchers ($F = 4.9, p < .01$).

Topic interest and topic familiarity were established through pre-task surveys, with participants asked to rate each factor on a scale of $1 - 10$. The median score ($\bar{x}$) is reported. Categorizing task-searchers based on their typing speed, there were no significant differences between different groups for topic interest ($F = 0.5, p = 0.6$), topic familiarity ($F = 0.1, p = 0.93$) or topic difficulty ($F = 2.4, p = 0.10$).

Limitations. In this study, we made an assumption that all documents saved were relevant - similar to the Click-through Hypothesis and did not record additional details about the documents saved. Auto-corrections and query suggestions were also excluded in the experimental design.

6 DISCUSSION AND CONCLUSIONS

Overall, our study participants demonstrated a range of typing speeds. On average, their speeds were comparable to that observed by Logan et al. [11] (48 vs 45 WPM). Our experimental data also showed that age may have contributed to differences in typing speed, which is a factor to consider for future experiments.

Framed within SET, we posit that higher typing cost is associated with lower typing speed and higher typing time. Regarding **RQ1**, as typing speed increased, more queries were issued and less time was spent per query, while slow task-searchers spent more time on both typing and assessments. Typing cost can be considered as one of the factors of total query cost, and is shown to support the cost-interaction hypothesis of SET. However, when typing cost increased, the total number of queries decreased, while the number of assessments per query did not change significantly. Allowing task-searchers to mark documents as relevant, without requiring document click-throughs, may be the cause of this artifact. On the other hand, for the time-based measures, fast task-searchers spent significantly less time on both queries and assessments.

For **RQ2**, fast task-searchers, as opposed to the average and slow ones, typed shorter queries, and entered a higher number of queries. We expected that as typing cost is reduced, then more characters would have been typed as a result; however, the results indicated the opposite. We conjecture that the shorter query lengths were balanced by the increased number of queries. In future work, we plan to study how different task-searcher types adapt their search strategies to changes in search system and document download delays.

For **RQ3**, while a relationship between topic familiarity, interest and typing speed was expected, we were not able to conclude that there is a difference in our study, based on typing speed. Given our sample size, there was not enough data for typing speed to reveal the differences in topic familiarity and interest.

We conjecture that the fast task-searchers were able to mark more documents as relevant because of the higher number of query reformulations they performed. This is because the average number

of documents marked did not differ significantly across different task-searcher types. In terms of propensity of typing errors, we observed that fast task-searchers made fewer typing errors than average or slow task-searchers (12% vs 19% and 26% error rates, respectively). For future work, we plan to investigate what contributed to differences in error rate, for example by studying the other aspects of typing, such as consistency and rhythm. We also plan to investigate how typing speed can be used as a signal to support different types of task-searchers, such as showing different forms of snippets for different task-searchers [3]. These findings support observations by Azzopardi et al. [2] and Maxwell and Azzopardi [12] that revision to SET is needed.

In conclusion, we show the relationship between task typing speed and search behavior. Fast task-searchers were younger. They also entered more queries with shorter lengths and marked more documents in total while slow and average task-searchers were more error-prone and spent more time per query. We did not observe a relationship between topic interest and familiarity with task typing speed, given our sample size.

7 ACKNOWLEDGEMENTS

This project is funded by ARC Discovery Grant, ref: DP140102655 and an APA scholarship. Travel funding is also provided by ACM SIGIR for the lead author to attend the conference.

REFERENCES

[1] Leif Azzopardi. 2011. The Economics in Interactive Information Retrieval. In *Proceedings of SIGIR*. 15–24.

[2] Leif Azzopardi, Diane Kelly, and Kathy Brennan. 2013. How Query Cost Affects Search Behavior. In *Proceedings of SIGIR*. 23–32.

[3] Ruey-Cheng Chen, J. Shane Culpepper, Tadele T. Damessie, Timothy Jones, Ahmed Mourad, Kevin Ong, Falk Scholer, and Evi Yulianti. 2015. RMIT at the TREC 2015 LiveQA Track. In *Proceedings of TREC*.

[4] Anita Crescenzi, Diane Kelly, and Leif Azzopardi. 2015. Time Pressure and System Delays in Information Search. In *Proceedings of CHIIR*. 767–770.

[5] Ashlee Edwards and Diane Kelly. 2017. Engaged or Frustrated?: Disambiguating Emotional State in Search. In *Proceedings of SIGIR*. 125–134.

[6] Anna Maria Feit, Daryl Weir, and Antti Oulasvirta. 2016. How We Type: Movement Strategies and Performance in Everyday Typing. In *Proceedings of CHI*. 4262–4273.

[7] Peter Ingwersen and Kalervo Järvelin. 2005. Information Retrieval in Context: IRiX. In *ACM SIGIR Forum*, Vol. 39. 31–39.

[8] Bonnie E. John. 1996. TYPIST: A Theory of Performance in Skilled Typing. *Human–Computer Interaction* 11, 4 (1996), 321–355.

[9] Diane Kelly and Colleen Cool. 2002. The Effects of Topic Familiarity on Information Search Behavior. In *Proceedings of JCDL*. 74–75.

[10] Yee Mei Lim, Aladdin Ayesh, and Martin Stacey. 2015. The Effects of Typing Demand on Emotional Stress, Mouse and Keystroke Behaviours. In *Intelligent Systems in Science and Information 2014*. 209–225.

[11] Gordon D. Logan, Jana E. Ulrich, and Dakota R. B. Lindsey. 2016. Different (Key)Strokes for Different Folks: How Standard and Nonstandard Typists Balance Fitts' Law and Hick's Law. *Journal of Experimental Psychology: Human Perception and Performance* 42, 12 (2016), 2084–2102.

[12] David Maxwell and Leif Azzopardi. 2014. Stuck in Traffic: How Temporal Delays Affect Search Behaviour. In *Proceedings of IIiX*. 155–164.

[13] Kevin Ong, Kalervo Järvelin, Mark Sanderson, and Falk Scholer. 2017. Using Information Scent to Understand Mobile and Desktop Web Search Behavior. In *Proceedings of SIGIR*. 295–304.

[14] Timothy Salthouse. 1984. Effects of Age and Skill in Typing. *Journal of Experimental Psychology: General* 113 (1984), 345–371.

[15] Eric Schurman and Jake Brutlag. 2009. Performance Related Changes and Their User Impacts. In *Velocity: Web Performance and Operations Conference*.

[16] Ben Shneiderman. 1984. Response Time and Display Rate in Human Performance with Computers. *Comput. Surveys* 16, 3 (1984), 265–285.

[17] Johanne R. Trippas, Damiano Spina, Mark Sanderson, and Lawrence Cavedon. 2015. Towards Understanding the Impact of Length in Web Search Result Summaries over a Speech-Only Communication Channel. In *Proceedings of SIGIR*. 991–994.

Exploring Online and Offline Search Behavior Based on the Varying Task Complexity

Manasa Rath, Souvick Ghosh, Chirag Shah

School of Communication and Information (SC&I),

Rutgers University

{manasa.rath,souvick.ghosh,chirags}@rutgers.edu

ABSTRACT

In an information seeking episode, users often look for sources in online and offline environments depending on the task at hand. However, at most times users consider factors such as ease, time taken to complete the task, and the number of sources to be consulted as the essential factors while fulfilling the information seeking task. In our study, we explore the role of different cost variables – ease, time taken to complete the task, and the number of sources consulted – as the factors to be explored based on different cognitive task complexity levels, from Bloom's taxonomy, by conducting a user study. We study the different search behaviors shown by users in online and offline environments based on the different cognitive task complexity levels and the three cost variables. We observed intriguing results that show factors such as ease, time, and the number of sources play a role in source selection while completing the tasks. Our study is a novel proposition in that we explore research in the direction of source selection based on different cognitive task complexity levels. The findings will contribute to shaping how tasks should be designed to use sources in a helpful and convenient manner. Moreover, the results also advance our understanding of the role that different affordances play in online and offline search behavior.

KEYWORDS

Information seeking; Search behavior; Sources; Task complexity

ACM Reference format:
Manasa Rath, Souvick Ghosh, Chirag Shah. 2018. Exploring Online and Offline Search Behavior Based on the Varying Task Complexity. In *Proceedings of 2018 Conference on Human Information Interaction & Retrieval, New Brunswick, NJ, USA, March 11–15, 2018 (CHIIR '18),* 4 pages.
https://doi.org/10.1145/3176349.3176890

1 INTRODUCTION

We are living in an age when information seeking is not limited to the Web but also occurs through social connections. Scholars in the field of Information Science have investigated the implications of fulfilling a task though Web and social connections [1, 8–10, 17, 25].

Research has also shown that social connections, along with Web sources, have contributed to not just fulfilling tasks but also help in learning processes. Studies have also investigated the role of source selection based on cognitive task complexity using the different cognitive levels of Bloom's taxonomy [1]. There are other forms of research that guide the source selection by the user, but in this study we triangulate the major concepts around the user, the source, and the task. The literature has primarily focused on the sources selected while fulfilling the tasks (based on the task fulfilled), without offering sufficient insights into the relationship between different cost variables that contribute to the fulfillment of the task in online and offline environments. To overcome this limitation, we adopted a mixed-method approach to examine the role of the cost variables – ease, time, number of sources consulted – in online and offline environments (shown in Tables 1 and 2.). In this work, 31 participants finished four tasks in a naturalistic setting in a two-week period using Web sources and in-person sources and detailed their information search in an online diary. The online diary experiences of the users, log data (collected using a browser plug-in), and the post-task questionnaires, were used for our analysis. To the best of our knowledge, this is the first mixed-method approach that investigates the online and offline behavior for different task complexity levels, based on Bloom's taxonomy, considering the online and offline search behavior. We specifically propose the following research question:

RQ: How can we compare the online and offline search behavior for different task complexity levels based on Bloom's Taxonomy?

To address the research question, the work reported here will present the analysis of the participants' online diary experiences and the browser log data collected while conducting the user study. This paper will proceed as follows: First, the paper will discuss the background of source selection while fulfilling tasks. Then, the paper will discuss the experimental method carried out by the authors to conduct the user study, followed by the analysis section. The paper concludes with the discussion and conclusion section.

2 BACKGROUND

Studies have emphasized information seeking research through a social and cultural context [7, 15, 22, 23] underlying the biological, physical, and anthropological layers, with respect to information seeking and searching [2], more like everyday information seeking in the context of "Way of Life" [23]. Furthermore, studies have investigated information seeking to the related task [5, 6, 11], along with the faceted approach, to conceptualize tasks in information seeking [16], characterizing Web-based information seeking tasks [14] in a field study setting. Morris [19] studied how online social tools could be better integrated with each other and with existing search facilities to fulfill exploratory search tasks.

Few studies have also explored how the role of quality and accessibility influence the selection of human information sources from a social capital perspective, the role of cost-benefit analysis in information seeking, along with the role of "Principle of Least Effort" in the information seeking process. In [13, 20], a study done by Borgatti and Cross [3], a formal model of information seeking was proposed and the relationship of probability of information seeking was studied as a function of knowing what the person knows, valuing what the person knows, being able to gain timely access to the person's thinking, and perceiving that seeking information will not be expensive. This has given way to several IR-based studies of using social networking tools to fill an information need, compared to a search engine [19], along with expressing an information need in a status message of a social networking site [21]. It seems clear from the literature that although studies exist on information seeking from Web and in-person sources and searching behavior, there still needs to be investigation on the comparison of online and offline searching behavior based on different task complexity levels.

3 METHOD

In this section, we explain the methodology that we used to address our research question. Thirty-one undergraduate students from Rutgers University, belonging to diverse academic backgrounds (18 from STEM and 13 from Arts and Humanities), took part in a two-week field study. Before beginning the user study, each participant was asked to fill out a questionnaire on their background and demographics. Then participants were provided instructions on how to install Coagmento [12, 18, 24], a Chrome browser plugin to record their browsing activity.[1] While designing the exploratory search tasks, we considered the literature from the field of education and developed tasks of different cognitive complexity levels using the Bloom's Taxonomy of Learning. Each of the four search tasks corresponded to the different cognitive complexity levels using Bloom's Taxonomy, revised by Anderson et al. [1] – Remember, Understand, Apply, Analyze, Evaluate, and Create. These exploratory search tasks belonged to the same topic but varied by levels of complexity. The four learning-oriented tasks provided to the participants were as follows:

Task 1: (Remember and Understand) *What is cyber bullying? How is it similar or different to other types of harassment (e.g. cyberbullying vs. traditional bullying)? What are some long-term/short-term risks involved with cyberbullying?*

Task 2: (Apply) *In 2010, Rutgers University witnessed the tragic incident of Tyler Clementi, whose case raised concerns about cyberbullying. Find out more about this case, and possibly some other cases. What does/do this/these case(s) show are some common characteristics of cyber bullying?*

Task 3: (Analyze) *Having heard some of the recent reports on cyberbullying, what seems to be the main cause of the bullying behavior online? How much is technology and the use of electronic communication associated with cyber bullying and why?*

Task 4: (Evaluate) *How effective are some of the currently available strategies to mitigate cyberbullying at schools and university campuses? Why? Which strategy/method do you think is best and why?*

The participants were asked to fulfill these learning-oriented tasks consulting the following online and offline sources: Web-searching the information using the search engines, friends, family members, and unknown sources, which included consulting information science professionals. Before beginning and submitting each of the learning tasks, the participants were compulsorily required to fill the pre-task and post-task questionnaires. Participants were then asked to write a report at the end of each search task on the topic:

You are among the main leaders of a student organization that raises awareness on the issue of cyberbullying. Teachers, educators and policymakers of your local community have recognized your efforts, and they have asked you to write a brief report on cyberbullying. Your report will be used as part of their training materials for the schoolteachers, educators and decision makers who will implement new practices and strategies within the local community.

Table 1: Cost variables with respect to search behavior in an online environment.

Cost variable	Search Behavior
Ease	Query Length, No. of queries
Time	Dwell Time
No. of sources	Unique pages saved

Table 2: Cost variables with respect to search behavior in an offline environment.

Cost variable	Search Behavior
Ease	Type of source referred
Time	Self-reported time to complete the task
No. of sources	Total number of sources consulted

The participants were also asked to write a report of at least 500 words on exploring and answering the exploratory search tasks. After the participants finished all four tasks, they were required to meet the researchers for a in-person 10-minute semi-structured interview. After the exit interview was conducted, a monetary compensation of $40 was paid to each participant, which marked the end of the user study.

4 DATA COLLECTION AND ANALYSIS

To answer our research question, we analyzed the data collected from the Chrome browser plug-in, post task questionnaires, and the online diaries of the participants. The participants provided detailed accounts of the URLs and the sources – offline or online – consulted

---

[1]Available from http://coagmento.org.

to fulfill the search tasks. We divided the sources consulted into online and offline sources. The online diaries consist of detailed self-reported experiences of how many sources – online and offline – were consulted by the participants. The data about the total time taken to finish the search tasks were collected from the post-task questionnaires.

While reviewing the literature, we found that users always consider the "go-to sources" [19] as the more preferred sources for the task at hand, keeping in mind the effort or the cost incurred in consulting them [13]. Therefore, on the basis of our user study design, we considered the following cost variables- ease, time, number of sources- which were considered by the participants while completing the task. While analyzing the log data, we found that participants occasionally digressed from performing the tasks by opening links unrelated to the tasks. Therefore, we had to manually remove those unrelated links. We then calculated the different search behavior measures based on the participants' log data, as follows:

- Query Length: The average length of the queries submitted for a task.
- Dwell Time: The average amount of time spent by the participants on the Web pages for a task.
- Unique pages saved: The total number of pages saved by the participants deemed useful for the completion of the task.
- Number of queries typed by the participants for the completion of the task.

We classified these search behaviors under the different cost variables – ease, time taken to finish the task, number of sources consulted – as the measures to evaluate online and offline search behavior. We mapped the online search behavior measures with the cost variables as follows: Query Length was associated with the ease variable, dwell time and the unique pages visited with the time taken to finish the task, and number of queries typed by the participant mapped with the number of sources consulted by the participant. We then analyzed the online diary accounts of each participant and categorized their experiences while consulting the different sources under three broad categories – ease, time, number of sources consulted – to complete the study through qualitative coding. We defined ease in obtaining the sources as the absence of difficulty or the state of being free from concern, whereas we defined the time variable as the time taken to finish the task, and the number of sources is defined as the total number of sources, consulted to complete the task.

The online diary accounts were personal experiences written by the participants, which did not have any structured categories showing time, ease, and number of sources. The researchers, therefore, reviewed the online diary accounts written by the participants and coded the three above-mentioned categories into high, medium, and low categories. After coding 25% of the data by the researchers, inter-coder reliability values were calculated. Once, the Cohen Kappa values were found greater than 0.7 for inter-coder reliability values of (reported in Table 3.), the researchers coded the rest of the data separately and came up with categorical variables such as High, Medium, and Low. For the variable ease, we coded the variable as "Low" when a friend or a family member was consulted to

complete the task, whereas a librarian was coded as "Medium" level of ease, and the stranger or an unknown source as coded as "High." Furthermore, we performed quartile analysis to code the amount of time taken for the participants to complete the four tasks from the post-task questionnaires. We performed quartile analysis and classified the time taken to complete the tasks into three categories: "Low" for less than 30 minutes, "Medium" for 30-90 minutes, "High" for greater than 90 minutes. The quartile analysis was also done for the web search behavior shown by the participants (reported in Table 4.). After performing the quartile analysis for the different search behaviors based shown by the participants' search behavior, we categorized them into three categories – High, Medium, and Low. We then built two logistic regression models to predict the search behavior based on the different cost variables considered in online and offline behavior to obtain meaningful insights from the different cost variables in the online and offline environment.

Table 3: Inter coder Reliability Scores for Ease and the Number of sources consulted.

Category	Inter coder reliability
Ease	0.782
No. of sources consulted	0.720

5 FINDINGS

Two logistic regression models were built on online and offline environments using the whole dataset to examine the possible association between the search behaviour – in terms of cost variables: ease, time, and number of sources. Akaike Information Criterion (AIC) values were compared, along with the standard error and p values. We report the coefficient of standard error and the $Pr(|z|)$ values for both online and offline models. The findings show no effects on the values for the different search behaviors in the online environment, whereas significant values were obtained for the number of sources consulted for the offline search behaviors (Table 6). However, considering our small dataset, a higher value of p, although increases the Type I error, also ensures that we do not miss the significant effects based on smaller dataset. The AIC values reported show the goodness of fit measures in the model that favor smaller residual errors found in the model [4, 26]. On the basis of the AIC values and the adjusted R squared values reported in Table 4., we can infer the model built on the offline sources were found to perform better compared to the online sources. The lower AIC values for the offline sources along with the higher adjusted R squared values are shown in the Table 7.

6 DISCUSSION

Our research presents intriguing findings that show why and how online and offline search behaviors differ based on different task complexity levels on the basis of the different cost variables – use, time, and number of sources. The cost variables based on offline search behavior played a major role compared to the online behavior in our study. Our results provide a significant contribution to the field of task complexity and source selection. This enhances our understanding on how users employed online and offline sources while completing the search tasks.

Table 4: Variables along with threshold values considered for Online and Offline Search Behavior

Variables	Quartile Values
Online	
Dwell Time	Q1<148, Q2: 149-1370, Q3>1370
Unique pages saved	Q1<2, Q2: 2-3, Q3>3
No. of queries	Q1<1, Q2: 1-3, Q3>3
Query Length	Q1<2.4, Q2: 2-4, Q3>4.7
Offline	
Time taken to finish task	Q1>30, Q2: 30-90, Q3>90
Ease	Q1<2, Q2: 2-3, Q3>3
No. of sources referred	Q1<1, Q2: 2-3, Q3>3

Table 5: Logistic Regression Model for the Online Search Behavior.

Category	Coefficient (Std Error)	Pr(>|z|)
Query Length	0.30	0.36
Dwell Time	-0.14	0.64
Unique pages saved	-0.40	0.18
No. of queries	-0.42	0.17

Table 6: Logistic Regression Model for the Offline Search Behavior.

Category	Coefficient (Std Error)	Pr(>|z|)
Time	-0.19	0.50
Ease	0.07	0.75
No. of sources	-0.87	0.018

Table 7: AIC values and adjusted R square values for the models.

Environment	AIC	R^2
Online	145.48	0.02
Offline	140.56	0.50

7 CONCLUSION AND FUTURE RESEARCH

Our research forms the basis to study online and offline behavior while studying information seeking behavior. The findings show that the number of sources have an effect in completing the tasks based on cognitive complexity levels. Our research is a contribution to the field of information science that takes into account source selection with the help of Bloom's taxonomy. Our future research will focus on studying the different modes of communication used while interacting with the source. We will also focus on studying the role of search systems while users complete the tasks at different cognitive complexity levels. Our research bridges the future research in the disciplines of Learning Sciences and Information Sciences. In our future research, we shall focus not just in developing a learning taxonomy, but also mapping the different sources that the user will select based on the task at hand on the basis of different cost variables- ease, time, and number of sources consulted in the online and offline environments.

8 ACKNOWLEDGMENTS

The authors wish to thank Matthew Mitsui and SeoYoon Sung for their help with conducting the study described here. The research reported in this paper is supported by US Institute of Museum and Library Services (IMLS) grant LG-81-16-0025-16.

REFERENCES

[1] L. W. Anderson, D. R. Krathwohl, P. Airasian, K. Cruikshank, R. Mayer, P. Pintrich, J. Raths, and M. Wittrock. A taxonomy for learning, teaching and assessing: A revision of bloom's taxonomy. *Development of a cognitive-metacognitive framework for protocol analysis of mathematical problem solving in small groups. Cognition and Instruction*, 9(2):137–175, 2001.

[2] M. J. Bates. Toward an integrated model of information seeking and searching. *The New Review of Information Behaviour Research*, 3:1–15, 2002.

[3] S. P. Borgatti and R. Cross. A relational view of information seeking and learning in social networks. *Management science*, 49(4):432–445, 2003.

[4] T. Byrt, J. Bishop, and J. B. Carlin. Bias, prevalence and kappa. *Journal of clinical epidemiology*, 46(5):423–429, 1993.

[5] K. Byström and K. Järvelin. Task complexity affects information seeking and use. *Information processing & management*, 31(2):191–213, 1995.

[6] D. J. Campbell and K. F. Gingrich. The interactive effects of task complexity and participation on task performance: A field experiment. *Organizational Behavior and Human Decision Processes*, 38(2):162–180, 1986.

[7] C. Courtright. Context in information behavior research. *Annual review of information science and technology*, 41(1):273–306, 2007.

[8] M. Dalal. Personalized social & real-time collaborative search. In *Proceedings of the 16th international conference on World Wide Web*, pages 1285–1286. ACM, 2007.

[9] B. M. Evans, S. Kairam, and P. Pirolli. Do your friends make you smarter?: An analysis of social strategies in online information seeking. *Information Processing & Management*, 46(6):679–692, 2010.

[10] J. Freyne and B. Smyth. An experiment in social search. In *Adaptive Hypermedia and Adaptive Web-Based Systems*, pages 95–103. Springer, 2004.

[11] S. Ghosh and C. Shah. Information seeking in learning-oriented search. *Proceedings of the Association for Information Science and Technology*, 54(1):682–684, 2017.

[12] R. González-Ibáñez and C. Shah. Coagmento: A system for supporting collaborative information seeking. *Proceedings of the ASIST*, 48(1):1–4, 2011.

[13] A. P. Hardy. The selection of channels when seeking information: Cost/benefit vs least-effort. *Information Processing & Management*, 18(6):289–293, 1982.

[14] M. Kellar, C. Watters, and M. Shepherd. A field study characterizing web-based information-seeking tasks. *Journal of the Association for Information Science and Technology*, 58(7):999–1018, 2007.

[15] D. Kelly, J. Arguello, A. Edwards, and W.-c. Wu. Development and evaluation of search tasks for iir experiments using a cognitive complexity framework. In *Proceedings of the 2015 International Conference on The Theory of Information Retrieval*, pages 101–110. ACM, 2015.

[16] Y. Li and N. J. Belkin. A faceted approach to conceptualizing tasks in information seeking. *Information Processing & Management*, 44(6):1822–1837, 2008.

[17] M. McDonnell and A. Shiri. Social search: A taxonomy of, and a user-centred approach to, social web search. *Program*, 45(1):6–28, 2011.

[18] M. Mitsui and C. Shah. Coagmento 2.0: A system for capturing individual and group information seeking behavior. In *Proceedings of the ACM/IEEE Joint Conference on Digital Libraries*, volume 2016-Septe, 2016.

[19] M. R. Morris, J. Teevan, and K. Panovich. A comparison of information seeking using search engines and social networks. *ICWSM*, 10:23–26, 2010.

[20] E. W. Morrison and J. B. Vancouver. Within-person analysis of information seeking: The effects of perceived costs and benefits. *Journal of Management*, 26(1):119–137, 2000.

[21] A. Oeldorf-Hirsch, B. Hecht, M. R. Morris, J. Teevan, and D. Gergle. To search or to ask: the routing of information needs between traditional search engines and social networks. In *Proceedings of the 17th ACM conference on Computer supported cooperative work & social computing*, pages 16–27. ACM, 2014.

[22] K. E. Pettigrew, R. Fidel, and H. Bruce. Conceptual frameworks in information behavior. *Annual review of information science and technology (ARIST)*, 35(43-78), 2001.

[23] R. Savolainen. Everyday life information seeking: Approaching information seeking in the context of "way of life". *Library & information science research*, 17(3):259–294, 1995.

[24] C. Shah. Coagmento-a collaborative information seeking, synthesis and sensemaking framework. *Integrated demo at CSCW*, 2010, 2010.

[25] P. Vakkari. Task-based information searching. *Annual review of information science and technology*, 37(1):413–464, 2003.

[26] E.-J. Wagenmakers and S. Farrell. Aic model selection using akaike weights. *Psychonomic bulletin & review*, 11(1):192–196, 2004.

Inter-Disciplinary Research on Inquiry and Learning: Information and Learning Sciences Perspectives

Rebecca Reynolds
Department of Library & Information Science
Rutgers University
Rebecca.reynolds@rutgers.edu

Preben Hansen
Department of Computer and Systems Sciences
Stockholm University
preben@dsv.su.se

ABSTRACT

This paper describes conceptual, technological and information environmental terrain across which scholarship in the inter-related disciplines of information and learning sciences occurs. The aim is to encourage researchers across these fields to find one another's work, as we engage in ongoing theory-building around inquiry and learning phenomena, to enrich scholarship and pragmatic design of learning innovations across both domains.

KEYWORDS

Learning; e-Learning; information-seeking; inquiry; search; information literacy

ACM Reference format:

R. Reynolds and P. Hansen. 2018. Inter-disciplinary Research on Inquiry and Learning: Information and Learning Sciences Perspectives. In *CHIIR '18: Conference on Human Information Interaction and Retrieval, March 11-15, 2018, New Brunswick, NJ, USA.* ACM, NY, NY, USA, 3 pages.
DOI: https://doi.org/10.1145/3176349.3176884

1 INTRODUCTION

Information science is the science and practice of effective collection, storage, retrieval, and use of information. It is concerned with recordable information and knowledge, as well as the technologies and related services that facilitate their management and use (e.g., Saracevic, 2009). Learning Sciences is the interdisciplinary study of teaching and learning in both formal and informal settings, drawing on a wealth of knowledge from various fields including cognitive science, educational psychology, computer science, information sciences, and design studies among others (e.g., Sawyer, 2014). From social science and "social constructivist" perspectives, learning starts with human actors. Researchers in both information and learning sciences aim to reach a deeper understanding of the cognitive and social processes that facilitate searching, learning, and knowledge co-construction, in order to advance theories of learning, information-seeking, and design of systems [1-11].

Information-seeking can inherently be seen as a human learning process; one that involves human inquiry. Special issues of leading scholarly journals in the field, and several international symposia, seminars and workshops in recent years have discussed these intersections in human information and learning behavior [4, 5, 8, 10, 11,

31, 32]. These advances have led to the development of a new Special Interest Group within ASIS&T, "SIG Information and Learning Sciences" (SIG InfoLearn) launched in 2016. At the 2017 annual meeting of ASIS&T, a pre-conference workshop will be offered by the SIG, featuring panelists whose work bridges both of these scholarly domains.

This paper builds upon the growing recognition of the ways in which the disciplines of information science and learning sciences stand to enrich one another theoretically, methodologically and empirically, for instance through design improvements within systems in which human learning is to be expected – including online information environments such as learning management systems, and search systems. The paper describes some of the technological terrain across which scholarship in the inter-related arenas of information and learning sciences occurs. The aim is to encourage researchers across these fields to find one another's work, as we engage in ongoing theory-building around inquiry and learning phenomena, to enrich scholarship and pragmatic design of learning innovations in both domains.

2 BACKGROUND

2.1 Growth of e-Learning innovations

The field of the learning sciences, or education sciences, is substantial, and many scholars within this field address the design and development of technological innovations for learning, and engage in theory-building around instruction and human learning that takes into consideration the presence and use by learners, of technological affordances. Such affordances have been encapsulated by an umbrella term in the literature: e-Learning.

2.1.1. Early definitions of e-Learning.. Earlier / narrower conceptualizations of e-learning were focused on the "learning management system" or "LMS" [12]. LMSs are web-based technologies that provide instructors with a way to create and deliver content, to monitor student participation and engagement, and to assess student performance online [13]. LMS platforms produced by commercial technology vendors are ubiquitous in higher education, with 99% of institutions having an LMS in place [14, 15]. In addition, one study found that 85% of faculty use an LMS, and 56% of faculty use it daily; 83% of students use an LMS and 56% say they use it in most or all courses [15]. Industry reports cite the K-12 LMS market as representing almost 100,000 individual US schools, compared to higher education's roughly 7000, which presents opportunities for continued growth among LMS providers pursuing K-12 [16]. Upside Learning [17] predicts that "...between the years 2017 and 2018, the LMS market will grow by about 23.17%, with an estimate of growth from $2.65 billion in 2013 to $7.8 billion in 2018, which is roughly an annual growth rate of 25.2%." Among 86 education publishing companies analyzed in one product market survey, the most frequently cited product medium for delivering instructional materials was online/digital delivery (82.6%), followed by print (65.2%), showing that electronic formats are growing in their prevalence [18].

For the time being at least, the major source for digitally formatted instructional materials in US schools continues to be commercial providers [18]. Blackboard is actively expanding from a focus on higher education to K-12, given the competition experienced by its LMS product at the university level [16]. Google is expanding upon its G Suite for Education, which is becoming ubiquitous at universities and colleges, placing emphasis on the reach of Google Classroom into K-12 schools. Google Classroom serves as a frontend to their productivity suite, which includes Google Docs and Google Drive [19].

Publishing companies hold longstanding ties to school districts, administrators, and state-level departments of education. Working alongside LMS platform vendors, they maintain their school relationships as well as their longstanding focus on content. We may increasingly see LMS platform providers partnering with publishing companies on content delivery. Across all of these platforms, varying types of search and inquiry behaviour among users are pervasive.

2.1.2. Expansion of e-Learning definitions. In contrast to definitions of e-Learning focusing on the LMS as a platform for dissemination of publisher curriculum content, Haythornthwaite & Andrews [12] define e-learning quite broadly, as a transformative movement in learning, not just the transfer of learning to an online stage. The authors embrace the ways in which learning flows across physical, geographical, and disciplinary borders [12]. They describe e-learning as perpetual, sustained over a lifetime, and enacted in multiple daily occurrences as we search for information to satisfy our learning needs and contribute content that promotes our and others' understanding [12]. They state that in e-learning, teachers and learners use technology to create the social space in which learning occurs, which includes psychological space that is sustained in learning across multiple devices and activities; cyberspace; and physical space, for instance using technology to connect learning to locations or objects in cities and museums [12, p. 2]. The broad definition they offer highlights the ways in which e-learning affordances are expanding; their aim is to make this concept inclusive of the existing and future range of innovations.

In an updated volume, Haythornthwaite, Andrews, Fransman & Meyers [20] highlight newer e-learning developments that have garnered recent attention. These include the following: Video-based resources for teaching and learning; games and gamification of learning; massive open online courses (MOOCs); enhanced means of helping learners navigate their way through materials, such as lecture recordings that can be annotated; adaptive learning systems that determine next steps according to learner progress and types of error; dashboards that show progress or effort in comparison to other learners; embedded tutors.

2.1.3. Challenges, opportunities in e-Learning design. When considering learning affordances, we must consider the ways in which e-learning technologies are tailored, structured and scaffolded to suit the given learning task, as well as the given learners and communities. At the K-12 level especially, where public education is a mandate, effective and personalized design and structure of e-learning becomes an equity issue, in that requiring use of an e-learning system that is unsuitable to particular learners *restricts their equitable access to learning.* Therefore, it is important that e-learning solutions be culturally responsive and adaptive to the needs of different students, teacher and school communities, focusing on *improving upon* the learning experience rather than simply replacing older modalities.

The design of instructional affordances, and how much structure is provided in such autonomy-supportive contexts, plays a role in students' success. Less-structured interventions have been critiqued due to their potential to tax cognitive load, frustrating or demotivating students [21]. Critiquing the rapid advance of digitized book materials through commercial learning management system infrastructure, Humphreys [22] challenges LMS companies' and publishers' focus on reaching and serving greater numbers of students in a given program offering quickly, rather than addressing *quality* of the learning experience and

improvement of teaching strategies and learning outcomes (both the *what* and *how* students are learning with these digital tools). Reynolds [10] explores the ways in which a more tailored, customized and scaffolded online learning solution designed to teach computer science education varies in its effectiveness in meeting the inquiry needs of learners, based on learning task difficulty, and inquiry strategy as adopted by the learner.

If well-conceived, designed, and researched, as well as executed and implemented, the technical and design features of e-learning offerings such as those discussed by Haythornthwaite, Andrews, Fransman & Meyers [20] have potential to be tailored and customized to meet the learning goals of the educator and the needs of the learner. Design affordances may address needs of student learner populations, groups and individuals, such as grade level, reading levels, and individual differences in prior knowledge, motivation, self-regulation and other dispositions. Despite the widespread and growing availability and use of more generic course shell environments in US schools, there is definitely more tailored and research-supported innovation in instructional design and e-learning development occurring. Haythornthwaite, et al [20] summarize the arenas where one may find high quality e-learning innovation, backed up by solid research development, design-based research, and rigorous evidence bases, as follows: learning sciences, computer-supported collaborative learning, networked learning, educational data mining, learning@scale, and learning analytics. "Design-based research" is one key method utilized in these domains.

These research domains often reside within university and non-profit educational technology innovation hubs funded by entities like the National Science Foundation, focusing on human computer interaction (HCI) research, design-based research (DBR), and learning sciences instructional theory and learning theory advances. Results of such research and development efforts can be found in the proceedings of the International Conference of the Learning Sciences (ICLS), the Journal of the Learning Sciences (JLS), and the Computer-Supported Collaborative Learning (CSCL) conference and journal by the same name, as well as the Journal of Learning Analytics, and the Learning Analytics and Knowledge annual conference.

2.2. Learning and search systems.

Information systems involving search are a mainstay central to information science scholarship. In the research literatures, search systems have been considered as a tool for querying and retrieving relevant information that satisfy a specific information needs. As such, the development and research on search and seeking technology have focused on the process of more efficient ways of improving the effectiveness of matching a given document with search queries. Regarding the search user interface, a ranked list of search results are still the most preferred way of displaying documents, and this matches what people expect of a search system today.

As discussed in [23] this kind of interface and information representation may work well for certain information tasks, while for others, this is not optimal. For example, task such as learning, creative processes or discovery requires other types of interaction that involves reflection, iteration, information merging, distillation and summarization [24, 33-35]. Search engines today can handle both very specific tasks – like acquiring factual knowledge. However, other learning aspects still need to be considered, such as supporting the users' analysis and synthesis, related to real work or everyday search tasks. Even though information search systems have evolved from text-based information retrieval tools to multimedia information-intensive systems, researchers have only just now begun to recognize information access and search systems as rich information and learning spaces. Not only can users very quickly retrieve and gather information, but they can also learn and discover new information while interacting with online content that eventually transform into new knowledge. The concept of learning has generally been assumed during the information search process, rather than clearly explicated, described and modeled when designing and building search systems. It has been something assumed to have taken place 'outside' the computational design of information access systems [8].

Learning effects can already now be studied using log data from search engines. These data may inform us about how to characterize, understand, explore and assess the nature of search-related learning. Log data have the ability to and can demonstrate aspects such as a) inferring the presence and the nature of learning-related tasks; b) estimating motivation to learn while browsing and searching; c) measuring change in expertise over time; d) log-based analysis and metrics for comprehensive search and e) process-related stages of information inspection. For example, '...This combination of user events and document relationship types could enable comprehensive search engines to use the resulting log data for learning the association between properties of comprehensive search trails and the estimated usefulness of documents for different learning outcomes...' [23, p.28].

In order to reconsider interactive search systems and the design of them as part of learning processes supporting humans engaging in learning activities, we may think of different directions. These search systems need to be designed to enable and support more diverse types of learning, that goes beyond merely knowledge acquisition. Rieh et al. [23] suggest four directions.

2.2.1. System: Developing a search system that supports sense-making and enhances learning. This direction should investigate how we may design systems that support people making sense of information. Research in this domain focuses on exploratory search and beyond [29, 30]. In this context, interactive information systems may be modeled and designed as search technologies with appropriate learning components. As such, it can support reflective thinking, critical thinking, argumentation, and creative learning processes. New and diverse models of user's information behavior will emerge, such as critical assessment and judgment of the usefulness of information, scoping, differentiating, comparing and making sense of information pieces.

2.2.2. Interaction: Supporting effective user interaction for searching as learning. Search systems today aim to support different ways of interacting and engaging with information [25]. A well-established knowledge is that information objects encountered during the search process may result in that the searcher shift or change their goal, intention or search tasks. O'Day and Jeffries [26] very early found that search results for a specific goal from time to time triggered additional or new goals. A similar phenomena was also discussed by Marcia Bates [27] Berry-picking model. O'Day and Jeffries [26] concluded that one of the main important values of searching was the very process of acquiring information and accumulating learning. This indicates that we should try to design new tools to facilitate implicit or explicit learning activities by prompting with additional query terms or asking questions for critical thinking and reasoning. Therefore, we argue that, when developing and designing, for example, new browsing and navigational structures, we also, at the same time need build support for learning behaviours.

2.2.3. Information literacy: Providing inquiry-based information literacy tool within a search system. As pointed out by Rieh et al. [23], we may consider developing an information literacy approach/model that integrates information literacy instructions into the design of a search system. Employing a scaffolding-guided inquiry framework has been suggested but there may be other such models. Scaffolding is about the practice of supporting learners in their activity by providing targeted assistance, either as a technical, informational or social aid (for example through peers). In this way, they could help learners engage in complex or difficult tasks that are beyond their current level of proficiency [28].

2.2.4. Learning assessment and comprehensive search: Assessing learning from online search behaviour. An interesting concept is discussed in Rieh et al [23], where the authors develop the notion of comprehensive search. Modeling comprehensive search progress will require richer representations of both information as well as learning and domain expertise. The situation that may be involved in such comprehensive search includes the situation when diverse perspectives are encountered along the learning path, or multiple sources of evidence are gathered in support of a conclusion. Searchers' trails can therefore indicate, form and contribute to an intrinsic learning resource.

In summary, advances has been made towards models for system design embedding learning motivation, intentions, knowledge levels, and different levels of content diversity, which can contribute to a richer representation of information and data, of information need and queries and about users in order to provide better learning opportunities and outcome. We may need to reconsider the design, utilities, qualities and values of search systems when supporting human knowledge exploration, creation and when facilitating human and organizational learning processes. Current search systems could be extended to foster and support learning by '...reconfiguring search systems from information-retrieval tools to rich learning spaces in which search experiences and learning experiences are intertwined and even synergized' [8].

2.3. Cross-disciplinary opportunities.

The presentation of two distinct sections in this paper describing e-Learning, and search system innovations for learning, demonstrates ways in which research has been occurring in parallel, but without intersection and cross-navigation. One can imagine a range of scenarios in learning sciences research, in which a researcher/developer may incorporate search tasks in the learning sequence. For instance, an e-Learning designer developing a learning management system might add a Google search widget enabling learners to search a given pre-curated corpus within the confines of the designed platform – but may grouse at the design limitations of the search results page, for having added to the cognitive load of the given learning sequence. Nonetheless, out of necessity, they simply "worked with what they had" with the search interface. How could the planned inquiry moment in the learning sequence be better conceptualized, developed and designed to enhance knowledge building without unduly taxing the user?

The research and development in these two domains has not been formally bridged. Search system designers have not identified the range of e-learning contexts, sequences, and modalities in which new forms of search may be better incorporated. For *information* researchers, it is important to understand the broad range and types of learning modalities in which resource uses are deployed sub-optimally. This is especially true as e-learning solutions continue to proliferate. Furthermore, *learning sciences* researchers can advance conceptualization of inquiry, resource uses, information-seeking and search engines. How could learners' resource needs *in situ*, be better met with a more intelligent systems? Conversations and collaborations herein, will help both sides advance their human learning and knowledge-building agendas to help advance inquiry and human information-seeking beyond the boundaries, limitations and confines of the million-record results page -- facilitating more seamless inquiry activity, in a broad scope of human learning contexts.

REFERENCES

[1]   Saracevic, T. "Information science." In M. J. Bates (Ed.), *Encyclopedia of library and information sciences* (3rd ed.) New York: Taylor and Francis. 2009, 2570-2585.

[2]   Sawyer. R. K. "Introduction: the new science of learning." In R. K. Sawyer (Ed.) *The Cambridge handbook of the learning sciences.* Cambridge University Press. 2014, 1-20.

[3]   Agosto, D. E., Abbas, J., & Naughton, R. "Relationships and social rules: Teens' social network and other ICT selection practices." *Journal of the American Society for Information Science & Technology,* 2012, *63*, 1108-1124.

[4]   Ahn, J., Erickson, I., & Meyers, E. "Connecting fields, connecting

scholars: Breaking down walls between learning and information sciences." *Led Workshop for iConference 2014*. Berlin, Germany. 2014.

[5]   Ahn, J. & Erickson, I. "Introduction to the special issue revealing mutually constitutive ties between the information and learning sciences." *The Information Society*, 2016, *32:2*.

[6]   Bowler, Leanne. "The self-regulation of curiosity and interest during the information search process of adolescent students." *Journal of the American Society for Information Science and Technology*, 2010, 61 (7). 1332-1344.

[7]   Chu, S.K.W., Reynolds, R.B., Tavares, N.J., Notari, M. & Lee., C.W.Y. *21st Century Skills Development through Inquiry-based Learning: From Theory to Practice*. 2017. New York: Springer Science.

[8]   Hansen, P. & Rieh, S. Y. "Editorial: Recent advances on searching as learning: An introduction to the special issue." *Journal of Information Science*. 2016, 42: 3-6.

[9]   Reynolds, R. & M. M. Chiu. "Reducing digital divide effects through student engagement in coordinated game design, online resource uses, and social computing activities in school." *Journal of the Association for Information Science and Technology*. 2016. 67: 8, 1822-1835.

[10]   Reynolds, R. "Relationships among tasks, collaborative inquiry processes, inquiry resolutions, and knowledge outcomes in adolescents during guided discovery-based game design in school." *Journal of Information Science*. 2016, 42: 35-58.

[11]   Vakkari, P. "Searching as learning: A systematization based on literature." *Journal of Information Science*. 2016, 42: 7-18.

[12]   Haythornthwaite, C., & Andrews, R. N. L. *E-learning theory and practice*. 2011. SAGE Publications Inc.

[13]   Venter, P., van Rensburg, M. J., & Davis, A. "Drivers of learning management system use in a South African open and distance learning institution." *Australasian Journal of Educational Technology*, 2012, *28* (2) 183-198

[14]   Dahlstrom, E., de Boor, T., Grunwald, P., & Vockley, M. *The ECAR National Study of Undergraduate Students and Information Technology*, EDUCAUSE, Boulder, CO. 2011.

[15]   Lang, L., & Pirani, J. *The Learning Management System Evolution*. Research bulletin. Louisville, CO: ECAR. 2014, May 20. http://www.educause.edu/ecar.

[16]   LMS Data, "Spring 2015 Updates." *Edutechnica.com*. 2015. http://edutechnica.com/2015/03/08/lms-data-spring-2015-updates/

[17]   Upside Learning. "LMS Selection Guide for SMBs." 2016. https://www.upsidelms.com/free-ebook-lms-selection-guide-for-smbs.asp

[18]   Simba Information. "The Complete K-12 Report." 2015. https://www.simbainformation.com/Complete-9588037/

[19]   Fenton, W. "Google classroom absent from college courses." *Inside Higher Ed*. 2017, June 21. https://www.insidehighered.com/digital-learning/article/2017/06/21/google-classroom-not-college-classroom

[20]   Haythornthwaite, C., Andrews, R., Fransman, J. & Meyers, E. *SAGE Handbook of E-Learning Research, 2nd edition*. 2016. London: Sage.

[21]   Kirschner, P.A., Sweller, J., & Clark, R.E., "Why minimal guidance during instruction does not work: An analysis of the failure of constructivist, discovery, problem-based, experiential, and inquiry-based teaching", *Educational Psychologist*, 2006, 41, 75–86.

[22]   Humphreys, D. "The questions we need to ask first." In D.G. Oblinger *'s Game Changers: Education and Information Technologies*. 2012, Educause.

[23]   Rieh, S.Y. Collins-Thompson, K. Hansen, P. & Lee H-J. "Towards searching as a learning process: A review of current perspectives and future directions." *Journal of Information Science*. 2016, 42: 19-34.

[24]   Marchionini G. "Exploratory search: From finding to understanding." *Communications of the ACM*, 2006; 49(4): 41–46.

[25]   Petrelli, D., Hansen, P., Beaulieu, M., Sanderson, M., Demetriou, G., and Herring, P. "Observing Users, Designing Clarity: A Case Study on the User-Centered Design of a Cross-Language Information Retrieval System". *Journal of the American Society for Information Science and Technology*, 2004, 55(10): 923-934.

[26]   O'Day V and Jeffries R. "Orienteering in an information landscape: How information seekers get from here to there." In: Proceedings of the *INTERCHI conference on human factors in computing systems* (CHI'93), 1993: 438–445.

[27]   Bates, M. "The design of browsing and berrypicking techniques for the online search interface", *Online Review*, 1989, 13(5): 407-424.

[28]   Zhang M and Quintana C. "Scaffolding strategies for supporting middle school students' online inquiry processes." *Computers and Education*, 2011; 58: 181–196.

[29]   White R and Roth R. "Exploratory search: Beyond the query-response paradigm." *Synthesis Lectures on Information Concepts, Retrieval, and Services*, 2009; 1(1): 1–98.

[30]   White R and Drucker S. "Supporting exploratory search." *Communications of the ACM*, 2006; 49(4): 36

[31]   Collins-Thompson, Hansen, Hauff, Klas. Searching as Learning. *Dagstuhl Seminar 17092*, 2017. March. http://www.dagstuhl.de/de/programm/kalender/semhp/?semnr=17092

[32]   Fisher, K., Davis, K., Yip, J., Dahya, N., Mills, JE., Eisenberg, M. "Digital Youth Think Tank White Paper." *Digital Youth Think Tank, 2016*. Seattle, WA.

[33]   Kuhlthau, C.C. "Seeking Meaning: A Process Approach to Library and Information Services." *The Library Quarterly*, 1994, 64, no. 4(Oct. 473-475.

[34]   Kuhlthau, C.C., LK. Maniotes, and Caspari, AK. *Guided Inquiry: Learning in the 21st Century*, 2007. Westport, Conn: Libraries Unlimited.

[35]   CC. Kuhlthau, Maniotes, LK., and Caspari AK. "Guided Inquiry: Design: A Framework for Inquiry in Your School." 2012. Santa Barbara, California: Libraries Unlimited.

Social Aspects of Task-Based Information Seeking Behavior

The Conceptual Integration of Cognitive Sociology and Practice Theory

Eun Youp Rha

School of Communication and Information, Rutgers University

New Brunswick, New Jersey

eunyoup.rha@rutgers.edu

ABSTRACT

The aim of this study is to introduce a conceptual approach to understand social effects on task-based information seeking behavior. This analytical work provides a new theoretical lens that will be potentially useful to identify the relationships between social communities and information behavior. Specifically, I suggest an integrated sociological view on human information behavior primarily influenced by cognitive sociology and practice theory, which emphasizes the roles of socially constructed cognition of individuals.

CCS CONCEPTS

• **Human-centered computing** → *User studies*; • **Social and professional topics** → *Cultural characteristics*;

KEYWORDS

Task-based information seeking; Social context of task; Cognitive sociology; Practice theory

ACM Reference Format:
Eun Youp Rha. 2018. Social Aspects of Task-Based Information Seeking Behavior: The Conceptual Integration of Cognitive Sociology and Practice Theory. In *CHIIR '18: 2018 Conference on Human Information Interaction Retrieval, March 11–15, 2018, New Brunswick, NJ, USA*. ACM, New York, NY, USA, 4 pages. https://doi.org/10.1145/3176349.3176882

1 INTRODUCTION

Task, an activity to be performed in order to accomplish a goal [31], is an important element in understanding information seeking reasons, information types, seeking methods and information uses [9]. It plays a fundamental role in motivating the start of information seeking by providing goals to be satisfied through information seeking processes. Scholars in information behavior studies have strived to determine relationships between a variety of tasks and associated information seeking behaviors. One aspect of task that has been little discussed is the social context in which it takes place. Accordingly, this work aims to propose an original conceptual framework for research into social effects on task-based information seeking.

2 TASK-BASED APPROACH IN INFORMATION STUDIES

Task is considered a key contextual factor influencing human information seeking behavior, and how task is associated with information seeking behavior has been examined in terms of certain aspects of task, such as task types and task doer's characteristics. Since a variety of tasks conducted either in everyday life or in the workplace can be characterized by certain types [9, 22], the effects of task types on information seeking behavior have been one of the key foci of research in this area. In such research, task is usually perceived as an activity performed in an individualistic mode, and the performance of task is considered dependent on a range of individual qualities, such as prior knowledge, skill, preference, motivation, mood, and so on [8]. For this reason, the relationships of individuals' cognitive states to information behavior in task have received a great deal of attention, specifically in terms of two types of cognition: perceived difficulty or complexity [2, 7, 10, 16] and prior knowledge, domain knowledge [19, 33, 34] or topical knowledge [1, 5, 21].

It is also worth noting that task is performed within a certain context which can determine task doers' recognition or interpretation of information problems and selection of information sources [30]. For instance, a number of researches explored task-based information behavior at authentic work environments [10, 15, 23, 26]. Moreover, a sociological lens to task-based information seeking behavior has emerged, which primarily stresses information behavior as the embodied process of the resolution of a problematic situation within a context [29]. Work task performance is placed into a context of activities constituting information practice as well as into a context of socio-cultural, historical and material-economic conditions that characterize the formation of the information practice [11]. These examples demonstrate that social contexts of task may play a critical role in affecting individuals' information behavior by providing them with social and cultural constructs and practices.

3 SOCIAL PERSPECTIVES ON INFORMATION BEHAVIOR

In information studies, applying a social lens has primarily meant paying attention to social contexts of people in relation to their information behavior over their cognitive or affective states. Taylor [30] proposed the information use environments (IUE) model, emphasizing that professional context plays a crucial role in not only providing individuals with a context of information uses, but also in establishing tasks and responsibilities from which information problems are triggered. Also, domain analysis [18] is a theoretical framework highlighting the role of social context (i.e. domain) in shaping human cognition leading to information behavior. In this view, information needs are generated from social and cultural factors since the information demanded by users is an expression of their subjective information needs after being socialized to the context, which may be different from their real or objective needs [17].

From a more socio-cultural perspective, Savolainen [27] developed a sociologically and contextually oriented model of information activity, Everyday Life Information Seeking (ELIS), which illustrates a socially and culturally determined system of thinking, perception, and evaluation. Also, Chatman's [12] theory of life in the round is a good example derived from the sociological roots to understand everyday information behavior. She maintained that human information interactions are influenced by a social community, named as a *small world* that holds specific social conditions and forces for people's thinking and acting when they seek and use information. Following Chatman's *small world*, Jaeger and Burnett [20] suggested *information worlds*, a social place where information needs and behaviors take place based on common interests, expectations and behaviors. This social world enables members to recognize *information value*, a shared sense of a scale of the importance of information, and it directs their way of talking about the differences in the worlds' perceptions not only of those things that are of importance in the world that they share, but also of the meaning and significance and provides a way of assessing how different worlds understand or interpret the phenomena or events with which they come into contact [20].

4 APPROACHES TO HUMAN BEHAVIOR IN SOCIOLOGY

The socio-cognitive and social perspectives on human information behavior demonstrate that human information behavior is influenced by various social aspects of context including material, environmental and cultural elements and different social groups may reveal different information behavior. Nevertheless, it is still insufficient to pinpoint why such differences of behavior occur. Cognitive sociology that mainly delineates social dimensions of individuals' cognition seems useful to articulate a new facet of the sociological view on information behavior, which can explain causes of behavior influenced by societies from a different angle. In addition, practice theory is reviewed to understand habitual unconscious cognition of individuals that affect their action. Therefore, this study attempts to integrate cognitive sociology and practice theory as theoretical stance in order to particularly approach how a social context influences individuals' mental acts in the process of information seeking.

4.1 Cognitive sociology

In cognitive sociology, how the individual human mind is constructed by the society(ies) of which it is a member, is the focal point. It mainly conceives individuals as social beings, who think not only individually and universally, but also socially, being affected as well as constrained in the way to interact with the world by a particular social environment [36]. It places the emphasis on individuals' socialization to their community, which enables them

to build a certain mental structure used for mental acts in everyday life.

4.1.1 Thought Communities. The sociology of cognition highlights that a group develops a particular style of thoughts, and that individuals within a group think in the manner in which their group thinks [24]. Fleck [14] introduced a *thought collective*, a community of persons mutually exchanging ideas and maintaining intellectual interaction, which offers a special carrier for the historical development and for the given stock of knowledge and level of culture. Within a thought collective, the thought style governs the members' cognitive processes, which makes possible the perception and establishment of facts in the community, whereas it renders recognition of other forms and other facts impossible [14]. Similarly, a *thought community* refers to a community in which people experience cognitive traditions and socializations. It is an intersubjective world, larger than the individual but smaller than the entire human race such as professions, generations, social classes, and status groups [6]. A thought community influences the members' ways of viewing the world, which make them understand and notice things similarly.

Importantly, it is not necessary that this be an official community that holds any formal structure [14]. Rather, social factors are essential in forming and maintaining it, which allow individuals to develop a certain *sociomental lens* [35] to see the reality so as to think and act in a more social manner; for instance, the knowledge socially and relatively constructed in the specific social context based on the taken-for-grantedness for what is real [3], culture, a major locus of cognition [36] that constrains people's capacity to imagine alternatives to existing arrangements [13], and social norms which create rules and standards of behavior within a community [13].

4.1.2 Optical Socialization. Cognitive sociology emphasizes that how individuals perceive the world is neither purely personal nor universal; rather it is social. They are socialized to a particular thought community (i.e., optical community: the social unit from within which the world looks the same), where they learn to look at things in unmistakably social ways [36]. The same object is often perceived somewhat differently by different people since there is always more than just a single mental stance from which something can be seen. For instance, cooking is viewed as just one of the domestic chores to be finished by a housewife, while it is considered a crucial task that helps improve and practice cooking skills by a prospective chef. Also, individuals in the same community perceive things somewhat similarly since they basically see the world through the same mental lenses, whereas they tend to be different from those of people who come from somewhat different social backgrounds (i.e., communities) and therefore use altogether different ones [36].

4.1.3 Attentional Socialization. A thought community also helps determine what actually enters our minds in the first place [36]. Members of the community have the ability to notice things that nonmembers tend to ignore as well as to ignore some of the things they attend to [37]. When individuals exclude certain parts of reality from their attention as irrelevant, they do so not just as human beings, but also as social beings, as members of particular thought communities that ignore certain things. For instance, one scholar focuses on publishing research papers in certain journals selectively, which never gain attention from other scholars in a different field. They may do so habitually, but they, in fact, have become accustomed to overlook journals irrelevant or less relevant within their social context as a result of cognitive habituation [37]. Each field of study, as a sub-culture of academia, creates specific cognitive biases which normally determine what scholarly activities are noticed and ignored by individual scholars in the realm. Their behavior of publishing a paper through a certain channel is a product of the particular way they focus their attention as a result of their professional socialization [37]. Thus, the ways we draw a line between relevance and irrelevance is neither inherent nor universal, but social as a consequence of learning restricted norms of focusing through socialization to a group.

4.2 Practice theory

Another approach is practice theory that views everyday life human actions as the outcome of social practices. Practice theory mainly understands individuals' behavior as a set of habitualized and routinized bodily actions shared within a society. Practices refer to shared actions among a particular group of people including the ways of doing and approaching things that are shared to some significant extent among members [32]. From the standpoint of practice theory, routines shared within a social boundary fundamentally constitute individuals' actions. For instance, Bourdieu [4] defined a practice as a logic organized by unconscious schemas and instantaneous intuitive judgments, emphasizing the routines of institutions in everyday activities. Schatzki [28] also argued practice is a routinized way in which bodies are moved, objects are handled, subjects are treated, things are described, and the world is understood. Similarly, Reckwitz [25] stressed routinized mental activities that encompass people's routinized ways of understanding the world, of desiring something, and of knowing how to do something in addition to embodied skillful performance of bodies. Overall, the practice-based perspective proposes that the social is located in embodied routinized activities and our decision and behavior are part of routines learned from communities of practice.

5 SOCIAL EFFECTS ON TASK-BASED INFORMATION SEEKING BEHAVIOR

5.1 A theoretical model

The review of the literature on cognitive sociology and practice theory identifies that human behavior is considerably shaped by both individuals' social cognition and routinized acts as a consequence of socialization to a certain community. It implies the necessity to assume cognition and behavior as social products rather than solely individualistic features. That is, individuals' information seeking behavior may be formed based not only on their sociomental lens which is used to recognize or interpret information problems and sources, but also on habitual activity in terms of dealing with information derived from practices, in that information seeking typically takes place in a certain social context including everyday life settings. Consequently, a theoretical model of task-based information seeking behavior has been built with particular focus on social variables.

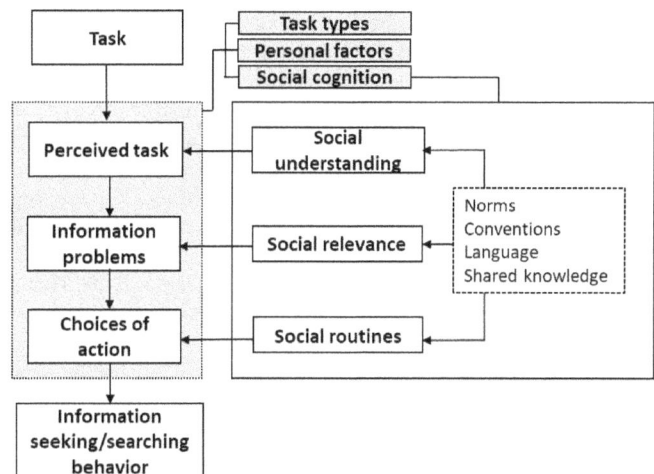

Figure 1: A theoretical model of task-based information seeking behavior

This model (figure 1), developed upon the existing model of information seeking in task [10], describes the process of how a task leads to information seeking behavior. Task types (e.g. fact-finding, decision making) and personal factors (e.g. motivation, attitude, mood) are important elements affecting information seeking behavior. This model highlights social cognition as another key variable to information seeking behavior in task. Three different cognitive acts, social understanding, social relevance and social routines, may intervene in the process of information seeking. An individual who belongs to a particular community perceives a given task and understands it in a social manner, and proceed to identifying information problems and possible solutions for the problems using social relevance. This step leads to a person's choices of certain actions to resolve the problems, which can be influenced by social routines of the community. Such social interventions may arise either consciously or unconsciously in the task performer' mind. Each of them is explained as follows:

- Social understanding: When individuals perceive a task, they understand it as a member of a certain thought community according to optical socialization in cognitive sociology; for instance, as a student, as a Christian, as a journalist, as a scientist, etc. Such social identity tends to direct how a person recognizes and interprets the reality. Thus, the same task can be understood in a different way by two individuals who are located in different thought communities due to their different sociomental lens used to view the task.
- Social relevance: Detailed information problems or needs can be defined socially based on social relevance which is concerned with social framing of attention that draws a line between relevant and irrelevant entities as a result of attentional socialization. Within a task, only relevant issues may be noticed as information problems by a person, whereas

irrelevant ones may be disattended. A person's thought community will influence ways of articulating specific information needs from the task since each community has a particular norm of focusing that can differ from other groups.

- Social routines: An individual may reveal routinized behaviors when he or she engages in information seeking in task and some of them are socially built by participating in a certain thought community. Such behaviors may include which bodies are moved, objects are handled, subjects are treated, things are described, and the world is understood [25]. Therefore, individuals' actions chosen to conduct a task can be derived from socially-oriented practices from the community.

- Norms, Conventions, Language, Shared knowledge: Social norms, conventions or traditions of a group, specialized language, terminology and symbols commonly used within a group, and shared knowledge and know-hows among members of a group will play a fundamental role not only in making the group exist and maintain, but also in leading the members to acquire social cognition.

6 CONCLUSION

Conducting information seeking has been considered an individualistic activity largely affected by individuals' cognitive attributes and their interactions with different task types. However, a social perspective on human cognition and behavior points to substantial impacts of social contexts on task-based information seeking since people may utilize a certain sociomental lens as well as embodied social practices when they perform the task and seek information. A sociological viewpoint that integrates cognitive sociology and practice theory can be a new social approach to information behavior to underpin the close relationships between a social community and information seeking behavior in task with the emphasis on influences of individuals' social thinking.

The conceptual model presented here identifies a novel way to investigate the effects of various types of social environments on individuals' information behavior, not only work environments but also everyday life settings, and sheds light on new variables that might have a significant association with human information behavior, such as social mind, social practice, norms and others. This framework could be also used to design effective strategies for inventing a practice-oriented information system that assists information seeking and searching in particular social communities or contexts.

REFERENCES

[1] B. Allen. Topic knowledge and online catalog search formulation. *The Library Quarterly*, 61(2):188–213, 1991.
[2] D. Bell and I. Ruthven. Searcherâ ÁŽs assessments of task complexity for web searching. *Advances in Information Retrieval*, pages 57–71, 2004.
[3] P. L. Berger and T. Luckmann. The social construction of reality. *New York*, 1966.
[4] P. Bourdieu. *The logic of practice*. Stanford University Press, 1990.
[5] S. Brand-Gruwel, Y. Kammerer, L. Meeuwen, and T. Gog. Source evaluation of domain experts and novices during web search. *Journal of Computer Assisted Learning*, 33(3):234–251, 2017.
[6] W. H. Brekhus. *Culture and Cognition: Patterns in the Social Construction of Reality*. John Wiley & Sons, 2015.
[7] K. Byström. Information and information sources in tasks of varying complexity. *Journal of the Association for Information Science and Technology*, 53(7):581–591, 2002.
[8] K. Byström. Approaches to" task" in contemporary information studies. *Information Research*, 12(4):12–4, 2007.
[9] K. Byström and P. Hansen. Conceptual framework for tasks in information studies. *Journal of the Association for Information Science and Technology*, 56(10):1050–1061, 2005.
[10] K. Byström and K. Järvelin. Task complexity affects information seeking and use. *Information processing & management*, 31(2):191–213, 1995.
[11] K. Byström and A. Lloyd. Practice theory and work task performance: How are they related and how can they contribute to a study of information practices. *Proceedings of the Association for Information Science and Technology*, 49(1):1–5, 2012.
[12] E. A. Chatman. A theory of life in the round. *Journal of the Association for Information Science and Technology*, 50(3):207, 1999.
[13] P. DiMaggio. Culture and cognition. *Annual review of sociology*, 23(1):263–287, 1997.
[14] L. Fleck. *Genesis and Development of a Scientific Fact*. University of Chicago Press, 1981.
[15] L. Freund, E. G. Toms, and C. L. Clarke. Modeling task-genre relationships for ir in the workplace. In *Proceedings of the 28th annual international ACM SIGIR conference on Research and development in information retrieval*, pages 441–448. ACM, 2005.
[16] J. Gwizdka and I. Spence. What can searching behavior tell us about the difficulty of information tasks? a study of web navigation. *Proceedings of the Association for Information Science and Technology*, 43(1):1–22, 2006.
[17] B. Hjørland. Epistemology and the socio-cognitive perspective in information science. *Journal of the Association for Information Science and Technology*, 53(4):257–270, 2002.
[18] B. Hjørland and H. Albrechtsen. Toward a new horizon in information science: Domain-analysis. *Journal of the Association for Information Science and Technology*, 46(6):400–425, 1995.
[19] I. Hsieh-Yee. Effects of search experience and subject knowledge on the search tactics of novice and experienced searchers. *Journal of the American Society for Information Science*, 44(3):161, 1993.
[20] P. T. Jaeger and G. Burnett. *Information worlds: Social context, technology, and information behavior in the age of the Internet*, volume 8. Routledge, 2010.
[21] D. Kelly and C. Cool. The effects of topic familiarity on information search behavior. In *Proceedings of the 2nd ACM/IEEE-CS joint conference on Digital libraries*, pages 74–75. ACM, 2002.
[22] Y. Li and N. J. Belkin. A faceted approach to conceptualizing tasks in information seeking. *Information Processing & Management*, 44(6):1822–1837, 2008.
[23] Y. Li and N. J. Belkin. An exploration of the relationships between work task and interactive information search behavior. *Journal of the Association for Information Science and Technology*, 61(9):1771–1789, 2010.
[24] K. Manheim. *Ideology and utopia: An Introduction to the Sociology of Knowledge*. Harcourt, Brace, 1949.
[25] A. Reckwitz. Toward a theory of social practices: a development in culturalist theorizing. *European journal of social theory*, 5(2):243–263, 2002.
[26] M. Saastamoinen and K. Järvelin. Search task features in work tasks of varying types and complexity. *Journal of the Association for Information Science and Technology*, 68(5):1111–1123, 2017.
[27] R. Savolainen. Everyday life information seeking: Approaching information seeking in the context of âÄIJway of lifeâÄİ. *Library & information science research*, 17(3):259–294, 1995.
[28] T. R. Schatzki. *The site of the social: A philosophical account of the constitution of social life and change*. Penn State Press, 2002.
[29] S. Talja and J. M. Nyce. The problem with problematic situations: Differences between practices, tasks, and situations as units of analysis. *Library & Information Science Research*, 37(1):61–67, 2015.
[30] R. S. Taylor. *Value-added processes in information systems*. Greenwood Publishing Group, 1986.
[31] P. Vakkari. Task-based information searching. *Annual review of information science and technology*, 37(1):413–464, 2003.
[32] E. Wenger. *Communities of practice: Learning, meaning, and identity*. Cambridge university press, 1998.
[33] R. W. White, S. T. Dumais, and J. Teevan. Characterizing the influence of domain expertise on web search behavior. In *Proceedings of the second ACM international conference on web search and data mining*, pages 132–141. ACM, 2009.
[34] B. M. Wildemuth. The effects of domain knowledge on search tactic formulation. *Journal of the Association for Information Science and Technology*, 55(3):246–258, 2004.
[35] E. Zerubavel. Horizons: on the sociomental foundations of relevance. *Social Research*, pages 397–413, 1993.
[36] E. Zerubavel. *Social mindscapes: An invitation to cognitive sociology*. Harvard University Press, 1997.
[37] E. Zerubavel. *Hidden in plain sight: The social structure of irrelevance*. Oxford University Press, 2015.

Redesigning a Document Viewer for Legal Documents

Adam Roegiest
Kira Systems
adam.roegiest@kirasystems.com

Winter Wei
Kira Systems
winter@kirasystems.com

ABSTRACT

In Mergers and Acquisition due diligence, lawyers are tasked with analyzing a collection of contracts and determine the level of risk that comes from a merger or acquisition. This process has historically been manual and resulted in only a small fraction of the collection being examined. This paper reports on the user-focused redesign of our document viewer that is used by clients to review documents and train machine learning algorithms to find pertinent information from these contracts.

We present an overview of the due diligence task and the user stories, generated through analysis of support tickets, user interviews, and usability testing sessions, that we used to redesign our document viewer to accommodate the variety of workflows that our clients employ. Additionally, we detail the important design decisions made and discuss the implications of our redesign beyond our particular use case.

CCS CONCEPTS

• **Information systems** → **Search interfaces**; *Information extraction*; *Structured text search*; • **Human-centered computing** → *Usability testing*;

KEYWORDS

Due diligence, document viewer, legal retrieval, usability study

ACM Reference Format:
Adam Roegiest and Winter Wei. 2018. Redesigning a Document Viewer for Legal Documents. In *CHIIR '18: 2018 Conference on Human Information Interaction & Retrieval, March 11–15, 2018, New Brunswick, NJ, USA*. ACM, New York, NY, USA, 4 pages. https://doi.org/10.1145/3176349.3176873

1 INTRODUCTION

In the due diligence process of Mergers and Acquisitions, lawyers are tasked with extracting and analyzing content from contracts (e.g., start date, value, what happens when one party is bought) to determine any potential risks that would result from a merger or acquisition. Due to the manual effort historically involved, a very small sample of the contracts is analyzed, and senior lawyers then extrapolate to the entire collection. There have been several cases where a failure in due diligence had substantial fiscal repercussions [1]. One of the most costly was HP's acquisition of Autonomy for $10B USD and the subsequent $8.8B loss reported by HP, which is largely believed to result from poor due diligence on HP's part regarding Autonomy's worth.

Accordingly, there is continued growth [2] of software companies aiming to target the due diligence use case with the goal of improving the review process (i.e., increasing efficiency and effectiveness). A crucial component to any such system is a full-featured document viewer, which allows users to view contracts, highlight relevant text, and summarize text that the system has identified as important to their use case.

In this paper, we describe the design and evolution of our company's document viewer. The original document viewer was based on the past experiences of company employees (former lawyers) and was largely created in an ad hoc manner. This resulted in the original document viewer having serious flaws: including, summary panels of extracted information overlaying the document; inability to zoom; hard to distinguish overlapping highlights; lack of contextual document navigation (i.e., navigation only took folder structure into account).

Through a combination of direct customer feedback, user interviews, and usability testing with clients, we developed a series of personas, each having different goals when using the document viewer. Using these personas, we developed a set of job stories (i.e., particular tasks to be completed) which formed the basis of our design and development process. With all this in mind, we present the evolution of our document viewer and the rationale behind these decisions. The result is, to the best of the our knowledge, one of the first attempts to qualitatively design an interface for document review in legal information retrieval. Indeed, we believe that the iterative design process used herein would benefit the design of UI and UX for other legal retrieval tasks.

In the following section, we place our work in context and distinguish the due diligence task from related legal retrieval tasks. Section 3 describes the old document viewer and the user stories, generated through various interactions with clients, that were the motivation behind the redesign. We then (Section 4) provide a description of the new document viewer and how it was designed and developed to meet these user needs. Section 5 discusses user feedback to the new document viewer, collected during and after the design process. We also provide a new set of user stories based on our goal of continual improvement to the document viewer. We conclude (Section 6) with a discussion of this work in the context of legal retrieval and the takeaways from this work.

---

[1]See https://www.firmex.com/thedealroom/top-10-due-diligence-disasters/. Accessed October 1, 2017.
[2]See https://www.artificiallawyer.com/2017/09/15/legal-ai-co-s-seal-kira-leverton-show-buoyant-growth. Accessed October 1, 2017.

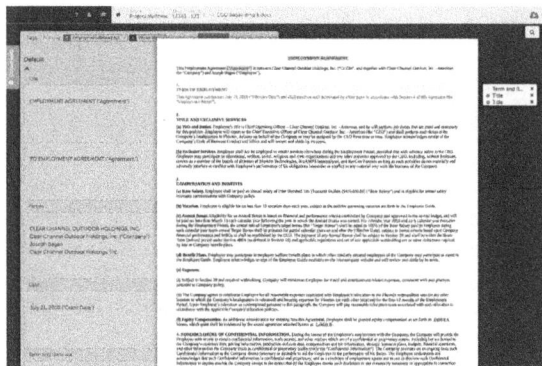

(a) The document pane displays an image representation of each page in the document and overlays any highlights that have been made on top of the corresponding text.

(b) The document navigation tab allows users to move from the current document to any document within the same directory. Navigation through other contexts (e.g., search results) required using browser history.

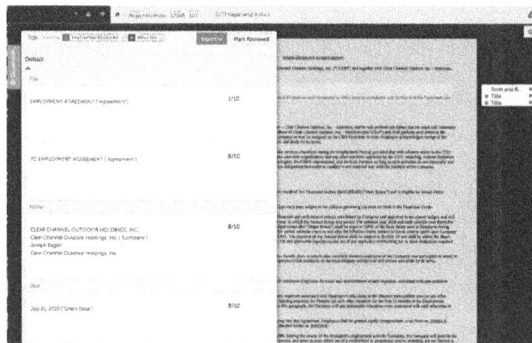

(c) The annotation summary pane displays highlighted text from the document grouped by topic with "jump to page" functionality.

Figure 1: Examples of the three panes of the original document viewer: the document pane, the summary (of annotations) pane, and the document navigation tab.

2 BACKGROUND

To the best of our knowledge, there has been little scientific research done on the due diligence problem; most published work is primarily for lawyers and other practitioners in legal journals [3, 7, 8]. This is in contrast to the large amount of work that has gone into the related field of electronic discovery from the scientific and legal communities (c.f., [2, 6]). While it is not clear why this is the case, we might speculate that the amount of data required to be processed and the stakes in failing to do it well, have traditionally been much higher in electronic discovery. More concretely, electronic discovery seeks to find all relevant material relating to a particular topic in hopes of finding a "smoking gun"; whereas, due diligence seeks to analyze risk inherit in a particular merger or acquisition through the extraction of relevant information from contracts, bills, etc. Furthermore, electronic discovery is usually a regulated process but due diligence is limited primarily by the effort that lawyers and their clients want to invest in the process.

Electronic discovery has had much more exposure in the scientific community but much of this discusses the trade-offs between manual versus technology-assisted review, the efficacy of

algorithms, or ways to measure performance [2, 4, 10]. Very little research has focused on what makes a good review platform and the human factors involved. While there has been work on sense-making in electronic discovery [1, 5, 9], which deals with understanding the document collection (e.g., through clustering or email threading), there has been little work done in tying this to a review workflow or platform.

Accordingly, the work we present herein is not only applicable to our particular use case but may help inform others in designing systems for related legal high-recall tasks that involve a component of document review. In particular, it would be an interesting study to see how much of the user interface presented here would be applicable to an electronic discovery use case.

3 OLD DOCUMENT VIEWER AND USER STORIES

Our original document viewer (Figure 1) had three constituent components: (a) a document pane that allowed users to read the documents themselves and annotate particular portions of text as being relevant to a particular need; (b) a summary pane that allowed users to view manually and automatically generated annotations;

and, (c) a document listing tab that allowed users to navigate from one document to the next using a directory structure. As seen above, these three components overlay each other in undesirable ways, creating numerous usability issues.

Additionally, it is worth noting that the document pane displayed a rendered image (to promote supporting a wide variety of file formats during ingestion) and overlaid transparent HTML on top of the image's text to facilitate highlighting and extraction. This approach, while effective, suffered from a serious flaw in that documents could not be zoomed or rotated since similar actions could not be performed on the HTML elements. While not a deal-breaker, such inability meant that users occasionally had to struggle when viewing poor quality scans of documents.

The old document viewer was filled with other usability issues including: the inability to toggle the active highlight when several overlapped, the inability to navigate through searched documents without returning to the search, a reliance on the browser's built-in search to look for keywords in a document, and difficulty in getting the summary and document panes to align correctly in the browser or swap between them.

Based upon customer feedback (e.g., support tickets, interviews, and usability sessions) on the original document viewer, we formulated the following user stories for how customers want to use our application in various scenarios:

- When I review the documents assigned to me, I want to go through the list without disruption, so I can keep in the flow.
- When I am reviewing documents, I want to read the document instantly once the document viewer is opened, so I can finish my job faster.
- When I read the documents that contains landscape and portrait pages, I want to zoom in to the document or rotate the pages, so I can read the text easily.
- When I read a document, I want to search by keywords as they are usually a good indication of where the important clauses are, so I can read and review them.
- When I review the summary, I want to only review the ones I care about so I can save time.

4 NEW DOCUMENT VIEWER

As several of our user stories were impeded by technical constraints in the old document viewer, the new document viewer was built from scratch. This allowed us to take completely different technical approaches to address these issues rather than trying to retrofit existing components. This also included changing how the document viewer fit users' mental model. For example, in opening a document, instead of being redirected to a new page, the document opens on top of the current page and its context, and the user can "exit" the document by closing it (i.e., the 'X' in Figure 2). When this feature was tested, experienced users often took a few seconds to realize they could utilize this functionality, while new users immediately took advantage of the new functionality.

Figure 2 depicts our new document viewer which maintains the document and summary panes from the original document viewer. However, they no longer overlap and are able to have their screen share adjusted or be collapsed. The choice to have an adjustable size for the two panes is relatively straightforward in that it allows users to customize the document viewer to their particular workflow (e.g., annotating documents versus reviewing annotations). Swapping the order of the panes was done to align more with how users have typically described using the viewer (i.e., document first) and with other web applications where comments/notes appear on the right-hand side (e.g., Google Docs). It is worth noting that the navigation tab was removed and replaced with navigation arrows (top right) which are modally dependent (e.g., using a search context) and fit more closely to the previous/next document workflow.

One of the main benefits of the new document viewer is that the user is able to zoom in on the document and still annotate text [3]. This was accomplished by utilizing the virtual DOM present in modern Web frameworks to tag portions of the image with associated metadata (e.g., bounding boxes for words) which facilitates the annotation under zoom with relatively simple maths.

Features like text annotation under zoom required several data migrations to ensure all necessary metadata was available in the virtual DOM. On the other hand, features such as overlapping highlights, were improved simply through better colour selection, improved CSS usage, and allowing the desired highlight to be brought to the forefront.

We followed an iterative design and development process to help determine what wasn't working for users and refine what was. To this end, we conducted 6 user testing sessions with a combination of in-house annotators, our support team (who have a strong understanding of user pain points), and mid-level associates during different stages of development.

5 RESPONSE TO THE REDESIGN

Generally, the reception to the new document viewer has been highly positive. One of the best examples of this occurred during the phased roll-out: a client firm had the new document viewer turned on a week prematurely, requested it to be turned off, then, three hours later, asked to have it turned back on due to internal user requests for it.

One of the glaring flaws that has persisted in measuring improvement to the document viewer, is a lack of instrumentation to determine how users *actually* use the viewer, primarily due to a lack of resources being allocated to the task.

While we lack quantitative feedback from the document viewer itself, we have some idea of the impact of the redesign on our clients and internal support team. Figure 3 depicts the number of support tickets submitted (pre- and post-redesign) since the company's inception. The release of the new document viewer was roughly August 2017, where we see a precipitous drop in document viewer issue tickets. The general downward trend is an indicator to us that many of the long standing issues have been addressed.

Of course, this isn't to say that all of the feedback we've received has been positive. Indeed, the following are some of the issues that users have had with the new document viewer:

- When I read a document that is too small, I want to *precisely* control the granularity of zoom so I can read the document comfortably according to my level of comfort.

---

[3]Rotation issues were solved by ensuring the rotation of the pages was consistent during the ingestion and OCR phase of document processing.

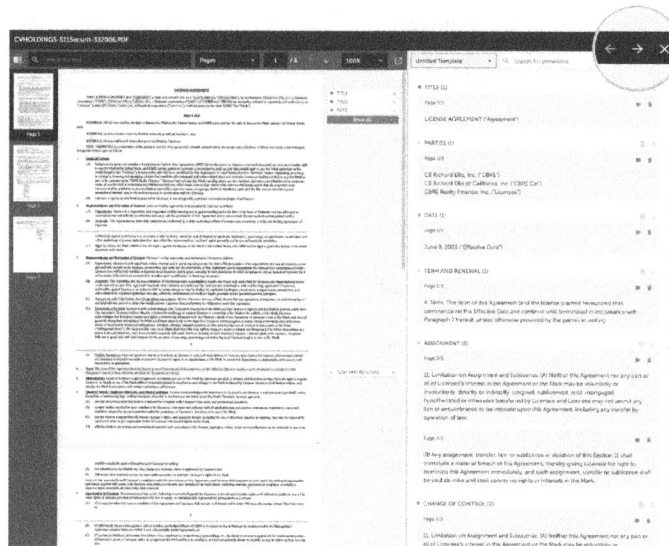

Figure 2: The new document viewer with the document pane on the left, the annotation summary on the right, and the navigation buttons (previous document, next document, and exit document) are magnified on the top-right bar.

- When I organize the summary, I want to re-order the results of certain provisions, so they fit the template I was given.
- When I have to manually add summary results, I want to do that in an intuitive and more discoverable way, so that the process is seamless.

6   DISCUSSION AND CONCLUSION

As part of this redesign it became increasingly obvious to us that when designing the UI and UX for complex workflows that the user is a necessary component throughout the design process. Trying to model the user's mental state when performing their daily tasks and the struggles that arise from conflicting workflows is crucial to making a usable and pleasurable design. While there will always be some trade-offs between focusing on micro- versus macro-interactions, the end goal ought to be an effective user experience.

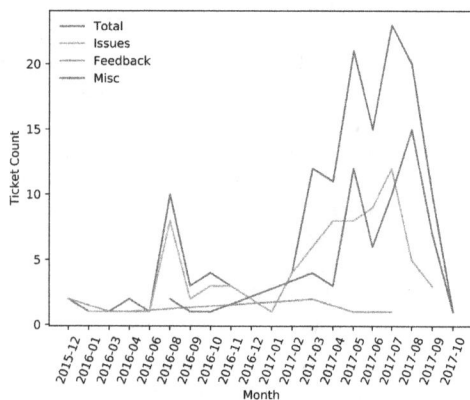

Figure 3: The number of tickets submitting to the support line regarding the document viewer over time as a total number of tickets, identified issues, feedback tickets, and tangential tickets to the document viewer.

While there has been substantial research on user experience in Web search and related tasks, there has been little on complex workflows that encompass legal retrieval and discovery tasks, like electronic discovery and due diligence. Accordingly, there was little to guide us in our initial development and design of the document viewer, but by utilizing user research we have been able to more fully understand and empathize with our users. Ensuring that they get their job done as efficiently and effectively as possible means they're more likely to continue to use our software and speak positively about it. Based upon interactions with our users, we have made great strides towards this but as with any design there is always more to be done.

REFERENCES

[1] S. Attfield and A. Blandford. Discovery-led refinement in e-discovery investigations: sensemaking, cognitive ergonomics and system design. *Artif. Intell. Law*, 18(4), 2010.

[2] G. V. Cormack and M. R. Grossman. Evaluation of Machine-Learning Protocols for Technology-Assisted Review in Electronic Discovery. In *SIGIR 2014*, 2014.

[3] B. Klaber. Artificial Intelligence and Transactional Law: Automated M&A Due Diligence, 2013.

[4] D. W. Oard, J. R. Baron, B. Hedin, D. D. Lewis, and S. Tomlinson. Evaluation of Information Retrieval for E-Discovery. *Artif. Intell. Law*, 18(4), 2010.

[5] M. Sathiyanarayanan and C. Turkay. Challenges and Opportunities in using Analytics Combined with Visualisation Techniques for Finding Anomalies in Digital Communications. In *ICAIL DESI VII Workshop*, 2017.

[6] K. Schieneman et al. The Implications of Rule 26 (g) on the use of Technology-Assisted Review. *Fed. Cts. L. Rev. 239*, 2013.

[7] J. A. Sherer, T. M. Hoffman, and E. E. Ortiz. Merger and Acquisition Due Diligence: A Proposed Framework to Incorporate Data Privacy, Information Security, E-Discovery, and Information Governance into Due Diligence Practices. *Rich. JL & Tech.*, 21, 2015.

[8] J. A. Sherer, T. M. Hoffman, K. M. Wallace, E. E. Ortiz, and T. J. Satnick. Merger and Acquisition Due Diligence Part II-The Devil in the Details. *Rich. JL & Tech.*, 22, 2016.

[9] D. van Dijk, D. Graus, Z. Ren, H. Henseler, and M. de Rijke. Who is Involved? Semantic Search for E-Discovery. In *ICAIL DESI VI Workshop*, 2015.

[10] W. Webber. Re-examining the Effectiveness of Manual Review. In *Proc. SIGIR Information Retrieval for E-Discovery Workshop*, 2011.

Term Relevance Feedback for Contextual Named Entity Retrieval

Sheikh Muhammad Sarwar, John Foley, and James Allan
Center for Intelligent Information Retrieval
College of Information and Computer Sciences
University of Massachusetts Amherst
{smsarwar,jfoley,allan}@cs.umass.edu

ABSTRACT

We address the role of a user in Contextual Named Entity Retrieval (CNER), showing (1) that user identification of important context-bearing terms is superior to automated approaches, and (2) that further gains are possible if the user indicates the relative importance of those terms. CNER is similar in spirit to List Question answering and Entity disambiguation. However, the main focus of CNER is to obtain user feedback for constructing a profile for a class of entities on the fly and use that to retrieve entities from free text. Given a sentence, and an entity selected from that sentence, CNER aims to retrieve sentences that have entities similar to query entity. This paper explores obtaining term relevance feedback and importance weighting from humans in order to improve a CNER system. We report our findings based on the efforts of IR researchers as well as crowdsourced workers.

ACM Reference Format:

Sheikh Muhammad Sarwar, John Foley, and James Allan. 2018. Term Relevance Feedback for Contextual Named Entity Retrieval. In *Proceedings of 2018 Conference on Human Information Interaction & Retrieval (CHIIR '18)*. ACM, New York, NY, USA, 4 pages. https://doi.org/10.1145/3176349.3176886

1 INTRODUCTION

Entity list retrieval is an important and well motivated problem that has been addressed for more than a decade by the IR community [1, 3–5, 13]. This problem assumes that a user has a well-defined information need that can be expressed using a set of keywords for submitting to an entity ranking system. Some variations allow the user to provide an example entity along with its textual description. The ranking system then returns a list of entities ordered by their relevance to the example entity as well as the user description.

We consider a scenario for list entity retrieval where the entity need is formed on-the-fly, for example, when a user finds an interesting entity in a text excerpt. Small touch-screen devices make this situation more likely as at any time a user can only view a small part of a document, perhaps a sentence or a paragraph. That focused region with an entity of user interest provides contextual clues for a system that would tackle the problem of finding related

entities given the example entity. Part of the challenge is that not every token in this short contextual window is important and some of them might hurt the system's performance by driving the entity retrieval system in the wrong direction.

As an example, consider a user who reads a document and comes across the sentence: *Carolyn and her twin sisters, Lauren and Lisa, were raised by their mother Ann Freeman, a teacher and administrator in the New York public schools, and their stepfather, orthopedic surgeon Richard Freeman.* [1] Assume that the user wants to know the name of all the family members of Carolyn Bessette, and she pointed out *Ann Freeman* as an example of the target entity class. The context terms related to family members in the given sentence are **sisters**, **mother**, and **stepfather**, and the terms from the entities of interest are **Lauren**, **Lisa**, **Ann**, **Freeman**, and **Richard**. Other terms – such as **teacher** or **surgeon** – might direct the search in a completely different direction; that is, away from family members by focusing on professions rather than family relationships.

This work addresses the above problem, and proposes context term selection using two approaches: (1) top-k keyword extraction from a sentence based on keyword and example entity similarity, and (2) weighted term relevance feedback (TRF) from users. We focus on the latter and use the former automated process as a baseline as we explore the following research questions:

RQ1. *Does a user's term-level relevance feedback provide improved results for the CNER task in comparison to fully automated baselines?*

RQ2. *Is the user feedback more effective for CNER if the user can indicate which of the terms is more important?*

Given a starting sentence and an identified entity, the output of CNER is a ranked list of sentences that are most likely to contain an instance of the desired entity class (as inferred from the query sentence). We impose a novelty requirement, also, such that a sentence is only relevant if it includes at least one relevant entity that has not already been seen in the ranked list.

We show that user feedback provides a 10.7% improvement in mAP over strong baselines and that there is an improvement of 14.9% if the user can provide weights on the selected terms.

2 RELATED WORK

CNER is broadly similar to tasks such as List QA, Entity Ranking, and list completion [1, 3–5, 13]. All of these tasks rely heavily upon external sources of information like Knowledge Bases (KB) to locate an entity of interest and then retrieve similar types of entities based on the contextual evidence present in a question or search query.

---

[1] Sentence taken from TREC List QA collection that we have used as dataset.

CNER differs from these tasks as it is focused on entities that are not popular enough to be found in a KB, requiring techniques based solely on the original source text. Moreover, typical solutions to the broad set of tasks do not allow for user interactivity, a specific goal for CNER.

There have been numerous attempts to use term feedback to improve retrieval tasks, but it can be quite a challenge to do so. Even though users desire to provide and control the set of terms for query expansion, in most cases it does not lead to better performance [8, 10, 11]. Kelly et al. showed that if a sentence is provided as an example use of an expansion term, users can slightly improve the precision of the retrieval system in comparison with a strong Pseudo Relevance Feedback (PRF) baseline [7]. Studies suggest that even if the improvement is not great, the availability of interactive TRF is considered a positive aspect of a system by users [2, 10]. We are inspired from the application of TRF on ad-hoc IR, and incorporated it as a context refinement technique for CNER.

Our problem is closely related to entity disambiguation that primarily aims to link an entity to a KB given a document about that entity [12]. Entity disambiguation has a different goal and we also assume that knowledge about a target entity might not be available in a structured form. Nevertheless, our challenge of finding related sentences could be useful for entity disambiguation.

3 METHODOLOGY

We discuss our method of obtaining term relevance feedback from a user for formulating a CNER query, and how we use those terms to obtain a better representation of the query.

3.1 Term Relevance Feedback Acquisition

3.1.1 Collection. We use a pool of queries from the TREC 2005 and 2006 List Question Answering (QA) datasets, where relevant entities relevant to each of the list questions are annotated by TREC assessors in several relevant documents. We combine those documents as well as other non-relevant documents from the dataset and break them into sentences. For each list question we then select a sentence that contains at least one entity relevant for that question. The selected sentence and entity becomes a CNER query seeking to find the remaining sentences that contain other relevant entities. Figure 1 shows two sample list questions and corresponding sentences that we selected from our dataset.

We selected 20 queries for which there are nine relevant entities (excluding the query entity) on an average and all sentences that contain those entities. We created two subsets of ten sentence queries and an interface that presents 10 queries to the user one by one (randomized for each user). The interface allows the user to select terms for each query-sentence pair (as described below). We chose 10 queries for a single session because we measured that on an average it takes around 12 minutes for a user to annotate 10 queries. We did this to ensure that users would not be overwhelmed by the length of the task, inspired by the 15 minute attention span limit often cited in education [14].

3.1.2 Interface for Query Generation. Each user was asked to look at a sentence containing an entity and then select the words within that sentence that seemed most likely to be useful as query words if someone wanted to find other examples of entities of the

"Who testified in defense of Susan McDougal?"
→ "Susan McDougal 's lawyer says she plans to attend the opening of Independent Counsel Kenneth Starr's latest case, the trial of a Virginia woman who provided helpful testimony for Mrs. McDougal a month ago."
"Programs sponsored by the Lions Club [International]"
→ "Lions Club International, the world's largest service club organization, plans to help more cataract sufferers in China as an example of blindness prevention for the rest of the world, according to Tam Wing Kun, chairman of the Sight First China Action (SFCA) project."

Figure 1: Example of List Question, and a corresponding sentence for annotation are presented below.

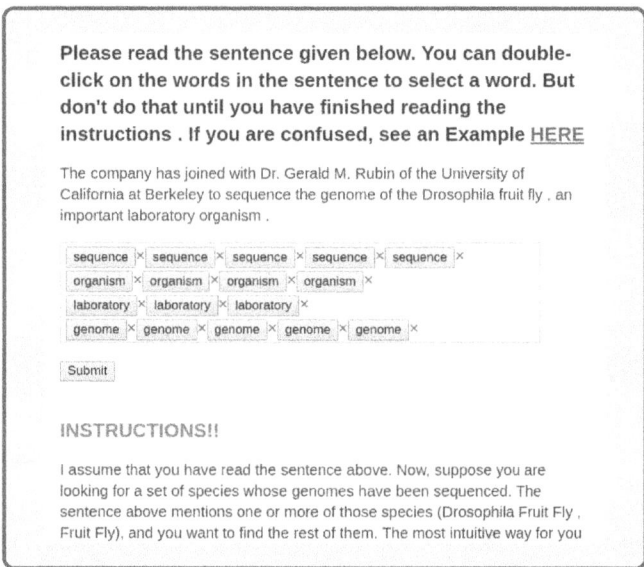

Figure 2: Interface for Obtaining Contextual Keywords

same type. The user was also asked to indicate relative importance of words by selecting the best words more often.

Figure 2 shows a screen-shot of the interface that we used to obtain this term relevance feedback. The interface does not return any search result, but it facilitates users' providing terms and their importance by double-clicking them. In the Figure, clicked words are shown in small grey boxes. More important words were clicked more often and appear multiple times. After the annotation process we processed the collected queries and all the baselines offline.

3.1.3 Subjects. We collected context word annotations for 20 queries. For each query we took annotation from six Mechanical Turk users from the United States and three lab researchers familiar with Information Retrieval and thus likely to be better at selecting terms and judging their relative importance.

3.2 Retrieval Method

Vocabulary mismatch is a problem that particularly affects short-text retrieval and semantic features are an effective way to alleviate this problem. Our retrieval task also demands the use of semantic similarity because we do not seek to find entities that appear exactly as described in the query sentence. We combine the effectiveness of both syntactic and semantic matching for computing sentence similarity. We use BM25 for keyword matching and Sentence Embedding (SE) [15] to compute semantic similarity. We assume that word matching is more important for the user selected words and semantic similarity is important for matching similar entities, and combine the benefits of both to create an effective model.

We capture semantic level matching between a sentence pair to retrieve and score the top k sentences against the query sentence. We use the average of word embedding to obtain sentence embedding for the query and candidate sentences. Word embedding methods learn a low-dimensional vector representation of words from a large, unstructured text corpus; we use the skip-gram model proposed by Mikolov et al. [9] to generate representations for words. Finally, we use cosine similarity to compute similarity between a query and a candidate sentence. Our approach is inspired by Wieting et al. [15], who showed that a simple averaging over the embedding of the words in a sentence provides an effective representation for that sentence and that representation is particularly helpful for sentence similarity task.

For all our ranking techniques, we use the Stanford Named Entity Recognizer [6] to reject candidate sentences that do not contain entities of the appropriate type. While this may introduce false-negatives, it greatly increases precision of our system, and allows our other techniques to focus on ranking and increasing recall.

3.3 Query Expansion (QE)

In order to obtain a broader and generalized representation of query sentence, we use Pseudo Relevance Feedback (PRF) for query expansion at the sentence level. We use BM25 to retrieve PRF sentences given the query sentence and compute the average over the embedding of those sentences to obtain a more robust representation of the query.

3.4 PRF with User Feedback

We make use of the context words selected by user for finding PRF sentences with BM25 technique. We expect that a keyword-based search technique would find sentences focusing on user selected terms. Suppose, our original query sentence Q_o contains a list of n terms, and user u has constructed a list, CW from Q_o, of k words, where each word appears there one or more times. Now, in order to get an expanded query Q_e, we simply concatenate all the terms in CW with Q_o. The goal of this process is to assign term importance in a query by repeating the term multiple times. Even though it is not a sophisticated method of incorporating user-provided term weights, it works well in practice. We search the sentence corpus with Q_e and use the top k retrieved sentences, S_{topk} for obtaining a better representation for Q_o. Finally, we compute the average of the sentence embeddings from the sentences in set $Q_f = \{Q_o \cup S_{topk}\}$, perform SE based search using Q_f and re-rank them using the method described in 3.2.

4 EXPERIMENTAL RESULTS

4.1 Evaluation Metrics and Relevance

We use novelty versions of recall and precision, standard measures modified so that only the first instance of a target entity is considered relevant. We use recall@k to measure the number of relevant (and unique) entities observed in the top k sentences and we use precision@k to measure the proportion of sentences in the top k that contain relevant (and unique) entities. We stress that the relevance of a sentence is determined by two properties: containing a relevant entity *and* being unique in the ranked list so far. We also report MAP@1000 and recall@1000, measures that are important because when we want to perform two-stage retrieval and ranking, retrieving most of the entities in the top 1000 sentences becomes crucial.

4.2 Baseline Methods

We compare the effectiveness of user feedback against three non-interactive baselines.

- **SE** is the Sentence Embedding (SE) based search described in Section 3.2 that assumes no information regarding term importance.
- **SE + PRF** is similar to the approach described in Section 3.4 that uses BM25 to retrieve the top k sentences using the sentence query and then combines those to obtain an expanded query that is used with SE.
- **SE + PRF + CW + Sim (Entity, Token)** is similar to the process of integrating user-selected context words into the query as mentioned in Section 3.4. However, the process of obtaining context word is not based on any human input. We use this baseline to check how better human input is compared to an automatic process that can generate context words. This method computes the similarity of each word in the query sentence with the query entity. Then it uses the five most similar words for performing PRF. Similarity between a word and query entity is computed using the similarity of their embedding. An entity embedding is constructed by the average of the embedding of the words in it.

4.3 Result Discussion

Table 1 summarizes the average performance of term relevance feedback for CNER across the queries that have been annotated by lab and Mechanical Turk participants. Across all forms of feedback, the lab participants created more effective queries than the crowd-source workers: this is reasonable as the lab participants are likely to be more expert searchers.

Overall, term feedback was helpful (10.7% improvement in mAP), and weighted term feedback was even more helpful (14.9% improvement in mAP). The means that our two research questions are both answered positively: user feedback provides improved results for CNER, and allowing users to specify an ordering or weighting on terms is helpful.

In addition, we analyze the impact of adding fewer keywords (and therefore minimizing user involvement). For each of the queries, we selected the top-$k = 1 \ldots 5$ terms based on the weights provided by the users, added them to the original query (with weights). Performance is presented in Figure 3 in terms of Precision@5, Recall@5 and mAP@1000. Although there is some noise, particularly in the

Table 1: Average performance of various methods. Measures are listed in the first row, with high-precision measures listed first. mAP and R are cut-off at depth 1000. The first section of the table presents baselines, then weighted feedback and finally unweighted feedback. The percentage improvement is shown over the Sentence Embedding (SE) baseline.

R@5	R@10	P@5	P@10	mAP	R	Method	Source of Context Words	Weighted?
0.145	0.234	0.180	0.180	0.188	0.891	SE	None	No
0.123	0.183	0.160	0.130	0.153	0.884	SE + PRF	None	No
0.147	0.177	0.200	0.150	0.162	0.865	SE + PRF + CW	Sim (Entity, Word)	No
0.183 (+26.3%)	0.244 (+4.3%)	0.231 (+28.4%)	0.184 (+2.3%)	0.216 (+14.9%)	0.910 (+2.2%)	SE + PRF + CW	Mturk + Lab Participants	Yes
0.204 (+40.7%)	0.267 (+14.2%)	0.237 (31.7%)	0.196 (+8.9%)	0.232 (+23.5%)	0.921 (+3.4%)	SE + PRF + CW	Lab Participants	Yes
0.171 (+18%)	0.229 (-2.2%)	0.222 (+23.4%)	0.176 (-2.3%)	0.205 (+9.1%)	0.900 (+1.1%)	SE + PRF + CW	Mturk Participants	Yes
0.175 (+20.7%)	0.234 (+0.0 %)	0.226 (+25.6%)	0.179 (-0.6%)	0.208 (+10.7%)	0.907 (+1.1%)	SE + PRF + CW	Mturk + Lab Participants	No
0.186 (+28.3%)	0.255 (+9.0%)	0.234 (+30%)	0.194 (+7.8%)	0.220 (+17.1%)	0.920 (+3.3%)	SE + PRF + CW	Lab Participants	No
0.166 (+14.5%)	0.219 (-6.5%)	0.217 (+20.6%)	0.168 (-6.7%)	0.199 (+5.9%)	0.897 (+0.7 %)	SE + PRF + CW	Mturk Participants	No

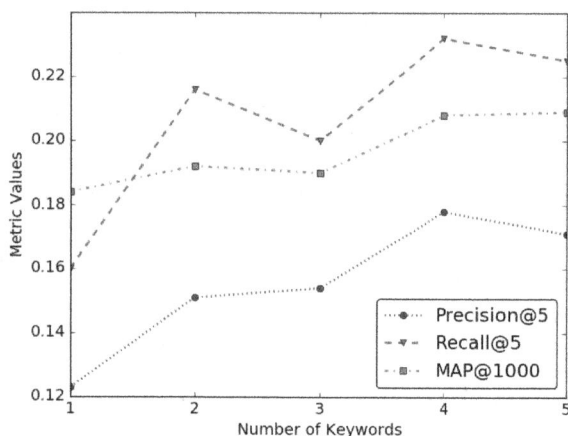

Figure 3: Performance Sensitivity with Keywords Addition

recall of the solution, it is clear that a handful of keywords can be effective (although it does depend on the user and the quality of the terms selected), but more terms do appear to be better.

5 CONCLUSION

We adopt a term relevance feedback technique for list query construction from a sentence and show its effectiveness in entity retrieval. We started this work with two research questions and answered them both affirmatively. We showed that (RQ1) users *can* select better query terms than automatic methods, and that (RQ2) it *is* helpful for the user to identify which terms are best. Our interface for collecting this information was rudimentary and we did not explore alternatives for this study. Future work will look at how an interface can best support a user in providing that information.

ACKNOWLEDGEMENT

This work was supported in part by the Center for Intelligent Information Retrieval and in part by NSF grant #IIS-1617408. Any opinions, findings and conclusions or recommendations expressed in this material are those of the authors and do not necessarily reflect those of the sponsors.

REFERENCES

[1] Krisztian Balog, Pavel Serdyukov, and Arjen P de Vries. 2010. *Overview of the TREC 2010 entity track*. Technical Report. DTIC Document.
[2] N. J. Belkin, C. Cool, D. Kelly, S.-J. Lin, S. Y. Park, J. Perez-Carballo, and C. Sikora. 2001. Iterative Exploration, Design and Evaluation of Support for Query Reformulation in Interactive Information Retrieval. *Inf. Process. Manage.* (2001).
[3] Bhavana Bharat Dalvi, Jamie Callan, and William W. Cohen. Entity List Completion Using Set Expansion Techniques. In *TREC'10*.
[4] Hoa Trang Dang, Jimmy Lin, and Diane Kelly. Overview of the TREC 2006 Question Answering Track. In *TREC'06*.
[5] Gianluca Demartini, Tereza Iofciu, and Arjen P. De Vries. Overview of the INEX 2009 Entity Ranking Track. In *INEX'09*.
[6] Jenny Rose Finkel, Trond Grenager, and Christopher Manning. Incorporating Non-local Information into Information Extraction Systems by Gibbs Sampling. In *ACL'05*.
[7] Diane Kelly and Xin Fu. Elicitation of Term Relevance Feedback: An Investigation of Term Source and Context. In *SIGIR'06*.
[8] Jürgen Koenemann and Nicholas J. Belkin. A Case for Interaction: A Study of Interactive Information Retrieval Behavior and Effectiveness. In *CHI'96*.
[9] Tomas Mikolov, Ilya Sutskever, Kai Chen, Greg Corrado, and Jeffrey Dean. Distributed Representations of Words and Phrases and Their Compositionality. In *NIPS'13*.
[10] Yael Nemeth, Bracha Shapira, and Meirav Taeib-Maimon. Evaluation of the Real and Perceived Value of Automatic and Interactive Query Expansion. In *SIGIR'04*.
[11] Ian Ruthven. Re-examining the Potential Effectiveness of Interactive Query Expansion. In *SIGIR'03*.
[12] Yaming Sun, Lei Lin, Duyu Tang, Nan Yang, Zhenzhou Ji, and Xiaolong Wang. Modeling Mention, Context and Entity with Neural Networks for Entity Disambiguation. In *IJCAI'15*.
[13] Ellen M Voorhees and Hoa Trang Dang. Overview of the TREC 2005 Question Answering Track. In *TREC'05*.
[14] P.C. Wankat. 2002. *The Effective, Efficient Professor: Teaching, Scholarship, and Service*. Allyn and Bacon.
[15] John Wieting, Mohit Bansal, Kevin Gimpel, and Karen Livescu. Towards Universal Paraphrastic Sentence Embeddings. In *ICLR'16*.

Column Major Pattern: How Users Process Spatially Fixed Items on Large, Tiled Displays

Anton Sigitov
Bonn-Rhein-Sieg Univ. of Applied Sciences
Sankt Augustin, Germany
anton.sigitov@h-brs.de

Oliver Staadt
University of Rostock
Rostock, Germany
oliver.staadt@uni-rostock.de

André Hinkenjann
Bonn-Rhein-Sieg Univ. of Applied Sciences
Sankt Augustin, Germany
andre.hinkenjann@h-brs.de

Ernst Kruijff
Bonn-Rhein-Sieg Univ. of Applied Sciences
Sankt Augustin, Germany
ernst.kruijff@h-brs.de

ABSTRACT

Large, high-resolution displays demonstrated their effectiveness in lab settings for cognitively demanding tasks in single user and collaborative scenarios. The effectiveness is mostly reached through inherent displays' properties - large display real estate and high resolution - that allow for visualization of complex datasets, and support of group work and embodied interaction. To raise users' efficiency, however, more sophisticated user support in the form of advanced user interfaces might be needed. For that we need profound understanding of how large, tiled displays impact users work and behavior. We need to extract behavioral patterns for different tasks and data types. This paper reports on study results of how users, while working collaboratively, process spatially fixed items on large, tiled displays. The results revealed a recurrent pattern showing that users prefer to process documents column wise rather than row wise or erratic.

CCS CONCEPTS

• **Human-centered computing** → **User studies**; **Empirical studies in HCI**;

KEYWORDS

Fixed spatial data; Information interaction; Tiled displays; Co-located work; User Study

ACM Reference Format:
Anton Sigitov, Oliver Staadt, André Hinkenjann, and Ernst Kruijff. 2018. Column Major Pattern: How Users Process Spatially Fixed Items on Large, Tiled Displays. In *CHIIR '18: 2018 Conference on Human Information Interaction & Retrieval, March 11–15, 2018, New Brunswick, NJ, USA*. ACM, New York, NY, USA, 4 pages. https://doi.org/10.1145/3176349.3176870

1 INTRODUCTION

Large display environments like high-resolution, tiled displays are highly suitable for co-located collaboration. The enlarged display real estate provides enough room to accommodate synchronous activities of multiple users. While approaching complex tasks, users can fluidly adjust the tightness of collaboration through allocation, shifting, merging, and splitting of physical and virtual workspace areas. The vast number of pixels allows for visualization of complex datasets making it possible to display high-resolution details in the context of an overview. Promoting embodied interaction by means of physical navigation and gestures, the displays enable (a) establishment and maintenance of correspondences between users' spatial position/orientation and visualized data elements, (b) the use of virtual and physical landmarks for objects finding, as well as (c) increasing of workspace awareness for better work coordination [1, 8]. Finally, systems incorporating large displays often implement a whiteboard or tabletop metaphor with novel interaction techniques and devices to resemble well-known collaboration principles used in real-life communication [6, 12].

Yet, datasets continue to grow in all application domains making analysis and sense making tasks even more complex, while displays' size and pixel density reach the limits of humans' visual acuity. This raises the need for new approaches of user support. One possibility to ensure such support is to improve user interfaces. For instance, intelligent user interfaces [10] driven by an artificial intelligence could be utilized. These interfaces will understand user activities in the context of the task and predict users' intentions. Based on the prediction, the system can pre-calculate complex visualizations, load necessary data, or pre-calculate possible next steps of the user and execute them beforehand. To build better interfaces for large, tiled displays, however, we need to acquire understanding of how such displays and their properties (e.g. display size, bezels, curvature, etc.) affect users' work, users' behavior, and user-information interaction.

In our study, we observed users working collaboratively on fixed-position data in front of a large, tiled display. Among other findings, we detected a virtual navigation pattern of how users process spatially fixed items. The analysis revealed that users navigated significantly more often column wise in comparison to row wise or erratic navigation. We believe this insight might help software engineers to implement better intelligent interfaces.

2 RELATED WORK

In this section we provide a brief overview of related studies that investigated effects of large, tiled displays on users' effectiveness, efficiency, and behavior.

Ball et. al [3] investigated what effect different display sizes have on users' behavior and task performance. They found that increased display size caused increase in physical navigation and better performance time, thus having impact on users' behavior.

Andrews et. al [1] compared how users conduct a sense making task in front of large, tiled displays and in front of a common desktop display. They observed that users made extensive use of space for management of documents and applications.

Liu et. al [9] investigated what effects display size and navigation type have on a classification task. They compared physical navigation in front of a large display with virtual navigation on a common desktop display. The study revealed that desktop displays are more suitable for easy tasks, while large, high-resolution displays is significantly more efficient for difficult tasks.

Bi et. al [4] investigated effects of tiled display interior bezels on user performance and behavior by visual search, straight-tunnel steering, and target selection tasks. Three types of large displays were simulated and compared with each other: 1x1 - display with no interior tiles; 2x2 - large, tiled display consisting of four 40" display units; 3x3 - large, tiled display consisting of nine 26" display units. They found that interior bezels did not have impact on visual search, and target selection performance. Both tasks utilized fixed-position items. On the other hand, interior bezels hindered straight-tunnel steering performance and affected steering behavior. Moreover, they observed that users tend to apply a grid-by-grid search strategy, as an entire surface was divided into grids.

Wallace et. al [15] investigated how bezels impact magnitude judgement, an important aspect of perception especially for applications with spatially fixed data. They detected an increase in judgement error for conditions where bezels were wider that 0.5 cm. In a subsequent study, Wallace et. al [14] investigated how the presence and width of interior bezels impacts visual search performance across tiled displays. They could not detect significant differences in visual search time, though, they found that participants were more accurate in test conditions where targets were split across a bezel. They hypothesized that this improved performance was ascribed to a change in the user's behavior: the participants performed more accurate two-phase search.

Ball and North [2] observed and analyzed users' actions in front of a high-resolution tiled display. They detected that most users have found bezels inconvenient and irritating. Yet, users tended to use bezels to partition the display into regions with specific semantics and dedicated these regions for certain applications.

There are several other studies that investigated effects of large, high-resolution displays on users' performance at different tasks (e.g. [13, 16]). In our study, however, we were more interested in how users interact with data so we could extract behavioral patterns. Such behavioral patterns might be useful for improving user interfaces that in a trivial case will provide a more thorough arrangement of visual elements, and in an advanced case will be able to predict users' next move.

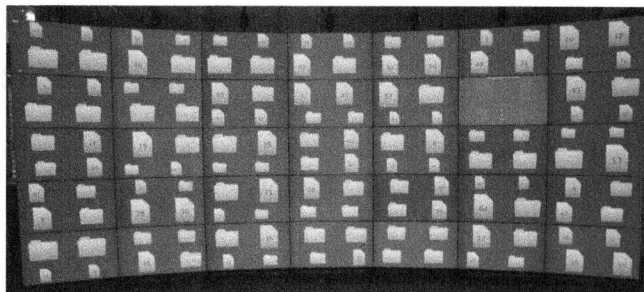

Figure 1: Visual representation of the task: 140 symbols of folders and documents representing unprocessed and processed question. The window in the top right corner shows a question with proposed answers.

3 STUDY

In our study, we investigated users' behavior during a collaborative task in front of a large, high-resolution, tiled display. In this paper, we present results regarding users' behavior in the context of fixed-position items processing. During the study, we gathered quantitative data encompassing participants' position in front of the display (logged every 100 milliseconds), pointer positions (logged on every position change), and task related system events like opening of a question, answering of a question, connection of documents etc.

3.1 Task

The task resembled the facts gathering activity. This activity is an integral part of a typical visual analytics task that involves processing of multiple documents (e.g. [1, 7]). Since our focus was on fixed spatial data, the documents in our task had fixed positions on the display. A real-world use case for such scenario, might be a situation, where analysts must investigate a series of events at specific geographic locations (e.g. investigation of home burglaries).

During the task, the participants had to process 70 documents. For each document the participants had to open it and answer the contained question. In total, 140 fixed-position symbols were shown to the participants: 70 symbols were folder symbols while other 70 symbols were document symbols with IDs (see Figure 1). Symbols varied in size and had fixed positions. Each display unit contained four symbols. The symbols were placed in a way that no bezels occluded any symbol. The folders represented unanswered questions, while documents represented answered questions. To answer a question the participants had to choose from four proposed answers the correct one. Alternatively, they could close the question to answer it later. Once a question was answered correctly its' folder symbol was exchanged for the document symbol with a correct ID, otherwise the document symbol with an incorrect ID was shown. The system did not allow to re-answer questions. No time constraint was set and the task ended as soon as all questions were answered. The system notified participants of task completion through background color change.

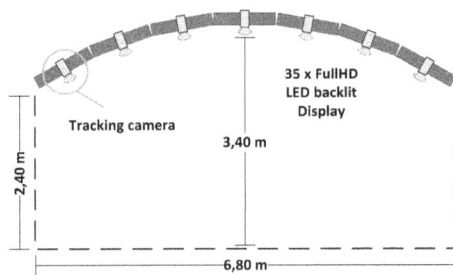

Figure 2: Apparatus: a curved display built of 35 Full HD displays with 7 tracking cameras on it that allow for tracking in front of the display within an area of around 20 square meters.

3.2 Apparatus

The study was performed at a large curved tiled display (henceforth display) comprising 35 LCD displays (henceforth display units) ordered through a seven (column) by five (row) grid. Each column had a relative angle difference of 10 degrees along the Y-axis to adjacent columns, as such creating a slight curvature (see Figure 2). Each display unit had a bezel of less than three millimeters, minimizing the visual rim effect. The displays units were 46" panels with a 1080p resolution, resulting in a total of 72 megapixels.

We used an array of seven infrared cameras (see Figure 2) together with head-worn helmets to track user positions within an area of around 20 square meters directly in front of the display. For interaction purposes, two available smartphones (LG Nexus 5X and Acer Liquid E700) with similar performance characteristics were utilized.

3.3 Participants

The experiment was performed with 12 groups with two randomly assigned participants each, aged between 18 and 39 years (M = 25.08; SD = 4.90), with normal or corrected-to-normal vision. There were 11 female participants and 13 male participants. The participants were paid for taking part in the experiment.

3.4 Results

At the beginning of the task, 2 out of 12 groups decided to work tightly and process the documents mutually. Both groups started on a random display unit, switched, however, soon to the most left/right column, and proceeded the documents in a column by column manner. Figure 3 (bottom) exemplifies the behavior, since the participants opened documents alternately the pointer position maps of individual users complement each other. The remaining 10 out of 12 groups went for divide and conquer strategy, and partitioned the display into the "left" and the "right" regions. Each participant oversaw one region depending on his spatial position relative to the display and to the partner. No distinct boundaries between these two regions were observed. Within the region. Figure 3 (top) depicts the behavior.

While participants proceeded with solving questions, we could recognize a recurrent behavior. Multiple participants tried to solve all questions inside one display unit before moving to the next one.

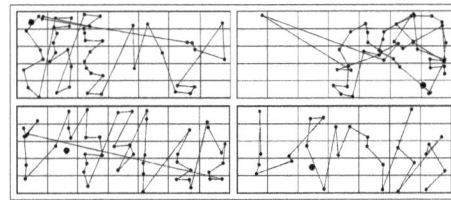

Figure 3: Logged pointers' positions during OpenTask-Events, each line connects two consecutive events: (top) participants A (left) and B (right) working loosely; (bottom) participants A (left) and B (right) working tightly.

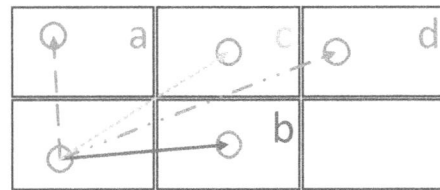

Figure 4: Transition types: (a) direct vertical neighbor; (b) direct horizontal neighbor; (c) indirect neighbor; (d) jump.

Moreover, movement between display units was column oriented. For example, the participant started with the topmost display unit of the leftmost column, solved all the questions inside it, and moved the pointer to the display unit beneath the current one. Working in this manner the column was processed. Next, the participant moved the pointer to the column on the right and continued in the same manner, starting either again from the top or staying at the bottom and working upwards.

However, within the groups that worked loosely the workflow did not last to the end of the task, but rather until participants met in the middle of the display. From there, participants either switched the sides to answer the questions left by their partner, or started to work tightly-coupled and answered remained questions mutually. To compare different strategies for virtual navigation we logged what documents on what display units and at what time were opened. We classified each transition from one display unit to another into four groups (see Figure 4):

- Direct vertical neighbor - the participant transitioned to a display unit direct above or beneath the current display unit.
- Direct horizontal neighbor - the participant transitioned to a display unit direct to the left or direct to the right of the current display unit.
- Indirect neighbor - the participant transitioned to a diagonally adjacent display unit.
- Jump - the participant transitioned to a non-adjacent display unit.

To examine if there are any differences between occurrences of individual virtual navigation strategies, a Friedman test was carried out. The result showed a significant difference, $\chi^2(3)=40.269$, p < 0.001. Dunn-Bonferroni post hoc tests were carried out and revealed significant differences between the types: indirect neighbor and jump (p = 0.026), indirect neighbor and direct vertical neighbor (p

OCCURRENCES OF TRANSITION TYPES

■ Jumps ■ Direct vertical neighbor
■ Direct horizontal neighbor ▫ Indirect Neighbor

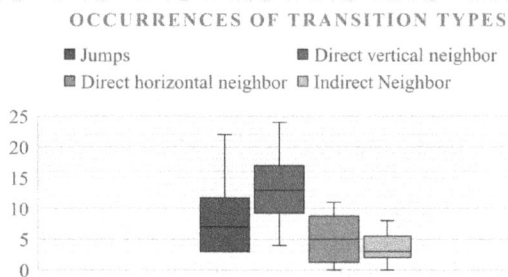

Figure 5: Occurrences of transition types: Y-axis represents number of transitions.

< 0.001), direct horizontal neighbor and direct vertical neighbor (p < 0.001), jump and direct vertical neighbor (p = 0.015). Thus, we can conclude that the participants navigated significantly more often vertically (direct vertical neighbor) in comparison to other patterns. The tendency for direct vertical neighbor pattern is also visible in the box plot diagram (see Figure 5). We also questioned the participants regarding interior bezels. 23 participant stated that the bezels were barely perceived and not distracting.

4 DISCUSSION

We have several explanations for the observed column major pattern. These are based on psychological and physical factors.

One possible explanation could be that visual boundaries of display regions formed by bezels induced feeling of element grouping according to the gestalt principle of common region [11]. Thus, participants would like to finish work in "one" region before moving to the next one. Similar perception of the display area was observed by Andrews et. al [1] and Grudin [5]. Such workflow would also ease tracking of progress for users, since the display could be used as external memory [1] in that case.

Column oriented movements could be motivated by large display size in conjunction with tendency to reduce physical navigation, as row oriented workflow would require more walking. Like with display units, column oriented movement allows easier tracking of progress for participants and reduces search activity. For example, the participant always knows that all questions left to the column she is currently working on are processed. Since the pattern was observed by tightly working groups as well as by loosely working groups, we can exclude the possibility of second user presence affecting the pattern.

Although, the interior bezels were barely perceived by most of the participants, they seemed to have a vigorous effect on the participants' behavior. Thus, interior bezels could be exploited by user interface designers to better support users or direct them in a desired way. For instance, one can group elements of a graph using bezels to highlight their relationship. Moreover, knowing what effect the bezels and display size have on the users' behavior, designers become able to predict users' actions, and as a result build more intelligent interfaces. For instance, the system can pre-load complex data, pre-calculate a complex visualization, or do some other pre-procession for those elements which the user will open next.

ACKNOWLEDGMENTS

The authors thank German Research Foundation (Deutsche Forschungsgemeinschaft,. DFG), which supported the given study by the grant HI 1615/2-1.

REFERENCES

[1] Christopher Andrews, Alex Endert, and Chris North. 2010. Space to think: large high-resolution displays for sensemaking. In *Proceedings of the 28th international conference on Human factors in computing systems - CHI '10*. ACM Press, New York, New York, USA, 55. https://doi.org/10.1145/1753326.1753336

[2] Robert Ball and Chris North. 2005. Analysis of user behavior on high-resolution tiled displays. *Lecture Notes in Computer Science (including subseries Lecture Notes in Artificial Intelligence and Lecture Notes in Bioinformatics)* 3585 LNCS (2005), 350–363. https://doi.org/10.1007/11555261_30

[3] Robert Ball, Chris North, and Doug A. Bowman. 2007. Move to improve: Promoting physical navigation to increase user performance with large displays. In *Proceedings of the SIGCHI conference on Human factors in computing systems - CHI '07*. ACM Press, New York, New York, USA, 191. https://doi.org/10.1145/1240624.1240656

[4] Xiaojun Bi, Seok-Hyung Bae, and Ravin Balakrishnan. 2010. Effects of interior bezels of tiled-monitor large displays on visual search, tunnel steering, and target selection. In *Proceedings of the 28th international conference on Human factors in computing systems - CHI '10*. ACM Press, New York, New York, USA, 65. https://doi.org/10.1145/1753326.1753337

[5] Jonathan Grudin. 2001. Partitioning DigitalWorlds: Focal and Peripheral Awareness in Multiple Monitor Use. In *Proceedings of the SIGCHI conference on Human factors in computing systems - CHI '01*. ACM Press, New York, New York, USA, 458–465. https://doi.org/10.1145/365024.365312

[6] Francois Guimbretière, Maureen Stone, and Terry Winograd. 2001. Fluid Interaction with High-resolution Wall-size Displays. In *Proceedings of the 14th Annual ACM Symposium on User Interface Software and Technology (UIST '01)*. ACM, Orlando, 21–30. https://doi.org/10.1145/502348.502353

[7] P. Isenberg, D. Fisher, S. A. Paul, M. R. Morris, K. Inkpen, and M. Czerwinski. 2012. Co-Located Collaborative Visual Analytics around a Tabletop Display. *IEEE Transactions on Visualization and Computer Graphics* 18, 5 (may 2012), 689–702. https://doi.org/10.1109/TVCG.2011.287

[8] Can Liu, Olivier Chapuis, Michel Beaudouin-Lafon, and Eric Lecolinet. 2017. CoReach: Cooperative Gestures for Data Manipulation onWall-sized Displays. In *Proceedings of the 2017 CHI Conference on Human Factors in Computing Systems - CHI '17*. ACM Press, New York, New York, USA, 6730–6741. https://doi.org/10.1145/3025453.3025594

[9] Can Liu, Olivier Chapuis, Michel Beaudouin-Lafon, Eric Lecolinet, and Wendy E. Mackay. 2014. Effects of display size and navigation type on a classification task. In *Proceedings of the 32nd annual ACM conference on Human factors in computing systems - CHI '14*. ACM Press, New York, New York, USA, 4147–4156. https://doi.org/10.1145/2556288.2557020

[10] Mark Maybury. 1999. Intelligent user interfaces. *Proceedings of the 4th international conference on Intelligent user interfaces - IUI '99* (1999), 3–4. https://doi.org/10.1145/291080.291081

[11] Stephen E Palmer. 1992. Common region: A new principle of perceptual grouping. *Cognitive Psychology* 24, 3 (jul 1992), 436–447. https://doi.org/10.1016/0010-0285(92)90014-S

[12] Stacey D. Scott, Karen D. Grant, and Regan L. Mandryk. 2003. System Guidelines for Co-located, Collaborative Work on a Tabletop Display. In *Proceedings of the eighth conference on European Conference on Computer Supported Cooperative Work - ECSCW'03*. Springer Netherlands, Dordrecht, 159–178. https://doi.org/10.1007/978-94-010-0068-0_9

[13] Desney S. Tan, Darren Gergle, Peter G. Scupelli, and Randy Pausch. 2004. Physically large displays improve path integration in 3D virtual navigation tasks. *Proceedings of the 2004 conference on Human factors in computing systems - CHI '04* 6, 1 (2004), 439–446. https://doi.org/10.1145/985692.985748

[14] James R. Wallace, Daniel Vogel, and Edward Lank. 2014. Effect of Bezel Presence and Width on Visual Search. *Proceedings of The International Symposium on Pervasive Displays (PerDis'14)* (2014), 118–123. https://doi.org/10.1145/2611009.2611019

[15] James R. Wallace, Daniel Vogel, and Edward Lank. 2014. The effect of interior bezel presence and width on magnitude judgement. In *Proceedings of Graphics Interface 2014*. 175–182. http://dl.acm.org/citation.cfm?id=2619648.2619678

[16] Beth Yost, Yonca Haciahmetoglu, and Chris North. 2007. Beyond visual acuity: The Perceptual Scalability of Information Visualizations for Large Displays. In *Proceedings of the SIGCHI conference on Human factors in computing systems - CHI '07*. ACM Press, New York, New York, USA, 101. https://doi.org/10.1145/1240624.1240639

Study of Relevance and Effort across Devices

Manisha Verma
University College London
m.verma@cs.ucl.ac.uk

Emine Yilmaz
University College London,
Alan Turing Institute
e.yilmaz@cs.ucl.ac.uk

Nick Craswell
Microsoft
nickcr@microsoft.com

ABSTRACT

Relevance judgments are essential for designing information retrieval systems. Traditionally, judgments have been gathered via desktop interfaces. However, with the rise in popularity of smaller devices for information access, it has become imperative to investigate whether desktop based judgments are different from mobile judgments. Recently, user effort and document usefulness have also emerged as important dimensions to optimize and evaluate information retrieval systems. Since existing work is limited to desktops, it remains to be seen how these judgments are affected by user's search device. In this paper, we address these shortcomings by collecting and analyzing relevance, usefulness and effort judgments on mobiles and desktops. Analysis of these judgments shows high agreement rate between desktop and mobile judges for relevance, followed by usefulness and findability. We also found that desktop judges are likely to spend more time and examine non-relevant/not-useful/difficult documents in greater depth compared to mobile judges. Based on our findings, we suggest that relevance judgments should be gathered via desktops and effort judgments should be collected on each device independently.

KEYWORDS

Effort, relevance judgments, search device, mobile

ACM Reference Format:
Manisha Verma, Emine Yilmaz, and Nick Craswell. 2018. Study of Relevance and Effort across Devices. In *CHIIR '18: 2018 Conference on Human Information Interaction & Retrieval, March 11–15, 2018, New Brunswick, NJ, USA.* ACM, New York, NY, USA, 4 pages. https://doi.org/10.1145/3176349.3176888

1 INTRODUCTION

Evaluation of Information retrieval (IR) systems is dependent on document relevance. IR Systems are built to optimize for relevance, where training data consists of documents either labeled manually or derived from dwell time. However, studies [2, 11] have shown that topical relevance is not the primary factor and that '*user effort*' also affects user satisfaction. Their findings suggest that besides relevance, the *ability to find information* i.e. *findability* in a web-page is highly correlated with user satisfaction. They showed that users prefer documents where information can be located *quickly* over documents where it takes *longer* to find relevant information. Given that people can access the same information from different devices, we posit that user's *search device* would also affect the

ability to locate relevant information. For instance, small viewport of mobile and limited touch-based input may affect how a user finds information on mobile. In this work, we investigate how document relevance and effort vary with search device.

Information access is no longer limited to stationary desktops. With constant rise in search queries from different mediums [3, 10], it has become imperative to understand whether desktop based relevance and effort judgments can be directly used for mobiles. Recent work [7] only gathered topical relevance labels and showed that relevance labels may differ across devices. We believe that the observed differences in the labels is a function of both *relevance* and *effort* required to label documents on both devices. Annotators may find it more difficult to label some documents on mobile and may give up or assign incorrect label to the document. Since, the authors in [7] only elicit relevance labels, it is difficult to examine role of judging effort across devices from their judgments.

We posit that the differences in relevance labels across devices [7] is a result of both *topical relevance* and *user effort required to extract useful information* from web-page. We investigate these differences further by gathering judgments for relevance *and* effort on both mediums. In this work, we perform a preliminary analysis of labels obtained via crowd-sourcing study on mobile and desktop. We specifically gather judgments for topical relevance, page utility [4] and effort [2, 11] to systematically understand the differences between mobile and desktop. For generalizability, we obtain judgments for documents of TREC Web track[1], a publicly available dataset.

Our work aims to further answer two research questions. First, we analyze whether judgments for relevance, page utility and effort required to find the information differ across two devices with help of judging time and annotator's actions on webpage. Secondly, we study how relevance, page utility and effort are correlated across devices. From these judgments, we observed highest agreement rate between desktop and mobile judges for relevance, followed by usefulness and findability. Second, we found that desktop and mobile usefulness labels are highly correlated, followed by relevance and findability labels. Finally, we found that desktop judges are likely to spend more time and examine non-relevant/not-useful/difficult documents in greater depth compared to mobile judges.

We provide a brief overview of related work and their short comings in Section 2. We describe adopted methodology and our dataset in Section 3. We describe our findings from crowd-sourced judgments in Section 4 and summarize our conclusion in Section 6.

2 RELATED WORK

Our work spans multiple areas of research. We review literature that addresses crowdsourcing judgments, user behavior on different mediums and assessor behavior. Several studies have looked into *when* does user search for information on mobile. Existing research [10] has shown that today mobiles are used extensively to satisfy information needs. Researchers have found [1, 5] that user search

[1]http://trec.nist.gov/data/webmain.html

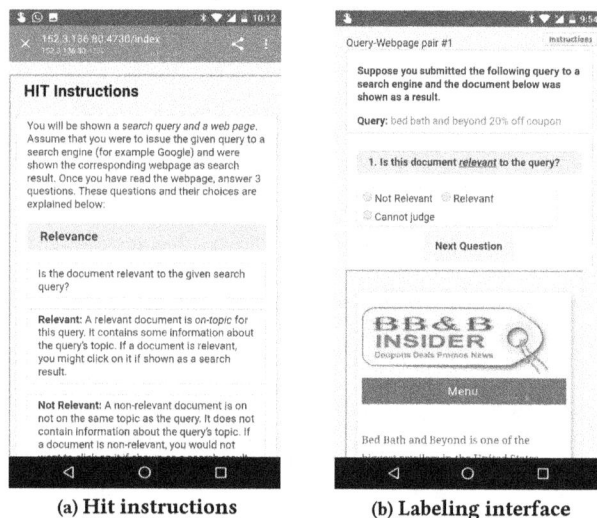

(a) Hit instructions   (b) Labeling interface

Figure 1: Sample Mobile hit

logs on mobiles and desktop differ in query length, click patterns and dwell time respectively. Kamvar *et al* [3] analyze large scale query logs to distinguish between queries issued from mobile. These studies found mobile queries to be short (2.3 - 2.5 terms) and high rate of query reformulation. Small scale studies like [6, 10] also report differences in search patterns across devices. One key result of Song *et al.* [5] studied mobile search patterns on three devices: mobile, desktop and tablets. Given significant differences between user search patterns on these platforms, their study suggested use of different web page ranking methodology for mobile and desktop.

Topical relevance has been the primary focus of evaluating documents. Xu *et al.* [9, 12] conducted a study to investigate criterion that users employ to make relevance judgments. They found that topicality and novelty are the most important relevance criteria for the users, followed by understandability and reliability. However, recent work has shown [11] that besides relevance, **user effort** also affects satisfaction. Users may have to invest significant effort in reading and extracting information from a relevant document. Several parameters have been investigated [8] to characterize user effort and it has been shown that users prefer documents where it is *easier to locate* required information. Recent work [7] collected judgments for topical relevance on mobile and desktop. They showed that relevance labels may differ across devices. We believe that these differences are an outcome of effort required to label documents. In this study, we gather labels for relevance, page utility *and* effort on mobile and desktop respectively to thoroughly investigate these differences.

3 METHODOLOGY

Primary aim of this study is to collect judgments and investigate differences across devices. We designed a judging interface for mobile and desktop respectively. Mobile based judging interface is shown in Figure 1. We sampled TREC Web track queries and documents to create TREC specific evaluation dataset. We recruited annotators via the crowd-sourcing platform Mechanical Turk[2].

---

[2]http://www.mturk.com

Table 1: Relevance label distribution

Desk↓/Mob→	NA	CJ	rel	not-rel	Total
NA	1	1	5	4	11
CJ	0	0	1	0	1
rel	12	0	65	21	98
not-rel	11	2	25	55	93
Total	24	3	96	80	**203**

Since Clueweb12 collection is an older snapshot of www, we crawled desktop and mobile versions of URLs judged in TREC Web track. We computed cosine similarity between term vectors of Clueweb12 document and crawled desktop/mobile webpage. In this study, we consider pages whose desktop/mobile cosine similarity is greater than 0.80. Each TREC web query has been assigned a class on basis of its underlying information need: *'faceted'*, *'single'* and *'ambiguous'*. We construct a sample of 203 documents for 45 queries from *'single'* category for query-url pairs as these topic represent a clear and atomic information need. For an in-depth analysis, judges label each document for 1) topical relevance (*relevance*), 2) ease of finding required information (*findability*)[8] and 3) utility of the page (*usefulness*)[4] with respect to the search query. The annotation interface with instructions is available online[3]. We gather binary labels for each parameter to reduce labeling overhead on both devices. We use the following scales for each label:

- **Relevance** (*rel*): Not relevant, relevant, cannot judge (CJ).
- **Findability** (*find*): Difficult and easy.
- **Usefulness** (*use*): Not useful and useful.

We allowed annotators to skip documents that they did not want to judge to reduce spurious labels in the dataset. We payed MTurk annotators 0.06 cents for annotating a single document. Each document was annotated by 3 judges and each judge was required to label at least 10 documents to get payed. This was to ensure that only annotators interested in the task completed it. Annotators that had acceptance rate of >95% and had completed over 5000 HITs could attempt our task on Mechanical Turk. We tracked mouse movements and touch events on both devices via Javascript.

4 RESULTS

In total, we obtained labels for 203 TREC Web documents for 44 queries by 90 and 42 judges on desktop and mobile respectively. Each query-document pair was labeled by three judges. We elicit labels from judges for 3 aspects: relevance, usefulness and findability. We begin by analyzing label distribution of each dimension.

4.1 Label Distribution

Since, each document was labeled by three judges, we use majority vote to compute the final label on both mediums. Documents with no majority vote are marked NA. Distribution of majority relevance, findability and usefulness labels is given in Table 1, Table 2 and Table 3 respectively. Overall, we obtain similar distribution of relevance labels on mobile and desktop. We observe that more documents have no majority on mobile than desktop. We obtain a similar distribution for usefulness labels on both devices with slightly more documents with no majority label on mobile. However, there is slightly more variation in findability labels, where more number of documents are *difficult* (85) on mobile than desktop where only 57 documents got labeled *difficult*.

---

[3]http://128.16.12.66:4730/index, batch:nxaa, workerid:userid

Table 2: Findability Label Distribution

Desk↓/Mob→	CJ	easy	difficult	Total
CJ	1	1	4	6
easy	12	79	49	140
difficult	5	30	22	57
Total	18	110	85	203

Table 3: Usefulness label distribution

Desk↓/Mob→	NA	CJ	use	not-use	Total
NA	0	1	5	7	13
CJ	1	0	0	0	1
use	8	0	64	23	95
not-use	15	4	15	60	94
Total	24	5	84	90	203

Table 4: Inter-rater agreement on binary judgments

	Desktop		Mobile		M/D	Random
	α	κ	α	κ	κ	κ
Useful	0.47	0.46 (0.02)	0.44	0.43 (0.02)	0.38	0.11 (0.06)
Rel	0.55	0.56 (0.02)	0.44	0.43 (0.02)	0.41	0.12 (0.05)
Find	0.22	0.23 (0.04)	0.11	0.11 (0.03)	0.17	0.06 (0.07)

We compute inter-rater agreement using Krippendorff's Alpha (α) and Cohen's kappa (κ) on binary judgments given in Table 4. Since three judges labeled each document, we report average (and standard deviation) Cohen's kappa over 50 trials. For each trial, we randomly sample two labels for each query-url pair and compute Cohen's kappa. We also report agreement within device (desktop and mobile), across devices (M/D) and agreement computed between randomly chosen desktop and mobile labels. It is worth noting that (M/D) is computed using document's majority label for mobile and desktop. Random Agreement (column 4 in Table 4) is the average agreement between randomly choose label from desktop and mobile respectively. We observed the high agreement rate for relevance on desktop, followed by usefulness and findability respectively. In mobile, we obtain similar agreement rates for relevance and usefulness but least agreement for findability. Agreement rate between mobile and desktop is also largest for relevance followed by usefulness and findability. Random agreement between mobile and desktop is expected to be lower than others. However, chance agreement of relevance labels is the highest amongst all other labels.

4.2 Judging time and Examination depth

We now compare the overall distribution of judging time of each annotator on Mobile and Desktop. Figure 2a shows the overall distribution of time it took any judge to label the same document on mobile and desktop. We also compare the percentage of document examined by any assessor on mobile and desktop before submitting the judgments. Note that y-axis reports the percentage of URL examined on mobile and x-axis depicts the percentage of same URL examined on desktop. The scroll percentage distribution is shown in Figure 2b. Here, judges examine more content on mobile as compare to desktop[4].

---

[4]Percentage is computed with respect to document length rendered on desktop/mobile screen to remove effect of screen size on calculation.

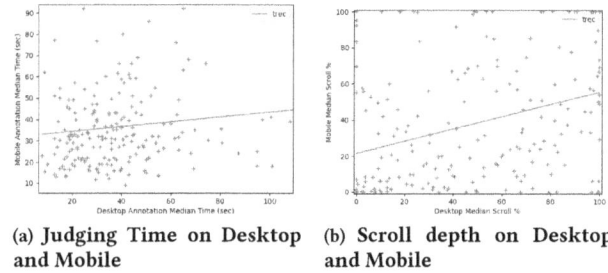

(a) Judging Time on Desktop and Mobile

(b) Scroll depth on Desktop and Mobile

Figure 2: Scroll Depth and Judging time on desktop and mobile

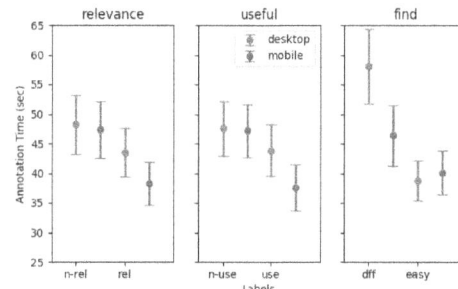

Figure 3: Judging Time on Mobile/Desktop

We observe that median judging time on desktop is weakly associated with median judging time on mobile. Pearson's correlation ρ between desktop and mobile judging time is 0.12 (p-val < 0.01). However, in Figure 2b we see stronger correlation between median scroll depth on mobile and desktop. Pearson's correlation ρ between desktop and mobile examination depth is 0.28 (p-val < 0.01), higher than that of judging time correlation.

We also examine whether relevance, usefulness and effort labels differ on basis of judging time and examination depth. We plot mean judging time and examination depth with 95% confidence intervals for each label in Figure 3 and Figure 4 respectively.

One key observation is that judges take more time to judge non-relevant/not-useful and difficult documents on mobile and desktop respectively. However, we find that desktop judging time distribution of relevant (useful) and non-relevant (not-useful) are not statistically different. On the contrary, mobile judging time of relevant (useful) and non-relevant (not-useful) documents is significantly different. Mobile judging time of relevant (and useful) documents is also significantly lower than desktop judging time which is in line with previous findings in [7].

We observe a different trend for findability labels. We found that mobile judges are much less likely to spend time examining difficult documents in comparison to desktop judges. We attribute this difference to limited input capabilities and touch interaction on mobile devices. Desktop judges can be more thorough as they can easily interact with a webpage via keyboard and mouse. Similar conclusion can be drawn from scrolling/swiping behavior in Figure 4. We find that desktop judges examine significantly more content than mobile judges regardless of document's relevance/usefulness/effort label.

Table 5: Correlation between all judgments

Desk↓/Mob→	relevance	usefulness	effort
relevance	0.23**	0.33**	0.21**
usefulness	0.28**	0.34**	0.20**
effort	0.16*	0.13	0.08

Figure 4: Examination Depth on Mobile/Desktop

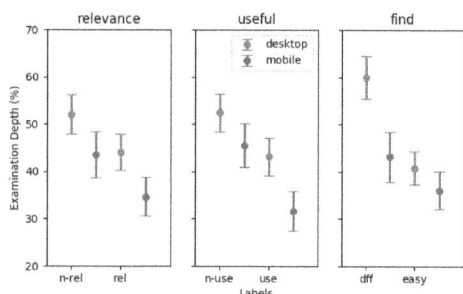

Figure 4 shows that judges examine non-relevant/not-useful/difficult documents in greater depth than relevant/useful/easy documents on both devices. This is expected, as judges would need to read difficult documents more carefully and thoroughly to find required information. This would result in higher examination depth on non-relevant/useful/difficult documents. We observe a significantly large difference in examination depth of difficult pages between mobile and desktop, in combination with judging time information, indicates that mobile judges may be less patient in looking for query specific information.

On analysis of judging time and examination depth information, in conjunction with agreement rates in Table 4 (column M/D) we believe that desktop judges are more thorough in labeling documents than mobile judges. They are likely to spend more time and examine the document in greater depth before assigning any label. Mobile judges, however, due to device and interface limitations, may be less patient in labeling a document with respect to a search query. However, low agreement of findability between mobile and desktop judges clearly elicits the need of device specific effort judgments.

5 LABELS CORRELATION

To investigate this further we can compute correlations between desktop and mobile relevance, usefulness and findability labels. Our hypothesis is that weak correlation of labels across both devices would indicate a disagreement between desktop and mobile judges while a stronger correlation would reflect higher agreement between judges.

We present the correlation between each label across devices in Table 5. Statistically significant entries are marked with * (p-val < 0.05) or ** (p-val < 0.01) respectively. Table 5 clearly indicates that relevance and usefulness have higher correlation than relevance and findability labels. Weak correlation between effort labels across devices suggests that effort labels differ across devices and should be gathered on per-device basis.

6 DISCUSSION AND CONCLUSION

Information retrieval (IR) is no longer limited to desktops. Today, users increasingly rely on IR systems to find information on devices such as mobiles or tablets. While prior work exists on designing, exploiting or evaluating IR systems across devices, little work has been done to investigate affect of user's search device on relevance judgments. Relevance judgments lie at the heart of IR systems and existing algorithms need large scale labeled data to be effective. Until recently, judgments have been collected via desktop interfaces. However, with advent of different devices, we need to investigate whether relevance judgments differ across devices.

Recently, researchers have also suggested to gather usefulness and effort based judgments along with relevance to train more effective systems. We believe that these judgments would be affected by user's search device. Existing work only analyzes these judgments for desktops. In this work, we address the above shortcomings in that we systematically collect and analyze device specific judgments for TREC dataset for three factors: relevance, usefulness and effort. Our analysis indicates three key trends. First, we observed highest agreement rate between desktop and mobile judges for relevance, followed by usefulness and findability. Second, we found that desktop and mobile usefulness labels are highly correlated, followed by relevance and findability labels. We also observed higher correlation between relevance and usefulness labels than between relevance and findability labels. Finally, we found that desktop judges are likely to spend more time and examine non-relevant/not-useful/difficult documents in greater depth compared to mobile judges.

Based on our findings, we suggest that relevance judgments should be gathered via desktops as desktop judges are more patient and thorough in assessing a webpage compared to mobile judges. However, effort based judgments should be collected on each device independently to account for affect of device specific properties on labels.

REFERENCES

[1] K. Church and B. Smyth. Understanding the intent behind mobile information needs. In *Proc. IUI*. ACM, 2009.
[2] J. Jiang, D. He, D. Kelly, and J. Allan. Understanding ephemeral state of relevance. In *CHIIR '17*, 2017.
[3] M. Kamvar, M. Kellar, R. Patel, and Y. Xu. Computers and iphones and mobile phones, oh my!: A logs-based comparison of search users on different devices. In *Proc. WWW*. ACM, 2009.
[4] J. Mao, Y. Liu, K. Zhou, J.-Y. Nie, J. Song, M. Zhang, S. Ma, J. Sun, and H. Luo. When does relevance mean usefulness and user satisfaction in web search? In *Proceedings of the 39th International ACM SIGIR Conference on Research and Development in Information Retrieval*, SIGIR '16, pages 463–472, New York, NY, USA, 2016. ACM.
[5] Y. Song, H. Ma, H. Wang, and K. Wang. Exploring and exploiting user search behavior on mobile and tablet devices to improve search relevance. In *Proc. WWW*, 2013.
[6] C. Tossell, P. Kortum, A. Rahmati, C. Shepard, and L. Zhong. Characterizing web use on smartphones. In *Proc. SIGCHI*. ACM, 2012.
[7] M. Verma and E. Yilmaz. Characterizing relevance on mobile and desktop. In *European Conference on Information Retrieval*, pages 212–223. Springer, 2016.
[8] M. Verma, E. Yilmaz, and N. Craswell. On obtaining effort based judgements for information retrieval. WSDM '16. ACM, 2016.
[9] Y. C. Xu and Z. Chen. Relevance judgment: What do information users consider beyond topicality? *Journal of the American Society for Information Science and Technology*, 57(7), 2006.
[10] J. Yi, F. Maghoul, and J. Pedersen. Deciphering mobile search patterns: A study of yahoo! mobile search queries. In *Proc. WWW*. ACM, 2008.
[11] E. Yilmaz, M. Verma, N. Craswell, F. Radlinski, and P. Bailey. Relevance and effort: an analysis of document utility. In *CIKM '14*. ACM, 2014.
[12] Y. Zhang, J. Zhang, M. Lease, and J. Gwizdka. Multidimensional relevance modeling via psychometrics and crowdsourcing. In *Proceedings of the 37th International ACM SIGIR Conference on Research & Development in Information Retrieval*, SIGIR '14. ACM, 2014.

Understanding Music Listening Intents During Daily Activities with Implications for Contextual Music Recommendation

Sergey Volokhin
Emory University
sergey.volokhin@emory.edu

Eugene Agichtein
Emory University
eugene.agichtein@emory.edu

ABSTRACT

Why do we listen to music? This question has as many answers as there are people, which may vary by time of day, and the activity of the listener. We envision a contextual music search and recommendation system, which could suggest appropriate music to the user in the current context. As an important step in this direction, we set out to understand what are the users' intents for listening to music, and how they relate to common daily activities. To accomplish this, we conduct and analyze a survey of why and when people of different ages and in different countries listen to music. The resulting categories of common musical intents, and the associations of intents and activities, could be helpful for guiding the development and evaluation of contextual music recommendation systems.

CCS CONCEPTS

• **Human-centered computing** → **User studies**; *HCI theory, concepts and models*;

KEYWORDS

contextual music recommendation; music listening intent

ACM Reference Format:
Sergey Volokhin and Eugene Agichtein. 2018. Understanding Music Listening Intents During Daily Activities with Implications for Contextual Music Recommendation. In *CHIIR '18: 2018 Conference on Human Information Interaction & Retrieval, March 11–15, 2018, New Brunswick, NJ, USA.* ACM, New Jersey, NJ, USA, 4 pages.

1 INTRODUCTION AND MOTIVATION

Music is an integral part of our life and accompanies us everywhere we go, from stores and cafes, to taxis and elevators. With almost ubiquitous smartphone and digital music player devices, listening to music continues to increase in popularity[18]. Hagreaves et al. [17] have surveyed people about their music listening habits, and concluded that people listen to music mainly during another activity (such as exercising or driving), rather than as a deliberate, exclusive process. This was true in 2004, and the trend has only increased in the following decade. 51.6% of people in the world (roughly 3.9 billion) and 82.6% of people in North America and Europe use the Internet [23], and 96% of Internet users consume licensed music, primarily (76%) via smartphones, which often accompany users

through their activities [18]. Furthermore, most people discover music to listen to through recommendation or search (e.g., via services like Pandora, Spotify, or YouTube). For all these reasons, music recommendation is a critical and impactful aspect of the users' online experience.

It is also widely known that people prefer different types of music for different activities [15, 17]. However, we hypothesize that even for the same activity, such as driving, people may want to listen to music for different reasons, for example, for relaxation, or for inspiration, or to aid concentration. Thus, in this paper, we introduce and study the concept of *music listening intent*, which we believe is an important component of contextual music recommendation. Specifically, our hypothesis is that there may be *multiple* music listening intents associated with each activity, and that in order to accurately recommend music to match the users' need, a recommendation system must take the music listening intent into account.

We further hypothesize a correlation between activities and associated intents. That is, we hypothesize that a small group of intents cover a vast majority of music listening needs for each activity. Identifying this association would allow for more accurate modeling of the latent factors, such as intent, for predicting the music to recommend to the user, and would naturally support generalization (exploration) and diversification of the recommendations.

Next, we describe existing work on music recommendation (2), to place our work in context. Next, in Section 3 we describe our study methodology and data. Section 4 presents our findings and analysis. Finally, in Section 5 we discuss the implications of our findings and promising directions for future work.

2 RELATED WORK

Music recommendation has been extensively studied from different angles, taking into account a variety of features and factors, that could influence the users' choices or preferences. The most common approaches are variations of collaborative filtering [21, 28, 29] and content-based filtering [12, 13, 27]. These methods perform satisfactory in the long run, but immediate preferences can be heavily influenced by a range of different factors and characteristics, which is generally referred to as 'context'.

Context-aware recommender systems can be effective for immediate or online recommendations [2]. Several context representations have been studied with regards to music recommendations, including emotions and mood [3, 7, 16, 22], time of day and microprofiling [4], location [6, 8], weather [19, 30], and demographic information [31]. One of the most effective contexts is 'activity', which have been previously studied [5, 10, 21, 26]. These works have focused on the activity itself, and do not ask about the intent of listening, but rather map music recommendation directly to the activity. We go a step further, aiming to understand the *intent* of the user, as the reason for music listening may differ even for the same activity.

Table 1: List of activities

Cleaning	Commuting	Cooking	Driving
Eating	Exercising	Shopping	Showering
Studying	Walking	Working	

Table 2: List of intents

Intent	Description
Concentration	sharpening attention and devoting it to task at hand, not to be distracted by anything
Distraction	entertainment, not to be bored by current activity, giving yourself something to do
Filtering background noise	pretty self-explanatory. block irritating or loud noises
Inspiration	clear one's mind and try to create something or come up with a solution
Mood and emotion control	evoking certain emotions or mood using music
Motivation	gathering strength and will to do what needs to be done
Relaxation	become less anxious and tense, rest

To address this problem, we build on the extensive work on studying Web search intent[9, 11, 20], and frame our study in the general area of online intent prediction. Specifically, using the taxonomy developed in reference[20], music recommendation can be viewed as "resource search", i.e., searching (or recommending) entertainment resources. Our goal, however, is to classify the *type* of music appropriate for a given situation, which is a more specialized task with different characteristics from general Web search intent. User intent was also previously studied for recommendation systems [25], but not specifically in the music recommendation field. To the best of our knowledge, this paper is the first to explicitly study music listening intent, and our work builds on the extensive research of intent classification in other domains.

3 METHODOLOGY

We now describe our survey-based methodology, which consisted of an initial pilot survey, followed by survey refinement and a large scale survey of a different, more diverse set of users, recruited via social media as well as through SurveyMonkey research panel.

To determine a list of relevant activities and intents or reasons, we used a pilot survey, using the SurveyMonkey platform, where we asked people why they listen to music, for what reasons, and during which activities. We provided a list of activities, during which we thought people might listen to music, and asked them to provide their intents for each one, or to add new intents or activities if none matched their experience. 20 respondents participated in the pilot survey, allowing us to formulate a comprehensive list of common activities and music intents.

Table 1 provides a list of the available activities and table 2 provides a list of intents with their brief descriptions. We specifically avoided 'pleasure' as an intent and 'listening to music' as an activity, as we are trying to maximize pleasure of user by default, so there is no need to distinguish them. After analyzing the pilot results, we refined the survey of activities and musical intents, which we then

posted on social media to recruit respondents. The responses were collected anonymously, and only after the respondents consented to participate in the survey as the first, required question.

The main part of the survey was the Activity-Intent matrix (Figure 2), for which the respondents were instructed to provide up to 3 intents for each activity. We also provided an empty field to add any other activity or intent we may have missed. Very few people proposed any new intents or activities, and those proposed activities or intents, were not directly applicable to our task. For example, two people mentioned 'listening to music to play it using musical instruments', which is a highly specialized intent applicable to only a small fraction of users who are seriously studying musical instruments. Thus, we are confident that our final survey captured the vast majority of common activities and music listening intents. We report the data collected with this survey, and the findings, in the next section.

4 RESULTS AND DISCUSSION

In this section we report the general user statistics and main distributions of intent and activity, followed by the more detailed analysis of intents for different activities and user demographics.

We received 166 responses from people 18-76 years old (average age: 37), responding from 12 countries: Belarus, Canada, Denmark, Germany, Hungary, Iran, Netherlands, Niger, Russian Federation, Spain, USA, and Ukraine. 81 of the respondents live in the Russian Federation (Russia for the rest of the paper), and 67 live in the USA. Thus, we report the results both for the whole dataset (N=166), as well as separately for subsets of respondents, namely those from Russia (N=81) and from the USA (N=67).

Figure 3b shows that younger people in Russia listen to more music than older respondents, with number of hours decreasing significantly with age. In contrast, respondents from the USA appear to listen to about the same amount of music across different age groups. Interestingly, ANOVA analysis shows that the difference between countries in terms of hours of listening per day is not significant enough ($p < 0.178$).

Figures 4 and 1 report the distribution by age of the music listening intents, and distribution of listening intents for different activities, for all participants.

4.1 Analysis of intent and activity popularity

Activities associated with music listening for Russia are distributed more uniformly than for the USA respondents: top activity for USA is driving, almost 2.5% more common than most popular activity in Russia – working. Interestingly, respondents from the USA do not report listen to music while eating, whether for concentration, motivation or inspiration, but primarily for relaxing (50%). In contrast, respondents from Russia listen during eating for distraction (26%), relaxing and mood control (23-24%). It is also interesting to note that shopping, eating, and showering are least popular activities for both countries, with 3% drop of popularity in Russia, and $\sim 1 - 1.5\%$ in USA. However, since these activities are rare, differences between countries may not be meaningful.

4.2 Most popular intents for different activites

First, we compare the overall distribution of the most popular intents for all activities, with responses from all countries combined, in Figure 5a. The figure shows that the dominant intents are Mood

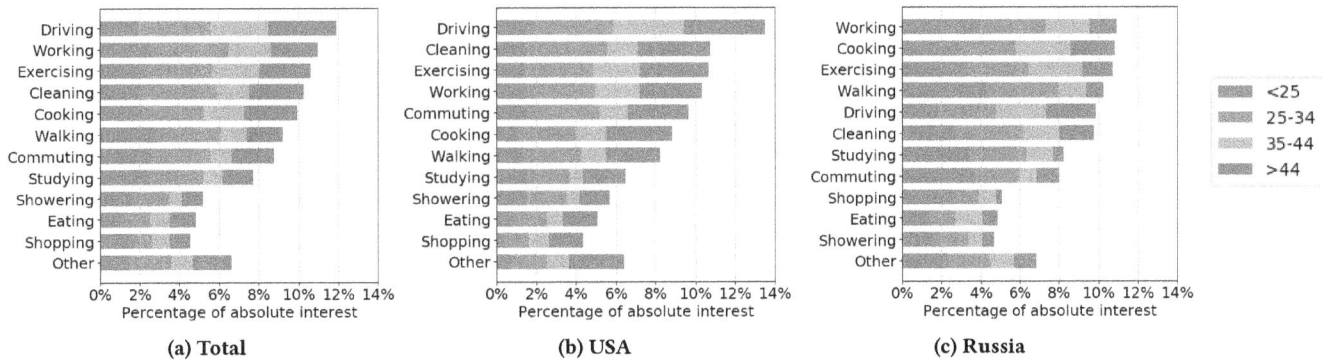

Figure 1: Music listening activity distribution for different age groups: overall (a), in the USA (b) and in Russia (c).

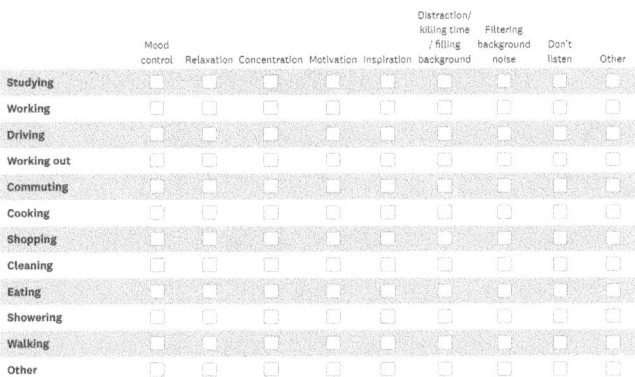

Figure 2: Activity and Music Intent Survey Interface

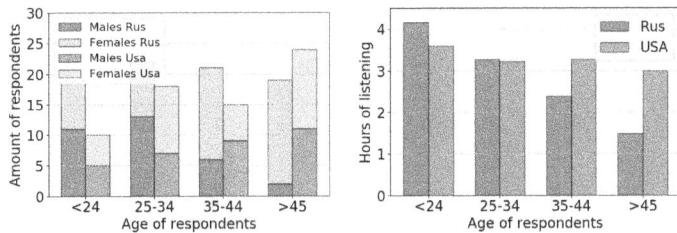

(a) Age and Gender distribution among respondents

(b) Average hours of listening to music per day respondents

Figure 3: Respondents statistics

control (9 times), Relaxation (7 times) and Distraction (7 times). They cover 54% of all reported music listening instances, according to 4a. Interestingly, ANOVA analysis shows a large overlap among these intents across activities and the differences are not significant and have a large overlap in meaning. However, the other 10 out of 21 pairs of intents (excluding 'Other') are indeed distinct according to ANOVA ($p < 0.05$).

However, some activities have different dominant intents for the different countries. Figure 5b reports the distribution of top-3 intents for such activities, separated by country. For example, respondents from the USA listen to music during exercising mostly for motivation ($\sim 40\%$), while respondents from Russia report Motivation intent for only $\sim 23\%$, with higher fraction of other intents (Concentration and Relaxation).

5 DISCUSSION AND FUTURE WORK

One limitation of the survey-based method is that people may not accurately recall their intent or motivation for listening to music. However, we believe that in aggregate, collecting a sufficiently large number of survey responses, as we report in this paper, identified the most common music intents for common activities.

If we are able to more accurately infer music listening intent, it would enable more accurate and effective music recommendation. A natural follow-up to this work is evaluating and quantifying the actual improvements that could be achieved by these additional factors, e.g., by reducing uncertainty about the most likely intents for a given activity. To accomplish this, we plan to build on existing work on recognizing activity [13, 24, 26] and matching music with activity [1, 14], but extending the model with the (latent) intent factor, informed by the prior intent distributions for each activity.

In summary, we introduced the concept of music listening intent, and showed intent to be distinct from the context (i.e., user's activity). Our empirical findings provide valuable initial data about musical intent distribution for different activities, which could be ultimately incorporated into more effective and accurate contextual music recommendation systems.

REFERENCES

[1] 2014. Google Activity Recognition Client. (2014). Retrieved October 22, 2017 from goo.gl/V98vUs
[2] Gediminas Adomavicius and Alexander Tuzhilin. 2011. *Context-Aware Recommender Systems*. Springer, 217–253. https://doi.org/10.1007/978-0-387-85820-3_7
[3] Ivana Andjelkovic, Denis Parra, and John O'Donovan. 2016. Moodplay: Interactive Mood-based Music Discovery and Recommendation. In *Proceedings of the 2016 Conference on User Modeling Adaptation and Personalization (UMAP '16)*. 275–279. https://doi.org/10.1145/2930238.2930280
[4] Linas Baltrunas and Xavier Amatriain. 2009. Towards Time-Dependant Recommendation based on Implicit Feedback. In *Proc. of RECSYS*.
[5] Fredrik Boström. 2017. *AndroMedia - Towards a Context-aware Mobile Music Recommender*. Master's thesis.
[6] Matthias Braunhofer, Marius Kaminskas, and Francesco Ricci. 2013. Location-aware music recommendation. *International Journal of Multimedia Information Retrieval* 2, 1 (01 Mar 2013), 31–44. https://doi.org/10.1007/s13735-012-0032-2
[7] Steven Brown and Michael et. al Martinez. 2004. Passive music listening spontaneously engages limbic and paralimbic systems. *Neuroreport* 15, 13 (2004).
[8] Zhiyong Cheng and Jialie Shen. 2016. On Effective Location-Aware Music Recommendation. *ACM Trans. Inf. Syst.* 34, 2, Article 13 (April 2016), 32 pages. https://doi.org/10.1145/2846092
[9] Hal Daumé, III and Eric Brill. 2004. Web Search Intent Induction via Automatic Query Reformulation. In *Proc. of HLT-NAACL 2004: Short Papers (HLT-NAACL-Short '04)*. ACM, 49–52. http://dl.acm.org/citation.cfm?id=1613984.1613997
[10] Ricardo Dias, Manuel J. Fonseca, and Ricardo Cunha. 2014. A User-centered Music Recommendation Approach for Daily Activities. In *CBRecSys@RecSys*.
[11] Bernard J Jansen, Danielle L Booth, and Amanda Spink. 2007. Determining the user intent of web search engine queries. In *Proceedings of the 16th international*

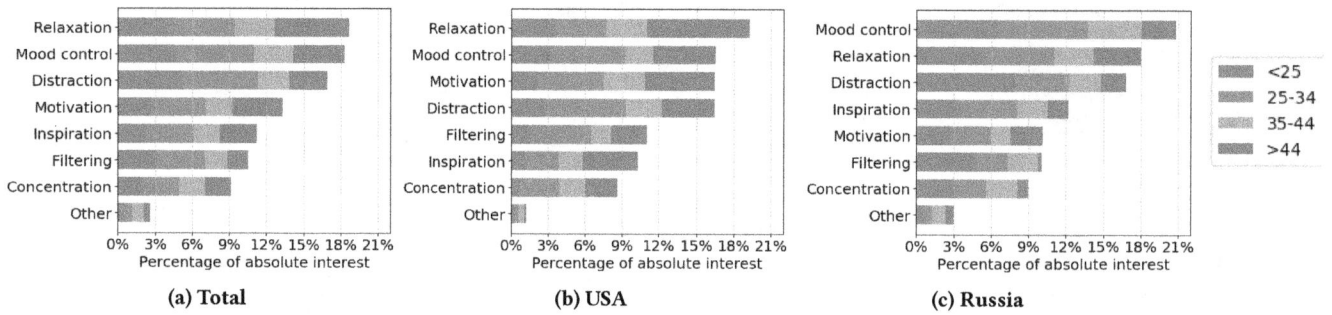

(a) Total

(b) USA

(c) Russia

Figure 4: Music listening intent distribution by age groups: overall (a), in the USA (b) and in Russia (c).

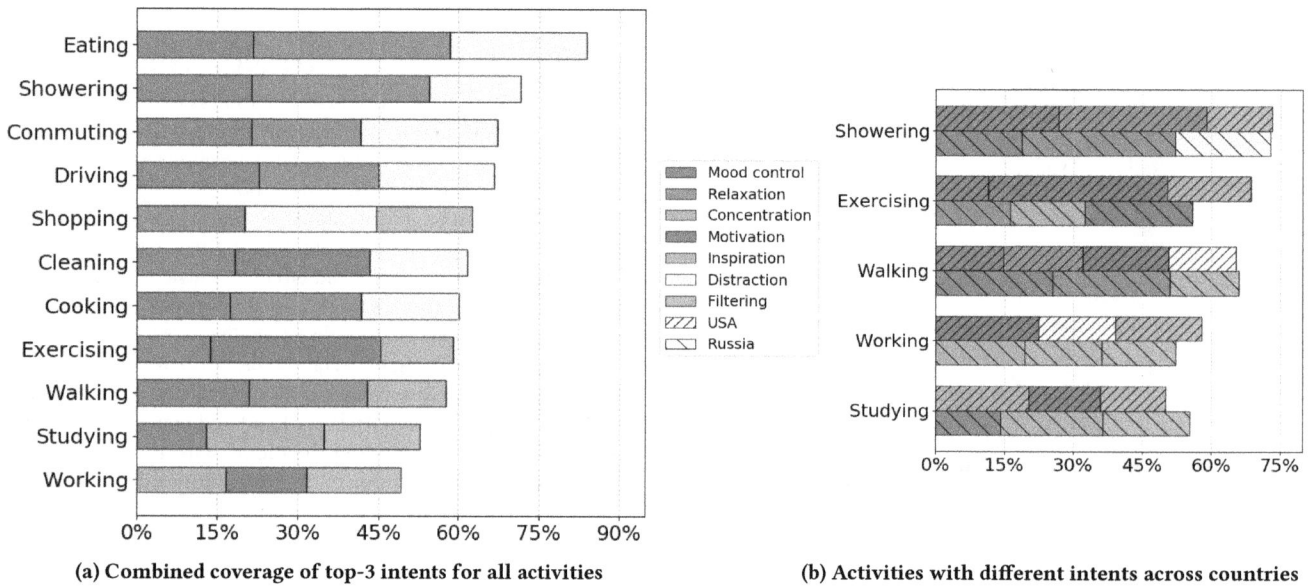

(a) Combined coverage of top-3 intents for all activities

(b) Activities with different intents across countries

Figure 5: Intent distribution across activities: for all respondents (a), separately for Russia and USA (b)

conference on World Wide Web. ACM, 1149–1150.

[12] Juuso Kaitila. 2017. A content-based music recommender system. (2017).

[13] Wei-Po Lee, Chun-Ting Chen, Jhih-Yuan Huang, and Jhen-Yi Liang. 2017. A smartphone-based activity-aware system for music streaming recommendation. *Knowledge-Based Systems* 131 (2017). https://doi.org/10.1016/j.knosys.2017.06.002

[14] Young-Seol Lee and Sung-Bae Cho. 2011. *Activity Recognition Using Hierarchical Hidden Markov Models on a Smartphone with 3D Accelerometer.* 460–467. https://doi.org/10.1007/978-3-642-21219-2_58

[15] Daniel J. Levitin and James McGill. 2007. Life Soundtracks: The uses of music in everyday life. (2007).

[16] Cathy Mckinney, Michael Antoni, Mahendra Kumar, Frederick C. Tims, and Philip Mccabe. 1997. Effects of Guided Imagery and Music (GIM) Therapy on Mood and Cortisol in Healthy Adults. 16 (08 1997), 390–400.

[17] Adrian C. North, David J. Hargreaves, and Jon J. Hargreaves. 2004. Uses of Music in Everyday Life. *Music Perception: An Interdisciplinary Journal* 22, 1 (2004), 41–77. https://doi.org/10.1525/mp.2004.22.1.41 arXiv:http://mp.ucpress.edu/content/22/1/41.full.pdf

[18] The International Federation of the Phonographic Industry. 2017. Connecting with music. Music consumer insight report. (2017). http://www.ifpi.org/downloads/Music-Consumer-Insight-Report-2017.pdf

[19] So-Hyun Park, Sun-Young Ihm, Wu-In Jang, Aziz Nasridinov, and Young-Ho Park. 2015. *A Music Recommendation Method with Emotion Recognition Using Ranked Attributes.* 1065–1070. https://doi.org/10.1007/978-3-662-45402-2_151

[20] Daniel E. Rose and Danny Levinson. 2004. Understanding User Goals in Web Search. In *Proc. of WWW.* 13–19. https://doi.org/10.1145/988672.988675

[21] Diego Sánchez-Moreno, Ana B. Gil González, M. Dolores Muñoz Vicente, Vivian F. López Batista, and María N. Moreno García. 2016. A collaborative filtering method for music recommendation using playing coefficients for artists and users. *Expert Systems with Applications* 66, Supplement C (2016), 234 – 244. https://doi.org/10.1016/j.eswa.2016.09.019

[22] Yading Song, Simon Dixon, and Marcus Pearce. 2012. A Survey of Music Recommendation Systems and Future Perspectives. In *9th International Symposium on Computer Music Modelling and Retrieval (CMMR 2012).* London.

[23] Internet World Stats. 2017. The Internet Big Picture. World Internet Users and 2017 Population Stats. (2017). http://www.internetworldstats.com/stats.htm

[24] Yonatan Vaizman, Katherine Ellis, and Gert R. G. Lanckriet. 2016. Recognizing Detailed Human Context In-the-Wild from Smartphones and Smartwatches. *CoRR* abs/1609.06354 (2016). http://arxiv.org/abs/1609.06354

[25] Saul Vargas, Pablo Castells, and David Vallet. 2011. Intent-oriented diversity in recommender systems. In *Proceedings of the 34th international ACM SIGIR conference on Research and development in Information Retrieval.* ACM, 1211.

[26] Xinxi Wang, David Rosenblum, and Ye Wang. 2012. Context-aware Mobile Music Recommendation for Daily Activities. In *Proc. of the ACM International Conference on Multimedia (MM '12).* ACM, New York, NY, USA, 99–108. https://doi.org/10.1145/2393347.2393368

[27] Xinxi Wang and Ye Wang. 2014. Improving Content-based and Hybrid Music Recommendation Using Deep Learning. In *Proc. of ACM International Conference on Multimedia (MM'14).* 627–636. https://doi.org/10.1145/2647868.2654940

[28] Zhe Xing, Xinxi Wang, and Ye Wang. 2014. Enhancing Collaborative Filtering Music Recommendation by Balancing Exploration and Exploitation.. In *Proc. of ISMIR.* 445–450.

[29] Yan Yan, Tianlong Liu, and Zhenyu Wang. 2015. *A Music Recommendation Algorithm Based on Hybrid Collaborative Filtering Technique.* Springer Singapore, Singapore, 233–240. https://doi.org/10.1007/978-981-10-0080-5_23

[30] Jinhyeok Yang, WooJoung Chae, SunYeob Kim, and Hyebong Choi. 2016. *Emotion-Aware Music Recommendation.* Springer International Publishing, Cham, 110–121. https://doi.org/10.1007/978-3-319-40355-7_11

[31] Billy Yapriady and Alexandra L. Uitdenbogerd. 2005. *Combining Demographic Data with Collaborative Filtering for Automatic Music Recommendation.* 201–207. https://doi.org/10.1007/11554028_29

Analysis of Open Answers to Survey Questions through Interactive Clustering and Theme Extraction

Fredrik Espinoza, Ola Hamfors, Jussi Karlgren, Fredrik Olsson, Per Persson, Lars Hamberg,
Magnus Sahlgren
Gavagai
Stockholm, Sweden

ABSTRACT

This paper describes design principles for and the implementation of Gavagai Explorer—a new application which builds on interactive text clustering to extract themes from topically coherent text sets such as open text answers to surveys or questionnaires.

An automated system is quick, consistent, and has full coverage over the study material. A system allows an analyst to analyze more answers in a given time period; provides the same initial results regardless of who does the analysis, reducing the risks of inter-rater discrepancy; and does not risk miss responses due to fatige or boredom. These factors reduce the cost and increase the reliability of the service. The most important feature, however, is relieving the human analyst from the frustrating aspects of the coding task, freeing the effort to the central challenge of understanding themes.

Gavagai Explorer is available on-line at http://explorer.gavagai.se

CCS CONCEPTS

•**Information systems** → **Clustering;** *Online analytical processing;* •**Human-centered computing** → User interface design;

ACM Reference format:
Fredrik Espinoza, Ola Hamfors, Jussi Karlgren, Fredrik Olsson, Per Persson, Lars Hamberg, Magnus Sahlgren. 2018. Analysis of Open Answers to Survey Questions through Interactive Clustering and Theme Extraction. In *Proceedings of Conference on Human Information Interaction & Retrieval, New Brunswick, NJ, USA, March 11–15, 2018 (CHIIR'18),* 4 pages.
DOI: http://dx.doi.org/10.1145/3176349.3176892

OPEN ANSWERS TO SURVEYS

Open answers in surveys and questionnaires are a challenge for analysts: how to report the collected responses together with more quantitative data elicited from respondents is not obvious. Typically a team of human analysts have been given the text responses together with a manually determined coding scheme, discussed and revised at intervals. The task of the analysts is to label the responses according to the coding scheme and to extract samples from the responses to anchor the labels in the data. In example (1) some extracts from reviews for a hotel are shown.

This coding procedure, converting the open responses into a structured form, requires time and expertise on the part of the analyst, both of which come at a cost. The effort involved in coding open answers is simultaneously intellectually non-trivial and demanding, but still monotonous: analyst fatigue and frustration risks leading to both between-analyst and within-analyst inconsistencies over time in reporting. This challenge is well-established both in the market research field and in scientific studies.[1] It takes about 1 minute for a human to categorise an abstract[2], when the categories are already given. If the task is to explore a set of responses and define and revise categories or labels as you go it will involve more effort and require more time per item.

(1)   a.   I would definately recommend this hotel, the location was great!
      b.   Had I known, I would NOT have chosen this hotel for my busy work visit in which I needed quiet time in hotel to do work.
      c.   Modern, stylish hotel with numerous, pretty decent restaurants in the area!

This paper describes a productivity tool for interactive coding, i.e. exploring and assigning thematic labels to open responses, based on a back-end technology which learns terminology and semantic relations from text.[3]

USE CASE

The purpose of including open questions in a survey is to explore the underlying motivations of the respondents with respect to some topic of interest. These motivations can be known in advance, they may be somewhat predictable, or they may be entirely unknown to the researcher. The resulting analysis, which is intended to give insights form the basis of e.g. strategic market decisions or other actions for the client, will be a set of such themes, with relevant quotes extracted from responses, reported together with their relative strengths and quantitative statistics on the numbers of respondents involved in discussing each theme.

The ambiguity, vagueness, and fluidity over time of human vocabulary is often described as a problem. This perspective does not do justice to the nature of human communication. The adaptability of human vocabulary and thus the entire human communication system is useful: it allows new terms to be coined, established terms

---

[1] E.g. O'Cathain and Thomas [9] and many others.
[2] As shown by e.g. Macskassy et al. [7], McCallum et al. [8], Schohn and Cohn [14].
[3] This approach builds on a long-standing strand of research in information retrieval which builds on interplay between similarity based clustering and end-user assessment of clusters, such as Cutting et al. [1], Jardine and van Rijsbergen [6], Pirolli et al. [10], Sanderson and Croft [13] and many others.

to be recruited into service ad hoc to fit the needs of some discourse, and various discourses to be associated or contrasted through term choice. The challenge for the analyst of our specific use case is in fact exactly the reason why open answers are useful: if the choice of words were entirely predictable, the information captured through open answers would be so much less rich and valuable.

A question on trustworthiness of text gave the answers given in (2), referring to the various qualities the readers take into account. [4]

(2) a. The appearance of the text, the quality of its design and polish.
     b. How enjoyable and fun it is, how it addresses its readers, and who has written it.
     c. Who wrote it and why.
     d. Does it speak to me?

There are at least two themes in these four responses: the *source* of the text and the *audience design* of the text. The first theme was an expected theme, the second somewhat unexpected, and it would have been difficult for an editor to instruct a coding scheme to make note of terms such as *speak*, and *address* before the fact.

This sort of information is exactly what the study was designed to find. The intention underlying the design presented here is to empower the analyst to fold together Xs and Ys into a topically coherent theme, retaining the variation found in the material, not to normalise the behaviour of the respondents into a uniform vocabulary given before the responses.

INTERACTIVITY, NOT AUTOMATION

Our design principles are based on human language being useful as is, and on automating drudgery, not creation of insights.

Design principle 1: Empowering analysts, not replacing them. A repetitive and frustrating task often is understood as a candidate for full automation. Our design is instead based on the work practice of human analysts, and intended to afford a human analyst tools to work with the text smoothly and painlessly, leaving the human effort to be expended on the most crucial and demanding task of content analysis, but freeing the analyst from keeping track of consistency.

Design principle 2: Incremental refinement in clustering pipeline. The assumption of interaction designers is often that users are best served by automation. Our design is a departure from that assumption. We want our system to go beyond a one-shot dialog. The dialog builds on incremental specialization of the analysis: in a few iterations of the data set, the analyst can achieve a stable clustering to save and report.

Design principle 3: Errors do not matter. The assumptions made by the system, however well its algorithms are designed and however well established its background knowledge is, are often daring and sometimes mistaken. The design is intended to display analyses, and to allow the analyst to correct misclusterings with little effort, with a high degree of interactivity. The above principle of incremental

refinement alleviates the presence of errors — the analyst is able to find themes in the texts, even if some of the first clusters were irrelevant or overlapping.

Design principle 4: Representation in surface terms. The end result of the analysis is a knowledge representation through which the set of texts can be understood better. This structure can be saved for future incoming data sets, e.g. a before-and-after study or a periodically repeated survey over some population. We want the knowledge representation to be inspectable, reportable, and editable by a human analyst without specialist knowledge. The representation is entirely in surface terms, for that purpose.

Design principle 5: No dependence on outside resources. We want the system to be portable to various languages, various domains of application, and various cultural areas. We do not want it to rely on costly or cumbersome lexical or encyclopædic resources which may not be available in all languages. The system is designed not to need anything but the texts under consideration and a larger sample of other background text written in the target language to tune term statistics.

IMPLEMENTATION

The functionality on which the system is built automatically clusters the documents into bins by lexical statistics. This creates clusters of documents that share topically important terms.

Text clustering. Lexical clustering builds on measures of term specificity to select which terms to use as clustering features, which requires general language data to be able to assess how specific or general a term is. Clustering by terms is fairly sensitive to genre-specific and topical usage, since a term which has high specificity in general language may have little utility in the context being examined.

Most standard lexically based clustering algorithms give similar results; we use a clustering algorithm based on insights from our previous research results on distributional semantics, [4] and we find that improving response speed and capacity of the system are more important to address (given Design principles 2 and 3 above) than marginal improvements in cluster quality. [5]

The example sentences from a hotel review data set given in (1) were all in the first iteration clustered together under the label *hotel.* A term such as *hotel* in hotel reviews does not appear to be a useful clustering feature. The texts should in most scenarios not end up being clustered on *hotel* but instead on *location* (for samples (1-a) and (1-c)) and *work* (for sample (1-b)) instead. Achieving this requires automatically reweighting term specificity during the clustering process, and, most importantly, as our system currently does, consulting the analyst to see if the clustering terms are appropriate and informative.

Manipulating clusters. Following the above design principles, the clusters are then displayed to the analyst for consideration. The main actions for the analyst are (1) joining existing closely related clusters, (2) discarding clusters that are of no interest, and

---

[4] The survey was performed in the Fall of 2016 to explore the attitudes to digital tools in teaching among students. http://www.berattarministeriet.se/undersokning/

[5] This is in keeping with earlier results comparing different text clustering systems, comparing their output with human assessments. There are differences, but they are comparatively small. [11]

(3) working on what terms characterise a cluster by approving synonyms suggested by the system or entering them manually.

The action of *joining* clusters into one common theme is a frequent operation to refine the end result, and our tool supports joining through simple direct manipulation. Similarly, clusters of low utility can be *discarded*, and the items constituting it are redistributed over other clusters instead. In this way, the content of the clusters are iteratively refined with simple and reversible point-and-click manipulation.

Synonyms. The nature of human language being as it is, we can expect many answers to diverge from the expected terminology. There will be many ways to say the same thing but you want them all in the same theme bin after the analysis process. The theme bin is represented by a set of terms which are prevalent in the texts clustered into that bin, and using a lexicon learned from text in the target language, [12] the system suggests synonyms to increase the coverage of that theme such as *friendly* for *pleasant* and related terms in a broad sense such as giving *coffee* and *pastry* for *breakfast* which will be of use in the example given in Figure (3). The analyst is also able to freely enter terms to enrich the representation of a theme.

(3) a. The staff were very *friendly* and *helpful.*
     b. The staff was *courteous* and *professional,* and they gave the impression that *hospitality* was something they enjoyed expressing.
     c. The staff was *personable* and demonstrated a true thankfulness for your business.
     d. The *breakfast* was always fine and we enjoyed a light *breakfast* every morning of a bowl of fruit together with a choice of a *bagel, toast* or *croissant.*
     e. However the hotel did offer free pastries, muffins, fruit, *coffee,* and juices every morning.
     f. There was no restaurant when we were there but they did offer *coffee* and *pastry* in the AM.

Multi-word terms. Most written languages build on white-space separated words, which is very convenient for tokenisation of the input stream in text processing. Many languages — and English is especially liberal in this respect — formulate multi-word compound terms quite freely, and all languages have set phrases such as *kick the bucket* and some degree of lexicalised multi-word terms, not least names such as *San Francisco* but also technical terms such as *linear accelerator* or *bed linen.* Our tool picks n-grams incrementally [12], as they appear in streaming data, and uses this to propose multi-word terms found in the text.

Handling several languages. Analysis of responses must as a rule be done in the language the responses were submitted. Our tool is built to be language agnostic and handles any human language (the only bottleneck being the quality of the synonym suggestions: to deliver reliable high-quality synonyms the system needs to have had access to some collection of general texts in the source language, such as a collection of newsprint, or a Wikipedia snapshot), and it still requires the analyst to be handy in the source language of the texts.

CASE STUDIES

We present here short abstracts of case studies where our tool as described above has been used. They serve to illustrate its versatility in application to multi-lingual and multi-cultural data, very open questions of wide-ranging themes, and drilling down into subthemes of customer reviews.

Attitude towards gender equality in seven cultural areas. In 2016, Gavagai was commissioned to execute a study in the Middle East, Latin America, Russia, and Sweden as part of an effort to monitor awareness of some aspects of Swedish society and Swedish foreign policy. The study collected 9800 free-text answers to open-ended survey questions in the various cultural areas and gave very various answers to questions such as the one given, with some sample answers, in (4). [5]

As one example we found a clear difference across cultural areas with respect to "feminism". The question as given in (4) gave very various attitudinal results. Explaining them by exploring the answers we found that feminism was associated with negative gender behavioural patterns such as machismo or with reverse discrimination in Latin American countries and in Russia, whereas it was accepted as a label for progressive policies and viewed comparatively positively in Middle Eastern countries. This analysis was made possible by identifying topical themes among the items with attitudinal loading.

(4) If a man or woman describes themselves as feminist, what would you think of that person? What kind of associations do you get? Is feminism positive or negative in your view? How would you describe feminism?

     a. *"Feminism is a positive concept, as women previously were discriminated against (earlier the world was sexist) whereas now women also find positions in areas which earlier were considered to be only for men."*
     b. *"Feminism is neutral until it has acquired a mass character."*
     c. *"I have a neutral view on this topic as each individual has their own perspective, as for me feminism shouldn't exist in today's world and education system."*
     d. *"I consider feminism to be negative that it is the opposite to machismo or am I wrong?"*

"What do you most wish for the coming year?". In order to better understand their customers' thoughts and wishes for the coming year one of our customers, AMF – a limited liability life insurance company, – sent out a survey to more than 100,000 senior citizens with 14,793 responses.[2] The survey included the open-ended question:

(5) What do you most wish for the coming year?

Two thirds of the senior citizens responding to the open-ended question wished for a better health for themselves, followed by concerns about their family, the global society and peace. The hopes were expressed using a manifold of formulations as might be expected from a broad sample of senior citizens from all walks of life. Clustering those into consistent themes would be a major challenge for any human operator, but with the terminology support we found

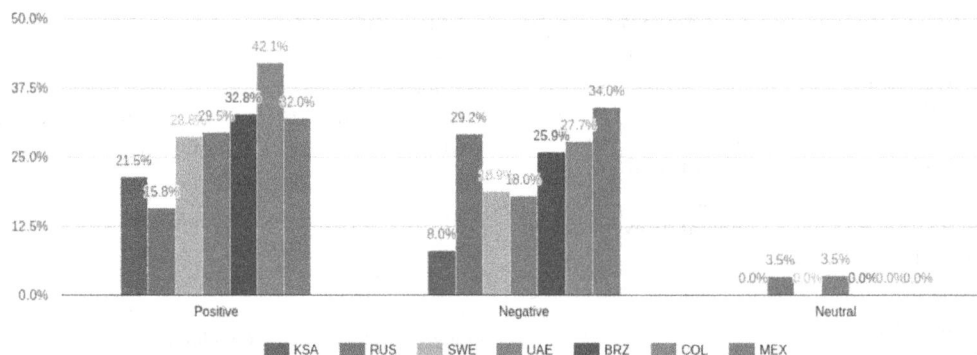

Figure 1: Attitude towards "feminism" in seven cultural areas.

handily that there were strong underlying topics in the content. Of the top ten themes expressed, three or even four concern various aspects of money and economy.

"What makes airline passengers happy?". We used our tool to analyse online consumer reviews of airlines published on an online consumer review site. [3] We collected 20 000 free text reviews of 22 airlines, with no quantitative data attached to them from the site. Attitude and topical themes are automatically identified and clustered. We measured how strongly opinionated reviewers are with regard to different aspects of their experience and we make these values comparable between different carriers. Some themes emerge from the text, with various degrees of prevalence for different airlines: Food, Drink, Seat, Service, Value, Inflight Entertainment, and so on and forth. Our main finding was that airline passengers seem to put up with almost anything, as long as they feel that they are being seen and looked after as individuals: the happiest passengers complained mostly about meals; the unhappiest about service. Satisfaction with staff service was a key driver for satisfaction with other aspects, such as the comfortability of the seat, the taste of the food, and for the overall passenger experience. This makes the results of review analyses much more actionable and shortens the path from attitude analysis to strategic business decisions.

LESSONS LEARNT

The advantages of using highly interactive automation for analysis is scale, speed, consistency, and saving human effort for the most important tasks.

An automated system has *full coverage*: all the above case studies would have been possible to do manually, if one single analyst or a very highly coordinated group of analysts had perused all the answers. This is impracticable at scale, unless automation is used.

An automated system is *quick*: an analyst is able to analyze more answers in a given time period which means that the number of responses to a survey can be larger which improves explanatory power. The granularity of the analysis can be increased to allow the analyst do drill down into more detailed and more actionable subtopics than before. The marginal effort for a larger survey increases sublinearly.

An automated system is *consistent*: it will allow one analyst to process more data, and provides the same initial results regardless

of who does the analysis, reducing inter-rater variation. If a coding scheme is retained for repeated use, e.g. in monthly surveys, the analysis will remain consistent over time.

These factors reduce cost and increase reliability. Most important, however, is relieving the human analyst from the frustrating aspects of the coding task, freeing human effort to the more central task of understanding themes.

REFERENCES

[1] Douglass R Cutting, David R Karger, Jan O Pedersen, and John W Tukey. 1992. Scatter/gather: A cluster-based approach to browsing large document collections. In *Proceedings of the 15th annual international ACM SIGIR conference on Research and development in information retrieval*. ACM.

[2] Gavagai. 2016. *What do you most wish for the coming year?* Stockholm. http://gavagai.se/wp-content/uploads/2016/03/AMFPension-CustomerCase.pdf

[3] Gavagai. 2017. *What makes airline passengers happy?* http://gavagai.se/blog/2017/04/24/what-makes-airline-passengers-happy/

[4] Amaru Cuba Gyllensten and Magnus Sahlgren. 2015. Navigating the Semantic Horizon using Relative Neighborhood Graphs. In *Proceedings of the Conference on Empirical Methods in Natural Language Processing, EMNLP*.

[5] Svenska institutet. 2016. *Feministisk utrikespolitik: rött skynke eller vit flagg?* Stockholm. https://si.se/wp-content/uploads/2016/12/Sverigebilden-Rapport-_om_synen_pa_-jamstalldhet.pdf (In Swedish; A slide deck with a summary in English is at http://gavagai.se/Gender_Equality_Study.pdf).

[6] Nick Jardine and Cornelis Joost van Rijsbergen. 1971. The use of hierarchic clustering in information retrieval. *Information storage and retrieval* 7, 5 (1971).

[7] Sofus A. Macskassy, Arunava Banerjee, Brian D. Davison, and Haym Hirsh. 1998. Human Performance on Clustering Web Pages: A Preliminary Study. In *Proceedings of the Conference on Knowledge Discovery and Data Mining (KDD)*.

[8] Andrew McCallum, Kamal Nigam, Jason Rennie, and Kristie Seymore. 1999. A machine learning approach to building domain-specific search engines. In *Proceedings of the International Joint Conference on Artificial Intelligence*. IJCAI.

[9] Alicia O'Cathain and Kate J Thomas. 2004. " Any other comments?" Open questions on questionnaires–a bane or a bonus to research? *BMC medical research methodology* 4, 1 (2004).

[10] Peter Pirolli, Patricia Schank, Marti Hearst, and Christine Diehl. 1996. Scatter/gather browsing communicates the topic structure of a very large text collection. In *Proceedings of the SIGCHI conference on Human factors in computing systems*. ACM.

[11] Dmitri G Roussinov and Hsinchun Chen. 1999. Document clustering for electronic meetings: an experimental comparison of two techniques. *Decision Support Systems* 27, 1 (1999).

[12] Magnus Sahlgren, Amaru Cuba Gyllensten, Fredrik Espinoza, Ola Hamfors, Jussi Karlgren, Fredrik Olsson, Per Persson, Akshay Viswanathan, and Anders Holst. 2016. The Gavagai Living Lexicon. In *Language Resources and Evaluation Conference*. ELRA.

[13] Mark Sanderson and Bruce Croft. 1999. Deriving concept hierarchies from text. In *Proceedings of the 22nd annual international ACM SIGIR conference on Research and development in information retrieval*. ACM.

[14] Greg Schohn and David Cohn. 2000. Less is More: Active Learning with Support Vector Machines. In *Proceedings of the International Conference on Machine Learning*. ACM.

Automatic Persona Generation (APG):
A Rationale and Demonstration

Soon-gyo Jung
Qatar Computing Research Institute
Hamad Bin Khalifa University
sjung@hbku.edu.qa

Joni Salminen
Qatar Computing Research Institute
Hamad Bin Khalifa University
jsaminen@hbku.edu.qa

Haewoon Kwak
Qatar Computing Research Institute
Hamad Bin Khalifa University
haewoon@acm.org

Jisun An
Qatar Computing Research Institute
Hamad Bin Khalifa University
jisun.an@acm.org

Bernard J. Jansen
Qatar Computing Research Institute
Hamad Bin Khalifa University
jjansen@acm.org

ABSTRACT

We present Automatic Persona Generation (APG), a methodology and system for quantitative persona generation using large amounts of online social media data. The system is operational, beta deployed with several client organizations in multiple industry verticals and ranging from small-to-medium sized enterprises to large multi-national corporations. Using a robust web framework and stable back-end database, APG is currently processing tens of millions of user interactions with thousands of online digital products on multiple social media platforms, such as Facebook and YouTube. APG identifies both distinct and impactful user segments and then creates persona descriptions by automatically adding pertinent features, such as names, photos, and personal attributes. We present the overall methodological approach, architecture development, and main system features. APG has a potential value for organizations distributing content via online platforms and is unique in its approach to persona generation. APG can be found online at https://persona.qcri.org.

CCS CONCEPTS

• **Human-centered computing** → **Human computer interaction (HCI)** → **Empirical studies in HCI**

KEYWORDS

Personas; User Experience Research; User Analytics

ACM Reference format:
Jung, S.G., Salminen, J., Kwak, H., An, J., and Jansen, B. J. Automatic Persona Generation (APG): A Rationale and Demonstration. In *Proceedings of ACM SIGIR Conference on Human Information Interaction and Retrieval, New Brunswick, NJ, USA, 11-15 March 2018 (CHIIR'18)*, 4 pages. DOI: https://doi.org/10.1145/3176349.3176893

1 INTRODUCTION

The instrument of personas is used in a wide range of domains from software development to system design to marketing in order to describe and communicate about core users and customers. A persona is a fictional individual embodying the attributes of a key market segment that could be users, audience, or customers. In simple terms, a persona is a representation of a group of people with similar behaviors and demographics. One can think of a persona as a mental shortcut that explains the who, what, and why of a set of individuals. Personas can help define organizational strategy, develop new products, and improve customer operations. Personas are integrated into many design and product development processes [1, 2].

However, personas have traditionally been challenging to create [3, 4], as their creation is an expensive and slow process, involving ethnographic studies, surveys, or focus group interviews. Given that these methods are one-time data collection events, the created personas can quickly stale requiring another round of data collection. Also, without the opportunity to verify the data collection process, end users of personas lack confirmation of whether or not the personas are representative of their current target users. These limitations are some of the motivations for our efforts to automate persona creation with system development and underlying research that addresses the major shortcomings of manual persona creation.

APG leverages privacy-preserving aggregated data of user interactions with product content posted on major online social media and other analytics platforms. APG collects, processes, and decomposes this actual user data and then enriches the results systematically with descriptive attributes to produce data-driven persona profiles. APG can generate personas from millions of user interactions within a couple of days versus the months it takes to create personas via traditional approaches [5].

Here, we provide an overview of APG, including architecture and development. Then, we highlight some of the many features of APG, focusing on the core features. We then discuss commercial efforts underway, followed by a conclusion presenting a brief recap.

2 SYSTEM OVERVIEW

APG is built using a stable, robust, and scalable structure employing (a) the Flask web framework to support the front-end applications, services, and application programing interfaces (APIs), (b) PostgreSQL database for back-end data storage, processing, and (c) Python libraries including Pandas and scikit-learn for data analysis.

For configuration and data collection, APG accesses the targeted online social media platforms, for example, Facebook or YouTube, via the analytics API provided to the account holders. Typical user profile data from these platforms are demographic variables of gender, age, country location, and which site the user comes from, although at an aggregated level. Via the social media platform's API, the APG system also collects the detailed interactions of users with the online content. This detailed level of data is accessible only to managers of a particular social media channel.

To automatically generate personas from this data, our methodology [6] requires a sequential approach, consisting of:

- identifying the distinct user interaction patterns from the data set,
- linking these distinct user interaction patterns to the set of user demographic groups,
- identifying impactful user demographic groups from the data set,
- creating shell personas via demographic attributes, and
- enriching these shell personas to create rich persona descriptions.

As the data from online platforms are aggregated, APG must disaggregate it. To do this, we develop a matrix representing users' interaction with the online content, such as videos. We denote by V the $g{\times}c$ matrix of g user groups (G_1, G_2, ..., G_g) and c contents (C_1, C_2 ,..., C_c). The element of the matrix V, V_{ij}, is any statistic that represents the interaction of user group G_i for content C_j. With this matrix as the basis, APG can identify first distinct user behavior patterns (which can be patterns of associations between users and contents) and then the impactful user segments from this set of distinct user patterns.

Once APG has the matrix V, the next step is discovering the underlying latent factors, i.e. the user interaction patterns, that become the basis of the personas. APG uses non-negative matrix factorization (NMF) [7] that can find multiple behavioral patterns even from a single group. As a behavioral pattern can be associated with multiple demographic groupings, APG selects the demographic group with the largest coefficient.

The result of NMF is a set of shell personas that we turn into rich personas by adding personal attributes. To generate a name for a persona, we build a dictionary of names by collecting popular names by gender and year from the 181 countries. Through <age group, gender, and country> of a representative group, APG can automatically assign an age, gender, and country appropriate name to a persona. To assign a photo to a persona, APG stores nearly 4,000 commercial stock photos of models for different ethnicities, genders, and ages, to which the copyrights were purchased. Through <age group, gender, ethnicity, country> of a

representative user segment, APG can assign an appropriate photo to a persona. APG can filter users based on topical interests by leveraging the collection of content consumed by that persona.

The final result of this attribute incorporation is rich insightful persona profiles automatically generated from aggregated, privacy preserving social media data, with the entire process outlined in Fig. 1.

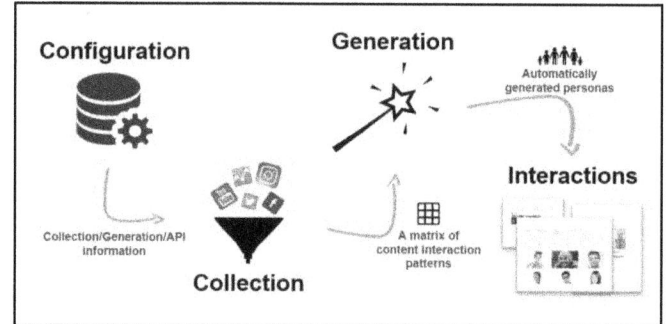

Figure 1: APG flowchart from server configuration to data collection, to persona generation, to users accessing the system.

We now present some of the main features of APG to demonstrate the capabilities of the system, with others shown during the live demonstration.

3 SYSTEM FEATURES

3.1 APG Interface and Persona Listing

3.1.1 APG Interface. As shown in Fig. 2, a user who wishes to generate personas can select the number to generate, with the system currently set for a minimum of 5 and a maximum of 15. The user can also select the desired platform and is provided options for viewing the personas. The user can generate the desired number of personas via the Show button.

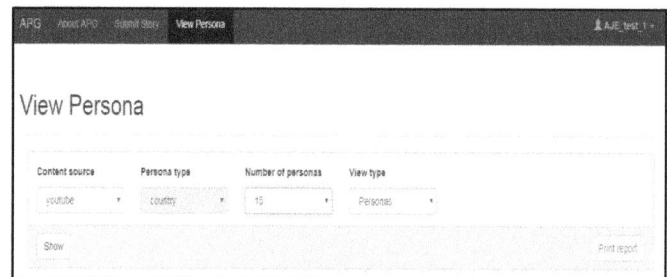

Figure 2: APG interface with options for selecting the content source platform (e.g., Facebook, YouTube), the number of personas to generate from the data (5 to 15), and the view type (various formats of viewing the relationship between content and personas). The options in the screen capture are set to YouTube and 15 personas.

3.1.2 APG Persona Listing. The listing of the personas, combined with the mouseovers, afford the user the ability to get an overview of the audience segments in terms of demographic information, as shown in Fig. 3. By hovering over one of the persona images, the basic persona attributes are displayed, in this case *'Andrew, United Kingdom, 31, Male'*. The user can also change content collections, change the number of personas, or apply different filterings, such as data set, topics of interest, ethnicity, country, age, or gender.

3.2 Persona Profile

Clicking on one of the images in the persona listing will display the corresponding persona profile, with one persona profile displayed in Fig. 4. Each of the displayed sections of the persona is discussed below.

3.2.1 Entire persona set. Along the top of the persona profile is a series of preview pictures permitting navigation to another of the persona profiles.

3.2.2 Image and base information. The persona profile contains an appropriate image along with the base information (i.e., name, age, country, and gender) of the persona.

3.2.3 About Persona. This section is a short snippet in paragraph form that recaps the base information, combined with topics of interest, the device used for the interaction with the online platform, and level of engagement with content (see Fig. 4). Clicking on the graph icon shown in the title bar displays the proportions of career, marriage, parenting, and educational status (see Fig. 5).

3.2.4 Topics of Interest. As part of the matrix decomposition, we can identify the specific pieces of content that a persona interacts with. APG topically classifies this content, displaying the most and least interesting topics for the persona (see Fig. 4), which is an on-going research efforts [8].

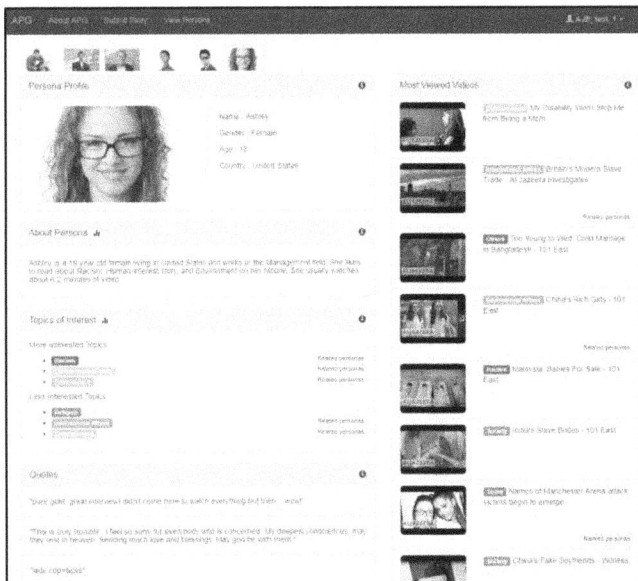

Figure 3: APG persona listings, with mouse-over data displayed for one persona. As APG archives all data collections, the user can change the data set. The user can also apply filters of Topic, Ethnicity, Country, Age, and Gender.

Figure 4: Persona profile for Ashley. The top ribbon presents the entire set of personas, in this case 6. The image is gender and age appropriate. There is an About section outlining device used and interaction time. Most liked and least liked topics are displayed, followed by social media comments left by those who are like Ashley. Along the right rail are top videos interacted with.

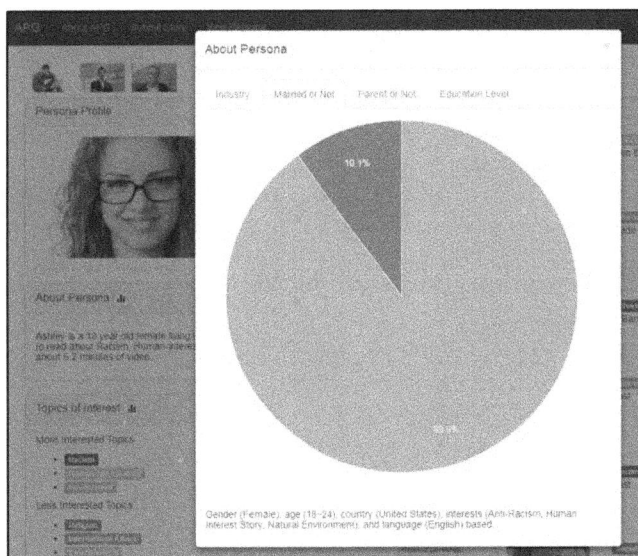

Figure 5: For the About section, clicking on the graph icon displays breakdown on career, marriage, parenting, and education of the persona. In this case, marital status.

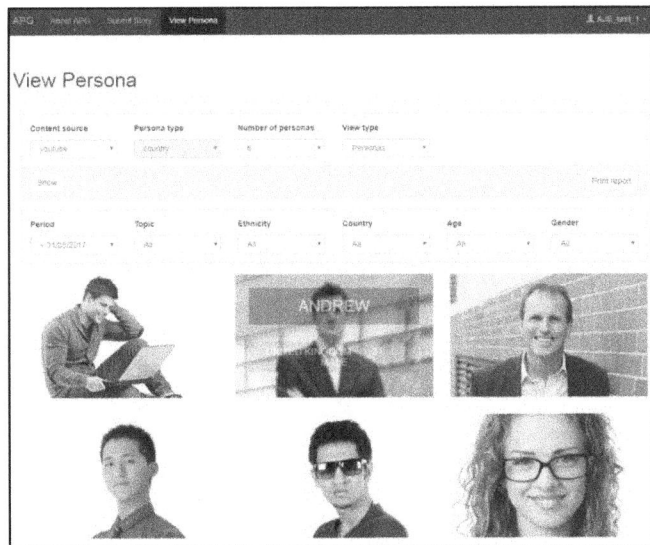

3.2.5 Quotes. To provide contextual and personal insights of the persona, social media comments aligned with the topics of interest are displayed in the persona profile (see Fig. 4).

3.2.6 Most Viewed Videos. The persona profile displays the top content most interacted with by this persona. Each content piece is linked to the actual online content (see Fig. 4).

3.2.7 Audience Size. The persona profile also displays the potential reach of the persona, which is the size of the user segment based on demographical attributes and topical interests. The potential reach numbers are generated via a series of Targeting Audiences API calls to the Facebook Marketing (see Fig. 6).

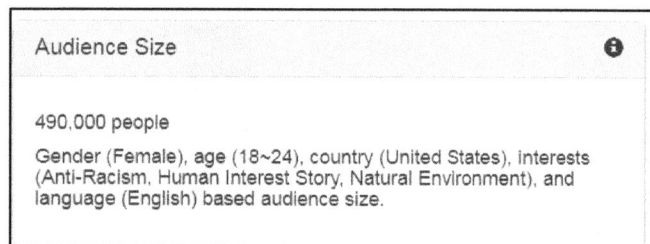

Figure 6: The Audience Size section of the persona profiles displays the number of people that match the persona's attributes, both demographically and behaviorally. This feature helps the end user of APG determine the potential impact of the user segment represented by this persona.

There are a multitude of other features and capabilities that will be presented during the live demonstration, including comparing personas between periods, comparing current user segment size for personas against potential audience size, and displaying personas related to each item of content [9].

4 RESULTS AND DISCUSSION

4.1 Comparison with Other Systems

As far as we know, APG is the first system to use large amounts of online behavioral user data for quantitative and automatic persona generation. Earlier efforts with data-driven personas [10] are more limited, as discussed in [5].

4.2 Commercialization Efforts

Currently, APG is in beta use with three major multi-national corporations, one major non-profit organization, and two SMEs in the retail vertical. Efforts are underway to expand the list of beta clients. The APG project has received funding for development,

which will take the system to a Technology Readiness Level 8 (TRL-8). The APG has one evaluation license in place and it participated in an Entrepreneur in Residence (EIR) program, with start-up funding in progress.

5 CONCLUSIONS

In this research, we demonstrate that APG can automatically create personas from large scale, quantitative, aggregated user data from major online social media platforms. The resulting personas are based on real data reflecting real user behavior and can be updated with ease. APG is flexible for application in a wide range of contexts.

REFERENCES

[1] Elina Eriksson, Henrik Artman, and Anna Swartling, "The Secret Life of a Persona: When the Personal Becomes Private," presented at the Proceedings of the SIGCHI Conference on Human Factors in Computing Systems, Paris, France, 2013.

[2] Erin Friess, "Personas and Decision Making in the Design Process: An Ethnographic Case Study," presented at the Proceedings of the SIGCHI Conference on Human Factors in Computing Systems, Austin, Texas, USA, 2012.

[3] K. Ronkko, "An Empirical Study Demonstrating How Different Design Constraints, Project Organization and Contexts Limited the Utility of Personas," in Proceedings of the 38th Annual Hawaii International Conference on System Sciences, 2005, pp. 220a-220a.

[4] Christopher N. Chapman and Russell P. Milham, "The Personas' New Clothes: Methodological and Practical Arguments against a Popular Method," in Human Factors and Ergonomics Society Annual Meeting, San Francisco, CA, 2006, pp. 634-636.

[5] Jung, S., An, J., Kwak, H. Ahmad, M., Nielsen, L., and Jansen, B. J. (2017) Persona Generation from Aggregated Social Media Data. ACM Conference on Human Factors in Computing Systems 2017 (CHI2017). P. 1748-1755.

[6] An, J., Kwak, H., and Jansen, B. J., (2017) Personas for Content Creators via Decomposed Aggregate Audience Statistics. Advances in Social Network Analysis and Mining (ASONAM 2017). Sydney, Australia, p. 632-635. Australia, 31 Jul – 3 Aug.

[7] Daniel D. Lee and Sebastian H. Seung, "Learning the Parts of Objects by Non-Negative Matrix Factorization," Nature, vol. 401, pp. 788-791, 1999.

[8] Zarrinkalam, F., Kahani, M., Bagheri, E. (2018) Mining user interests over active topics on social networks, Information Processing & Management, 54(2) 339-357.

[9] Salminen, J., Nielsen, L., An, J., Jung, S.G., Kwak, H., and Jansen, B. J. (2018) Is More Better?": Impact of Multiple Photos on Perception of Persona Profiles. ACM CHI Conference on Human Factors in Computing Systems (CHI2018), Montréal, Canada, 21-26 April.

[10] McGinn and N. Kotamraju, "Data-driven persona development," in Proceedings of the SIGCHI Conference on Human Factors in Computing Systems, 2008, pp. 1521–1524.

Coagmento: Past, Present, and Future of an Individual and Collaborative Information Seeking Platform

Matthew Mitsui
Department of Computer Science
Rutgers University
mmitsui@cs.rutgers.edu

Jiqun Liu, Chirag Shah
School of Communication & Information
Rutgers University
{jl2033,chirags}@rutgers.edu

ABSTRACT

In this demo, we present *Coagmento*, a Web-based, open-source tool for information seeking projects that collects information for individuals and groups and helps facilitate collaborative information seeking. *Coagmento* has been used in information retrieval and human-computer interaction studies to investigate individual and group information seeking behaviors in a lab or a field setting. In this demo, we discuss what *Coagmento* is, its past uses in prior studies, and its present state. We also discuss current work in progress. With *Coagmento* recently passing its 10th anniversary, we discuss our intention to make it a tool that is easy to configure for a human information behavior researcher with little programming skill.

CCS CONCEPTS

• **Information systems** → **Collaborative search**; Open source software; • **Human-centered computing** → **Computer supported cooperative work**; Open source software;

KEYWORDS

collaborative information seeking; user studies; human-computer interaction; web search behavior;

ACM Reference Format:
Matthew Mitsui and Jiqun Liu, Chirag Shah. 2018. Coagmento: Past, Present, and Future of an Individual and Collaborative Information Seeking Platform. In *CHIIR '18: 2018 Conference on Human Information Interaction Retrieval, March 11–15, 2018, New Brunswick, NJ, USA*. ACM, New York, NY, USA, Article 4, 4 pages. https://doi.org/10.1145/3176349.3176896

1 BACKGROUND

Over decades of interactive information retrieval research, there has been much work linking interactive information retrieval behaviors to interesting phenomena, such as the type of task a person is working on or a person's task/topic familiarity. Such works have also attempted to use a searcher's information seeking behavior to support their overall search experience, for instance by providing live suggestions. Behind each of these data-driven studies about information seeking behavior is a great data collection tool. Other data collection tools include recent works by He and Yilmaz [6] and

Huurdeman et al [8]. Such tools collect an individual's behaviors as they browse through the web and/or a custom search engine web portal on a desktop browser such as Firefox or Chrome. Such infrastructure offers the flexibility of allowing researchers to choose whether to conduct a laboratory study or a field study.

Some information retrieval researchers have focused particularly on collaborative information seeking (CIS) efforts where people work in groups. Corresponding tools to study and support CIS include Ariadne [17], Cerchiamo [3], CoSearch [1], and SearchTogether [12]. *Coagmento*, inspired by these past systems, has been in development and use since 2007 as a tool for supporting collaborative information seeking [2]. It made its public debut in 2009 [16] with subsequent versions demonstrated at various places (e.g., [5, 11]). Some of the design lessons in developing a system like this were presented by Shah [13]. *Coagmento* fundamentally differs by supporting both individual and collaborative work in both synchronous and asynchronous contexts. It has been used in several studies.

Coagmento has recently passed its 10-year anniversary, and it has since undergone several foundational shifts. We will present the current state of *Coagmento*, future work, and the implications towards future research in individual and collaborative information seeking.

2 WHAT IS COAGMENTO?

2.1 As a Researcher's Tool

While much focus on Coagmento has been the types of interface support it provides, at its core it is also a browser logger. It logs the pages and queries of users as they search for information. This functionality has been utilized in a variety of studies purely for the sake of recording and analyzing log data. Hendahewa and Shah[7] used these recording capabilities on top of traditional browser logging methods to forecast how well a person will perform in a session-based Web search task. In addition, components of the collection have been modified and utilized to create new interfaces. For instance, Mitsui et al.[10] incorporated Coagmento and other tools to record study query-level information seeking intentions in search sessions to study interactive IR. Other traditional data capture methods can of course be incorporated with Coagmento, such as diary studies in Shah and Leeder[15], commercial video capture tools such as Morae in Mitsui et al.[10], and also face capture in González-Ibáñez et al.[4]. Of course, Coagmento is intended for studying CIS, for which it has also been utilized as in Shah et al.[14] and Knight et al.[9]. Shah et al. [14] directly examined the effect of crowd size on search performance, assigning Web search tasks to synchronously working groups of dyads and triads. Knight et al.[9]

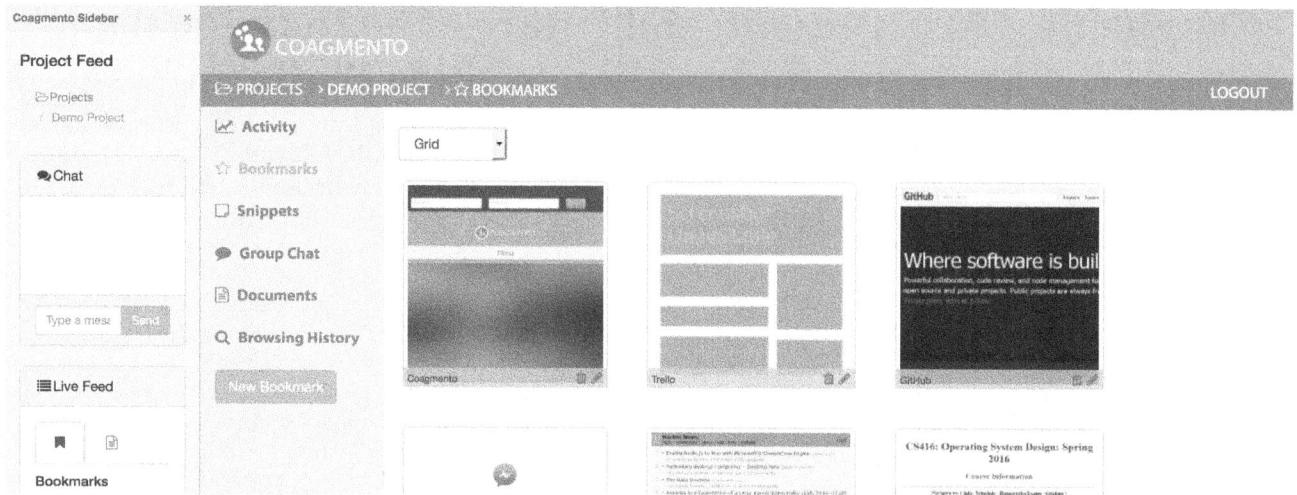

Figure 1: Coagmento web interface, including sidebar (left) and project page with thumbnails of collected bookmarks (center).

examined groups' assessments of expertise and document trust in a collaborative task. Moreover, it has also been used for several laboratory studies, such as in Hendahewa and Shah[7]. In such studies, a traditional linear flow of "stages" is incorporated into the base version of Coagmento. Stages are a linear flow of pages typical to an IR-based laboratory study, such as a demographic survey, a pre-task questionnaire, tutorial videos, and a post-task questionnaire. While Coagmento has largely been used for small-scale studies, it has also been used for larger ones. Knight et al.[9] and Hendahewa and Shah[7] examined the logs of over 1000 and 200 participants, respectively, engaged in a controlled study, with browser log data collected through Coagmento.

2.2 As a System

Coagmento comprises of two parts. The first and main component is the browser plugin. This is installed on individual machines where a researcher wants to collect a study participant's information seeking behavior. Installation may occur on a person's private machine in a field study or on a lab machine for a lab study. The public version of the plugin is available in several flavors, including Firefox, Chrome, and even Android and iOS[1]. It includes several buttons, a toolbar and a sidebar. The toolbar is typically used to house buttons for bookmarking pages or saving snippets of text. The sidebar is used to display these things as well as to interact with the chat. More importantly, these are overlaid on the browser window so that a participant may seamlessly interact with Coagmento while searching for information in parallel. While a person may engage with the web service as in Figure 1, they may alternatively engage with the sidebar in parallel searching on Google or browsing the news. The plugin is also the main component that collects browsing and searching behavior of users. The sidebar is given in Figure 2. An example of the main web-based interface - programmed in PHP - is also shown in Figure 1, where a user can edit their browsing history.

This front-end functionality is supported by several back-end services. First is the core functionality for storing and retrieving data. This was once programmed in vanilla PHP but is now built on a framework called Laravel[2]. It is a Model-View-Controller PHP framework that offers several constructs that make further Coagmento development more manageable. Laravel follows modern web development conventions, such as defining routes and following RESTful APIs. It also provides support for several common functions useful to any web service and also Coagmento, such as authentication middleware, administrator privileges, and form validation. While Coagmento is traditionally built on MySQL, Laravel supports the use of several other types of SQL databases. Coagmento is additionally supported by real-time functionality using Node.js[3]. Real-time functionality is necessary for any interactive study, especially one where there is synchronous collaboration such as in Shah et al.[14] and Knight et al.[9]. Node.js provides this through "push notifications", which are common in mobile applications like Twitter where real-time reactivity is desirable but computational resources are scarce. Push notifications push live updates to project collaborators, such as when a collaborator creates a new bookmark.

The expected installation workflow of Coagmento is given in Figure 3. To summarize, any computer with PHP, Laravel, Node.js and a SQL database could be a *Coagmento* server.

3 WORK IN PROGRESS

The largest hurdle in accessibility to Coagmento is that it still requires programming experience to be modified. Coagmento comes with many features out of the box, but not all researchers are interested in using the full suite of tools. In such a case Coagmento needs to be modified, which currently requires at least some navigation of code. Various data collection processes and visualization components all need to be modified or omitted for new studies. Other options that need configuration include database credentials

---

[1]http://coagmento.org/download.php

[2]https://laravel.com/
[3]https://nodejs.org/en/

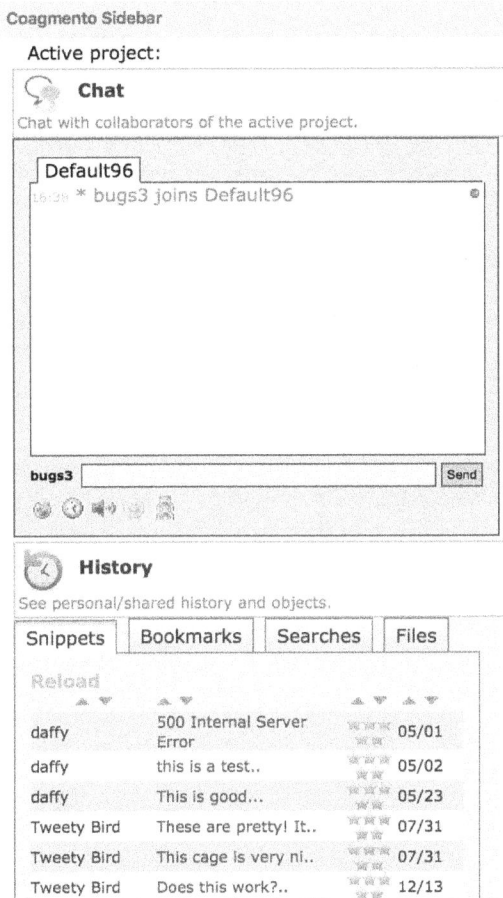

Figure 2: Sidebar.

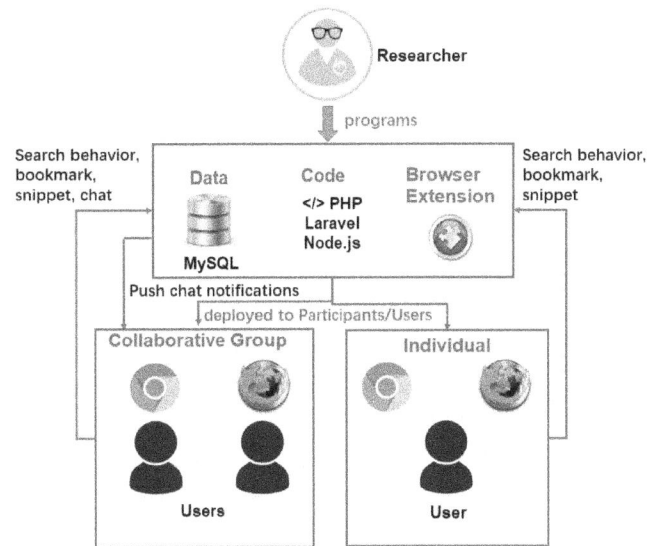

Figure 3: Overview of the flow of data and software for Co-agmento. Researchers program the main code and distribute plugin instances to participants.

4 WHAT'S IN THE DEMO?

In this demo, we will show some of the basic front-end functionality for out-of-the-box Coagmento. This includes the functionality of the web-based service and also the desktop browser plugin. We can show interested parties how to download and install Coagmento on their machines. We can also walk interested programmers through the basics of the code base, and we can help interested parties create a fresh installation of Coagmento on their machines. The tool is currently available for public use at the footnote below.[4]

ACKNOWLEDGMENTS

Work on Coagmento is supported through the Institute of Museum and Library Services (IMLS) grant LG-81-16-0025-16 and the National Science Foundation (NSF) grant IIS-1717488.

REFERENCES

[1] Saleema Amershi and Meredith Ringel Morris. 2008. CoSearch: A System for Co-located Collaborative Web Search. In *Proceedings of CHI '08*. ACM, New York, NY, USA, 1647–1656. https://doi.org/10.1145/1357054.1357311
[2] Xin Fu, Diane Kelly, and Chirag Shah. 2007. Using Collaborative Queries to Improve Retrieval for Difficult Topics. In *Proceedings of ACM SIGIR '07*. ACM, New York, NY, USA, 2. https://doi.org/10.1145/1277741.1277955
[3] Gene Golovchinsky, John Adcock, Jeremy Pickens, Pernilla Qvarfordt, and Maribeth Back. 2008. Cerchiamo: a collaborative exploratory search tool. *Proceedings of CSCW* (2008), 8–12.
[4] Roberto González-Ibáñez, Chirag Shah, and Natalia Cordova-Rubio. 2011. Smile! Studying expressivity of happiness as a synergic factor in collaborative information seeking. *Proceedings of the American Society for Information Science and Technology* 48, 1 (2011), 1–10. https://doi.org/10.1002/meet.2011.14504801171
[5] Roberto González-ibáñez and Chirag Shah. 2011. Coagmento: A System for Supporting Collaborative Information Seeking. *The74th Annual Meeting of the American Society for Information Science and Technology ASIST 2011* (2011).
[6] Jiyin He and Emine Yilmaz. 2017. User Behaviour and Task Characteristics: A Field Study of Daily Information Behaviour. In *Proceedings of the 2017 Conference*

to which data is committed and administrative credentials for researchers. If a researcher wants to design a questionnaire for a human-computer interaction study (e.g. "How was your experience using this tool?", "How satisfied were you in finding information?"), this is an extra step that needs deliberate programming effort.

Understandably, not everyone who has used Coagmento (or will ever want to use it) has a background in Computer Science, let alone computer programming. The main goal of human behavior research is to generate and investigate questions and to publish the answers. It is not to generate, investigate, and publish code. Therefore, any extra steps from question generation to answer are a barrier to research. Our current work is in breaking down this barrier so that human behavior researchers with little to no programming experience can quickly investigate their research questions. Future work in this regard includes:

- Questionnaire generation through a GUI
- Stage generation through a GUI, for a study that contains stages such as consent forms, pre-task questionnaires and post-task questionnaires
- Toggling existing components in a configuration file
- A (official) Chrome extension

---

[4]https://github.com/InfoSeeking/Coagmento

on Conference Human Information Interaction and Retrieval (CHIIR '17). ACM, New York, NY, USA, 67–76. https://doi.org/10.1145/3020165.3020188

[7] Chathra Hendahewa and Chirag Shah. 2017. Evaluating User Search Trails in Exploratory Search Tasks. *Inf. Process. Manage.* 53, 4 (July 2017), 905–922. https://doi.org/10.1016/j.ipm.2017.04.001

[8] Hugo C. Huurdeman, Max L. Wilson, and Jaap Kamps. 2016. Active and Passive Utility of Search Interface Features in Different Information Seeking Task Stages. In *Proceedings of the 2016 ACM on Conference on Human Information Interaction and Retrieval (CHIIR '16)*. ACM, New York, NY, USA, 3–12. https://doi.org/10.1145/2854946.2854957

[9] Simon Knight, Bart Rienties, Karen Littleton, Matthew Mitsui, Dirk Tempelaar, and Chirag Shah. 2017. The relationship of (perceived) epistemic cognition to interaction with resources on the internet. *Computers in Human Behavior* 73, Supplement C (2017), 507 – 518. https://doi.org/10.1016/j.chb.2017.04.014

[10] Matthew Mitsui, Jiqun Liu, Nicholas J. Belkin, and Chirag Shah. 2017. Predicting Information Seeking Intentions from Search Behaviors. In *Proceedings of the 40th International ACM SIGIR Conference on Research and Development in Information Retrieval (SIGIR '17)*. ACM, New York, NY, USA, 1121–1124. https://doi.org/10.1145/3077136.3080737

[11] M. Mitsui and C. Shah. 2016. Coagmento 2.0: A system for capturing individual and group information seeking behavior. In *Proceedings of the ACM/IEEE Joint Conference on Digital Libraries*, Vol. 2016-Septe. https://doi.org/10.1145/2910896.2925447

[12] Meredith Ringel Morris and Eric Horvitz. 2007. SearchTogether: An Interface for Collaborative Web Search. In *Proceedings of the 20th ACM UIST Symposium (UIST '07)*. ACM, New York, NY, USA, 3–12. https://doi.org/10.1145/1294211.1294215

[13] Chirag Shah. 2012. Coagmento âĂŞ A Case Study in Designing User-Centric Collaborative Information Seeking System. In *System Science and Collaborative Information Systems: Theories, Practices and New Research*, Emilia Currás and Nuria Lloret (Eds.). IGI Global, 242–257.

[14] Chirag Shah, Chathra Hendahewa, and Roberto González-Ibá nez. 2015. Two's company, but three's no crowd: Evaluating exploratory web search for individuals and teams. *Aslib Journal of Information Management* 67, 6 (2015), 636–662. https://doi.org/10.1108/AJIM-05-2015-0082 arXiv:https://doi.org/10.1108/AJIM-05-2015-0082

[15] Chirag Shah and Chris Leeder. 2016. Exploring collaborative work among graduate students through the C5 model of collaboration: A diary study. *Journal of Information Science* 42, 5 (2016), 609–629. https://doi.org/10.1177/0165551515603322 arXiv:https://doi.org/10.1177/0165551515603322

[16] Chirag Shah, Gary Marchionini, and Diane Kelly. 2009. Learning Design Principles for a Collaborative Information Seeking System. In *CHI '09 Extended Abstracts on Human Factors in Computing Systems (CHI EA '09)*. ACM, New York, NY, USA, 3419–3424. https://doi.org/10.1145/1520340.1520496

[17] Michael B. Twidale, David M. Nichols, and Chris D. Paice. 1997. Browsing is a collaborative process. *Information Processing Management* 33, 6 (1997). https://doi.org/10.1016/S0306-4573(97)00040-X

HealthTalks — A Mobile App to Improve Health Communication and Personal Information Management

João M. Monteiro

Institute for Systems and Computer Engineering, Technology and Science (INESC TEC)

Porto, Portugal

joao.m.lopes@inesctec.pt

Carla Teixeira Lopes

INESC TEC

Faculty of Engineering of the University of Porto

Porto, Portugal

ctl@fe.up.pt

ABSTRACT

A patient's health literacy has a direct impact on their health, but more than a third of the USA population has "basic" or "below basic" levels of health literacy. An individual's wellbeing is also affected by the communication with their physician, as the use of technical terminology may hinder the patient's understanding. A patient's ability to, later on, recall or retrieve helpful information could reduce these comprehension problems and this can be improved by a good management of personal health information. To help overcome some of these problems, we created HealthTalks, a mobile app that empowers the patients, easing their daily health tasks and self-care ability. It does so by recording the audio of a medical appointment, transcribing its dialogue, giving more information about medical concepts employed, and allowing information associated with medical appointments to be easily managed by the patient. Usability tests were conducted with elderly people, ranging from the icons used to the general user experience. Results were very positive, with users accomplishing most tasks successfully and often with the least amount of clicks. We also evaluated the speech recognition software used, Google Cloud Speech API, reaching an error rate of 12 percent in medical texts.

CCS CONCEPTS

• **Human-centered computing** → **HCI design and evaluation methods**; *Human computer interaction (HCI)*; *Ubiquitous and mobile computing*; • **Applied computing** → **Health care information systems**; *Life and medical sciences*; • **Information systems** → Information systems applications; Mobile information processing systems; Information retrieval;

KEYWORDS

Health literacy, Physician-patient communication, Personal information management, Speech-to-text, Mobile application

ACM Reference Format:

João M. Monteiro and Carla Teixeira Lopes. 2018. HealthTalks — A Mobile App to Improve Health Communication and Personal Information Management. In *CHIIR '18: 2018 Conference on Human Information Interaction & Retrieval, March 11–15, 2018, New Brunswick, NJ, USA*. ACM, New York, NY, USA, 4 pages. https://doi.org/10.1145/3176349.3176894

1 INTRODUCTION

Health literacy is the ability of an individual to acquire and understand health information, as well as applying it to obtain a better health condition for themselves and their communities [8, 12]. Individuals with low health literacy are more likely to misinterpret their health professional [2] and medication instructions [9], which may result in inadequate treatments and self-care. In 2003, more than a third of Americans had "basic" or "below basic" levels of health literacy, with the majority of the country having an intermediate level [15].

A patient can acquire health information from different ways: their doctors, their community, or sources such as the Internet. A patient's health literacy level will affect their dialogue with medical professionals, as well as the terminology gap between them, which may hinder their communication [7]. Physicians should actively listen to their patients, not interrupting them, asking questions, and creating a friendly environment for the patients to do the same, as that will lead to better treatments [1].

A proper personal health information management (PHIM) may help patients overcome comprehension problems and contributes to a more efficient health management. Among others, it enables patients to identify points of discussion during consultations and to, later on, recall what was discussed and retrieve additional information. However, this usually fails due to human errors such as recording information incorrectly [6].

In order to tackle some of these problems we created HealthTalks. It is an Android app able to a) record the physician's speech; b) link each recording to an appointment; c) transcribe each recording; d) detect medical concepts used in the transcription and provide additional information for each of them; e) allow an easy management of appointments through custom fields such as medical specialty and the physician's name; and f) allow the association of notes to each appointment.

This makes it both a personal health information management tool with customizable and searchable appointment pages; and a health information repository that explains the physician's medical vocabulary. Any patient can benefit from this app, but it should be most helpful to those with lower levels of health literacy.

2 RELATED WORK

Some solutions such as HealthTranslator [3] aim at reducing the terminology gap between patients and physicians by providing easy access to databases with technical concepts. But these systems cannot circumvent a patient's forgetfulness or incomprehension, which means that they may not help patients to better understand their doctors. Moreover, to the best of our knowledge, no existing solution focuses on the physician's speech and their dialogue with the patient to recognize the terms that are more relevant to the patient.

There are several different implementations of systems that store electronic health records, though many do not require any input from the patient as they are aimed at their health professionals [19]. This, in our opinion, is a limitation since it ignores the patient's health literacy and PHIM methods, negating any potential improvement in those areas. On the other hand, relying exclusively on the patient's input can lead to unreliable accounts of health conditions due to the limitations of the patient's knowledge [20]. Patient's understanding of their own health condition can then be seen as an obstacle to an efficient management of personal health information [14], so it is paramount to circumvent that aspect when building a PHIM app.

In terms of existing mobile apps for health consumers, we can highlight "Patient Journey App", "Patient.info" and "Patient Access". They are all health information sources, the first of which requires the physician's input. They are all restricted to a few select countries and languages and when serving as a glossary they depend on the patient correctly remembering the term they are looking for. Other apps such as "Apple Health" and "S Health" focus on personal health information management, but have very limited features concerning self-care.

3 HEALTHTALKS

HealthTalks is beneficial in any medical field, being versatile and customizable. Moreover, it was developed with a user-centric approach in order to facilitate its use by people less adapted to technology. It will be adapted to recognize Portuguese and English.

3.1 Interface

The interface was created with a minimalist approach, mostly following Google's Material Design guidelines and with a color palette of blue tones with orange accents. Some examples can be seen in Figure 1.

A good user experience is achieved by making adaptations for different types of users [13]. Hence, we added some features to allow for a more efficient use of the app by advanced users, such as Android 7.1 Nougat's "App Shortcuts" feature, which allows a user to press on the app's icon for longer than usual in order to access shortcuts to specific pages inside the app. We also relay information at a glance, such as by showing a microphone icon in appointments that have associated recordings.

We also tried to decrease frustration and repetitiveness by allowing a user to set the name of the default patient, which is automatically used in all appointments and can be changed at any time; and to avoid the need to write a title for each appointment we also create automatic titles based on other fields such as the date,

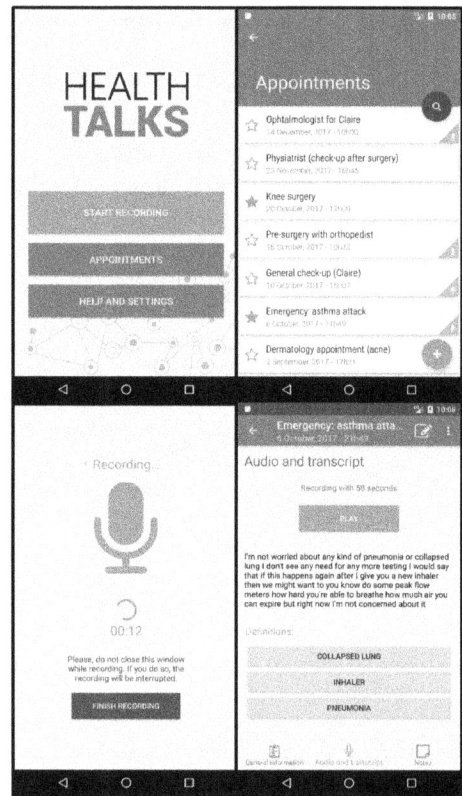

Figure 1: Views of HealthTalks. From left to right and top to bottom: landing page, appointment list, recording screen, and appointment with transcription.

medical specialty, and physician, allowing those to be changed as well.

The icons used throughout the app were chosen after asking testers to select from a list the most appropriate options to define a certain list of concepts. This was done in order to understand which icons better correlated with each concept in the testers' minds, both for ideas with standard icons (such as "settings") and more complex concepts (such as "health establishment", "medical appointment", "medical specialty", and "physician").

3.2 Architecture

HealthTalks uses two external APIs to provide specific services: a speech recognition solution to transcribe the appointment recordings, and a content scrapper to retrieve the necessary definitions of medical concepts. Those will interact with the app's business logic, which in turn will be responsible to control all of the interfaces and user interactions. The app's architecture can be seen in Figure 2.

3.3 Speech Recognition

To choose which speech recognition solution we would use, we first ran a simple elimination process to select two options from the existing ones. The criteria included: available languages, price (paid apps were discarded), and ease-of-use (mostly based on the

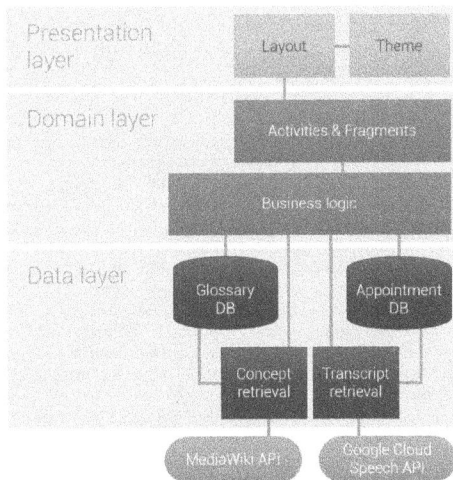

Figure 2: HealthTalks' architecture.

amount of documentation available). In the end, we chose Google Cloud Speech API (GCSA) and Bing Speech API (BSA).

To compare them, we started by using Fiscus' definition for word error rate (WER): the sum of all deletions, insertions, and modifications of words divided by the total number of words in the original text [4]. We used two texts: one with medical terms and another one with generic vocabulary. After analyzing the results, we came to the conclusion that some errors were more justifiable than others: transcribing a homophone of the original word, for example, is understandable when the software is not context-aware. Because of that, we developed our own method for discriminating between different error types and divided them into intonation errors (such as homophones or words with the same root word as the original) and meaningful errors (all others).

The tests showed that GCSA had a WER 20 to 24% lower than BSA, and often with a higher ratio of intonation errors (which we considered less severe). A summary of the results can be seen in Figure 3.

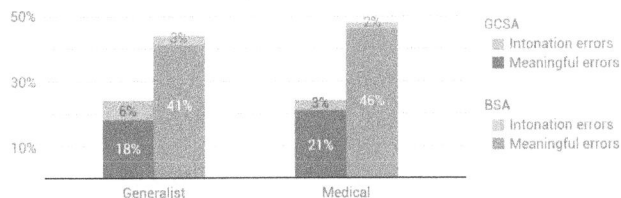

Figure 3: Comparison of the word error rates of Google Cloud Speech API and Bing Speech API for different texts.

The final solution implements GCSA through gRPC, an open-source remote procedure call framework which is faster than alternatives such as REST [10] and relies on protocol buffers. These are a way of structuring serialized data, and are more condensed than their equivalents, which means that they tend to be smaller in size (up to 10 times smaller than XML [5]). Unlike JSON or XML, they are not intended to be read by humans, which means that if they are intercepted, they will most likely be impossible to interpret without access to the schema used for their encoding [16]. This is an important aspect of the implementation since the information to be sent and received will be sensitive and private. To minimize the risk of privacy breaches we do not send any information to the cloud at any other moment during the app's use.

3.4 Medical concepts

For the vocabulary definitions, we used the MediaWiki API (MWA) to collect articles related to medicine, anatomy, illnesses, and other medical issues from Wikipedia. Since Wikipedia's language is usually colloquial, its articles are categorized, and it is regularly updated, it made sense to use it as a data source for the definitions. Wikipedia is referenced as an accurate and comprehensive source on mental health topics [18] and pharmacology [11]. Moreover, the MWA has a lot of flexibility, allowing for requests in different languages and a high degree of customization of the kind of results we want to retrieve.

We hope that the information we present to the patients will be a good starting point for them to learn more about specific topics by doing their searches online. In the app, we present the first lines of an article and a link to open the respective Wikipedia page so that the user can learn more about that subject.

4 EVALUATION

4.1 Transcription Quality

After the development of the app, we tested GCSA again with eight excerpts of simulated medical appointments of around one minute each in English. These were then translated to Portuguese and tested in that language as well. These excerpts included voiced dialogue by two or more people, acronyms, background noises, non-lexical conversation sounds and interjections, as well as occasional dialogue overlaps.

We used Fiscus' word error definition [4] as we had done before. The results show an average word error rate of 18% in English and 30% in Portuguese. The lowest and highest values in English were 11% and 29%, while in Portuguese were 10% and 42%. These values might indicate that GCSA works better in English than in Portuguese, even though in some cases they may get comparable error rates.

4.2 User Experience

4.2.1 Participants. Although the app is meant for the general adult population, we conducted usability tests exclusively with elderly users. This is a target group that is expected to greatly benefit from this solution, while at the same time assumed to be less receptive to it.

4.2.2 Procedure. To determine how technology-savvy the participants were, we decided to use Parasuraman's TRI 2.0 scale [17]. This scale measures the technology readiness index (TRI) of an individual, which represents their willingness to try and use new technologies.

The usability tests were done with a prototype of the app using a Think Aloud Protocol, which means that the testers were incentivized to express their thoughts and reasoning while completing the tasks [21]. Both the dialogue and the smartphone screen were recorded.

We asked the volunteers to complete seven tasks in the following order: firstly, to record an appointment; then to check that recording after it is finished; to create a new appointment without creating a recording; to edit an appointment's details; to transcribe a recording; to take notes on an appointment; and to find the app's privacy statement. This order was deliberately devised to introduce the tester to the functionalities in an increasing order of complexity and logical usage of the app. These tasks did not have any time limit, although there were occasions where the volunteers gave up and did not finish the task. We annotated the time each volunteer spent on a task and the number of clicks needed to reach the correct final state. After the test, we asked a few broad questions to gauge the volunteers' opinions on the app.

4.2.3 Results. The testers accomplished the vast majority of tasks with reasonable speed and often with the minimum number of clicks (MNC) required. This number corresponds to the least amount of clicks needed to complete a certain task. Creating a new appointment without an associated recording was generally the most difficult task. The average TRI of the volunteers was 3.1 in a scale from 1 to 5. A summary of the results for each tester (T1-T5) can be seen in Table 1.

Table 1: Results of the usability test for each volunteer.

Parameter	T1	T2	T3	T4	T5
Age	66	69	84	74	80
TRI 2.0 result	3.6	3.9	3.1	2.4	2.6
Tasks completed successfully	5/7	7/7	7/7	7/7	7/7
Tasks completed with the MNC	4/5	6/7	7/7	7/7	5/7
Seconds spent in each task	16	12	28	17	17

4.2.4 Discussion. We noticed how some elements of Google's Material Design such as the floating icon were not easily understood due to the testers' lack of experience with mobile apps. However, the removal of such elements would alienate many other users, so we opted to retain them. Some of the changes done after the tests were an increase in contrast and font size in some of the texts, and the addition of instructions in the app.

5 CONCLUSION

HealthTalks is an app that caters to both the most efficient users and the less experienced population, empowering all patients with the tools they need to provide a better self-care. We hope to disrupt the current dynamics of medical appointments by holding patients more accountable for their own health situation and helping them understand their physician's message.

Our goal in the future is to understand how receptive physicians are to HealthTalks, since its use depends on their acceptance. We also wish to test it in a real-world scenario, and add more features that complement the current goals of the app.

6 ACKNOWLEDGMENTS

Project "NORTE-01-0145-FEDER-000016" (NanoSTIMA) is financed by the North Portugal Regional Operational Programme (NORTE2020), under the PORTUGAL 2020 Partnership Agreement, and through the European Regional Development Fund (ERDF).

REFERENCES

[1] Neeraj K. Arora. 2003. Interacting with cancer patients: the significance of physicians' communication behavior. *Social Science & Medicine* 57, 5 (sep 2003), 791–806. https://doi.org/10.1016/S0277-9536(02)00449-5

[2] Richard H. Carmona. 2006. Health literacy: A national priority. *Journal of General Internal Medicine* 21, 8 (aug 2006), 803–803.

[3] Hugo Miguel Ribeiro de Sousa. 2016. *HealthTranslator: automatic annotation of Web documents in order to assist health consumer's searches.* M.Sc. Thesis. Universidade do Porto.

[4] Jonathan G. Fiscus, Jerome Ajot, and John S. Garofolo. 2008. The Rich Transcription 2007 Meeting Recognition Evaluation. In *Multimodal Technologies for Perception of Humans*, Rainer Stiefelhagen, Rachel Bowers, and Jonathan Fiscus (Eds.). Springer-Verlag, Chapter The Rich T, 373–389. https://doi.org/10.1007/978-3-540-68585-2_36

[5] Google. 2017. Developer Guide - Protocol Buffers. (2017). https://developers.google.com/protocol-buffers/docs/overview

[6] Burkay Gur. 2012. *Improving Speech Recognition Accuracy for Clinical Conversations.* M.Sc. Thesis. Massachusetts Institute of Technology.

[7] Jane Harrington, Lorraine M. Noble, and Stanton P. Newman. 2004. Improving patients' communication with doctors: a systematic review of intervention studies. *Patient Education and Counseling* 52, 1 (jan 2004), 7–16. https://doi.org/10.1016/S0738-3991(03)00017-X

[8] Monique Heijmans, Ellen Uiters, Tamsin Rose, Jolien Hofstede, Walter Devillé, Iris van der Heide, Hendriek Boshuisen, and Jany Rademakers. 2015. *Study on sound evidence for a better understanding of health literacy in the European Union.* Technical Report. Consumers, Health and Food Executive Agency (Chafea), Luxembourg. https://doi.org/10.2818/150402

[9] Inkyoung Hur, Ronald Lee, and J.J. Schmidt. 2015. How Healthcare Technology Shapes Health Literacy? A Systematic Review. In *AMCIS 2015 Proceedings.* http://aisel.aisnet.org/amcis2015/HealthIS/GeneralPresentations/3

[10] Husobee. 2016. REST v. gRPC. (2016). https://husobee.github.io/golang/rest/grpc/2016/05/28/golang-rest-v-grpc.html

[11] Jona Kräenbring, Tika Monzon Penza, Joanna Gutmann, Susanne Muehlich, Oliver Zolk, Leszek Wojnowski, Renke Maas, Stefan Engelhardt, and Antonio Sarikas. 2014. Accuracy and Completeness of Drug Information in Wikipedia: A Comparison with Standard Textbooks of Pharmacology. *PLoS ONE* 9, 9 (sep 2014), e106930. https://doi.org/10.1371/journal.pone.0106930

[12] Mark Kutner, Elizabeth Greenberg, Ying Jin, and Christine Paulsen. 2006. *The Health Literacy of America's Adults: Results From the 2003 National Assessment of Adult Literacy.* Technical Report. National Center for Education Statistics, Washington, DC.

[13] Jakob Nielsen. 1994. *Usability Engineering* (1 ed.). Morgan Kaufmann, San Francisco, CA, USA.

[14] Alice M Noblin, Thomas T H Wan, and Myron Fottler. 2012. The impact of health literacy on a patient's decision to adopt a personal health record. *Perspectives in health information management* 9, Fall (2012), 1–13. http://www.ncbi.nlm.nih.gov/pubmed/23209454http://www.pubmedcentral.nih.gov/articlerender.fcgi?artid=PMC3510648

[15] Office of Disease Prevention and Health Promotion. 2008. America's Health Literacy: Why We Need Accessible Health Information. (2008). https://health.gov/communication/literacy/issuebrief/

[16] Hamish Ogilvy. 2016. gRPC and the displacement of REST based APIs. (2016). https://www.sajari.com/blog/grpc-and-displacement-of-rest-apis

[17] A. Parasuraman and Charles L. Colby. 2015. An Updated and Streamlined Technology Readiness Index. *Journal of Service Research* 18, 1 (2015), 59–74. https://doi.org/10.1177/1094670514539730

[18] N. J. Reavley, A. J. Mackinnon, A. J. Morgan, M. Alvarez-Jimenez, S. E. Hetrick, E. Killackey, B. Nelson, R. Purcell, M. B. H. Yap, and A. F. Jorm. 2012. Quality of information sources about mental disorders: a comparison of Wikipedia with centrally controlled web and printed sources. *Psychological Medicine* 42, 08 (aug 2012), 1753–1762. https://doi.org/10.1017/S003329171100287X

[19] Alex Roehrs, Cristiano André da Costa, Rodrigo da Rosa Righi, and Kleinner Silva Farias de Oliveira. 2017. Personal Health Records: A Systematic Literature Review. *Journal of medical Internet research* 19, 1 (jan 2017), e13. http://www.jmir.org/2017/1/e13/http://www.ncbi.nlm.nih.gov/pubmed/28062391http://www.pubmedcentral.nih.gov/articlerender.fcgi?artid=PMC5251169

[20] Paul C Tang, Joan S Ash, David W Bates, J Marc Overhage, and Daniel Z Sands. 2006. Personal health records: definitions, benefits, and strategies for overcoming barriers to adoption. *Journal of the American Medical Informatics Association : JAMIA* 13, 2 (2006), 121–6. https://doi.org/10.1197/jamia.M2025

[21] U.S. Department of Health and Human Services. 2014. Running a Usability Test. (may 2014). https://www.usability.gov/how-to-and-tools/methods/running-usability-tests.html

Information Retrieval and Interaction System (IRIS): A Toolkit for Investigating Information Retrieval and Interaction Activities

Jonathan Pulliza and Chirag Shah
School of Communication and Information
Rutgers University
{jonathan.pulliza, chirags}@rutgers.edu

ABSTRACT

In this demo we present IRIS, an open-source framework that provides a set of simple and modular document operators that can be combined in various ways to create more interesting and advanced functionality otherwise unavailable during most information search sessions. Those functionalities include summarization, ranking, filtering and query. The goal is to support users looking for, collecting, and synthesizing information. The system is also easily extendable, allowing for customized functionality for users during information sessions and researchers studying higher levels of abstraction for information retrieval. The demo shows the front end interactions using a browser plug-in that offers new interactions with documents during search sessions, as well as the back-end components driving the system.

KEYWORDS

Interactive search; Exploratory search; Information synthesis; Sensemaking;

ACM Reference format:

Jonathan Pulliza and Chirag Shah. 2018. Information Retrieval and Interaction System (IRIS): A toolkit for investigating information retrieval and interaction activities. In *Proceedings of 2018 Conference on Human Information Interaction & Retrieval, New Brunswick, NJ, USA, March 11-15, 2018, New Brunswick, NJ, USA*. ACM, NY, NY, USA, 3 pages.
DOI: https://doi.org/10.1145/3176349.3176895

1 INTRODUCTION

The Information Retrieval and Interaction System (IRIS) is built with the understanding that simple and modular functions, which we refer to as operators, can be combined in various ways to create more interesting and advanced functionality for users

to explore documents. Each operator performs a specific function on a single document or a created collection, including ranking, clustering, and summarization. By building with modularity in mind, the system encourages the development of new operators that then can be easily integrated into the system, further expanding the complexity of possible requests and outcomes. Front-end users can access this functionality through a browser plug-in, which extends possible interactions with documents in real-time, or by making requests to a publicly hosted API. The complete back-end code and requirements are available in a public repository, which allows those interested to quickly host their own local IRIS instance for further exploration, as well as encouraging further development from the information science research community. The open-source project has been available to the community since 2013 and has served as a component of the Coagmento system, a platform for collaborative information seeking [1, 2, 3].

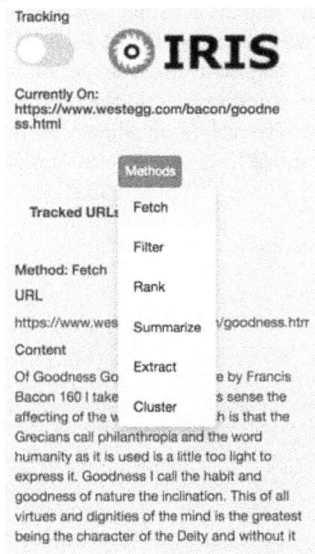

Figure 1 IRIS web browser extension sidebar displaying possible user methods for transforming documents

2 WEB BROWSER PLUG-IN

The IRIS web browser plug-in is designed to provide increased functionality as users try to make sense out of information they encounter on the Web. It monitors users' current activity and keeps track of documents that users collect, which then become the basis for the various operators available through IRIS. The sidebar gives users a snapshot of the current state of their IRIS session, including information on the current webpage as well as documents saved to a Saved Stack. Users can then use the available operators to explore these documents in ways usually unavailable to them, including extracting key terms and summarizing documents into a requested number of sentences, as shown in Figure 1. The browser plug-in is also context-aware, so in the case of search result pages IRIS can be called on to cluster the links together sharing common content and themes. Users can then make judgments on similar documents as a group and move forward appropriately instead of judging links individually in a linear manner. Selected documents can then be added to a Saved Stack where other operators can be used, such as extracting certain terms or ranking documents.

3 ACCESSING THE IRIS PUBLIC API

A publicly hosted instance of IRIS is available for those who wish to access the API programmatically through requests. Users can then send properly formatted XML as laid out by the API guidelines, providing the appropriate documents or URLs to be processed by the indicated operators on the IRIS server. All IRIS operators are available to users making requests through the API, with the added benefit of the UNIX-like pipe feeding the output of one command into the input of another. Conditional requests can also be handled through the use of IF/Then/Else tags, further expanding the possible complexity of output. The request is then processed and returned as an XML object defined by the API guide. This allows users the ability to create and integrate complex workflows into their projects that expand beyond document retrieval to an almost unlimited amount of operations. An example XML response to summarize the content of two webpages is shown graphically in Figure 2.

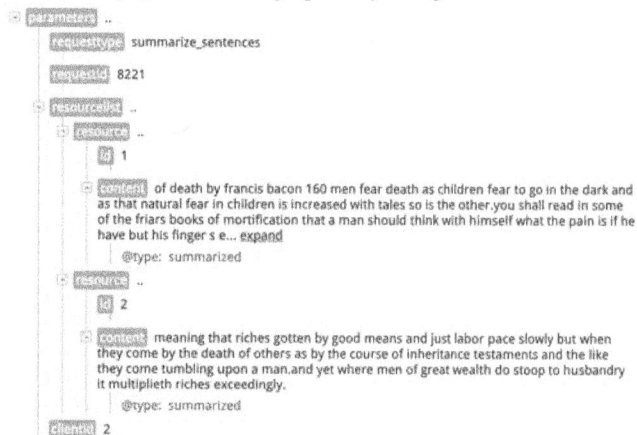

Figure 2 Example XML request for IRIS to summarize the content of a set of webpages

An example user scenario is a Ph.D. student writing a thesis and who would like to utilize previously written essays, but is

unsure of which are relevant to the thesis. Using a current draft of the thesis, the user wants to select the old essays that are the most relevant to the thesis topic. The user begins by utilizing the "extract" operator to find the most frequent words in the current thesis, with the assumption that these relate to the most important concepts. These terms then become the basis for ranking the old essays regarding their similarity to the thesis. A "rank" request is made on the old essays in respect to the extracted keywords, and the result is a ranked list indicating which essays are the most relevant to the user's thesis. From a collection of documents the user can select the most relevant based on a single target document, and can now further query and manipulate the resulting documents as needed.

Another example outside of academia is a user that is a parent of a 7-year old daughter who wants to learn about sharks, specifically pertaining to their body size and speed. The user collects a list of URLs that relate to sharks and instead of going through each URL, the user decides to upload the URLs to IRIS and query for the terms "body" and "speed." IRIS returns the documents with those terms, but the user is looking for just the relevant blocks of texts related to body and speed. The user can then request to extract the blocks of text from these documents related only to shark bodies and speed, which the parent can now quickly read over or further process and manipulate. From a list of raw URLs IRIS can extract and transform relevant information into the desired format.

4 HOSTING AN IRIS INSTANCE

The back-end of IRIS is comprised of a PHP server connected to a MySQL database, with queries handled through the Indri Query Language. All of the text processing extensions which correspond to operators in IRIS are written and compiled in C and then called by the PHP instance when necessary. Adding a new operator then means simply creating a new file in the Controllers directory and adding that operator to the top-level PHP config file. This design not only makes adding new operators straightforward but allows for previous extensions to be easily augmented and improved as better techniques and algorithms become available.

To further encourage community contributions to the project the entire IRIS codebase is available GitHub as an open source tool. The repository also contains a guide to the requirements necessary for setting up a local instance of IRIS, as well as example requests and responses. We will continue to host our own instance of IRIS open to the public for API use, but we hope researchers will explore their own custom instances for experimentation and user studies. We hope this will lead to an active community dedicated to IRIS development and further exploration of information abstraction and interaction.

5 DEMONSTRATION

In this demo, we will show some of the front-end functionality of IRIS through the web browser plug-in as well as through API requests. This will include going through some example user sessions and possible outcomes with the assistance of IRIS. Next, we will show how to install and run a local instance of IRIS locally, as well as creating and utilizing an example custom operator.

ACKNOWLEDGEMENT

This work is supported by the National Science Foundation (NSF) grant IIS-1717488.

REFERENCES

[1] X. Fu, D. Kelly, and C. Shah. Using collaborative queries to improve retrieval for difficult topics. In Proceedings of ACM SIGIR '07, New York, NY, USA, 2007. ACM.

[2] C. Shah, G. Marchionini, and D. Kelly. Learning design principles for a collaborative information seeking system. In CHI '09 Extended Abstracts on Human Factors in Computing Systems, CHI EA '09, pages 3419–3424, New York, NY, USA, 2009. ACM.

[3] M. Mitsui, C. Shah. Coagmento 2.0: A system for capturing individual and group information seeking behavior. In Digital Libraries (JCDL), 2016 IEEE/ACM Joint Conference on (pp. 233-234). IEEE.

Serendipity in the Research Literature: A Phenomenology of Serendipity Reporting

Carla M. Allen

2nd year PhD. Candidate

Information Sciences and Learning Technologies, University of Missouri

allencar@health.missouri.edu

Sanda Erdelez, PhD, Dissertation Supervisor

Abstract

The role of information sciences is to connect people with the information they need to accomplish the tasks that contribute to the greater societal good. While evidence of the wonderful contributions arising from serendipitous events abound, the framework describing the information behaviors exhibited during a serendipitous experience is just emerging and additional detail regarding the factors influencing those behaviors is needed in order to support these experiences effectively. Furthermore, it is important to understand the whole process of serendipity to fully appreciate the impact of research policies, disciplinary traditions and academic reporting practices on this unique type of information behavior. This study addresses those need by examining the phenomenon of serendipity as it is reported by biomedical and radiography researchers. A mixed method content analysis of existing research reports will be incorporated with semi-structured interviews of serendipity reporters to gain a robust understanding of the phenomenon of serendipity, and provide detail that may inform the design of information environments.

ACM Reference format:

Carla M. Allen. 2018. Serendipity in the Research Literature: A Phenomenology of Serendipity Reporting. In *CHIIR '18: Conference on Human Information Interaction and Retrieval, March 11-15, 2018, New Brunswick, NJ, USA*. ACM, NY, NY, USA, 3 pages. DOI: https://doi.org/10.1145/3176349.3176358

1. INTRODUCTION

Serendipity is a phenomenon that has the potential to connect disparate ideas and produce outcomes that improve our quality of life. If we can develop information systems that support the factors that promote serendipity, we could increase the realization of these improvements. A clear understanding of the factors that mediate the serendipity experience is necessary to the development of these systems. Research on serendipity as an information behavior has increased dramatically over the past 25 years[4]. While some researchers have focused on the features of serendipitous events, information, or individuals [8],

others have focused on the entire process or experience of serendipity[7]. In studying serendipity as a holistic experience, the prominent theories share similarities in the linear elements of the process they identify, beginning with the information encounter itself, progressing through a follow-up period, and culminating with the achievement and reporting of the valuable output [12:24]. Following a meta-analysis of these studies, McCay-Peet and Toms [10] have advanced a model of serendipity that consists of three major stages, each with its own mediating factors (See Figure 1). This model was synthesized from five different conceptions [3,7,9,14,16] and provides a framework for understanding the experience of serendipity.

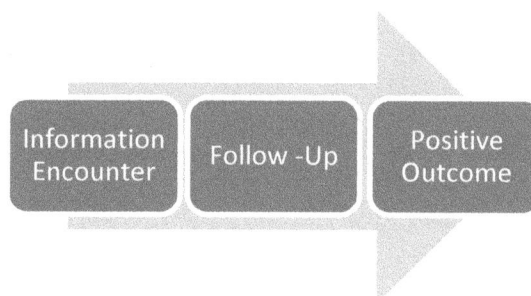

Figure 1: Basic Model of Serendipitous Experiences

Quite a bit is known about the initial triggering phase of the experience. It was first described in the information sciences literature as information encountering [5] and mediating factors have been described in a number of studies [11,12,17,18]. Much less attention has been directed toward the other two stages of the process. McCay-Peet and Toms [10] note the need for greater understanding of the factors and influences related to each stage of the serendipity experience. They also note that inconsistencies in definitions and terminology complicates the development of theory. Empirical studies are needed to validate these conceptions of the final stage of serendipity.

2. MOTIVATION & RESEARCH QUESTIONS

This study focuses on understanding serendipity as it occurs in the context of biomedical and diagnostic imaging research. From the discovery of x-rays [15] to the development of Viagra [2], serendipity has shaped medical practice and improved healthcare outcomes. As healthcare increasingly embraces evidence-based practice, biomedical research and the information behaviors involved in completion of those studies hold the potential to enhance well-being world-wide. By examining reports of serendipity in published biomedical reports and exploring those experiences with the authors, we can better understand the process of serendipity and the terminology used to convey aspects of the serendipity experience.

In addition to analyzing the experience of serendipity across the fields that comprise biomedical research, this study will investigate serendipitous experiences in the narrow area of radiography research. According to Leckie's General Model of the Information Seeking of Professionals [6], professional role influences the tasks undertaken, and the associated information behaviors. Therefore, professional domains may have specific facilitating and inhibiting factors associated with information behavior in the field. By comparing findings in a narrow discipline to the findings across the broader biomedical field, it may be possible to uncover patterns of serendipity and terminology use that are discipline-specific. Furthermore, the field of radiography as a research discipline is just emerging and may provide a contrast to other, more established disciplinary cultures.

The following research questions will be addressed.

Research Question 1 (RQ1): How do researchers represent and report their experiences of serendipity that occur in the context of research investigations?

- Subquestion 1.1: In the biomedical research literature, what is the correlation between use of synonyms for serendipity, location of term use within the report and actual serendipitous experiences?
- *Subquestion 1.2:* How do the themes identified relate to current models of serendipity?

Research Question 2 (RQ2): How do researchers in radiography represent and report their experiences of serendipity that occur in the context of research investigations?

- Subquestion 2.1: In the radiography research literature, what is the correlation between use of synonyms for serendipity, location of term use within the report and actual serendipitous experiences?
- Subquestion 2.2: How do the themes identified relate to current models of serendipity?
- Subquestion 2.3: How are discipline-specific terms related to serendipity identified?

Research Question 3 (RQ3): How do researchers describe their experiences with identifying and reporting instances of serendipity?

- Subquestion 3.1: What factors influence their reporting decisions?
- Subquestion 3.2: How do the serendipitous experiences of radiography researchers compare with those of researchers across a wide variety of disciplinary fields?
- Subquestion 3.3: How do the themes identified relate to current models of serendipity

3 METHODOLOGY

The overall research approach for this study is phenomenological, in that phenomenology seeks to consciously examine an experience, both objectively and subjectively, and through systematic reflection, determine the essential properties and structures of the experience. The purpose of this study is to understand the shared experiences of serendipity for biomedical researchers, particularly focusing on the reporting phase of the process. In achieving this purpose, both document analysis and interview data will be collected. This study builds on a pilot study [1] in which it was determined that document analysis of full-text journal articles could provide evidence of serendipity. In analyzing the data, an *exploratory concurrent mixed methods approach* will be applied. The study will be conducted in three phases.

RQ1 & 2: Document Analysis In the first and second phases of the study, content analysis will be employed involving both qualitative and statistical analysis of full-text research articles, mining for synonyms for serendipity.

Context Units The first step of a content analysis involves the identification of the context units, i.e. the synonyms related to the idea of serendipity. Search for these synonyms was undertaken through a process of chaining – identifying the synonyms of serendipity, and then identifying the synonyms of the synonyms until the possibilities were exhausted. Terms identified through this chaining process include: accidental, chance, fortuitous, happenstance, incidental, serendipitous, serendipity, surprising, unanticipated, unexpected, and unforeseen.

Population For RQ1 the articles will be drawn from reports indexed by PubMed Central, a free full-text archive of biomedical and life sciences journal literature at the U.S. National Institutes of Health's National Library of Medicine, which currently archives over 4.3 million articles. The articles for RQ2 will be drawn from the four major radiography journals as indexed in Scopus, the largest abstract and citation database of peer-reviewed literature, which currently indexes over 69 million articles.

Sampling Once the population size is known, a random sample that provides a 95% confidence with a precision (half-width interval) of 0.1 will be drawn based on a table of recommended sample sizes [13:179]. Stratified sampling will also be used to maintain the distribution of the sample across the search terms and to accurately represent the entirety of articles within the selected population.

Preliminary Coding A text search for each of the context units will be performed using qualitative analysis software, and all references to serendipity will be coded regardless of the strata assigned. Each identified synonym will be coded using the schema for term use developed in the pilot study[1]. This content analysis will used to identify instances of term use related to actual serendipitous events. The location of the term within the article will also be identified.

Data Analysis In applying the exploratory concurrent mixed methods approach, both quantitative analysis and qualitative analysis will be performed. A factorial logistic regression will be performed to determine if a predictive relationship exists between relevance to serendipitous events (DV) and serendipity synonym used (IV) or location of term use within the article (IV). Additional qualitative analysis will be performed on the units identified as reporting serendipitous events to identify information behaviors and intervening factors described in the articles. These themes will form the basis for comparison to the existing models of serendipity.

RQ3: Semi-Structured Interviews Participants will be recruited from authors of articles coded in the previous two phases as containing references to actual serendipitous experiences. Target sample size will be determined once the number of serendipity revealing articles is known. Once the research protocol is approved by the institutional review process, semi-structured, open-ended, telephone interviews will be conducted. Interviews will be audio recorded and transcribed to facilitate content analysis. Content analysis will be applied to the transcripts. Each transcript will be analyzed and inductively coded for information behaviors and intervening factors discussed by the authors. These themes will form the basis of a comparison to the existing models of serendipity. Comparison of themes between the biomedical and radiography groups will be made.

4 PROGRESS

RQ1: Full text search for 11 single-word synonyms for serendipity returned 552,288 articles. A random stratified sample of 459 articles was drawn. The text search for serendipity synonyms returned 624 unique instances of serendipity term use. Preliminary coding of the term use and location within the article has been performed. This analysis identified 249 instances that reported an actual serendipitous event. Statistical analysis and in-depth qualitative analysis are pending.

RQ2: 8,228 articles were returned for the four major radiography journals. Title, abstract and keyword search for the serendipity synonyms returned 108 unique articles. Because full text searching is not available for articles indexed in the Scopus database, a random sample was used to estimate the incidence of synonyms for serendipity within the total population. From this estimate it was determined that a sample of 184 articles containing serendipity terms would be needed to accurately represent the number of articles in the population. Those articles have been selected and full-text copies of the articles have been obtained. Preliminary coding has not yet been conducted.

5 FUTURE PLANS

This project involves three research phases: (i) Completing the content analysis of biomedical journal articles across themes indexed by PubMed Central with quantitative analysis (1 month remaining); (ii) conducting the content analysis of radiography journal articles, including completing coding and associated inter-rater reliability activities and performing both qualitative and quantitative analyses (3 months); and (iii) conducting interviews with researchers identified in steps 1 and 2, analyzing the transcripts for themes and relating findings to the existing research base (3 months). After these stages I will present my findings to my dissertation committee for revisions and defense. I plan to continue my study of serendipity by focusing on the ways serendipity may play a role in image analysis and evidence-based practice.

6 REFERENCES

[1] C. Allen, S. Erdelez, and M. Marinov. 2013. Looking for Opportunistic Discovery of Information in Recent Biomedical Research – A Content Analysis. In *Proceedings of the 76th ASIS&T Annual Meeting.*

[2] Thomas A. Ban. 2006. The role of serendipity in drug discovery. *Dialogues Clin. Neurosci.* 8, 3 (September 2006), 335–344.

[3] Joseph Corneli, Anna Jordanous, Christian Guckelsberger, Alison Pease, and Simon Colton. 2014. Modelling serendipity in a computational context. *ArXiv14110440 Cs* (November 2014). Retrieved from http://arxiv.org/abs/1411.0440

[4] S. Erdelez, J. Heinström, S. Makri, L. Björneborn, J. Beheshti, E. Toms, and N.K. Agarwal. 2016. Research perspectives on serendipity and information encountering. *Proc. Assoc. Inf. Sci. Technol.* 53, 1 (2016), 1–5. DOI:https://doi.org/10.1002/pra2.2016.14505301011

[5] Sanda Erdelez. 1997. Information encountering: a conceptual framework for accidental information discovery. 412–421. Retrieved from http://portal.acm.org/citation.cfm?id=267217

[6] Gloria J. Leckie, Karen E. Pettigrew, and Christian Sylvain. 1996. Modeling the Information Seeking of Professionals: A General Model Derived from Research on Engineers, Health Care Professionals, and Lawyers. *Libr. Q. Inf. Community Policy* 66, 2 (1996), 161–193.

[7] Stephann Makri and Ann Blandford. 2012. Coming across information serendipitously – Part 1: A process model. *J. Doc.* 68, 5 (August 2012), 684–705. DOI:https://doi.org/10.1108/00220411211256030

[8] Lori McCay-Peet and Elaine Toms. 2018. *Researching serendipity in digital information environments.* Retrieved October 25, 2017 from http://dx.doi.org/10.2200/S00790ED1V01Y201707ICR059

[9] Lori McCay-Peet and Elaine G. Toms. 2015. Investigating serendipity: How it unfolds and what may influence it. *J. Assoc. Inf. Sci. Technol.* 66, 7 (July 2015), 1463–1476. DOI:https://doi.org/10.1002/asi.23273

[10] Lori McCay-Peet and Elaine G. Toms. 2017. Researching Serendipity in Digital Information Environments. *Synth. Lect. Inf. Concepts Retr. Serv.* 9, 6 (September 2017), i-91. DOI:https://doi.org/10.2200/S00790ED1V01Y201707ICR059

[11] A.J. Million, S. O'Hare, N. Lowrance, and S. Erdelez. 2013. Opportunistic discovery of information and millennials: An exploratory survey. *Proc. ASIST Annu. Meet.* 50, 1 (2013). DOI:https://doi.org/10.1002/meet.14505001096

[12] Á. Pálsdóttir. 2010. The connection between purposive information seeking and information encountering: A study of Icelanders' health and lifestyle information seeking. *J. Doc.* 66, 2 (2010), 224–244.

[13] Mildred L Patten. 2005. *Understanding research methods: an overview of the essentials.* Pyrczak Pub., Glendale, Calif.

[14] Victoria L. Rubin, Jacquelyn Burkell, and Anabel Quan-Haase. 2011. Facets of serendipity in everyday chance encounters: a grounded theory approach to blog analysis. *Inf. Res.* 16, 3 (September 2011), 27–27.

[15] Gilbert Shapiro. 1986. *A skeleton in the darkroom: stories of serendipity in science* (1st ed ed.). Harper & Row, San Francisco.

[16] X. Sun, S. Sharples, and S. Makri. 2011. A user-centred mobile diary study approach to understanding serendipity in information research. *Inf. Res.- Int. Electron. J.* 16, 3 (September 2011). Retrieved June 22, 2017 from http://informationr.net/ir/16-3/paper492.html

[17] Bazilah A. Talip. 2015. IT Professionals' Information Behaviour on Twitter. *Libr. Libr. Inf. Sci. Res. Electron. J.* 25, 2 (December 2015), 86–102.

[18] Kirsty Williamson. 1998. Discovered by chance: The role of incidental information acquisition in an ecological model of information use. *Libr. Inf. Sci. Res.* 20, 1 (January 1998), 23–40. DOI:https://doi.org/10.1016/S0740-8188(98)90004-4

On the Interplay Between Search Behavior and Collections in Digital Libraries and Archives

Tessel Bogaard

2nd Year PhD

Supervisors: Lynda Hardman, Laura Hollink, Jacco van Ossenbruggen, Jan Wielemaker

Centrum Wiskunde & Informatica (CWI)

Amsterdam, The Netherlands

Tessel.Bogaard@cwi.nl

ABSTRACT

Log analysis is an unobtrusive technique used to better understand search behavior and evaluate search systems. However, in contrast with open web search, in a vertical search system such as a digital library or media archive the collection is known and central to its purpose. This drives different, more collection-oriented questions when studying the logs. For example, whether users need different support in different parts of the collection.

In a digital library, the collection is categorized using professionally curated metadata. We conjecture that using this metadata can improve and extend the methods and techniques for log analysis. We investigate how to identify different types of search behavior using the metadata explicitly, how to explain and predict user interactions for the different types of behavior found, and finally how to communicate our research results to domain experts.

CCS CONCEPTS

• **Information systems** → **Digital libraries and archives**; *Query log analysis*; Search interfaces; • **Human-centered computing** → *Visual analytics*;

KEYWORDS

Log analysis, Search behavior, Faceted search, Metadata

ACM Reference format:
Tessel Bogaard. 2018. On the Interplay Between Search Behavior and Collections in Digital Libraries and Archives. In *Proceedings of 2018 Conference on Human Information Interaction & Retrieval, New Brunswick, NJ, USA, March 11–15, 2018 (CHIIR '18)*, 3 pages.
https://doi.org/10.1145/3176349.3176350

1 MOTIVATION

Search log analysis is an unobtrusive technique used to better understand user behavior in search systems [1, 3, 5, 6, 8, 9, 11, 12, 19]. It can be used to evaluate search algorithms or user interfaces, or to (re-)design systems.

Traditional log analysis focuses on queries and clicks [1, 3, 8, 10–13, 16, 19]. This focus poses some disadvantages. First, queries are

ambiguous, as they form an uncontrolled vocabulary and have little context to interpret the information need. Second, most queries are in the *long tail*; they occur infrequently making it hard to find recurring patterns. Third, queries may contain privacy-sensitive information such as names and personal information [7, 14, 15], and thus are seldom shared among researchers.

In a closed, vertical search system such as a digital library or archive other data is available in addition to the logs: the documents in the collection and their categorizations using professionally curated metadata. This metadata is often reflected in the search interface in facets, acting as a filter over the search results. This extra information is normally not an integral part of a log analysis.

We conjecture that using the metadata of the collection explicitly can improve and extend analytical methods for logs collected in such search systems, in order to be able to examine detailed types of search behavior in relation to specific subsets in the collection. The collection inspires some of the questions relevant here: What parts of the collection have a high user interest? Do users search differently in different parts of the collection? Do they need different support for different parts of the collection? Are there potential gaps in the collection or are some parts of the collection harder to find? A focus on the metadata of the collection, both with respect to the facets used in search and the metadata of clicked documents, makes it possible to answer these type of questions. For example, we can identify gaps in the collection where people search for certain categories of documents but have difficulties finding them. Or we may discover that search behavior within specific subsets of the collection is different, suggesting the need for a different kind of support from the search system. Additionally, with this shift away from the query to the metadata of facet use and clicked documents, we alleviate the disadvantages previously mentioned. First, facet and document metadata is not ambiguous, as it forms a controlled vocabulary. Second, we can group infrequent queries based on shared metadata. Third, the metadata is less privacy-sensitive.

In our research we investigate how to identify different types of search behavior based on metadata of search and clicked documents, how to explain and predict user interactions for these types of behavior, and how to communicate our research results to the domain experts.

2 RESEARCH GOALS AND METHODOLOGY

The main goal of this research is to improve the understanding of different types of user search behavior in vertical search systems where the content is known, by studying the interplay between search behavior and the collection in digital libraries and media archives. We investigate specific and detailed types of behavior and their relation to the subsets present in the collection. We expect this to lead to better support for the user (such as dynamic facet presentation or generation, or the development of different search interfaces for different types of use), and help the curators of a collection to provide better access to their documents.

We address the following research questions:

(1) How can we identify different types of search behavior in relation to the metadata of facets used and documents clicked?

(2) How can we explain and predict user interactions for each type of search behavior to gain a better understanding of the different types of search behavior?

(3) How can we communicate the research results of **RQ1** and **RQ2** to domain experts?

Central to our methodology is the investigation of correlations between metadata-based subsets in the collection and certain types of user search behavior. In the next sections we describe the methods and techniques that we (plan to) use to answer these questions: (1a) a descriptive, comparative analysis, (1b) clustering, (2) sequential modeling and (3) graph visualization.

We do our research in the context of the search interface, logs, and content of the search platform curated by the National Library of the Netherlands. This collection can be accessed using an advanced, faceted search interface[1]. We have been given access to data from the National Library. This includes ten months of log records (October 2015-March 2016, April-July 2017, and we expect to receive more logs in the future), and the complete historical newspaper collection, described in metadata records (400 years, over 100M documents) with full text available as well.

For the evaluation of the techniques and methods we are looking for a second dataset. We are currently investigating the possible use of logs of the collections of Europeana[2].

3 PROGRESS

3.1 Comparative Log Analysis

In the first year, an approach for a comparative log analysis using metadata to observe usage patterns has been developed and executed. The main research question addressed here is **RQ1**. Concretely we focus on the following question:

How can we discover specific usage patterns by comparing (1) subsets of sessions, in which certain facets were used, to (2) clicked documents, and (3) the collection?

In addition, we address **RQ3**, in particular the question whether we can provide recommendations to the curators of a digital library based on our results.

The applied methodology is to automatically label the sessions identified in the logs with the (different categories of) metadata of facets used, and then to explore if and how subsets, based on those metadata labels, correlate with specific usage patterns.

We found distinct usage patterns based on the metadata. For example, the results showed that the family announcement facet

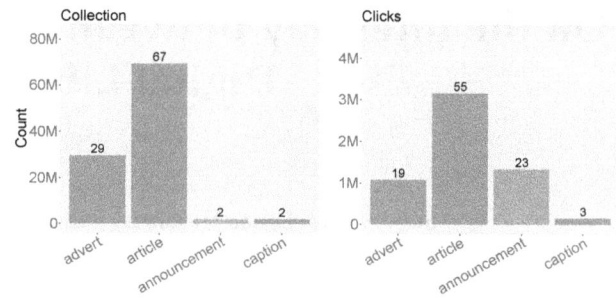

Figure 1: Item types in the collection, and of clicks in search sessions. Percentages given above the bars.

(relating to birth, death and marriage announcements) was the most frequent choice of the item type facets. The facet was used in 19% of all search sessions, with the percentage of clicks on announcements at 23%, even though announcements represent only 2% of the collection (Fig. 1). Sessions using the announcement facet are comparatively short, with fewer clicked results per session than for the other facets, even if the number of search interactions is similar. Perhaps users can more easily assess the relevance of the documents from their snippets on the results page. A recommendation given to the National Library is to give the snippets for these items extra attention.

3.2 Clustering Search Behavior

Following this, ongoing work started in the second year, we approach **RQ1** again, this time from another angle, addressing the question:

How can we identify different types of search behavior by clustering sessions based on facet use and metadata of clicked documents, as well as traditional query and click features?

We want to explore if and how characteristics of a clustering of different types of behavior correlate with search within certain subsets in the collection.

The sessions are represented using a set of features based on the interactions within the search interface, similar to the variables in [5]. In addition, the sessions are represented using a second set of features based on the metadata of the facets used and clicked documents. We then cluster the sessions two times, based on (1) the interactions with the search interface and based on (2) the metadata of facets used and clicked documents. Investigating the two resulting clusterings makes it possible to explore if and how general search behavior correlates with specific facets and metadata of clicked documents.

Since the normality assumption does not hold for our data, the CLARANS algorithm is chosen for the clustering [17]. The silhouette method is used to choose the number of clusters [18], and the stability of the clusters over different samples of the dataset to evaluate the validity of the clustering [20]. For the description and labeling of the clusters we use both feature sets for each clustering. In addition, we believe it will be insightful to investigate what type of information tactics are used within the clusters [2], and to label them according to an existing information seeking behavior model, such as those described in [21].

---

[1]http://www.delpher.nl provides access to collections from the National Library of the Netherlands and other heritage institutions, comprising newspapers, magazines, radio bulletins, and books. Our focus is on the well-curated historical newspaper collection, which amounts to more than 90% of all HTTP page requests on Delpher.

[2]https://www.europeana.eu/portal/en provides access to different collections from European cultural heritage institutions

4 FUTURE PLANS

After identifying different types of behavior using the clustering technique, we plan to address the second research question, **RQ2:** How can we explain and predict user interactions for each type of search behavior to gain a better understanding of the different types of search behavior? We will use a data mining technique to find the common sequential patterns within the clusters. The methodology envisioned here is Markov chain analysis to find the sequential patterns for each cluster. We will use the facets and metadata of clicked documents, labeling the type of search interaction or click. We are planning to use two evaluation methods for this stage of the research. First, we will use the predictive accuracy of the patterns discovered in the analysis. Second, we will use a test for statistical significance of the differences found between the patterns, like the Chi-squared test used for the work in [6].

In parallel to the first two research questions, we focus on **RQ3:** How can we communicate the results of **RQ1** and **RQ2** to domain experts? The domain experts are both curators and developers of digital libraries. In an ongoing development, started in the first year, we created what we call a *session graph*, a graph visualization that represents the user interactions in their search session. This visualization is already part of a method of an iterative, transparent data cleaning process, where the session graphs function as a sanity check as to whether the processed logs make sense and represent valid user interactions [4]. We will investigate how this visualization can help interpret and understand search behavior and how it can improve the analysis of search logs. An important aspect of this visualization technique is to try and create prototype session graphs. This type of graph will visualize a virtual session graph that is most typical for a cluster, creating what amounts to an aggregated central graph for the cluster. This graph visualization will – like the session graphs – be designed to help the curators of a collection, to visually inspect aggregated common search behavior in their search system. The visualization techniques we develop will be evaluated in a user study among curators and developers of a digital library.

ACKNOWLEDGMENTS

I would like to thank the National Library of the Netherlands for their support.

This research is partially supported by the VRE4EIC project, a project that has received funding from the European Union's Horizon 2020 research and innovation program under grant agreement No 676247.

REFERENCES

[1] Ricardo Baeza-Yates, Carlos Hurtado, and Marcelo Mendoza. 2005. Query Recommendation Using Query Logs in Search Engines. In *Current Trends in Database Technology - EDBT 2004 Workshops: EDBT 2004 Workshops PhD, DataX, PIM, P2P&DB, and ClustWeb, Heraklion, Crete, Greece, March 14-18, 2004. Revised Selected Papers*, Wolfgang Lindner, Marco Mesiti, Can Türker, Yannis Tzitzikas, and Athena I Vakali (Eds.). Springer Berlin Heidelberg, Berlin, Heidelberg, 588–596. https://doi.org/10.1007/978-3-540-30192-9{_}58

[2] Marcia J. Bates. 1979. Information search tactics. *Journal of the American Society for Information Science* 30, 4 (7 1979), 205–214. https://doi.org/10.1002/asi.4630300406

[3] Steven M Beitzel, Eric C Jensen, Abdur Chowdhury, David A Grossman, and Ophir Frieder. 2004. Hourly analysis of a very large topically categorized web query log. In *SIGIR 2004: Proceedings of the 27th Annual International ACM SIGIR Conference on Research and Development in Information Retrieval, Sheffield, UK, July 25-29,*

2004, Kalervo Järvelin, James Allan, Peter Bruza, and Mark Sanderson (Eds.). ACM, 321–328. https://doi.org/10.1145/1008992.1009048

[4] T. Bogaard, J. Wielemaker, L. Hollink, and J. van Ossenbruggen. 2017. SWISH DataLab: A web interface for data exploration and analysis. In *BNAIC 2016: Artificial Intelligence: 28th Benelux Conference on Artificial Intelligence, Amsterdam, The Netherlands, November 10-11, 2016, Revised Selected Papers*, Tibor Bosse and Bert Bredeweg (Eds.). Vol. 765. Chapter 13, 181–187. https://doi.org/10.1007/978-3-319-67468-1_13

[5] Hui-Min Chen and Michael D Cooper. 2001. Using Clustering Techniques to Detect Usage Patterns in a Web-Based Information System. *Journal of the American Society for Information Science and Technology* 52, 11 (2001), 888–904. https://doi.org/10.1002/asi.1159

[6] Hui-Min Chen and Michael D. Cooper. 2002. Stochastic modeling of usage patterns in a web-based information system. *Journal of the American Society for Information Science and Technology* (2002). https://doi.org/10.1002/asi.10076

[7] Alissa Cooper. 2008. A Survey of Query Log Privacy-enhancing Techniques from a Policy Perspective. *ACM Trans. Web* 2, 4 (10 2008), 19:1Ã¢ÂÂÂ§19:27. https://doi.org/10.1145/1409220.1409222

[8] Carsten Eickhoff, Jaime Teevan, Ryen White, and Susan Dumais. 2014. Lessons from the Journey: A Query Log Analysis of Within-session Learning. In *Proceedings of the 7th ACM International Conference on Web Search and Data Mining (WSDM '14)*. ACM, New York, NY, USA, 223–232. https://doi.org/10.1145/2556195.2556217

[9] Jiyin He, Pernilla Qvarfordt, Martin Halvey, and Gene Golovchinsky. 2016. Beyond actions: Exploring the discovery of tactics from user logs. *Information Processing & Management* 52, 6 (2016), 1200 – 1226. https://doi.org/10.1016/j.ipm.2016.05.007

[10] Laura Hollink, Peter Mika, and Roi Blanco. 2013. Web Usage Mining with Semantic Analysis. In *Proceedings of the 22Nd International Conference on World Wide Web (WWW '13)*. ACM, New York, NY, USA, 561–570. https://doi.org/10.1145/2488388.2488438

[11] Vera Hollink, Theodora Tsikrika, and Arjen P de Vries. 2011. Semantic search log analysis: A method and a study on professional image search. *Journal of the American Society for Information Science and Technology* 62, 4 (6 2011), 691–713. https://doi.org/10.1002/asi.21484

[12] Bouke Huurnink, Laura Hollink, Wietske Den Van Heuvel, and Maarten De Rijke. 2010. Search Behavior of Media Professionals at an Audiovisual Archive: A Transaction Log Analysis. *Journal of the American Society for Information Science and Technology* (2010). https://doi.org/10.1002/asi.21327

[13] Bernard J Jansen, Amanda Spink, and Tefko Saracevic. 2000. Real life, real users, and real needs: a study and analysis of user queries on the web. *Information Processing and Management* 36, 2 (2000), 207–227.

[14] Rosie Jones, Ravi Kumar, Bo Pang, and Andrew Tomkins. 2007. "I Know What You Did Last Summer": Query Logs and User Privacy. In *Proceedings of the Sixteenth ACM Conference on Conference on Information and Knowledge Management (CIKM '07)*. ACM, New York, NY, USA, 909–914. https://doi.org/10.1145/1321440.1321573

[15] Rosie Jones, Ravi Kumar, Bo Pang, and Andrew Tomkins. 2008. Vanity Fair: Privacy in Querylog Bundles. In *Proceedings of the 17th ACM Conference on Information and Knowledge Management (CIKM '08)*. ACM, New York, NY, USA, 853–862. https://doi.org/10.1145/1458082.1458195

[16] Edgar Meij, Marc Bron, Laura Hollink, Bouke Huurnink, and Maarten de Rijke. 2011. Mapping queries to the Linking Open Data cloud: A case study using DBpedia. *Web Semantics: Science, Services and Agents on the World Wide Web* 9, 4 (2011), 418 – 433. https://doi.org/10.1016/j.websem.2011.04.001

[17] Raymond T Ng and Jiawei Han. 2002. CLARANS: A Method for Clustering Objects for Spatial Data Mining. *IEEE Trans. Knowl. Data Eng.* 14, 5 (2002), 1003–1016. https://doi.org/10.1109/TKDE.2002.1033770

[18] Peter J Rousseeuw. 1987. Silhouettes: A graphical aid to the interpretation and validation of cluster analysis. *J. Comput. Appl. Math.* 20, Supplement C (1987), 53 – 65. https://doi.org/10.1016/0377-0427(87)90125-7

[19] Amanda Spink and Bernard J Jansen. 2006. *Web search: Public searching of the Web*. Vol. 6. Springer Science & Business Media.

[20] Robert Tibshirani and Guenther Walther. 2005. Cluster Validation by Prediction Strength. *Journal of Computational and Graphical Statistics* 14, 3 (2005), 511–528. http://www.jstor.org/stable/27594130

[21] Peiling Wang. 2011. Information Behavior and Seeking. In *Interactive Information Seeking, Behaviour and Retrieval*, Ian Ruthven and Diane Kelly (Eds.). Facet Publishing, London, Chapter 2, 15–41.

Distant Voices in the Dark: Understanding the Incongruent Information Needs of Fiction Authors and Readers

Carol Butler
City, University of London
London, United Kingdom
carol.butler@city.ac.uk

ABSTRACT

Online tools enable authors and readers to share information, questions and feedback about a written work without the mediation of a publisher or agent. Little is known about how the two groups interact online around works of fiction, using either specialist social reading platforms e.g. GoodReads or Wattpad, or popular social media tools like Twitter. A better understanding of the interplay between them and the role technology plays as mediator can help inform the development of next-generation tools to suit their needs. We describe findings from interviews conducted with genre fiction authors and readers about how and why they interact and share information online. Interviews revealed that the social dynamics between the groups are complex, and that intercommunication can be both limited and somewhat unwanted. This shifted our focus from identifying how they interact to understanding why they do not. We found that communication patterns established by the traditional publishing industry create barriers between the groups, made visible, and exacerbated, by their retrofit to online social platforms where readers and authors are treated as equal. We discuss our key findings and highlight opportunities to better support the incongruent information needs of the groups.

ACM Reference format:

Carol Butler. 2018. Distant Voices in the Dark: Understanding the Incongruent Information Needs of Fiction Authors and Readers. In *CHIIR '18: Conference on Human Information Interaction and Retrieval, March 11-15, 2018, New Brunswick, NJ, USA.* ACM, NY, NY, USA, 3 pages.
DOI: https://doi.org/10.1145/3176349.3176359

1. INTRODUCTION

Historically, authors and readers have interacted only through the written book, with further communication limited to letters mediated by agent or publisher, or through events such as book signings. When reading fiction, readers apply their own knowledge and experiences to interpret its meaning [1], and often seek confirmation that their views match the intentions of the author and the experience of other readers [6]. Obtaining feedback from readers has often helped inform an author's writing, suggesting that direct interaction through online social communication tools may be mutually beneficial to both parties

[5]. The use of popular social media or specialist social reading platforms allows authors to promote their work, and for readers to discuss it. Although often viewed as an isolated activity, reading is influenced by wider social and cultural practices, and by the institutions who promote it [4]. Research has highlighted how people use institutions such as libraries and bookshops socially to chat, kill time, discuss their reading and share recommendations [2, 3]. Little is known, however, about how these social reading practices translate to an online environment, without specific institutional controls in place. Online, users are vulnerable to negative interactions, making them wary of sharing information publically [7]. How this affects authors, who are expected to maintain a public-facing profile, often attracting thousands of followers, is unknown.

This empirical study, undertaken in the first year of my PhD in collaboration with the British Library, examines the social interplay between authors and readers, and how this is influenced by the technology they use. We plan to use these findings to generate theory explaining their behaviour, and to expose design implications to assist the development of future tools to support it. The British Library intend to use this research to inform their policies and service design.

2. METHOD

We recruited twelve participants through a mix of referrals and advertisement on social networking tools. Participants formed of six genre fiction authors (three male, three female) and six readers (five female, one male), all adults over eighteen. Semi-structured interviews were conducted, with data collected and analysed using an inductive Grounded Theory approach, using constant comparisons to inform an evolving theoretical sample of participants. A participant-led approach to interview helped uncover information needs and interaction behaviours and sparked a gradual shift in focus from uncovering how authors and readers interact together, to understanding why they do not.

3. FINDINGS

Interviews revealed that neither party see real benefit to discourse with each other, and so do not seek it. The complex social dynamics between author and reader online are influenced by a legacy system of communication created by historic publishing traditions. Designed for top-down information distribution the retrofit of this system to an online, democratic environment reveals discordances in communication between authors and readers. Differing aims, timings, locations and needs create missed opportunities to help each other with their information sharing goals.

3.1. Different Aims

Online interactions focused on connection to information about books, rather than to each other. The authors key aim online is to share information about their book, e.g. release dates or reviews. Although such information appears to target readers, authors expressed that their intended audience was instead industry professionals, in support of their career: *"[because] they buy books and they give it to people (...) every time you write a new book it's a new job. And you have to keep working on that CV."*(A5). Readers interact online primarily to find good books to read. This search is not limited to any one author, as many books may fit their taste and needs. However all readers described an interest in tracking releases by some favoured authors, and used the information they shared online, even if it had not been intentionally shared for them.

3.2. Different Timing

Writing a book takes time - often years. Once written, it can take a further year to be published, during which time authors work on their next book. Two distinct patterns of information dissemination were identified: 1) promotional information about a new book at the time of release and 2) sharing information about related activity, between releases, to maintain visibility. Reading, too, takes time, with busy lives and conflicting priorities making it an infrequent activity for many. All of the readers regularly sought information about new releases across the genre, and by specific authors. When they do this depends on their readiness to obtain a new book, which does not often correspond with when an author promotes a new release: *"my use of it really fluctuates. It depends if I'm reading something or not (...)"* (R1).

3.3. Different Places

Most commonly, authors used popular social media tools Twitter, Facebook and Instagram, to share information. A fear that not being online could be detrimental to their career was shared: *"[We] live in an age where everything is in public. And if you don't have some kind of public [profile], you're invisible." (A5).* In the absence of best-practice guidance, they chose which tools to use by following the example of other popular authors, or chose tools they already used to connect with family and peers. An obligation to manage multiple profiles was expressed: *"you need to be on, like ,all of them, but it's just, like, deciding how much energy you're gonna spend on which [and] not to spread yourself so thinly."*(A4). Many described a passive observation of reader activity in other tools too, primarily to monitor what was said about them (*"I track all the things they are saying about me on all the various media (...) I'm very easy to ego surf."* (A1)), rather than through a desire to interact. Some of the readers confirmed they did visit the tools authors used and observed, however none consistently - and some never - used them to join in with public discourse, making their presence in the tools invisible, and their interactions difficult for the authors to see, let alone understand.

3.4. Different Interaction Needs for Information

Both parties described information needs to support their understanding of a book. Authors sought help with narrative choices or procedural information about the publishing process, best obtained from peers and domain experts. Readers looked to confirm or enrich their understanding of a book to help decide whether to read it in the first instance, or to compare their understanding, having read it, with that of others. This comparison helped them choose whether to commit to further books by the same author- a decision that could also be influenced by what they could learn about that author online. Impressions gleaned from an author's profile could influence their decision to read more of their books either negatively (*"I don't wanna attach my heart-blood to somebody, or somebody's work, when [they seem a bad person] (...) there's loads of other things I could be reading."* (R6)), or positively (*"I think it's given me a fondness for [the author] that means I might buy things that I wouldn't have otherwise."* (R4)). Both groups preferred to limit direct interaction to peers, feeling greater safety, comfort and relevance to communicating with those in a similar position to them. Although the readers felt an author's insight could enrich their experience, issues such as an aversion to spoilers, embarrassment about asking questions, and an uncertainty of whether responses were truly from the author, rather than from their agent or personal assistant, meant that they did not feel it truly necessary. Where they had contacted an author, a response was not always anticipated. Learning from the views of other readers, rather than the author was generally considered more likely (*"you can ask a question and even if the author doesn't answer it someone else might"* (R5)), and also more helpful to developing their skills of literary critique, as they could learn from the questioning of others. However, readers who did receive useful response from authors found it positively influenced their understanding: *"I still had some questions about it, and the author [responded] saying '(...) this is what I'm implying' [and] what she said was satisfactory and made sense and answered my question."*(R1). Despite an aversion to reader contact, most authors noted positive experiences of reader interaction, which boosted their confidence: *"that kind of buoyancy you get [is] really fantastic"* (A6).

3.5. The Impact of Technology in Information Interaction

That authors must self-promote is not new- the internet is simply a new forum for it. However, the expectation for authors to be public facing online was described as at times overwhelming, and all made attempts to distance themselves from unsolicited contact, e.g. by locking-down their profile or ignoring direct messages. To block contact, however, is difficult when using tools deliberately designed for open connectivity. A sense of reluctant resignation was expressed as a result (*"sometimes it's not appropriate, so I've tried to block him but (...) he still comes through and now I realise that doesn't matter so much"* (A3)) and an assertion that it comes with the territory- an unavoidable part of their job.

Most found the volume of direct contact to be manageable, however expressed unease, as it could sometimes be invasive (*"people think you're a friend – 'I know you on the internet, I've seen (...) what you had for breakfast' and... so it becomes this kind of false intimacy"* (A2)), or potentially damaging to their career. A resultant caution in presentation online was taken: *"quite a lot of people know you and they do care about your opinions and stuff so you have to be therefore careful about what you say."* (A1). All chose to maintain a positive tone, to avoid negative repercussions, as the relationship between reputational damage and repair online is asymmetric, and rebuttal risky. A view that *"Anything you post online never really disappears"* (R2), heightened fears. Readers shared this concern, and so chose to stay anonymous where possible, to minimise risk- a luxury not afforded by the authors, who needed to stay publically visible.

Where authors invite reader contact through controlled Q&A's online, it is largely timed with new releases, meaning that readers have often not yet read the book. Readers, therefore, do not know what to ask, and so often turn to stock questions to fill the void: *"When I haven't read it (...) you're kind of under pressure to ask a question (...), so you just write something (...) general"* (R2). The trivial appearance of these questions fed a belief amongst authors that there is little benefit to increased discourse opportunities, noting that readers had always used standard questions at live events too- events that are also aligned with releases. In these offline events, there is a sense that the author is on show (*"When you go to a convention you are there as an attraction (...) and it behoves you professionally to make a good impression"* (A1)), but online, they feel less pressure to please or participate, feeding an expectation by readers of no response: *"sometimes they'll answer them, and sometimes they won't"* (R1).

Finding useful information shared by authors, too, was difficult, as search functionality was poor in all tools discussed, and it was often buried in lengthy threaded conversations. Tool algorithms caused problems too, dictating the visibility of information- e.g. Facebook prioritises activity by specific friends, but does not enable readers to give preference to author page updates.

4. DISCUSSION AND DESIGN ISSUES

That author and reader operate in different tools, without understanding of each other's needs and behaviours, makes it difficult for them to see a benefit to interacting directly with each other about a book. Both groups prefer to learn from peers, with whom they feel they can have safer, more relevant interactions. However, glimmers of positive experiences and of a shared interest in each other's activity, even if passively, indicate that there is benefit to enabling interactions.

Whilst many of the problems uncovered derive from the legacy practices of the traditional publishing industry, e.g. sharing information around book releases, which is often incongruent to readers timing needs, improvements to technology could serve to tackle existing barriers to communication. Better enabling readers to access information about an author's book at the opportune time, and by helping to protect authors from unwanted or damaging contact could improve their perception of each other and lay the foundations to facilitate increased interaction and richer dialogue. Through dialogue, they could potentially enrich each other's understanding and experience of fiction books.

Future work will build on these findings to generate theory to explain current behaviours, and to develop suggestions for design interventions for more suitable future tools. Ideas for next steps include an analysis of the types of discourses currently held at different times, such as during or between publications, which are currently treated equally by the tools. Alternatively, an investigation into the social reading practices of readers- how they connect with each other, and online information to navigate the breadth of literature available to them through online search, without the influence of a specific institution to aid or direct their decisions. This can help us to better support their search efforts.

About the author: Carol is a 2nd yr PhD Student (approx.. 1/3 through the PhD, in month 15) Supervised jointly by Dr Stephann Makri (City, University of London) and Ian Cooke (British Library)

5. REFERENCES

[1] Roland Barthes. 1967. The Death of the Author. Retrieved November 25, 2016 from http://www.tbook.constantvzw.org/wp-content/death_authorbarthes.pdf

[2] George Buchanan and Dana Mckay. 2011. In the Bookshop: Examining Popular Search Strategies. *Proceedings of the 11th ACM/IEEE-CS Joint Conference on Digital Libraries*: 269–278. https://doi.org/10.1145/1998076.1998127

[3] Sally Jo Cunningham, Nicholas Vanderschantz, Claire Timpany, Annika Hinze, and George Buchanan. 2013. Social information behaviour in Bookshops: implications for digital libraries. *Lecture Notes in Computer Science* 8092 LNCS: 84–95. https://doi.org/10.1007/978-3-642-40501-3_9

[4] Danielle Fuller and DeNel Rehberg Sedo. 2013. *Reading beyond the book: The social practices of contemporary literary culture.* Routledge, New York. https://doi.org/10.4324/9780203067741

[5] Thomas Keymer and Peter Sabor. 2005. *Pamela in the marketplace: literary controversy and print culture in eighteenth-century Britain and Ireland.* Cambridge University Press, Cambridge.

[6] Peter L. Shillingsburg. 2006. Script Act Theory. In *From Gutenberg to Google: Electronic Representations of Literary Texts.* 40–79. https://doi.org/10.1017/CBO9780511617942.004

[7] Allison Woodruff. Necessary, Unpleasant, and Disempowering: Reputation Management in the Internet Age. https://doi.org/10.1145/2556288.2557126

The Moderator Effect of Working Memory and Emotion on the Relationship between Information Overload and Online Health Information Quality Judgment

Yung-Sheng Chang
2nd year Ph.D.
School of Information, University of Texas at Austin
yscchang@utexas.edu
Supervisor: Jacek Gwizdka

ABSTRACT

I aim to investigate how information overload (IO) affects participants' judgment of online health information quality. The moderator effects of working memory capacity and elicited emotion on the relationship between IO and online health information quality judgment will also be studied. I will also investigate how individuals with different working memory (WM) capacities perceive IO. Hence, I propose to conduct a lab-based, two-factor (task topics and levels of IO) within-subject experiment to investigate the research questions. Eye-tracking data, retrospective think-aloud (RTA), search outcomes, and perceived information overload will be collected and analyzed. The results of the experiment will help to better understand how health consumers make quality judgment under different levels of IO, working memory capacities, and elicited emotions.

KEYWORDS

Information overload; working memory; information processing theory; health information; quality judgment.

ACM Reference Format

Yung-Sheng Chang. 2018. The Moderator Effect of Working Memory and Emotion on the Relationship between Information Overload and Online Health Information Quality Judgment, CHIIR'18, March 11-15, 2017, New Brunswick, NJ USA,   3 pages. DOI: https://doi.org/10.1145/3176349.3176355.

1 MOTIVATION

The amount of health information on the internet has increased tremendously ever since the invention of the internet. In the field of biomedical, the citations added per year on MEDLINE have doubled between 2000 and 2014, reaching nearly a million new citations per year [17]. Instead of traditionally seeking health information from healthcare providers, health consumers nowadays are more likely to self-diagnose their symptoms and seek health information on the internet [12]. A recent survey found that about 72% of the American adult had used the internet to search for a range of health-related issues [4]. Although seeking health information online is convenient, it may have its drawback for health consumers: the experience of IO. IO is defined as "the experience of feeling burdened by large amounts of information received at a rate too high to be processed efficiently or used effectively" [11]. The experience of IO can cause behavioral, psychological, and health-related burden to information seekers [11]. [15] found that the experience of IO would predict psychological ill-being, such as depression and anxiety, which would then cause health information seeker to discontinue their online health information search. The experience of negative emotion would also affect one's decision making [14], which is a critical cognitive process for information seeking [13]: to decide what information to receive. Although [15] has investigated the relationship between IO, emotion, and information seeking intention, the result was merely based on participants recalling their past experience through questionnaires. Furthermore, in past research on IO, few studies have taken one's WM capacity (or mental workload, cognitive load) into account. The capacity for a human brain to process and handle information is limited and varies across individuals. Hence, it could also affect how one perceives a given amount of information as IO. In my doctoral research proposal, I will be using information processing theory to investigate the relationship between IO and quality judgment of health information. Working memory capacity and elicited emotion will be investigated as moderator variables. Overall, the research questions I proposed to investigate are as follow:

Q1: How does IO affect health consumers' quality judgment of online health information?

Q2: How does people with different working memory capacities subjectively perceive information overload?

Q3: How does working memory capacity affect the relationship between IO and quality judgment of online health information?

Q4: How does emotions elicited by IO affect the relationship between IO and quality judgment of online health information?

2 THEORETICAL FRAMEWORK

2.1 Information processing theory

The information processing theory (IPT) is a cognitive approach to understand how the human brain processes sensory input [1]. In IPT, the human brain is compared to how digital computer operates and processes information: receiving input, processing information, and executing output. For the human brain, the input is multisensory inputs from the environment, while the output is viewed as the human brain selecting and executing responses after processing the information. For information processing, the sensory memory will first filter relevant information to the working (or short-term) memory. Working memory is where the information is being processed, such as categorizing, comparing, or combining new information with retrieved information from the long-term memory. The IPT can universally explain how the human brain processes information. However, past study [9] revealed that there are individual differences in working memory capacities, which could affect how one processes information and executes information search [7,8].

2.2 Information overload

Due to the invention of the internet, countless of information is being produced daily. Given that an individual has limited memory capacity, IO represents when one's efficiency in using information is hindered by the huge amount of potentially available and relevant information [2]. IO could affect an individual's ability to find thorough, high quality information. The measure of IO could be objective and subjective. [16] used a formula to explain objective information overload: information processing requirements > information processing capacities. Requirements can be measured as a given amount of information that has to be processed within a time period, while capacity is one's processed information in the available time slot. On the other hand, since there are individual differences in WM, IO can be perceived differently between users. Hence, the subjective term perceived IO is defined as "a form of psychological stress that occurs when the environmental demands perceived by an individual exceeds his or her perceived capacity to cope with them" [11]. In this proposal, the definition of objective and subjective IO will be applied to manipulate objective IO and measure subjective participants' perception of it.

3 RELATED WORK

3.1 Working memory capacity

In a series of studies [7,8], Gwizdka examined how the capacity of WM affected one's searching behavior. In [7], the study found that users with high-WM span performed more actions to find information in more demanding search tasks, whereas users with low-WM decreased documents visit. In [8], the results of the study found that users with high-WM have longer absolute reading time and time relative to the task length on the search engine results pages (SERPs). [3] also investigated WM under different term (workload) and found that various cognitive abilities have different effect on users' search behaviors.

3.2 Emotion and information seeking behavior

Based on the definition of perceived information overload, IO would cause one to experience stress. Other studies also shown that IO would negatively affect one's health status and psychological well-being [11,15]. When one's emotion is being elicited, either positively or negatively, it would affect an individual's information searching behavior [6,15]. For example, [6] found that when participants were in negative moods and perceived their search performance as poor, it would encourage them to seek more information. [15] found that psychological ill-being (negative affect, depression, and anger) can predict one's intention to stop searching for health information online. Although pass studies have investigated the relationship between emotion and information searching behavior in general, there is lack of research studying how emotion elicited by IO affects quality judgment of online health information.

3.3 Quality judgment of health information

With the abundance amount of health information online, it is critical to understand how health consumers evaluate the quality of online health information. [19] did a systematic literature review to understand what criteria health consumers use to evaluate the quality of online health information. Based on different webpages' elements, they summarized eleven criteria, such as accuracy and credibility. In a research project I was involved [18], we used eye-tracking device and RTA to understand how health consumers with different e-Health literacy evaluate online health information derived from governmental, commercial, and user-generated websites. Although there have been many research studying quality evaluation of online health information, up to date little research has investigated how IO, WM capacity, and elicited emotion affect health consumers' quality judgment of online health information. Hence, in my doctoral research I will use eye-tracking device, emotion detection, and RTA to answer the research questions.

4 METHODOLOGY
4.1 Participants

I will recruit 45 native English speakers, age range from 18 to 24 years old (college-aged students), as participants, which will be recruited through the university' mailing system. The defined age range is set to avoid age as a confounding factor that affects participants' WM and online information seeking behavior. Due to eye-tracking and facial expression detection, participants need to have normal vision and without beard. Participants need to rate their familiarity of the task topics as below medium-level.

4.2 Experiment design

A two-factor within-subject experiment will be designed. The independent variables are the search task and levels of IO. Participants will search on two health-related topics: healthcare provider and medical treatment. The levels of IO will be manipulated by asking participants to search for 3 and 7 items regarding the search topics (details provided in procedure).

Working memory capacity and elicited emotions are two moderator variables. A standard memory span test from a cognitive lab textbook [5] is used to measure participants' WM capacity. Only two sub-scores that measure memory span for short and long words will be analyzed. Participants elicited emotion will be detected by using facial expression analysis (Affective AFFDEX: https://www.affectiva.com), which could detect seven emotions: anger, surprise, sadness, disgust, fear, contempt, engagement.

Four major dependent variables will be measured: eye-tracking data, RTA, perceived information overload, and search outcomes. Eye-tracking data includes: fixation duration, count, and rate; time to first fixation; and number of regressions. RTA, which is a method used to record participants' searching session and then ask them to elaborate their thinking process, will be analyzed to generate the quality criteria participants used to evaluate online health information. Perceived information overload will be measured by using a questionnaire derive from [6]. Search outcomes include: time spends on SERPs and webpages, number of generated queries, number of visited webpages. Thematic content analysis will be used to analyze data derived from RTA. Qualitative data analysis will be used to analyze eye-tracking data, perceived IO, and search outcomes.

4.4 Search system

Participants will search via Google in a naturalistic setting. An add-on sidebar for web browser will be used to bookmark and annotate webpages participants found relevant to the task. Participants can delete and modify the added annotations, and review the prompt. The bookmarks and annotations are timestamped and saved in the experiment data database. Tobii TX-300 eye-tracker will be used for eyes movement measurement.

4.5 Procedure

Participants will read the study instruction and sign the consent form. Then they will fill in demographic information. The experiment will be conducted by using iMotions software. Participants will perform a training task to guide them through the procedure. First, participants will measure pre-task WM capacity and emotional state. Then they will calibrate their eye movement. Next, a scenario will be displayed and participants are asked to search for a list of items about different healthcare providers/medical treatments. The number of items will be unknown to the participants and the items will be presented one at a time. After participants finish searching information on the first item, the next item will then be provided. During the search, participants have to save and annotate webpages they think are relevant. The topics and the order of the items will be randomly presented. After conducting all the search on the list, participants need to provide reasons why they think a certain healthcare provider/medical treatment is the best, and measure post-task WM capacity. Participants' elicited emotions will be recorded during the search. Following each search task, RTA will be conducted so that participants can explain their thoughts and actions. There will be a 5-minute break between the two search tasks. After both search tasks are completed, participants will finish the perceived information overload questionnaire. Camtasia software will be used to record the RTA sessions.

5 PROGRESS AND FUTURE PLAN

My previous experience in conducting the experiment [18] had led me to my interests of how health consumer evaluate the quality of online health information. During the experiment, I noticed how some participants will make quality judgment differently depends on the amount of information provided. Up to date, little studies have investigated how IO affects one's health information quality judgment. [15] only investigate participants' intention to continue searching for health information, which the result is based on questionnaire. Furthermore, pass research did not take WM capacity into account. As a result, I am interested to know the relationship between IO and quality judgment of online health information, and the moderator effect of WM capacity and elicited emotion on it. Hence, I aim to conduct a pilot study to preliminary investigate my proposed research questions.

REFERENCES

[1] Atkinson, R.C. and Shiffrin, R.M., 1968. Human memory: A proposed system and its control processes. *Psychology of learning and motivation 2*, 89-195.

[2] Bawden, D. and Robinson, L., 2009. The dark side of information: overload, anxiety and other paradoxes and pathologies. *Journal of information science 35*, 2, 180-191.

[3] Brennan, K., Kelly, D., and Arguello, J., 2014. The effect of cognitive abilities on information search for tasks of varying levels of complexity. In *proceedings of the 5th information interaction in context symposium* ACM, 165-174.

[4] Fox, S., 2014. The social life of health information, Pew Research Center.

[5] Francis, G., Mackewn, A., and Goldthwaite, D., 2004. *CogLab on a CD*. Wadsworth Publishing Company.

[6] Gasper, K. and Zawadzki, M.J., 2013. Want information? How mood and performance perceptions alter the perceived value of information and influence information-seeking behaviors. *Motivation and Emotion 37*, 2, 308-322.

[7] Gwizdka, J., 2013. Effects of working memory capacity on users' search effort. In *Proceedings of the International Conference on Multimedia, Interaction, Design and Innovation* ACM, 11.

[8] Gwizdka, J., 2017. I Can and So I Search More: Effects Of Memory Span On Search Behavior. In *Proceedings of the 2017 Conference on Conference Human Information Interaction and Retrieval* ACM, 341-344.

[9] Just, M.A. and Carpenter, P.A., 1992. A capacity theory of comprehension: individual differences in working memory. *Psychological review 99*, 1, 122.

[10] Liu, C.-F. and Kuo, K.-M., 2016. Does information overload prevent chronic patients from reading self-management educational materials? *International journal of medical informatics 89*, 1-8.

[11] Misra, S. and Stokols, D., 2012. Psychological and health outcomes of perceived information overload. *Environment and behavior 44*, 6, 737-759.

[12] Ryan, A. and Wilson, S., 2008. Internet healthcare: do self-diagnosis sites do more harm than good? *Expert opinion on drug safety 7*, 3, 227-229.

[13] Savolainen, R., 2014. Emotions as motivators for information seeking: A conceptual analysis. *Library & Information Science Research 36*, 1, 59-65.

[14] Schwarz, N., 2000. Emotion, cognition, and decision making. *Cognition & Emotion 14*, 4, 433-440.

[15] Swar, B., Hameed, T., and Reychav, I., 2017. Information overload, psychological ill-being, & behavioral intention to continue online healthcare information search. *Computers in Human Behavior 70*, 416-425.

[16] Tushman, M.L. and Nadler, D.A., 1978. Information processing as an integrating concept in organizational design. *Academy of management review 3*, 3, 613-624.

[17] U.S. National Library of Medicine. Key MEDLINE Indicators 2014. Available from: http://www.nlm.nih.gov/bsd/bsd key.html

[18] Ye, Z., Gwizdka, J., Lopes, C.T., and Zhang, Y., 2017. Towards understanding consumers' quality evaluation of online health information: A case study. *Proceedings of the Association for Information Science and Technology, 54*(1), 838-8

[19] Zhang, Y., Sun, Y., and Xie, B., 2015. Quality of health information for consumers on the web: a systematic review of indicators, criteria, tools, and evaluation results. *Journal of the Association for Information Science and Technology 66*, 10, 2071-2084.

Towards Human-Like Conversational Search Systems

Mateusz Dubiel (2nd Year PhD Student)
Supervised by Dr. Martin Halvey and Dr. Leif Azzopardi
Department of Computer and Information Sciences, The University of Strathclyde
18 Richmond Street, Glasgow
mateusz.dubiel@strath.ac.uk

ABSTRACT

Voice search is currently widely available on the majority of mobile devices via use of Virtual Personal Assistants. However, despite its general availability, the use of voice interaction remains sporadic and is limited to basic search tasks such as checking weather updates and looking up answers to factual queries. Present-day voice search systems struggle to use relevant contextual information to maintain conversational state, and lack conversational initiative needed to clarify user's intent, which hampers their usability and prevents users from engaging in more complex interaction activities. This research investigates the potential of a hypothesised interactive information retrieval system with human-like conversational abilities. To this end, we propose a series of usability studies that involve a working prototype of a conversational system that uses real time speech synthesis. The proposed experiments seek to provide empirical evidence that enabling a voice search system with human-like conversational abilities can lead to increased likelihood of its adoption.

KEYWORDS

Conversational Search; Interactive Voice Interfaces; Usability Testing

ACM Reference format:

Mateusz Dubiel. 2018. Towards Human-Like Conversational Search Systems. In *CHIIR'18: 2018 Conference on Human Information Interaction & Retrieval, New Brunswick, NJ, USA, March 11-15, 2018*, 3 pages.
DOI: 10.1145/3176349.3176360

1 MOTIVATION

The recent technological advances in speech technology have contributed to the proliferation of devices that support voice search. Currently, the performance of automatic speech recognition (ASR) is reported to be on a par with human performance [25; 26], while high quality synthetic voices generated with deep neural networks (WaveNet Model) can sound almost indistinguishable from natural speech [2; 18]. Another

argument in favour of using speech for information retrieval is its speed (reportedly voice interaction is 3 times faster than texting [21]) and overlearned character [19].

However, regardless of technological improvements and potential to facilitate information retrieval, voice-based interaction with search systems remains sporadic [3; 4] and limited to simple functionalities such as looking for factual information or checking weather updates [7]. Recent evaluation studies of voice search systems [5; 11-13; 16; 24] highlight a number of problems that lead to users' dissatisfaction with voice interaction. Firstly, present day conversational systems struggle with preserving contextual meaning [11; 12; 24], which makes tasks that require several conversational turns either very cumbersome, or impossible to complete. Secondly, voice technology is perceived as unreliable as device does not understand user's intent and irrelevant returns [5; 17]. Finally, users tend to have unrealistic expectations regarding capabilities of voice search systems and lack awareness on how to communicate with them in order to obtain required results, which discourages frequent use of the system and limits its scope[13; 16]

Moore et al. suggested that by making voice search to resemble human-human dialogue it can become a viable alternative of text-based information retrieval [14; 15]. In a similar vein, Radlinski and Craswell [20] suggested a set of conditions that a search system needs to meet in order to be considered conversational. The two main features suggested are (1) 'Conversational Memory', which is required to maintain conversational state and (2) 'Mixed Initiative' that can be used to clarify user's intent and make necessary repairs during the conversation.. In recent years we have seen several attempts to create a conversational system with human-like capabilities [9; 23]. While implementation of deep learning methods resulted in improvement of voice search systems, their performance is still far from human conversational abilities.

The goal of my PhD is to investigate whether enabling voice search systems with human-like conversational abilities can improve their usability. The project is empirical in nature and seeks to provide data obtained via evaluation experiments with real users. My research is expected to advance the knowledge on voice search by:

- Helping to understand users requirements regarding conversational system
- Validating proposed theoretical framework for conversational search
- Providing evidence that systems enabled with conversational memory and initiative can lead to more frequent usage and more functions being explored.

2 RESEARCH QUESTIONS

In my research, I seek to gain a better understanding of implications of enabling voice search systems with human-like conversational systems on their perceived usability. In particular, the questions that I seek to answer are:

- **RQ1**: Do users expect their interaction with voice search system to reflect 'human-human dialogue'?
- **RQ2**: Is voice search system with conversational memory perceived as more usable as compared with current state of the art system?
- **RQ3**: Can we improve user's satisfaction with the voice search system by enabling it with conversational initiative, (i.e. making it more inquisitive)?
- **RQ4**: Can real-life implementation of conversational system with human-like capabilities (memory and initiative) lead to improved usability and extend the scope of system's applications to tasks that go beyond checking weather and answering factual queries?

The anticipated contributions of my research are: firstly to elicit users' expectations towards conversational search system, and secondly, based on the obtained results, to propose a set of design guidelines for future conversational interfaces to make them more usable, and, in turn, to improve the prospect of their adoption in the future. Although the focus of the project is currently anticipated to be on contextual awareness and frequency of turn-taking in conversation, features of speech such as, speed and prosody may be included in the analysis (if time permits).

3 RESEARCH METHODOLOGY AND PROPOSED EXPERIMENTS

The methodology applied in my PhD project comprises of both qualitative and quantitative methods gathered from a survey, semi-structured interviews and usability studies. The project consists of 3 main parts: (1) 'Gathering Users' Requirements', (2) 'Voice Interaction Studies', and (3) 'Creating a Prototype of a Closed Domain Conversational Search System'. The goal of Part 1 (already completed) is to elicit users' requirements of conversational systems. Part 2 (currently in progress) is based on usability studies in which a hypothesised conversational system is tested by using a Wizard of Oz (WOZ) framework [6]. Finally, in Stage 3, a prototype of a closed domain conversational search system will be developed based on feedback obtained from Stages 1 and 2, and tested in a usability study.

3.1 Results so Far

3.1.1 Part 1 – Online Opinion Survey. The results of our opinion survey (N = 178) [7] have provided the answer to **RQ1**. The feedback provided by respondents, presented in Figure 1, indicates that the majority of people want their interaction with voice search system to be more human like. However, the opinions are divided when it comes to system's conversational initiative - with less than 50% of respondents who agreed that voice search system should ask more questions. In the answers provided to open

questions, many respondents expressed need to for conversational system to have memory of their past interactions, and to ask follow up questions in order to clarify their intent. The insights obtained from the survey informed the design and the scope of 'Voice Interaction Studies' used in Part2 of the project.

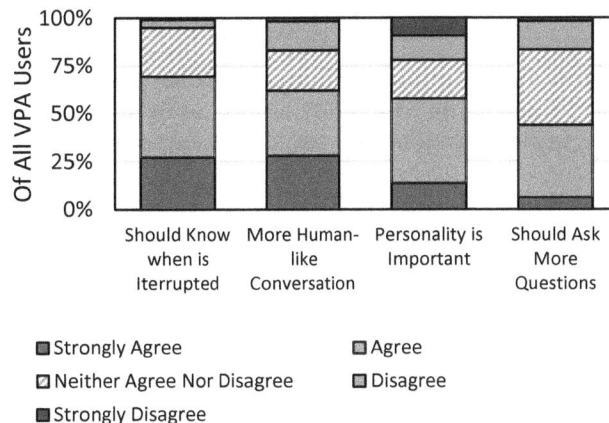

Figure 1: Users' expectations regarding performance of voice search systems. Note: blue highlights correspond to respondents who 'agree' or 'strongly agree' with presented statements. NOTE: 'VPA'= 'Virtual Personal Assistant' (Used as a synonym of voice search system)

3.1.2 Part 2 - Voice Interaction Study Conversational System with Memory Component. We carried out a lab based experiment (N = 12) [8] in which participants were asked to complete four search tasks on two voice search systems (two tasks per system). One of the systems was designed to reflect the performance of current state of the art voice search systems that are based on slot-filling architecture, while the other one was a hypothesised conversational system with memory component. Participants were given two questionnaires, i.e. NASA TLX [10] to assess their cognitive load for each of the system, and System Usability Questionnaire (SUS) [1] to evaluate systems' usability. The findings obtained from the experiment provided us with the answer to **RQ2**, indicating that our proposed conversational system was both more usable and less taxing to use than current state of the art system. The experimental results are provided in Table 1 and Table 2.

Table 1: Comparison of Cognitive Impact of Baseline System and Proposed Conversational System. The Scores are measures on a 0-100 scale, the lower score the better. * – indicates p <0.05, ** - indicates p < 0.01.

	Baseline (M/SD)	Conv. (M/SD)
TLX Score*	**23.26/11.53**	**13.19/10.38**
Mental Demand**	**29.11/6**	**14.21/3.68**
Effort*	30.8/5.9	14.6/3.5
Frustration	30.4/6.5	17.5/5.85
Temporal Demand	17/2.9	16.25/3.69
Performance[1]	16.9/5.8	9.1/2.67

---

[1] Values for performance have been inverted for comparability reasons

Table 2: Comparison of Usability of Baseline System and Proposed Conversational System. The Scores are measures on a 0-100 scale, the higher the score the better the performance. * – indicates p <0.05,

	Baseline (M/SD)	Conv. (M/SD)
SUS Score*	77.91/21.31	89.37/16.17

Note: The score of Baseline system falls between the 30th and 25th percentile of top SUS scores, while the score of Conv. system corresponds to the 5th percentile.

3.2 Planned Experiments

During the remaining part of my PhD (Years 2 and 3), I plan to carry out another lab-based experiment that will involve comparing usability of a baseline voice search system with a system enabled with conversational initiative. The experiment will conclude Part 2 of my PhD project. Once the data gathered in Part 2 has been analysed and conclusions drawn, I will proceed to the final stage of my project in which I will create a prototype of a conversational search system and evaluate it in a usability study.

The remaining research activities with brief descriptions and approximate timelines are provided below.

3.2.1 Part 2: Conversational System with Conversational Initiative. The experiment will follow the pattern explained in *Section 3.1.2.* (study designed in WOZ framework). The main focus of the study will be on creating a system that will use incremental dialogue approach, i.e. the system that will actively interact with participants without waiting for their conversational turn to be over, and likewise, the participants will be able to barge in at any point of the conversation. Real time reactive speech synthesis will be used to increase the naturalness of interaction [22]. The goal of the experiment will be to test if increased conversational initiative of the system can improve error recovery and ability to recover from misunderstandings during search task. The results obtained from the experiment are expected to provide the answer to **RQ3**. The experimental part of the study is planned to run between November 2017 to May 2018 with the aim to write a journal paper by June 2018.

3.2.2 Part 3: Prototype of Human-Like Conversational System. Finally, having investigated both memory component and turn taking aspects of conversational system, I will move on to develop a prototype of a conversational system. The system will be designed based on feedback obtained from both experiments carried out in Part2 and then evaluated in a usability study. Prototyping is expected to be the most time consuming part of my project that is expected to run from summer 2018 to autumn 2019. During that time I will use machine learning techniques to analyse the data gathered in Part 2 of the project and use state of art spoken language understanding, and dialogue management modules (using neural network models e.g. Google Speech API) to create the prototype. The results of prototype evaluation are expected to provide answer to **RQ4,** and conclude my PhD project.

4 REFERENCES

[1] Brook, J., 1996. SUS-A quick and dirty usability scale. *Usability evaluation in industry 189*, 194, 4-7.

[2] CABRAL, J.P., COWAN, B.R., ZIBREK, K., and MCDONNELL, R., 2017. The Influence of Synthetic Voice on the Evaluation of a Virtual Character. *Proc. Interspeech 2017*, 229-233.

[3] CAROLINA, M., 2017. Voice Assistant Anyone? Yes please, but not in public! In *Creative Strategies*.

[4] COWAN, B.R., 2014. Understanding speech and language interactions in HCI: The importance of theory-based human-human dialogue research. In *Designing speech and language interactions workshop, ACM conference on human factors in computing systems, CHI*.

[5] COWAN, B.R., PANTIDI, N., COYLE, D., MORRISSEY, K., CLARKE, P., AL-SHEHRI, S., EARLEY, D., and BANDEIRA, N., 2017. What can i help you with?: infrequent users' experiences of intelligent personal assistants. In *Proceedings of the 19th International Conference on Human-Computer Interaction with Mobile Devices and Services* ACM, 43.

[6] DAHLBÄCK, N., JÖNSSON, A., and AHRENBERG, L., 1993. Wizard of Oz studies—why and how. *Knowledge-based systems 6*, 4, 258-266.

[7] DUBIEL, M., HALVEY, M., and AZZOPARDI, L., 2018. What Stops People from Speaking to Machines? A Survey Investigating Barriers to Adoption of Virtual Personal Assistants *(Under Review)* (2018).

[8] DUBIEL, M., HALVEY, M., and AZZOPARDI, L., and DARONNAT, S., 2018. Towards Conversational Search Agents: Investigating how natural language dialogue affects search behaviour, performance and satisfaction. *(Under Review)* (2018).

[9] FUJITA, T., BAI, W., and QUAN, C., 2017. Long short-term memory networks for automatic generation of conversations. In *Software Engineering, Artificial Intelligence, Networking and Parallel/Distributed Computing (SNPD), 2017 18th IEEE/ACIS Conference on* IEEE, 483-487.

[10] HART, S.G. and STAVELAND, L.E., 1988. Development of NASA-TLX (Task Load Index): Results of empirical and theoretical research. *Advances in psychology 52*, 139-183.

[11] KISELEVA, J., WILLIAMS, K., HASSAN AWADALLAH, A., CROOK, A.C., ZITOUNI, I., and ANASTASAKOS, T., 2016. Predicting user satisfaction with intelligent assistants. In *Proceedings of the 39th International ACM SIGIR conference* ACM, 45-54.

[12] KISELEVA, J., WILLIAMS, K., JIANG, J., HASSAN AWADALLAH, A., CROOK, A.C., ZITOUNI, I., and ANASTASAKOS, T., 2016. Understanding User Satisfaction with Intelligent Assistants, 121-130. DOI= http://dx.doi.org/10.1145/2854946.2854961.

[13] LUGER, E. and SELLEN, A., 2016. Like Having a Really Bad PA: The Gulf between User Expectation and Experience of Conversational Agents. In *Proceedings of the 2016 CHI Conference on Human Factors in Computing Systems* ACM, 5286-5297.

[14] MOORE, R.K., 2015. From talking and listening robots to intelligent communicative machines. *Robots that Talk and Listen—Technology and Social Impact*, 317-336.

[15] MOORE, R.K., 2017. Is spoken language all-or-nothing? Implications for future speech-based human-machine interaction. In *Dialogues with Social Robots* Springer, 281-291.

[16] MOORE, R.K., LI, H., and LIAO, S.-H., 2016. Progress and Prospects for Spoken Language Technology: What Ordinary People Think. In *INTERSPEECH*, 3007-3011.

[17] MOORE, R.K. and MARXER, R., 2016. Progress and Prospects for Spoken Language Technology: Results from Four Sexennial Surveys. In *INTERSPEECH*, 3012-3016.

[18] OORD, A.V.D., DIELEMAN, S., ZEN, H., SIMONYAN, K., VINYALS, O., GRAVES, A., KALCHBRENNER, N., SENIOR, A., and KAVUKCUOGLU, K., 2016. Wavenet: A generative model for raw audio. *arXiv preprint arXiv:1609.03499*.

[19] PIERACCINI, R. and RABINER, L., 2012. *The voice in the machine: building computers that understand speech*. MIT Press.

[20] RADLINSKI, F. and CRASWELL, N., 2017. A theoretical framework for conversational search CHIIR.

[21] RUAN, S., WOBBROCK, J.O., LIOU, K., NG, A., and LANDAY, J., 2016. Speech Is 3x Faster than Typing for English and Mandarin Text Entry on Mobile Devices. *arXiv preprint arXiv:1608.07323*.

[22] WESTER, M., BRAUDE, D.A., POTARD, B., AYLETT, M.P., and SHAW, F., 2017. Real-time reactive speech synthesis: incorporating interruptions. *Proc. Interspeech 2017*, 3996-4000

[23] WESTON, J.E., SZLAM, A.D., FERGUS, R.D., and SUKHBAATAR, S., 2017. End-to-end memory networks Google Patents.

[24] WILLIAMS, K., KISELEVA, J., CROOK, A.C., ZITOUNI, I., AWADALLAH, A.H., and KHABSA, M., 2016. Is This Your Final Answer?, 889-892. DOI= http://dx.doi.org/10.1145/2911451.2914736.

[25] XIONG, W., DROPPO, J., HUANG, X., SEIDE, F., SELTZER, M., STOLCKE, A., YU, D., and ZWEIG, G., 2016. Achieving human parity in conversational speech recognition. *arXiv preprint arXiv:1610.05256*.

[26] XIONG, W., DROPPO, J., HUANG, X., SEIDE, F., SELTZER, M., STOLCKE, A., YU, D., and ZWEIG, G., 2017. The Microsoft 2016 conversational speech recognition system. In *Acoustics, Speech and Signal Processing (ICASSP), 2017 IEEE International Conference on* IEEE, 5255-5259.

With Maps and Mobs: Searching for Trustworthiness using Belief Spaces

Philip Feldman
UMBC
feld1@umbc.edu

ABSTRACT

The detection of echo chambers and information bubbles is becoming increasingly relevant in this era of polarized information. It may be possible to evaluate information trustworthiness by examining the behavior of individuals in belief space rather than evaluating the information itself, which is a harder problem. To explore this, I propose to research a model for information retrieval that integrates two levels of information interaction. On the individual level, I leverage Munson and Resnick's[10] *diversity-seeker, confirmer,* and *avoider* patterns. At a group level, I integrate individual behaviors according to Moskivici's work on crowd polarization [9]. These perspectives have been integrated in a simulation that employs insights from animal collective behavior to model agent groups, which enable the systematic exploration of belief navigation behaviors that can be detected algorithmically. Viewing information retrieval from the perspective of belief spaces may shed light on current practices and lay out consideration for future design work.

ACM Reference Format:

Philip Feldman. 2018. With Maps and Mobs: Searching for Trustworthiness using Belief Spaces. In *Proceedings of Conference on Human Information Interaction Retrieval (CHIIR'18).* ACM, New York, NY, USA, 3 pages. https://doi.org/10.1145/3176349.3176353

Figure 1: Elk group interaction with physical environment

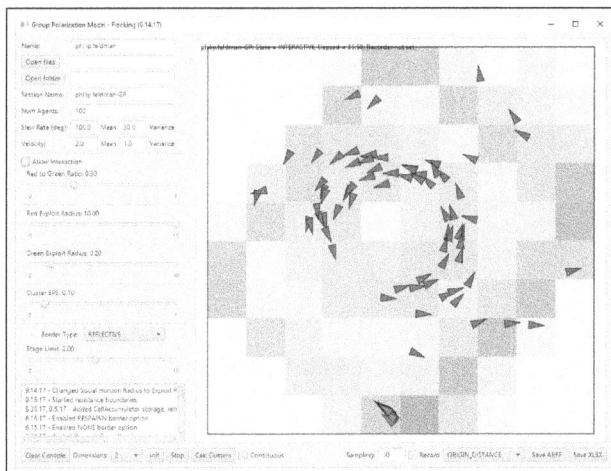

Figure 2: Agent interaction with belief environment

1 SITUATION

I am currently a post-proposal candidate in the UMBC HCC program. My advisor is Dr. Wayne Lutters.

2 MOTIVATION

The initial motivation for this work arises from contemplating the synergy between Information Systems and echo chambers - a self referential data entity that does not depend on additional outside information for continued viability [4].

In polarizing news items such as climate change and gun control [6], the facts are well known but there are groups who interact with this information in dramatically different ways, ranging from deep exploration of the available information, to the creation of [3] alternate "facts" [2]. Even outside of "hot-button" issues, echo chambers arise easily. This can happen in two ways. In the first, we select sources of information that are most agreeable to us. In the second a system or person that we trust learns our information biases and preferences, and begins to tailor the information we receive to fit with that perspective. The former could be the intentional selection of a set particular news sources from cable, radio and the internet. The latter tailors its delivery of results to the user [11]. This could take the nefarious form of an Iago-like advisor, or as a more innocuous information recommender system which customizes returns based on personalized observations and generally invisible decisions.

In both cases, an echo chamber may be created, but the first is the result of *explicit* action on the part of the user while the second is an *implicit* choice to accept the selection of others, be

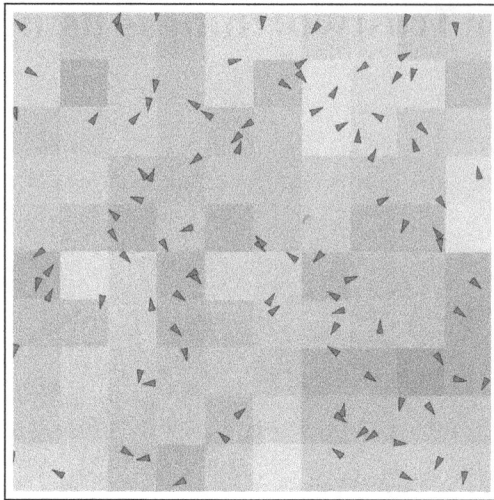

Figure 3: Explorer phase

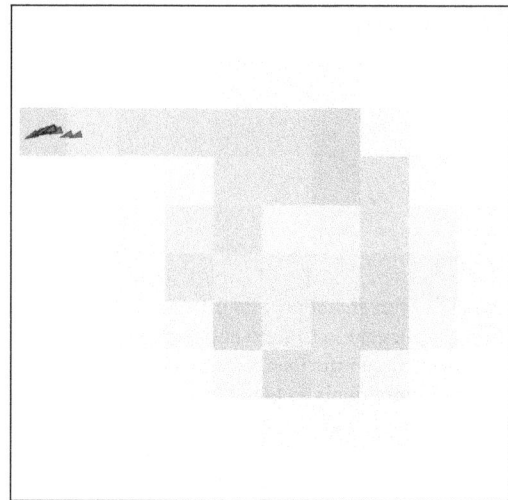

Figure 5: Echo chamber phase

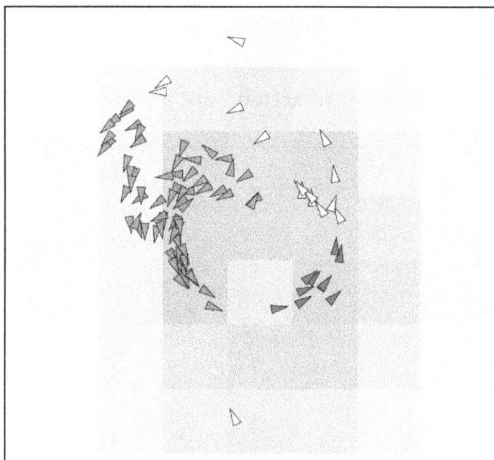

Figure 4: Flocking phase

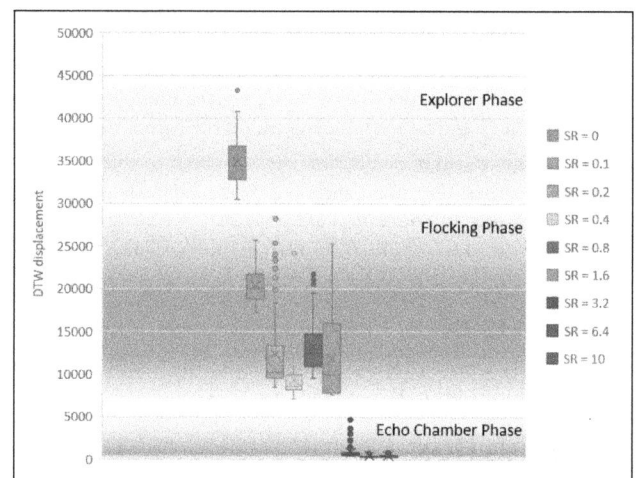

Figure 6: DTW detection of populations

they people or systems. This implicit choice has deep implications, since we are unlikely to realize the ramifications of such implicit choices. In either case, the implication to the user is that they are being presented all pertinent information while in fact being led directions that reflect the provider's underlying bias.

3 RESEARCH QUESTIONS

- RQ1: What is a simple model that can serve as a proxy for behaviors that indicate Group Polarization? Within the model, what behavior can be determined to be most trustworthy? Is it possible to adjust the degree of polarization by making changes to the social network, such as varying degree?
- RQ2: What are the design considerations for an information browsing display that affords exploring/diversity-seeking behavior? How does an interface that supports diversity-seeking behavior support search?

4 METHODS

The key insight of this work is the idea that human navigation through *belief space* (a subset of information space that contains items associated with opinions) is analogous to animal motion through physical space (figures 1 and 2). Long before we as humans needed to cognitively navigate belief space 2, we had to coordinate as groups. To study this, I built a stand-alone program using Java that created the multidimensional belief environment and then populated it with agents. The model is based on the Reynolds[12] flocking and herding algorithm modified for belief spaces and can run in interactive or batch mode. Sampled output was saved to Excel files that were then analyzed offline. Analysis beyond the capabilities of Excel, such as network analytics, were done using Python scripts.

5 RESULTS

For two through ten dimensions, three phases of agent behavior emerged by varying only the parameter that controlled the "social influence horizon", or the range of agent's awareness. The influence of neighboring agents falls off linearly as a function of distance until the social influence horizon is reached. These three phases can be seen in Figures 3 (*Explorer*), 4 (*Flocking*) and 5 (*Echo Chamber*).

The number of dimensions did subtly alter agent behaviors. The social influence horizon had to be multiplied by the square root of the number of dimensions to produce the same agent behaviors. This is an example of the "curse of dimensionality"[1] which refers to the difficulty in calculating meaningful Euclidean distance in high-dimensional space. This may explain why polarization only happens after concepts have been simplified - essentially a form of dimension reduction[5][9]. Based on this result, the majority of simulations were run in two dimensions as this appears to reflect observed human behavior and supports visualization.

Dynamic time warping (DTW)[13] was used to find the lowest distance that one set of agent coordinates need to be moved to exactly match another sequence of coordinates. The distribution of DTW distance by agent social influence horizon is shown in Figure 6. The phase changes (random, flocking, polarized) are distinctive and *non-overlapping* in our datasets.

6 FUTURE PLAN

I am currently modeling how external forces can be applied to these populations to force echo chambers simulating mechanisms described for "Troll Farms". Once these simulation steps are complete, The next phase of the project includes building an online discussion "game" to study how groups create normative alignment while coming to consensus along the lines of those studied by Moscovici [9] and McGuire et. al. [8]. Text will be logged and analyzed from multiple runs to develop "normative maps" to see if discussion trajectories can be plotted on them. A subsequent study will use these maps and other *explorer* affordances to see if such interfaces provide sufficient instrumentation to detect the patterns discovered in the current phase.

The model and UI will then be iteratively refined to develop a "Research Browser" (RB) proof-of-concept that will provided to the public (mockup shown in figure 7). As anticipated, the RB will be a thick client or browser plugin that will provide 1) "traditional" and explorer interfaces for multi-session search, 2) cooperative pinning, marking and tagging of returned results, and 3) human-in-the-loop machine learning[7] to support augmented search and tagging capabilities.

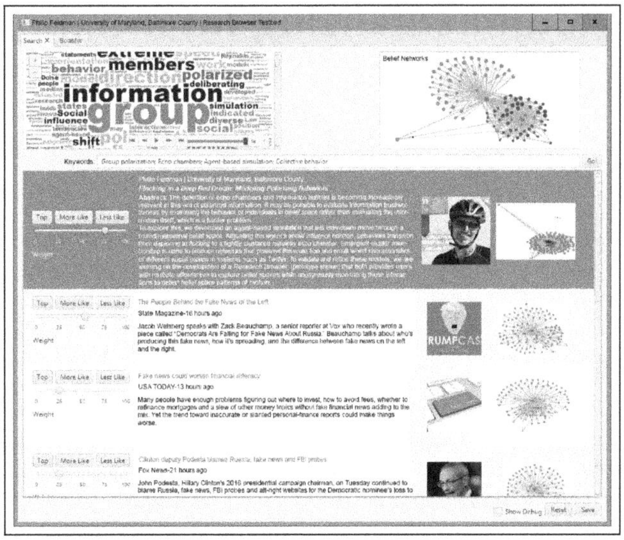

Figure 7: Research Browser mockup

REFERENCES

[1] Richard Bellman. 1957. *Dynamic programming.* Courier Corporation.
[2] R Kelly Garrett, Brian E Weeks, and Rachel L Neo. 2016. Driving a wedge between evidence and beliefs: How online ideological news exposure promotes political misperceptions. *Journal of Computer-Mediated Communication* 21, 5 (2016), 331–348.
[3] Kersty Hobson and Simon Niemeyer. 2013. "What sceptics believe": The effects of information and deliberation on climate change scepticism. *Public understanding of science* 22, 4 (2013), 396–412.
[4] Valdimer Orlando Key. 1968. *The responsible electorate* (third ed.).
[5] Nicolas Lanchier. 2010. Opinion dynamics with confidence threshold: an alternative to the Axelrod model. *arXiv preprint arXiv:1003.0115* (2010).
[6] Stephan Lewandowsky, Ullrich KH Ecker, Colleen M Seifert, Norbert Schwarz, and John Cook. 2012. Misinformation and its correction: Continued influence and successful debiasing. *Psychological Science in the Public Interest* 13, 3 (2012), 106–131.
[7] Travis Mandel, Yun-En Liu, Emma Brunskill, and Zoran Popovic. 2017. Where to Add Actions in Human-in-the-Loop Reinforcement Learning.. In *AAAI*. 2322–2328.
[8] Timothy W McGuire, Sara Kiesler, and Jane Siegel. 1987. Group and computer-mediated discussion effects in risk decision making. *Journal of personality and social psychology* 52, 5 (1987), 917.
[9] Serge Moscovici and Willem Doise. 1994. *Conflict and consensus: A general theory of collective decisions.* Sage.
[10] Sean A Munson and Paul Resnick. 2010. Presenting diverse political opinions: how and how much. In *Proceedings of the SIGCHI conference on human factors in computing systems.* ACM, 1457–1466.
[11] Eli Pariser. 2011. *The filter bubble: How the new personalized web is changing what we read and how we think.* Penguin.
[12] Craig W Reynolds. 1987. Flocks, herds and schools: A distributed behavioral model. *ACM SIGGRAPH computer graphics* 21, 4 (1987), 25–34.
[13] Stan Salvador and Philip Chan. 2007. Toward accurate dynamic time warping in linear time and space. *Intelligent Data Analysis* 11, 5 (2007), 561–580.

Contextualizing Information Needs of Patients with Chronic Conditions Using Smartphones

Henna Kim

School of Information
University of Texas at Austin
1616 Guadalupe St. Suite #5.546
Austin, TX 78701
USA
henna@utexas.edu

ABSTRACT

Having become integral to daily life, smartphones become a main tool in addressing daily information needs. Smartphones provide immediate and ubiquitous access to the internet. Mobile apps are becoming popular resources for the general public and patients to obtain health-related information and to self-manage their health. Little is known about patients' needs for information in the context of their phone use. Thus, this study investigates the context of emergence of information needs of diabetes patients using smartphones. This study focuses on the chronic disease type 2 diabetes because patients with this condition are required to take an active role in managing their condition on a daily basis. This study employs employ a web-based survey using the critical incident technique. This study has theoretical significance and practical implications. Information needs should be conceptualized in the contexts that give rise to them. This study will enrich our understanding of multi-faceted information needs related to chronic disease self-care in daily life. Understanding the information needs of diabetes patients and the contexts for the needs is necessary to help researchers and designers develop mobile services to satisfy patients' needs and requirements.

ACM Reference format:

Henna Kim. 2018. Contextualizing Information Needs of Patients with Chronic Conditions Using Smartphones. In *CHIIR '18: Conference on Human Information Interaction and Retrieval, March 11-15, 2018, New Brunswick, NJ, USA.* ACM, NY, NY, USA, 3 pages.
DOI: https://doi.org/10.1145/3176349.3176352

1 MOTIVATION

Mobile technology, including mobile devices, networks, services, and applications (apps), has dramatically changed how people access and use online information. Almost 95% of American adults own a cell phone and 77% have smartphones [1]. As of May 2015, 75% of adult mobile phone owners used their phones to go online; 34% of mobile internet users go online solely using their phones instead of desktops, laptops, or other devices [2].

Mobile phones in general and smartphones in particular provide immediate and ubiquitous access to the internet. They have become a main tool in addressing people's daily information needs. Nevertheless, researchers have paid limited attention to patients' health information needs in the mobile environments where they carry and use their phones. To achieve a better understanding of patient health information needs, we need to better understand the contexts in which the needs arise and are addressed. This knowledge is important for providing health information services through mobile phones to meet patients' needs.

Mobile apps have become popular resources for obtaining health information [3]. Despite the popularity of apps, however, prior studies have shown that apps targeting a given health condition are limited in the quantity and quality of information provided [4]. For example, many apps for diabetes do not include reliable information such as medical reference and the apps provide only general information about symptoms, management, and prevention of the disease [5]. Few diabetes apps offer adequate resources such as psychosocial support, disease-related alerts/reminders, and healthcare providers or facilities to meet patients' need for health information [6]. Mobile apps for diabetes self-management tend to focus primarily on self-monitoring of signs, symptoms, and lifestyle behavior. If we are to provide patients adequate, accurate, relevant, and timely information through mobile apps or phones, it is critical to understand patient information needs.

Prior studies have reported on patients' unmet information needs—the gap between information perceived as provided and information perceived as received [7]. Meeting patient information needs results in increased patient involvement in decision-making, increased self-care abilities and adherence to treatment, improved communication with healthcare professionals, and reduced anxiety and mood disturbances [8-11]. To narrow the information need gap, information sources such as healthcare professionals and the internet play an important role in offering health information to meet patients' needs.

In the existing literature, health information needs have been explored in response to the situations in which health-related incidences occur and patients are involved in their self-management, such as utilizing healthcare facilities and making treatment decisions. For example, studies have examined health information needs in situations such as when patients are newly diagnosed with a health condition and when symptoms have progressed [12]. Little is known, however, about health information needs in contexts of daily smartphone use, specifically, when smartphones are nearly always with patients and various online resources for health care are easily accessible.

This study focuses on patients with type 2 diabetes as a case of chronic disease. Information and knowledge play an important role in effectively self-managing this condition on a day-to-day basis and over the course of a lifetime [13]. Diabetic patients may need information to address both immediate and long-term issues for their self-management. In particular, many everyday situations and activities might require diabetic patients to cope with healthcare-related issues. Few studies focus on the context that the information needs of diabetes patients arise in their daily lives, even if some studies have identified their needs in the specific contexts, including at home and at the time of diagnosis [14-15]. Thus, understanding the context of the emergence of diabetes patients' information needs is required in that the context can provide multi-faceted information needs related to their self-management in daily life.

The objectives of this study are to contextualize information needs of patients with type 2 diabetes in the mobile environments where they carry and use their smartphones.

2 CONCEPTUAL FRAMEWORK AND RESEARCH QUESTIONS

2.1 Conceptual Framework

Fig. 1 shows a conceptual framework that guides this study. It was developed based on two theoretical perspectives—context-aware mobile computing and task-based information needs.

Information needs arise in the context in which people are embedded. In mobile computing area, context generally can be characterized by these five factors; time, location, activity (task), social surroundings, and information technology environment. People's smartphone use, including information behavior, is strongly shaped and influenced by these factors. Time refers to "the non-spatial continuum in which actions and events occur" [16]. Location refers to the physical position or place of the user [17]. Social surroundings represent the presence or co-location of others around users, or the users' social networks [18]. Information technology environment includes computer ownership, access to Wi-Fi, and data subscriptions for wireless broadband internet access [19].

Activity refers to goal-directed actions [20]. To better understand the activity in relation to chronic disease patients' smartphone use for information, I will utilize the concept of tasks, defined as activities performed in order to achieve goals [21]. I will focus on examining work and search tasks. Patients' health-related activities, called "patient work" [22], constitute a type of non-job-related work. More specifically, the goals and actions of patient work tasks and search tasks will be examined.

The attributes of work and search tasks would influence task performance and information search behavior [23]. This study will utilize attributes related to individuals' perception of tasks:

the importance, urgency, and difficulty of a task, subjective task complexity, and knowledge of task topic and procedure.

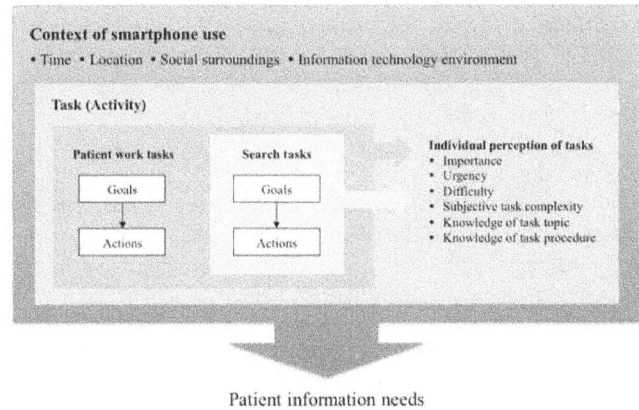

Figure 1: Framework of the Information Needs of Patients Using Smartphones

2.2 Research Questions

While tasks provide the analytic lens to understand the context of patient information needs, I will examine work and search tasks that diabetes patients perform for their self-care. Furthermore, I will examine the attributes related to an individual's perception of patient work and search tasks. I will characterize work and search tasks in terms of the following contextual factors: time, location, social surroundings, and information technology environment. I will explore the following research questions:

1. What goals do diabetes patients want to achieve while performing work tasks for their self-care? What actions do diabetes patients take to accomplish these goals?

2. What topics do diabetes patients search? What actions do diabetes patients take to search for information?

3. What perceived attributes of work and search tasks affect patients' smartphone use?

4. What are the characteristics of contextual factors (including time, location, social surroundings, and information environment) when performing the work tasks and searching for information using smartphones?

3 METHODOLOGY

To explore the research questions, I will employ a web-based survey using the critical incident technique [24].

3.1 Participants

This study will employ a convenient sampling strategy. Participants will (1) be over 18 years old, (2) have a diagnosis of type 2 diabetes, and (3) possess a smartphone. The sample size is expected to be between 150 and 200 participants. Participants will be recruited through two methods: the university's email listserv and the online forums of health websites.

3.2 Data Collection: Instruments and Process

A web-based questionnaire has been developed to collect data and consists of six sections: 1) smartphone use, 2) health conditions, 3) health information sources, 4) diabetes-related tasks, 5) health information needs and seeking, and 6) demographics. The questionnaire items have been adapted from existing instruments and developed from the literature.

At the beginning of the survey, potential participants will be screened to make sure they are eligible for this study. If volunteers are over 18, have a diagnosis of type 2 diabetes, and possess a smartphone, they can continue to the next page, which is a consent form. On the consent form page, approved by the Human Subjects and Institutional Review Board (IRB) at the University of Texas at Austin, volunteers will be informed of the purpose of this study and the data collection process. They will be asked to agree to participate in this study. Participants who agree to participation will go the next page, a survey questionnaire. At the end of the survey, participants will be asked to enter their email address for a $20 eGift card drawing. Ten participants will be selected randomly at the end of this study. This survey will take about 20 minutes to complete.

3.3 Data Analysis

Data collected from the survey will be analyzed using descriptive statistics and content analysis. Descriptive statistics will be used to summarize the characteristics of participants and their use of smartphones and health information sources. SPSS version 25 will be used for descriptive statistics. Data about diabetes-related tasks and health information needs and seeking will be imported into the Nvivo 11.0 software and analyzed using content analysis. This study will incorporate quantitative and qualitative approaches of content analysis.

4 PROGRESS MADE

An initial coding schema has been developed from the conceptual framework and the literature. After all the data has been coded, through the constant comparison approach, the emerging relationships and categories will be continually refined and documented.

5 FUTURE PLANS

This study will provide the foundation to further explore the changing and evolving information behavior in today's mobile technology environment. The follow-up future research will explore health information practices using mobile phones to satisfy their information needs.

REFERENCES

[1] Pew Research Center. (2017). Mobile Fact Sheet. Retrieved from http://www.pewinternet.org/fact-sheet/mobile/

[2] Smith, A. (2015). U.S. Smartphone Use in 2015. Pew Research Center. Retrieved from http://www.pewinternet.org/2015/04/01/us-smartphone-use-in-2015/

[3] Fox, S., & Duggan, M. (2013). Health Online 2013. Pew Internet & American Life Project. Retrieved from http://www.pewinternet.org/Reports/2013/Health-online.aspx

[4] Boulos, M.N., Brewer, A.C., Karimkhani, C., Buller, D.B., & Dellavalle, R.P. (2014). Mobile medical and health apps: state of the art, concerns, regulatory control and certification. Online Journal of Public Health Informatics, 5(3), e229.

[5] El-Gayar, O., Timsina, P., Nawar, N., & Eid, W. (2013a). Mobile Applications for Diabetes Self-Management: Status and Potential. Journal of Diabetes Science and Technology, 7(1), 247–262.

[6] Nie, L., Xie, B., Yang, Y., & Shan, Y. M. (2016). Characteristics of Chinese m-Health Applications for Diabetes Self-Management. Telemedicine and E-Health, 22(7), 614–619.

[7] Faller, H., Koch, U., Brähler, E., Härter, M., Keller, M., Schulz, H., ... Mehnert, A. (2016). Satisfaction with information and unmet information needs in men and women with cancer. Journal of Cancer Survivorship, 10(1), 62–70.

[8] Rooks, R. N., Wiltshire, J. C., Elder, K., BeLue, R., & Gary, L. C. (2012). Health information seeking and use outside of the medical encounter: Is it associated with race and ethnicity? Social Science & Medicine, 74(2), 176–184.

[9] Samal, L., Saha, S., Chander, G., Korthuis, P. T., Sharma, R. K., Sharp, V., ... Beach, M. C. (2011). Internet Health Information Seeking Behavior and Antiretroviral Adherence in Persons Living with HIV/AIDS. AIDS Patient Care and STDs, 25(7), 445–449.

[10] Hong, T. (2008). Internet Health Information in the Patient–Provider Dialogue. CyberPsychology & Behavior, 11(5), 587–589.

[11] Sairanen, A., & Savolainen, R. (2010). Avoiding health information in the context of uncertainty management. Information Research, 15(4).

[12] Halkett, G. K. B., Kristjanson, L. J., Lobb, E., Little, J., Shaw, T., Taylor, M., & Spry, N. (2012). Information needs and preferences of women as they proceed through radiotherapy for breast cancer. Patient Education and Counseling, 86(3), 396–404.

[13] Kalantzi, S., Kostagiolas, P., Kechagias, G., Niakas, D., & Makrilakis, K. (2015). Information seeking behavior of patients with diabetes mellitus: a cross-sectional study in an outpatient clinic of a university-affiliated hospital in Athens, Greece. BMC Research Notes, 8(1), 48.

[14] Whetstone, M. (2013). Information needs of adults living with type 2 diabetes: When cookbooks are more than just recipes. In Proceedings of the American Society for Information Science and Technology, 50(1), 1–4.

[15] Longo, D.R., Schubert, S., Wright, B., LeMaster, J., Williams, C. & Clore, J. (2010). Health Information Seeking, Receipt, and Use in Diabetes Self-Management. Ann Fam Med. 8(4). 334-340.

[16] Sonnenwald, D. H. & Iivonen, M. (1999). An integrated human behavior research framework for information studies. Library & Information Science Research, 21(3), 429–457.

[17] Bellavista, P., Corradi, A., Montanari, R. & Stefanelli, C. (2006). A mobile computing middleware for location- and context-aware internet data services. Journal ACM Transactions on Internet Technology (TOIT). 6(4). 356-380.

[18] Absar, R., O'Brien, H. L., & Webster, E. T. (2014). Exploring Social Context in Mobile Information Behavior. In Proceedings of the Association for Information Science and Technology. 51(1), 1-10.

[19] Kim, H., & Zhang, Y. (2015). Health information seeking of low socioeconomic status Hispanic adults using smartphones. Aslib Journal of Information Management, 67(5), 542 - 561.

[20] Leont'ev, A.N. (1981). The problem of activity in psychology. In: Wertsch, J.V. (Ed.), The Concept of Activity in Soviet Psychology. M.E. Sharpe, Armonk, NY.

[21] Vakkari, P. (2003), Task-based information searching. Ann. Rev. Info. Sci. Tech., 37, 413–464.

[22] Valdez, R.S., Holden, R.J., Novak, L.L., & Veinot, T.C. (2015). Transforming consumer health informatics through a patient work framework: connecting patients to context. JAMIA, 22(1), 2–10.

[23] Li, Y., & Belkin, N.J. (2008). A Faceted Approach to Conceptualizing Tasks in Information Seeking. Information Processing & Management, 44(6), 1822-1837.

[24] Flanagan, J. C. (1954). The critical incident technique. Psychological Bulletin, 51(4), 327-358.

Exploring the Effects of Social Contexts on Task-Based Information Seeking Behavior

Eun Youp Rha
4th year PhD candidate
School of Communication and Information, Rutgers University
New Brunswick, New Jersey
eunyoup.rha@rutgers.edu

ABSTRACT

The aim of this study is to identify social effects on task-based information seeking behavior. Task has been studied for understanding information seeking behavior in relation to task properties and task performers' characteristics. However, there has been little attention to social contexts of task. This work focuses on social aspects of task performance and information seeking behavior by analyzing effects of a social context in which task is generated and conducted on cognition of individual performers. A novel theoretical framework has been designed based on literature on information science and sociology. In the future, data will be collected using self-recorded diaries and subsequent in-depth interviews.

KEYWORDS

Task-based information seeking; Social context of task; Cognitive sociology; Practice theory

ACM Reference Format:
Eun Youp Rha. 2018. Exploring the Effects of Social Contexts on Task-Based Information Seeking Behavior. In *CHIIR '18: 2018 Conference on Human Information Interaction Retrieval, March 11–15, 2018, New Brunswick, NJ, USA*. ACM, New York, NY, USA, 3 pages. https://doi.org/10.1145/3176349.3176356

1 MOTIVATION

Task, an activity to be performed in order to accomplish a goal [23], is an important element in understanding information seeking reasons, information types, seeking methods and information uses [8]. Scholars in information behavior studies have examined relationships between a variety of tasks and associated information seeking behaviors since it plays a fundamental role in motivating the start of information seeking. However, there is one aspect of task that has been little discussed: the social context in which it takes place. Although work task studies could be an example of embracing a social context of tasks, especially professional contexts, the major emphasis is still placed on individualistic qualities of work task performers rather than on socially shaped behavior of the performers. Accordingly, my research aims to identify social aspects of information seeking behavior when people conduct a task by looking

at how their social community influences task performance and information seeking activity.

In information studies, a social framework to analyze information behavior has emerged, paying attention to social contexts of people in relation to their information behavior over their cognitive or affective states (e.g. Taylor's information use environments [22], Chatman's small world [11], Jaeger and Burnett's information worlds [15]). Some studies have suggested applying a sociological viewpoint to study task-based information seeking behavior, viewing information behavior as the embodied process of the resolution of a problematic situation within a socio-cultural and historical context [10, 20]. My research also lies in this emerging interest in social aspects of task, how individuals' ways of performing a task and of seeking information are affected by their social context.

For the study, I have examined two theoretical lenses in sociology: cognitive sociology and practice theory. Cognitive sociology is a sub-field of sociology that defines human cognition as a product of social interventions to the individuals. From this view, an emphasis is placed on the relationships between the self and the social boundary, especially on roles of *thought communities* in shaping individuals' cognition [26]. A thought community is an intersubjective world, larger than the individual but smaller than the entire human race; for instance, professions, generations, social classes and status groups, in which similar thought styles and norms of focusing are shared and exchanged [14, 26]. Within this community, individuals experience distinctive cognitive traditions and socialization and obtain a certain *sociomental lens* [26]. The sociomental lens enables members to develop specialized cultures of perception and attention leading to certain ways of seeing and rules for filtering and framing information as relevant or irrelevant [6]. Therefore, cognitive sociology highlights that the way we perceive things and the way we focus on things are mainly achieved in a social manner more than in a purely sensory manner, since our perception and attention are normally filtered through interpretive frameworks that are built through our socialization to a particular thought community [26, 27].

Furthermore, practice theory, which views human actions as the outcome of social practices, also discusses roles of social context in shaping human behavior. Practices refer to shared actions among a particular group of people including the ways of doing and approaching things that are shared to some significant extent among members [25]. From this perspective, individuals' behavior is construed as a set of habitualized and routinized bodily actions shared within a society [4, 16, 18]. Thus, routines shared within a social boundary, for instance routinized ways of understanding worlds and desiring something [16, 18], fundamentally constitute individuals' actions.

The examination of cognitive sociology and practice theory leads to the conclusion that information seeking behavior may be formed based not only on their sociomental lens used to recognize or interpret information problems, information sources, or information itself, but also on social habits or routines with respect to dealing with task and information. Therefore, in this study, how individuals' socially constructed cognition and actions influence task-based information seeking behavior will be analyzed.

2 RESEARCH QUESTIONS

The main objective of the study is to understand the relationships between social contexts and individuals' cognition and actions in a circumstance in which tasks are conducted. Specific research questions are as follows:

- RQ1. Are there differences of individuals' understanding of a task in different thought communities?
  - 1-1. What are the differences?
  - 1-2. What are the reasons for the differences?
- RQ2. Are there differences of individuals' information problems and possible solutions of a task in different thought communities?
  - 2-1. What are the differences?
  - 2-2. What are the reasons for the differences?
- RQ3. Are there differences of individuals' choices of actions to resolve the information problems in different thought communities?
  - 3-1. What are the differences?
  - 3-2. What are the reasons for the differences?

3 METHODOLOGIES

The Zerubavelian cognitive sociologist on which I mainly rely for studying information seeking behavior collects evidence across multiple contexts and uses a comparative method to generate analysis across these disparate social contexts [5]. Therefore, this study will also conduct cross-cultural comparative analysis, examining two different thought communities and comparing their characteristics or patterns of socially mediated cognition in order to uncover the cognitive structures and conventions that the members use to socially construct their actions.

Methods of the study will consist of self-recorded diaries and in-depth interviews. Diaries will be used to collect data about individuals' information seeking processes and activities in detail. Diary study has been used for analysis of task-based information seeking behavior, particularly in the natural setting of information seeking [7, 13], because it is known as an unobtrusive method which enables researchers to increase reliability and completeness of the data [9]. This study will be also conducted in a naturalistic environment of task performers. Therefore, a diary method will be suitable to gain authentic real-time data from participants in this study.

In-depth semi-structured interviews will be performed after task diary sessions are complete. This stage aims to acquire more details about participants' thoughts and behaviors based on data from self-recorded diaries. The subsequent interviews will be essential in this study as a means for not only clarifying any unclear data from the diaries, but also articulating whether participants' thoughts and actions for completing a task are associated with their thought community or with individualistic components.

3.1 Thought communities

Academic communities will be chosen as a thought community of this study, in which a scholar has cultivated a professional vision and routines by learning specialized knowledge and interacting with colleagues. In particular, humanists and natural scientists will be compared as two subcultures of academia. Prior study has shown different research cultures of these groups (e.g. knowledge validation [12], research styles [2]). Also, their information behavior is considered fairly different (e.g. information source choices [17, 19, 21], data management/sharing behavior [1, 3, 24]). Given the existence of different information behavior between Humanities and Natural sciences, the two groups will be proper as subjects to be tested if such differences come from members' social cognition and practices.

3.2 Procedure

Expected participants are post-tenured faculty members in Humanities and Natural sciences. Presumably, graduate students are unable to fully socialize to a certain knowledge domain as a scholar, whereas being a post-tenured faculty member in a certain field of study in higher education can prove sufficient time for his or her socialization to the field. Thus, this study will recruit post-tenured professors in two disciplines in a single institution to minimize other factors that could affect information seeking behavior, such as professional age and institutional culture. There may be other factors that need to be controlled for recruitment (e.g. gender), which has yet to be identified at this point.

In order to control a possible effect of task types on information seeking behavior, I will assign a particular task type to be performed in participants' real world setting, writing a research proposal. Writing a research proposal is a common, major academic task entailing various information seeking and/or searching activities although specific targets or formats may vary across disciplines. Participants will choose their own task of research proposal writing for study participation. Detailed structures of a diary and an interview are tentatively developed based on the research questions and are still open for discussion.

Participants will need to write a diary throughout the process of proposal writing. At first, a short description about the main task and detailed sub-tasks should be identified. Second, for each of the sub-tasks articulated, specific information problems and possible solutions for those problems should be described. Then actions taken to resolve the information problems need to be explained. After the completion of a diary session, in-depth interviews will be held based on the preliminary analysis of data from diaries. The primary goal of this step is to distinguish between actions from individualistic motivations, goals or styles and socially-driven actions. The questions will be concerned with reasons motivating each activity in the diaries such as selecting sub-tasks, describing problems and possible solutions, and choosing certain actions for problem solving, and their field's imperatives and principles with regard to proposal writing. The specific period of time for data collection has yet been determined.

4 PROGRESS SO FAR

I have achieved the holistic review of the literature on social perspectives on information behavior and human behavior in sociology. This process was a fundamental step of the entire research since it led to developing a novel conceptual framework for understanding social factors that may be involved in information seeking.

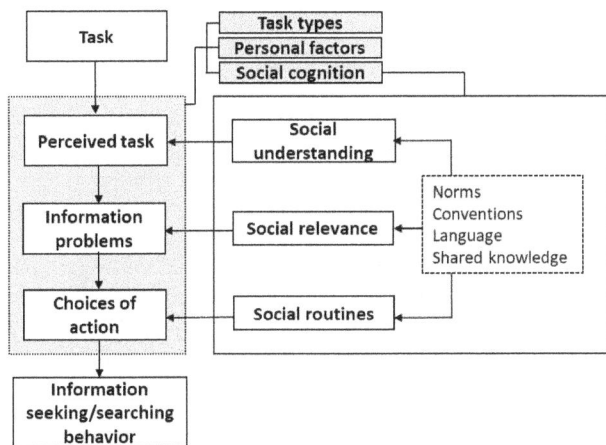

Figure 1: A theoretical model on task-based information seeking behavior

Figure 1 demonstrates the process of how a task leads to information seeking behavior. It focuses primarily on how social cognition may affect the process of information seeking and searching behavior in task. This model is developed upon the existing model of information seeking in task [9].

Through the process of information seeking for task, various kinds of information seeking/searching behavior may occur for the purpose of accomplishing an initial task. During this procedure, there will be social interventions, similar to influences of task types and personal factors on information seeking behavior. Specifically, when an individual perceives a given task, he or she may understand it socially. Then specific information problems of the task can be identified based on social relevance that exists in a social environment. The information problems will be resolved by certain actions chosen by a person who may be influenced by social routines of a certain group to which he or she belongs.

5 FUTURE PLAN

The immediate plan is to finalize the methods by developing task diary structures and interview questions and specifying a data collection period. After finishing the study design, pilot study will be carried out with three people to evaluate feasibility and reliability of the overall process and instruments of the study. Also, a specific sample size will be determined according to the data obtained from the pilot study. I hope that this study will be able to successfully test whether a social context of task is a key variable of information seeking behavior. This study could suggest a new direction for

research into information seeking and searching in a certain social and cultural context by providing a theoretical framework that allows for the analysis of sociological cognition and behavior of individuals. Ultimately, understanding various social factors affecting information seeking behavior will be helpful to design information systems that assist practice-oriented information seeking behaviors of individuals in a certain social and cultural context.

REFERENCES

[1] K. G. Akers and J. Doty. Disciplinary differences in faculty research data management practices and perspectives. *International Journal of Digital Curation*, 8(2):5–26, 2013.
[2] T. Becher. The significance of disciplinary differences. *Studies in Higher education*, 19(2):151–161, 1994.
[3] C. L. Borgman. The conundrum of sharing research data. *Journal of the Association for Information Science and Technology*, 63(6):1059–1078, 2012.
[4] P. Bourdieu. *The logic of practice*. Stanford University Press, 1990.
[5] W. Brekhus. The rutgers school: A zerubavelian culturalist cognitive sociology. *European Journal of Social Theory*, 10(3):448–464, 2007.
[6] W. H. Brekhus. *Culture and Cognition: Patterns in the Social Construction of Reality*. John Wiley & Sons, 2015.
[7] K. ByströM. Information and information sources in tasks of varying complexity. *Journal of the Association for Information Science and Technology*, 53(7):581–591, 2002.
[8] K. Byström and P. Hansen. Conceptual framework for tasks in information studies. *Journal of the Association for Information Science and Technology*, 56(10):1050–1061, 2005.
[9] K. Byström and K. Järvelin. Task complexity affects information seeking and use. *Information processing & management*, 31(2):191–213, 1995.
[10] K. Byström and A. Lloyd. Practice theory and work task performance: How are they related and how can they contribute to a study of information practices. *Proceedings of the Association for Information Science and Technology*, 49(1):1–5, 2012.
[11] E. A. Chatman. A theory of life in the round. *Journal of the Association for Information Science and Technology*, 50(3):207, 1999.
[12] J. G. Donald. Disciplinary differences in knowledge validation. *New directions for teaching and learning*, 1995(64):6–17, 1995.
[13] J. T. Du. The information journey of marketing professionals: Incorporating work task-driven information seeking, information judgments, information use, and information sharing. *Journal of the Association for Information Science and Technology*, 65(9):1850–1869, 2014.
[14] L. Fleck. *Genesis and Development of a Scientific Fact*. University of Chicago Press, 1981.
[15] P. T. Jaeger and G. Burnett. *Information worlds: Social context, technology, and information behavior in the age of the Internet*, volume 8. Routledge, 2010.
[16] A. Reckwitz. Toward a theory of social practices: a development in culturalist theorizing. *European journal of social theory*, 5(2):243–263, 2002.
[17] R. S. Rosenbloom and F. W. Wolek. Technology, information and organization; information transfer in industrial r and d. 1967.
[18] T. R. Schatzki. *The site of the social: A philosophical account of the constitution of social life and change*. Penn State Press, 2002.
[19] S. Talja and H. Maula. Reasons for the use and non-use of electronic journals and databases: A domain analytic study in four scholarly disciplines. *Journal of documentation*, 59(6):673–691, 2003.
[20] S. Talja and J. M. Nyce. The problem with problematic situations: Differences between practices, tasks, and situations as units of analysis. *Library & Information Science Research*, 37(1):61–67, 2015.
[21] S. Talja, R. Savolainen, and H. Maula. Field differences in the use and perceived usefulness of scholarly mailing lists. *Information Research: an international electronic journal*, 10(1):n1, 2004.
[22] R. S. Taylor. Information use environments. *Progress in communication sciences*, 10(217):55, 1991.
[23] P. Vakkari. Task-based information searching. *Annual review of information science and technology*, 37(1):413–464, 2003.
[24] T. Weller and A. Monroe-Gulick. Understanding methodological and disciplinary differences in the data practices of academic researchers. *Library Hi Tech*, 32(3):467–482, 2014.
[25] E. Wenger. *Communities of practice: Learning, meaning, and identity*. Cambridge university press, 1998.
[26] E. Zerubavel. *Social mindscapes: An invitation to cognitive sociology*. Harvard University Press, 1997.
[27] E. Zerubavel. *Hidden in plain sight: The social structure of irrelevance*. Oxford University Press, 2015.

Diversity-Enhanced Recommendation Interface and Evaluation

Chun-Hua Tsai
University of Pittsburgh
Pittsburgh, PA 15260
cht77@pitt.edu

ABSTRACT

The beyond accuracy user experience of using recommender system is drawing more and more attention. For example, the system interface has been shown to associate positively with overall levels of user satisfaction. However, little is known about how the interfaces can constitute the user experience and the social interactions. In this paper, I plan to propose a visual diversity-enhanced interface that supports the user to inspect and control the multi-relevance recommendations. The goal is to let the users explore the different relevance prospects of recommended items in parallel and to stress their diversity. Two preliminary user studies with real-life tasks were conducted to compare the visual interface to a standard ranked list interface. The users' subjective evaluations show significant improvement in many metrics. I further show that the users explored a diverse set of recommended items while experiencing an increase in overall user satisfaction. A user-centered evaluation was used to reveal the mediating effects between the subjective and objective conceptual components. The future plans are discussed to extend the current findings.

KEYWORDS

Recommender System; Diversity; Beyond Relevance; User control

ACM Reference format:
Chun-Hua Tsai. 2018. Diversity-Enhanced Recommendation Interface and Evaluation. In *Proceedings of CHIIR'18, March 11-15, 2018, New Brunswick, NJ, USA.*, , 3 pages.
DOI: http://dx.doi.org/10.1145/3176349.3176357

1 MOTIVATION

The mainstream research on recommender system (RS) focuses on improving recommendation accuracy which determines the quality of a predictive model. The model is usually trained with user-generated data (e.g., bookmarking and rating) for optimizing a recommendation list in descending order. An accurate predictive model can filter the recommendations by relevance to the user. This approach has been proven useful for further eliciting users' interests or preference which reduces the effort of decision making and choice difficulties [20]. However, since the users interact with the complete RS interface instead of the relevance scores, the predictive model only partially constitutes the **user experience** [9]. The finding implies that high accuracy of the predictive model may not always be equivalent to user's perceived recommendation quality [9, 11]. There are more factors, e.g., control, transparency, trust, that need user-centric approaches to RS evaluation.

One challenge of the accuracy-oriented RS is to generate a "one fit for all" recommendation list for various user needs, which is not realistic in many real-world scenarios. For instance, a hybrid recommender system that fuses several recommendation sources can be diversified. Each source, which is considered as one-dimension relevance, may be preferred for different needs. In [4], the study showed the social-based similarity works best for finding known friends while content-based similarity could be used to find unknown people with similar interests. We can add some variation to the recommendation list, but it may be accompanied by the risk of lowering the user satisfaction due to the exposure of the beyond-expectation items [21]. To solve this issue, several authors argued to offer **user controllability** to fuse the multi-relevance features by choosing various algorithms [5] or data sources [1]. Providing a visual interface could make the fusing process more transparent; for example, showing recommender sources and their overlaps as set diagrams [12, 17] can further address this problem. However, it is not clear how the user interacts with the control functions and interfaces in the exploration tasks with multi-relevance. The effects on user experience, in this case, is also unknown.

The other challenge of a relevance-driven RS is to deliver a narrow set of recommendations to the user. All the recommended item are highly similar to the user's profile, which is a well-known over-specification (lack of diversity) problem that leads to a poor user experience [9]. Critics argued the personalized algorithm causes filter bubble effect, which shields the user from other viewpoints [2], facilitates an adverse effect in social fragmentation and creates an ideological polarization of discussions on social issues [10]. In response to those issues, the factor of **beyond relevance** are attracting more and more attention in the recent RS studies. The diversity-enhanced recommendations can be generated based on users' personality for broader exposure [19] and balance choice between novelty & similarity items [18]. Many studies further leveraged visual interfaces to enhance recommendation diversity [16], e.g., adopting a visual discovery interface [14] or organization interfaces [6] in a RS can increase the selection diversity. However, little research efforts have been focused on understanding how the user interactions can moderate the user experience.

My work is to propose a diversity-enhanced interface which supports the user perception of the multi-dimension social recommendation. An user-centric evaluation framework would be conducted using Structural Equation Modeling (SEM) method [9]. This framework aims to explain the user experience in multiple systems and user aspects. The primary goal of my proposal can be seen in three-fold: First, this proposal seeks to uncover the moderators which explaining the user experience while interacting the interface. It can help ground out the casualty between the interface design and user experience outcome. Second, this proposal aims to explain the mediation between the proposed interface and the recommendation diversity. It can help to explain the effects of adopting the interface on multi-relevance tasks. Third, this proposal aims to explain the social implications of applying an RS. The framework helps to investigate the issues of causing the filter bubble effects and how to react with a proper interface design.

2 RESEARCH QUESTIONS

My work focus on answering questions regarding user-centered evaluation of social recommender system. **RQ1:** How do objective system aspects (OSAs) affect the user perception (SSA) with a social recommender system? **RQ2:** How do OSAs affect the user experience (EXP) with a social recommender system? **RQ3:** How do OSAs affect the user interaction (INT) with a social recommender system? **RQ4:** How do personal and situational characteristics (PCs and SCs) affect the SSAs, EXPs, and INTs with a social recommender system? **RQ5:** How do the mediation effects help to explain the SSAs, EXPs, and INTs with a social recommender system?

3 PLANNED METHODOLOGY

To assess the value of the proposed interface, I plan to conduct user experiments to compare the proposed interface with differently controlled manipulation. The study is scheduled in a within-subject design; all participants were asked to use the interface for three designed tasks and to fill out a (pre) post-stage questionnaire at the (beginning) end of each manipulation. At the end of the study, participants were asked to compare interfaces regarding their explicit preference and situational awareness. The order of manipulation was randomized to control for the effect of ordering. The interface is embedded in the Conference Navigator System (CN3), a social support system for academic conferences [3]. To minimize the learning effect (becoming familiar with data), we used conference data from multiple years.

I plan to extend the User-Centric Evaluation Framework for Recommender systems from [8] on explaining the user experience. The framework represents as five interrelated conceptual components. **1) Objective System Aspects (OSAs):** the aspects of the proposed system that are currently being evaluated. In this proposal, the OSA represents the diversity-enhanced interface with different manipulations; **2) Subjective System Aspects (SSA):** the effects that mediating between EXPs, INTs and the OSAs. SSAs help to establish connections through user perception of certain system aspects; **3) User Experience (EXP):** the EXP is the subjective evaluation from the users. It helps to understand the user feedback on different system aspects. **4) Interaction (INT):** the INT is representing the logged data the user interaction with the system; **5) Personal and Situational Characteristics (PCs and SCs):** the PCs and SCs are used to test the influence of the user's characteristics and the situation on using the system. The factors are beyond system aspects but with a significant impact on EXPs.

4 PROGRESS MADE

Two attempts have been made to test the design of diversity-enhanced interface [15]. First, we proposed a recommender interface that

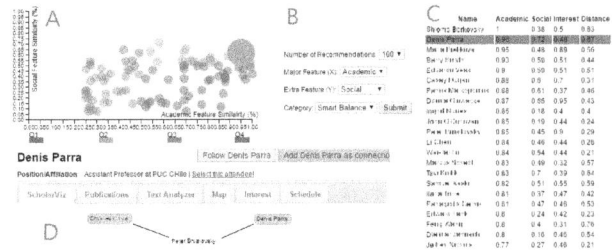

Figure 1: The design of Scatter Viz: (A) Scatter Plot; (B) Control Panel; (C) Ranked List; (D) User Profile Page. The user can select (or inspect) the recommendations with two relevance dimensions in the scatter plot.

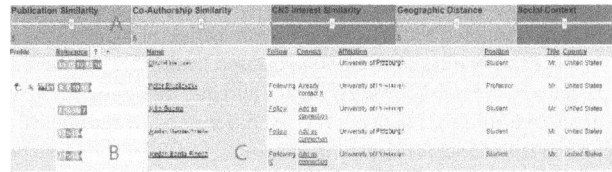

Figure 2: The design of the Relevance Tuner: (a) Relevance Slides; (b) Stackable Score Bar; (c) User Profiles. The user can inspect the recommendations with multi-relevance dimensions while controlling the weightings.

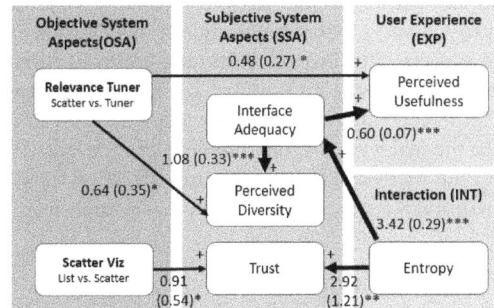

Figure 3: The structural equation model of the experiments. The number (thickness) on the arrows represents the β coefficients and standard error of the effect. Significance: *** $p < 0.01$, ** $p < 0.05$, * $p < 0.1$. The model fit the statistics of $\chi^2(96) = 234.68$, $p < 0.01$, $RMSEA = 0.18$, $90\%CI : [0.152, 0.211]$, $CFI = 0.941$, $TLI = 0.922$.

explores the value of a two-dimensional scatter plot visualization to present recommendations with several dimensions of relevance (shown in Figure 1). In our context, the scatter plot interface was used to help users combine different aspects of relevance for recommended items as well as providing inspectability to the users. Second, we proposed a recommender interface that enhances the fusion control function within a ranked list with meaningful visual encoding for multiple dimensions of relevance (shown in Figure 2). The users can adjust the relevance weightings to customize the recommendation results, which provides the user with a higher level of control over their results.

The two interfaces were designed to explore the value of user-controllable and diversity-aware interfaces in a social recommender system. Each of the interfaces has been evaluated in a controlled field study in the target context (assigned exploration tasks in a conference), with 25 and 20 subjective respectively. The results show that the new visual interfaces reduce exploration efforts for a set of realistic tasks, and also make the users more aware of the diversity of recommended items. Also, the users' subjective evaluation shows a significant improvement in subjective metrics, i.e., perceiving useful and satisfaction. The experiments further showed the effects of the proposed interfaces for the users' interaction. We measure the user's selection diversity using information entropy [15]. The experiment results supported the two proposed interface can facilitate the user with higher selection diversity.

To better understand the mediation effects across the two interfaces, we conducted a structural equation model (SEM) analysis [7] to inspect the results of the two proposed interfaces on the user experiences. We used the logged data and questionnaire feedback from the two studies. There are two conditions and five summarized factors in the model (as shown in Figure 3). In OSAs, there are two manipulations based on the proposed interfaces. In SSAs and EXPs, we introduced four factors based on the classification by [13] and our post-experiment questions. In INT, we listed the entropy of the participant's selection diversity. The model shows that the two manipulations have different positive effects on the system, which helps to explain the EXP by the meditating impacts of SSA and INT.

The progress can be summarized as threefold: 1) we propose two interfaces that support the continuously controlled fusion of several relevance aspects with inspectability and controllability. 2) we provide evidence that the diversity-aware interface not only helps the user to perceive diversity but also helps the user to improve usability in the real world beyond simple relevance tasks. 3) finally, we discuss the user experience mediating effects on the proposed interfaces through a structural equation model analysis.

5 FUTURE PLANS

The preliminary study supports the two interfaces were useful in different aspects. The Scatter Viz is helpful on perceiving trust of the recommendations due to it reveals the relative relations of the multi-relevance, which may help to gain the transparency of the RS. The Relevance Tuner is let the user perceive usefulness and diversity due to the better inspectability and controllability. The next move is to consider the synergy of the two proposed interfaces designs. My plan can be summarized in three folds. **1) Full Design:** the two proposed interfaces were contributing to the different subjective system aspects (SSAs), i.e., perceived diversity and trust, which means they are useful in different contexts. I plan to combine the two designs as a Full Design, so a total four manipulations (Basic List, Scatter Plot, Relevance Tuner and Full Design) would be tested in a within-subject user study. The participants would be asked to find (explore) the scholars in academic conferences with specific criteria. **2) Generalizability:** one of the limitations of the two proposed studies is the small sample size, which decreased the robustness of the findings. A more extensive scale (size = 50) controlled study is scheduled to explain the conceptual components, which mentioned in the research questions section above. **3) Social**

Interactions: I plan to extend the INTs with more diversity and usability metrics, e.g., the Gini index of the exploration diversity, the user's rating and the engagement on time spending. The goal is to correlate the logged user interactions to the user-centered evaluation framework, which aims to explain the causality through the conceptual components [9].

REFERENCES

[1] Svetlin Bostandjiev, John O'Donovan, and Tobias Höllerer. 2012. TasteWeights: a visual interactive hybrid recommender system. In *Proceedings of the sixth ACM conference on Recommender systems*. ACM, 35–42.

[2] Engin Bozdag and Jeroen van den Hoven. 2015. Breaking the filter bubble: democracy and design. *Ethics and Information Technology* 17, 4 (2015), 249–265.

[3] Peter Brusilovsky, Jung Sun Oh, Claudia López, Denis Parra, and Wei Jeng. 2016. Linking information and people in a social system for academic conferences. *New Review of Hypermedia and Multimedia* (2016), 1–31.

[4] Jilin Chen, Werner Geyer, Casey Dugan, Michael Muller, and Ido Guy. 2009. Make new friends, but keep the old: recommending people on social networking sites. In *Proceedings of the SIGCHI Conference on Human Factors in Computing Systems*. ACM, 201–210.

[5] Michael D Ekstrand, Daniel Kluver, F Maxwell Harper, and Joseph A Konstan. 2015. Letting users choose recommender algorithms: An experimental study. In *Proceedings of the 9th ACM Conference on Recommender Systems*. ACM, 11–18.

[6] Rong Hu and Pearl Pu. 2011. Enhancing recommendation diversity with organization interfaces. In *Proceedings of the 16th international conference on Intelligent user interfaces*. ACM, 347–350.

[7] Bart P. Knijnenburg, Svetlin Bostandjiev, John O'Donovan, and Alfred Kobsa. 2012. Inspectability and Control in Social Recommenders. In *6th ACM Conference on Recommender System*. 43–50. http://dl.acm.org/citation.cfm?id=2365966

[8] Bart P Knijnenburg and Martijn C Willemsen. 2015. Evaluating recommender systems with user experiments. In *Recommender Systems Handbook*. Springer, 309–352.

[9] Bart P Knijnenburg, Martijn C Willemsen, Zeno Gantner, Hakan Soncu, and Chris Newell. 2012. Explaining the user experience of recommender systems. *User Modeling and User-Adapted Interaction* 22, 4-5 (2012), 441–504.

[10] Q Vera Liao and Wai-Tat Fu. 2013. Beyond the filter bubble: interactive effects of perceived threat and topic involvement on selective exposure to information. In *Proceedings of the SIGCHI conference on human factors in computing systems*. ACM, 2359–2368.

[11] Sean M McNee, John Riedl, and Joseph A Konstan. 2006. Being accurate is not enough: how accuracy metrics have hurt recommender systems. In *CHI'06 extended abstracts on Human factors in computing systems*. ACM, 1097–1101.

[12] Denis Parra and Peter Brusilovsky. 2015. User-controllable personalization: A case study with SetFusion. *International Journal of Human-Computer Studies* 78 (2015), 43–67.

[13] Pearl Pu, Li Chen, and Rong Hu. 2011. A user-centric evaluation framework for recommender systems. In *Proceedings of the fifth ACM conference on Recommender systems*. ACM, 157–164.

[14] Choon Hui Teo, Houssam Nassif, Daniel Hill, Sriram Srinivasan, Mitchell Goodman, Vijai Mohan, and SVN Vishwanathan. 2016. Adaptive, Personalized Diversity for Visual Discovery. In *Proceedings of the 10th ACM Conference on Recommender Systems*. ACM, 35–38.

[15] Chun-Hua Tsai and Peter Brusilovsky. 2017. Enhancing Recommendation Diversity Through a Dual Recommendation Interface. In *Workshop on Interfaces and Human Decision Making for Recommender Systems*.

[16] Chun-Hua Tsai and Peter Brusilovsky. 2017. Leveraging Interfaces to Improve Recommendation Diversity. In *Adjunct Publication of the 25th Conference on User Modeling, Adaptation and Personalization*. ACM, 65–70.

[17] Katrien Verbert, Denis Parra, Peter Brusilovsky, and Erik Duval. 2013. Visualizing recommendations to support exploration, transparency and controllability. In *Proceedings of the 2013 international conference on Intelligent user interfaces*. ACM, 351–362.

[18] Jacek Wasilewski and Neil Hurley. 2016. Intent-Aware Diversification Using a Constrained PLSA. In *Proceedings of the 10th ACM Conference on Recommender Systems*. ACM, 39–42.

[19] Wen Wu, Li Chen, and Liang He. 2013. Using personality to adjust diversity in recommender systems. In *Proceedings of the 24th ACM Conference on Hypertext and Social Media*. ACM, 225–229.

[20] Bo Xiao and Izak Benbasat. 2007. E-commerce product recommendation agents: use, characteristics, and impact. *MIS quarterly* 31, 1 (2007), 137–209.

[21] Yuan Cao Zhang, Diarmuid Ó Séaghdha, Daniele Quercia, and Tamas Jambor. 2012. Auralist: introducing serendipity into music recommendation. In *Proceedings of the fifth ACM international conference on WSDM*. ACM, 13–22.

Task-based Information Seeking in Different Study Settings

Yiwei Wang

School of Communication and Information, Rutgers University

New Brunswick, NJ

yw498@scarletmail.rutgers.edu

ABSTRACT

Existing studies have presented the relationships between task characteristics and individuals' information seeking and searching behaviors. Some task characteristics are found to have predictable influences on information seeking behaviors. However, most studies took place in lab settings and focused on individuals' interactions with information systems. How a laboratory environment affects individuals' natural information seeking behaviors is open to question. This paper proposes a study investigating the differences between information seeking behaviors in a lab setting where individuals' activities and resources are controlled and in naturalistic settings where individuals have access to all types of sources.

KEYWORDS

Task-based information seeking; Lab study; Field study

ACM Reference format:

Yiwei Wang. 2018. Task-based Information Seeking in Different Study Settings. In *Proceedings of 2018 Conference on Human Information Interaction Retrieval, New Brunswick, NJ, USA, March 11–15, 2018 (CHIIR '18)*, 3 pages.

https://doi.org/10.1145/3176349.3176351

1 INTRODUCTION AND MOTIVATION

Tasks, as a driving force of information seeking, have been identified as essential elements of context affecting information seeking behavior [6]. The literature has presented a variety of task facets or characteristics that influence information seeking behaviors such as task complexity (e.g., [3]), task difficulty (e.g., [4]), task goal (e.g., [7]), task product (e.g., [17]), and task stage (e.g., [9]). Tasks and individuals' information seeking behaviors under the influence of task characteristics subsequently influence information seeking outcomes (i.e., successes) [16].

Empirical studies in task-based information seeking have heavily focused on the online environment and most of them were conducted in lab settings. Specifically, observable browsing and searching behaviors have drawn continuous attention. For example, Gwizdka and Spence [4] discovered positive correlations between subjective post-task difficulty and various searching behaviors such as the number of Web pages visited and page dwell time in factual task performance. Li and Belkin [11] suggested that product and complexity played different roles in influencing search behavior. A few researchers have also examined task characteristics and

information seeking behaviors by conducting field studies that use authentic work tasks. For example, Byström' [2] study of two Finnish local governmental organizations revealed that the increase of task complexity increased the number of types of information needed, which in turn increased the use of people as sources. Saastamoinen and Järvelin [12] reported from their field study in city administration that increased perceived task complexity was associated with more searches and the use of more networked sources instead of organizational systems.

As Saastamoinen and Järvelin [13] have pointed out, naturalistic field studies of task-based information seeking are rare. Studies that include both online and offline sources (particularly human sources) are even scarcer. The literature has shown that individuals may behave differently in different study settings. For instance, they may digress from the tasks at hand (e.g., conducting irrelevant searches) when they are allowed to work in the field [5, 15]. As a result, sorting out task-related actions may be challenging. They are more likely to stay focused in a lab setting. Kelly and Gyllstrom [8] examined participants' search behavioral differences in remote and lab settings. They did not find significant differences in two settings for most measures, though greater variances were observed for the number of documents opened and saved by remote participants and for the amount of time taken by remote participants to complete the study. However, they instructed remote participants to finish the study in one uninterrupted session with all other applications on their computer closed. This set-up did not entirely resemble real-life scenarios where multi-tasking and less strict time constraint are common. We are not entirely clear about how a controlled setting affects individuals' natural information seeking behavior as well as how it affects the relationships between task characteristics and information seeking behavior. Distraction from task performance and utilizing non-Web sources are real parts of everyday life information seeking that should not be ignored. To fill in this gap, I propose a study that explores and compares individuals' information seeking behaviors in different study settings (i.e., lab setting, naturalistic settings) and in different types of tasks (i.e., simulated tasks, authentic tasks).

2 RESEARCH QUESTIONS

I hope to address the differences between a lab setting where individuals' activities and resources are controlled and naturalistic settings where individuals could decide when to work on their tasks and have access to all the sources that are available to them. I also hope to explore individuals' behavioral differences in performing simulated tasks and authentic tasks. This study will attempt to provide implications both problem-wise and methodology-wise for the understanding of task-based information seeking and the design of future research. If we are to use behavioral variables to predict task characteristics, it is essential to know if the data we collect in lab settings resemble information seekers' real behavior. This study will also provide implications for information system design. Participants in naturalistic settings will have access to non-Web sources. Thus, we may be able to see how offline sources complement online sources. Information seeking is not always limited to online environment. I argue that it is also important to consider users' offline behaviors and to provide support accordingly in system design. I propose the following research questions:

RQ1: If and how individuals' online searching behaviors are different in lab settings and naturalistic settings?

RQ2: How do individuals utilize non-Web information sources in naturalistic settings and how having these sources affect their online information seeking activities?

RQ3: If and how individuals' online searching behaviors are different in performing simulated tasks and authentic tasks?

3 PROPOSED METHODOLOGY

3.1 Recruitment and Participants

I propose to recruit 40 participants from Rutgers for this study through university email lists and Facebook groups. Twenty will be assigned to each study group. Participants in each group should represent a variety of majors and professions. Each gender should also be equally represented in each group.

3.2 Task Design

I will assign four information seeking tasks related to everyday health topics (e.g., physical exercises, diet) to each participant. A simulated task should be tailored to a situation that participants can relate to and find topically interesting [1]. Everyday life tasks are more suitable for participants from various educational backgrounds, as school-related or work-related tasks are more likely to be relevant to only individuals from one field. Health topics concern almost everyone so participants may find them relevant to their lives. The simulated tasks will be designed along three dimensions, according to Li and Belkin's faceted classification [10]: **Product:** a factual task locates facts, data, or other similar information items; an intellectual task produces new ideas or findings; **Quality:** a specific task has explicit or concrete goals; an amorphous task has abstract goals; **Objective Complexity:** a highly complex task involves significantly more paths during engaging in the task; a lowly complex task involves a single path.

These facets are chosen primarily because they were proven to have important roles in past studies [11]. Further, as the tasks are not real-life tasks, some facets are determined by the study design and will remain constant during the study such as source of task (externally assigned), task doer (individual), and length (short-term). Participants' subjective perceptions of the tasks (e.g., perceived difficulty, topical knowledge) will be solicited by questionnaires. To design tasks that mimic authentic everyday life tasks, a qualitative questionnaire will first be sent out through various university email lists to collect students' everyday tasks involving health information seeking. In the questionnaire, I will ask questions about two of their recent health information needs and the reasons motivating them to seek the information. The simulated tasks assigned to participants will be designed based on the real-life information needs collected. In addition to the simulated tasks, I will also ask each participant to bring one of their own health information needs that has not been fulfilled (authentic information seeking task).

3.3 Study Procedure

After signing up for the study, each participant will be assigned to one of the two conditions (lab vs. naturalistic settings). They will receive study instructions based on their assigned group. I will collect a combination of log data, diary data, and interview data to learn about participants' information seeking experiences from multiple angles and to allow data triangulation. The detailed procedure is proposed as follows.

3.3.1 Lab Group. Each participant in the lab group will come to a computer lab to finish five information seeking tasks on a desktop computer (four simulated tasks and one authentic task). A study system will be developed as a Web application to present the tasks and questionnaires. During their search for each task, a text box will be provided for them to record any information or answers. They will be asked to describe their prepared authentic task in a text box before searching for the task. The tasks (including the authentic task) will be permuted to exclude any ordering effects. Participants will not be given a time constraint. Each simulated task should not take more than 15 minutes if finished without interruption. Before and after each task, a pre-search questionnaire and a post-search questionnaire will ask about their perceptions of the tasks (e.g., perceived task difficulty). The post-search questionnaire will also ask if they have encountered any barriers in a session. All of their actions (e.g., queries, pages) will be collected by a Coagmento browser plugin [14] (http://coagmento.org/). Their screen will be recorded by Morae and be monitored in another room during task performance. In addition, each participant will be interviewed at the end of the lab study regarding their search experiences, particularly mental activities that cannot be captured by log data or Morae.

3.3.2 Semi-naturalistic Group. Each participant in the semi-naturalistic group will perform the same four information seeking tasks and one authentic task on their personal devices at any location of their choice. Here, this setting is not entirely naturalistic, as participants will be assigned simulated tasks (i.e., semi-naturalistic). However, performing the same set of tasks is essential for statistical comparisons between and within groups. After signing up, they will receive an email containing instructions to install the Coagmento plugin on their browser (used to collect log data) and to log into the study system. The set-up in the naturalistic group aims to capture individuals' natural information seeking behavior by giving as little constraint as possible. Therefore, participants will have access to all the sources available to them in normal circumstances. They may consult physical books or ask other people for information when necessary. They will be given up to two days to finish the tasks and they can approach the tasks at any time. Two days should be plenty for participants to finish the tasks so they would not feel the pressure they usually have in lab settings. They will fill out the same questionnaires as the lab group. In addition, as I will not observe their behaviors and offline activities will not be captured by any devices, they will detail their information seeking experiences, particularly mental activities and offline activities including sources consulted and channels used, in a structured online diary.

When they do search online, their search actions will be captured by Coagmento. Although self-reported data may not be completely accurate, the diary method can capture the activities that would not otherwise have been easily accessible (e.g., face-to-face communication). Allowing participants to use non-Web sources will examine if having other sources affect their online information behaviors. It is possible that, when participants could use online and offline sources jointly, their online searching and browsing behaviors are different. Having this design will also help me explore how offline sources interact with online sources in some scenarios.

3.4 Behavioral Measurements

To explicate participants' behaviors in different groups and different tasks, I will measure information seeking behaviors on three levels: 1. **Person Level:** average task completion time (for semi-naturalistic group, only the time they spend on the tasks will be counted), total number of query issued, total number of pages visited, total number of unique pages visited; 2. **Task Level:** task completion time, number of queries issued in a task session, number of SERPs visited, number of content pages visited, number of unique content pages visited; 3. **Query Segment Level (all that occur from one query to the next):** query length (number of words), query segment time (total time spent in a query segment), number of SERPs visited, number of content pages visited, number of unique content pages visited, average content page dwell time.

I will also categorize participants' offline information seeking sources and methods and draw connections between their online and offline information seeking.

3.5 Data Analysis

I will take a mixed methods approach in analyzing the data with quantitative analysis as the primary method. In quantitative analysis, I will conduct statistical tests (e.g., ANOVA) to examine 1) if online search behaviors are different across two study settings; and 2) if online search behaviors are different in simulated task performance and authentic task performance. Qualitative analysis will be used 1) as a supplement to quantitative analysis to help explain why some quantitative observations take place, and 2) to present how having access to non-Web sources influence individuals' task-based information seeking as compared to when they only use Web sources.

4 ANTICIPATED CHALLENGES AND LIMITATIONS

This study has several anticipated challenges and limitations. First, four out of five tasks will be simulated tasks that do not belong to participants' everyday lives. Although the extent to which they will encourage natural information seeking behaviors is unknown, simulated tasks are necessary here to compare participants' search behaviors. A series of steps (i.e., qualitative survey, pilot test) will be taken to create simulated tasks similar to authentic everyday life tasks. Second, I will rely on participants to report any offline activities and I cannot verify if their reports are completely accurate. It is critical to make the diary questions structured and clear so

they are guided through their reports. Third, there may be occasional technical difficulties. Pilot tests will be conducted to test the reliability of the study system.

5 PROGRESS MADE AND FUTURE PLANS

Previously, I have conducted a series of studies examining individuals' selection and use of information sources and their information seeking barriers (e.g., [15]). The structured diary, codebook, Coagmento plugin, and questionnaires developed from these studies may be modified and used for the proposed study. My next step will be finalizing the study design, preparing the study instruments, and starting pilot tests. A first round of pilot tests with eight participants will be conducted to test the study instruments and procedure. Each pilot test participant will be interviewed after the test regarding their experiences. After revising the instruments and procedure based on feedback collected from pilot tests, a second round of pilot tests may be arranged if necessary.

ACKNOWLEDGMENTS

I would like to thank my advisor, Dr. Chirag Shah. The work reported here is supported by the Institute of Museum and Library Services (IMLS) grant no. LG-81-16-0025-16.

REFERENCES

[1] Pia Borlund. 2016. A study of the use of simulated work task situations in interactive information retrieval evaluations: A meta-evaluation. *Journal of Documentation* 72, 3 (2016), 394–413.
[2] Katriina Byström. 2002. Information and information sources in tasks of varying complexity. *JASIST* 53, 7 (2002), 581–591.
[3] Katriina Byström and Kalervo Järvelin. 1995. Task complexity affects information seeking and use. *Information Processing and Management* 31, 2 (1995), 191–213.
[4] Jacek Gwizdka and Ian Spence. 2006. What can searching behavior tell us about the difficulty of information tasks? A study of Web navigation. *Proceedings of the ASIST* 43, 1 (2006), 1–22.
[5] Chathra Hasini Hendahewa. 2016. *Implicit search feature based approach to assist users in exploratory search tasks.* Ph.D. Dissertation. Rutgers University, New Brunswick, United States.
[6] Peter Ingwersen and Kalervo Järvelin. 2005. *The Turn: Integration of Information Seeking and Retrieval in Context.* Springer, Dortrecht, NL.
[7] Jiepu Jiang, Daqing He, and James Allan. 2014. Searching, browsing, and clicking in a search session: Changes in user behavior by task and over time. *Proceedings of the SIGIR 2014 Conference* (2014), 607–616.
[8] Diane Kelly and Karl Gyllstrom. 2011. An examination of two delivery modes for interactive search system experiments: Remote and laboratory. In *Proceedings of the SIGCHI Conference on Human Factors in Computing Systems.*
[9] Carol C. Kuhlthau. 1991. Inside the search process: Information seeking from the user's perspective. *JASIST* 42, 5 (1991), 361–371.
[10] Yuelin Li and Nicholas J. Belkin. 2008. A faceted approach to conceptualizing tasks in information seeking. *Information Processing and Management* 44, 6 (2008), 1822–1837.
[11] Yuelin Li and Nicholas J. Belkin. 2010. An exploration of the relationships between work task and interactive information search behavior. *JASIST* 61, 9 (2010), 1771–1789.
[12] Miamaria Saastamoinen and Kalervo Järvelin. 2012. Task complexity and information searching in administrative tasks revisited. In *Proceeding of the Fourth Information Interaction in Context Symposium.*
[13] Miamaria Saastamoinen and Kalervo Järvelin. 2017. Search task features in work tasks of varying types and complexity. *JASIST* 68, 5 (2017), 1111–1123.
[14] Chirag Shah. 2010. Coagmento-a collaborative information seeking, synthesis and sense-making framework. *Integrated demo at CSCW* 2010 (2010).
[15] Yiwei Wang, Jiqun Liu, Mandal Soumik, and Shah Chirag. 2017. Search successes and failures in query segments and search tasks: A field study. In *Proceedings of the 80th Annual Meeting of the Association for Information Science and Technology.*
[16] Werner Wirth, Katharina Sommer, Thilo von Pape, and Veronika Karnowski. 2016. Success in online searches: Differences between evaluation and finding tasks. *Journal of the Association for Information Science and Technology* 67, 12 (2016), 2897–2908.
[17] Iris Xie. 2009. Dimensions of tasks: Influences on information-seeking and retrieving process. *Journal of Documentation* 65, 3 (2009), 339–366.

Creative Search: Using Search to Leverage Your Everyday Creativity

Yinglong Zhang
School of Information and Library Science
Chapel Hill, North Carolina
yinglongz@unc.edu

ABSTRACT

By highlighting the values of creativity to a society and individuals, we argue the importance of investigating people's daily creativity and the necessity of designing user interfaces to support the creative process. In this paper, moreover, we propose a dissertation study to examine people's creative process in the context of information search. The implications of this research will inform the future design of a novel search interface for supporting people's creativity.

KEYWORDS

Creativity, Creative Process, Information Search

ACM Reference Format:
Yinglong Zhang. 2018. Creative Search: Using Search to Leverage Your Everyday Creativity. In *CHIIR '18: 2018 Conference on Human Information Interaction & Retrieval, March 11–15, 2018, New Brunswick, NJ, USA*. ACM, New York, NY, USA, Article 4, 3 pages. https://doi.org/10.1145/3176349.3176354

1 INTRODUCTION

Creativity and innovation are highly valued characteristics in different fields, such as science, commerce, education, and the arts. Sawyer [13] argues that creativity will continue to increase in importance because of increased global competitiveness, shorter product development cycles, decreasing number of jobs that do not involve creativity, and increasing demand for products of creative industries.

In addition to these social values, creativity has been regarded as a universal quality that helps people survive. As Richards highlighted in her seminal paper on everyday creativity, "Throughout our day, whether at home or at work, we humans adapt and innovate, improvise flexibly, at times acting from our 'gut feelings', at times from options we imagine and systematically try out, one after the other. Our creativity may involve anything from making breakfast to solving a major conflict with one's boss." [11, p. 190]. In fact, much previous research has shown that creativity is a process that is trainable [4, 9, 12]. The Stanford d.school[1] is a good example of showing the feasibility of teaching people the design thinking method to help them develop their creative abilities.

[1] https://dschool.stanford.edu

In the realms of human-computer interaction (HCI) and information science (IS), Shneiderman is one of the earliest scholars who advocated the importance of supporting people's creativity using information technologies. In 1999, he published a paper emphasizing the significance of developing user interfaces that support creativity. In the paper, he described ways that information tools and interfaces could support users during phases in a creative process and proposed a framework for helping to design interfaces to support creative work.

However, to the best of our knowledge, very few efforts have been made to understand the creative process in the context of information search. In White's book, he highlights the importance of supporting creativity and also points out that "searching and information seeking can be creative process" [18, p. 135]. Although prior work has explored ways to support serendipity in the area of information retrieval, it should be noted that the creative process and serendipity are not identical. In other words, inducing serendipity is just one of the possible ways to support the creative process.

In the dissertation research proposed here, a primary goal is to gain a better understanding of the creative process in the context of information search. We are particularly interested in investigating how people use search systems to perform creative tasks in their everyday life and work, and how search systems might better support creative endeavors.

2 RELATED WORK

2.1 Creativity

What is creativity? In the literature, creativity has been mainly defined and investigated through two different lenses: the individualist approach and the sociocultural approach. From the individualist point of view, creativity was referred to "a new combination that is expressed in the world." [12, p. 7] Richards operationally defined creativity using two product criteria: ***originality*** (how rare is the product with a given reference group?) and ***meaningfulness*** (is this product comprehensible to others?) [11]. Most of the researchers advocating the individualist approach hold the belief that everyone has a potential of being creative.

Different from the individualist approach, the sociocultural approach adopts a more strict way to look at creativity. Socioculturalists consider creativity as "the generation of a product that is judged to be novel and also to be appropriate, useful, or valuable by a suitably knowledge social group" [12, p. 8]. An idea or action can be considered creative only if it solves a tough problem or results in significant works of genius. In the proposed dissertation, the individualist approach will be adopted to scope and define the "everyday creativity" that we intend to investigate.

2.2 Creativity Process

In many decades of research, psychology research has demonstrated that creativity tends to occur in a sequence of stages. For example, Wallas [17] developed a four-stage model, assuming that the creative process involves four stages: preparation, incubation, illumination, and verification. In the **preparation stage**, individuals define and set up a problem by consciously drawing on their education, analytical skills, and problem-relevant knowledge. During **incubation stage**, individuals take a break from the problem or work consciously on other problems. After taking a break, individuals are very likely to enter the **illumination stage** where they feel a sudden enlightenment. Hypothetically, the illumination phase is very delicate and can be easily disrupted by outside interruptions or the time pressure of generating the merging idea. Following the illumination stage, the fourth is the **verification stage** where individuals evaluate, redefine, and develop their ideas. Inspired by Wallas' system, many variants emerged in the creativity research, such as Amabile's five-stage model [1], Geneplore model [5], Mumford's eight-stage model [9], and Sawyer's eight-stage framework [13].

In the context of HCI and IS, Shneiderman [14] defined a four-phase *genex* framework for "generating excellence", which included: "**collect** (learn from previous works stored in digital libraries, the web, etc.); **relate** (consult with peers and mentors at early, middle and late stages); **create** (explore, compose, evaluate possible solutions); and **donate** (disseminate the results and contribute to the digital libraries)" [14, p. 15].

2.3 Creativity and Search

In addition to the four-phase genex framework aforementioned, Shneiderman advanced to provide several contexts that existing technologies could play a role in supporting creativity [14]. One of the contexts that had been mentioned is to use existing web search engines and digital library interfaces to support creativity. In previous research in IS, there are few studies carried out to investigate how to support creativity using search engines. However, some efforts have been made to investigate and design ways to deliberately induce serendipity. In 2000, Toms [16] proposed four possible approaches to support serendipitous retrieval:

(1) Enhance chance or "blind luck" by a random information node generator;
(2) Use a user profile to enhance the chance that are more likely to meet the user's expectation (using Pasteur principle);
(3) Enhance anomalies and exception by using poor similarity measures;
(4) Support reasoning by analogy.

In a recent theoretical study, by interviewing 14 creative professionals, Makri identified some strategies that the creatives used to enhance the likelihood of serendipity, such as "vary your routine, be observant, make mental space, relax your boundaries, draw on previous experiences, look for patterns, and seize opportunities." [8]

Several systems or tools have been developed to support serendipity in web browsing. For instance, Beale [3] developed two systems for supporting users' serendipity by using ambient intelligence, which can incorporate information about the user's actions and environment.

The first system was a tool for interactive data exploration and the second was a tool that incorporated a user's web browsing interactions to 'look ahead' to find additional pages of possible interest. In a more recent study, Rahman and Wilson [10] have developed a search engine that could match search results with recorded Facebook "Like" data. This novel search system did not re-rank SERP results based on interests specified by participants, but it would highlight results to provide a secondary notion of potential relevance to ranking.

However, some authors have argued that focusing on the "chance encounters" aspect of serendipity will not necessarily result in significant discoveries or support creativity. As André, scraefel, Teevan, and Dumais empathized in their paper, "discovery is never by chance" [2]. A system could increase users' chances of encountering the "dots" of information that might result in discoveries, but knowing how to connect these dots is a different story. Without sufficient domain knowledge and expertise, it could be challenging for people to synthesize and make use of this encountered information.

3 RESEARCH QUESTIONS

The proposed dissertation will address the following research goals:

RG1: Identify the *types* of creative tasks for which people use information searches, and understand their characteristics. Search tasks have been categorized and studied along different dimensions (e.g., fact-finding, comparative, exploratory, etc.) [6]. In this work, we are interested in exploring and understanding the types and range of creative tasks for which people incorporate information searches. As with exploratory search tasks, we anticipate that these creative search tasks may be ill-defined and the searcher may have unclear goals at the beginning of the task. However, there may be other important characteristics and dimensions that are important to understand about these tasks in order to provide search support for them. Some prior research has been conducted to examine ill-defined tasks. Wilson and Elsweiler [19], for instance, developed a new search task scenario, called "causal-leisure searching" to characterize the users who browse information without an explicit information need to solve. However, "causal-leisure searching" tasks and creative tasks are not the same. Only certain types of "causal-leisure searching" tasks are creative tasks. Their relationship is shown in **Figure 1**. In this dissertation, we will investigate the creative tasks that people perform in their everyday life and then identify the creative tasks that search engines can support.

RG2: The second goal of this dissertation is to understand how people use search engines to complete their creative tasks. In previous research, many efforts have been made to study users' searching behaviors and information needs in a variety of contexts and across different types of information seeking tasks. However, little research has been conducted to specifically understand how the information seeking process relates to and is used as part of a creative process. Findings of previous creativity studies have demonstrated that creative tasks require more mental effort

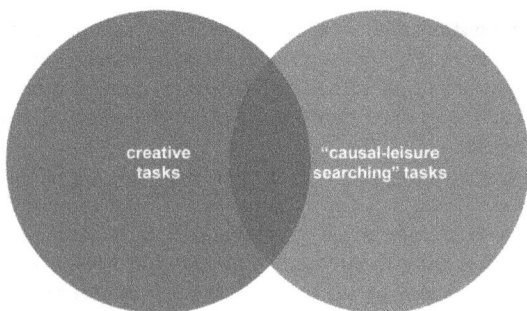

Figure 1: Relationship between creative tasks and "causal-leisure searching" tasks

and different types of thinking skills compared to standard problem-solving tasks [7, 9]. These differences suggests searchers' behaviors may differ when they perform creative search tasks and that it could be valuable to understand these in the context of existing models of information seeking.

RG3: The last goal of our research is to explore ways to design a search interface for supporting people's creativity. In a report from a U.S. National Science Foundation Sponsored Workshop [15], a set of design principles has been proposed for guiding the development of new creative support tools. In the dissertation, we attempt to figure out how to apply these principles to design search interfaces.

4 STUDY DESIGN AND METHODS

The proposed dissertation project involves three phases. Firstly, we will conduct a survey study to investigate the creative tasks that people conduct in their everyday life and situations in which they use search as part of these creative tasks (**RG1**). Based on results of the survey study, secondly, we will select specific types of creative tasks and then design a diary study to investigate how people use search engines to complete these tasks (**RG2**). In this phase, we will recruit participants and ask each to log regular diary entries while they complete a creative task that involves searches. Participants will be asked to record information about relevant activities in their task. For the study, we will also ask participants to use a tool to automatically log their searching behaviors (such as URLs, queries, web pages, etc.). We expect the diary study to provide us a better understanding of users' information needs and their searching strategies in creative tasks. Based on results of the second study, in the last phase, we will develop a set of design guidelines for search system to help support creative search tasks (**RG3**).

5 PROGRESS AND FUTURE PLAN

Using Amazon Mechanical Turk, We have conducted a survey study to investigate the creative tasks that people perform in everyday life. Next, we will analyze the quantitative and qualitative data in this survey to identify the types and range of the creative tasks that information search process are involved.

REFERENCES

[1] Teresa M Amabile. 1988. A model of creativity and innovation in organizations. *Research in organizational behavior* 10, 1 (1988), 123–167.
[2] Paul André, Jaime Teevan, and Susan T Dumais. 2009. Discovery is never by chance: designing for (un) serendipity. In *Proceedings of the seventh ACM conference on Creativity and cognition*. ACM, 305–314.
[3] Russell Beale. 2007. Supporting serendipity: Using ambient intelligence to augment user exploration for data mining and web browsing. *International Journal of Human-Computer Studies* 65, 5 (2007), 421–433.
[4] Mihaly Csikszentmihalyi. 1996. *Flow and the psychology of discovery and invention.* New York: Harper Collins.
[5] Ronald A Finke, Thomas B Ward, and Steven M Smith. 1992. Creative cognition: Theory, research, and applications. (1992).
[6] Yuelin Li and Nicholas J Belkin. 2010. An exploration of the relationships between work task and interactive information search behavior. *Journal of the Association for Information Science and Technology* 61, 9 (2010), 1771–1789.
[7] Todd I Lubart. 2001. Models of the creative process: Past, present and future. *Creativity Research Journal* 13, 3-4 (2001), 295–308.
[8] Stephann Makri, Ann Blandford, Mel Woods, Sarah Sharples, and Deborah Maxwell. 2014. âĂIJMaking my own luckâĂİ: Serendipity strategies and how to support them in digital information environments. *Journal of the Association for Information Science and Technology* 65, 11 (2014), 2179–2194.
[9] Michael D Mumford, Michele I Mobley, Roni Reiter-Palmon, Charles E Uhlman, and Lesli M Doares. 1991. Process analytic models of creative capacities. *Creativity Research Journal* 4, 2 (1991), 91–122.
[10] Ataur Rahman and Max L Wilson. 2015. Exploring opportunities to facilitate serendipity in search. In *Proceedings of the 38th International ACM SIGIR Conference on Research and Development in Information Retrieval*. ACM, 939–942.
[11] Ruth Richards. 2010. Everyday creativity. In *The Cambridge handbook of creativity*. 189–215.
[12] Badrul Sarwar, George Karypis, Joseph Konstan, and John Riedl. 2001. Item-based collaborative filtering recommendation algorithms. In *Proceedings of the 10th international conference on World Wide Web*. ACM, 285–295.
[13] R Keith Sawyer. 2011. *Explaining creativity: The science of human innovation.* Oxford University Press.
[14] Ben Shneiderman. 1999. User interfaces for creativity support tools. In *Proceedings of the 3rd conference on Creativity & cognition*. ACM, 15–22.
[15] Ben Shneiderman, Gerhard Fischer, Mary Czerwinski, Mitch Resnick, Brad Myers, Linda Candy, Ernest Edmonds, Mike Eisenberg, Elisa Giaccardi, and Tom Hewett. 2006. Creativity support tools: Report from a US National Science Foundation sponsored workshop. *International Journal of Human-Computer Interaction* 20, 2 (2006), 61–77.
[16] Elaine G Toms. 2000. Serendipitous Information Retrieval. In *DELOS Workshop: Information Seeking, Searching and Querying in Digital Libraries*. Zurich, 17–20.
[17] G Wallas. 1926. The art of thought. (1926).
[18] Ryen W. White. 2016. *Interactions with Search Systems.* Cambridge University Press, Cambridge.
[19] Max L Wilson and David Elsweiler. 2010. Casual-leisure Searching: the Exploratory Search scenarios that break our current models. *HCIR 2010* (2010), 28.

Visualizing and Exploring Scientific Literature with CiteSpace

An Introduction to a Half-day Tutorial

Chaomei Chen
College of Computing and Informatics
Drexel University
USA
chaomei.chen@drexel.edu

ABSTRACT

This half-day tutorial aims to introduce the fundamental concepts, principles and methods of visualizing and exploring the development of a scientific knowledge domain. The tutorial explains the design rationale and various applications of CiteSpace – a freely available tool for interactive and exploratory analysis of the evolution of a scientific domain, ranging from a single specialty to multiple interrelated scientific frontiers. The tutorial demonstrates the analytic procedure of applying CiteSpace to a diverse range of examples and how one may interpret various patterns and trends revealed by interactive visual analytics.magnetic field, applied along the easy axis of the elements[1].

CCS CONCEPTS

• **Human-centered computing** → **Visual analytics**; • **Information systems** → Information integration

KEYWORDS

CiteSpace, visual analytics, mapping scientific frontiers, visual exploration of scientific literature

ACM Reference format:

C. Chen. 2018. Visualizing and exploring scientific literature with CiteSpace: An introduction to a half-day tutorial. In *Proceedings of ACM CHIIR conference, New Brunswick, NJ, USA, March 11-15, 2018 (CHIIR'18)*, 2 pages.DOI: 10.1145/3176349.3176897

1 INTRODUCTION

This half-day tutorial aims to introduce the fundamental concepts, principles and methods of visualizing and exploring

the development of a scientific knowledge domain. The tutorial explains the design rationale and various applications of CiteSpace – a freely available tool for interactive and exploratory analysis of the evolution of a scientific domain, ranging from a single specialty to multiple interrelated scientific frontiers [1,2,8]. The tutorial demonstrates the analytic procedure of applying CiteSpace to a diverse range of examples and how one may interpret various patterns and trends revealed by interactive visual analytics.magnetic field, applied along the easy axis of the elements.

Figure 1: A network visualization showing citation burstness in CiteSpace.

The tutorial is suitable for anyone who is interested in learning and applying an effective method to generate a systematic review of the history and the state of the art of a scientific field. For example, doctoral students may gain an insightful understanding of a research topic by identifying landmark studies in the development of the field, critical contributions in the past, and potentially transformative ideas. Experienced researchers may repeatedly apply the same procedure to keep abreast new developments in a new field as well as in the field where they have established expertise.

CiteSpace has been applied to the study of numerous scientific disciplines. CiteSpace has been instrumental in revealing insightful patterns from a set of relevant scholarly publications (Fig. 1-5). On the other hand, users may considerably improve the efficiency and effectiveness of the application of such a visual analytic procedure through demonstrations and interpretations offered by the tutorial.

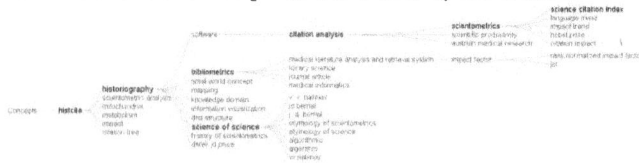

Figure 2: A visualization of a tree of keywords in CiteSpace.

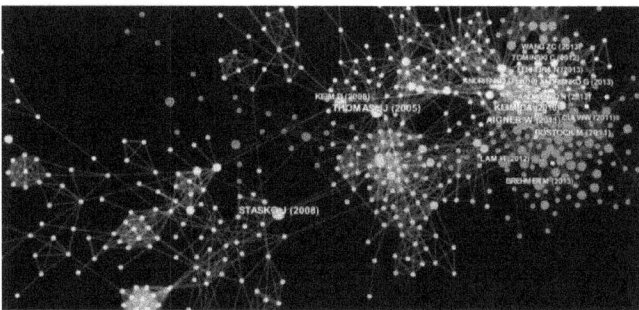

Figure 3: A visualization of clusters in CiteSpace.

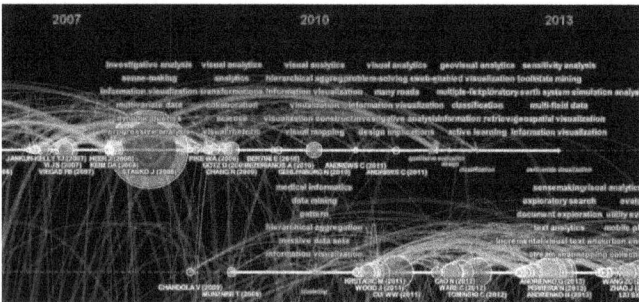

Figure 4: A timeline visualization in CiteSpace.

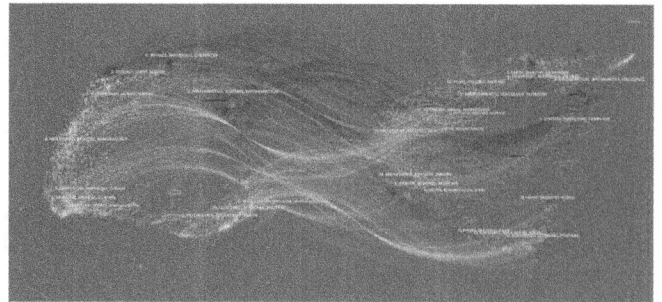

Figure 5: A dual-map overlay visualization in CiteSpace [5].

The half-day tutorial first introduces the basic concepts, relevant theories, and design rationale. Then the tutorial demonstrates several representative cases produced by CiteSpace, such as [3–7], so as to illustrate the breadth and depth of CiteSpace applications. Next, the tutorial guides the participants through step-by-step demonstrations from retrieving the initial input data to interpreting and summarizing the findings. On completion of the tutorial, participants should be able to apply the procedure to a domain of their own choice.

ACKNOWLEDGMENTS

This work was partially supported by the Science of Science and Innovation Policy (SciSIP) Program of the National Science Foundation (#1633286). .

REFERENCES

[1] Chen, C. (2017). Science Mapping: A Systematic Review of the Literature. Journal of Data and Information Science, 2(2), 1–40. DOI: 10.1515/jdis-2017-0006

[2] Chen, C. (2016) CiteSpace: A Practical Guide for Mapping Scientific Literature. Nova Publishers. ISBN: 978-1-53610-280-2.

[3] Chen, C., Dubin, R., Kim, M. C. (2014) Emerging trends and new developments in regenerative medicine: A scientometric update (2000-2014). Expert Opinion on Biological Therapy, 14 (9), 1295-1317.

[4] Chen, C., Dubin, R., Kim, M. C. (2014) Orphan drugs and rare diseases: A scientometric review (2000-2014). Expert Opinion on Orphan Drugs, 2(7), 1-16.

[5] Chen, C., Leydesdorff, L. (2014) Patterns of connections and movements in dual-map overlays: A new method of publication portfolio analysis.Journal of the American Society for Information Science and Technology, 65(2), 334-351.

[6] Chen, C., Hu, Z., Liu, S., Tseng, H. (2012) Emerging trends in regenerative medicine: A scientometric analysis in CiteSpace. Expert Opinions on Biological Therapy, 12(5), 593-608.

[7] Chen, C., Ibekwe-SanJuan, F., & Hou, J. (2010) The structure and dynamics of co-citation clusters: A multiple-perspective co-citation analysis. Journal of the American Society for Information Science and Technology, 61(7), 1386-1409. DOI: 10.1002/asi.21309.

[8] Chen, C. (2006) CiteSpace II: Detecting and visualizing emerging trends and transient patterns in scientific literature. Journal of the American Society for Information Science and Technology, 57(3), 359-377.

Information Visualization for Interactive Information Retrieval

Orland Hoeber
Department of Computer Science
University of Regina
Regina, SK, Canada
orland.hoeber@uregina.ca

ABSTRACT

As search tasks move beyond targeted search and into the domain of complex search, a substantial cognitive burden is placed on the searcher to craft and refine their queries, evaluate and explore among the search results, and ultimately make use of what is found. In such cases, information visualization techniques may be leveraged to enable searchers to perceive, interpret, and make sense of the information available throughout the search process. This tutorial will establish the fundamental principles and theories of information visualization, explain how information visualization can support interactive information retrieval, and survey search interfaces from my own research that leverage information visualization techniques. The goal of this tutorial will be to encourage researchers to make informed design decisions for how to integrate information visualization into their own interactive information retrieval projects.

CCS CONCEPTS

• **Information systems** → **Search interfaces**; • **Human-centered computing** → **Visualization techniques**;

KEYWORDS

information visualization; pre-attentive processing; Opponent Process Theory of Colour; Gestalt Principles; interactive information retrieval; information scent; exploratory search; sensemaking

ACM Reference Format:
Orland Hoeber. 2018. Information Visualization for Interactive Information Retrieval. In *CHIIR '18: 2018 Conference on Human Information Interaction & Retrieval, March 11–15, 2018, New Brunswick, NJ, USA*. ACM, New York, NY, USA, 4 pages. https://doi.org/10.1145/3176349.3176898

1 INTRODUCTION

In recent years, the importance of the human-centred and interactive nature of information retrieval has been well studied [3, 5, 7, 20–22]. While a substantial focus has been placed on the features of the search interface [5, 21, 22] and the interactive behaviour associated with searching [3, 7, 20], relatively little work has sought to study how information visualization methods can be leveraged to support search tasks and activities [9].

Although the textual nature of queries and search results make them inherently visual, reading requires focus and attention. Automatic statistical and machine learning approaches may be leveraged to extract features from such text, which may then be visualized [1]. However, such visual text analytics research is seldom applied to information retrieval settings.

This tutorial will provide graduate students and researchers with fundamental knowledge on information visualization principles and theories, discuss how information visualization can support interactive information retrieval processes and behaviours, and survey various approaches for using information visualization within search interfaces. The goal is to inspire others to investigate how information visualization techniques may be used to enhance the search interfaces they develop, and to encourage them to make wise design decisions supported by established theories and principles.

2 PRIMARY TOPICS

2.1 Fundamentals of Information Visualization

Information visualization research focuses on the design, development, and study of methods for visually representing information. By considering both the features of the data and the needs of the users, visual encodings can be chosen that enable users to perceive, interpret, and make sense of the information presented to them [18, 19]. There are a number of different visual variables that can be manipulated by mapping these to specific dimensions or attributes of the data, including position, shape, size, brightness, hue, texture, and orientation. Choosing which aspects of the data to map to which visual variables requires awareness of both the data type (quantitative, ordinal, qualitative) [15] and the user's primary visual task (association, selection, order, quantity) [4].

Choosing an appropriate visual encoding also requires awareness of the fundamental principles and theories of information visualization. Under constrained conditions, certain visual variables can be perceived without focus or attention. Such pre-attentive processing of visual stimuli occurs in a fraction of a second, and is done in parallel in the human mind [18]. Visual encodings of information that can be pre-attentively processed require minimal effort to see what is being shown.

The use of colour in information visualization is not as straightforward as one might assume. Although colour can readily be decomposed into wavelengths of light, or values of red, green, and blue, this is not the way the human mind perceives colour. The Opponent Process Theory of Colour proposes a model of colour perception along three opposing colour channels: red-green, yellow-blue, and back-white [6]. The human vision system can readily perceive differences in colour along these channels (e.g., red apples among the green leafs of an apple tree). Knowledge of this theory supports the design of different colour maps, depending on whether the information to convey is categorical, sequential, or divergent.

The Gestalt School of Psychology focuses on the study of how the human mind decomposes the whole of what is seen into its constituent parts, and how these parts are perceived to be related to one another [14]. From this theory, a set of design principles have been established for creating visualizations that convey relationships, called the Gestalt Principles [19]. The most useful of these for interface design are the Gestalt Principles of similarity, proximity, closure, and connectedness. Understanding how the human mind perceives relationships among visual objects enables the creation of effective visual representations, and avoiding accidentally implying relationships that do not exist in the data.

2.2 Information Visualization Support for Interactive Information Retrieval

Given the importance of the searcher's active involvement in interactive information retrieval, the use of information visualization techniques in this context should be done in consideration of the support they can provide for information seeking behaviours and strategies. While there is a broad range of such behaviours and strategies [5], this tutorial will focus on three that are particularly receptive to information visualization techniques.

Information foraging theory and the concept of information scent [16] explain processed by which people collect and consume information. The theory is inspired by the foraging activities of wild animals, and the influence of scent for attracting animals to new sources of food. Humans seeking information will make implicit decisions on whether to continue with their current information seeking sub-tasks, or move on to new sub-tasks (e.g., continue assessing the search results list, click on a link to view a document, return to the search results, issue a new query). Information visualization techniques may be used to conveying information scent, enabling searchers to see previews or overviews of the new information they might gain by viewing particular search results. For example, it may be possible to measure the new knowledge in each of the search results, and present this visually within the search results list; or when complex queries are issued, visualization techniques may be used to show the relationships between the search results and different aspects of the query.

Exploratory search behaviour is often employed when the information need is open-ended and multi-faceted [20], or when the task is complex in nature [2]. It is highly interactive, with the searcher issuing queries, developing knowledge on the topic, and using this knowledge to further refine their search activities. Software that supports exploratory search should provide guidance to the searcher and help them to make sense of unfamiliar information spaces [20]. In this regard, information visualization can be very valuable, providing visual overviews that enable searchers to quickly assess the overall makeup of the search results, visual comparisons that allow searchers to assess the search results in relation to what they have previously found, and visual cues regarding query suggestions.

Sensemaking is a critical element in information seeking, enabling the searcher to develop an understanding of complex information in relation to the situation that motivated the information seeking activities. Sensemaking can be supported in software by providing meaningful representations and rich interaction mechanisms [17]. Information visualization techniques may be used to illustrate the relationships between search results, and connect these to well-known events. Perhaps more importantly, the interactive nature of information visualization approaches allow searchers to exert control over the visual representations, enabling them to create personalized views of the search results that are specific to their existing knowledge and information seeking goals.

2.3 Survey of Visual Search Interfaces

This tutorial will provide a survey of visual search interfaces that have been developed within my research group and by collaborators, focusing on a broad range of information seeking settings. These will include searching within the web [8] (see Figure 1), social media [10] (see Figure 2), online encyclopedias [11] (see Figure 3), digital libraries [13] (see Figure 4), and image collections [12] (see Figure 5). Each of these examples will be considered in terms of the information visualization techniques employed, the type of information that is to be conveyed, the support provided for information seeking behaviours and strategies, and the interactive nature of the visualization.

For those attending the tutorial who already have been integrating information visualization techniques into their interactive information retrieval research, an opportunity will be given to have their work serve as further examples for discussing the value of information visualization and how it can enable and support information seeking behaviours. This activity will assist other researchers in ensuring that their use of information visualization is properly grounded in established theories and principles, and support information seeking tasks that can benefit from visual representations of underlying data.

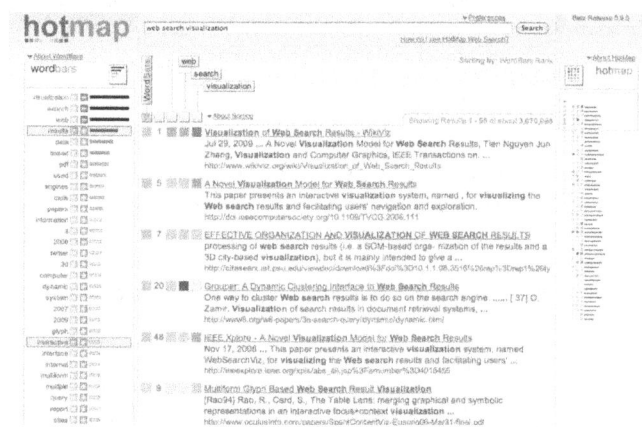

Figure 1: A screenshot from HotMap Web Search, using visualization to show the correspondence between query terms and search results, and the makeup of the top terms among the search results [8].

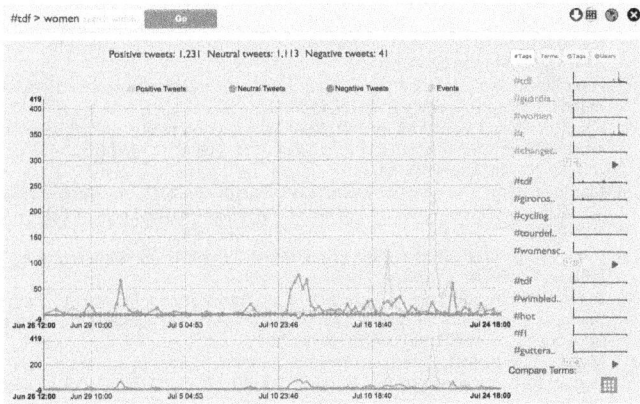

Figure 2: A screenshot from Vista, showing the temporal pattern of tweets and information about the top hashtags, terms, user mentions, and authors [10].

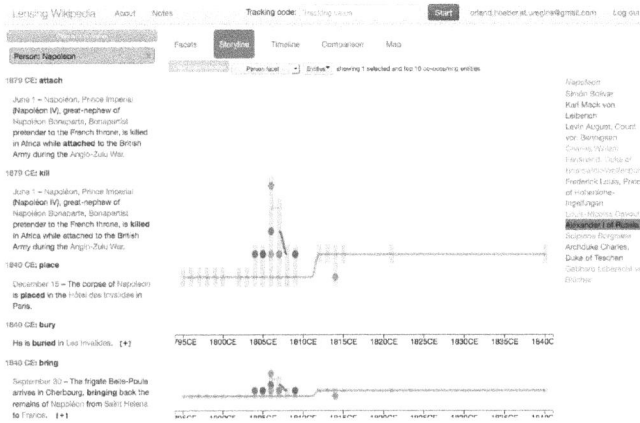

Figure 3: A screenshot from Lensing Wikipedia, illustrating the relationships between historical figures over time [11].

Figure 4: A screenshot from Bow Tie Academic Search, using visualization to show the pattern of forward and backward citations, and the relationships between search results and keywords [13].

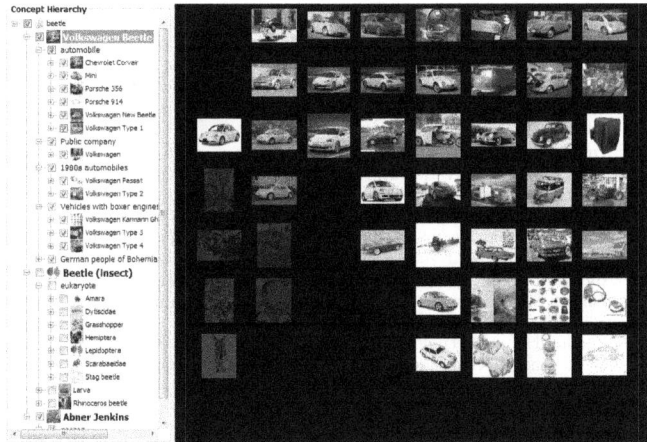

Figure 5: A screenshot from Cider, showing both visual and conceptual organization of search results, and a hierarchy of related concepts used for query expansions [12].

3 LEARNING OUTCOMES

The primary learning outcomes for this tutorial are to develop: (1) an understanding of the fundamental principles and theories of information visualization, (2) an appreciation for how information visualization can enable and support various interactive information retrieval processes, and (3) the ability to apply this knowledge to the study and analysis of visual search interfaces. With this knowledge, graduate students and researchers will be set on a path to study how information visualization techniques may be used to support interactive information retrieval processes within their own research projects.

4 CONCLUSION

This tutorial will serve the interactive information retrieval research community by educating about and advocating for the use of information visualization techniques within the development of new search interfaces. Such research, with a basis in established theories and principles, will enable further study on how information visualization can support information seeking behaviours and strategies.

REFERENCES

[1] Aretha B. Alencar, Maria Cristina F. de Oliveira, and Fernando V. Paulovich. 2012. Seeing beyond reading: A survey on visual text analytics. *Wiley Interdisciplinary Reviews: Data Mining and Knowledge Discovery* 2, 6 (2012), 476–492. https://doi.org/10.1002/widm.1071
[2] Ahmed Hassan Awadallah, Ryen W. White, Patrick Pantel, Susan T. Dumais, and Yi-Min Wang. 2014. Supporting complex search tasks. In *Proceedings of the ACM International Conference on Information and Knowledge Management.* 829–838. https://doi.org/10.1145/2661829.2661912
[3] Nicholas J. Belkin. 2015. People, Interacting with Information. *ACM SIGIR Forum* 49, 2 (2015), 13–27. https://doi.org/10.1145/2766462.2767854
[4] Jaques Bertin. 1983. *Semiology of Graphics.* University of Wisconsin Press, Madison, WI.
[5] Marti Hearst. 2009. *Search User Interfaces.* Cambridge University Press, Cambridge, UK.
[6] Ewald Hering. 1964. *Outlines of a Theory of Light Sense (Grundzge der Lehr von Lichtsinn, 1920).* Harvard University Press.
[7] Orland Hoeber. 2012. Human-centred web search. In *Next Generation Search Engines: Advanced Models for Information Retrieval,* C. Jouis, I. Biskri, J.-G. Ganascia, and M. Roux (Eds.). IGI Global, 217–238.

[8] Orland Hoeber. 2013. A longitudinal study of HotMap web search. *Online Information Review* 37, 2 (2013), 252–267. https://doi.org/10.1108/OIR-09-2011-0153

[9] O. Hoeber. 2014. Visual search analytics: Combining machine learning and interactive visualization to support human-centred search. In *Proceedings of Beyond Single-Shot Text Queries: Bridging the Gap(s) Between Research Communities Workshop*. 37–43.

[10] Orland Hoeber, Larena Hoeber, Maha El Meseery, Kenneth Odoh, and Radhika Gopi. 2016. Visual Twitter analytics (Vista): Temporally changing sentiment and the discovery of emergent themes within sport event tweets. *Online Information Review* 40, 1 (2016), 25–41. https://doi.org/10.1108/OIR-02-2015-0067

[11] Orland Hoeber, Anoop Sarkar, Andrei Vacariu, Max Whitney, Manali Gaikwad, and Gursimran Kaur. 2017. Evaluating the value of Lensing Wikipedia during the information seeking process. In *Proceedings of the ACM SIGIR Conference on Human Information Interaction and Retrieval*. 77–87. https://doi.org/10.1145/3020165.3020178

[12] Enamul Hoque, Orland Hoeber, and Minglun Gong. 2013. CIDER: Concept-based image diversification, exploration, and retrieval. *Information Processing & Management* 49, 5 (2013), 1122–1138. https://doi.org/10.1016/j.ipm.2012.12.001

[13] Taraneh Khazaei and Orland Hoeber. 2017. Supporting academic search tasks through citation visualization and exploration. *International Journal on Digital Libraries* 18, 1 (2017), 59–72. https://doi.org/10.1007/s00799-016-0170-x

[14] Kurt Koffka. 1935. *Principles of Gestalt Psychology*. Harcourt-Brace, New York.

[15] Jock Mackinlay. 1986. Automating the design of graphical presentations of relational information. *ACM Transactions on Graphics* 5, 2 (1986), 110–141. https://doi.org/10.1145/22949.22950

[16] Peter Pirolli. 2007. *Information Foraging Theory: Adaptive Interaction with Information*. Oxford University Press, New York.

[17] Peter Pirolli and Daniel M. Russell. 2011. Introduction to this special issue on sensemaking. *Human-Computer Interaction* 26, 1-2 (2011), 1–8. https://doi.org/10.1080/07370024.2011.556557

[18] Matthew Ward, Georges Grinstein, and Daniel Keim. 2015. *Interactive Data Visualization: Foundations, Techniques, and Applications* (2nd ed.). A K Peters, Natick, MA.

[19] Colin Ware. 2013. *Information Visualization: Perception for Design* (3rd ed.). Morgan Kaufmann, Waltham, MA.

[20] Ryen W. White and Resa A. Roth. 2009. *Exploratory Search: Beyond the Query-Response Paradigm*. Morgan & Claypool Publisher, San Rafael, CA. https://doi.org/10.2200/S00174ED1V01Y200901ICR003

[21] Max L. Wilson. 2011. Interfaces for information retrieval. In *Interactive Information Seeking, Behaviour and Retrieval*, I. Ruthvan and D. Kelly (Eds.). Facet Publishing.

[22] Max L. Wilson, m. c. schraefel, and Ben Shneiderman. 2010. From keyword search to exploration: Designing future search interfaces for the web. *Foundations and Trends in Web Science* 2, 1 (2010), 1–97. https://doi.org/10.1561/1800000003

Estimating Models Combining Latent and Measured Variables

A Tutorial on Basics, Applications and Current Developments in Structural Equation Models and their Estimation using PLS Path Modeling

Markus Kattenbeck
Chair for Information Science
University of Regensburg
markus.kattenbeck@ur.de

David Elsweiler
Chair for Information Science
University of Regensburg
david.elsweiler@ur.de

ABSTRACT

Structural Equation Modeling is a powerful statistical approach where measured variables and those which are latent can be combined in a single model. In this half-day tutorial participants learned about the statistical technique, its theoretical underpinnings and gained sufficient insight to apply this technique in a practical sense to their own research problems.

CCS CONCEPTS

• **Information systems** → **Users and interactive retrieval**; **Evaluation of retrieval results**;

KEYWORDS

structural equation models, pls path modeling, interactive information retrieval, quantitative data analysis method

ACM Reference Format:
Markus Kattenbeck and David Elsweiler. 2018. Estimating Models Combining Latent and Measured Variables: A Tutorial on Basics, Applications and Current Developments in Structural Equation Models and their Estimation using PLS Path Modeling. In *Proceedings of CHIIR '18*. ACM, New York, NY, USA, Article 4, 3 pages. https://doi.org/10.1145/3176349.3176899

1 THEME & MOTIVATION

The half-day tutorial introduced participants to Structural Equation Models and their estimation using Partial Least Squares Path Modeling. Structural Equation Models are a statistical technique to simultaneously assess the relationships between unobserved factors (i.e. latent variables) and the way these factors are measured based on observable variables. This is useful, for example, for researchers in our community interested in learning about how different factors influence human information behavior and as a means to validate and optimize measurement instruments for subjective concepts important in IIR, such as engagement, satisfaction, trust etc. The following, simple example illustrates why:

Suppose one wants to study the trust users have in the results of an interactive information retrieval (IIR) system. Typically, trust in the results presented on a Search Engine Result Page is a concept which cannot be observed directly, but can be measured, e.g., using survey questions. These so-called items are subsequently used to impute a latent variable score. Suppose further, researchers hypothesize that trust in the results a search engine presents is influenced by the perceived helpfulness of these results as well as by their reliability and that both aspects are correlated. Both of these aspects can be regarded as latent variables, too. Figure 1 shows the structural model reflecting these hypotheses, where unobservable constructs (latent variables, LVs) are depicted using ellipses and measured variables (MVs) imputing latent variable scores are shown using rectangles.

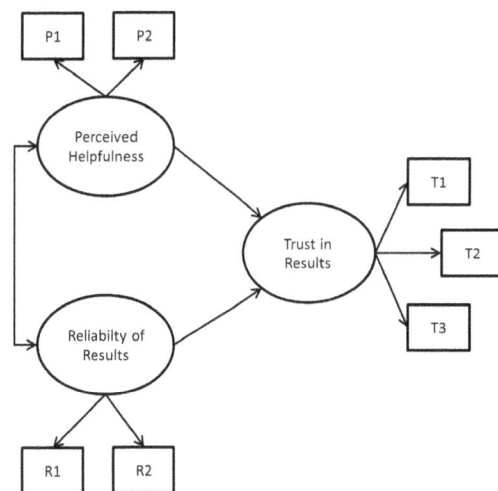

Figure 1: A pictorial representation of the structural equation model reflecting the aforementioned hypotheses. Measured (i.e. observable) variables are shown as rectangles, latent (i.e. non-observable variables) are shown as ellipses. One-headed arrows denote the direction of impact, two-headed arrows denote correlations.

Estimating this structural equation model using empirical data can now yield two important results simultaneously. First, it provides insight into whether the questions devised for each construct are a suitable way to measure this construct (i.e. the measurement model can be examined). Second, the estimated model provides evidence for the hypotheses leading to the way, LVs are connected (i.e. the structural model can be examined). This means, in case of the given SEM, examining whether helpfulness of the results and reliability of the results have a positive impact on the trust users show in the search engine results. It is important to note, however, that the way variables are measured is by no means fixed to survey questions but may be gained from a variety of sources – including behavioral log data.

2   INTENDED AUDIENCE & RELEVANCE

Our tutorial complemented a series of efforts to improve the empirical practices within the community. At IIiX 2014, Diane Kelly offered insights into power analysis as one important step to ensure statistical validity of result reported. At CHIIR 2016 Pia Borlund dedicated her keynote to the the proper design of IR experiments (see [1]). Heather O'Brien focused on proper ways of survey design in her perspectives paper in 2017 (see [14]).

We view SEM as a tool which offers researchers in our community great utility. In our opinion, the researchers who would benefit most are those focused on studying human-aspects and the examples in the tutorial reflected this.

The tutorial demonstrated how Structural Equation Models can be estimated using PLS Path Modeling and showed participants how to combine LVs and MVs. As this estimation technique focuses on prediction it has the potential to contribute to our field in at least three ways:

(1) It provide a statistically solid option to use ad-hoc surveys. This is important as questionnaires form a major method of data acquisition in our field.

(2) It is suitable to assess the degree to which latent variables impact each other. This means, it can foster the development of theories with a solid base in empirical data.

(3) It can incorporate formative measurement variables, thereby providing the possibility to combine log data with survey-based data in a single model.

The tutorial was introductory in nature and assumed audience members only had basic knowledge in statistics.

3   STRUCTURAL EQUATION MODELS & PARTIAL LEAST SQUARES PATH MODELING – WHAT'S IN A NAME?

Structural Equation Modeling as a statistical technique has the unique capability to use all information available, concurrently. This means, by using Structural Equation Models (SEM) the relations between several latent variables in a so-called structural model can be assessed simultaneously accompanied by the measurement models proposed for each of these constructs [5]. This is in sharp contrast to other multivariate techniques such as factor analysis, multiple regression or multivariate analysis of variance involving multivariate sample means and more than one dependent variables. In contrast to exploratory factor analysis, where no measurement model specification is required at all [6, p. 641], SEM analysis requires a specification of dependencies according to theory. Using latent, i.e. not directly measured, variables to build a model is particularly sensible as the use of multiple indicators for a

single latent variable reduces measurement error [6, p. 635]. While covariance- (commonly referred to as LISREL, [10]) and variance-based methods (commonly referred to as PLS Path Modeling, [16]) to assess SEMs exist, the variance-based approach, i.e. PLS Path Modeling, is the focus of this tutorial. This descision was taken reflecting to two important properties of the approach: First, it is focused on prediction, i.e. coefficients are estimated in a way such that the amount of variance explained in endogenous constructs (e.g. Trust in Results in the example above) is maximized [7, p. 140]. Second, it makes no assumptions regarding the distribution of the data [2].

4   TOPICS

Topics covered in this tutorial included:

- Refresher of basic statistical approaches
- Basic ideas of Structural Equation Modeling in general and PLS Path Modeling in particular including the ways of depicting SEMs graphically, measurement model theory and the PLS algorithm
- Recent methodological advancement leading to consistent PLS Path Modeling (see [3, 4, 8])
- Important measures in applying PLS Path Modeling covering measures to assess measurement model fit (e.g. composite reliability, see [15], discriminant validity based on the Heterotrait-Monotrait-Ratio of correlations, see [9]), as well as structural model fit (e.g. based on a bootstrapped analysis of overall model fit, see [3])
- Use Case: Measuring Users' Trust in Search Engine Results

5   EXPECTED OUTCOMES

On completing the tutorial participants were able to

- understand different modes of measurement and how these must be taken into account during data acquisition;
- name the advantages and disadvantages of the PLS Path Modeling as compared to LISREL estimation techniques;
- to draw diagrams representing structural and measurement model relationships which reflect a set of hypotheses under analysis;
- to know and understand the different steps needed to estimate Structural Equation Models using PLS Path Modeling;
- to interpret several important figures commonly reported in PLS Path Modeling;
- to name and understand different methodological advancements in PLS Path Modeling recently made.

6   EXPERTISE OF AUTHORS & SUPPORT BY THE COMMUNITY

David Elsweiler is a professor at the Chair for Information Science at the University of Regensburg. David's research focuses on understanding information behavior with the main aim of designing information systems that align with the way people think and behave naturally. He received his PhD from the University of Strathclyde, Glasgow in 2007. David has published more than 65 conference papers, journal articles and book chapters on search and recommender systems, personal information management, as well as user studies investigating what users want from such systems and how they behave to achieve their aims.

David has won several awards including Best Paper Award Honorable Mention at WWW'17, ACM SIGIR Outstanding Paper Award (2011), an Alexander von Humboldt Fellowship (2009) and an Emerald Outstanding Author Contribution Award for best book chapter (2011). In 2014 David was general co-chair for the Information Interaction in Context Conference (IIiX) and he has previously co-organized successful workshops at ACM SIGIR, CIKM, CSCW and RecSys.

Markus Kattenbeck is a post-doctoral researcher and lecturer at the Chair for Information Science at the University of Regensburg. He applied PLS Path Modeling extensively during his PhD [12], which he defended successfully in 2016 in Regensburg. The results of his thesis have been published at presitigous venues such as SIGSPATIAL [11] and COSIT [13]. His scientific interest in how people navigate on the web has recently gained momentum. He has been teaching empirical methods classes as well as data analysis classes at both, bachelor and master level, for more than 7 years.

David and Markus have jointly taught the empirical methods class in Regensburg for 6 years and have extensive experience in teaching statistics and data analysis. The idea for this tutorial was discussed with several members of the CHIIR community. We would like to extend our gratitude to Ian Ruthven, Pia Borlund and Heather O'Brien who were all very supportive about the idea, as well as Diane Kelly and Anita Crescenzi, who provided helpful suggestions for the content.

REFERENCES

[1] Pia Borlund. 2016. Interactive Information Retrieval: An Evaluation Perspective. In *Proceedings of the 2016 ACM on Conference on Human Information Interaction and Retrieval (CHIIR '16)*. ACM, New York, NY, USA, 151–151. https://doi.org/10.1145/2854946.2870648

[2] C. Cassel, P. Hackl, and A. H. Westlund. 1999. Robustness of partial least squares method for estimating latent variable quality structures. *Journal of Applied Statistics* 26, 4 (1999), 435–446.

[3] Theo K. Dijkstra and Jörg Henseler. 2015. Consistent and asymptotically normal PLS estimators for linear structural equations. *Computational Statistics & Data Analysis* 81 (2015), 10–23.

[4] Theo K. Dijkstra and Jörg Henseler. 2015. Consistent Partial Least Squares Path Modeling. *Management Information Systems Quarterly* 39, 2 (2015), 297–316.

[5] David Gefen, Detmar Straub, and Marie-Claude Boudreau. 2000. Structural Equation Modeling and Regression: Guidelines for Research Practice. *Communications of the Association for Information Systems* 4 (2000), Article 7.

[6] Joseph F. Hair, William C. Black, Barry J. Babin, and Rolph E. Anderson. 2010. *Multivariate Data Analysis. A Global Perspective* (7th ed.). Person Education, Upper Saddle River, NJ.

[7] Joe F. Hair, Christian M. Ringle, and Marko Sarstedt. 2011. PLS-SEM: Indeed a Silver Bullet. *Journal of Marketing Theory and Practice* 19, 2 (2011), 139–151.

[8] Jörg Henseler, Geoffrey Hubona, and Pauline Ash Ray. 2016. Using PLS path modeling in new technology research: updated guidelines. *Industrial Managment & Data Systems* 116, 1 (2016), 2–20.

[9] Jörg Henseler, Christian M. Ringle, and Marko Sarstedt. 2015. A new criterion for assessing discriminant validity in variance-based structural equation modeling. *Journal of the Academy of Marketing Science* 43, 1 (2015), 115–135.

[10] Karl Jöreskog. 1971. SIMULTANEOUS FACTOR ANALYSIS IN SEVERAL POPULATIONS. *Psychometrika* 36 (1971), 409–426.

[11] Markus Kattenbeck. 2015. Empirically Measuring Salience of Objects for Use in Pedestrian Navigation. In *Proceedings of the 23rd SIGSPATIAL International Conference on Advances in Geographic Information Systems (GIS '15)*. ACM, New York, NY, USA, Article 3, 10 pages.

[12] Markus Kattenbeck. 2016. *Empirically Measuring Salience of Objects for Use in Pedestrian Navigation*. Dissertation. Lehrstuhl für Informationswissenschaft, Universität Regensburg. http://nbn-resolving.de/urn/resolver.pl?urn=urn:nbn:de:bvb:355-epub-341450

[13] Markus Kattenbeck. 2017. How Subdimensions of Salience Influence Each Other. Comparing Models Based on Empirical Data. In *13th International Conference on Spatial Information Theory, COSIT 2017, September 4-8, 2017, L'Aquila, Italy (LIPIcs)*, Eliseo Clementini, Maureen Donnelly, May Yuan, Christian Kray, Paolo Fogliaroni, and Andrea Ballatore (Eds.), Vol. 86. Schloss Dagstuhl - Leibniz-Zentrum fuer Informatik, 10:1–10:13. http://www.dagstuhl.de/dagpub/978-3-95977-043-9

[14] Heather L. O'Brien and Lori McCay-Peet. 2017. Asking "Good" Questions: Questionnaire Design and Analysis in Interactive Information Retrieval Research. In *Proceedings of the 2017 Conference on Conference Human Information Interaction and Retrieval (CHIIR '17)*. ACM, New York, NY, USA, 27–36. https://doi.org/10.1145/3020165.3020167

[15] C.E. Werts, R.L. Linn, and K.G. Jöreskog. 1974. Intraclass Reliability Estimates: Testing Structural Assumptions. *Educational and Psychological Measurement* 34, 1 (1974), 25–33. arXiv:http://epm.sagepub.com/content/34/1/25.full.pdf+html

[16] Herman Ole Andreas Wold. 1975. Path models with latent variables: The NIPALS approach. In *Quantitative sociology: International perspectives on mathematical and statistical modeling*, H. M. Blalock, A. Aganbegian, F. M. Borodkin, R. Boudon, and V. Capecchi (Eds.). Academic Press, New York, 307–357.

Practical Representation Learning for Recommender Systems

Oleksandr Zakharchuk
Cograma
zakharchuk@cograma.com

ABSTRACT

The ability to provide high quality personalized recommendations is among the most significant types of competitive advantage an online business can have. However, even having vast amounts of data, creating a recommender system is far from being trivial. This tutorial covers applying deep learning models for creating robust item and user representations for personalized recommender systems, as well as some of the typical problems encountered when working on production recommender systems and possible solutions for these problems.

CCS CONCEPTS

• **Information systems** → **Recommender systems**; *Personalization*; • **Computing methodologies** → *Neural networks*; Transfer learning;

KEYWORDS

personalized recommendations; representation learning; deep learning

ACM Reference Format:
Oleksandr Zakharchuk. 2018. Practical Representation Learning for Recommender Systems. In *CHIIR '18: 2018 Conference on Human Information Interaction & Retrieval, March 11–15, 2018, New Brunswick, NJ, USA*. ACM, New York, NY, USA, 1 page. https://doi.org/10.1145/3176349.3176900

1 TUTORIAL OUTLINE

1.1 Basic Collaborative Filtering

The tutorial starts with introducing the basic collaborative filtering setting where item and user representations are created using linear dimensionality reduction techniques.

1.2 Deep Learning Overview

In this part of the tutorial we introduce the basic concepts of deep learning and discuss deep neural networks as mechanisms for representation learning.

1.3 Item and User Representations

This part views recommender systems from the perspective of predictive modelling. We try to come up with representations that describe user behavior sufficiently well without having to deal with the possible user experience implications.

1.4 Taking the User Perspective

This part goes beyond predictive interpretation of RecSys, primarily focusing on user experience and possible interactions between the recommender system and the world.

2 INTENDED AUDIENCE

This tutorial is aimed primarily at researchers and professionals considering building their own recommender systems and looking for a hands-on introduction to the subject. A considerable part of the tutorial is devoted to the practical aspects rarely covered in research literature. At the same time, we hope that some of the concepts borrowed from other applications of representation learning would be interesting even for the seasoned practitioners in the RecSys domain. We do not anticipate any prior knowledge of deep learning or of recommender systems.

Health Data on the Front Lines: Data-Driven Decision-Making for New York City's Opioid Overdose Epidemic

Grace M. Begany
Department of Information Science
University at Albany, SUNY
Albany, NY 12222
gbegany@albany.edu

InduShobha Chengalur-Smith
Department of Information
Technology Management
University at Albany, SUNY
Albany, NY 12222
shobha@albany.edu

Erika G. Martin
Rockefeller Institute of Government,
SUNY; and Department of Public
Administration and Policy,
University at Albany, SUNY
Albany, NY 12222
emartin@albany.edu

Chad Stecher
Department of Economics
Rensselaer Polytechnic Institute
Troy, NY 12180
stechc@rpi.edu

Xiaojun (Jenny) Yuan
Department of Information Science
University at Albany, SUNY
Albany, NY 12222
xyuan@albany.edu

WORKSHOP ABSTRACT

Since 2000, fatal drug-related overdoses in the United States have increased by 137%, and almost two-thirds of drug overdose deaths now involve opioids including prescription medications and heroin. The opioid epidemic could result in the deaths of nearly a half million Americans over the next decade and is currently the leading cause of death among Americans under 50 years old. A barrier to addressing this problem is that the causes and consequences of opioid misuse affect multiple policy domains and addressing contributing factors in isolation may have adverse consequences: for example, interventions to prevent "doctor shopping" could increase deaths by pushing consumers to purchase opioids on the black market that may be contaminated with fentanyl. In 2012, New York City Mayor Michael Bloomberg convened a task force to address the abuse of painkillers. This initial formation led to the development of the RxStat data collaborative, a network of over 20 city, state, and federal public health and public safety agencies who examine local data to monitor population-level indicators and perform data analytics for evidence-based decision-making. Using these data also helps these stakeholders develop shared understandings of the local opioid overdose epidemics, thereby enabling creative policy approaches and improving implementation. In this full-day, interactive workshop, we will use RxStat as a case study to explore various perspectives, challenges, and opportunities to use diverse health data to convene stakeholders and develop tailored solutions to intractable health issues.

CHIIR '18, March 11–15, 2018, New Brunswick, NJ, USA
© 2018 Association for Computing Machinery.
ACM ISBN 978-1-4503-4925-3/18/03...$15.00
https://doi.org/10.1145/3176349.3176902

WORKSHOP LEARNING OUTCOMES

As a workshop attendee, you will be able to:

- Illustrate how diverse administrative, surveillance, and other data sources can be synthesized to understand different dimensions of critical health issues
- Identify existing data analytic tools to use public data to hot-spot disease outbreaks and tailor policy solutions
- Understand how data collaboratives such as RxStat can lead to knowledge transformation across sectors
- Share your ideas for additional data-driven approaches to analyze public data across sectors to develop innovative solutions to health issues
- Exchange ideas on the design and development of health search systems
- Network with other data experts interested in developing data collaboratives

2 WORKSHOP SESSIONS AT-A-GLANCE

2.1 Morning Session (~9:00 am – 12:00 pm)

- Workshop Welcome, Goals, and Agenda Review
- RxStat 101: A Data Collaborative for Public Health and Public Safety Partnerships
- Repurposing Data to Advance Evidence-Based Decision-Making
- Fostering Effective Data Ecosystems to Improve Engagement with Public Data
- From Correlation to Causation: Social Network Analytic Methods for Causal Inference
- Developing Health Search Systems: Understanding the Needs of Consumers and Stakeholders

- Information Quality: Navigating Imperfect Information in the Real World

2.2 Lunch and Networking

2.3 Afternoon Session (~1:00 pm – 4:00 pm)

- Interactive Session: Opportunities for Data Collaboratives to Tackle Wicked Policy Problems
- Interactive Session: Barriers to Data Analytics for Policy Analysis, Insight, and Implementation
- Interactive Session: Research Priorities and Future Directions
- Closing Remarks and Next Steps

3 WORKSHOP SESSION DETAILS

3.1 Morning Session (~9:00 am – 12:00 pm)

3.1.1 Welcome, Workshop Goals, and Agenda Review. Attendees will be welcomed and provided details regarding the workshop goals and overall agenda. The morning session will cover presentations by researchers and practitioners with diverse expertise in public health practice, policy analysis, data ecosystems, social network analysis, health search systems and information quality. Presentations will run approximately 30 minutes each, including Q&A.

3.1.2 RxStat 101. This presentation will describe New York City's RxStat data collaborative. Topics will include: a brief history of its initial formulation, its guiding principles, participating stakeholders, data sources currently used to measure and understand opioid misuse and problem drug use, early successes, and strategies to make similar initiatives successful in other jurisdictions. This context will set the stage for the subsequent presentations and afternoon break-out sessions.

3.1.3 Repurposing Data to Advance Evidence-Based Decision-Making. Many government-produced data are collected for one purpose and then reused for another. For example, New York's comprehensive all-payer hospital discharge data contains claims information that is used for medical billing. However, this rich data source is also a valuable asset that is frequently repurposed for monitoring, evaluation, and research. In the case of opioid overdose, these data have been repurposed to develop a core indicator of opioid-related emergency department visits that is reported quarterly. At the local level, these data can be analyzed to identify trends, hot-spot neighborhoods with disproportionate rates of opioid-related hospitalizations, and determine whether rates decline after implementing new interventions. This session will describe benefits and challenges to repurposing data for evidence-based decision-making and best practices from the RxStat case.

3.1.4 Fostering Effective Data Ecosystems to Improve Engagement with Public Data. Public, or "open" data are data that are released by all levels of government on publicly-accessible platforms. The hope and perceived benefit in releasing these data are that they will be used – to encourage more efficient public health operations, improve health literacy, support data-driven changes in healthcare, and empower healthcare consumers – and, their value ultimately realized. However, there is little known about who is using open data or in what ways it is used, especially in the domain of health. As such, developing a deeper understanding of ecosystems and communities around health data is crucial to the success of initiatives reliant upon these data. In this presentation, core concepts of open health data ecosystems will be discussed and related to the case of RxStat. Topics will include the roles, responsibilities, and activities of data facilitators and other health data ecosystem members, ways of interacting with data, and data communities. Further, strategies to foster effective data ecosystems that can support and improve engagement with and use of potentially valuable public data will be highlighted.

3.1.5 From Correlation to Causation: Social Network Analytic Methods for Causal Inference. The success of many public health initiatives and campaigns, such as RxStat, require effective communication and collaboration between multiple healthcare organizations and community partners. Similarly, the professional relationships among physicians are instrumental for disseminating new medical knowledge, and social networks between patients can foster greater adherence to treatment protocols. These examples illustrate the importance of social network analyses for understanding and promoting a wide range of health policies. To introduce these analytic methods, this presentation will first describe several forms of data that are commonly used to construct networks among healthcare regions, organizations, and individuals. Then we will discuss network visualization algorithms, descriptive statistics (e.g. diameter, density, and clustering), and measurements of network centrality. Finally, this presentation will introduce novel econometric techniques for identifying the causal impact of network relationships on health outcomes.

3.1.6 Developing Health Search Systems - Understanding the Needs of Consumers and Stakeholders. In the field of information retrieval and human computer interaction, health search has been drawing much attention by researchers. How do we leverage consumers' health needs and stakeholders' information needs? What are the most challenging issues in developing a health search system? What can we learn from the RxStat collaborative? How can the analysis of health data help us better understand consumers and inform the design of health search systems? How can we help consumers engage actively with existing health data? This session will explore these questions and introduce current methodologies and techniques, evaluation resources, as well as future directions and promising research areas.

3.1.7 Information Quality: Navigating Imperfect Information in the Real World. A large part of any data analytics effort is cleaning and preparing the data for analysis. This part of the workshop will illustrate common data integrity issues in health data and discuss methods to scrub data. Perfect data is not attainable but data governance plays a big role in improving data quality. As the costs of improving data quality increase the further we get from the source, the ultimate goal is to establish processes for data collection that will result in data that meets given quality thresholds.

3.2 Afternoon Session (~1:00 pm – 4:00 pm)

3.2.1 Interactive Workshops. The afternoon sessions will allow participants opportunities to network and share their ideas for additional data-driven approaches to analyze public data across sectors to develop innovative solutions to health issues. Prior to the workshop, participants will complete a short survey describing their interests and areas of expertise. This information will be used to assign participants to tables. An effort will be made to create groups that have common interests in specific health topics, such as obesity or infectious disease, and with a range of expertise and technical skills, such as big data analytics or human-computer interaction. Each interactive session will start with guiding questions for participants to discuss at their tables, followed by report-outs to other workshop attendees. In the first interactive session, participants will reflect on the RxStat case to identify other potential use cases in other health domains where data collaboratives could be implemented to promote evidence-based decision-making and improve policy implementation. In the second interactive session, participants will reflect on key barriers to organizing and sustaining data collaboratives, and brainstorm possible solutions and best practices that can be used to overcome these challenges. In the final interactive session, participants will draw on their own expertise to identify future directions for the field of human information interaction and retrieval that can enhance capabilities to leverage data collaboratives to solve health problems of consequence. Each interactive session will run approximately 45 minutes.

3.2.2 Closing Remarks and Next Steps. This final session will summarize the highlights of the workshop and explain to participants how the organizers will synthesize the findings from the afternoon sessions to share with participants after the workshop.

Workshop on Barriers to Interactive IR Resources Re-use (BIIRRR 2018)

Toine Bogers
Aalborg University Copenhagen
Denmark
toine@hum.aau.dk

Maria Gäde
Humboldt-Universität zu Berlin
Germany
maria.gaede@ibi.hu-berlin.de

Luanne Freund
University of British Columbia
Canada
luanne.freund@ubc.ca

Mark Hall
Martin-Luther-Universität
Halle-Wittenberg
Germany
mark.hall@informatik.uni-halle.de

Marijn Koolen
Royal Netherlands Academy of Arts
and Sciences
Netherlands
marijn.koolen@huygens.knaw.nl

Vivien Petras
Humboldt-Universität zu Berlin
Germany
vivien.petras@ibi.hu-berlin.de

Mette Skov
Aalborg University
Denmark
skov@hum.aau.dk

ACM Reference Format:
Toine Bogers, Maria Gäde, Luanne Freund, Mark Hall, Marijn Koolen, Vivien Petras, and Mette Skov. 2018. Workshop on Barriers to Interactive IR Resources Re-use (BIIRRR 2018). In *CHIIR '18: 2018 Conference on Human Information Interaction & Retrieval, March 11–15, 2018, New Brunswick, NJ, USA.* ACM, New York, NY, USA, 4 pages. https://doi.org/10.1145/3176349.3176901

1 DESCRIPTION

The goal of the BIIRRR 2018 workshop is to serve as a starting point for a community-driven effort to design and implement a platform for the collection, organization, maintenance, and sharing of resources for interactive information retrieval (IIR) experimentation. In 2016, Pia Borlund calls in her CHIIR keynote:"Interactive Information Retrieval: An Evaluation Perspective" for a IIR (evaluation) framework [2].

As in all scientific endeavors, progress in IIR research is contingent on the ability to build on previous ideas, approaches, and resources. Current trends towards open science and funding mandates to preserve and share research data lend support and even urgency to the notion of establishing a shared disciplinary repository of research tools and data for IIR. Components from IIR experiments, which could be valuable to archive for re-use, include:

- the systems or platforms used for experimentation
- the content or resources of the experimental platform (data collections)
- the search tasks or work situation

- the experimental context and other important aspects of the test design
- experimental protocols, questionnaire designs, etc.
- the gathered user and system interaction data
- the tools used for analysis
- the results and measures of the analysis

However, we believe there to be a number of barriers to reproducibility and re-use of resources in IIR research: the fragmentary nature of how the community's resources are organized, the lack of awareness of their existence, insufficient documentation and organization of the resources, the nature of the typical research publication cycle, and the effort required to make such resources available.

One such problem is the **fragmentary nature** of how the resources are organized. The experimental components that are used in the design and implementation of IIR studies are not always made available to the community for re-use. If they are, they are nearly always stored in different locations, making it cumbersome to gain access to and an overview of all relevant resources, as well as build upon them when designing new studies. The TREC initiative [1] has provided a single access point for the system-based evaluation of many different IR tasks by offering a repository for test collections, topic sets and relevance judgments. A TREC Interactive Track did run from 1997 to 2002 [10], which contributed to the standardization of protocols for experimental search studies, and involved the use of shared tasks and systems. However, due to the large differences between system-based and user-based evaluation, the fit between IIR tracks and TREC has not been an overly successful one.

As a result of this fragmentation, IIR resources are often underutilized due to a **lack of awareness** of their existence, leading to them falling in disuse. Apart from being publicized in research talks and linked to in publications (with often less-than-persistent links), no dedicated promotion channel or platform exists for these type of resources. Another issue is with the **documentation and**

[1] http://trec.nist.gov/

organization of IIR resources. While most IIR resources are documented sufficiently, they are typically only documented from the perspective of the researcher who originally used them. However, the metadata used to describe such resources may not match the needs of other IIR researchers and thereby hinder re-use. Given that the notion of context plays such a central role in IIR research, rich documentation is needed to serve the needs of the community, but such documentation can be very time-consuming to produce. This is exacerbated by the **typical research publication cycle** in the field: working from one submission deadline to the next means there is little time left to properly document and maintain these resources after publication. The lack of flexibility also hinders the recruitment of participants for IIR studies.

We believe that an online platform dedicated to the collection and organization of IIR resources could be a promising way of overcoming these barriers. This single access point, henceforth referred to as the iRepository, could be used to collect, manage and enable and promote the re-use of a variety of components of IIR experiments. The means by which components such as search tasks, experimental protocols, questionnaire designs, reporting standards, evaluation procedures, data collections, and the search interaction data produced in such experiments could be archived and made accessible for re-use is an unsolved challenge, which needs to consider data modeling and description as well as rights, data security and privacy issues.

While the idea of collecting such resources in a central location is perhaps not a new one, we are aware that the effort required in designing, implementing, and maintaining such a platform can only be borne by the community as a **collective effort**. The BIIRRR 2018 workshop therefore aims to serve both as a brainstorming opportunity about the shape this iRepository should take, as well as a way of building support in the community for its implementation.

2 RELATED EFFORTS

Recent years have seen several evaluation campaigns and workshops dedicated to aspects related to this workshop's topic. The TREC Interactive Track (1997-2002) [11], the INEX Interactive Track (2004-2010) [12, 13] as well the Cultural Heritage in CLEF (CHiC) Interactive Task (2013) [14] followed by the interactive Social Book Search (SBS) task (2014-2016) [5–7] have attempted to provide settings for long-term IIR evaluation. Several workshops have accompanied these IIR campaigns, bringing together community members, discussing challenges and future direction. At least one of BIIRRR's workshop chairs has been involved in each of these previous workshops. Examples include the SCST (Supporting Complex Search Tasks) workshop series (2015, 2017) [1, 4] organized in conjunction with ECIR and CHIIR.

While an extensive interest in IIR studies can be observed [9], these studies still tend to be quite fragmentary, and establishing and maintaining a collaborative platform for re-use is still an open issue. The complexity of IIR studies requires a combination of system- and user-centered evaluation approaches [8]. At the same time, this complexity requires the coordination of participants, search contexts, tasks, processes, systems, data sets and evaluation measures. A first step towards the systematic collection and registration of existing IIR research components has been taken in the form of

RepAST[2], the Repository of Assigned Search Tasks, which collects, analyzes and shares search tasks that have been used in previous IIR studies. It contains bibliographic data and abstracts from approximately 750 published papers, as well as a list of author-identified search task types (e.g. complex, simple, subject, known-item, factual), and the full text of any assigned search tasks reported in the papers [3]. RepAST serves as a library of tasks to encourage reuse of well-designed tasks and it enables analysis and comparison of task descriptions, which reveals the current lack of consistency and consensus in how assigned search tasks are used. While RepAST is valuable, it has been underutilized to date, likely due to a lack of awareness.

With the proposed iRepository, we wish to build upon and extend these previous efforts through a community-wide effort to coordinate, consolidate and build awareness.

3 WORKSHOP ACTIVITIES

The BIIRRR 2018 workshop will be a highly interactive, full-day workshop, which will intersperse keynotes, discussion lead-ins, and break-out discussions. We will start the day with a full round of introductions of all participants, asking them to identify their interest in the workshop. Two keynotes will present the challenges for IIR standardization and previous attempts and experiences with IIR evaluation campaigns. The keynotes will lead towards break-out discussions, which will be prepared by the workshop leads as well as invited participants. The morning break-out session will ask participants to discuss their experiences and viewpoints on the barriers to the re-use of IIR resources. The afternoon break-out session will be used to discuss plans, features, and characteristics for a platform for IIR data or other standardization activities. The workshop will close with a concrete mission statement and a clear view of future work in this area.

To take stock of current efforts, resources, and interest, the workshop will also feature a pre-workshop activity. Around the early-bird registration deadline, we aim to distribute a survey to potential participants and interested IIR researchers to gather their views of, experiences with, and requirements for breaking down the barriers to re-use of IIR resources. This will serve as a basis for further discussions and will also inform us of efforts, which we might not be aware of.

Ideally, the results of the survey will represent a variety of IIR research approaches and can be leveraged to seed the starting points of the different breakout groups. However, the workshop does not depend on the quantity of respondents but will be enriched by a multi-level analysis using information derived from the survey in combination with previous investigations and results from the breakout sessions.

3.1 Workshop Discussion Themes

With the survey and our collaborative discussions during the workshop we specifically aim at addressing the following aspects and exemplary questions:

(1) **Resources / Data sets**: "What kind of data has been used before?"; "Is the data reusable and documented?"; "What domains have been studied?"

---

[2]https://ils.unc.edu/searchtasks/search.php

(2) **Systems**: "What systems and features were investigated?"; "Can systems / prototypes be adapted for individual research questions?"

(3) **Experimental protocols**: "Which experimental designs were used?"; "Can protocols be re-used in other contexts?"

(4) **Metrics and Measures**: "Are comparable measures or metrics used?"; "How are task descriptions realized / comparable?"

(5) **Experimental data**: "What kind of experimental data was collected?"; "Is the data documented and archived for re-use?"; "How can we facilitate citation of data and shared resources?"; "Which rights or privacy issues could arise when re-using the data?"

(6) **Challenges or Problems**: "What are the main challenges for (long-term) IIR projects?"; "What problems can we identify and address based on previous projects?"; "What are challenges to re-use of IIR studies and materials?".

(7) **Potential solutions**: "What are potential ways to improve long-term IIR projects and re-use of existing IIR studies and materials?"; "What should an open, long-term accessible iRepository consist of?"; "Which challenges cannot be addressed by an iRepository?".

3.2 Tentative timeline for workshop activities

The workshop activities will extend before and after the actual workshop. While the survey will focus and shape the discussion, the momentum from the workshop will be used to plan and execute further activities (see section 4).

- First call for participation: January 15, 2018
- Deployment of IIR resources survey: February 1, 2018
- Finalization of workshop programme: March 1, 2018
- Workshop (at CHIIR 2018): March 15, 2018
- Workshop results statement: March 25, 2018
- Planning for future activities: starting April 2018

3.3 Planned workshop program

This overview paper was written before the survey results were analyzed or keynote speakers have been recruited. Therefore, the program may change during the actual workshop as the planning is adjusted accordingly.

The workshop is planned as an all-day workshop. The break-out discussions will have smaller groups discussion particular topics in each round. The number of groups and topics depends on the number of participants. Written comments and minutes for the workshop will be solicited by a shared and constantly updated document, which will be available from the workshop website. Via this document, Twitter and other available social media channels, interested IIR researchers may participate remotely if they cannot attend the workshop in person.

- Introductions:
  - Short introductions by participants (all participants)
  - Introduction of workshop purpose, goals and planned activities (workshop leads)
- Keynote 1: *The importance and challenges for standardization in IIR Evaluation - Basis for an iRepository* (keynote speaker 1)

- Break-out Session 1:
  - Introduction to break-out discussions round 1: *Viewpoints on standardization and IIR re-usable experimental components*, as previously defined through workshop call for participation (workshop leads)
  - Break-out discussions round 1: *Viewpoints on standardization: which components of IIR experiments could be re-used?* (all participants in break-out groups)
  - Feedback round 1: feedback from each break-out group (all participants)
- Lunch break
- Keynote 2: *Previous experiences at IIR evaluation campaigns: INEX, TREC, CLEF, RepAST* (keynote speaker 2)
- Break-out Session 2:
  - Introduction to break-out discussions round 2: *Requirements for IIR re-use – towards an iRepository based on survey results and previous discussion* (workshop leads)
  - Break-out discussions round 2: *Requirements for IIR re-use – towards an iRepository. How can documentation and archiving be standardized?* (all participants in break-out groups)
  - Feedback round 2: feedback from each break-out group (all participants)
- Closing:
  - Summary of insights (workshop leads)
  - Discussion & task assignment for next steps (all participants)
  - Composition & publication of closing statement (workshop leads)

4 DESIRED OUTCOMES & CONTINUING ACTIVITIES

Breaking down the barriers to re-use in the IIR field is not an activity that can be completed within a full-day workshop and this shapes the proposed workshop outcomes. The outcomes are thus centered around follow-on activities to move the community forward towards a shared iRepository.

The main, initial outcome will be a set of requirements and activities that the community needs to commit to in order to develop an iRepository that is likely to see actual uptake within the community. The requirements and activities will be developed in the breakout groups and draw on the responses from the IIR resources survey. They will be published in the form of a short report that will be available from the workshop's web-site. Ideally for some or all of the activities identified within the report participants at the workshop will express their interest in participating in or leading some of these activities and that way aspects of the work can be advanced independently. This also provides an opportunity for groups to form around potential grant applications in this area.

At the same time, a community-wide repository requires a certain amount of discussion and co-ordination of all its development. To achieve this we envisage a more extensive activity, such as a Dagstuhl Seminar, which will provide the time to discuss the requirements and solutions in more detail. In parallel to that, smaller hackathon-style events could be organized that focus on developing technical solutions for aspects of the problem. The central aspect of these is that the workshop's discussions will enable us to develop concrete requirements and plans for these future events, rather than having follow-on activities that each time start from fresh, which will enable them to be more productive and also integrate with each other.

To achieve these outcomes, wide dissemination to the community is a key activity. One of the issues we have experienced with past workshops is that there is a loss of momentum directly after the workshop. To counteract this we propose to provide more dissemination activities on the workshop's website directly after the workshop's completion. The main focus of this will initially be a short statement of intent that is produced and discussed at the end of the workshop and published within a few days of the workshop. This statement of intent will not be comprehensive, but indicate the direction of the initiative and providing a point of reference that participants can state their commitment to. This will be followed by the more extensive report described above.

Building on this initial statement of intent, in the medium term we plan to further analyze the workshop's discussions and then disseminate this to the wider IR community via a SIGIR Forum workshop report or an article describing our vision in an appropriate journal. Finally, to ensure that the discussions from the workshop continue and that the momentum and interaction between participants is maintained, we propose setting up a public mailing list as well as responsibilities. This will not only allow the discussions to continue after the workshop completes, it will also enable researchers who could not attend the workshop to engage in the discussion, increasing the likelihood that the workshop achieves its aims.

REFERENCES

[1] Nicholas Belkin, Toine Bogers, Jaap Kamps, Diane Kelly, Marijn Koolen, and Emine Yilmaz. 2017. Second Workshop on Supporting Complex Search Tasks. In *Proceedings of the 2017 Conference on Conference Human Information Interaction and Retrieval (CHIIR '17)*. ACM, New York, NY, USA, 433–435. DOI : http://dx.doi.org/10.1145/3020165.3022163

[2] Pia Borlund. 2016. Interactive Information Retrieval: An Evaluation Perspective. In *CHIIR '16: Proceedings of the 2016 ACM on Conference on Human Information Interaction and Retrieval*. ACM, New York, NY, USA, 151–151.

[3] Luanne Freund and Barbara M. Wildemuth. 2014. Documenting and studying the use of assigned search tasks: RepAST. *Proceedings of the American Society for Information Science and Technology* 51, 1 (2014), 1–4. DOI : http://dx.doi.org/10.1002/meet.2014.14505101122

[4] Maria Gäde, Mark M. Hall, Hugo Huurdeman, Jaap Kamps, Marijn Koolen, Mette Skove, Elaine Toms, and David Walsh. 2015. Report on the First Workshop on Supporting Complex Search Tasks. *SIGIR Forum* 49, 1 (June 2015), 50–56. DOI : http://dx.doi.org/10.1145/2795403.2795415

[5] Maria Gäde, Mark Michael Hall, Hugo C. Huurdeman, Jaap Kamps, Marijn Koolen, Mette Skov, Toine Bogers, and David Walsh. 2016. Overview of the SBS 2016 Interactive Track. In *Working Notes of the CLEF 2016 Conference (CEUR Workshop Proceedings)*, Krisztian Balog, Linda Cappellato, Nicola Ferro, and Craig Macdonald (Eds.), Vol. 1609. CEUR-WS.org, 1024–1038.

[6] Maria Gäde, Mark Michael Hall, Hugo C. Huurdeman, Jaap Kamps, Marijn Koolen, Mette Skov, Elaine Toms, and David Walsh. 2015. Overview of the SBS 2015 Interactive Track. In *Working Notes of the CLEF 2015 Conference (CEUR Workshop Proceedings)*, Linda Cappellato, Nicola Ferro, Gareth J. F. Jones, and Eric SanJuan (Eds.), Vol. 1391. CEUR-WS.org.

[7] Mark Michael Hall, Hugo C. Huurdeman, Marijn Koolen, Mette Skov, and David Walsh. 2014. Overview of the INEX 2014 Interactive Social Book Search Track. In *Working Notes of the CLEF 2014 Conference (CEUR Workshop Proceedings)*, Linda Cappellato, Nicola Ferro, Martin Halvey, and Wessel Kraaij (Eds.), Vol. 1180. CEUR-WS.org, 480–493.

[8] Diane Kelly. 2009. Methods for Evaluating Interactive Information Retrieval Systems with Users. *Foundations and Trends in Information Retrieval* 3, 1–2 (2009), 1–224.

[9] Diane Kelly and Cassidy R Sugimoto. 2013. A Systematic Review of Interactive Information Retrieval Evaluation Studies, 1967–2006. *Journal of the American Society for Information Science and Technology* 64, 4 (2013), 745–770.

[10] Paul Over. 2001. The TREC interactive track: an annotated bibliography. *Information Processing & Management* 37, 3 (2001), 369–381. DOI : http://dx.doi.org/https://doi.org/10.1016/S0306-4573(00)00053-4 Interactivity at the Text Retrieval Conference (TREC).

[11] Paul Over. 2001. The TREC Interactive Track: An Annotated Bibliography. *Information Processing & Management* 37, 3 (2001), 369–381.

[12] Nils Pharo, Thomas Beckers, Ragnar Nordlie, and Norbert Fuhr. 2011. Overview of the INEX 2010 Interactive Track. In *INEX '10: Proceedings of the Ninth International Workshop of the Initiative for the Evaluation of XML Retrieval*, Shlomo Geva, Jaap Kamps, Ralf Schenkel, and Andrew Trotman (Eds.). Springer, Berlin, Heidelberg, 227–235.

[13] Anastasios Tombros, Birger Larsen, and Saadia Malik. 2005. The Interactive Track at INEX 2004. In *INEX '04: Proceedings of the Third International Workshop of the Initiative for the Evaluation of XML Retrieval*, Norbert Fuhr, Mounia Lalmas, Saadia Malik, and Zoltán Szlávik (Eds.). Springer, Berlin, Heidelberg, 410–423.

[14] Elaine G. Toms and Mark M. Hall. 2013. The CHiC Interactive Task (CHiCi) at CLEF 2013. In *Working Notes of the CLEF 2013 Conference (CEUR Workshop Proceedings)*, Pamela Forner, Roberto Navigli, Dan Tufis, and Nicola Ferro (Eds.), Vol. 1179. CEUR-WS.org.

WEPIR 2018: Workshop on Evaluation of Personalisation in Information Retrieval

Gareth J. F. Jones
ADAPT Centre, School of Computing
Dublin City University
Dublin 9, Ireland
Gareth.Jones@dcu.ie

Nicholas J. Belkin
School of Communication & Information
Rutgers University,
New Brunswick, NJ, USA
belkin@rutgers.edu

Séamus Lawless
ADAPT Centre, School of Computer Science & Statistics
Trinity College Dublin
Dublin, Ireland
seamus.lawless@scss.tcd.ie

Gabriella Pasi
Department of Informatics, Systems & Communication
University of Milano-Bicocca
Milan, Italy
pasi@disco.unimib.it

ABSTRACT

The purpose of the WEPIR 2018 workshop is to bring together researchers from different backgrounds, interested in advancing the evaluation of personalisation in information retrieval. The workshop focus is on the development of a common understanding of the challenges, requirements and practical limitations of meaningful evaluation of personalisation in information retrieval. The planned outcome of the workshop is the proposal of methodologies to support evaluation of personalised information retrieval from both the perspectives of the user experience in interactive search settings, and of user models for personalised information retrieval and their algorithmic incorporation in the search process.

CCS CONCEPTS

• **Information systems** → **Users and interactive retrieval**; **Personalization**; **Task models**; **Evaluation of retrieval results**; *Web searching and information discovery*; *Search interfaces*; *Retrieval tasks and goals*;

KEYWORDS

information retrieval; personalisation; user models; interaction; evaluation

ACM Reference Format:
Gareth J. F. Jones, Nicholas J. Belkin, Séamus Lawless, and Gabriella Pasi. 2018. WEPIR 2018: Workshop on Evaluation of Personalisation in Information Retrieval. In *CHIIR '18: 2018 Conference on Human Information Interaction & Retrieval, March 11–15, 2018, New Brunswick, NJ, USA.* ACM, New York, NY, USA, Article 4, 3 pages. https://doi.org/10.1145/3176349.3176903

1 INTRODUCTION

One of the key goals of information retrieval research is to advance the development of search applications which enable searchers to satisfy their information needs more effectively and efficiently. Given that the information need underlying their engagement with a search application relates to a personal need for information, it makes intuitive sense that in addition to the searcher's stated search request, a search application should make use of all available information about the user in order to return content most likely to be relevant to them.

Information relating to the user of a search application can be gathered from logs of their previous search activities, and also from monitoring their other online activities with various applications and their context. A user can also be requested to explicitly provide information to complete a personal profile. Given the very large amounts of information available from these different sources, an important research question is how to utilize it within the search process [3]. It might for example be used to populate personal profiles of characteristics and interests or more general user models, which can then be used within a personalised information retrieval application to return documents more likely to be relevant to the user than those returned by an equivalent, but not personalised search application.

There are many ways in which personal information might be modeled and represented within some form of user model and how this model might be used within the information retrieval process. In order to determine how best to implement a personalised information application, an evaluation strategy is required.

While it is potentially relatively straightforward to evaluate the impact of a personalisation model on retrieval effectiveness for a "single shot" search by applying the same query to multiple instances of a search engine incorporating alternative personalisation methods, much more interesting is the incorporation of personalisation in session based settings incorporating multiple queries expressing the evolution of an information need as the searcher progresses through the session, and further the use of personalisation across multiple sessions where the user model is updated in response to developments in the searcher's interests. Evaluation in this setting is a highly complex problem.

This workshop will seek to develop a shared understanding of the challenges involved in evaluating personalised information retrieval in interactive search settings and seek to establish an agreed overall framework for both user-centered studies and laboratory-based algorithmic research for personalisation in information retrieval.

2 BACKGROUND

A number of current and previous initiatives and workshops have focused on topics relevant to this workshop. While each of these has aspects relevant to the WEPIE 2018: Workshop on Evaluation of Personalisation in Information Retrieval, none of them directly addresses the focus of this workshop or encompasses the scope of this workshop.

The key relevant activity exploring this topic from the perspective of the user is the Interactive Track at the TREC conferences, which ran for twelve years [5], and is of relevance to this workshop for several reasons. One is that it developed methods for evaluating various aspects of system performance over entire search sessions, a crucial aspect of evaluation of personalisation. Another is that one of the main findings of this track was the difficulty, perhaps impossibility, of applying the general TREC/Cranfield evaluation model to the dynamic situation of interactive information retrieval, again, a key aspect of the personalisation situation.

More recently the TREC Session Track held from 2010 to 2014, sought to provide test collections and evaluation measures for studying information retrieval over user sessions with multiple stages of query reformulation rather than one-time queries. This track introduced modified evaluation metrics for session based search [6], but had the limitation that the information need was assumed to remain static for a query across the session.

The 2012 NII-Shonan Seminar on Whole-Session Evaluation of Interactive Information Retrieval Systems [2], and the 2013 Dagstuhl Seminar on Evaluation Methodologies in Information Retrieval [1], each addressed evaluation issues relevant to this workshop, including evaluation measures for entire search sessions, and user modeling for evaluation, but stopped short of the problem of evaluation of personalization of information retrieval.

The recent interest in conversational information retrieval is also related to the topic of this proposed workshop. The International Workshop on Conversational Approaches to Information Retrieval, held at the 2107 ACM SIGIR conference in Tokyo (CAIR, 2017) addressed some personalization issues, including system adaptation and clarification dialogues, but discussion of evaluation of such techniques was minimal.

Introduced at CLEF 2017, the Personalised Information Retrieval (PIR-CLEF) task is seeking to develop a framework for the repeatable evaluation of user models and search algorithms for personalised information retrieval (PIR) [7]. The PIR-CLEF 2017 task introduced a Pilot Task that provided data gathered during a single search session by ten users; these data are related to various activities undertaken during their search session by each participant, including details of relevant documents as marked by the searchers [8]. The Pilot task is the preliminary edition of a Lab dedicated to the theme of personalised search that is planned to officially start at CLEF 2018.

Unlike the Information Retrieval research community, the User Modeling research community has traditionally not had a significant focus on comparative evaluation or shared evaluation tasks. However, this situation is changing with the emergence of the Eval-UMAP workshop series exploring the evaluation of user modeling, adaptation and personalization' which began at the UMAP 2016 conference [4], and is currently being held on an annual basis.

3 WORKSHOP FORMAT

The topic of evaluation of the incorporation of personalisation within search applications and algorithms and their impact on user engagement and experience of search is currently underexplored within the information retrieval community. This is particularly the case from the perspective of comparative evaluation of interactive and algorithmic elements of personalised search systems, and the representation and exploitation of user models. To reflect this, the workshop will focus on establishing and exploring the principles working towards the outcome of a proposed framework.

The workshop will have the following elements:

- Invited talks: focusing on user-centered interactive issues, and on evaluation of the algorithmic component of search.
- Presentations of papers submitted in response to an open call for research and position papers. Papers will be presented as short oral and poster format. The number of oral presentations will be limited to allow for the maximum of time for interactive activities, with other papers being presented as posters.
- Working groups focusing on relevant topics for the evaluation of personalised information retrieval, including experimental protocols, test collection development, evaluation metrics.
- Consolidation session: integration of the activities of the working groups, and proposal of agreed framework or frameworks for the evaluation of personalised information retrieval.

4 ORGANISERS

The organisers of the workshop have a broad range of relevant expertise in the topics of the workshop including benchmark evaluation task development, interactive information retrieval, search algorithm design, user modeling, and personalised information retrieval, as well as extensive experience in organising and running successful workshops.

Gareth Jones is Professor of Computing in the School of Computing, and a Principal Investigator in the ADAPT Research Centre, Dublin City University, Ireland, His research focuses on multiple topics in information retrieval including adaptive search, multimedia information retrieval (particularly for spoken content), multilingual information retrieval, interactive and algorithm search for lifelogging, A particular focus in much of this work has been the development of evaluation frameworks including task design, test collection specification and construction, and the introduction of new task specific evaluation metrics. With Gabriella Pasi he is currently leading the development of the PIR-CLEF Lab for the comparative evaluation of personalisation algorithms in information retrieval. He is co-founder of the MediaEVal multimedia benchmark evaluation initiative, and since 2002 has coordinated a variety of benchmark tasks at CLEF, FIRE, NTCIR and TRECVid. He regularly serves on of programme committees leading conferences in information retrieval, multimedia, natural language processing and human-computer interaction. He served as Programme co-Chair for CIKM 2010 amd ECIR 2010, and as General co-Chair for SIGIR 2013 and CLEF 2017.

Nicholas Belkin is a Distinguished Professor in the Department of Library and Information Science at Rutgers University. He was the initiator of the Interactive Track in TREC, and variously chaired and participated in that Track for its twelve years. He was also a key participant in the TREC Session Track, devising the task classification system used in that Track. He was the organizer of the NII Shonan Seminar on Evaluation of Whole Session Information Retrieval, and of the Dagstuhl Seminar on Interactive Information Retrieval. His research group has been engaged in studies of personalization of interactive information retrieval since 2010, with funding from the US Institute for Museum and Library Services, the US National Science Foundation, and Google. His proposal that the best criterion for evaluation of interactive information retrieval is usefulness, rather than relevance, has been adopted, and validated, by several different research groups throughout the world. Professor Belkin holds the ACM SIGIR Salton Award, the ASIS&T Award of Merit, and has been the Chair of the ACM SIGIR, and the President of the ASIS&T.

Seámus Lawless is Assistant Professor in the Knowledge and Data Engineering Group in the School of Computer Science and Statistics at Trinity College Dublin. He is also a Funded Investigator in the ADAPT Centre for Digital Content and Media Innovation. His research interests are in the areas of information retrieval, information management and digital humanities with a particular focus on adaptivity and personalisation. The common focus of this research is the application of technology to support enhanced, personalised access to knowledge. He was General co-Chair of the 23rd Conference on User Modelling, Adaptation and Personalization (UMAP 2015) and of CLEF 2017. He is a co-organiser of the EvalUMAP Workshop series which began at UMAP 2016 focusing on "Comparative evaluation in user modeling, adaptation and personalization".

Gabriella Pasi is Full Professor at the University of Milano-Bicocca, Italy where she leads the Information Retrieval Lab within the Department of Informatics, Systems and Communication. Her research activities mainly concern the modeling and design of flexible and context-aware systems for the management and access to huge collections of documents (such as Information Retrieval Systems and Information Filtering Systems). Recently, within CLEF 2017, she led the introduction of the PIR-CLEF initiative for the evaluation of Personalised Search. She has also contributed to the organization of several international events, in both roles of General and Program Chair (e.g. for ECIR 2018). She is Associate Editor or member of the Editorial Board of several International Journals in her domains of expertise.

5 ACKNOWLEDGEMENTS

This work was partially supported by Science Foundation Ireland as part of the ADAPT Centre (Grant No. 13/RC/2106) (www.adaptcentre. ie), and by the US National Science Foundation under grant IIS-1423239.

REFERENCES

[1] Maristella Agosti, Norbert Fuhr, Elaine Toms, and Perti Vakkari. 2014. *Evaluation methodologies in information retrieval.* Dagstuhl Seminar 13441. Schloss Dagstuhl - Leibniz-Zentrum fuer Informatik, Schloss Dagstuhl, Germany.
[2] Nicholas J. Belkin, Susan Dumais, Noriko Kando, and Mark Sanderson. 2016. *Whole-session evaluation of interactive information retrieval systems.* NII Shonan Meeting Report 2012-7. National Institute of Informatics, Japan, Tokyo, Japan.
[3] Paul N. Bennett, Filip Radlinski, Ryen W. White, and Emine Yilmaz. 2011. Inferring and Using Location Metadata to Personalize Web Search. In *Proceedings of the 34th International ACM SIGIR Conference on Research and Development in Information Retrieval (SIGIR 2011).* ACM, Beijing, China, 135–144.
[4] Owen Conlan, Liadh Kelly, Kevin Koidl, Seamus Lawless, Killian Levacher, and Athanasios Staikopoulos (Eds.). 2016. *EvalUMAP2016: Towards Comparative Evaluation in the User Modelling, Adaptation and Personalization.* Halifax, Canada.
[5] Susan Dumais and Nicholas J. Belkin. 2005. The TREC interactive tracks: Putting the user into search. In *TREC. Experiment and evaluation in information retrieval,* Ellen M. Voorhees and Donna K. Harman (Eds.). MIT Press, Cambridge, MA, 123 – 152.
[6] Evangelos Kanoulas, Ben Carterette, Paul D. Clough, and Mark Sanderson. 2011. Evaluating Multi-query Sessions. In *Proceedings of the 34th International ACM SIGIR Conference on Research and Development in Information Retrieval (SIGIR 2011).* ACM, Beijing, China, 1053–1062.
[7] Gabriella Pasi, Gareth J. F. Jones, Stefania Marrara, Camilla Sanvitto, Debasis Ganguly, and Prochzta Sen. 2017. Overview of the CLEF 2017 Personalised Information Retrieval Pilot Lab (PIR-CLEF 2017). In *Proceedings of CLEF 2017.* Springer, Dublin, Ireland.
[8] Camilla Sanvitto, Debasis Ganguly, Gareth J. F. Jones, and Gabriella Pasi. 2016. A Laboratory-Based Method for the Evaluation of Personalised Search. In *Proceedings of The Seventh International Workshop on Evaluating Information Access (EVIA 2016).* Tokyo, Japan.

Author Index

www.ingramcontent.com/pod-product-compliance
Lightning Source LLC
Chambersburg PA
CBHW080659220326
41598CB00033B/5262